Blackstone's

Student Police Office‌ ‌book

Blackstone's

Student Police Officer Handbook

Second Edition

Edited by

Dr Robin Bryant

Contributors:

Dr Bryn Caless, Kevin Lawton-Barrett, Robert Underwood, and Dr Dominic Wood

OXFORD
UNIVERSITY PRESS

Great Clarendon Street, Oxford OX2 6DP

Oxford University Press is a department of the University of Oxford.
It furthers the University's objective of excellence in research, scholarship,
and education by publishing worldwide in

Oxford New York

Auckland Cape Town Dar es Salaam Hong Kong Karachi
Kuala Lumpur Madrid Melbourne Mexico City Nairobi
New Delhi Shanghai Taipei Toronto

With offices in

Argentina Austria Brazil Chile Czech Republic France Greece
Guatemala Hungary Italy Japan Poland Portugal Singapore
South Korea Switzerland Thailand Turkey Ukraine Vietnam

Oxford is a registered trademark of Oxford University Press
in the UK and in certain other countries

Published in the United States
by Oxford University Press Inc., New York

© Oxford University Press 2007

British Library Cataloguing in Publication Data

Data available

Library of Congress Cataloging in Publication Data

Blackstone's student police officer handbook/edited by Robin Bryant; contributors: Bryn Caless . . . [et al.].
    p. cm.
    Includes bibliographical references and index.
    ISBN 978-0-19-923841-5 (pbk.: alk. paper) 1. Police—Great Britain—Handbooks, manuals, etc. 2. Police
training—Great Britain. I. Bryant, Robin, Dr. II. Caless, Bryn. III. Title: Student police officer handbook.
    HV8196.A4B548 2008
363.20941—dc22   2007048033

Typeset by Laserwords Private Limited, Chennai, India
Printed in Great Britain
on acid-free paper by
Ashford Colour Press Limited, Gosport, Hampshire

ISBN 978–0–19–923841–5

10 9 8 7 6 5 4 3 2

Foreword

The usefulness and application of the Blackstone's series is well known to police officers. They have provided sound support for many years. This latest addition to the series maintains this excellent tradition and provides vital support to new police officers embarking on a career. Now in its second edition with many updates, including the Fraud Act 2006, new Standards, and Code H this very useful book remains extremely relevant.

Policing is changing at an astonishing rate. It may be too slow for some, too fast for others, but there is no question that it is changing faster than it has ever done so in its history. This Handbook starts you running in the right direction.

The Handbook reflects the new pattern of police training. It introduces you to National Occupational Standards which now form the basis for recruitment, selection, development, and appraisal. These clearly set out the competencies you will need—the knowledge and understanding you need to store away, the skills you will need to handle your role, even the attitudes and behaviours expected of you. This will allow you to develop quickly into a modern police officer. The new approach will drive out the bigots or the demonstrably incompetent. It will ensure the nation has the police service it wants and, in short, it will enable you to become what you want to be—the best!

Robin Bryant and his team have drawn on their years of experience to put together this excellent publication. Up to date, accurate, and very readable—I heartily commend it to you.

Richard Winterton
Managing Director
City & Guilds Awards

Acknowledgements

Robin Bryant

I would like to thank my colleagues Roy Murphy, Martin O'Neill, Leo Raznovich, and Ben Waters for reviewing parts of the Handbook and offering their professional advice; to my wife Sarah Bryant, for her ability to make sense out of convoluted prose and for her major contribution to the writing of this handbook.

Bryn Caless

Clare because she lived with it for so long and read so much of it; Madryn for the computer (occasionally); Helen, Sally, and Kit (even if they thought fiction preferable...) for their support; Allyn Thomas for his wit and wisdom, Hugh Martyn and Angus Kerr for many happy arguments, Jean Craft for the European experiences, my Kent Police College colleagues for many hours of conversations about the police and how they got that way, and the K&S and St Thomas' for bringing me back, more than once.

Kevin Lawton-Barrett

My wife, Zoë, deserves thanks for her patience and photography, and all my colleagues at Crime Scene Training from 1990 onwards for the background material and unknowing guidance: all are simply known as 'Reg'. Thanks also to Andrew Turner at LGC Ltd for the images of drugs. Not least of all, to Paul Clark for discussions on science and for fixing my laptop which, at one stage, contained everything.

Robert Underwood

To my wife Vuka. Thank you for your continued support, guidance, advice, and dedication. Neither of us quite understood the enormity of the task in the beginning, but you have remained determined to produce work of the highest quality throughout some exceedingly difficult times. Thank you for remaining so patient. I would also like to thank my colleague Malcolm Underdown for taking the time to review sections of the Handbook and for making a number of professional recommendations.

Dominic Wood

Thanks for the ongoing, patient support from my wife, Tanya.

Contents

Contents

Table of Cases

Table of Legislation

Introduction

This is the second edition of Blackstone's Student Police Officer Handbook. All the material contained in the first edition has been reviewed and updated where necessary. New material has also been added, particularly in terms of legislation introduced since the first edition and changes to the structure of initial police training. Some changes have also been made as a result of feedback from individual readers and police organizations both in terms of structure and at the level of content. We are grateful for both this feedback and for the identification of the occasional error.

The authors of this Handbook have taken care to ensure the accuracy of the information contained within. However, neither the authors nor the publisher can accept any responsibility for any actions taken, or not taken, as a consequence of the information it contains.

We would be grateful for feedback on the contents of this Handbook, including any proposed corrections.

References throughout the Handbook to IPLDP materials have not been reviewed or endorsed by the IPLDP Central Authority Executive Services.

Introduction to the First Edition

It is now more than 170 years since the formation of the 'new police' in London, arising from Robert Peel's notion of a civilian organization that would uphold the peace and only use coercion as a last resort. By the mid nineteenth century every county and every city and town had acquired a police 'presence' whose organization, approach, and even uniforms we would still easily recognize today as being drawn from the traditions of the British police. The so-called 'Golden Age' of policing (an indeterminate age, somewhere in the 1950s, of apparent public peace and tranquillity and unquestioning respect for the institutions of state) still resonates in the minds of many, if only as a symbolic representation of supposedly better times. Because of this, and because most of us have grown up with the police as a given in our society, there is a tendency to assume that the police are permanent. But they have not 'always been there' and there is no guarantee at all that they will continue to exist, at least as we know them now. There is also no guarantee that the public will continue to maintain its apparently high regard for the police. In a 2002 BBC poll, police officers were only tenth in a list of the most respected professions, behind doctors, nurses, teachers, fire fighters, paramedics, military personnel, scientists, and ambulance personnel (BBC, 2002). It must also be of some concern to the service that public confidence in the ability of the police to do a good job actually diminishes after an individual has been in contact with the police, in contrast to most other public services (Office of Public Services Reform, 2004). We note too, that even the definition of a police officer is losing clarity with the growth of the private security industry, police community support officers (PCSOs), wardens, both rural and parish, and other members of the extended police family. The warrant card may soon be the only meaningful distinction between the police officer and all the other agencies and groups who contribute to policing.

It is against this background of change that you will join the police, not at the outset as a confirmed police constable but as a student police officer. Police training, as with public policing itself, is in a phase of significant flux. Until recently, the initial training of police officers involved a co-operation between the national organization Centrex (previously National Police Training or NPT and now the NPIA) and local police forces. The programmes were often known as 'probationary', 'probationer', or 'foundation training'. This national model of police training typically consisted of an induction course (the responsibility of the local police force), 15 weeks' training at a regional Centrex police training centre alongside students from other police forces, followed by a series of further training courses within a two year probationary period. (The exception was the Metropolitan Police Service that delivered its own training at the Hendon Police College). All this has now changed. One impetus for change was the HMIC 'Training Matters' thematic inspection report published in 2002. The inspection examined initial police training at both national (Centrex) and local (force) levels and made a total of 59 recommendations one of which was that 'A complete review of probation training is undertaken, as HMIC considers the present arrangements no longer fit for purpose' (HMIC, 2002). The reaction to the screening of *The Secret Policeman* programme on BBC television in October 2003, which uncovered racism at a regional police training centre, added urgency to these calls for change. The programme was followed by the HMIC 'Diversity Matters' report in 2003 and the 2005 Commission for Racial Equality report into the 'Police Service in England and Wales', both critical of the existing arrangements.

Subsequently, the Home Office determined that the responsibility for ensuring the delivery of probationary training should lie with police forces. Forces now have the option of contracting with Centrex (now incorporated within the NPIA), or working in partnership with education and training providers (such as further education colleges or universities), or using their own training facilities, or collaborating with each other, or combinations of these approaches, to deliver their own initial police training. The process of reform of police training is being implemented through the Initial Police Learning and Development Programme (IPLDP) linked in turn to the Wider Police Learning and Development Programme (WPLDP). Now the training of student police officers has become the responsibility of local forces which are delivering a new 'modernized' curriculum based on National Occupational Standards. There is a renewed emphasis on respect for diversity and for students to engage with their local communities, including 'hard to reach' groups. The gates to the 'secret garden' of police training are to be opened, and for the first time student police officers who successfully complete their training will gain a qualification. That, at least, is the vision.

For many police forces, the new era of the IPLDP began in April 2006. At the time of writing, only a small number of student police officers have completed the new form of training. Many aspects of the new approach are untested: the National Occupational Standards, the Student Officer Learning and Assessment Portfolio, and the Police Action Checklist to name a few. This Handbook is a response to these systemic changes to initial police training and to the advent of the IPLDP in particular. The chapters that follow reflect the new IPLDP curriculum.

The onset of the IPLDP is one reason, amongst others, that you will not find yourself (unlike generations of 'probationers' before you) staying at a residential training centre separated from the rest of society (in an environment that some critics described as a 'boot camp'). Instead, you are likely to be 'trained in the community' which might even mean that you attend your local college or university alongside other students. Initial police training is at an interesting crossroads in other respects too. In some ways it retains its links with the 'military model' of policing (Bowling and Foster, 2002) in that 'probationers' are expected to know how to address police officers superior in rank (as Sir or Ma'am), wear a uniform, and carry a warrant card almost from the beginning of training (even though they have yet to gain the skills and knowledge to back this up), be subject to Police Regulations that know only the masculine personal pronoun ('he') and, most tellingly of all, soon after joining, be attested and immediately considered as part of the police 'complement', that is a person to be deployed during times of crisis if need dictates. You have joined a police force.

But in many other respects your training will be in keeping with a more liberal model of policing. You will probably be referred to as a 'student police officer' rather than 'probationer' (that is, until you undertake your first Supervised Patrol and encounter more seasoned colleagues), and the support staff you meet will no longer be referred to as 'civilians', and you will be encouraged to reflect on your own values and ideas and be expected to learn from, and to respect, the diverse communities that make up the UK population. You will probably attend college out of uniform. You will learn that reassurance is often as important as law enforcement. You have joined the police service.

No doubt you have already framed a number of questions in your mind, both about the police organization that you are joining, and the whole process of becoming a police officer. Amongst them may be: 'What am I joining? What do I have to do to pass my training? What do I have to know? What will it be like in ten or twenty years' time?'

Our powers of prediction are no more accurate or far-seeing than anyone else's, although we have all been in and around British policing for a long time. Our predictions may very well be wrong, and we have no monopoly on the truth. This Handbook paints a detailed picture of policing in the twenty-first century, and on occasions we discuss what perhaps the police aspire to be, rather than what they actually are. At times, we look ahead to where the police service is going—particularly in 'Developing as a Police Officer' in Chapter 14, and consider larger societal changes, such as the shifting demographics of our UK population. But let us take a moment now, right at the beginning of this Handbook, to talk about what being a police officer may mean to you, and to your family and friends, as you start your training.

At the outset it is obvious that you will not simply be performing one role and one role alone. The police undertake many jobs, and some of them are by no means obvious to the outside observer. However, to start with the obvious, there is the responsibility to tackle crime. However, what is meant by 'tackle' is far from obvious. Do we mean that you are to maintain order, so that crime does not occur, and people can undertake their 'lawful business'? Or do we mean that you are to investigate and detect crime, given that even the most optimistic of us acknowledges that a certain level of crime is inevitable? Or, most likely, do we mean both? If we mean both, which of these is more important: maintaining order or fighting crime?

We would not be the first to ask such questions. One answer was provided in 1829 by Sir Richard Mayne, one of the first two jointly-appointed Commissioners of the Metropolitan Police (Metropolitan Police, 2006):

> The primary object of an efficient police is the prevention of crime: the next that of detection and punishment of offenders if crime is committed. To these ends all the efforts of police must be directed. The protection of life and property, the preservation of public tranquillity, and the absence of crime, will alone prove whether those efforts have been successful and whether the objects for which the police were appointed have been attained.

So important was this definition of the role of the police that it was required reading for all new recruits to the Metropolitan Police Service from 1829 until the mid 1980s.

But the prevention and detection of crime is not all that you will be called on to do. Indeed, you will probably spend most of your time on tasks not related to crime (Waddington, 1999). You are also a key member of the emergency services; you will often be the first person to arrive at the scene of a road traffic collision or a critical incident. Finally, people will often turn to you for help on matters entirely unrelated to crime, because there is simply no one else left to turn to who might listen and do something.

All this means that policing today is probably more complex, and more demanding, than at any time since 1829. For example, there have been over a thousand new criminal offences created since 1997 alone (Miles, 2005), some of which feature in Chapter 9. The Government's Police Reform initiatives have led to a whole series of changes to the organization of policing and the responsibilities of police officers. How should the police respond? (We put aside at this point the debate about whether the police should be more of a 'profession'.) What is clear is that, as a student police officer, you will be required to learn more, to develop your skills more rapidly and in greater depth, and to demonstrate your knowledge and skills more thoroughly than any previous generation of new recruits.

The job itself will also sometimes send you on a roller-coaster of emotions, from anger when watching a suspect walk free from the court on a technicality, to exhilaration when a missing child is found safe and well because of your actions. You will be expected keep a lid on your emotions; it is easy to say, 'Don't let your emotions affect the way you work', but it is much, much harder to achieve.

You probably already suspect that there will be more tedium than variety in the job, whatever the fictional portrayal. Policing is not about grumpy loners following hunches in grimy backstreets, nor is it a soap opera about sexual conflict in uniform. There is plenty of painstaking routine in police work of any kind, whether in road traffic policing or in serious crime investigation. The reality of police work is a constant attention to detail, the prosaic need to follow procedure and that, throughout your shift, there is the inescapable requirement to write up your pocket notebook.

You probably have not joined the police to become rich, or because you have a burning need to promote social justice, or because you like wearing uniforms, or because you are manically power-hungry (although all these reasons are possible). You have probably joined the police because you have concerns about society, about the way that people behave towards each other, about the vulnerability of the weak and the disadvantaged, and you want to do something about it. Yes, you could be naïve in your reasons for joining the police, but do not let an accumulated shell of cynicism and disillusionment so burden you that eventually you cannot remember why you are there. Your colleagues will also have doubts about what they are doing, they too will have crises of confidence in the police service, and have moments when they feel utterly defeated. Like you, they will bounce back, try again, wake refreshed, and do whatever it takes to get back to normal duty. Some of your colleagues will be ambitious, some selfish, some lazy; a very small number may be corrupt. But most will put themselves on the line for you, as they expect that you would for them. And if, as cynics will claim, that is not the case at all, how can we explain the fact that all those police officers came in off-duty and on rest days when a probationer police officer was shot dead in January 2006? No one ordered that; it was spontaneous action by people who cared for each other.

As you face the uncertainties of the future, of changes to the organization of policing, single-issue politics, ambiguity about the essence of policing itself, evidence of growing violence in society, perhaps even a feeling that you are an anonymous cog in a large and impersonal machine, what can you hold on to? What could sustain you in your role? What could lead you, day after day, to face abuse, being spat on, being sworn at, being vilified, being criticized, and being alternately demonized and lauded in the media and finally being left to face a hard reality on your own?

Perhaps it is the fact that you are there to uphold the law, to support the vulnerable and to protect democratic values for the benefit of us all. Admittedly these commendable ambitions will not be at the forefront of your mind at the start of every late shift. But cumulatively, over the years to come, with occasional highs (and some lows), **you will make a difference**. All we would ask, as members of the society that has given you powers denied the ordinary citizen, is that you are worthy of our trust.

1 Reference Material

1.1 Chapter Briefing

This chapter contains reference material likely to be of value to you during your initial training as a student police officer.

It is not necessary to memorize all of the information contained in this chapter—instead view it as a source of reference material that you may wish to return to from time to time during your training. For example, you may encounter more experienced police colleagues using an acronym or a form of jargon that you have not encountered. Section 1.2 of this chapter might well provide an answer.

1.1.1 Aim of the Chapter

The aim of this chapter of the Handbook is to provide you with some important background information as a reference point during your initial training. The chapter includes a glossary of terms used in policing, a brief chronology of police history, a summary of the IPLDP phases and modules, a list of the National Occupational Standards (NOS) relevant to the student police officer, and finally a look at the IPLDP Learning Requirement.

This chapter will enable you to:

- refer to a glossary of terms used in policing when needed;
- assimilate some of the key dates and events in the history of policing in England and Wales;
- gain an overview of the IPLDP phases and modules;
- refer to a summary of the NOS and Learning Requirements for initial police training.

1.1.2 National Occupational Standards

This chapter will provide you with the knowledge required to demonstrate aspects of the following NOS elements:

> **National Occupational Standard Elements**
>
> 1A2.1   Communicate effectively with members of communities.
> 4C1.2   Synthesise new knowledge into the development of one's own practice.

You should refer to Chapter 6 for general information and advice concerning the NOS elements.

1.1.3   IPLDP Induction and Law, Policy, and Procedures Modules

This chapter will provide you with resources to support the Induction Module IND 4 to 'Develop effective relationships with colleagues' (and IND 4.1 in particular) and aspects of LPG 1 ('Police communication' in particular).

1.1.4   SOLAP

The contents of this chapter are relevant to the knowledge evidence requirements of CARs 1A2 and 4C1.

1.1.5   The Learning Requirement

This chapter is relevant to section 2.6 of the IPLDP Learning Requirement.

1.2   Glossary of Terms Used in Policing

You will meet many acronyms and forms of jargon during your training as a police officer. The following glossary of terms may assist you in understanding some of the often bewildering words and phrases used within policing. Note also that many police forces also publish their own glossary of terms.

ABC (1) Acceptable Behaviour Contract. (2) Activity-Based Costing, a finance/budgeting methodology that enables costs of an activity to be calculated (as opposed to a value which can only be assessed).

ABH Assault resulting in actual bodily harm.

ACC Assistant Chief Constable, a command rank (see sections 7.3 and 7.4 below).

ACPO The Association of Chief Police Officers. The term ACPO is also sometimes used as a vernacular proper noun for a chief officer (qv). The future shape of ACPO is currently under discussion.

ACMU Area Crime Management Unit.

Active Defence A proactive approach to defence which involves a rigorous examination of police investigation procedures and the prosecution case. The title of an influential book by Roger Ede and Eric Shepherd.

Ad hoc A Latin phrase meaning 'for this special purpose', but has come to mean 'off the cuff' or 'unrehearsed'.

ADVOKATE Mnemonic used in police training to assist the recollection of the so-called 'Turnbull' rules for witness recall where (usually) A is the Amount of time under observation, D is Distance, V is Visibility, O is Obstruction, K is Known, A is Any reason to recall, T is Time that has lapsed, and E is Error.

AIC Area Intelligence Co-ordinator (sometimes referred to as Area Intelligence Controller).

Airwave The digital national police radio communication system, replacing the previous (and less secure) VHF system.

Alpha/Bravo/etc The phonetic alphabet used in police communication (see Section 7.5).

ALI Adult Learning Inspectorate.

AMU Administration Management Unit.

Analyst A professional police staff member whose role (usually) is to analyse and assess crime data and intelligence, and present research.

ANPR Automatic Number Plate Recognition system, see 'Nexus'.

AO Authorizing Officer (for an intelligence operation).

APA Association of Police Authorities.

APACS Association of Payments and Clearing Services (the Financial Services' fraud group).

APL Accreditation of Prior Learning.

APEL Accreditation of Prior Experiential Learning.

ARA Assets Recovery Agency.

Area Commander A uniformed superintendent who commands an area, or BCU (qv).

ARV Armed Response Vehicle.

ASBO Anti-Social Behaviour Order.

ASP An informal term for an extendable metal baton.

Attestation The formal point at which the powers and responsibilities of the office of constable are assumed, accompanied by the swearing of an oath. The phasing of attestation is currently under discussion.

Awarding Bodies Organizations permitted to issue awards and qualifications such as NVQs (qv).

Baton A side-handled self-protection weapon carried by uniformed police officers.

Baton-round Known popularly as the rubber or plastic bullet.

BAWP British Association for Women in Policing.

BCU Basic Command Unit (Area, Division) or sometimes Borough Command Unit, particularly amongst MPS officers (qv).

Biometrics The use of unique physical characteristics (such as the iris of the eye) as identifiers.

Bolt-on ASBO An informal term for an ASBO (qv) ordered after a conviction (it is bolted on), usually by a magistrate.

BPA Black Police Association.

BTP British Transport Police.

CAP Common Approach Path.

Cat A/B/C murders Categories of homicide. 'A' is a serious or series of 'stranger' killing(s), 'B' a serious or cross force murder where the offender is not known, and 'C' a local or domestic murder, where the offender is usually known.

CCTV Closed-Circuit Television.

CDRP Crime and Disorder Reduction Partnership.

Centrex Centrex was the short-hand name for the 'Central Police Training and Development Authority' and has now been replaced by the NPIA (qv).

cf Latin for compare.

Chief Officer A police officer with the rank of assistant chief constable and above, command rank.

CHIS Covert Human Intelligence Source (informant).

CI (1) Cognitive Interview. (2) Cell Intervention.

CID Criminal Investigations Department, now replaced in many police forces by Specialist Crime Investigations, SCI, or similar.

CJPOA Criminal Justice and Public Order Act 1994.

CJ(S) A common acronym, referring to a process or unit concerned with Criminal Justice (Systems).

CLUE2 A case-tracking data system.

Collar To make an arrest (vernacular).

Compromise When a criminal target (a suspect) detects covert surveillance.

Continuity Continuity of evidence: an audited and continuous trail from crime scene or suspect to court, such that evidential items can be accounted for at all times en route, to prevent interference or contamination.

Confirmation The final stage of successful initial training, normally after a period of two years, when a student police officer is confirmed as a police constable.

CNC Civil Nuclear Constabulary

CPA (1) Crime Pattern Analysis. (2) Child Protection Agency.

CPIA Criminal Procedures Investigation Act 1996.

CPS Crown Prosecution Service, the governmental body of qualified lawyers who prosecute criminal cases before the courts. CPS agreement to proceed is a mandatory factor in any criminal case. If the CPS believes that a conviction is unlikely, then a public prosecution will not proceed, unless more compelling evidence is discovered.

CRE Commission for Racial Equality.

CRFP Council for the Registration of Forensic Practitioners.

CRO (1) Criminal Records Office. (2) Criminal (vernacular).

CROPS Close Rural Observation Posts (or Points).

CSI Crime Scene Investigator.

CSP Communications Service Provider.

CTM Contact Trace Material.

Cuff (1) Police vernacular for not doing something which one is supposed to do as a matter of duty or obligation. (2) To handcuff (vernacular).

Custody or custody suite A designated area in a police station (usually where the cells are located), where arrested persons are logged and processed by trained custody staff.

Dabs Colloquial term for fingerprints.

Doctrine A body of knowledge and procedure concerned with police practice, notably criminal investigation—for example, as expressed in the MIM (qv) and Volume Crime Investigation Manuals of NCPE (qv).

DC Detective Constable.

DCC Deputy Chief Constable.

DCI Detective Chief Inspector.

DCS Detective Chief Superintendent, command rank.

DDA Normally a reference to the Disability Discrimination Act 1995.

De minimis Latin for at the least risk meaning the law is not concerned with trifles.

DfES Department for Education and Skills.

DI Detective Inspector.

DIC Drunk in charge.

Dicker A person who records vehicle registration plates; often outside law enforcement agency premises, with obvious potential to compromise the security of covert teams (vernacular). Thought to originate from Northern Ireland.

Dippers/Dips Vernacular term for pickpockets.

Disclosure A reference to the requirement on the police and the prosecution to provide the defence with certain information and documents which may be pertinent to a criminal case.

DoB/DOB Date of birth.

DNA Deoxyribonucleic Acid (genetic material used to obtain a genetic fingerprint).

DS Detective Sergeant.

DVLA Driver, Vehicle and Licensing Authority.

ed(s) Editor(s).

DWP Department for Work and Pensions.

EAW European Arrest Warrant.

ECHR European Convention on Human Rights.

Element (of a Unit of an NOS) Units of NOS (qv) are usually divided into two or more elements which more precisely describe the skill or competence to be attained and measured.

ERO Evidence Review Officer.

ESDA Electrostatic Detection Apparatus.

esp Especially.

ETA Estimated time of arrival.

et al Latin for and others.

Europol The European Union Law Enforcement Organisation.

Extended Police Family A reference to the wider group of law enforcement and public order staff, beyond the traditional full-time police—for example, special constables and PCSOs (qv).

FA Forensic Alliance (an independent forensic science laboratory and service).

Family of Forces Term once used by the HMIC to describe those police forces which were considered to be very alike in structure, size, budget, and so on. Now largely replaced by the Home Office's designation of 'Most Similar Forces' (MSF, qv)

FCA Forensic computer analyst.

FCC Force Communications (or Control) Centre.

Federation The police staff association (resembling a trade union), covering ranks from constable to chief inspector.

Fence Person to whom stolen goods are sold or exchanged.

FIND Facial Images National Database, currently being developed on a project basis.

FIO Field Intelligence Officer meaning either: (1) source-handler; or (2) R&D officer (qv).

Fishing Police vernacular for any speculative attempt, particularly where the intention is to try to recover evidence of potential value in a criminal case but the grounds for doing so (and the form of evidence to be seized) are uncertain.

5 x 5 x 5 A '5 by 5 by 5' is an intelligence report. The numbers refer to a scale that is used to attempt to measure the reliability, access, and other factors about the source providing the intelligence.

FLINTS Forensic Linked Intelligence System, a database and comparative analysis system developed by West Midlands Police.

FLO Family Liaison Officer.

Force Orders A reference to the practice of issuing directions and clarifications of force policy to employees including police officers, often issued using the closed force intranet (qv). Also referred to as 'General Orders' (borrowed from the military).

Foundation degree/FD A qualification at higher education level. There are a number of foundation degrees in Policing, many incorporating the NOS (qv) for initial Policing.

FPN Fixed Penalty Notice.

FSS (1) Forensic Science Service. (2) Forensic Science Society.

FTS Forensic Telecommunications Services.

FY Financial year (1 April to 31 March).

GBH Grievous Bodily Harm, category of assault.

GCHQ Government Communications Headquarters.

GMP Greater Manchester Police.

GPA Gay Police Association.

Handling Taking illegal ownership of stolen or otherwise illegally obtained goods.

Handler Vernacular term for police officer responsible for liaising with and tasking CHISs (qv).

Hearsay A reference to information which is not given directly (orally) to the court, but is somehow second-hand. Hearsay evidence is generally not usable in a court as evidence, although there are many notable common law and other exceptions to this general rule.

Hit A DNA sample which can be matched with an identified person (not always criminal).

HMCE Her Majesty's Customs and Excise, now HMRC (qv).

HMIC Her Majesty's Inspectorate of Constabulary (HMIC) has the responsibility for examining and improving the efficiency of the Police Service in England and Wales. It inspects at BCU (qv) and force levels and also carries out thematic inspections (for example, into police training).

HMIS Her Majesty's Immigration Service, now IND (qv).

HMPS Her Majesty's Prison Service.

HMRC Her Majesty's Revenue and Customs.

HMSO Her Majesty's Stationery Office.

Home Office A government department responsible for policy relating to policing and crime. The Home Office is responsible for the Government's programme of police reform, including the IPLDP (cf).

HORTIES Police vernacular reference to driving document production records HO/RT/1 and HO/RT/2.

HOLMES, HOLMES2 Home Office Large Major Enquiry System, an information system designed to support large-scale police investigations (for example, homicide).

HOSDB Home Office Scientific Development Branch.

Hot spot A geographical location where there is a high incidence (or a perceived high incidence) of current crime and criminality.

HRA Human Rights Act 1998.

HSE Health and Safety Executive.

HQ Headquarters.

HYDRA A simulation system, used by some police organizations, to assist in the training of police commanders and others in the response to critical incidents.

ibid Latin for in the same place.

IC1, IC2 to IC9 A reference to Identity Codes used when police officers record ethnicity. IC1 is White European.

ICF Integrated Competency Framework. This combines descriptions of behavioural requirements with the National Occupational Standards (NOS (qv)) and profiles for a number of policing roles such as patrol constable.

ICV Incident Command Vehicle used in situations where public order might be a problem.

IDENT ONE The fingerprint database which replaced NAFIS (qv) in late 2004.

Idents Identifications (vernacular).

ILP/ILPM Intelligence-Led Policing and hence Intelligence-Led Policing Model.

IND Immigration and Nationality Directorate.

Independent Patrol The ability of a student police officer to conduct police patrol without the constant supervision of a qualified police officer. Usually achieved after successful completion of the PAC (qv).

INDIS Immigration and Nationality Directorate Intelligence Service.

Informant A person who passes intelligence to a source handler, see CHIS. Often a criminal, an informant is known in criminal argot by a variety of unflattering soubriquets, such as snout, grass, and nark.

Institutional racism A term used in 1999 during the Macpherson Inquiry (qv) which claims that institutions, through their policies and procedures (both written and unwritten) can unintentionally behave in a manner prejudicial to the position of ethnic minorities. The suggestion was that the MPS (qv) was institutionally racist.

Interagency A term often employed in policing to describe approaches to crime investigation and reduction that involve partnership with non-police agencies. For example, collaboration with the probation service and social services. See also CDRP.

Inter alia Latin for among other things.

Intranet Often refers in police circles to a police internal electronic information system, with restricted access rights.

Interpol The International Criminal Police Organisation.

IO Investigating (police) officer, usually a detective officer (for a crime), but can be a uniformed officer (for example, for traffic collisions).

IP Injured person or party (often literally the injured person in a crime involving personal violence).

IPCC Independent Police Complaints Commission.

IPLDP Initial Police Learning and Development Programme; the programme of modernization of initial police training managed by the Home Office (qv). From April 2006 all new student police officers were expected to undertake 'IPLDP compliant' programmes of training in order to qualify as police officers.

IPLDP Central Authority Responsible for the implementation and policy direction of IPLDP (qv) and includes representation from the Home Office, Police Federation, Superintendents' Association, and the NPIA (qv).

ISO Individual Support Order. An ISO may be imposed upon a young person between the ages of 10 and 17 as a form of positive inducement to end anti-social behaviour.

JRFT Job Related Fitness Test.

KUSAB *K*nowledge, *U*nderstanding, *S*kills, *A*ttitudes, and *B*ehaviours as developed in the training of student police officers.

Lantern A portable electronic device which automatically scans and sends the fingerprints of a person (currently being trialled by a number of police forces, including BTP (qv)).

Latent prints Fingerprints (or even earprints) which are invisible to the naked eye but which can be revealed by dusting or other techniques.

LCN Low Copy Number; a minute DNA trace which can be recovered through advanced scientific processes.

LDR Learning Development Review. These are regular reviews (typically three in the course of training) as part of the IPLDP (qv) approach to monitoring achievement of a student police officer's skills and behaviour.

Learning Diary Under IPLDP (qv) student police officers are expected to keep a learning diary as part of the process of reflective learning. The learning diary may form part of the SOLAP (qv).

Learning Requirement A set of learning requirements underpin the IPLDP (qv) curriculum designed by Professors John Elliott, Saville Kushner, and others (Elliott et al, 2003).

Level 1 Local crime signifier (used within NIM, qv). Examples of level 1 crimes or criminals are crimes such as illegal possession of a controlled drug.

Level 2 Cross-BCU or cross-force crime signifier (used within NIM, qv). Examples of level 2 crimes or criminals are crimes such as dealing in illegal drugs.

Level 3 National or international crime signifier (used within NIM, qv). Examples of level 3 crimes or criminals are crimes such as organizing the importation or distribution of illegal drugs.

LGC Laboratory of Government Chemists (service provider for scientific analysis).

LIVESCAN Commercial computerized database used to take fingerprints digitally.

LOCARD Forensic database system.

Loc cit Latin for at the place quoted.

MAPPA Multi-Agency Public Protection Arrangements (part of the joint agency approach to managing violent and sex offenders).

Match An identified DNA (qv) sample.

MBPA Metropolitan Black Police Association.

Meet Vernacular term for covert physical contact with an informant (CHIS, qv).

Met or Mets Vernacular for the Metropolitan Police Service (qv).

MG3 A form used to report to the CPS (qv) for an initial charging decision.

MG11 Statement form.

MIM Murder Investigation Manual (sometimes called the 'Murder Manual'), distributed by ACPO (qv). The MIM was the first example of a comprehensive doctrine (qv) to assist in the investigation of serious crime (in this case, murder). It sets out the various investigative strategies that may be employed (for example, the forensic strategy and the interview strategy). The MIM was written partly as a result of the enquiry into the death of Stephen Lawrence (qv).

Minutiae Latin for of small parts, the individuality of a fingerprint through examination of its ridge characteristics (anywhere up to 150 characteristics in a single fingerprint).

Misper Missing person or missing person forms.

M. O. or MO Modus operandi is Latin for a characteristic way of doing something. Often used to refer to a particular way of committing a crime.

MOD or MoD Ministry of Defence.

Modus vivendi Latin for a practical way to co-exist (between those who differ).

MOPI Management of Police Information.

Morris Inquiry Reference to the inquiry conducted by Sir William (Bill) Morris in 2004 into professional standards and employment issues in the MPS (qv).

MoPI Management of Police Information.

MOU Memorandum of Understanding.

MPS Metropolitan Police Service. London's police force.

MSF Most Similar Force (for comparison).

NACRO National Association for the Care and Resettlement of Offenders.

NAFIS National Automated Fingerprint Identification System.

NB Latin for take especial note of.

NBPA National Black Police Association.

NCALT National Centre for Applied Learning Technology. NCALT is a password-protected internet based learning portal for the police service.

NCOF/NCF The National Crime and Operations Faculty, previously the National Crime Faculty. It is based in the Police Staff College at Bramshill in Hampshire.

NCIS National Criminal Intelligence Service. Now subsumed within SOCA (qv).

NCPE National Centre for Policing Excellence. Likely to become part of the NPIA (qv).

NCS National Crime Squad. Now subsumed within SOCA (qv).

Nexus A combined computer database system.

NFA (1) No Further (police or CPS) Action. (2) No Fixed Abode.

NHTCU National High Tech Crime Unit, now part of SOCA (qv).

Nick Vernacular for: (1) A police station. (2) To arrest a person.

NIM National Intelligence Model. All police forces are required to follow the NIM. It is sometimes described as a business model for policing. The focus is largely, but by no means exclusively, on crime and criminality. The NIM describes both strategic (for example, threat assessment) and tactical (for example, the use of informants) approaches to both police and interagency (qv) responses to crime and public disorder.

Nominals Vernacular police term for those perceived to be active and often recidivist and high-volume criminals.

Non-Home Office forces Somewhat misleading term that refers to police forces that are not one of the 43 county or city based forces. Examples of non-Home Office forces include BTP (qv).

NOS National Occupational Standards. The National Occupational Standards for policing were developed by Skills for Justice (qv). For student police officers there is a subset of 23 NOS which are required before Confirmation (qv).

NPIA National Police Improvement Agency—the new body that has replaced various other policing organizations, including Centrex (qv) and PITO (qv).

NPP National Policing Plan.

NPT National Police Training, a defunct organization whose responsibilities are now subsumed within the NPIA (qv).

NSLEC National Specialist Law Enforcement Centre, a consortium of representatives of national policing bodies which seeks excellence in policing, principally in covert operations (a part of NCPE).

NTSU National Technical Services Unit.

NVQ National Vocational Qualification. There are NVQs at Levels 3 and 4 in Policing, incorporating the relevant NOS (qv).

OP Observation Post (or Point).

Op Operation. Usually taken as referring to a targeted police operation against a criminal problem and given names such as 'Op. Damocles'. Note that the name of the operation is simply taken from a list and does not reflect the particular circumstances of that operation (indeed, police forces consider it better that the operational name has no connection with the operation it signifies).

Op cit Latin for see the work cited.

OSPRE Objective Structured Performance Related Examination, from Centrex, now replaced by the NPIA (qv). The OSPRE examination process is undertaken by those who wish to become police sergeants or inspectors.

OPSY Operational security officer.

OSC Office of the Surveillance Commissioner.

OST Officer Safety Training (a term not used by all police forces).

p or pp Page or pages.

PAC Police Action Checklist. Satisfactory completion is one of the criteria for the right to undertake Independent Patrol (qv).

PACE Police and Criminal Evidence Act 1984.

PAS Police Advisers' (or Advisory) Service.

Passim Latin for everywhere, but used in the sense of throughout.

PC or Pc Police constable.

PCSO Police Community Support Officer: a member of police staff in a police force whose role is nominally to support operational policing, but who usually patrols a small geographical area and deals with low level civic nuisance.

PDP The Professional Development Portfolio is a tool to record an individual police officer's professional development. The PDP for student police officers is effectively the Student Officer Learning and Assessment Portfolio (SOLAP, qv).

PDU A dedicated Professional Development Unit for the development of student police officers, police officers, and other police employees.

PEACE Acronym for an interviewing model, adopted by police forces in the UK. The letters represent the stages of an interview: *P*lanning and preparation; *E*ngage and explain; *A*ccount, clarification and challenge; *C*losure; and *E*valuation.

PI Performance Indicator, a type of quantitative measure which the Home Office often uses to assess the police service.

PIMS Performance Indicator Management System.

PIP (levels 1, 2, 3, and 4) 'Professionalizing Investigation Programme' or sometimes 'Professionalizing Investigations Programme' or even 'Professional Investigation Programme', originally developed by NCPE (qv). Level 1 is embedded in the initial training of student police officers, through mapping to the NOS, namely 2G2, 2H1, and 2H2 (qv).

PITO Police Information Technology Organisation, now subsumed within the NPIA (qv).

PLO Prison Liaison Officer (a police officer).

PM Apart from its more common meaning (post meridian or afternoon), used to mean a post-mortem examination.

PNC Police National Computer.

PNLD Police National Legal Database.

POCA Proceeds of Crime Act 2002.

Police Staff Official designation of support (civilian) staff, some of whom are operational but who do not have warranted powers like police officers. Includes PCSOs (qv).

PolSA/POLSA Police Search Adviser.

POP/BritPOP Problem Oriented Policing and its UK derivative.

PPU Prisoner Process Unit.

PRDLPD Police Race and Diversity Learning and Development Programme.

Profiling/Profilers An informal term often used in policing (as in 'offender profiling' and 'geographical profiling') but of uncertain meaning. Most often used to describe psychological profiling of an unknown offender (for example, when used to support the investigation into a linked serial rape case). However, the official ACPO (qv) term for those engaged in this latter form of activity is behavioural analyst or behavioural adviser.

Probationer An informal term for a police officer in initial training in the first two years of service, and a reference to the probationary period. Now usually replaced by student police officer or student officer, but you will still often hear the term used.

PS or Ps Police sergeant.

PSD Professional Standards Department.

PSDB Police Scientific Development Branch, now the Home Office Scientific Development Branch (qv).

PSNI Police Service of Northern Ireland (previously called the RUC, Royal Ulster Constabulary).

PSSO Police Skills and Standards Organization. Now subsumed within Skills for Justice (qv).

PSU Policing Standards Unit (Home Office). Likely to be subsumed within the NPIA (qv).

PTDB Police Training and Development Board, led by the Home Office (qv).

QPM Queen's Policing Medal.

qv Latin for which see—reference to another item or word.

RAIF Recovered Assets Incentivisation Fund: a national agency set up under POCA (qv), using seizures and forfeitures from criminals to fund a host of community-based schemes.

R&D Research and Development Unit (usually used of intelligence analysis and tasking at BCU level).

Refs A vernacular reference to having a break and eating and drinking during a tour of duty.

Reg 12 and Reg 13 Reference to the Regulations surrounding police conduct and dismissal.

RCS The (now defunct) Regional Crime Squads.

Re-coursing/Back-coursing An informal term for the process of student police officers repeating elements of initial training, normally as a result of failure or personal reasons.

Reflex Nationally funded project to deal with organized immigration crime.

RIC Regional Intelligence Cell.

RIG Regional Intelligence Group.

Ridge and furrow Identifying features in fingerprints.

RIPA Regulation of Investigatory Powers Act 2000.

RTA (1) Road Traffic Act. (2) Road Traffic Accident, now largely replaced by RTC (qv).

RTC Road Traffic Collision. The term collision is preferred to the previous accident as it is more suggestive of the fact that most accidents are due to human error, negligence, or a criminal act rather than a chance event.

Sanitized Used to describe intelligence from which the identifying features and origins have been omitted.

SB Special Branch. A part of every police force that specializes in matters of national security and made up of non-uniformed police officers.

Scarman/Scarman Report A reference to the influential 1981 report by Lord Scarman into the Brixton riots of the previous year.

SCAS Serious Crime Analysis Section. A database of homicides and stranger rapes housed at the Police College, Bramshill.

Secret Policeman Reference to the video documentary made in 2003 by an undercover reporter and subsequently aired by BBC television. The documentary produced evidence of racist behaviour by police recruits at a police regional training centre.

SFO Serious Fraud Office.

SGM Second Generation Multiplex, a DNA profiling system using seven areas for discrimination between people (1 in 50 million). See STR.

SGM+ A similar DNA profiling system to SGM, using 11 areas for discrimination (1 in 1,000 million). See STR.

Sheehy A reference to the Sheehy Report of 1993 which made a number of recommendations on police conditions, pay, and rank, most of which were not implemented at the time.

Shoemarks Informal term for footwear prints which can match a suspect to a crime scene, in the same way as DNA and fingerprints can.

Show out A vernacular reference to a security problem on a surveillance operation when the suspect realizes that he/she is being observed.

SH(U) Source Handler (or Handling Unit). See also Handler.

SIA Security Industry Association.

sic Latin for as it is written.

SIO Senior Investigating Officer (usually a detective officer) investigating a serious or major crime, such as a Category A or B murder (qv), or a rape or series of rapes.

SIU Special Investigation Unit (for child abuse and child protection investigations).

16+1 Reference to the system used to record self-defined (as distinct from officer-defined) ethnicity, for example A1 is used for Indian. See IC1.

Skills for Justice/SfJ/S4J The Sector Skills Council (SSC) for Criminal Justice, including policing. Skills for Justice is also responsible for the National Occupational Standards for policing and other justice related bodies and organizations (such as the Probation Service).

Skillsmark Quality assurance scheme introduced by Skills for Justice (qv).

SLA Service Level Agreement.

SMART(ER) Used in reference to objectives: *S*pecific, *M*easurable, *A*chievable, *R*ealistic, *T*imely (and *E*valuated and *R*eviewed) or abstract nouns to the same effect.

SMT Senior Management Team (on a BCU, it usually consists of the Commander, a Superintendent, or, on large BCUs, a Chief Superintendent, together with one or more Chief Inspectors (Crime and Operations) and a Business Manager).

SO 19 Firearms unit in the MPS (qv).

SOCA Serious Organised Crime Agency, established by the Government in 2005 to embrace the work of NCS, NCIS, SFO, and parts of HMCE (Investigation and Intelligence Divisions) and HM Immigration Service staff.

SOCO Scenes of Crime Officer. A somewhat outmoded term replaced in many police forces by CSI (qv).

SOLAP Student Officer Learning Assessment Portfolio. In many forces this is replacing the PDP (qv) for student police officers.

SOLO Sex Offender Liaison Officer.

SOP Standard Operating Procedure.

SPoC/SPOC/spoc Single Point of Contact.

Stephen Lawrence/the Lawrence Inquiry/the Macpherson Inquiry References to the death of the black teenager Stephen Lawrence in 1993, the subsequent investigation conducted by the MPS (qv), and the reports that followed (for example, as conducted by Lord Macpherson, 1999).

Stinger Device used to stop a speeding car by puncturing the tyres.

Supervised Patrol Pre-Independent Patrol (qv) undertaken by student police officers under the supervision of a qualified police officer or officers.

STR Short Tandem Repeat, a DNA profiling methodology which replaces the SGM and SGM+ terms (qv).

T&CG Tasking and Co-ordinating Group.

Tac team (1) Tactical Support Team—for example, used to serve a warrant. (2) Terrorism and Crime Team (MPS, qv).

TDA or TADA Taking and Driving Away, a reference to a form of vehicle crime. Also known as TWOC (qv).

Tenprint A fingerprinting process whereby all 10 digits of a suspect or other individual are recorded.

Test Purchase The authorized purchase of drugs, alcohol, or other items (by an undercover police officer or another person) to provide evidence of illegal activity.

TIE Trace, Implicate, and/or Eliminate (in investigations).

TFIO Technical field intelligence officer.

TIC Acronym for offences 'taken into consideration' by a court.

TNA Training Needs Analysis.

TWOC Taken WithOut (or Without Owner's) Consent—normally used in reference to a motor vehicle. Also known as TDA or TADA (qv).

UKIS UK Immigration Service (see HMIS).

UKTA UK Threat Assessment (NCIS derived).

Unit (of an NOS) The NOS (qv) for initial policing are made of 22 Units, for example Unit 2I1 to 'Search Individuals'. Unit 2I1 has just one element (qv).

UVP Ultra-Violet (Light) Photography.

VCSE Volume Crime Scene Examiner (forensic).

VEM Visible Ethnic Minority, used of both the individual and of the community from which he/she comes.

VIPER Video Identification Parade Electronic Recording.

ViSOR Violent Offender and Sex Offender Register, accessed by all police forces in the UK.

Vol Volume.

'Whorl' With 'loop' and 'delta' etc, names given to fingerprint characteristics.

WPLDP Wider Police Learning and Development Programme, a programme of learning and skills development introduced to support the training of members of the extended police family (qv), for example, PCSOs (qv).

TASK 1

There could well be terms, acronyms, and jargon particular to your own police organization and hence not on the list above. Forces often have lists of their own, on the force intranet, sometimes on publicly-available websites, and occasionally in published form. Ask around to find out if such a list is available.

1.3 Chronology of Policing

An understanding of the past is an important precursor to understanding the present. There are no IPLDP learning outcomes that are explicitly concerned with the history of policing but there is an argument that, say, 'Understanding and being in the community' and 'Understanding Social change' (both part of IND 11) benefit from placing what we currently do in an historical context.

This section of the Handbook is not a comprehensive history of the police in the UK, nor does it offer much in the way of analysis, but it does provide you with some of the background that explains how we have arrived at the police service that you joined and a number of key dates that are milestones in that journey. It is surprising to note that the police (in the UK and elsewhere) are a relatively modern phenomenon and there have been a number of notable occasions when their very existence has been contested. Perhaps this is the key observation to take away from this section: the police service as we would recognize it today is barely 180 years old and remains subject to continuing fundamental changes to its purpose and structure.

1.3.1 Background

If there is one key date in modern day policing it is probably 1829 when Sir Robert Peel, then Home Secretary, introduced a Bill in Parliament for the establishment of a Metropolitan Police Force to police the city of London. The Bill was passed, became an Act, and the foundations of the modern police service were established. Initially, the police existed only in the greater part of London (the City of London Police Force, separately constituted and referring only to the square mile of the capital's commercial centre, came into being 10 years later). Prior to 1829, the main official ways of keeping law and order rested, in serious instances, with the military and in less serious cases, with parish constables appointed by local Justices of the Peace.

What is hard for us to imagine is the way in which society was ordered in pre-industrial Britain. That we created a genuine civil police force only after the end of the Napoleonic Wars, and eight years before Queen Victoria came to the throne, suggests that there was probably no perceived official need for an integrated independent arm of criminal justice in a Britain which was still largely rural.

In fact, the origins of enforcing the law probably date back to the Saxons, or even earlier. The Saxons may well have brought with them the notion of dividing society into groups ('tythings' or 'tenths', which were organized into hundreds) which would then assume some responsibility for social organization, acting under the control or oversight of a 'Shire Reeve', a man responsible for law and order and deriving his authority from the King. Our modern word 'sheriff' is believed to come from this ancient title. Shire Reeves controlled shires or large geographical districts (or towns, such as Nottingham) and were often military men who had undertaken service with the King. They could call upon able-bodied men in the community to hunt for fugitives or criminals by raising a 'hue and cry', and each landowner had the obligation of providing men for both military and local service. Since many of the landowners were also Justices of the Peace, there was seldom any problem for the Shire Reeve to find men to track those on the run.

After the Norman invasion in 1066, rural communities were dominated by Norman placemen (those rewarded by King William with land and people to serve the land), who regularized the old shire system with parish constables and the migration of the Shire Reeve himself to be a Justice of the Peace. 'Constable' is a Norman French word (deriving from Latin) meaning 'count of the stable', an official who supervised the care of horses and who was thus of considerable social rank. Again the name survives in its old meaning with honorary roles such as High Constable, Constable of the Tower, or Constable of Dover. However, the role of parish constable, though membership was originally drawn from members of the propertied classes, was often performed by the very poor (and very old) as substitutes, under the control of the magistrate. The office of constable was symbolized by the carrying of a painted or engraved 'stave' or 'truncheon', which in time developed into the wooden truncheon used in the first 150 years of official policing as a self-defence weapon. The parish constable system by the late eighteenth century had become widely acknowledged as inadequate, but survived despite its inefficiency, largely because there was apparently neither the will nor the imperative to change. The provision of law and order was largely performed by pressure of social opinion in the small rural communities together with harsh criminal law (including capital punishment and transportation) which persisted until the end of the eighteenth century. It was the war with Napoleon and the increasing industrialization of Britain which showed up the inefficiencies of the old system and the need for a non-military power, acting on behalf of the Crown, though with its roots in the local community, to keep the peace and uphold the law.

The use of military force was not a satisfactory way of dealing with the public. You may well have heard of the 'Peterloo Massacre' of 1819, named ironically (echoing 'Waterloo') after St Peter's Fields, a district of Manchester, in which a largely peaceable and unarmed crowd of 50,000 or more people, gathered in political protest to hear a radical MP, Henry Hunt, speak on parliamentary reform. Despite the crowd being peaceable, local magistrates ordered the yeomanry to disperse the crowd and arrest Hunt. The crowd was charged by the mounted militia with drawn swords. A number of people, including women, were killed and over 400 were wounded; there was a major public outcry.

Allied to this was increasing lawlessness in the new towns and suburbs springing up throughout the UK and the perceived ever-present danger of mob rule. Large crowds formed in the towns and cities on slight pretexts, from the oratory of a radical or the perceived shortcomings of government. The crowd would sometimes stampede through the cities for a few days, looting and killing, and the resultant disorder led to much criticism of the government of the day. The conditions appeared at least to some to be ripe for anarchy, and the inadequacy of the military to deal with either mob rule or peaceable demonstration led the authorities to introduce a different kind of peace-keeping force.

So Peel's Police Force, at first only in London, was established. Very soon, counties, cities, and towns followed suit and established their own police forces, using the Metropolitan Police Act as the basis for their authority (see below). Police officers were 'sworn officers' responsible to the Crown, as they are to this day. That responsibility, exercised on behalf of the Sovereign, stretches back to link with the notion of the Shire Reeve ten or more centuries earlier.

1.3.2 Chronology

There now follows a brief **chronology** (time-line) of the significant developments in the history of the police service of England and Wales, dominated (at least in the nineteenth century) by the Metropolitan Police in London.

1829 **Sir Robert Peel** established the first civilian police force in London. Sir Charles Rowan and Sir Richard Mayne were appointed as Justices of the Peace in charge of the force.

1831 Period of considerable unrest and **mob violence**, especially in the north of England and in London, where a crowd attacked the home of the Duke of Wellington and broke all the windows. The new police eventually imposed order.

1835 The Municipal Corporations Act established watch committees to oversee policing of areas outside London. The term 'watch committee' comes, not from the idea of having a watch over the police, but from the older meaning of a watch being the provision of law and order at night, established by the Statute of Winchester in 1285.

1839/1840 Various pieces of legislation allowed the setting up of provincial constabularies under a local police committee of magistrates, based on the Metropolitan Police model. An important difference was that the Metropolitan Police was answerable directly to the Home Secretary through its Commissioners (of which there were two at first), whereas provincial police forces were answerable to their local authorities through the magistrates' committee.

1842 Establishment of a **detective force** at Scotland Yard (Metropolitan Police HQ), but investigation was in its infancy and the numbers very small (it was only increased to ten in 1856). At first, formation of a detective branch was resisted at borough and county level because of a distaste for spies and informers. A major corruption scandal (the 'Turf Fraud') among detectives in London in 1877 led to the formation of the **Criminal Investigation Department** (CID) in 1878, a pattern followed with greater or lesser success across provincial forces during the next thirty years. Scotland Yard detectives were still called in by county forces to lead criminal investigations well into the 1930s, but after the Second World War, most county forces had their own CIDs.

1840s–50s A period of considerable hostility to the new police, particularly in the boroughs and counties, where there was widespread resentment about the cost of supporting the police, a belief that a police force was illiberal and that there was a lack of visibility of police officers when needed (this last is a remarkably modern complaint).

1856 The **County and Borough Police Act** made it mandatory on local government bodies to set up police forces. These were often shoe-string affairs organized on a parochial basis, but the introduction of **inspections** of constabularies to assess efficiency did much to improve standards and to ensure consistency in applying what were proper actions for a police force to undertake. Financial support in the form of **Exchequer Grants** were centrally awarded to those forces which proved to be efficient and reliable, paving the way for the modern inspection regime by the HMIC (qv).

1860 A survey in this year established that there were more than 200 borough and county police forces in England and Wales, with similar arrangements being put in place in Scotland. Unrest and armed disaffection in Ireland (then a single colonial possession) led to the formation of the **Royal Irish Constabulary**, which was paramilitary from the outset. The RIC, later, after the creation of Eire in 1922, became the **Royal Ulster Constabulary** (RUC) before changing again to the **Police Service of Northern Ireland** (PSNI), following the Patten Inquiry and Report of 1999. The RIC served as a model for the establishment of colonial police forces in places like Kenya and South Africa in the late nineteenth century.

1872 Police officers went on **strike** for the first time.

1883 The **Special Irish Branch** formed in the Metropolitan Police to deal with attacks by Irish republicans in London. This later became known simply as Special Branch and many of the larger police forces had their own branches by 1918, largely as a result of MI5's urging of the police to deal with German spies and saboteurs during the First World War.

1888 An important change was the transfer of oversight of local police from the committee of magistrates to a joint committee of magistrates and elected councillors. (This arrangement endured until around 2005, when Police Authorities changed their composition to the wholly elected.)

1890 The **Police Act**, which came into law in this year, provided for the first time a police pension payable after twenty-five years' service, together with other benefits such as one rest day off each week and regularized pay systems (see below). We tend now to think of pensions as perfectly normal (if expensive) adjuncts to employment, but at the time of their introduction to the police, such notions were comparatively rare and a pension was a genuine inducement to join the police. The Police Act also brought in the concept in law of 'mutual aid' between police forces.

1900 Lord Belper headed a committee to ascertain the best system of identifying suspects as criminals. A year later, Scotland Yard's **Fingerprint Bureau** was formed and, by 1905, many of the larger provincial forces had their own fingerprint bureaux.

1910 **Radio telegraphy** was used to apprehend Dr Crippen who had fled by ship from Britain after killing his wife.

1911 A siege of armed anarchists in a house in Sidney Street, London, and overseen by the Home Secretary (Winston Churchill), resulted in police officers being **armed** and working with the military to end the siege.

1912 Establishment of **Special Constables** on a permanent basis both in London and in the larger provincial forces.

1914 The first (unofficial) Police **Union** (NUPPO) was formed, following unrest and dissatisfaction about pay and conditions, but was not recognized by the authorities. The **Women Police** were founded (see below).

1914–18 The First World War put enormous pressure on the police. Not only were numbers of male officers severely depleted by enlistment in the armed forces but recruitment was suspended. New tasks such as the pursuit of deserters, new roles such as the protection of vulnerable points and new laws, such as the Defence of the Realm Act (DORA) of 1915, added considerably to police responsibilities. As a consequence, morale appeared to suffer, pay and conditions were comparatively poor, and the police became increasingly vocal in demands for reform and a pay rise.

1916 The Commissioner of the Metropolitan Police ruled that any officer joining a union rendered himself liable to dismissal.

1918–19 The police, particularly in Liverpool and London, embarked on a series of **strikes** for better pay and conditions and for recognition of police trades unions. This resulted in another Police Act of 1919 which prohibited the formation of police trades unions and denied the police the right to strike, but allowed the formation of the **Police Federation** to represent the ranks from constable to chief inspector in negotiations over pay, conditions of service, and Police Regulations. Many of those who had been dismissed for having leading roles in the strike were never reinstated.

1918 Women had filled various police roles during the First World War, owing to the absence of many male officers in the armed forces. The regularizing of **women police officers** as equal members of the force is generally dated from 1916, though many would argue that women were not fully accepted in the police service until the Second World War, and even then, attitudes to female police officers were often negative. The Police Federation (qv), for example, took until 1948 to admit female officers as members.

1921 The first **motorcycle patrols** took place and the Police Pensions Act fixed an age limit for each police rank at which time retirement was compulsory.

1930s The period between the Wars saw a major development of personal **motor transport** and for the first time brought the police into conflict with the middle class who could afford cars. The love/hate relationship between motorists and the law persists to this day.

1931 Lord **Trenchard** appointed as Metropolitan Police Commissioner. Founder of the Royal Air Force in 1918 (previously the Royal Flying Corps), Trenchard believed in a **two-tier entry system** to the police, based on the officer/non-commissioned ranks recruitment in the armed forces. He established a Police College at **Hendon** in 1934 to train police officers, but his experiment with 'officer entry' was short-lived. The system remained that all police officers would enter the service as constables. It was only in the early twenty-first century that the possibility of multiple entry points into the police service was raised again as a serious proposition.

1935 The first police **forensic laboratory** was opened by the Metropolitan Police, paving the way for adoption of more scientific detection processes throughout the police service.

1937 The emergency telephone number **999** was introduced.

1946 Another Police Act **amalgamated** police forces which served populations of fewer than 10,000. This reduced the number of forces to 125.

1951 **Police Cadets** (aged sixteen–eighteen) were introduced as a pathway to become police officers. They wore distinctive pale blue bands on their caps.

1950s The so-called **Golden Age** of policing in the UK (although less so in Northern Ireland) characterized by apparent widespread acceptance of the legitimacy of the police and relatively low levels of crime and disorder. However, the very existence of the Golden Age is the subject of some debate. Our popular belief in the existence of the Golden Age probably derives at least in part from a television series at the time called *Dixon of Dock Green* in which an elderly actor played an elderly police officer who appeared infinitely wise, able to talk to anyone, calm, inordinately knowledgeable, honest, and trusted, it seemed, by the entire nation.

1964 Although the Government abolished some small police forces during the Second World War, it was the Police Act of 1964 which brought about major **amalgamations** of police forces, reducing the overall number of separate and distinct forces from 117 to 49. In the same Act, the borough watch committees and county force joint committees were abolished and replaced with **Police Authorities** based on a county or city force.

1965 Police officers first had **personal radios** to maintain communication during their beat patrols.

1973 **Women police officers** were integrated directly into the police service.

1978 Lord Edmund-Davies headed an enquiry into **police pay** which improved pay and allowances. Similar increases occurred for the armed forces.

1984–5 Miners' Strike. The National Union of Mineworkers (NUM) organized a strike in protest at pit closures and there were numerous clashes between picket lines and police with allegations of heavy-handed behaviour by the police and political intervention by the Conservative Government.

1984 The **Police and Criminal Evidence Act** (PACE) created the **Police Complaints Authority** (PCA), through which complaints about the police from members of the public were investigated. The PCA was formed in response to criticism of the police 'acting as judge and jury in their own cases' because police officers from another force always investigated serious complaints. However, in the majority of cases, the PCA simply monitored investigations conducted by the police themselves.

1990 The Association of Chief Police Officers (ACPO) published its '**Statement of Common Purpose and Values**', which emphasized that the police was more a service than a force.

1991 The police service as a whole claimed to clear up 26% of all recorded crime, which appeared to be an impressive record. However, it was estimated in 1991 that recorded crime represented only 7% of all crime committed. Indeed, data from 2002 suggests that, from 100% of actual crimes, 47% are reported, 27% are recorded, 5% are cleared up, and 2% result in conviction (Wright, 2002). In 1771, the clear-up rate for crime was estimated at 24.6% (Emsley, 1996).

1994 Creation of a centralized computer database for **criminal records**.

1997 **NAFIS**, the National Automated Fingerprint Identification System, was launched which allowed forces to access the national database for fingerprint records.

1999 The **Macpherson Inquiry** into the death of Stephen Lawrence (a black teenager murdered in London in 1993) criticized the whole police service as **institutionally racist** and major efforts were made, and continue to be made, both to communicate with diverse communities and to increase the proportions of ethnic minority communities within police ranks.

2002 Introduction of **Police Community Support Officers** (PCSOs) under the provisions of the Police Reform Act 2002. PCSOs are not sworn officers, but are support staff and are the most visible part of an extending security industry, which some commentators argue runs the risk of marginalizing the police and usurping their functions. Others argue that society is becoming more complex and policing has to match a need for flexible responses; this results in policing also being undertaken by people other than the public police themselves.

2003 TV airing by the BBC of *The Secret Policeman* video uncovering racism at a regional police training centre.

2003 The **Independent Police Complaints Commission** was established to replace the Police Complaints Authority.

2005 Formation of the **Serious Organised Crime Agency** which brought together the National Crime Squad, the National Criminal Intelligence Service, parts of HM Immigration Department, the Serious Fraud Office, and the Investigation Branch of HM Customs and Excise into one body with federal powers to counter level 3 crime and criminality.

2006 Following a 2005 report by HMIC, a further **amalgamation** of police forces was proposed, using 6,000 staff as the minimum stand-alone benchmark for a single force. The aim was to produce a police force having a critical mass which could respond both to local policing needs and to terrorism or civil emergency. It is estimated that amalgamation, if carried through, would result eventually in a total of about twenty police forces in England and Wales, one-tenth the number of police forces in 1860. Amalgamation was abandoned, at least temporarily, in July 2006. The **National Police Improvement Agency** (NPIA) was formed, incorporating the previous organization Centrex (police training) and other agencies such as the Police Information Technology Organization (PITO).

2007 It was proposed that the Home Office be divided into two parts: the 'justice' element incorporated into a Ministry of Justice whilst the 'security' element (including the police) would remain part of the existing Home Office.

TASK 2

What is the history of your own force? See if you can establish the dates of a few key events in the last 200 years or so.

1.4 IPLDP Phases and Modules

The Initial Police Learning and Development Programme (IPLDP) is the new form of police probationary training that all forces had introduced by April 2006. The following is presented as an overview of the IPLDP Phases and Modules for reference purposes.

The IPLDP describes training for student police officers in terms of four phases, taking approximately twenty-four months to complete (when undertaken on a full-time basis):

Phase 1—Induction
Phase 2—Community Safety & Partnerships
Phase 3—Supervised Patrol
Phase 4—Independent Patrol

There are eleven Induction Modules, nine Operational Modules, and three Legislation, Policing and Guidelines Modules (although module LPG 0 is optional):

IPLDP Phases and Modules

Module | Title

IND 1 | Underpinning ethics/values of the police service
IND 2 | Foster people's equality, diversity and rights
IND 3 | Develop one's own knowledge and practice
IND 4 | Develop effective relationships with colleagues
IND 5 | Ensure your own actions reduce the risks to health and safety
IND 6 | Assess the needs of individuals and provide advice and support
IND 7 | Develop effective partnerships with members of the community and other agencies
IND 8 | Operation of information technology systems
IND 9 | Administer first aid
IND 10 | Use police actions in a fair and justified way
IND 11 | Social, community issues and Neighbourhood Policing

OP 1 | Deal with aggressive and abusive behaviour
OP 2 | Obtain, evaluate and submit information and intelligence to support local priorities
OP 3 | Respond to incidents, conduct and evaluate investigations
OP 4 | Participate in planned operations
OP 5 | Search individuals and premises
OP 6 | Prepare, conduct and evaluate interviews
OP 7 | Arrest and report suspects
OP 8 | Escort suspects and present to custody
OP 9 | Prepare and present case information, present evidence and finalise investigations

LPG 0 | Underpinning Legislation Policy and Guidelines (Phases 3 and 4)
LPG 1 | Underpinning Legislation Policy and Guidelines (Phase 3)
LPG 2 | Underpinning Legislation Policy and Guidelines (Phase 4)

Note, however, that forces:

- may decide to structure their own training (as long as they remain IPLDP compliant);
- may not use the same terminology as above. For example, instead of using the term 'modules' they may use 'courses' and they may not use 'phases' in the same way as the IPLDP.

1.5 The National Occupational Standards

There are a number of National Occupational Standards (NOS) for initial policing that underpin the training of student police officers, developed by Skills for Justice, a Sector Skills Council. The standards feature extensively throughout the Handbook and the following is a list of the headings of the twenty-two relevant Units.

Relevant NOS Units

Unit | Title

1A1 | Use police actions in a fair and justified way
AB1 | Communicate effectively with people
AA1 | Promote equality and value diversity

Unit	Title
BE1	Provide initial support to victims, survivors and witnesses and assess their needs for further support
2A1	Gather and submit information that has the potential to support policing objectives
2C1	Provide an initial police response to incidents
2C2	Prepare for, and participate in, planned policing operations
2C3	Arrest, detain or report individuals
2C4	Apply conflict management
2G2	Conduct priority and volume investigations
2G4	Finalise investigations
2H1	Interview victims and witnesses
2H2	Interview suspects
2I1	Search individuals
2I2	Search vehicles, premises and open spaces
2J1	Prepare and submit case files
2J2	Present evidence in court and at other hearings
2K1	Escort detained persons
2K2	Present detained persons to custody
AE1	Maintain and develop your own knowledge, skills and competence
AF1	Ensure your own actions reduce risks to health and safety
4G4	Administer First Aid

In addition, you may be assessed against Unit 1D4 to 'Contribute to the protection of children and young people from abuse'.

TASK 3

What are the three barriers to communication identified within the NOS Unit AB1, to 'communicate effectively with people'? (Descriptions of NOS units for the justice sector are available via the Skills for Justice website <www.skillsforjustice.com>).

1.6 The IPLDP Learning Requirement

The Learning Requirement for initial police training was developed by Professors John Elliott, Saville Kushner, and others and is reproduced below (Elliott et al, 2003). It is referred to throughout the Handbook. References to probationary officers should be taken as referring to student police officers.

1. Understanding and Engaging with the Local Community

Learning to position oneself appropriately as a police officer in the local community. In this context local community includes temporary residential, Gypsy and Traveller groups.

In learning to position themselves appropriately as police officers in their particular communities Probationary Officers should:

A. Learning Through Experience

1.1 engage with real policing situations, incidents and events either directly or indirectly via observational or vicarious experiences.

1.2 be able to contextualise their knowledge by engaging with a range of methods and media for representing real policing situations, in addition to direct practical experience.

B. Social Awareness and Understanding

1.3   develop their awareness and understanding of the needs of society generally, and of its most vulnerable members in particular, and how they and the service as a whole can help to meet them.

1.4   develop their understanding of the ways in which the authority, power, leadership, attitudes and behaviour of police officers may either create or undermine public trust and confidence in the police service, and thereby either improve or diminish access to knowledge of the local community. And further, help counter the effects of fear of crime by positive display of such attitudes and behaviour.

1.5   come to appreciate the significance and value of gathering community information and intelligence (in addition to criminal intelligence) for effective police practice and the quality of the service provided.

1.6   understand how the changing nature of society and community living gives rise to changing forms of crime.

1.7   develop their understanding of the complexity of community life, including that of temporary residential, Gypsy and Traveller groups, and the calls for a multiplicity of roles and relationships that are not shaped only by the technical demands of operational policing.

1.8   develop their understanding of the community as a learning site and as the source of its own 'learning requirements' in addition to those which originate at the national level and from within the police organisation.

1.9   develop their awareness and understanding of the role of community support groups in mediating relationships between the police and community and the importance/significance of such groups for informing policing decisions.

1.10   deepen and extend their understanding of a range of emotional, psychological, cultural, religious and physical conditions associated with the effects of crime on a victim, and be able to devise appropriate police responses to these conditions in terms of both personal action and referral to external sources of support and advice.

C. Multi-Agency Co-operation

1.11   develop a critical understanding of the importance of co-operation and collaboration with other local services and agencies, including how those services and agencies perform their different roles and functions and work together for the benefit of the whole.

1.12   develop the ability to work effectively in multi-agency and community groups (public, private and voluntary) by focussing on the ways policing knowledge and skills can complement those of other agencies.

1.13   develop knowledge and sensitivity to the range of professional values and procedures in other agencies and how they overlap with or diverge from policing values and priorities.

1.14   become aware of key aspects of law and procedures that govern the work of others in the public, private and voluntary sectors so as to interact with them in an informed way.

D. Improving Social Cohesion

1.15   act in ways which proactively seek to improve and not undermine community cohesion, rather than reacting to situations that display diversity and social tension.

1.16   come to understand how policing practices can help to shape community cohesion rather than be shaped by its absence.

1.17   be able to create opportunities for conversation, discussion and collaboration with, and between, people from diverse groups, so as to understand how community cohesion can sustain difference.

1.18   develop the ability to communicate effectively and empathetically with people of all age groups and from different faiths, cultures and backgrounds and come to appreciate their potential as catalysts or resources for improving community cohesion.

1.19 develop the ability to conduct investigations without discrimination (for example on the grounds of age, gender, sexuality, race, health or disability) to the stage where they determine an appropriate course of action and can justify it as such, including being aware of relevant law and procedures that govern interactions in all circumstances.

2. Enforcing the Law and Following Police Procedures

In learning to use the law appropriately in the context of professional judgement and learning to follow appropriate police procedures Probationary Officers should:

2.1 become able to demonstrate a thorough knowledge of police powers, relevant legislation, statutory instruments and regulations in relation to particular situations and to discern how they may need to be applied differently with appropriate discretion in different contexts.

2.2 become capable of undertaking the initial stages of a criminal investigation, understanding the concept of 'evidence', its use in the judicial process, and the important implications for operational policing.

2.3 become able to recognise the sources and characteristics, and effectively deal with, hate crime.

2.4 develop the capacity to empathize with the thoughts and feelings of members of the public when applying police procedures in potentially sensitive situations, e.g. 'stop and search', public order situations.

2.5 develop their knowledge and understanding of law and procedures that are specific to investigating crimes against children and other vulnerable groups, and become capable of using it to investigate cases that involve inter-agency collaboration.

2.6 become able and disposed to implement the law without bias or prejudice and thereby to avoid discriminating among victims of crime when investigating or carrying out their primary roles or duties.

2.7 develop their ability to write reports and complete documentation in accordance with established protocols, procedures and systems.

2.8 develop the confidence to address dilemmas in practice where the law/procedures may be insufficient to effecting a satisfactory resolution.

3. Responding to Human and Social Diversity

Learning to act appropriately in responding to human and social diversity, including but not exclusive to race, in a) the community, and b) the police family.

In learning to respond to human and social diversity in their particular communities and within the service itself Probationary Officers should:

3.1 Deepen and elaborate their understanding of the diversity of lifestyles within the community and the police service, and of the factors which shape them.

3.2 become increasingly aware of, and equally responsive to, the diverse needs of different groups and sections within both the community and the police service, and refrain from 'problematising' particular groups.

3.3 become able to adapt investigative and incident-processing procedures where appropriate to meet the special language, social, cultural, political or personal characteristics of minority groups and individuals.

3.4 become able to distinguish between (a) acknowledgement of diversity (as a rational informed view) and (b) stereotyping of minority groups (as a personal disposition), and develop personal learning strategies to counter the latter and encourage the former.

3.5 develop their understanding of the nature, manifestations and causes of 'social prejudice', 'social discrimination', and 'racism'. Enact such understandings within the police role in ways that neither condones such acts nor provokes hostile confrontation leading to a breakdown of relationships within the local community or the police family.

3.6 develop an understanding that where personal prejudice may exist this need not lead to personal bias in practice. This implies the ability to detach their personal prejudices from their actions based on an overriding commitment to professional principles.

3.7 become able to identify and understand the factors operating in the organisational and community context of policing that enhance and diminish their capacity to effectively engage with all sections of the community.

3.8 develop interpersonal skills and dispositions towards others that facilitate safe, trusting and positive relationships between themselves and their colleagues and the public in complex and sensitive situations.

3.9 develop their understanding of how the police role responds to social change and the growth of complex national and cultural identities arising out of migration, dual citizenship and different religious affiliations.

3.10 learn how to calculate and assess the risks associated with police action in relations to themselves, the police organisation and plural communities.

3.11 learn how to construct productive working partnerships with local agencies when dealing with racist crime and incidents.

3.12 develop an understanding of how to support, and handle sensitively and effectively victims of all types, including the victims of crimes arising from prejudice.

3.13 develop an understanding of how to handle effectively, and in collaboration with appropriate local community and agency support, the interviewing of sensitive witnesses, paying attention to special demands of language, culture, politics and personal identity.

4. Positioning Oneself in the Role of a Police Officer Inside the Police Organisation

Learning to position oneself appropriately as a police officer in relation to the organisation and the occupational culture.

In learning to position themselves appropriately as police officers in relation to the organisation and the occupational culture probationary officers should:

4.1 become aware of national policing priorities and how these may be reflected in particular local circumstances. Where they enjoy discretion they should develop the ability to prioritise between national and local targets and to justify their judgement.

4.2 develop their awareness and understanding of policing as a cost-bearing activity and be able to demonstrate an awareness of best value in their practical decision-making and responses to policing situations and incidents.

4.3 develop the ability to identify and recognise stress in oneself and in others, and to balance their personal commitment to the police role with the preservation of their psychological and physical health to prescribed minimum standards.

4.4 become able to integrate the different components of professional learning into a holistic conception of police action eg knowledge of powers, law and procedures; understanding of individual behaviour and reaction; skills of communication, ICT, problem-solving, investigation, team-working; crime prevention techniques; using evidence to inform judgement.

4.5 develop their understanding of the distinctive leadership responsibilities of a police officer with respect to crime prevention and detection in a multi-agency system together with those policing skills and personal dispositions that enable them to enact these responsibilities.

4.6 develop an understanding of the distribution of responsibilities and skills across the policing family, of how to locate their own practice within that range and when it is appropriate to refer cases.

4.7 become aware of how police officers are perceived by community and collaborating agencies and be able to exercise the personal skills and dispositions to counter unproductive stereotyping of policing as a whole.

4.8   develop an understanding of where it may be legitimate and appropriate to challenge management decisions, culture and procedures.

5. Professional Standards and Ethical Conduct

Learning to live up to one's service ideals and standards.

In learning to live up to service ideals and standards Probationary Officers should:

5.1   become able and disposed to consistently demonstrate in practice their ability to uphold the police code of conduct and their duty of care to the public and to each other.

5.2   become able to maintain their responsibility to uphold the law, perform their police roles and duties, and follow procedures while working with the community and in multi-agency environments.

5.3   deepen their understanding of the meaning and significance of police ethics, become aware of the ways in which organisational and personal ethics can sometimes diverge, and begin to develop an appropriate policing ethic of their own consistent with the police code of conduct.

6. Learning to Learn and Creating a Basis for Career-long Learning

Learning to learn about one's role as a police officer in the community and the police organisation.

Learning to access, make sense of, and use appropriate information as a police officer.

In learning to learn Probationary Officers should:

6.1   develop the ability to reflect about policing problems and to self-monitor and improve the quality of their actions in relation to them on a regular basis in the light of service values, using formal and informal feed-back from colleagues, supervisors and peers, and members of the public.

6.2   be evolving a personal learning agenda that enables them to seek out opportunities to develop their skills, knowledge and experience, both in the context of their initial training and throughout their careers.

6.3   develop their ability to identify their learning or support needs including when in stressful situations or predicaments.

6.4   know how to request and use guidance, help or support from supervisory, peer, social or spiritual sources as an integral part of their continuing professional development process.

6.5   become aware of the limits of formal instruction for their professional learning, and come to understand that their learning needs to emanate from a range of sources, people and contexts.

6.6   be able to assess their current levels of capability and skills and their learning needs generally, and the relationship of these to the NOS/NCF frameworks.

6.7   actively contribute to a workplace environment where learning is valued and supported.

6.8   seek out and respond to learning opportunities throughout their careers in ways that are commensurate with their role or aspirations and the needs of their organisation.

6.9   develop their ability and motivation to use ICT for learning, communication and information more effectively.

7. Qualities of Professional Judgement and Decision-Making

In learning to cultivate capacities for judgement and decision-making Probationary Officers should:

7.1   develop the ability to integrate all elements of their training—including relevant legal procedural knowledge, skills of communication, skills of detection, investigation and apprehension, using information and communication technology

(ICT), problem solving, team working, crime reduction—into a form of practice which enhances the quality of professional judgement and decision-making.

7.2   demonstrate qualities of professional judgement and decision-making in upholding their responsibilities to the law when working in situations that require collaboration with other agencies.

7.3   exercise sufficient rigour and diligence (eg in gathering evidence and taking witness statements) during the conduct of an investigation to achieve an appropriate and defensible course of action based on sound professional judgement and decision-making.

7.4   become aware of how their authority is perceived, how it relates to other forms of authority in the police family and know how to use it effectively.

7.5   develop the ability to locate individual incidents in a context of recurring patterns.

1.7   Answers to Tasks

TASK 1

Police forces often publish a glossary of terms that they use in their documentation which they make available under the Freedom of Information Act 2000. An example is Cheshire Constabulary whose glossary may be found at <http://www.cheshire.police.uk/showcontent.php ?pageid=264> (follow the links on the right hand side of the page).

TASK 2

Police organizations sometimes describe their history on their websites (for example, the extensive MPS site at <http://www.met.police.uk/history/>). Many also have museums (for example, the Essex Police museum at Police HQ in Chelmsford) and some forces may also have a comprehensive and published written history (for example Ingleton, 2002).

TASK 3

You should have found that the three barriers to communication identified were:

a) environmental (eg noise, lack of privacy),

b) personal (eg language differences, gender differences, ethnic differences, age differences, religious beliefs, health and wellbeing of the individuals involved, literacy levels, personal experiences etc),

c) social (eg violent and abusive situations).

<http://www.skillsforjustice.com/websitefiles/NOS_POLICE06_AB1.doc>

2 | How to Use the Handbook

2.1   Chapter Briefing

In this chapter we provide advice about how to use the Handbook. We are familiar with the wide range of experiences that new entrants bring to the police service and the Handbook has been designed and written to be both accessible and of value to a wide range of readers.

2.1.1   Aim of the Chapter

This aim of this chapter is to provide you with guidance on how to use the Handbook, how it relates to your training, the NOS, the PAC and the Learning Requirement, and the importance of further reading.

This chapter will enable you to:

- understand how the Handbook has been set out;
- appreciate the reasons for including tasks for you to undertake;
- see the links between the Handbook, the IPLDP curriculum, the NOS, the PAC, and the Learning Requirement;
- understand the importance of referring to local force policy when appropriate;
- follow our approach to referencing and how we quote from legislation, circulars, and codes;
- appreciate the necessity and benefits of undertaking further reading.

2.2   Survival First

When you joined the police service as a student police officer you probably did so with the intention of 'walking the walk' and not 'talking the talk'. Naturally you would prefer to be practising your profession rather than simply learning about it, particularly if you have spent the last two or three years studying at college or university or have waited some time to join the police. However, many would see it is as important that you first earn the right to exercise your powers and that you do so with professional judgement and with due respect to the rights and diversity of the citizens of the United Kingdom. Your training, and this Handbook, are designed to help you do just that.

The Handbook is designed as a form of survival guide to assist you in qualifying as a police officer. For example, in order to help you learn, we have omitted some of the more detailed aspects of the law and police procedure and instead provided a simplified version. Yet even this can look pretty daunting in places. This is based upon our experience of teaching trainee police officers. Of course, this does not mean that the detail is not important; it is just that learning is usually easier when moving from the simple to the complex, so we start you off with the simple. In the case of the law, the full complexity will normally be introduced and explained to you by your police tutors and trainers using a variety of teaching and learning methods. However, you may be expected to learn new material for yourself, and if this is so then you are likely to find Chapter 4 particularly useful. You will also find the detail of legislation covered in other publications and sources including:

- the original legislation itself. Most recent legislation is now available from the government website <http://www.opsi.gov.uk/legislation/index.htm>. However, note that it can be confusing when attempting to understand original legislation as it may have been subject to amendment and changed by subsequent legislation. This is not always obvious when reading the original. For example, the definition of a religiously aggravated offence (see section 8.10) to be found in the Crime and Disorder Act 1998 was subsequently added to by the Anti-terrorism, Crime and Society Act of 2002. The 2002 legislation added a new subsection 28(5) to the four original subsections of the 1998 legislation. The new government website at <http://www.statutelaw.gov.uk/Home.aspx> provides 'updated' versions of original legislation;
- publications such as Butterworth's Police Law and the Blackstone's publications (notably the Police Operational Handbook and the annual Police Manuals);
- the NCALT learning portal for the police service at <http://www.ncalt.com>;
- the PNLD website at <http://www.pnld.co.uk/pnld/welcome.asp>;
- legal guidance from the CPS at <http://www.cps.gov.uk/legal/index.html>;
- the NPIA digests at <http://www.npia.police.uk/digest>;
- your own police force resources (for example, the force intranet).

TASK 1

Use the internet to identify the definition of the 'designated area' in the law governing demonstrations in the vicinity of Parliament. It is defined within the Serious Organised Crime and Police Act 2005.

The content of the Handbook is arranged to reflect this survivalist approach. The order of chapters, particularly from Chapter 8 onwards, reflects the usual order of police training and Supervised Patrol as practised by many forces. For example, your first Supervised Patrol might well include observing a response to a report of shoplifting. This requires a basic understanding of the crime of theft and police powers of arrest. These are covered in Chapters 9 and 11. You also require certain skills in almost every policing situation, notably forensic awareness, communication skills, and a respect for diversity. These are addressed at an introductory level from Chapter 7 onwards. For this and other reasons you may find that you use the Handbook in a non-linear way and do not read it in the conventional fashion from beginning to end. In this respect the index at the end of the Handbook may be your best guide.

Finally, the style of the Handbook represents a judgement concerning the best ways of introducing and describing a subject area. For many aspects of the law (for example, as covered in Chapters 8 to 11 inclusive) we have adopted a bite-size approach with the legislation and police practice. We have simplified and condensed the topics into relatively short sections of text and diagrams dealing with that subject and that subject alone. This would seem to suit the subject matter and the need for you, on many occasions, to assimilate and be able to reproduce the facts. In other parts of the book we have adopted a more holistic approach—for example to interviewing, covered in Chapter 12. This reflects the reality that learning the skills of interviewing involves more than adherence to codes and legislation. You will also need, for example, to appreciate the structure an interview can take, the forms of communication used (particularly for questioning), and the role of the interview within a wider criminal investigation.

2.3 Tasks

In many chapters you are asked to undertake tasks, which occur within the sections of each chapter rather than, as is more traditional, at the end of the whole chapter. In some cases these tasks will also be useful to you as stimulus material for your SOLAP or Learning Diary. Answers are provided at the end of each chapter.

In many cases the tasks also provide further ideas for you to explore or point you in the direction of additional reading and study to undertake. For this reason it is helpful to read the answers to the tasks even though you may already be confident that you have a clear understanding of the answer to a question.

2.4 Links with the IPLDP

A typical pattern of training for student police officers in their probationary period is described in Chapter 3. Police forces have some flexibility and can vary these patterns in order to reflect local need and their own particular circumstances (for example, they may be in partnership with a local FE College or University and this might affect the pattern of delivery). However, in all cases, forces are required to be 'IPLDP-compliant'—that is, to demonstrate how their curriculum delivers the learning outcomes of the modules of the IPLDP (Home Office, 2005b).

There are three clusters of modules in the IPLDP (Home Office, 2005f).

The **Induction modules** are referred to as the IND modules and there are eleven of them. Induction would seem to suggest that these modules are all covered in the first few weeks of service. Although partly the case (for example, you are likely to undertake IND 9: to 'Administer First Aid' early on) this is not wholly true. In some cases these modules are introduced during the induction process but then developed and revisited during the remainder of your training. An example of this is IND 10. to 'use police actions in a fair and justified way'.

This Handbook covers most, but not all, of the content of the IND modules. Some aspects of your training, such as First Aid, are more suited to specialist publications and others such as IND 8: the 'Operation of information technology systems' are very dependent on individual force policy and equipment. In these cases we provide an overview of the kind of training you are likely to receive rather than describing the detail. Similarly, a subject such as the multicultural nature of modern Britain and the diverse communities that you will police, is, we would wish to argue, better studied using textbooks or other learning material specifically devoted to this task rather than in sections of this Handbook or even pages from your Centrex notes.

The **Operational modules** are referred to as the OP modules and there are nine of them. As you have probably guessed, these nine modules are concerned with the routine but vital operational tasks of the police officer, often (but not exclusively) those most closely associated with patrol. For example, OP 5 is concerned with your ability to 'search individuals and premises'. This Handbook covers, at an introductory level, the knowledge required for **most** of the OP modules.

The **Legislation, Policy, and Guidelines modules** of the IPLDP are referred to as the LPG modules and there are three of them. These are the modules that are most closely linked with the acquisition of knowledge of the law, policy, and procedures that we often associate with initial policing. This Handbook provides you with much of the basic knowledge required for

LPG 1 and LPG 2. Most of the aspects of LPG 1 and LPG 2 that we do not cover are related to local force policy and therefore inappropriate for a general textbook of this kind.

Curriculum areas of LPG 1 and 2 not covered	
LPG 1.2(1) Standard of operating procedures for dealing with cannabis	See local force policy
LPG 1.2(1) Control measures and sources of assistance	See local force policy
LPG 1.3(1) Their role in addressing anti-social behaviour within the community	See local force policy
LPG 1.3(1) Individual Support Orders	Not covered
LPG 1.3(1) Acceptable Behaviour Contracts	Not covered
LPG 1.3(1) Parenting Contracts	Not covered
LPG 1.3(1) Parenting Orders	Not covered
LPG 1.3 (1) Penalty Notice for Night Noise	Not covered
LPG 1.3 (1) Crack House Closure Powers	Not covered
LPG 1.3 (1) Anti-social behaviour and the TOGETHER campaign	Not covered
LPG 1.3(2) Community safety units	See local force policy
LPG 1.3(7) Meeting victims' needs	See local force policy
LPG 1.3(11) Solvent abuse	Not covered
LPG 1.3(12) Victim support	See local force policy
LPG 1.3(13) Youth offending teams	See local force policy
LPG 1.3(21) Welfare (eg positional asphyxia)	Part of force staff safety training
LPG1.3 (23) Firearms and Support	See local force policy
LPG1.3 (23) Priorities in Relation to Spontaneous Incidents	See local force policy
LPG1.3 (23) Responsibilities in Relation to Spontaneous Incidents	See local force policy
LPG 1.4(1) Transportation of detained persons	See local force policy
LPG 1.4(3) Methods of briefing/de-briefing	Not covered
LPG 1.4(3) Crime reporting	See local force policy
LPG 1.4(6) Stopping lost or stolen vehicles (Officer Safety Training (OST) issues)	Part of staff safety training
LPG 1.4(7) Use of personal radios	See local force policy
LPG 1.4(7) PNC source input documents	See local force policy
LPG 1.4(9) Welfare matters (facilities and accountability)	See local force policy
LPG 1.4(14) Police personnel procedures	See local force policy
LPG 1.5(2) Police action at civil disputes	Not covered
LPG 1.5(3) Civil trespass	See local force policy
LPG 1.5(5) Illness in the street	Part of force first aid training
LPG 1.5(6) Lost and found property	Local force policy
LPG 1.5(8) The social effects of alcohol	Not covered
LPG 1.7 (3) Explain the SARA model and its application	Not covered
LPG 1.7 (3) Explain the PAT model and its application	Not covered
LPG 1.7(4) Completion of street ID procedures documentation	See local force policy
LPG 1.7(15) Personal descriptions	Not covered
LPG 1.7(18) Reporting lost or stolen vehicles	See local force policy

LPG 1.8(1) Collision scene management	See local force policy
LPG 2.1(3) Section 5 of the Sexual Offences Act 2003—Rape of a child under 13 years	Not covered—detail of sexual offences legislation
LPG 2.1(3) Section 6 of the Sexual Offences Act 2003—Assault of a child under 13 by penetration	Not covered—detail of sexual offences legislation
LPG 2.1(3) Section 8 of the Sexual Offences Act 2003—Causing or inciting a child under 13 to engage in sexual activity	Not covered—detail of sexual offences legislation
LPG 2.1(3) Section 10 of the Sexual Offences Act 2003—Causing or inciting a child to engage in sexual activity	Not covered—detail of sexual offences legislation
LPG 2.1(3) Section 11 of the Sexual Offences Act 2003—Engaging in sexual activity in the presence of a child	Not covered—detail of sexual offences legislation
LPG 2.1(3) Section 12 of the Sexual Offences Act 2003—Causing a child to watch a sexual act	Not covered—detail of sexual offences legislation
LPG 2.1(3) Section 63 of the Sexual Offences Act 2003—Trespass with intent to commit a sexual offence	Not covered—detail of sexual offences legislation
LPG 2.1(3) Section 69 of the Sexual Offences Act 2003—Intercourse with an animal	Not covered—detail of sexual offences legislation
LPG 2.1(3) Section 70 of the Sexual Offences Act 2003—Sexual penetration of a corpse	Not covered—detail of sexual offences legislation
LPG 2.1(3) Section 71 of the Sexual Offences Act 2003—Sexual activity in a public lavatory	Not covered—detail of sexual offences legislation
LPG 2.3 (1) Early Evidence Kits	See local force policy
LPG 2.3 (1) Rape Trauma Syndrome	Not covered
LPG 2.3 (1) Havens/Safe Houses	See local force policy

We do not cover all the content of the LPG 0 module; we cover only those areas we regard as essential for the student police officer, despite the fact that they are designated as optional under the IPLDP.

Note that a new IPLDP curriculum is expected during the second half of 2007 and hence there may be changes in the content of the modules.

2.5 Links with the NOS, the PAC, and the Learning Requirement

The Handbook is linked throughout to the National Occupational Standards for initial policing (the NOS) and the Police Action Checklist (the PAC). You will find explicit reference to them at the beginning of many chapters and sometimes within the text itself. The underlying knowledge requirements of a number of headings of the PAC (a key requirement of Independent Patrol) are also covered. However, bear in mind that both the NOS and the PAC are concerned with performance and competence, and although an understanding of the theory is a necessary condition, it is not by itself sufficient for their attainment. The NOS and PAC are examined in more detail in Chapter 3.

The Learning Requirement for student police officers (as developed by Professors John Elliott, Saville Kushner, and others) is also referenced on a number of occasions.

The Learning Requirement is based around seven core learning goals (Elliott et al, 2003):

1. Understanding and engaging with the community.
2. Enforcing the law and following police procedures.
3. Responding to human and social diversity.

4. Positioning oneself in the role of a police officer inside the police organization.
5. Professional standards and ethical conduct.
6. Learning to learn and creating a base for career-long learning.
7. Qualities of professional judgement and decision-making.

A summary of the Learning Requirement is given in Chapter 1.

2.6   Local Force Policy

Each of the forty-three Home Office police forces in England and Wales has its own local policies, often to be found on the organization's intranet and usually expressed as 'Force Orders', 'Standard Operating Procedures (SOP)', 'Policies' and likewise. This Handbook should always be read in conjunction with local force policies, particularly when the Handbook describes procedures such as writing a statement or making a pocket notebook entry.

Your force may also wish you to learn verbatim definitions whilst you are a student police officer. These definitions are often concerned with the law, for example the definition of what constitutes theft. In this case we advise you to use the definitions given to you by your force rather than those reproduced in this Handbook or, indeed, in other textbooks. This is because there is sometimes a slight variation between forces in definitions of the same terms—for example, whether 'he' in the original Act (a common occurrence) is replaced with 'he/she' or 'they' in the definition you are given to learn, or is left in its original form.

2.7   References and Further Reading

Referencing is a standard academic system for producing evidence for your arguments or for directing the reader towards further information. We have deliberately kept the volume of referencing in this Handbook to a minimum, and largely restricted referencing to where it is necessary to indicate to you the sources of our ideas and information. This is a common courtesy to those authors whose work we have utilized. It is also respect for the intellectual property rights of others. The main reason for minimizing the number of references is to try and make the Handbook more accessible to a wider range of readers; the flow is not disturbed by frequent references to other material. This is not to undermine the importance of referencing—far from it. In fact you may well be required to reference your own work, particularly if your training is linked with a higher education foundation degree.

We would also encourage you to undertake further reading (and on some occasions indicate so in the body of the Handbook or in the answers to tasks). As explained in section 2.2 of this chapter, the Handbook is very much a survival guide and you will find more detail and further explanation in many other textbooks, in your NPIA (Centrex) or force notes, and via the NCALT and other websites. A small technical point—many internet sites will use the Adobe Acrobat format for documents and written reports (particularly the Home Office), so ensure that you have the software available to view the pdf formats (it is free and is also built in to later versions of MS Internet Explorer).

2.8   Extracts from Legislation, Circulars, and Codes

Throughout the Handbook there are numerous extracts from primary legislation or Codes—often from Acts of Parliament. These are quoted as the original but sometimes with minor changes. Often an explanation in everyday language is also given, normally in a text box to the right of the original legislation. Quotations are signified by the use of a different font while explanations and comments are in ordinary text, like this:

| if when not at [his/her] place of abode. | The term place of abode means the place or site where someone lives. It normally includes the garage and garden of a house and should be given its normal meaning, but it will be a question of fact for the court to decide. If a homeless person sleeps in his or her car, the car counts as an abode while he/she is asleep. However, when the same car is being driven by the same person, it is not considered as a place of abode for the purposes of the offence of going equipped (see *R v Bundy* 1977). |

When changes have been made this is usually because legislation tends to use the personal pronoun 'he' to cover also 'he or she'. (There are some circumstances, however, particularly in legislation that covers sexual offences, when 'he' really does just mean 'he'.) We have changed 'he' to 'he/she' 'him' to 'him/her', etc. A change of this kind can also have follow-on effects in the remainder of the sentence. We have also occasionally changed a word so that a sentence makes more sense when quoted alone. Minor changes to the wording of legislation or codes in the Handbook are signified by the use of square brackets as in the following example. The original, from s 74 of the Sexual Offences Act 2003 states that:

> For the purposes of this Part, a person consents if he agrees by choice, and has the freedom and capacity to make that choice.

Our revised version reads:

> For the purposes of this [offence], a person consents if [he/she] agrees by choice, and has the freedom and capacity to make that choice.

As you can see in this example the changes made to the wording of the original legislation were as follows:

- Part was changed to [offence];
- he was changed to [he/she].

2.9 Answer to Task 1

The Serious Organised Crime and Police Act (SOCPA) 2005 can be located at <http://www.opsi.gov.uk/ACTS/acts2005/20050015.htm>. Demonstrations in the vicinity of Parliament are dealt with in Part 4 of the Act, 'Public Order and Conduct In Public Places etc.' and in ss 132 to 138 inclusive. You should find a hypertext link to s 132. Subsection (7) of s 132 explains that designated area means 'the area specified in an order under section 138'. Hence we now need to look at s 138 which states, in effect, that it is the responsibility of the Secretary of State to specify the area but that 'no point in the area so specified may be more than one kilometre in a straight line from the point nearest to it in Parliament Square'. This needs some thinking about. The SOCPA sets the limits to the maximum area that the Secretary of State can specify (essentially a buffer zone, 1 km wide, around the edge of Parliament Square) but allows some flexibility within this. Normally in these kinds of circumstances the Secretary of State will issue a Statutory Instrument which provides the detail of the decisions made. (The use of Statutory Instruments enables changes to be made on a frequent basis if required without having to make adjustments to the Act itself. See section 5.11 of this Handbook.) Sure enough, a little detective work locates Statutory Instrument 2005 No 1537, the Serious Organised Crime and Police Act 2005 (Designated Area) Order 2005 at <http://www.opsi.gov.uk/si/si2005/20051537.htm> which informs us that the designated area from 1 July 2005 was:

> ...the area bounded by an imaginary line starting at the point where Hungerford Bridge crosses Victoria Embankment, continuing along Hungerford Bridge to the point where it crosses Belvedere Road, rightwards along Belvedere Road as far as Chicheley Street...

and so on.

3 Qualifying as a Police Officer

3.1 Chapter Briefing

This chapter examines the process of qualification as a police officer. We use the word qualification in its wider sense of having the knowledge and skills to undertake professional responsibilities and to exercise judgement and discretion.

3.1.1 Aim of the Chapter

The aim of this chapter is to assist in your understanding of the route map from student police officer to full Confirmation as a police officer. Your Confirmation will normally be at the end of two years' probationary service.

This chapter will enable you to:

- reflect on your reasons for joining the police service and why these reasons are important;
- observe a typical pattern of training in the first two years of service;
- appreciate the professional and legal context to training whilst on probation;
- appreciate the links between the NOS, the PAC, Independent Patrol, and the stages of qualification;
- develop the underpinning knowledge required for a number of NOS elements, entries for your Learning Diary Phase 1 and a CAR of your SOLAP.

3.1.2 National Occupational Standards

This chapter will provide you with the knowledge required to demonstrate the following NOS elements, either within the first few months of service or during the remaining period of probation:

> **National Occupational Standards Element**
>
> AE1.1 Maintain and develop your own knowledge, skills and competence.

You should refer to Chapter 6 for general information and advice concerning the NOS elements.

3.1.3 IPLDP Induction Modules

This chapter will provide you with resources to support the following induction modules of the IPLDP:

> IND 1 Underpinning ethics/values of the police service.
>
> IND 3 Develop one's own knowledge and practice.

3.1.4 SOLAP

The contents of this chapter are relevant to the knowledge evidence requirements of CAR 4C1.

3.1.5 Learning Diary Phases

The contents of this chapter may provide you with stimulus material for completion of your Learning Diary (Phase 1) and the following headings in particular:

- Introduction to the Organisation;
- IPLDP.

3.2 Why Did You Join the Police?

This may seem an obvious question but spend a few moments thinking about this as Task 1.

> **TASK 1**
>
> List your reasons for joining the police service. If possible, put these into some kind of order with the most important reason first.

You were obviously motivated to join the police. A common way of thinking about motivation is to subdivide it into **extrinsic** and **intrinsic** motivation (although the distinction is not always clear cut). As the phrase suggests, extrinsic motivation comes from without and involves pull factors on our behaviour and actions. Examples of extrinsic motives for joining the police might include:

- a good wage (particularly in terms of the initial salary, one of the largest in the public sector);
- ample career opportunities, both in terms of rank and role;
- the prospect of early retirement (compared with most occupations) and a good pension.

Intrinsic factors on the other hand come from within and can be thought of as push factors. Examples of intrinsic motives for joining the police might include:

- the desire to do something to improve our society (for example, to protect the weak and the vulnerable);
- to have an interesting and exciting working life;
- to feel more important and to exercise power over others.

(We pass no value judgement on these.)

Extrinsic motivation, although a powerful factor, is probably not enough to guarantee your successful qualification as a police officer. Indeed, there is a debate in academic circles on whether tangible rewards that increase external motivation actually have a reverse effect of undermining intrinsic motivation.

TASK 2

Revisit your list in Task 1 and try to reclassify your reasons as either extrinsic or intrinsic (not always easy!).

Your intrinsic motivation for joining the police might have to sustain you through the first difficult months of training until the extrinsic motivation reasons begin to deliver. Joining the police will mean many changes in your working and personal circumstances and the challenge of juggling training with the rest of your life, possible family commitments, and travel can prove very demanding. Remember, though it might seem obvious, you do not suddenly become a different person the moment you join the police.

3.3   Training

In Chapter 4 we will look in more detail at how the personal and educational history you bring with you can affect your learning as a student police officer. It is obvious that no student police officer is a blank canvas on which their trainers and assessors are able to paint the idealized picture of a perfect modern day police officer. For example, the average age of entry to a police force in the UK is in the mid twenties. It is likely therefore that student police officers bring with them a significant personal and employment history, which is not abandoned the moment they join.

It may be a cliché, but undoubtedly policing is not just any other job. When you become a student police officer profound changes occur which inevitably affect your relationships with family and friends. For example, studies have shown that, in western Europe, about one-third of people have used cannabis on at least one occasion. Many young people have also downloaded copyrighted music from the internet (usually in the form of mp3 files), which is, like illegal cannabis use, an offence. It is highly likely therefore that within any particular group of student police officers there will be those who have tried cannabis, or illegally downloaded copyrighted music, or committed some other relatively minor offence which has not been detected or prosecuted. You may choose, like a number of politicians, not to reveal whether you have smoked a cannabis joint, or taken Ecstasy or not. However, if you have, then this behaviour is certainly known to at least some of those around you, including colleagues, family, and friends. In all likelihood, those with whom the student police officer may have shared illegally downloaded music are still around and may indeed still feature amongst his/her circle of friends. How the student officer now responds may take a number of forms:

- to change his/her circle of friends;
- if questioned, to diplomatically explain that his/her own personal behaviour, and expectations of others, has changed as a result of joining the police;
- to continue the behaviour, even though it is against the law; or
- to avoid thinking about the issue.

There is of course a multitude of other solutions. You will no doubt explore your own personal solution to this—after all, you enter the police service with approximately one-third of your life behind you and with all the baggage this brings.

However, it is vital for you to establish and maintain a moral authority (see Chapter 5). This might sound a rather outmoded way of viewing police officers but it remains an important source of your legitimacy (see Chapter 5) in terms of the exercise of powers not available to the rest of society. Establishing and maintaining your moral authority is not the same as claiming that you are better than the rest of society or that you have some special claim on judging what is right or wrong. Rather, it is an acknowledgement of the responsibility of the privileged position that you are placed in and is part, some would argue, of the social contract between the police and the communities they serve.

3.3.1 Pattern of Training

The IPLDP has proposed that there should be **four phases to the initial training of police officers**, with the following suggested content and activities (Home Office, 2004c):

Phase	Typical Activities
Phase 1—Induction	• Introduction to your police force • Practical and organizational needs, eg uniform, Federation, etc • Learning about IPLDP, ethics, and diversity • Undertaking First Aid and Officer Safety Training (eg self-protection) • Introduction to the use of technology, eg radio, PNC, etc • Job Related Fitness Test
Phase 2—Community Safety and Partnerships	• Receiving a crime and disorder 'package' • Community safety • Undertaking a community engagement
Phase 3—Supervised Patrol	• Learning legislation, policies, and guidelines • Operating the 'Crime Investigation Model' • Undertaking Supervised Patrol
Phase 4—Independent Patrol	• Learning legislation, policies, and guidelines • Developing police practice (particularly local practice) • Undertaking Independent Patrol

However, the exact pattern of training will vary from force to force, (for example when you undertake your 'Community Engagement', your 'Personal Safety Training', your 'Supervised Patrol', or your first introduction to the law). The following diagram, however, describes a *typical* arrangement:

Time line	Stage	IPLDP Phases	Typical duration	Activities	Milestones
Weeks 1–2	Induction	1	2 weeks	Learning about the organization, Health & Safety, Personal Safety Training, First Aid, etc.	Undertaking the Job Related Fitness Test. Completion of first Learning Diary entries. **Attestation**
Week 3	Community Engagement	2	1 week	Placement with a community group.	Completion of first SOLAP entry.
Week 4	Area familiarization	1	1 week	The work of a BCU.	Completion of more Learning Diary and SOLAP entries.
Weeks 5–10	Taught courses	1 and 3	6 weeks	Legislation, procedures, and other subjects.	Successful completion of assessments.
Weeks 11–12	Supervised Patrol	3	2 weeks	Coaching & assessment.	Beginning **Supervised Patrol**. Completion of some NOS.
Weeks 13–18	Taught courses	1 and 3	6 weeks	Legislation, procedures and other subjects.	Successful completion of assessments.

Time line	Stage	IPLDP Phases	Typical duration	Activities	Milestones
Weeks 19–21	Supervised Patrol	3	3 weeks	Coaching & assessment.	Completion of some NOS.
Weeks 22–27	Taught courses	4	6 weeks	Legislation, procedures and other subjects.	Successful completion of assessments.
Week 28	Supervised Investigation	3	1 week	Coaching & assessment.	Completion of some NOS.
Weeks 29–32	Taught courses	4	4 weeks	Legislation, procedures and other subjects.	Successful completion of assessments. Completion of NOS units relevant to PAC. Satisfactory completion of PAC. Satisfactory Learning Development Review. **Independent Patrol status**
Weeks 33–35	Supervised Patrol and Supervised Investigation	3	3 weeks	Coaching & assessment.	**Beginning Independent Patrol**. Completion of some NOS.
Weeks 36–69	Independent Patrol	4	34 weeks	Patrol and or investigation. Assessment against NOS units. Taught courses.	Completion of some NOS.
Week 70	Independent Patrol	4	Part of 1 week	Meeting with supervisor.	Second Learning Development Review.
Weeks 71–104	Independent Patrol	4	34 weeks	Patrol and/or investigation. Assessment against NOS units.	Completion of remaining NOS units. Completion of SOLAP. Final Learning Development Review. **Confirmation**

Note that for Supervised Patrol, Independent Patrol, and Confirmation there are significant variations between forces. For example, in some forces Supervised Patrol occurs earlier than we suggest above, and may also occur more frequently and contain a greater coaching dimension. Similarly, Attestation and Independent Patrol may happen earlier or later than in this typical model. More profound differences include the decision by some forces to concentrate most of the taught elements of training in the first fifty-two weeks. You should perhaps also note that a number of the forces that adopted the IPLDP at an earlier pilot stage are now changing their existing pattern of training to meet the new requirements of the four phases.

Forces often elect to organize their training in terms of a series of 'courses' or 'modules' that deliver the requirements of the IPLDP. For example, Thames Valley Police structures its training in the following way:

A typical structure for training (Thames Valley Police)

Students undertake 14 modules of study. The modules are divided across four distinct phases: Induction, Community, Basic Police Skills (including three weeks of programmed leave), and Independent Patrol Skills (including one week of programmed leave).

1st Year	2nd Year
Induction	Sexual crimes and vulnerable witnesses
Community placement	(Thames Valley Police, 2006)
Introduction to policing	Standard Driving Course
Patrol	Crime
Theft	PACE
Burglary	Warrants
Public safety	
Policing of roads	
Neighbourhood policing	

TASK 3

Establish the pattern of training in your force and how it relates to IPLDP Phases 1 to 4 inclusive.

3.4 Probationary Period

The probationary period refers to the time that you are technically under or in probation; that is, you are not a confirmed constable, you are still undertaking training and you are subject to the regulations that apply to probationers (see section 3.8). The normal probationary period for full-time student police officers is two years. There are very few student police officers undertaking training on a part-time basis; this option is rarely available. Where they exist, part-time student police officers have an extended probationary period calculated according to Annex C of the Police Regulations 2003. For example, training at half the full-time rate will take twice as long.

As with many aspects of initial training, the length of the probationary period may soon change. It is expected that accredited prior learning (APL) or prior experiential learning (APEL) will shorten the length of training and the probationary period for some student police officers. This may be particularly important for PCSOs and special constables who join in future years, although foreshortened training through APL and APEL might also be open to others.

3.5 Independent Patrol

Attaining the right to undertake Independent Patrol is a key milestone in your development as a student police officer. It means that, although your training is far from over, you can undertake many police functions associated with fully qualified (Confirmed) police officers without the need for constant supervision. Independent Patrol normally occurs after about week thirty in training, although this does vary significantly from force to force (from about twenty-eight weeks in some forces to a proposed thirty-seven in others). As with many aspects of initial police training, the timing of Independent Patrol is currently under discussion. The traditional approach was simply to say that it would, all other criteria being satisfied, happen on a certain week. This makes less sense in an era of competence-based occupational standards.

Your suitability for Independent Patrol is assessed against various criteria, including the Police Action Checklist (the PAC, see section 6.8 below) and normally after a Learning Development Review (see Chapter 6). As you would expect, the principles involved are used as an attempt to ensure that you are competent and safe and that you hold the appropriate values and behaviour to undertake Independent Patrol (for example, in the seven core behavioural areas of respect for race and diversity, team working, community and customer focus, effective communication, problem solving, personal responsibility, and resilience). Although the PAC is a key component in this, it is important to realize that the PAC is described by the IPLDP as only one trigger for Independent Patrol and does not automatically lead to it. The PAC is described in more detail in Chapter 6 and consists of 10 main headings:

The Police Action Checklist headings

1. Safety First
2. Information Management
3. Patrol
4. Search
5. Investigation
6. Disposal
7. Custody Officer Procedures
8. Finalise Investigations
9. Road Policing
10. Property

You will receive confirmation of competence from your Professional Development Unit (PDU) supervisor/assessor against the PAC during phases 1, 2, and 3 of your training (using the IPLDP terminology). In addition some forces may also expect the acquisition of advanced driving skills before you are granted Independent Patrol status.

Finally, note that you will probably receive a pay rise when you achieve Independent Patrol status!

3.6 Confirmation

After two years (104 weeks) you should expect to be deemed 'fit for confirmation of appointment'. That is, you've made it! In our view, the criteria for Confirmation under the IPLDP are currently less than clear and so you should look towards your own employer for a definitive statement of what is required. However, some or all of the following are likely to be involved:

- the attainment of all, or a subset of, the NOS for initial police training (see section 3.9 and Chapter 6);
- the attainment of the core responsibilities of a student police officer (see section 6.3);
- the satisfactory completion of the SOLAP (see section 6.6);
- the satisfactory completion of the PAC (see section 6.8);
- a 'successful' final Learning Development Review;
- a minimum academic attainment;
- other requirements such as a level of fitness (the Job Related Fitness Test), ability to administer first aid, and being able to drive a car to a certain standard.

(Note that these requirements are not mutually exclusive but instead interrelate and overlap. For example, the SOLAP is likely to at least cross-reference the PAC, the Learning Development Review will involve the seven core behavioural areas, and so on. The list could also be summarized in IPLDP language as the successful completion of Phases 1 to 4 inclusive.)

This Confirmation may also be linked to the attainment of a qualification, such as an NVQ Level 3 or 4 or a foundation degree. The Government have declared their intention that there will be a national minimum qualification (NMQ) for all successful student police officers who reach Confirmation (see section 3.10). The IPLDP Central Authority has decided that the NMQ shall be NVQ Levels 3 and 4 in Policing.

3.7 Assessment

In our view assessment is currently one of the most confused and ambiguous aspects of the IPLDP. For this reason you are strongly advised to read carefully the information your force provides about assessment. Ask questions about the assessment strategies and criteria if you are unclear. A key question to ask is *'How do I qualify for confirmation as a police officer'*? Do not expect a simple answer.

In essence you may be assessed in the following ways:

Assessment focus	How likely is it to happen?
Against the 22 NOS, or a subset of them, (see section 3.9 and Chapter 6).	Almost certain.
Against the PAC headings (see Chapter 6).	Almost certain.
Grading in your Learning Development Review against skills and the core behavioural areas (see Chapter 7).	Likely; grades used may be 'exceptional', 'competent', or 'not yet displayed'.
Your practical skills such as Officer Safety and advanced driving and your physical fitness (a follow up to the Job Related Fitness Test undertaken during induction).	Very likely although the detail will vary.
Satisfactory completion of the SOLAP against certain criteria.	A completion requirement is very likely, but the standard of work required may vary.
Against some other criteria, linked with knowledge attainment.	Not certain. If you are tested in this way, the assessment instruments used are likely to include MCQs (multiple choice questions), unseen examinations, or assignments. You need to ask your trainers the following questions: • Is there a pass mark? • What is the pass mark? • What happens if I don't pass?

Whatever the forms of assessment it is important that you are clear on **what** is being formally assessed. For example, there are over 250 learning outcomes in the IPLDP Induction Modules alone and the LPG 1 module has over seventy-five!

3.8   What Can Go Wrong?

We have no wish to be negative, but, things **can** sometimes go wrong.

3.8.1   Could I Get Sacked?

At the outset it is important to note that most student police officers, as with qualified police officers, are not employees in the usual sense of the term. Technically they are 'holders of public office' (note, however, some even more complicated variations, such as British Transport Police). This means that the conditions of employment for student police officers are particularly complex. In terms of aspects such as dismissal (officially called dispensing with your services) and resignation (called retirement), the main source of definitive information is the Police Regulations 2003, Statutory Instrument No 527 (see section 5.11 for an explanation of the Statutory Instrument and the task in Chapter 2). The Regulations may be found at <http://www.opsi.gov.uk/si/si2003/20030527.htm>. Note that there are a number of Annexes to the Determinants which set out the important detail.

As with many aspects of police training, the position regarding probation, the regulations, and complaints may well be reviewed. The Morris Enquiry in particular highlighted the complexity of current arrangements (Morris et al, 2004).

Probably the most important paragraphs in the Police Regulations 2003 for the student police officer are Regulations 12 and 13 often known colloquially as Reg 12 and Reg 13.

Regulation 12 provides for an extension to the usual probationary period of two years for full-time student police officers. Details are given in Annex C to the Regulations. Normally the probationary period is extended for the following reasons:

- training has been interrupted for some reason—for example illness or personal problems; or
- a student police officer has been 'back coursed' (that is, required to retake a stage of training), perhaps because of failure.

Forces are unlikely to allow an indefinite extension to the probationary period and will usually provide you with detailed information concerning the implementation of 'Reg 12' on the local level.

Regulation 13 allows for your dismissal. It is worth quoting in full:

Regulation 13

(1) Subject to the provisions of this regulation, during [his/her] period of probation in the force the services of a constable may be dispensed with at any time if the chief officer considers that [he/she] is not fitted, physically or mentally, to perform the duties of his office, or that [he/she] is not likely to become an efficient or well conducted constable.

(2) A constable whose services are dispensed with under this regulation shall be entitled to receive a month's notice or a month's pay in lieu thereof.

(3) A constable's services shall not be dispensed with in accordance with this regulation and any notice given for the purposes thereof shall cease to have effect if [he/she] gives written notice to the police authority of [his/her] intention to retire and retires in pursuance of the said notice on or before the date on which [his/her] services would otherwise be dispensed with; and such a notice taking effect on that date shall be accepted by the police authority notwithstanding that less than a month's notice is given.

(4) Where a constable has received a notice under this regulation that [his/her] services are to be dispensed with and [he/she] gives written notice of [his/her] intention to retire and retires under paragraph (3), [he/she] shall nevertheless be entitled to receive pay up to and until the date on which the month's notice [he/she] has received would have expired or where [he/she] has received or is due to receive a month's pay in lieu of notice [he/she] shall remain entitled to that pay notwithstanding the notice [he/she] has given under paragraph (3).

In practice Reg 13 dismissals are rare and are normally the end of a long process during which you would have been offered support and guidance. If you are issued with a Reg 13 notice then you are advised to contact your JBB (the Police Federation, see section 7.17) representative if you are paying subscriptions to the Federation or otherwise take advice.

Note that the grounds for dismissal ('not fitted, physically or mentally, to perform the duties of his office, or that [he/she] is not likely to become an efficient or well conducted constable') are quite broad. For example, persistent failure in assessments or examinations could be considered grounds to consider you not *mentally* fit to continue training. However, more common reasons for being dismissed or resigning are examples of inappropriate behaviour, an inability to maintain a certain level of fitness and so on.

Further, note that the regulation allows the possibility of retirement (voluntary resignation) before dispensing (dismissal), although this does not mean that an individual would escape prosecution if the grounds for dispensing arose from a criminal act of the individual concerned. There are obvious reasons why you may wish to resign before being dismissed in terms of your future employment prospects.

3.9 National Occupational Standards

Your progression to full qualification as a police officer is inextricably linked with the gaining of the National Occupational Standards in initial policing. The NOS are examined in detail in Chapter 6. The standards set out the skills and abilities that you will need to demonstrate before being Confirmed, although the detail of this is subject to local force policy.

3.10 Qualifications

Your force may link your initial training to:

- a foundation degree or other higher education (HE) award;
- an NVQ Level 3 and an NVQ Level 4;
- a combination of the above;
- a Modern Apprenticeship, Advanced Apprenticeship, or Apprenticeship;
- no external qualification.

The qualifications in the list above are not necessarily mutually exclusive. For example, some HE qualifications have NVQs embedded within them as confirmation of professional competence. Trainee probation officers, for example, are now required to achieve an NVQ Level 4 and a degree. It could also be that only certain parts of your training are linked with qualifications rather than the whole probationary period—for example, your first aid training (part of IND 1).

In some cases Confirmation (see section 3.6) may depend on the minimum attainment of one of these qualifications, or a staged award with the qualification (for example, a Certificate in Higher Education as Level 1 of a foundation degree).

The Home Office has declared its intention that there shall be a **single** national qualification for student police officers who successfully complete their probation (section 4.54 of the White Paper, 'Building Communities, Beating Crime'). However, the IPLDP Central Authority (the body now responsible for probationary training) has stated that this will be a **minimum** level of qualification, that forces may 'gold plate' if they so wish (Home Office, 2005b, para 17). The IPLDP has decided that this will be an NVQ Level 3 and NVQ Level 4 qualification in Policing. In any eventuality, it would appear reasonably obvious that whatever qualification your force offers, it should, and in all likelihood will be, linked with the NOS for initial policing and be approved by Skills for Justice (see Chapter 6).

We now examine each possible form of qualification.

3.10.1 Foundation Degree or Other HE Award

If a foundation degree or other HE award (for example, a Cert HE, a Dip HE, or an HE Certificate) is part of your training then your force will be working in partnership with a higher education institution (HEI), possibly a university, a university college, or a further education (FE) college with links to an HEI. This also probably means that you have a form of 'dual nationality' where you are both a student of the HEI or FE college and an employee of your police force. There are advantages and disadvantages to this. On the one hand you will gain a qualification still held in relatively high esteem around the world (useful for that second career after policing). You will also be able to access the learning facilities (library, open learning centres, and so on) on the same basis as any other student of that HEI or FE college. Finally, in many cases, you will be able to study alongside students engaged in training in parallel occupations such as nursing and social work (both part of higher education). This is particularly important in terms of the inter-agency approaches to policing.

On the other hand there is no gain without pain. By this we mean that the gaining of higher education qualifications will require you to demonstrate your knowledge and understanding in distinctive ways, and not just your professional competence in the field. You will almost certainly be required to undertake formal assessment, such as examinations and assignments that will have predetermined pass marks and strict rules concerning re-submission, missing deadlines, and so on. For example, failing an examination, after all re-submission possibilities have been exhausted, may result in you being re-coursed if that is the policy of your force.

You should note however, the foundation degrees in particular are not just another degree from a university. You are not undertaking, say, an undergraduate programme in history; foundation degrees are **meant** to be different and to be linked inextricably with the practical skills needed for the occupation concerned and for initial policing this means, at least in part, the NOS. It is unlikely therefore that you will be set essays asking you to 'Discuss the history of the use of police dog' but instead your assignments will be professionally related and often linked with your Supervised and Independent Patrol experiences. However, they **are** higher education awards and carry credit in many cases to honours degrees such as a BSc (Hons) in Policing (this is meant to be a design feature common to all foundation degrees). This linkage to an honours degree could be important in terms of your subsequent professional development (see Chapter 14).

3.10.2 NVQs

National Vocational Qualifications (NVQs; SVQs in Scotland) are offered at Levels 1 to 5 and are available for a wide range of occupations including policing. For student police officers, NVQ Levels 3 and 4 in Policing are the most relevant. NVQs are approved by the Qualifications and Curriculum Authority (QCA), a national body. The QCA does not issue awards—this is undertaken by the Awarding Bodies. NVQs in Policing are offered by a number of familiar Awarding Bodies, including Edexcel and OCR. Some Awarding Bodies, for example City & Guilds, suggest that the Level 4 NVQ is appropriate for 'those individuals undertaking Independent Patrol' (City & Guilds, 2005, p 1) but the rationale for this advice is unclear.

The following is the likely composition of the NVQ Level 3 in terms of the eleven mandatory NOS Units (note that the NOS Units were revised in 2006 and hence some of the following may change):

NVQ Level 3

Unit 1A1	Use police actions in a fair and justified way.
Unit AA1	Promote equality and value diversity.
Unit 2C1	Provide an initial police response to incidents.
Unit 2C3	Arrest, detain, or report individuals.
Unit 2C4	Apply conflict management.
Unit 2H1	Interview victims and witnesses.
Unit 2I1	Search individuals.
Unit 2K2	Present detained persons to custody.
Unit AE1	Maintain and develop your own knowledge, skills and competence.
Unit AF1	Ensure your own actions reduce risks to health and safety.
Unit 4G4	Administer first aid.

The following Units are required for the NVQ Level 4 in policing (as with Level 3, note that the NOS Units were revised in 2006 and hence some of the following may change):

NVQ Level 4

Unit AB1	Communicate effectively with people.
Unit BE1	Provide initial support to victims, survivors and witnesses and assess their needs for further support.
Unit 2A1	Gather and submit information that has the potential to support policing objectives.
Unit 2C2	Prepare for, and participate in, planned policing operations.
Unit 2G2	Conduct priority and volume investigations.
Unit 2G4	Finalise investigations.
Unit 2H2	Interview suspects.
Unit 2I2	Search vehicles, premises and open spaces.
Unit 2J1	Prepare and submit case files.
Unit 2J2	Present evidence in court and at other hearings.
Unit 2K1	Escort detained persons.

Your force will either be an approved centre of an Awarding Body, giving it the right to offer NVQs directly or your force may be working in partnership with another education or training body that is an approved centre. A typical partner might be a local FE college. However, if your force offers an NVQ at Levels 3 or 4, it must subscribe to the assessment strategy of Skills for Justice. For example, the force will need to have certain safeguards in place to ensure that its assessors are suitably skilled. You will sometimes hear mention of 'A1 assessors' which is reference to a qualification that your assessors are undertaking or one that they have already gained (it is also the case with foundation degrees linked to NOS that the assessors are required to have certain skills).

As with foundation degrees, there are advantages and disadvantages to linking initial police training with NVQs. In terms of advantages, the NVQ is now an established and widely recognized qualification. It also lends itself naturally to occupational standards (not surprisingly, as it is based upon them) and therefore has the potential to be seamlessly interwoven within your training. Finally, if other aspects of police training become linked with NVQs (this is certainly possible) then you will be already well-versed in the philosophy and approach of NVQs. The disadvantages are that NVQs do not necessarily carry the same weight with other professional groups. Remember the Home Office IPLDP comment above about gold plating? This is not, we think, just about some kind of educational snobbery but a realistic reflection of the historical development of the professions in the UK. Ask the police surgeon, the defence solicitor, or even the custody nurse about their qualifications and you are unlikely to hear much at the moment about NVQs.

3.10.3 Apprenticeships

To our knowledge there are no police forces currently offering Apprenticeships, Modern Apprenticeships, or Advanced Apprenticeships as part of their IPLDP-compliant training. Advanced Apprenticeships consist of an NVQ, key skills, occupational specific requirements (for example, officer safety training in policing), and a technical certificate. (Note that the title of these programmes has changed over the years and so you will also find references to Advanced Modern Apprenticeships and you may also find variations of title and rules within the UK.) The absence of apprenticeships for the police service may be partly due to apprenticeship schemes being restricted in the past to people between the ages of 16 to 24, although Adult Apprenticeships for those aged 25 or over are being designed.

3.11 Answers to Tasks

TASK 1

Possible answers are discussed in the text that follows immediately after Task 1.

Well, you have made it this far. On average for your one success there are six others who failed to even reach the first day of training. Statistically, you are likely to be male, aged in your mid twenties, and white. There again you are probably not (look up 'ecological fallacy' on <http://en.wikipedia.org/wiki/Main_Page>).

Disturbingly, if you are an ethnic minority recruit you are twice as likely to drop out of training as your white counterparts (Woolcock, 2006). The police service seems serious about tackling this issue.

TASK 2

This task is not easy because it is not always obvious whether a motivation is extrinsic or intrinsic in nature. On the surface they may appear one way or the other to us but it is evident that human motivation is highly complex (look at the number of psychology textbooks devoted to this subject alone). What is perhaps more important than classification is that you spend time thinking about your motivation for joining and how you might respond to the challenges presented by two years' training.

TASK 3

Well, how does it compare? Do not be surprised (or concerned) to find significant variation with the national template.

The internet will give you access to brief descriptions of a number of force approaches to structuring initial training, and it is surprising how varied these can be. Norfolk Constabulary, for example, has adopted the following approach, indicating clearly the links with the IPLDP (Norfolk Constabulary, 2006). Note the decision to include some subjects from the optional LPG 0 module relevant to local circumstances.

Training and Development (Norfolk Constabulary)

Phase 1—Induction

Three weeks in duration.

Modules covered in this phase include health and safety, first aid, race and diversity, ethics and values and information technology.

Students have three days' basic personal safety training and start looking at social, community and neighbourhood policing in order to prepare them for Phase 2.

Phase 2—Community Engagement

Two weeks—based in Professional Development Units (PDUs).

Students spend the first two days of this phase getting to know their tutor, supervisor, PDU staff and station, and receive information on the local community make-up and the role the local police play.

The remainder of the time is spent on attachment to a local community group.

Phase 3, Part 1—Legislation, Procedures, and Guidelines

12 weeks—based at OCC operations and communications centre.

Students are given the knowledge they need before going out on Supervised Patrol. The timetable will follow a natural progression through the subjects, eg giving the input on theft and burglary before going on to initial investigation methods and the first input from crime scene investigators on what to do at the scene of a burglary and how to preserve evidence. There are also several occasions during the timetable when members of the community will be involved as guest speakers or role players.

Also included are a day of public support unit training and the remainder of their personal safety and information technology training.

There will be regular knowledge checks during these weeks with a final knowledge check at the end.

There is then one week of annual leave.

Phase 3, Part 2—Supervised Patrol

12 weeks—based at the PDUs.

The student officer is assigned a tutor on a one-to-one basis. At completion of this period the tutor will probably remain as the student's assessor for the remainder of the probationary period. The modules to be assessed are the ones that cover the day to day operational elements.

The students will work alongside a shift on a twelve hour shift pattern but will only be fully operational for ten of those twelve hours to allow time for completion of the Student Officer Learning and Development Portfolio (SOLAP). At the end of the twelve weeks it will be decided by the assessor/tutor whether the officer is fit for Independent Patrol.

There will also be a classroom based course of 5x8 hour days at the PDU when officers will be taught the legislation on subjects such as Anti Social Behaviour Orders (ASBOs) using live local data.

Phase 4—Independent patrol

Return to OCC for a critical/major Incident course of one week's duration.

Foot Patrol/Neighbourhood Policing

Four weeks—based at PDU.

If the area where the officer is based has a neighbourhood policing scheme then the officer will spend some time attached to it.

Driving Course

Three weeks—based at OCC.

Protected Independence

Six weeks—based at the area PDU before transferring to the officer's designated station at forty-five weeks' service.

During the remaining fifty-nine weeks, students will complete the SOLAP, an attachment programme and attend two courses at OCC in order to gain the legislation contained in the LPG two modules. These include sexual offences, drugs and any optional subjects that it is felt are relevant to our area, such as wildlife and countryside. In line with these subjects officers will have another four/five days of community involvement in areas that are more demanding than those in phase two.

4 | Learning as a Student Police Officer

4.1 Chapter Briefing

This chapter discusses how to build upon the ways you learn best in order to make learning easier for you. It demonstrates how you can use a route map of learning to find out what point you have reached. The chapter describes tips on how to recall facts and how to apply reflective practice in your Learning Diary. Undertaking your community engagement and learning whilst with your Professional Development Unit are also examined and this is followed by a look at diversity training in the police.

Finally, the chapter examines forms of reasoning and argument that are relevant to learning for student police officers, together with the ways in which we can sometimes commit errors in reasoning—logical fallacies.

4.1.1 Aim of the Chapter

The aim of this chapter is to develop your understanding of learning as a student police officer and the forms of teaching you will receive, and to assist in the development of your skills for studying, reasoning, and argument.

This chapter will enable you to:

- understand the approaches to learning and teaching adopted by many police forces;
- appreciate the value of the experiential learning cycle;
- understand and, if appropriate, adopt the role of the reflective practitioner;

- place the community engagement stage of training into context;
- understand how a PDU supports your professional development;
- consider some of the questions and issues that surround diversity training in the police;
- develop skills of reasoning and argument;
- identify common logical errors.

4.1.2   National Occupational Standards

This chapter will provide you with some of the knowledge required to demonstrate the following NOS elements:

National Occupational Standards Element

AE1.1 Maintain and develop your own knowledge, skills and competence.

You should refer to chapter 6 for general information and advice concerning the NOS elements.

4.1.3   IPLDP Phases and Modules

This chapter will provide you with resources to support the IPLDP Induction Module IND 3 to 'Develop one's own knowledge and practice'.

4.1.4   SOLAP

The contents of this chapter are relevant to the 'knowledge' evidence requirements of CAR 4C1.

4.1.5   IPLDP Learning Requirement

This chapter is relevant to the following sections of the IPLDP Learning Requirement: 1.4, 1.8, 1.9, 1.10, 1.11, 1.12, 1.13, 1.17, 1.18, 2.7, 3.1, 3.2, 3.8, 4.2, 4.3, and 4.5 (many of these will be met through an effective community engagement—see section 4.8 of this chapter).

4.2   Introduction

In many respects a student police officer is just that: a student. You should not be expected to know everything from the start although you will almost certainly encounter members of the public and even fellow police officers that believe that you should. Indeed, you will probably come to the conclusion that the end of your training is just the beginning of a career-long need to continue learning.

It is perhaps illuminating to compare the transition from student to qualified police officer with the parallel progression through nurse training; that is from **novice** nurse to **expert** nurse (Benner, 1984).

In many of the models of nurse training in the UK there are five levels of proficiency, which we have adapted to police training:

> **Novice**—the new student police officer
> Decision-making is limited and based upon strict rules out of context—'just tell me what to **do**!'
> You are largely exposed to policing but play little active part.
> No occupational standards have been achieved.

> **Advanced beginner**—the student police officer on Supervised Patrol
> Enough competence has been demonstrated, in knowledge checks, real situations, and role play,
> to allow limited autonomy although skills and knowledge are viewed as if in separate boxes
> (the Theft Act, diversity, forensic awareness, ABH)—'let me have a go!'
> Some occupational standards have been achieved.

> **Competent**—the student police officer on Independent Patrol
> Mastery of many of the skills and competences of policing, although they are still compartmentalized
> and not yet joined up and they are still not second nature—'I think I can do this'.
> The PAC has been achieved.

> **Proficient**—the student police officer at Confirmation
> Situations are viewed as a whole and patterns are discerned and analysed and subtleties recognized—
> 'I've been here before'.
> All required occupational standards have been achieved.

> **Expert**—the confirmed police officer after two or three years service
> An apparently intuitive grasp of situations, confident but now also questioning—
> 'Perhaps there is more to learn?'

When you start your training you are probably at the novice stage (unless you have joined after being a special constable or PCSO). This is to be expected. All being well, in two years you will be proficient and perhaps even expert. Your training will have been designed to support your transition from novice to advanced beginner to competent and finally to proficient. This chapter has been written to provide you with some understanding of the processes involved.

Finally, note that there are a number of IPLDP requirements for police forces, in terms of the way they organize and deliver their teaching and assist in your learning. For example, the recommendation is that there is a maximum ratio of sixteen student police officers to one trainer for taught training room activities but one to one for Supervised Patrol (Home Office, 2005d). This is not to say that you will not sometimes be taught in larger groups in a classroom (it could make sound pedagogical sense to do so) but rather the norm should be no more than sixteen to one. Although your trainers are expected to be 'occupationally competent' (Home Office, 2005d), bear in mind that police training is still often viewed as the remit of the 'generalist'. Your trainers, for example, might be expected to know and teach (or facilitate) everything from the detail of the Sexual Offences Act 2003 to theories concerning human communication.

4.3   Teaching and Learning Styles

To understand how you will learn in police training, you will need to understand **how you learn as an adult**. The educational backgrounds of those who read this Handbook are likely to be as varied as the people themselves. Some of you will have entered the police family earlier in another police-related role (eg as a PCSO), some of you will have become student police officers almost straight from school, some of you will have recently left full-time further or higher education (up to 30% in recent years), whilst a number of you may not have undertaken training or studied for a long time.

Whatever your previous educational background, police training should be innovative, diverse, and exciting. The IPLDP philosophy is to encourage police forces to adopt educational principles and practices that suit adults, and principles and practices which are flexible and diverse enough to accommodate the learning styles of most students, whatever their personal educational backgrounds. It is worth noting that police training has been taking place in the UK for over 150 years, and hundreds of thousands of student police officers have been successfully trained before you. This does not mean, of course, that police training was perfect in the past nor, indeed, that it is now (HMIC, 2002). After all, we tend not to hear much from those who have been unsuccessful in their police training, but we often witness the self-fulfilling prophecy of those who **do** succeed. What it does mean, however, is that many people like you have successfully trained to become police officers and moved on to rewarding careers in policing.

4.3.1   Safe Learning Environment

A phrase that you might well hear your trainers use (if not to you, then to each other) is 'safe learning environment'. The phrase is used in reference to Professional Development Units (see section 4.10) as well as the training room. There is no official definition of what safe learning environment actually means but it probably contains elements of some or all of the following:

- **physically** safe—that is, the training room or the officer safety training facilities meet appropriate health and safety requirements (your trainers will often consider this as the first stage of 'Maslow's hierarchy of needs');
- **psychologically** safe—that is, establishing a climate in the classroom where you feel free to express your ideas and feelings without fear of ridicule from others. Bear in mind, however, that your trainers may also have a role in the requirement to assess your attitudes and behaviour;
- the existence of **well-defined parameters** that specify the boundaries of acceptable behaviour and actions in the classroom and other learning environments. These parameters sometimes form part of a learning agreement that you might even be asked to sign, signifying that you will demonstrate an awareness of the needs of others and so on.

4.3.2   Domains of Learning

Many of our day-to-day actions centre on three main areas of activity and so it follows that these three areas are the ones in which learning or education often take place. An understanding of these areas will help you to assess your own competences and evaluate your own training needs. You will find it easier to learn and revise for exams and it will provide you with a route map through any of your learning experiences.

These areas are referred to as the **learning domains** (eg Bloom, 1964 and subsequent publications in this series), and you will no doubt hear your trainers refer to them from time to time.

1. The first one is linked to the area of cognition associated with the ability to **reason**, and will include learning subject matter such as law, legislation, policy, and procedure, about which we have to **think**. We can therefore associate this domain with our **heads** but it is often referred to in academic literature as the **cognitive domain**.

2. The next domain is associated with your feelings and emotions, for example, the way you react to situations (such as provocation), and what your values and prejudices are. A cliché in police training is that 'attitudes can be caught or taught', and therefore a great deal of your training will involve learning to adopt appropriate **attitudes** and behaviours towards the public and your colleagues, in areas such as respect, race and diversity, team working, community and customer focus, effective communication, problem-solving, personal responsibility, and resilience. You can think of this domain as being associated with the **heart**, but it is more formally referred to as the **affective domain**.

3. The third domain is associated with **physical dexterity**, for example, personal safety training, first-aid training, using a breath test machine, and traffic control. You can consider this domain as being associated with the use of your **hands**, but it could easily be associated with your legs, arms, or any part of your body you use to carry out an action. It is called the **psychomotor domain**.

Within these domains there are levels of complexity, beginning with the easiest and progressively becoming more difficult. In the table below these are read from left to right.

For the cognitive domain (the head):

Knowledge ➝	Comprehension ➝	Application
The ability to recall facts, words, or phrases, eg a definition of an Act or a section of law.	To understand and be able to explain component parts of policy, procedure, or legislation, eg the meanings of words within definitions, the variations and exceptions.	To use this knowledge and understanding to apply previous learning to a set task which is either simulated, paper-based or in the work place.

For the affective domain (the heart):

Receives ➝	Responds ➝	Values
Listens to or sees demonstrated an attitude which is to be learned, eg 'We want you to be a non-discriminator, regardless of the prejudices you may actually have.'.	Outwardly shows the learned attitude or behaviour, but does not necessarily believe in it, eg 'I have prejudices, but I will not discriminate because I've been told I must not.'.	Adopts the learned attitude or behaviour and, without request and prompting, owns the feeling personally, eg 'Even though I have prejudices I believe it is wrong to discriminate and therefore I will not do so.'.

For the psychomotor domain (the hands):

Imitation ➝	Manipulation ➝	Precision
Performs the skill as a result of copying or repeating what has been observed, eg resuscitation techniques in first aid.	Executes the skill with some instruction or coaching.	Carries out the skill alone without copying instruction or the necessity for coaching.

It is almost an orthodoxy in police training that learning in one domain cannot easily be separated from learning in another. This is particularly the case in terms of cognitive and affective learning. Hence you will find your trainers often working simultaneously on these dimensions. For example, in a session on the police response to domestic violence, your trainer might well start with a group discussion on attitudes to domestic violence and through this encourage you to explore your own feelings and preconceptions (is it just a domestic that the police should keep out of? Is it always male on female violence? What about elderly people as victims of their children?).

For a session involving the cognitive domain, you will probably be asked to assimilate at least some of the knowledge about the subjects involved before entering the training room, for example during the evening before. This will probably be referred to as organizing in advance or even an advanced organizer. At this stage, you may be tasked with learning an offence, Act, or section, perhaps in the form of a definition. The content could come from this Handbook, your NPIA (Centrex) or force notes, a virtual learning environment, or from a handout issued to you. This process is sometimes referred to in police training as a 'pre-read'; perhaps this could be misleading as you are required to learn material, and not just read it!

The next stage of the lesson will possibly involve a knowledge check to assess whether or not you have gained the appropriate level of understanding of the material. This will be carried out before the next classroom session or at the start of it. A trainer or tutor will then probably be intent on moving you on to the next level in the cognitive domain (from knowledge to comprehension) by asking you to take part in one of the teaching and learning activities listed in section 4.4 below, in order to check your understanding and clarify any misunderstandings.

Finally, again in the classroom, you will be given an opportunity to develop your learning further, using one or more of the methods listed in section 4.4 below. This will involve the third level of the domain (from comprehension to application) when you apply your learning.

Similar activities will be used in the other two domains for attitudinal and skills-based subjects, but each time you will probably start at the simplest level and move incrementally to the more complex (this is a very common approach in police training, often paraphrased as 'from simple to complex'). Then, whether it is through assimilation or work-based learning in your Professional Development Unit, you will be coached and mentored by your tutor to a level of competency in preparation for assessment against the National Occupational Standards (see section 6.4).

4.3.3 Preferred Learning Styles

It will probably come as no surprise, and probably as a reassurance in many respects, that people prefer to learn in different ways (Kolb, 1984). Each way may be unique to that learner but many researchers have discerned the existence of four main families of learning styles which most people relate to in some way. However, before we describe these learning styles, undertake the following four tasks. In each case, answer the questions 'yes' or 'no'. Of course, you probably wish to qualify your answers with 'sometimes' or 'mostly' but it will work better if you can just give a straight answer! (Note that answers are not provided to these four tasks at the end of the chapter, because this is all about you.)

TASK 1
- Do I like to be animated in my learning and do best when I am actively involved with a task?
- Do I prefer, for example, computer-based activities, over simply reading something?
- Do I normally like taking part in simulations or role-plays, but rarely like just to observe them?

If you answered mostly 'yes', here are some tips for you:
- Set yourself tasks, write your own questions or case studies involving the subject matter you are learning.
- Take part in computer-based learning, which is interactive and visual, for example through the NCALT portal at <www.ncalt.com>.
- Use pre-formed questions before sessions which will keep you active and enable you to continually check your learning.
- Do your learning in bite-sized chunks, and never stay too long without a break.
- At revision time, do not only rely on reading your notes, but engage yourself in activities that allow you to look back at the subject in more depth, such as setting yourself questions to answer.

TASK 2

- Do I like to have a logical outlook to my learning, with set outcomes for me to work towards?
- Do I like to produce a theory or attach an idea to the subject?
- Do I like reading about a subject and drawing my own conclusions as to its structure and adaptation?
- Do I like to challenge or question the underlying assumptions in subject matter presented to me?

If you answered mostly 'yes', here are some tips for you:

- Establish the reasoning behind the subject matter. If there does not seem to be a clear theory which relates to the subject, research this for yourself. It might exist, even though you may not have been taught it in the training room.
- If you are learning a law-based subject, look for its origins in terms of the crimes or situations it is intended to prevent. Look for the period in time when it was written and introduced, and why.
- Whilst revising for an assessment process, design your own logical diagrams which summarize the subject matter as a sequence of points to be learned.

TASK 3

- Do I like to learn by thinking or dealing with the problem in a practical way, rather than using theory or abstract principles?
- Do I look at the learning requirements on me in a pragmatic way; for example, just how much of a new subject I need to learn, and why?
- When introduced to new subjects, do I almost immediately look for the practical applications and where I can use the learning in the work place?

If you answered mostly 'yes', here are some tips for you:

- Adapt the material you are learning into a form with which you are more comfortable by making links with the practical applications.
- Produce examples to clarify your own understanding of the subject, construct flow-charts (like the ones to be found in Chapter 8 and elsewhere in this Handbook) or mind-maps on paper to make connections between the subject matter.
- Involve yourself in the assessment of others, so that you are learning at the same time.

TASK 4

- Do I like to learn in a slow, deliberate way, and would rather take my time to reinforce what I have learned before moving on and risk possibly forgetting something?
- Do I like to take a step back and look at the subject from all angles before drawing a conclusion?
- Do I like to discuss issues, so that I fully understand what it is that I need to learn?
- Do I try to hide sometimes during simulations or role-plays and prefer to observe but then fully participate in the debrief afterwards?

If you answered mostly 'yes', here are some tips for you:

- Most of your learning will take place towards the end of a lesson or later on the same day. Organize your time so that you have the opportunity to look back over material you have learned earlier.
- Expose yourself to pre-formed questions, but allow yourself time to carry them out effectively.
- Use reinforcement tools, such as question and answer books, and try not to feel embarrassed if you want to do an exercise more than once.

So which group do you belong to, or perhaps (most likely) are your responses spread across two (or more) groups? The following task may provide you with a more precise measure of your preferred learning style.

TASK 5

One way to find out what kind of learning style you have is to take part in an online questionnaire, so go to the Learning Styles interactive website at Canterbury Christ Church University: <http://orientation.canterbury.ac.uk/studying/learning_styles.shtml>.

4.4 Learning from Trainers and Others

If you are in a class of up to sixteen people, there is every chance that each of you will have a different preferred learning style. Therefore, it is obviously a challenge to the training staff to accommodate each student police officer with an appropriate learning activity best suited to his or her preferred learning style. A popular approach in police training is that of facilitation where trainers adopt styles and techniques to bring out (you may hear the phrase 'tease out') ideas and views from the group whilst at the same time reducing their own role as conventional didactic 'stand at the front and talk' teachers.

A number of activities commonly employed by trainers are described below. They are used to engage all members of the group at least once during a session.

The **'boardblast'** is a very popular teaching method used by police trainers. The tutor will invite responses from some or all of you which will be written down on a pen board (whiteboard) or flip-chart and are then discussed. The content of the boardblast will be assessed by the tutor and revisited at different stages of the lesson. This is often a very effective method. However, it might be worth you and your fellow students making it known (diplomatically) that you would like to try some different ways of discussing ideas if it seems to you that you have contributed to rather too many boardblasts recently. Another occasional disadvantage to the boardblast approach is that most of the class will be at the level of novice or advanced beginner (see section 4.2) and hence the suggestions from the class may not cover all the aspects of the topic required for that session.

Case studies involve a practical example of a police-related problem which will be given to you as an individual or a group activity. You will be invited to read the material and form conclusions about its content to show your understanding of the subject.

The NPIA (formerly Centrex) has developed a number of case studies and extensive associated materials (including e-learning content) to support the delivery of the IPLDP curriculum. These include case studies concerned with robbery, theft, missing persons, burglary, terrorism and so on.

Demonstration can be used if the subject matter involves the use of the body in the psycho-motor domain. The tutor will demonstrate how your body should move in order that you can repeat the activity afterwards.

Small group work is a very common method in police training. You will be invited to work in small groups and share ideas between the group. For this approach to work well, it is very important that each member of the group is actively involved in the task and that nobody sits back allowing the rest to carry the main burden. It is important also that concentration is maintained on the task in hand, and that your mind does not wander to unconnected matters; important, but not easy to achieve (see section 7.18.2 which is concerned with listening skills). When the group reports back its findings, the trainer or trainers will probably be in facilitator mode and see their main task as teasing out the learning.

Large group work usually involves you being sent away in smaller numbers to research a subject using books, reference material, and computer-based learning. You will then be asked to come back as a large group and present all your small group findings as one coherent piece. On the other hand, as a large group you may be presented with information on a large scale, perhaps from a specialist or guest speaker or by watching a video clip, for example.

Individual work provides an opportunity for you to work alone. You will be set work to do on your own, perhaps under exam conditions or, less informally, during lessons. This may take the format of knowledge checks, assignments, case building, or interviewing.

Electronic learning often uses computer-based learning (CBL) packages which are now available both nationally and locally. They provide you with an opportunity to interact with the resources available. CBL activity can be carried out individually or in small groups, both inside and outside the classroom environment. For example, CBL material supporting the IPLDP is to be found at <www.ncalt.com>. As a police officer, you should have access to the resources on the NCALT website through the use of a username and password.

Facilitated discussions are particularly useful for exploring attitudes and behaviour. Your trainers will encourage you to share your own thoughts with others in the safe learning environment they hope to have established (see section 4.3.1). You should be prepared to maintain confidentiality as you and your colleagues may disclose private and sensitive matters (you will certainly be reminded of this need on numerous occasions). From the discussion you will have the opportunity to draw your own conclusions. The discussion may be initiated by watching a video or DVD, or by reflecting on the presentation of a guest speaker. Finally, as a student police officer you should remember throughout discussions that you are probably under observation by your tutors. Confidentiality does not protect you from disciplinary action against inappropriate language, attitudes, or behaviour.

Presentations are used for some topics. If the subject matter is appropriate for this form of delivery (for example, an introduction to the Theft Act 1968), or time is short, your trainers may well deliver a presentation, often using Microsoft PowerPoint software. Throughout the presentation, you will be given the opportunity to ask questions and make notes. Your trainer might well direct questions towards you. Different trainers will have different approaches to delivering presentations which may or may not coincide with your learning style. For example, some may use the technique of progressively revealing bullet points which, although it will keep your attention, can be irritating to some. Most trainers welcome feedback on matters such as this, possibly in the evaluation sheets you might be asked to complete and submit. Finally, if your organization uses Virtual Learning Environments (such as Blackboard) then you may well find copies of the presentations are available to you in an electronic format.

Role plays are where you adopt or play given roles in a certain situation. For example, one of you may act the police officer and the other a member of the public in a simulated 'stop and account' scenario. Role plays are normally used when you have gained sufficient knowledge and skills (particularly in terms of police procedure) to make them meaningful. Some police forces use semi-professional actors or volunteers from the local community to play roles. The latter approach may also have certain added advantages in terms of your diversity training. One underlying principle to the role play approach is that adult learners are able to draw upon previous experiences to enhance their learning. Just as significant for your learning as the role play itself is the debrief that normally happens later (you could even be videoed to assist with this). In all cases the brief for the role play should be carefully explained to you at the outset. Note that, as we discuss in Chapter 6, role plays and simulations cannot normally be used as evidence against achievement of the NOS. However, your experiences can certainly feature in your Learning Diary Phase 3.

Undertaking a **community engagement** is seen as an important way in which you will learn both about the diverse communities that you will police and your attitudes towards these communities. This is considered in more detail in section 4.8. However, at this point note the importance that the IPLDP places on a **self-critical** approach to be adopted (Home Office, 2004c). This means an active self-questioning of your existing beliefs and attitudes. Your force will probably expect to see evidence of this self-criticality in your Learning Diary Phase 2 entries under headings such as 'What challenged you during the engagement, in what ways and how did you respond?'

Syndicate exercises involve you working in small groups. You will first be divided into syndicates by your trainers. A syndicate is a group of people where each assumes a certain role. For example, in a syndicate exercise you might be a member of the public with a particular problem with anti-social behaviour in your neighbourhood. Other members of the syndicate may play the role of the local Pc, the police area (BCU) commander, and so on. The exercise then takes place and you explore the various issues involved. Syndicate exercises can be useful learning devices but need to be carefully organized and managed by your trainers, with detailed instructions and briefing on the roles you will play. For example, if the syndicate group is quite large (six or more) then there is the danger that certain members of the group may come to dominate and because of time constraints issues are examined in token and ineffective ways.

4.5 The Experiential Learning Cycle (ELC)

You have undoubtedly heard of the sayings, 'If you don't succeed the first time, then try, try again' or 'We all learn by our mistakes'. Much of your learning will take place through your own experiences, and as adults we can actually teach ourselves, at least in part. How many times have you mentally said to yourself, 'I won't do that again!' or 'That didn't work! Is there another way?' or 'When I do that again, I'll do it better and safer!'?

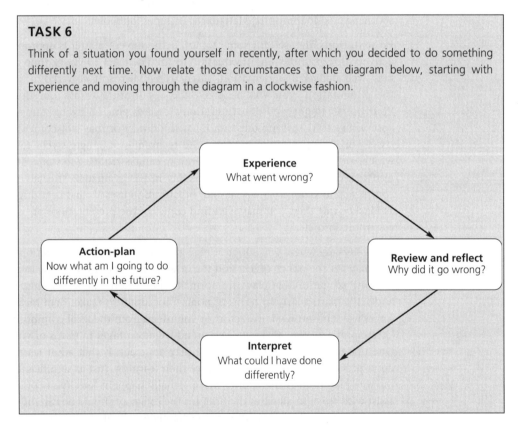

TASK 6

Think of a situation you found yourself in recently, after which you decided to do something differently next time. Now relate those circumstances to the diagram below, starting with Experience and moving through the diagram in a clockwise fashion.

Experience
What went wrong?

Review and reflect
Why did it go wrong?

Interpret
What could I have done differently?

Action-plan
Now what am I going to do differently in the future?

This diagram in Task 6 shows the **experiential learning cycle** (ELC) and has been adapted from the work of David Kolb (Kolb, 1984). It has been widely adopted (but is not without its critics) as an integral part of police learning and hence you will find it extensively used on an individual basis, to inform your Learning Diary (all phases), and in the teaching environment in an attempt to develop greater learning of individuals or groups. Many of your trainers are likely to have used the cycle to inform the way in which they have structured and organized your taught sessions. The cycle can also be viewed as a dynamic (on-the-spot) assessment of how to carry out tasks in a manner that meets health and safety considerations, thereby informing safer working practices.

The four stages to the cycle are as follows:

- **Experience** (called 'Concrete Experience' in the Kolb original). This is **direct** experience, often through practical application. As a student police officer you will often want to know what the practical applications of the session will be. You may want to get hands on as soon as possible. The trainer may provide 'hooks' for you to hang on to—for example, by asking the question 'think of times in your own life when you have been subject to bullying or harassment'.
- **Review and reflect** ('Reflection'). What does the experience mean to me? This stage is the beginning of understanding through review and reflection. A question such as 'describe your feelings when you were bullied or harassed' may be asked.
- **Interpret** ('Abstract Conceptualization'). This involves placing the experiences in some form of theoretical and more abstract framework. 'How then do victims feel about this?'
- **Action-plan** ('Active Experimentation'). The stage of action-planning on how we take this learning forward and test it against reality. 'How then do we act as a police service to support victims of harassment?'

The cycle is also used by trainers during other forms of learning. For example, after a role play (see section 4.4), the participants will be asked, amongst other things: 'What did not go quite so well? So what was the outcome of that? Now what are you going to do differently in the future?'

Many police trainers are taught to link the learning cycle with the styles of learning that we described in the latter part of section 4.3—for example, by devising approaches for activist learners to help them through the interpret stage of the ELC. This is part of the facilitation tradition in police training that we described earlier.

Finally, note that learning to use the ELC is not the same as unstructured discovery learning. Your trainers are not likely to ask you, in small group work, to discover the Theft Act 1968 for yourself. However, if you feel uncomfortable with this way of learning (perhaps through unfamiliarity) then make your feelings known so your trainers will be more able to help you.

TASK 7

A student police officer, whilst undertaking Personal Safety Training, starts learning how to handcuff a suspect by taking part in supervised practice using a mannikin (dummy). The trainer, observing the student practise and testing the results, then asked: 'Were there any risks to you during the cuffing? How tight did that feel for the suspect? What might you have done differently?'

That night the student police officer consults notes on how to handcuff suspects and reads about the reasons for doing it in particular ways, including force procedure and the human rights of the suspect. The next day, presented with a fellow student officer to handcuff, the student thinks: 'Now what did I do wrong yesterday and what did it say in those notes I read? I'll try it like this today.'

Identify in the above, each of the four stages of Kolb's ELC.

4.6 Studying

To begin with we should perhaps acknowledge that learning policing is sometimes a confusing and disorientating experience. In some cases we even have to **unlearn** before we can learn. For example, if you do not know that there are major legal differences between the offences of robbery and theft, you will have to unlearn what you thought you knew already! We tend not to view differences in definition as being particularly important in everyday life, but they are when you are dealing with the law. Taylor (1986) suggests that this discomfort we experience is actually a necessary part of adult learning. In particular, she discerned four distinct phases of the learning experience:

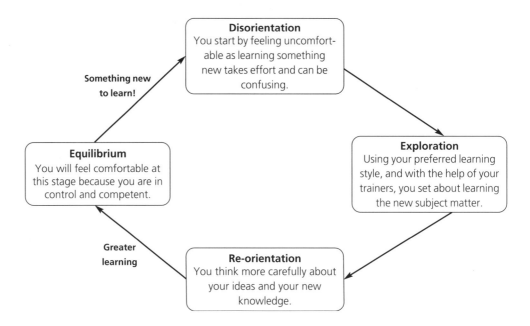

In summary, learning something new is often initially characterized by feelings of discomfort and anxiety. So, do not worry if you feel like this from time to time. Bear this in mind when studying and it will help you cope; it is quite normal to have some ups and downs as you learn.

4.6.1 Study Skills

There are numerous guides, books, and websites which can be used to help develop your ability to study. For example, if you are also undertaking a higher education award as part of your training then you may find it useful to work through Stella Cottrell's *Study Skills Handbook* (Cottrell, 2003). If you are also based for part of your training at an FE college or university then you will almost certainly find that your host organization offers support for study skills. Broadly, the following skills are normally involved in studying as a student police officer:

- Reading skills.
- Note taking.
- Memorizing.
- Using libraries and learning centres.
- Researching.
- Writing skills.
- Time management.
- Revising for assessments.

Finally, note that you may have undiagnosed difficulties in learning which could affect your ability to study. If you are based with an FE college or university then they will probably offer screening for these problems (normally at the outset of the programme).

> **TASK 8**
>
> Find out about the reading technique SQ3R, perhaps by using Google or another internet search engine. This will also prove useful to you if you undertake further training as an investigator over the next few years.

4.7   The Learning Requirement

When Her Majesty's Inspectorate of Constabulary (HMIC) published a report called '**Training Matters**' in 2002, it recommended fifty-nine ways to improve the training of student police officers (HMIC, 2002).

As one response to the recommendations, the Home Office sponsored an independent review by the University of the West of England and the University of East Anglia. Two of the co-authors of the review were Professors John Elliott and Saville Kushner, who have extensive experience in the on-going reform of initial police training. Their resulting 'Learning Requirement for Police Probationer Training in England and Wales' was described as 'society's validated expectation of what a police officer needs to know, to do and be disposed to do in the 21st century' (Elliott et al, 2003, p 2).

The Learning Requirement has played a major part in the design of the IPLDP curriculum, and has helped produce a framework of principles upon which the expectations of the knowledge, understanding, skills, attitudes, and behaviour (often called KUSAB, see Chapter 6) of a student police officer have been developed. It is also of importance in terms of informing your organization's approach to community engagement and PDUs (see sections 4.8 and 4.10 below respectively).

The Learning Requirement is divided into seven main headings:

1. Understanding and Engaging with the Local Community

Learning to position oneself appropriately as a police officer in the local community. In this context, local community includes temporary residential, Gypsy, and Traveller groups.

2. Enforcing the Law and Following Police Procedures

Learning to use the law appropriately in the context of professional judgement and learning to follow appropriate police procedures.

3. Responding to Human and Social Diversity

Learning to act appropriately in responding to human and social diversity, including but not exclusive to race, in (a) the community and (b) the police family.

4. Positioning oneself in the Role of a Police Officer inside the Police Organization

Learning to position oneself appropriately as a police officer in relation to the organization and the occupational culture.

5. Professional Standards and Ethical Conduct

Learning to live up to one's service ideals and standards.

6. Learning to Learn and Creating a Basis for Career-long Learning

Learning to learn about one's role as a police officer in the community and the police organization.

7. Qualities of Professional Judgement and Decision-Making

Full details of the Learning Requirement are given in Chapter 1.

4.8   Learning from the Community

Under the IPLDP, all student police officers are expected to undertake at least eighty hours of community engagement in the first few months of their service (normally as part of Phase 2 or Phase 3, if your force uses this terminology). These hours could be a continuous week of block placement or perhaps one or two days per week for a number of months. You will be based with a community group or a public, private, or voluntary organization such as a care home, a refugee support centre, or a youth-offending team. A particular emphasis is placed on the opportunities the placement provides for you to experience and explore issues around ethnicity and diversity (by 'issues around diversity' the police service normally means gender, disability, gay and lesbian groups, and age). However, the community engagement can also be used to give you an insight into the community's expectations of the police. Examples of these latter kinds of placements include being based in local supermarkets, hospitals, schools, and housing authority units.

You are not likely to be in uniform (or carrying personal safety equipment) whilst undertaking the community engagement. Your force and the community organization concerned may decide that it is best not to reveal to others involved that you are a student police officer in training. This is normally to allow you to interact as naturally as possible with the clients of the organization, particularly if some of these clients may be hostile to the police. If this is the case, bear the following in mind:

- your force will have conducted a risk assessment concerning the placement but, if you feel uncomfortable in terms of your own personal safety, then you should make this known to your force. If the problem persists then you may wish to contact your Police Federation representative (see section 7.17);
- there will be standard operating procedures (SOPs) in place to govern the relationships between your force and the organizations involved and also what you should do under certain circumstances—for example, in the case of questions concerning health and safety. Familiarize yourself with these SOPs.

TASK 9

You are on community engagement at a centre that provides support for young people who have been excluded from full-time secondary education. The young people at the day centre have been told that you are a student undertaking training and that you are at the centre in order to learn about their experiences and the work of the support group. However, they have not been told that you are a student police officer. During a break you observe one young person selling another what appears to be Ecstasy, a class B drug (see section 9.13). What do you do?

4.8.1   Making the Most of Your Community Engagement

The following are some suggestions on making the most of your community engagement:

- **find out about the organization** you are to be based with before you start your placement. For example, do they have a website setting out their aims and objectives? How are they funded? Are they inspected in some way? If so, you might find copies of inspection reports on the net;
- when on your placement, **engage** with people—for example, staff and clients of the organization. They will be as interested in you as you are in them and so you will probably find that any attempt on your part to learn more will be enthusiastically reciprocated;
- keep in mind the **objectives** of the community placement. It is easy to return to your initial police training extolling the benefits of engaging with a community group but with a less clear idea of what you actually achieved in terms of **learning** about community issues. Think also of ways in which you can evidence the skills and knowledge gained whilst on the placement and on reflection;

• consider ways to demonstrate how your understanding of the **ethics and values** of the police service has been enhanced through engagement with the community.

You are sometimes required to present your findings to fellow student officers and perhaps even members of the BCU that you are based with for Supervised Patrol. Your experiences whilst on community placements will also form the basis of a number of entries for your Learning Diary in the SOLAP (see section 6.6), perhaps through the mechanism of a professional assignment that you be asked to undertake. The community engagement is also likely to be relevant to some of the NOS and in particular Unit AA1 to 'promote equality and value diversity'.

Your experience of learning from the community is unlikely to be restricted to the community engagement alone. As noted earlier, you will also receive inputs from guest speakers and community representatives whilst you undertake your training. It is perhaps important to realize that these speakers are not necessarily experienced or qualified as teachers. Instead they are normally invited to contribute to your programme as a form of professional witness. You should make a real effort as a learner to engage with the guest speakers and achieve as much as possible from the session.

4.9   Diversity Training in the Police

One of the reasons for undertaking a community engagement see (section 4.8) is that it provides real and complex opportunities for you to witness and learn from the views and experiences of members of the diverse communities that make up the UK.

In general terms, diversity is about the range of features found in human life and culture including ethnicity, religion, gender, physical ability, age, sexual orientation, customs, and language. We ought perhaps to celebrate diversity as part of the richness of human cultures, but diversity is sometimes thought as a form of 'otherness'—that is, qualities that make 'them' different to 'us'.

As a student police officer, you will be asked think carefully about your own experiences and attitudes, and how these might affect the way you relate to the diverse range of people you will encounter in your work. What skills do you need to work effectively in the community, and how can diversity training help you develop these skills?

This section about diversity training in the police service explains why diversity training is important, how it takes place, and what it is that you will probably learn.

This part of the Handbook relates to NOS element AA1.1 which requires you to 'promote equality and value diversity'. As with most NOS elements, assessment of AA1.1 is most likely through direct observation of your actions, the records you keep, and testimony from witnesses. You are likely to encounter diversity training within IPLDP module IND 2, one of the Induction Modules. We also examine diversity as a key theme in policing in Chapter 5.

There is a tendency in some police environments to view diversity training as a form of inoculation. In fact, you sometimes hear police officers saying that they have 'had' their diversity training as if it were some form of one-off injection that would protect them for the rest of their careers. Perhaps it would be more appropriate to see diversity training as just the start of a process that will continue throughout your career.

4.9.1   Questions You Might Need to Consider

You might need to consider the following questions when undertaking your diversity training.

• What are my existing beliefs and attitudes about diversity?
• How will my beliefs and attitudes affect the way that I behave during my everyday and professional life?
• How will my behaviour affect other people around me?

But at the outset, why is it important to consider these questions? This is a crucial starting point because many (but not all) argue that our beliefs, attitudes, and values can spill over into our work whilst on duty as a police officer. Hence if you hold prejudices and bias towards certain groups of people (as most of us do), you are more likely to act upon your prejudices if you are not aware of them, and your conduct may fall short of the standards expected of police officers.

There have been a number of reports in recent years about the policing of diverse communities, and in particular the relationship between the police and ethnic minorities. Most student police officers will have heard of the Macpherson Inquiry into the circumstances surrounding the death of the black teenager Stephen Lawrence.

The police service and the community as a whole will expect you to adopt acceptable attitudes and behaviours. You should aim to satisfy their expectations because you are part of a public service for the communities you work in. On close examination of your own beliefs, you may find that you feel that there are some parts of the community who seem less deserving of a good level of service, especially if they are antagonistic towards the police. You will need to think carefully about this.

Finally, respect for diversity makes good policing sense. You are more likely to gain the co-operation of others, to secure information and intelligence, and hence to progress an investigation, if you are aware of the pluralistic nature of the communities within the UK and know how best to work with them.

4.9.2 The Aim of Diversity Training within the Police Service

The aim of diversity training within the police service is usually to help you to meet the expectations of the public you serve and of your organization regarding your attitude and behaviour towards other people and members of diverse communities.

Perhaps your own personal objective should be that you not only satisfy the expectations of your police force and the communities it serves, but more importantly that you actually believe in the value of diversity and respectful behaviour. In other words, not only should you behave appropriately because you have been trained to do so, but you should also appreciate the value of such behaviour on a personal level.

4.9.3 Looking Inwards

As an individual, you will view the world in your own way, but you also need to remember that other individuals will have their own view of the world too. Their views may well be different from yours, but their views still deserve respect, and have as much value as your own. To consider these issues fully, you will need to genuinely engage with your trainers, your colleagues and most of all, yourself.

In particular you will need to examine what you know about yourself in relation to diversity and the following issues:

> What I know about myself as an individual:
> - how I currently behave;
> - my current beliefs;
> - my current values;
> - my present attitudes;
> - how my background has influenced me.
>
> What I know about myself as a student police officer:
> - my responsibilities;
> - the duties I have to perform;
> - my career history;
> - the policies I have to follow;
> - how the law affects me.

TASK 10

Take the time to think, then take a plain piece of paper and jot down your thoughts about the points above—you might find it quite hard to see yourself in these ways. Reflect upon your ideas—which parts have you found easy, and which parts have been more puzzling? Do you know why? Through asking yourself these questions, you will be preparing yourself for genuine engagement with police service diversity training.

TASK 11

Consider:

- your experiences in life so far and those you are likely to have in the near future;
- your prejudices and their influence on what you do;
- your assumptions and stereotypical views, and their consequences;
- your view of the world you live in and the people within it;
- your ability to mix well in a social environment with people from other backgrounds and cultures to your own.

Again, take some time to think about each point in turn. Make brief notes on a plain piece of paper and reflect upon your answers.

4.9.4 Diversity and the Experiential Learning Cycle

We discussed the experiential learning cycle, and its use in police training and education, earlier in this chapter. A similar approach can be used to help you learn about your own attitudes and behaviour and how diversity can be valued. This is illustrated in the diagram below.

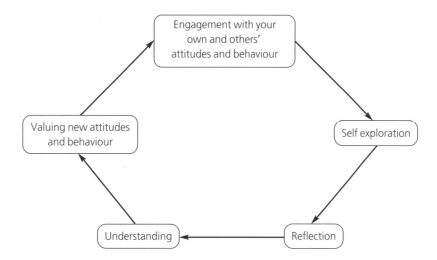

One starting point in the cycle could be **Engagement with Your Own and Others' Attitudes and Behaviour.** You will have the opportunity to observe diversity in a variety of locations:

- in your training during role plays and discussions;
- during your community engagement (see section 4.8);
- during simulations and work place situations;
- off duty, with friends, colleagues, and relatives.

Use these experiences to observe diversity; what differences do you see in how people behave and their attitudes and beliefs? Try to be open to feedback and discussion; remember that other people probably feel as certain about their beliefs and attitudes as you feel about yours!

The next stage of the cycle is **self-exploration**. Whatever environment you find yourself in, use the time to observe and think about yourself. Consider how you arrived at your existing values, attitudes, and beliefs:

- What part of your history contributed towards how you behave now?
- Did you arrive at your existing beliefs as a result of influences in your background or from self-teaching? In other words, was your attitude 'caught' or 'taught'?

The **reflection** phase of the cycle might make you feel uncomfortable, frustrated, anxious, or even confused. After all, you may not have ever questioned your own values and beliefs, and now that you have, you might be feeling some self-doubt. You might also feel uneasy about the people around you if they hold differing views to you. Remind yourself why you are exploring the way you think and the future benefits of all your hard work. Remind yourself of what you want to achieve and begin to work towards it.

After a period of disorientation, you will begin to have some **understanding** and feel more comfortable. You will have recognized during your training that much of how you think and what you do is as a result of the environment you have been living in. You will have faced your own prejudices and seen that you can live with them, as long as you do not treat anybody differently as a result. You may well change some, if not all, of your prejudices by facing them head-on and seeing how self-defeating they can be.

With time, you may come to **value your new attitudes and behaviours**. The journey may be a slow one, and you may have sudden moments of insight at unexpected times. Whatever happens to you, as long as you have remained open-minded, open to change and taken part with enthusiasm and professionalism, you will have achieved greater understanding.

TASK 12

After completing the various suggested activities above, consider writing up your reflections as evidence towards the knowledge requirement of CAR1A4 within your SOLAP.

4.10 Professional Development Units (PDUs)

Earlier you read about the three learning domains and that your learning as a student police officer is often designed by your trainers to begin with relatively simple tasks. This might involve acquiring largely factual knowledge, and once this has been assimilated your learning will become progressively more developed until you are able to **apply** your learning.

It will sometimes be appropriate therefore to perform the simpler tasks away from other influences, such as the general public, so that you can easily rectify mistakes and clarify any misunderstandings. In this way, you will apply your learning in simulated situations at first which makes things more controllable and hence safer for all concerned. Eventually though, it will be appropriate for you to go onto the streets of your town or city and begin the process of policing your community, first on Supervised Patrol and then later on Independent Patrol. As this is a daunting prospect at first for anyone, you will be allocated a tutor, coach, or mentor to support you during your initial training and probably also be attached to a Professional Development Unit (PDU).

4.10.1 PDUs

Professional Development Units (also known occasionally as Probationer Development Units) are a relatively new phenomenon in policing. In some forces PDUs have only been established in the last year or so, and this might partly explain why some force BCUs struggle to support a large number of student police officers (HMIC, 2005a, p 17). PDUs are usually physically based within the BCU and they often carry out a large number of tasks. These include assisting police officers who have transferred from other forces, supporting police officers back into reactive policing duties (for example, after a period of illness) as well as providing important aspects of initial police training—the training of student police officers. However, practice does vary significantly from force to force. In some forces there may be PDUs in every BCU whilst in others a single PDU serves the whole force. Staffing also varies, as does the management structure and the type of resources available to the PDU, so it is difficult to describe a typical PDU. However, a BCU police officer of inspector rank or above is likely to carry responsibility for a PDU, line-managing sergeants, and Pcs (sometimes referred to as training officers) based with the PDU itself.

The PDU is likely to work alongside the other departments in your organization and might be part of your training department (in fact you might receive all your training at the PDU, including classroom-based teaching). You can expect your tutor at the PDU (sometimes called a tutor constable or assessor constable) to be an experienced officer with skills in coaching and assessment and with the ability to deliver a service in a professional manner including the application of safe working practices. Whatever the particular arrangements, the PDU is likely to be of crucial importance to you during your two years' training towards Confirmation, an observation supported by the Home Office (2005c, p 22): 'The importance of the role of the Professional Development Unit in providing and supporting…learning experiences throughout the whole of the probationary period cannot be overstated.'

4.10.2 What Are the Advantages of the PDU?

PDUs provide you with the opportunity to apply the learning you have gained previously in the training room at university, college, or training school in a controlled environment. So, instead of being immersed straight away in a world of reactive policing, you can reinforce selected aspects of your learning in simulations of genuine policing tasks, chosen for you by your trainer or tutor.

The further advantages of this system include the opportunity for your tutor and you to carry out activities, usually on a one-to-one basis (Home Office, 2005c). You will be able to discuss what you intend to do and say at an incident (a **pre-brief**). You will then be able to deal with the incident itself in an effective, safe, and professional manner, albeit in a monitored or co-pilot fashion with your tutor/coach, and then discuss the incident afterwards in a safe environment (**debrief**). This will help you learn, and you will find yourself moving through the different stages of the learning cycle (the ELC, see section 4.5). As further reinforcement, you will probably be asked to make entries in your Learning Diary (see section 4.12), which will provide you with further opportunities for self-assessment and reflection.

Within the PDU, there will be staff members who will assess your competence against the NOS and PAC, and this might involve your own tutor. In turn, the Home Office expects these people to be competent to perform this task, perhaps demonstrated through undertaking an assessor's award although this is not compulsory (Home Office, 2005c). Both your tutor and your line manager will take responsibility for your development and you will be advised by your force to use every opportunity to prove your competency by collecting evidence in your SOLAP (see section 6.6).

You may find yourself wondering if you could learn everything you need to by being out on the streets. There are one or two police forces that may believe this too, but most subscribe to the view that you will succeed best through a combination of learning in the training room (and through reading and study) and learning in practice, through the support of your PDU and others. How would you feel if you discovered that your newly-qualified GP had spent seven years practising on patients but had never actually formally learned anatomy and physiology? In most police forces therefore, the training will combine both the theory and the practice.

4.11 Coaching

In police training, coaching is normally carried out on a one coach to one student basis with the aim of assisting individuals to perform a task competently. Coaching will be one of the responsibilities of your tutor or mentor, and particularly so when you are based with a PDU (see section 4.10).

As soon as you have been given details of your tutor(s), try to arrange a meeting at the earliest opportunity; make contact via your organization's e-mail system or by telephone. When you meet, you may find yourself talking about your background, how you came to join the police, and what you are aiming for. Do not say too much if it makes you feel uncomfortable, and remember to tell your tutor the name by which you wish to be referred to. Take with you your SOLAP if it contains any feedback from your training staff at university or training centre, so that your tutor can start to get to know you.

Be prepared to explain your own preferred learning style having completed the first five tasks of this chapter. Show them entries from your Learning Diary (see section 4.12) to help illustrate your strengths and weaknesses, so that together you can create a development plan for the future. Take with you a list of subjects that you have already learned in theory, so that you can agree upon a development plan of how to apply your learning in the work place.

4.11.1 The Coaching Process

Your tutor will use a variety of techniques to help you learn.

Questioning is a valuable technique. Your tutor may use closed questions or check information from you. He/she will use open questions to receive full answers from you, and will use reflective questions to check understanding of what you have said. If they use multiple questions you need to answer one question at a time to avoid confusion. Watch out for leading questions as they might also confuse you; value-loaded ones could lead you to agree with them when you might have a different opinion. Remember, these observations could equally well apply to your own use of questions, so you should be aware of what style of questions to ask your tutor.

Coaching often takes place before and after you attend an incident as part of Supervised Patrol. These incidents may have been cherry picked by the PDU, that is they wait for a particular incident to be reported (such as a suspected shoplifting incident) and then accompany you to that incident. In some cases, for practical or other reasons, you may attend any incident that day, regardless of its nature. In either eventuality, your response to incidents (but not necessarily on the first occasion) will be important in terms of your subsequent assessment against the NOS (see Chapter 6).

Pre-briefs are a good way of preparing for attending an incident. Your tutor will question you about the theory you have learned in the training room and then ask you how you intend to deal with the incident.

Debriefs take place after an incident. Your tutor will choose a suitable environment in which to debrief you. You will probably be asked to reflect on the incident and make notes (which you can use later for your Learning Diary) of what went well for you at the incident, and what did not go quite so well for you. Using these points, your tutor may employ the ELC we described in section 4.5 to develop greater learning by asking questions such as 'What happened at the incident? So what was the outcome of that? Now what are you going to do differently (or better) in the future?'

The **feedback** your tutor offers you serves two main purposes; first to reassure you that your contribution has been recognized and noted, and secondly to help you develop the skills and abilities required. When giving feedback your tutor might well use the following guidelines:

1. Giving feedback only on things that can be changed.
2. Only describing what they have observed.
3. Being specific.
4. Resisting the temptation to make judgements.
5. Choosing the most appropriate time to give the feedback.
6. Giving the feedback as soon as possible after making the observation.
7. Remembering they cannot force an individual to change.

A common technique employed is to structure the feedback as a kind of sandwich, by first making an observation on something you did well, then discussing a developmental point, and then returning to something you did well.

Identifying your learning needs helps you and your tutor plan for the future. As a result of the pre-brief, your performance during the incident, and the debrief, both you and your tutor will be able to identify your learning needs for the future and these can be entered in your Learning Diary. You may need to revise the theory once more, or take part in a simulated exercise or it may be that you simply need more practice.

After time you may come to the conclusion that some aspects of policing are largely based upon using a 'reference library' of previous experiences that you can call upon and select when dealing with incidents as they are presented to you. Eventually, incidents, calls, and circumstances will begin to look familiar and you will feel more confident in dealing with situations—the stage of proficiency that we described in section 4.2 above.

4.12 The Learning Diary

The place of the Learning Diary in the SOLAP and its function within Learning Development Reviews are described in Chapter 6. You will be asked to keep a Learning Diary throughout your training, but the format of the diary is likely to reflect the particular phase of training (for example, the style used for community engagement will not be the same as that used for Supervised Patrol). This should be explained to you during the induction phase of your training. Your Learning Diary is meant to provide you with an opportunity to write down personal reflections, so that you will be able to make judgements on your progress, evidence competency for assessment purposes, and plan future development. Consider structuring your diary entries to follow the four stages of the ELC which we described earlier in section 4.5. You should therefore seek to answer the following questions in each Learning Diary entry, such as:

- What happened?
- How did you, and the others around you, respond?
- What was the outcome of the events?
- What could you do differently, or better, in the future?

During the first two phases of training you will probably be asked to make weekly entries in your Learning Diary and then on a monthly basis.

The following is an example of a number of (fictitious) Learning Diary entries.

Student Police Officer: Pc Phillips

Crime

Whilst on night duty on mobile patrol, my tutor and I were sent along with other patrols to an audible alarm activation at a newsagents on a housing estate where suspects had been seen to make off on foot with cigarettes and alcohol.

Key learning points:

Choosing the right search parameters when called to incidents.

What surprised me?

My tutor did not drive us straight to the newsagents but began an area search for the suspects some distance away having judged how long it took for the alarm to be notified to control, how long it took for us to be sent to the call and how far the suspects could have travelled on foot in that time.

How will I put this learning into practice?

In the future, if appropriate I will also notify control of my intention not to go straight to the scene, but to judge how long it has been since the incident took place, taking into consideration direction of travel of the suspect(s) and begin my search some distance away from the scene. I will also consider sitting up in a static location with the engine of the car switched off, waiting and listening as well as requesting a dog patrol to attend to track the suspect.

Intelligence

Today in our briefing we were given intelligence about a known criminal who is suspected of committing burglaries in our area during the day time. The MO of the suspect is to gain entry via insecure windows at the back of terraced houses, make an untidy search and take high value electronic equipment in pillow cases from the house and leave via the front door.

Key learning points:

The importance of intelligence to police operations.

What surprised me?

Whilst on foot patrol today, my tutor and I saw the same suspect from the briefing on a housing estate, apparently trying to hide from us in the back garden of a house. We confirmed with the homeowner that the suspect did not have permission to be in the garden. His behaviour, the existence of information, time of day, and location were our grounds to look for stolen property and we carried out a s1 PACE search. In a pillow case just a few feet from the suspect we found an iPod, another make of MP3 player and a DVD recorder. I arrested the suspect as his arrest was necessary for one of the reasons we learnt about during training.

How will I put this learning into practice?

This incident reinforced the importance of intelligence. I will pay more attention to briefings as the information in them helps my patrol skills and gives me the opportunity to pay attention to specific areas and to specific people. I see now that intelligence-led policing can really work and help me to add to my reasonable suspicion to carry out s1 PACE searches. I will also go to the Intel unit by myself from time to time to get current information on disqual drivers and their cars.

Investigation and interview

While observing my tutor constable interviewing a shoplifter I had arrested in the shopping centre, I saw how to prove the offence by interview.

Key learning points:

Questioning techniques for interviewing.

What surprised me?

I was expecting my tutor to use the words like "Did you dishonestly appropriate the property from the shop with the intention of keeping it?" What actually happened was that my tutor used open questions and everyday language and kind of managed the conversation. Questions were used such as "Why did you go into the shop"? "What were you thinking about when you picked up the bottle of scotch"? "How much money did you take to go shopping today"? "What did you want to do with the scotch"?

How will I put this learning into practice?

In my interviews I will attempt to establish the truth not by using the words in the legislation so much as general conversation which will get a better response from the suspect for the points we may need to prove. I will attempt to use open questions when appropriate to get as much information from the suspect and begin my questions with "Tell me about . . .". This appeared to me to be a better way of interviewing a suspect.

Non-crime incidents

Today my tutor and I were requested to attend a misper call which involved a 10 year old child who had gone missing from the parental home.

Key learning points:

An appropriate initial response to child mispers.

What surprised me?

Before we started to complete the misper form my tutor asked the parents if they had looked for the child themselves. They said they had searched the whole house but even so, my tutor said that another search would have to be done. I observed my tutor searching the house and gardens of the misper looking for anywhere that a child of that age could hide. We looked for any voids or spaces which could contain a child. After a little while, we went to an old shed at the bottom of the garden and found the child hiding. My tutor then asked some questions of the parents and the child about why he might have chosen to hide in the way he did.

How will I put this learning into practice?

When I receive the report of a misper, especially a child, I will normally consider starting the enquiry by making a thorough search of the home address, even if the family have said they have already done one. This might save a lot of time in the long run and might prevent a large scale search involving lots of time and people. I will look for any spaces which would contain a child and concentrate my efforts to locate these spaces in the first place.

Police policies and procedures

Today we attended the scene of a road traffic collision between two cars. Neither of the drivers were accompanied nor injured. The vehicles themselves had very slight damage and the collision took place at a t-junction at very slow speed.

Key learning points:

The importance of following force policy.

What surprised me?

I did not have any suspicion that either of the drivers had been drinking, but even so, my tutor reminded me of our force policy to give a breath test to every driver involved in road traffic collision using the powers under the Road Traffic Act. I was surprised to discover that, even though it was only 8.30 am, one of the drivers proved positive and I arrested him.

How will I put this learning into practice?

In the future I will take care to implement force policy and breathalyse every driver involved in a crash whether I suspect them of having been drinking or not. This will be the case in whatever circumstances the crash takes place and whether or not any other driving offences are suspected or not.

Protecting people

Whilst on foot patrol in the shopping centre today, my tutor asked me to imagine I was a thief, to look around at the shoppers and to consider who is most likely to become a victim of a crime whilst out shopping.

Key learning points:

Crime prevention is just as important as crime detection.

What surprised me?

When I looked around I saw people paying very little attention to their valuable property. I saw people of all ages carrying mobile telephones very insecurely in their hands, giving a thief the opportunity to snatch them out of their hands. This was a similar thing for others with their iPods, it was if they didn't see the dangers. There were also a number of people holding large amounts of money in their hands and a great number of older and more vulnerable women carrying their purses very high up in handbags which could easily be snatched. Together with my tutor we began advising some of these people about the possible consequences of their actions.

How will I put this learning into practice?

Whenever it is appropriate to offer crime prevention advice I will do so. For example, If I observe a vulnerable person keeping their purse near the top of their bag I will take the opportunity to tell them that it could be snatched and that they should think about fixing a chain onto the purse at one end and attaching the other end to their bag.

Stops and searches

While out with my tutor today I saw a number of searches being carried out by other officers. Some of the searches did not go quite as well as the others and in some of them the suspects were clearly not as compliant.

Key learning points:

The importance of following a professional 'stop, account and search' routine.

What surprised me?

Most of the searches in which the suspects had been more compliant were the ones where the searching officers gave the suspect the PACE Codes of Practice requirements for searching. What I saw was the searching officers going through the requirements using the mnemonic GOWISELY. The effect of this seemed to be that the suspects thought the searching officers really knew their powers and so they did not try to obstruct or interfere in the process.

How will I put this learning into practice?

When I carry out my searches I will do exactly the same thing and use the mnemonic GOWISELY to remind me of what to say. Before today, I have to say that I thought I was taught it only to help me remember what was in the code for my exam, but now I realise how important it is and the effect it has on people that are being searched.

Traffic

Today on mobile patrol, we must have stopped between 10 and 20 vehicles at various times of the day. Each time we stopped a vehicle it was to give some advice to the driver.

Key learning points:

The need to address driver and passenger safety.

What surprised me?

The reasons why we stopped the vehicles did not appear to be major issues as far as I was concerned. The stops were for no seat belts, children that were too short to be in the front seat of a car, parking near crossings and minor speeding. Then, after speaking to my tutor, I realised that we have a responsibility towards road safety and that it is part of our job to prevent injury to drivers, passengers or pedestrians, not just to 'catch criminals'. After all if we can prevent someone's head hitting the windscreen or the head of another passenger when the vehicle is involved in a crash by reminding them to wear their seat belt or wearing it properly, then we might have saved a lot of pain and misery. Equally, parking near crossings cannot take place as it endangers the lives of pedestrians using the crossings. Finally, we learnt recently in class that 30 mph areas are there for a purpose and exceeding the speed limit by even a small amount may mean the difference between life and death for a pedestrian.

How will I put this learning into practice?

Even when I am over-worked with calls to attend, I will try to take the time to give advice to road users as there are thousands of deaths and injuries on the road each year as a result of bad driving, not wearing seatbelts, bad parking and insecure children. I will point out that the problem lies in the unexpected situations that can arise within split seconds that cannot be avoided. It will be difficult for me sometimes to be motivated to give advice to a road user when I am tired and hungry, but I must remember that one day I might not take up the opportunity to say something and a moment or two later that same road user is involved in a crash and is injured or possibly dies. I would find that very hard to cope with.

> **TASK 13**
>
> Use the theories we have discussed in this chapter to plan a number of entries in your Learning Diary related to your experiences when being coached or taught, using the following suggestions:
>
> - Make reference to your preferred learning style.
> - Determine which learning domain(s) you have been working within for any particular incident and what level of that domain you reached.
> - Assess what level of the domain you need to return to if it was acknowledged that you were not competent to carry out the task, and produce a plan in your diary to develop greater learning.
> - Use the diagnosis of your preferred learning style to create a methodology which you prefer.
> - Describe how you will enhance your ability to recall facts by employing memory tools.
> - Use the outcomes of pre-briefs and debriefs held with your tutor to make diary entries and use the ELC process within the entry to make an action plan for yourself for the future.
> - During the taught part of your course at college, university, training centre, or PDU, reflect on the legislation, policy, and procedure you have learned and consider how you will put the theory into practice and make subsequent diary entries.
> - During your placements in the community and within the extended police family, reflect on the benefit of interacting with these groups and how you will use the learning you have gained from the placements in the work place in the future.
> - During the periods with your tutor, reflect on your ability to satisfy the performance criteria of the NOS and assess yourself against the PAC and make diary entries accordingly (see Chapter 6).

4.13 Forms of Reasoning and Argument

An important aspect of learning, either as a student police officer undertaking training, or as an experienced police officer, is a **logical and structured** approach to problem solving. This is not to deny the use of intuition as a problem solving approach; many cases of intuition in fact rest on rational thought processes, but the person is unaware of this because their reasoning is not part of their conscious thought. We are not suggesting that we should all behave like the Star Trek character Mr Spock with his absolute adherence to purely logical argument; we must always leave room for creativity. Many people would also probably claim to be naturally logical, and hence not require any particular training or, indeed, any particular need to read this part of the Handbook. However, logical ways of thinking are skills that need to be nurtured and developed and not simply assumed to already exist at the appropriate level.

Logic underpins the development of sound arguments which we use to express ourselves (sometimes in a formal context, such as a courtroom, on other occasions in our Learning Diaries). Perhaps just as important, in the policing context, is the ability to identify **fallacious** (incorrect) lines of argument. On occasions these have, at least in part, led to miscarriages of justice and to innocent people enduring long prison sentences.

Reasoning is also an important skill to develop within investigation and you will find references to investigative reasoning in the IPLDP Crime Investigation Model during your training (see Chapter 12).

4.13.1 Inductive Reasoning

Inductive reasoning involves generalizing from a number of previous examples to establish a rule or theory. This form of reasoning is very common in everyday life and, indeed, was the basis for much scientific discovery in the past. (There are some suggestions that this form of reasoning is hardwired into our brains, as most people appear able to use this reasoning without any training.) For example, early humans undoubtedly realized that there is a cycle consisting of day-night-day-night and generalized from this pattern to conclude that, in all future events, night would follow day. On a certain intellectual level most of us are probably content that induction is sufficient grounds for us to retain our acceptance of the day-night-day cycle. We do not necessarily require convincing with the use of cosmological arguments concerning the motions of the Earth, Sun, and the entropy of the Solar System. The more this confidence is reinforced by subsequent events, the more we are persuaded by the truth of the generalization. This is known as the **rule of inductive generalization**.

However, despite being a widespread technique for reasoning, induction has an inherent weakness. As Bertrand Russell, Karl Popper, and others have demonstrated (Popper, 1990), there is no **logical reason** why the generalization should follow from the observations. A famous example concerns swans. If every example of a swan that we have seen is coloured white then we (not unnaturally) conclude that **all** swans are white. This is all very well until we observe our first black swan. (They occur in the southern hemisphere.)

This is not to say that inductive reasoning has no value, but simply that we should be cautious in its application. The danger for student police officers (and indeed, for all of us) when using inductive methods resides in the problem of generalization from observation, particularly if these observations are limited in number or unrepresentative. For example, consider the white detective investigating gun crime within inner London. In all likelihood, given the social demography of the area (there are significant numbers of ethnic minority people living in inner London), these crimes are likely to involve members of ethnic minorities to an extent that might appear disproportionate to a detective new to the area. However, these parts of Britain also tend to feature amongst some of the poorest (as do parts of Manchester and Birmingham). A false generalization here would be for our detective to conclude, using induction, that gun crime is some how endemically black in nature rather than symptomatic of some other social phenomena that have independent links with gun crime and being black. There is no evidence to show that ethnicity can cause gun crime. In some senses the incorrect reasoning of the detective is a natural response and this demonstrates the need for an understanding of the nature and limitations of inductive reasoning. The detective's error in judgement is not helped by some parts of the media referring to gun crime in London as a 'black on black' phenomenon. In summary, the mistake made here by our detective is to mistake association for causality and he or she does so by the incorrect application of inductive reasoning.

Similarly, unless unchecked, we all have a tendency to look for evidence which supports our generalized inductive theories and to ignore other evidence. This is particularly problematic in investigations. (The proper scientific approach is to look for evidence which might contradict our theories.)

It helps, particularly if you move on later to more advanced training in investigation, to be aware that there are a number of forms of inductive reasoning. A very common form of inductive reasoning used within criminal investigation is the so-called 'argument from analogy'. Note that in the following example:

- **Premises** does not have its usual everyday or legal meanings (such as a building). In this context, premises refer to starting points for the argument.
- The letters A, B, C, and so on are shorthand for observations or other known facts.
- **Has the property of** is a technical term meaning that the two listed items share a quality in common.

Argument from Analogy

- A has the property of C
- B has the property of C
- B has the property of D

(Together, these statements are called the **premises**)

Therefore (and this is the **argument** part)

- A has the property of D (the **conclusion**)

In fact, there are usually more than three premises as illustrated with this example, adapted from <http://faculty.ncwc.edu/TOConnor/315/315lect03.htm>:

- Tuesday's burglary was committed during the night (T has the property of N).
- Wednesday's burglary was committed during the night (W has the property of N).

- Tuesday's burglary took place in Acacia Gardens (T has the property of A).
- Wednesday's burglary took place in Acacia Gardens (W has the property of A).
- Tuesday's burglary involved forcing a window (T has the property of F).
- Wednesday's burglary involved forcing a window (W has the property of F).
- Tuesday's burglary involved a careful search for property (T has the property of C).
- Wednesday's burglary involved a careful search for property (W has the property of C).

Suppose we now know that:

- Tuesday's burglary was committed by Bill (T has the property of B).

Therefore our conclusion is that:

- Wednesday's burglary was also probably committed by Bill (W has the property of B).

Note that we cannot be **certain** that Bill committed the burglary on Wednesday, as this is inductive reasoning. It is also true that we could probably work out that Bill is a suspect (due to the similarities in circumstances) without knowing about 'arguments from analogy'. However, formalizing the reasoning used in this way has two main advantages:

- we know where this reasoning comes from;
- we know its strengths and limitations.

TASK 14

You are given the numbers 2, 4, 8, and 16.
What is the next number in the pattern?
(Check the answer—it is not 32!).

4.13.2 Deductive Reasoning

In contrast with inductive reasoning, deductive approaches start with assumptions (or a general rule) and **deduce** other conclusions from these starting points. For example, we may assume that all human beings have DNA. If we arrest John, a human being, then we can conclude that John has DNA. Deductive reasoning forms part of a wider set of concepts and methods known as logic. In fact there are two main schools of logic known as formal logic or sometimes symbolic logic which is mathematically derived (using, for example, set theory) and informal logic which uses everyday language. We will examine informal logic in this Handbook. We can use deductive logic to draw conclusions from initial assumptions. For example, in terms of John and DNA we can describe our logical process in the following ways:

- All humans have DNA
- John is a human
- Therefore John has DNA

This is known as an **argument** (see section 4.13.4).

Deductive reasoning also has its drawbacks. In essence, it helps us to extend what we already know by demonstrating the consequences of our assumptions rather than adding directly to the pool of new knowledge. Further, although the logic is impeccable the value of our conclusions is entirely dependent on the truth of our assumptions (see section 4.13.5).

4.13.3 Inductive and Deductive Reasoning: The Debate

In conclusion, inductive reasoning is a useful means of adding to our knowledge, but is inherently untrustworthy. On the other hand, deductive reasoning is logically watertight but only extends what we already know. The two approaches are not in competition or contradiction (as some writers claim) but perhaps should be viewed as complementary ways of reasoning. A good example is falling from a building. We can observe that on every occasion somebody jumps or is pushed from a building then they fall a distance before they are stopped (usually by the ground). Inductive reasoning tells us that this will always be the case. Deductive reasoning would use Newton's Laws, with the added advantage of being able to predict, say, the velocity on impact. The two approaches are not contradictory. Indeed, the starting points for deductive reasoning are often determined inductively.

TASK 15

Classify the following statements as examples of inductive or deductive reasoning or a combination of the two (use only the statements given to you—make no other assumptions).

(a) Every person's fingerprint is unique to him/her, as no two fingerprints have ever been found to match.

(b) If anything made up largely of water boils at approximately 100°C, and blood is mostly water, then it must boil at roughly 100°C.

(c) You need to take care when searching the clothes of a suspect as many criminals are drug addicts and they may have syringe needles hidden somewhere.

(d) Defence barristers cannot have a conscience, because they are prepared to defend somebody like Myra Hindley (she was a notorious child killer).

(e) Anyone who works long and difficult hours in their job should be paid well. Police officers work long and difficult hours, so they should be paid well.

(f) If DNA is entirely inherited and two people are found with the same DNA profile then they must be identical twins.

4.13.4 Arguments

Technically speaking, an **argument** is a group of propositions of which one is claimed to follow from the others—the process known as **inference**.

Consider the following simple example of an argument:

- All humans have DNA.
- John is human.

(We now draw the inference).
- Therefore John has DNA (the conclusion).

Of course, in everyday policing, arguments are not usually expressed in this way. Instead they are incorporated into sentences, sometimes with information extraneous to the argument, and often with the conclusion presented first. Written arguments often contain hidden premises (see section 4.13.1 for a description of premises) which are not immediately obvious to the untrained eye. It requires skill (derived from practice) to identify the premises, forms of argument, and the conclusions and, most importantly, to decide whether these arguments are logically justified or not.

There are however, various key words which give clues to the structure of the argument, in terms of the premises and the conclusions:

Examples of premises	Examples of conclusions
Because	eg
All	It follows that
Since	Therefore
Firstly	Thus
However	We can conclude that
For the reason that	Only
Obviously	
Let's assume	

TASK 16

Just for fun, try the following Critical Thinkers' Questionnaire (some questions are adapted from Facione (1998), most are original). Answer each question with an Agree or a Disagree. Then calculate your critical thinker index by turning to the answer to Task 16 at the end of this chapter.

(a) I dislike those parts of talk shows where people just state their opinions but never give any reasons at all.

(b) I'm entitled to my opinions.

(c) If a person's DNA is found at the scene of a crime then they must have been there.

(d) No matter how complex the problem there is probably a simple solution.

(e) God either exists or doesn't exist. Therefore the chances that he exists are 50:50.

(f) Rather than relying on someone else's notes, I prefer to read the material myself.

(g) Working out what people really mean by what they say is important to me.

(h) If somebody is really sincere in their arguments then the case they are making is more likely to be correct.

(i) I prefer not to make decisions until I've thought through my options.

(j) I try to see merit in other people's opinions even if I disagree with them.

(k) The reason why the US has such a high murder rate is because of the widespread availability of guns.

(l) The validity of an idea is enhanced by effective communication skills.

(m) A theory is always false if it is incorrectly argued.

(n) I dislike it when tutors discuss problems rather than just giving the answers.

(o) You can't disprove the existence of leprechauns.

4.13.5 Forms of Argument and Proof

As you have seen, an argument is the process of drawing inferences from premises. As well as logic, arguments also tend to take certain assumptions as being inherently true. For example, the 'law of the excluded middle' which states that it is not possible for something to be and not be at the same time. So a person committed arson or they did not. Similarly we have the 'law of identity': if A is the same as B, and B is the same as A, then A and B are the same. So if a substance is tested by a forensic laboratory and has the same chemical composition as diamorphine then it is diamorphine.

There are many forms of argument which are logically justifiable and we will examine those most relevant to both learning as a student police officer and more widely in policing itself. Likewise, there are some forms of arguments which are not valid arguments at all and, unfortunately, these are very common and are referred to as **fallacies** (see section 4.13.7). In order to learn, it is important that we avoid fallacies and so we need to be able to spot them.

The most famous forms of deductive argument are drawn from a family of arguments referred to as **syllogisms** (eg categorical, disjunctive, and hypothetical syllogisms). For example, the categorical syllogism is an argument consisting of two premises and a conclusion; usually employing the concepts of 'all', 'some', and 'none'. Probably the most famous example is as follows:

A famous syllogism

• All men are mortal (called the major premise).
• Socrates was a man (called minor premise).

Therefore (as before, this is the inference)
• Socrates was mortal (conclusion).

In general terms, the categorical syllogism goes something like this:

- All As are Bs.
- C is an A.

Therefore:
- C is a B.

As another example of a syllogism, consider the famous logic of Conan-Doyle's Sherlock Holmes (paraphrased as 'the dog that didn't bark'):

> The Simpson incident had shown me that a dog was kept in the stables, and yet, though someone had been in and had fetched out a horse, he had not barked enough to arouse the two lads in the loft. Obviously the midnight visitor was someone whom the dog knew well (Conan-Doyle, 1894, p 9).

However, there are many other forms of argument beyond the syllogisms (some of which are potentially probably more useful to you). An example is the **modus tollens** form of argument:

- If P then Q (a premise).
- Q is false (a premise).

We conclude:
- P is false (the conclusion).

As an everyday example (adapted from <http://faculty.ncwc.edu/TOConnor/315/315lect03 .htm>) of modus tollens might occur during an investigation into homicide:

- If Mary's boyfriend deserves to be a suspect, he must have a motive (a premise).
- Mary's boyfriend does not have an apparent motive (a premise).

We then have a conclusion:
- Mary's boyfriend is probably not the offender (the conclusion).

Note that the first premise ('If Mary's boyfriend deserves to be a suspect, he must have a motive') might well have been established using inductive reasoning (see section 4.13.1) as most victims of murder are murdered by those they know, and there is normally a motive for the murder.

It is important to note that, if we begin our arguments with correct premises and then argue logically, we can be assured that our conclusions are also correct. However, if we start with false premises then, although we may use a logical and deductive argument, **we cannot say anything** about the truth of our conclusions: they may be true or untrue. This is an important observation in the context of policing.

For example, consider the following argument:

- All humans are self-centred (a premise).
- Criminals are humans (a premise).

Therefore:
- Criminals are self-centred (the conclusion).

This is a perfectly valid **argument** but the validity of the **conclusion** depends entirely upon the truth of the premises. The premise that 'All humans are self-centred' might not be correct.

The relationship between premises, arguments, and conclusions is summarized in the table below:

Premises	Argument	Conclusion
Valid	Valid	Valid
Invalid	Valid	Valid or invalid (we do not know)
Valid	Invalid	Valid or invalid (we do not know)
Invalid	Invalid	Valid or invalid (we do not know)

As an example, consider the following written argument taken from a report in the late 1990s:

> Human rights training in the RUC also lags behind other police organizations we have spoken to. In the new curriculum (introduced only this year), of 700 sessions of training there are only 2 sessions dedicated to human rights, compared with 40 of drill and 63 of firearms training (Patten Commission, 1999, para 4.5).

We can summarize this argument as follows:

- The proportion of time taken in training a skill or subject reflects its relative importance (a premise).
- A new curriculum provided an opportunity for the RUC to reassess the relative importance of these skills and subjects (a premise).
- The RUC spends proportionally more time training drill than human rights compared with others (a premise).
- The RUC spends proportionally more time training firearms than human rights compared with others (a premise).

Therefore

- Human rights training in the RUC lags behind other police forces (the conclusion).

How valid is the conclusion based upon the premises?

Well, we can probably take issue with a number of the premises. For example, the first—that the time taken is proportional to the relative importance. What else could it be proportional to? Drill is an example of a psychomotor skill (see section 4.3.2 above). Psychomotor skills quite often take longer to perfect than others. (For example, a carpenter/joiner could explain the theory concerning the dove-tail joint to you relatively easily. Constructing such a joint from wood is an entirely different matter.) Taking longer to perfect a skill does not, by itself, prove that we attach more importance to it. So, even though the argument is a valid one, if we have serious doubts concerning the premises then we must also have doubts concerning the validity of the conclusion.

(Remember, we are not saying that Patten's conclusion concerning human rights in the RUC was **wrong**, rather that it is not justified on the grounds that were given. The Commission could well have been correct on this point, but perhaps should have used a different set of premises.)

Understanding the reasoning used (or sometimes the lack of it!) is an important tool in learning. As a trainee police officer you will be presented with many arguments: on the streets, in the training room, and by fellow student officers. Without making yourself too unpopular, you may wish to subject some of these arguments to scrutiny in terms of the validity of their premises and arguments and hence the validity of the conclusions.

TASK 17

Which of the following are arguments?

(a) The registration numbers of all cars can be found on the Police National Computer (PNC). Hence if I stop a car I should be able to check its details on the PNC.

> (b) Forensic investigators have a particularly stressful occupation. They are an important part of the criminal justice system. Some work for police forces, whilst others work in the private sector.
>
> (c) I'm tall, so the sight of blood doesn't worry me.

4.13.6 Proof

Within logic, **proof** is the means by which we demonstrate that a deductive argument is valid. In mathematics there are many such proofs. In everyday life, and criminal investigation in particular, it is rare to be in possession of such a proof.

Indeed, within criminal investigation and policing in general the word proof may also assume other meanings beyond a strictly formal meaning, and is often related to the level of certainty. After all, we speak of proving a person's guilt beyond reasonable doubt. Osterburg and Ward (2004) have provided a useful summary of the levels of certainty that may be involved within criminal investigation:

Levels of Certainty and Levels of Proof

Proof	Intuition	Probable Cause	Preponderance of Evidence	Clear and Convincing	Beyond Reasonable Doubt	Scientific Certainty
Evidence	Hunch, guess, or gut feeling	Facts a reasonable person would accept	Corroborated facts, eyewitness testimony, physical evidence, or evidence interpreted by an expert			Precise facts with known accuracy
Quantity	Articulable suspicion about possible facts	Prima facie, presumptive but rebuttable facts	Over 50% of facts are in support	Slightly less facts than beyond reasonable doubt	Sufficient facts to preclude every reasonable alternative hypothesis	Overwhelming facts
Certainty	Apparent	Possible	Basis for hypothesis formulation		Basis for theory construction	Seldom achieved
Law	Suppressed	Basis for binding over to next stage	Civil law standard of proof	International law standard of proof	Criminal law standard of proof	Seldom used
Investigation	Useful during early stages	Basis for arrest or search warrant	Basis for confession and informant law		Basis for conviction	Seldom used

(Reprinted from Criminal Investigation, 4th edition, with permission. Copyright 2004 Matthew Bender and Company Inc, a member of the Lexis Nexis Group. All rights reserved).

4.13.7 Fallacies

Fallacies (the full technical term is 'informal logical fallacies') are incorrect forms of argument. At the risk of stating the obvious, fallacies are a bad thing and should be avoided. There are dozens of fallacies, some of which are so infamous that they have been given Latin names. Indeed, it is quite a long list; here are just a few:

- affirmation of the consequent;
- anecdotal evidence;
- argumentum ad antiquitatem;
- argumentum ad baculum.

There are many websites and books which will explain the meaning of these terms. We will concentrate here on some of the more **common fallacies**. It should perhaps be noted at the outset that these fallacies are not necessarily mutually exclusive: it is perfectly possible, for example, that a single statement may contain more than one logical fallacy. Bear in mind that in what follows, the conclusions may or may not be valid (most are not): what we are interested in here is the **validity of the argument** not the conclusions. We have used everyday language as the name for the fallacy but have also included their more traditional Latin names where appropriate. If nothing else, this may impress your family and friends.

Anecdotal evidence. One of the most common fallacies is to use personal experience or hearsay as a form of argument. There are a number of problems with this, not least of which is the fact that each of our experiences is unique to us. An example of the anecdotal evidence fallacy is:

> Miscarriages of justice are more common today as evidenced by increased coverage in the media.

Appeal to force ('Argumentum ad baculum'). Appealing to force is the fallacy of using force (or more usually simply the threat of force) in order to try and win an argument. An example of the appeal to force fallacy is:

> If you are innocent you shouldn't be concerned about having your fingerprints taken. However, your consent is really irrelevant as the authorities can force you to give your fingerprints anyway. So, the most sensible policy is co-operation.

Attacking the person ('Argumentum ad hominem'). This is a particularly common form of fallacy. In fact it divides into two distinct forms: **abusive** and **circumstantial**. The abusive form is the fallacious argument that seeks to undermine the position of an opposing view by attacking the person or people that hold that view. An example of the abusive form is:

> It is the policy of the British National Party that we should re-introduce corporal punishment for petty criminals (BNP, 2005) and this demonstrates how wrong the policy is.

The circumstantial form is an attempt to undermine a particular conclusion by drawing attention to the (irrelevant) personal circumstances of the person constructing the argument. An example would be:

> Naturally you are against speed cameras as you drive a fast car.

Argument from ignorance ('Argumentum ad ignorantiam'). This fallacy takes two forms: arguing that since something has not been proven false, it is must be true and the converse (the argument that since something has not been proven true, it is therefore false). An example of an argument from ignorance is:

> Of course taking an intimate forensic sample from a victim is psychologically damaging. Nobody has proved otherwise.

Appeal to pity ('Argumentum ad misericordiam'). With this fallacy we try to persuade somebody of our argument by appealing to their pity, often the dire consequences that will follow if the argument is not accepted. An example of an appeal to pity is:

> The Government must accept the recommendations of the HMIC report on the FSS. The report took many months and thousands of pounds to produce and this will all be wasted if the recommendations are not accepted.

Appealing to the people ('Argumentum ad populum'). This is the fallacy of claiming that a proposition is true because it is subscribed to by popular opinion. An example would be:

> The most appropriate penalty for child murder committed by paedophiles is the death sentence. Opinion poll after opinion poll demonstrates that the British people believe this to be the case.

Appeal to authority ('Argumentum ad verecundiam'). This fallacy needs to be carefully distinguished from the acceptable argument of referring to an authority in a particular field of study as evidence to support an argument **within** that field. The fallacy occurs when an authority is invoked in an irrelevant context. This is sometimes quite subtle. An example of an appeal to authority would be:

> Sir Alec Jeffries invented the DNA profile. His support in 2001 for a National DNA database for all UK citizens lends credibility to the idea.

(Sir Alec is an undoubted expert on DNA genetic fingerprinting, but is he an expert on the implications of a national DNA database?)

Accident ('Dicto simpliciter'). This fallacy occurs when a generalized rule is applied in circumstances for which it was not intended or designed. An example would be:

> The law states that we are not allowed to 'jump' the red lights at a set of traffic lights. It is therefore wrong for the police to be allowed to do so, even in an emergency.

Converse accident. Needless to say, this is the converse of the fallacy of accident. It occurs when a generalization is based upon an exceptional case. An example is:

> The government is being asked to consider allowing patients with MS to use cannabis for pain relief. If this happens it is only right that they should legalize cannabis for everyone's use.

False cause and effect ('Non causa pro causa'). This fallacy often occurs when we assume association (often measured as mathematical correlation) is the same as causation. Just because two events occur together does not automatically mean that one caused the other. To assume so is a fallacy. An example of an argument that assumes association and causation are the same would be:

> The widespread availability of guns is a major contributory factor to the murder rate of a country. This is demonstrated by the fact that the countries with the highest gun ownership (such as the US) also have the highest rates of homicide.

There is also the fallacy of assuming an event to be the cause of another event simply because it happened before that event. An example would be:

> Since the availability of hard core gay pornography on the internet we have witnessed a significant increase in the incidence of anal rape of men.

Begging the question ('Petitio principii'). This fallacy may take various forms, some of which are quite difficult to spot. In its simplest form a begging the question fallacy starts with a questionable premise before making a deduction or sometimes repeating the premise in different words. In more subtle cases the premises are actually a consequence of the conclusion rather than the converse (as it should be). The fallacy often takes the form of circular argument. An example of begging the question would be:

> Freedom of speech is an essential right in a police service, since every police employee should have the right to express him or herself with complete freedom.

An even more subtle example would be:

> Gays should not be encouraged to join the police. The reason is that any police officer who is 'outed' as gay would find it very difficult to remain in the police after it was revealed that he kept this secret from his fellow officers. Therefore gay police officers will do anything to keep their sexuality secret and will thus be open to blackmail. Therefore gays should not be allowed to join the police.

Irrelevant conclusion ('Ignoratio elenchi'). This is a fallacious argument which sets out to prove a certain conclusion but instead proves a somewhat different conclusion. An example would be:

> Hundreds of rare bird's eggs are stolen each year, even though we have the Wildlife and Countryside Act. Clearly, we should repeal the Act.

Non sequitur. This is a particularly infamous fallacy, which probably accounts for why there is no common equivalent English phrase. A non sequitur is an argument where the conclusion is derived from a set of premises which are not logically connected with the conclusion. The non sequitur fallacy happens more often in spoken arguments rather than in a written form. An example would be:

> We should return to 'bobbies on the beat' in this country. If the police need additional powers then they should receive them.

TASK 18

Identify the fallacies in the following statements (remember, **this is not an exercise on the validity of the statement**, but on identifying errors in argument):

(a) We must introduce a 'Sarah's Law' against paedophiles in this country in memory of the young girl who was tragically killed.

(b) The police use of test purchasing is wrong. The law states that 'impersonating another for gain' is unlawful and this is exactly what test purchasing involves.

(c) The Intelligence-led Policing model was a mistake. The vast majority of people prefer 'bobbies on the beat' instead of the emphasis on intelligence.

(d) Since the recent increase in asylum-seeker numbers in the UK we have witnessed a big increase in the prostitution problems in Maidbury.

(e) The police reform process is self-evidently moving us in the right direction as evidenced by the support of the Home Office, ACPO and the 'rank and file' police officers themselves.

(f) Fingerprints are one the most trusted forms of forensic evidence. DNA is sometimes difficult to collect.

(g) When investigating child abuse allegations if we must err, then we must err on the side of the child.

(h) It is well-known that the Prime Minister, Tony Blair, is a practising Christian. So there must be something in Christianity.

(i) Dr Shipman was able to kill his patients because he was permitted to prescribe diamorphine. We should therefore legislate to stop GPs having this power.

(j) Capital punishment deters crime because it ensures criminals do not recommit murder.

4.14 Answers to Tasks

TASKS 1–4 INCLUSIVE

Possible responses and interpretations are given immediately after these tasks.

TASK 5

You will find that the site will describe each of the categories that we explored in Tasks 1, 2, 3, and 4 as 'activist', 'theorist', 'pragmatist', and 'reflector' and undertaking the online questionnaire would have placed your preferred learning style into a grid:

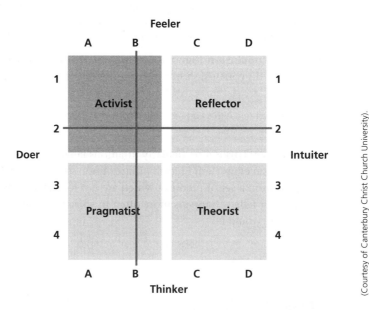

(Courtesy of Canterbury Christ Church University).

Where the two lines intersect gives you some measure of your preferred learning style. It shows that I am a predominantly activist learner, which the site then explains means that I seek hidden possibilities; I learn by talking with others; I get totally involved; I take risks; I am enthusiastic, working quickly and involving others and my favourite question is 'What if'?

The site is not the only way of exploring your preferred learning styles. A popular method in police training is to use Honey and Mumford's Learning Styles Questionnaire. Further details may be found at <http://www.peterhoney.com/>.

TASK 6

Not everybody finds that the Kolb process works for them. Indeed, there are a number of more general critiques of the underlining theory to ELC. Rogers for example, has argued that 'learning includes goals, purposes, intentions, choice and decision-making, and it is not at all clear where these elements fit into the learning cycle' (Rogers, 1996, p 108).

TASK 7

A student police officer, whilst undertaking Personal Safety Training, starts learning how to handcuff a suspect by taking part in supervised practice with a dummy—this is the **experience** stage.

The trainer, observing the practice of the student and testing the results, then asked, 'Were there any risks to you during the cuffing? How tight did that feel for the suspect? What might you have done differently?'—this is the **review and reflect** stage.

That night the student police officer consults his/her notes on how to handcuff suspects and reads about the reasons for doing it in particular ways, including force procedure and the human rights of the suspect—this is the **interpret** stage.

Next day, presented with a fellow student officer to handcuff, the student thinks, 'As a result of what happened yesterday, and because of what I read last night I ought to do it like this'—this is the **action planning** stage.

TASK 8

SQ3R stands for:

- **S**urvey/Skim the material you need to read;
- formulate **Q**uestions that you expect the material to answer;
- do the **R**eading;
- **R**ecall what you have read; and
- **R**eview.

In terms of investigation (particularly preparing for interview), you may wish to read Eric Shepherd's book *SE3R A Resource Book* (Shepherd, 2001) where SE3R stands for 'Survey, Extract, Read, Review and Respond'.

TASK 9

This is a difficult issue for you. You have probably been attested, and hence have assumed the full responsibilities and powers of a constable and yet you are barely trained and even less experienced. You are with the organizations to learn from them and their students, not to disrupt their usual ways of working. However, dealing in drugs is a serious offence.

Your force will have standing operating procedures to help you decide what to do and these often involve you taking advice from your supervisor and referring to the policies of the organization concerned. The important point is not to keep this to yourself.

TASKS 10, 11, & 12

Your answers will reflect your own particular experiences and thoughts.

As background reading you might wish to consider downloading the 2003 HMIC thematic inspection 'Diversity Matters' which examined training on matters of race and diversity in the police service. It is freely available from the HMIC website via <http://inspectorates. homeoffice.gov.uk/hmic/inspections/ptd/thematic/diversity-matters/>. The 2005 CRE report on the 'Police Service of England and Wales' is also available from <http://www.cre.gov.uk/ policefi_final.pdf>. You will find (in Chapter 5 of the report) that the CRE were quite critical of the early versions of the proposed IPLDP curriculum.

TASK 13

Your responses should have provided some stimulus material to help with Learning Diary entries.

TASK 14

We gave you 2, 4, 8, and 16 to look at and asked you the next number. You would probably have given the answer as 32, if we had not ruled this out. The answer we were thinking of is 31. This is not a trick question!

To explain this, consider the following ways of cutting a pie (technically, dissecting a circle):

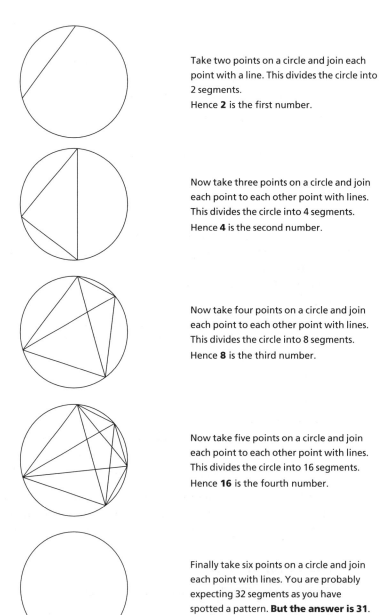

Take two points on a circle and join each point with a line. This divides the circle into 2 segments.
Hence **2** is the first number.

Now take three points on a circle and join each point to each other point with lines. This divides the circle into 4 segments.
Hence **4** is the second number.

Now take four points on a circle and join each point to each other point with lines. This divides the circle into 8 segments.
Hence **8** is the third number.

Now take five points on a circle and join each point to each other point with lines. This divides the circle into 16 segments.
Hence **16** is the fourth number.

Finally take six points on a circle and join each point with lines. You are probably expecting 32 segments as you have spotted a pattern. **But the answer is 31**. Try it and see.

(If you want to know the next numbers in the list then look up 'Moser's circle').

By this stage you might well be thinking, 'What has all this got to do with training as a student police officer?' There are a couple of points here:

- Guessing 32 is a form of inductive reasoning—we are generalizing from past events and making predictions about the future. As explained in this chapter, there are inherent dangers in this that we should be aware of—for example, the likelihood of being wrong. This is easy to spot with 2, 4, 8, 16, and 31 but less easy to identify when we encounter our third example in a week of arresting a member of a minority community for theft.
- When establishing a hypothesis it is tempting to look for evidence which supports the hypothesis rather than refutes it. Remember that when investigating and interviewing, your main objective is to establish the truth, not to prove a point.

TASK 15

(a) Inductive reasoning
(b) Deductive reasoning
(c) Inductive reasoning
(d) Deductive reasoning
(e) Deductive reasoning
(f) Deductive reasoning

TASK 16

Score 1 for each of the following answers, otherwise score 0. Total your score.

(a) Agree
(b) Disagree
(c) Disagree
(d) Disagree
(e) Disagree
(f) Agree
(g) Agree
(h) Disagree
(i) Agree
(j) Agree
(k) Disagree
(l) Disagree
(m) Disagree
(n) Disagree
(o) Disagree

Remember, this is just for fun.

If you scored:

12–15   You are already a critical thinker.
6–11   You are close to being a critical thinker, but there is room to develop your skills.
0–5   Consider developing your critical thinking skills.

Whatever you scored, you might find it useful to look at Stella Cottrell's *Critical Thinking Skills* (Cottrell, 2005). A 'taster' can be located at <http://www.palgrave.com/PDFs/1403996857 .Pdf.>.

TASK 17

(a) This is an argument.
(b) This is not an argument.
(c) The basis of an argument, but as it stands, not really an argument.

TASK 18

(a) Appeal to pity.
(b) Accident.

(c) Appealing to the people.

(d) False cause and effect.

(e) To some extent appeal to authority but also begging the question (the Home Office are the originators of the formal police reform process).

(f) Non sequitur.

(g) To some extent appeal to pity but also some element of begging the question.

(h) Appeal to authority.

(i) Converse accident.

(j) Begging the question.

5 | Key Themes in Policing

5.1   Chapter Briefing

This chapter brings together a number of the underpinning concepts and theories that are important to initial police training.

5.1.1   Aim of the Chapter

The aim of this chapter is to explore a number of key themes in policing that are relevant to the student police officer, through both an analysis of the underlying theory and an examination of the application of those theories.

This chapter will enable you to:

- understand a number of key themes important to policing as a profession, in particular ethics and policing, the nature of personal authority, legitimacy, and discretion;
- comprehend the nature of different models of policing used elsewhere in Europe and in other parts of the world;
- place crime reduction within the context of contemporary policing;
- discern the basic building blocks of the law and relationship of the police with the CJS;

- appreciate how an understanding of crime, criminality, and criminology can support your development towards becoming a qualified police officer;
- understand how a respect for diversity and the needs of all communities in the UK is central to your professional role;
- understand the particular challenge of domestic violence;
- appreciate the importance of the extended policing family to your role, but also the issues that arise with this extension of private and public policing;
- develop the underpinning knowledge required for a number of NOS elements, entries for your Learning Diary (Phase 3) and a number of CARs of your SOLAP.

5.1.2 National Occupational Standards

This chapter will provide you with the knowledge required to demonstrate aspects of the following NOS elements:

National Occupational Standards Elements

1A1.1 Apply principles of reasonable suspicion or belief.
1A1.2 Use police actions proportionately.
1A1.3 Use police actions fairly.
AE1.1 Maintain and develop your own knowledge, skills and competence.

5.1.3 IPLDP Phases and Modules

This chapter will provide you with resources to support the following Induction Modules of the IPLDP:

IND 1 Underpinning ethics/values of the police service (particularly IND 1.2, Applying police ethics).
IND 2 Foster people's equality, diversity and rights.
IND 4 Assess the needs of individuals and provide advice and support (particularly IND 4.5, Challenging inappropriate behaviour).
IND 10 Use police actions in a fair and justified way (particularly IND 10.2, Use police actions fairly).
IND 11 Social, community issues and neighbourhood policing (particularly IND 11.6, Crime reduction).

It also provides support for the following topic areas of LPG 1:

- Discretion (LPG 1.7);
- Domestic Violence (LPG 1.3).

5.1.4 SOLAP

The contents of this chapter are relevant to the knowledge evidence requirements of CARs 1A1 and 4C1.

5.1.5 Learning Diary Phases

The contents of this chapter may provide you with stimulus material for completion of your Learning Diary (Phase 3) and the following headings in particular:

- Police policies and procedures;
- Protecting people.

5.1.6 IPLDP Learning Requirement

This chapter is relevant to the following sections of the IPLDP Learning Requirement: 1.3, 1.4, 1.5, 1.6, 1.13, 1.15, 2.1, 2.8, 3.10, 5.1, 5.3, 5.4, and 6.4.

5.2 Introduction

On occasions some of the content of this chapter may appear abstract and even unrelated to the day-to-day work of a student police officer. However, much of what follows could form the basis of any claim that policing is a profession. As we shall discuss in section 5.3, one hallmark of a profession is the existence of a corpus of knowledge that influences, in more or less subtle ways, the actions and decisions of the members of that profession. The principles of law would naturally feature within any such corpus of knowledge. However, we would also argue for the inclusion of authority, legitimacy, and discretion as being key areas that help to establish policing as a distinct profession. Crime and criminality must also surely feature, as should their ancillary concerns of how we model, plan, and implement our policing. Domestic violence, as one of the largest contributors to the statistics of volume crime, is also worthy of special consideration. All these matters are considered, alongside more recent developments such as the need for our police forces to better represent our pluralisms of communities and the continuing growth of the extended policing family.

5.3 Policing as a Profession

You will often hear references during training to 'adopting a professional attitude' or the need for student police officers to 'behave in a professional manner'. But what does this actually mean? Can we really think of policing as a profession? This section considers the extent to which policing can be considered a profession and what this means for the student police officer.

Before we examine the idea that policing is a profession, we need to consider what we might mean by the term 'profession'.

TASK 1

Make a list of professions. What features do you look for in an occupation that makes it a profession? Are there any common features that are found in all the professions you have listed?

5.3.1 What Is a Profession?

We encounter the word profession in many different contexts and applied to numerous occupational groups. You might have already suspected that there is not a universally accepted definition of the meaning of profession, though there is a general agreement that not all occupations qualify as professions. What is confusing is that the word professional is often appended to an activity simply to acknowledge that its practitioners receive some form of payment or it that is undertaken more seriously. For example, we know that a reference to a 'professional computer games player' means that the person concerned probably earns a living from what most see as a hobby. However, there is likely to be more to a profession (as distinct from adding professional to an activity) than simply earning money through it.

Traditionally, there were just four professions; law, medicine, the church, and the military. Later, accountancy came to be seen as a profession, and now there are many more occupations commonly regarded as professions.

There is a broad consensus in the academic world that at least some of the following are required for an occupation to also be a profession:

- an accepted corpus of knowledge and theory underpinning the practice of the profession;
- controls on entry to the profession, normally through qualification, coupled with a need to maintain the currency of qualification;
- autonomy, discretion, and a degree of self-regulation;
- its practitioners have a form of vocational calling;
- a code of ethics.

For most professions, many of the control and regulatory functions are carried out by a professional body.

To illustrate these ideas, and to explore them further, we now consider medical practice as an example of a profession and measure it against our list above.

Requirements of a profession	The medical profession
Corpus of knowledge and theory	The scientific basis to medical practice (eg physiology and biochemistry), knowledge of clinical practice (eg conducting physical examinations), aspects of the behavioural and social sciences.
Controls on entry to the profession and continuing professional development	Completing a recognized medical degree, followed by a period of supervised practice (eg foundation training followed by postgraduate training). There is a need to demonstrate regular Continuous Professional Development under seven headings in order to maintain a place on the professional register.
Autonomy, discretion, and self-regulation	Medical doctors have significant autonomy and discretion. Their conducted is regulated by the General Medical Council (GMC). Their representative body is the British Medical Association (BMA). Their authority is largely epistemic in nature (see section 5.5).
Vocational calling	Difficult to prove, as no clear definitions of a vocation exist. However, interviews for entry to medical degrees often attempt to test this.
Code of ethics	A code is published by the GMC. It includes the need for doctors to 'make the care of your patient their first concern', to 'respect patients' dignity and privacy', and 'to give patients information in a way they can understand'.

We can see that medicine matches our working definition of a profession very closely.

5.3.2 Is Policing a Profession?

First attempt the following task.

TASK 2

Complete the following table for the occupation of policing:

Requirements of a profession	The policing profession
Corpus of knowledge and theory	?
Controls on entry to the profession and maintenance of position	?
Autonomy, discretion and self-regulation	?
Vocational calling	?
Code of ethics	?

You probably found that policing in the UK meets some of our criteria for being a profession. Skills for Justice and the NPIA (which now incorporates Centrex) are currently participating in a consultation with the criminal justice sector on the establishment of a professional body for policing and the introduction of a professional register (Skills for Justice, 2005). If these are put in place, then policing will match the definition of a profession more closely.

5.3.3 Does It Matter If Policing Is Not a Profession?

As a student police officer, the debate concerning policing as a profession is probably not at the forefront of your thinking. You are almost certainly more concerned with assimilating the corpus of knowledge rather than debating its importance or its constituents. However, some would argue that establishing and maintaining policing as a profession is important for the following reasons:

- to develop the body of knowledge (for example, doctrine) and skills required for modern-day policing. Professions usually take the lead in determining what research and development best suits the needs of the clients;
- to protect the right of the police, in certain key respects, to regulate themselves;
- to improve public confidence in the work of the police. For example, a professional register would almost certainly imply the need for the membership to regularly demonstrate that they have met the requirement to maintain their skills and knowledge;
- to distinguish the work and the professional standing of the police officer from other members of the extended police family (see section 5.17) and other law enforcers (you might not agree that this is a good reason, but it is certainly behind some thinking).

There are, of course, alternative arguments. Many of the traditional professions, such as the law, are not noted for their inclusivity (in fact, some may be regarded as closed shops to the majority of citizens of this country) and there are some concerns that the striving for a professional status may only serve to reduce the representative nature of the policing family.

5.4 Ethics and Policing

We saw in section 5.3 that a code of ethics is often a hallmark of a profession.

5.4.1 Introduction

Ethics is concerned with analysing the moral principles that govern human conduct. We can think of individuals as operating according to moral principles that may be derived from two main sources:

- their own assumptions, ideas, and principles;
- external sources, such as cultural norms, religion, or other rules imposed by society.

A consideration of ethics is important for the student police officer, because a key function of a police service is to uphold the law, and laws generally reflect our society's ethics (that is, the things which society, over time, values or places above other matters as being of high mutual value). It follows that for the police to be credible, their methods and procedures should meet the same ethical standards as the ethics of law.

If police methods and procedures do **not** meet the same ethical standards as the ethics of law, the authority of the police will be undermined, and the public may well have less trust in the police and the law. For example, many East Germans feared and distrusted their secretive and repressive police force, the STASI, before the reunification of Germany in the 1990s. Conversely, a police force that shows respect for human rights will encourage ordinary citizens to support the police. This has been demonstrated on a large scale in the UK, for example:

- public assistance with hate crime investigations;
- significant public support for the MPS in the aftermath of terrorist bombings in London in July 2005.

Such conduct by the police is closely bound up with ethical standards and what is morally right.

For the student police officer, the standards of behaviour expected are clearly defined in existing documents—you are expected to act according to these externally imposed rules; you will be introduced to some of the key principles in the course of this chapter. We will also consider later how ethics are linked with notions of moral authority. But ethics is also about your own ideas, and if your actions as a police officer are to ring true, your own personal rules of moral behaviour (your ethics) need to be in line with the formal requirements of the police force you work for. Diversity training (see section 4.9) will provide you with further opportunities to consider your own views and feelings about your role in society, both as an individual and as a student police officer.

TASK 3

All student police officers **attest** their responsibility to uphold the law and keep the peace (the twin aspects of the office of constable) at an early point in their first year (see Chapter 7). But is there more to the moral role of a police officer than this? Does the public expect more? Or is it not enough just to say to the student police officer to be honest? Should we really concern ourselves about notions like proportion, trust, and the duty of care?

5.4.2 Documents Containing Guidance About Police Ethics and Behaviour

There are a number of official documents that set out, in varying degrees of detail, guidance concerning police ethics and behaviour.

The Police (Conduct) Regulations 2004 stipulate that police officers:

- should respect confidentiality and not use information for personal benefit nor disclose it unless authorized.
- must act with fairness and impartiality in all their dealings with the public and their colleagues.
- should avoid being improperly beholden to any person or institution.
- should be open and truthful in their dealings.
- should discharge their duties with integrity.
- must obey all lawful orders.
- should oppose any improper behaviour, reporting it where appropriate.
- should treat members of the public with courtesy and respect, avoiding abusive or deriding attitudes or behaviour. In particular, officers must avoid all forms of harassment, victimization, or unreasonable discrimination, and favouritism of an individual or group.
- should treat all colleagues with courtesy and respect, and avoid overbearing conduct, particularly to a colleague of junior rank.
- must never knowingly use more force than is reasonable.
- should never abuse their authority.

Aside from a few other cautions against drinking on or before duty, exhortations to take care of property, to dress smartly, and to attend promptly to duties, the bullet points above encapsulate the range of expected behaviours and attitudes of any police officer in England and Wales. One assumes that these regulations cover support staff too, but this would not have the force of law (except in employment law) and may vary from force to force. As well as containing ethical behaviour standards, the discipline code is also included within the Police Regulations (see sections 7.13 and 7.14).

Most police forces in Britain also have **codes of conduct**, setting out the expected standards of behaviour for:

- treatment of the public;
- treatment of suspects;
- preparation of case files;
- giving of evidence;
- interaction with colleagues.

The codes of conduct also offer guidance on how police officers should conduct themselves when off duty. Their activities should not impact adversely on their ability to discharge public office without fear or favour.

We now also have the seven core behavioural areas for student police officers as a result of the IPLDP. These are described in section 6.5.

The **European Code of Police Ethics** was published in 2001, and noted that:

- The police help to safeguard the law.
- The police depend upon the public for support (consensual policing).
- Public confidence in the police, in any country, is tightly bound up with how the police treat the public, especially over fundamental rights, such as those set out in the Human Rights Act 1998.

Finally, there are also general statements made within police services' mission statements and policy guidelines relating to particular aims and aspects of police work. For example, the Home Secretary John Reid sent a letter to all police services in England Wales on 6th March 2007 outlining what he felt summed up 'the mission, values, goals and aspirations…essential to successful policing' (Reid, 2007). The values he expected to see were:

- Fairness and impartiality;
- Integrity;
- Freedom from corruption;
- Respect for liberty and compassion;
- Freedom from racism;
- Equality of service to all communities;
- A commitment to the protection and well-being of all individuals.

5.4.3 Ethics and Policing in a Changing World

It would seem misguided to suppose that ethical standards never change. As society and technologies change people develop new activities, and our attitudes may change too. Some of these changes provide new opportunities for crime, and present new challenges for policing.

5.4.4 Changes in Society and New Crimes

The inter-relationships between new technologies and changing social attitudes might look like this:

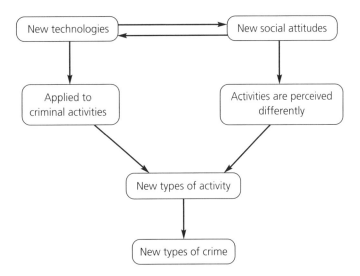

5.4.4.1 New technologies and new social attitudes

We can all list many forms of new technologies and suggest some examples of new social attitudes. What is more interesting however, is the interaction between the two. For example, how can technology affect social attitudes? It is more straightforward to see how social attitudes affect technology—after all, if people want a certain product or service, a company will usually try and provide it for them—a feature of business.

> **TASK 4**
> 1. Make a list of six new technologies (new during the past 30 years).
> 2. Make a list of changes in social attitudes (limit yourself to no more than 10!).
> 3. Try and find links between the new technologies and social attitudes—you might find it helpful to discuss this with your colleagues, friends, or family.

5.4.4.2 New activities and new crimes

The availability of new technologies and changes in social attitudes have led to the development of new activities such as downloading mp3 file format music from the internet. At least some of this music is copyright protected. This particular example illustrates a number of interesting points. This activity was made possible by commonly available computers and the internet, and (when it involves copyrighted music) has only recently been classified as a crime.

As we have seen in this example, it takes time for some new activities to be classified in law as crimes. Some new activities are clearly existing crimes carried out in a new way, for example using computers to illegally transfer money out of your employer's bank account into your own bank account (the so-called 're-tooling' of a crime for the electronic age). This is theft, and it does not require much thought to see it as such. But other activities, such as 'phishing' are new types of activity, and it is difficult to find a precedent for this in existing law. So, new laws have to be made, laws which classify some of the new activities as new types of crime.

A hundred years ago, police actions at the operational level were almost entirely parish or county based, or limited to the boroughs of a large city. Now, the policing horizon is much wider, partly because at least some crime has become internationalized. Fraud is a good example of this. Up to about twenty years ago, the majority of frauds were local: committed locally and investigated locally. Only occasionally did such frauds or embezzlements reach beyond national boundaries. With the advent of the internet, the electronic transfer of money, and the widespread use of bank accounts in different countries, fraud has rapidly become global. A recent case of international fraud began with the arrest of an individual who had drawn out large sums of cash from an account (the presumption being that this was to pay off an illegal drugs shipment). The bank became suspicious when large sums were deposited in the account just before the large withdrawal took place, and informed the police. Within hours of the criminal investigation beginning, enquiries had spread to the USA, Switzerland, Liechtenstein, Thailand, and Oman. The essence of the crime had not changed, but the size, range, and complexity of the financial transactions certainly had changed the scope of the investigation, as well as impacting on the skills expected of the investigator.

5.4.5 Ethics and Changes in Policing

Just as new technologies and changing social attitudes influence crime, these changes also influence the police methods and attitudes. These changes are due to different types of influence:

- new crimes and behaviours present new challenges, and the police react to these particular challenges, in order to facilitate the fight against crime. These changes are **demand-led**; the changes are in direct response to changing patterns of crime;
- the police are part of society so they are directly affected by any changes, in the same way that other organizations and people are affected. These changes do not occur in response to any particular demand.

Demand-led responses to the challenge of coping with new crimes and changing behaviours occur on a number of different levels. They occur informally, at the level of the individual (for example, officers may find themselves modifying the way they speak to certain aggressive individuals in order to facilitate an arrest). The police also respond as an organization; new approaches will be imposed formally within the organization through new procedures, laws, codes, and conduct. This inevitably takes time, as formal changes have to be carefully planned and implemented. These demand-led changes in police practice are part of a pragmatic response.

The police are also directly affected by changes in society, as we all are. For example, in today's society, great emphasis is placed on accountability, and the police will be exposed to this new idea, just like the rest of society. So even if crime and criminals remained unchanged, and therefore presented no new challenges to policing, the police might still look for ways of making individuals and the whole organization more accountable.

TASK 5

Consider the following three changes in police practice:

1. Increased use of computer databases. The police can access more information about individuals than previously through centralized databanks such as the National Fingerprint Identification System (NAFIS) and the Police National Computer (PNC) for vehicle registration plates, or a central criminal records bureau to trace criminal histories.
2. Intelligence-led policing.
3. Developing more community links.

For each one, suggest how:

- might an individual police officer have contributed to planning the changes;
- would each new practice help the police solve or prevent crime;
- each new practice reflects general changes in society.

You may be able to see what some of these factors have to do with policing, but what have they to do with ethics? One answer could be that it may be considered as ethical for policing practice to respond to changing patterns of crime in order that laws (which are ethical themselves) are upheld. We have observed that the police as part of society are exposed to changes in society and those changes include changes in ethical values.

5.4.6 Ethics and Demand-led Changes in Policing Practice

We have noted that it can be argued that it is inherently ethical that the police seek to solve and prevent crime. However, new police methods and procedures adopted in order to further this aim may also present ethical dilemmas. For example, there are concerns about the large amount of information stored about individuals on police computers. Is it right for information to be held about innocent individuals, and does the storage of information about criminals and suspects need further regulation? This is a new problem; the technology to store and retrieve information simply did not exist until recently, so although there are undoubtedly huge benefits in terms of solving and preventing crime, there is a danger of abusing the rights of individuals and invading their privacy. Questions arise about the ethics of holding information about individuals, and about who should vet its contents for accuracy, probity, and the way it is recorded. There are safeguards in place, but these need to be interpreted with care—after the Soham murders, the Chief Constable of Humberside was criticized because his force did not retain sufficient information about suspects; information that could have prevented Huntley working with the children he subsequently killed. Clearly, this issue raises significant ethical questions, and the rights of suspects need to be balanced against the rights of other members of the public. It is interesting that the report by Sir Michael Bichard (2004) (into the recording of police information about suspect individuals) dealt only marginally with the ethics of the situation and placed far more emphasis on the mechanisms for recording the information.

Round-the-clock criminal activity is now commonplace, in line with the 24/7 society, and the police have to keep up with these changes. This has led to an expansion of the policing role and a blurring of the boundaries between **sworn officers** (those in the office of constable, see section 7.12) and those who have some limited powers (acting in support of sworn officers) such as community support officers, rural or parish wardens, crime scene investigators, detention officers, and many other civilian roles within a police force. These police support staff must also have ethical codes, standards of behaviour and action, honesty, and probity, to the same extent as police officers. Yet there is no agreed national standard, such as those in the Police Regulations, no ratified code of behaviour, no national guidance to 'morality in public office' with which all such support staff must comply. This is despite the deliberations of Lord Nolan and his report on 'Standards in Public Life' (Nolan, 1995).

Consider international peace-keeping. Alongside the military presence, there may be a host of supporting agencies, including the police. If the peace-keepers are to have moral (rather than imposed or forced) authority (see section 5.5), there must be an ethical consistency in their behaviours—all the more so if they are police officers. If there is no code of conduct and no consistent guidance is provided, should we be surprised that problems sometimes occur? Partly as a consequence of round-the-clock crime, the British police operate in conjunction with other police forces around the world. British police may be dealing with people who do not share common behavioural boundaries or shared cultural identities with those commonly associated with British people. In other countries there may be:

- widespread corruption;
- routine bribery of public officials;
- governments using their police as a political arm;
- very low rates of pay for police officers;
- very low status for police officers;
- paramilitary style force employed by the police.

TASK 6

Consider the bullet points listed above. Draw a flow diagram showing how these factors might interact. Use arrows to show how one factor causes another. (An example of this particular use of arrows is shown in the diagram below; the arrow shows that poor pay leads to low status.)

Note there are no certain answers to this exercise; you might argue that it is the low status that is causing the low pay.

5.4.7   Ethics and Non Demand-led Changes in Police Practice

Along with the changes in society and societal norms, there is renewed debate about policing methods. There is even some ambiguity about what the police are for. This may be seen, for example, in organizational name changes; some counties now have Police Service titles, others have retained the original Police Force in their title. Is the use of force a fundamental part of policing? Some commentators argue that, increasingly, the use of force by the police, particularly deadly force in the use of firearms, is not tolerable in modern society. Others assert that, as society seems to be becoming more violent, especially with gun crime, police officers should be routinely armed, like their colleagues in Continental Europe or the USA. Clearly the more frequent use of firearms by the police is to some extent a demand-led response stimulated by the increasing level of gun crime in Britain.

The debate can be widened to include changes in the public perception of the police. Some of the questions raised are very general, and others are more specific, such as:

- Are the police still the repositories of authority? If so, on whose authority?
- Is the use of force sanctioned by law (and therefore at the mercy of political changes and amendments) or is the use of force sanctioned by society as necessary for public protection?
- Should the police target teenage vandals and graffiti artists rather than fraudsters?
- Should car thieves or burglars be made a higher priority for police action than catching speeding drivers on the basis that theft and burglary have a bigger negative impact than speeding on the supposedly-peaceful lives of ordinary citizens?
- What does society fear most, and should the police be responsive to that fear?

The public perception of the police is clearly an issue here. Can the public trust the police to know best, and may the police therefore set their own priorities, such as tackling invisible crimes like fraud or drug smuggling? Or are the police morally obliged to focus on issues of immediate public concern, such as minor vandalism and dispersing groups of youths hanging about on street corners? Despite the fact that public anxiety is not fully justified by available data, the public perception of the level of crime is widely regarded as one of the many factors police need to take into account when considering their priorities.

5.4.8 Managerialism, Ethics, and the Police

The police have faced a dilemma in recent years between the official structuring of its responses to crime and criminality (the Government's approach) and the impatience within its ranks concerning measurement systems (the internalized approach). This has led to accusations of managerialism, and the suggestion that the police are more concerned with reaching targets set by the Government than they are with maintaining order, protecting the vulnerable, and catching criminals. Others argue that the police, like any other public service, should be seen to be providing value for money and that the best way to ascertain that is to set targets for the reduction of specific crimes. Others still argue that 'what gets measured gets done' and this leads the police into mechanistic and target-driven responses to society's problems, avoiding consideration of wider and more complex general issues.

The targets and tick-boxes of managerialism are probably unavoidable. Some would argue that accountability is a central part of any programme for change in all public services, not just the police, and that it is the best way to improve standards. However, critics of such changes assert that the drive for accountability disrupts effective practice within most organizations. We can see at least some of the consequences of such an approach in the health services where performance targets have led, allegedly, to redefinitions of illness (so waiting lists appear shorter), a shortage of hospital beds, competition for resources, and a 'postal lottery' for prescribing expensive medication. Critics of recent changes in policing suggest that increased managerialism in police forces has fundamentally changed the nature of policing, including its ethical position.

Performance and delivery of outcomes against measurable targets are increasingly used to determine whether or not a police force is effective, efficient, and economic. In 2002, the link between police performance and police budgets was made explicit by the Home Office. The controversy over the rights and wrongs of managerialism is not within the scope of this Handbook, but the whole issue presents forces with a real dilemma and is the subject of active debate; should forces concentrate on achieving what gets measured (and nothing else) in order to meet their targets, or should they instead aim to deliver the whole spectrum of policing (which includes the specified targets and measures, but only as a by-product of good policing practice)? A decision to concentrate on meeting targets, rather than providing an effective police service per se will impact on individual moral behaviour as much as it impacts on community or societal behaviour.

We do not offer solutions to these complex issues, but they are important parts of the context in which we can discuss ethics and police codes of conduct. It follows that you should know a little about these issues and be prepared to think about what is involved. The ethical dilemmas are likely to increase rather than recede during your service as a police officer.

5.4.9 Ethics and Your Everyday Work

Looking back to the documents quoted at the start of this section of the chapter, you may feel that the principles are sound, but you might also be wondering how the rather abstract principles might actually apply in day-to-day situations. Even in these short summaries, you may have noted the variations between must and should; some elements of the Regulations specify **action** ('you must') and others specify **expectation** ('you should'). Also, there are some words used without qualification, such as integrity and knowingly. There appears to be a subjective flavour to the guidance and an assumption of shared or implicit understanding about concepts and how they relate to conduct. Do you know what all the words mean? Does everyone else already know what these terms mean? What is meant by a lawful order or improperly beholden? (This last point is a curiously old-fashioned use of language, it actually means that officers should not be under an obligation to anyone, by taking gifts or payments in kind.)

This part of Chapter 5 looks at some of the qualities required of individual officers, and the practical impact of ethics on everyday policing.

TASK 7

Take a moment to think about the meaning of the terms:

- must
- should
- integrity
- knowingly

in the context of police ethics. Write down your reflections and consider making a Learning Diary Phase 1 entry under the 'Ethics and values of the police' heading.

5.4.10   Ethics and Police Discretion

We examine discretion in detail in section 5.7. At this point, we look at the exercise of discretion in the context of police ethics.

One of the key skills you will be required to develop whilst training as a student police officer is the ability to apply **discretion**. Some might imagine that the language used to frame our laws is pretty cut and dried and that your subsequent role as a qualified police officer will involve merely deciding which laws and offences apply to whatever activity you are investigating. However, you may know already that it is not that simple! In exercising discretion, you will need to decide when to act on a law and when to ignore certain acts that might be viewed as law-breaking. Further, in making these choices, you may have to justify the reasons for your decision.

The code of conduct contained within Police Regulations (see sections 5.4.2 above and 7.14 below) does not try to restrict the discretion of police officers, but it does define the parameters of conduct within which a police officer can exercise discretion. Police officers, once sworn, have powers not granted to the ordinary citizen. It is expected that police officers will exercise judgement whether to use those powers or not as circumstances, common sense, or experience dictate.

A practical example may be drawn from a recent skills exercise, in which student police officers on Supervised Patrol were called to deal with a theft at a supermarket, with instructions to investigate the matter and decide upon a course of action. The student police officers attended the scene of the alleged crime; the offender was a confused, ninety-four-year-old man who had apparently picked up a bag of sweets and wandered out of the store, pursued by store detectives. What would you do in these circumstances?

The exercise brings home to the police officers that their powers need to be tempered with a mixture of good sense and humanity. Yes, the elderly person had technically committed a crime, but there were **mitigating circumstances**; his age and frailty must be taken into account, and proving 'intention permanently to deprive' (the basis of the Theft Act 1968, see section 9.3 below) would be somewhat difficult.

Discretion is not simply the exercise of good sense; it is a matter of making **judgements**, some of which can only come with experience. Two important situations requiring the use of discretion are:

- **Making an arrest**—no other police officer, not even a chief constable, can command another officer to make an arrest. This is because the responsibility for an arrest is that of the arresting officer alone, who may have to answer for his or her actions in court (see section 11.11 below);

- **Opening fire**—no police officer can order another police officer to open fire with a weapon (a gun, baton round, or Taser). The personal responsibility to open fire is a judgement exercised by the officer on his or her own. However, a police officer receiving a lawful order **not** to open fire **must** obey (since a commander of a firearms incident may be in possession of knowledge not possessed by other officers at the scene).

From the beginnings of policing in Britain more than 170 years ago, great emphasis has been placed on the individual officer's responsibility for behaviour and conduct, concerning what actions should be refrained from as well as what actions should be taken. The Regulations, in effect, set out this key responsibility of the 'office of constable' in detail.

However, we should not assume that the daily life of a police officer is constantly beset with moral ambiguity and that there is a need to make fundamental ethical judgements all the time. In fact, most of the complexity of policing lies in the technical or legal requirements for evidence, which are dealt with extensively throughout this Handbook.

5.4.11 Respect for Personal Autonomy

Citizens have the right to dignity and respect and police officers should treat all people they encounter with the same imperturbable impartiality and show respect for possible differences of culture and belief. The police should do nothing to threaten citizens' rights to be treated decently whatever a person might have done (or had done to them by others). It also follows that police officers should not exploit people as a means to an end (such as putting people in danger in order to secure a conviction).

5.4.12 Beneficence and Non-Malificence

Police officers are obliged, by their duty and by their office, to help people (beneficence), and this should be done so that others are not hurt or harmed (non-malificence). Thus a firearms officer has a moral and civic, as well as a legal duty to ensure that bystanders, victims, and hostages are not harmed when he or she uses a weapon as a last resort. It almost (but not quite) goes without saying that no police officer should knowingly try to harm someone maliciously.

5.4.13 Justice

A police officer must apply the law fairly and equitably, having due respect for people's rights. This principle actually extends beyond policing into the whole criminal justice system, because the law itself must be morally respectable. In other words, you cannot be selective about whom you will punish and whom you will not. The law must apply equally to all, and the police must uphold that law equally (however much police officers may privately dislike a particular law or a judicial outcome). We might note that applying the law equally ('without fear or favour') may not mean that people receive justice equally; there are ambiguities around affording justice which are beyond the scope of this Handbook, but about which you are no doubt aware.

5.4.14 Responsibility

This principle requires police officers to justify actions they take and to take personal ownership of these actions. This may present moral ambiguities which some police officers find difficult. Take our example from above: a police firearms officer opening fire on a suspect. The rules of engagement say that a police officer may open fire only if he/she believes his/her life to be in danger or that the lives of others are in danger. A split-second decision may result in every action of that officer being scrutinized, analysed, and judged. There are many such examples, such as when officers fired on a man carrying a chair leg in a plastic bag, or the more recent case of MPS firearms officers shooting dead an unarmed Brazilian man in the aftermath of the bombings in London in July 2005. Many firearms officers find it unacceptable (and unethical?) that their decisions and actions are scrutinized by people with little or no personal experience of taking life and death decisions.

These difficulties do not, of course, absolve a firearms officer from the moral or legal responsibility of the judgement to fire; no one else can take that responsibility, as we noted above. The media do not make it any easier, dominated as they are by the need to sell stories that may be sensational and often without great regard for the circumstances or context of what happened.

You should note that such ethical difficulties accompany many specialist roles in policing, not just firearms, and in your career as a police officer, you could be called to account for your actions (or lack of action), and asked to justify your decisions at any time.

5.4.15 Care

This principle derives from the inter-dependence of police officers with the community they serve, and is at the heart of the consensual debate. You will read (in section 5.8) that there are many styles and models of policing. In the UK, we operate a model of policing by consent; policing derives its legitimacy from the **consent of the public** to be policed. If this is the dominant model, then the relationship between the police and the policed has to be based on moral principles. In addition, the police owe a special duty of care to the vulnerable and the weak in society; remember the example of the old man in the supermarket we looked at earlier? There are many others, from missing persons' enquiries (often called 'mispers') to road safety advice for children, where the police directly demonstrate the care which they owe to the community, and for which, by and large, the community seems grateful. However, such interdependence and trust can be eroded quickly by the unthinking and foolish actions of just a few officers; some community relationships, especially in areas of high social tension, are balanced on a knife-edge and the ethical principle must be consciously reinforced if reasonable relations are to be sustained.

5.4.16 Honesty

Described by Neyroud and Beckley (2001) as 'a key virtue', honesty is central to public confidence in the police (or indeed any public office); yet, as we noted above, it needs only a few instances of dishonesty, cheating, or evasion in the police for that confidence to be eroded very quickly. We not only expect honesty in our day to day dealings with the police; we also expect the police to be honest in the gathering and submission of evidence. A police officer's testimony, case preparation, and conduct must be above reproach, and there can be no compromise about this.

5.4.17 Stewardship

Stewardship is about the role of the police in protecting the weak and the vulnerable, and it is often a motivation for people to join the police in the first instance. Trust and reliance are moral behaviours which the public has every right to expect from its police officers. Stewardship encompasses a positive regard for the whole community as well as the disposition to care for individuals within that community.

5.4.18 Ethics and the Student Police Officer

You may be thinking by this point in the discussion that policing is full of 'should' and 'must' and difficult ethical choices.

These virtues are fundamental to the profession of policing, but the real value of this discussion of ethics in policing is to focus your attention on how you perceive yourself, as a police officer in the making, and how others see you. The public pays police officers to do a difficult and often dangerous job. High on the list of musts is protection of the public, helping the helpless, protecting the vulnerable, and differentiating between coercion and persuasion. These are issues we have already discussed. You are joining a profession in which people all around you expect you to be fair, impartial, skilled, and sensible. These issues are not easily resolved; in fact they can never be fully resolved as there are too many different factors and too many unknowns.

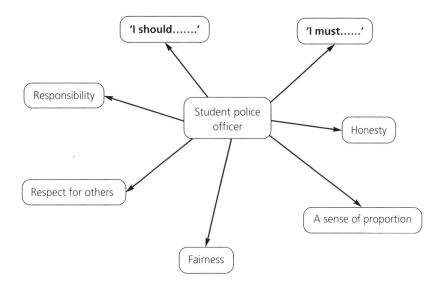

To define the ethics of policing and ethical behaviour more clearly it is necessary to consider one of the ever-present threats to ethical policing, namely corruption. We devote a considerable part of this chapter to the topic of corruption. This is not to suggest that police officers (including you as a student police officer) are any more or less likely to become corrupt than any other person in the UK. We devote attention to corruption because the consequences of police corruption are so damaging, and because maintaining police integrity requires the active engagement of every new generation of police officers.

5.4.19 Police Corruption

In March 2003, Surrey Police mounted an operation to 'test purchase' a supply of drugs, leading to the arrest of three drug dealers and the recovery of drugs to the street value of £2 million. Police also seized a loaded sawn-off shotgun and a pistol, 14 kilos of cocaine, 200,000 ecstasy tablets, 180 kilos of cannabis, over a kilo of amphetamines, false bank account details, and presses for cocaine production. A total of four men were arrested and later sentenced to prison terms.

So far, this might be considered a fairly routine case, though officers were confident they had significantly undermined serious organized crime in Surrey. However, what made this case unusual was that two other arrests were carried out by the police in connection with the drugs importation and that one of those arrested was a former police officer and the other was a staff member in the call-handling centre of the local police force. Both arrests followed standard security audits and intelligence leads; both suspects had been under surveillance for several months before the main arrest operation. The former police officer involved had accessed the force computer system, as had a female member of staff through the call centre. In this way, they were able to track the investigation of the importation of controlled drugs. Both members of staff were found guilty and each was subsequently sentenced to a term of imprisonment.

Any investigation into criminality by the police is made more difficult when insiders are involved. There is the danger that the details of the investigation will become known and that the criminals involved will be tipped off. This did not happen in the Surrey case because the force knew already that the two people concerned were acting inappropriately, and the investigators were able to keep details of the investigation secure.

Is Surrey Police unique in having members of staff involved in corruption? Was this a one-off event or are other police forces likely to have similar problems? If so, how widespread are such activities, and what can be done about them?

Surrey Police is by no means unique; there are probably small numbers of corrupt or corruptible officers and staff in any police force. If so, we need to understand how widespread corruption is likely to be and how we might prevent it. But we must start at the beginning.

TASK 8

Consider the following questions:

- What is corruption?
- What are the theories about corruption?
- Why does corruption happen?
- What makes a police officer or police staff member act corruptly?
- Can we predict who is likely to act corruptly?
- Can theories help tackle corruption?

5.4.20 The Definition of Corruption

Consider the following definition of corruption:

> Corruption exists when a member of a police force illegally puts personal interests, or the interests of others, above those of the people he or she is pledged to serve. (Adapted from Klitgaard, 1988.)

No doubt there are some problems with this definition, but we will take it as a working definition for the purposes of our discussion here. You need also to be aware of technical and legal definitions of some aspects of corruption in a public office. These are:

Definitions of corruption

- Non-feasance   (not doing what you should)
- Misfeasance   (doing what you should not do)
- Malfeasance   (the commission of indictable crimes)

In the case study given above, the ex-police officer was charged with **misfeasance** (in his case, improper use of a police computer). Misfeasance includes all aspects of doing something contrary to your duty—such as failing to charge someone with an offence or impeding an investigation. It is implicit that the act is knowingly done; in other words, it is presumed that an offender knew the difference between what he or she **should** do and the actions he or she actually carried out. This should not be confused with the exercise of initiative and discretion, which we looked at in the discussion about ethics. In the case of the elderly man at the supermarket in section 5.4.10, no one would argue that the offence had not occurred (the old man had taken the bag of sweets without paying), but there were many mitigating factors, and it would be difficult to prove that he knew such an act was wrong, given his confused state.

In **non-feasance**, the reverse applies (and it is, to some extent, a lesser charge) because an individual has failed to do something which his or her duty would normally oblige them to do. Examples of this might include not reporting someone for a traffic offence or, more seriously, not intervening when there is a fight in a pub. There is frequently some ambiguity about some aspects of non-feasance. For instance, the decision whether or not to charge a suspect (with an offence) requires the use of discretion. In general terms though, police officers and staff should know what they are supposed to do in the proper discharge of their duties. As emphasized in section 5.4.14, it is a matter of **making a judgement** and being able to **justify your decision**. Most student police officers could justify not charging the elderly man in the supermarket but few could justify not intervening to stop a fight.

If we take Klitgaard's definition of corruption and the legal descriptions of offences as our starting point, we should now turn to the question: what makes a police officer act corruptly?

5.4.21 The Causes of Corruption

We all have the potential for corruption, even if we generally behave ethically. We have all been tempted at some time or other to do something we know is wrong. The crisis occurs when we give way to that temptation and actually carry out actions we know to be wrong.

Many people use a formal belief system such as a religion to help guide their actions, though in some cultures it is more common for people to use their own personal code of ethics. Others rely on what the law proscribes and will refrain from certain acts for fear of being caught. It is likely that the majority of people are influenced by a combination of external and internal factors, and it may be difficult for an individual to account for a particular stance. Whatever the general proscription, we need to find out what tempts an individual to ignore religious, cultural, social, or legal restraints.

It does not seem that officers begin their careers with a conscious disposition to be corrupt. Indeed, Sir John Woodcock (cited in Morton, 1993), then HM Inspector of Constabulary, said in 1992, when looking at people who join the police:

> I see young men and women who join the police service. Invariably, they join out of a sense of idealism, to serve their society. I find it very unlikely that many individuals join so that they can give perjured evidence against fellow citizens and send them to prison.

The use of the word invariably is possibly unjustified as there is some evidence that a few people join the police service at the instigation of criminal colleagues, but such instances are really very rare. Most police officers join to serve, not to steal. Sir John Woodcock was referring to a genuine concern of his time, that police officers had falsified evidence or invented confessions in order that known criminals would receive a prison term. This form of behaviour was given the title 'noble cause corruption'. The idea that such actions were noble stemmed from police officers believing that a particular person was guilty of a crime or crimes and, because suitably incriminating evidence was not available, they would invent, embellish, or plant evidence, or lie when giving their own evidence in court, all for the noble cause of convicting a known criminal. It did not seem to matter that the person concerned had not carried out that particular crime; the officers felt their actions were justified for the greater good—the end justified the means. What thought processes or experiences could lead them to act this way?

If we return to our earlier premise that most police recruits are not corrupt when they join the police, then there must be particular circumstances or experiences which convert them from Woodcock's idealists to cynical law-breakers. What sorts of experiences might cause these disturbing changes in attitude?

We suggest the following could be potentially corrupting factors, which any new police officer might encounter in the first five years of service. It is not exhaustive and only partly based upon research (there is very little to draw upon in this field).

- Corrupt police officers providing a role model.
- The pressure for results.
- Rigorous and humiliating cross-examination in court.
- Abuse or assault from members of the public.
- Observing that much crime actually does seem to pay for some people.
- The difficulties in securing convictions.
- Belief that sentencing was not adequate for the crime committed.
- Occasions when the plainly guilty escape justice, particularly when as a consequence of a legal technicality.
- The first arrival at the scene of a crime, when cash or goods are lying about.
- Personal financial pressures.
- Handling and storing drugs from police investigations.
- The 'long hours, low reward' culture, leading to envy of others more fortunately placed.
- The 'enclave mentality' which sees the police as a beleaguered and misunderstood group in society pitted against the glamorous criminal, or even against the apparently uncaring public ('them and us').
- Lack of effective supervision.
- The excessive exercise of discretion without challenge.
- Feelings of bitterness or resentment at not receiving expected promotion.
- Animosity towards their police force as the result of other disciplinary offences.
- Managing informants without adequate supervision or scrutiny.

So far we have considered factors that might result in the **predisposition** to act corruptly. Any or all of the experiences outlined above could be enough to make someone think about acting corruptly, but an **opportunity** is also required.

> ### TASK 9
>
> Look at the list of factors above that might contribute to an officer's decision to act corruptly. Most of them are about predisposition—motivations for an officer to act corruptly. But as well as predisposition, an opportunity is also required. List the five factors from the list above which are **opportunities** to act corruptly.

5.4.21.1 Theories about the causes of corruption

There are a number of theories about the causes of corruption. In some cases these theories are largely descriptive in nature: that is, they set out a typical sequence of events leading to corruption but do not really provide much in the way of explanation. One such theory is that the metaphorical (in some cases, actual) **free cup of coffee** is enough to start a police officer on the **slippery slope** to corruption. The suggestion is that once a police officer accepts a free cup of coffee, it is but a short step to a free meal, then free entry to a club, then preferential treatment, then provision of goods and inducements and finally the offer to engage in joint criminal exploits. By accepting the free cup of coffee the officer signals his or her willingness to be corrupted. One commentator noted that:

> a free cup of coffee may not in itself constitute a bribe, but the taking of it might condition a police officer to accept other larger gratuities which were indeed intended as bribes (Feldberg, 1985, p 267).

> ### TASK 10
>
> How convinced are you by the 'free cup of coffee' theory? Can you see any flaws in it? Can you think of examples that might challenge the theory? Jot down three scenarios (these may be real or imaginary) that illustrate any problems with this theory.

As with most complex issues, there are other theories to consider. One of these is the **bad apple theory**, often put forward by those who appear to have a vested interest in hushing matters up or in trying to make things look better, at least on the surface. The argument here is that a corrupt police officer or staff member is an isolated instance, different from the norm and by no means typical. Keeping the bad apple could infect the whole barrel, so you have to remove the individual officer; the problem and threat are simultaneously solved.

How convincing do you find this theory? What does it presume or imply?

Who is likely to put forward such an explanation of corruption? Why should he or she do so?

> ### TASK 11
>
> Try to put yourself in the shoes of the bad apple officer (difficult, but try!). What sort of events or feelings would make you, the bad apple, more likely to act corruptly? Why would other officers not succumb to the same pressures or temptations?

The **bent for the job** theory is a third explanation for corruption. According to this account, the law does not give the police sufficient powers, so the police themselves have to invent ways to circumvent the criminal justice system. A former Commissioner of the Metropolitan Police, Sir David McNee, said:

> Many police officers have, early in their careers, learned to use methods bordering on trickery or stealth in their investigations because they were deprived of proper powers by the legislature (McNee, 1983, p 180).

This may have been a quite widespread perception in 1983 when McNee wrote his book; it was argued that the law was so inadequately structured that substantial numbers of the guilty went unpunished and that officers were forced to be devious and underhand because that was the only way in which they could achieve results.

> **TASK 12**
>
> How convinced are you by this theory? Do you accept that the end is more important than the means, and, if so, does that mean that inexperienced officers have to be taught trickery or stealth?

You can see from these three theories that there is a wide range of ideas about corruption and why it happens, but we hope that you have some scepticism concerning their adequacy as explanations. We now examine some of the problems encountered when applying these theories to reality.

5.4.21.2 Testing the theories against reality

The free cup of coffee/slippery slope theory depicts a gradual and inevitable decline into full-blown criminality and is favoured by moral absolutists and those who believe that people (including police officers) are infinitely corruptible. But if that is true, why are the vast majority of police officers patently **not** corrupt? If all corruption starts small and grows big, then we should all be wary of accepting anything from anyone, ever. The main flaw in this theory is the premise that the first step entails the second, the second the third and so on. This is probably not the case; people can (and do) say no at any point. One step does not **necessarily** entail the next.

The bad apple theory is in some respects the opposite of the free cup of coffee theory. Whereas the slippery slope is open to all, and anyone could be corrupted on the slightest pretext, the bad apple theory only applies to the select few. It begins and ends with one bad person being caught and punished. However, there is evidence to suggest that corruption breeds corruption and that corrupt officers often act together. In London in the late 1990s, there was a series of successful prosecutions of police officers who were acting together for corrupt purposes. One of the principal cases involved a serving police detective and an ex-officer conspiring to steal drugs and re-sell them. Another case involved a police officer in the Flying Squad who was prosecuted for theft (and sentenced to a substantial prison sentence). He claimed that the pressures of joining an elite squad and wanting to fit in had corrupted him. Other corrupt officers effectively tested him by providing opportunities for him to demonstrate his corruptibility and, when he succumbed, he was 'in'. This demonstrates the inadequacy of the bad apple theory, at least in the UK context.

What of the bent for the job theory of corruption? There is plenty of evidence to suggest that these were widespread practices in the 1970s and 1980s. However, it is still not clear whether the corrupt police officers used falsified evidence or corrupt testimony in order to get around a poor law or whether poor law occasioned the corrupt officers' actions. This is not to say that miscarriages of justice do not happen today, but there appear to be fewer opportunities. There is closer scrutiny of the evidence-gathering process; detailed procedures are specified in a series of laws, such as the Police and Criminal Evidence Act 1984. Internal police procedures have changed; it is now recognized that elite squads, unchanged over time, unsupervised and free to do more or less what they want, are conducive to corrupt practices. Limited tenure, obtrusive supervision, and stronger countermeasures have all blunted the power of such elites, and there are very few forces, if any, where secretive squads function without oversight and appropriate challenge.

Is there then a persuasive theory of police corruption to which we might all sign up? We know that corruption flourishes when **predisposition** coincides with **opportunity**, and the individual or group succumbs to the temptation. However, it could be argued that there are as many variants of corruption as there are variants of human character. You might try discussing with your colleagues and friends whether any theory (or theories) can account for human criminal behaviour and the specific nature of corruption in the police and, if such a theory or theories do exist, whether they can be used predictively.

5.4.22 Levels of Corruption

We could classify episodes of corruption in terms of two factors:

- the seriousness of the offence;
- the context of the offence.

5.4.22.1 The seriousness of the offence

The table below gives examples of corrupt acts. The seriousness increases as you move down the table.

Examples of Corrupt Acts

Seriousness	Descriptor
Corruption of authority	This can range from the relatively minor, such as not being assertive enough to take charge of a situation or allowing undue familiarity, through to turning a blind eye to the relatively minor misdemeanours of friends or colleagues. It might entail a free dinner or free entry to an event. It gives a handle to the unscrupulous to exploit any predisposition to corruption. Blackmailable behaviour, especially of a sexual kind, comes into this category.
Favours	A wide spectrum of activities, from letting someone know that a lucrative maintenance contract is in the offing, through to using a particular crash recovery service for motorway accidents and taking a percentage of the resulting business.
Bribery	This includes accepting cash not to book a motorist for speeding or having defective tyres, taking money to lose a file or a report, or taking a holiday paid for by someone to whom the corrupt officer has given valuable information.
Protection of criminals	Overlapping with bribery (because it inevitably involves payment of some sort) but even more serious; informing criminals about police investigations into their activities, warnings about raids, seizures, sting operations or intelligence information, perverting the course of justice to ensure that the criminal is not convicted.
Direct criminal activities	Pimping for prostitutes, theft, embezzlement, violence, resale of stolen drugs, intimidation of witnesses. All entail the commission of indictable offences for which the penalty at law would be a sentence of not less than two years' imprisonment.

5.4.22.2 The context

You will recall that part of the discussion above included the notion of the context for corruption. The second part of our classification system for corruption is a list of activities to show the context of an episode of corruption.

- **Actions** We have noted that there must be a decision taken by the individual when opportunity meets predisposition.
- **Peer group** Most human actions, particularly at work, are modulated or modified by the people we work with and whose respect we value. The peer group for police officers could be officers of the same rank or other officers we work with. Whatever the group, it will have a direct influence on actions. If an individual felt that his or her peer group would thoroughly disapprove of a corrupt action, that disapproval might act as an inhibitor. If, on the other hand, a peer group approved of a corrupt action and deliberately inveigled an individual into joining in, then resistance to corruption would be much harder.
- **Authority** We have noted the role of the obtrusive supervisor, the sergeant, or inspector who wants to know what is going on and has a thorough understanding of the tricks and misdemeanours that people can get up to. Such a supervisor can be a potent force in the inhibition of police corruption. The classic case is supervision of the handling of informants: where supervision is lax or inept, instances occur where the informant 'turns' the handler and corrupts him/her. Where supervision is tight and vigilant, any such signs would be quickly noted and acted on so that a professional relationship could be re-established or the handler moved away. This proper use of supervising authority goes all the way up the chain of command in a police force. It reduces opportunity and inhibits temptation.

- **Conspiracy** Two or more police officers or police staff acting together form a conspiracy. The advantage to a corrupt individual is that someone is watching his or her back, and there is a further protection against discovery or suspicion. We noted above that it was a characteristic of the old-style remote, secretive, and elite squads, but it need only involve two officers to be effective.
- **Likely outcome** The debate essentially is about how likely it is that corruption will be discovered. Where the likelihood is high, corruption will be more difficult to accomplish. Where the likely outcome is a warning or a ponderous, inconclusive investigation, then corruption may be encouraged. There have been instances when juries have found it hard to credit that police officers could act corruptly.

5.4.23   A Corruption Matrix

If we put the **seriousness levels** (section 5.4.22.1) and the **contexts** (section 5.4.22.2) together in a matrix, it might look like this:

	Actions	Peer group	Authority	Conspiracy	Likely outcome
Corruption of authority					
Favours					
Bribery					
Protection of criminals					
Direct criminal activities					

This is not a mathematical matrix (as it contains only one continuous variable) but it does provide a structure for analysing and comparing different instances of corruption.

TASK 13

Based on what you have read and discussed in these analyses of ethics and corruption, attempt short responses to the following:

- Bent coppers are so rare that it is hardly worth all the machinery to inhibit or catch them. Do you agree?
- Do you accept that anyone defaulting, even in a minor way, from expected ethical standards should be dismissed from the police?
- Populate the corruption matrix with a published case.

5.5   Personal Authority

Authority may seem a somewhat old-fashioned concept in the era of supposed late modernity. It conjures up images of strict Victorian fathers and the arbitrary exercise of power by officials (civil servants, teachers, and the like) and may even seem to run contrary to the desire of a modern police force to serve the community. However, we would argue that authority is a key concept for the police and of particular interest and concern to the student police officer. The exercise of authority is often viewed as a mark of a professional although it is often expressed or described instead as autonomy or credibility and related concepts.

5.5.1   Introduction

As a student police officer your authority (to act in certain ways, to exercise discretion, to arrest somebody) will no doubt be challenged and you will also find yourself thinking deeply about where your authority comes from. There are a number of behaviours that you need to exhibit before completing training (see section 6.3) and some of these are clearly related to your personal authority.

In the 1960s and 70s, the educational philosopher Richard Peters (often referred to as 'RS Peters' and who usually wrote and worked in collaboration with Paul Hirst) argued that there are different forms of authority which nonetheless interrelate (Peters, 1973). Although Peters' focus was authority in education we have adapted his work here to apply to policing.

5.5.2 The Main Forms of Authority

The main forms of authority are considered to be:

- **Epistemic**—authority from knowledge (knowing more than the next person).
- **Natural** sometimes called 'charismatic authority'—derived from personality, demeanour (non-verbal communication).
- **De facto**—(from fact) authority that exists through convention rather than as a matter of right.
- **De jure**—(from right) authority as a matter of right.
- **Moral**—authority that arises from a moral high ground.

Note that these categories are not intended to be mutually exclusive. As we shall note below, de facto and moral authorities, for example, are often linked. It is also important to note that authority here can relate to two distinct concepts. There is the general authority of the police service, often thought about in terms of legitimacy and which is discussed in section 5.6 in this chapter. The second is the authority of the individual police officer, which may and will vary from individual to individual and which concerns us here.

5.5.2.1 What do these mean in policing terms?

As a student police officer your **epistemic** authority stems from knowledge of the law and procedure. The public expect you to know the rudiments of the law. Although members of the public may know that an offence has occurred (by applying their common sense), they will expect you to know which particular law or laws have been broken. In part, this expectation is fed by media portrayals of the police which often feature a police officer using the words 'I arrest you for [specifics of the offence]'. (Indeed, you may find that your friends and family will expect you to become an expert on the law overnight, even though they know you have only just commenced training!) Therefore, if in certain situations your grasp of the law or proper procedure seems uncertain, then your epistemic authority declines in the opinion of those around you. The law, policy, and guidelines that you study as a student police officer (for example, the IPLDP LPG modules, see section 1.4) are the basis for establishing your epistemic authority. This form of authority needs to be worked on throughout your subsequent career and in some respects the proposal for a professional register (see section 5.3) is a response to this need.

Some people appear to have more **natural** authority, through sheer presence (charisma) than others and hence seem more able to take control when required, to direct others and so on. This is a form of authority that comes from within and it would appear that it is more natural to some than it is to others. Note that natural authority is not necessarily related to physical size or appearance. Being over six feet tall with a powerful physique may go some way to enhancing your natural authority but is certainly no guarantee. We have all witnessed other people without these physical advantages who exercise natural authority in abundance. However, the word 'natural' is possibly misleading in this context and implies somehow that this form of authority resembles other aspects of our being, such as the shape of our ears which we can do little about. However, natural authority **can** be developed and you will receive training on your demeanour, on your use of language, on your non-verbal communication (body language) and other more subtle ways in which your natural authority can be enhanced. Other aspects of your appearance, such as your clothing, can also either enhance or undermine your natural authority. Being smartly dressed (that is polished shoes, clean and tidy uniform, etc) may seem a strangely old-fashioned topic for a Handbook of this kind but, as we shall discuss in section 12.8, they are important aspects of your authority when, for example, giving evidence in court.

Police officers are seen to have **de facto** authority in certain circumstances, for example, in the aftermath of a road traffic collision. This authority comes, not just from the law, but through custom. A more controversial example (in some eyes) is the common practice of other road users moving out of the way of police patrol cars using their sirens and lights. Police cars also frequently pass red lights at junctions in order to respond to emergency calls. All this is common knowledge and accepted by most of the public as a de facto right of the police. However, this form of authority is easily lost if abused or even if simply perceived as being abused. Your friends and family will still carry on making wry comments about the police using their sirens and lights to get back to the station more quickly for their cup of cocoa and a biscuit!

It is a simple fact that police officers have powers that other members of society do not, and many of those powers feature in this Handbook. These powers are the main source of your **de jure** authority. The wearing of a uniform symbolizes this form of authority, to separate you from the rest of society, as does the possession of a warrant card, which you show people to establish both your credentials and your authority.

Police officers are expected to subscribe to a code of ethics and behaviour which is of a higher standard than the rest of society, and this gives them a **moral** authority. Some may dispute this claim. After all, the police code (see section 7.14 below) makes reference to judging the behaviour of police officers whilst off duty by the 'generally accepted standards of the day' which would suggest that higher than average standards are not required. However, there are certainly greater moral obligations on the police when compared to many other occupational or professional groups; for example, in terms of honesty, integrity, fairness, impartiality, politeness, and general conduct. Gross examples of inappropriate police behaviour (such as the ill-treatment of prisoners) undermine the moral authority of the police service as a whole, but there are other less dramatic examples that happen at the level of the individual. Put simply, members of the public do not expect to witness police officers swearing in public, smoking on duty, or acting other than seriously in the role. More challengingly, these restrictions on the personal behaviour of police officers, and the effect on moral authority, also extend to off-duty life. Where is the moral authority of a police officer who arrests an acquaintance for possession of cocaine during a raid on Saturday, having shared a cannabis joint with the same person the previous evening? How is your moral authority affected if you use your police warrant card to gain free entry to a nightclub?

5.5.3 Development of Personal Authority

It is likely that there will be opportunities for you to develop your personal authority during your initial training. These may include:

- preparing and delivering presentations to others, including groups of students and training staff;
- increasing your knowledge and recall of the law and procedure;
- observing your own behaviour, including your demeanour and use of language, for example, by analysing video of your performance whilst undertaking a particular task;
- feedback from others including your trainers, assessors, fellow student police officers, representatives of community groups (for example, whilst undertaking your community attachment).

TASK 14

You have arrested a woman on suspicion of assault and theft in a shopping centre. The victim has identified the woman to you and the suspect cannot explain her possession of the victim's mobile phone. Give examples of how the five forms of personal authority would feature in this particular scenario.

5.6 Legitimacy

The issue of legitimacy is central to debates about the police role in democratic societies. The existence of police authority requires individuals to willingly sacrifice a degree of personal freedom and liberty in order to secure a greater degree of collective freedom and liberty. The logic behind this way of thinking is made explicit in the writings of the seventeenth-century English philosopher Thomas Hobbes: that without authority in society there would exist 'a war of all against all'. For Hobbes, therefore, the existence of any authority is preferable to none at all. This is an important point to note because, as Nozick (1974) and Simmons (2001) argued, the necessity for authority must be considered before questioning the legitimacy of authority. The difficulty in justifying police authority is illustrated by the fact that it took six attempts (from 1785 onwards) to pass a Police Bill through the Houses of Parliament, finally leading to the creation of the 'new' police in 1829. Clearly there was opposition at the time to the very existence of a professional standing body of police in England and Wales. Today, we largely take the existence of the police for granted and few in society seriously question whether we would be better without any police. Indeed there are more police officers in the UK today than there have ever been before, and there appears to be an appetite for swelling the ranks still further.

Nonetheless, in terms of civil liberties, it is important to be able to justify a police presence, especially given the extent to which we could argue that such a presence may be disproportionate (for example at football matches) or expensive (such as in shopping malls). We may even go beyond justifying the existence of the police to consider a more pressing and ongoing 'libertarian' concern: the legitimacy of the police. Here it is worth noting two distinct ways in which the police obtain legitimacy: consensual and moral.

5.6.1 Consensual Legitimacy of the Police

Consensual legitimacy is gained through the support of those who are being policed. It is reflected in the notion of 'policing by consent' (Reiner, 2000). Discussion about legitimacy in the early years of the police was almost exclusively concerned with this aspect. The Home Office's (2004a) recent focus on Neighbourhood Policing has also stressed the importance of this issue.

From the perspective of those advocating consensual legitimacy, the police are legitimate to the extent that they are consented to by the public. Of course there are differing degrees to which we might say the public consents to the police. One view is to say that the public consents **passively** by not opposing what the police do. On the other hand we might insist on the public having an ongoing engagement with the police in order for consent to be given **actively**. In practice, the kind of consent gained will be dependent upon the type of police response and the particular problem it is addressing. For example, if the police are required to deal with a serious threat of terrorism then the consent will have to be passive in order to allow the police to be effective. The more the public know about how the police intend to counter the terrorists, the more the terrorists will also know and the police intervention might fail as a consequence. Conversely, when the police are required to resolve low level but persistent offending, there is a greater need for the police to communicate adequately with the local community to establish and agree the most appropriate means of addressing the problem. In this latter case, the consent must be active and ongoing. The police need to negotiate their response to the problem and ensure that the community supports, as much as is possible, any police interventions. In this respect, the process for ensuring the consensual legitimacy of the police involves making sure that the public involvement in negotiating police responses is appropriate and that the response deals effectively with the problem at hand.

5.6.1.1 The limits of consensual legitimacy

Consensual legitimacy is important but it is possible for the police to be **too** responsive to the views of the communities being policed. As Waddington (1999a) has noted, the police are required to deal with conflicts in society and in the exercise of this function they may have to police 'against' sections of the community. A real concern exists that the police might be overly responsive to one section of the community against another. This could lead to the exclusion and/or targeting of groups of individuals who are seen to be on the periphery of a community. Put another way, the popularity of the police, which is effectively what consent measures, is no guarantee that the police are acting in a legitimate way.

There are various ways of establishing the legitimacy of police authority, and approval from citizens is just one. As Simmons (2001) observes, this particular way of establishing legitimacy focuses on how an authority is perceived rather than what it does. In other words it measures the attitudes of the recipients of the authority rather than the authority itself.

5.6.2   The Moral Legitimacy of the Police

For police services to be legitimate they must also adhere to the rule of law. We discussed this in section 5.5 in the context of personal moral authority at the level of the individual police officer, but it also applies at the level of the police service as a whole. It is illegitimate for the police to break the law simply to please the community. Furthermore, in addition to legal constraints, it is also becoming increasingly important for the police to 'do the right thing', from a moral perspective. The popular police option is not always the correct one. Conversely the police will not always be able to gain consensual support when called upon, for example, to protect a known paedophile living within a residential area or to allow a racist organization to march through the centre of the town. However, the reason why the police do what they do is often a matter of moral legitimacy, rather than consensual legitimacy. As far as possible, the police will try to achieve both moral and consensual legitimacy, but this is not always possible. The former Chief Constable of Devon and Cornwall, John Alderson, has been an advocate of what he refers to as 'principled policing' for a number of years (see Alderson, 1998). He has argued that policing should be more firmly founded upon moral principles rather than pragmatic concerns. The Human Rights Act 1998 has given legislative support to this point of view. Increasingly, police officers must take into account a number of (often different or contradictory) moral considerations in order to make professional judgements. Policing by consent remains an important part of police legitimacy, but the police must operate primarily within both legal and moral boundaries if they are to be truly legitimate.

TASK 15

What judgements would you make if you had to control a march by the British National Party through your town, knowing that the Anti-Nazi League was planning to turn up in large numbers to oppose the march? (Note that our interest here is in judgements based on police legitimacy rather than the detail of operational orders.)

5.7   Discretion

In this section we extend the discussion of discretion. We have already looked briefly at discretion (in section 5.4) and considered its fundamental place in modern policing in relation to ethics and corruption.

Police officers are not robots, programmed to respond to every crime they encounter (however trivial) by arrest and charging. There are a number of reasons for this:

- It is not practically feasible (the police officer would have no time to respond to more serious offences or to undertake more important work).
- It is not fair (it would undermine the relationship between police and public).
- It is not effective (it is not likely to have any significant impact on levels of crime, although see Zero Tolerance Policing models and also the association between offences and criminality).

Thus the exercise of discretion may be seen as an important, we might even say, fundamental policing skill. Indeed, Lord Scarman, saw it in this way:

> the exercise of discretion lies at the heart of the policing function. It is undeniable that there is only one law for all: and it is right that this should be so. But it is equally well recognised that successful policing depends on the exercise of discretion on how the law is enforced. … Discretion is the art of suiting action to particular circumstances (Scarman, 1981, para 4.58).

Chan (2003) has noted that in the early stages of initial police training, officers are hungry for basic technical knowledge, a statement you might agree with. This is understandable; police officers require the basic know-how skills in order to feel confident enough to perform duties (under the supervision of a tutor) in operational settings such as Supervised Patrol. Police discretion is a subject that does not fit easily under the umbrella of basic technical knowledge and in this respect it differs from much of the other initial learning of student police officers. Nonetheless, it is important that student police officers understand what police discretion is and what it is not, because discretion informs (to a large extent) everything that a police officer does. It is, as this discussion will try to demonstrate, the vital ingredient that allows police work to be presented as a profession, or in Neyroud and Beckley's (2001, p 86) words, discretion is 'the essence of informed professionalism in policing'. We noted this earlier in section 5.3.

This section is organized in two parts. The first (section 5.7.1) defines police discretion and then identifies ways in which it is commonly misunderstood. The second part (section 5.7.2) develops the argument that discretion is a vital weapon in the professional police officer's armoury.

5.7.1 Defining Discretion

Police discretion does not apply only to front-line officers but also to the kinds of decisions that police managers and chief officers must make. These were defined by Neyroud and Beckley (2001) as **prioritizing decisions** and **tactical decisions**. The former relates primarily to the allocation of limited resources and the latter relates to the balancing of liberty and order in a democratic society.

In a similar vein, Delattre (2002) discusses the need for senior investigative officers to make anticipatory and planning decisions about, for example, when to identify and release information concerning a serial killer. These are all good examples of police discretionary decisions and it is important for new police officers to be aware of why and how these kinds of decisions are made. However, the focus here will be on the discretion of front-line officers; in other words, the kind of decisions that patrol constables (and therefore student police officers) are expected to make on a daily basis.

It is also important to note that discretion often involves choosing between different law enforcement options. For example, officers are regularly confronted with minor offences that present a choice of issuing fixed penalty tickets or making an arrest and taking the suspect to the police station. 'Under-enforcement as opposed to choosing how to enforce the law, has led to concerns because it is seen by some to occur as a consequence of either an officer's "misappropriation of judicial power" or an officer's "discrimination"' (Neyroud and Beckley, 2001, pp 85–6). Clearly those people that do not have the law enforced against them but are instead given a verbal warning or reprimand, are unlikely to complain about it. At the same time, what defence can the perpetrator of an offence have when subjected to law enforcement? It could be argued that they have no defence; they have committed an offence and therefore merit the law's full weight of sanction. But, if one person deserves to be punished for committing an offence, why do not all persons (committing identical offences) also deserve to be punished in the same way? The unfairness of this situation is not so much that some are having the law enforced against them, but rather that others are not. Critics of under-enforcement therefore point to the inconsistency in applying the law which may result. As a consequence, the fundamental right of the police to employ discretionary powers is called into question.

One simple answer (proposed by the critics of police discretion) is to remove police discretion altogether or at least to reduce the extent to which officers can draw upon it. There are practical problems that prevent this from happening completely. For instance, the Criminal

Justice System (CJS) already struggles to cope with the existing load presented to it; how would it cope if the police enforced the law without discretion? Another example is that police work is extremely difficult to manage (Reiner, 2000, Chapter 2). Most officers operate alone or with a partner and as Crawshaw et al (1998, p 24) note, police supervision tends to occur after the event. These examples illustrate the amount of discretion police officers have, but they are not arguments for keeping it.

Governments have periodically introduced legislation and guidelines to restrict the amount of discretion a police officer has. This may be reflected in force policies as well, for example in relation to the policing of domestic violence. Positive action policies (which would include an arrest when attending a domestic incident) have been applied across the UK. If police discretion is to be maintained, it is important that we make a positive case for it. As part of the argument for discretion we need to identify a number of ways in which police discretion is often misrepresented. We begin by considering the view that police discretion is nothing more than applying common sense.

5.7.2 Discretion as Common Sense

The view that police discretion is a matter of applying common sense to policing situations would appear to have some merit. It helps police officers understand how real operational experiences complement the necessarily theoretical and abstract learning which takes place during the initial period of police training. Importantly, officers learn in this way to use the law as a means to an end rather than as an end in itself. However, the problem with viewing police discretion as the application of common sense is that it is too simplistic. It suggests that discretionary decisions are straightforward and could be applied by anyone. This view also fails to distinguish between decisions that are just simple common sense decisions and decisions that genuinely require the use of discretion. As Davis (1996) notes, not all choices are discretionary. This is an important point. Police discretion cannot be reduced simply to being a matter of making choices or decisions.

5.7.3 Police Discretion as Subjectivity

Another way of understanding discretion is to consider the view that every police officer has a unique subjectivity that produces different approaches to how the law is interpreted and enforced. Within this perspective, police discretion is understood as the means by which individual subjectivity can be realized. It is undoubtedly true to say that the individual subjectivities of officers play an important role in how they police, but this should not be confused with police discretion. Indeed, police discretion is necessary precisely because it provides a way of curbing the influence of individual subjectivity.

To illustrate what this point means, consider the following question: should we expect all police officers to make the same decision in identical circumstances? Student police officers answer this question in different ways; some answer that there will be as many different decisions as there are officers making them, but at the other extreme others answer that every officer should make the same decision. So what is the correct answer? Well, first we should note that the question is not entirely fair because different contexts would probably produce different answers (in reality no two sets of circumstances are ever identical). Nonetheless, the existence of police discretion implies that we should anticipate neither of the extreme answers presented above. If we expect every officer to make the same decision then why are we considering discretion at all? Alternatively, if every officer makes a different decision, in what sense are these decisions connected? That is, in what sense are these decisions related to policing principles and practice?

The answer is that we should expect officers' decisions to differ, but that there will be a finite number of decision categories, normally two or three. Ideally, each of these categories would represent good police decisions that could be justified and explained. (More realistically, we might expect a few officers to make decisions that fall into another separate category, one that represents bad police decisions.) In other words, police discretion assumes that on the one hand there is more than one way to deal with most situations, but at the same time, there are a limited number of valid options open for consideration to the officer. So what is it that limits the options open to the officer and thereby the individual subjectivity of each officer?

The answer to this question is that decisions are discretionary but only to the extent that they relate to professional standards, integrity, the law, and force policy. The legal philosopher Ronald Dworkin has explained this point by referring to discretion as the 'hole in the doughnut' (see Neyroud and Beckley, 2001, p 83). The doughnut analogy suggests that discretion is given meaning by the professionalism surrounding it in the same way that the hole in a ring doughnut is given meaning by the dough surrounding it. If we eat the ring, the hole disappears; likewise, without professional standards, discretion becomes meaningless; discretion has to exist and has to be applied within a policing context.

Just as professional standards limit the number of options available to officers, the same standards also allow for different responses. So in answering how we explain different responses, we can say that subjectivity is not an adequate answer because it would mean law enforcement is too arbitrary. It is not acceptable that an individual is arrested only because he/she encountered officer A rather than officer B or officer C. All police responses are only valid to the extent that they can be explained and justified and this has to be in relation to professional standards, not as a product of a subjective perspective. To reiterate and emphasise the point, discretion curbs subjectivity by providing an objective, professional guide.

5.7.4 Discretion as Judicial Misappropriation

It was noted earlier that for some critics, police discretion is seen as nothing more than an individual officer's misappropriation of judicial power. The reasoning behind this view is that when officers decide not to enforce the law against an individual who has clearly committed an offence, they are effectively acting as judge and jury as well. This view is based upon a misconception of the police officer's role, that the police are merely law enforcers. This view is summarized by Waddington (1999b) with reference to the surprise expressed by researchers (into policing) in the 1960s. He says:

> the prevailing assumption had been that policing was little more than the application of the law...Criminals committed crimes and the police captured the criminals who were tried and convicted by the courts (Waddington, 1999b, p 31).

Indeed such was the surprise of these early researchers that Waddington refers to the discretionary powers of the police as being 'discovered' in the 1960s. Of course police officers had been exercising discretion since at least the creation of the modern police in 1829 but it was not an aspect of police work that had received much attention. As more research was conducted, it was found that the police would consistently enforce the law against certain sections of society and not others (see section 5.7.5). There can be no defence for the police discriminating against certain sections of society; nonetheless, it is wrong to suggest that the police should therefore have their discretion removed. Instead, what needs to be learnt from these experiences is that the police officers are not so much law enforcers as peace officers (Banton, 1964). Waddington (1999b) has argued that the police use the law as and when appropriate in order to bring about a greater sense of peace and order in society. He refers also to Lord Scarman's warning following the Brixton riots in 1981 'that the maintenance of "public tranquillity" was a higher priority than "law enforcement"' (Waddington, 1999b, p 42).

The police make law enforcement decisions based upon their interpretation of what is in the public interest. It is this balancing act between law enforcement and the needs of society that gives rise to police discretion. The police are expected to use the law to maintain order, and therefore they need discretionary powers in order to use the law as effectively as possible. This does not mean that the police can operate outside the law; of course they must work within legal boundaries, but they should not be required to enforce the law in every circumstance. In this respect the police are not only accountable to the law but also to the people they police.

5.7.5   Discretion and Discrimination

The view that discretion is the means by which certain sections of society are discriminated against has arisen from research conducted since the 1960s. So why are some sections of society more likely to have the law enforced against them? In their defence, police officers have argued that they do not discriminate against any sections of society but respond to each individual they encounter according to how that individual responds to them. This is referred to in police circles as the **attitude test**. (You will no doubt hear more experienced police officers using this phrase, or more colloquial versions.) Quite simply, if an individual is polite and repentant, they are less likely to have the law enforced against them. The reason for this is that the individual has learnt a lesson and is judged unlikely to re-offend. An intervention by a police officer is in itself an effective form of remonstration and helps prevent repeat offending. It may not be in the public interest to pursue certain cases any further as it would contribute nothing towards achieving a more ordered society (and apart from the wasted expense, it could have a negative effect on the individual stopped). On the other hand, if the individual stopped by the police officer is rude, abusive, and unrepentant then it is assumed that further action needs to be taken against them in order to make sure they feel sufficiently reprimanded.

The problem with this defence is that it perpetuates problems that exist in society. It is likely that those who regularly come into contact with the police will be immune to police warnings and will feel more confident in challenging the police officer's authority. They are more likely to be abusive and to have an existing antagonistic relationship with the police. Historically, individuals from certain ethnic minority groupings have had a disproportionately high interaction with the police and so the attitude test does nothing to break this cycle; indeed it helps perpetuate it.

This kind of information needs to be absorbed into police culture and recognized as an issue to be rectified; this is precisely what has been happening over the past 40 years, though with mixed results. There have undoubtedly been some low points during that time (see Macpherson, 1999 and *The Secret Policeman* programme, 2003), but police officers today are in a better position to understand the cycle and to respond accordingly. The important difference between discriminatory decisions and discretionary decisions is that discrimination is based upon prejudice, whereas discretion is premised upon professional judgement (which incorporates many different factors, including the prevalence of discrimination in previous times). This requires officers to go beyond simply providing a common standard by which every individual encounter is measured. We now recognize that this measurement would favour some sections of society and discriminate unfairly against others. Officers are thus required to respond to each encounter individually, taking into account the specifics of each situation. As Rowe (2002) has noted, since the Macpherson Report (1999) policing no longer treats everyone equally but rather pursues specific policies aimed at reducing discrimination, eg by actively promoting an anti-racist agenda. It is now part of the police officer's role to break the cycle of discrimination.

TASK 16

In the following task you are given two scenarios to consider. The first is taken from the National Police Training notes issued to student police officers in 1995 and the second is our own invention.

1. You see a woman, who appears to be slightly drunk, pick up a street sign that has fallen from a wall, conceal it under her raincoat and walk off. When stopped, she readily admits that she intends to keep it as a trophy. She is a medical student who is celebrating passing her final exam (NPT, 1995, p 4).

2. You are on duty outside a football ground when you observe a young man, clutching a can of super strength lager, pick up an 'Away Supporters' sign that has fallen from a wall, conceal it under his hoodie and walk off. When stopped, he readily admits that he intends to keep it to start a collection. He is a football fan who is celebrating his club's victory in an important match.

In each case consider what discretion, if any, you would exercise.

5.8   Models of Policing

We all have the tendency to think that systems which are familiar are the norm, and that all good systems will be just about the same as ours. In Chapter 12, you will encounter references to different criminal justice systems such as the Continental **inquisitorial** system, which is different from our **adversarial** system. In the same way, the organization of policing and police forces varies between different countries.

We are going to take a few moments now to look at different **models** for policing: these will refer not only to the way that the police are structured and organized but to fundamental differences in function. This is known as comparative study; it involves comparing and making comparisons, usually between practices in different countries. It is used by academics (and other commentators on police systems) to identify differences as well as similarities. You may have already noticed how most criminologists and writers about police matters tend to look to the USA rather than to Europe. This is partly a matter of language (not many criminologists are linguists as well), but is also to do with their familiarity with the systems. For example, many policing methodologies (such as 'zero tolerance') are imported directly into the UK from the USA. In 2002, the Home Office even went so far as to appoint a North American as the Head of the Police Standards Unit. The FBI's federalist approach to crime has influenced, we think, the British government's decision to set up the **Serious and Organised Crime Agency** (SOCA) in 2005.

TASK 17

Can you think of an instance when, with similar speed, we adopted an idea about criminal justice from Europe?

It is difficult to find examples—except perhaps the incorporation of the European Convention on Human Rights (ECHR), which became the Human Rights Act in 1998. But that was in the context of the whole of human rights, including freedom from torture, rather than matters specifically related to policing or criminal justice.

At the moment though, importations from the USA (such as increased use of litigation, the dominance of the defence, and televising of trials) may be influencing our view of what policing and criminal justice systems are best suited to the UK. But let us make a confident assertion: in matters such as **jury trial** and **continuity of evidence**, the early signs are that England and Wales may well incline more to the Continental models than to North American ones. Although unthinkable ten years ago, trial without a jury for complex fraud cases is now being openly considered. The increasingly interventionist role of the Crown Prosecution Service (CPS) in criminal investigations is actually closer to the European model (the *juge d'instruction* or 'investigating magistrate') than it is to any US model.

So, what different types of policing models might we consider? Well, let us start by looking at our own model for England and Wales (with apologies to readers from Northern Ireland and Scotland).

TASK 18

What do you think characterizes our approach to policing? What can you point to which is essentially British about it?

If you want to read further into this aspect of policing, we refer you to the bibliography at the end of the Handbook. In any case, much of the British model is likely to change, and is changing already in some respects.

Why do you think the Government considered amalgamating police forces in England and Wales? Is it wholly and entirely to do with greater 'critical mass', efficiency, and resilience? Is it so that police forces are large enough to provide neighbourhood teams and a professional response to the investigation of terrorism? All this may be true, but there might be more to it than that. Might it be that the Government wishes to exercise greater central control over previously independent and autonomous police forces (and chief constables) and that a smaller number of forces will be easier to manage? Although amalgamation is off the agenda for the moment, the government undoubtedly wants to control a smaller number of police forces.

In England and Wales each chief constable can decide (to some extent) which operational model of policing best suits his/her force. In practice, a force is likely to adopt a combination of models. You may be able to identify several forces which have tried to do all of them simultaneously and where the police officers themselves are confused about what particular model is operating at any one moment. We also know of forces which have implemented intelligence-led policing alongside community-based policing and have done so very efficiently and effectively. Much depends on the conceptual planning of the individual chief constable and his or her Police Authority.

TASK 19

Examine in detail three operational models of British policing, namely:

- intelligence-led policing;
- problem-oriented policing; and
- community-based policing.

(You will find information on these models from various sources, including the internet and Nick Tilley's chapter in Newburn, 2003.)

How would each of these models, adopted in their purest form (that is, to the exclusion of all other approaches), deal with the phenomenon of anti-social behaviour?

We do not have to look very far afield to see differences in policing approaches: there are minor ones in Scotland, and, in the recent past, we had an essentially paramilitary police force in the Royal Ulster Constabulary (RUC). The change to the Police Service of Northern Ireland (PSNI) has to some degree moved away from the paramilitary model (in line with an increasingly peaceful province) but PSNI officers are still armed routinely, which their counterparts in Scotland, England, and Wales are not.

5.8.1 Models of Policing in Western Europe

We do not expect you to know the detail of the policing models in Europe but you may well have been to France, Germany, Spain, or Italy on business trips or holidays and observed some fundamental differences.

TASK 20

Consider individual countries in Western Europe. What do you know about their police organizations and cultures? What characterizes their approach to policing? Do they respond in the same way (after all they face many of the same problems and difficulties we experience in the UK)?

The table below shows some of the characteristics of police organizations in a range of European countries. Compare your response to Task 20 with the information provided in the table.

Comparative Western European Policing Models—A table of essential differences in a sample of states

Member State	Public prosecutor investigates?	Admissibility of evidence	Jury system?	Adversarial	Inquisitorial	Comment
Belgium	Yes; state role, the PP is *officier de police judiciaire* and works with the examining magistrate.	No right to silence. Investigating judge examines evidence. Intercept product is not admissible.	Yes, in some trials, the role of lay judges is used rather than the Anglo-Saxon system.	Yes, but only at the trial. There has been much internal criticism. There is no cross-examination.	Yes; the investigating judge applies inquisitorial process to pre-trial investigation.	Confessional evidence is the norm.
Denmark	Yes; in practice delegates investigation through the police.	There is disclosure to the defence. Intercept product is admissible.	Yes, 8 out of 12 needed to secure conviction, and the jurors sit with 4 judges to share sentencing. No jury in fraud cases. Widespread criticism of jury system and could be abolished.	No	Inquisition is for pre-trial process, then accusatorial.	Confessional evidence seldom challenged.
England & Wales	No, though the Crown Prosecution Service (CPS) is playing a more prominent role in investigations and will alone decide whether criminal case to answer.	Disclosure of evidence to defence is norm. Intercept not admissible. Very liberal use of non-intrusive visual surveillance in evidence. Defence sit in on police interviews with suspect.	Yes, though Government plans to remove for fraud cases.	Yes, on 'not guilty' plea.	No	Confessional evidence is widely discredited and under PACE may be excluded. Plea-bargaining is common (though not as widespread as in the USA)
France	Yes, either acting as *officier de police judiciaire* or in support of investigating judge *(juge d'instruction).*	Intercept evidence is admissible on a judge's authority.	In some trials, 9 jurors will deliberate with the Bench (3 judges).	No	Yes	No plea-bargaining and defence lawyers not allowed presence in police interviews. Confessional evidence is the norm.
Germany	Yes, at both Federal and local *(Länder)* levels. PP brings charges to court and has state monopoly on criminal prosecution.	Seizure of mail only on a judge's authority. Telephonic intercept can be used in evidence but covert bugging cannot.	No. Norm is 3 judges sitting as tribunal.	No	Yes, but defence has no burden of proof.	No plea-bargaining.
Greece	Yes, either through own office or through the police.	Intercept evidence is generally not admissible, but some exceptions have been made in espionage trials.	Mix of professional and lay judges, no ordinary people as in the English and Welsh model.	Some elements in defence at trial, but largely accusatorial.	Yes in the pre-trial and early investigations stages. Trial itself is accusatorial.	Confessional evidence is the norm.
Italy	Yes, on own authority or through the police. New criminal code has abolished the investigating judge role.	Intercept evidence is permitted on the authority of a judge, exceptionally on the authority of the PP.	No jury, but lay and professional judges. Strong move to get rid of the lay element.	Yes; full adversarial model, but without jury.	No.	Suspect cannot defend self—must have defence advocate.

Comparative Western European Policing Models—A table of essential differences in a sample of states (*continued*)

Member State	Public prosecutor investigates?	Admissibility of evidence	Jury system?	Adversarial	Inquisitorial	Comment
Luxembourg	Very similar system to Belgium, with some important differences. Police investigate crime acting under the authority either of the PP or an investigating judge.	Investigating judge can authorize intercepts, the product of which is then admissible.	Jury system 'stuttered' a little in early part of 19th century, then fully implemented. Juries finally abolished in 1987.	No	Yes, trials are conducted by tribunal judges.	Commentators say that Luxembourg's system is more favourable to the accused than the Belgian system. Confession is the most common form of guilty evidence.
Malta	No, police have primacy in criminal investigations. There is no judicial direction of enquiries.	Intercept evidence is not admissible. Status of non-intrusive visual surveillance is unclear.	Yes, along British lines.	Yes, on the British model.	No	Malta's constitution dates from British occupation in 1851 and was modified with independence in 1964. All magistrates are stipendiary.
The Netherlands	Yes, but the prosecution of criminal offences is separated from the judiciary.	Widespread use of intercept material but restrictions on the use of both intrusive and non-visual images.	No, juries were abolished in 1813.	No	Pre-trial is inquisitorial but trial itself is accusational, directed by a judge who examines suspects and witnesses.	The Netherlands is developing role for victim to testify at trial or give statement. Some problems around prejudicial evidence to be resolved.

5.8.2 Other Models of Policing

In other parts of the world we find a wide range of models of policing, and a detailed consideration of these is beyond the scope of this Handbook. However, we consider a few illustrative examples here.

The **proliferation model** is to be found in the USA and in Canada where local approaches to policing are widespread. Both countries have the rough equivalent of a national police (the Federal Bureau of Investigation (the FBI) and the Royal Canadian Mounted Police (RCMP)), but there are separate police departments for each city (such as the Los Angeles Police Department, or the Vancouver City Police), municipal or small town police forces, as well as county organizations such as sheriffs' departments and cross-boundary organizations such as the Highway Patrol. The RCMP has a national remit in Canada but local jurisdiction can be fraught even though the RCMP administers and polices territories such as the Yukon in its own right. If you think that this proliferation model is sometimes problematic, you would be right; consider for example the Waco massacre where 74 people died, partly as a result of confusion arising from poor co-ordination between the multitude of police organizations in attendance. The **state police model** involves a national police force run on state lines, such as the *Garda Siochana* in Eire and the Swedish National Police Force. Even here, the notion of a monolithic, monopolist police system organized on national lines is not necessarily uniform. The Swedish and Irish examples are largely rural in location and performance, and, whilst there is a national remit for terrorism and civil emergency, the majority of the policing takes place locally.

The old **Soviet style** policing model consisted of a repressive and secretive police force which was the arm of the state used in part to stifle criticism or dissent about the regime in power. They placed restrictions on internal movements of the populace, and the use of informants and eavesdropping techniques was widespread.

5.8.3   The Influence of History on Policing Models

One point we should emphasize, perhaps, is that history plays a prominent part in any country's policing system or criminal justice process. We will consider just one example here to illustrate this point.

In the late nineteenth century, the dominance of Napoleon's troops over most of Europe also ushered in a French administrative and legal system. So we find that, in The Netherlands, the Royal Protection Unit is called the *maréchaussée*, a direct importation of the French term for highway or traffic police (horse-drawn; this was before the internal combustion engine). More fundamentally, the civil and legal **Code Napoléon** was imposed on the conquered countries. The Code merely embellished what the revolutionary idealists had created ten or so years earlier to replace the old French legal system. The Code introduced the notion that the accused must prove their innocence before the state inquisitor(s) (rather than the prosecution having to prove guilt as we have in English law). It was the French Revolution which created the examining magistrate or judge (*juge d'instruction*) who oversees the criminal investigation and directs the police. In other words, the widespread use of the inquisitorial criminal justice system in Western Europe is a direct legacy of the Napoleonic occupation. One of the reasons that we have a different system in the UK is because we were not subject to Napoleonic rule.

We may conclude that the policing models which we see in Europe are partly derived from the French Revolution (the *gendarmerie* and *carabinieri* directly so) and partly in reaction to the Napoleonic and subsequent occupations. The triangle of power in The Netherlands is directly derived from the Dutch experience of the misuse of power by the state, first under Napoleonic rule and latterly under the Nazis. The purpose of the triangle between mayor, police chief, and chief prosecutor in any locality is to prevent any one of these office-holders from having too much power. Similar systems exist in Italy, Spain, and Belgium (though in Italy it is complicated by the need to deal with organized crime). Belgium recently abolished its *gendarmerie* and created a national (Federal) police instead, moving away from the French policing model for the first time in its history. In West Germany, the post-war organization of the police gave more power and autonomy to regional districts (*Länder*) and much less to a centralized civil power. This derives directly from rejection of the state police model, as a result of experiences during the Nazi era.

5.8.3.1   Reactive models: the lessons of history

Especially amongst those countries of Eastern and Central Europe (and indeed of the Baltic States) who wanted to become members of the EU, there has been an official embracing of the European Convention on Human Rights and a liberalizing of police organization and structure coupled with checks and balances in an attempt to ensure that there is no further abuse of power. The modern East and Central European police forces are the product of reaction against the previous state model. They are heavily influenced by policing models in The Netherlands, France, and Eire (indeed, some of these countries have exercised considerable influence in redesigning policing models and structures) but also by the USA which has been supplying funding, expertise, training, and inducements to the former Soviet Bloc countries in a campaign against crime and terrorism. However, it may be some time before the reformed police models of Central and Eastern Europe find their own identity and gain the unconditional trust of the citizens.

In Japan, the organization of the police is very much on local lines in reaction against the state police (the *Kempitei*) which existed before and during the Second World War. Subordinate only to the ruling military caste during the War, the *Kempitei* was pervasive, repressive, and brutal. Despite the inevitable inefficiencies of local focus, the modern Japanese people appears to prefer its police to be relatively subordinate to the elected bodies in the regional Prefectures. That said, there is increasing evidence that national control is being exercised in an attempt to gain consistency and to move away from the often inordinately long and drawn-out protocols which govern local administrations.

5.8.4 Conclusions

This has been a canter at some speed through the principal models of policing and, inevitably, detail has suffered and in-depth comparisons have not been possible. The main points which you need to take away and remember are:

- the policing model for England and Wales is not the only model there is (nor is Scotland's or Northern Ireland's);
- within the UK there are a number of operational models, such as intelligence-led policing, community-based policing, and problem-oriented policing which are not necessarily mutually exclusive and rarely occur in their purest forms;
- numerous variations on other models are to be found in Europe;
- the proliferation model has major drawbacks as well as strengths.

5.9 Policing Plans

In this part of Chapter 5 we consider the Policing Plans that forces are expected to construct and deliver.

5.9.1 Introduction

Every police force in England and Wales has a Policing Plan which outlines its commitments and what it expects to be able to deliver during the forthcoming three or so years. Scotland and Northern Ireland have very similar policing plans to those for the police forces of England and Wales. However, there are important regional differences too and individual priorities which a blanket plan cannot cover. The Plan in England and Wales is an amalgam of the directives from the Government (that is, from the Home Secretary, in whose name the Minister with responsibility for Policing and Prisons will act) and whatever constitutes local priorities for the individual force, as agreed with its Police Authority. This sounds straightforward but is actually rather complex especially if the national priorities do not accord with local perceptions and priorities or where national priorities run directly counter to local feeling and opinion (for example, applying the law which outlaws hunting foxes with dogs).

> **TASK 21**
> What do you think the value of a Policing Plan may be? Write down a few bullet points.

5.9.2 National Policing Plans

To help you to appreciate what is being said and to demonstrate how a National Policing Plan (NPP) will impact on your day-to-day deployment as a student police officer, we will examine the elements that make up a typical Policing Plan (concentrating on the current government targets and priorities).

We begin at the top, looking at what the current National Policing Plan says. The NPP is part of the Government's **National Community Safety Plan** which incorporates strategies for the work of a number of Departments of State, including Health and Employment. The NPP in its (updated 2006) current form covers the years 2006–09 and it sets out the Home Secretary's strategic priorities and the key performance indicators for those years.

The Home Secretary has set five key priorities for the police service of England and Wales by 2009 (Home Office, 2005g):

- Reduce overall crime by 15% (more in high crime areas).
- Bring more offences to justice.
- Provide 'dedicated, visible, accessible and responsive' neighbourhood policing teams in 'every area' and 'reduce public perceptions of anti-social behaviour'.

- Tackle serious and organized crime (including improved intelligence and information-sharing between partners).
- Protect the UK from both terrorism and domestic extremism.

We shall now look at each of these in detail, noting how these key priorities will affect you as a student police officer.

5.9.2.1 Reduce overall crime by 15% and more in high crime areas

The Government argues that volume crimes, such as burglary, theft from vehicles, theft of vehicles, and robbery are linked to the supply and misuse of drugs. Thus dealing with drugs issues through enforcement, education, and drug treatment is given a high priority. Criminal damage also figures in the priorities if only because the British Crime Survey (BCS), published annually, deals with public perceptions about crime. Criminal damage makes up nearly a quarter of BCS crime and consequent public concerns.

The measures in the **Violent Crime Reduction Act** are designed to ensure that the police and local authorities have more powers to deal with guns, knives, and alcohol-related violence. This focuses on crime hot spots, particularly alcohol-related crime and domestic violence.

Other priorities (which will therefore find expression in your force's Policing Plan), are:

- Working with force-wide **Crime and Disorder Reduction Partnerships** to deliver local crime reduction goals, which will contribute towards the Government's target of a 15% reduction in all crime.
- Integrating the principles in the Government's 'tackling violent crime programme' into local initiatives to drive down violent crime. This will be undertaken at BCU level.
- Applying national intelligence-model (NIM) approaches to tackling crime and anti-social behaviour (see section 12.3 for a description of the NIM).

5.9.2.2 Bring more offences to justice

The Government has the goal of bringing 1.25 million offences to justice by 2008. This will entail a national sanction detection rate of 25%. Local targets at BCU level and force level will need to be set, especially through the **Local Criminal Justice Boards** in which the police play a key role. The current sanction detection rates across England and Wales stand at about 22%, so raising the detection rates by the equivalent of 1% year on year to 2008–09 is quite a challenge (especially for a high-performing force).

Actions for your police force's Policing Plan will therefore include:

- working with Local Criminal Justice Boards to deliver locally-agreed 'brought to justice' targets and the implied sanction detection rates which underpin them;
- making best use of alternative sanction detection disposal means (such as fixed penalty notices), whilst also working with the CPS to increase the proportion of offences which result in prosecution;
- improving frontline investigation skills by rolling out nationally the Professionalising the Investigative Programme (PIP) at Level 1. In your case PIP Level 1 is already built into your training.

5.9.2.3 Provide every area in England and Wales with dedicated, visible, accessible, and responsive neighbourhood policing teams and reduce public perception of anti-social behaviour

Part of the funding for the emphasis on neighbourhood teams will be used to recruit a total of 16,000 **Police Community Support Officers** (PCSOs) across the country, the majority of whom will be in London (see section 5.17). There are also specially funded 'pathfinder' BCUs, across both England and Wales, which provide communities with access to policing services and with influence over policing priorities in their neighbourhood. Interventions through joint actions with partners and communities help to provide the answers to their problems through sustainable solutions and feedback. It is intended that what has been learned from the forty-three pathfinder BCUs (one in each force as currently structured) is shared with the rest of the police service in order to support neighbourhood policing teams. Forces and their police authorities are expected to take these proposals into account when drawing up their local policing plans.

The Government notes that neighbourhood policing is only one part of a broader programme to answer the public's concern about policing. That broad programme has targets which cover matters such as local confidence in the police and ways to increase victim and witness satisfaction across the whole criminal justice system. A Quality of Service Commitment underpins forces' responses to these targets, which include standards for call-handling and a single non-emergency number to deal with anti-social behaviour issues.

Here the National Policing Plan has focussed on anti-social behaviour (most of which is not criminal) as a primary concern of communities, but the phraseology used in the Government's NPP is ambiguous. It seems to suggest that only the perception of anti-social behaviour must be modified, rather than the anti-social behaviour itself.

Actions for the police, which will find expression in your force's Policing Plans, are:

- developing a pathfinder BCU;
- complying with minimum standards in the Quality of Service Commitment;
- implementing a single non-emergency telephone number;
- working with local agencies to tackle anti-social behaviour.

5.9.2.4 Tackle serious and organized crime including improved intelligence and information-sharing between partners

The Serious Organised Crime Agency, or SOCA, was created by combining the National Crime Squad, the National Criminal Intelligence Service, the Serious Fraud Office, and the Investigation Division of Customs and Excise, with elements of other agencies. It investigates serious organized crime at national and international levels. The Government also asserts that tackling organized crime is just as much of a priority for local police forces, especially 'where its impact extends into neighbourhoods of every kind and its harmful consequences manifest themselves in local communities' (Home Office, 2005g, p 28).

This is because lifestyle criminals and the development of organized crime such as drug-trafficking or the sex trade have an impact at a local level. Criminals at all levels choose to live somewhere and that somewhere is within a BCU. The Government does not mean that forces can investigate serious and organized crime alone but that the local level may be just as fertile an area for investigation as the international level. The reality of the emphasis on tackling serious and organized crime means that, like now, the national agency will look outwards to national and international levels, while forces do the best they can at local levels. The criminal who moves between force boundaries, however extensive or restricted they are, will continue to be problematic for local police forces unless the police service focusses—as the NIM says it should—upon the crime and not upon the criminal. The potential problems with this are revealed by the language in which the idea is couched:

> forces and authorities . . . are encouraged to take on any investigations not falling within the Serious Fraud Office's remit . . . (Home Office, 2005g, p 29).

In effect this means that your police force will be expected to take up the slack on investigations not considered appropriate for action by the national agencies. Such cases can be just as tangled, complex, international in effect and method, and almost as costly to investigate as those the SOCA will handle. There will still be a gap at Level 2 for most forces, and a frustration will still exist for the detectives in your force.

Inadequacies in forces' and other agencies' sharing of intelligence and information was highlighted by the Bichard enquiry into the Soham murders (Bichard, 2004). The framework for such co-operation and sharing is therefore the third proposition in this key priority. It will have a direct influence on how forces record and access information about criminals or criminal intelligence. Through the Impact Programme, new systems and technical facilities to support information-sharing across policing and between forces and other agencies should have been rolled out to all forces by the end of 2007. Predictably, however, producing a coherent system which can apply to all forces has proved very difficult; it seems unlikely that the programme can make much impact before 2011.

The actions for your police force related to key priority 4 are likely to be:

- police force restructuring to increase capacity and resilience;
- establishing and maintaining effective partnerships with SOCA;
- using the 'Impact Programme' for information-sharing between forces and other agencies;
- enhancing intelligence through a number of means (such as ANPR);
- implementing the roads' policing strategy and the Code of Practice on information management.

5.9.2.5 Counter-terrorism

The Government acknowledges that the threat posed by terrorism is not new. However, the attacks in London in July 2005 followed by the arrest and trial of other 'home-grown' extremists in 2006–07 stimulated a new need for co-ordination of effort and intelligence. The Government strategy entails:

- preventing young people from being drawn into extremism and violence;
- pursuing the existing generation of terrorists and disrupting their networks;
- protecting citizens and the national infrastructure from attack; and
- preparing to deal with the consequences should such an attack occur.

The strategy itself is based upon assessments of the threat, the risk, and the UK's vulnerabilities. The strategy translates into actions around legislation, the exercise programme for counter-terrorism, effective use of science and technology and the resilience programme to counter chemical, biological, radiological, and nuclear attacks.

The Government insists that police forces and authorities are vital partners in the delivery of all parts of this strategy. They believe it is particularly important to build relationships with communities which will enhance intelligence gathering. The Government wants all police forces to have specialist capabilities through their Special Branches, but this clearly entails larger forces that must be strategically able to deliver such capabilities, rather than small forces operating with slim resources.

In concert with counter-terrorism, the Government is concerned about domestic extremism such as the work of animal rights extremists, with their threats of intimidation and violence against law-abiding citizens and businesses. These groups work within a smaller compass, of course, and the principal counters to their activities are likely to be locally based.

The actions for your police force are likely to include:

- allocating resources to Special Branch and to regional intelligence cells to support intelligence-gathering requirements;
- making best use of counter-terrorist exercises;
- targeting the activities of domestic extremists.

5.9.3 Local Delivery

In its National Policing Plan, the Government emphasizes that the delivery of these key priorities is critical at all levels, from the neighbourhood teams, the BCUs, at force level, and thence to national and international levels through the SOCA and other agencies. What remains to be seen is precisely how the Plan is to be funded.

This then is the updated government strategy for the police service in England and Wales until 2009. How will it impact on your force's Policing Plan and local priorities? Your force is likely to have incorporated the provisions of the National Policing Plan and the need for partnership working outlined in the National Community Safety Plan into its own local plan. Recent developments have tied local planning into the same business cycle as the national plan. Most force Policing Plans will be based on a three-year cycle (though updated and refreshed annually) to reflect the provisions in the NPP from 2006–09 and beyond.

We cannot predict what your force will do because there are too many variations between forces and too many local considerations to take into account. However, some recurrent themes will no doubt figure in the planning for all forces. These in turn will influence the way that you do your job.

TASK 22

Can you suggest what some of those themes or subjects will be?

5.10   Principles of Law

Although policing involves more than upholding the law (and criminal law in particular), we saw in section 5.5 how an understanding of the law is an important factor of a police officer's personal authority. Here we will examine some of the basic principles of the law that are relevant to the work of the student police officer, and these principles will be built upon in subsequent chapters.

5.10.1   Criminal Liability

Student police officers will find themselves thinking about more than just the laws relevant to crime—for example, you may become involved in policing a picket line established during a strike, and this is not a criminal matter. However, most of the law relevant to your first few years of service undoubtedly is of the criminal rather than the civil form. Indeed, if you look at the list of subjects in the IPLDP LPG modules you will find the list dominated by criminal law.

We begin with the notion of 'criminal liability'—how do we know and then prove that a person has broken the law? There is a cardinal rule in the criminal law of England and Wales born out of a Latin proverb or short saying which is '*Actus non facit reus, nisi sit mens rea*'. For those of you (like some of the authors) who did not take Latin at school, this means 'An act does not make a person criminally liable unless it is accompanied by a guilty mind'. There are therefore two elements of criminal liability:

1. The **action** that the defendant undertook, which must always be proved beyond reasonable doubt (see section 5.10.2 below)—commonly known as *actus reus*.
2. The **guilty mindset** that the defendant had at the time the action was taken which also must be proved, that is they intended to commit the crime—commonly known as *mens rea*.

Although the use of Latin can seem off-putting and exclusionary to some people, these terms are still used quite extensively in policing and so are worth remembering. (See also the discussion about interviewing in section 12.5 below.) We will now look at these two building blocks of criminal liability in more detail.

5.10.1.1   *Actus reus*

If a person is to be found guilty of a criminal offence, then it must be proved that he/she either:

* acted criminally in some way, for example committed murder;
* omitted to do an act which brought about a criminal outcome, such as knowing that someone was going to commit a crime but doing nothing to stop it or report it;
* caused a state of affairs to happen, like being found drunk and incapable at the wheel of a car; or
* failed to do an act which brought about a criminal outcome; for example, by failing to ensure that a vehicle was roadworthy when offering it for hire.

5.10.1.2   *Mens rea*

Although the Latin term appears to be very narrow in its meaning, in reality there are a number of thought processes which can meet the points to prove in many offences other than just having guilty knowledge. You will find these states of mind listed under different terms in a number of offences. The most common words are:

- dishonestly: such as theft;
- wilfully: such as in neglect of children;
- reckless: as in causing criminal damage;
- intent: as in burglary with intent to steal.

The level of *mens rea* in criminal offences can generally be grouped in three main levels of intent. These are described below, starting with the lowest level.

1. Offences requiring an element of negligence

The defendant's negligence is usually measured against the standards of a reasonable person (usually a hypothetical person in the mind of a jury member or magistrate). An example of an offence that uses such a test is careless or inconsiderate driving.

2. Offences requiring a low level of intent

A defendant's low-level intention is only that required to achieve their objective in carrying out a criminal offence. When some offences are committed therefore, it is relatively straightforward to prove that the defendant had a low level of intent, such as when they are caught outside a building with stolen property from a burglary. Such offences therefore include theft, and driving with excess breath/blood alcohol.

3. Offences requiring a particular *mens rea*

There are two groups of offences requiring a particular *mens rea*:

- The first group of offences involves **specific** intent. This is where the defendant is proved to have a specific aim to achieve a specific objective. Offences involving specific intention include murder and 'wounding or inflicting grievous bodily harm with intent'.
- The second group of offences involves **ulterior** intent. This is where the defendant is proved to have a second or hidden intention other than the main criminal act. An example of this would be when a defendant is charged with burglary with intent. Under these circumstances it must be proved that the defendant did not only intend to enter a building as a trespasser but also to inflict grievous bodily harm, cause damage, or steal.

5.10.2   Burden of Proof

How do we prove that a person is guilty of a criminal offence?

> Throughout the web of the English criminal law one golden thread is always to be seen; that it is the duty of the prosecution to prove the prisoner's guilt (*Woolmington v DPP* [1935] AC 462).

This duty deserves thinking about in some depth. What it means is that, in criminal proceedings:

1. The onus is on the prosecution to prove the guilt of the defendant, not for the defendant to prove his or her innocence.
2. Further, the degree of proof (in criminal cases) is that of **beyond reasonable doubt**. This was famously expressed by Geoffrey Lawrence (cited in Johnston and Hutton, 2005, p 133) in the following way:

> The possibility of guilt is not enough, suspicion is not enough, probability is not enough, likelihood is not. A criminal matter is not a question of balancing probabilities and deciding in favour of probability.

5.11   The Law in England and Wales

An understanding of the law in England and Wales, if only at the level required to exercise your day-to-day responsibilities as a student police officer, is an important aspect of the **epistemic authority** that you will exercise as a Confirmed police officer (see section 5.5 above).

In section 5.10 above, we examined the basic principles that underpin the law in England and Wales. Although we have noted on a number of occasions that policing is much more than simply enforcing the law, we devote this section to examining in more detail the basic aspects of the criminal law that are particularly relevant to police work. This understanding is a necessary condition for you to be able to demonstrate the achievement of a large number of the NOS elements. Law also features extensively during most Operational Modules and in LPG 1 and LPG 2.

5.11.1 The Law

There are several different forms of law: common law, statute law, case law, Acts of Parliament, Statutory Intruments, and bye-laws. These all interrelate in a number of ways, but first we consider each one individually in turn.

5.11.1.1 Common law

In the past, when laws were not written down, courts made decisions that were then passed by word of mouth to other courts. These were known as **precedents** or decisions. An example would be of a court that decided that for one human being to kill another is unlawful. This decision was then accepted by other courts throughout the country and, from that point onwards, such a killing would be contrary to common law. No new common law offences are created now since, apart from the setting of precedents by the courts, the making of new laws is undertaken by Parliament through the enactment of statutes.

Examples of common law offences which remain today are:

* murder;
* manslaughter;
* perverting the course of justice;
* escape from lawful custody.

5.11.1.2 Statute law

Statute law is written law and it is the foundation of the current legal system in England and Wales. It is made up of **Acts of Parliament** (see below) which begin their lives as documents called **Bills** or **draft law**.

The Bill is written by ministry officials as a proposal and then submitted to the Houses of Parliament for a decision. If it is accepted, it is given Royal Assent before becoming an Act of Parliament. For student police officers, commonly encountered Acts of Parliament in criminal law include:

* The Theft Act 1968 (principal offences of dishonesty).
* The Criminal Damage Act 1971 (some offences of damage).
* The Misuse of Drugs Act 1971 (the principal drug-related offences).
* The Public Order Act 1986 (the main offences of public disorder).

5.11.1.3 Case law

Case law helps establish the precise meaning of legislation. Decisions made by a particular court about legislation are then accepted by the judicial system throughout the country. An example of this would be a decision that was made about identification evidence in the case *R v Turnbull* [1976] 3 All ER 549.

(Note the system for referencing cases: 'R' is an abbreviation for Regina (the Crown as prosecutor), 'v' for versus, and 'Turnbull' is the name of the defendant. This case can be found in Volume 3 of the 1976 All England Law Reports on page 549.)

5.11.1.4 Acts of Parliament

Acts of Parliament are divided into sections that may contain definitions, offences, powers of arrest, exemptions, and interpretations of words and expressions used. An Act is a complex document that often requires technical details, such as fines and penalties, which may need frequent revision and updating. Sorting out these details is often left to government ministers in order to reduce the pressure on parliamentary time. These details are provided in the form of Orders, Regulations, and Rules, known as Statutory Instruments.

5.11.1.5 Statutory Instruments

Statutory Instruments (SIs) make it possible for details of an Act to be revised without having to be subjected to parliamentary procedures every time. Importantly, they are as much part of the law of England and Wales as is the main body of the Act of Parliament. An example is the Road Vehicles (Construction and Use) (Amendment) (No 2) Regulations 2001. The Home Secretary, using powers given to him by s 41 of the Road Traffic Act 1988, introduced a number of detailed provisions regarding seat belts in road vehicles. As with Acts of Parliament, SIs are given a number as well as a title, so the number of these Regulations is SI 2001 No 1043.

5.11.1.6 Bye-laws

Bye-laws are local laws which have been made by a local authority and approved by a Secretary of State of the government. These are passed by a local authority and normally deal with local matters, for example dogs on leads in recreational areas

> **TASK 23**
>
> Under s 41 of the Road Traffic Act 1988, the Statutory Instruments Road Vehicle Lighting Regulations 1989 (SI 1989 No 1796) were introduced. Use *Blackstone's Police Manual: Volume 3 Road Policing*, the internet, or other publications to determine what regs 11–22 inclusive cover in relation to a motor vehicle.

5.12 The Criminal Justice System

The **Criminal Justice System**, or **CJS**, is defined by the government as the police, the courts, the Prison Service, the Crown Prosecution Service (CPS), and the National Probation Service. In this section, we will concentrate on the police, the courts, and the CPS.

Inevitably the focus of the CJS is on crime the consequences of crime, and punishment. How we define crime (or perhaps, more accurately, criminal offences) is discussed elsewhere, most notably in section 5.13. The remainder of this section presupposes that a crime has been committed and reported to the police.

As a student police officer, you will soon come into contact with the CJS. Indeed, in many forces a criminal justice placement forms part of IPLDP Phase 2 of training, and this provides an opportunity for you to meet other professionals working within the CJS. Many of these professionals are also undertaking programmes of education and training linked to NOS elements determined by Skills for Justice. There are likely to be numerous opportunities for you to demonstrate achievement of NOS when involved in such collaborative activities. Remember that some of these fellow professionals may also be A1 assessors (see Chapter 6) and hence capable of signing off elements of standards relevant to their areas of expertise.

5.12.1 Investigation and Prosecution

Once an alleged crime has been reported, the police undertake most of the tasks involved in an investigation. Any subsequent prosecution is formally undertaken on behalf of the Crown (the State) and is handled by an official agency called the Crown Prosecution Service (CPS). A decision to prosecute means that the courts are likely to be involved. Depending on their seriousness, the cases are dealt with at different courts (see section 5.12.3). The defendant may represent his/her own case, though he/she is usually represented by a solicitor or barrister. The courts may be assisted by Social Services and the Probation Service.

A number of the NOS elements relate to carrying out investigations, preparing cases, and appearing in court (covered in more detail in section 12.8), for example:

National Occupational Standards Elements

2J1.1 Prepare case files.

2J1.2 Submit case files and progress enquiries.

2J2.1 Prepare for court or other hearings.

2J2.2 Present evidence to court or other hearings.

The PAC heading 'Finalise investigations' also requires you to demonstrate your ability to 'adhere to court procedures' and 'give evidence at court' before you are declared fit to undertake Independent Patrol.

5.12.2 Criminal Offences

Offences are classified according to their seriousness and at which court they can be tried. Note that the term arrestable offence is no longer used as offences are no longer classified in this way. This can be confusing if you are already familiar with the term (through, for example, undertaking special constable training). Offences are now classified as either 'summary' offences, 'indictment only' offences, or 'either way' offences. There is a further term of 'indictable' offence which is a collective name for both 'indictable only' and 'either way' offences.

5.12.2.1 Summary offences

Summary offences can only be tried in the magistrates' court. Examples are: common assault, assaulting a police officer in the execution of his/her duty, most motoring offences.

5.12.2.2 Indictment only offences

Indictment only offences can only be dealt with at the Crown Court and are the most serious cases. Examples are: murder, manslaughter, causing death by dangerous driving, rape, robbery, aggravated burglary, wounding with intent.

5.12.2.3 Either way offences

Either way offences may be tried either in the magistrates' court or at the Crown Court. The magistrate decides initially where the case is most suitably tried. Examples are theft, obtaining by deception, assault occasioning actual bodily harm, indecent assault.

5.12.2.4 Indictable offences

This is a collective term for both 'indictment only' and 'either way' offences. The term 'indictable offences' is used extensively in the legislation and codes surrounding stop and search (see section 8.5).

Two questions may occur at this stage:

- Where will I find the classification for each criminal offence?
- Where will I find the mode of trial and penalty for each of these offences?

The answers will be found either by reference to the legal texts themselves (for example, through the Home Office website) or secondary sources such as *Blackstone's Police Manuals*. For example, for the offence of theft, the following will be found:

- **Section 1 of the Theft Act 1968**;
- **Mode of trial**: triable either way;
- **Maximum penalty for a person found guilty**: seven years' imprisonment on indictment (Crown Court); six months' imprisonment and/or a fine summarily (magistrates' court).

TASK 24

Use an appropriate textbook, or the internet, with the offence of robbery to determine the:

- relevant Act, including section;
- mode of trial;
- maximum penalty for a person found guilty.

5.12.3   The Courts

As you probably guessed from section 5.12.2, the structure of the courts in England and Wales tends to be arranged according to the subject matter and seriousness of the cases brought before them.

Below is a simplified diagram of the court system in England and Wales:

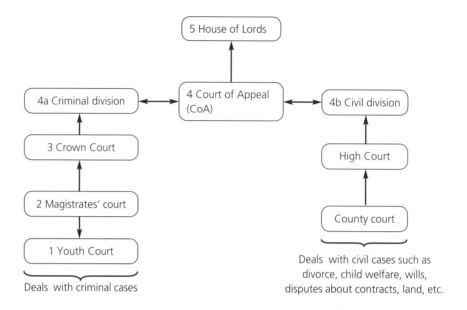

Deals with criminal cases

Deals with civil cases such as divorce, child welfare, wills, disputes about contracts, land, etc.

For student police officers, the courts dealing with criminal offences are the most important, as there are only rare occasions when a police officer would be giving evidence at a court dealing with civil cases.

5.12.3.1   Youth court

Young people aged ten to seventeen years would normally have their cases dealt with at the youth court (unless they are being charged jointly with an adult or they are charged for murder or manslaughter). Procedures in the youth court are very similar to those in the magistrates' court; indeed within the magistrates' courts, certain courts are formally designated as youth courts. Their procedures are adapted to take account of age of the defendant, and they are not open to the public.

5.12.3.2   Magistrates' court

Less serious criminal cases (which comprise over 90% of criminal cases) are sent for summary trial in one of over 400 magistrates' courts. A summary trial means there is no committal (that is, no transfer is necessary to the Crown Court) and no jury. The trial is before a bench of magistrates. In most cases, there are three magistrates who are lay persons—in other words, they are not professional judges nor are they lawyers, but they are people drawn from the local community. However, there are now an increasing number of stipendiary magistrates—paid magistrates who are qualified lawyers.

Because of the nature of the criminal cases dealt with by the magistrates' court, they cannot order sentences that exceed six months for a single offence, twelve months for consecutive sentences, or fines exceeding £5,000 (at the time of writing). If an offence is triable either way (see section 5.12.2), and the magistrates believe that a more severe sentence is necessary, the magistrates' court can commit the offender to the Crown Court for sentence. If a defendant is dissatisfied by the verdict from the magistrates' courts, he or she may appeal to the Crown Court.

5.12.3.3   Crown court

The Crown Court deals with more serious criminal cases such as murder, rape, or robbery. Other cases in the Crown Court may be on appeal or may have been referred from magistrates' courts. These cases are tried on the basis of a document called an **indictment** (see section 5.12.2). The trial takes place before a judge and a twelve person jury. Members of the public are selected for jury service. Other members of the public may have to attend court as witnesses.

In summary, the Crown Courts deal with the relatively small proportion of offences triable only on indictment. They also deal with:

- cases transferred from the magistrates' courts;
- cases sent for sentence from the magistrates' courts;
- appeals against decisions from the magistrates' courts.

5.12.3.4 Court of Appeal

The Court of Appeal is the highest court within the Supreme Court of Judicature, which also includes the High Court and the Crown Court. It normally sits in up to twelve courts in the Royal Courts of Justice in London. On matters of fact and law, it is possible to appeal from the Crown Court to the criminal division of the Court of Appeal. Likewise, appeals from the High Court would go to the civil division of this Court.

5.12.3.5 House of Lords

The House of Lords is the final Court of Appeal on points of law and important legal dispute for criminal cases in England, Wales, and Northern Ireland, and civil cases for the whole of the United Kingdom. This work is carried out by the Law Lords.

5.12.4 Summary of the Courts

Courts	Deals with offences	Features	Appeals go to
Youth courts	Offences involving persons aged 10 to 17	Usually not open to public	Crown Court
Magistrates' courts	Offences triable summarily only Offences triable either way	Bench of magistrates Local, over 400 of them Usually open to public Over 95% of cases dealt with here Sentence cannot exceed 6 months (or 12 months for consecutive sentences), or £5,000 fines More serious offences committed to Crown Courts	Crown Court
Crown Courts	Offences triable only on indictment Offences triable either way (cases referred from magistrates' court for trial or sentence) Appeals from magistrates' court	Judge and jury Regional c. 90 of them	Court of Appeal
Court of Appeal	Appeals from Crown Court	Criminal and civil division	House of Lords
House of Lords	Appeals from Court of Appeal	Law Lords	Final point of appeal

---

TASK 25

Find out the exact location of your nearest magistrates' and Crown Courts. Use as many resources as necessary including the web and local telephone directories. (Cross-check the results, identifying any inconsistencies in spelling, postcodes, and so on, if they are present.) When off duty, consider visiting one of the courts and sitting in the public gallery to observe proceedings.

5.13   Crime and Criminality

In this section we will take a brief look at the nature of crime and criminality in the UK and try to synthesize some modern thinking about crime. Every day, the contents of news bulletins on TV and radio and the pages of newspapers are dominated by crime, ranging from fraud investigations in the City through to muggings on housing estates; from the sadistic torture of young children through to the murder of a solicitor for his watch and mobile phone. Many articles and research papers are devoted to trying to understand criminal motivations, why people commit crimes and why certain crimes are more prevalent than others. You will read some of these criminological texts and papers in the course of your own work as a student police officer or through your participation in a higher education programme.

We have deliberately simplified these issues because this is not a Handbook of crime or criminology, and the issues are very complex, drawing on psychological, philosophical, sociological, and political perspectives. In a very real sense, they are issues with which you will be grappling with for the whole of your time in the police and certainly include matters on which you will have to reflect during your time as a student police officer.

> ### TASK 26
> - What makes a crime sensational?
> - What makes a crime of little apparent interest?
> - What makes a crime impact on a community?

Increasingly over the past forty years, criminologists have become interested in studying the police. This has produced numerous publications concerning the organization, administration, and general understanding of police work. However, beyond this, criminology has also provided the police with a number of important theories about the nature of crime and criminal behaviour that can be of great assistance to the police in different ways. For example, the move towards proactive policing has been assisted by developments in criminological theories concerning crime prevention, the study of victims, and the spatial movements of criminals. Indeed the scope of criminological studies is too vast to cover here but by providing a selection of important ways in which criminology informs contemporary policing, it is hoped that you will be encouraged to consult the growing body of criminological research concerning many different policing matters. But first we will consider some more basic questions, some possible definitions of crime, and some possible causes of crime.

5.13.1   Definitions of Crime

What is crime? We tend to think we know the answer until we begin to think through the details and test out our general ideas on some specific examples. We might say that crime is what is forbidden, that crime is activity which society wants to stop happening, or that crime is a measure of society's health: the more unbalanced the society, the more the crimes on the statute book. Technically, an activity is a crime because the law defines it as such. But remember that laws are made by people so, in the end, we are back to where we started; people, albeit only certain categories of people such as judges and MPs, decide which activities are crimes. Without reference to existing concepts of crime and laws there is nothing about an activity in itself that marks it out as a crime. Consider, for example, how some forms of gay sexual activity between consenting adult men were treated as crimes in the recent past but are no longer treated as such. There are a very few acts that have been consistently considered crimes throughout modern history (try Task 27). Other types and definitions of crime are mutable (they change as society changes). Think about our attitudes to the environment in which we live: how activities like collecting birds' eggs or hunting foxes with dogs are now seen by many as unacceptable and how laws have followed suit.

In this section we look first at defining crime narrowly by what it is not—that is, in terms of those acts sanctioned by the law. This provides us with a definitive statement but does not really explain why particular acts and behaviours are treated as criminal whilst others are not. However, if we look beyond the law as part of the definition of crime, we then find that the task becomes no easier. Finally, we consider the thoughts of Mill, a nineteenth-century philosopher who proposed that deviant behaviour might have a role in promoting beneficial changes in society, though some deviant behaviours would be classed as crime if they caused harm to other people.

5.13.1.1 Crimes are defined by law

Originally, the word crime actually meant judgement or accusation (from Latin *crimen*, a judgement), later coming to be associated with the act of offence or wrong-doing. By the Middle Ages, crime was something against the law, and thus a crime was an action punishable by law. On one level, we now simply define crime as action which is against the law, and clearly the act needs to be against a specific criminal law. Critics of this definition of crime point to an obvious tautology—we are essentially saying the same thing twice but in a different form. Using such a circular argument, that crime is defined by law, takes us no further forward in our understanding.

5.13.1.2 Crimes are defined by society

Others have argued conversely that crime is a social construction. By this they mean that no act or behaviour is in itself wrong but rather that different societies will identify different crimes according to the specific needs of a given society at particular points in history. This challenges the notion that there are fixed laws that classify certain acts as crimes and argues instead that laws are created by humans in social situations in order to bring greater cohesion and order to those situations.

> **TASK 27**
> - List three crimes that would appear to be universal.
> - List three offences that are considered criminal in the UK today but were not 100 years ago.
> - List three offences that are considered criminal in other parts of the world but not in the UK.

On the other hand, crime is defined more broadly by some as **all social wrong-doings and anti-social behaviour**. This sociological approach to understanding crime addresses the question from the perspective of why certain acts are criminalized but can lose the clarity of legal definitions. A current example of this kind of dispute occurs in debates about how we deal with anti-social behaviour. Some have argued that the use of Anti-Social Behaviour Orders (ASBOs) is a way of criminalizing behaviour through the back door. This is because ASBOs are a civil procedure at the outset but the breaking of the terms of an order may invoke criminal proceedings. Others have argued that ASBOs represent a civil procedure against criminal activities that are not readily and effectively dealt with by existing criminal proceedings.

5.13.1.3 Mill's principle of 'harm to others'

John Stuart Mill was an English philosopher writing in the nineteenth century. For Mill it was important to allow individuals as much freedom as possible for the development of a healthy society. This is primarily because a society needs individuals to deviate from the norm if it is to advance. The problem confronting any authority is establishing when a deviation from the norm might be beneficial and when it is not. In other words, it is not always possible to decide whether an individual acting differently is being innovative or criminal.

There are numerous examples throughout history of individuals (some of whom we now celebrate as heroes) who were considered a threat to society at an earlier time. Think, for example, about the suppression of scientific thinkers, such as Galileo, who were considered heretics or more recently civil rights protesters, like Martin Luther King in the USA. In the UK today there are many examples of people willing to break the law for causes that they see as being a future morality, ranging from animal rights activists, Fathers for Justice, anti-abortionists, and environmentalists. What these different groups have in common is a belief that they represent values that are not normal today but will become so in the future, in the same way that those fighting at previous times in history for equal rights for women or the abolition of the slave trade eventually came to be recognized as heroic figures.

For Mill, the way to permit individuals or groups to deviate from existing norms, and indeed to challenge them, is to allow people to make mistakes and act immorally providing these acts do not harm others. This is Mill's famous 'harm to others' principle. It is largely from this perspective that we have established a separation between the law and morality where it is argued the law pertains to public matters and morality to private individual concerns. This view was supported in the 1957 Wolfenden Report into homosexuality and prostitution in which it was argued that private acts between consenting adults should not be the concern of law enforcement (Wolfenden Report, 1957). Campaigners for gay rights have criticized this finding for putting too much emphasis on the word private as this suggests that public expressions of homosexuality should be regulated and controlled.

However, other criticisms have challenged the view that law and morality can be so neatly separated. These critics argue that there is a significant grey area which we might characterize as social morality and that it is simply not possible completely to insulate our private activities: that there will always be leakage and our actions will always have consequences in ways that we could not have predicted. This challenges Mill's harm to others principle because it suggests that others are harmed by our actions even if this was not our intention. Perhaps a good example of this to illustrate the point is passive smoking. For many years it has been argued that smokers are harming themselves and campaigns have encouraged smokers to stop for their own sakes. However, until recently, little was done to prohibit smokers. Increasingly though, smoking has come to be regulated on grounds of others' health and safety. In many parts of the world smoking is banned in public places, including bars and restaurants, and the bans are justified in terms of the health of employees working in these public places.

This also illustrates that harm is more widely defined today than when John Stuart Mill was writing. We have become more sophisticated in identifying different forms of harm. For example, consider the extent to which we have broadened our understanding of domestic violence to include psychological, emotional, and financial harm in addition to physical damage.

5.13.2 The Causes of Crime

When examining the causes of crime an important starting point is to acknowledge some fundamental differences in how we might understand crime and how these differences in turn can inform police work. Indeed, as we have seen in section 5.13.1, an important question to begin with is to ask what we think crime is.

Blackburn (1995) makes a distinction between crimes and criminality. Crimes are seen to be a rational response to the environment in which people find themselves. Criminality, on the other hand, is a characteristic of an individual and emphasizes the propensity of an individual to commit crimes.

5.13.2.1 Crimes—a rational response?

Some crimes are apparently easily explained as a product of the social situation in which they occur. For example, an unemployed single mother shoplifting nappies for her baby is certainly committing a crime, but it could be said that a more serious problem is that she should be in such a difficult position in the first place. Others will point out that not all mothers in the same situation would resort to shoplifting but would find a legal solution to the problem. Irrespective of which moral position is adopted, from a policing perspective this particular crime can be understood better as a social response rather than an individual failing. This view is associated with what is referred to as classical criminology, which emerged in the late eighteenth century and informed the thinking of law reformers at this time (eg Bentham, Howard, Beccaria). This view of crime suggests that anyone could become a criminal given the right circumstances, and that punishment is required to act as a deterrent to crime.

5.13.2.2 **Criminals—a breed apart?**

Conversely, it is difficult to understand the actions of a violent serial murderer as the consequence of injustices in society. No matter how bad society is, it is hard to view such brutality as a reasonable response in any sense. A contrasting explanation for the causes of crime is the concept of **criminality**. This view developed from what is referred to as the positivist school of criminology, associated with Cesare Lombroso's *L'Uomo Delinquente* (The Criminal Man) published in 1876. Positivists differed from the classical approach to criminology by arguing that:

- criminality is determined by factors beyond the immediate control of an individual and is not a product of his or her free will;
- criminals are a certain type of individual distinct from non-criminal individuals;
- criminals are pathological (see Jones and Newburn, 1998, pp 101–2).

5.13.2.3 **Nature and nurture**

We have debated these kinds of questions for centuries. It is often referred to as the nature/nurture debate. Nature refers to what we are born with or, in recent terms, our genetic make-up. Nurture relates to the environmental contexts in which we develop. This includes everything from our schooling, how our parents raised us, whom we chose to associate with and every arbitrary experience that has good, bad or indifferent outcomes. However, this dichotomy can often be misleading. The debates have often been polemical and exclusionary; that is, those favouring nature explanations would dismiss nurture as an influence and those supporting nurture explanations would exclude completely the view that nature has any part to play. Increasingly today we recognize that both nature **and** nurture form part of the explanation and indeed that it is not always easy to distinguish one from the other. Modern biology continues to uncover examples of genetic predispositions being either masked or revealed by environmental factors. We cannot hope for simple answers; both nature and nurture have to be taken into account.

5.13.3 **Hate Crime**

A consideration of hate crime certainly raises interesting and thorny issues around the definition of crime and its causes. Interestingly, hate crime (including homophobic or racist crimes) can be defined by the victim(s) or any other person, as such, irrespective of the views of the police officer dealing with it. This amendment arose from the enquiry into the death of the black London teenager Stephen Lawrence and a subsequent report into the police investigation chaired by Sir William MacPherson. (This report famously branded the police service as 'institutionally racist'.) The following question then arises: 'if any person present can define a crime as a "hate crime", why cannot *any* individual define *any* incident in which they feel disadvantaged, wronged or frightened, as a "crime"?' The law provides the answer. There must have been an identifiable criminal offence (such as assault) before the qualification of whether or not it is homophobic or racist can be considered. It is the hate which is defined by the individual and not the crime. Once again, the close interrelationship between the law, society, and individuals is a key factor in understanding crime.

5.13.4 **Measuring Crime**

There are various means of measuring crime, through the police and criminal justice statistical records, large-scale, mostly government-sponsored surveys, and small-scale academic studies. However, we know that the problems of under-reporting, under-recording, political interest, intellectual bias and/or perspective all contribute to distortions in actually determining the levels of crime at any given time. This is particularly so if we wish to make comparisons with the past. The problems of under-reporting and under-recording are particularly problematic for the police and are factors that have been given much attention in recent years.

Discovering a truer picture of the extent of crime and ensuring that it is recorded properly are important aspects of modern policing. However, what exactly needs to be reported and recorded?

5.13.4.1   Reported and recorded

An important distinction is between **reported** crime-related incidents and **recorded** crime. It is obvious that not all crimes that occur will be reported to the police. Given our discussion earlier concerning the definition of crime it is not difficult to see the major methodological issues that surround this subject. Often the police prefer to start instead with the idea of an incident. Imagine that I have witnessed an incident of a heated argument in the street, perhaps with some pushing, shoving, and screaming. I phone the police and report this. At this stage the police will register the contents of my call. This registration is what most commentators mean when they refer to 'reported'. However, the police then have to decide whether this reported incident should be **recorded** as a crime (a so-called 'notifiable offence'). They are required to use the Home Office criteria which state that if, on the balance of probability, the circumstances as reported amount to a crime defined by law, and there is no credible evidence to the contrary, then it should be recorded as a crime (Home Office, 2005a).

As our incident described above illustrates, the decision is far from simple. In response to my call the police are required to make all reasonable enquiries to identify specific victims and secure any supporting evidence. Although pushing and shoving could technically be an offence of assault or battery (see section 9.15) or a public order offence (see section 8.12) this would depend on the circumstances, and these would probably not be clear from my account over the phone. More importantly, a victim is unlikely to be identified and then located and found on the basis of my call. The basic recording rule of 'no victim, no crime' would be applied. Hence in my example, it is highly unlikely that the pushing and shoving that I witnessed, although registered as an incident, would actually result in the police recording a notifiable offence.

Crime recording and counting methods (currently under review by the Government) have in recent times been made more consistent across police organizations and are audited for accuracy and reliability. The **three main group headings** for classifying the status of a crime, following its recording, are:

- Undetected
- Detected
- No crime

The processes of reporting and recording crime are complex and you will find the full detail at <http://www.homeoffice.gov.uk/rds/countrules.html>. Bear in mind that the system might well change.

5.13.4.2   The perception of crime

There is a general acceptance that the fear of crime and disorder has increased in the last decade or so, despite the fact that most forms of recorded crime have shown a decrease in the same period (although see Farrall & Gadd, 2004, for a critique). As Walker et al (2006, p 34) note, 'despite the total number of crimes estimated by the BCS [British Crime Survey] falling over recent years, comparatively high proportions of people continue to believe crime has risen across the country as a whole and in their local area'. It would also appear that particular communities are more likely to believe that crime has risen significantly when compared to others and also to worry more about crime. For example, the British Crime Survey for 2005/2006 suggests the following demographic factors are significant in terms of perceptions and worry about crime:

- Gender. Women are more likely than men to feel that burglary and violent crime has risen.
- Age. Young people worry more about violence and car crime than other age groups (although men and women in the 65–74 age group are most likely to perceive that there has been a significant increase in crime overall).
- Ethnicity. People from non-white ethnic groups are more likely to be concerned about crime than those from white.
- Accommodation. Those living in the social rented sector were more likely to worry about crime when compared with those who rented privately or owned their own homes.

• Newspapers read. Readers of the 'red top' newspapers were more likely to worry about crime when compared to those that read the 'broadsheets'.

(Walker et al pp 35–36 and Table 3.01).

However, it is important to note that those who feel most worried about crime or who perceive crime to be increasing are not necessarily those, according to official statistics, who are actually the most likely to become victims of recorded crime. Having said this, it could be argued that fear of crime alone is a form of harm to an individual, regardless of the statistical reality. It is also the case that for some of our communities that fear crime the most, the implications of crime can be profound. To put this another way, an elderly person's statistically 'irrational' fears about crime are in fact quite rational if the effect of crime on this person is factored in. Think of this as some kind of calculation: the risk may be low but the negative consequences are very high (eg in terms of recovery from an injury) and so overall the product is one of significant size for the individual concerned.

One possible reason for this apparently irrational overestimation of the volume of crime and disorder is that many of us may make our judgments concerning the level of insecurity of our communities based not only on those 'invisible' but often very serious crimes (such as domestic violence, burglary, sexual crimes etc) but also on the more obvious and usually less serious local examples of incivility such as repeated vandalism and graffiti, groups of young people that shout abuse at passers-by and so on. These latter forms of incivility are examples of 'signal crimes' (Innes, 2004) or 'signal disorders' which are, in effect, warning signals to people about the level of insecurity in their neighbourhoods. As Innes (2005, p 192) notes, 'major crimes such as homicides can and do function as signals, but ... for most people, most of the time, the signals that they attend to and that assume particular salience for them are what have tended to be treated by the criminal justice agencies as less serious'. The signals may arise from other people's behaviour (eg 'rowdy' groups of people) and physical signs such as damage to public amenities.

Possible examples of signal crimes and disorder, particularly when a number of these examples coincide in a local community, include:

• Public drinking, swearing, rowdy and uncivil behaviour by groups of individuals.
• Graffiti and other forms of damage and vandalism, litter.
• Evidence of drug taking and dealing, prostitution.
• Speeding.
• Rubbish dumped in the street or outside houses, burnt-out cars and other vehicles.

Once spotted, these signals can give rise to a heightened sense of awareness amongst individuals of other similar examples—a form of non-virtuous feedback loop.

5.13.5 Modelling Crime and Criminality

In section 5.13.2 we provided an overview of some of the theories that attempt to explain the existence of crime and criminality. In this section we move from these general theories (often concerned with human nature and society) to more detailed models that in some ways explain the existence of crime or criminality and also provide some possible responses for the police and others.

5.13.5.1 Opportunities for crime

Pease (2002) notes three different ways in which crime has been understood which he defines in terms of structure, human psyche, and circumstance. The first of these, structure, can be characterized in terms of the major social issues that are seen to be linked to crime, eg poverty and inequality. Human psyche concerns the attributes of the criminal, in other words the reasons why he/she has a propensity to commit offences. However, Pease proposes that it is the circumstance dimension of crime, or the opportunity for crime to occur, that is the key factor for causing crime.

Rational choice theory assumes that when criminals decide to commit offences they go through the same kind of thought process used by non-criminals when making everyday, non-criminal decisions:

It is not the case (except for a tiny handful of pathological personalities) that criminals are so unlike the rest of us as to be indifferent to the costs and benefits of the opportunities open to them (Wilson, 1996, p 312).

This suggests that crimes occur if and when they are easy to commit and the results are sufficiently rewarding.

Routine activity theory is also predicated upon an understanding of the relationship between an individual's everyday experiences and his or her criminal behaviour. Importantly, it defines criminal opportunities in terms of three interrelated and necessary components:

- a motivated offender;
- a suitable target; and
- the absence of a guardian.

Criminal opportunities arise when these three components coincide. We may observe that the number of offences might increase even if there is no increase in the number of motivated offenders. This occurs if a small number of motivated offenders are in situations where there are few guardians and plenty of suitable targets. Schools are a prime example of this kind of scenario: there are significant numbers of vulnerable children with mobile phones, computer games, and mp3 players largely unsupervised, and there are other children who are keen to take these items.

5.13.5.2 The 'hot' model

One way to consider the phenomenon of crime in society is to think about some of its constituent elements as being hot; that is, both frequently occurring and worthy of attention. (The following owes much to Clarke, 1999, although terms such as 'hot offender' are ours.)

Hot Spots are places that are particularly prone to crime, such as railway station concourses, shopping malls, town centres, particular shops, houses, post offices, or flats. This may have to do with easy pickings for the criminal intent on theft, shop-lifting, mugging, or similar. It may have much to do with opportunity, because this is a place where people may be carrying large quantities of cash (railway stations close to race courses for example, or streets leading away from ATMs or cash machines). This leads to an unevenness of crime distribution, across a city say, where some particular and precise geographical areas can be pinpointed as always or nearly always productive of crime (of all types), whilst others will be virtually crime free. Until some preventive action is taken, these hot spots will persist. The hot spots may even return some time after action is taken (see 5.14.1.2).

Hot Offenders are defined as the relatively small number of people that are responsible for the majority of crime. There is, however, considerable debate concerning just what proportion of offenders are responsible for what proportion of crimes—for example, see Heaton, 2000. But we need to be careful about what we deduce from such a statement; the majority of crimes in numerical terms are relatively minor crimes (volume crime), not single crimes of violence, nor one-off assaults, nor large-scale robbery. So the hot offender profile has less significance for the more serious crimes.

The typical hot offender, a volume crime offender, often steals or burgles to feed a drug habit, or because he/she is a lifestyle or career criminal. Many high-volume offenders start committing crimes at a relatively young age; they make what is called an early debut into crime. Initial offences may be stealing from cars or shoplifting or theft (for example, Svensson, 2002, although this is Scandinavian research and may not be applicable to the UK).

Hot Products are the items we know are more attractive to thieves or burglars or muggers (street robbers) than others and there is a form of logic to what is stolen or snatched. Currently, car SatNavs, mobile phones, jewellery, and small electronic products like DVD players, iPods, laptops, and minidiscs are popular, but these things go in fashions. Once it was televisions (which were heavy and bulky and difficult to steal without a car or van to transport them). Indeed, plasma screens are still objects of desire for house breakers and burglars but the average, small-time, drugs-abusing, volume criminal will go for small items of value which are easily transportable and not easily traced. This is why cash (pre-eminently) and jewellery are popular targets for thieves. Cash, of course, is easily disposed of and generally untraceable. Jewellery is somewhat harder to fence, and some items can be so individual as to be easily traced, but the bulk of rings and watches are easily converted into money.

As you might suppose with police training, there is a mnemonic (Clarke, 1999) used to estimate the hotness of products: it is **CRAVED**, which stands for:

> C Concealable
> R Removable
> A Available
> V Valuable
> E Enjoyable
> D Disposable

The CRAVED model may be used as a means of judging just how attractive an object will be in terms of its stealability. Imagine assigning a score to each heading in turn and totalling these scores. Those objects with high CRAVED scores are more likely to be stolen. (Granted, it is not as simple as this, but the scoring system gives a relatively easy way of using the checklist.)

Above all, thieves prefer things which they can get rid of quickly and without fuss to a trusted fence, or receiver of stolen goods, in all probability taking only a tenth or a fifth of the actual value of the item from the fence. In the original work by Clarke (1999) disposability was considered to be one of the most important factors in determining the stealability of items.

TASK 28

Estimate how CRAVED the following articles might be:

- an iPod;
- a Blackberry or equivalent hand-held computer;
- a laptop;
- £642.89p in coins;
- a computer with separate screen and keyboard;
- a CRT (conventional) television;
- a mobile phone;
- £350 in £50 notes;
- A manuscript copy of *The Lindisfarne Gospels*;
- twelve Japanese ivory *netsuke* dating from the late sixteenth century;
- a Rolex watch, engraved and dated;
- an unframed oil painting by Rubens, measuring 23 ×19 cm.

(Older readers may have a flashback to the BBC's *Generation Game*).

Hot Victims are perhaps the least studied and least understood part of the equation. Intuitively, it could be expected that old age, frailty, and naivety would make a person more vulnerable than the average person, but there is little empirical evidence to support this other than in the particular case of distraction burglary (sometimes called 'burglary artifice') that we mention later in section 9.5. However, studies have shown that once someone has been a victim of certain types of crime (the classic example is burglary) on one occasion, they are more likely than other people to be a victim again even if all other variables have been taken into account. If repeat victimization is planned or contemplated, we know it will happen again pretty quickly and that often high crime rates and hot spots exist precisely because of repeat victimization (if not the same person, then the same address or the same street).

Why some people, or some premises or some organizations should be repeat victims of crime is not always clear. There is some evidence (although not conclusive) that it is the same offenders that tend to return to the same places and re-offend. Some of it may have to do with the notion inside the thieves' heads that 'it worked once and will work again'. Some of it could be a clever thieves' strategy: give a house owner time to claim on insurance for a valuable item, and return when the house is restocked to steal the replacement. (See for example Bowers et al, 1998.) Whatever the explanation, we should emphasize that people who do not take elementary precautions after having been victims of crime once should not be surprised if they are targeted again. This is particularly the case with domestic burglary—it is simply not the case that if it has happened once, then it is unlikely to happen again. The reverse is true.

Finally, we know that those who repeatedly victimize the same target tend to be more established as lifestyle or career criminals than those who do not. All this should suggest that intelligence about the nature of a crime, why it is repeated in the same spot with the same victim, should enable police forces to predict, with a limited degree of accuracy, where, when, and by whom the next attempt will be made (see for example Bowers et al, 2004). In terms of operational practice however, this would appear to be a long way off.

TASK 29

Following what we have said about hot victims, what operational strategies do you think that the police should employ to help reduce repeat victimization?

Clearly, there are many possible **interactions** between hot spots, hot offenders, hot products, and hot victims. Hot offenders are more likely to want hot products. Hot victims are more likely to be in hot spots, and this is certainly the case for domestic burglary. Hot offenders are likely to target hot spots because, as we noted above, there are relatively easy opportunities for crime and relatively little chance of being caught. And, as mentioned above, the same offenders may return to burgle the same house again. It is hard to disentangle cause and effect, but the unevenness of the distribution of crime cannot be ignored.

TASK 30

What are the practical policing implications that can be derived from the following quotation, assuming that the argument being made is valid?

Becoming criminal can be explained in much the same way we explain becoming a carpenter or buying a car (Wilson, 1996, p 307).

5.14 Crime Reduction

We often hear the terms crime prevention, crime reduction, and community safety used both within policing and more widely. Ekblom (2001) draws subtle distinctions between these concepts whereas Pease (2002) suggests they are different expressions of the same thing, but that the use of different terms is an indication of different political perspectives. We will follow Pease and use the terms interchangeably.

The focus within police work is increasingly oriented towards reducing crime. This can be achieved to some extent through detecting crimes that have occurred and if the offender is then imprisoned, he or she will be prevented from committing further crimes. However, it is also acknowledged that preventing crimes from happening in the first place represents a far more rational approach. Of course it is hard to imagine a situation where the police are not required to investigate crimes that have occurred. Nonetheless, reducing crime through earlier prevention techniques provides clear benefits to society. In other words, it can be assumed that prevention is better than cure.

A crime reduction agenda has also been bolstered by the move towards partnership approaches in policing, and in this respect the increasing emphasis on crime prevention entails a relative decline in the role of the police:

One of the key messages put out by the government and the police ... was that the police could not be expected to carry responsibility for the prevention of crime unaided (Morgan and Newburn, 1997, p 58).

The partnership approach towards tackling crime had already been strengthened in the Crime and Disorder Act 1998 and reflects the current Government's commitment to a joined up approach to tackling crime and disorder.

5.14.1 Crime Reduction in Practice

In order to prevent and reduce crime we need to understand as much as possible about why and how crime occurs. Pease (2002) focuses on the circumstance dimension of crime or the opportunity for crime to occur (see section 5.13.5.1 above).

5.14.1.1 Reducing the opportunities for crime

Routine activity theory and rational choice theory are also used to explain the causes of crime (section 5.13.5.1). Using these different factors we can suggest that preventative techniques could be organized under three headings:

- increasing the effort (eg target hardening);
- increasing the risks (eg CCTV);
- reducing the rewards (eg marking property).

Pease (2002) also adds a fourth heading of 'reducing the excuses'. The relative significance of each of these strategies depends upon the particular crime in question; which strategy is most likely to have the greatest deterrent impact on the potential criminal? These ideas are illustrated in Task 31.

TASK 31

Consider the following scenarios and identify whether increasing the effort, increasing the risk, or reducing the reward would be the most effective preventative measure. (We acknowledge that, to some extent, all three would be appropriate but try to identify the one that you think addresses the problem most directly.)

1. There have been a number of thefts from vehicles in a supermarket car park. The cars targeted have had valuable items stolen from them.
2. A shop is being repeatedly targeted at night by a group of known drug addicts.
3. Small amounts of money are being stolen by a member of staff from within a bank.

A consideration of routine activity theory suggests some other approaches that may be used in crime reduction, for example by ensuring that motivated offenders are not left unobserved where there are easy criminal targets. From this perspective, we do not have to reduce the number of motivated offenders in order to reduce crime; we simply need to ensure that they are monitored more closely or that we design goods in a way that makes them less attractive as criminal targets.

5.14.1.2 The prevention of hot spots

A persistent police presence would undoubtedly have a deterrent effect, but that cannot be sustained over the long or even the medium term. The use of PCSOs or Wardens as a visible deterrent is costly, intermittent at best, and dubious as other than a temporary solution. **CCTV** cameras are a possible short-term solution especially if co-ordinated with police action on the ground such as 'blitzes' on pickpockets for example, but if the CCTV is to be effective it needs twenty-four-hour live monitoring—which is expensive and is only really cost-effective in town centres.

A longer-term (but potentially very effective) solution is to 'design out' crime through the use of features such as more carefully designed walkways and better street lighting. Allied to CCTV and unpredictable police presence, this could be an effective combination. The use of intelligence (see Chapter 12) is likely to be an important part of any approach to dealing with hot spots. The kinds of crime, the times when the crimes take place, the sorts of people who commit those crimes, the seasonal impact, if any, upon the nature of the crime, and the likelihood of achieving a result will all be important considerations for the intelligence analyst. It is this intensity of knowledge, allied to detailed understanding about the hot spot and other contributory factors, which may bring a hot spot down several degrees in temperature.

5.14.2 Displacement

One problem that has been identified with crime prevention is that it leads to crime displacement; crimes are not prevented but merely displaced to other places or other times. New types of crime may also occur through criminal innovation (see below). Displacement is often explained as a consequence of criminality: those with a disposition to commit crimes will adapt and find different ways in which to realize their criminal disposition.

The following types of displacement have been identified:

Temporal displacement—the crime takes place at a later time. As an example consider the depot that introduces a security guard overnight to counter a number of burglaries that have occurred during the night-time hours. However, there is a one-hour gap between the security guard finishing and the day staff arriving so criminals adapt and choose this time to commit the offence.

Spatial displacement—the crime happens somewhere else. In this case imagine that in police force Area 1, a high police presence is introduced to curb the incidents of anti-social behaviour from a group of teenagers. The teenagers move to force Area 2 to avoid the police presence.

Displacement by type of crime—the criminals turn to different crimes. Suppose that the local council introduces better street lighting on an estate that has seen a high number of street robberies. This reduces the number of these offences but there is an increase in the number of burglaries in the area.

Displacement by innovation—the criminals become better at what they do. An example is credit cards which allow people to spend relatively large sums of money without having to carry large amounts of cash with them thus reducing the reward for potential muggers. Criminals develop ways of using credit cards fraudulently thereby gaining access to even larger sums of money.

5.14.2.1 The consequences of displacement

Displacement is clearly a problem that needs to be considered within crime prevention strategies. However, Pease (1997) has suggested that the extent to which displacement is a problem is often exaggerated. He suggests that there are ideological rather than empirical grounds for raising the issue of displacement and in this respect it is used as an excuse for doing nothing.

Furthermore, Pease argues that displacement is never likely to be 100% and he also illustrates ways in which it can be benevolent. For example, it might be beneficial to move a crime from one area to another to reduce its overall impact on society or to change the type of crimes that offenders are committing. Take for example a scenario in which prostitutes are operating in a residential area where many children live. We could assume that a high police presence in the area would move the prostitutes on to another area. The question would then be to establish whether this movement is beneficial or not. If the prostitutes move to a non-residential area it would clearly reduce the concern that children would be affected, although this might need to be balanced against a separate concern for the safety of the prostitutes. We might also consider that some of the prostitutes would potentially turn to other forms of crime, for example, shoplifting, whilst others would innovate and use more discreet means of operating as a prostitute, for example, by using cards in telephone boxes to advertise their services. We might also assume that some of the prostitutes will desist from any kind of criminal activity. The important point is that an assessment can be made as to what are the likely consequences following from anticipated displacement, which can then also be tested empirically in order to establish what the effect actually was. As Pease puts it, displacement is positive as long as 'the deflected crime causes less harm and misery than the original crime' (Pease, 1997, p 978).

5.14.3 The Advantages and Disadvantages of Crime Reduction Strategies

A final consideration in this section follows from the recognition that the consequences of crime prevention strategies can be to varying degrees either benevolent or malevolent. This raises a fundamental question and challenges our initial premise that prevention is necessarily better than cure.

By seeking to reduce crime we are intending to make society better in some way. However, intervening in the lives of individuals will not always make things better and there are occasions when we have to accept that doing nothing is actually preferable to taking action. This may be hard to accept because we do not want to feel as though we are ignoring problems in society and just standing by, letting bad things happen. Police officers (especially) have a duty of care and they respond to problems. Nonetheless, it is important that any intervention is properly evaluated. To this end, policing in general (and crime reduction in particular) is increasingly subjected to research and evaluation. The results of this research will help ensure that any claims used to justify preventative strategies are based on firm evidence (see for example Smith and Tilley, 2005).

The view that crimes are informed by rational considerations has been an important feature of situational crime prevention programmes. There are many examples of how this understanding has led to reductions in crime through architectural design and other measures aimed at making it more difficult for criminals to operate and more likely that they will be identified, caught, and prosecuted if they commit an offence. We have also introduced measures to reduce potential rewards of committing offences, for example the introduction of phone cards in place of the old coin-operated public telephone boxes.

However, critics of the rational view of crime argue that all crime prevention measures result in displacement. As we noted earlier, this criticism has been widely acknowledged but is countered by evidence that suggests displacement is never 100%. In other words we might expect some individuals to stop committing crime altogether as a consequence of crime prevention measures because the extra effort and risk makes the proposition less attractive. In this respect we begin to see a distinction between criminals who are driven by favourable opportunities and more prolific offenders who are driven by a desire to commit an offence. This can allow the police to concentrate resources against those offenders least affected by general crime prevention strategies.

5.15 Domestic Violence

At the outset, you should note that there is no legal definition of domestic violence nor is it a legally separate and distinct category of crime (although it involves criminal activity, such as unlawful violence). The term domestic violence relates to the **context** within which various crimes and acts of violence occur.

The boundaries of what constitutes domestic violence are continually refined and reconsidered in terms of the meanings we attribute to both domestic and violence. These boundaries have varied historically from force to force. Some have adopted narrower definitions, for example, emphasizing married heterosexual couples where there is evidence of physical violence. Others have broadened the definition to include same sex and cohabiting couples outside marriage. Violence could also include emotional and psychological abuse. Likewise, the term domestic could be restricted to activities within the home or include violence between partners wherever it happens, in public as well as in private. A definition provided by the Home Office Violent Crime Unit in 2004 demonstrates the extent to which a broad understanding of domestic violence is favoured:

Any incident of threatening behaviour, violence or abuse (psychological, physical, sexual, financial or emotional) between adults who are or have been intimate partners or family members, regardless of gender or sexuality (Home Office, 2004e, p 12).

It has been noted by a number of commentators that in the past domestic violence had been seen by police officers as 'messy, unproductive, and not "real" police work' (Reiner, 1997, p 1012). This attitude is not officially accepted today and the Crime and Disorder Act 1998 established in legislation the need for the police and local authorities to work through partnerships with appropriate local bodies to address the problem of domestic violence locally.

5.15.1 Policing Domestic Violence

Despite the political commitment to deal with domestic violence it remains a difficult area in practical terms for the police. This is partly because of the relationship of the offender to the victim. By definition, the offender and victim within a domestic context are part of a more complex relationship than is the case in most non-domestic crimes. There will be, or at least will have been, a loving and caring aspect of the relationship and there will be many shared memories, friends, family, and possibly children involved.

This partly explains the difficulty of establishing the true prevalence of domestic violence in our society. The problem of under-reporting is particularly acute for domestic violence: research suggests that women are abused up to thirty-five times before reporting the abuse to the police. Additionally, in the past the police were guilty of under-recording because their experience suggested victims of domestic abuse would withdraw complaints and drop the charges against their spouse offender.

However, despite not having precise figures on domestic violence (varying accounts estimate that domestic violence comprises 16%–25% of all violent offences), we do know that an average of **two women die every week** in domestic violence incidents (Home Office, 2003, p 6). It is not always an easy crime to identify, yet the consequences are potentially fatal; policing domestic violence is clearly one of the most serious and pressing aspects of police work.

5.15.2 Factors Involved in Domestic Violence

The violence that occurs in domestic settings will often be triggered by the same factors as in other violent offences, such as alcohol and jealousy. However, in domestic contexts, the stresses and strains of everyday life can become exaggerated. As with other crimes, the circumstances in which the crime occurs can provide a better explanation for why it occurred rather than the characteristics of the offender or, more controversially, the characteristics of the victim. In this respect we might make a distinction between one-off acts of violence that occur in the heat of the moment during exceptionally bad family circumstances and persistent acts of abuse that occur regularly and in which offenders actively seek opportunities to inflict violence upon their partners.

In cases where the violence is persistent, domestic violence is often seen as part of a cycle of abuse: some victims of domestic violence and/or children who witness domestic violence, may become domestic violence victims and/or offenders at a later date. Knowledge of this cycle of abuse links domestic violence to child protection. The cycle is not simply historical. There is also evidence to suggest that where a man is beating his spouse, he may also be beating his children. Alternatively, where a man is beating his wife, his wife may in turn be beating the children. This raises questions as to how the policing of domestic violence should be organized. The benefits of linking it to child protection units is that duplication of work can be avoided and risk factors can be identified and responded to earlier.

5.15.3 Domestic Violence and the Position of Women in Society

Another key factor identified in domestic violence is that general discrimination against women leads to abuse. Gelles and Cornell (1990) refer to Blackstone's codification of English common law in 1768 which asserted that a husband has the right to 'physically chastise' his wife provided that the stick was no thicker than his thumb. This piece of common law was not abolished until 1891. Zedner (2002) notes the influence of the women's movement in the late 1960s and 1970s in raising the profile of domestic violence as a serious issue that required immediate attention. In particular, Erin Pizzey's campaigning resulted in the establishment of the first refuge for battered women in the UK in Chiswick, London in 1972.

5.15.4 The Government Response

The late 1980s and early 1990s also witnessed a significant change in the attitude of the Home Office and police towards domestic violence. The Home Office Circular 60/1990 (revised in HO Circular 19/2000) is seen as an important influence upon the development of a proactive policing policy towards domestic violence (see Grace, 1995; Plotnikoff and Woolfson, 1998). There were three main recommendations of Circular 60/90:

1. The police should take a more interventionist approach to domestic violence cases, with a presumption in favour of arrest

All forces have adopted positive action policies to ensure that officers attending the scene of a domestic incident treat it with the utmost seriousness. Although there is an assumption of arrest in all cases and the officer's discretion would appear (on the surface at least) to have been completely removed, it should be stressed that positive action, not arrest, is required. Indeed always making an arrest could be counterproductive. Levi (1997) suggests that far from reducing the violence, arrests can lead to an increase in the rate of recidivism amongst certain social groupings. Likewise, Waddington (1999a) refers to studies in the USA that show a difference in this deterrent's effectiveness depending upon the social class of those involved. Elsewhere, Waddington (1999b) supports this with reference to Hoyle's (1998) research which suggests women tend to want nothing more than an immediate break from the violence and a warning given to their partners. A fear is that making arrests could stop women from calling the police because they feel that the action they take goes too far.

2. Domestic violence crimes are recorded in the same way as other violent crimes

The problem of under-recording has already been mentioned but this recommendation suggests that not only should all incidents of domestic violence be recorded but also that they should be recorded in a way that clearly identifies the level of seriousness of the alleged offence. A good example of research that looked at how the recording of domestic violence could be improved, is provided in the Killinbeck Project (Hanmer et al, 1999), which focussed on reducing repeat victimization in domestic violence by establishing appropriate responses to domestic incidents according to the severity of each case and the extent to which repeat victimization could be established.

3. The police adopt a more sympathetic and understanding attitude towards victims of domestic violence

As far as victims of domestic abuse are concerned, the circular emphasized the need for the police to adopt a duty of care. In this respect the policing of domestic violence should be less concerned with instrumental goals and more concerned with doing the right thing (see section 5.4 and Neyroud and Beckley, 2001, for a discussion of different ethical approaches in policing).

However, this presents us with an important question: should the police give greater priority to tackling domestic violence (and treat it as a core mandate of police work) or should other agencies become more involved? Likewise, what happens when there is a clash between supporting the wishes of a victim who decides not to press charges and responding to a perceived social need to punish domestic offenders? The answer to this question is largely dependent on the varying roles and status of the domestic violence unit (DVU) and domestic violence officer (DVO) within the force, eg whether the DVU/DVO is part of the criminal investigation department or not.

In addition to those works cited in the text above, there are many documents dealing with different aspects of policing domestic violence available online at the Home Office 'Violence against Women' section at <http://www.homeoffice.gov.uk/rds/violencewomen.html>.

5.16   Diversity and the Police

It would be advisable to read this section in conjunction with section 4.9 above, where we discuss diversity training for the police.

We have noted throughout this Handbook that one of the characteristics of policing in this country is that it is undertaken by **consent**. You and I (as citizens) accept, or consent, that some of our individual freedoms will be curtailed or limited for the common good. We allow some of our citizens greater powers than the rest of us in order that they may police our society. We expect in exchange to be protected and that our society will be ordered and peaceful under the law. When that security or law and order is disturbed, we expect the 'citizen police' to find the likely perpetrators and the criminal justice system to determine guilt or innocence on the basis of fair process. In essence, this is the social contract view of the relationship between the police and society.

If you accept the social contract model, it follows that if the police service needs to have the consent of the populace in order to do its work effectively then, in turn, the police should represent that populace in all its variety and permutations. This is where the issue of **diversity**, and what it means to the police, becomes important.

5.16.1   What is Important About Diversity?

A whole book could be written on this subject alone and we have to compress the issue into a few pages, but the essential point is that, as a student police officer, you will come into contact with all kinds of people in the course of your job. Some will be vulnerable because they are very young or very old; some will be vulnerable because they come from a minority group in the community and may have been targeted because of the colour of their skins, or because they are female, or because they are gay; some may be vulnerable and confused because of impaired hearing or failing vision; some may have been harassed because they have different beliefs from the majority and some may have mental illnesses which isolate them from normal relationships.

All such people are vulnerable in one way or another, and your job as a police officer is to protect them. Society looks to the police to protect the weak or vulnerable wherever they may be found. In other words, as a police officer and as a member of society, it is considered your duty to recognize and embrace diversity and to sustain it wherever possible.

5.16.2   What is Diversity?

Put simply, **diversity is recognizing and understanding difference**. The fact that someone (compared with you) has a differently coloured skin, or a different belief system, or different sexual orientation, or is older or younger, or is disabled in a way that you are not, does not make that person worse, better, weird, mad, or scary; only different. It is the mark of a truly benevolent society that difference between its members is a cause for celebration rather than a cause for anxiety or hatred. Of course, we do not have a truly benevolent society but perhaps we ought to, just as we ought to be stimulated by difference rather than feeling threatened by it. You may recollect the controversy about *The Secret Policeman* programme from the BBC in 2003. We have made reference to this on previous occasions in the Handbook. The attitudes to black people and others exhibited by some of the student police officers in that film have no place anywhere in modern policing. It not only does a disservice to the training system for the police, and to the police service as a whole, but it does a disservice to society as it reinforces the stereotypes on which our prejudices are based. Remember: diversity is about **difference**, not about better or worse.

> ### TASK 32
> As we have already suggested in the examples used above, there are perhaps six strands to diversity. Can you suggest what they are?

Several of the strands of diversity are subject to law. **It is unlawful to discriminate on the ground of race, disability, age, sexual orientation, and gender**. The Government has tried to introduce legislation to outlaw discrimination on the grounds of **belief** (that is, hatred against someone based on religion) but the subject is fraught with difficulty and it may be some time before a law is comprehensively framed which can allow criticism of belief but which prohibits actions that discriminate against belief systems. There is now legislation (2006) which makes discrimination on the grounds of **age** unlawful, but this is also a complex area since age discrimination applies to the young as well as to the old (or indeed any age). In practical terms, trying to prevent discrimination on the grounds of age has much to do with the laws of employment and a progressively 'greying' population. It is more likely to be an issue about employing people who are past the conventional retirement age rather than discriminating against people because they are young (though note in this context the decisions by some shopping malls, notably Bluewater in Kent, to ban the wearing of baseball caps and hoodies, which are currently the dress preferences for some young people, because they are perceived by some to be associated with theft and violence).

Let us look at what the integrated competency framework (ICF) says about 'respect for race and diversity' behaviours. You are expected to:

- consider and show respect for the opinions, circumstances, and feelings of colleagues and members of the public, no matter what their race, religion, position, background, circumstances, status, or appearance;
- understand other people's views and take them into account;
- [be] tactful and diplomatic when dealing with people, treating them with dignity and respect at all times;
- understand and [be] sensitive to social, cultural, and racial differences.

The behavioural competency goes on to note that there are positive indicators about how you deal with diversity and negative indicators.

TASK 33

Without referring to the competency, what do you think would be some of the positive and what would be some of the negative behaviours? (The answers are provided below rather than at the end of the chapter.)

You might have referred to all or any of these **negative** indicators:

- not considering other people's feelings;
- not encouraging people to talk about personal issues;
- criticizing people without considering their feelings and motivation;
- making situations worse with inappropriate remarks, language, or behaviour;
- being thoughtless and tactless when dealing with people;
- being dismissive and impatient with people;
- not respecting confidentiality;
- unnecessarily emphasizing power and control in situations where this is not appropriate;
- intimidating others in an aggressive and overpowering way;
- using humour inappropriately;
- showing bias and prejudice when dealing with people.

You might have included all or any of these in the **positive** indicators:

- seeing issues from other people's viewpoints;
- [being] polite, tolerant, and patient when dealing with people, treating them with respect and dignity;
- respecting the needs of everyone involved when sorting out disagreements;
- showing understanding and sensitivity to people's problems, vulnerabilities and needs;
- dealing with diversity issues and giving positive, practical support to staff who may feel vulnerable;
- making people feel valued by listening to and supporting their needs and interests;

- using language in an appropriate way and [being] sensitive to the way that your use of language may affect people;
- identifying and respecting other people's values *within the law*;
- acknowledging and respecting a broad range of social and cultural customs and beliefs;
- respecting confidentiality, wherever appropriate;
- delivering difficult messages;
- challenging attitudes and behaviour(s) which are abusive, aggressive, and (or) discriminatory.

You can see from these specific indicators that your assessors will be looking at your negative behaviours as much as at your positive behaviours. In other words, you can fail this competency rather than simply not reach the required standard.

There is one other thing you should know: if your behaviour is proven to show racial, sexual, gender, or other kinds of discrimination and brings the police service into disrepute, you might be disciplined and dismissed. Worse, you could be charged with a criminal offence. Your force will be serious about the standards it expects from you.

5.16.3   Diversity and Being 'Politically Correct'

You might well hear the claim during your training that diversity is just about being politically correct. Recognizing diversity is more about being tolerant of those who are different and about trying to understand them. For example, police officers when questioning should ask for a given name or first name instead of a Christian name because this has nothing to do with politics or appearing to be conventionally correct but everything to do with being professional and sensitive to others.

Sensitivity towards gay people and understanding that many still feel vulnerable in a society which is often aggressively heterosexual can pay dividends in terms of police work, as well as building bridges between the police and minority communities. We know of several forces where gay or lesbian officers have linked into the gay and lesbian communities and that, subsequently, police investigators have been helped by the gay community when homophobic and other crimes have occurred. It takes time to build up trust of this kind, and it can be undone in one unthinking moment. That is why the police service as a whole deplored *The Secret Policeman* and why it welcomed the dismissal of the officers who expressed racist opinions in the film.

However, we have to accept that if the police service is to be broadly representative of society as a whole, there will be some officers who are prejudiced against black people and other officers who dislike gays, lesbians, or transsexuals or who resent dealing with people who are mentally ill. But what really matters here is what such discriminators actually **do**.

Your police force will not (and indeed, cannot) dictate to you what you should believe or think about in the private recesses of your mind, and nor can anyone else. But these beliefs and feelings must stay inside your mind and must not become translated into action or behaviour. As we discussed in section 4.9, this is often difficult to do. If, in your dealings with the public, including people from ethnic minorities and gay communities, you act fairly, honestly, and impartially you will have fulfilled your duty.

A parallel issue is how the police deal with the arrest and detention of a paedophile. Most would deplore what paedophiles do (or try to do) to vulnerable children, but you know that detained suspects have to be treated with the same courtesy and consideration as anyone else, and that extends to paedophiles as well as to those who commit rape or domestic violence, or any of the other myriad crimes of violence in which the vulnerable are exploited or hurt.

If we sound passionate about this aspect of your work as a police officer, it is because we are. Professional tolerance can be important in defusing rows, calming situations, understanding motivations, and communicating to members of the public who might be frightened and abused. Private intolerance, once expressed publicly, damages the police service in ways far beyond the merely individual. If you police with society's consent, you cannot afford to break trust with those whom you police. Once the trust goes, so does the legitimacy of what you do as a police officer (see sections 5.5 and 5.6). There is little enough trust about and precious little in the way of consent. You need all the trust and consent you can get if you are to be an effective officer. That is why there is such emphasis upon the proper, proportionate, and fair treatment of people, without abusing those powers entrusted to you.

5.17 The Extended Police Family

This Handbook is aimed primarily at the student police officer, but it is worth taking a moment now to look at the wider police family especially as there are many people engaged in law enforcement and what could loosely be called policing in addition to sworn officers.

5.17.1 Special Constables

You will probably be familiar already with special constables (known in-force as 'specials') who are volunteers, but sworn officers with powers, who undertake police duties on a part-time basis. Most have day jobs; the specials function very much in the same way as the Territorial Army, or RAF or Naval volunteer reserve forces, applying themselves to the reserve task with whatever hours each week that they can afford. Some use the specials as a route into the regular police force. The days have gone when specials only turned out at weekends to marshal car parking at village fetes. Now, in most forces, they work alongside regular officers, go out on patrol and deal with the range of activities which a patrol constable would encounter during an ordinary shift. The number of specials in England and Wales has been in decline in recent years (from approximately 20,000 in 1997 to 11,000 in 2004, although there have been slight increases since). At the time of writing, it seems likely that during their training, specials will be assessed using a subset of the NOS that are also used to assess you during your training.

5.17.2 Police Support Staff

Another part of the immediate police family and which you will encounter from your first day in the job is the police support staff member. These used to be termed 'civilian' and the word was often associated with administration or work which was 'non-police'. Those days are long gone in most police forces. Indeed, in many forces, support staff can make up to a third of total numbers, and they undertake a wide range of tasks which used to be performed by police officers (more or less amateurishly) or which never existed before about 1980.

TASK 34

Can you think of examples of the types of work which the (58,000 in England and Wales) police support staff do?

You might have included the following (which vary from force to force, of course, but which most forces have most support staff engaged in):

- **Crime Scene Investigators.** (CSIs, who used to be called 'scenes of crime officers' or SOCOs.) An operational role which used to be undertaken exclusively by police officers, modern CSIs are often well-qualified in forensic investigation (see section 13.6).
- **Statement takers.** Many of the statements taken from witnesses and victims of crime, particularly volume crime, are taken, not by police officers but by support staff. The reason is that such statements do not have to be taken under caution (unlike statements by suspects) and therefore do not have to be taken by sworn officers. This can free up a great deal of time for police officers to pursue the investigation, and there can be a marked increase in the professionalism with which victims and witnesses are interviewed because the support staff involved are undertaking these tasks all the time.
- **Volume Crime Scene Examiners (VCSEs).** This role may not exist in all forces, but VCSEs are employed to undertake specialist forensic examination of extended areas of crime on a large scale. They are particularly used in vehicle crimes.

- **Detention officers (jailers).** These are support staff trained in custody and holding prisoners.
- **Human resources (HR).** HR can include the whole range of specialist people management from recruitment, through promotions and postings, training, assessment and appraisal, to retirement, secondment, dismissal, or capability issues. HR also deal with all matters to do with police support staff, including negotiations with staff associations and the like.
- **Information technology.** This embraces everything from AIRWAVE communications to laptops, databases to PCs; these specialists are almost exclusively support staff, though some forces retain police officers in areas like the force communication centres or control rooms where there is direct interface with police officers on patrol. IT often includes telephony and wireless communications (including personal radios) within its remit.
- **Lawyers.** Force legal advice (civil and/or criminal) is now seen as an important resource particularly for the chief officer team and the Police Authority and in dealing with complaints from the public or litigation by employees (for example employment tribunals).
- **Estates.** Police forces occupy considerable numbers of buildings and possess vast stocks of property which need specialists to handle, particularly in negotiations with planning authorities.
- **Finance.** With police budgets in the hundreds of millions of pounds annually, there is a need for specialist financial and budget management. In most forces, 80% or more of the budget goes on salaries or pensions, leaving a relatively small operational revenue budget to which is added the capital budget for aspects such as the estate and buildings, the vehicle fleet or projects.
- **Administration.** From paper files to computerized records, from sickness certificates to awards ceremonies, from shotgun certificates to booking training courses, the administrative tasks in a police force are complex and numerous. The bureaucratic nature of policing (meaning that things have to be formalized in a process) lends itself to a large administrative tail. We have left the days when police officers had to type reports with two fingers and forces now employ trained in-putters and clerks who can do the work. Nonetheless, the modern police force, however computerized, relies heavily on a corps of administrators who assume responsibility for the burden of recording and processing.

You may be able to think of other police support staff roles (such as training) which exist in your force, but the above are the principal functions which are now carried out in support of the operational policing side of the work. The original intention was to free up all police officers to return to front-line duties (though this was always somewhat tenuous), but the situation now is that no police force can do without its specialist support staff—from HR to estates manager—because of the complexity of the work, the fact that police officers could not master the breadth of knowledge entailed and because litigation is at such a pitch generally that punitive awards against a force for the amateur handling of a specialist process may cost it dear. There are still some areas in policing where it may be more appropriate to employ specialist support staff (high-tech crime and fraud being two obvious examples) than relying on 'omnicompetent' officers, but this is part of a wider debate about what is the purpose of sworn officers and where police powers are needed and where they are not. We continue this debate in looking at other roles below.

5.17.3   Other Police Forces

There are police forces apart from the Home Office forces of England and Wales, such as the British Transport Police and military police forces. You will come across some of them during your career in the police (you may even be a member of one) and it is worth noting why they exist separately from your own force.

British Transport Police are responsible for policing the railway network in the UK over- and underground rather than other forms of transport such as roads, sea, or air. With its headquarters in London, BTP has officers in uniform and in plain clothes travelling on the railways and performing police functions in upholding law and order, preventing and detecting crime and so on. BTP figured very prominently in co-operation with the MPS in the wake of the tube train bombings in London on 7 July 2005.

The **Ministry of Defence Police** polices and guards MoD establishments such as naval dock-yards, airfields, and army regimental depots. It operates across the UK (that is, including Scotland).

Other police forces within the armed forces are the **Royal Military Police** (RMP) and the RAF's **Provost and Security Services** (P&SS). These have jurisdiction only within their force establishments and then only for crimes which are not classified as major crimes. Murders and serious assaults are usually investigated by the local police force. You have no doubt read about the civil police investigations into allegations of bullying at Deepcut Barracks in Surrey which emerged after several young soldiers died. The official verdict was that the soldiers had killed themselves but some of the families of the soldiers believed that a bullying culture may have resulted in their sons or daughters being murdered or driven to kill themselves. Repeated investigations have failed to support the parents' contentions but have served to underline the sometimes rather difficult relationships between a local police force and the military or air force equivalent.

Finally, there is one police force with an unusual function: the **Civil Nuclear Constabulary** (the CNC), under the Energy Act 2004, protects civil nuclear installations and fuels in shipment and storage. Unusually, all of its officers are firearms trained.

5.17.4 Other Law Enforcement Agencies

There are other agencies with investigative powers which can also prosecute their own cases and agencies which investigate and then turn their findings over to the police to take to court. Prior to the formation of the **Serious Organised Crimes Agency** (SOCA) in 2005, **HM Revenue and Customs** had its own Investigation Division which looked at smuggling, especially of contraband and drugs. It mounted its own operations sometimes independently and sometimes in conjunction with the **National Crime Squad.** It has now become part of SOCA, but we understand that HM Revenue and Customs retains powers to investigate other crimes such as evasion of VAT or other taxes, improper importation, and other matters.

The **Immigration and Nationality Directorate** has a component which investigates illegal entry to the UK, and this includes the crime of people-trafficking. Again, parts of the Immigration and Nationality Directorate's investigation capability have been absorbed into SOCA. The rump may become the UK's 'border police' (August 2006).

HM Prison Service has powers in dealing with convicted criminals who have been sent to prison, as well as those on remand awaiting their trials.

Other state departments, such as **Social Services** and the **Department of Health** have small teams which investigate matters such as fraud, false documents, and fraudulent claims.

5.17.5 Regulatory Bodies

These are bodies which have a particular interest in a specialized matter such as public health or environmental crime. They can prosecute offenders. This category includes bodies which regulate, such as:

- the Health and Safety Executive (HSE);
- Trading Standards Authorities;
- the National Society for the Prevention of Cruelty to Children (NSPCC);
- the Royal Society for the Prevention of Cruelty to Animals (RSPCA); and
- the Royal Society for the Protection of Birds (RSPB).

In a sense, most of these bodies focus on niche crime, such as maltreatment of animals, stealing birds' eggs, and the like. It is only the HSE and the NSPCC which impact on police work substantially, in terms of sanctions for safe working and the prevention or detection of child abuse.

5.17.6 Police Community Support Officers (PCSOs)

The concept of a visible, non-police patrol function originated with Sir Ian Blair, among others, when he was Deputy Commissioner of the Metropolitan Police in 2001–02. PCSOs were introduced partly in response to public pressure to have bobbies on the beat, a supposed desire particularly echoed by politicians and harking back to the (probably mythical) Golden Age of policing (see section 1.3).

Sir Ian's concept was an achievable and imaginative one and it immediately found favour with the government of the day especially when sufficient numbers of volunteers were found who wanted to become PCSOs or Wardens (the latter on rural beats particularly).

The Community Support Officer soon acquired the prefix 'Police' to show that the officer was part of the extended police family, though the PCSO was without any special police powers and initially did not have a police function other than the supposed prevention of crime by the deterrent effect of visible presence.

However, the PCSO, despite some initial hostility from quarters within the police themselves, appears popular with the public, particularly in London. PCSOs were encouraged to engage with the public, to walk or travel on a limited beat where they could be seen and spoken to, and there was an emphasis on their meeting and talking to young people. So popular indeed has the concept become that, in 2005, the Government announced that the overall numbers for PCSOs in England and Wales would increase to 24,000 by 2008. However, in 2007 the Government revised its PCSO targets to 16,000 and suggested that forces completed recruitment to those targets within 2007. The signal was clear: funding for PCSOs from central government cannot be guaranteed beyond 2008. Consequently, some forces felt let down by the Government and realized that, if central funding dries up, forces will be saddled with the whole PCSO bill. That might mean fewer police officers recruited in future years (Caless, 2007).

Although it would seem that PCSOs are initially funded by the Home Office for a limited period, other organizations have been encouraged to part-fund. This approach has had some success with a number of authorities and organizations part-funding the PCSO, usually on a yearly basis. A proportion of the officer's time is then spent working in support of the part-funder, for example, patrolling shopping centres or working in local crime reduction partnerships (the PCSO's beat would include local housing estates and so on). It is debatable whether local part-funding of PCSOs will continue beyond 2008, especially if central government funding dries up.

We noted above that PCSOs do not receive anything like the same kind of training which a police officer would receive. However, it is likely that at some time in the future they will be assessed against a subset of the NOS used for initial police training, in a similar way to the training and assessment of special constables.

TASK 35

What training do you think that PCSOs should have, and for how long?

Police forces have remained uneasy about the precise long-term role of PCSOs and their cousins, the local and rural wardens (and indeed some forces have proved remarkably reluctant to embrace the concept at all). This does not simply reflect the professional unease of police officers (or the complaint from the Police Federation that this may represent a form of 'policing on the cheap'). It is also to do with how the PCSO as a concept can be sustained over a period, especially since the Government has promised funding only until 2008. There may be some unease expressed by the partner agencies and organizations which part-fund some of the posts.

Should forces accept their proportion of the 16,000 PCSOs planned under the government expansion? This would mean that a medium-sized force of about 8,000 staff would be expected to assimilate a further 370 PCSOs; where will funding come from if the Government withdraws financial support after 2008? PCSOs are support staff in employment terms so they have security of tenure in the sense that they cannot be arbitrarily sacked just because direct earmarked government funding ceases. This may mean that forces will have to continue funding PCSO posts from their own resources.

It seems to us that the Government (and indeed chief constables and police authorities) have not thought through carefully enough the long-term function and funding of the PCSO.

There is talk of extending PCSO powers beyond that of detaining a person for thirty minutes pending the arrival of regular police. If that happens, will there not be implications for the training regime? PCSOs will require further and more expensive training if their powers are extended, and forces may have to look for different qualities in the person for recruitment, concentrating more on physical fitness, strength, stamina, and the ability to perform heavier tasks such as lifting than has been the case until now. There is also the potential for the gibe about 'policing on the cheap' to be brought one step nearer to reality. It is possible that over time, there will be blurring between the role of PCSO and that of police officer. Alternatively, we may witness an increase in the specialization of the traditional uniformed police officer, with the PCSO occupying the more traditional role of providing a presence in public places.

That said, PCSOs appear to be popular with the public and have quickly become a part of each force's 'reassurance agenda'. Reactions to PCSOs and wardens has been largely positive in the media. What is not clear at this stage is whether PCSOs have actually had an effect on crime and criminality (for example, has a force's sanction detection rate improved?) or do they simply provide a reassurance factor for the public who want to see uniforms in public places and to have someone to address their concerns to in the face of anti-social behaviour?

5.17.7 Agencies and Partnerships

The extended police family has developed in recent years to include a number of agencies and service providers on a local basis. You will look at some of these in more detail during your initial training because such partnerships vary from force to force. This variation is because of differences in emphasis placed on them by your chief constable and your police authority. In general terms, your force is likely to have the following:

- **Crime Reduction Partnerships.** These are sometimes called Crime and Disorder Reduction Partnerships (CDRPs) and are based within local, municipal, or unitary authorities. They include representatives from housing, social services, education as well as the police, the Probation Service, and others.
- **Multi-Agency Public Protection Arrangements.** MAPPA are much concerned with the control of violent and sexual offenders, especially their re-integration into society on release from prison. MAPPA work on plans for assimilation and control of such offenders.
- **Partnerships with local councils or authorities over fixed penalty notices.** Fixed penalty notices are often issued for parking infringements or driving offences (such as those recorded by speed cameras). This partnership is likely to include close co-operation with local authority CCTV monitoring, especially of city centres and popular club or pub venues.

5.17.8 The Private Sector

This section concerns the expanding private security industry.

TASK 36

What do you think is meant by the 'private security industry' and can you think of some examples?

You may have thought straight away about bouncers at clubs, or, to give them one of their more official titles, door stewards. Other examples include security guards who control access to buildings or who patrol areas frequented by the public. But there are many others who are engaged in the business of giving security reassurance to the private and propertied sectors. There has been a growth in the last few years of the 'gated community' (following a US model) in which access to a group of private and exclusive dwellings is controlled by uniformed guards, twenty-four hours a day. This not only reassures the householder that his or her privacy is guaranteed, but it also increases physical security, making burglaries, robberies, and assaults more difficult to attempt.

Security extends outwards to the community through people like bailiffs, who recover property not (fully) paid for or seize goods in lieu of debt. Bailiffs can work on behalf of private companies seeking to recover debts or can work on their own behalf as a debt collection agency. On some occasions, particularly with evictions, or where there is concern about public order, bailiffs work with the police.

Our high streets and shopping malls are monitored through a network of CCTV cameras. It is estimated that the average person on an hour's shopping trip is photographed fifty-seven times in an average high street. There are now nearly three million CCTV cameras operating in the UK, the majority of which are on private property such as shops, offices, and warehouses. The police have become used to routine seizure of CCTV footage in the initial investigations of nearly any kind of crime (excepting perhaps domestic violence). We are among the most monitored people in the world, and we seem content to surrender at least some of our privacy in exchange for the greater security which CCTV offers, or appears to offer.

There is little current regulation of the operation of CCTV cameras, though licensing was introduced for CCTV cameras in public spaces from March 2006. Most CCTV cameras are automatic and many are actually unmonitored, with tapes being renewed on average about every seven days. Some are monitored, and these include surveillance cameras operated by local authorities in places like town centres and other areas where people gather, such as outside clubs and pubs. The human monitors of such public areas are often able to co-ordinate with the police when there is a disturbance in a city centre. Furthermore, the new 'Sprint 2' technology enables some police forces to access CCTV coverage of town and city centres remotely and thus directly respond to any incidents unfolding on the screens. We may conclude that the extension of the police family includes the large surveillance system which now cobwebs the whole of the urban geography of the UK. The movement of vehicles in rural areas and on motorways can also be monitored through automated number plate readers (ANPR) linked to cameras mounted on bridges and gantries.

When considering the steady growth of private security, we should not ignore the successful security companies, such as Group4 and Securitas AB. They are involved in all aspects of private security, such as cash collection from businesses, 'cash in transit' arrangements, the provision of physical security and guarding, and latterly, prison management and the transportation of prisoners. Thus, even the public sector is not immune to contracting out security tasks to the private sector. Indeed, there is a blurring of roles between public policing and private policing when such companies are used to provide security for organizations which engage in live animal research and which, consequently, find themselves the target of animal rights' protesters. At places like Huntingdon Life Sciences, for example, external security seems to be run by the police whilst internal security seems to be managed by a private company. The degree of co-operation that exists between the two is not clear, but there must be some and therefore the distinctions between 'accountable police activity' and 'unaccountable police activity' remain blurred.

Finally (though we have by no means exhausted the examples of the private security industry), we may look at private investigators. These are small-scale enquiry companies, usually staffed by ex-police officers, which seldom exceed half a dozen employees. They are principally engaged in matters such as gathering evidence for presentation in divorce cases or tracking down missing persons. They present little in the way of conflict with the regular police, except when attempts are made to access official records or data (such as vehicle number plates). The world of the private investigator has always been one where small budgets rather than large profits operate, and that is probably the reason why they remain small-scale and somewhat under-developed. They do not operate in the UK on anything like the scale of the USA, nor do they conform with the exciting image beloved of pulp fiction. It remains a fact that the private detective is seldom likely to detect public crime.

5.17.8.1 Unregulated private security activities

Commentators have not been slow to look at the extension of the police family. One of them, Professor Adam Crawford, (cited in Newburn, 2003, p 148) asserts that:

> A pluralized, fragmented and differentiated patchwork has replaced the idea of the police as monopolistic guardians of public order.

What Crawford is arguing is that in the past the police provided the only form of public order, but now this has been multiplied into many different providers. He goes on to ask what regulation there is of the private security industry; this is a good question which the Government appears to have been slow to answer. Professor Crawford (p 149) also shows us the size of this industry by quoting some figures compiled by the British Security Industry Association (BSIA, now the SIA) for 2001:

- The commercial security industry employs 350,000 people.
- There are estimated to be 8,000 security companies in the UK market.
- The industry turnover in staffed security services (excluding in-house security) was estimated at £1.68 billion in 2001.

This is growth on a serious scale. Employees in security exceed police officers by nearly three to one which is food for thought, especially since such employees are not answerable in the same way that police officers are. After all, such employees would probably detain you, hold you, or eject you if you caused any kind of disturbance on premises which they were guarding. They have no more rights of detention or arrest or use of physical force than any other citizen, but when did you last see a prosecution of such a guard (or his/her company) for such an action?

The SIA is introducing codes of practice, but there are many companies (most of which operate on a small scale) who are not members and there is no compulsion on anyone setting up or managing a security company to register it or to join the Association. These companies are therefore unregulated and it is this which worries commentators like Professor Crawford and some police officers. If the security industry is unregulated and not subject to mandatory government control of standards, how can it be trusted? It gains more and more power over private space and has functions of prevention and deterrence, but no obligation to investigate. Indeed, its interests are largely with its stakeholders and these interests do not necessarily coincide with the greater public good.

5.17.9 Policing Cyberspace

What about the policing of the internet? The monitoring of criminal, or potentially criminal, activity in cyberspace does not fall to a single jurisdiction; activities that might lead to prosecution in the UK cannot necessarily be prosecuted in Namibia or Chile. The internationalism of the internet, its global quality, is precisely what makes it attractive to some criminals and equally hard to police. You will be familiar with the kinds of crime which the internet has spawned (identity theft, fraud, scams, paedophile grooming of children in chat rooms, hacking into organizations' databases, creation of viruses which then infect and destroy databases, and so on). However, many of the Internet Service Providers (ISPs) have responded to calls for surveillance of the use of the internet. A group called The Internet Watch Foundation works extensively in this area and it is expected that ISPs will respond more readily to pressure to monitor and regulate the use of the internet if threatened with civil litigation. Police forces in the UK are already monitoring the internet for signs of grooming by paedophiles and have participated in chat rooms in plain clothes, as it were, to detect or investigate approaches to children. Other than sexual crimes, the biggest private threat from the internet is probably the infection of an individual database by a virus which is akin to housebreaking. Yet for the PC owner at home, there is little in the way of effective counter-action and not much the police can do until the perpetrator is identified or at least isolated. What fills this void is the private sector; there has been a proliferation of security systems against spam and viruses, systems that the individual can purchase for protection and a sense of security. The virus-makers persist however, and there is no such thing as a foolproof security system.

5.17.10 Conclusions

If we were to summarize the implications of the growth of the extended police family, we might formulate the trends and developments like this:

- The conventional police roles are being narrowed and more focussed upon responses to crime and criminality.

- Specialist knowledge which does not require a warrant holder is increasingly being provided within police forces by support staff, but the expected 'release to the front-line' of police officers does not appear to be happening in quite the way hoped for.
- The creation and expansion of the PCSO role has reassured the public but presents a challenge to the traditional autonomy of police patrol.
- There are large numbers of law enforcement agencies which work independently of the police as well as in co-operation with them.
- There are regulatory or single-issue bodies which monitor and investigate criminal activity within their areas of responsibility. These may impinge upon policing or require police action in the latter stages.
- There has been a boom in the private provision of security and policing. Such provision currently lacks mandatory regulation.

5.18 Answers to Tasks

TASK 1

It is highly likely that you included some of the following under the list of professions:

- Medicine (eg a doctor).
- Law (eg a barrister).
- Church (eg a vicar).
- Teaching (eg a school teacher).

It is less likely, but still possible, that you listed the following:

- Military (eg a General).
- Nursing.
- Accountancy.

Did you include policing?

Professions are occupations that normally have the following qualities:

- They provide an income which is normally referred to as a salary. Interestingly, in many respects police officers are paid a wage rather than a salary—for example, below certain ranks they qualify for overtime payments calculated at an hourly rate.
- Entry to the profession is regulated and controlled. Quite often a higher education degree in an approved area of study is required. Members of the profession are then licensed to practise but there are also procedures for the removal of this licence (which in some professions is referred to as being struck off). Others are prohibited from practising the profession unless they are licensed. (The title may even be legally controlled, as in the case of the medical profession.)
- There is a code of ethics and behaviour that members of the profession subscribe to.

TASK 2

Some possible answers are:

Requirements of a profession	The policing profession
Corpus of knowledge and theory	There is underpinning knowledge and theory for some aspects of policing, for example the law. There is also doctrinal development undertaken by the NCPE. However, there is no universally accepted corpus of knowledge which is unique to policing.
Controls on entry to the profession and maintenance of position	Entry is controlled through the national selection process. However, there are no formal academic requirements to enter the profession, beyond relatively simple tests of English and numeracy. There is currently little formal requirement on the maintenance of skills.

Autonomy, discretion, and self-regulation	Police officers enjoy relatively high levels of autonomy and discretion. The title of police constable is controlled so that only those that qualify are entitled to use it.
	Self-regulation of policing exists in a restricted form but is increasingly under challenge.
Vocational calling	Policing is more than just a job and affects many aspects of an individual's life.
Code of ethics	There is an established code of ethics.

TASK 3

There are two major problems with simply **telling** student police officers to be honest:

- Telling people is no guarantee that they will internalize the values that underpin the police service.
- Honesty is too vague a term. As we have discussed, in certain forms of police corruption, the officers themselves probably feel that they **are** being honest, at a deeper level.

The relationship between our values, attitudes, beliefs, and actions is obviously a complex one. (See, for example, just about any textbook in social psychology.) The concepts themselves are also particularly slippery and hence difficult to pin down. Then following is an overview of the usual meaning of the terms:

Concept	Meaning
Values	Concerned with the **relative worth** or **importance** of people, groups, objects. Those things that we value most we put first in our priorities. Our values can be drawn, inter alia, from: • ourselves; • those around us; • social norms and expectations; • religious and cultural belief systems.
Attitudes	An overall tendency to view matters in certain ways, either positively or negatively—for example to like or dislike something or somebody. We are not always aware of our attitudes.
Beliefs	Convictions about the truth of assumptions that we hold. Belief, however, does not have to be blind. We can base our beliefs on inductive reasoning (see section 4.13) or sound evidence. Belief in a religious context often refers to faith.

The relationship between values, attitudes, beliefs, and **actions** is a fraught one in police training. Some may argue that our actions do not **by necessity** follow from our values, attitudes, and beliefs. In an earlier chapter we discussed *The Secret Policeman* documentary of 2003. In that case a police recruit was heard to **claim** that he exercised his discretion in a racist manner against members of ethic minorities. However, there was no clear evidence that this had actually occurred. In his case there did not appear to be a clear link between his beliefs and his actions.

TASKS 4 & 5

No doubt you found it easy to answer parts 1 and 2 of Task 4. Less easy is 3. In the following we provide some suggested responses to Tasks 4 and 5.

These changes are very rapid, even though it may seem to us that society changes imperceptibly. By way of illustration, we can point to a few things which have developed enormously quickly in the last couple of decades and which impact on policing.

The twenty-four hour economy: clubs, pubs, bars, and places of entertainment are now open for much longer, stretching the commercial world across twenty-four hours. Additionally, people expect to be able to access services such as shops, supermarkets, banking, cash machines, and insurance at any time.

Disposable income: most people earn more and therefore spend more.

Profits from crime: some of the profits from drug-taking, contraband, and criminal businesses are immense and criminals re-invest such sums in legitimate business ventures where dirty money can be laundered with clean (legitimate) money. Paradoxically, the illegal money helps to fuel economic growth, thus creating greater criminal opportunity.

Variety of social conventions: conventional marriages no longer dominate social structures. More older people are living alone and for longer; partners live together rather than marrying; divorce is higher than ever before (which has contributed to the rise of single-parent families); social groupings are more flexible and smaller, so that the nuclear family is more common than an extended family. This, combined with earlier economic independence enjoyed by some young people, has changed many social conventions.

Some commentators have suggested that changing social conventions have led to lack of respect for authority (including the police) and to the abandoning of parental controls. Others think that more emphasis on freedom has encouraged society to question authority more freely and that the police, among others, should rethink its role in controlling and perhaps emphasize more its capacity for enabling.

Single-issue politics: some people who had previously confined their political activities to voting are becoming active in single issues, such as live animal exports, ecological issues, animal experimentation, abortion, and so on. The mass spectrum of party politics does not appear to interest them, nor do they necessarily support a single party. At one end of the scale, this may involve well-planned peaceful demonstrations with strong media coverage. At the other end of the scale it can entail violence and threatening behaviour (such as with some animal rights' groups).

Travel and personal mobility: there has been a major increase in travel over the past twenty years. People regularly travel hundreds of miles in the course of their work, and more leisure time is spent travelling than ever before. The number of cars and drivers on our roads has increased dramatically.

Credit-based consumerism: there is more debt now than there has ever been, and calculations by economists have indicated that the average personal debt in the UK is in excess of £4,000 (not including mortgages on property). It is not necessarily just the fault of the individual that we all owe more, because credit is often easy to obtain. This has fuelled a buoyant market for goods: more people own things than ever before (and, as a corollary, have more that is worth stealing). Correspondingly, there are more insolvencies, bankruptcies, and defaulting on debts than at any time since the Great Depression of 1926–9.

Communication: from the internet to the mobile phone, from computer to Blackberry, the communications revolution is perhaps the most profound change in modern society. Put simply, more information on more subjects is available to more people more quickly than ever before. We do not need to labour this point, but information technology of all kinds has changed our lives. It has also changed policing irrevocably. A couple of simple examples: a few years ago, people had to find a static phone (landline) to report a crime or an accident. The emergency services could cope (just) with responses to 999 calls. Now, when there is a road traffic accident or a street brawl, as many as fifty 999 mobile phone calls may be made virtually simultaneously to the police concerning one event. Even computer-based force communication centres find it difficult to cope at such times. Correspondingly, the police can access more information about individuals than previously, through centralized databanks such as the National Fingerprint Identification System (NAFIS) and the Police National Computer (PNC) for vehicle registration plates or a central criminal records bureau to trace criminal histories. The overall result is that the police have more information about people than ever before.

TASK 6

As we suggested, there are no certain answers to this task.

There are interesting examples of attempts by a number of countries to tackle, for example, corruption amongst their police officers through using the kind of analysis that you have just undertaken. For example, in Kenya, police wages in 2004 were almost doubled and corruption subsequently fell. (However, proving that the two events are cause and effect is somewhat more difficult.)

TASK 7

No doubt you have your own impressions of the meanings of these terms in the context of police ethics.

TASK 8

We discuss the meanings of these terms in the text that follows.

Drugs policing, in particular, gives rise to a number of opportunities for corruption both in type and frequency (Lee, 2003). These include:

- theft (stealing from arrested drug dealers);
- planting drugs (to imply guilt);
- illegally protecting drug dealers (eg by classifying them as a CHIS);
- participation in dealing.

TASK 9

The five opportunities from the list are:

- first arrival at the scene of a crime, when cash or goods are lying about;
- handling and storing drugs from police investigations;
- the excessive exercise of discretion without challenge;
- managing informants without adequate supervision or scrutiny;
- lack of effective supervision.

TASK 10

The free cup of coffee theory may seem to you to be an unlikely explanation. However, think about those circumstances in the past where police officers (including student police officers) used their warrant cards to secure financial advantage—for example, to gain free entry to a club. No doubt most of the officers justified this to themselves on the grounds that their (non-uniformed) presence would somehow be to the benefit of the club concerned. But did this not lead to at least a small sense of obligation on the side of the police officer and a potential compromise of their position? As they say in the USA, 'nobody ever gave a cop something for nothing'. The situation is made even more complex when a police officer has a second job (with the approval of his/her force). For example, the *Observer* newspaper reported in February 2006 that almost eighty police officers in Norfolk held second jobs, including at least one as a car salesman (*Observer*, 5 February 2006).

This is not to say that accepting gratuities is always wrong. The circumstances will be a guide, as will force policy. For example, you may well be offered cups of tea (or coffee!) by well-meaning members of the public if you are engaged in long and tiring public order duties. There would appear to be little to be lost and much to be gained by accepting the offer on those occasions.

TASK 11

Remember that this theory assumes that you have a predisposition towards corruption or deviant behaviour. In this case you are likely to find many reasons that will **justify** undertaking corrupt acts.

TASK 12

For a comprehensive discussion of this and other aspects of police corruption you might want to read Tim Newburn's 'Understanding and Preventing Police Corruption: Lessons from the Literature' (Newburn, 1999) and Joel Miller's 'Police Corruption in England and Wales: An Assessment of Current Evidence' (Miller, 2003). Both are downloadable from the Home Office website.

TASK 13

When thinking about these questions you might like to read at least parts of the 1999 HMIC report into police integrity (HMIC, 1999). The report gave rise to the introduction of integrity tests. These are situations designed to test the integrity (eg corruption, behaviour) of police officers. Note, however, that they are not usually directed at police officers in general (blanket testing) but are targeted at an individual or individuals as a result of information or intelligence. However, consult your force policy on this.

In terms of the corruption matrix, you might like to examine the 1998 case of DCI Elmore Davies, Merseyside Police, jailed for five years for corruption and perverting the course of justice. You should be able to find the details on the internet.

TASK 14

The following are examples of how the five forms of authority might feature in the scenario:

Form of authority	Examples
Epistemic	You have a clear understanding of the definition of the possible offences involved in this incident. You have knowledge of the appropriate procedures to be followed and this is conveyed in speech to those present, including the victim and the offender.
Natural	You use your demeanour and language to take control of the situation, including indicating when you wish a person to answer a question and in which order.
De facto	Your right to question those involved is probably accepted without challenge (but not necessarily with co-operation!).
De jure	You have the authority to arrest if the circumstances require this.
Moral	You demonstrate, through your behaviour and attitudes, that you do not immediately jump to conclusions concerning the sequence of events and attributing guilt or otherwise.

TASK 15

You would have had to arbitrate between the rights of freedom of expression (however extreme such views may be) and the need to sustain law and order. The legitimacy of your presence may not be consensual, but it may be both legitimized in law and necessary for preservation of the peace. The police would endeavour to control the marchers by determining the safest route for the parade to follow whilst also ensuring that direct clashes with the protesters were avoided. Someone, somewhere, would have individual freedoms circumscribed (even if only the rights of Saturday shoppers to go about their lawful business) however you managed the event, and thus the police are using moral as well as legal legitimacy in the policing of the march.

TASK 16

You would have quickly spotted our intentions with this task. The two situations are very similar. Indeed, if anything, the first scenario is the more serious in policing terms as you are told that that the woman appears to be slightly drunk whereas the young man is simply clutching a can of lager. In the first case the fact that she is a medical student who will soon (presumably) join the medical profession may well have influenced your thinking towards exercising discretion. However, you were **not** appointed to be a moral guardian of society and the place that a person holds in society should not feature in your decision whether or not to exercise discretion.

In terms of your answer you might well have considered other aspects such as the intent of each person concerned, the precise nature of the apparent offence and so on. The problem with presenting these scenarios in a written form (or as simulations in training) is the lack of this context, so important when making decisions.

When exercising discretion it is important that you are able to justify your actions to an outsider looking in—that is, to show how discretion is the result of rational decision-making rather than instinct or some other gut reaction. Doing so will also help you meet the evidence requirements of the NOS elements. What is important is that during training you evidence your decision-making. What your assessor cannot do is read your mind.

Taylor (1999) has produced a useful checklist for the exercise of discretion. You are asked to consider issues such as:

- fairness;
- justice;
- accountability;
- consistency;
- wider community interests and expectations.

TASK 17

We discuss this in the paragraphs that follow the task.

TASK 18

You might have included things like:

- It is **decentralized**. Public policing is still largely local, autonomous, and non-political (with shades of grey, viz the Miners' Strike in 1982–3).
- Policing is **consensual**: it cannot operate without the active support of the public.
- Approaches to policing are characterized by provisions in the Human Rights Act 1998 and the Police and Criminal Evidence Act 1984, which **respect human dignity and ensure fairness of process**.
- Police officers, for the most part and on most occasions, are **unarmed**.
- Police officers have **independence** in conducting investigations; they may still exercise initiative in whether to investigate or not.
- We have an adversarial criminal justice system (see section 12.8), which requires the prosecution to **disclose evidence**.
- There is a **presumption of innocence** until proven guilty; the burden of proof lies with the prosecution.

TASK 19

As suggested, an excellent starting point to find out more concerning these operational models is Nick Tilley's chapter in Newburn's *Handbook of Policing* (Newburn, 2003). It is perhaps misleading to suggest that these three models are somehow in competition or are mutually exclusive although there are significant points of departure between them. Rather, they have different foci. Intelligence-led policing tends to be seen as a response to the inevitable and unavoidable existence of criminals in society and the existence of high volume recidivist criminals at that (see section 12.3 and the NIM). Problem-oriented policing on the other hand, as the label suggests, attempts to model crime or disorder in terms of problems that we analyse and attempt to solve. Finally, community-based policing posits that crime and disorder must always be viewed in the wider context of the community or communities from which it originates.

In terms of anti-social behaviour (and with our caveat about not treating the models as being in some form of competition) you might have suggested the following:

- **Intelligence-led policing.** Target the most active and serious contributors to the anti-social behaviour. This might require the use of informants and surveillance. When these individuals have been identified then examine all appropriate means, within the law, of removing them from exercising leadership and direction over the rest. For example, consider what offences they may have committed, whether ASBOs might be suitable, what other agencies may be engaged to bring pressure to bear (for example, do we have information that they are illegally claiming benefits?), what evidence we will need and so on. If we cannot detect the crime, then disrupt it.

- **Problem-oriented policing.** What is the fundamental problem here? The anti-social behaviour may simply be the visible manifestation of a less obvious problem or change. For example, has the removal of fences between the gardens of publicly-owned houses meant that spaces are no longer as defensible for those living in the area? This might mean involving other agencies in an agreed and concerted strategy to address the underlying problem.

- **Community-based policing.** First we need to talk to those that can really help us: members and representatives of the local community, and the patrol officers who work with them. If young people are involved then how can we mobilize their parents and others in the community to address both the anti-social behaviour **and** its underlying causes? What support can be offered? In summary, do not simply view this as a question of law enforcement but more as a wider question concerning the stability and cohesion of the local community.

TASK 20

You might have noticed that:

- Uniformed police officers routinely and openly carry **arms** (so do detectives, but concealed).
- **Stop and search** can be more widespread than in the UK. Also, European citizens routinely carry an **identification card** or identifying papers.
- There are often several **kinds of police officer** (*gendarmes, carabinieri, guarda civil, police municipale*, city police as well as national police) in the same country.
- Most European police forces are **nationally organized**, even when they have variations in police types (such as the paramilitary *gendarmes*, as against the *agents de police* in France).
- Particularly in Eastern Europe and Russia, as well as further afield, you may have detected a **hostility** to the police or even a fear of them, especially at border controls. This is a legacy and, in some cases, a continuation of the role of the **police as an arm of the state** (in the case of the ex-USSR, as an arm of the Communist Party) and is associated with repression and denial of freedom. Citizens in countries which have suffered under occupation or tight state control may show contempt and loathing of the police to a degree you seldom find in the UK.

There are other differences which you will find only by close comparative study or by investigation into the individual country's criminal justice system. Did you know, for example, that the Dutch abolished the jury system in 1804 and never reinstated it? Or that Italy has provision for a jury trial system but has never used it?

TASK 21

Remember that a major theme in policing is that you **police by consent**, that is, through the active co-operation and tolerance of the majority of the populace. It is important that your force shows, in its Policing Plan, how it intends to respond to local concerns and how it will meet criticisms of its actions (such as faster responses to 999 calls or more neighbourhood police action to counter criminal damage). It is also a communication exercise which shows how the budget is allocated, sets out what the priorities are, and also shows that some aspects of policing are not determined locally but nationally. Finally, it is a document, revised and rewritten approximately annually, which is potentially a good promotional tool for the force and for the Police Authority. Most force Policing Plans are quite glossy, expensively-produced publications or web page designs which, naturally enough, put a positive spin on what the force does. You might consult your own Policing Plan for detail specific to your force.

TASK 22

You might include the provisions of the National Policing Plan, which we looked at in detail above, as modified or amended to fit local conditions. However, you could also have included themes such as:

- citizen focus, including engagement with the public and responsiveness to public fears about crime, anti-social behaviour, criminal damage, and alcohol-initiated violence or disorder;
- developing witness and victim care programmes (see also 'providing assistance' below);
- building and sustaining good relationships with the communities which you police;
- reducing crimes, with especial focus on reducing those crimes which adversely affect local communities such as domestic burglary, vehicle crime, drugs misuse, and street robberies;
- partnership working, especially in the fields of combating illegal drugs and domestic violence;
- crime investigation, particularly in improving the 'brought to justice' statistics, identifying and dealing with persistent and prolific offenders and in seizing criminals' assets;
- reducing the incidence of violent crime, especially the abuse of children, crimes involving guns and knives, sexually motivated crimes, and hate crime;
- promoting public safety, such as reducing anti-social behaviour, dealing with abandoned, unlicensed, and nuisance vehicles, crime prevention strategies, Crimestoppers and Neighbourhood Watch initiatives, and roads policing;
- providing assistance through effective call handling, case investigations, liaison with partner agencies, 'visible policing', witness protection, and victim support;
- effective use of resources, especially those of the force itself through effective budgeting, financial management and accountability, managing people from recruitment to retirement, healthy workforce initiatives, race and diversity equality issues, training and skills acquisition, the retention and development of a representative work force, and the effective use of information technology.

If you managed to include all these points in your answer, you may very well be asked to help with the force Policing Plan in future years! The essential point for you is that, although the National Policing Plan and the aspirations of the Government (or even the closer-to-home joint planning by your force and your Police Authority) may seem somewhat remote, these things constantly affect you and the way that you do your job.

TASK 23

You should have found that these regulations cover the fitting of lights, reflectors, and rear markings on vehicles.

TASK 24

You should have found:

Offence: The act of **robbery**.

- **Theft Act 1968, s 8(1)**;
- **Mode of trial**: triable on indictment only;
- **Maximum penalty for a person found guilty**: life imprisonment.

(Crown Court).

TASK 25

You will find the website <http://www.hmcourts-service.gov.uk/HMCSCourtFinder> a useful resource.

Note, however, that in some cases postcodes are given but not in others (you may need to use your investigative skills).

TASK 26

There are many different explanations for what registers as a crime, or series of crimes, in public imagination through the media. A sensational crime is often one which has something out of the ordinary, something different, even a little outrageous, to make it stand out.

Some violent crimes involving children may feature highly in media and thus public consciousness (possibly because many of us are expected to identify with the parents of the victim, or because the vulnerability of a child evokes sympathy and pity in us), as may crimes in which single young women are involved. (There is some suggestion of an ethnic bias in reporting crimes of this type, with victims of ethnic minorities less likely to receive extensive media coverage that their white counterparts. However, the discussion is beyond the scope of this Handbook.)

Crimes which tend not to make the headlines, unless really bizarre or huge, are the so-called victimless crimes such as defrauding a large company or embezzling insurance money. There are victims, of course, with any crime (because that helps to define the nature of a crime), but what frightens a community or spreads anxiety is the thought that some sort of terror or dread is stalking the streets. A series of rapes can do this, especially in a small community like a town or at a college. The abduction of children is another.

TASK 27

There are a large number of possible answers, and we provide some examples below. The answer for 'universal crimes' is somewhat speculative.

Crimes	Examples
Universal	Theft, murder, and rape.
In the UK now, but not 100 years ago	Stalking, computer crimes (eg hacking), and holding illegal raves.
In other parts of the world, but not in the UK	Adultery (Nigeria), consuming alcohol (Saudi Arabia), keeping African Pygmy Hedgehogs (some States of the USA).

TASK 28

There is a difference between **intrinsic value** and '**CRAVED**'. The thieves would probably leave the **coins** behind because they are bulky and very heavy, but they would pocket the £350 in **notes** immediately. The **PC** would probably be left; again it is bulky and heavy and could even be secured by steel straps to its desk or to the wall. Thieves would not want to waste valuable time cutting the cables. The **laptop** would be easily picked up and sold on, as would the **iPod, Blackberry, mobile phone**, and the **Rolex**. Beware though, traffic in electronic goods is transient and short-lived. It is often the next generation white goods that the fences demand. Steal a mobile phone which is out of date and you could get nothing. (This does not include those thieves who use stolen mobiles to set up other crimes or who want them to use abroad.) The Rolex might later cause problems because of the engraving (which potentially makes it traceable), but in snatching or mugging for it the thieves would not stop to check. Only when the fence jibbed at the engraving and date, and knocked pounds off the price, would the thieves realize that they had lost out. They would get something though; the fence could always file the engraving out.

As to the rest, well, they are small but would be very difficult to sell on. The Gospel and Rubens' painting would be worth several million pounds and enormously hard to fence on any art market. (For all that, we know that organized drugs importers and traffickers have used valuable art such as paintings or sculptures as 'cash' for their transactions—the more so since the **Proceeds of Crime Act 2002** made depositing large amounts of cash in a bank account subject to scrutiny and investigation.)

The *netsuke*, which are small carved figures, would be worth several thousand pounds each but only through an expert dealer. It is doubtful that the average fence would know what they were. That said, some thieves steal to order and may target such items specifically, but these are not likely to be volume criminals working on hot spots.

TASK 29

In this task you were asked to consider police strategies to combat repeat victimization. A useful starting point is the Government's crime reduction website concerned with 'RV' at <http://www.crimereduction.gov.uk/repeatvictimisation02.htm>. There is a popular phrase, 'once bitten, twice shy', which suggests that we become more vigilant after an unpleasant incident such as being the victim of a crime. Whilst it might be true that we become more wary, it is certainly not the case that we become less vulnerable. As we suggested in terms of burglary, by far the best predictor of future victimization is whether we have been a victim in the recent past. Put another way, if you knew the following about a person:

(a) age
(b) sex
(c) ethnicity
(d) income
(e) the football club, if any, that he supports
(f) whether he had been the victim of a burglary in the previous month
(g) height
(h) annual investment in household security devices
(i) whether he has previous convictions or not

then by far the best way of predicting whether he/she is more or less likely than average to be burgled in the next month would be (f), that is, whether he/she has been the victim of burglary in the last month.

TASK 30

The quotation assumes that criminal behaviour will follow a rational pattern thus allowing the police to anticipate appropriate points at which to intervene. We can anticipate hot products that will be targeted in hot spots; markets will exist for the products of crime.

TASK 31

1. Reducing the reward. The fact that the cars targeted have valuables on show suggests that the offenders are looking for easy rewards. Increasing the risk by introducing better lighting, CCTV cameras, or security guards would also be beneficial but the most cost-effective measure is likely to be encouraging people not to leave valuables in the car.
2. Increasing the effort. We can assume that these particular offenders are desperate and therefore unlikely to be overly concerned at being caught (increasing the risk) and will be prepared to take risks for small rewards (reducing the reward). Therefore making it physically difficult to break in by installing metal bars and stronger locks is likely to be the most effective measure.
3. Increasing the risk. The rewards are already limited and making it more difficult to take the money is impractical because of the need for employees to handle money. Therefore increasing the risk, for example by installing CCTV, is likely to have a deterrent effect because the employees have much to lose if they are caught.

TASK 32

You would probably have picked up on **race** and **gender**, but did you get **sexual orientation**? What about **age**? Did you remember **belief**? And, mindful of the references throughout this Handbook to the Disability Discrimination Act (the DDA), did you get **disability**?

TASK 33

The negative behaviours are discussed in the paragraphs that follow the task.

TASK 34

We provide a comprehensive list immediately after the task.

Force websites often provide descriptions of the roles undertaken by police staff. A good example is Essex Police and its website <http://www.essex.police.uk/recruitment/r_sta_07.php>.

TASK 35

The volume and exact nature of the training is very much up to the directions set by your chief constable in your force, or even to the local BCU Commander in terms of any specific training. There is still debate about the outline of a training package which all PCSOs should receive. In most forces it would look something like this:

Training for PCSOs

Training lasts for five weeks.

Week 1 is an induction course, which contains health and safety instruction, learning about diversity and some introduction to the general nature of being a community support officer.

Weeks 2–4 include attitude and behaviour development, combined with knowledge of outside agencies and other tools for successful community problem solving.

Week 5 is the 'Powers' week where PCSOs are provided with knowledge of their existing powers and their practical effectiveness. This would also include some rudimentary safety training and training to defuse potentially dangerous situations and how to calm angry people.

Finally, there will be BCU or beat training and familiarization until independent patrol.

TASK 36

We provide some examples of the work of the private security industry in the paragraphs that follow the task. We also discuss the regulation of the industry. Licensing is being introduced to a raft of security occupations such as door supervision (bouncers), vehicle immobilisers (clampers), and so on. You can find a complete list of licensed activities and timetables for introduction of licences at the SIA website at <http://www.the-sia.org.uk/home>. You could well find that the law and regulation surrounding private security features more extensively in your work as a police officer in the years to come.

6 | Competence and Assessment

6.1   Chapter Briefing

In this chapter we examine the various ways in which your competence is measured and how other aspects of your attainment of skills, knowledge, and behavioural qualities are likely to be assessed. Note when reading this chapter that some aspects of assessment of initial policing have yet to be determined.

6.1.1   Aim of the Chapter

The aim of this chapter is to assist your understanding of what competence means in initial policing, how this relates to national occupational standards, how you are likely to be assessed against these standards, and how your achievements and progress are recorded.

This chapter will enable you to:

- understand the nature of competence and competencies in respect to initial policing and the place of the Integrated Competency Framework in your training;
- comprehend the importance of the National Occupational Standards within the broader context of your training programme;
- identify the relationship between Units, Elements, and Range within the NOS;
- know how to claim the achievement of elements and units of the NOS;
- understand how your achievements and plans for future development are identified and recorded;
- appreciate the position of the PAC in terms of the decision to grant you Independent Patrol status;
- develop the underpinning knowledge required for a number of entries for your Learning Diary Phase 1.

6.1.2 Learning Diary Phase

The contents of this chapter may provide you with stimulus material for completion of your Learning Diary Phase 1 and the heading 'IPLDP Content' in particular.

6.1.3 IPLDP Learning Requirement

This part is relevant to sections 4.6 and 6.1 of the IPLDP Learning Requirement (see Chapter 1 for details of the Learning Requirement).

6.2 Introduction

As we discussed in Chapter 3, your ability to undertake the tasks and assume the responsibilities of a police officer will be judged against a number of criteria, including the occupational standards set down for initial policing. Occupational standards are a relatively new concept in policing. There are, however, existing National Occupational Standards (NOS) in many vocational areas, including homeopathy, early years care and education, and mechanical engineering. The NOS define what a person working in a certain occupation is expected to be able to do. As the National part of NOS implies, these standards are meant to be the same throughout the country. In this way, despite variations between forces in terms of training delivery or qualifications structure, the public can have reasonable confidence that a Confirmed police officer, after achieving the NOS, has reached at least the same level of competence in Morecombe as in Maidstone.

If you are used to being assessed through recent experience at college or university then the approach adopted for the NOS may be unfamiliar to you. The assessment used is much more like taking a driving test than it is sitting an examination in biology. First, the emphasis is on evidence of **knowing how to do something**. When you take a driving test, the examiner is not overly concerned with how you managed to gain the skills but that you can actually drive; that you possess those skills. You could have been taught by the most expensive driving school in the country, or by your sister, or (most unlikely) have simply paid close attention to car chase sequences in films. What matters instead is your ability to drive safely, competently, and to agreed standards. Although the standards for initial policing do not work in quite the same way as they do for driving, nonetheless the emphasis is very much on the **assessment of the end product** rather than on the process you used to achieve the result. This is not to suggest that you will not be assessed and judged in other ways; for example, your attitudes and behaviour will come under close scrutiny against the core behavioural areas (see section 6.3 below) and you might well be expected to demonstrate that you have reached a certain level in your understanding of legislation and procedure. It is just that the main emphasis in your formal assessment is likely to focus on the final 'threshold' standards that you need to achieve to be confirmed as a constable.

Secondly, you will find nothing on timescales in the description of an NOS Unit. The philosophy is that you achieve an element or Unit when you are competent to do so, and this may be at different times for different people. Indeed, you could be given credit if you can already meet a standard (perhaps through working as a special constable before joining as a full-time student police officer) through a process called the accreditation of prior learning (APL), or prior experiential learning (APEL), but to date this has been difficult to implement in practice. However, your force will almost certainly have systems in place to encourage (and even require) you to plan the phasing of your assessment against the units, according to a given schedule. This is relatively uncharted territory for the police service and the 'tying' of at least a subset of the NOS to Confirmation (see section 3.6 above) may well give rise to some adjustments to timescales. However, in some forces you may be expected, for example, to achieve 11 of the standards in the first year of training and the remainder in the second and final year.

Thirdly, assessment of competence is not based on pass marks. There is no pass mark such as 40%, 50%, or 90% for a standard. Instead, you achieve the standard when it has been confirmed that you have provided reliable, valid, and sufficient evidence (in the correct format) to demonstrate your competence. Think of the analogy with the burden of proof in the courts—we are talking here of beyond reasonable doubt and **not** the balance of probabilities, but remember also that it is the quality of evidence that is important, not the volume.

Finally, and contrary to some impressions, the NOS do not automatically lead to a National Vocational Qualification (NVQ), although some forces do provide access to NVQs at levels 3 and/or 4 in Policing. Reaching at least level 3 may become a requirement in the future. Instead of NVQs, your police force may have chosen to link the attainment of the standards to the gaining of a Foundation Degree, often in association with a local university or college. Current examples of this approach include Kent Police, West Yorkshire Police, and Cleveland Police. Some other forces have decided, at least for the time being, against the need for any form of academic or vocational accreditation for their student police officers. The Home Office is, however, committed to requiring a minimum qualification for student police officers (see Chapter 3).

This chapter therefore examines in some depth the National Occupational Standards for initial police training. These standards are placed within the context of the Integrated Competency Framework (ICF). We also examine other key aspects of the way your competence is measured and how you are assessed, including the Student Officer Learning and Assessment Portfolio (the SOLAP) and the Police Action Checklist (the PAC).

6.3 Competence, Competencies, and the ICF

In this section, we will briefly examine the **Integrated Competency Framework** and look at the way the competencies against which you will be assessed as a student police officer are integrated with the National Occupational Standards. As with many of these things, it all may appear at first to be far more complicated than it is. It is important, however, to understand the material in this section because your future as a police officer will depend on your assessments against the NOS and the ICF during your probation. Failure to attain the overall standard required may mean that you have to repeat modules or even whole phases (in IPLDP speak) where your performance has been below par (sometimes called re-coursing), or your probationary period may have to be extended (see section 3.4), or, worst of all, you may have to leave policing altogether.

Putting aside these dire warnings, let us begin with an understanding of what the concepts **competence** and **competencies** mean, because you will be meeting them frequently.

> **TASK 1**
>
> Look **competence** and **competencies** up in a dictionary (such as the Shorter Oxford English Dictionary, or an internet site such as Wikipedia at <http://en.wikipedia.org>).

For competence, you should have found something which conveyed the sense of fitness, of 'sufficiency of qualification' (Shorter OED, 2002) or of capacity (meaning ability). But there is a much simpler sense in which the police use the term. By competence they mean generally your ability to do the job.

On the other hand, **competencies** are the assessed skills or assets you have for the job. When we refer to the **Integrated Competency Framework**, we mean all the skills you have learned, the qualities which you have, and your attitudes and behaviours, and how they all come together. The integrated part simply means that the competencies are bedded into the **requirements** (or NOS, see section 6.4) for a particular role. The role we are going to examine in depth is obviously that of the **student police officer**.

You trainers may sometimes use the acronym **KUSAB** when discussing your learning, which is short for:

> K Knowledge
> U Understanding
> S Skills
> A Attitudes
> B Behaviours

KUSAB (introduced to the police by the Police Training Council) is linked with competencies in the sense that your competence in any field (that is, your ability to do the job asked of you) will be the product of how much you know, how much you understand, what skills you have which fit what is needed, and the attitudes and behaviours you show.

Remember the discussions about **diversity** in sections 4.9 and 5.16? These discussions were very much geared to how you, as a trainee police officer, demonstrated your attitudes and what behaviours you showed when dealing with people who in some way were different to you. But before the attitudes and behaviours can be developed, the knowledge and understanding need to be in place, informed by the skills for the job. You cannot have one without the other, and it is only relatively recently that the police service came to the conclusion that all parts of KUSAB are interdependent which means that all aspects of KUSAB are needed if you are to demonstrate the required level of competence.

You are currently a student police officer and are developing the core responsibilities needed of a police officer (a confirmed constable). The Skills for Justice ICF defines your core responsibilities in the following way:

Core Responsibilities for a student police officer

Core Responsibilities	Activities
Community Safety	Conduct patrol.
Police Operations	Prepare for and participate in planned policing operations.
	Provide an initial response to incidents.
Investigation	Conduct investigation.
	Interview suspects.
	Interview victims and witnesses.
	Provide care for victims and witnesses.
	Search person(s) or personal property.
	Search vehicles, premises, and land.
Custody and Prosecution	Complete prosecution procedures.
	Conduct custody reception procedures (as arresting officer).
	Prepare and present case files.
	Present evidence in court and at other hearings.
Personal Responsibility	Comply with Health and Safety legislation.
	Maintain standards for security of information.
	Maintain standards of professional practice.
	Promote equality, diversity and human rights in working practices.
	Provide an effective response recognizing the needs of all communities.
Intelligence	Use intelligence to support policing objectives.
Health, Safety and Welfare	Provide first aid.

You will see from the various entries in the table above that KUSAB is woven through all elements which make up the competencies. In practice, each of the entries has to be evidenced through a portfolio of work so that assessment may be made of your achievements.

Correspondingly, areas for improvement can be identified as can areas requiring development (after all, if you have not yet assisted at, or managed, a road traffic collision (RTC), there is going to be a gap in your competence).

You will also have noticed that some of the elements represent **continuous themes** (the 'golden thread'), whatever the particular task you are doing. A good example is Health and Safety. Whether you are dealing with an RTC and moving vehicles on to the hard shoulder or searching premises you have to be cognizant of the Health and Safety legal requirements as well as safe practice. This means that you have to be aware of potential risks, such as the chance encounter of a needle hidden in clothing or in a pocket when searching a drug addict, and you also need to know what to do in such a situation. Some elements seem to mask the depth of KUSAB which you have to demonstrate, such as 'interview suspects'; this is covered by a whole mass of legislation and also involves a complex battery of skills that you will be expected to deploy to a high standard. Look, for example, at section 12.5 below for a detailed and exhaustive examination of what is involved in interviewing suspects.

In summary, the table above represents only the 'headlines' of the skills and understanding, the knowledge and the attributes, which you will be expected to demonstrate in full and detailed measure as a police officer. Many of the components of the core responsibilities are dealt with in detail in the pages which follow, but also remember that these are the competencies of a student police officer only; there are different as well as overlapping sets of competencies for all other roles.

The ICF is linked inextricably with the NOS for initial policing and we examine these now.

6.4 The NOS for Initial Policing

There are currently twenty-two Units of National Occupational Standards that underpin the initial training for student police officers. Note that an additional Unit 1D4, concerned with protecting children, may or may not feature in your assessment although you will certainly learn about the underlying knowledge and skills required for this Unit. (If you are not assessed against 1D4 you almost certainly will be assessed against **most**, if not all of the remaining twenty-two Units.) Indeed, in general terms, you should be aware that the requirements can change quite quickly, and you should check the current situation with your force, in terms of the number of Units and their content.

The following is a list of all the relevant Units and their constituent elements:

Relevant NOS Units for Initial Policing

NOS Unit	Unit title	Elements
1A1	Use police actions in a fair and justified way	1A1.1 Apply principles of reasonable suspicion or belief
		1A1.2 Use police actions proportionately
		1A1.3 Use police actions fairly
AB1	Communicate effectively with people	AB1.1 Develop and maintain communication with people
		AB1.2 Maintain the security of information
AA1	Promote equality and value diversity	AA1.1 Promote equality and value diversity
BE1	Provide initial support to victims, survivors and witnesses and assess their needs for further support	BE1.1 Provide initial support to victims, survivors and witnesses
		BE1.2 Assess the needs and wishes of victims, survivors and witnesses for further support
2A1	Gather and submit information that has the potential to support policing objectives	2A1.1 Gather and submit information that has the potential to support policing objectives

NOS Unit	Unit title	Elements
2C1	Provide an initial police response to incidents	2C1.1 Gather information and plan a response
		2C1.2 Respond to incidents
2C2	Prepare for, and participate in, planned policing operations	2C2.1 Prepare for, and participate in, planned policing operations
2C3	Arrest, detain, or report individuals	2C3.1 Arrest, detain, or report individuals
2C4	Apply conflict management	2C4.1 Defuse aggressive and abusive behaviour
		2C4.2 Use personal safety and restraint techniques
2G2	Conduct priority and volume investigations	2G2.1 Conduct priority and volume investigations
2G4	Finalize investigations	2G4.1 Finalize investigations
2H1	Interview victims and witnesses	2H1.1 Plan and prepare interviews with victims and witnesses
		2H1.2 Conduct interviews with victims and witnesses
		2H1.3 Evaluate interviews with victims and witnesses
2H2	Interview suspects	2H2.1 Plan and prepare interviews with suspects
		2H2.2 Conduct interviews with suspects
		2H2.3 Evaluate interviews with suspects
2I1	Search individuals	2I1.1 Search individuals
2I2	Search vehicles, premises, and open spaces	2I2.1 Prepare to search vehicles, premises, and open spaces
		2I2.2 Conduct searches of vehicles, premises, and open spaces
2J1	Prepare and submit case files	2J1.1 Prepare case files
		2J1.2 Submit case files and progress enquiries
2J2	Present evidence in court and at other hearings	2J2.1 Prepare for court or other hearings
		2J2.2 Present evidence to court or other hearings
2K1	Escort detained persons	2K1.1 Escort detained persons
2K2	Present detained persons to custody	2K2.1 Present detained persons for custody process
		2K2.2 Conduct initial custody reception actions
AE1	Maintain and develop your own knowledge, skills and competence	AE1.1 Maintain and develop your own knowledge, skills and competence
AF1	Ensure your own actions reduce risks to health and safety	AF1.1 Identify the hazards and evaluate the risks in the workplace
		AF1.2 Reduce the risks to health and safety in the workplace.
4G4	Administer First Aid	4G4.1 Respond to the needs of casualties with minor injuries
		4G4.2 Respond to the needs of casualties with major injuries
		4G4.3 Respond to the needs of unconscious casualties
		4G4.4 Perform cardio-pulmonary resuscitation (CPR)

In some cases these Units are the same as those used by other occupational groups—for example, those in Health and Safety and First Aid (which partly explains the unusual numbering system). This makes sense as a number of tasks performed by a police officer will be similar to those performed by parallel occupational groups, and indeed there are likely to be many circumstances when you find yourself working alongside other professionals trained to the same occupational standard. You will also find that some other professional requirements on you, for example the CARs and PIP Level 1, are also linked closely with a subset of the NOS.

Each Unit is a self-contained and self-standing expression of a particular part of the role of police constable, together with a description of how competence for this part of the role can be assessed. The Units are not just concerned with 'can do' activities but (implicitly at least) also attempt to infer attitudes and behaviours. For example, Unit AA1 is concerned with your ability to 'promote equality and value diversity'. Without being unduly pedantic, we suggest that to 'promote and value' is a different type of skill from being able to 'apply handcuffs to a prisoner in a safe and secure manner'. So you need to be aware of the wide-ranging nature of the Units, particularly in terms of the evidence you must produce.

Unit AA1 is also an example of a holistic Unit which you will be assessed against during the whole period of training. These holistic units link to the more technically-oriented units and tend not to be assessed in isolation but alongside the other Units. For example, your force is likely to look for evidence against Unit AA1 whilst you are also engaged with Unit 2C1.

Units are subdivided into a number of **elements**. For example, Unit 1A1 is subdivided into three elements:

Unit 1A1 Use police actions in a fair and justified way

1A1.1 Apply principles of reasonable suspicion or belief.

1A1.2 Use police actions proportionately.

1A1.3 Use police actions fairly.

To gain unit 1A1, it follows that you need to achieve each of the three elements. There are a total of forty elements for initial policing, with between one and four elements to a unit.

You are unlikely to achieve elements (or whole Units) early on in your training (although this is not impossible). Most forces appear to have structured their programmes to enable you to achieve elements and then standards after a few months, with the majority of Units being achieved in the second year of training.

6.4.1 Units and Elements

In this section we look in detail at one particular Unit and its elements. We have chosen Unit 2C1:

Unit 2C1 Provide an initial police response to incidents

2C1.1 Gather information and plan a response.

2C1.2 Respond to incidents.

As you can see, this Unit has two elements, 2C1.1 and 2C1.2, and the attainment of these two elements will lead to the attainment of the Unit itself.

We have chosen 2C1 for a number of reasons:

• You are likely to encounter this Unit relatively early in your training (although not achieve it until sometime later).
• It has more than one element and so the interrelationship between elements is more easily illustrated.
• It demonstrates the links between the NOS and other aspects of your training, for example the PACs.
• It links with one of the holistic Units, AA1.

First, an overview of the Unit itself. Skills for Justice provide the following summary:

Unit 2C1

This unit covers providing an initial police response to incidents. The unit is not rank specific and applies to all persons responding to incidents. The incidents covered by this unit include crime, non-crime, and traffic incidents. You must be able to deal with these types of incidents.

You will need to be able to gather information on the incident. Such information may include, for example, history, dangers, and witness information. Based on the information you have obtained you will need to be able to establish the nature of the incident and plan your actions accordingly. This process will often happen fairly quickly en route to the incident.

You will need to take into account the health and safety of self and others during the incident. If it is a major or critical incident, and you are the first on the scene, you will need to take interim control until relieved by the appropriate person (Skills for Justice, 2007).

As you can see, it is a wide-ranging Unit and central to the work of a student police officer. The summary of a Unit usually contains the following information:

- A general description of the Unit, in terms of the kind of activities involved.
- Any links with any other Units. In this case there are certainly implicit links with other Units in the suite for initial policing, but none are explicitly specified.
- The target group for the Unit—who is it for? The summary makes it clear that the 'Unit is not rank specific and applies to all persons responding to incidents'. This obviously includes student police officers training to be confirmed constables.

You can probably also see that much learning is required on your part (acquiring knowledge and understanding, and practising skills) before you will be able to demonstrate your attainment of Unit 2C1, probably during Supervised or Independent Patrol.

First, there is knowledge of legislation and police procedure surrounding a whole range of incidents; 'crime, non-crime and traffic incidents'. Hence you will need at least a working knowledge of the legislation surrounding public order offences (eg s 4 of the Public Order Act 1986), violent incidents (eg s 47 of the Offences Against the Person Act 1861—Actual Bodily Harm) and so on. You will also need to be familiar with:

- police procedure, such as the correct use of your pocket notebook and making police statements—'you will need to be able to gather information on the incident';
- health and safety—'take into account the health and safety of self and others';
- critical incident management—'take interim control' and 'establish the nature of the incident, and plan your actions accordingly';
- intelligence—'history'; and
- human rights and respect for diversity (as always).

This knowledge and understanding is likely to be incrementally achieved during your first year or so of training (and is covered throughout this Handbook).

In terms of skills, you will certainly need to know how to communicate with the control room and your fellow officers, and you might need your personal safety training too. You may also need to know how to support witnesses and victims, how to protect the scene (for forensic purposes) and possibly how to administer first aid.

It is now probably obvious to you that a Unit such as 2C1 is not achieved overnight. It is a major milestone towards your Confirmation as a competent police officer.

Unit 2C1 has two elements:

> **Elements of 2C1**
>
> 2C1.1   Gather information and plan a response.
>
> 2C1.2   Respond to incidents.

These effectively subdivide 2C1 into logical stages within the Unit itself. Think of element 2C1.1 as being concerned with all those actions (mental as well as physical) that lead up to actual attendance at an incident—for example between the report of an incident being passed to you and your actual arrival at the scene. Element 2C1.2 then takes over at this point and is concerned with your response to the incident itself. It makes sense to group these two elements together since the quality of your response is likely to partly depend on the quality of your planning. The Unit is quite realistic about when this planning is likely to occur—'this process will often happen fairly quickly en route to the incident'. This is a reflection of the fact that much of the work of the student police officer, particularly whilst on Supervised Patrol, is involved with so-called 'reactive' policing.

> **TASK 2**
>
> Use the internet to locate and download the specifications for Unit 4G4 'Administer First Aid' (you might want to start at the site <http://www.skillsforjustice.com>). What are the knowledge and understanding requirements?

6.4.2   Evidence Towards an Element and Unit

The evidence for attainment of a Unit features at the level of the element (although Units occasionally consist of a single element). There are three important concepts to be grasped here: **performance criteria**, **range**, and **evidence requirements**.

6.4.2.1   Performance criteria

For each element, the performance criteria are the basic building blocks of the element and more closely describe what actually has to be demonstrated. They tend towards behavioural descriptions of the 'can do' kind but are by no means always of this nature.

In terms of Unit 2C1, element 2C1.1 has the following performance criteria:

> **Performance Criteria of 2C1.1—Gather information and plan a response**
>
> To meet the standard, you should:
>
> 1. identify and assess relevant information on the **incident**;
> 2. establish the nature of the **incident** based on the available information;
> 3. obtain any necessary additional information for the response to the **incident**;
> 4. prioritize and plan your actions according to the nature of the **incident**;
> 5. respond to the **incident** within the appropriate timescales and according to current policy;
> 6. provide the necessary information to **others** regarding the incident.

Notice the use of words such as identify, establish, obtain, prioritize, respond, and provide. These are more concrete in nature and hence considered more susceptible to direct observation and measurement. In this way, element 2C1.1 has been opened up and made less abstract and more detailed. In practice, each performance criterion is also put into context. For example, suppose you are undertaking Supervised Patrol and you and your supervisor were called to a road traffic collision (RTC). What does performance criteria 1 mean in this context? You would need to 'identify and assess relevant information on the incident'. Well, remember that this is 2C1.1 and is concerned therefore with gathering information and planning a response (you are not at the incident yet). Looking in more detail at performance criteria 1, we can list a number of important phrases or words:

First, you need to **identify** relevant information. What is it that you need to know in advance of attending this RTC? Has all this information been given to you? Probably most of the relevant information has been provided already, for example, location, number of vehicles, and so on but you need to identify precisely what is needed and to ensure that, if available, you have all this information. This might mean that you need to ask the control room or colleagues for more information (see 'others' in the description of the range below). For example, what are the weather conditions like at the incident itself? If there is thick fog, then how should you take this into account? Remember, you will not (or should not) be on your own during these circumstances; you will be under the supervision of more experienced colleagues.

Secondly, you need to **assess** the relevant information. Assessing information involves establishing its value. For example, on assessing the information given, you might decide that there are ambiguities concerning the location of the incident that need to be clarified. Of course, it is possible that exact locations are simply not known at this stage because of the confusion surrounding the event—what is important however, in the context of element 2C1.1, is that you have **demonstrated** that you have assessed the information and identified the problem.

6.4.2.2 Range

The range helps you understand the meaning of the performance criteria. It is a description of the kind of circumstances in which you need to demonstrate each performance criterion. You would have noted that Skills for Justice highlighted the words 'incident' and 'others' in their description of the performance criteria for 2C1.1. This was a reference to the range.

In terms of our example of 2C1.1 the range is specified by Skills for Justice as follows:

> **Range of 2C1.1**
> 1. **Incident**
>   (a) crime
>   (b) non-crime
>   (c) traffic
> 2. **Others**
>   (a) members of the public
>   (b) line management
>   (c) other specialists, including external agencies
>   (d) colleagues
>   (e) control room

Specifying the range in this way means that, in practice, it is rare that evidence from a single incident will be sufficient to prove 2C1.1. Instead, you will be expected to demonstrate competence in a number of different situations—for example, domestic violence, road traffic incidents, public order incidents, and so on. You will also be required to show how this competence is employed when dealing with others—for example, the control room and members of the public. In this way, it can be reasonably certain that your demonstration of competence is not down to chance or limited to just certain types of incident.

6.4.2.3 Evidence requirements

A Unit also specifies the **evidence requirements**, setting out in detail how much and the sort of evidence you will need (for example you might be able to use some evidence from simulated incidents or role plays). Evidence requirements are particularly important if your training is linked to an NVQ, although even forces that do not link initial training to NVQs will still pay attention to the evidence requirements.

In terms of our example element 2C1.1, Skills for Justice specify the following evidence requirements:

Evidence Requirements for 2C1.1

For element 2C1.1 Gather information and plan a response.

From the range . . . you must show that you:

— have planned a response to five types of incidents*
— have provided the necessary information to all others

* Items from the range not covered by performance evidence should be supported by knowledge evidence

---

Note here the reference to the range that we described earlier. The evidence requirements are such that you need to document or otherwise evidence your planning for **at least five** of the following types of incident:

(a) crime;
(b) non-crime;
(c) traffic.

(We specify 'at least five' rather than exactly five as any additional examples can be used to provide the necessary information required for the remainder.)

For the attainment of the overall unit 2C1, Skills for Justice specify the following:

Evidence Requirements for Unit 2C1

1. Where simulations are used for performance evidence, these should properly reflect the requirements of real working situations.
2. You must practically demonstrate in your work that you have met the standard for providing an initial police response to incidents on at least three separate occasions.

Hence you need to have both elements 2C1.1 and 2C1.2 signed off (as successfully achieved) on at least three separate occasions in order to be awarded Unit 2C1. Further, the emphasis here is very much on real examples rather than the use of simulation, although the latter is permitted within limits.

6.4.3 Types of Evidence

You will need to produce evidence that you have met the requirements of an element and Unit. This is regardless of whether your training is linked with an NVQ, a foundation degree, or has no formal link with a qualification.

Producing evidence demonstrates that, as far as can be judged, you have attained the competence described. Unless properly organized, this can be a tedious process, particularly if it involves documenting aspects of your training and Supervised Patrol which would not normally require documenting. Your more experienced colleagues will be making decisions in their heads and, in some cases at least, will not be asked to document and evidence the reasons for their actions. You may think that there is enough paperwork in policing as it is. However, it is perhaps important to acknowledge that it is almost impossible to evidence and validate thought processes in isolation. During the period in which you are proving your competence, you need to document the evidence that supports your claims of 'knowing how to do the job' so that others can see how you are progressing. After all, they cannot read your mind.

You may well be assisted in the process of identifying evidence against a Unit through the use of a Professional Discussion. This is a form of case discussion with your assessor when you look at a particular Unit or Units and discuss the evidence you have assembled.

The type and form of evidence depends in part on the particular element but is likely to include at least some of the following:

6.4.3.1 Direct observation

This is a very common form of evidence. Put simply, a suitably qualified person, normally your assessor constable or PDU assessor (the terms vary from force to force), observes you doing something and confirms that it meets the standard. Your assessors will be working to criteria that enable them to decide whether the evidence is appropriate and sufficient. Normally an assessor will explain what is happening (and may also question you before and after the event) but during the period of observation assessors are meant to remain unobtrusive (you are their 'co-pilot'), though they are likely to intervene if your plane is about to crash!

6.4.3.2 Questioning by an assessor

Questioning is often used to test your underpinning knowledge relevant to the element under consideration. The questions are not always verbal questions but are sometimes written, although most assessors avoid referring to this as a test.

6.4.3.3 Testimony from witnesses

(Possibly a confusing phrase in the context of police training but you are likely to hear it used.) The witnesses in this case are most likely to be your more experienced and qualified police colleagues, and they can produce supporting evidence that you have met the requirements of an element. Even fellow student police officers (who have already achieved the element concerned) are able to provide witness testimony. However, in all cases the witnesses need to be credible and for the more technical units, occupationally competent.

6.4.3.4 Written evidence or 'work products'

(Again, the first phrase is potentially confusing, but widely used.) These come in a wide variety of forms. Common sources of written evidence will be police statements that you have written, your PNB entries, proformae that you have completed (for example, FPNs) and reports. The assessor will obviously be interested in how far these products demonstrate the performance criteria of an element but will also be checking on aspects such as authenticity (checking that it is your work and not 'borrowed' from elsewhere).

6.4.3.5 'Artefacts'

These are tangible objects such as photographs of a cordon that you have established or tape recordings of an interaction with a member of the public. This evidence is indexed and cross-referenced in your SOLAP. This form of evidence requires contextualization—that is, the object alone will not normally provide sufficient evidence and you will be expected to also provide a written description of the background and context. This is an art form in itself and we look at how it is done later in this chapter.

6.4.4 Claiming Achievement of an Element or Unit

Finally, a few pointers on claiming achievement of an element or Unit:

- **Be proactive** in claiming competence towards an element. Familiarize yourself with the performance criteria. It is in your own interest to do so. Do not slip into thinking that the standards are things that happen **to** you; think of them as opportunities to demonstrate your skills. Remember that the elements of certain Units may be demonstrated outside the context of traditional policing—for example, during a community placement in the second year of training. Although policy does differ from force to force, ask whether a suitably qualified person outside your force is also able to confirm competence.
- **Let somebody know** (for example, one of your tutors) if you feel that you do not have sufficient opportunity (particularly on Supervised Patrol) to demonstrate attainment of an element or that your assessor has it wrong. Forces are required to follow certain quality assurance procedures in terms of the NOS and these will almost certainly include the right to appeal against an assessment decision.

- **Be as efficient as possible.** A single incident that you have attended or task that you have completed could potentially be used as the basis of evidence for a whole range of elements and Units.
- **Do not leave it to the last minute.** If you leave it too long, you will discover that, like stamp collecting, you will have many 'doubles' for 2C3.1 but you are still looking for the elusive 2G4.1!
- **Consider appealing if you consider a decision to be unfair or unreasonable.** All police forces will have a published policy concerning appeals against assessment decisions which set out the grounds for an appeal and the processes involved. Normally the appeal is made to the person responsible for the PDU where the decision was made rather than to the assessor who made the decision.

6.4.5 Simulation

In some circumstances your force may consider it more appropriate to test your competence by using a simulation or role play (although this is more often used as a learning method) rather than by observing you in a real life situation. This is not just because of any safety considerations but sometimes because of the difficulty in arranging the necessary circumstances for you whilst on Supervised Patrol or because some situations are just so complex it makes sense to separate elements out for simulation. It is also the case that certain first aid skills (for example the use of realistic mannequins) are more appropriately practised through simulation than for real.

Be aware however, that, according to the rules of Skills for Justice, the scope for simulation is very limited (only certain elements of Units BE1, 2C1, 2C4, 2J1, 2J2, and 4G4 allow for any kind of simulation). Many elements of Units will not permit simulation to be used in lieu of the real thing (and in the case of NVQs these rules are mandatory). If simulation is used to assess you against an element then you may need to think about this a little differently. Simulations, unless particularly carefully designed and organized, always run the risks of any hypothetical situation (recollect those difficult interview questions that began with 'imagine the following')—that is, missing the rich detail of real-life contexts. Bear this in mind if undertaking an assessed simulation.

> **TASK 3**
>
> Is simulation allowed as evidence towards element 2K2.2, to 'conduct initial custody reception actions'?

6.4.6 When Should I Achieve a Unit?

There is no simple answer to this question; when you achieve a Unit will depend on your own circumstances and the arrangements put into place by your force. However, the IPLDP suggests the following timetable (we have used IPLDP notation but bear in mind that your force might use other means of describing the phases of training):

> **NOS Units and IPLDP Phases**
>
> **Phase 1 Induction**
> Evidence of the knowledge aspects (not the whole Unit) of Units AB1, AA1, 2C4, AE1, and AF1 and the whole of Unit 4G4 (the First Aid Unit).
> **Phase 2 Community Safety and Partnerships**
> Evidence towards the knowledge, performance criteria, and range of Units AB1 and AA1.
> **Phase 3 Supervised Patrol**
> Evidence towards completion of all remaining Units.
> **Phase 4 Independent Patrol**
> The emphasis during this phase is towards completion of all required NOS Units.

The advice of your police force is likely to be more detailed.

6.5   The Student Officer Role Profile

In section 6.3, we glanced at the competences and KUSAB that are used for the assessment of your capability in a range of jobs but principally in the role of patrol constable. We noted then that the first part of the integrated competency framework (ICF), shown in the table of core responsibilities, covers the Knowledge, Understanding and Skills part of your learning. This part (the second part of the ICF) deals with **attitudes** and **behaviours**: the last elements of KUSAB.

We refer you to Chapter 14 which deals with your potential development as a police officer once your initial training is over. You might also look at sections 4.9 and 5.16, where the discussions about diversity examine the detail of the attitudes and behaviours expected of a police officer dealing with people who are different to you and who may be vulnerable. You should also read that part of the discussion about interviewing in section 12.5 which deals with how to approach and obtain responses from vulnerable victims and witnesses. As you can see, the principles embodied in KUSAB and the integrated competencies are woven tightly into this Handbook, and you can dip into relevant parts of the framework in nearly all of the sections.

6.5.1   Attitudes and Behaviours

To follow our theme, we shall now look at the behavioural areas designated for the role of **patrol constable**. However, unlike specific job requirements which may change between roles, or have different emphases placed upon them (such as investigation for detectives, or driving competencies for traffic officers), the specified behaviours do not vary very much between roles. This is because they are seen as **generic** (constant or part of the standard parcel) and will require consistent application of the sorts of responses we have already discussed. The key behavioural areas are shown below:

Patrol Constable—Key behaviour areas

Behaviour area	Behaviour	Minimum grade required
Achieving results	Problem solving	C
	Personal responsibility	B
	Resilience	A
Working with others	Respect for race and diversity	A
	Team working	C
	Community and customer focus	C
	Effective communication	B

It is important that we look behind the headlines at this point, and discuss what forms of behaviours are expected.

> **TASK 4**
>
> Look back briefly at the discussion on diversity (in section 5.16) and remind yourself of the structure for assessing behaviours; then write it down.

You will see that each element of the behaviour (or behavioural area) is given **two evidence sections** together with **positive** and **negative indicators**. (Note, however, that the use of element here is a little different from the meaning of element in the NOS.)

These should not only inform how you structure the presentation of evidence of your competence in your SOLAP but also indicate to you precisely where the assessment of your performance will be focussed. Thus, if we look at **problem solving** (where your standard is expected to be C), the detail looks like this:

> **Behaviour: Problem solving**
>
> 1. Gathers information from a range of sources. Analyses information to identify problems and issues, and makes effective decisions.
> 2. Gathers enough relevant information to understand specific issues and events. Uses information to identify problems and draw logical conclusions. Makes good decisions.

What sort of evidence will help assessors in these areas? Both positive and negative indicators are used:

6.5.1.1 Positive indicators

- Identifies where to access information and retrieves it.
- Retrieves as much information as is appropriate on all aspects of a problem.
- Separates relevant information from irrelevant information, and important information from unimportant information.
- Takes in information quickly and accurately.
- Reviews all the information gathered to understand the situation and draw logical conclusions.
- Identifies and links causes and effects.
- Identifies what can and cannot be changed.
- Takes a systematic approach to solving problems.
- Remains impartial and avoids jumping to conclusions.
- Refers to procedures and precedents as necessary before making decisions.
- Makes good decisions that take account of all relevant factors.

(Adapted from Skills for Justice, 2003)

6.5.1.2 Negative indicators

On the other hand, negative indicators show where you will be marked down or assessed as less than adequate:

- Does not deal with problems in detail and does not identify underlying issues.
- Does not gather enough information before coming to conclusions.
- Does not consult other people who may have extra information.
- Does not research background.
- Shows no interest in gathering or using intelligence.
- Does not gather evidence.
- Makes assumptions about the facts of a situation.
- Does not notice problems until they have become significant issues.
- Becomes enmeshed in the detail of complex situations and cannot see the main issues.
- Reacts without considering all the angles.
- Becomes distracted by minor issues.
- Leaves others to solve problems and does not see it as part of the role.

(As before, adapted from Skills for Justice, 2003)

You can see from this that the negative indicators are not simply the opposite of the positive indicators, such as merely refraining from doing something you should. Rather it is about how well you understand what is required of you and how you respond to that expectation. Some of the negative indicators have to do with **passivity** too; the downside of sitting back and letting things happen around you, such as leaving it to others to solve problems, instead of attempting to take control of a situation and addressing matters.

It is not difficult to see why such emphasis is placed on problem-solving behaviour: very often, police arrive when a situation is chaotic, confused, or muddled. Much of the initial police response is concerned with bringing order to the situation and sorting out who did what to whom and who was involved. You will encounter this from your very first patrols at night, near pubs and clubs, where you will be expected to sort any problems out there and then, quickly and decisively, having regard for all the circumstances (or initially at least, observe more experienced colleagues doing so).

Let us look at another example which is considered of equal importance. These are the behavioural areas for **team working** (again, Grade C):

Behaviour: Team working

1. Develops strong working relationships inside and outside the team to achieve common goals. Breaks down barriers between groups and involves others in discussions and decisions.
2. Works effectively as a team member and helps [to] build relationships within [the team]. Actively helps and supports others to achieve team goals.

Again, these behaviours are underpinned by negative and positive indicators:

6.5.1.3 Negative indicators

- Does not volunteer to help team members.
- Is only interested in taking part in high-profile and interesting activities.
- Takes credit for successes without recognizing the contribution of others.
- Works to own agenda rather than contributing to team performance.
- Allows small exclusive groups of people to develop.
- Plays one person off against another.
- Restricts and controls what information is shared.
- Does not let people say what they think.
- Does not offer advice or get advice from others.
- Shows little interest in working jointly with other groups to meet the goals of everyone involved.
- Does not discourage conflict within the organization.

(Adapted from Skills for Justice, 2003)

We have all met people with some or all of these attributes. It is interesting and reassuring to note that these are precisely the behaviours which are **not** encouraged or rewarded in the police service. It is especially reassuring to those who may one day have to rely on members of the team pulling together. In a very real sense, entering a conflict situation with a colleague who does not contribute appropriately can be positively dangerous. Whilst many police forces encourage individuality, the exercise of initiative, and independence of thought and attitude, there is a fine dividing line between those attributes and selfish self-regard. You perhaps need to understand that co-operation does not mean that the individual is suppressed or diminished but that each person has the right to be heard and to make a contribution.

So much for the negative side. What positive things should you be striving for in order to do your job well? What tangible factors should outweigh the selfish?

6.5.1.4 Positive indicators

- Understands own role in a team.
- Actively takes part in team tasks in the workplace.
- Is open and approachable.
- Makes time to get to know people.
- Co-operates with and supports others.
- Offers help to other people.
- Asks for and accepts help when needed.
- Develops mutual trust and confidence in others.
- Willingly takes on unpopular or routine tasks.
- Contributes to team objectives no matter what the direct personal benefit may be.
- Acknowledges that there is often a need to be a member of more than one team.

(Adapted from Skills for Justice, 2003)

To the extent that these are ideal behaviours, we all should try to attain them, but they are especially important in the policing context. Much police work is repetitive, painstaking, and sometimes even boring. However, these tasks have to be done because otherwise some significant fact might be overlooked or some vital piece of evidence ignored. That is the reason why so much emphasis is placed on the behaviours which demonstrate that you can cope with complex and demanding tasks.

We have examined two of the key behavioural areas for patrol constable, but there are others and you should read the rest yourself. Ask your training staff for the Skills for Justice CD-ROM or for hard copies which you can look at in your own time.

6.6 The SOLAP

The SOLAP is the Student Officer Learning and Assessment Portfolio, a form of record of achievement that you will keep during your initial training. The SOLAP was an innovation of IPLDP, although every police force had something similar before April 2006 (usually called a PDP, and not universally popular). Forces sometimes emphasize that it is **your** portfolio, although you are no doubt aware that this does not make the portfolio confidential to you, nor does this ownership necessarily offer you any kind of protection in the case of legal action. These are early days for SOLAP and there is some uncertainty concerning the status of the contents of the document—for example, in terms of recording any disciplinary action that may be taken against you.

The SOLAP is either a physical document, or an electronic document stored in a folder on the force intranet or housed on a Virtual Learning Environment such as Blackboard. Although the SOLAP has to follow certain national requirements, forces are permitted to customize it for their own purposes: from the relatively trivial act of adding their own logos to the more significant step of deciding to release the SOLAP requirements to you in parts, rather than as a whole at the outset.

The SOLAP is likely to be a key document for you as it charts your claim to be a professional and competent student police officer who is ready for Confirmation as a constable. If your force offers an NVQ as part of its training, then the SOLAP also performs important functions in terms of accountability to an Awarding Body (see section 3.10).

6.6.1 Components of the SOLAP

A typical SOLAP will be made up of the following (the format may vary from force to force):

The SOLAP

Section	Contents	Comments
Chapter 1	Student Officer Personal Profile	You provide brief biographical details (name, DoB etc) together with a list of your prior educational and other achievements. You are expected to keep this up-to-date.
Chapter 2	Student Officer Role Profile	Information concerning the Student Officer Role Profile (see 6.5 above); including the ICF, the NOS, the PACs, assessment and appeals.
Chapter 3	Introduction to the Phases of Learning	A description of the four IPLDP phases (see 3.3.1).
Chapter 4	The Learning Modules	A description of the three sets of IPLDP Learning Modules (the IND, OP and LPG modules described in 2.4) and how the curriculum is structured.
Chapter 5	Learner Development Framework	A description of Learning Diaries (see 6.6.1.1 below) and Learning Development Reviews (see 6.6.1.2 below). You will be expected to keep a Learning Diary and take part in the Learning Development Reviews.
Chapter 6	Police Action Checklists	Information concerning the PACs (see 6.8 below). You need to achieve the PACs before Independent Patrol.

Section	Contents	Comments
Chapter 7	National Occupational Standards	Detailed information concerning the NOS for initial policing (see 6.4 above), at the level of Units and elements and also how these will be assessed. You need to achieve the twenty-two NOS Units to qualify.
Chapter 8	Assessment Process	Information concerning competence, collecting evidence, the assessment process (induction, planning etc) and a useful detailed example of an assessment activity.
Chapter 9	Overview of Assessment Methods	Note that this chapter is concerned with the assessment of your competence rather than more generally.
Chapter 10	Overview of Assessment	A description of the main forms of documentation involved in the assessment process. These include induction records, witness testimony forms, the evidence index and the CARs (see 6.6.1.3 below).
Chapter 11	Glossary of terms	A 'jargon-buster' of acronyms used in the IPLDP assessment process.

In addition there are a number of appendices which either contain additional information or templates for use to use in order to complete your SOLAP.

We now examine some of the key components of the SOLAP in more detail.

6.6.1.1 **The Learning Diary**

The **Learning Diary** is a structured account of your learning during your probationary period. It is, however, unlikely to consist of entries beginning 'and then I did this'. Instead most forces will expect you to write in a more reflective and evidenced manner and use given sub-headings. (Some forces emphasize the need for structure and criticality by renaming the Learning Diary a Reflective Diary or Reflective Journal.)

Under the IPLDP, the Learning Diary sub-headings normally reflect your stage of training (Home Office, 2004c). For example, during the initial induction phase in the first few weeks you might well be required to address sub-headings related to your introduction to the organization; during your community placement you will be asked to reflect on what you learned during the placement, and so on. Under IPLDP the Learning Diary is related to the first three phases of training (up to Independent Patrol) in the following way (Home Office, 2004c updated with Home Office, 2005d):

Learning Diary and IPLDP Phases

Phase	Learning Diary activities
1. Induction	Critical reflections on, for example, the introduction to your police force and the IPLDP, the training you received on Health & Safety, OST, the PNC, etc. How you are going to balance work with the other demands on your time, your relationship with others in training, the ethics and values of policing.
2. Community Safety & Partnerships	Critical reflections on, for example, working with the community, your experiences and learning during the community placement and how you will develop in the future.
3. Supervised Patrol	The entries may feature under seven headings that mirror the content of LPG 1: • Crime • Stop & Search • Protecting People • Police Policies and Procedures • Non-crime Incidents • Investigation and Interview • Road Policing You may be asked to summarize the main learning points and reflect on how this learning will be put into practice.

In most cases the Learning Diaries also have a 'golden thread' running through them in the shape of respect for diversity, ethics, relationships with colleagues, and health and safety. There is also normally a section for your trainers to complete. This is not only useful feedback but is also a way in which your force can monitor your completion of the diary. Although your Learning Diary is not formally assessed (in the way that a written examination would be) there is some scope for using the entries as partial evidence towards completion of some of the NOS elements. Section 4.12 of the Handbook provides a (fictitious) example of a possible Learning Diary entry.

6.6.1.2 Learning Development Reviews

The **Learning Development Reviews** and other forms of self-assessment give rise to more formal documents than the Learning Diary. The documents are based on structured meetings with your tutors and assessors. The meetings consist of reviews and critical self-assessment which you then write up as a formal document, based on the behavioural requirements and role profile of student police officers. The number of Learning Development Reviews that you take part in will differ from force to force but you will probably have around ten during your training. The reviews are documented in the SOLAP. However, there are **three key reviews** during your training which are of particular note:

* One for **Independent Patrol**, involving completion of the PAC (see sections 3.5 and 6.8).
* An **interim review**, for example after the first year of training.
* The final review for **Confirmation** (see section 3.6), probably involving completion of the NOS plus other professional requirements.

These reviews are essentially a progress report and an agreement of what actions you may need to take within a specified timescale. The SMART model of objective setting may be used when agreeing targets for future development: that is, you are expected to make your targets Specific, Measurable, Relevant, Achievable, and Timed. Note also that you might be asked to link the objectives you set for yourself with the behavioural areas of the ICF that we discussed earlier in this chapter.

It has also been suggested that this part of the SOLAP could also contain a record of any disciplinary matters. Chapter 7 of this Handbook describes the role of the Police Federation in representing the position of student police officers in matters of discipline.

6.6.1.3 Recording assessment

This is the final part of the SOLAP and it usually consists of a large number of documents related to your assessment. Perhaps the most important documents are the Assessment Reports, the Evidence Index, and the CARs.

Assessment Reports are completed by your assessor and are likely to form the bulk of your evidence for competence. An assessment plan is agreed in advance with you, and the assessment then undertaken. The plan is subsequently used and completed in terms of feedback and action planning. Assessors will complete a report for each NOS Unit that they assess and also make a note of what actions they directly observed (for example, how you may have treated a suspect when making an arrest). They will also make a note of what written evidence they may have examined (for example, your PNB), what questions they may have asked you (for example, to probe your knowledge or to discover your reasons for taking a certain action) and the responses that you made. You will be asked to countersign this record as a fair and accurate summary so you should make sure that you read it carefully.

The **Evidence Index** sets out clearly where the evidence for the claims of competence can be found. Each piece of evidence (for example, a PNB entry) may give rise to more than one claim for competence according to the performance criteria of the particular NOS Unit. Note, however, that the evidence itself is not normally kept in the SOLAP. You may well be asked to reference where this evidence may be found, due to both the volume and confidentiality of the material.

Cumulative Assessment Records (**CARs**) are records of the achievement of elements and Units of the NOS for initial policing. They are usually annotated through reference to the parallel

NOS Unit. For example, CAR 2A1 relates to Unit 2A1—'Gather and submit information that has the potential to support policing objectives', and hence will also be subdivided into the constituent elements of the Unit. The CAR describes where the evidence will be found that (in the case of 2A1.1) links with the nine performance criteria and the range (see section 6.4.2).

6.7 Assessment in Practice

In this part of chapter 6 we illustrate, in the form of an example, the links between the NOS (see section 6.4) and the SOLAP (see section 6.6).

Imagine that you are Sam Palmer, and whilst on Supervised Patrol you attend an incident of suspected shoplifting and make an arrest. You were accompanied by your assessor/tutor Pc Navarro. You complete a PNB entry concerning the circumstances of the incident, the arrest, and the other relevant details (see section 11.5). This one event could in fact be used as evidence against a number of the NOS elements—for example, potentially elements of AA1, 2C1, 2C3, 2C4, 2I1, and so on.

In fact the PNB entry in particular provides evidence that Sam has met performance criterion 7 of element 1A1.2, namely to 'record any **police actions** correctly and within the required time':

Element 1A1.2 Use police actions proportionately

Performance Criteria

(1 to 6 omitted) 7. Record any **police actions** correctly and within the required time.

The phrase 'police actions' is in bold which means that Sam also needs to consider the range statement for police actions:

Element 1A1.2 Use police actions proportionately

Range Statement

1. **Police Actions**
    1. Police Powers (statutory, non-statutory).
    2. Procedures.

In this case, the PNB entry is an example of range 1b 'Procedures' and so this too can be evidenced.

Sam then makes an entry in the Evidence Index (this is her 23rd entry):

Candidate: Sam Palmer

Assessor: Pc Navarro

Reference	Description of evidence
23	PNB entry made on 01/09/07

Note that Pc Navarro might well also complete a full assessment report concerning Sam's competence in responding to the incident and carrying out the arrest, although this would have been agreed with Sam in advance using an assessment plan. Sam would keep a copy of the report, give it a reference and add it to her Evidence Index. It is also possible that others involved, if suitably qualified to do so (for example, a more experienced student police officer who has already gained 1A1), could produce Witness Testimony that could also be referenced in the Evidence Index.

It is important to note that simply referencing and recording evidence is not sufficient to prove competence. Sam's evidence from the PNB entry will require signing off by an assessor.

The CAR for 1A1 under element 1A1.2 is then completed (this is the second piece of evidence that Sam has so far accumulated for performance criterion 7):

CAR for Element 1A1.2

Performance Criteria	Ref 1	Ref 2	Ref 3
1. Consider options . . .			
2. Balance the . . .			
3. Use the . . .			
4. Deal with..			
5. Use legitimate . . .			
6. Ensure that..			
7. Record any police actions correctly and within the required time	09	23	

(Unfortunately some police force CARs also use the word 'ref' as in 'reference' when making a reference to the reference in the Evidence Index which can be confusing!)

There are then usually a number of summative documents largely concerned with the achievement of the NOS, including **Unit Assessment Summary Sheets** (for each of the NOS units) and a **Summative Assessment Record** (sometimes Summative Assessment **Report**) that confirms that all of the NOS Units have been met and confirmed by the assessor, the internal verifier (a suitably qualified person that checks the decision-making of the assessor) and the external verifier.

6.8 The PAC

The Police Action Checklist (the PAC) is part of the system for checking if you are ready to begin Independent Patrol, that is to undertake the duties of a police officer without the need for constant supervision by more experienced colleagues. It does not, of course, mean that you have now reached the end of your training, but it does mean that you know enough and have sufficient skills to be able to conduct many activities without the presence of an assessor constable. In many forces you will still attend formal training and in all forces you will certainly be continuing to collect evidence towards completion of the remaining NOS. (Under the IPLDP for example, you are meant to have at least thirty days of 'protected learning time' after being granted Independent Patrol and before Confirmation.)

The PAC is cross-referenced to a subset of the NOS. For example, the requirement that you are able to 'obtain a DNA sample' is linked to NOS Unit 2K2 that you are able to 'present detained persons for custody'. It follows that completing your PAC is a process that complements the achievement of the NOS and is not in competition or separate from this process.

The Police Action Checklist has ten main headings and each heading is broken into a number of specific requirements.

Police Action Checklist

Safety first

- First Aid
- Health and Safety—Dynamic assessment

- Health and Safety—Reporting
- Personal Safety Training (PST/OST etc)
- Fitness test—according to force policy

Information management

- Utilize the PNC.
- Utilize force information management systems (eg intelligence/crime reporting/command and despatch).

Patrol

- Demonstrate patrol priorities in accordance with NIM.
- Demonstrate communication with control rooms.

Search

- Conduct stops.
- Demonstrate lawful search—persons.
- Demonstrate lawful search—premises.
- Demonstrate lawful search—vehicles.

Investigation

- Use CCTV during an investigation.
- Demonstrate initial crime scene management.
- Conduct the initial investigation and report of missing persons.
- Conduct the initial investigation and report of volume crime according to National Policing Plan.
- Conduct the initial investigation and report of volume crime according to Local Policing Plan.
- Conduct the initial investigation and report of a domestic incident.
- Conduct the initial investigation and report of racist and/or hate crime.
- Conduct the initial investigation and report in relation to a child protection and/or vulnerable person incident.
- Conduct the initial investigation and report of a sudden death.
- Demonstrate initial RTC scene management.
- Interview—conduct a witness interview using the PEACE model.
- Interview—conduct a suspect interview using the PEACE model.
- Demonstrate correct handling of exhibits.
- Provide support and advice to victims and witnesses.
- Respond to developments during an investigation.

Disposal

- Report for summons.
- Make lawful arrests.
- Convey a suspect into custody.

Custody office procedures

- Present suspect to custody in accordance with force procedures.
- Obtain fingerprints.
- Obtain photographs.
- Obtain DNA sample.
- Complete pre-charge procedures.

Finalize investigations

- Complete case files (eg summons and post charge files).
- Prepare for court or other hearings.
- Present evidence to court or other hearings.

Road policing

- Check driving documents.
- Demonstrate vehicle stops.
- Complete traffic documents—including HO/RT1/FPN(E)/CLE2/VDRS.
- Demonstrate correct administration of the appropriate tests for drink/drugs driving offences.

Property

- Complete property register.

The PACs are largely concerned with performance and, as the term 'checklist' suggests, it is not generally used as a tool for student officer development. The checklist is also usually contextualized—that is, your performance is also judged in the light of your behaviour, the role profile for a student police officer (see section 6.5) and, in particular, your ability to communicate with others and your understanding of the needs of policing diverse communities.

Before you can be considered for Independent Patrol an assessor will confirm your competence against all forty-four or so headings in the checklist. Note that successful completion of the PAC does not necessarily **guarantee** that you will be eligible for Independent Patrol. Some police forces will expect more from you—for example, to have reached a certain level in terms of driving skills.

6.9 PIP Level 1

In 2004, the Home Office and ACPO commissioned the NCPE to construct a Professionalising Investigation Programme (PIP) in response to a widespread perceived need to improve the quality of police investigation of crime (Centrex, 2005). A total of four levels are envisaged:

Professionalising Investigation Programme

Investigative Level	Example of Role	Description of Typical Investigative Activity
Level 1	**Patrol Constable**/Police Staff/Supervisors	Investigation of volume crime
Level 2	Dedicated Investigator, eg CID officer	Substantive investigation into more serious and problem offences, including road traffic deaths
Level 3	Senior Investigating Officer	Lead investigator in cases of murder, stranger rape, kidnap, or crimes of complexity. Category A, B–C
Level 4	Principal Investigating Officer/Officer in Overall Command (OIOC)	Critical, complex, protracted, and/or linked serious crime. Category A +

(Derived from Centrex, 2005, our emphasis)

It follows that during your training you will be assessed against PIP Level 1. In a sense this should be automatic as PIP Level 1 is integrated into the IPLDP curriculum and has also been mapped against a subset of the NOS—Units 2G2 to 'Conduct priority and volume investigations', 2H1 to 'Interview victims and witnesses', and 2H2 to 'Interview suspects'. These standards feature within the operational modules of the IPLDP—for example, 2H1 and 2H2 have been mapped against OP6 to 'Prepare, conduct and evaluate interviews'. It is therefore not likely that you will achieve PIP Level 1 until the end of the first year of training at the earliest and more likely it will be during the second year.

After you have successfully completed PIP Level 1 you will be 'signed off' as a Level 1 investigator and be registered with your force as having reached this standard. (Level 3 PIP investigators will be registered at the national level.) However, it is likely that you will have to demonstrate on a regular basis (perhaps annually) how you have maintained the level of your skills and knowledge in order to remain registered. At the time of writing the system for doing so has not been agreed but may take the form of evidence in the PDP which replaces your SOLAP after you have been Confirmed.

6.10 Answers to Tasks

TASK 1

We give a variety of definitions in the text immediately after the task.

TASK 2

You should have found that the knowledge and understanding requirements of Unit 4G4 are:

1. Limitations and risks of applying first aid to others.
2. How to detect an obstructed airway and methods of clearing obstruction.
3. How to check for signs of life and for life-threatening conditions.
4. Methods of CPR and how to use this appropriately.
5. How to manage an unconscious casualty and the main causes of unconsciousness.
6. Precautions to be taken when performing CPR.
7. Different types of wound and their treatment.
8. Methods for controlling bleeding.
9. Signs and symptoms of shock.
10. Recognition and treatment of sprains, strains, and fractures.
11. Main safety considerations when dealing with burns or scalds.
12. How to recognize and assess the severity and extent of injuries.
13. Appropriate treatments for hypothermia, frostbite, heat-stroke and heat exhaustion.
14. How to recognize and respond to local danger and risks when dealing with casualties.

TASK 3

No, simulation is not permitted for element 2K2.2.

TASK 4

You were asked to read an earlier part of the Handbook.

7 | Induction into a Police Organization

7.1   Chapter Briefing

This chapter will assist you during your induction into your police organization. The process of induction involves an understanding of your position within the organization together with an appreciation of your own responsibilities and the responsibilities of those around you. Normally the formal stage of induction occupies the first three to five weeks of your training (IPLDP Phase 1) although a number of aspects are likely to be revisited at later stages during your two-year probationary period.

7.1.1   Aims of the Chapter

This chapter will enable you to:

- understand the basic configuration of the rank structure in policing;
- gain an overview of a typical police force organizational structure;

- learn the phonetic alphabet when required by your trainers;
- understand the fundamentals of safe police practice;
- learn something of the background to the use of Information Technology systems by police organizations, particularly the PNC;
- appreciate the need to respect confidentiality but also acknowledge the need to make information available;
- understand the milestone of attestation, whilst appreciating that the staging of attestation has proved problematic for the service;
- understand the role of the attested student police officer as a constable in terms of the codes, rules, and regulations governing conduct;
- further develop understanding of interpersonal skills such as communication and listening;
- develop the underpinning knowledge required for a number of NOS elements, several of the PAC headings and entries for your Learning Diary Phase 1 and the CARs of your SOLAP.

7.1.2 Police Action Checklist

This chapter will provide you with some of the underlying knowledge and theory to meet aspects of the following requirements of the Police Action Checklist:

7.1.2.1 Safety First

- First Aid.
- Health and Safety—Dynamic assessment.
- Personal Safety Training (PST/OST etc).

7.1.2.2 Information Management

Utilize the PNC.

7.1.3 National Occupational Standards

This chapter will provide you with some of the knowledge required to demonstrate the following NOS elements.

> **National Occupational Standard Units and Elements**
>
> Unit 4G4 Administer First Aid
> Unit AE1 Maintain and develop your own knowledge, skills and competence
> AB1.2 Maintain the security of information.
> 2C4.1 Defuse aggressive and abusive behaviour.
> 2C4.2 Use personal safety and restraint techniques.
> AF1.1 Identify the hazards and evaluate the risks in your workplace.
>
> You should refer to Chapter 6 for general information and advice concerning the NOS elements. There is a possibility that you may be able to gain the whole of Unit 4G4 during the induction period of training.

7.1.4 IPLDP Phases and Modules

This chapter will provide you with resources to support the following Induction Modules of the IPLDP.

> IND 1 Underpinning ethics/values of the police service (particularly IND 1.2 Applying police ethics).
> IND 2 Foster people's equality, diversity and rights (particularly IND 2.4 Provide information about the complaints system; IND 2.8 Demonstrate confidentiality of information and IND 2.9 Disclosing information to others).
> IND 5 Ensure your own actions reduce the risk to health and safety.
> IND 8 Operation of information technology systems.
> IND 9 Administer First Aid.

Much of the content of this chapter relates to IPLDP Phase 1 Induction.

7.1.5 SOLAP

The contents of this chapter are relevant to the knowledge evidence requirements of CARs 1A4, 2C4, 4G2, and 4G4.

7.1.6 Learning Diary Phases

The contents of this chapter may provide you with stimulus material for completion of your Learning Diary (Phase 1) and the following headings in particular:

- Introduction to the Organisation;
- Information and Communication Technology;
- Health and Safety;
- Ethics and values of the police;
- Rights and responsibilities.

7.1.7 IPLDP Learning Requirement

This chapter is relevant to the following sections of the IPLDP Learning Requirement: 2.6, 4.9, 5.1, and 5.2.

7.2 Introduction

Induction is the process of 'bringing in' or initiation. In some senses it also refers to a kind of transformation—in this case from being a member of the public to becoming both a member of the public and a police constable. Normally, this transformation will take a significant length of time. Although it is suggested that the induction phase of IPLDP should take between three and five weeks (Home Office, 2004c), the actual process of induction is more likely to be measured in months. This is because it is more than simply learning the rules of the organization: it involves more fundamental shifts in the way that you organize both your personal and professional life, and the ways in which you think about those individuals and communities around you.

You will discover that there are certain symbolic aspects to this induction, such as the ceremony that surrounds attestation. In many cases though, induction takes more tangible forms, such as learning your way around the organization in terms of its structures, locations, and people. Perhaps another way of explaining what induction really means is to describe it as an assimilation into an organizational culture or cultures. In policing, the process of 'buying into' the existing organizational culture has not been without controversy. For some observers, the prevailing cultures within the police have often been characterized as male-dominated and exclusionary. Allied to this view is the suggestion that initial police training moves you from being an individual to being part of a group, and into a group where it is 'dangerous to be different'. (This is the so-called police 'canteen culture' that you may hear or read about.) The police service is aware of these criticisms and one of the driving forces behind recent changes to initial police training is to create a learning environment which is more inclusive.

In this chapter, you will learn some of the small but important details which make up the organization you are joining: the police service. It may be that you are familiar with the police already, perhaps by working as a special constable, or as a member of the police support staff, even as a PCSO or as a family member or friend of a police officer before joining 'the regulars'. You may have had some of the material which we are about to look at, in briefing packs when you applied to join, and some elements, especially police rank structures, may have been part of the student police officer package when you received your acceptance letter. It may be that your force is well organized and proactive, so much so that you already know at least some of what follows.

However, we are going to work on the assumption that you know little about this police organization that you are joining. We begin your induction by examining the rank structure, where badges denoting rank for uniformed officers are shown on epaulettes and cap peak-decorations denote rank more generally (the more silver braid on show, the higher the rank, as a general rule). From looking at the rank structure, we move on to examine how a typical police force is structured and organized. Your own force will probably vary in detail from the general picture we present here, but most forces will have most of what we describe. Then we look at the phonetic alphabet, which assigns words to letters of the alphabet. This is used so that letters—for example, registration plates or the spelling of a surname—may be accurately communicated when using a radio or mobile phone. The purpose of giving each letter a different name is to avoid confusion over letters which sound the same, such as 'P', 'B', and 'D'; no-one can confuse Papa, Bravo, and Delta because they all sound so different.

Understanding the role of Health and Safety is an important part of a police officer's ability to make risk assessments, both for yourself and for others, and this is often covered in conjunction with First Aid, a vital skill for patrol constables. Your own safety and that of others will be covered in Personal Safety Training (the title varies between forces), where you will learn self-defence, how to manage angry and tense situations, and the appropriate use of rigid pattern handcuffs, the ASP baton, and incapacitant spray.

From these tools we move to look at operating IT systems (an increasingly important part of information management) and what is done with information, including matters covering confidentiality as well as the implications of the Freedom of Information Act. Finally, we look at your attestation and role as a constable. We look at the Code of Conduct (and refer you again to the discussions about ethics and corruption which we covered in section 5.4) and Police Regulations, and we talk about conduct, misconduct, discipline, and complaints. We then introduce your staff association, the Police Federation, as well as looking at specialist support groups such as the British Association of Women Police officers, the National Black Police Association, and the Gay Police Association. Finally we look at the importance of effective communication and your engagement with the community which you will police.

7.3   Police Ranks

You may sometimes hear your police force referred to as a 'disciplined organization'. This refers not only to the need for self-discipline and restraint but also to the fact that at least parts of the organization (those parts concerned with police officers) are organized into ranks in a hierarchical fashion, involving the issuing and receiving of orders. Apart from the MPS and one or two other forces, the rank structure (and the associated badges on the epaulettes of uniforms) are as follows:

Rank Structure

In order of increasing superiority:

- Constable
- Sergeant
- Inspector
- Chief Inspector
- Superintendent
- Chief Superintendent
- Assistant Chief Constable
- Deputy Chief Constable
- Chief Constable

In the non-uniformed equivalents Detective often precedes the rank, eg Detective Chief Inspector.

The insignia of the ranks are as follows (as before, this may vary from force to force, as, for example, in the case of the PSNI):

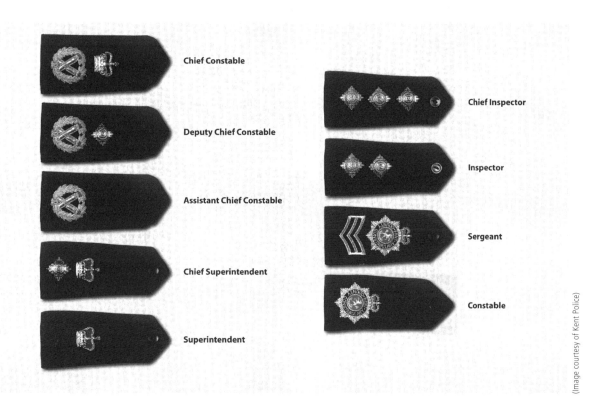

(Image courtesy of Kent Police)

In the MPS the rank structure has three additional tiers, shown in bold below:

MPS Rank Structure

- Constable
- Sergeant
- Inspector
- Chief Inspector
- Superintendent
- Chief Superintendent
- **Commander**
- **Deputy Assistant Commissioner**
- **Assistant Commissioner**
- Deputy Commissioner
- Commissioner

The City of London Police is a little different again.

You should also take the time to familiarize yourself with the insignia of uniformed members of the extended police family, such as special constables and PCSOs (see section 5.17).

TASK 1

Construct some memory cards to help you learn the police ranks and their associated insignia. Memory cards are best made from thick paper or cardboard (you may have used them as a child!). On one side of card put the rank, the other side the associated insignia, like so:

Superintendent

Now take cards at random from your collection. If the name of the rank is given then describe the insignia. Reverse the card and check your answer. If the insignia is given, then you need to name the rank. As before, turn over to check your answer.

Keep playing (alone or in a group) until you have memorized all the ranks and insignia.

(Image courtesy of Kent Police)

7.4 Typical Police Organizational Structure

The following is a typical police force structure for organizations with 6,000 plus staff (although remember that variations on this basic structure are probable):

Typical police force structure

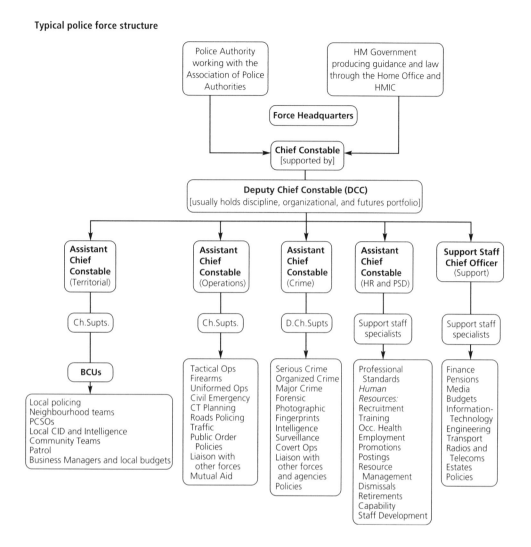

TASK 2

Learn the names and ranks of the individuals important to your training. For example, who is the ACC responsible for training? Who are the superintendents or chief superintendents responsible for the BCUs where you are likely to undertake Supervised Patrol?

7.5   The Phonetic Alphabet

If you have ever attempted to spell out a word on the phone to another person you have probably experienced the difficulty of clarifying the difference between 'm' and 'n', 's' and 'f' and so on. Mistakes made in the context of ordinary phone calls are seldom life-threatening, but if these same mistakes were made during a police communication it could prove costly, both in time and in terms of your safety and the safety of others. For this reason the 'phonetic alphabet' (sometimes referred to as the 'radio alphabet') was developed and subsequently adopted by police forces throughout the UK. Instead of using the letters themselves, you use instead the phonetic equivalent. So instead of saying 'a' you say 'alpha'. (There are similar problems when using numbers—for example, five and nine. These are sometimes replaced by 'fyfe' and 'niner' respectively).

The following is a list of the phonetic alphabet as normally employed by police forces in the UK (and beyond). You may well be asked to memorize and use it.

The phonetic alphabet					
a	Alpha	j	Juliet	s	Sierra
b	Bravo	k	Kilo	t	Tango
c	Charlie	l	Lima	u	Uniform
d	Delta	m	Mike	v	Victor
e	Echo	n	November	w	Whisky, Whiskie or Whiskey
f	Foxtrot	o	Oscar		(but same pronunciation)
g	Golf	p	Papa	x	X-ray
h	Hotel	q	Quebec	y	Yankee
i	India	r	Romeo	z	Zulu

(For a time 'Indigo' was used instead of 'India' but this practice is now very uncommon in police circles.)

TASK 3

Learn the phonetic alphabet. There are various ways of doing this, including using memory cards as in Task 2. One way of testing yourself is to spell out the names of family and friends.

7.6   Fitness Training

In order to join the police you will have undertaken the Police Initial Recruitment Test. As part of the test, your level of fitness will have been assessed in two main areas, namely endurance and dynamic strength ('push and pull'). The process of fitness testing is known as the Job Related Fitness Test (JRFT). As a student police officer, your force will expect you to maintain a minimum standard of fitness that will probably be based upon the JRFT. (If, after Confirmation, you subsequently join specialist departments such as Firearms then there may be an ongoing fitness requirement.)

Soon after joining you may be required to take a new fitness test, using the JRFT. This typically happens after about week three of training. At this time you will be tested again for endurance and dynamic strength.

7.6.1   Endurance

If your new endurance assessment is based upon the JRFT, then you will be required to run a 'bleep test' between two fifteen metre points in time with a series of bleeps played to you while you carry out the exercise. The amount of time between the bleeps will decrease successively through a series of five levels and therefore you will need to run faster as the exercise progresses.

7.6.2   Dynamic Strength

You may need to pass another test in dynamic strength which will involve using the Dyno ergometer ('push and pull') machine. In the pushing exercise you will be required to perform three warm-up pushes, and then the test will consist of five pushes at maximum effort with three seconds break in between each one. You will need an average of 34 kg to pass.

The pulling exercise will take place at the other end of the machine where you will be required to warm up with three pulls and then give maximum effort to five further pulls reaching an average of 35 kg to pass. The machine will calculate the average for you.

If you fail the fitness test then you will be given an opportunity to re-take the test, probably at about week nine. Obviously, if this happens then you will be well advised to attempt to improve your fitness in the intervening weeks. Forces are normally supportive in this matter (they appreciate that there may have been a long period between you undertaking the JRFT as part of the recruitment process and then starting). They may suggest a programme of activities such as swimming, road running, gymnasium circuits, rowing, or cycling, together with aerobic exercise.

If you fail a second time, you will probably be given a final attempt. Failure at the third and final attempt may lead to you being 'Reg 13'ed' and dismissed from the force (see section 3.8 above). However, policy can vary and you should consult your force on this and perhaps also your Police Federation representative (see section 7.17 below.)

7.7 Health and Safety

By its very nature, policing has always been and will continue to be a potentially hazardous occupation. Whilst risks are present in all work activities, operational staff are more frequently exposed to risks, whether dealing with environmental incidents or disorderly behaviour. Therefore, health and safety is not just another bureaucratic burden, but an issue you must consider and have in mind at all times during your day-to-day work to prevent people getting injured or becoming ill. After all, ill health or an accident could reduce the quality of your life and adversely affect the lives of those around you. Health and safety duties are covered by sections 2 to 7 of the Health and Safety at Work Act etc 1974, becoming applicable to police officers, special constabulary officers and cadets, by virtue of the Police (Health and Safety) Act 1997. Home Office publications from 1996 provide guidance for police managers. Your force will also have its own published health and safety policy.

All employers have a duty to ensure (as far as is reasonably practicable) the health, safety, and welfare of their employees. Each employee has a duty to take reasonable care for their own health and safety and that of other persons who may be affected by their acts or omissions. In other words, you are expected to look after yourself and the people around you.

This section will provide some of the knowledge required to attain the following NOS elements:

National Occupational Standard Elements

AF1.1   Identify the hazards and evaluate the risks in your workplace.

AF1.2   Reduce the risks to health and safety in your workplace.

This section is also linked with PAC heading 'Safety First' and in particular the sub-headings:

- Health & Safety—Legislation;
- Health & Safety—Dynamic assessment.

You will also find health and safety addressed during the IPLDP Induction Module IND 5 'Ensure your own actions reduce the risks to health and safety'.

7.7.1 The Employer's Role in Health and Safety

Section 2(2) of the Health and Safety at Work etc Act (HSWA) sets out the role of employers in relation to the health and safety of their employees, and states that employers are responsible for:

- providing and maintaining plant and systems of work that are, so far as is reasonably practicable, safe, and without risks to health;
- making safe arrangements for the use, handling, storage, and transport of articles and substances;
- providing necessary information, instruction, training, and supervision for ensuring, so far as is reasonably practicable, the health and safety at work of employees;
- maintaining places of work under the employer's control in a condition which is safe and free from health risks, with safe means of entry and exit;

- providing and maintaining a working environment for employees that is, so far as is reasonably practicable, safe, without risks to health, and has adequate facilities for their welfare at work.

(Adapted from the Home Office publication *A Guide for Police Managers*, 1997)

7.7.2 The Employee's Role in Health and Safety

Health and safety legislation places general duties on employees while they are at work. It requires an employee:

- to take reasonable care for their own health and safety and that of other persons who may be affected by his or her acts or omissions (s 7(a));
- to co-operate with their employer to enable the employer to comply with statutory duties for health and safety (s 7(b));
- to use correctly all work items provided by their employer, in accordance with their training and instructions received (Reg 14(1) Management of Health and Safety etc Work Regulations 1999);
- to inform their employer, or the person responsible for health and safety, of any work situation which might present a serious and imminent danger and any shortcoming in the health and safety arrangements (Reg 14(2) Management of Health and Safety etc Work Regulations 1999);.

(Adapted from the Home Office publication *A Guide for Police Managers*, 1997)

7.7.3 Hazards, Risks, and Threat Level

Consider a student police officer on foot patrol. What are the potential threats to the health and safety of a student police officer on foot?

You have probably thought of several scenarios in which the student police officer could be harmed. But how much harm, and how likely is it to happen? This is a matter of judgement for each different situation, but it makes it easier to judge if you think of each type of harm in terms of the **hazard**, the **risk**, and the **threat level**.

A **hazard** is something with a potential to cause harm, for example:

- slipping over on a wet surface;
- being hit by moving traffic;
- seizing drugs and used needles;
- falling from a height;
- being hit by a meteorite;
- being in proximity to a person with an infectious disease.

The **risk** is the likelihood of such an event actually happening. You might have already thought that some hazards are more likely to happen than others and that the likelihood of such events needs to be taken into account when assessing the overall threat of an activity.

The **threat level** (sometimes referred to as overall risk) is a combination of the hazard and the risk. (Note the possibility of confusing risk and overall risk. You will find the word risk may be used in these two different ways, and you will need to seek clarification from someone using the term risk if the context does not make their meaning clear.)

Some examples will help you see the interaction between hazard, risk, and threat level.

1. Death by meteorite—the hazard is very high as meteorites are heavy and fall from the sky at high speeds. But the risk is low as this event is very unlikely to occur. So the threat level is low.
2. Bruising from arresting a drunken suspect—the hazard is minor. However, the risk is high as this is quite likely to occur. But the threat level is low as the consequences are unlikely to be serious.
3. Gun-shot wounds when pursuing armed suspects—the hazard is serious, and there is quite a high risk of shots being fired. In this situation the threat level is high (and special precautions should be taken).

So there are varying levels of hazard and risk; each may be formally rated as high, medium, or low. The combined effect of the hazard and risk is the threat level.

7.7.4   Hazard Criteria

Remember, the hazard level is about how serious the consequences would be if the event occurs. The formal levels of hazard level classification are:

- High   Death, major injury, or serious illness may result
- Medium   Serious injuries or ill health; off work for more than three days
- Low   Less serious illness or injury; off work for less than three days

7.7.5   Risk Criteria

The risk level is about how likely it is to occur, and the levels are described as follows:

- High   It is very likely or near certain to occur
- Medium   It is likely to occur
- Low   It is very unlikely to occur

7.7.6   Threat Level Grid

The level of hazard and risk both need to be taken into account when assessing the threat level. The grid below shows different combinations of hazard and risk, and the resulting threat levels.

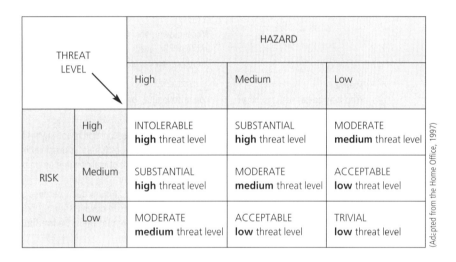

Another way of looking at assessing the threat level is to multiply the hazard and risk in an equation: **hazard × risk = threat level.**

(For those of you who are more mathematically minded, this is not the conventional kind of formula—after all there are no numbers to put into the formula—but just a way of helping you to remember the relationship.)

This shows clearly that it is the **combination** of hazard and risk that determines the threat level.

Consider another example. You are on duty at the scene of a road traffic crash. Your crew member is dealing with an injured person in one of the vehicles and you direct the traffic.

Hazards	You could be struck by a motor vehicle and your crew member could also be hit whilst attending to the injured person, therefore the hazard level is high, as death or major injury is likely to occur if another vehicle collides with you or your colleague.
Risk	Take into account day or night time, volume of traffic, weather conditions, and location. The risk level is medium as it is likely or possible that you may be struck by a vehicle.
Threat level	The threat level is therefore calculated to be substantial.

7.7.7 Control Measures

Control measures are steps that you can take to lower the risk and therefore reduce the threat level. You could use a five-step approach to assess the threat level and the control measures required.

Threat level assessment

Step 1 Identify the hazards.
Step 2 Who may be harmed and how?
Step 3 Evaluate the risks.
Step 4 Record your findings.
Step 5 Review your assessment from time to time and revise it if necessary.

Let us look again at the earlier example of foot patrol in section 7.7.3 and make an assessment of the risks involved so that we can put control measures into place to lower the threat level.

Threat level assessment example

Step 1	
Identify the hazards	Whilst you use the road network as a pedestrian you are exposed to danger from moving vehicles, and if a collision takes place, death or major injury is likely to occur.
	Whilst moving about on foot you face unpredictable confrontation with members of the public, and if a weapon is used, death or major injury is likely to occur. Therefore the hazard level would be **high**.
Step 2	
Who may be harmed and how?	You, a colleague, or a member of the public.
Step 3	
Evaluate the risks	Your up-to-the minute location is not always known and you are sometimes alone, as a result of which harm is possible/likely to occur.
	You are always at risk of walking into an unexpected situation in which harm is possible/likely to occur.
	You may face radio communication, reception and transmission difficulties, or faulty systems as a result of which harm is possible/likely to occur.
	Therefore the risk potential would be **medium** as there is a likely or possible risk that harm would occur.
Step 4	
Record your findings	Using the threat level grid, the threat level is assessed as **high** and therefore you should use control measures to lower the threat level.
Step 5	
Review your assessment from time to time, and revise it if necessary	

What control measures could be used to lower the threat level?

You may have considered the following:

- adopting the correct procedures that you have been trained in in relation to the road network, wearing the correct personal protective equipment (fluorescent), and using your first aid training if required;
- applying what you have learnt: control and restraint techniques, firearms training and knife awareness, and using personal protection equipment;
- keeping the Control Room updated with your location;
- using your local knowledge and requesting all available information to assess situations;
- being aware of the limitations of communications equipment.

TASK 4

We are not always good at judging risk. As an exercise, arrange the following risks in order of their likelihood for the average person in the UK, putting the most likely first. They are given to you in a random order.

The likelihood of death in the next year:

- by falling down stairs;
- through being struck by lightning;
- in an aircraft crash;
- in a train crash;
- in a cycling accident;
- as the victim of homicide;
- by drowning in a bath;
- as a consequence of lung cancer.

(Adapted from Haigh, 2006)

TASK 5

You are carrying out a search of a person (under s 1 of the PACE Act 1984, see section 8.5). What are your considerations in relation to yourself and your colleagues' safety whilst carrying out this search? What is your estimation of the threat level and what, if anything, is required to lower this level?

Completion of Task 5 will assist you in preparing to meet NOS standard AF1.1 'Identify the hazards and evaluate the risks in your workplace'. In turn, this links with PAC heading 'Safety First' and the checklist sub-headings 'Health & Safety—Legislation' and 'Health & Safety—Dynamic assessment'.

7.8 First Aid Training

It is the duty of every police officer to 'protect life' (see section 7.13 below). Inevitably you will find yourself attending accidents or scenes of crimes where there are seriously injured people. You may also be called upon by members of the public to assist in helping family members, friends, or strangers who are suffering medical conditions ranging from a sprained ankle or scalding by hot water through to heart attacks or epileptic seizures. The public will expect you to know what to do. Although you can expect specialized medical personnel to be present (or on their way) on most occasions, you will almost certainly encounter situations where not only are you the 'first officer on the scene' but also the first person on the scene with any kind of training for dealing with emergencies.

It is for this reason that, during the induction phase of your training, you will receive instruction in how to administer basic first aid. It is likely that you will be assessed against NOS Unit 4G4 ('Administer First Aid') which has four elements:

Elements of Unit 4G4—Administer First Aid

4G4.1 Respond to the needs of casualties with minor injuries.
4G4.2 Respond to the needs of casualties with major injuries.
4G4.3 Respond to the needs of unconscious casualties.
4G4.4 Perform cardio-pulmonary resuscitation (CPR).

Skills for Justice inform us that that the unit has been 'imported' from the Royal Marines Public Services NOS (Unit 4) and was developed by the British Red Cross in consultation with the St John Ambulance Service.

First Aid is also one of the headings in the Police Action Checklist and hence the successful completion of First Aid Training is likely to be a necessary condition of achieving Independent Patrol (see section 3.5 above). At the time of writing, the precise content of IPLDP-compliant First Aid training was not known. However, it is likely to contain some or all of the following:

- **Managing scenes and casualties:** for example, assessing the extent of casualties, communicating with others.
- **Basic Life Support (BLS) for Adults:** an algorithm of actions to administer immediate life support including the need to first ensure the safety of yourself and others, to check for a response from the injured person, the actions required in the event of a response or no response, the checking of airways and breathing and actions in the event of breathing (eg recovery position) and no breathing (eg chest compression, rescue breaths), performing cardio-pulmonary resuscitation (CPR).
- **Basic Life Support (BLS) for Infants and Children:** variations on the system used for adults.
- **Specific critical medical conditions:** this may include shock, bleeding, spinal injuries, heart attacks, and epilepsy.
- **Choking:** techniques employed to counter choking.
- **Sprains, strains, and fractures:** dealing with broken bones and similar injuries.
- **Scalds and burns:** methods of dealing with possibly life-threatening injuries in the short term before more specialist medical treatment can be obtained.
- **Hypothermia, frostbite, heat-stroke, and heat exhaustion:** ways to treat potentially difficult medical conditions especially when the individuals concerned are vulnerable.

TASK 6

Read and reflect on the contents of Chapter 10 ('First Aid') of the 1999 Macpherson Inquiry into the death of Stephen Lawrence. It is freely available on the internet at the site:

<http://www.archive.official-documents.co.uk/document/cm42/4262/sli-10.htm>.

Undertaking this task may provide you with stimulus material for completing an entry in your Learning Diary, Phase 1 under the 'Health and Safety' heading.

7.9 Personal Safety Training

Police officers are permitted to use reasonable force if necessary to prevent crime or to arrest a person. This right exists under common law and s 3 of the Criminal Law Act 1967. Section 117 of the PACE Act 1984 also allows a police officer to use reasonable force to exercise powers granted by that Act. You may also use reasonable force in your own self-defence (see *R v McInnes* [1971] 1 WLR 1600(CA)). However, in all cases the force used must be **proportionate** and exercised with due regard to the human rights of the individuals concerned.

You will receive practical training in both protecting yourself and others from attack and also how to use reasonable force against others. In most police forces this is referred to as Personal Safety Training (PST) or the Personal Safety Programme although you might also hear reference to Officer Safety Training (OST). (One reason why PST is now preferred as a title is that the training, or at least parts of it, is also undertaken by some members of the extended police family, see section 5.17.) The relevant NOS element is 2C4.2, to 'use personal safety and restraint techniques'.

The training you receive will take place in specialist facilities and will probably last for five to ten days.

As further reading, you might like to consult the ACPO Centrex 'Personal Safety Manual' and the ACPO 'Guidelines on the use of Handcuffs and Incapacitant Spray' available from your force.

These are the typical components of PST:

- **Conflict management:** for example, typical signs of potential conflict.
- **Searching people and places:** for example, health and safety when searching people with hidden weapons.
- **Protective equipment:** for example, body armour, baton, and 'less lethal weaponry' such as the Tazer.
- **Use of handcuffs and limb restraints:** for example, the use of the 'Speedcuff' rigid handcuffs and leg restraints.
- **'Unarmed' skills of self-protection:** for example, 'distraction strikes'.
- **Particular considerations when attending scenes:** for example, possible actions to be taken in the event of attending a person experiencing problems in water.
- **Edged weapon skills:** for example, the appropriate responses to those carrying edged weapons such as knives.
- **Incapacitant sprays:** for example, the use of PAVA (Captor spray).
- **Use of batons and ASPs:** for example, the use of the 21 inch expandable baton (the ASP) and the Arnold baton.

Successful completion of PST is a target within the PAC (under the 'Safety First' heading) and hence has to be achieved before Independent Patrol. Indeed, your force will probably expect you successfully to complete your PST before your first Supervised Patrol and, in many cases, before your community engagement.

TASK 7

Your police force will have officers trained in the use of equipment used to protect against a CBRN (Chemical, Biological, Radiological or Nuclear) incident. What is the standard CBRN personal protective equipment used by police officers in the UK?

7.10 Operating IT Systems

Throughout your training you will be expected to operate IT systems on both a general level (such as basic word-processing tasks and sending e-mails) and in specific police-related ways such as communicating with the Police National Computer (PNC) and using your own force information systems. Some police forces encourage their staff to take advantage of schemes such as the European Computer Driving Licence (ECDL). It is likely that you already have many generic IT skills, gained before joining the police service. You should certainly consider having a PC with internet connection at home; it is likely to be a good investment in terms of your future training and career development.

Check that you know how to do at least the following with your own preferred operating system (Windows XP, Mac OS X, Linux, or other):

- search the internet;
- create folders;
- manage files (eg naming, saving, and retrieving files);
- word-process documents;
- print documents;
- use presentational software (such as MS Powerpoint);
- send and receive e-mails.

We put 'search the internet' first because once you are able to do this you will find numerous internet sites that will help you with the other basic IT skills.

The ability to use 'force information management systems' is one of the requirements of the PAC under the 'Information Management' heading.

7.10.1 **The PNC**

You are likely to be given training on the use of the Police National Computer (PNC) at a relatively early stage in your training. In IPLDP language, use of the PNC is part of LPG 1. The ability to utilize PNC is also listed under the Information Management heading of the PAC. Hence you will need to demonstrate this ability before you can undertake Independent Patrol.

The PNC is a large database containing information on, amongst other things, people (for example, those with criminal records), vehicles, and property. The police service is not the only agency to access the PNC—it is also used by other agencies such as the Crown Courts (for checking potential jurors) and the Forensic Science Service. You will normally use the PNC to establish important information, such as checking that a driver is not disqualified from driving or assessing the potential for the behaviour of a particular suspect to be problematic. However, the PNC can do more than perform these relatively simple checks. You can also use the PNC to search for more 'fuzzy' information such as nicknames used by offenders, tattoos, scars, hair colour, and similar distinguishing features. (Try Task 8).

During your training you will be instructed in how to use the PNC. You will normally access the PNC by contacting an operator based at the Force Control Room using your radio. You will need to master the routine; this involves following a particular sequence of requests made to the operator. For example, you will probably be taught that you first specify your request (eg a vehicle check) then give your name and force number, and then the reason for the check, and so on. You will often need to use the phonetic alphabet to spell out words to ensure there is no mistake in transmitting the information (see section 7.5 above). Always make a note in your pocket notebook of the details of the checks you have carried out so that your work is auditable (see section 11.5 below).

What is sure to be emphasized during your training is the requirement to access the PNC in a responsible and professional manner. Inappropriate use of the PNC is viewed by police forces as a serious matter and could well lead to the dismissal of a student police officer found to be abusing the system. (Not only is it a contravention of the PNC code of practice; it is also against the law.) Unfortunately, examples of inappropriate use are only too easy to find. In the past these have included:

- checking on a daughter's new boyfriend (Wadham, 2004);
- accessing information about 'Soap Stars' to sell to the red-top press (Guardian, 2005);
- selling information to private investigators (Wadham, 2004).

Alleged misuse of the PNC can be the subject of an IPCC inquiry (see section 7.16 below).

TASK 8

1. What are VODS and QUEST? (You may need to use the internet or ask more experienced colleagues to answer this question).
2. The HMIC is carrying out PNC compliance inspections of police forces. These may be viewed via the HMIC <http://inspectorates.homeoffice.gov.uk/hmic> internet site. Check whether your force has yet been inspected. If so, read the report. If not, read one from your Most Similar Force (MSF) comparitor.

7.11 **Confidentiality, Management of Police Information, and Freedom of Information**

This section examines the need to both protect the confidentiality of information or data, and the sharing of some information under the requirements of the Freedom of Information Act 2000.

7.11.1 Confidentiality

During your training and in your subsequent career as a police officer, you will frequently encounter information of a sensitive and confidential nature. It is probably obvious but you are expected to maintain the confidentiality of the information you access. Individual force policies may also make reference to the Data Protection Act 1998 and perhaps to the Human Rights Act 1998 (particularly those sections relevant to the right to privacy). Confidentiality is a requirement of the Code of Conduct for police officers (as described in the Police (Conduct) Regulations 2004, see section 7.14 below).

Your respect for confidentiality can be evidenced through achievement of NOS element AB1.2 'to maintain the security of information'. To meet this element of the standard, you need to:

1. comply with relevant legislation, policies and procedures related to the security of information;
2. disclose information only to those who have the right and need to know it;
3. take the appropriate precautions when communicating confidential or sensitive information;
4. maintain the security of records when handling and storing them;
5. alert the appropriate person when you think the security of information is not being maintained or information is being misused.

(Skills for Justice, 2007a)

Your main source of evidence for meeting element AB1.2 is likely to come from your Supervised Patrol in the workplace. The evidence could take the form of artefacts such as records, or direct observation by your assessor (normally your tutor constable) or witness statements. It is very unlikely that simulations in a classroom environment would meet the requirements for element AB1.2.

7.11.2 Management of Police Information (MOPI)

How the police collect, record, share, and retain information has been the subject of some controversy in recent years, most notably as a result of the inquiry into the circumstances surrounding the murders at Soham and the subsequent police investigations (see Bichard, 2004). A new statutory Code of Practice on the Management of Police Information was published in 2005 (followed by Guidance in 2006) and sets out the basic principles that police organizations should adopt for the collection, recording, sharing, and retaining of information that is relevant to their usual work. At the level of the individual police officer, this information may take the form of intelligence and evidence gathering, details concerning domestic crime, search form completion, and pocket note book entries.

Further, the Human Rights Act 1998 (see section 11.3) requires all UK legislation to be matched with the European Convention on Human Rights. Any act by a public authority, such as the police, that contravenes the rights of the Convention will be unlawful. An individual's rights to privacy and family life (Article 8) can be 'interfered' with by the collection of personal information, and this interference is only permitted under certain circumstances (see 11.3.2.3).

Further constraints are placed upon holding personal data by the Data Protection Act 1998. The Act defines personal data as any information which can identify a living person from the data. However, when data is used for the prevention or detection of crime or the apprehension or prosecution of offenders, exemptions are permitted.

Finally, ACPO have also published their own Manual of Guidance on Data Protection (2006) with a greater level of detail than provided by the Code.

The Code, the Human Rights Act 1998, the Data Protection Act 1998, and ACPO's Manual all mean that there is an obligation to manage police information in ways that are both effective and which meet certain ethical and professional standards. Many of these obligations are at the level of the organization rather than the individual and manifest themselves in the form of standing orders, policies, strategies (the force 'Information Management Strategy'), and similar instruments. However, the principles involved also apply at all levels of police staff, regardless of rank or role and are likely to feature in your training. For example, there is the need to ensure that the information that you record is necessary (it is for policing purposes), accurate (check your facts), adequate (you do not omit important information), relevant (address the facts, record opinions only if necessary and clearly mark as such), and timely (make the entry as soon as possible).

7.11.3   Freedom of Information

The Freedom of Information Act 2000 (FoI) gives a general right of access to all types of recorded information held by public authorities. Police forces are included under the definition of public authorities. (On the other hand, ACPO, as a private company, is not.) Your force will publish, normally on the internet, details concerning the public's right under the FoI to access recorded information kept by the organization and the process that needs to be followed to receive that information. They will also have a publication scheme that, amongst other details, describes what information is available as a matter of routine. This avoids the need for repeated requests to be made for the same information. Not all requests for information will be successful—there are obvious exceptions, for example, requests that relate to matters such as the identity of a CHIS. However, it is important to note that the right to information is the **norm** rather than the exception. Requests can be made, and are made, on all kinds of subjects. For example, we learn from a FoI request to Sussex Police the rather unremarkable fact that the Chief Constable's expenses included £4.99 for a car wash on 6 December 2004. (Sussex Police, 2006).

There are two main ways that the FoI might directly affect you. Firstly, you may personally receive a request for information under the FoI, perhaps in the form of a letter addressed to you or by e-mail. (Many people will know, for example, that your work e-mail is likely to be of the form x.y@force.pnn.police.uk where x is your first name, y is your surname and 'force' is a shortened version of the name of your force, for example btp.) In this case you should not respond yourself but should promptly pass the request to the person designated as responsible for FoI requests in your force.

Secondly, and put simply, you should be aware at all times that if you are recording information as a police officer then somebody, some day, may apply under the FoI to view the record you have made. Unless there are very good reasons not to, this will be permitted, so choose your words accurately and carefully.

7.12   Attestation

Attestation is the stage at which a student police officer is formally given the powers of a police constable—for example, he or she is able to arrest somebody according to the law and codes of practice. The legal detail is set out in Sch 4 to the Police Act 1996, as substituted by s 83 of the Police Reform Act 2002. Attestation often coincides with the issuing of a warrant card, although practice may vary from force to force (some forces instead issue a form of 'trainee police officer identity card' at attestation). In many police organizations, attestation happens early on in a student officer's career—sometimes on initial appointment and certainly within the first few weeks.

Compared to other professional groups, this is an unusual and perhaps anomalous position. It is as if a trainee doctor were given a right to treat patients after a few weeks' training even though they still had almost five years of study and practice to complete. The timing of attestation is currently under review, partly as a result of the HMIC thematic inspection report 'Training Matters', the recommendations of the Morris Inquiry, and the Commission for Racial Equality report into police training (Morris, 2004). The timing of attestation might well change as a consequence.

You also begin your training on one of the highest initial wages for an unqualified public sector professional. For example, nurses start their training on a bursary of about £5,500 per annum, less than a third of your starting wage. (They also have to pass their training **before** they can undertake full-time work.) Again, it seems inevitable, at a time when police forces have assumed greater responsibility for their own training, that the employment status and pay of student police officers is likely to be reviewed.

At the moment at attestation you will make a formal declaration. This is described in section 7.15.1.

7.13 The Role of the Constable

After attestation (see section 7.12 above) you will hold the office of probationary **constable**, with your position being confirmed after about two calendar years. The origins of the office of constable within law enforcement in the UK can be traced back hundreds of years, although many commentators consider the most significant starting point for the modern-day police service as the year 1829 (see section 1.3 above).

In recent years, constables have become just one of many members of the extended police family; they no longer have a monopoly on certain traditional policing powers. They nonetheless continue to hold a special position within a police organization, as you will discover when working through this chapter and those that follow. This privilege brings additional responsibilities to the role of constable, particularly in terms of attitudes, values, and professional knowledge. Many of the NOS elements for initial policing are concerned with the need for you to demonstrate the appropriate attitudes and values, and, by extension, to have gained the appropriate underpinning skills and knowledge.

For example, you are likely to be required to achieve the following NOS elements before confirmation as a constable:

National Occupational Standard Unit and Elements

1A1.3   Use police actions fairly.
AA1.1   Promote equality and value diversity.
AB1.2   Maintain the security of information.
AE1.1   Maintain and develop your own knowledge, skills and competence.

Similarly, one of the Induction Modules of the IPLDP is concerned with the 'Underpinning Ethics/Values of the Police Service' (IND 1).

There has been much discussion about the possible effects of an individual's personal beliefs and values, and the manner in which these are expressed in their day-to-day actions and decisions. Student police officers may sometimes say (somewhat defensively) that they are 'entitled to their opinions' with the implication that their attitudes have no bearing on their actions, even if their personal opinions were to be at odds with their actual behaviour. This is obviously an important question for those engaged in police training and education, and is addressed on occasions in other parts of this Handbook. However, in this section we are concerned with how your own professional development as a student police officer (and your progress to Confirmation as constable) links up with the wider common purpose and values of the police service.

We noted in section 5.3 above that the existence of a code of professional conduct was a common feature of the professions. The **Police Service Statement of Common Purpose and Values** was first issued by ACPO in 1990 and is reflected today, almost word for word, in most police forces' own statements. It is a relatively consistent declaration of the guiding principles of the police service, and all police officers, including student police officers, are required to work towards the achievement of this statement.

According to this statement, the purpose of the police service is to:

'...uphold the law firmly and fairly...'	neither too weak or too aggressive, and with no bias
'...prevent crime...'	not to let it happen if it can be stopped first
'...pursue and bring to justice those who break the law...'	and hence we need to understand the requirements of the criminal justice system
'...keep the Queen's peace...'	not to allow public disorder and criminality to occur unchallenged
'...protect, help and reassure the community...'	that is, all our communities and not just those that appear to support the police or those that we belong to

We have already referred to *The Secret Policeman* documentary, first screened on BBC television in October 2003. An undercover journalist, Mark Daly, joined Greater Manchester Police as a student police officer and then spent fifteen weeks in training at the Bruche Centrex regional Police Training Centre, near Warrington. During his time at Bruche, Daly secretly filmed some of the behaviour of his fellow students and the trainers delivering the course. He uncovered evidence of racist language and attitudes amongst some of his fellow student police officers and inappropriate behaviour by some of his trainers. However, as Daly himself noted in 2003:

> The majority of the officers I met will undoubtedly turn out to be good, non-prejudiced ones intent on doing the job properly. But the next generation of officers from one of Britain's top police colleges contains a significant minority of people who are holding the progress of the police service back (Daly, 2003).

Examples of inappropriate behaviour by some student police officers at Bruche included:

- use of offensive racist terms to describe members of ethnic minorities, including unsubstantiated slurs on the character of the family of murdered black teenager Stephen Lawrence;
- donning an imitation Ku Klux Klan hood and threatening to knock on the door of a fellow student police officer of British Asian heritage;
- claims that they used police powers in a discriminating way against ethnic minorities.

One Centrex police trainer was also secretly filmed expressing his happiness to his group of students that the single British Asian heritage police recruit had been re-coursed (required to retake certain aspects of his training), although there was no suggestion that this was as a result of racism.

TASK 9

Now take a moment to consider why the Police Service Statement of Common Purpose and Values is important to you as a student police officer.

Write up your reflections so that they can be used as evidence for your SOLAP—for example, as evidence cross-referenced to the knowledge requirement of your Cumulative Assessment Record (CAR) for element AE1.1. Your reflections could also feature in your Learning Diary, under the heading 'Police Policies & Procedures'.

7.14 Code of Conduct

Much of your time as a student police officer will involve direct contact with both the public and fellow members of the extended policing family (for example, police community support officers). Many of the NOS elements for initial policing are concerned with the nature and quality of these interactions.

Whether the person you encounter is a victim, suspect, fellow police employee, partner, relative, friend, or any other member of the community, they all have expectations of you in terms of your conduct and integrity. If these expectations are reasonable but are not met then the consequences can be damaging for both the individuals concerned and for the reputation and standing of the police service as a whole. There may be accusations of double standards and a breakdown in the ability to police by consent. This is discussed in further detail in Chapter 5.

For this reason, all police officers have a **Code of Conduct** or ethics that they must work towards, and these are outlined below in section 7.14.1. We noted in section 5.5 that the existence of a code of conduct is an integral part of your personal moral authority as a trainee police officer. The code also relates directly to the following NOS elements:

National Occupational Standard Elements

1A1.1   Apply principles of reasonable suspicion or belief.
1A1.2   Use police actions proportionately.
1A1.3   Use police actions fairly.
AA1.1   Promote equality and value diversity.
AB1.2   Maintain the security of information.
AE1.1   Maintain and develop your own knowledge, skills and competence.

The following sections also contain material likely to be relevant to Phase 3 of the IPLDP and the Induction Module IND 1: 'Underpinning Ethics/Values of the Police Service'.

The legal standing of the Code is complex and links in turn with the Police Regulations. A number of legal texts, including *Blackstone's Police Manual: Volume 4 General Police Duties* consider this in more detail.

Note that there is also a European Code of Police Ethics, as mentioned in section 5.4.

TASK 10

Write down examples of the kinds of conduct the public should expect from police officers. Compare your answers to the table below.

7.14.1   Conduct Expected of a Police Officer

The following is a summary of the Code of Conduct taken from the Police (Conduct) Regulations 2004 (SI 2004 645).

Code of Conduct

Honesty and integrity	It is of paramount importance that the public has confidence in the honesty and integrity of police officers. Officers should therefore be open and truthful in their dealings, avoid being improperly accountable to any person or institution and discharge their duties with integrity.
Fairness and impartiality	Police officers have a particular responsibility to act with fairness and impartiality in all their dealings with the public and their colleagues.
Politeness and tolerance	Officers should treat members of the public and colleagues with courtesy and respect, avoiding abusive or deriding attitudes or behaviour. In particular, officers must avoid: • favouritism of an individual group; • all forms of harassment, victimisation or unreasonable discrimination; • overbearing conduct to a colleague, particularly to a junior in rank or service.
Use of force and abuse of authority	Officers must never knowingly use more force than is reasonable, nor should they abuse their authority.
Performance of duties	Officers should be conscientious and diligent in the performance of their duties. Officers should attend work promptly when rostered for duty. If absent through sickness or injury, they should avoid activities likely to retard their return to duty.
Lawful orders	The police service is a disciplined organisation. Unless there is good and sufficient cause to do otherwise, officers must obey all lawful orders and abide by the provisions of Police Regulations. Officers should

	support their colleagues in the execution of their lawful duties, and oppose any improper behaviour, reporting it where appropriate.
Confidentiality	Information which comes into the possession of the police should be treated as confidential. It should not be used for personal benefit and nor should it be divulged to other parties, except in the proper course of police duty.
Criminal offences	Officers must report any proceedings of a criminal offence taken against them. Conviction of a criminal offence may itself result in further action being taken.
Property	Officers must exercise reasonable care to prevent loss of or damage to property (excluding their own personal property, but including police property).
Sobriety	While on duty officers must be sober. Officers should not consume alcohol when on duty unless specifically authorised to do so, or it becomes necessary for the proper discharge of police duty.
General conduct	Whether on or off duty, police officers should not behave in a way which is likely to bring discredit upon the police service.

Note that the Police Service of Northern Ireland (PSNI) has its own code of ethics.

TASK 11

Ask yourself why the public has the right to expect police officers to behave in an ethical way and what the consequences are if their expectations are not met.

The Code of Conduct sets out the principles which guide police officers' conduct. The Police (Conduct) Regulations 2004 make it clear that:

> it does not seek to restrict the proper exercise of police officers' discretion: rather, it aims to define the parameters of conduct within which that discretion should be exercised (Note (b) to Sch 1 of the Police (Conduct) Regulations 2004).

Discretion is discussed fully in section 5.7 of the Handbook. However, it is important to note, as the Police (Conduct) Regulations 2004 emphasize, that 'any breach of the principles in this Code may result in action being taken by the organisation, which, in serious cases, could involve dismissal' (ibid).

Finally, note (c) to Sch 1 to the Police (Conduct) Regulations 2004 explains that 'police behaviour, **whether on or off duty**, affects public confidence in the police service' (our emphasis).

TASK 12

In January 2005, an off-duty police officer from South Wales Police was suspended from duty after allegedly taking a police car without permission, subsequently crashing the car, and then testing positive for alcohol.

Take a moment to consider and then list which parts of the Code of Conduct may have been breached during the alleged incidents. What are the consequences of this neglect for both the individual concerned and the police service as a whole?

Your written reflections may be relevant to the knowledge requirements of the 'Underpinning Ethics/Values of the Police Service' sections of your SOLAP.

Adherence to the code can also be evidenced, at least in part, through the achievement of the appropriate NOS. For example, the need to ensure fairness and impartiality can be evidenced through achievement of Unit 1A1 to 'use police actions in a fair and justified way and the 3 elements 1A1.1 to 'apply principles of reasonable suspicion or belief, 1A1.2 to 'use police actions proportionately, and 1A1.3 to 'use police actions fairly'.

> **TASK 13**
>
> For each of the first seven sections of the table of the Code of Conduct (see section 7.14.1), list the element of the NOS Unit that is most relevant. Give some thought to how you are likely to able to produce evidence that you have met these elements. Bear in mind that evidence usually takes the form of tangible objects such as written documents that you cross-reference in the relevant CAR of your SOLAP and by direct observation and questioning by your assessor (See chapter 6).

7.14.2 New Code of Professional Standards for Police Officers

Following the Taylor Report into police misconduct in 2006 the Home Office announced its intention to introduce a new Code of Professional Standards for Police Officers to replace the existing Code of Conduct described in 7.14.1 above. The ten proposed principles of the new Code are:

- Responsibility and Accountability
- Honesty and Integrity
- Lawful Orders
- Use of Force
- Authority, Respect and Courtesy
- Equality
- Confidentiality
- Fitness for Duty
- General Conduct
- Challenging and Reporting Improper Conduct

As you may have noted, there is some similarity here with the existing Code of Conduct but with the significant additional requirement to challenge and report improper conduct by others.

7.15 Conduct, Misconduct, and Regulations

Attested student police officers are not employees in the conventional meaning of the term, instead they are **holders of public office**. One consequence is that the activities of student police officers, both on and off duty, are regulated by law.

For this reason, references to conduct, complaints, and misconduct, as well as a number of restrictions and expectations are contained in Police Acts and the Police Regulations. Because of their length and complexity these will not be dealt with in their entirety here, but they are presented in a summarized and simplified form over the next three sections. Full details may be found in other textbooks such as *Blackstone's Police Manual: Volume 4 General Police Duties* and via the internet.

At the moment of attestation you become subject to the various regulations.

7.15.1 Declaration at Attestation

We described attestation earlier in section 7.12. Formally, s 29 of the Police Act 1996 requires that:

> Every member of a police force maintained for a police area and every special constable appointed for a police area shall, on appointment, be attested as a constable by making a declaration

as follows:

> I . . . of . . . do solemnly and sincerely declare and affirm that I will well and truly serve the Queen in the office of constable, with fairness, integrity, diligence and impartiality, upholding fundamental human rights and according equal respect to all people; and that I will, to the best of my power, cause the peace to be kept and preserved and prevent all offences against people and property; and that while

I continue to hold the said office I will, to the best of my skill and knowledge, discharge all the duties thereof faithfully according to law.

There is an alternative Welsh language version which may be used by student police officers in Dyfed-Powys, Gwent, North Wales, or South Wales:

Rwyf I...o...yn datgan ac yn cadarnhau yn ddifrifol ac yn ddiffuant y byddaf yn gwasanaethu'r Frenhines yn dda ac yn gywir yn fy swydd o heddwas (heddferch), yn deg, yn onest, yn ddiwyd ac yn ddiduedd, gan gynnal hawliau dynol sylfaenol a chan roddi'r un parch i bob person; ac y byddaf i, hyd eithaf fy ngallu, yn achosi i'r heddwch gael ei gadw a'i ddiogelu ac yn atal pob trosedd yn erbyn pobl ac eiddo; a thra byddaf yn parhau i ddal y swydd ddywededig y byddaf i, hyd eithaf fy sgil a'm gwybodaeth, yn cyflawni'r holl ddyletswyddau sy'n gysylltiedig â hi yn ffyddlon yn unol â'r gyfraith.

For a number of reasons, the declaration in Northern Ireland is somewhat different:

I hereby do solemnly and sincerely and truly declare and affirm that I will faithfully discharge the duties of the office of constable, with fairness, integrity, diligence and impartiality, upholding fundamental human rights and according equal respect to all individuals and their traditions and beliefs; and that while I continue to hold the said office I will to the best of my skill and knowledge discharge all the duties thereof according to law.

At attestation, and comparatively early in your training, you will be asked to read out one of the declarations above. The making of a declaration may seem somewhat old-fashioned. However, it is worth bearing in mind that the declaration you make has a statutory basis in law and its symbolic importance remains strong both within police culture and in the wider political and social world.

TASK 14

Learn the attestation declaration word for word! Note that you will probably be given an aide memoir to read from at actual attestation, or be asked to follow another's lead. However, you are likely to be required to memorize information on a number of occasions during training (for example, definitions) and this task is good practice.

Sections 7.15.2 to 7.15.8 that follow are extracts from the Police Act 1996 and the Police Regulations 2003. We have added additional explanations.

7.15.2 Restrictions on the Private Life of Members of Police Forces

These are set out in Sch 1 to the Police Regulations 2003 which state that:

The restrictions on private life...shall apply to all members of a police force (reg 6(1)).

A member of a police force shall at all times abstain from any activity which is likely to interfere with the impartial discharge of [his/her] duties or which is likely to give rise to the impression amongst members of the public that it may so interfere; and in particular a member of a police force shall not take any active part in politics (Sch 1, para 1).

In other words, that means that a police officer must not pursue a course of conduct which members of the public will perceive as favouritism and especially must not be active in politics.

A member of a police force shall not wilfully refuse or neglect to discharge any lawful debt (Sch 1, para 4).

This does not mean to say you cannot have a mortgage or a car loan, but any other debt which could place you in danger of being coerced is unacceptable.

7.15.3 Business Interests Incompatible with Membership of a Police Force

Regulation 7 of the Police Regulations 2003 states that:

If a member of a police force or a relative included in [his/her] family proposes to have, or has, a business interest within the meaning of this regulation, the member shall forthwith give written notice of that interest to the chief officer unless that business interest was disclosed at the time of [his/her] appointment as a member of the force.

For the purposes of their integrity and credibility, police officers must disclose business interests for checking whether such interests are compatible with the role of a constable.

TASK 15

What is the procedure used in your force for declaring business interests?

7.15.4 Discharge of a Student Police Officer

The procedure for discharge is set out in reg 13 of the Police Regulations 2003 which states that:

> Subject to the provisions of this regulation, during [his/her] period of probation in the force the services of a constable may be dispensed with at any time if the chief officer considers that [he/she] is not fitted, physically or mentally, to perform the duties of [his/her] office, or that [he/she] is not likely to become an efficient or well-conducted constable.

The first two years of your service are crucial to your Confirmation of appointment at the end of that period. However, under the same regulation, before being discharged, you can give notice of retirement (in other words, resign). See also section 3.8 for a discussion of this.

7.15.5 Contents of Personal Records

Regulation 15 of the Police Regulations 2003 states that:

> The chief officer of a police force shall cause a personal record of each member of the police force to be kept.

Throughout your service a personal record will be maintained, containing details of you and your relatives, as well as a history of courses that you have attended, expertise that you have gained, and promotions that you have achieved. It will also contain outcomes of any disciplinary investigations.

7.15.6 Fingerprints

Regulation 18 of the Police Regulations 2003 states that:

> Every member of a police force shall in accordance with the directions of the chief officer have [his/her] fingerprints taken.

For the purposes of eliminating you from any forensic investigation, a record of your fingerprints will be kept. Quite often this takes place early on in your training and sometimes as part of your training on forensic awareness.

7.15.7 Samples

Regulation 19 of the Police Regulations 2003 states that:

> Every member of a police force, except those members appointed following their transfer from another police force, shall on appointment and in accordance with the directions of the chief officer have a sample taken.

Once again, for the purposes of elimination, each officer will supply a sample, such as a mouth swab for DNA.

7.15.8 Duty to Carry out Lawful Orders

Regulation 20 of the Police Regulations 2003 states that:

> Every member of a police force shall carry out all lawful orders and shall at all times punctually and promptly perform all appointed duties and attend to all matters within the scope of [his/her] office as a constable.

The police service has a rank structure in which supervisors and managers may require certain actions to be carried out. It is an expectation that will you carry out these orders, but only if they are lawful.

7.15.9 New Police Misconduct Procedures

From 2008 it is expected that (subject to Parliamentary approval) new police misconduct procedures will replace those described above, as part of wider reform which also includes an Unsatisfactory Performance Procedure and Standards of Professional Behaviour (see 7.14.2 above). The new procedures are expected to be based on the current ACAS (Advisory, Conciliation and Arbitration Service) approach and involve two levels—minor and gross.

TASK 16

Take the opportunity to reflect upon these Regulations and how you are going to work within them. Which areas do you think are going to be easy for you to satisfy, and which areas do you need to consider at greater length?

The PSNI Code of Ethics, article 1.5 states that:

> A police officer should carry out orders properly issued by [his/her] superior, but [he/she] shall refrain from carrying out any order [he/she] knows, or ought to know, is unlawful.

How would you know that an order was unlawful?

This task will support you in preparing to demonstrate NOS element 4C1.1 ('Reflect on and evaluate one's own values, priorities, interests and effectiveness') and particularly the performance criterion that asks you to 'Identify your own values, interests and priorities in relation to the work you are undertaking'.

7.16 The Police Complaints System

A complaint against the police can be made by a member of the public (externally) or by a member of the police organization (internally). The kind of external complaints that are made against student police officers include complaints from a member of the public concerning the conduct or behaviour of an officer, for example rudeness or the use of excessive force, unjustified arrest, and the like. The person making the complaint could also be a witness or a relative of the aggrieved person.

When a complaint is made, or a police officer is suspected of misconduct, the process used to deal with the matter is known as the Police Complaints System. The diagram below shows the different ways in which complaints are handled. Many complaints against the police are dealt with by the police themselves through local resolution or local police investigation.

6 IPCC independent investigation
5 IPCC managed investigation
4 IPCC supervised investigation
3 Local police investigation
2 Local resolution
1 Dispensation / withdrawn

IPCC stands for **Independent Police Complaints Commission**

7.16.1 Dispensation and Withdrawal

There are situations when a specific complaint has already been made, or it has been made more than once by the same person, or it has been made anonymously. The investigation of the complaint may be stopped in such cases and is referred to as a dispensation. Similarly, if the person making the complaint decides he/she no longer wants to proceed with the matter, the complaint can also be withdrawn.

7.16.2 Local Resolution

Of the many ways of dealing with a complaint, local resolution is often the best outcome for all those involved. Regulation 9 notices (see section 7.16.3 below) are not required, and there is no blame attached or need to involve disciplinary procedures. The process will not affect a student police officer's personal development plan (usually the SOLAP, then the PDR), staff appraisal, or any subsequent misconduct hearing. Note that a police force cannot make an apology to the complainant unless the officer concerned (the officer against whom the complaint was made) authorizes such an apology.

7.16.3 Local Police Investigation and the Regulation 9 Notice

If an investigation is necessary, it will be in proportion to the seriousness of the complaint or allegation of misconduct. The investigation is usually carried out by personnel from the Professional Standards Department within your force, and the complainant has the right of appeal against the decision to the **Independent Police Complaints Commission**.

Regulation 9 of the Police (Conduct) Regulations 2004 outlines the requirement for a notice to be issued to the officer concerned, to safeguard his/her rights and inform him/her that he/she is under investigation. You will hear the notice being referred to in police circles as a 'reg 9'. The notice will be issued as soon as practicable after the investigation begins in order that the officer is better able to recall the incident.

If an officer receives a reg 9 notice, the Police Federation advises him/her not to say anything at that stage and to seek the advice of a Federation representative. Similarly, if the officer is told that he/she is about to be interviewed, once again he/she is strongly advised to contact a Federation representative who will arrange to attend the interview or, in some circumstances, arrange for legal representation.

7.16.4 Investigations Involving the IPCC

Depending on the seriousness of the allegations, the investigation can take a number of different forms.

An **IPCC Supervised Investigation** is used for complaints or allegations of misconduct which are of considerable significance and probable public concern. The investigation is supervised by an IPCC commissioner but is still conducted, directed, and controlled by the police. The complainant has the right of appeal to the IPCC.

An **IPCC Managed Investigation** is used when the alleged incident is more serious and likely to cause higher levels of public concern, and therefore the subsequent investigation must have an independent element. The IPCC direct and control the process, whilst the police conduct the investigation.

An **Independent Investigation** is used for incidents that cause the greatest level of public concern or have the greatest potential to impact on communities or have serious implications for the reputation of the police service. These require a wholly independent investigation conducted in its entirety by IPCC staff. Examples of such incidents include deaths in custody.

There is no right of appeal against an IPCC managed or independent investigation except through judicial review. This is a form of court proceedings which checks that the correct procedures have been used.

7.16.5 Further Action

If, for example, a procedure has been breached in a way that calls for no further action and no sanctions are required (see below), then the IPCC may decide the officer should receive advice, but the matter cannot be referred to in a personal development plan or staff appraisal. If the officer has admitted to the complaint, a formal warning may be issued by his/her superintendent. In a few cases, the IPCC may request that an officer appears before a misconduct panel. If this happens, the officer is advised to contact a Police Federation representative to provide support throughout this process.

7.16.6 Sanctions

There are a variety of sanctions if found guilty after an investigation:

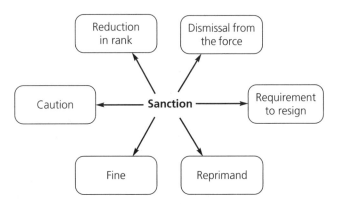

Note that for a student police officer no reduction in rank is possible although he/she may be re-coursed, or required to retake some part of training.

7.16.7 Reporting of Concerns by the Police

There may be occasions when you witness possible wrongdoings by a colleague. Normally you would report this to your supervisor or your force's Professional Standards Department. However, you can also raise concerns confidentially with the IPCC as it is designated as an official body for the purposes of public interest disclosure.

7.17 The Police Federation, the BAWP, the NBPA, and the GPA

When you join the police service as a student police officer you also join the Police Federation. This is automatic. You may decide, additionally, to join one or more of the following organizations: the British Association for Women in Policing (BAWP), the National Black Police Association UK (NBPA), the Gay Police Association (GPA). There are links between the Federation and these other organizations. For example, the BAWP is represented on the Equality Sub-Committee of the Police Federation.

7.17.1 The Police Federation

England and Wales have a single Police Federation, (s 64(1) of the Police Act 1996, Membership of Trades Unions) as does each of Northern Ireland and Scotland. This part of the Handbook describes the Police Federation of England and Wales, but many of the observations also apply to Scotland and Northern Ireland.

It is important to realize that the Federation is not a trades union in the usual sense of the term. Indeed, as a student police officer (and also when you become a Confirmed constable) you are forbidden to join a trades union:

> Subject to the following provisions of this section, a member of a police force shall not be a member of any trades union, or of any association having for its objects, or one of its objects, to control or

influence the pay, pensions or conditions of service of any police force (s 64(1) of the Police Act 1996, Membership of Trades Unions).

The Federation therefore does not have the right to call for any kind of industrial action such as a strike and cannot affiliate itself to the Labour Party or any other political organization.

However, in many other respects the Federation has been established to represent the views of its members (police officers below the rank of superintendent) on local, regional, and national levels in much the same way as any other staff association.

7.17.1.1   Structure of the Police Federation

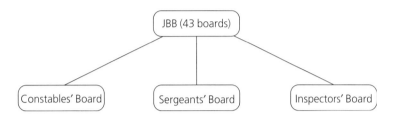

Each of the police forces in England and Wales has a Joint Branch Board (JBB). Within the JBB there are separate boards, representing the interests of constables, sergeants, and inspectors. These are known as, naturally enough, the Constables' Branch Board, the Sergeants' Branch Board, and the Inspectors' Branch Board. These boards each have separate agendas and meetings but also combine together to form the force JBB. The JBB represents the views of police officers to the chief constable or commissioner, others in positions of responsibility, and members of the police authority.

The Federation of England and Wales has eight regions, with each region electing representatives to form the national Joint Central Committee. For example, Region No 2 of the Federation consists of the police forces of Cleveland, Durham, Humberside, Northumbria, North Yorkshire, South Yorkshire, and West Yorkshire. The Joint Central Committee is responsible for the national policy of the Federation.

7.17.1.2   Pay, pensions, and allowances

On behalf of its members, the Police Federation negotiates aspects of pay, pensions, and allowances through a National Police Negotiating Board. The board consists of representatives from the Police Federations (England and Wales, Scotland and Northern Ireland), the Superintendents' Association, and ACPO. These meet with representatives of the government ministers responsible for the police: the Home Secretary, the Scottish Secretary, the Northern Ireland Secretary, and representatives of the local authorities and magistrates.

The Police Negotiating Board has an independent chairperson (appointed by the Prime Minister).

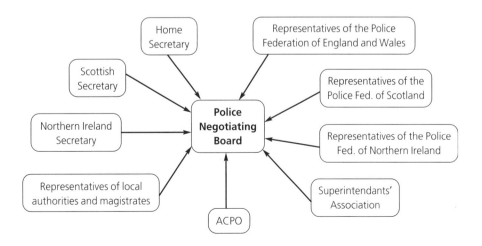

7.17.1.3 Training, promotion, and discipline

Under the chairmanship of the Home Secretary, the Federation is represented on the Police Advisory Board which meets to discuss professional subjects such as training, promotion, and discipline. After taking these discussions into account, the Home Secretary may then make proposals to amend Police Regulations.

7.17.1.4 Student officer personal discipline

One of the primary functions of the Federation is to give advice and assistance to its members when they are the subject of a formal complaint or internal investigation. If you are the subject of a complaint (see section 7.16), the Federation advises you to remain calm and, if you are unsure of the procedure or what to do next, to contact your local Federation representative. The Federation has produced a leaflet concerning complaints which is downloadable from <www.polfed.org/IPCC_PoliceStaff_LR2.pdf>.

7.17.1.5 Personal injury

The Federation offers advice and assistance to police officers (including student police officers) who sustain injuries while on duty and who wish to claim compensation from the Criminal Injuries Compensation Authority (CICA).

7.17.1.6 Personal conditions of service

The Federation also offers advice and assistance to police officers (including student police officers) on matters arising from the conditions of service set out in the various Acts and regulations governing the police service.

TASK 17

- Which Federation Region does your force belong to?
- Who is the Chair and Secretary of your force JBB?
- How are your concerns addressed and your views canvassed?

7.17.2 The BAWP

The British Association for Women in Policing seeks to address women's issues in policing and not simply to represent women; membership is open to both men and women. Further information is to be found at <www.bawp.org>.

7.17.3 The NBPA

The National Black Police Association UK is an independent charitable organization. The NBPA seeks to further the position of all police officers of 'African, African-Caribbean, Middle-Eastern, Asian or Asian sub-continent origin'. You join the NBPA through membership of your local Black Police Association or BPA. There are approximately 40 BPAs throughout the UK. Further information concerning the NBPA is to be found at <www.nbpa.co.uk>.

TASK 18

Does your force have a BPA? If not, why not?

7.17.4 The GPA

The Gay Police Association seeks to represent the interests of gay and lesbian police staff in the UK. Membership is on an individual basis and you join by contacting the national GPA. The GPA has a website to be found at <www.gay.police.uk>.

7.18   Effective Communication

As a student police officer you will need to be aware of how you speak to everybody you come into contact with, so that you can adjust accordingly what you say and how you say it.

This section links with the NOS element:

National Occupational Standards Element

AB1.1 Develop and maintain communication with people and in particular, performance criteria 2, 3 and 4 (see 7.18.3 below).

Performance criterion 2—to communicate with people in a form and manner and using language that:

- is open and respectful of them as individuals;
- is consistent with their level of understanding, culture, background and preferred ways of communicating;
- is appropriate to the context in which the communication is taking place;
- promotes equality and values diversity.

Performance criterion 3—to give people opportunities to check their understanding of the information you have given to them and ask questions.

Performance criterion 4—to take the appropriate action to reduce any barriers to effective communication (Skills for Justice, 2007a).

The chapter also supports the Learning Requirements of the IPLDP (3.8) and is typically introduced during module IND 4 of IDLDP.

The purpose of this section is to help you become more aware of the way you speak, and the effect it has on other people. In turn, this will help you develop strategies to help you communicate more clearly in the future, and to choose the most appropriate way to speak to another person. This is obviously of critical importance both during the induction period and during the rest of your subsequent career as a police officer. In section 7.18.2 we will also examine the other side of the communication equation—listening skills.

It is important to note that the ideas presented here are based on **only one particular theory** concerning human communication. This theory is known as transactional analysis which originated from the psychodynamic tradition in psychology. This does not mean that other theories concerning human communication are not equally valid for the student police officer; indeed, you may encounter quite different approaches during your training—for example, Shannon and Weaver's Information Theory. We are not asking you to buy into transactional analysis to the exclusion of other theories; instead we use it in this part of the Handbook as an example of the benefits that may flow from a careful and structured analysis of patterns of communication.

7.18.1   Transactional Analysis

Transactional analysis was originally developed by Eric Berne, (for an introduction see Berne, 1968) and is based upon the assumption that people tend to adopt the characteristics or ego states of a **parent** (critical or nurturing), **adult**, or **child** (adapted or free). This affects their attitudes and the way they speak to each other.

The typical attitudes, behaviour, and words or phrases that people use when adopting one of these ego states can be roughly categorized as follows:

Ego state	Typical words/phrases	Typical behaviour	Typical attitudes
Critical parent	'That's disgraceful!' 'You ought to . . . !' 'Always do it!'	Furrowed brow, pointed finger.	Condescending, judgemental.
Nurturing parent	'Well done, that's clever!'	Benevolent smile, pat on back.	Caring, permissive.
Adult	'How . . . '? 'When . . . '? 'Where . . . '? 'What . . . '?	Relaxed, logical, attentive.	Open-minded, clear-thinking, interested.
Adapted child	'Please can I'? 'I'll try harder'	Vigorous, nodding head, downcast eyes, whiny voice.	Compliant, defiant, complaining
Free child	'I want' 'I feel great'	Laughing with someone, uninhibited.	Curious, fun-loving, spontaneous.

Note that no one operates in one or other of these states on a permanent basis. Instead, once you become more aware of it, you may find yourself switching between states even within the course of a single conversation.

> **TASK 19**
>
> If this Handbook were a person, which of the ego states would fit best and most often?

7.18.1.1 Types of transaction

According to this theory, the response of the person you are speaking to will vary, partly due to the way you spoke to him/her and the ego state you were in. As a student police officer, you need to be able to analyse (to some extent) the way that **you** speak and respond and the way that **others** speak and respond, and to be able to identify the most appropriate way to manage the conversation. Having identified the ego states, the next task is to recognize the category of conversation or transaction, ie whether it is **complementary**, **crossed**, or **ulterior**.

7.18.1.2 Complementary transactions

Complementary transactions occur when the ego state of each side of the conversation makes a pair with the other. Here is an example of a complementary transaction. For the purpose of this example, let us call the student police officer 'SPO' and the member of public 'M'.

> The SPO stops a car to give advice to the driver.
>
> **M**   I don't know why you've stopped me, haven't you got anything better to do?
>
> **SPO**   Is this your car? I've stopped you because I've got the right, and what's your problem anyway?
>
> **M**   Get lost.
>
> **SPO**   You can't say that; any more lip and I'll report you.

So, how could you try and make sure that unsatisfactory exchanges like the one above do not happen to you? To start with, you need to analyse the way it happened, then you will be able to see more easily how it could be done differently.

In the above example, the opening transaction is from M in the child ego state, 'I don't know why you've stopped me, haven't you got anything better to do?' The SPO responds in parent mode 'Is this your car? I've stopped you because I've got the right, and what's your problem anyway?' The response of the SPO is in the ego state of parent and is directed at M's child ego state. The transaction therefore forms a complementary transaction sequence of:

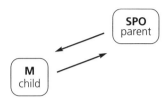

The exchange will continue in this way as long as the transactions are complementary. In the next section you will see how to interrupt and change the flow of the conversation by changing **your** ego state.

7.18.1.3 Crossed transactions

The last example showed how transactions can flow back and forth when they are complementary. They are likely to continue in the same style, with each person rather unproductively locked into their ego state. To interrupt this flow, and to change the style of the transaction, either SPO or M could employ a crossed transaction.

> Let us begin the conversation again, but with a subtle difference.
>
> **M**   I don't know why you've stopped me, haven't you got anything better to do?
>
> **SPO**   Hello, let me introduce myself, I'm PC Williams from Lewes police station and I've stopped you because I need to give you some advice about your car. Did you know that one of your brake lights isn't working? This could affect your safety as well as the safety of others.
>
> **M**   Oh right, I didn't realise about my lights—thanks for telling me—I'll get them fixed straight away.
>
> **PC**   Thanks for your co-operation. Good afternoon.

In this case M is still in the child ego state but the reply by SPO is different; it is now from the adult ego state. It is a reply that has reasoning in its content, which has an affect on M, who may not have expected this type of response. M responds accordingly in the adult ego state which brings about a satisfactory conclusion. This is referred to as a crossed transaction as the SPO's response has broken the adult-child-adult pattern, and the transaction has crossed over into a different style.

7.18.1.4 Ulterior transactions

In an ulterior transaction there are actually two different messages, an open message and a hidden message. Frequently with ulterior transactions, the open message is adult to adult, but the **hidden message** is parent to child or child to parent.

> For example M begins the transaction sarcastically, and emphasizes the word 'such'.
>
> **M**   It's nice to see the local police making **such** good use of their time.
>
> **SPO**   Yeah, it's all part of the service to **you**.

In this transaction it is not just about words; it is also about body language and the tone of voice. The opening transaction has a hidden meaning; M dislikes the police (or at least SPO); M feels the police (or SPO in particular) waste his or her time rather than catching real criminals; and hence the sarcastic emphasis on the word 'such'. SPO's response also has a hidden meaning; hence it is said with a smirk and an emphasis on the word 'you'. Each component is complementary. So, unless one of the participants crosses a transaction, the dialogue will continue in this manner. Your skill, therefore, is to be aware of what is happening, respond accordingly to break the transaction, and thereby change the ego state of the other person.

Try using these ideas to help you understand your own and other people's styles of communication, and then choose the most appropriate way of saying what it is that you want to say.

> **TASK 20**
>
> Over the next two days, listen carefully to conversations around you. What ego states are operating and what type of transactions are taking place? Write down three brief extracts and explain what is happening in terms of transactional analysis.

7.18.2 Listening Skills

Of all the skills that we develop during our lives, the ability to **listen** is probably the most difficult of all. We hear, but we do not always listen; this ability has to be learned and practised. (Interestingly, we teach children how to speak and write but we place less emphasis on how to listen.) Most of us will learn just enough to function successfully as social beings. However, as a student police officer, the ability to listen has to be developed more fully. What people tell us may be of critical importance when dealing with a public order situation or when investigating a crime.

In this section we shall simply offer some basic advice on listening. During the two years of your training you will no doubt receive more detailed advice on listening skills.

- Pay full attention to the person you are listening to. Do not look away when the person is talking to you (think what it feels like for **you**, if the person you are speaking to keeps glancing away). You should give verbal and non-verbal feedback (for example nodding) to the speaker that says, in effect, 'I'm listening'.
- Train yourself to let the speaker finish before you ask another question or make a comment—don't interrupt. Most of us think we already do this but research shows that this is normally not the case! (However, there may be occasions why there are sound operational reasons why you must interrupt.) A good way of training yourself to let someone finish is to mentally count a few seconds after he/she has finished talking before you respond. You may also notice that he/she then fills this silence, and carries on speaking, almost as an afterthought. Sometimes, this extra information is of critical importance. Family doctors have long known this; often the most important part of the surgery consultation is when the patient stands to leave and then remarks, 'Oh yes doctor, there is one more thing...'.
- Try echoing back if you need to clarify something being said, for example by using a phrase already used by the speaker—'You said, "He asked me for a cigarette,"...'

7.18.3 NOS Element AB1.1

The NOS element AB1.1, to 'develop and maintain communication with people', requires that you:

1. communicate in a manner that is consistent with relevant legislation, policies and procedures;
2. communicate with people in a form and manner and using language that:
- is open and respectful of them as individuals;
- is consistent with their level of understanding, culture, background, and preferred ways of communicating;

- is appropriate to the context in which the communication is taking place;
- promotes equality and values diversity;
3. give people opportunities to check their understanding of the information you have given to them and ask questions;
4. take the appropriate action to reduce any barriers to effective communication;
5. make records that:
- are accurate, legible, and complete;
- contain only the information necessary for the record's purpose;
- are free from labelling and discrimination;
6. seek support when you are having difficulty communicating effectively.

(Skills for Justice, 2007a)

TASK 21

List some examples of questions that you might ask people with reference to performance criterion 2.

7.19   Answers to Tasks

TASK 1

It might seem childish to use memory cards but they work!

TASK 2

Many police websites have a Who's Who section (although not always up to date), particularly for their Senior Management Team. Kent Police SMT for example is described at this site: <http://www.kent.police.uk/About%20Kent%20Police/How%20We%20Are%20Structured/How%20we%20are%20structured.html>.

TASK 3

You might like to test yourself by trying the NASA online phonetic alphabet tester available at <http://virtualskies.arc.nasa.gov/alphabet/alphabetIntro.htm>.

TASK 4

The correct order (from most likely to least), based upon statistics for 2004, is:

(1) as a consequence of lung cancer;
(2) as the victim of homicide;
(3) by falling down stairs;
(4) in a cycling accident;
(5) by drowning in a bath;
(6) in a train crash;
(7) in an aircraft crash;
(8) through being struck by lightning.

TASK 5

What hazards would you identify? The person you are searching could cause you injury as a result of using:

- physical force;
- weapon he/she is carrying;
- weapon he/she picks up;

- an object that he/she takes from you such as your own personal safety equipment;
- infection such as hepatitis C, tuberculosis (TB) or influenza (flu);
- infestation such as scabies;
- needle injury.

Therefore the hazard level is medium, as you could receive serious injuries or ill health and as a result could be absent from work for more than three days if the person does attack you.

What are the risks involved? Take into account the:

- person's level of agitation;
- length of time it takes you to carry out the search;
- level of aggression shown by the person towards you;
- opportunity you give to the person to use force against you.

Also take into consideration:

- the locality of the search in terms of its proximity to other members of the public;
- how well lit the area is if it is carried out in the dark;
- whether or not you are alone when you carry out the search.

The risk level is medium as it is likely or possible that you may be injured. What therefore is the threat level? The threat level is calculated to be moderate.

What control measures can you take? There are many more but, for example, request a cover officer if you are alone. Carry out personal safety techniques such as searching from the side of the person; be aware of the movements of the person you are searching at all times; keep him or her in conversation (because it is difficult to think of answers to questions and do other things at the same time); wear gloves to reduce the risk of injury and consider your own personal hygiene and wash exposed body parts such as your hands; consider carrying out the search in the sight line of a town CCTV camera and remain alert at all times.

TASK 6

Naturally, much media attention at the time of the Macpherson Inquiry report centred on the charge of institutional racism. Unfortunately, this inadvertently diverted national attention from the very serious issue of the training of police officers in first aid and the need for them to maintain their skills, throughout their careers and at all ranks. Although the Report is clear that Stephen Lawrence's death from his injuries was probably unavoidable, Chapter 10 remains a shocking catalogue of incompetence and ineptitude.

The Report concludes Chapter 10 with the observation that:

> This evidence reinforced the Inquiry's views as to the lack of satisfactory and proper training in First Aid for officers of all ranks. Not only should officers be properly trained and be given proper refresher training at regular intervals, but it must be made plain that more senior officers need instruction just as much as junior officers. An officer in the position of [name] must be able to ensure that what is being done by his juniors is proper and satisfactory and in accordance with well co-ordinated and directed training. The notion that it may be good enough simply to wait for the ambulance and the paramedics must be exploded (Macpherson, 1999, s 10.6).

TASK 7

The new standard CBRN personal protection equipment issued to trained police officers in the event of an incident is the CR1 (CR stands for Civil Responder; the military are issued with their own version). The CR1 replaces the older Mk4 equipment. In the MPS there are 1,400 CBRN trained and equipped officers, 500 with the new CR1 equipment and 900 with the older Mk4 kit (Safer London Committee, 2005). The CR1 is identical to that used by the fire service in similar circumstances.

You should be able to find the CBRN procedures 'Aide Memoire' on your force intranet.

TASK 8

1. VODS and QUEST are both functionalities of the PNC. VODS is a Vehicle Online Descriptive Search application that assists in identifying vehicles. Combinations of details such as make and model, colour and VIN (see section 10.7 below) can be searched. QUEST is a Query Using Extended Search Techniques facility within PNC. This is the fuzzy capability we referred to earlier. The operator can input partial descriptions of people and produce a list of names that match the characteristics. HMIC have reported the following example of a successful outcome when using QUEST:

> In the West Midlands, counterfeit currency was used in a public house. A search was carried out on the description of a white male, 6′ tall, thin build with a skinhead haircut, brown hair, aged 20–22 years. The offender had a tattoo of a swallow on his left hand. Enquiries at the scene suggested he lived in Solihull and may have been called 'Barry'. A QUEST search produced one suspect who was dealt with for the offence (HMIC, 2005b, p 36).

You might like to conduct further research on the use of 'Boolean' search techniques that use AND, OR, and NOT. These are also useful for conducting internet searches.

There is some evidence that knowledge of these aspects of PNC is not widespread amongst police officers in some forces (HMIC, 2006, p 9). However, you can find out more by visiting the NPIA website at <http://www.npia.police.uk/en/5977.htm>.

2. HMIC is interested in many aspects of a force's use of PNC including:
   - Accuracy
   - Timeliness
   - Completeness
   - Relevancy

   The overall security of the system will also be of interest to HMIC.

TASK 9

The circumstances surrounding the documentary and the political fallout are well-documented on the internet and elsewhere. Many commentators have argued that the documentary gave added impetus to the reforms contained within the IPLDP, and particularly those aspects concerned with the values and attitudes of police officers.

The reasons you gave in response to the task may well have been centred on one or more of the following:

- **Ethical or moral reasons.** You subscribe to the values of the Statement as they coincide (more or less) with your own values. Indeed, the reason you joined the police was perhaps in order to '...protect, help and reassure the community...'.
- **Professional reasons.** You have chosen to join a profession of your own free will and so should abide by the rules of that profession.
- **Instrumental reasons.** For example, in order to do my job properly (or indeed, to keep my job) I need to subscribe to, and implement, the requirements of the Statement.

TASK 10

You will know how closely your own guesses coincided with Police (Conduct) Regulations 2004 Code of Conduct.

TASK 11

On one level, the public should expect a certain level of service from police officers as they pay their wages! More fundamentally (as we have discussed in section 5.6) the police represent the most obvious forms of State legitimacy and still retain a monopoly of certain forms of power and the use of force. In simplistic terms there is always a delicate balance between a police service and a police force. If standards of service are undermined then there is a danger that the public will start to question your legitimacy.

TASK 12

Although the police officer concerned was off duty when the alleged incidents took place you have probably noted that the Code surrounding general conduct applies whether you are on or off duty. There may also have been an abuse of authority in gaining access to the police car.

TASK 13

The most appropriate elements of the NOS would appear to be:

Conduct	Relevant NOS elements
Honesty and integrity	AE1.1
Fairness and impartiality	1A1.3
Politeness and tolerance	2C4.1
Use of force and abuse of authority	Elements of NOS 1A1 and AA1
Performance of duties	AE1.1
Lawful orders	2C2.2
Confidentiality	AB1.2

(However, some alternative answers are entirely possible.)

TASK 14

There are many techniques for memorizing information (the author Tony Buzan, for example, has written extensively on the subject).

One technique for memorizing the declaration is as follows:

(a) First gather together ample supplies of blank paper!
(b) Now write out (or word-process) the declaration on a blank piece of paper by copying the original. Check and double check that you have the words **exactly** as they should be.
(c) Now read the first sentence several times (not the whole paragraph) and try to commit this to memory.
(d) Now turn the page and write down (or word-process), from memory, the first sentence on another piece of paper.
(e) Check your recollected version against the original, correct, version word for word.
(f) Repeat stages (c) to (e) above until you have the sentence completely correct.
(g Now attempt to memorize the first two sentences (not just the second sentence, but the first two together in order).
(h) Repeat the process above until you have the first two sentences completely correct.
(i) Now add the third sentence and so on.
(j) Continue until you have committed the complete declaration to memory.

This may take you some hours to achieve. The same technique can be used for memorizing other information—for example your 'definitions' if your force request so.

TASK 15

In many police forces, such as West Midlands Police, you will need to gain the permission of at least your area commander.

> The chief constable has delegated responsibility for the approval of Business Interests to Operational Command Unit (OCU) Commanders/Heads of Department, who will decide whether a business interest is compatible with an individual's position as a West Midlands officer, taking into account the requirement for officers to discharge and be seen to discharge their duties impartially (<http://www.west-midlands.police.uk/publications/freedom-of-information/policy.asp?id = 82>).

In many forces, the person with delegated responsibility over monitoring of police officers and police staff having 'secondary business interests' is the professional Head of HR.

TASK 16

You will have your own response to the first part of the task.

You are not likely to receive an unlawful order. The part of the PSNI Code of Ethics referred to in the task was inspired by the Council of Europe Declaration on the police, paras A(4) and A(7). This Declaration makes the case that obeying a superior's orders to undertake unlawful actions such as the ill-treatment of an individual, or to carry out an unlawful killing, would be no defence for the individual concerned. Similarly, the Basic Principles on the Use of Force and Firearms by Law Enforcement Officials as adapted by the Eighth Crime Congress of the UNCJIN (the United Nations Criminal Justice Information Network) in 1990 make it clear that:

> Obedience to superior orders shall be no defence if law enforcement officials knew that an order to use force and firearms resulting in the death or serious injury of a person was manifestly unlawful **and** had a reasonable opportunity to refuse to follow it. (Our emphasis.)

TASK 17

The National Police Federation has a website as do a number of branch boards. For example, the Kent Police Federation may be found at <http://www.kentpolfed.org.uk/>. These may well provide you with the information that you need.

TASK 18

You can establish whether your local force has a branch of the BPA by searching the database at <http://www.nationalbpa.com/>.

TASK 19

Agreed, this task requires a gross oversimplification of the theory. However, on most occasions the Handbook would appear to be in adult mode. However, there are certainly also aspects of the critical and nurturing parent.

TASK 20

We obviously provide a simplified version of transactional analysis (TA). You might want to read further. A good starting point is Berne's very readable 1968 book *Games People Play* (re-issued in the late 1990s) which you can pick up second-hand on eBay or at boot fairs for very little. The games that Berne refers to are transactions that lead inevitably to predictable outcomes.

Note that TA is not without its critics and some of its academic standing has been damaged by popularized and over-simplified accounts. Another frequent approach (in police training) to analysing the interactions between individuals (or groups) is the use of the so-called 'Johari' window. The unusual name Johari originates from its two inventors, Joseph Luft and **Har**ry Ingham (Luft, 1970). This proposes that one way of analysing aspects of human interaction is to identify areas of personal awareness and ignorance:

	Known to self	Not known to self
Known to others	**Open area**	**Blind area**
Not known to others	**Hidden area**	**Unknown area**

For example, the blind area includes aspects which are unknown by the person about him/herself but which others know. This can range from straightforward information (such as a medical complaint like halitosis) to more developed personality features, such as feelings of inadequacy, which are barely discerned by the individuals concerned and yet can be seen by others.

TASK 21

The kind of questions you might ask are with reference to actions such as entering a person's home, touching them when conducting a search, and religious requirements for the treatment of the dead.

8 | Police Procedures and Duties

8.1 Chapter Briefing

This chapter describes police procedures and duties relevant to policing of your local communities. It covers a wide amount of material, from your powers and responsibilities when stopping members of the public to the legislation concerning anti-social behaviour. You will probably be expected to meet many of the responsibilities described in this chapter whilst on Supervised and Independent Patrol.

Much of the content of this chapter concerns legislation. As we explained in Chapter 2, we often provide a simplified and abbreviated version of the law, and use flow charts to explain points when appropriate. If you require the detail then you may also need to consult the original legislation, other textbooks, or websites.

8.1.1 Aims of the Chapter

This chapter will enable you to:

- understand your rights and responsibilities when stopping people, asking them for an account, and searching them;
- implement, when appropriate, the law concerned with the use and purchase of alcohol;
- understand how an aggravating feature of some offences can be a racially or religiously motivated intention;
- exercise the powers concerning 'breach of the peace' and deliver the policing of public order in a professional manner;
- learn how the police may support those experiencing harassment from others;
- understand the range of legislation and powers available to counter anti-social behaviour;
- note the law surrounding the ownership and use of firearms, shotguns, and air weapons;
- comprehend the particular legislative and procedural issues surrounding the behaviour of those with 'mental disorders';
- develop the underpinning knowledge required for a number of NOS elements, several of the PAC headings and entries for your Learning Diary Phases 3 and 4 and the CARs of your SOLAP.

8.1.2 Police Action Checklist

This chapter will provide you with the underlying knowledge and theory to meet the following requirements of the Police Action Checklist:

8.1.2.1 Search

Conduct stops.
Demonstrate lawful search—persons.
Demonstrate lawful search—premises.
Demonstrate lawful search—vehicles.

8.1.3 National Occupational Standards

This chapter will provide you with some of the knowledge required to demonstrate aspects of the following NOS elements:

National Occupational Standard Elements

1A1.1   Apply principles of reasonable suspicion or belief.
1A1.2   Use police actions proportionately.
1A1.3   Use police actions fairly.
AA1.1   Promote equality and value diversity.
BE1.1   Provide initial support to victims, survivors and witnesses.
2I1.1   Search individuals.
2I2.2   Conduct searches of vehicles, premises and open spaces.

You should refer to Chapter 6 for general information and advice concerning the NOS elements.

8.1.4 IPLDP Phases and Modules

This chapter will provide you with resources to support the following Operational Modules of the IPLDP:

> OP 3 Respond to incidents, conduct and evaluate investigations.
> OP 5 Search individuals and premises.

It will also cover aspects of the following topic areas of Legislation, Policy and Guidelines of the IPLDP.

- Crime (LPG 1.1);
- Stop and Search (LPG 1.2);
- Protecting People (LPG 1.3);
- Police Policies and Procedures (LPG 1.4);
- Non-Crime Incidents (LPG 1.5).

Much of the content of this chapter relates to IPLDP Phase 3 'Supervised Patrol' and Phase 4 'Independent Patrol'.

8.1.5 SOLAP

The contents of this chapter are relevant to the knowledge evidence requirements of CARs 1A1, AA1, BE1, 2I1, and 2I2.

8.1.6 Learning Diary Phases

The contents of this chapter may provide you with stimulus material for completion of your Learning Diary Phase 3, particularly for the following headings:

- Crime;
- Non-crime incidents;
- Police policies and procedures;
- Protecting people;
- Stop and searches.

8.1.7 IPLDP Learning Requirement

This chapter is relevant to 3.12, 7.1, and 7.4 of the IPLDP Learning Requirement.

8.2 Introduction

In this chapter, we shall be looking at what you do, more or less routinely, as part of your general police duties. As usual, we have to generalize somewhat because we are discussing a typical police force, and yours may possibly vary in details from the average force described in this chapter. This might apply particularly to the applications of force policies, though the essence of what we talk about will hold for all forces. Not all the police procedures and duties expected of you are covered in this chapter, but you will find most of the remainder elsewhere in the Handbook. It is a long chapter too, and you may not want to read it all through in one sitting. You are more likely to dip into it to cover what you need, but we think, all the same, that there is a coherence to what is being described and discussed here.

We are considering your powers and responsibilities **other** than in the investigation of a crime (though there is some overlap). This chapter covers offences and the actions you can take to address these offences. This is not to say that offences described and analysed in this chapter would not lead on to a criminal investigation nor that some things (for example, possession of a bladed knife) may not result in arrest. They may well. But these will be ancillary offences, arising from original offences.

Consider, for example, the power to confiscate alcohol. If, on patrol, you decide that it would be sensible to take alcohol away from a young person in a town centre, the individual (if intoxicated) may try to hit you for depriving him or her of the bottle or can. This assault would be an ancillary offence (criminally grave enough in its own right) which followed from your intervention.

We should perhaps have a general word about '**Stop and Account**' and '**Stop and Search**' to put both in context. The power to stop someone and ask for an account of his or her movements or purpose, or the power to stop and search someone, are very traditional constabulary powers. However, you are probably already aware of the considerable sensitivities around the exercise of these powers. Stop and search has been particularly associated with racial harassment; it is claimed that ethnic minority members of the public have been stopped and searched disproportionately, compared with their proportion in the general population. There are, however, arguments concerning the statistical basis for this claim, which highlight the difference between the 'resident' and 'available' populations that you police. For example, see Waddington et al, 2004. Problems arise when there are no justifiable grounds for the stop and search and this has led to charges that the police are racist. As a rule, you should ask yourself whether you have a justification (within the context of the powers of search that you employ) to stop and search someone. In other words, are you sure of your grounds? Are you stopping this person for a reason that will withstand scrutiny?

The record of all stops and searches and stops and accounts is a conventional quantitative measurement of police performance, and you may find that your own force has very clear policy guidelines on when you may and when you may not exercise these powers. You should not be concerned if such policies are not available; just remember that whatever search power you use, it must conform to the guidelines of the PACE Act 1984 Codes of Practice relating to searches.

Public order offences are considered in some detail, and these will apply whether you are policing a large rally in a town centre or an individual breach of the peace. You will study your powers under the Public Order Act 1986, and even more importantly, the exercise of discretion (which we discussed extensively in Chapter 5). It is as important to you as a student police officer to know when **not** to make an issue of something as when you should. There are plenty of examples where the intelligent use of police discretion can defuse situations which might otherwise get out of hand. Take, for example, a demonstration with placards demanding the death of some individual for some supposed offence (this is not restricted to recent matters of race and religion; there was a well-known vigilante case in Hampshire in the 1990s where an alleged paedophile was subject to such public death threats). Technically, the placards are incitements to kill and therefore a criminal offence. But what might happen if you go in forcibly and wrest the placards from people's hands? Might it not make an inflamed situation even worse? Might you not provoke some really serious rioting or criminal damage by intervening so publicly and aggressively?

Certainly, some commentators (and some senior police officers) believe that such actions will only make things worse. The priority for the police at a heated demonstration of this kind is to keep the peace and prevent serious disorder. The intelligent things to do would be to monitor such events carefully and take action, if justified, after the event when temperatures have cooled.

That is not to say that the police should not intervene decisively and in force if serious rioting seems likely. Most of the time, in most situations of public order, arresting people for criminal intent can be carried out once the event itself is controlled or has ended. Such judgements come with experience, and even now not all senior officers get the tactics right every time, so you should not expect to be infallible.

The latter part of the chapter concerns possession of **offensive weapons** and, in particular, knives and firearms. Socially, and in terms of media attention, the illegal possession of such items is a source of considerable (and understandable) anxiety for the public. The notion that, particularly in schools, knives and bladed articles are almost a commonplace concerns many parents. Unlicensed and replica guns are also matters of concern in society. Hardly a year goes by when one of the police forces in England and Wales is not being investigated for a fatal shooting of someone subsequently found to be carrying a replica weapon. You should be aware of this context when you are looking into matters concerning such weaponry, and aware too of your powers. If you note that the use of a firearm in the commission of a crime carries a substantially heavier sentence, and that police officers themselves are at risk from criminals who can show themselves to be ruthless in their attempts to avoid arrest or detection, then you will be convinced of the importance of preventive action wherever possible. Your own force will have clear policies on licensed and unlicensed weapons.

Lastly, when using the powers which are described in this chapter remember the provisions of the **Human Rights Act 1998** (see section 11.3 below). When you exercise your powers, you must be able to justify what you do as proportionate and necessary. You must know what your powers are and under what authority you operate. Above all, ask yourself if you would be able to defend your actions in court or in an enquiry.

8.3 Stop and Account

There are a large number of statutes that provide you with the power to stop a person or vehicle, including such diverse legislation as s 6 of the Public Stores Act 1875, s 4 of the Crossbows Act 1987, and s 43 of the Terrorism Act 2000. Where appropriate we deal elsewhere in this Handbook with powers to stop and search that arise from specific legislation (for example, see section 8.22.3).

This section is about the recording of encounters with the public which are **not** governed by statutory powers. It is concerned with the more general circumstances where you interact with members of the public. One such interaction is the so-called 'Stop and Account' where members of the public are stopped and asked to account for their behaviour, actions, or presence in a public place or for their possession of anything. It does not involve searching. 'Stop and Account' is covered in the Police and Criminal Evidence (PACE) Act 1984, Code A, paras 3.1 and 4.12–4.19. As we noted in the introduction, there exists some controversy surrounding the use of stop, account, and search powers by the police, and in particular the claims made that these powers are used disproportionately against members of the ethnic minority communities. The debate is beyond the scope of this Handbook. However, if you wish to read further on this, see Waddington et al (2004) as a starting point. The PACE Act 1984 Codes of Practice state that when carrying out your duties:

> . . . all stops and searches should be carried out with courtesy, consideration and respect for the person concerned. This has a significant impact on public confidence in the police . . . (Code A, para 3.1).

To help you achieve this, the Codes regulate chance meetings with the public. These situations include general conversations with any member of the public. In some circumstances you are required to make a record of what happened and what was said, (see Code A, paras 4.12 to 4.19).

8.3.1 Recording of Encounters not Governed by Statutory Powers

These are covered in the PACE Act 1984, Code A, para 4.12 and state that:

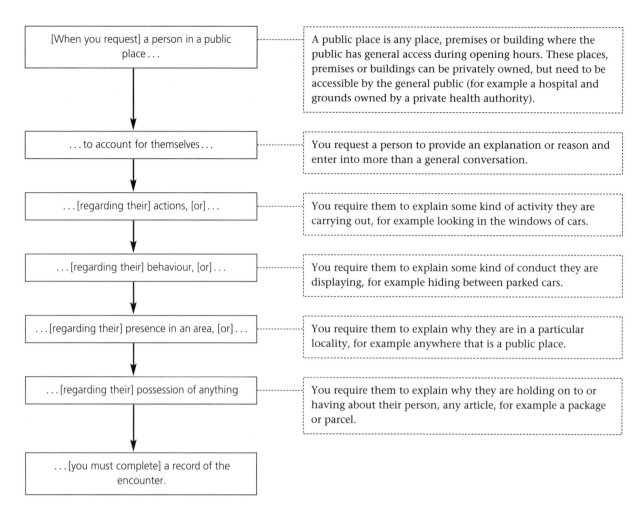

You must complete the form (record) at the time of the encounter and offer a copy to the person unless it is completely out of the question to do so (for example in a serious public order situation). In such difficult situations, you should provide the person with details (for example on a business card) of the date of the stop and the station the person can go to for a record. You should complete a form as soon as possible.

8.3.2 Exceptions

These are listed in Code A, para 4.13. You do not have to complete a form:

- if in general conversation;
- if you give directions;
- if you are looking for witnesses;
- if seeking general information;
- if questioning people in order to establish the background to incidents which have required you to become involved, for example in order to resolve a dispute or to restore order.

You also do not have to complete a form if you are issuing a person with a Penalty Notice for an offence or issuing them with another form requesting them to:

- produce their driving documents;
- rectify a defect on their vehicle;
- pay a fixed penalty;
- supply a specimen of breath for an alcohol screening test.

However, if the encounter or chance meeting does not satisfy the conditions to make it recordable (see Code A, para 4.12 above) but the person **requests** a record, you should still provide them with a copy of a stop form. However, make sure that you write on the form that the encounter did not meet the criteria to make the stop recordable in terms of Code A, para 4.12.

If the encounter or chance meeting does not meet the conditions to make it recordable, you can refuse to issue the form if you reasonably believe that the purpose of the request is deliberately aimed at **frustrating** or **delaying legitimate police activity.** An example would include if you are being talked to, or shouted at, in a public order situation (such as a large demonstration) by an individual or group of people who are trying distract you from the 'lawful execution of your duty'. So long as you have not initiated or engaged in contact with the person about their individual circumstances (such as why the person is there, what they are doing, where they have been or are going) then there is no need to issue a form (see Code A, para 4.19, note 20).

8.3.3   Summary of What to Do after Speaking with a Member of the Public

8.4   Road Checks (Section 4 of the PACE Act 1984)

In Chapter 10 you will read that you have the power, under s 163 of the Road Traffic Act (RTA) 1988 to stop a 'mechanically propelled vehicle' on a road. In addition, s 4 of the PACE Act 1984 provides a senior officer with the power to authorize a 'road check' for the specific purpose of determining whether a vehicle is carrying people connected with indictable offences (other than road traffic or vehicle excise offences), or people who are unlawfully at large. The authorization of a senior officer for a 's 4 road check' is necessary because every vehicle will be stopped in a certain area for the purposes of locating a specific person, and the rights of the individual must be considered when a significant disruption of usual public activity is likely to occur as a result of the check.

Section 4 of the PACE Act 1984 sets out the circumstances under which a road check can take place for the purposes of stopping vehicles which are selected to be stopped using s 163 of the RTA 1988, in a specified locality, during a specified time, for a specific reason. Section 4 does not affect your power to stop vehicles at any other time using s 163 of the RTA 1988 as described later in Chapter 10.

So, to summarize, you **set up road checks** under s 4 of the PACE Act 1984 and **stop the vehicles** under s 163 of the RTA 1988.

8.4.1 Purpose of a Road Check

Section 4 of the PACE Act 1984 states that the purpose of the road check must be to find:

a person who has committed an indictable offence other than a road traffic offence or a vehicle excise offence; [or] a person who is a witness to such an offence . . . . [or] . . . . a person intending to commit such an offence . . . [or] . . . a person who is unlawfully at large.

The suspected offence involved must be an indictable offence, and there must be reasonable grounds for suspecting that the person is, or is about to be, in the locality of the road check.

8.4.2 Authorization for a Road Check

A police officer of the rank of superintendent or above must authorize a s 4 road check in writing. If such a police officer is not available, a road check may be authorized by an officer below the rank of superintendent (see s 4(5)). Any use of the power to impose a road check must be conducted in accordance with the PACE Act 1984, Code of Practice A (concerned with stop and search).

TASK 1

Give thought to the health and safety implications of holding a road check.

What are the considerations in terms of you, your colleagues, and the general public?

8.5 Stop and Search

Sections 1 and 2 of the PACE Act 1984 give you the power to stop, search, and detain individuals and vehicles under the circumstances described below. As we noted in the introduction to section 8.3, it is by no means the only power to search people, as there are a further twenty or so, but for all of them, the Codes of Practice provide rules to safeguard the rights of an individual while you carry out a search. This part of the Handbook provides information about 'Stop and Search' (or, more precisely, 'Stop, Search and Detain') under s 1 of the PACE Act 1984. Note at the outset that you do not have to be in uniform to carry out such a search.

The ability to 'conduct stops' and to 'demonstrate lawful search of persons, premises and vehicles' are requirements within the PAC 'Search' heading and can contribute evidence for the attainment of NOS element 2I1.1:

National Occupational Standard Element

2I1.1 Search individuals.

Note that element 2I1.1 requires that you conduct the search on the appropriate 'grounds and legal authority' and that you also identify and deal with any potential risks. These risks may include offensive weapons, assault, sharps (eg hypodermic needles), or hazardous substances (see section 7.7 above). As with most NOS elements, you will achieve 2I1.1 largely through direct observation by your assessor when you carry out a search for real. The requirement is that you successfully complete a minimum of five searches in a variety of circumstances.

8.5.1 Appropriate Locations for 'Stop, Search and Detain'

Section 1(1) of the PACE Act 1984 states that you may search:

(a) in any place to which . . . the public or any section of the public has access, on payment or otherwise, as of right, or by virtue of express or implied permission;
(b) in any other place to which people have ready access at the time when [you propose] to exercise the power but which is not a dwelling.

The public have a **right** to use roads and footpaths and other public areas during opening hours. They have **express permission** to enter cinemas, theatres, or football grounds having paid an entrance fee and they can remain there until that particular entertainment is over, when permission to be there ends. There is an **implied permission** for persons to enter buildings to carry out business transactions with the owners, and even to use a footpath to a dwelling-house for the purposes of paying a lawful call upon the householder. That implied permission remains until withdrawn by the householder or the owner of the business premises. Places to which the public has **ready access** include places such as a private field, if that field is regularly used by trespassers. It definitely does not include inside a place of residence (dwelling). If the search is to be carried out in a garden, yard, or other land attached to a dwelling, then there are restrictions. You can still use the power in these places because the public can still gain access to them, for example in order to hide by jumping over a wall, but there are restrictions. These are shown in the flow chart below.

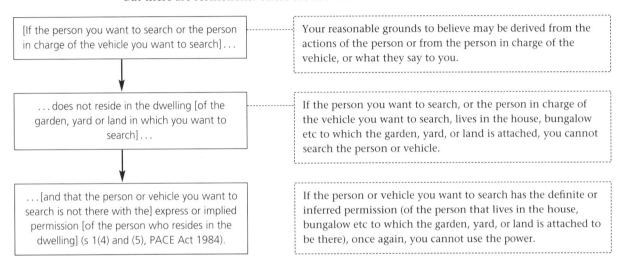

8.5.2 Who or What Can Be 'Stopped, Searched and Detained'?

Having made sure that you first of all satisfy the above requirements concerning the location, under s 1(2)(a) of the PACE Act 1984 you can search:

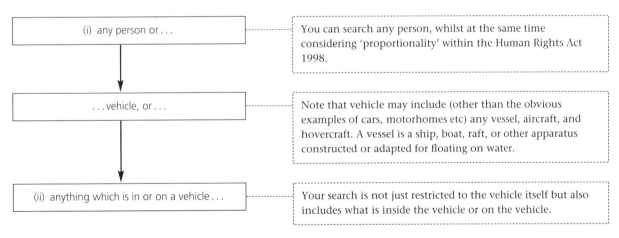

8.5.3 Items You May Search for under 'Stop, Search and Detain'

Section 1 of the PACE Act 1984 can only be used for searching for stolen or prohibited articles. You may search for stolen articles, including any article which you have reasonable grounds for suspecting to be stolen. You may also search for prohibited articles, including:

- offensive weapons which are made, intended, or adapted for causing injury to a person;
- articles with a blade or which are sharply pointed;

- articles made or adapted for use in burglary, theft, taking a conveyance without consent, fraud, or criminal damage;
- any firework possessed in breach of a prohibition imposed by any of the firework regulations.

Note that some items, drugs for example, are not prohibited articles. Instead, there are other statutory powers of search available to use for searching for other items such as drugs and firearms (see Code A, Annex A).

You may detain a person or vehicle for the purpose of such a search, but the length of time the person or vehicle is detained must be reasonable and kept to a minimum (Code A, para 3.3).

8.5.4 Grounds for 'Stop, Search and Detain'

Under s 1(3) of the PACE Act 1984, you do not have the power to search unless you have **reasonable grounds** for suspecting that you will find stolen or prohibited articles. Reasonable grounds for suspicion depend on the circumstances in each case (see Code A, para 2.2), but the following factors can all be considered:

- a suspect's behaviour, for example trying to hide something;
- accurate and current intelligence or information;
- reliable information that members of a group habitually carry prohibited articles.

Reasonable grounds do **not** include personal factors, such as ethnicity, age, appearance, or previous convictions either singly or in combination.

If you discover an article which you have reasonable grounds to suspect to be stolen or prohibited, you can seize it (s 1(6), PACE Act).

8.5.5 Requirements Regarding the Search of Persons and Vehicles

These requirements are explained in s 2 of the PACE Act 1984. Briefly, they state that you must take reasonable steps to provide certain information to the person to be searched or the person in charge of the vehicle to be searched. The information you must provide is shown in the table below and can be best remembered by the use of the mnemonic GO WISELY:

G	Grounds of the suspicion for the search
O	Object/purpose of search
W	Warrant card (if in plain clothes or requested)
I	Identity of officer
S	Station to which attached
E	Entitlement to a copy of the search record
L	Legal power used
Y	You are detained for the purposes of a search

You can carry out the search either:

- at the place where the person or vehicle was first detained; or
- near (within a reasonable travelling distance of) the place where the person or vehicle was first detained (see Code A, para 3.4, note 6).

After searching an **unattended vehicle**, you must leave a search form inside the vehicle (unless it is not reasonable or practical to do so without causing damage, see s 2(6), PACE Act).

When searching persons:

- You must seek the **co-operation** of the person to be searched every time. Reasonable force may be used as a last resort to conduct a search, but only after you have been met with resistance from the person to be searched (see Code A, para 3.2).
- You cannot require any person to remove any **clothing** in public other than an outer jacket and gloves. You can search a person's hair as well, but only if the removal of headgear is not required (see Code A, para 3.5).

- You can place your hands inside the pockets of outer clothing and feel round the inside of collars, socks, and shoes (see Code A, para 3.5).
- You cannot search a member of the **opposite sex** if it involves removal of more than outer coat, jacket, gloves, headgear, or footwear, and you cannot be present at such a search unless the person being searched specifically requests it (see Code A, para 3.6).
- You can carry out a more thorough search, for example requiring the removal of a T-shirt, but it must be undertaken out of **public view**, for example in a police van or police station (see Code A, para 3.6).
- You must make a **record** of the search and give a copy to the person you have searched unless it is impracticable to do so (see Code A, paras 4.1 and 4.2). In this case, provide the person with the date of the search and details of the police station where they can obtain the record of the search (see Code A, note 21).
- You must keep the search **relevant;** the extent of the search must relate to the object you are searching for, and if the suspicion relates to a certain pocket, then only that pocket can be searched (see Code A, para 3.3).

TASK 2

As you have seen, there are a number of requirements that you must follow when making a search under s 1 of the PACE Act 1984. Some of these relate to what you must tell the person you are searching. In order for this to become second nature, write down the list of things you have to say in a way that you will remember them. For example, make a mind-map or a mnemonic to help you remember.

Completion of this task will help you towards meeting the knowledge requirements of CAR2I1 in your SOLAP under the headings 'Legal and organisational requirements', and 'Searching individuals'.

8.6 Stop and Search for Offensive Weapons

If you find yourself in a situation where it seems likely that a serious breakdown in public order might occur, s 60 of the Criminal Justice and Public Order Act 1994 empowers a senior police officer to authorize you to stop and search people for offensive weapons or other dangerous instruments. Under s 60(5), you do **not** have to have grounds for suspecting that the person or vehicle is carrying weapons or dangerous articles.

Section 60(1) of the Criminal Justice and Public Order Act 1994 states that,

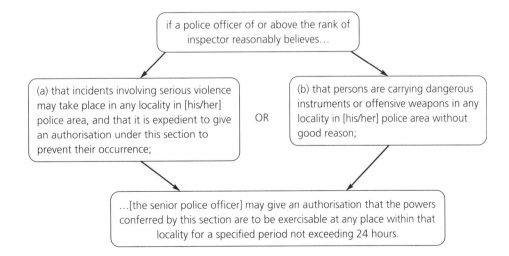

if a police officer of or above the rank of inspector reasonably believes…

(a) that incidents involving serious violence may take place in any locality in [his/her] police area, and that it is expedient to give an authorisation under this section to prevent their occurrence;

OR

(b) that persons are carrying dangerous instruments or offensive weapons in any locality in [his/her] police area without good reason;

…[the senior police officer] may give an authorisation that the powers conferred by this section are to be exercisable at any place within that locality for a specified period not exceeding 24 hours.

8.6.1   Authorization

The authorization can only be given by a police officer above the rank of inspector. The following points are also to be noted:

- 'If an inspector gives an authorisation under subsection (1) [he/she] must, as soon as it is practicable to do so, cause an officer of or above the rank of superintendent to be informed' (s 60(3A)).
- An officer of or above the rank of superintendent may direct that the authorization shall continue in being for a further 24 hours (s 60(3)).

8.6.2   Implementation

The search must comply with s 2 of the PACE Act 1984. Under s 60(4) of the Criminal Justice and Public Order Act 1994, the authorization provides you with the power to:

(a) stop any pedestrian and search [him/her] or anything carried by [him/her] for offensive weapons or dangerous instruments, and

(b) stop any vehicle and search the vehicle, its driver and any passenger for offensive weapons or dangerous instruments.

If, in the course of such a search under this power, you discover a dangerous instrument or an article which you have reasonable grounds for suspecting to be an offensive weapon, you may seize it (s 60(6)).

It is an offence (s 60(8)) for a person to fail to stop (or to stop his/her vehicle) when required to do so by you in the exercise of your stop and search powers under s 60(4).

This offence is triable summarily and the penalty is one month's imprisonment and/or a fine.

8.6.3   Searches Involving the Removal of Clothing

You can only ask someone to remove clothing if it seems to you that he/she is using that clothing in an attempt to conceal his/her identity. When carrying out a search under s 60, you have the power under s 60AA(2) to:

(a) require any person to remove any item which [you] reasonably [believe] that person is wearing wholly or mainly for the purpose of concealing [his/her] identity;

(b) to seize any item which [you] reasonably [believe] any person intends to wear wholly or mainly for that purpose.

A person who fails to remove an item worn by [him/her] when required to do so by a constable in the exercise of [his/her] power under this section, commits an offence (s 60AA(7)).

This offence is triable summarily and the penalty is six months' imprisonment and/or a fine.

TASK 3

A town has recently experienced several outbreaks of serious public disorder between two rival gangs. The disorder has mainly occurred in the local park. Subsequently, an order is in force under s 60 of the Criminal Justice and Public Order Act 1984.

You are on patrol in the local park when you see a person wearing a full face ski mask which is concealing his or her face. Under what circumstances can you ask the person to remove their mask? Choose one of the following:

1. If you reasonably believe that the person was carrying a dangerous instrument or an offensive weapon.
2. You reasonably believe that the person was attempting to conceal his or her identity.
3. No further circumstances are required as a s 60 order is in force.
4. If you reasonably believe that the person was likely to be involved in violence.

8.7 Alcohol-related Offences

It is likely that many of the incidents you will investigate whilst on Supervised and Independent Patrol will be alcohol-related, and particularly so if you are on late shift. Remember, you must consider your own health and safety and the health and safety of everybody around you when dealing with incidents fuelled by alcohol. Drunken people are sometimes subject to rapid mood swings, happy one minute and then violent the next. People who are normally quite reserved may lose some of their normal social inhibitions, and the potential for injury can be very high. During your training you will be helped to develop skills to defuse potentially dangerous situations involving people under the influence of alcohol.

Alcohol-related offences are dealt with under the following legislation:

* s 12 of the Licensing Act 1872;
* s 2 of the Licensing Act 1902;
* s 91(1) of the Criminal Justice Act 1967.

8.7.1 The Definition of 'Being Drunk'

The terms drunk and drunkenness are not defined in law. As a precedent, the case of *R v Tagg* [2002] 1 Cr App R 2 determined that the everyday meaning of 'drunk' should be used. The Court of Appeal also accepted that the *Collins Dictionary* definition (used by the Judge in the original case under appeal) and the *Shorter Oxford English Dictionary* (1933) definitions were essentially the same and were helpful in determining the existence of a state of drunkenness. For example, the OED defines drunk as 'having drunk intoxicating liquor to an extent which affects steady self-control' (*Shorter Oxford English Dictionary*, 1933, cited in *R v Tagg* [2002] 1 Cr App R 2).

The court itself must decide whether or not a suspect was drunk. The general rule that the opinion of a witness is inadmissible does not apply in this particular context; a competent witness may give evidence that, in his/her opinion, a person was drunk (*R v Davies* [1962] 1 WLR 1111). A competent witness is a person who understands questions put to them and gives answers that can be understood. As a police officer, you can therefore state your opinion (as a competent witness) on whether a particular person was drunk. You should also be able to give the facts on which your opinion is based, such as:

* he was unsteady on his feet;
* her eyes were glazed;
* his speech was slurred; or
* you could smell intoxicating liquor on her breath.

8.7.2 Drunkenness as an Offence

Section 12 of the Licensing Act 1872 states that it is an offence for a person to be:

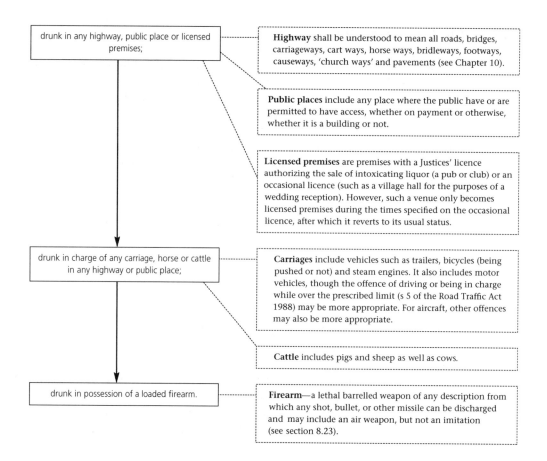

This offence is triable summarily and the penalty is one month's imprisonment or a fine. It is also a penalty offence for the purposes of s 1 of the Criminal Justice and Public Order Act 2001 (see section 11.21 below).

8.7.3 Drunk and Disorderly Behaviour

The precise meaning of the term 'disorderly behaviour' is not defined by statute but its everyday meaning is 'unruly or offensive behaviour'. Under s 91(1) of the Criminal Justice Act 1967, it is an offence for any person to display such behaviour whilst drunk in any highway, public place, or licensed premises.

This offence is triable summarily and the penalty is one month's imprisonment or a fine. It is also a penalty offence for the purposes of s 1 of the Criminal Justice and Public order Act 2001 (see section 11.21 below).

8.7.4 Drunk in Charge of Children

Under s 2 of the Licensing Act 1902, it is an offence for a person to be drunk while having charge of a child under the age of seven years, in any highway, public place, or licensed premises.

The precise meaning of 'having charge' is not defined by statute, but probably means some sort of care or control over the child(ren); for this offence the suspect must be the only person with the child, or alternatively everyone in the group with the child must be drunk.

This offence is triable summarily and the penalty is one month's imprisonment or a fine.

8.7.5 Drinking Alcohol in Designated Public Places

Under s 12(1) of the Criminal Justice and Police Act 2001, if you reasonably believe that a person is, or has been consuming, or intends to consume alcohol in a designated public place (designated by a local authority), you may require the person:

- not to consume in that place anything which is, or which [you] reasonably believe [. . .] to be, alcohol;
- to surrender anything in [his/her] possession which is, or which [you] reasonably believe [. . .] to be, alcohol or a container for alcohol.

You must inform the person that under s 12(4) of the Criminal Justice and Police Act 2001 it is an offence to fail to comply (without reasonable excuse) with your requirement not to consume or to surrender alcohol.

You may dispose of anything surrendered to you under this section in such a manner as you consider appropriate (s 12(3)). Your own force policies will be very clear about what you should do under these circumstances, therefore refer to these in order to establish a suitable course of action.

This offence is triable summarily and the penalty is a fine. It is also a penalty offence for the purposes of s 1 of the Criminal Justice and Public Order Act 2001 (see section 11.21 below).

8.7.6 Power to Direct a Person Away from an Area of Alcohol-related Crime and Disorder

Under s 27 of the Violent Crime Reduction Act 2006, you may give a direction to an individual aged sixteen or over who is in a public place (which includes a place on a means of transport) to leave the locality, and to prohibit the individual from returning to that locality for such a period (not exceeding forty-eight hours) from the giving of the direction as you may specify.

You may give the direction if the presence of the individual in that locality is likely, in all the circumstances, to cause or to contribute to:

- the occurrence of alcohol-related crime or disorder, or
- a repetition or continuance of such crime or disorder,

and the direction is necessary for the purpose of removing or reducing the likelihood of there being such crime or disorder or there being a repetition or continuance of such crime or disorder in that locality during the period for which the direction has effect.

The direction you give **must**:

(a) be given in writing;
(b) clearly identify the locality to which it relates;
(c) specify the period for which the individual is prohibited from returning to that locality.

The direction you give may:

(a) require the individual to whom it is given to leave the locality in question either immediately or by such time as you may specify;
(b) impose requirements as to the manner in which that individual leaves the locality, including his/her route; and
(c) be withdrawn or varied (but not extended so as to apply for a period of more than 48 hours) by you.

The direction you give must **not** prevent the individual from:

(a) having access to a place where he/she resides;
(b) attending at any place which he/she is required to attend for the purposes of any employment of his/hers or of any contract of services to which he/she is a party;
(c) attending at any place which he/she is expected to attend during the period to which the direction applies for the purposes of education or training or for the purpose of receiving medical treatment; or
(d) attending at any place which he/she is required to attend by any obligation imposed on him/her by or under an enactment or by the order of a court or tribunal.

Having given the direction, you must make a record of:

(a) the terms of the direction and the locality to which it relates;
(b) the individual to whom it is given;

(c) the time at which it is given;

(d) the period during which that individual is required not to return to the locality.

Under s 27(6) Violent Crime Reduction Act 2006 it is an offence for a person to fail to comply with such a direction.

This offence is triable summarily and the penalty is a fine.

8.7.7   Banning Orders

Under s 1 of the Violent Crime Reduction Act 2006 a court may order a person aged sixteen or over to be excluded from pubs and clubs in a defined geographic area for a given length of time.

It is an offence under s 11 Violent Crime Reduction Act 2006 if the subject of a drinking banning order or of an interim order does, without reasonable excuse, anything that he is prohibited from doing by the order.

This offence is triable summarily and the penalty is a fine.

TASK 4

In your area you often see a habitual drunk who often drinks large quantities of very strong lager and then becomes very abusive to members of the public passing by. Today, you have been requested to deal with this problem. How will you approach this person and what long-term solution will you consider to resolve the situation? Look at s 34(1) of the Criminal Justice Act 1972 to help you work out a suitable course of action.

8.8   Confiscation of Alcohol

Concern about young people drinking alcohol has increased considerably over the past few years. Section 1 of the Confiscation of Alcohol (Young Persons) Act 1997 does not make it illegal for young people to consume alcohol, but its effect is to prevent the consumption of alcohol in public (except in licensed premises where other legislation applies). Alcohol can also be confiscated from young people in private residences if they have unlawfully gained access.

However, you **cannot** require the surrender of a **sealed** container unless you can justify your belief that the person is:

*   currently consuming alcohol, or
*   has been recently consuming alcohol, or
*   is going to consume alcohol in the near future

in a relevant place.

A relevant place includes:

*   any public place, eg streets, parks, and shopping centres (but not licensed premises such as pubs or clubs);
*   any place, other than a public place, to which the person has unlawfully gained access, such as gate-crashing a party at a private house where the trespasser did not have the consent of the homeowner to gain entry.

Section 1 of the Confiscation of Alcohol (Young Persons) Act 1997 states that . . .

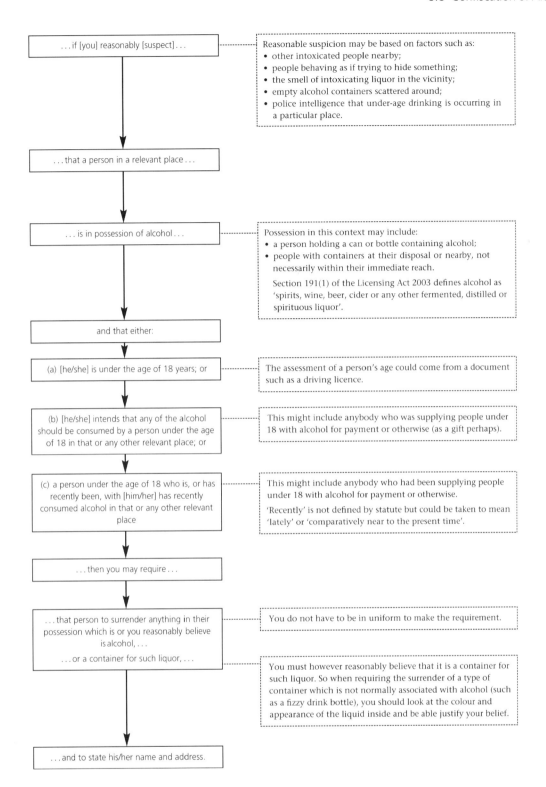

You must inform the person that it is an offence to fail to comply (without reasonable excuse) with your requirement to surrender alcohol, under s 1(14) of the Confiscation of Alcohol (Young Persons) Act 1997.

You may dispose of anything surrendered to you under s 1(1) in such manner as you consider appropriate (s 1(2)). Your own force policies will be very clear about what you should do under these circumstances, therefore refer to these in order to establish a suitable course of action.

Under the Police Reform Act 2002, a suitably designated police community support officer (PCSO) also has the power to make a requirement to surrender alcohol as described above.

8.8.1 Failing to Comply with a Requirement

It is an offence under s 1(3) of the Confiscation of Alcohol (Young Persons) Act 1997 for a person to fail (without reasonable excuse) to comply with a requirement imposed on him/her under s 1(1). But remember, for the person to commit this offence you must have **informed** the person that failure without reasonable excuse to comply with your requirement is an offence (s 1(4)).

This offence is triable summarily and the penalty is a fine.

8.8.2 Wider Considerations

This legislation will be a useful addition to your toolbox of policing skills. If you find a child carrying unopened cans of alcohol and you do not have grounds to reasonably believe that he/she has been consuming alcohol (or is about to consume it) at a relevant place, then at least consider where s/he bought the cans, the welfare of the child, and take action accordingly.

> **TASK 13**
>
> You have identified a group of sixteen-year-olds drinking alcohol in a 'relevant place'. Write down a list of things you would say to the young people involved in order to make your requirements lawful, and which will give you the opportunity to act.

8.9 Offences and Powers Relating to Licensed Premises

The Licensing Act 2003 includes legislation to try and address drunkenness in 'relevant premises'. Staff working in places where alcohol is served have a legal responsibility to try prevent drunkenness and disorder.

People with these **responsibilities** are listed in s 140(1) of the Licensing Act 2003, and are referred to from now on as **responsible staff** (a term of our own invention, not a legal term).

Responsible staff include:

- any person who works at the premises in a capacity which authorizes him or her to prevent disorderly conduct;
- the holder of a premises licence;
- the designated premises' supervisor of a licensed premises;

and for premises with a **club premises certificate**:

- any member or officer of the club with the capacity to prevent disorderly behaviour;
- the premises' user of premises with a permitted temporary activity;

and for premises with only **temporary permitted activity**:

- the premises' user.

Relevant premises within this legislation are:

- licensed premises, eg a pub;
- club premises with club premises certificate, eg a working men's club;
- premises such as village halls with permitted temporary activity such as a wedding reception.

8.9.1 Allowing Disorderly Conduct

An offence is committed by responsible staff who knowingly allow disorderly conduct on licensed premises. This offence is triable summarily and the penalty is a fine.

8.9.2 Selling Intoxicating Liquor to a Drunk Person

An offence is committed under s 141(1) of the Licensing Act 2003 by a licensee or responsible staff who knowingly sell or attempt to sell alcohol to a person who is drunk on relevant premises. This offence is triable summarily and the penalty is a fine. It is also a penalty offence for the purposes of s 1 of the Criminal Justice and Public Order Act 2001 (see section 11.21 below).

8.9.3   Obtaining Alcohol for a Drunk Person

An offence is committed under s 142(1) of the Licensing Act 2003 by a person who knowingly obtains or attempts to obtain alcohol for consumption on relevant premises by a person who is drunk. This offence is triable summarily and the penalty is a fine. It is also a penalty offence for the purposes of s 1 of the Criminal Justice and Public Order Act 2001 (see section 11.21 below).

8.9.4   Entering or Leaving Premises when Drunk or Disorderly

If a person is drunk or disorderly and fails to leave relevant premises when requested to do so, he/she has committed an offence under s 143(1) of the Licensing Act 2003. Such a person may be requested to leave by a constable or responsible staff. This offence is triable summarily and the penalty is a fine.

As a police officer, you have a responsibility to respond to requests for help from responsible staff to help expel or refuse entry to a drunk person, s 143(4) of the Licensing Act 2003.

8.9.5   Powers of Entry for Licensed Premises

You can use reasonable force to gain entry to premises for the purposes of detecting an offence under s 180(1) of the Licensing Act 2003.

Under s 97(1) of the Licensing Act 2003 you have the power to enter a **club** (with a club premises certificate) if you have reasonable cause to believe that an offence of:

(a) . . . supplying, or offering to supply, or being concerned in supplying, or making an offer to supply a **controlled drug** has been, is being, or is about to be committed there; or
(b) that there is likely to be a breach of the peace there.

Whilst exercising this power you may, if necessary, use reasonable force (s 97(2)). See section 9.13 for a discussion of 'controlled drugs'.

For premises with **permitted temporary activities**, you may (under s 108(1) of the Licensing Act 2003) at any reasonable time, enter the premises to assess the effect of the event in terms of:

- the prevention of crime and disorder;
- public safety;
- the prevention of public nuisance;
- the protection of children from harm.

There is no specific offence of obstructing a police officer under this section, so if this occurs, you should consider the offence of obstruction in the lawful execution of your duties under the Police Act 1996.

8.9.6   Selling Alcohol to Children

- An offence is committed under s 146(1) of the Licensing Act 2003 by a person who sells alcohol anywhere to a person under eighteen. This is a penalty offence under s 1 of the Criminal Justice and Public Order Act 2001 (see section 11.21 below).
- An offence is committed under s 147(1) of the Licensing Act 2003 by a person who knowingly allows the sale of alcohol on relevant premises to an individual aged under eighteen.
- An offence is committed under s 147A of the Licensing Act 2003 by a person where on three or more different occasions within a period of three consecutive months alcohol is unlawfully sold on the same licensed premises to an individual aged under eighteen.

These offences are triable summarily and the penalty is a fine.

> **TASK 6**
>
> In the course of your investigations into offences concerning public disorder, public in-decency, criminal damage and theft, you may discover that many of these offences are committed by people who have consumed large amounts of intoxicating liquor on relevant

premises. This intake of alcohol may have contributed towards these offences being committed.

Look up your force policy to establish how you will inform the licensing authority of the premises about such activities.

8.10 Racially or Religiously Aggravated Offences

The term 'racially or religiously aggravated' is defined by s 28 of the Crime and Disorder Act 1998. In everyday language certain offences, such as a s 29 assault, can be aggravated (regarded as more serious, and hence carrying a heavier sentence on conviction) by being motivated, at least in part, by racial or religious factors.

The following categories of offence can be racially or religiously aggravated:

- assaults (s 29);
- criminal damage (s 30);
- public order offences (s 31);
- harassment (s 32).

Such an offence without racial or religious aggravation is sometimes referred to as a 'basic offence' in order to distinguish it from the aggravated form of the offence.

8.10.1 The Definition of Racially or Religiously Aggravated

The definition is provided in s 28(1) of the Crime and Disorder Act 1998. An offence becomes racially or religiously aggravated for the purposes of ss 29 to 32 if:

(a) . . . the offender demonstrates . . . hostility [on racial or religious grounds]; or
(b) the offender is motivated . . . by hostility [on racial or religious grounds].

Clearly, it is easier to prove that an aggravated offence has been committed if the hostility has actually been demonstrated through the suspect's behaviour.

For s 28(1)(a), the offender demonstrates hostility if:

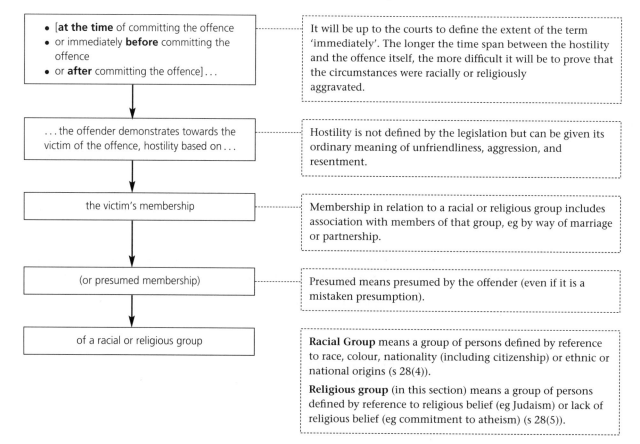

• **[at the time** of committing the offence • or immediately **before** committing the offence • or **after** committing the offence] . . .	It will be up to the courts to define the extent of the term 'immediately'. The longer the time span between the hostility and the offence itself, the more difficult it will be to prove that the circumstances were racially or religiously aggravated.
. . . the offender demonstrates towards the victim of the offence, hostility based on . . .	Hostility is not defined by the legislation but can be given its ordinary meaning of unfriendliness, aggression, and resentment.
the victim's membership	Membership in relation to a racial or religious group includes association with members of that group, eg by way of marriage or partnership.
(or presumed membership)	Presumed means presumed by the offender (even if it is a mistaken presumption).
of a racial or religious group	**Racial Group** means a group of persons defined by reference to race, colour, nationality (including citizenship) or ethnic or national origins (s 28(4)). **Religious group** (in this section) means a group of persons defined by reference to religious belief (eg Judaism) or lack of religious belief (eg commitment to atheism) (s 28(5)).

The person's behaviour might be motivated or partly motivated by other factors with no racial or religious basis. However, it is immaterial for this offence whether or not the person's hostility is partly related to any other non-racial or non-religious factor (s 28(3) Crime and Disorder Act).

As a police officer you are as entitled as anyone else to protection from any racial or religious aggravation.

8.10.2 Racially or Religiously Aggravated Assaults

Under s 29(1) of the Crime and Disorder Act 1998, the following types of basic offence can be racially or religiously aggravated.

Basic offence	Notes
Any offence under s 20 of the Offences Against the Person Act 1861	Includes malicious wounding or grievous bodily harm, but excludes s 18 'with intent' (see section 9.16).
Any offence under s 47 of the Offences Against the Person Act 1861	See section 9.15 on occasioning actual bodily harm.
Common assault	See section 9.15 on unlawful personal violence.

The motivation for the basic offence must be taken into account—it must be racially motivated or based on racial hostility. For example, in the case of *DPP v Roshan Kumar Pal* (unreported, 3 February 2000) the charge of racially aggravated common assault was not proved. Even though the assault on an Asian heritage caretaker was accompanied by abuse, it was not held to be motivated by racism but by the perceived low status of the victim's job.

If the racial or religious aggravation aspect of the offence charged is not proved, the basic offence may be substituted by the court in most cases.

8.10.2.1 Modes of trial and penalty

For s 29(1) (aggravated s 20 and s 47 offences), triable either way:

- Summarily; six months' imprisonment and/or a fine.
- On indictment; seven years' imprisonment and/or a fine.

For s 29(1) (aggravated common assault), triable either way:

- Summarily; six months' imprisonment and/or a fine.
- On indictment; two years' imprisonment and/or a fine.

8.10.3 Racially or Religiously Aggravated Criminal Damage

These offences are covered in s 30 of the Crime and Disorder Act 1998.

A person is guilty of an offence if he/she:

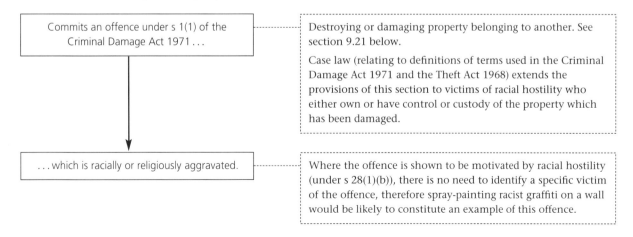

Commits an offence under s 1(1) of the Criminal Damage Act 1971 . . .	Destroying or damaging property belonging to another. See section 9.21 below. Case law (relating to definitions of terms used in the Criminal Damage Act 1971 and the Theft Act 1968) extends the provisions of this section to victims of racial hostility who either own or have control or custody of the property which has been damaged.
. . . which is racially or religiously aggravated.	Where the offence is shown to be motivated by racial hostility (under s 28(1)(b)), there is no need to identify a specific victim of the offence, therefore spray-painting racist graffiti on a wall would be likely to constitute an example of this offence.

Unlike the basic offence under s 1(1) of the 1971 Criminal Damage Act, the racially aggravated offence is triable either way regardless of the value of the property damaged:

- Summarily; six months' imprisonment and/or a fine.
- On indictment; imprisonment (not exceeding 14 years) and/or a fine.

8.10.4 Racially or Religiously Aggravated Public Order Offences

These offences are covered in s 31 of the Crime and Disorder Act 1998.

The table below lists the public order offences (see section 8.12 below) that may be racially or religiously aggravated.

Section number of the Public Order Act 1986	Type of public order offence
Section 4	Fear or provocation of violence.
Section 4A	Intentional harassment, alarm, or distress.
Section 5	Causing harassment, alarm, or distress (see *Norwood v DPP* [2003] EWHC 1564).

8.10.4.1 Mode of trial and penalty

For s 31(1)(a) (for s 4 Public Order Act 1986 offences, triable either way:

- Summarily; six months' imprisonment and/or a fine.
- On indictment; two years' imprisonment and/or a fine.

For s 31(1)(b) (for s 4A Public Order offences, triable either way:

- Summarily; six months' imprisonment and/or a fine.
- On indictment; two years' imprisonment and/or a fine.

For trials on indictment of a person charged with a racially aggravated s 4 or s 4A public order offence, if the jury find him/her not guilty, the jury may still find him/her guilty of the basic (public order) offence (s 31(6)).

For s 31(1)(C) (for s 5 Public Order Act offences):

- Triable summarily, and the penalty is a fine. This offence (relating to s 5 of the Public Order Act) being a summary only offence, has no alternative verdict.

8.10.5 Racially or Religiously Aggravated Harassment

These offences are covered in s 32 of the Crime and Disorder Act 1998. They relate to racially and religiously aggravated offences committed under the Protection from Harassment Act 1997, s 2 (harassment) and s 4 (putting people in fear of violence) (see section 8.14 of the Handbook).

8.10.5.1 Mode of trial and penalty

Section 32(1)(a) (harassment) offences are triable either way:

- Summarily; six months' imprisonment and/or a fine.
- On indictment; two years' imprisonment and/or a fine.

For trials on indictment of a person charged with racially aggravated harassment, if the jury finds the person not guilty, the jury may still find the person guilty of harassment (s 32(5)).

Section 32(1)(b) (putting people in fear of violence) offences are triable either way:

- Summarily; six months' imprisonment and/or a fine.
- On indictment; seven years' imprisonment and/or a fine.

For trials on indictment of a person charged with the racially aggravated form of this offence, if the jury finds the person not guilty, the jury may still find the person guilty of the basic offence (s 32(6)).

8.11 Breach of the Peace

You have no doubt heard of the phrase 'breach of the peace'. However, there is some considerable debate concerning both its meaning and whether it should still be dealt with by the police. Part of the reason for this debate is that the law surrounding a breach of the peace is somewhat unusual as it is not a criminal offence or part of statute law (see section 5.11 above). It is however part of common law, and case law has set a precedent in defining its meaning (see section 8.11.1 below).

Any person committing a breach of the peace can be arrested by any other person, and this includes you as a student police officer. Having been arrested, individuals can be detained until there is no likelihood of a breach of the peace happening again. Alternatively, a police officer can 'lay a complaint upon them' and place a person before a criminal court. (A complaint is similar to the process of charge.) The court can 'bind the person over' for a sum of money, which they will have to pay to the court if they breach the peace again in the future.

8.11.1 Breach of the Peace

The case of *R v Howell* [1981] 3 All ER 383, provides a definition of the meaning of breach of the peace.

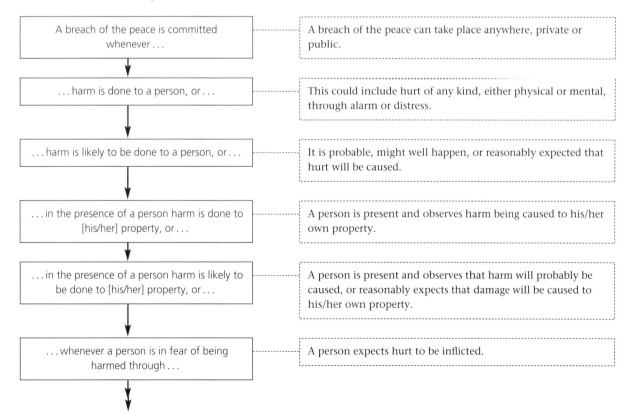

A breach of the peace is committed whenever . . .	A breach of the peace can take place anywhere, private or public.
. . . harm is done to a person, or . . .	This could include hurt of any kind, either physical or mental, through alarm or distress.
. . . harm is likely to be done to a person, or . . .	It is probable, might well happen, or reasonably expected that hurt will be caused.
. . . in the presence of a person harm is done to [his/her] property, or . . .	A person is present and observes harm being caused to his/her own property.
. . . in the presence of a person harm is likely to be done to [his/her] property, or . . .	A person is present and observes that harm will probably be caused, or reasonably expects that damage will be caused to his/her own property.
. . . whenever a person is in fear of being harmed through . . .	A person expects hurt to be inflicted.

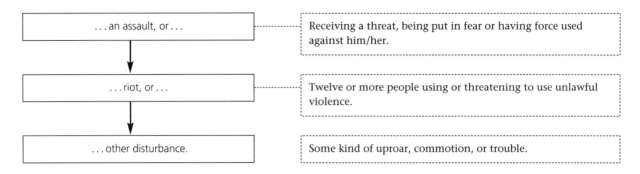

8.11.2 Powers of Arrest for Breach of the Peace

R v Howell also provides guidance on your powers of arrest in the case of a breach of the peace.

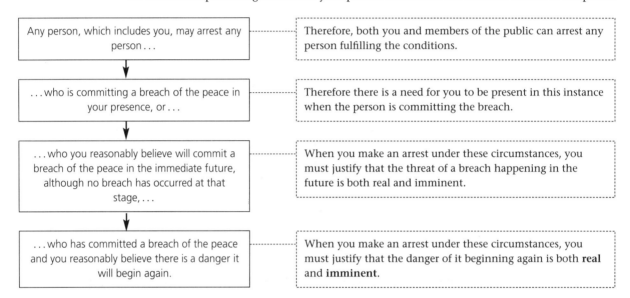

Breach of the peace is unique. You can use it in all manner of circumstances but you must apply the precedent set by the case *R v Howell* and satisfy its elements rigorously. Before making an arrest, always locate the all-important ingredients of harm and compare the circumstances in front of you with the definition. Afterwards, make sure that the breach took place in your presence or that the threat or renewal is both real and imminent.

> **TASK 8**
>
> In November 2003, a 61-year-old woman climbed the gates of Buckingham Palace to protest at the visit of US President George Bush. She then unfurled the Stars and Stripes flag on top of the gates with the words "ELIZABETH WINDSOR AND CO...HE'S NOT WELCOME' written on the flag. After about two hours she voluntarily climbed down from the gates and was reported as being arrested by the police on suspicion of criminal damage and breach of the peace.
>
> Explain how the conditions for breach of the peace were likely to have been met, or not, by the circumstances of this incident.

8.12 The Public Order Act 1986

Sections 1 to 5 of the Public Order Act 1986 deal with a wide range of behaviours and offences. The diagram below shows these clearly, with the more serious and rare offence of riot (s 1) at the top of the triangle, and the less serious but more common offences of harassment, alarm, or distress (ss 5 and 4A) at the base of the triangle.

S 1 Riot

S 2 Violent disorder

S 3 Affray

S 4 Fear or provocation of violence

S 4A Intentional harassment,
alarm or distress

S 5 Harassment, alarm or
distress

8.12.1 Intoxication Is Not a Defence

Some people accused of Public Order Act 1986 offences may claim in their defence that they were very drunk at the time that they committed public order offences. However, s 6(5) of the Public Order Act 1986 specifically states that a person whose awareness is impaired by:

- intoxication
- drink
- drugs
- other means, or a combination of means

will be taken by the court to have the same level of awareness had they not been intoxicated unless they show either that:

- their intoxication was not self-induced (eg 'spiked' drinks), or
- it was caused solely by the taking or administration of a substance in the course of medical treatment (eg prescribed medicine).

Note that s 6(5) does not apply to s 4A of the Act, as s 4A was introduced at a later date.

8.12.2 Locations for Public Order Offences

The more serious public order offences (riot, violent disorder, and affray) can take place in private, as well as in public places.

Offences under ss 4, 4A, and 5 of the Public Order Act 1986 can occur in a public or private place. However, if the conduct takes place inside a dwelling (a private place of residence excluding communal parts), then the person who is harassed, alarmed, or distressed cannot be inside the same or another dwelling but must be outside in a public place. For example, if a neighbour attaches an offensive poster to the inside of a window, which is then seen by a person from the street outside, the offence has been committed. However, if the poster is seen by the same person who is now inside their own house next door (perhaps through a window), then the offence has not been committed. The reason for this is simply that this is the **Public** Order Act, and there is other legislation available for circumstances which are completely private.

8.12.3 Offences under Sections 5, 4A, and 4

Members of the public generally want to be able to walk along the street without being intimidated, frightened, or stressed by other people's actions. Sections 5 and 4A of the Public Order Act 1986 offer safeguards against relatively minor forms of public disorder, such as persistent swearing, shouting, and other anti-social behaviour. Section 4, on the other hand, deals with a more serious type of public disorder, involving fear or provocation of violence.

Before looking at the sections in detail, you might find it useful to consider the following terms and definitions used in the legislation. The distinctions between offences under ss 5, 4A, and 4 require careful consideration and still cause some debate in legal and police circles. The offences will be described individually, and then compared in order to highlight important differences between them.

Definitions

Threatening	A physical or verbal act which indicates harm will be inflicted. It can also include violent conduct.
Abusive	Using or containing insulting or degrading language.
Insulting	Disrespectful, especially if done in a way that is offensive or with feeling that a person is beneath consideration, but in a way that is more than annoyance or causing bitterness.
Harassment	A feeling of annoyance, persecution, irritation, and aggravation.
Alarm	A state of surprise, fright, fear, terror, and panic.
Distress	A feeling of suffering, anguish, and misery.
Words	Spoken or shouted.
Behaviour	Display of conduct involving the treatment of others.
Disorderly behaviour	Rowdy, unruly, boisterous, loud, raucous, or unrestrained conduct.
To display	To show or exhibit for all to see, such as placing a sign or poster in a window.
Distribute	To hand out, share out, give out, or issue to a particular person or people, not just simply left 'lying about'.
Writing, sign, or other visual representation	A notice containing lettering or other visible form of copied picture, text or image, leaflet, pamphlet or fly-poster.

8.12.3.1 Section 5 of the Public Order Act 1986

The offence is also referred to as **non-intentional** harassment, alarm, or distress.

Section 5 of the Public Order Act 1986 states that:

> A person is guilty of [this] offence if [he/she]
>
> (a) uses threatening, abusive or insulting words or behaviour, or disorderly behaviour, or
> (b) displays any writing sign or other visible representation which is threatening, abusive or insulting,
>
> within the hearing or sight of a person likely to be caused harassment, alarm or distress thereby.

These are the main points of s 5 offences:

- The conduct does not have to be aimed towards a specific person.
- The conduct must take place within the presence of a person who can see or hear the conduct, but that person does not need to be identifiable.
- The type of conduct must be likely to cause harassment, alarm, or distress.
- The material (if used) is not distributed.
- The suspect must intend or be aware that their conduct is threatening, abusive, or insulting in general terms.
- However, there is no need to prove he/she actually intended to cause any person to be harassed, alarmed, or distressed.

You may feel that the last two bullet points appear contradictory, but consider the example below and the precise nature of a s 5 offence will become clear.

> In an interview with the suspect (S), you (SPO) might have the following exchange:
>
> **SPO** Why did you behave the way you did back there in the street?
> **S** I was trying to be hard in front of my mates.
> **SPO** Didn't you think about the effect it might have on other people?
> **S** Not really, it didn't even cross my mind they'd take any notice—I was only messing about.

SPO	What was the point of it all then?

SPO What was the point of it all then?

S Not a lot—I was showing off, I'd had a couple of drinks, but I wasn't drunk. I knew what I was doing and I wanted to be as loud and proud as I could, just to show my mates I could do it. In the end they just laughed and made out I was acting stupid.

SPO Yes, and you might have upset a few elderly people passing by; how do you think they felt hearing that lot?

S I just didn't think—yeah, I knew they were there... But if I did, I didn't mean to upset them...

It might now be clear from this example how a suspect might intend his/her conduct to be threatening, abusive, or insulting but still have no intention to make any person harassed, alarmed or distressed.

There are three defences to this offence (listed in s 5(3)):

• that he/she had no reason to believe, whilst **in public**, that anybody could hear or see his/her conduct and had become harassed, alarmed, or distressed as a result. In other words the suspect believed that his/her poster or behaviour could not be seen or his/her voices could not be heard by anybody else;

• that he/she had no reason to believe, whilst **inside a dwelling** (place of residence), that his/her words, behaviour, or conduct could be seen or heard by a person outside that same or another dwelling, for example a poster was hanging on an inside wall within a house which could not be seen clearly from the road outside;

• that his/her conduct was **reasonable** and did not cause anybody to be harassed, alarmed, or distressed, for example if he/she shouted at a group of people who were carrying out an unlawful act outside his/her home.

This offence is triable summarily and the penalty is a fine. This offence can be racially or religiously aggravated (see s 31(1)(C) of the Crime and Disorder Act 1998).

TASK 9

Take a moment now to consider what evidence you would need to obtain before making a decision to deal with a person for a s 5 Public Order Act 1986 offence.

• Who would you be able to collect evidence from?
• What evidence would they be able to provide?
• What evidence would you be able to provide?

8.12.3.2 Section 4A of the Public Order Act 1986

A s 4A offence is also often referred to as causing **intentional** harassment, alarm, or distress.

Section 4A(1) of the Public Order Act 1986 states that:

A person is guilty of [this] offence if, with intent to cause a person harassment, alarm or distress, [he/she]

(a) uses threatening, abusive or insulting words or behaviour, or disorderly behaviour, or
(b) displays any writing, sign or other visible representation which is threatening, abusive or insulting,

thereby causing that or another person harassment, alarm or distress.

These are the main points of S 4A offences:

• The suspect **intends** the conduct to be threatening, abusive, or insulting and to cause a person harassment, alarm, or distress.
• The conduct does **not** have to be aimed towards a specific person.
• At least one **identifiable person** must be harassed, alarmed, or distressed.
• Material (if used) cannot be distributed.

This piece of legislation is aimed at supporting the most vulnerable members of the community, who may be specifically targeted because of their inability to respond appropriately to intentionally directed acts which cause them harassment, alarm, or distress. These victims may feel particularly uncomfortable as witnesses, so you should take every opportunity to support them throughout any police or legal process.

As a possible defence, a suspect could demonstrate that:

- he/she had no reason to believe his/her words, behaviour, or conduct made **inside** a dwelling (place of residence) could be seen or heard by a person **outside** that same or another dwelling, eg a poster hanging on an inside wall within a house was not able to be seen from the road outside (s 4A(3)(a));
- his/her conduct was reasonable, eg if a person shouted at a group of people who were carrying out an unlawful act outside their home (s 4A(3)(b)).

This offence is triable summarily and the penalty is six months' imprisonment and/or a fine. This offence can be racially or religiously aggravated (see s 31(1)(b) of the Crime and Disorder Act 1998).

8.12.3.3 **Section 4 of the Public Order Act 1986**

A s 4 offence is also referred to as **fear or provocation of violence**.

Section 4 of the Public Order Act states that:

> A person is guilty of [this] offence if [he/she]
>
> (a) uses towards another person threatening, abusive or insulting words or behaviour, or
> (b) distributes or displays to another person any writing, sign or other visible representation which is threatening, abusive or insulting,
>
> with intent to cause that person to believe that immediate unlawful violence will be used against [him/her] or another by any person, or to provoke the immediate use of unlawful violence by that person or another, or whereby that person is likely to believe that such violence will be used or it is likely that such violence will be provoked.

For this offence, the **intentions** of the suspect are the key issue; the actual effect of the behaviour on other people is not relevant. Their intention must be to make the person (or persons) to whom the conduct is addressed (from this point onwards referred to as the recipient) feel fear or to provoke anyone to be violent. Despite the fact that the effect of the conduct is not relevant for this offence, for the intentions of the suspect to be held to be genuine, his/her conduct must be **directed** towards a recipient who must be present at the time when the words or behaviour are used. The recipient must be able to see or hear the conduct; alternatively, the suspect must believe that the recipient is able to see or hear the conduct (see *Atkin v DPP* [1989] Crim LR 581).

The suspect's intentions may be to cause **fear of violence**. If so, the suspect must intend the recipient to fear that violence will be used (or is likely to be used). The violent acts could be threatened by the suspect against the recipient. Or the suspect can intend to put the recipient in fear that violence will be used not against the recipient, but against another person instead. Also the suspect can intend to cause fear in the recipient that violent acts will be carried out by another person, rather than by the suspect, and that those violent acts could be against anyone at all. The key point is that if the suspect is intent on causing fear, the fear must be experienced by the recipient. The violent acts threatened by the suspect may or may not involve the suspect or the recipient directly, but it must be the intention of the suspect that the recipient should feel the fear.

Alternatively, if the suspect does not to intend to cause fear of violence in the mind of the recipient, there is a need to prove that the suspect had an intention (a determined state of mind) to **provoke violence**. The intention can be to provoke any person to use violence. For example, an extremist shouts at an animal research worker at a demonstration, 'A dog is for life, not just for you to torture and experiment on, you sadist! You'll get the same, I promise you that!'. If the intention is to provoke immediate violence on the part of a group of animal rights activists who are nearby, the offence is committed.

These are the main points of s 4 offences:

- The conduct must be directed towards a person or persons present at the scene.
- Material (if used) is distributed and not just displayed.
- The suspect must intend or be aware that his/her conduct is potentially threatening, abusive, or insulting (but it does not matter if the recipient does not actually feel threatened, abused, or insulted).
- The suspect may intend to cause fear or provoke a reaction of violence (but it does not matter if the conduct does not actually have either of these effects).
- If the suspect intends to cause fear (that violence will be or is likely to be used), the intention to cause fear need only concern the recipient.
- If the suspect intends to provoke violence, the intention can be to provoke any person present and not just the recipient.

You may enter any premises to arrest any person you reasonably suspect is committing an offence under this Act and section (s 17, PACE Act, see section 11.10 of the Handbook).

This offence is triable summarily and the penalty is six months' imprisonment and/or a fine. This offence can be racially aggravated (see s 31(2)(b) of the Crime and Disorder Act 1998).

8.12.3.4 Comparing sections 4, 4A, and 5 of the Public Order Act 1986

The diagram below enables the precise wording for each of the sections of the Public Order Act 1986 to be easily compared.

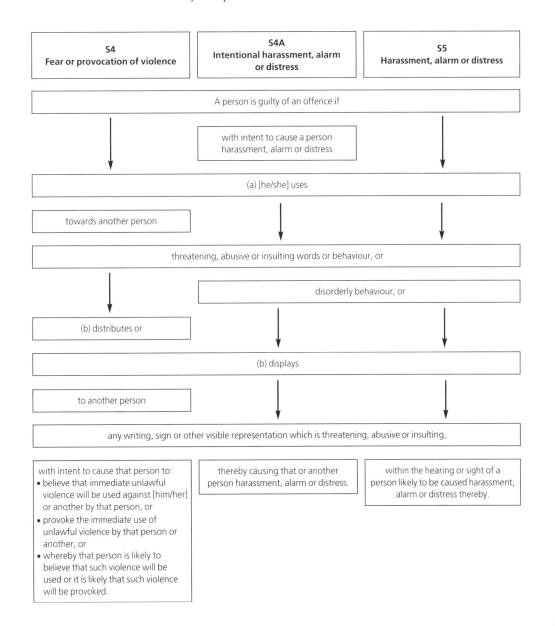

The table below identifies some important differences between ss 4, 4A, and 5:

	S4	S4A	S5
Intentions of the suspect	Intends or is aware that the conduct is threatening, abusive or insulting.	Intends the conduct to be threatening, abusive or insulting.	Intends or is aware that the conduct is threatening, abusive or insulting.
Recipient of the conduct	Conduct aimed towards a specific person.	Conduct does not have to be aimed towards a specific person.	Conduct does not have to be aimed towards a specific person (but has to be carried out in the hearing or sight of a person likely to be caused harassment, alarm or distress).
Includes disorderly behaviour?	Does not include disorderly behaviour.	Includes disorderly behaviour	
Distribution of material?	Includes distribution of material	Does not include distribution of material	
Outcome of the behaviour	Intends to cause fear or provocation of immediate unlawful violence. No requirement that someone experiences that fear, or that violence is provoked.	Evidence required that an identifiable person has been harassed, alarmed or distressed.	Evidence is **not** required that an identifiable person has been harassed, alarmed or distressed.

TASK 10

Often whilst on Independent Patrol, you may well be within the sight or hearing of a person whom you suspect by his or her behaviour to be causing harassment, alarm, or distress. Consider how you will deal with a situation such as this if there is nobody else in the area at the time to whom this conduct is aimed and hence it appears to be directed at you.

While drawing your conclusions, refer to *DPP v Orum* [1988] Crim LR 848.

TASK 11

You are on Independent Patrol when you see a man walk up to the door of a club and subsequently adopt an aggressive posture towards the door supervisor. You are about two metres away. The aggressive person has clenched fists, bulging eyes, and has taken up a 'boxing' position. The suspect then pushes his shoulder into the door supervisor's chest causing the door supervisor to move back. You hear the suspect say 'You're a dead man'. You believe that the door supervisor is about to be attacked and so arrest the suspect under s 4 of the Public Order Act 1986.

When you return to the club to obtain a statement from the door supervisor, you are informed that he is not willing to make a statement. In your opinion could a successful prosecution be brought against the suspect under these circumstances?

When drawing a conclusion, consider *Swanston v DPP* [1997] 161 JP 203.

8.12.4   Serious Public Order Offences

These offences under the Public Order Act 1986 are, in increasing order of seriousness:

- affray (s 3);
- violent disorder (s 2);
- riot (s 1).

Remember, these more serious public order offences can be committed in private as well as in public. Offences under ss 1 to 3 all involve **unlawful violence**.

Briefly, violence is aggressive or hostile conduct towards property or persons, and includes acts capable of causing injury, even if no injury or damage is caused.

Section 8 of the Public Order Act offers guidance on the meaning of unlawful violence:

(a) except in the context of affray, it includes violent conduct towards property as well as violent conduct towards persons, and

(b) it is not restricted to conduct causing or intended to cause injury or damage but includes any other violent conduct (for example, throwing at or towards a person a missile of a kind capable of causing injury which does not hit or falls short).

The legislation describing offences under ss 1 to 3 also uses the term a 'person of reasonable firmness' (sometimes referred to as the 'hypothetical bystander' for some offences). This is not defined under law but can be taken to mean an average person in terms of their reaction to violent incidents around them (that is, not somebody who is unduly frightened by the most minor of incidents, nor somebody who is completely 'hardened' to the witnessing of acts of violent behaviour).

8.12.4.1 Affray

For an affray (s 3, Public Order Act 1986), the threat of violence needs to be capable of affecting others. The primary objective of the law is to protect the general public around the affray, not the participants themselves.

If an individual is simply threatening another and no one else is involved or likely to be worried by the incident, then other offences such as common assault are available to deal with the situation. For an affray, the level of the threat of violence needs to be capable of affecting others and the court will consider how a hypothetical person of reasonable firmness (see above) witnessing the incident would feel (*R v Sanchez, The Times*, 6 March 1996).

Therefore, there are in effect three parties involved in an affray:

1. The individual making the threats.
2. The person subject to the threats.
3. Any bystander(s).

Section 3(1) of the Public Order Act 1986 states:

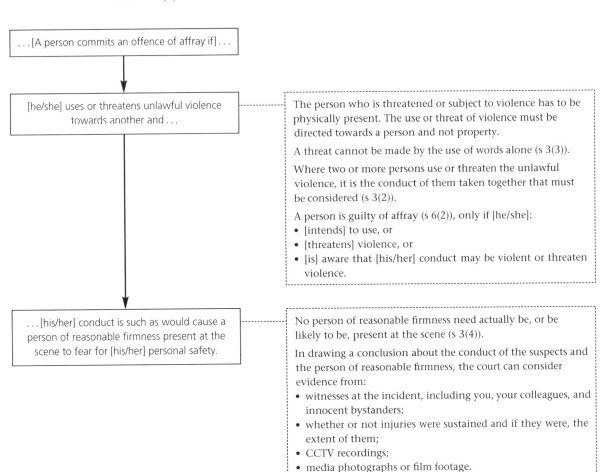

...[A person commits an offence of affray if]...

[he/she] uses or threatens unlawful violence towards another and...

The person who is threatened or subject to violence has to be physically present. The use or threat of violence must be directed towards a person and not property.

A threat cannot be made by the use of words alone (s 3(3)).

Where two or more persons use or threaten the unlawful violence, it is the conduct of them taken together that must be considered (s 3(2)).

A person is guilty of affray (s 6(2)), only if [he/she]:
• [intends] to use, or
• [threatens] violence, or
• [is] aware that [his/her] conduct may be violent or threaten violence.

...[his/her] conduct is such as would cause a person of reasonable firmness present at the scene to fear for [his/her] personal safety.

No person of reasonable firmness need actually be, or be likely to be, present at the scene (s 3(4)).

In drawing a conclusion about the conduct of the suspects and the person of reasonable firmness, the court can consider evidence from:
• witnesses at the incident, including you, your colleagues, and innocent bystanders;
• whether or not injuries were sustained and if they were, the extent of them;
• CCTV recordings;
• media photographs or film footage.

This offence is triable either way:

- Summarily; six months' imprisonment and/or a fine.
- On indictment; three years' imprisonment.

8.12.4.2 Violent disorder

For this offence under s 2 of the Public Order Act 1986, three or more persons must be present together and use, or threaten to use, unlawful violence. If only one of the three or more persons present together was able to be arrested and subsequently investigated then that person can still be charged with this offence. However, it must still be proved that at least two other people were present and that they were also using or threatening violence. The additional people must also be mentioned in the charge.

Section 6(2) states that 'a person is guilty of violent disorder only if [he/she]

- [intends] to use, or
- [threatens] violence, or
- [is] aware that [his/her] conduct may be violent or threaten violence

Section 2(1) of the Public Order Act 1986 states an offence of violent disorder is committed:

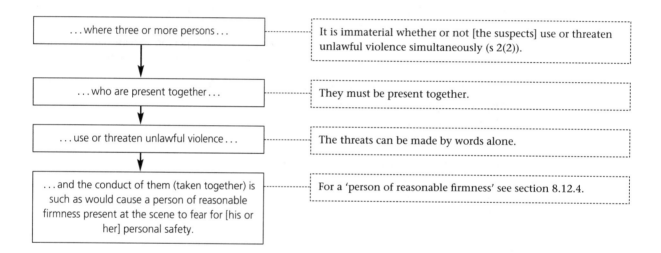

...where three or more persons...	It is immaterial whether or not [the suspects] use or threaten unlawful violence simultaneously (s 2(2)).
...who are present together...	They must be present together.
...use or threaten unlawful violence...	The threats can be made by words alone.
...and the conduct of them (taken together) is such as would cause a person of reasonable firmness present at the scene to fear for [his or her] personal safety.	For a 'person of reasonable firmness' see section 8.12.4.

This offence is triable either way:

- Summarily; six months' imprisonment and/or a fine.
- On indictment; five years' imprisonment.

8.12.4.3 Riot

A person who takes part in a riot using unlawful violence commits an offence under s 1(1) of the Public Order Act 1986. Charges of riot are very rare.

An offence is committed:

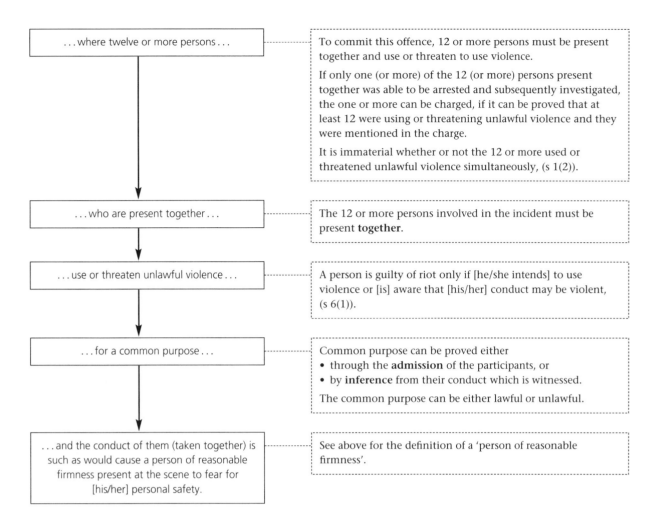

...where twelve or more persons...	To commit this offence, 12 or more persons must be present together and use or threaten to use violence.
	If only one (or more) of the 12 (or more) persons present together was able to be arrested and subsequently investigated, the one or more can be charged, if it can be proved that at least 12 were using or threatening unlawful violence and they were mentioned in the charge.
	It is immaterial whether or not the 12 or more used or threatened unlawful violence simultaneously, (s 1(2)).
...who are present together...	The 12 or more persons involved in the incident must be present **together**.
...use or threaten unlawful violence...	A person is guilty of riot only if [he/she intends] to use violence or [is] aware that [his/her] conduct may be violent, (s 6(1)).
...for a common purpose...	Common purpose can be proved either • through the **admission** of the participants, or • by **inference** from their conduct which is witnessed. The common purpose can be either lawful or unlawful.
...and the conduct of them (taken together) is such as would cause a person of reasonable firmness present at the scene to fear for [his/her] personal safety.	See above for the definition of a 'person of reasonable firmness'.

This offence is triable on indictment only and the penalty is 10 years' imprisonment.

8.12.5 Racial and Religious Hatred

Within the Public Order Act 1986 (added to by the Racial and Religious Hatred Act 2006), offences have been created to address the 'stirring up' (the phrase used in the legislation) or the inciting of hatred against a group of people on racial or religious grounds.

These offences include:

• using threatening words or behaviour, or displaying written material with intent to stir up racial (s 18) or religious (s 29B) hatred;
• publishing or distributing written material which may stir up racial (s 19) or religious (s 29C) hatred;
• distributing, showing or playing a recording, with intent to stir up racial (s 21) or religious (s 29E) hatred;
• possessing racially inflammatory material which is intended or likely to stir up racial (s 23) or religious (s 29G) hatred.

'Racial hatred' is defined by the Act to mean hatred against a group of persons defined by reference to colour, race, nationality (including citizenship), or ethnic or national origins.

'Religious hatred' is defined by the Act to mean hatred against a group of persons defined by reference to:

- religious belief, for example Christianity, Islam, Hinduism, Judaism, Buddhism, Sikhism, Rastafarianism, Baha'ism, Zoroastrianism, and Jainism (but not likely to include Satanism or Scientology, although this is untested); or
- lack of religious belief, for example atheists and humanists.

TASK 12

Whilst on Independent Patrol you respond to a call from a customer of a local nightclub which alleges that a member of the door staff has pushed a female customer out of the night club doorway. It is claimed that the female customer fell over as a result of the push. There are no other witnesses to the incident and no CCTV footage. Disregarding the investigation of the assault, could an investigation into an affray be sustained? Refer to *R v Plavecz* [2002] Crim LR 837 for your answer.

8.13 Using Violence to Secure Entry to Premises

It is an offence, under s 6 of the Criminal Law Act 1977 to use violence to gain entry into premises which are being occupied by a person opposing the entry. Under the law, it makes no difference that the person using the violence has a right or interest in the property. For example, a person trying to force his way into his own flat is committing an offence if his live-in partner is inside the flat and she does not want him to come in. Originally, forced entry was identified as an offence in order to prevent the owners, tenants, or occupiers of premises from using violence to gain entry into those premises while they were being occupied by squatters.

Under s 6 of the Criminal Law Act 1977 it is an offence:

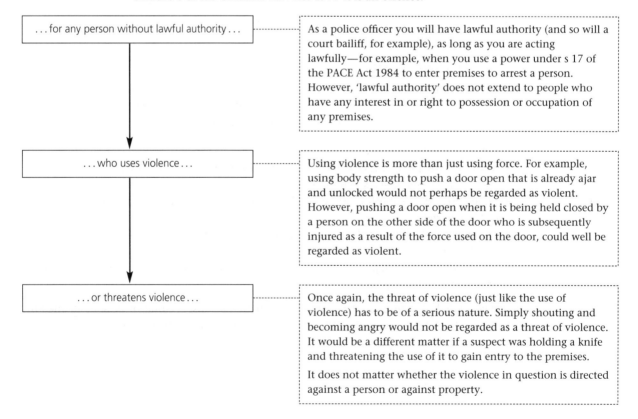

... for any person without lawful authority ...

As a police officer you will have lawful authority (and so will a court bailiff, for example), as long as you are acting lawfully—for example, when you use a power under s 17 of the PACE Act 1984 to enter premises to arrest a person. However, 'lawful authority' does not extend to people who have any interest in or right to possession or occupation of any premises.

... who uses violence ...

Using violence is more than just using force. For example, using body strength to push a door open that is already ajar and unlocked would not perhaps be regarded as violent. However, pushing a door open when it is being held closed by a person on the other side of the door who is subsequently injured as a result of the force used on the door, could well be regarded as violent.

... or threatens violence ...

Once again, the threat of violence (just like the use of violence) has to be of a serious nature. Simply shouting and becoming angry would not be regarded as a threat of violence. It would be a different matter if a suspect was holding a knife and threatening the use of it to gain entry to the premises.

It does not matter whether the violence in question is directed against a person or against property.

So for this offence, the suspect must not have lawful authority, and must either use violence or threaten to use violence:

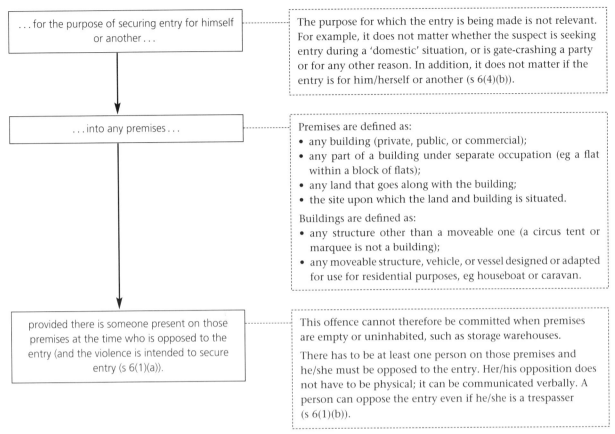

| ... for the purpose of securing entry for himself or another ... | The purpose for which the entry is being made is not relevant. For example, it does not matter whether the suspect is seeking entry during a 'domestic' situation, or is gate-crashing a party or for any other reason. In addition, it does not matter if the entry is for him/herself or another (s 6(4)(b)). |

...into any premises...

Premises are defined as:
- any building (private, public, or commercial);
- any part of a building under separate occupation (eg a flat within a block of flats);
- any land that goes along with the building;
- the site upon which the land and building is situated.

Buildings are defined as:
- any structure other than a moveable one (a circus tent or marquee is not a building);
- any moveable structure, vehicle, or vessel designed or adapted for use for residential purposes, eg houseboat or caravan.

provided there is someone present on those premises at the time who is opposed to the entry (and the violence is intended to secure entry (s 6(1)(a)).

This offence cannot therefore be committed when premises are empty or uninhabited, such as storage warehouses.

There has to be at least one person on those premises and he/she must be opposed to the entry. Her/his opposition does not have to be physical; it can be communicated verbally. A person can oppose the entry even if he/she is a trespasser (s 6(1)(b)).

A home owner may enter by force if there are trespassers inside but only if the home owners are:

- **Displaced Residential Occupiers** (defined in s 12 of the Criminal Law Act 1977): this would include people who leave the home they live in for a short while, and during the time they are away, a person or persons enter the premises as trespassers to take up residence themselves. This does not give the owners the right to carry out unlawful acts (such as assault) in relation to the trespassers; it only means they do not commit the particular offence of violence to secure entry (under s 6 of the Criminal Law Act 1977) if they use violence to enter their own home.
- **Protected Intended Occupiers** (defined in s 12A of the Criminal Law Act 1977): this would include people who do not live in their homes yet, because they have only just bought the premises or only just agreed to rent them. Therefore they are intending to take up occupancy. However, they must have completed a legal process to reach this stage.

This offence is triable summarily and the penalty is six months' imprisonment and/or a fine. There is a power of entry to arrest someone for this offence under s 17 of the PACE Act 1984.

This offence occurs frequently, in a wide range of situations. If you suspect that such an offence may have been committed you need to run through a mental checklist before you act. Check that the events you are considering match all the requirements of the legislation describing this offence.

> **TASK 13**
>
> Charlie and partner Sam have been facing up to the fact that their three-year relationship is drawing to an end. Recently there have been several episodes where they shouted angrily at each other and then one or both went out separately and got very drunk.
>
> They share a house which is owned jointly. One evening Charlie stays at home while Sam goes to a club nearby. Sam arrives home in the early hours of the following morning, very drunk, to find the front door will not open with the key. Sam begins to hammer on the door and wakes the neighbours up and down the street. The neighbours can clearly hear Charlie shouting from inside the house telling Sam the door will not be unlocked. One of the neighbours calls the police and you attend the scene to find Sam still hammering on the door. In relation to s 6(1) of the Criminal Law Act 1977, has Sam committed an offence?

8.14 Protection from Harassment

Sections 1 to 5 of the Protection from Harassment Act 1997 can be applied in a wide range of situations, including the investigation of disputes between partners in a relationship and disputes between neighbours. More recently, the Government has made additions to the Act to protect people from extremist campaigns, and it is now an offence to harass two or more people on separate occasions.

The definition of harassment is in terms of the effect it has on the victim rather than the actual events that took place. The victim must be distressed and the perpetrator must know that his/her actions are likely to cause distress. However, the behaviour must be consistent with the behaviour that a **reasonable person** would see as harassing (s 1(2), Protection from Harassment Act 1997). The final decision of whether or not particular behaviour led to a person being alarmed or distressed is taken by the court.

Only individuals can suffer harassment under the Act. Companies or corporate bodies cannot be harassed, but their employees can. References to 'a person', in the context of harassment, means references to a person or persons as **individuals** (s 7(5), Protection from Harassment Act 1997).

The harassment must consist of a **course of conduct** (s 7(3)(a)(b), Protection from Harassment Act 1997). Harassment is not just a one-off event; it must occur on more than one occasion. A course of conduct exists when conduct is directed towards:

- an individual on at least two occasions (s 7(3)(a)); or
- two or more people, and on at least one occasion in relation to **each** of those persons (s 7(3)(b)).

By precedent it has been decided that it is not just the number of incidents that are important, but whether those incidents are connected (*Lau v DPP* [2000] All ER (D) 224). However, it is less likely that the court will accept that behaviour constitutes a course of conduct if there is a long period of time between each event under consideration. The course of conduct does not have to comprise similar types of conduct; indeed it is often not obvious that separate incidents are connected, so be aware of this during any investigation. Conduct includes speech, letters, and e-mails so you will need to gather evidence from a wide range of sources such as diary entries, e-mails, letters, photographs, and interviews with witnesses. The conduct can involve a third person. For example, person A asks person B to give a threatening letter to the victim, person C, in which case both A and B are guilty of the offence if B has guilty knowledge of the harassment.

Harassment can also be caused by a person (as well a group of people) taking part in the planning or otherwise assisting with a course of conduct, but not actually carrying it out him/herself, on more than one occasion. An example of where a group of people could be guilty of harassment would involve three people, X, Y, and Z, who stand along the route which A takes to and from work, in order to give A some threatening letters. They give the letters to A, and later Z makes a threatening phone call to A. Provided A feels alarmed or distressed, and X, Y, and Z knew (or ought to know) that their actions were likely to be alarming or distressing, X,Y, and Z would all be committing an offence (s 7(3A), Protection from Harassment Act 1997).

Two of the offences described in the Protection from Harassment Act 1997 are:

- harassment (without violence) (ss 1 and 2);
- putting people in fear of violence (s 4).

8.14.1 Harassment

It is an offence under ss 1 and 2 of the Protection from Harassment Act 1997 for a person:

- to pursue a course of conduct (s 1(1)); or
- to aid, abet, counsel, or procure the pursuance of a course of conduct (s 7(3A))

which involves harassment of one or more persons (s 1(1) and s 1(1A)) which they know (or ought to know) amounts to harassment of the other(s) (s 1(1A)(b)).

It will be up to the court or jury to decide whether they believe a reasonable person would have considered the conduct was alarming or distressing in the particular circumstances. Otherwise, it would be relatively simple for the suspect(s) to claim a defence that they did not know their actions amounted to harassment (s1(2)) (see also s 1(3)(c) of the Act which we describe below).

In addition to the harassment of two or more persons in s 1(1A)(a), an offence can also be committed when the course of conduct is intended to persuade any person to change his/her current routine (s 1(1A)(c)(i) and (ii)). Such attempts to persuade may form part of a wider campaign about political or social issues. The attempt to persuade any person must:

- be directed towards two or more person(s) in the first instance; and
- must occur on at least one occasion in relation to **each** of those persons.

This offence can be also be committed when there is an intention to persuade any person (not only the two or more persons to whom it is directed) **not** to do something that they are entitled or required to do (s 1(1A)(c)(i)). For example, an animal rights' extremist may pressurize employees to stop working for a company that uses animals for research by:

- sending a threatening e-mail to an individual who works for that company;
- sending a threatening e-mail to an individual who works for another similar company.

If the extremist intends to persuade both individuals to resign because they both work for companies that supply animals for scientific research, the extremist would have committed an offence.

This offence can be also be committed when there is an intention to persuade any person (not only the two or more persons to whom it is directed) **to do something that they are not under any obligation to do** (s 1(1A)(c)(ii)). For example, an animal rights' extremist may pressurize employees to supply information by:

- making a threatening phone call to an individual who works for a company using animals for scientific research;
- verbally abusing another individual working for the same company.

If the intention is to persuade both individuals that they should supply information about other employees, suppliers, or clients, then the extremist has committed an offence.

As a possible defence, the suspect could try and show on the balance of probabilities that his/her course of conduct was pursued:

(a) 'for the purpose of preventing or detecting crime' (eg police officers, customs officers, and other personnel from law enforcement agencies working in the lawful execution of their duties);

(b) 'under any enactment or rule of law or to comply with any condition or requirement imposed by any person under any enactment' (eg court officers acting on behalf of a court and carrying out legislated and lawful court procedures such as locating a person for the purposes of serving a warrant);

(c) in reasonable circumstances: this will be for the court to decide on the basis of the facts which are presented before them and will probably be undertaken in a similar way to the 'reasonable person' test in s 1(2): '[...] the person whose course of conduct is in question ought to know that it amounts to or involves harassment of another if a reasonable person in possession of the same information would think the course of conduct amounted to or involved harassment of the other';

(d) 'on certain government business' (the police, customs, and the security services).

These offences are triable summarily and the penalty is six months' imprisonment and/or a fine. This offence can be racially or religiously aggravated (see section 8.10).

8.14.2 Isolated Events Causing Distress

If distress is only caused on one occasion then, under the Protection from Harassment Act 1997, this does not constitute a course of conduct. Instead an actual or apprehended harassment may be the subject of a claim in **civil proceedings** by the distressed or alarmed person under s 3(1) of the same Act.

The main points of this option are:

- A 'course of conduct' is not necessary.
- The result of such a civil claim can be damages (a court order to pay money) and/or an injunction (a court order to impose sanctions on a person) against the offender.
- A company can apply for an injunction (rather than individuals).

If such an injunction is breached, the offence is triable either way:

- On indictment; five years' imprisonment and/or a fine.
- Summarily; six months' imprisonment and/or a fine.

Within the Crime and Disorder Act 1997, there are no racially or religiously aggravated versions of the civil proceedings under s 3 of the Protection from Harassment Act 1997.

8.14.3 Putting People in Fear of Violence

This offence is described under s 4 of the Protection of Harassment Act 1997 and involves more than sending threatening letters or e-mails. The victim must experience a real fear of violence, and they must believe that whatever they are frightened of will happen as opposed to the possibility that it might happen.

There are several key differences from the harassment (s 2) offence we described earlier. In s 4 offences:

- the victim must believe the violence will happen as opposed to believing it might happen;
- the victim must fear the violence personally, not on behalf of somebody else, such as a family member (*Mohammed Ali Caurti v DPP* [2002] Crime LR 131);
- the fear of violence cannot be achieved through a third party. In other words, an individual cannot be put in fear of violence via an intermediary.

In most other ways, the conditions for this offence are similar to those for the offence of harassment (s 2) described in detail above; it is an offence to pursue or assist the conduct, there must be a course of conduct, and the court decides what is reasonable. The defences to this offence are similar to the defences for s 2 but with one major addition: the course of conduct was pursued reasonably for the protection of themselves (or another), or for the protection of their (or another's) property. For example, a group of people threaten to damage person G's house. Person G threatens retributions should they do so but, as he/she is acting to protect property, he/she is not guilty of the offence of putting people in fear of violence.

This offence is triable either way:

- Summarily; six months' imprisonment and/or a fine.
- On indictment; five years' imprisonment and/or a fine.

This offence can be racially or religiously aggravated (see section 8.10).

8.14.4 Restraining Orders

A court may make a restraining order under s 5 of the Protection from Harassment Act 1997 against a person convicted of the offences described above. A restraining order will place restrictions on a defendant's future behaviour and in particular attempt to inhibit any further harassment of the victim. The order may last indefinitely or for a period stated by the court. You can use the PNC to find out if a person is subject to a restraining order (see section 7.10 above).

If such a restraining order is breached an offence is committed which is triable either way:

- Summarily; six months' imprisonment an/or a fine.
- On indictment; five years' imprisonment and/or a fine.

Clearly, the Protection from Harassment Act 1997 is a potentially valuable piece of legislation which offers a number of options to support victims of harassment. Victims will want to see results, or be given advice on how to put an end to current problems they are facing. However, note the amount of evidence required to secure a successful prosecution within this Act and be very clear about what can constitute a course of conduct, what proof is required, and the collection of evidence. You may need to seek advice from the CPS at an early stage.

TASK 14

You are requested to attend an address in your area where a complaint of harassment has been made. Write brief answers to the following questions:

1. If appropriate, what evidence will you need to collect to prove either an offence under s 2, or under s 4, of the Protection from Harassment Act 1997?
2. What other methods could be used to stop the conduct?
3. How can future evidence be recorded?
4. What reason(s) would make an arrest necessary in these circumstances?

8.15   Harassment of Persons in Their Homes

Harassing or intimidating behaviour by individuals towards a person in his/her home is an offence under ss 42 and 42A of the Criminal Justice and Police Act 2001. The Act also enables you to give directions to a person to leave a particular area, and can be used, if appropriate, with protesters. You can subsequently arrest a person if they knowingly contravene a direction.

The following section outlines the offence and the power to direct a person to leave who is harassing someone in his/her home.

(a) ...they are present outside or in the vicinity of any premises that are used... as a dwelling...	There is no legal definition of 'vicinity'. It is for the courts to decide what is meant by it as a matter of fact and degree in the particular circumstances of each case. Vicinity is not simply determined by distance, it can also be measured by the impact on the householder. For example, someone protesting at the end of a quarter-mile long drive which is the only access road for the inhabitants may be out of sight and sound, but they could still have the ability to cause harassment, alarm, or distress to the residents.
(b) ...[they are] there for the purpose of representing to the resident or another individual or persuading the resident or another individual (i) [that he/she] should not do something they are entitled...to do; [or] (ii) [that he/she] should do something they are not under any obligation to do;	For example to try and persuade a person to resign from an animal research company or not to take up employment with such a company.
(c) ...the person intends [his/her] presence to amount to the harassment of, or to cause alarm or distress to the resident; [or knows or ought to know that their presence is likely to do so; and]	This could mean climbing onto the roof of a dwelling belonging to a person who is the employee of an animal research organization, thereby intending harassment, alarm, or distress. Courts will use the 'reasonable person' test to decide whether a person would find the presence so disturbing.
(d) ...[their] presence amounts to the harassment of, or causes alarm or distress to the resident, [or is likely to result in the harassment of, or cause alarm or distress of any such person.]	This could mean aggressive or abusive conduct such as shouting, heckling, or shouting abusive slogans (such as 'animal killer!') or continuous loud chanting at persons coming into or out of a dwelling, or any visitors to that dwelling. Such conduct could also be accompanied by the aggressive use of banners or placards. For example, they could be used to block or impede vehicular or pedestrian access to another dwelling which shares a drive.

As well as causing distress to the resident, other categories of people can also be affected, such as other people in the resident's dwelling or a person living nearby.

Courts will use the reasonable person test to decide whether a person would find the presence and activities significantly disturbing. Behaviour that may cause harassment, alarm, or distress includes:

• persistent, sustained, and aggressive hammering on the doors;
• ringing doorbells or shouting through letter boxes;
• climbing onto the roof of a dwelling;
• shouting abusive slogans;
• continuous loud chanting;
• aggressive use of banners or placards used to block or impede access.

You do not have to be present when the behaviour occurs. If the resident has CCTV evidence of particular individuals on the roof of his/her house, and he/she had been harassed, alarmed, or distressed by the presence of the protesters, you could arrest the suspects for the offence.

This offence is triable summarily and the penalty is six months' imprisonment and/or a fine.

8.15.1 Giving Directions in Order to Prevent Harassment, Alarm, or Distress

You have powers under s 42(1) of the Criminal Justice and Police 2001 Act to give 'directions' to people in order to prevent them from causing harassment, alarm, or distress to residents (or other people in the vicinity). By directions it is meant instructions such as, 'You have caused harassment and distress to people living in this area. I therefore require you to leave immediately'. However, your ability to give directions to protesters (and to arrest them if they knowingly contravene a direction) is only effective if you are in attendance at the scene of a protest. It does not cover a situation where, for example, a resident makes a complaint about the presence of protesters outside his or her home, but the protesters leave the scene before you arrive. Note that giving directions will not serve any purpose if you do not have the resources to enforce them at the scene.

A direction under s 42(2) may require the person to whom it is given:

to do all such things as the constable giving it may specify as the things [he/she] considers necessary to prevent one or both of the following:

(a) the harassment of the resident; or
(b) the causing of any alarm or distress to the resident.

The direction can be given:

- orally;
- to a group, as individuals or all together;
- to instruct the person(s) to leave the vicinity and for any period not exceeding three months;
- along with conditions.

It must not be given by you when a senior officer is present or to a person exercising the right to peacefully picket a workplace.

8.15.2 Failure to Comply with a Direction

An offence is committed under s 42(7) and (7A) of the Criminal Justice and Police Act 2001 by any person:

- who knowingly fails to comply with a requirement (other than to leave and not return for a period not exceeding three months) (s 42(7));
- to whom a constable has given a direction (including a requirement to leave and not return for a period not exceeding three months) who then returns to the vicinity of the premises in question within the specified period, for the purpose of attempting to persuade.

This offence is triable summarily and the penalty is six months' imprisonment and/or a fine.

These sections of the Act should not be seen as a way of stopping people carrying out their lawful rights to protest peacefully. Similarly, they should not be viewed as a way of restricting people who have a particularly strong view they want to voice. Nor are they meant to stop a fan from standing outside the home of his/her favourite television celebrity or to stop media commentators from trying to record first hand comments from people in the news. Instead the sections are intended to establish a balance between all those issues and the right of individuals to be protected from harassment, alarm, or distress in their own homes.

This legislation gives you more than one tool to deal with this type of situation. The direction to leave is useful, but of course it does not prevent the same protesters from returning time after time to increase the harassment, alarm, or distress of the residents. The offence (causing harassment, distress, or alarm), however, is more final, and therefore you will need to consider carefully which of the powers to use. This will depend on various issues such as the number of people in the vicinity of the person's home, the behaviour of those individuals, the purpose for which they have gathered there, and the impact of their presence on the resident and on anyone living with them and on people in the surrounding area.

> **TASK 15**
>
> Whilst on Supervised Patrol you have been asked to attend the address of a person who claims to be harassed by people in the street outside their house. What factors are you going to consider in order to decide:
>
> - whether or not to direct anybody away from the house;
> - whether you will investigate the offence in relation to the harassment?

8.16 Management of Difficult People in the Community

In this section, we examine three relatively new approaches to countering anti-social behaviour that may adversely affect the lives of others living in the wider community. Areas with particular problems can be targeted by the police, who can provide support for communities seeking to improve their lives by reducing intimidation and anti-social behaviour. The target area can be as small as a parking area or as large as a whole housing estate.

8.16.1 Local Child Curfews

Local child curfews are intended to prevent children of under sixteen years being in certain areas during specified hours without a responsible adult. This legislation is covered under s 14 nof the Crime and Disorder Act 1998. A local authority or a chief officer of police may introduce a local child curfew scheme for a specified period not exceeding ninety days. The schemes ban children under sixteen from being in a specified area of a public place between 9pm and 6am unless they are under the effective control of a parent or a responsible person aged eighteen or over.

Before making a local child curfew scheme, the applicant will consult with the chief officer of police in the area and with appropriate bodies such as the local authority. A local child curfew scheme will not come into effect until it is confirmed by the Secretary of State. The notice will be given by displaying it in the area or by any other suitable method.

Section 15 of the Crime and Disorder Act 1998 describes the action you should take if you find a child contravening a local child curfew. If you have reasonable cause to believe that a child is in contravention of a ban imposed by a curfew notice you must inform the local authority (s 15(1)). You may take the child back to his or her home unless you have reasonable cause to believe that the child would be likely to suffer significant harm (s 15(3)).

8.16.2 Anti-Social Behaviour Orders

Anti-social behaviour orders (or ASBOs as they are commonly known) may be used for individuals over ten years of age who continually behave in such a way as to cause harassment, alarm, or distress to members of the local community. Section 1 of the Crime and Disorder Act 1998 enables a magistrates' court to make an ASBO against such an individual. An ASBO is intended to prevent problem behaviour in the future rather than punishing behaviour that has already occurred; if the individual breaches their ASBO, they commit a criminal offence and this is intended to act as a deterrent.

An ASBO lists the types of behaviour that are prohibited for that particular individual and:

- is made following a complaint about a behaviour that occurred in the preceding six months;
- lasts at least two years;
- can be discharged (discontinued) if both parties agree;
- may be varied (changed) if new and different complaints are made.

In some situations, a banned behaviour might not be in breach of the ASBO if it can be proved that the behaviour was reasonable under those particular circumstances. A breach of such an order is an offence under s 1(1) of the Crime and Disorder Act 1998.

This offence is triable either way;

- Summarily; six months' imprisonment and/or a fine.
- On indictment; five years' imprisonment and/or a fine.

TASK 16

What power is available to you to help identify a person who you believe has been acting, or is acting, in an anti-social manner?

8.16.3 Dispersal of Groups

Section 30 of the Anti-Social Behaviour Act 2003 describes police powers to disperse groups of two or more young people aged under sixteen who are unsupervised in public places after 9pm, requiring the young people to return to their place of residence. The term 'group' is not defined in the legislation but has been held to include protesters (see *R (on the application of Singh and another) v CC of West Midlands Police* [2006] EWCA Civ 1118). You must be in uniform to use this power.

The authorization must be made by an officer of at least the rank of superintendent in regard to a designated area. Under s 30(1), if a police officer of, or above the rank of, superintendent:

has reasonable grounds for believing . . .

(a) that any members of the public have been intimidated, harassed, alarmed or distressed as a result of the presence or behaviour of groups of two or more persons in public places in any locality in [his/her] police area (the relevant locality), and

(b) that anti-social behaviour is a significant and persistent problem in the relevant locality . . .

the senior officer may give an authorization (s 30(2)) that empowers you with powers (3), (4), and (6) below, for a period specified in the authorization which does not exceed six months.

Section 30 Anti-Social Behaviour Act 2003 powers

Section	Power
S 30(3)	If [you have] reasonable grounds for believing that the presence or behaviour of a group of two or more persons in any public place in the relevant locality has resulted, or is likely to result, in any members of the public being intimidated, harassed, alarmed or distressed.
S 30(4)	[You] may give one or more of the following directions, namely— (a) a direction requiring the persons in the group to disperse either • immediately or • by such time as [you] may specify and in such way as [you] may specify; (b) a direction requiring any of those persons whose place of residence is not within the relevant locality to leave the relevant locality or any part of the relevant locality either • immediately or • by such time as [you] may specify and in such a way as [you] may specify; (c) a direction prohibiting any of those persons whose place of residence is not within the relevant locality, from returning to the relevant locality or any part of the relevant locality for such period (not exceeding 24 hours) from the giving of the direction as [you] may specify.
S 30(6)	If, between the hours of 9pm and 6am, [you find] a person in any public place in the relevant locality who [you have] reasonable grounds for believing— (a) is under the age of 16, and (b) is not under the effective control of a parent or a responsible person aged 18 or over, [you] may remove the person to the person's place of residence unless [you] have reasonable grounds for believing that the person would, if removed to that place, be likely to suffer significant harm. If the young person is unwilling to go voluntarily, the word remove has been held to mean 'take away using reasonable force if necessary' (*R (W) v Commissioner of Police for the Metropolis and another, Secretary of State for the Home Department, interested party* [2004] EWCA Civ 458).

8.16.4 Using Directions

Section 32 of the Anti-Social Behaviour Act 2003 provides more guidance on directions and how to use directions. Under s 32(1):

> a direction may be:
>
> (a) given orally;
>
> (b) given to any person individually or to two or more persons together, and
>
> (c) withdrawn or varied by the person who gave it.

Section 32(2) states that it is an offence to knowingly contravene a direction.

This offence is triable summarily and the penalty is three months' imprisonment and/or a fine.

8.16.5 Power to Require Name and Address of a Person Acting in an Anti-Social Manner

Section 50(1) of the Police Reform Act 2002 states that if you have 'reason to believe that a person has been acting, or is acting, in an anti-social manner [you may] require that person to give [his/her] name and address [to you]'.

Section 1 Crime and Disorder Act 1998 states an anti-social manner is that which 'caused or was likely to cause harassment, alarm or distress to one or more persons not of the same household as [him/herself]'.

Section 50(2) Police Reform Act states that it is an offence for any person who:

> (a) fails to give his name and address when required to do so under [the above] subsection (1), or
>
> (b) gives a false or inaccurate name or address in response to a requirement under that subsection.

This offence is triable summarily and the penalty is a fine.

8.16.6 Smoking in a Smoke-Free Place

Under s 7 of the Health Act 2006, a person commits an offence if he/she smokes in a smoke-free place.

Smoking includes the smoking of cigarettes (hand-rolled and manufactured), pipes, cigars, herbal cigarettes, and waterpipes (for example, 'hubble-bubble' pipes).

Smoke-free places include 'enclosed or substantially enclosed premises which are open to the public, and shared workplaces'. The Smoke-free (Premises and Enforcement) Regulations 2006 define enclosed and substantially enclosed premises as follows:

- Enclosed premises have a ceiling or roof and, except for doors, windows, or passageways, are wholly enclosed, whether on a permanent or temporary basis.
- Substantially enclosed premises have a ceiling or roof, but there are permanent openings in the walls which are less than half of the total areas of walls, including other structures which serve the purpose of walls and constitute the perimeter of premises (known as the '50% rule').

Roof includes any fixed or moveable structure or device which is capable of covering all or part of the premises as a roof, including, for example, a canvas awning.

This offence is triable summarily and the penalty is a fine.

TASK 17

You are on Supervised Patrol in a part of a city in which an order has been given under s 30 of the Anti-Social Behaviour Act 2003, enabling you to disperse people from the locality because anti-social behaviour is a significant and persistent problem there. During your patrol, you see a group of about a dozen or so young people who appear to be local residents. A member of the group appears to intimidate a passer-by. What powers do you have to deal with the young people involved?

8.17 Trespassers or Travellers Using Land Owned by Others

Travelling people with no fixed abode sometimes find temporary places to live on land that is privately owned by others. This may cause anxiety and distress for the owners of the land or for local residents. A senior police officer attending the scene has the power under the Criminal Justice and Public Order Act 1994 to order the trespassers and their vehicles to leave as soon as reasonably practicable, if that officer believes the trespassers are there for the common purpose of residing on the land.

8.17.1 Trespass or Nuisance on Land

Section 61(1) of the Criminal Justice and Public Order Act 1994 states that:

> If the senior police officer present at the scene reasonably believes that two or more persons are trespassing on land with the common purpose of residing there for any period and reasonable steps have been taken by or on behalf of the occupier of the land to ask them to leave, and . . .
>
> (a) that any of those persons has caused damage to the land or to property on the land or used threatening, abusive or insulting words or behaviour towards the occupier, a member of his family or an employee or agent of his, or
> (b) that those persons have between them six or more vehicles on the land (vehicle includes a caravan, and unroadworthy vehicles),
>
> [the senior police officer] may direct those persons, or any of them, to leave the land and to remove any vehicles or other property they have with them on the land.

It is an offence (s 61(4)) for a person to:

- fail to leave the land as soon as reasonably practicable; or
- enter again within the period of three months.

These offences are triable summarily and the penalty is three months' imprisonment and/or a fine.

8.17.2 Seizing and Removing Vehicles

If the trespassers will not leave (having been given an order to leave), s 62 of the Criminal Justice and Public Order Act 1994 gives you the power to seize and remove vehicles. Under s 62(1), if a person fails to remove any vehicle on the land or again enters the land as a trespasser within the period of three months, you may seize and remove the vehicle.

8.18 Open-air Gatherings with Music

Although complaints about excessive noise coming from residential properties are often dealt with by staff from local authorities, larger gatherings in the open air may sometimes require police action. You may need to use ss 63, 64, and 65 of the Criminal Justice and Public Order Act 1994 to deal with such situations. These sections include the power for you to give directions to people present at such gatherings (and to people travelling there). There are some predictable exemptions; the following categories of people cannot be given directions under ss 63 to 65:

- the occupier of the land;
- any member of his or her family;
- any employee or agent of his or hers; and
- any person whose home is situated on the land.

'Occupier' means (in England and Wales): 'the person entitled to possession of the land by virtue of an estate or interest held by him [or her]' (s 61(9)).

8.18.1 Powers of Entry and Seizure

Section 63 of the Criminal Justice and Public Order Act 1994 gives you powers of entry and seizure for musical gatherings on land in the open air at night (also referred to as 'open-air raves'). Under s 63, the gathering does not have to involve trespass, and therefore, if you wanted to hold such a gathering on your own land, this legislation would still apply. The following conditions, however, **must all be met** for s 63 to apply. The gathering must:

- take place on land in the open air;
- take place at night;
- involve 20 or more people;
- involve amplified music with repetitive beats;
- involve music that is either loud or goes on for a long time;
- be likely to cause serious distress to local residents.

8.18.2   Powers to Remove Persons at a Gathering in the Open Air

This power (under s 63(2)), applies to people preparing for such a gathering as well as to people attending.

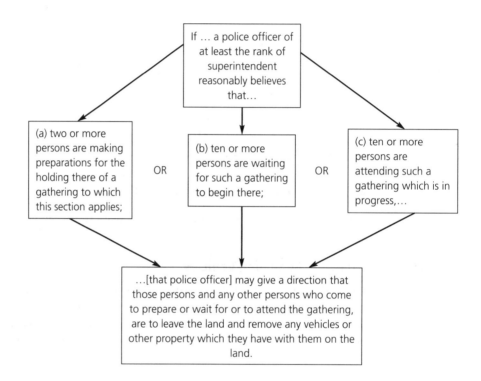

Such a direction, if not communicated by the police officer giving the direction, may be communicated by any constable at the scene (s 63(3)).

Persons shall be treated as having had the direction communicated to them if reasonable steps have been taken to bring it to their attention (s 63(4)). It is an offence (s 63(6)) for a person (knowing that a direction has been given which applies to them) who then:

(a) fails to leave the land as soon as reasonably practicable or
(b) having left, again enters the land within the period of 7 days . . .

If the suspect can show that he/she had a reasonable excuse for either failing to leave the land as soon as reasonably practicable, or for entering the land again he/she has not committed an offence (s 63(7)).

8.18.3   Moving on to Another Gathering

A person who has been directed to leave a gathering who then moves on to another similar gathering within twenty-four hours commits an offence under s 63(7A). A person commits an offence if:

(a) [he/she] knows that a direction under subsection (2) above has been given which applies to [him/her], and
(b) [he/she makes] preparations for, or [attends] a gathering to which this section applies within the period of 24 hours starting when the direction was given.

These offences are triable summarily and the penalty is three months' imprisonment and/or a fine.

8.18.4 Powers of Entry and Seizure for Outdoor Musical Gatherings at Night

Section 64 of the Criminal Justice and Public Order Act 1994 gives powers of entry to the police when dealing with musical gatherings on land in the open air at night. Police officers may need to be deployed to find out what is happening at such gatherings; a warrant is not required (s 64(3)). Under s 64(1) if a police officer of at least the rank of superintendent reasonably believes:

that circumstances exist in relation to any land which would justify the giving of a direction under s 63 in relation to a gathering to which that section applies, [he/she] may authorise any constable to enter the land

to ascertain whether such circumstances exist and to exercise any power conferred on a constable by s 63 or s 64(4).

Vehicles and sound equipment may be seized if a direction has been given under s 63 and a constable reasonably suspects that any person to whom the direction applies has, without reasonable excuse:

(a) failed to remove any vehicle or sound equipment on the land, which appears to the constable to belong to [him/her] or to be in [his/her] possession or under [his or her] control, or
(b) entered the land as a trespasser with a vehicle or sound equipment within the period of 7 days beginning with the day on which the direction was given.

8.18.5 Directing People not to Proceed Towards a Gathering

Section 65 of the Criminal Justice and Public Order Act 1994 gives you powers to direct persons **not to proceed** towards a gathering to which s 63 applies. You must be in uniform and within five miles of the gathering. It is an offence (s 65(1)) for a person not to comply with such a direction.

This offence is triable summarily and the penalty is a fine.

8.19 Aggravated Trespass

This offence and the police powers to deal with it are covered in ss 68 and 69 of the Criminal Justice and Public Order Act 1994. The legislation is intended to deal with trespassers who disrupt or obstruct any lawful activity taking place on land or adjoining land, such as protesters at military bases (and hence the 'aggravated' nature of the trespass).

8.19.1 Disrupting Lawful Activity

A person commits the offence of aggravated trespass under s 68(1) of the Criminal Justice and Public Order Act 1994 if:

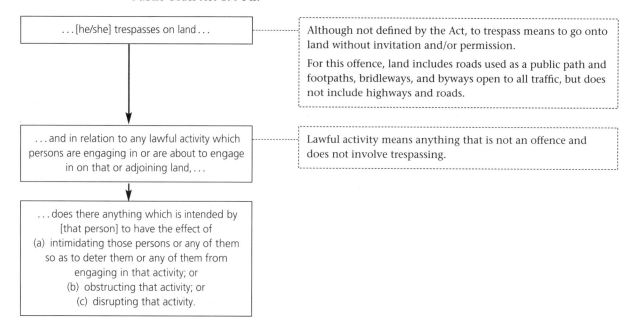

...[he/she] trespasses on land...	Although not defined by the Act, to trespass means to go onto land without invitation and/or permission. For this offence, land includes roads used as a public path and footpaths, bridleways, and byways open to all traffic, but does not include highways and roads.
...and in relation to any lawful activity which persons are engaging in or are about to engage in on that or adjoining land,...	Lawful activity means anything that is not an offence and does not involve trespassing.

...does there anything which is intended by [that person] to have the effect of
(a) intimidating those persons or any of them so as to deter them or any of them from engaging in that activity; or
(b) obstructing that activity; or
(c) disrupting that activity.

This offence is triable summarily and the penalty is three months' imprisonment and/or a fine.

8.19.2 Powers to Direct Trespassers to Leave the Land

Section 69 of the Criminal Justice and Public Order Act 1994 provides the senior police officer at the scene of an aggravated trespass with the power to direct a person to leave the land. The senior police officer must reasonably believe that the person is committing, has committed, or intends to commit the offence of aggravated trespass.

Under s 69(1) of the Criminal Justice and Public Order Act 1994:

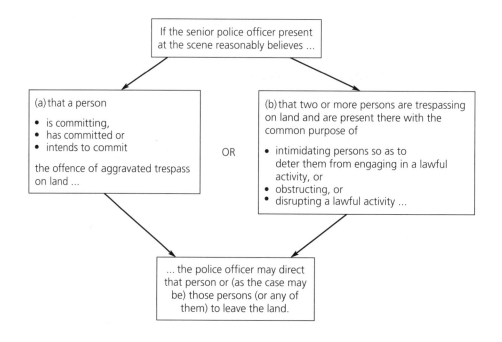

If the senior police officer present at the scene reasonably believes ...

(a) that a person
- is committing,
- has committed or
- intends to commit

the offence of aggravated trespass on land ...

OR

(b) that two or more persons are trespassing on land and are present there with the common purpose of
- intimidating persons so as to deter them from engaging in a lawful activity, or
- obstructing, or
- disrupting a lawful activity ...

... the police officer may direct that person or (as the case may be) those persons (or any of them) to leave the land.

Under s 69(3), It is an offence for a person who has been directed to leave if he or she:

(a) [fails] to leave the land as soon as practicable, or
(b) having left, again [enters] the land as a trespasser within the period of three months beginning with the day on which the direction was given.

It is a defence if the accused can show that he/she:

• was not trespassing on the land, or
• had a reasonable excuse for failing to leave the land as soon as practicable or for again entering the land as a trespasser.

This offence is triable summarily and the penalty is three months' imprisonment (maximum) and/or a fine.

8.20 Offensive Weapons, Bladed, and Sharply Pointed Articles

Serious wounding and possibly death can result from the use of these items, but you will hear numerous excuses from people found in possession of such articles. In some cases, the individuals concerned may be genuinely vulnerable to attack by others. However, whatever the circumstances, it is your responsibility to attempt to prevent any crimes from taking place involving the use of these weapons, and it is a police officer's responsibility, if at all possible, to detect their presence before they are used.

The legislation covered in this section concerns offensive weapons, bladed, and sharply pointed articles in public places and on school premises, and is to be found in:

• s 1 of the Prevention of Crime Act 1953;
• s 139A(2) of the Criminal Justice Act 1984; and
• s 139 of the Criminal Justice Act 1988.

You have the power to search for offensive weapons or bladed or sharply pointed articles under s 1 of the PACE Act 1984.

8.20.1 Offensive Weapons in a Public Place

Section 1 of the Prevention of Crime Act 1953 is an important piece of legislation that will assist you in circumstances where you discover an offensive weapon in the possession of a member of the public.

When searching for offensive weapons always consider health and safety implications the PAC Safety First checklist is relevant as is NOS element AF1.1—'to identify the hazards and evaluate the risks in your workplace' (see section 7.7 of the Handbook).

Section 1(1) of the Prevention of Crime Act 1953 states that it is an offence for:

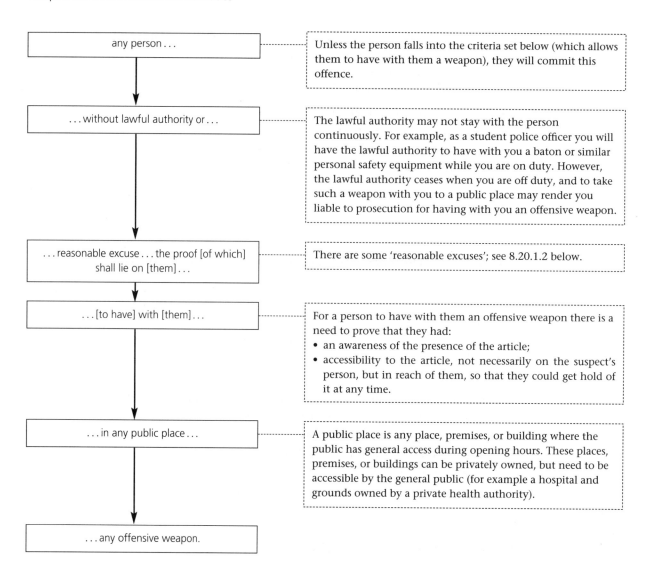

any person . . .

Unless the person falls into the criteria set below (which allows them to have with them a weapon), they will commit this offence.

. . . without lawful authority or . . .

The lawful authority may not stay with the person continuously. For example, as a student police officer you will have the lawful authority to have with you a baton or similar personal safety equipment while you are on duty. However, the lawful authority ceases when you are off duty, and to take such a weapon with you to a public place may render you liable to prosecution for having with you an offensive weapon.

. . . reasonable excuse . . . the proof [of which] shall lie on [them] . . .

There are some 'reasonable excuses'; see 8.20.1.2 below.

. . . [to have] with [them] . . .

For a person to have with them an offensive weapon there is a need to prove that they had:
• an awareness of the presence of the article;
• accessibility to the article, not necessarily on the suspect's person, but in reach of them, so that they could get hold of it at any time.

. . . in any public place . . .

A public place is any place, premises, or building where the public has general access during opening hours. These places, premises, or buildings can be privately owned, but need to be accessible by the general public (for example a hospital and grounds owned by a private health authority).

. . . any offensive weapon.

8.20.1.1 Definition of an offensive weapon

An offensive weapon (s 1(4)) is any article made, adapted, or intended for causing injury. **Made** articles include any article which has been made or manufactured with the intention of causing injury to people, for example flick knives or telescopic batons. These are offensive weapons per se. In other words, the courts need no further proof of what they are intended for, only that the defendant did not have reasonable excuse to have them. **Adapted** articles include any articles which have been altered or modified in some way, with the intention of causing injury, for example a broken bottle with sharp edges or a potato with razor blades sticking out. **Intended** articles include **any** articles which a suspect has with them, with which they intend to cause injury. The precise nature of the article is not important: it is what the suspect intends to do with it. A pillow could become an offensive weapon if it can be proved that the suspect intended to use it to cause injury to his elderly relative. Once again, gathering evidence through interview is important here.

Of course some items that may be classed as an offensive weapon may have innocent uses, and the person would therefore have a reasonable excuse for carrying such an item.

8.20.1.2 Reasonable and unreasonable excuses

A person **may** have a reasonable excuse if s/he fears for his/her safety from an **unprovoked** or **unlawful attack**, for example a security guard picking up or dropping off money at a bank. A person **may** have a reasonable excuse if **he/she fears for his/her safety**. For example a person feels he/she is about to be assaulted, and before he/she can receive help or can escape, he/she picks up a chair to defend him or herself. Other reasonable excuses include having an **innocent reason**, such as a chef carrying knives.

Unreasonable excuses include:

- **Forgetfulness**—a person may not have a reasonable excuse if he/she has forgotten he/she has an offensive weapon with him/her, for example forgetting that there is one in the car.
- **Ignorance**—a person may not have a reasonable excuse if he/she does not know the true identity of the item, for example thinking a truncheon is a telescope.
- **General self-defence**—a person does **not** have reasonable excuse to have an offensive weapon with him/her generally, for self-defence, 'just in case' he/she is attacked.

In any prosecution the burden of proving reasonable excuse to have with them an offensive weapon lies with the defendants themselves; if the defendants can persuade the court to consider the likelihood that they had a reasonable excuse, that could be enough to find them not guilty. Therefore, when you investigate a person for this offence, be prepared to counteract later defences by gathering together as much evidence as possible; before, during, and after interview under caution.

This offence is triable either way:

- Summarily; six months' imprisonment and/or a fine.
- On indictment; four years' imprisonment and/or a fine.

8.20.2 Bladed or Sharply Pointed Articles in a Public Place

The offence of having a bladed or sharply pointed article (s 139(1), Criminal Justice Act 1988) was created in an attempt to prevent more serious crime taking place through the use of everyday items. Historically, under the Prevention of Crimes Act 1953, if the defendant was able to persuade the court on the balance of probabilities that he/she had reasonable excuse for having an offensive weapon with them, he/she would not be found guilty (see above). Therefore it was difficult for the prosecution to prove a case when the article was an everyday item, such as a kitchen knife, pair of scissors, or large pocket knife. Section 139(1) of the Criminal Justice Act 1988 states that an offence is committed by any person who possesses a bladed and sharply pointed article in a public place.

8.20.2.1 The definition of bladed and sharply pointed articles

The definition of '**bladed**' includes any kind of bladed article, for example kitchen knife, scissors, craft knife, pocket knife, daggers, and any other article which has been given a cutting edge or blade. Pocket knives with a blade less than 7.62 cm long which cannot be locked in the open position are not classed as bladed under this legislation.

The definition of '**sharply pointed**' includes any kind of sharply pointed article, for example needles, pins, geometry compasses, and any other article which has been given a sharp point. This is in contrast to the Prevention of Crimes Act 1953 which is more concerned with objects that are more obviously only 'offensive weapons' rather than everyday articles. A court must decide whether or not an article has a blade or is sharply pointed, so the prosecution must be able to prove that the article fits this description. In *R v Davis* [1998] Crim LR 564 the suspect was carrying a screwdriver which the court was asked to consider was a bladed article capable of causing injury. The court decided that that it was more important to decide whether the screwdriver had a cutting edge or point, than to consider whether it was capable of causing injury. Therefore, unless a screwdriver has a pointed end or has been sharpened to make a blade, it is still not an article for the purposes of this Act.

8.20.2.2 Defences for having bladed or sharply pointed articles

There may be a good reason for a person having a bladed or sharply pointed article in their possession, such as a carpet layer carrying a specialist knife for cutting carpet at work. But general self-defence, ignorance, and forgetfulness are not a suitable defence; see the description of reasonable excuses for carrying an offensive weapon in section 8.20.1.2 above.

Other grounds for defence (s 139 of the Criminal Justice Act 1988)

Defence	Example
Lawful authority	The lawful authority may not stay with the person continuously. For example, as a student police officer you will have the lawful authority to have with you a bladed or sharply pointed article after seizure and before placing it into a special property store. Members of the armed services will also have lawful authority to carry articles, such as bayonets, whilst they are on duty, but if they carry such articles whilst they are not on duty, this may make them liable for prosecution.
For use at work	A joiner uses wood chisels with very sharp cutting edges during the course of his or her work and may need to carry them in a bag in the street while moving between jobs. He/she would, however, not be able to use this claim if he/she had chisels in a night club whilst socializing.
Religious reasons	Genuine followers of the Sikh religion carry kirpans (a small rigid knife) for religious reasons.
Part of any national costume	Whilst wearing national costume, some Scots carry a skean dhu (a small dagger, in the top of their socks). However, this defence could not be used if the person was still carrying the knife and was not wearing national costume.

As before, when you investigate a person for this offence, be prepared to counteract later defences by gathering together as much evidence as possible; before, during, and after interview under caution.

This offence is triable either way:

- Summarily; six months' imprisonment and/or a fine.
- On indictment; four years' imprisonment and/or a fine.

TASK 18

Whilst on duty during Supervised and Independent Patrol there will be many occasions when you have the opportunity to see inside vehicles. What will be your reaction to the occupants of those vehicles when you see everyday utensils and tools inside, including scissors and craft (Stanley) knives lying on the floor?

8.20.3 School Premises and Offensive Weapons, Bladed, or Sharply Pointed Articles

The Criminal Justice Act 1998 states that it is an offence for any person to have with them on school premises an offensive weapon (s 139 A(2)) or a bladed or sharply pointed article (s 139A(1)). School premises are defined (by s 4 of the Education Act 1996) as land and buildings used for the purposes of:

- primary education;
- secondary education;
- combined primary and secondary education.

Further or higher education institutes, for example FE colleges or universities, are not covered by this Act.

The classification of these offences and powers of search are the same as s 1(1) of the Prevention of Crime Act 1953 above. You do not have to be in uniform to enter such premises if you believe an offence under this section is being or has been committed, and you may use reasonable force to secure an entry. If you find offensive weapons or bladed or sharply pointed articles on school premises, you may seize them (s 139B of the Criminal Justice Act 1988).

8.20.4 Using Someone to Mind a Weapon

Under s 28 of the Violent Crime Reduction Act 2006, a person commits an offence if she/he:

- uses another to look after, hide or transport a dangerous weapon for [him/her]; and
- does so under arrangements or in circumstances that facilitate, or are intended to facilitate, the weapon's being available to [him/her] for an unlawful purpose.

A dangerous weapon is to be regarded as available to a person for an unlawful purpose including any case where:

(a) the weapon is available for [him/her] to take possession of it at a time and place; and

(b) his/her possession of the weapon at that time and place would constitute, or be likely to involve or to lead to, the commission by [him/her] of an offence.

This offence is triable either way.

The table below lists those items which are classified as dangerous weapons for the purposes of s 28. Some descriptions (in quotes) are taken from the relevant Acts and Statutory Instruments.

Dangerous Weapon	Comments
Bladed or sharply pointed article	'Any article which has a blade or which is sharply pointed and which is made or adapted for use for causing injury to [a] person.'
Firearm	'Other than an air weapon or a component part of, or accessory to, an air weapon' (see 8.2 below).
Axe	The usual meaning of the term.
Knife	With the exception of a 'folding pocket-knife if the cutting edge of its blade does not exceed 7.62 centimetres (3 inches)'.
Disguised knife	'Any knife which has a concealed blade or concealed sharp point and is designed to appear to be an everyday object of a kind commonly carried on the person or in a handbag, briefcase, or other hand luggage (such as a comb, brush, writing instrument, cigarette lighter, key, lipstick or telephone)'.
Stealth knife	'A knife or spike, which has a blade, or sharp point, made from a material that is not readily detectable by apparatus used for detecting metal and which is not designed for domestic use or for use in the processing, preparation or consumption of food or as a toy.'
Razor blades	With the exception of 'razor blades permanently enclosed in a cartridge or housing where less than 2 millimetres of any blade is exposed beyond the plane which intersects the highest point of the surfaces preceding and following such blades'.
Knuckleduster	'Band of metal or other hard material worn on one or more fingers, and designed to cause injury.'
Telescopic truncheon	'A truncheon which extends automatically by hand pressure applied to a button, spring or other device in or attached to its handle.'
Baton	'A straight, side-handled or friction-lock truncheon.'
Shuriken, Shaken or Death Star	'A hard non-flexible plate having three or more sharp radiating points and designed to be thrown.'
Push dagger	'A knife the handle of which fits within a clenched fist and the blade of which protrudes from between two fingers.'
Belt buckle knife	'A buckle which incorporates or conceals a knife.'
Swordstick	'A hollow walking-stick or cane containing a blade which may be used as a sword.'
Handclaw	'A band of metal or other hard material from which a number of sharp spikes protrude, and worn around the hand.'
Hollow kubotan	'A cylindrical container containing a number of sharp spikes.'
Footclaw	'A bar of metal or other hard material from which a number of sharp spikes protrude, and worn strapped to the foot.'
Balisong or Butterfly knife	'A blade enclosed by its handle, which is designed to split down the middle, without the operation of a spring or other mechanical means, to reveal the blade.'
Blowpipe or Blow gun	'A hollow tube out of which hard pellets or darts are shot by the use of breath.'
Kusari gama	'A length of rope, cord, wire or chain fastened at one end to a sickle.'
Kyoketsu shoge	'A length of rope, cord, wire or chain fastened at one end to a hooked knife.'
Manrikigusari or kusari	'A length of rope, cord, wire or chain fastened at each end to a hard weight or hand grip.'

Your ability to search for and discover offensive weapons may prevent further and perhaps more serious offences taking place. Many offensive weapons have been cleverly disguised, and what you initially recognize as an everyday item, may possibly be concealing a weapon. The law regarding weapons is different in some other countries, and therefore certain weapons are easily obtainable elsewhere and then brought into the UK.

TASK 19

Ahmed, a seveteen-year-old at a local FE College, is under genuine threat from others at the college and has good grounds to fear for his safety. He carries a knife for his own personal protection.

Put aside any discussion whether Ahmed has a reasonable excuse; what other actions by you would be appropriate in this case?

Note that your reflections may be relevant to the knowledge requirement of NOS element BE1.1 'Provide initial support to victims, survivors and witnesses' and the C3 Cumulative Assessment Record of your SOLAP.

8.21 Football-related Offences

Football-related offences do not feature within the compulsory LPG modules of the IPLDP. We cover them here since the policing of football matches often features as part of the training of student police officers whilst on Supervised or Independent Patrol. Hence, although the policing of football matches is not a common occurrence for every police officer in England and Wales, you might well be involved in it during your training, particularly if you are a student police officer within a force responsible for the policing of large towns and cities.

The offences described in this section are covered under two Acts:

- Sporting Events (Control of Alcohol etc) Act 1985.
- The Football (Offences) Act 1991.

The Sporting Events (Control of Alcohol etc) Act 1985 applies only to sports grounds, certain sporting events, and designated periods relating to those sporting events. Currently the only sport which is considered necessary to control is football, and therefore no restrictions have been placed upon the people attending other sporting events such as rugby or cricket matches.

Many football clubs will take steps to inform their supporters of the main points of the law and the regulations governing behaviour. A good example is Ipswich Town Football Club: <http://www.itfc.premiumtv.co.uk/page/TicketNews/0,,10272~513056,00.html>.

The two Acts above specify certain offences associated with the behaviour of supporters at particular types of football matches, including the consumption of alcohol. These are described below, but in the case of alcohol, apply only to so-called 'designated' matches.

8.21.1 The Sports Grounds and Sporting Events (Designation) Order 2005

The Sporting Events (Control of Alcohol etc) Act 1985 only applies if **both** the sports (in our case football) ground **and** the sporting event (in our case football match) have been **designated** as such by the Secretary of State.

Schedule 1, art 2(1) of Statutory Instrument 2005 No 3204 states that designated sports grounds (football grounds) will include **any sports ground in England or Wales**.

The same Statutory Instrument includes the following as **designated sporting events** (football matches):

1. Association football matches in which one or both of the participating teams represent a club which is for the time being a member (whether a full or associate member) of:
   - the Football League, [or]
   - the Football Association Premier League, [or]
   - the Football Conference National Division, [or]

- the Scottish Football League or Welsh Premier League, [or]
- represents a country or territory.

2. Association football matches in competition for the Football Association Cup (other than in a preliminary or qualifying round.

Note that the list may vary from year to year to reflect changes in the organization of football leagues. The 2005 Statutory Instrument may be found at <http://www.opsi.gov.uk/si/si2005/20053204.htm>.

The following events are examples of matches which would be likely to be **designated** for the purposes of the Sporting Events (Control of Alcohol etc) Act 1985, as they meet both the ground and the match (teams) criteria:

- A football match played between Bristol City and Scunthorpe United at Bristol City's ground, Ashton Gate. This is because Ashton Gate is, a designated sports ground and both teams are currently members of the Football League.
- A match played between Dover Athletic and Manchester United at Dover Athletic's Crabble ground. This is because the Crabble is a designated sports ground and Manchester United is a currently member of the Football Association Premier League (although Dover Athletic is not).

So, in these cases the Sporting Events (Control of Alcohol etc) Act 1985 would apply for a certain period of time (see section 8.21.2).

The following events are examples of matches which are **not designated** for the purposes of the Sporting Events (Control of Alcohol etc) Act 1985:

- An international hockey match being played at the Millennium Stadium in Cardiff, because although the stadium is a sports ground and will therefore be designated, it is not hosting one of the type of football matches listed above.
- A football match played between Dover Athletic and the Metropolitan Police at Dover because although the Crabble ground at Dover is a sports ground and therefore designated, both teams are currently in the Ryman League Division One which is not designated.

Further, the Statutory Instrument explains that the Act does not apply to any sporting event in which players are not paid and if spectators are admitted free of charge, such as amateur weekend football matches which take place on school sports fields or recreation grounds.

8.21.2 Period of a Designated Sporting Event (Football Match)

Offences under the Sporting Events (Control of Alcohol etc) Act 1985 can only be considered if they occur during the period commencing two hours before the start of a football match and one hour after the end of the match, inclusive.

The designated period is determined as follows: a football match is scheduled to start at 7.45pm, and there are 45 minutes play in the first half (up to approximately 8.30pm), 15 minutes half time (8.45pm), 45 minutes of second half play and the match ends at approximately 9.30pm. The period of this designated football match would be from 5.45pm to 10.30pm. (We ignore here the added complexity of added time being played to compensate for stoppages, or extra time to decide a match, or the match itself starting late.)

We now consider a number of offences covered by the Act.

8.21.3 Vehicles Transporting Passengers to Sports Events

Drivers, owners, and passengers of some types of vehicle used to transport fans to sports events are subject to legislation under s 1 of the Sporting Events (Control of Alcohol etc) Act 1985.

8.21.3.1 Public service vehicles

The type of vehicle affected by this legislation (s 1 of the Sporting Events (Control of Alcohol etc) Act 1985) is referred to as a **specified vehicle** and is:

(a) a public service vehicle or railway passenger vehicle; [and]
(b) is being used for the principal purpose of carrying passengers for the whole or part of a journey to or from a designated sporting event.

It is an offence under s 1(2) for the following persons to knowingly cause or permit intoxicating liquor to be carried on a specified vehicle:

- the operator of a public service vehicle (or the servant or agent of the operator); [or]
- a person who has hired a vehicle (or the servant or agent of that person).

It is also an offence for such a person to have intoxicating liquor in their possession while on a specified vehicle (s 1(3)) or to be drunk on a vehicle to which this section applies (s 1(4)).

This offence is triable summarily only and the penalty depends on the subsection:

- Subsection 1(2)—a fine;
- Subsection 1(3)—three months' imprisonment and/or a fine;
- Subsection 1(4)—a fine.

8.21.3.2 Vehicles other than public service vehicles

Under s 1A of the Sporting Events (Control of Alcohol etc) Act 1985, a 'specified motor vehicle' is defined as a vehicle which is 'mechanically propelled and intended or adapted for use on the road' which is:

- not a public service vehicle

[but]

- is adapted to carry more than 8 passengers; [and] is being used for the principal purpose of carrying two or more passengers for the whole or part of a journey to or from a designated sporting event.

Under s 1A(2), it is an offence for the following persons to knowingly cause or permit intoxicating liquor to be carried on a specified (s 1A) motor vehicle:

- the driver;
- the vehicle's keeper;
- 'the servant or agent of its keeper';
- 'a person to whom it is made available (by hire, loan or otherwise) by its keeper or the keeper's servant or agent, or the servant or agent of a person to whom it is so made available'.

It is an offence for such a person to have intoxicating liquor in his or her possession while on a specified vehicle (s 1A(3)) or to be drunk on a vehicle to which this section applies (s 1A(4)).

This offence is triable summarily only and the penalty depends on the subsection:

- Subsection 1A(2)—a fine;
- Subsection 1A(3)—three months' imprisonment and/or a fine;
- Subsection 1A(4)—a fine.

8.21.4 Alcohol and Drinks Containers at a Designated Sporting Event

Section 2(1) of the Sporting Events (Control of Alcohol etc) Act 1985 is generally imposed for football matches where there is a potential for disorder. Under this legislation it is an offence to possess alcohol or drinks containers likely to contain alcohol.

Drinks containers are referred to as specified articles (s 2(3)), and are defined as:

any article capable of causing injury to a person struck by it, being:—

(a) a bottle, can or other portable container (including such an article when crushed or broken) which:—
  (i) is for holding any drink, and
  (ii) is of a kind which, when empty, is normally discarded or returned to, or left to be recovered by the supplier, or
(b) part of an article falling within paragraph (a) above, but does not apply to anything that is for holding any medicinal product (within the meaning of the Medicines Act 1968).

Section 2(1) of the Sporting Events (Control of Alcohol etc) Act 1985 states that it is an offence for a person to possess intoxicating liquor (or 'specified articles'):

(a) at any time during the period of a designated sporting event when [he/she is] in any area of a designated sports ground from which the event may be directly viewed, or

(b) while entering or trying to enter a designated sports ground at any time during the period of a designated sporting event at that ground.

It is also an offence under s 2(2) of the same Act for a person to be drunk inside the ground, or to be drunk while entering or trying to enter such a ground at any time during the period of a designated sporting event at that ground.

This offence is triable summarily and the penalty is three months' imprisonment and/or a fine.

8.21.5 Fireworks, Flares, and Similar Articles During a Designated Sporting Event

Section 2A of the Sporting Events (Control of Alcohol etc) Act 1985 controls the possession of fireworks and similar objects at designated sporting events. The prohibited objects (s 2A(3) and (4)) include fireworks, rockets, distress flares, fog signals, pellets and capsules intended to be used as fumigators or for testing pipes, and any other item which is for 'the emission of a flare for purposes of illuminating or signalling, or the emission of smoke or a visible gas'. It does not include matches, cigarette lighters or heaters.

Section 2A of the Sporting Events (Control of Alcohol etc) Act 1985 states that a person is guilty of an offence if he/she has an article or substance to which this section applies:

(a) at any time during the period of a designated sporting event when [he/she is] in any area of a designated sports ground from which the event may be directly viewed, or

(b) while entering or trying to enter a designated sports ground at any time during the period of a designated sporting event at the ground.

This offence is triable summarily and the penalty is three months' imprisonment and/or a fine.

8.21.6 Powers of Entry for Sports Grounds

Section 7 of the Sporting Events (Control of Alcohol etc) Act 1985 allows you to enter and search any part of the ground if you have reasonable grounds to suspect that an offence under the Act is being committed or is about to be committed or to enforce the provisions of the Act.

Under s 7(1) you may:

at any time during the period of a designated sporting event at any designated sports ground, enter any part of the ground for the purpose of enforcing the provisions of this Act.

This applies to the possession of alcohol, fireworks, and similar articles.

Section 7 states that you may search a person (s 7(2)) or a vehicle (s 7(3)) if you have reasonable grounds to suspect that an offence under this Act has been committed or is about to be committed. However, remember that you must carry out any searches in line with the relevant PACE Act 1984, Code of Practice.

8.21.7 Designated Football Matches and the Throwing of Objects

The Football (Offences) Act 1991 also deals with forms of misbehaviour at football matches. It too uses the notions of a 'designated match' and time periods discussed earlier in sections 8.21.1 and 8.21.2 but with a number of quite subtle differences. The Football (Offences) Act 1991 defines a designated match as a match in which one or both of the participating teams either represent a country (or territory) or are members (full or associate) of:

• the Football League;
• the Football Association Premier League;
• the Football Conference; or
• the League of Wales.

Subsequent Statutory Instruments and Orders have made it clear that the Football Conference includes the two feeder leagues (Conference North and Conference South) as well as the Conference National Division. The League of Wales is taken to refer to the Welsh Premier League.

Section 1(2) of the Football (Offences) Act 1991 states that:

> references in this Act to things done at a designated football match include anything done at the ground:—
>
> (a) within the period beginning two hours before the start of the match or (if earlier) two hours before the time at which it is advertised to start, and ending one hour after the end of the match; or
>
> (b) where the match is advertised to start at a particular time on a particular day, but does not take place on that day, within the period beginning two hours before and ending one hour after the advertised starting time.

Section 2 of the Football (Offences) Act 1991 states that it is an offence for a person at a designated football match to throw anything at or towards:

> (a) the playing area, or any area adjacent to the playing area to which spectators are not generally admitted, or
>
> (b) any area in which spectators or other persons are or may be present,
>
> without lawful authority or lawful excuse (which shall be for [him or her] to prove).

This offence is triable summarily and the penalty will be a fine.

8.21.8 Indecent or Racist Chanting at a Designated Football Match

Section 3(1) of the Football (Offences) Act 1991 states that it is an offence to engage or take part in chanting of an indecent or racialist nature at a designated football match. Section 3(2) goes on to clarify that:

- 'chanting' means the repeated uttering of any words or sounds (whether alone or in concert with one or more others); and
- of 'racialist nature' means consisting of or including matter which is threatening, abusive or insulting to a person by reason of [his/her] colour, race, nationality (including citizenship) or ethnic or national origins.

This offence is triable summarily and the penalty is a fine.

8.21.9 Spectators on the Playing Area at a Designated Football Match

Section 4 of the Football (Offences) Act 1991 states that:

> it is an offence for a person at a designated football match to go onto the playing area, or any area adjacent to the playing area to which spectators are not generally admitted, without lawful authority or lawful excuse (which shall be for [the suspect] to prove).

This offence is triable summarily and the penalty is a fine.

TASK 20

As a student police officer you are deployed whilst on Supervised Patrol to a football match. The club concerned plays within the Football Conference National Division, so you can therefore assume that both the ground and the matches played in the ground are designated under both the Sporting Events (Control of Alcohol etc) Act 1985 and the Football (Offences) Act 1991. Consider each of the following offences and match them against the situations given below by putting the appropriate letter(s) in the right hand column. The first answer has been given to you. You may need to consult the original legislation for the detail.

a— s 2(1) of the Sporting Events (Control of Alcohol etc) Act 1985
b— s 2(2) of the Sporting Events (Control of Alcohol etc) Act 1985
c— s 2 of the Football (Offences) Act 1991
d— s 3 of the Football (Offences) Act 1991
e— s 4 of the Football (Offences) Act 1991
f— s 1(2) of the Sporting Events (Control of Alcohol etc) Act 1985
g— s 1(3) of the Sporting Events (Control of Alcohol etc) Act 1985
h— s 1(4) of the Sporting Events (Control of Alcohol etc) Act 1985
i— s 2A of the Sporting Events (Control of Alcohol etc) Act 1985

1. You see a fan fumbling for money to pay for a cup of tea from the refreshment stand. When you approach, the fan is hardly able to stand. The fan's breath smells of intoxicating liquor, his eyes are glazed, and his speech is slurred.	**b**
2. You are on duty at the edge of the pitch near the entrance to the players' tunnel as the teams enter after half time. Whilst observing the crowd, you see a dark metal object hit the ground near your feet and see one of the players stop in his stride and grab his head in pain. You look up and see a youth in the crowd raising his right hand and arm in a throwing action.	
3. A mid-field player is black. Every time he receives the ball you hear opposition supporters make derogatory 'monkey' sounds and shout racist abuse.	
4. Whilst on duty outside the ground you see a fan arrive waiting to get a ticket and enter. Under his arm you clearly see a four-pack of lager cans.	
5. Before the start of a match you see a supporter waiting to purchase a ticket to enter the ground. The fan finishes drinking from a can, drops it to the ground, and stands on it to crush it. The fan is now at the front of the queue to get in, looks around, picks up the crushed tin, and puts it in a coat pocket out of view.	
6. One of your responsibilities is to monitor the away supporters arriving by coaches and mini-buses hired for the occasion. On one of the mini-buses you observe an away fan drinking from a bottle of cider. As the vehicle stops, the door of the mini-bus is opened by the driver just as one of the other passengers offers the driver a can of lager. Just then a third passenger gets up from a seat and falls down the steps of the mini-bus, apparently drunk.	
7. At the end of one of the matches when the final whistle is blown, the two teams leave the pitch and a group of fans go on to the pitch to follow the players and congratulate them.	
8. At the end of a match close to 5 November, as the crowd are leaving the ground, you see a youth reach into his pocket. As he withdraws his hand from his pocket, a firework falls to the ground.	

8.22 Introduction to Firearms

Your safety and the safety of others around you is paramount in relation to firearms. Your force will have specially trained and equipped personnel to deal with all firearms incidents and your control room must consider the deployment of firearms officers to all firearms incidents. However, there always remains the possibility that you could find yourself unexpectedly at the scene of a firearms incident.

In addition, there may be occasions, perhaps during a search of premises, when you will find firearms, or you will be deployed to investigate people using air weapons. You will need to investigate whether the firearms are legally owned or not.

For the forensic aspects of firearms see section 13.6.16.

8.22.1 What is a Firearm?

A firearm is 'a lethal barrelled weapon of any description from which any shot, bullet or other missile can be discharged' (s 57(1) of the Firearms Act 1968).

Firearms are loosely grouped into four categories under the Act:

1. Section 1 firearms (s 1 of the Firearms Act 1968).
2. a Shotguns.
3. Air weapons.
4. Prohibited weapons.

Imitation firearms form a fifth and separate category, which we examine in section 8.27.

In detail, a firearm is:

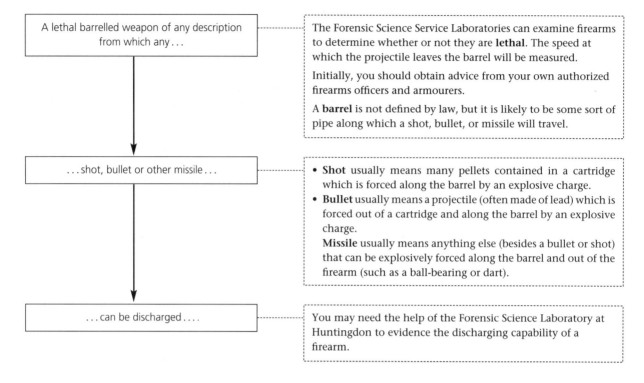

Definition of a firearm

Item	Notes
(a) any prohibited weapon whether it is such a lethal weapon [. . .] or not	See section 8.26 below on prohibited weapons.
(b) any component part of such a lethal or prohibited weapon; and	Component parts includes all the working parts of the firearm, the trigger mechanism, the firing pin, and so on, but does not include the additions such as the trigger guard.
(c) any accessory to any such weapon designed or adapted to diminish the noise or flash caused by firing the weapon.	A court will decide whether the silencer or flash eliminator could be used with the firearm in question, and whether the suspect had the accessory for that purpose.

8.22.2 Requesting a Person to Hand Over a Firearm or Ammunition

Remember your health and safety!

Section 47(1) of the Act authorizes you to require any person whom you have:

reasonable cause to suspect . . .
- of having a firearm, with or without ammunition, with [them] in a public place; or
- to be committing or about to commit, elsewhere than in a public place, an offence relevant [see below] for the purposes of this section,
to hand over the firearm or ammunition for examination by [you].

Remember, a public place includes any highway and any other premises or place to which (at the relevant time) the public have access.

Relevant offences for the purposes of this legislation include:

- Carrying a firearm with criminal intent (s 18 of the Firearms Act 1968).
- Trespassing in a building with a firearm (s 20(1) of the Firearms Act 1968).
- Trespassing on land with a firearm (s 20(2) of the Firearms Act 1968).

It is an offence for a person in possession of a firearm or ammunition to fail to hand it over when required to do so (s 47(2)).

This offence is triable summarily and the penalty is three months' imprisonment and/or a fine.

8.22.3 Stop and Search for Firearms

You can stop and search a person (s 47(3) of the Firearms Act 1968) or a vehicle (s 47(4)) if you suspect that a firearms offence has been committed or is about to be committed, but, as ever, first and foremost remember your own and others' health and safety.

In order to carry out such a search, you must follow the PACE Act 1984 Codes of Practice and provide the following information to the person you are searching:

> G Grounds of the suspicion for the search
> O Object/purpose of search
> W Warrant card (if in plain clothes or requested)
> I Identity as a police officer
> S Station to which you are attached
> E Entitlement to a copy of the search record
> L Legal power used
> Y 'You are detained for the purposes of a search'

This mnemonic is widely used in police training and is also employed in a variety of other circumstances (you first saw it as a response to an earlier task). You also have power of entry (s 47(5)) to search for firearms.

8.22.4 Requesting to See a Firearms Certificate

A firearms certificate is needed for s 1 firearms (which includes most types of firearms) and for shotguns. Other categories of firearms such as air weapons and imitation firearms do not require certificates.

Under s 48(1) of the Firearms Act 1968 [you]:

may demand, from any person whom [you believe] to be in possession of

- a firearm, firearms or ammunition
- ammunition to which the holding of a valid firearm certificate is necessary, or
- a shotgun,

the production of [his/her] firearm or [shotgun certificate] (s 48(1)).

You need to check your force's interpretation of the term 'demand'. In some forces 'demand' could mean 'demand on the spot', though in others it would mean the certificate could be produced at some specified time in the future.

Section 48(2) states that if a person upon whom a demand is made fails to:

- produce the certificate/document; or
- permit you to read it; or
- show that he/she is entitled to have the firearm, ammunition, or shot gun in his/her possession without holding a certificate

you may

- seize and detain the firearm, ammunition, or shot gun; and
- require the person to declare to you immediately his/her name and address.

8.22.5 Possessing Firearms in a Public Place

Section 19 of the Firearms Act 1968 states that a person commits an offence if:

without lawful authority or reasonable excuse [he/she has] *with* [him or her] *in a public place*

(a) a loaded shotgun, or

(b) an air weapon (whether loaded or not), or

(c) any other firearm (whether loaded or not) together with ammunition suitable for use in that firearm, or

(d) an imitation firearm.

The offence of possessing an air weapon ((b) above) is triable summarily and the penalty is six months' imprisonment and/or a fine.

The offence of possessing (a), (c), or (d) above is triable either way:

- On indictment in the case of (a) or (c) above; seven years' imprisonment and/or a fine.
- On indictment in the case of (d) above; twelve months' imprisonment and/or a fine.
- Summarily; six months' imprisonment and/or a fine.

8.22.6 Overview of Age Restrictions in Relation to Firearms

The table below shows the age restrictions for firearms certificates; this applies to s 1 firearms. An empty box in the table means the activity is not permitted. The age restrictions for shotguns are slightly different; see section 8.24. Other categories of firearms such as air weapons and imitation firearms do not require certificates.

Firearms certificates—age restrictions

	Under 14	Age 14+	Age 15+	Age 17+
Hold a shotgun certificate	✓	✓	✓	✓
Hold a firearm certificate		✓	✓	✓
Own a shotgun (received as a gift)			✓	✓
Own a s 1 firearm (received as a gift)	✓	✓	✓	✓
Purchase or hire a shotgun				✓
Purchase or hire a s 1 firearm				✓

8.23 Section 1 Firearms

Section 1 firearms are defined in s 1 of the Firearms Act 1968 and include all firearms **except**:

(a) shotguns;

(b) legal air weapons;

(c) prohibited weapons;

(d) imitation firearms.

8.23.1 Certificate for a s 1 Firearm

Under s 1 of the Firearms Act 1968 a certificate is required for all s 1 firearms; it is an offence for a person:

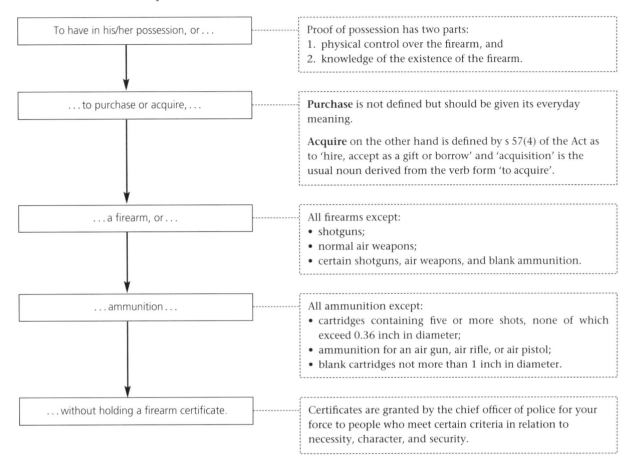

To have in his/her possession, or...	Proof of possession has two parts: 1. physical control over the firearm, and 2. knowledge of the existence of the firearm.
...to purchase or acquire,...	**Purchase** is not defined but should be given its everyday meaning. **Acquire** on the other hand is defined by s 57(4) of the Act as to 'hire, accept as a gift or borrow' and 'acquisition' is the usual noun derived from the verb form 'to acquire'.
...a firearm, or...	All firearms except: • shotguns; • normal air weapons; • certain shotguns, air weapons, and blank ammunition.
...ammunition...	All ammunition except: • cartridges containing five or more shots, none of which exceed 0.36 inch in diameter; • ammunition for an air gun, air rifle, or air pistol; • blank cartridges not more than 1 inch in diameter.
...without holding a firearm certificate.	Certificates are granted by the chief officer of police for your force to people who meet certain criteria in relation to necessity, character, and security.

This offence is triable either way:

• Summarily; imprisonment for six months and/or a fine.
• On indictment; imprisonment for five years and/or a fine (seven years for a sawn-off shotgun (classed as a s 1 firearm)).

There are special arrangements which may mean that a s 1 firearm certificate is not required. This is a complex area, but special arrangements are in place for certain types of firearm including antique firearms and handguns used for killing animals. Rifle and pistol clubs, visiting overseas forces, and even theatrical performances are also excluded from the requirement for a firearms certificate.

8.23.2 Age Restrictions and s 1 Firearms

The table below shows the age restrictions for s 1 firearms. An empty box in the table means the activity is not permitted. As noted earlier, the age restrictions for shotguns are slightly different (see section 8.24 below).

Age restrictions for s 1 firearms

	Under 14	Age 15+	Age 17+
Hold a firearm certificate	✓	✓	✓
Receive a s 1 firearm as a gift	✓	✓	✓
Purchase or hire a s 1 firearm			✓

8.24 Shotguns

Subsection 1(3)(a) of the Firearms Act 1968 describes shotguns as separate group of firearms and states that:

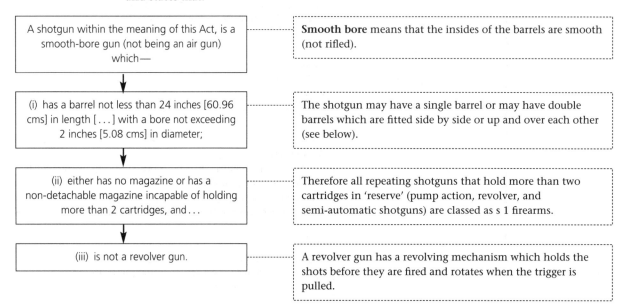

A shotgun within the meaning of this Act, is a smooth-bore gun (not being an air gun) which—	**Smooth bore** means that the insides of the barrels are smooth (not rifled).
(i) has a barrel not less than 24 inches [60.96 cms] in length [...] with a bore not exceeding 2 inches [5.08 cms] in diameter;	The shotgun may have a single barrel or may have double barrels which are fitted side by side or up and over each other (see below).
(ii) either has no magazine or has a non-detachable magazine incapable of holding more than 2 cartridges, and...	Therefore all repeating shotguns that hold more than two cartridges in 'reserve' (pump action, revolver, and semi-automatic shotguns) are classed as s 1 firearms.
(iii) is not a revolver gun.	A revolver gun has a revolving mechanism which holds the shots before they are fired and rotates when the trigger is pulled.

Note that a sawn-off shotgun cannot be classed as a shotgun because (having been sawn off) its barrel length is too short.

Main types of barrel configuration for shotguns.

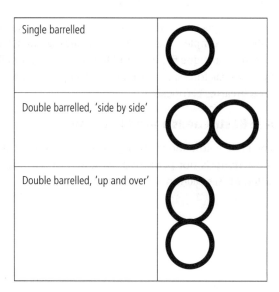

Single barrelled	
Double barrelled, 'side by side'	
Double barrelled, 'up and over'	

8.24.1 Shotgun Certificates

Individuals possessing, purchasing, or acquiring a shotgun without holding a relevant certificate commit an offence under s 2(1) of the Firearms Act 1968. In certain circumstances however, a person may have an ordinary shotgun without a shotgun certificate, such as when he/she borrows it from a person who holds a certificate, and uses it on that person's premises (including land) and in his/her presence.

A certificate is not required in order to possess shotgun ammunition, providing it contains five or more shot pellets in a cartridge and none of the pellets is larger than 0.36 inch in diameter.

A shotgun certificate (also referred to as a licence) is granted by the chief police officer of the force in which the applicant lives. Shotguns are frequently used for sporting purposes (eg clay pigeon shooting) and for shooting game. Therefore, unless there is a specific reason to refuse the application it will normally be granted, in marked contrast to the issue of s 1 firearms certificates.

This offence (of not holding the relevant certificate) is triable either way:

- Summarily; six months' imprisonment and/or a fine.
- On indictment; five years' imprisonment and/or a fine.

8.24.2 Conditions Placed upon the Holder of a Shotgun Certificate

A number of conditions are placed upon the holder of a shotgun certificate. An important requirement is that shotguns will be kept secure when not in use, for example in a specially designed steel gun cabinet. It is an offence for a person to fail to comply with a condition relating to a shotgun certificate (s 2(2)).

This offence is triable summarily and the penalty is six months' imprisonment and/or a fine.

8.24.3 Age Restrictions for Shotguns

The following table summarizes the age limits for shotguns. An empty box in the table means the activity is not permitted.

The person may	Under 14	Age 14 +	Age 15 +	Age 17 +
Hold a shotgun certificate	✓	✓	✓	✓
Possess a shotgun (received as a gift)			✓	✓
Purchase or hire a shotgun				✓

8.25 Air Weapons

An air weapon is usually less dangerous to other people than many other firearms because the pellets are discharged from the barrel relatively slowly and have less mass than, for example, a handgun bullet. (Remember from your science lessons at school or college that kinetic energy is related to both the square of the speed and the mass.) The velocity is relatively low because the pellets are propelled by air pressure only, rather than by an explosive charge. Air weapons include air pistols, air guns, and air rifles which are different in shape and size.

However, air weapons are capable of producing serious injury and most years there are cases of people being blinded through the criminal use of air weapons. Indeed, air weapon offences make up more than half of all recorded firearms offences. Fatalities are also not unknown, particularly with children. It is clear that air weapon offences should be taken very seriously and no doubt this message will be reinforced during your training.

8.25.1 Definition of Lawful Air Weapons

The missiles (pellets) from this category of weapons are propelled by air. The kinetic energy rate (the energy used to fire the pellet) must not exceed 6 ft lb (for air pistols only), or 12 ft lb (for air weapons other than air pistols).

A lawful air weapon does not require a certificate under s 1 of the Firearms Act 1968. If the air weapon exceeds the authorized kinetic energy, it becomes a s 1 firearm and must be certificated as such. The forensic laboratories will be able to measure the kinetic energy of the pellets produced by an air weapon. Note that weapons that use a self-contained gas cartridge system (the cartridge contains both a charge of compressed air or other gas as well as the pellet) are not classified as lawful air weapons. They are prohibited weapons under s 5 of the Firearms Act (see section 8.26 below).

8.25.2 Age Limits for the Possession of an Air Weapon and Firing Restrictions

Section 22(4) of the Firearms Act 1968 states that it is an offence for a person under the age of eighteen to possess an air weapon or ammunition for an air weapon unless (s 23) the child or young person:

- is accompanied by someone over twenty-one years of age in which case the child or young person can be allowed to fire the air weapon, but the missiles must not go beyond those premises (otherwise the firer and the supervisor commit an offence); or
- is aged fourteen years or over, in which case he/she may possess the weapon on premises with the permission of the occupier, and can fire the air weapon, but the missiles must not go beyond the premises; or
- is a member of an approved club for target shooting; or
- is at a shooting gallery where only air weapons or miniature rifles not exceeding .23 calibre are used.

It is an offence under s 21A Firearms Act 1968 for a person who has with him/her an air weapon on any premises if he/she uses it for firing beyond those premises.

In either of the above offences it will be a defence for the firer or the supervisor to show that the occupier of the premises, into or across which the missile was fired, had consented to the firing of the missile (whether specifically or by way of a general consent).

'Premises' is not defined in this Act but examples will include houses and gardens and other private places which are enclosed.

Both these offences are triable summarily and the penalty is a fine.

8.25.3 Selling and Purchasing Air Weapons

It is an offence for a person who is not a registered firearms dealer (or an airweapon-only registered firearms dealer) to:

- sell
- transfer
- expose for sale or transfer
- have in his/her possession for sale or transfer

an air weapon (s 3(1) of the Firearms Act 1968).

This offence is triable either way:

- Summarily; six months' imprisonment and/or a fine.
- On indictment; five years' imprisonment.

It is an offence for a person under the age of eighteen to purchase or hire an air weapon or ammunition (s 22(1) of the Firearms Act 1968).

It is an offence to sell or hire an air weapon or ammunition to a person under the age of eighteen (s 24(1) of the Firearms Act 1968).

These offences are triable summarily and the penalty is six months' imprisonment and/or a fine.

8.25.4 Air Weapons as Gifts

It is an offence under s 24(4) of the Firearms Act 1968:

(a) to make a gift of an air weapon or ammunition for an air weapon to a person under the age of 18; or

(b) to part with the possession of an air weapon or ammunition for an air weapon to a person under the age of 18 except where by virtue of s 23 of this Act the person is not prohibited from having it.

This offence is triable summarily and the penalty is a fine.

8.26 Prohibited Weapons

Parliament decided that the general public have no reasonable need to possess a group of potentially highly dangerous weapons such as machine guns, PAVA (an incapacitating spray) or CS spray. Under s 5 of the Firearms Act 1968, no one may possess them, or make them, without special authority.

Prohibited weapons and exceptions

Type of weapon	Exceptions (ie allowed)
The barrel is less than 30 cm long	• None
The weapon is less than 60 cm long overall	• an air weapon; • a muzzle loading gun; or • a firearm designed as signalling apparatus.
Two or more missiles can be successively discharged without repeated pressure on the trigger	• None
Self-loading or pump-action rifled gun	• chambered for .22 inch rim fire cartridges
Any self-loading or pump-action smooth-bore gun which • has a barrel less than 60.96 cm (24 inches) long, or • is less than 101.6 cm (40 inches) long overall.	• chambered for .22 inch rim fire cartridges; • air weapon.
Smooth-bore revolver gun	• chambered for 9 mm rim fire cartridges; • muzzle-loading gun.
Rocket launcher or any mortar for projecting a stabilized missile	For the following purposes: • line throwing; or • pyrotechnics; or • as signalling.

(Images courtesy of Kent Police)

The two canisters on the left are examples of CS Spray and those on the right, pepper spray. All are examples of s 5 prohibited weapons.

There are other categories of weapons which are prohibited with no exceptions. Some of these are listed below:

- Any weapon of whatever description designed or adapted for the discharge of any **noxious** liquid, gas, or other thing.
- Any **ammunition** containing or designed or adapted to contain any such noxious thing as is mentioned above.
- Any **cartridge with a bullet designed to explode** on or immediately before impact.
- Any **explosive object** such as grenades, bombs, rockets, or shells, if capable of being used with a firearm of any description.
- Any air weapon that uses, or is designed or adapted for use with, a self-contained **gas cartridge** system.
- Any firearm which is **disguised** as another object.

A person commits an offence under s 5(1) of the Firearms Act 1968 if, without the written authority of the Defence Council (which consists of the Secretary of State for Defence, other MoD Ministers, the Chiefs of Staff, and senior civil servants), he/she:

- has in his/her possession;
- purchases;
- acquires;
- manufactures;
- sells; or
- transfers a prohibited weapon or ammunition.

This offence is triable either way:

- Summarily; six months' imprisonment and/or a fine.
- On indictment; 10 years' imprisonment and/or a fine.

8.27   Imitation Firearms

The definition of an imitation firearm provided in s 57(4) of the Firearms Act 1968 is

> . . . anything which has the appearance of being a firearm [other than a prohibited weapon] whether or not it is capable of discharging any shot, bullet or other missile.

Imitation or replica firearms will generally fall into two categories:

- imitations that **can be readily converted** into a firearm of a type requiring a firearm certificate under s 1 of the Firearms Act 1968;
- imitations that **cannot** be readily converted into a firearm to which s 1 of the 1968 Act applies. These are not required to be licensed or certificated and are therefore not subject to

most of the regulations regarding firearms. To all intents and purposes, they are treated as toys or collectibles.

As you may know, it is often difficult to distinguish an imitation firearm from the 'real thing'.

(Images courtesy of Kent Police)

On the left a real Mauser, on the right the imitation

8.27.1 The Meaning of 'Readily Convertible'

The meaning of 'readily convertible' is explained in s 1(6) of the Firearms Act 1982. An imitation firearm is regarded as readily convertible if it can be converted **without** special skill or special tools. Special tools are defined as tools that would not generally be used by people for construction and maintenance in their homes. So if the conversion required the simple use of a normal screwdriver, the imitation firearm could be described as readily convertible.

8.27.2 Control of Readily Converted Imitation Firearms

Section 1 of the Firearms Act 1982 provides for legal control of imitation firearms which are readily convertible and therefore become a s 1 firearm under the Firearms Act 1968. Such imitation weapons will require a firearms certificate.

Any such converted firearm would normally need to be submitted for testing at a forensic laboratory before any lawful proceedings were undertaken. Ultimately, only a court can decide whether or not a particular imitation firearm requires a firearms certificate.

It may be a defence if the accused can 'show that [he/she] did not know and had no reason to suspect that the imitation firearm was so constructed or adapted as to be readily convertible' (s 1(5) of the Firearms Act 1982).

Any such imitation firearm that is converted into a firearm to which s 1 of the Act applies will therefore require a s 1 certificate. If no certificate is held, an offence will be committed.

8.27.3 Offences Relating to Imitation Firearms

A person commits an offence under s 24A of the Firearms Act 1968 if he/she

* is under the age of eighteen years and purchases an imitation firearm;
* sells an imitation firearm to a person under the age of eighteen.

This offence is triable summarily and the penalty is twelve months' imprisonment and/or a fine.

A person commits an offence under s 19 of the Firearms Act 1968 if he/she:

* without lawful authority or reasonable excuse has with him/her an imitation firearm in a public place (see section 8.22.5 above).

8.27.4 Ball Bearing ('BB') Guns

These are guns that fire ball bearings (small round objects made of plastic or aluminum) powered by a spring, electricity (via a battery), or gas (for example, carbon dioxide) from an external aerosol canister. They are low-powered and do not require a license. A typical BB gun will not be classified as a firearm within the definition as it is not 'lethal'. In other words, power generated by the spring or other means will not be sufficient to force the projectile out of the gun and kill. However, you should consider the following:

- If the gun appears more powerful than a typical BB gun or has large projectiles, the power level and classification may need to be assessed by the Forensic Science Service. In such a case, the gun may be sufficiently lethal to be classified as a firearm and could be an air weapon or a 'section 1 firearm' (see section 8.23 above).
- If the projectile of the BB gun is forced out of the weapon by a self-contained gas cartridge (similar in appearance to a bullet and casing) but not an external aerosol cartridge, then the BB gun is a prohibited weapon (see section 8.26 above).

Finally, note that BB guns can easily resemble lethal firearms and carrying an imitation gun in public is an offence (see 8.27.3 above). In 2006 over 80% of all firearms incidents dealt with by Derbyshire police involved BB guns.

TASK 21

1. Describe the general characteristics of a firearm.
2. What are your powers to demand production of certificates?
3. Under what circumstances may you require a person to hand over a firearm or ammunition for examination?
4. What firearms are covered by s 1 and so require a s 1 certificate?
5. What ammunition is covered by s 1 and so requires a s 1 certificate?
6. What shotguns need a certificate?

TASK 22

1. You attend an incident where a sixteen-year-old boy has been firing an air rifle from his parents' bedroom window at baked bean cans on top of their garden wall. The pellets have clearly gone into the next door neighbour's garden. What offence has the boy committed?
2. You see a boy carrying an air rifle along the High Street (the rifle is not in a gun cover). After questioning you establish that he is seventeen years old. What offence, if any, has he committed?

TASK 23

Find out about the firearms incident in Hungerford, Berkshire in 1987 (there are numerous websites that will provide the details). Consider also the subsequent White Paper, *Firearms Act 1968: Proposals for Reform* (Cm 261, 1987) and the amendment to the 1968 Act which was effected by s 1 of the Firearms (Amendment) Act 1988. Why was a change in the list of prohibited weapons thought to be necessary at this time?

TASK 24

Whilst on Independent Patrol you are tasked with attending the local park where an adult has detained a young person who is apparently carrying an imitation firearm. What offence are you going to consider?

8.28 Mentally Disordered Persons in Private and Public Places

During the course of your duties, you will frequently find yourself in situations involving people with 'mental disorders' (this is the term that the legislation uses). A common misconception is that many people who suffer from mental disorders are also violent. This is not the case; most pose no physical threat to others, but they may also be confused or unable to cope. You need to learn how to recognize the symptoms of mental disorder and how to support a very vulnerable section of the community in a professional and caring manner. You will receive information and advice on this during your training. Here we examine the relevant legislative considerations. When attending an incident involving a person suffering from mental disorder you have a number of options available, and these are outlined below. Note when reading this part of the Handbook that the main intent of the legislation is that mentally disordered people should receive psychiatric assessment and care as soon as is possible.

Section 136 of the Mental Health Act 1983 states that if you find:

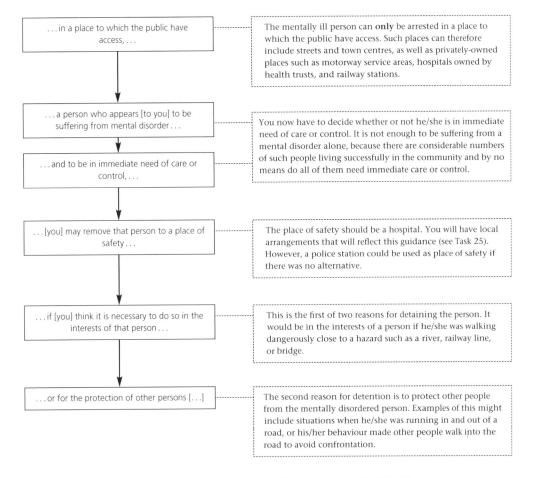

. . . in a place to which the public have access, . . .	The mentally ill person can **only** be arrested in a place to which the public have access. Such places can therefore include streets and town centres, as well as privately-owned places such as motorway service areas, hospitals owned by health trusts, and railway stations.
. . . a person who appears [to you] to be suffering from mental disorder . . . . . . and to be in immediate need of care or control, . . .	You now have to decide whether or not he/she is in immediate need of care or control. It is not enough to be suffering from a mental disorder alone, because there are considerable numbers of such people living successfully in the community and by no means do all of them need immediate care or control.
. . . [you] may remove that person to a place of safety . . .	The place of safety should be a hospital. You will have local arrangements that will reflect this guidance (see Task 25). However, a police station could be used as place of safety if there was no alternative.
. . . if [you] think it is necessary to do so in the interests of that person . . .	This is the first of two reasons for detaining the person. It would be in the interests of a person if he/she was walking dangerously close to a hazard such as a river, railway line, or bridge.
. . . or for the protection of other persons [. . .]	The second reason for detention is to protect other people from the mentally disordered person. Examples of this might include situations when he/she was running in and out of a road, or his/her behaviour made other people walk into the road to avoid confrontation.

8.28.1 Detaining a Mentally Disordered Person in a Public Place

Note that it is **not an offence** to be mentally disordered in a place to which the public have access. However, you have the power to detain such a person and take him or her to a place of safety. Section 136 of the Mental Health Act 1983 provides you with the power to detain only; your powers of arrest under s 24 of the PACE Act 1984 cannot be used because no offence has been committed.

8.28.2 Detention in a Place of Safety

A person removed to a place of safety may be detained there:

- for a period not exceeding 72 hours;
- for the purpose of enabling him or her to be examined and assessed by a registered medical practitioner; and
- to be interviewed by an approved social worker; and
- for making any necessary arrangements for his or her treatment or care.

8.28.3   Mentally Disordered Persons in Their Own Homes

You might need to help or restrain mentally disordered persons in their own homes. If they refuse to let you in and there is nobody else present to grant you entry, you might have to use force. Under the Mental Health Act 1983, there is no power to force entry in such circumstances, other than with a warrant. There are, however, three other justifications for the use of force in this situation:

- if there is a breach of the peace (see section 8.11);
- to save life or limb (s 17(1)(e) of the PACE Act 1984);
- to prevent serious damage to property (s 17(1)(e) of the PACE Act 1984).

You can detain the person in order to prevent a breach of the peace, but remember there are conditions which have to be met relating to the use of force, which we discussed in section 8.11. There may be other reasons to arrest the person for an offence, but arrest will not necessarily be the most appropriate way of dealing with a mentally disordered person who is suspected of committing one of these offences.

8.28.4   Removing the Person to a Place of Safety from His or Her Home

If there is no breach of the peace and no offences have been committed, there is no power available under the Mental Health Act 1983 for you to detain or convey a person from a private place to a hospital or other place of safety unless at least one of the following conditions is met:

- the person consents;
- the person is sectioned for admission to hospital. This has to be authorized by at least an approved social worker and a doctor. It is essential that a Section Application form is written out and signed prior to police action;
- a magistrate's warrant already exists for that private place. This is a warrant (granted under s 135 of the Mental Health Act 1983) authorizing you to search for and remove persons believed to be suffering from mental disorder.

Clearly, the most satisfactory solution is to gain the co-operation and agreement of the person concerned. However, if you think that a person needs to be sectioned you should contact your control room and request the attendance of an approved social worker. It is the responsibility of Social Services to assess and progress these matters from this point forward, with the police providing any necessary assistance. You should remain at the scene until the approved social worker arrives. Once you have explained the situation to the social worker you may then leave, unless the social worker requests your further assistance. You may be asked to provide help to remove the person to hospital, by force if necessary, if the person is, indeed, sectioned (s 6, Mental Health Act 1983).

Whatever his or her state of mind, a person must be treated with the utmost respect and professionalism. Whatever the circumstances, a mentally disordered person is vulnerable and it will be necessary for you to treat him/her with care just like any other person suffering from injury or illness.

TASK 25

1. What is your force policy in terms of the use of s 136 powers?
2. You are requested to attend the home of the parents of a twenty-year-old person who seems to be suffering from a mental disorder. On arrival the parents inform you that their son is inside the house in his bedroom holding on to the door handle so that nobody can come in or out. Using the minimum force necessary:
   (a) how are you going to gain entrance for the parents, and
   (b) what options are available to you should you decide the person is in need of medical attention in relation to his or her apparent mental disorder?

8.29   Searches and Examinations of Suspects under the PACE Act 1984, Code D

At the beginning of the chapter we looked at your powers and responsibilities when stopping, searching, and detaining people. We have also noted on a number of occasions that the Police and Criminal Evidence (PACE) Act 1984, and its associated Codes, are the main sources of legislation that define the way the police should behave toward suspects or volunteers assisting the police. Sections 4 to 6 of **Code D** of the PACE Act 1984 cover the forensic intelligence and evidence taken or recorded from a person. This will involve a search and examination of a person and his/her clothing. There are two main reasons why we may wish to collect material of a forensic value from a person: to identify an individual and to provide material for comparison to that found at a crime scene. Obviously, DNA and fingerprint samples are also normally subsequently retained in databases for 'speculative' (untargeted) searches, but some samples are destroyed.

The legislation quoted in full can be found in the Appendix. It is taken from the Codes of Practice, which took effect on 1 January 2006 (there were significant changes as a result of the Serious Organised Crime and Police Act (SOCPA 2005)). The table below shows the main sections included in the Appendix to help you find your way through the large number of sections and subsections.

Main sections of the PACE Act 1984, Code D

Section	Contents	
4	**Identification by fingerprints and footwear impressions**	
	A Taking fingerprints in connection with a criminal investigation	4.1–4.9
	B Taking fingerprints in connection with immigration enquiries	4.10–4.15
	C Taking footwear impressions in connection with a criminal investigation	4.16–4.21
	Notes for guidance	4A–4B
5	**Examinations to establish identity and the taking of photographs**	
	A Detainees at police stations	5.1–5.18
	B Persons at police stations not detained	5.19–5.24
	Notes for guidance	5A–5F
6	**Identification by body samples and impressions**	
	A General	6.1
	B Action	6.2–6.12
	Notes for guidance	6A–6F

We have added comments in plain text where we feel additional explanation or emphasis is required. Comments added should be taken only as a general guide: refer to a full copy of the PACE Act 1984 for the full wording and context of the Act. It is available from <http://police.homeoffice.gov.uk/operational-policing/powers-pace-codes/pace-codes.html> (along with the other Codes).

Some of the key points from ss 4 to 6 are:

- Remember that samples should be **relevant** and should be proportional to the offence (unless they are for speculative searching and are covered by blanket policies, such as DNA and fingerprints).
- **Appropriate adults** are required in many circumstances, including where juveniles, the mentally disordered, or visually impaired are concerned.
- A number of **records** are to be kept concerning consent, authority, and warnings to the detained person. It is vital that these procedures are followed.

8.29.1 Intimate and Non-Intimate Samples

Samples under Code D fall into several categories, but two are particularly important: intimate and non-intimate samples.

A **non-intimate** sample is:

- a sample of hair, other than pubic hair, which includes hair plucked with the root;
- a sample taken from a nail or from under a nail;
- a swab taken from any part of a person's body other than a part from which a swab taken would be an intimate sample;
- saliva;
- a skin impression, which means any record, other than a fingerprint, which is a record, in any form and produced by any method, of a skin pattern and other physical characteristics or features of the whole, or any part of, a person's foot or of any other part of [his/her] body.

An **intimate** sample is:

- a dental impression;
- a sample of blood, semen, or any other tissue fluid;
- urine;
- pubic hair;
- a swab taken from any part of a person's genitals or from a person's body orifices other than the mouth.

A police officer may take a non-intimate sample from a detained person but must call for the assistance of a **registered** medical practitioner (a doctor, dentist, nurse, or paramedic) for intimate samples.

8.29.2 Fingerprints and Footwear Impressions

The table shows the parts of s 4 of Code D which are relevant to taking fingerprints and footwear impressions.

Main sections of the PACE Act 1984, Code D

Identification by fingerprints and footwear impressions

A Taking fingerprints in connection with a criminal investigation	4.1–4.9
B Taking fingerprints in connection with immigration enquiries	4.10–4.15
C Taking footwear impressions in connection with a criminal investigation	4.16–4.21
Notes for guidance	4A–4B

Fingerprints means any record of the fingers or palms taken by any means, such as using traditional ink and paper or electronically, by a device such as Livescan. (This digitized method has been installed in most main police stations. Smaller police stations, and those with limited opening hours, might not have this and may rely on inked impressions.)

Importantly, fingerprint and digital technology has moved on since the PACE Act 1984 was first enacted. It is now possible to scan a fingerprint on portable equipment and transmit this to a Fingerprint Bureau direct from a handheld unit.

You will see from what follows that you can require people to provide their fingerprints when those taken previously have proved unsatisfactory for analytical use. The advent of Livescan makes this less likely, but for the police it is an important right that directly affects the performance of NAFIS.

Impressions taken of footwear are important intelligence tools since they may be compared to a database or file of marks recovered from crime scenes. This might lead to a full shoe to shoemark comparison. Hence, one arrest might lead to other crimes also being considered. In essence, the data recovered provide an indication that the detained person may be involved in other offences. This is particularly relevant where property crime is considered, but a well-populated database can also be valuable to Major Crime as an intelligence tool.

Taking footwear impressions was previously an ill-defined area, since many forces wished to take images or prints of a suspect's shoes covertly, particularly after a number of observations made by the HMIC about using forensic intelligence. A change was brought about by s 118(3) of the SOCPA 2005, which amended s 63a of the PACE Act 1984 by including references to 'impressions of footwear' as well as fingerprints.

8.29.3 Conducting a Search or Examination and Taking Photographs

The table below shows the parts of s 5 of Code D which are relevant to conducting a search or examination of a suspect or volunteer and the taking of photographs.

Examinations to establish identity and the taking of photographs

A Detainees at police stations (details about conducting the search or examination and taking photographs)	5.1–5.18
B Persons at police stations not detained (details about conducting the search or examination and taking photographs)	5.19–5.24
Notes for guidance	5A–5F

Certain features, such as tattoos and scars, provide valuable identification evidence, and a recent injury may indicate a suspect's involvement in an offence. The Code is not explicit regarding injuries. However, it is common, especially in major crimes, for suspects to be examined by a doctor (or nurse) and to be photographed by a suitable person in connection with injury evidence. Such injuries can include burns from arson attacks and bruises or lacerations caused by one or both or more parties defending themselves.

Note that when PACE refers to somebody attending a police station voluntarily (s 5.19 of the Code reproduced below), it is not just referring to a 'volunteer' who is a victim of crime. CSIs, in particular, may use the term volunteer for an entirely innocent person who is attending to supply an elimination sample, or set of fingerprints.

Section 5 is quoted in full in the Appendix.

8.29.4 Taking Body Samples and Impressions

The table shows the parts of s 6 of Code D which are relevant to the taking of both intimate and non-intimate body samples and impressions. This is the section of the Code that covers DNA swabs and pulled hair for use by the NDNAD.

Identification by body samples and impressions

A General (a brief introduction giving the definitions quoted above for intimate and non-intimate samples)	6.1
B Action (details about taking the samples, the use of reasonable force and documentation required)	6.2–6.12
Notes for guidance	6A–6F

Intimate samples are essential when the investigator is attempting to prove a sexual assault or rape and other serious offences against the person. It is especially important in these offences to attempt to discover the existence, or otherwise, of a 'two-way transfer' to and from both parties (see section 13.6). You should attempt to recover intimate samples as quickly as possible after the incident. Failure to secure these samples can hamper an investigation. However, even if intimate samples are not available, your CSI may be able to assist in some circumstances, since DNA and other trace evidence can be sourced from a variety of non-intimate sampling procedures.

Non-intimate samples typically yield DNA and trace material from the hair, nails, and skin in addition to prints taken of, say, the bare feet and ears. Whilst somewhat unusual, Code D covers these body impressions and other forms of evidence comprehensively, but this section of the Code does not permit the taking of impressions from an intimate area.

Finally, note that although s 6.7 of the Code refers to the use of 'reasonable' force to take a buccal swab, you should not do so since the undue use of force in the mouth areas could be dangerous and swabs can fall apart if force is used.

Section 6 is quoted in full in the Appendix.

8.30   The Prevention of Harm to Animals

The history of the use of legislation to protect animals in the UK stretches back as far as 1822 with an Act to Prevent the Cruel and Improper Treatment of Cattle. This became the first animal welfare legislation passed by parliament anywhere in the world. More recently research findings summarized by the organization 'People for the Ethical Treatment of Animals' (PETA) have indicated that there may be links between animal abuse and human abuse. (See http://www.peta.org.uk/factsheet/files/FactsheetDisplay.asp?ID=172.) The Animal Welfare Act 2006 (which came into force on 6 April 2007) has brought together a raft of previous legislation and introduced new offences relating to the care and treatment of animals. The new legislation introduces a 'duty of care' on animal owners (including owners of pets) in an attempt to ensure the basic needs of animals are met as well as outlawing certain forms of suffering. Other parties involved in investigating possible animal welfare offences include Local Authorities and the State Veterinary Service.

Offences which can be committed under the Animal Welfare Act 2006 include:

1. Unnecessary suffering (s 4)
2. Mutilation (s 5)
3. Docking of dog tails (s 6)
4. Administration of poisons (s 7)
5. Fighting (s 8)
6. Duty of person responsible for animal to ensure welfare (s 9)
7. Transfer of animals by way of sale or prize to persons under 16 (s 11).

8.30.1 Unnecessary Suffering

Section 4 (1) of the Animal Welfare Act 2006 states that a person commits an offence if:

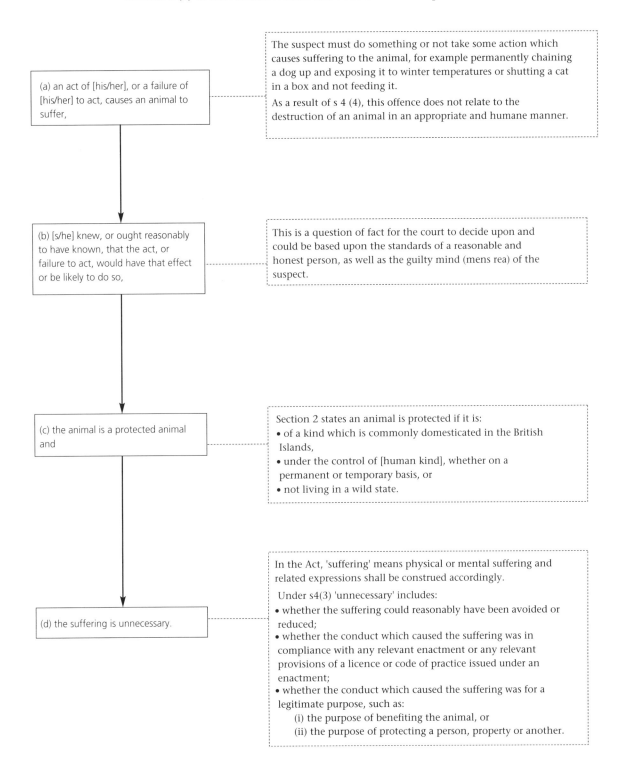

(a) an act of [his/her], or a failure of [his/her] to act, causes an animal to suffer,

The suspect must do something or not take some action which causes suffering to the animal, for example permanently chaining a dog up and exposing it to winter temperatures or shutting a cat in a box and not feeding it.

As a result of s 4 (4), this offence does not relate to the destruction of an animal in an appropriate and humane manner.

(b) [s/he] knew, or ought reasonably to have known, that the act, or failure to act, would have that effect or be likely to do so,

This is a question of fact for the court to decide upon and could be based upon the standards of a reasonable and honest person, as well as the guilty mind (mens rea) of the suspect.

(c) the animal is a protected animal and

Section 2 states an animal is protected if it is:
• of a kind which is commonly domesticated in the British Islands,
• under the control of [human kind], whether on a permanent or temporary basis, or
• not living in a wild state.

(d) the suffering is unnecessary.

In the Act, 'suffering' means physical or mental suffering and related expressions shall be construed accordingly.

Under s4(3) 'unnecessary' includes:
• whether the suffering could reasonably have been avoided or reduced;
• whether the conduct which caused the suffering was in compliance with any relevant enactment or any relevant provisions of a licence or code of practice issued under an enactment;
• whether the conduct which caused the suffering was for a legitimate purpose, such as:
    (i) the purpose of benefiting the animal, or
    (ii) the purpose of protecting a person, property or another.

Section 4(2) Animal Welfare Act 2006 states that a person commits an offence through the actions of another if s/he:

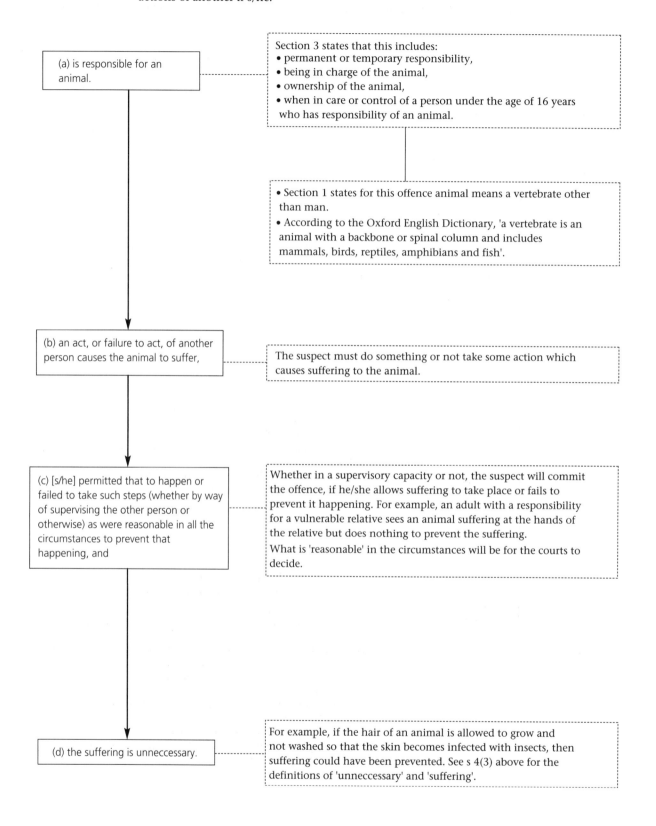

(a) is responsible for an animal.

Section 3 states that this includes:
• permanent or temporary responsibility,
• being in charge of the animal,
• ownership of the animal,
• when in care or control of a person under the age of 16 years who has responsibility of an animal.

• Section 1 states for this offence animal means a vertebrate other than man.
• According to the Oxford English Dictionary, 'a vertebrate is an animal with a backbone or spinal column and includes mammals, birds, reptiles, amphibians and fish'.

(b) an act, or failure to act, of another person causes the animal to suffer,

The suspect must do something or not take some action which causes suffering to the animal.

(c) [s/he] permitted that to happen or failed to take such steps (whether by way of supervising the other person or otherwise) as were reasonable in all the circumstances to prevent that happening, and

Whether in a supervisory capacity or not, the suspect will commit the offence, if he/she allows suffering to take place or fails to prevent it happening. For example, an adult with a responsibility for a vulnerable relative sees an animal suffering at the hands of the relative but does nothing to prevent the suffering.
What is 'reasonable' in the circumstances will be for the courts to decide.

(d) the suffering is unneccessary.

For example, if the hair of an animal is allowed to grow and not washed so that the skin becomes infected with insects, then suffering could have been prevented. See s 4(3) above for the definitions of 'unneccessary' and 'suffering'.

8.30.2 Mutilation

Section 5(1) of the Animal Welfare Act 2006 states that a person commits an offence if s/he:

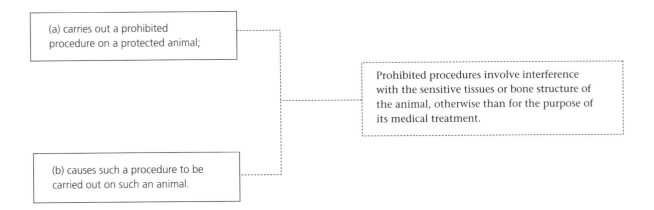

Section 5(2) of the Animal Welfare Act 2006 states that a person commits an offence through the actions of another if:

(a) [s/he] is responsible for an animal,

(b) another person carries out a prohibited procedure on the animal, and

(c) s/he permitted the prohibited procedure to happen or failed to take such steps (whether by way of supervising the other person or otherwise) as were reasonable in all the circumstances to prevent that happening.

The following are applicable to both s 5(1) and s 5(2):

- Neither sub-sections are applicable in such circumstances as the appropriate national authority (for example the armed services) may specify by regulations.
- Prohibited procedures do not include the removal of a dog's tail or part of it as this is dealt with in s6 below.

8.30.3 Docking of Dogs' Tails

Section 6(1) and (2) of the Animal Welfare Act 2006 states that a person commits an offence if he/she:

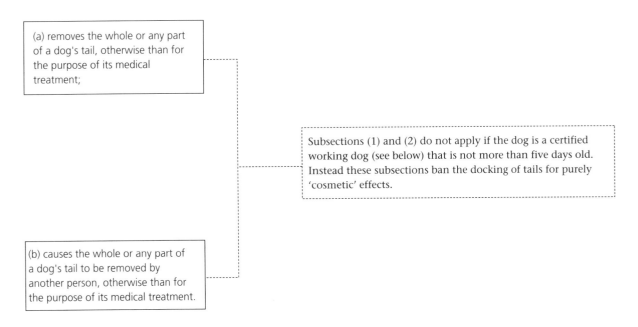

A dog is a certified working dog if:

- evidence has been given to a vet;
- a national authority has proved the dog will be used for work;
- the dog is of a specified working type.

National authority work includes:

- law enforcement,
- emergency rescue,
- lawful pest control, or
- the lawful shooting of animals.

Section 6(2) of the Animal Welfare Act 2006 states that a person commits an offence through the actions of another if:

(a) [s/he] is responsible for a dog,

(b) another person removes the whole or any part of the dog's tail, otherwise than for the purpose of its medical treatment, and

(c) [s/he] permitted that to happen or failed to take such steps (whether by way of supervising the other person or otherwise) as were reasonable in all the circumstances to prevent that happening.

8.30.4 Administration of Poisons

Section 7(1) of the Animal Welfare Act 2006 states that a person commits an offence if without lawful authority or reasonable excuse if s/he:

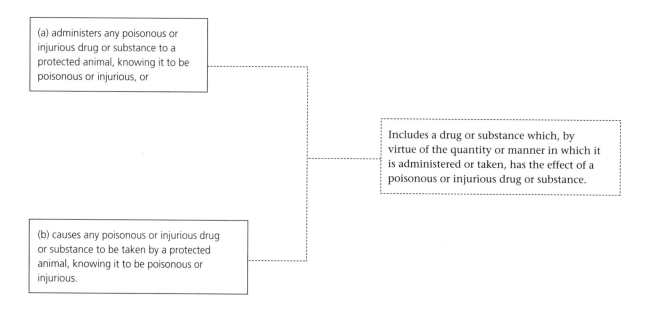

(a) administers any poisonous or injurious drug or substance to a protected animal, knowing it to be poisonous or injurious, or

Includes a drug or substance which, by virtue of the quantity or manner in which it is administered or taken, has the effect of a poisonous or injurious drug or substance.

(b) causes any poisonous or injurious drug or substance to be taken by a protected animal, knowing it to be poisonous or injurious.

Section 7(2) of the Animal Welfare Act 2006 states that a person commits an offence through the actions of another if:

(a) [s/he] is responsible for an animal,

(b) without lawful authority or reasonable excuse, another person administers a poisonous or injurious drug or substance to the animal or causes the animal to take such a drug or substance, and

(c) [s/he] permitted that to happen or, knowing the drug or substance to be poisonous or injurious, [s/he] failed to take such steps (whether by way of supervising the other person or otherwise) as were reasonable in all the circumstances to prevent that happening.

8.30.5 Animal Fighting

Section 8(1) of the Animal Welfare Act 2006 states that a person commits an offence if s/he:

a) causes an animal fight to take place, or attempts to do so;

b) knowingly receives money for admission to an animal fight;

c) knowingly publicises a proposed animal fight;

d) provides information about an animal fight to another with the intention of enabling or encouraging attendance at the fight;

e) makes or accepts a bet on the outcome of an animal fight or on the likelihood of anything occurring or not occurring in the course of an animal fight;

f) takes part in an animal fight;

g) has in [his/her] possession anything designed or adapted for use in connection with an animal fight with the intention of its being so used;

h) keeps or trains an animal for use for in connection with an animal fight;

i) keeps any premises for use for an animal fight.

Section 8 states that 'a person commits an offence if, without lawful authority or reasonable excuse [s/he]:

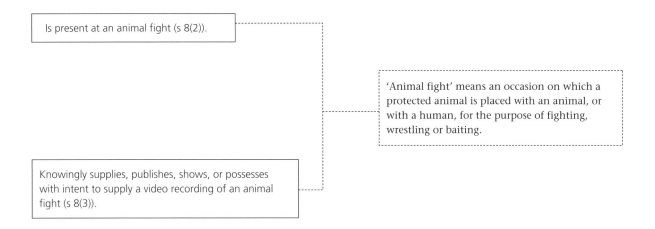

Sections 4, 5, 6(1) and (2), 7 and 8 are triable summarily and the penalty is imprisonment not exceeding fifty-one weeks and/or a fine.

8.30.6 Power of Search to Arrest a Suspect under ss 4, 5, 6 (1), 6(2), 7, 8(1), and 8(2)

You may enter and search any premises to arrest any person you reasonably suspect of committing an offence under sections 4, 5, 6 (1) and (2), 7, and 8 (1) and (2) of this Act (s17 of the PACE Act 1984, see section 11.10 of the Handbook).

8.30.7 Power of Entry and Seizure of Animals Involved in s 8 Fighting Offences

Section 22(1) of the Animal Welfare Act 2006 states you may seize an animal if it appears to you 'that it is one in relation to which an offence under section 8(1) or (2) has been committed'.

Section 22(2) states you may enter and search premises (not a private dwelling) for the purpose of exercising the power under subsection (1) if you reasonably believe:

(a) that there is an animal on the premises, and

(b) that the animal is one in relation to which the power under subsection (1) is exercisable.

8.30.8 Duty of Person Responsible for Animal to Ensure Welfare

Section 9(1) of the Animal Welfare Act 2006 states that a person commits an offence if s/he '... does not take such steps as are reasonable in all the circumstances to ensure that the needs of an animal for which [s/he] is responsible are met to the extent required by good practice'.

Under s 9(2) an animal's needs shall be taken to include:

• its need for a suitable environment,
• its need for a suitable diet,
• its need to be able to exhibit normal behaviour patterns,
• any need it has to be housed with, or apart from, other animals, and
• its need to be protected from pain, suffering, injury and disease.

8.30.9 Transfer of Animals by way of Sale or Prize to Persons under 16

Section 11(1) of the Animal Welfare Act 2006 states that a person commits an offence if s/he:

> ...sells an animal to a person whom [s/he] has reasonable cause to believe to be under the age of 16 years where selling an animal includes transferring, or agreeing to transfer, ownership of the animal in consideration of entry by the transferee into another transaction (s 11(2)).

Section 11(3) of the Animal Welfare Act 2006 states that a person commits an offence if s/he

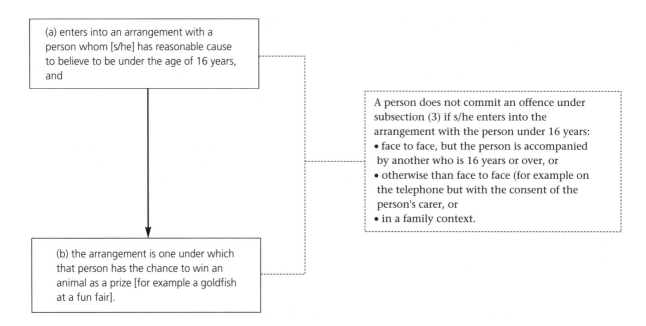

(a) enters into an arrangement with a person whom [s/he] has reasonable cause to believe to be under the age of 16 years, and

(b) the arrangement is one under which that person has the chance to win an animal as a prize [for example a goldfish at a fun fair].

A person does not commit an offence under subsection (3) if s/he enters into the arrangement with the person under 16 years:
• face to face, but the person is accompanied by another who is 16 years or over, or
• otherwise than face to face (for example on the telephone but with the consent of the person's carer, or
• in a family context.

Sections 9 and 11 are triable summarily and the penalty is imprisonment not exceeding fifty-one weeks and/or a fine.

8.30.10 Section 18 Powers in Relation to Animals in Distress

You should refer to your own force policy in relation to the use of s 18 powers.

Subsection 18(1) of the Animal Welfare Act 2006 states that if you reasonably believe that a protected animal is suffering,

• [you] may take, or
• arrange for the taking of

such steps as appear to [you] to be immediately necessary to alleviate the animal's suffering.

Note that this does not authorize destruction of an animal by itself (s18 (2)).

Subsection 18(3) states that if a veterinary surgeon certifies that the condition of a protected animal is such that it should in its own interests be destroyed, you may:

• destroy the animal where it is or
• take it to another place and destroy it there, or

arrange for either to take place.

Subsection 18(4) states you may act under s 18(3) without the certificate of a veterinary surgeon if it appears to you:

• that the condition of the animal is such that there is no reasonable alternative to destroying it, and that the need for action is
• such that it is not reasonably practicable to wait for a veterinary surgeon.

Subsection 18(5) states you may take a protected animal into possession if a veterinary surgeon certifies:

- that it is suffering, or
- that it is likely to suffer if its circumstances do not change.

Section 18(6) states you may act under s18(5) without the certificate of a veterinary surgeon if it appears to you:

- that the animal is suffering or that it is likely to do so if its circumstances do not change, and that the need for action is such that it is not
- reasonably practicable to wait for a veterinary surgeon.

Subsection 18(7) includes power to take into possession dependent offspring of an animal taken into possession under subsection 18(5).

Subsection 18(8) states that 'where an animal is taken into possession under subsection (5)' you may:

- remove it, or arrange for it to be removed, to a place of safety;
- care for it, or arrange for it to be cared for:
  (i) on the premises where it was being kept when it was taken into possession and use any equipment there, or
  (ii) at such other place as you think fit;
- mark it, or arrange for it to be marked, for identification purposes.

Section 18(12) states that a person commits an offence if s/he intentionally obstructs a person in the exercise of power conferred by s18 of the Animal Welfare Act 2006.

Subsection 18(12) is triable summarily and the penalty is imprisonment not exceeding fifty-one weeks and/or a fine.

8.30.11 Power of Entry for s 18 Purposes

Subsection 19(1) of the Animal Welfare Act 2006 states that you may enter premises for the purpose of searching for a protected animal and of exercising any power under section 18 in relation to it if you reasonably believe:

- that there is a protected animal on the premises, and
- that the animal is suffering or, if the circumstances of the animal do not change, it is likely to suffer.

  [You] may (if necessary) use reasonable force in exercising the power conferred by s19(1), but only if it appears to [you] that entry is required before a warrant under subsection (4) can be obtained and executed.

This subsection does not authorize entry to any part of premises which is used as a private dwelling. Under these circumstances a warrant will need to be obtained under subsection 19(4).

8.30.12 Power to Stop and Detain Vehicles for s 19 Purposes

Subsection 54(1) of the Animal Welfare Act 2006 states that, whilst in uniform, you may stop and detain a vehicle for the purpose of entering and searching it in the exercise of a power conferred by s 19(1) (suffering animal) and 22(2) (seizing an animal) of the Act.

Section 54(4) states a vehicle may be detained for as long as is reasonably required to permit a search or inspection to be carried out (including the exercise of any related power under this Act) either at the place where the vehicle was first detained or nearby.

8.30.13 Fishing

The provisions of the Animal Welfare Act 2006 do not apply to the sports of sea, freshwater, game, or coarse fishing (angling) or to commercial fishing.

The Act does, however, apply to the keeping of fish, for example in an ornamental pond.

8.30.14   Cruelty to a Wild Animal

The law surrounding cruelty to wild animals is to be found largely in the Wild Mammals (Protection) Act 1996 and the Wildlife and Countryside Act 1981.

In terms of wild mammals, s 1 of the Wild Mammals (Protection) Act 1996 states that a person commits an offence if s/he mutilates, kicks, beats, nails or otherwise impales, stabs, burns, stones, crushes, drowns, drags, or asphyxiates any wild mammal with intent to inflict unnecessary suffering.

The scientific definition of a mammal is a vertebrate animal whose female produces milk for the nourishment of its young. Examples of wild mammals include rabbits, foxes, squirrels, and hedgehogs. This means that cruelty to wild animals such as birds, frogs, toads, fish, insects, or snakes is not covered by this Act (however, see the Wildlife and Countryside Act 1981 below).

Similarly, animals that are:

- of a kind which is commonly domesticated in the British Islands, or
- under the control of human kind whether on a permanent or temporary basis,

are not covered by the Wild Mammals (Protection) Act 1996 but instead by the Animal Welfare Act 2006 (see above).

Note that actions which are **not** offences under the Wild Mammals (Protection) Act 1996 include:

- mercy and attempted mercy killing, for example the action of putting an injured wild animal 'out of its misery',
- actions under authorization, for example by a vet,
- lawful killing by traps, dogs, or birds,
- lawful use of poisons.

The offence is triable summarily only with a penalty of six months' imprisonment and/or a fine.

8.30.14.1   Powers to stop, search, and seize under the Wild Mammals (Protection) Act 1996

Where [you] have reasonable grounds for suspecting that a person has committed an offence under [. . .] this Act and that evidence of the commission of the offence may be found on that person or in or on any vehicle [he/she] may have with [him/her], [you] may-

- stop and search that person and any vehicle or article [he/she] may have with [him/her]; and
- seize and detain for the purposes of proceedings [. . .] anything which may be evidence of the commission of the offence.

Code A of the PACE Act 1984 Codes of Practice apply to this search, for example GOWISELY (see 8.5.5 Requirements Regarding the Search of Persons and Vehicles).

8.30.14.2   Killing, injuring, or taking a wild bird or egg

Section 1 of the Wildlife and Countryside Act 1981 states a person commits an offence if s/he intentionally:

- kills, injures or takes any wild bird;
- takes, damages or destroys the nest of a wild bird;
- takes, damages or destroys the nest of any wild bird while that nest is in use or being built; or
- takes or destroys an egg of any wild bird.

A 'wild bird' is any bird of a species that is resident in or is a visitor to the European Territory of any member state in a wild state. Game birds (such as pheasants) are not considered as wild birds for the purposes of this Act, and there are also other current exceptions (as determined by the Secretary of State for the Environment) such as wood pigeons and herring gulls.

The offence is triable summarily only with a penalty of six months' imprisonment and/or a fine.

8.30.14.3   Killing, injuring, or taking a wild animal

Section 9 of the Wildlife and Countryside Act 1981 states a person commits an offence if he/she intentionally kills, injures or takes any wild animal.

According to the Act, wild animal means any animal (other than a bird) which is or was (before it was killed or taken) living wild. The definition of wild animal does not apply to captive bred animals being held in captivity. However, the schedules and various amendments to the Act specify yet more precisely the wild animals that are protected from killing, injuring or taking. These include hedgehogs, bats, dormice, otters and red squirrels. Wild animals such as rabbits and rats are not included.

The offence is triable summarily only with a penalty of six months' imprisonment and/or a fine.

8.30.15   Powers to Stop, Search, Seize, or Enter under the Wildlife and Countryside Act 1981

Section 19 of the Wildlife and Countryside Act states if you suspect with reasonable cause that any person has committed an offence under this Act you may:

- stop and search a person;
- search and examine anything the person has in his/her possession;
- seize and detain evidence;
- enter premises other than a dwelling to arrest a person.

Code A of the PACE Act 1984 Codes of Practice apply to these searches.

TASK 26

1. In the Animal Welfare Act 2006 an animal can only 'suffer' physically. True or false?
2. What are the three component parts that define a 'protected animal' under the Animal Welfare Act 2006?
3. You are resourced by control to a flat in which it has been anonymously reported that the pet cat and dog have been suffering from long periods of starvation and physical mistreatment by the flat owners. Restricting your answer to s19 of the Animal Welfare Act 2006 (entering for the purpose of searching for a protected animal and of exercising any power under section 18 in relation to it), could you enter the premises under this section?
4. You are resourced by control to a housing estate where a cat has been found with a discharged firework taped to its body which had been recently ignited. The cat is still alive but badly injured. The suspects were seen running into a nearby house. Restricting your answer to the Animal Welfare Act 2006, what power of entry, if any, could you use if required to enter and arrest the suspects?

8.31   Firework Offences

Under the law, fireworks are any device intended for use as a form of entertainment which burn and/or explode to produce a visual and/or audible effect. Some offences relating to fireworks are about misuse, and relate to the time of year or relate to the age of the person buying fireworks. Of particular concern in recent years has been:

- the use of powerful fireworks which distress others because of their force and loudness. These include 'aerial shells, aerial maroons, shells-in-mortar and maroons-in-mortar' which can register sound levels above 120 dB—about the noise level of a jet aircraft from 100 metres away. The sale of these products to the public are now banned but you might find the people have purchased these products abroad (where the law is different) and have brought them back to the UK;
- the use of fireworks in constrained areas to damage or even destroy objects such as phone boxes or cars.

It is for these reasons that we include fireworks as a subject for the Handbook. Relevant legislation includes the Explosives Act 1875, the Fireworks Act 2003, the Fireworks Regulations 2004 (as amended, and the Fireworks (Safety) Regulations 1997 (as amended).

It is an offence for any person:

- 'to throw, cast or fire any fireworks in or into any highway, street, thoroughfare or public place' (s 80, Explosives Act 1875);
- to wantonly (deliberately) throw or set fire to a firework in the street to the obstruction, annoyance, or danger of residents or passengers (s 28, Town Police Clauses Act 1847);
- under the age of eighteen years to possess fireworks in a public place, except for indoor fireworks (see below) (reg 4, Fireworks Regulations 2004).

A **public place** includes 'any place to which at the material time the public have or are permitted access, whether on payment or otherwise' (reg 4(2), Fireworks Regulations 2004).

Indoor fireworks include: a cap, cracker snap, novelty match, party popper, serpent, sparkler or 'throwdown'. (A throwdown is a firework containing impact-sensitive explosive and grains of inert material (wrapped in paper or foil) which produces a sound when thrown onto the ground.)

These offences are triable summarily.

Offences (except for the s 28 of the Town Police Clauses Act 1847 offence) can be dealt with by way of a Penalty Notice for Disorder (upper tier, see section 11.21.2).

8.31.1 Period of Sale

Fireworks may only be sold by traders to members of the public during the following periods:

- First day of Chinese New Year and three days prior to this.
- Diwali and three days prior to this.
- Between 15 October and 10 November.
- Between 26 and 31 December.

However, a trader may have a special licence to sell outside these periods.

8.31.2 Fireworks in Public Displays

Public displays frequently use large fireworks, known as category 4 fireworks. They may only be used by a professionally-qualified, trained person (reg 5, Fireworks Regulations 2004). The general public are prohibited from possessing such fireworks, except for any person who is employed by a local authority, or who is involved in public or commercial firework displays. A breach of reg 4 or 5 is a criminal offence, under s 11 of the Fireworks Act 2003.

This offence is triable summarily, and the penalty is a fine.

8.31.3 Supplying Fireworks to Persons under 18

Under s 12(1) of the Consumer Protection Act 1987 it is an offence to supply fireworks (including sparklers but excluding all other indoor fireworks) to persons under the age of eighteen years.

This offence is triable summarily, and the penalty is a fine.

8.31.4 Firework Curfews

A 'firework curfew' is a period of time where the general use of fireworks is not permitted. Under reg 7(1) of the Fireworks Regulations 2004 it is an offence for a person to use an 'adult firework' (essentially all fireworks other than indoor fireworks) between 2300 and 0700 hrs the next day except during the following periods:

Event	Finish
First day of the Chinese New Year	0100 hrs the following day
5 November ('Guy Fawkes Day')	Midnight
Diwali	0100 hrs the following day
31 December	0100 hrs the following day

There are exemptions for people employed by a local authority using a firework during a local authority display or national commemorative event.

This offence is triable summarily and the penalty is six months' imprisonment and/or a fine.

The breaking of a firework curfew can be addressed through a Penalty Notice for Disorder (upper tier, see section 11.21.2).

8.32   Answers to Tasks

TASK 1

Considerations at road checks:

1. Wear your personal safety equipment including high visibility clothing.
2. Carry out the road check in an area which is well lit by street lamps.
3. Use signs to reduce the speed of vehicles entering the checking area.
4. Remain alert to the presence of vehicles at all times.
5. Reduce the risk to the general public by asking them to stay in or near their vehicles.
6. Bear in mind the possibility that a vehicle may fail to stop at the road check.
7. Only use the techniques that you have been trained in to bring a vehicle to a halt which has failed to stop.
8. Give clear indications to drivers of what you want them to do.
9. Communicate with your colleagues and do not become detached from the main group involved in the check.
10. Select a location with clear views of oncoming traffic.
11. Select a location which is suitable to stop vehicles, particularly large ones such as a lay-by.
12. Provide the opportunity for vehicles to return to the traffic flow safely.
13. Consider the classification of the road and the speed of oncoming traffic if it is part of the 'fast road network' such as a dual carriageway.
14. Make allowances for the safe stopping distances of moving traffic during periods of adverse weather conditions.
15. Avoid certain locations if practicable, such as road junctions, bends, the brow of a hill and crossings.

TASK 2

An example mnemonic would be:

> **G** Grounds of the suspicion for the search
> **O** Object/purpose of search
> **W** Warrant card (if in plain clothes or requested)
> **I** Identity of police officer
> **S** Station to which attached
> **E** Entitlement to a copy of the search record
> **L** Legal power used
> **Y** 'You are detained for the purposes of a search'

We discuss this mnemonic later in the chapter.

TASK 3

The power is not absolute and cannot be exercised unless you reasonably believe that the person is wearing the item to conceal his or her identity, so response 3 is incorrect.

There is no reason to believe the person was carrying a dangerous instrument or an offensive weapon or that the person was likely to be involved in violence, so numbers 1 and 4 are incorrect.

Therefore, the answer is 2. You reasonably believe that the person was attempting to conceal his or her identity.

TASK 4

Look at s 34(1) of the Criminal Justice Act 1972 to help with the answer.

- The health and safety of the individual is paramount—is he or she injured in any way?
- How drunk is the individual?
- What offence has he/she committed? Is he/she drunk? Or drunk and disorderly?
- Is arrest necessary therefore to prevent him/her from causing physical injury (to self or others)?
- Can the matter be dealt with by another process?
- What other agencies should you involve?
- Does your force have a local agreement whereby the person can be taken to an approved treatment centre for alcoholism and therefore you can treat him/her as being in lawful custody for the purposes of the journey under s 34(1) Criminal Justice Act 1972?

TASK 5

- Introduce yourself and the station you are from.
- Explain to the person that you suspect he/she is under eighteen years of age.
- State to the person that he/she is in a public place or where he/she has gained unlawful access.
- Make clear to the person that you wish him/her to surrender anything in his/her possession which is intoxicating liquor, and to state his/her name and address, and that failure without reasonable excuse to comply with your requirement is an offence.

TASK 6

Your own force may have staff whose responsibility it is to represent the police at applications for premises licences or renewals. If this is the case, then notify the relevant person of incidents where suspects have been drinking excessively. This will enable the licensing authority to have sufficient information in order to make an informed decision about the granting of the licence (or its renewal), or otherwise.

TASK 7

The answers are:

1. Ethnic origin and religious group.
2. Not an ethnic group but a religious one.
3. Not a racial group but a religious one.
4. Racial group.

TASK 8

You probably considered the following:

(i) There was no evidence in the description given of harm being done to a person.
(ii) There was no evidence in the description given of harm likely to be done to a person.

(iii) There was no evidence in the description given that, in the presence of a person, harm was done to their property.

(iv) There was no evidence in the description given of a person fearing being harmed through assault, riot, or other disturbance.

It would therefore be very difficult from the information in the description alone to prove a breach of the peace.

TASK 9

You probably considered the following:

1. That the suspect was aware that while he/she was in public anybody could hear or see his/her conduct and would become harassed, alarmed, or distressed as a result.
2. That the suspect was aware that if the behaviour took place inside a dwelling it could be heard outside that same or another dwelling.
3. That the suspect was aware that his/her conduct was unreasonable and caused harassment, alarm, or distress.

Evidence could be gathered from people in the public area at the time confirming that they felt alarmed or distressed.

You could provide evidence of what you saw and heard in relation to the suspect's conduct and that there were other people in the public area at the time.

TASK 10

As a police officer you can also be harassed, alarmed, or distressed, but remember that this is a question of fact to be decided in each case by the magistrates. In determining this, the magistrates may take into account the familiarity which police officers have with the words and conduct typically seen in incidents of disorderly conduct. The evidence of other people in the area is an important factor.

TASK 11

In the case of *Swanston v DPP* [1997] 161 JP 203, the incident had occurred in a very small area and the officer was within five feet (about 1.5 m) of the suspect. Unless the door supervisor had impaired hearing or sight, he could not have failed to understand what was said and the actions committed by the suspect. In the *Swanston* case, the prosecution proved that the suspect had the intention of causing the door supervisor to fear that violence was going to be used against him. Those facts were proved by the admissible evidence including evidence of the police officer who was a witness to the incident.

TASK 12

In *R v Plavecz* [2002] Crim LR 837, having been found guilty of affray, the defendant appealed and the court decided that affray was a public order offence and was inappropriate where the incident was essentially 'one on one'. The conviction was therefore quashed. It is doubtful therefore, given these circumstances, that an investigation for affray could be sustained, but always seek guidance from the CPS in such matters.

TASK 13

Section 6(1) of the Criminal Law Act 1977 states that:

any person who, without lawful authority, uses or threatens violence for the purpose of securing entry into any premises for him/her self or for any other person is guilty of an offence provided:

- that there is someone present on those premises at the time who is opposed to the entry which the violence is intended to secure; and
- the person using violence or threatening the violence knows that that is the case.

In the circumstances it appears that Sam is only hammering on the door and therefore the actions of Sam fall short of the 'violence' that is required for this offence. If Sam's actions escalate to the likelihood of damage being caused, or threats or use of violence, then the offence would be committed provided that Sam knew Charlie was on the premises and opposed the entry.

TASK 14

1. As with any other offence, in order to secure a successful prosecution, you must obtain evidence. For either of these two offences to be proven, you must investigate what evidence exists to prove a course of conduct; for example are there any letters, photographs, or eye-witness accounts?
   - If the harassment consists of calls over the phone, you should seek the assistance of your own department to liaise with the service provider in order to obtain evidence of the calls.
   - Clarify with the victim whether there have been any previous instances of harassment or being put in fear of violence and whether the police were informed or any civil remedy taken under s 3 of the Act.
   - Collect statements from colleagues who have seen the victim on previous occasions.
   - Collect evidence from any other witnesses, paperwork, letters, and photographs from the victim and exhibit them in a statement.
   - Consider discussing the case with a CPS Evidence Review representative or anyone involved in the investigation in an advisory capacity.
2. If the suspect(s) is (are) known and a course of conduct cannot be proved, but the victim has been harassed or put in fear of violence, then consider warning the suspect and recording what you did in your pocket book in the way that your force prescribes and make sure it is recorded on your force database for future reference. This may be evidence towards proving a course of conduct in the future.
   - Advise the victim to seek legal advice if it is appropriate for him/her to pursue a civil remedy under s 3 of the Act.
   - Advise the victim to contact Victim Support representatives in your area.
   - Advise the victim to contact his/her service provider if the phone is being used to harass or put the victim in fear of violence, in order that a block can be placed on incoming 'number withheld' calls.
3. Future events can be recorded by advising the victim to maintain a diary of events, to retain physical evidence (such as letters), and take photographs of any visible evidence.
4. If a course of conduct can be proved or suspected, then consideration must be given to the most appropriate course of action. If an arrest is considered, then examples of the reasons for the arrest being necessary may be to protect a child or other vulnerable victim, to allow the prompt and effective investigation of the offence or of the conduct of the person in question, or to prevent any prosecution for the offence being hindered by the disappearance of the person in question.

TASK 15

The following are factors for consideration:
- How many times has the victim been harassed by people outside his/her own home?
- Have the people been asked to leave the area by the person who lives there?
- What is the severity of the harassment?
- How many people are in the vicinity?
- What is their behaviour?
- What is the purpose of their gathering?
- What is the impact on the person in his/her home?
- Have the people causing the harassment been told on a previous occasion to leave and have they returned subsequently?

- Is there sufficient evidence to investigate the offence because of the circumstances above, or can the situation be better resolved in its early stages by directing the people to leave the area?

TASK 16

Section 50(1) of the Police Reform Act 2002 states that if a constable in uniform has reason to believe that a person has been acting, or is acting, in an anti-social manner (within the meaning of s 1 of the Crime and Disorder Act 1998 which deals with anti-social behaviour orders), then the constable may require that person to give his or her name and address.

Further, s 50(2) states any person who—

    (a) fails to give [his or her] name and address when required to do so under subsection (1), or
    (b) gives a false or inaccurate name or address in response to a requirement under that subsection,

is guilty of an offence.

TASK 17

Since the young people in the group appear to be local residents, you will only be able to require the people in the group to disperse immediately or by a time as you may specify. As they are all local residents, you will not be able to prohibit them from returning within twenty-four hours. Even though only one of the group was actually apparently intimidating a member of the public, you have the power to disperse the whole group as two or more persons were present.

TASK 18

You probably considered the following:

(i) Do the occupants have a reasonable excuse for the presence of the items?
(ii) Who do the items belong to?
(iv) Will you be preventing a crime from taking place if you investigate the matter further?
(v) How will you progress this matter further? Do the circumstances (and a reason to make an arrest) exist?
(vi) Can you deal with the matter by way of reporting the suspect?

TASK 19

You probably considered the following:

(i) Is Ahmed above the age of criminal responsibility?
(ii) How is Ahmed carrying the knife?
(iii) What type of knife is Ahmed in possession of?
(iv) Has it been made, adapted or intended to cause injury?
(v) How long has Ahmed carried the knife?
(vi) Will Ahmed give you the knife or do you need to use a power of search?

TASK 20

The answers are as follows:

1 b, 2 c, 3 d, 4 a, 5 a, 6 f g h, 7 e, 8 i.

TASK 21

1. Any lethal barrelled weapon of any description from which any shot, bullet, or other missile can be discharged and includes: a prohibited weapon, whether it is a lethal weapon or not; any component part of such a lethal or prohibited weapon, and any accessory to

any such weapon, designed or adapted to diminish the noise or flash caused by firing the weapon.

2. You may demand from any person whom you believe to be in possession of a s 1 firearm or ammunition or a shotgun the production of their firearm or shotgun certificate.

3. When you have reasonable cause to suspect a person of having a firearm with or without ammunition in a public place or to be committing or about to commit elsewhere than in a public place an offence relevant to the Firearms Act 1968.

4. All firearms except shotguns, prohibited weapons, air weapons (unless 'specially dangerous'), or imitation firearms (unless converted).

5. Any ammunition for a firearm except: cartridges containing five or more shot none of which exceeds .36 inch in diameter, ammunition for an air gun, air rifle or air pistol and blank cartridges not more than 1 inch in diameter.

6. A smooth bore gun which has a barrel not less than 60.96 cm long and a barrel bore not exceeding 5.08 cm, which either has no magazine or has a non-detachable magazine incapable of holding more than two cartridges and is not a revolver gun.

TASK 22

1. It is an offence for a person under the age of seventeen to have with him or her an air weapon or ammunition for an air weapon. There are exceptions. For example it is not an offence if the person is fourteen years or over to possess the air weapon on private premises with the consent of the occupier, and he/she does not have to be supervised.
However, under s 21A of the Firearms Act 1968 that a person commits an offence if:

   (a) [he/she has] with [him or her] an air weapon on any premises; and
   (b) [he/she uses] it for firing a missile beyond those premises.

2. A person commits an offence if, without lawful authority or reasonable excuse, he/she has with him/her in a public place any loaded or unloaded air weapon (s 19 of the Firearms Act 1968).

TASK 23

As a result of the shootings at Hungerford on 12 August 1987, it was considered that certain firearms were so dangerous as to justify their inclusion in the class of prohibited weapons. These included self-loading and pump-action rifles, other than those chambered for .22 rimfire and certain self-loading and pump-action shotguns (see the White Paper, Firearms Act 1968: Proposals for Reform (Cm 261, 1987) and the amendment to the 1968 Act which was effected by s 1 of the Firearms (Amendment) Act 1988). Similarly the 1968 Act was also amended so as to extend the level of control on certain shot guns to the extent that a firearm certificate was required.

TASK 24

Section 19 of the Firearms Act 1968 states that a person commits an offence if, without lawful authority or reasonable excuse (the proof whereof lies on him or her), he or she has with him or her, in a public place, an imitation firearm.

TASK 25

1. There are likely to be policy agreements with local Social Services and the Healthcare Trusts.

2. A dynamic risk assessment of the situation should be made first. Can you safely enter the room or should you seek the assistance of other officers with appropriate personal safety equipment? Entrance can be gained by seeking the permission of the parents/owners of the property to unscrew the door handle, withdrawing the bar sufficiently to enable you to turn the handle from your side of the door and using the element of surprise to enter the room safely.

Does the person want to go voluntarily to hospital or do you need to call an approved social worker to begin the process of determining if the person can be taken into hospital under one of the sections within the Mental Health Act 1983?

TASK 26

1. False. In the Act, 'suffering' means physical or mental suffering and related expressions shall be construed accordingly.
2. Section 2 states an animal is protected if it is:
   • of a kind which is commonly domesticated in the British Islands,
   • under the control of [human kind] whether on a permanent or temporary basis, or
   • not living in a wild state.
3. Section 19 does not authorize entry to any part of premises which is used as a private dwelling. Under these circumstances a warrant will need to be obtained under section 19(4).
4. You may enter and search any premises to arrest any person you reasonably suspect of committing an offence under s 4 Animal Welfare Act 2006 using s 17 of the PACE Act 1984 (see section 11.10 of the Handbook). Always follow your force policy in relation to using force to gain entry in such circumstances.

9 | Criminal Law and Procedure

9.1 Chapter Briefing

This chapter examines the law and procedure concerned with a number of criminal offences. We present the basic knowledge of the criminal law required by student police officers whilst undertaking initial training.

9.1.1 Aim of the Chapter

The aim of this chapter is to introduce you to the legislation and police practice associated with the application of the criminal law and the investigation of crime. You are likely to encounter this aspect of policing whilst undertaking Supervised and Independent Patrol and whilst studying the IPLDP LPG modules.

This chapter will enable you to:

- understand the legislation surrounding theft, acts of violence and cruelty, and fraud;
- identify a number of sexual offences;
- understand some of the law surrounding criminal damage and criminal attempts;
- develop the underpinning knowledge required for a number of NOS elements, entries for your Learning Diary Phase 3 and a CAR of your SOLAP.

9.1.2 Police Action Checklist

This chapter will assist in meeting the following requirements of the Police Action Checklist under the Investigation heading; that you are able to:

- conduct the initial investigation and report of volume crime according to Local/National Policing plan;
- conduct the initial investigation and report in relation to a child protection and/or vulnerable person incident.

9.1.3 National Occupational Standards

This chapter will provide you with some of the knowledge required to demonstrate aspects of the following NOS elements:

National Occupational Standards Elements

2C1.1 Gather information and plan a response.
2C1.2 Respond to incidents.
2G2.1 Conduct priority and volume investigations.

9.1.4 IPLDP Phases and Modules

This chapter will provide you with resources to support the following Operational Modules, LPGs, and Phases of the IPLDP:

OP 3 Respond to incidents, conduct and evaluate investigations.
LPG 1.1 Crime.
Phase 3 Supervised Patrol.

As we noted in Chapter 2, we cover in this Handbook the material which we believe is of critical importance to you at this stage of your policing career. This means that the Handbook does not correspond exactly with the current IPLDP syllabus. For example, a compulsory IPLDP subject is the law contained within s 70 of the Sexual Offences Act 2003 concerned with the offence of 'sexual penetration of a corpse'. We judge that you are unlikely to require knowledge of this kind of detail at this stage of your training. On the other hand, 'aggravated burglary' is an optional subject within IPLDP but we include it in this Handbook because we think it important to understand the difference between the basic offence of burglary and its aggravated form.

9.1.5 SOLAP

The contents of this chapter are relevant to the knowledge evidence requirement of CAR 2C1.

9.1.6 Learning Diary Phases

The contents of this chapter may provide you with stimulus material for completion of your Learning Diary (Phase 3) and the 'Crime' heading in particular.

9.2 Introduction

In this chapter, we look at your role as a student police officer in the application of the criminal law. We must repeat that, although this Handbook will provide you with the essence of the individual law and some interpretations (both academic and from case law or precedent), there is no substitute for reading and understanding the law itself.

The process of criminal law (and its associated procedures) is different, in kind and in application, from the offences considered in the previous chapter. If you remember, we said in the introduction to Chapter 8 that offences could sometimes bring criminal matters into play as ancillary offences (not that they are any the less serious). In this chapter, we are considering the criminal law itself and therefore it is the crime which takes precedence. It also tends to be the area upon which the effectiveness and professionalism of your police force is judged.

We maintain consistently in this Handbook our reservations about a wholly quantitative methodology for measuring police performance. We understand why the Home Office and HMIC focus so much on the 'countable': it must be, at least in part, because the quantitative data are relatively straightforward to gather and at least the gathering appears objective; thus allowing comparisons between forces on specific aspects of policing. What we find inadequate about this measurement methodology is that it is very limited and it is open to many different kinds of interpretation. Force X may have detected and brought to justice fifteen homicides out of twenty-one in the course of a year, whilst Force Y has detected 'only' nineteen out of forty-seven. On the face of it, Force X is the more effective and efficient force, at least in terms of the investigation of homicide. What we do not know, from these bald figures alone, is the relative seriousness of each homicide. We do not know, for example, how many of each force's homicides were Cat A or B or C (see section 12.3). If Force X's were all, or mostly, Cat C, then it is not surprising that the crimes were brought to justice. If Force Y's homicides had a higher proportion of stranger killings (Cat A), then a lower success rate is understandable because of the inherent difficulty of detecting stranger murders. In other words, we have insufficient information on which to base meaningful comparisons.

Our reason for discussing our reservations about the Home Office's performance regime at this point (though we do refer to it elsewhere) is that it is directly relevant to the prevention and detection of crime, and the bringing of offenders to justice. (The performance of a force is measured in other ways too, but their performances in reducing crime and the fear of crime, as well as specified offences, are paramount in any assessment.) Your performance, your team's performance, your BCU's performance, and ultimately your force's performance, all depend on the interpretation of quantitative statistics, not upon qualitative or inferential statistics or other forms of more sophisticated measurement.

Keep this in your mind when you read about the criminal law and our discussion of its applications to policing in the pages which follow. How you detect and bring offenders to justice in theft, robbery, vehicle crime, other types of volume crime, drugs crimes, violent crime, and sexual crime are efficiency measures by which you and your force are judged annually. Your force's performance ought to have a direct impact on public confidence in the police and on the public's fear of crime, but repeated surveys show that this is not the case. For example, in 2004–5, 61% of people surveyed as part of the British Crime Survey believed that crime had increased in the previous two years despite the fact that it had actually fallen (Nicholas et al, 2005). You might like to consider the reasons for this as you read and learn what follows.

Actually, at the high end of seriousness, such as crimes against children, or homicide, public confidence (at least temporarily) is directly related to force performance (think of the Stephen Lawrence, Damilola Taylor, Jamie Bulger murders, and many others). That is certainly the case if we view public confidence through the prisms of the media. However, the public generally does not make detailed distinctions between crimes and other anti-social acts, so that the fear of vulnerability to local crime, or something as simple as the fear of groups of youngsters who might cause criminal damage, can worry people considerably, even if the force statistics show that crime is going down. The public is most concerned about violent crime (for sound and obvious reasons), but anti-social behaviour, theft from vehicles, and burglary all figure highly in public consciousness and their concerns about a force's capability to reduce crime. You could look at the annual publications of the British Crime Survey for more details on this. The latest survey is freely available from <http://www.homeoffice.gov.uk/rds/pdfs05/hosb1105.pdf>.

9.3 Theft

Theft is a so-called 'volume crime'. Of all the dishonest criminal offences you will deal with, theft will probably be the most common. The primary source of legislation relating to theft is to found in ss 1 to 6 of the Theft Act 1968. This section is therefore relevant to the PAC requirement that you conduct the Initial Investigation & Report of Volume Crime according to National/Local Policing Plans.

You are likely to encounter theft early on in your career as a student police officer. Offences of theft include shoplifting and stealing from an employer, as well as a number of other similar crimes. There are many legal complexities surrounding theft and in this section we will simply examine the basic principles involved. However, it is worth clarifying at this point two particular examples of theft that occur commonly but are examined separately in this Handbook, and are therefore not covered here. These are robbery (theft from a person, accompanied by violence or the threat of violence) and burglary (theft or the intention of theft from a building). These are covered in sections 9.4 and 9.5 below.

9.3.1 The Definition of Theft

Section 1 of the Theft Act 1968 states that a person is guilty of theft if he/she 'dishonestly [appropriates] property'. We examine each of the concepts of dishonesty, appropriation, and property in turn.

9.3.1.1 Dishonesty

Dishonesty is not defined by the Act, but s 2(1) of the Theft Act 1968 defines where a person will **not** be treated as dishonest. The person is not acting dishonestly if he/she believes:

• that he/she had the lawful right to take the item (for example a person mistakenly taking the wrong coat in a changing room believing it was his or her own);
• that he/she would have had the owner's consent if the owner knew of the circumstances (for example a person's lawnmower breaks down and whilst looking after the property of the neighbour who is on holiday, he/she takes the neighbour's);
• that the owner cannot be discovered by taking reasonable steps (for example a person finds cash in the street).

But s 2(2) of the Theft Act 1968 states that a person may be treated as dishonest even though he/she was willing to pay for the property (for example a person wants to buy a particular garden ornament, but the shopkeeper cannot be found, so the person takes the ornament and leaves behind what he/she thinks it is worth in money). In the end, a court must decide if a person acted dishonestly or not.

9.3.1.2 Appropriation

With reference to theft, the term **appropriate** is given the following meaning in the Theft Act 1968, s 3(1):

• assuming the rights of an owner of property by stealing it (for example, by shoplifting); or
• obtaining property innocently and later keeping it and using it as his or her own (for example hiring a piece of machinery and not returning it).

However, when an innocent purchaser pays the right price to a person who is selling some kind of property which later turns out to be stolen, the innocent purchaser will not have committed theft. For example, if a person buys a second-hand bicycle in good faith and then discovers it is stolen, the innocent purchaser will not have committed theft. This will be a matter for the civil court to decide (s 3(2), Theft Act 1968).

9.3.1.3 Property

The definition of **property** (s 4, Theft Act 1968) is not straightforward. Property is:

- money;
- personal property, for example personal effects and pets;
- real property, for example land and things forming part of the land, such as plants and buildings. However, land can only be stolen:
  - by a trustee (someone who has the legal control over the land) for example during its transfer in some kind of a legal process;
  - by persons who do not own the land, for example by removing turf, top soil, or digging up cultivated trees and shrubs;
  - by tenants, for example by removing fixtures and fittings;
- things in action, for example patents, copyrights, and trademarks;
- plants or fungi growing wild, but only if they are picked for sale, reward, or a commercial purpose (but always consider other legislation that might prohibit such activities such as the Wildlife and Countryside Act 1981);
- wild creatures, but only if they are tamed and have not been lost or abandoned since they were kept in captivity;
- tangible property, for example gas.

(Note that electricity is not legally property, so it cannot be stolen; see section 9.10.)

9.3.2 Summary of theft

So, a person is guilty of theft if he/she **dishonestly appropriates property**:

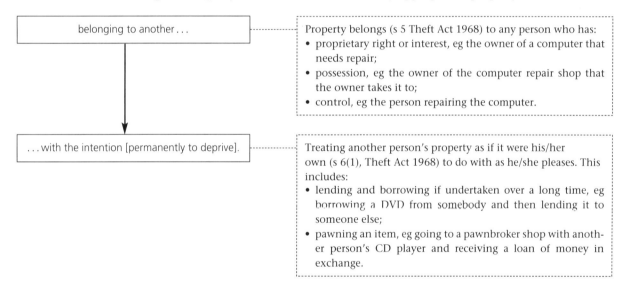

The offence of theft is triable either way:

- Summarily; six months' imprisonment and/or a fine.
- On indictment; seven years' imprisonment.

TASK 1

Now that you know what constitutes a theft, think of three incidents of theft that you are aware of, either through the media or other means, and consider where the elements of theft were within those incidents.

9.4 Robbery

Robbery is the act of stealing from a person whilst using (or threatening the use of) force or violence. It is an aggravated form of the primary offence of theft and therefore, for robbery to be proved, theft has to be proved first.

Robbery is covered in s 8 of the Theft Act 1968.

First, note that two key points about robbery are that:

- force, or the threat of force, must be used for the theft to be carried out;
- there must be an attempt to make the victim fearful.

There are two main ways of establishing the 'put in fear' element of the offence:

- Actually to put in fear; this can be proved from the victim's statement. The fear of being subjected to force must be genuine. The fear could be evidenced by what he/she saw the suspect do and the way that made the victim feel as a result.
- To seek to put in fear; the state of mind of the offender is what is important, and this could be evidenced from the suspect's statement. The suspect must seek to put some person in fear of force. However, it is not necessary to prove that any person was actually put in fear; if the victim is not intimidated by the suspect, it is enough that the suspect tried to frighten the victim. This might be proved by either the evidence of other witnesses or circumstantial evidence, such as the suspect wielding an offensive weapon.

The offence of robbery is defined by s 8(1) of the Theft Act 1968 which states that a person is guilty of robbery if:

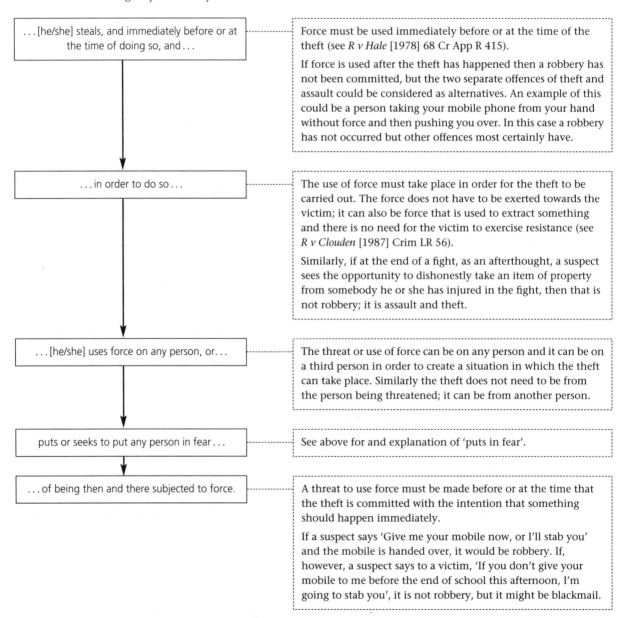

...[he/she] steals, and immediately before or at the time of doing so, and...	Force must be used immediately before or at the time of the theft (see *R v Hale* [1978] 68 Cr App R 415).
	If force is used after the theft has happened then a robbery has not been committed, but the two separate offences of theft and assault could be considered as alternatives. An example of this could be a person taking your mobile phone from your hand without force and then pushing you over. In this case a robbery has not occurred but other offences most certainly have.
...in order to do so...	The use of force must take place in order for the theft to be carried out. The force does not have to be exerted towards the victim; it can also be force that is used to extract something and there is no need for the victim to exercise resistance (see *R v Clouden* [1987] Crim LR 56).
	Similarly, if at the end of a fight, as an afterthought, a suspect sees the opportunity to dishonestly take an item of property from somebody he or she has injured in the fight, then that is not robbery; it is assault and theft.
...[he/she] uses force on any person, or...	The threat or use of force can be on any person and it can be on a third person in order to create a situation in which the theft can take place. Similarly the theft does not need to be from the person being threatened; it can be from another person.
puts or seeks to put any person in fear...	See above for and explanation of 'puts in fear'.
...of being then and there subjected to force.	A threat to use force must be made before or at the time that the theft is committed with the intention that something should happen immediately.
	If a suspect says 'Give me your mobile now, or I'll stab you' and the mobile is handed over, it would be robbery. If, however, a suspect says to a victim, 'If you don't give your mobile to me before the end of school this afternoon, I'm going to stab you', it is not robbery, but it might be blackmail.

The offence of robbery is triable by indictment only and the maximum penalty is life imprisonment.

> **TASK 2**
>
> Chris is walking in Maidbury shopping centre when she drops a bag full of shopping by accident. Jo, happening by, grabs the dropped bag and makes off, but the bag breaks spilling all its contents onto the floor of the shopping centre. Throwing down the empty bag, Jo picks up one of the items from the dropped bag which is on the ground, changes direction quickly and runs into Chris causing her to fall over heavily and break her arm. Has Jo committed the offence of robbery?

9.5 Burglary and Trespassing

Burglary is a so-called 'volume crime' and you will undoubtedly encounter crimes of burglary whilst on Supervised and Independent Patrol. Indeed, burglary may feature as one of your case studies during Phase 3 of the IPLDP (if your force uses that approach).

Despite being a volume crime, burglary is a serious offence; aggravated burglary (see section 9.5.4) for example, carries a maximum sentence of life imprisonment. There is also the phenomenon of distraction burglary (in some forces called 'burglary by artifice') where entry is gained to the home of a person (usually an elderly person) by an offender pretending to be an official such as the gasman.

The legislation concerning burglary is to be found in ss 9–10 of the Theft Act 1968. We look separately at the basic offence of burglary, then at aggravated burglary, and finally at various aspects of trespass associated with this type of crime.

9.5.1 The Basic Offence

The basic offence of burglary is set out in s 9 of the Theft Act 1968 which states that:

> A person is guilty of burglary if—
>
> (a) [he/she] enters any building or part of a building as a trespasser and with intent to commit any such offence as is mentioned in subsection 2 below; or
> (b) having entered into any building or part of a building as a trespasser [he/she] steals or attempts to steal anything in the building or that part of it or inflicts or attempts to inflict on any person therein any grievous bodily harm.

The subsection 2 offences (referred to in the quoted law above) are listed in s 9(2) of the Theft Act 1968; they are:

- 'stealing anything in the building or part of a building in question'; or
- 'inflicting on any person therein any grievous bodily harm'; the entry has to be with intent to inflict GBH and thus enough evidence to satisfy a charge under s 18 of the Offences Against the Person Act 1861 is required (see sections 9.15 and 9.16 below); or
- 'doing unlawful damage to the building or anything therein' (see section 9.21 of the Handbook and s 9(2), Theft Act 1968).

Note that part (a) offences involve a person entering a building with the **intent** to steal or cause injury or damage (but these actions do not actually need to be carried out). For part (b) offences, the theft, injury, or damage must be **carried out** or at least attempted.

9.5.2 Part (a) Burglary

Certain terms, such as 'entry', 'building', and 'intent' need to be carefully defined in order to fully appreciate the range of activities that might count as burglary under s 9(1)(a) of the Theft Act 1968.

9.5.2.1 Entry as a trespasser

Trespass means entering without the consent of the owner. **Entry** can be gained in a number of clearly defined ways:

- **In person** by walking or climbing into a building either completely or by inserting a body part such as an arm or a leg through a letter box. However, there must be more than minimal insertion; sliding a hand between a window and frame from the outside of a building in order to release the catch would be insufficient.

- **Using a tool or article** as an extension of the human body to carry out one of the relevant offences. In these circumstances no part of the body needs to be inserted, only the article that is being used. However, the article must be used for more than just gaining entry. Using a crowbar just to prise open a door would not qualify as the full offence, but a length of garden cane pushed through a letter box of a shop to hook a scarf from a display would qualify as the full offence.
- **Using a blameless accomplice** in a similar way to using an article as an extension of the suspect's body. Here, for example, a child below the age of criminal responsibility (ten years of age) could be lifted through a small window to obtain property from inside. However, if the child is used only to gain entry for the burglar, then the full offence is not committed; it has only been attempted.

Trespass involves a person entering a building or part of a building (for the purpose of committing one of the relevant offences) in one of the following ways:

- **Entering a building** for a purpose other than the intended purpose of that building, for example going into a shop with the intention to steal (rather than an intent to browse or buy).
- **Entering by some kind of deception**, for example pretending to represent a utility company for the purpose of reading a meter and being invited into the building ('burglary by artifice', referred to earlier).
- **Crossing over a demarcation line** of some kind, unlawfully and without invitation or permission, whether or not the owner knows he/she is trespassing.

The person must have guilty knowledge ('mens rea' see section 5.10) that what he/she is doing amounts to trespass, or alternatively, he/she does not care about whether they are trespassing or not.

(Image © Kevin Lawton-Barrett)

Burglary involves entering a building as a trespasser

9.5.2.2 Building or part of a building

The term 'building' is not defined in the Theft Act 1968, although 'dwelling' is. However, case law is reasonably well established for a building:

- Building is an ordinary word, which is a matter of fact (*Brutus v Cozens* [1973] AC 854, 861);
- 'A structure of considerable size and intended to be permanent or at least to endure for a considerable time' (*Stevens v Gourley* (1859) 7 CBNS 99);
- An unfinished building becomes a building when it reaches a point at which it has all its walls and a roof, because 'a building need not necessarily be a completed structure; it is sufficient that it should be a connected and entire structure' (Judge Lush in *R v Manning & Rogers* (1871) CA).

Examples of buildings other than houses include garages and garden sheds, but see your force policy or procedure for an interpretation of burglary from different types of buildings.

A **dwelling** is defined as:

- an inhabited building; or
- a vehicle or vessel which is, at the time of the offence, inhabited (irrespective of whether or not the person who occupies the vehicle/vessel is present at the time of the burglary). For example, a houseboat which is moored up alongside a river bank, and is inhabited by its owners, is regarded as a building for the purposes of the Theft Act 1968. Similarly, a motor home or caravan, if inhabited during a holiday, is a building (though it is not regarded as a building when parked and empty during the winter). However, even during the holiday season and inhabited, a tent would not be included, since it is not a semi-permanent structure.

This legislation also covers the circumstances where a person is in a building lawfully but enters part of it that he/she is not meant to enter. For example:

- a customer who leaves the front of a shop where purchases take place and walks through to the back, past a sign clearly stating 'Staff Only—No Unauthorized Entry' and into a storeroom;
- a customer in a pub who hides behind the bar at closing time;
- a student at evening classes in a centre for adult education who, during a break in lessons, goes into the administrative offices of the centre which are only staffed during the day.

9.5.2.3 Intent

The suspect must intend to commit certain specified offences. The intent can be proved in a number of ways or in combination:

- during the interview of the suspect when he/she admits to having guilty knowledge or criminal intent to commit the offence;
- during the interview of other suspects involved in committing the offence, who name his/her accomplices and the part they played in its commission;
- circumstantial evidence.

Circumstantial evidence may include:

- witness statements;
- observations of the arresting officer(s) in relation to the suspect's proximity to the crime scene when he/she was arrested;
- the retrieval of stolen property from the crime scene, subsequently found in the possession of the suspect when arrested;
- the results of forensic examination of the suspect's clothes indicating he/she was present at the crime scene, or the retrieval of fingerprint evidence demonstrating the same (see sections 8.29, 11.18, and 13.6 of this Handbook).

In summary, for a part (a) burglary, the suspect does not actually need to have committed any of the acts described below.

9.5.3   Part (b) Burglary

Under s 9(1)(b) of the Theft Act 1968, burglary involves acts (or attempted acts) of theft, injury, or damage committed by a trespasser:

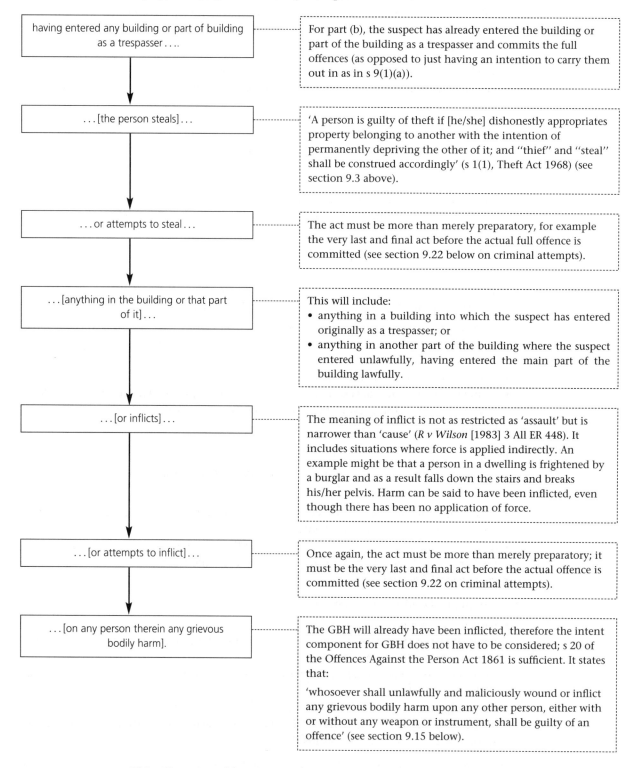

having entered any building or part of building as a trespasser....	For part (b), the suspect has already entered the building or part of the building as a trespasser and commits the full offences (as opposed to just having an intention to carry them out in as in s 9(1)(a)).
...[the person steals]...	'A person is guilty of theft if [he/she] dishonestly appropriates property belonging to another with the intention of permanently depriving the other of it; and "thief" and "steal" shall be construed accordingly' (s 1(1), Theft Act 1968) (see section 9.3 above).
...or attempts to steal...	The act must be more than merely preparatory, for example the very last and final act before the actual full offence is committed (see section 9.22 below on criminal attempts).
...[anything in the building or that part of it]...	This will include: • anything in a building into which the suspect has entered originally as a trespasser; or • anything in another part of the building where the suspect entered unlawfully, having entered the main part of the building lawfully.
...[or inflicts]...	The meaning of inflict is not as restricted as 'assault' but is narrower than 'cause' (*R v Wilson* [1983] 3 All ER 448). It includes situations where force is applied indirectly. An example might be that a person in a dwelling is frightened by a burglar and as a result falls down the stairs and breaks his/her pelvis. Harm can be said to have been inflicted, even though there has been no application of force.
...[or attempts to inflict]...	Once again, the act must be more than merely preparatory; it must be the very last and final act before the actual offence is committed (see section 9.22 on criminal attempts).
...[on any person therein any grievous bodily harm].	The GBH will already have been inflicted, therefore the intent component for GBH does not have to be considered; s 20 of the Offences Against the Person Act 1861 is sufficient. It states that: 'whosoever shall unlawfully and maliciously wound or inflict any grievous bodily harm upon any other person, either with or without any weapon or instrument, shall be guilty of an offence' (see section 9.15 below).

This offence is triable either way:

- Summarily: six months' imprisonment and/or a fine.
- On indictment: ten years' imprisonment (fourteen years' imprisonment if the building or part of the building was a dwelling) and three years' minimum imprisonment on conviction for a third domestic burglary.

9.5.4 Aggravated Burglary

Aggravated burglary (s 10, Theft Act 1968) is a more serious offence than burglary, and may involve the use of weapons or explosives. The types of weapons or explosives (articles) covered by this legislation are shown in the table below.

Articles within the definition of aggravated burglary

Article	Details	Theft Act 1968
Firearm	Includes an airgun or air pistol (see section 8.22).	s 10(1)(a)
Imitation firearm	Anything which has the appearance of being a firearm, whether capable of being discharged or not.	s 10(1)(a)
Weapon of offence	Any article made or adapted for use for causing injury to or incapacitating a person, or intended by the person having it with him for such use (see section 8.20).	s 10(1)(b)
Explosive	Any article manufactured for the purpose of producing a practical effect by explosion, or intended by the person having it with [him/her] for that purpose.	s 10(1)(c)

A person commits an offence of aggravated burglary if he/she:

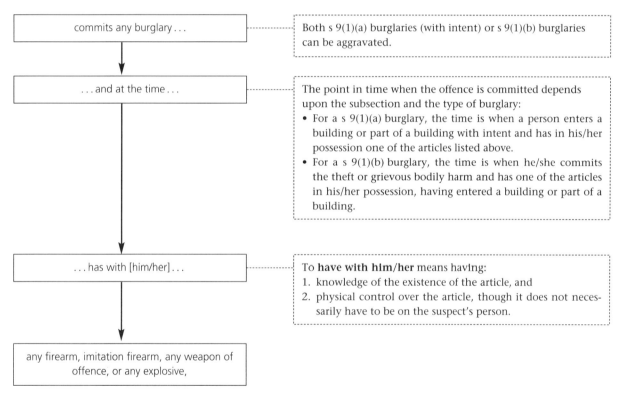

This offence is triable by indictment only and the penalty is life imprisonment.

9.5.4.1 Trespassing with a weapon of offence

If the suspect has no criminal intention other than trespassing with a weapon, he/she still commits an offence. To commit this offence, the entry must have been as a trespasser. Therefore a person will not commit this offence having innocently entered but then subsequently been asked to leave, even if he/she possesses the weapon of offence. Section 8 of the Criminal Law Act 1977 states:

> A person who is on any premises as a trespasser, after having entered as such, is guilty of an offence if, without lawful authority or reasonable excuse, [he/she] has with [him/her] on the premises any weapon of offence.

This offence is triable summarily and the penalty is three months' imprisonment and/or a fine.

9.5.5 Vagrancy and Trespassing

Where a suspect is found on enclosed premises, perhaps preparing to commit a burglary or theft, he/she can be investigated for offences under the Vagrancy Act 1824. It may also be useful to read at this point section 8.17 which explores the concept of trespass.

Section 4 of the Vagrancy Act 1824 states it is an offence for every person found:

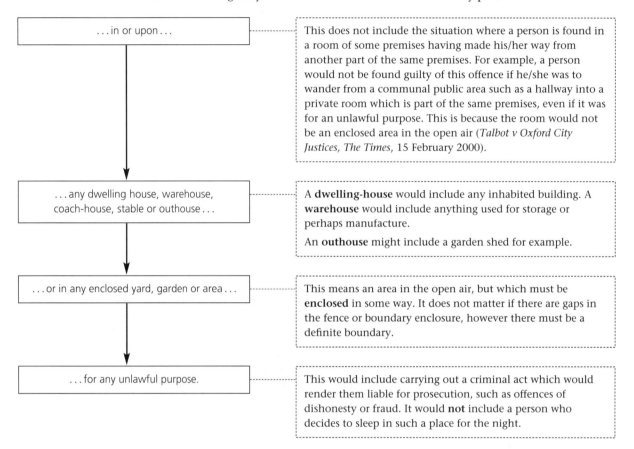

. . . in or upon . . .	This does not include the situation where a person is found in a room of some premises having made his/her way from another part of the same premises. For example, a person would not be found guilty of this offence if he/she was to wander from a communal public area such as a hallway into a private room which is part of the same premises, even if it was for an unlawful purpose. This is because the room would not be an enclosed area in the open air (*Talbot v Oxford City Justices, The Times*, 15 February 2000).
. . . any dwelling house, warehouse, coach-house, stable or outhouse . . .	A **dwelling-house** would include any inhabited building. A **warehouse** would include anything used for storage or perhaps manufacture. An **outhouse** might include a garden shed for example.
. . . or in any enclosed yard, garden or area . . .	This means an area in the open air, but which must be **enclosed** in some way. It does not matter if there are gaps in the fence or boundary enclosure, however there must be a definite boundary.
. . . for any unlawful purpose.	This would include carrying out a criminal act which would render them liable for prosecution, such as offences of dishonesty or fraud. It would **not** include a person who decides to sleep in such a place for the night.

This offence is triable summarily and the penalty is three months' imprisonment and/or a fine.

TASK 3

In which of the cases set out below has burglary been committed? Give reasons for your answers.

(a) On the way home from a nightclub in the early hours of the morning, Jo walks through an industrial estate where there are a number of storage warehouses. Jo decides to go in one of the warehouses without permission, through an open door, with the intention of finding somewhere to sleep for the night. Having entered the warehouse, Jo forces open a door to another room and in so doing damages the lock. Once inside the room, Jo switches on an electric fire to keep warm and falls asleep until awoken by a security guard patrolling the industrial estate.

(b) Terri enters a house as a trespasser with intent to steal small items of electrical equipment for which there is a demand at local car boot sales. While Terri is on the premises, and as a precaution against capture, Terri takes a screwdriver from a drawer underneath the stairs where some tools are kept and continues the search for electrical goods, still with the screwdriver. Twenty minutes later, the occupier returns and Terri stabs the homeowner causing serious injury. (Consider only the offences relating to burglary here.)

9.6   Vehicle Crime

Every year thousands of cars are stolen in England and Wales. Where do they go and why are they stolen? How do we identify stolen vehicles? This section examines some of the legal aspects and police procedures surrounding a number of vehicle crimes.

9.6.1   Why are Cars Stolen?

There are a number of possible reasons why cars are stolen:

Reasons for Car Theft

Joyriding	Cars are stolen to be used for a usually brief period of excitement and as a means of transport. However, joyriders often abandon and set alight cars they have stolen, possibly in order to destroy forensic evidence.
Parts	After it reaches a certain age, the resale value of a vehicle is often much higher if it is broken down into parts. The total value of the parts may be more than the value of the intact vehicle.
Insurance claims	The cost of repairing or maintaining a vehicle sometimes means that people fraudulently claim that their vehicle has been stolen, or actually get somebody to 'steal' it, so that the owner can claim on the insurance.
Export	For some vehicles there is a ready market in other countries, so these vehicles are either driven or shipped out through UK ports.

9.6.2   Innocent Purchase of a Stolen Vehicle

There are a number of ways in which an innocent purchaser could take possession of a stolen vehicle. The most common method is:

1. the thief obtains the identifying features of a vehicle (see below) which has been declared uneconomical to repair (see below regarding DVLA V23 form);
2. the thief steals a similar vehicle;
3. the thief removes the identifying features from the stolen vehicle and replaces them with those from the badly damaged vehicle;
4. the stolen vehicle (with its new identity) is then sold to an innocent purchaser.

A **V23 form** is used either by insurance companies to notify the DVLA about a vehicle when it makes a total loss payment on a vehicle, or by a police officer to make a report on a vehicle written off in an accident. These vehicles may, however, be subsequently repaired and used on the roads.

9.6.3   The Identifying Features of a Vehicle

Vehicles normally have a number of identifying features unique to each vehicle. Consider using the police mnemonic VICE to remember what the identifying features of a vehicle are:

Feature	Description
Vehicle Identification Number (VIN)	All vehicles used on or after 1 April 1980 have a plate in a conspicuous and readily accessible position, on a part not normally subject to replacement. On the plate will be a 17 character VIN unique to that vehicle.
Index number or registration plate	All mechanically-propelled vehicles used on public roads require a registration mark (number).
Chassis number (same as VIN)	All vehicles used on or after 1 April 1980 will have their 17 character VIN stamped into the chassis or frame of the car. It will be the same number as on the VIN plate.
Engine number	Not always as easy to find as the VIN since engine numbers are often tucked away in locations most easily seen when (or if) the engine is taken out of the vehicle. Engines are also sometimes replaced, so the fact that you cannot see an engine number should not in itself be a cause for suspicion.

If you have difficulty finding the identifying features on a vehicle, contact your control room with details of the make and model of the car you want to check. Control-room staff have access to databases listing the positions of the stamped-in VIN, the VIN plate, and the engine number, for each make and model of vehicle.

Example of a VIN on the chassis of a VW camper van

(Image © Kevin Lawton-Barrett)

9.6.4 Detection of Stolen Vehicles

You might need to consider the following points to help you decide if the vehicle in front of you is a stolen vehicle:

* Is the car reported lost or stolen? You can identify a stolen vehicle relatively easily by undertaking a PNC check on the registration number or, if the car is without registration plates, finding the VIN plate or stamped-in number and doing a PNC check on the VIN.
* Does it belong to a group of vehicles more likely to be stolen? Increase your chances of finding a stolen car by undertaking Task 5 in this chapter and researching police intelligence, noting which cars are stolen most often in your area.
* Does the PNC show that a DVLA form V23 has been submitted on the car? If someone nonetheless has gone ahead with repairs, those repairs will be extensive and may be easy to see, for example, welding. If there are no indications of major repairs, the vehicle displaying the VICE details may not be the original, but a stolen one.
* Is the vehicle displaying the correct registration plates? Do the plates look as though they have been replaced or have new plates been stuck over the old plates? Do the plates have a completely different character from the rest of the car—for example, is the car clean and the plates old and dirty, or the other way round; or are the plates plain, rather than also advertising the dealership that sold the car?

In other situations it will be less obvious that the vehicle has been stolen. You might need to check if there any differences between the identifying marks of the car (VICE) and the details of the identifying features which appear on PNC. In training, you may be asked to follow the procedure outlined below.

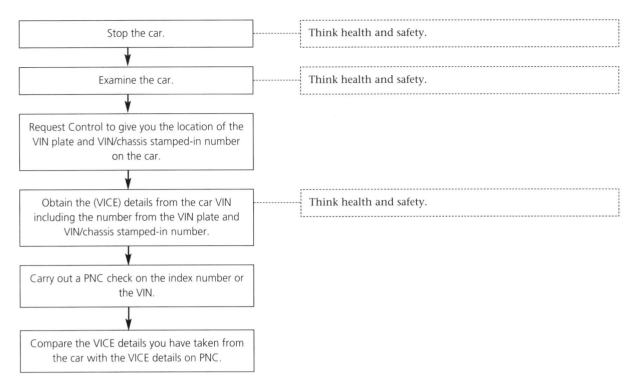

Are there any differences in the:

- colour;
- model;
- make;
- VICE identifying features?

If there are any differences, then you may have detected a stolen vehicle. If you need the vehicle examined still further, you may need to request attendance from a force vehicle examiner.

TASK 4

In the above flow chart, references are made to:

- stopping the car;
- examining the car;
- locating the VIN and VIN/chassis number.

Find out:

1. what powers or regulations allow you to stop and examine a car;
2. what regulations require the car to be equipped with a VIN or chassis number.

9.7 Taking a Conveyance Without the Owner's Consent or Authority (TWOC)

This offence is described within s 12 of the Theft Act 1968. Taking a conveyance is a very common offence in England and Wales and unfortunately, modern technology has so far failed to deter criminals from this activity. The offence is often referred to as joyriding, especially in the media. It was created as a separate offence (from theft itself) in the Theft Act 1968, because although the suspects take the vehicle, they do not have the intention permanently to deprive the owner of it, so they cannot be committing the offence of s 1 theft. The offence may also result in damage and injury, so we also describe a second offence of 'aggravated vehicle taking'.

Some of the relevant legislation refers to 'conveyances'. A **conveyance** is any equipment constructed or adapted for the carriage of a person or persons whether by land, water, or air. It does not include a conveyance constructed or adapted for carrying items other than people, such as the pedestrian-controlled vehicle used by postal workers to transport mail. Pedal cycles are not included under this legislation either; cycle theft is covered by separate legislation described in section 9.7.2 below.

Other legislation refers to **mechanically-propelled vehicles**. A mechanically-propelled vehicle is not defined in law but would include any vehicle which is:

- powered by a mechanical means; and
- does **not** have to be intended or adapted for use on the roads, examples might be an off-road quad bike or a scrambler.

A mechanically-propelled vehicle should not be confused with a **motor vehicle**, defined under s 185 of the Road Traffic Act 1968 as 'a mechanically-propelled vehicle intended or adapted for use on the road'.

Section 12 of the Theft Act 1968 states it is an offence for a person:

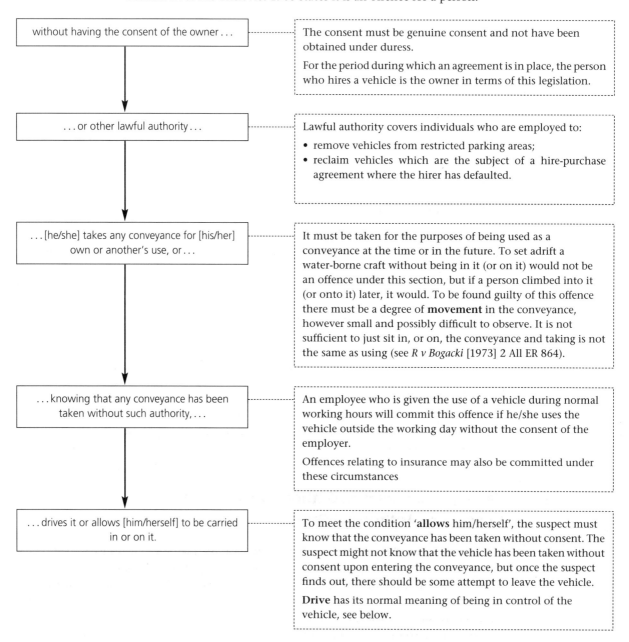

| without having the consent of the owner... | The consent must be genuine consent and not have been obtained under duress.

For the period during which an agreement is in place, the person who hires a vehicle is the owner in terms of this legislation. |

| ...or other lawful authority... | Lawful authority covers individuals who are employed to:

• remove vehicles from restricted parking areas;
• reclaim vehicles which are the subject of a hire-purchase agreement where the hirer has defaulted. |

| ...[he/she] takes any conveyance for [his/her] own or another's use, or... | It must be taken for the purposes of being used as a conveyance at the time or in the future. To set adrift a water-borne craft without being in it (or on it) would not be an offence under this section, but if a person climbed into it (or onto it) later, it would. To be found guilty of this offence there must be a degree of **movement** in the conveyance, however small and possibly difficult to observe. It is not sufficient to just sit in, or on, the conveyance and taking is not the same as using (see *R v Bogacki* [1973] 2 All ER 864). |

| ...knowing that any conveyance has been taken without such authority,... | An employee who is given the use of a vehicle during normal working hours will commit this offence if he/she uses the vehicle outside the working day without the consent of the employer.

Offences relating to insurance may also be committed under these circumstances |

| ...drives it or allows [him/herself] to be carried in or on it. | To meet the condition '**allows** him/herself', the suspect must know that the conveyance has been taken without consent. The suspect might not know that the vehicle has been taken without consent upon entering the conveyance, but once the suspect finds out, there should be some attempt to leave the vehicle.

Drive has its normal meaning of being in control of the vehicle, see below. |

There is no definition of **driving** or **driven** within the legislation but there are precedents which provide guidelines. The decision finally rests with the court and is a question of fact. The court will consider:

- the degree to which the person had control over the direction and movement of the vehicle;
- the period of time during which the person had control;
- the point at which the person stopped the driving;
- the use of the vehicle's controls by the person in order to direct its movement.

As a possible defence, s 12(6) of the Theft Act 1968 states that a person does not commit this offence if he/she

(1) believes that [he/she] has the consent of
  - the owner, or
  - other lawful authority to do it, or
(2) has a mistaken belief of such lawful authority or consent of the owner.

This offence is triable summarily and the penalty is six months' imprisonment and/or a fine.

The basic offence of taking a conveyance cannot be attempted (see section 9.22 of this Handbook), as the offence is not indictable; more appropriate offences might include vehicle interference or tampering with a motor vehicle (see section 9.8). Note that theft is an indictable offence, so the offence of theft could also be considered if some form of attempt has taken place.

9.7.1 Aggravated Vehicle-Taking

A further offence may have been committed under s 12A(1) of the Theft Act 1968 if damage or injury is caused when a vehicle is taken without consent. Injuries may also include shock. Damage includes any damage caused during the whole incident and does not have to be deliberately-inflicted damage; it could be accidental damage. Note that the damage can be caused to any property including the vehicle itself.

Section 12(A)(1) of the Theft Act 1968 states that a person commits the offence of aggravated vehicle-taking if he/she first of all commits:

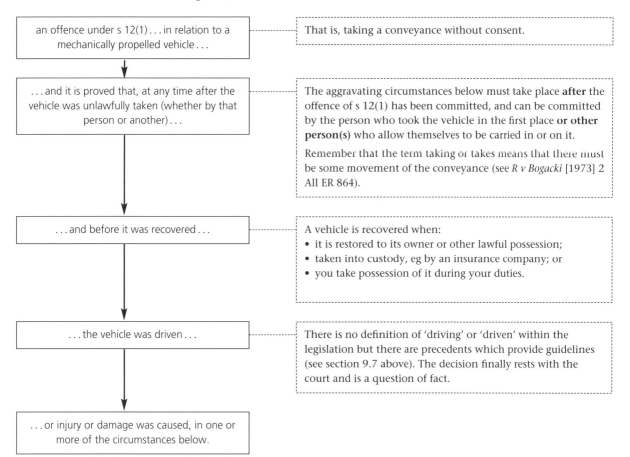

| an offence under s 12(1)...in relation to a mechanically propelled vehicle... | That is, taking a conveyance without consent. |

| ...and it is proved that, at any time after the vehicle was unlawfully taken (whether by that person or another)... | The aggravating circumstances below must take place **after** the offence of s 12(1) has been committed, and can be committed by the person who took the vehicle in the first place **or other person(s)** who allow themselves to be carried in or on it. Remember that the term taking or takes means that there must be some movement of the conveyance (see *R v Bogacki* [1973] 2 All ER 864). |

| ...and before it was recovered... | A vehicle is recovered when: • it is restored to its owner or other lawful possession; • taken into custody, eg by an insurance company; or • you take possession of it during your duties. |

| ...the vehicle was driven... | There is no definition of 'driving' or 'driven' within the legislation but there are precedents which provide guidelines (see section 9.7 above). The decision finally rests with the court and is a question of fact. |

| ...or injury or damage was caused, in one or more of the circumstances below. | |

The aggravating circumstances for this offence are that:

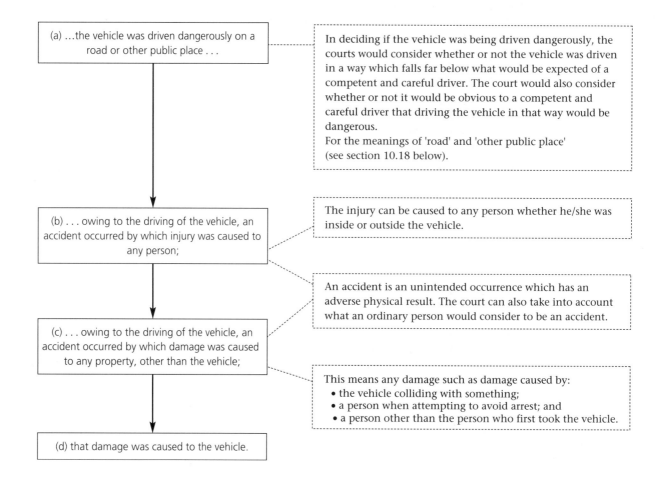

| (a) ...the vehicle was driven dangerously on a road or other public place . . . | In deciding if the vehicle was being driven dangerously, the courts would consider whether or not the vehicle was driven in a way which falls far below what would be expected of a competent and careful driver. The court would also consider whether or not it would be obvious to a competent and careful driver that driving the vehicle in that way would be dangerous.
For the meanings of 'road' and 'other public place' (see section 10.18 below). |

| (b) . . . owing to the driving of the vehicle, an accident occurred by which injury was caused to any person; | The injury can be caused to any person whether he/she was inside or outside the vehicle. |
| | An accident is an unintended occurrence which has an adverse physical result. The court can also take into account what an ordinary person would consider to be an accident. |

| (c) . . . owing to the driving of the vehicle, an accident occurred by which damage was caused to any property, other than the vehicle; | This means any damage such as damage caused by:
• the vehicle colliding with something;
• a person when attempting to avoid arrest; and
• a person other than the person who first took the vehicle. |

(d) that damage was caused to the vehicle.

Possible defences include:

- the aggravating circumstances occurred before the suspect committed the basic offence of taking the vehicle;
- the suspect was not in, on, or in the immediate vicinity of the vehicle when that driving, accident, or damage occurred.

Immediate vicinity is not defined by the legislation and therefore it will be for the court to determine in each case.

The suspect will need to demonstrate on the balance of probabilities that the aggravating factors occurred before he/she committed the basic offence of 'taking a conveyance'. Even if the suspect can disprove aggravating factors, he/she can still be found guilty of the basic offence.

This offence is triable either way:

- Summarily; six months' imprisonment and/or a fine.
- On indictment; two years' imprisonment and/or a fine.

If the accident (under s 12A(2)(b)) caused death, the penalty is 14 years' imprisonment.

9.7.2 Theft of Pedal Cycles

A pedal cycle is not a conveyance for the purposes of s 12(1) of the Theft Act 1968, so the theft of cycles cannot be covered by s 12(1) (taking a conveyance without consent). However, s 12(5) of the Theft Act 1968 states it is an offence for a person:

> without having the consent of the owner or other lawful authority [to take] a pedal cycle for [his/her] own or another's use, or to ride a pedal cycle knowing it to have been taken without such authority.

The defence for this offence is the same as for ss 12(1) and 12A(1) of the Theft Act 1968.

The penalty for this offence is six months' imprisonment and/or a fine.

TASK 5

Approximately 1,000 vehicles are taken without the owner's consent in the UK every day. Find out the answers to the following questions from your area to assist you to trace stolen vehicles:

- What type of vehicle is most often taken in your area?
- What time of the day are these vehicles taken?
- Where are they taken from?
- Where are they abandoned?

9.8 Interference and Tampering with Motor Vehicles

When a suspect takes a conveyance without the consent of the owner, in many cases he/she will go through a process of selecting a vehicle, gaining entry either forcibly or by trying door handles, overcoming anti-theft devices such as alarms and steering locks, and then applying a technique such as hot wiring to start the engine. This process inevitably takes time, and sometimes the suspect can be apprehended before the vehicle is taken. However, TWOC is a summary offence (and therefore cannot be attempted under s 1(1) of the Criminal Attempts Act 1981, see section 9.22). Therefore, the Criminal Attempts Act 1981 Act includes a specific offence of 'interference and tampering with motor vehicles'.

9.8.1 Interference

The law surrounding offences concerned with interfering with motor vehicles is largely to be found in s 9 of the Criminal Attempts Act 1981. In everyday language, a person is interfering with a motor vehicle when it is apparent that he/she is attempting to commit a crime such as stealing the car. However, actually proving intent is tricky. In section 5.10, we discussed the two main building blocks to a criminal act: actus reus, that is the act itself, and mens rea, an intention to commit an act. In this case, the act cannot simply be preparation but needs to go further than this. Unfortunately, case law provides us with little guidance on what interference actually means in practice.

Nonetheless, s 9(1) of the Criminal Attempts Act 1981 states that it is an offence for a person to interfere:

- 'with a motor vehicle or trailer'; or
- 'with anything carried in or on a motor vehicle or trailer';

with the intention of committing:

- 'theft of the motor vehicle or part of it';
- 'theft of anything carried in or on the motor vehicle or trailer'; and
- the offence of taking a conveyance.

Note that although you need to prove that the suspect had one of the three intentions, you do not need to prove which particular one.

This is a summary offence and the penalty is three months' imprisonment and/or a fine.

9.8.2 Tampering

The act of tampering is more readily understood than interference. Section 25(1) of the Road Traffic Act 1988 states it is an offence for a person:

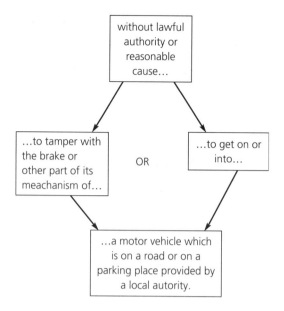

This is a summary offence and the penalty is a fine.

9.8.3 Holding or Getting onto a Motor Vehicle

The final offence in this section concerns 'holding or getting onto a vehicle in order to be towed or carried'. Section 26(1) of the Road Traffic Act 1988 states it is an offence for a person who:

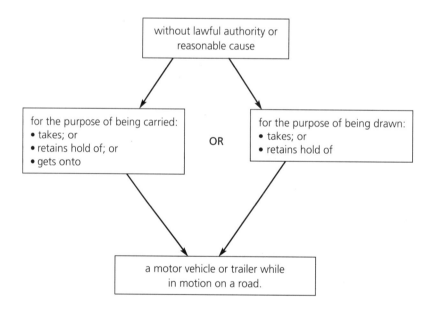

This is a summary offence and the penalty is a fine.

TASK 6

Which of the following would constitute an offence of interfering with a motor vehicle?

1. Trying to removing a horse box from the tow bar of a vehicle in order to steal the horse box.
2. Attempting to remove a go-kart from the garden of a house in order to steal it.
3. Opening the unlocked front driver's door of a car to steal a CD player in the dashboard.
4. Putting super glue in a car door lock to prevent the owner from opening the door.

9.9 Handling Stolen Goods

Section 22 of the Theft Act 1968 states that:

> a person [handles stolen goods] if otherwise than in the course of stealing knowing or believing them to be stolen goods [he/she]
>
> i. dishonestly receives the goods, or
> ii. dishonestly undertakes their retention, removal, disposal or realisation by or for the benefit of another person, or
> iii. dishonestly assists in their retention, removal, disposal or realisation by or for the benefit of another person, or
>
> arranges to do (i), (ii) or (iii) above.

There are three types of offences for which goods are considered to be stolen within the meaning of handling stolen goods. These are:

1. Blackmail (s 21, Theft Act 1968);
2. Fraud (s1, Fraud Act 2006); and
3. Theft (s 1, Theft Act 1968).

Let us first consider the meaning of the terms 'handling', 'stolen', and 'goods'. The meanings of some other terms used in the Act are shown later.

9.9.1 The Distinction between 'Handling' and 'Theft'

It is important to distinguish clearly between 'handling' and 'theft'. To help you decide whether or not the goods were handled (otherwise than in the course of stealing), you have to decide whether or not the actions of the suspect followed on from the theft continuously, that is without a break, and consider whether:

- the theft was complete; and
- there was a break in the proceedings; and
- the suspect became involved only after the theft had occurred.

For example, Jo (a prolific shoplifter), goes to The White Goods electrical store in the High Street. Jo manages to steal two digital radios from the store, goes outside, and hides them in a rubbish bin to evade detection. An accomplice then takes the radios. The table below presents a number of different scenarios and shows whether the activity amounts to handling or theft.

Offences committed by an accomplice to theft?

The accomplice	Offence committed by the accomplice	Other factors to be taken into account
Is waiting by pre-arrangement and takes the radios away.	Theft	
Arrives half an hour later, by pre-arrangement, and takes the radios away.	Theft	Particularly if the proceeds are to be shared out between Jo and the accomplice.
	Handling	May be considered if the accomplice subsequently pays Jo for the goods.
Is told where the radios are, but only after they have been stolen. The accomplice then goes to collect the radios. The accomplice is not involved until after the radios have been taken.	Handling	

A thief can become a handler of the property that he/she originally stole, but only if he/she loses control of the property and later decides (whilst the goods can still be referred to as stolen goods) to have dealings with the property once again.

9.9.2 Knowing or Believing that Goods are Stolen Goods

Another key issue for this offence is that the person handling the stolen goods must know or believe that the goods are stolen. In the legislation, if someone knows or believes that the goods are stolen, he/she is said to be handling the goods dishonestly. The court has to decide what is dishonest by everyday standards, and whether the suspect was aware he/she was dishonest by those standards. Dishonesty in relation to handling goods would **not** include:

• believing he/she has a right to the property in law;
• believing he/she would have the owner's consent;
• believing that the owner cannot be traced.

The difference between knowing and believing is not clear cut; the following points could be considered:

• **Knowing** them to be stolen goods means having actually been told that the goods are stolen by the thief or burglar or someone with first-hand knowledge.
• **Believing** them to be stolen goods means being uncertain as to whether or not the goods are stolen, but then thinking there is no other likely explanation in those particular circumstances (see *R v Hall* [1985] 1 QB 496).

Knowledge or belief could be proved by:

• direct evidence from the thief;
• admission by the handler; or
• circumstantial evidence, such as non-standard packaging or where they were being sold.

9.9.3 The Meaning of Goods

The Theft Act (s 34(2)(b)) extends the definition of goods to:

> include money and every other description of property, except land, and includes things severed from the land by stealing.

Under s 24(2) of the Theft Act 1968, goods are also the proceeds of the disposal of the original stolen items. The proceeds could be money or other items which have been received in exchange for the items that were originally stolen. After the original theft there is often a whole chain of events, and each of the handlers in this process commits the offence of handling stolen goods, so long as each has guilty knowledge (*mens rea*) that the goods he/she is handling represent the original stolen goods. The chain will only be broken when a person is **unaware** that the goods he/she receives represent the original stolen goods. If, for example, a person who is unaware of the origin of the goods sells or exchanges those goods, whatever he/she receives cannot be considered stolen goods because without the person having guilty knowledge, the proceeds can no longer represent the original stolen goods.

Section 22 of the Theft Act 1968 states:

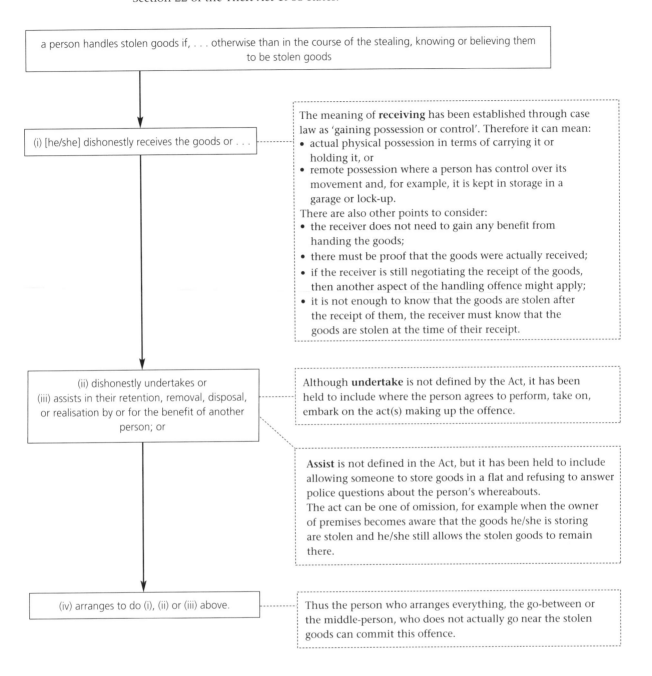

a person handles stolen goods if, . . . otherwise than in the course of the stealing, knowing or believing them to be stolen goods

(i) [he/she] dishonestly receives the goods or . . .

The meaning of **receiving** has been established through case law as 'gaining possession or control'. Therefore it can mean:
- actual physical possession in terms of carrying it or holding it, or
- remote possession where a person has control over its movement and, for example, it is kept in storage in a garage or lock-up.

There are also other points to consider:
- the receiver does not need to gain any benefit from handing the goods;
- there must be proof that the goods were actually received;
- if the receiver is still negotiating the receipt of the goods, then another aspect of the handling offence might apply;
- it is not enough to know that the goods are stolen after the receipt of them, the receiver must know that the goods are stolen at the time of their receipt.

(ii) dishonestly undertakes or
(iii) assists in their retention, removal, disposal, or realisation by or for the benefit of another person; or

Although **undertake** is not defined by the Act, it has been held to include where the person agrees to perform, take on, embark on the act(s) making up the offence.

Assist is not defined in the Act, but it has been held to include allowing someone to store goods in a flat and refusing to answer police questions about the person's whereabouts.

The act can be one of omission, for example when the owner of premises becomes aware that the goods he/she is storing are stolen and he/she still allows the stolen goods to remain there.

(iv) arranges to do (i), (ii) or (iii) above.

Thus the person who arranges everything, the go-between or the middle-person, who does not actually go near the stolen goods can commit this offence.

The following is an explanation of the various key terms used within the Act:

Benefit	Some kind of an advantage, although the person does not have to be aware of it at the time, nor it does not have to be financial.
Another	The term 'another' must refer to someone who is not the defendant or one of the co-accused.
Retention	Continuing to possess something (especially when someone else wants it).
Removal	Take something away from the place where it was.
Disposal	Passing on, getting rid of, giving away.
Realization	To obtain an amount of money or profit by selling something.

349

To prove 'undertaking' or 'assisting' (or arranging to undertake or assist), you must prove that the actions taken were for the benefit of another person. This does not have to be proved for a charge of **receiving** stolen goods.

This offence is triable either way:

- Summarily; six months' imprisonment and/or a fine.
- On indictment; fourteen years' imprisonment.

TASK 7

With regard to handling stolen goods, which, if either, of the following statements is true?

1. For the purposes of committing an offence of handling, 'stolen goods' include money and every other description of property, except land, and include things severed from the land by stealing.
2. Property obtained as a result of a fraud under s 1 of the Fraud Act 2006 is considered to be 'stolen goods' for the purposes of the offence of handling.

Choose one of the following responses:

1. statement 1 only;
2. statement 2 only;
3. both statements;
4. neither statement.

9.10 Abstracting Electricity

Electricity does not fall within the definition of property in the Theft Act 1968, and therefore, in legal terms, it cannot be stolen. Instead, 'abstracting' is the legal term used for the offence of illegally taking and using electricity, and is covered under s 13 of the Theft Act 1968. As electricity is not property within the Theft Act 1968, an entry into premises with the sole intention of abstracting electricity will not amount to burglary.

Section 13 of the Theft Act 1968 states that it is an offence for a person:

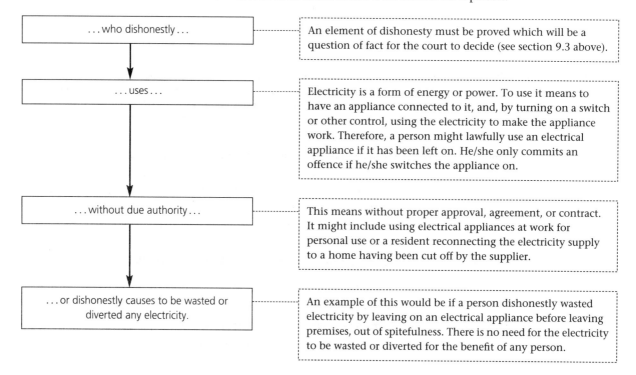

. . . who dishonestly . . .	An element of dishonesty must be proved which will be a question of fact for the court to decide (see section 9.3 above).
. . . uses . . .	Electricity is a form of energy or power. To use it means to have an appliance connected to it, and, by turning on a switch or other control, using the electricity to make the appliance work. Therefore, a person might lawfully use an electrical appliance if it has been left on. He/she only commits an offence if he/she switches the appliance on.
. . . without due authority . . .	This means without proper approval, agreement, or contract. It might include using electrical appliances at work for personal use or a resident reconnecting the electricity supply to a home having been cut off by the supplier.
. . . or dishonestly causes to be wasted or diverted any electricity.	An example of this would be if a person dishonestly wasted electricity by leaving on an electrical appliance before leaving premises, out of spitefulness. There is no need for the electricity to be wasted or diverted for the benefit of any person.

The electricity does not have to be mains electricity to be abstracted. It can be electricity from a battery in a caravan for example.

This offence is triable either way:

- Summarily; six months' imprisonment and/or a fine.
- On indictment; five years' imprisonment.

9.11 Going Equipped

This offence is described in s 25 of the Theft Act 1968. A wide range of articles are used to carry out burglary, or theft, such as:

- items used for the removal of security tags on clothing;
- instruments used for gaining entry to vehicles, including keys;
- tools used to gain entry to buildings or vehicles.

The offence is not committed simply by the suspect being in possession of the articles. In order to commit the offence of going equipped, the suspect must have possession of the articles **and** be on his/her way to carry out the theft or burglary (see *R v Ellames* [1974] 3 All ER 130). The offence cannot be committed when coming away from the crime. A direct connection to a specific burglary or theft does not need to be established. The only proof that is required is that the article is intended to be used to commit crime by the suspect (or another person).

Section 25(1) of the Theft Act 1968 states it is an offence for a person:

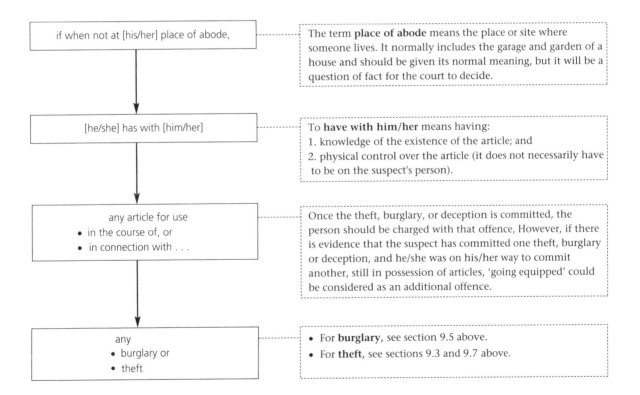

if when not at [his/her] place of abode, — The term **place of abode** means the place or site where someone lives. It normally includes the garage and garden of a house and should be given its normal meaning, but it will be a question of fact for the court to decide.

[he/she] has with [him/her] — To **have with him/her** means having:
1. knowledge of the existence of the article; and
2. physical control over the article (it does not necessarily have to be on the suspect's person).

any article for use
- in the course of, or
- in connection with . . .

Once the theft, burglary, or deception is committed, the person should be charged with that offence, However, if there is evidence that the suspect has committed one theft, burglary or deception, and he/she was on his/her way to commit another, still in possession of articles, 'going equipped' could be considered as an additional offence.

any
- burglary or
- theft

- For **burglary**, see section 9.5 above.
- For **theft**, see sections 9.3 and 9.7 above.

This offence is triable either way:

- Summarily; six months' imprisonment and/or a fine.
- On indictment; three years' imprisonment.

TASK 8

1. At each of your BCU briefings throughout the past week, you have been informed about a series of car thefts in your area. One night, you are on patrol when you enter the street in which you know a prolific car thief lives. You see someone in a car switch off its lights and park in the street outside the home of the known car thief. You speak to the person in the car and notice gloves, a large bunch of approximately 40 car keys and a short length of scaffolding pole on the passenger's seat.

   What will you say to the driver? Could the offence of 'going equipped' have been committed? What questions do you need to ask in order to establish if this offence has actually been committed?

2. Which of the following offences match the definitions of 'theft' or 'burglary':
   (a) robbery;
   (b) taking a conveyance;
   (c) abstracting electricity?

   Is it:
   (i)   (a) and (b) only
   (ii) (a) and (c) only
   (iii) (b) and (c) only
   (iv) (a), (b), and (c)?

9.12   Fraud Offences

As we discussed in section 9.3, theft involves the dishonest appropriation of property belonging to another. In addition to theft itself, the various Theft Acts (1968, 1978, and 1996) also contained sections addressing aspects of what we tend to call fraud and deception. This proved confusing and much of the law surrounding the crime of fraud is now encapsulated instead in the Fraud Act 2006, which came into effect in January 2007. (Given its recency, note that there are as yet no precedents to help with a deeper understanding of some parts of the new fraud legislation. For example, it might well be that an intention to carry out a 'phishing' crime could be prosecuted as a s2(4) offence but this has not yet been tested.)

Section 1 of the Fraud Act 2006 states that the offence of fraud can be committed in one or more of three distinctive ways:

1. By **false representation**, eg returning stolen goods to a shop to try to obtain a refund (s2 Fraud Act 2006).
2. By **failing to disclose information** eg omitting important information when applying for a job or health insurance (s3 Fraud Act 2006).
3. Through **abuse of position**, eg whilst driving a local authority mini-bus, demanding fares from local residents when the service is actually free (s2 Fraud Act 2006).

9.12.1   False Representation

Section 2 Fraud Act 2006 states that a person commits an offence if s/he:

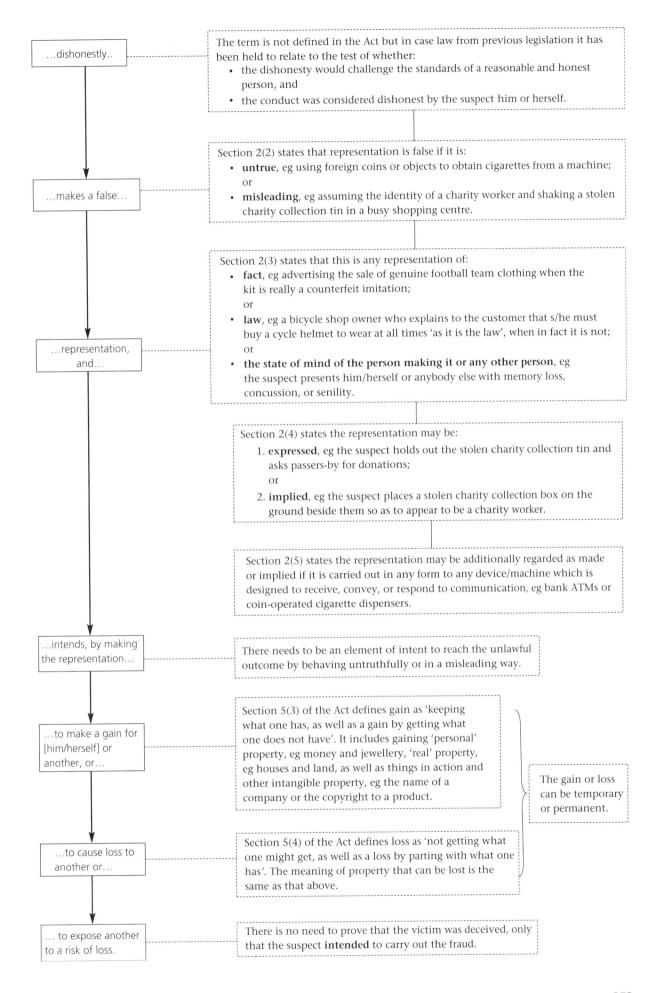

...dishonestly..

The term is not defined in the Act but in case law from previous legislation it has been held to relate to the test of whether:
- the dishonesty would challenge the standards of a reasonable and honest person, and
- the conduct was considered dishonest by the suspect him or herself.

...makes a false...

Section 2(2) states that representation is false if it is:
- **untrue**, eg using foreign coins or objects to obtain cigarettes from a machine; or
- **misleading**, eg assuming the identity of a charity worker and shaking a stolen charity collection tin in a busy shopping centre.

...representation, and...

Section 2(3) states that this is any representation of:
- **fact**, eg advertising the sale of genuine football team clothing when the kit is really a counterfeit imitation; or
- **law**, eg a bicycle shop owner who explains to the customer that s/he must buy a cycle helmet to wear at all times 'as it is the law', when in fact it is not; or
- **the state of mind of the person making it or any other person**, eg the suspect presents him/herself or anybody else with memory loss, concussion, or senility.

Section 2(4) states the representation may be:
1. **expressed**, eg the suspect holds out the stolen charity collection tin and asks passers-by for donations; or
2. **implied**, eg the suspect places a stolen charity collection box on the ground beside them so as to appear to be a charity worker.

Section 2(5) states the representation may be additionally regarded as made or implied if it is carried out in any form to any device/machine which is designed to receive, convey, or respond to communication, eg bank ATMs or coin-operated cigarette dispensers.

...intends, by making the representation...

There needs to be an element of intent to reach the unlawful outcome by behaving untruthfully or in a misleading way.

...to make a gain for [him/herself] or another, or...

Section 5(3) of the Act defines gain as 'keeping what one has, as well as a gain by getting what one does not have'. It includes gaining 'personal' property, eg money and jewellery, 'real' property, eg houses and land, as well as things in action and other intangible property, eg the name of a company or the copyright to a product.

The gain or loss can be temporary or permanent.

...to cause loss to another or...

Section 5(4) of the Act defines loss as 'not getting what one might get, as well as a loss by parting with what one has'. The meaning of property that can be lost is the same as that above.

... to expose another to a risk of loss.

There is no need to prove that the victim was deceived, only that the suspect **intended** to carry out the fraud.

9.12.2   Failure to Disclose Information

Section 3 of the Fraud Act 2006 states that a person commits an offence if s/he:

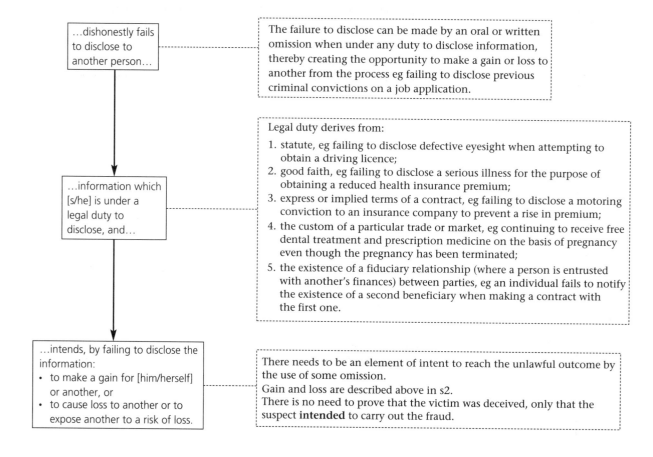

...dishonestly fails to disclose to another person...

The failure to disclose can be made by an oral or written omission when under any duty to disclose information, thereby creating the opportunity to make a gain or loss to another from the process eg failing to disclose previous criminal convictions on a job application.

...information which [s/he] is under a legal duty to disclose, and...

Legal duty derives from:

1. statute, eg failing to disclose defective eyesight when attempting to obtain a driving licence;
2. good faith, eg failing to disclose a serious illness for the purpose of obtaining a reduced health insurance premium;
3. express or implied terms of a contract, eg failing to disclose a motoring conviction to an insurance company to prevent a rise in premium;
4. the custom of a particular trade or market, eg continuing to receive free dental treatment and prescription medicine on the basis of pregnancy even though the pregnancy has been terminated;
5. the existence of a fiduciary relationship (where a person is entrusted with another's finances) between parties, eg an individual fails to notify the existence of a second beneficiary when making a contract with the first one.

...intends, by failing to disclose the information:
- to make a gain for [him/herself] or another, or
- to cause loss to another or to expose another to a risk of loss.

There needs to be an element of intent to reach the unlawful outcome by the use of some omission.
Gain and loss are described above in s2.
There is no need to prove that the victim was deceived, only that the suspect **intended** to carry out the fraud.

9.12.3 Abuse of Position

Section 4 of the Fraud Act 2006 states that a person commits an offence if s/he occupies a position in which h/she:

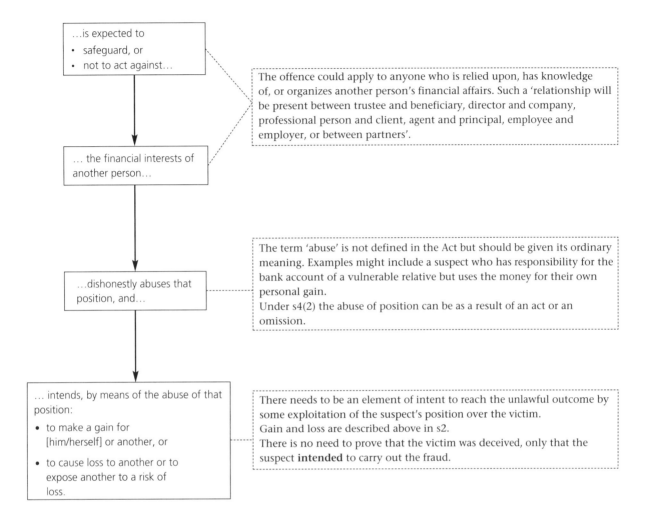

This offence is triable either way:

- Summarily; twelve months imprisonment and/or a fine;
- On indictment; ten years imprisonment and/or a fine.

9.12.4 Possession, Making or Supplying of Articles

Just as with burglary (see 9.11), it is also possible for a person to commit an offence if they are 'going equipped' to carry out a fraud, rather than actually having committed the fraud itself. In this context, going equipped means either:

1. Possession or control of articles for use in frauds (s 6 of the Fraud Act 2006).
2. Making or supplying articles for use in frauds (s 7 of the Fraud Act 2006).

Section 6 of the Fraud Act 2006 states that a person commits an offence if s/he:

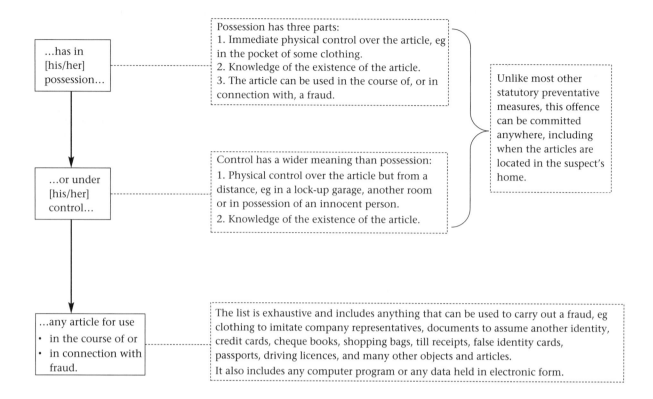

...has in [his/her] possession...

Possession has three parts:
1. Immediate physical control over the article, eg in the pocket of some clothing.
2. Knowledge of the existence of the article.
3. The article can be used in the course of, or in connection with, a fraud.

...or under [his/her] control...

Control has a wider meaning than possession:
1. Physical control over the article but from a distance, eg in a lock-up garage, another room or in possession of an innocent person.
2. Knowledge of the existence of the article.

Unlike most other statutory preventative measures, this offence can be committed anywhere, including when the articles are located in the suspect's home.

...any article for use
• in the course of or
• in connection with fraud.

The list is exhaustive and includes anything that can be used to carry out a fraud, eg clothing to imitate company representatives, documents to assume another identity, credit cards, cheque books, shopping bags, till receipts, false identity cards, passports, driving licences, and many other objects and articles.
It also includes any computer program or any data held in electronic form.

This offence is triable either way:

• Summarily; twelve months' imprisonment and/or a fine;
• On indictment; five years' imprisonment and/or a fine.

Section 7 of the Fraud Act 2006 states that a person commits an offence if s/he:

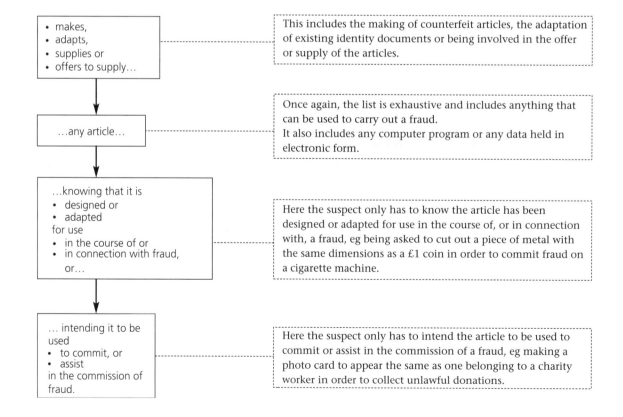

• makes,
• adapts,
• supplies or
• offers to supply...

This includes the making of counterfeit articles, the adaptation of existing identity documents or being involved in the offer or supply of the articles.

...any article...

Once again, the list is exhaustive and includes anything that can be used to carry out a fraud.
It also includes any computer program or any data held in electronic form.

...knowing that it is
• designed or
• adapted
for use
• in the course of or
• in connection with fraud,
  or...

Here the suspect only has to know the article has been designed or adapted for use in the course of, or in connection with, a fraud, eg being asked to cut out a piece of metal with the same dimensions as a £1 coin in order to commit fraud on a cigarette machine.

... intending it to be used
• to commit, or
• assist
in the commission of fraud.

Here the suspect only has to intend the article to be used to commit or assist in the commission of a fraud, eg making a photo card to appear the same as one belonging to a charity worker in order to collect unlawful donations.

Under s 1 of the PACE Act 1984, you have the power to search for articles made or adapted for use in fraud (see 8.5.3 Items You May Search for under 'Stop, Search and Detain').

This offence is triable either way:

- Summarily; twelve months' imprisonment and/or a fine;
- On indictment; ten years' imprisonment and/or a fine.

9.12.5 Fraudulent Obtaining of Services

In the previous fraud offences of false representation, failing to disclose information, and abuse of position, the gain or loss related to tangible and intangible property. However, in circumstances where a service has been provided, eg a taxi ride or a stay in a hotel room, there is no gain or loss of property, only the provision of a facility or service. For this reason, an additional offence is provided for by the Fraud Act 2006 when a service is obtained by dishonest means.

Section 11 of the Fraud Act 2006 states that a person commits an offence if s/he:

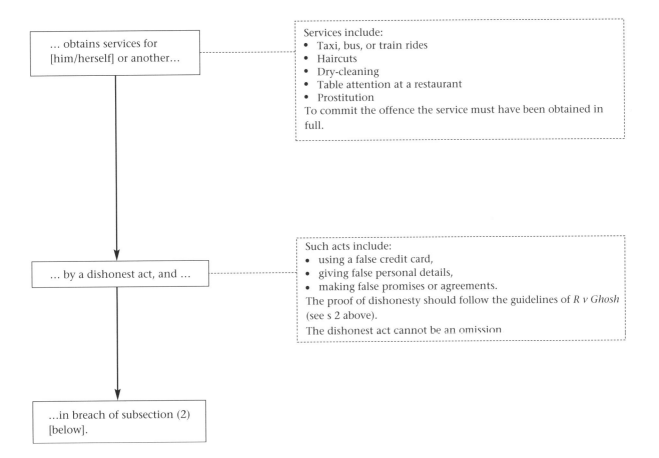

... obtains services for [him/herself] or another...

Services include:
- Taxi, bus, or train rides
- Haircuts
- Dry-cleaning
- Table attention at a restaurant
- Prostitution

To commit the offence the service must have been obtained in full.

... by a dishonest act, and ...

Such acts include:
- using a false credit card,
- giving false personal details,
- making false promises or agreements.

The proof of dishonesty should follow the guidelines of *R v Ghosh* (see s 2 above).

The dishonest act cannot be an omission

...in breach of subsection (2) [below].

Subsection (2) of s 11 of the Fraud Act 2006 states that a person obtains services in breach of this subsection if:

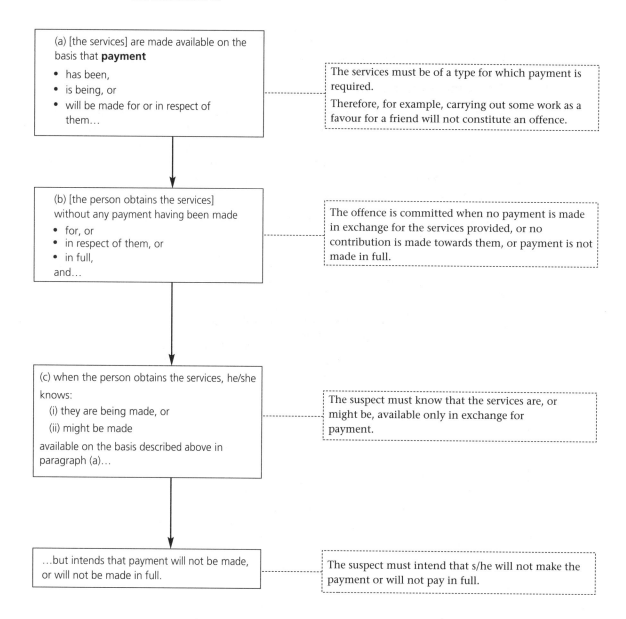

(a) [the services] are made available on the basis that **payment**
- has been,
- is being, or
- will be made for or in respect of them...

The services must be of a type for which payment is required.

Therefore, for example, carrying out some work as a favour for a friend will not constitute an offence.

(b) [the person obtains the services] without any payment having been made
- for, or
- in respect of them, or
- in full,
and...

The offence is committed when no payment is made in exchange for the services provided, or no contribution is made towards them, or payment is not made in full.

(c) when the person obtains the services, he/she knows:
  (i) they are being made, or
  (ii) might be made
available on the basis described above in paragraph (a)...

The suspect must know that the services are, or might be, available only in exchange for payment.

...but intends that payment will not be made, or will not be made in full.

The suspect must intend that s/he will not make the payment or will not pay in full.

This offence is triable either way:

- Summarily; twelve months' imprisonment and/or a fine;
- On indictment; five years' imprisonment and/or a fine.

9.12.6 Making Off Without Payment ('Bilking')

If no fraud is practised but goods are still obtained dishonestly and without payment, it is an offence under s 3 of the Theft Act 1978 rather than fraud under s 1 of the Fraud Act 2006. For example, a person might fill up with petrol on the forecourt of a filling station with every intention of paying for the petrol, but on seeing the staff otherwise engaged and no other customers around, decide to drive off without paying. This particular offence is often referred to as 'bilking', a slang term which means to avoid payment.

Note that this offence only applies if 'payment on the spot' is the norm in that particular situation, such as collecting goods on which work has been done (for example, shoe repairs) or paying for a service which has been provided (for example, a restaurant meal). This offence does not cover circumstances in which a customer has a credit arrangement or a 'tab' with the service provider.

Section 3 of the Theft Act 1978, states that it is an offence for a person:

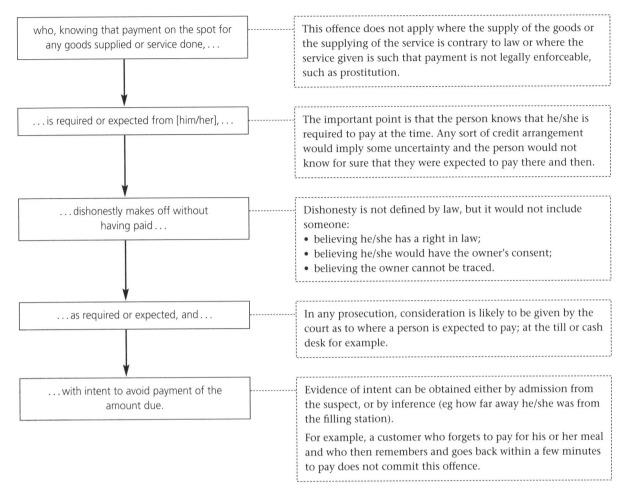

who, knowing that payment on the spot for any goods supplied or service done, . . .	This offence does not apply where the supply of the goods or the supplying of the service is contrary to law or where the service given is such that payment is not legally enforceable, such as prostitution.
. . . is required or expected from [him/her], . . .	The important point is that the person knows that he/she is required to pay at the time. Any sort of credit arrangement would imply some uncertainty and the person would not know for sure that they were expected to pay there and then.
. . . dishonestly makes off without having paid . . .	Dishonesty is not defined by law, but it would not include someone: • believing he/she has a right in law; • believing he/she would have the owner's consent; • believing the owner cannot be traced.
. . . as required or expected, and . . .	In any prosecution, consideration is likely to be given by the court as to where a person is expected to pay; at the till or cash desk for example.
. . . with intent to avoid payment of the amount due.	Evidence of intent can be obtained either by admission from the suspect, or by inference (eg how far away he/she was from the filling station). For example, a customer who forgets to pay for his or her meal and who then remembers and goes back within a few minutes to pay does not commit this offence.

This offence is triable either way and the penalty is:

• Summarily; six months' imprisonment and/or a fine.
• On indictment; two years' imprisonment and/or a fine.

TASK 9

At what stage of a visit to a restaurant are the following offences potentially committed by people who fail to pay for a meal?

• s 1 Fraud Act 2006;
• s 3 of the Theft Act 1978;
• s 11 Fraud Act 2006.

To answer the question, complete the table below by describing in the right hand column the likely actions and thought processes of the customers at each stage of the visit to the restaurant, linking these to s 1 and s 11 of the Fraud Act 2006 and s 3 of the Theft Act 1978. The case of *DPP v Ray* [1974] AC 370 may assist.

People enter the restaurant and order a meal.	
Having ordered the meal, they wait at the table for it to be served.	
The meal is served to the table.	
Having consumed the meal, they are expected to pay.	
They leave the restaurant.	

9.13 Unlawful Possession of a Controlled Drug

In this part of Chapter 9, we examine the most important piece of legislation available to the police and the CJS in countering the street-level use and distribution of illegal drugs. The legislation for the offence of 'unlawful possession of a controlled drug' is covered in s 5(2) of the Misuse of Drugs Act 1971. Drugs that are subject to legal control are referred to as **controlled drugs.** Some controlled drugs are addictive and/or dangerous, and the results of their misuse are obvious to us all. The Misuse of Drugs Act 1971 was enacted to curb the use of controlled drugs and to outlaw various actions by those people who are unlawfully in possession of them.

Unless you have a great deal of experience in relation to controlled drugs, you will initially find recognizing them very difficult as there are so many different shapes, colours, and sizes including pills, tablets, liquids, powders, and resins. Therefore, your first thoughts when finding such substances without pharmaceutical company packaging, is not to try and work out exactly what drug it is, but to suspect that the person may be in possession of controlled drugs.

A great number of criminal procedures are linked to drug-related activities, so you will be frequently faced with such situations. Remember, you must assess risk and hazard levels when dealing with people who have been taking drugs as they may behave unpredictably. Always be prepared to use your personal safety equipment; remember the possible consequences of contamination from bodily fluids or equipment used by a drug addict. The merest micro-cut from a sharp article contaminated by a transferable virus could infect you and cause a serious illness. Demonstration of appropriate health and safety measures will also help you meet the Safety First requirements of the PAC and NOS elements in Unit AF1.

9.13.1 What Is a Controlled Drug?

Drugs are controlled because of their effect on the human body, and are divided into classes A, B, and C (Misuse of Drugs Act 1971) according to the potential for harm they are thought to present to individuals and to society at large:

> **Class A** eg Ecstasy, Heroin, Cocaine, Crack Cocaine, 'Magic Mushrooms (containing Psilocin) and LSD.
> **Class B** eg Amphetamines and barbiturates.
> **Class C** eg Cannabis leaves, Cannabis resin, tranquilizers (such as Temazepan), and some painkillers.
>
> You will find a full list of controlled drugs via the website <http://www.drugs.gov.uk>.

A block of cannabis resin is normally the size of a glasses case and weighs about 9 ounces. Cannabis users normally buy an eighth (1/8) of an ounce at a time, with a street cost of approximately £15.

A wrap of coke (cocaine) with a street cost of about £45.

Crack cocaine is a form of cocaine. The street price is about £10 per 'rock'. A crack rock is about the size of a raisin.

(Photographs copyright LGC Limited 2007. Reproduced with permission)

9.13.2 Unlawful Possession

As a police officer in training, the most common offence that you will deal with in relation to the misuse of drugs is that of **unlawful possession**.

The Misuse of Drugs Regulations 2001 exempts some workers from the main offence of possession of a controlled drug. Regulation 5 provides a licence for some categories of worker that allows them to have drugs in their possession, for example a drug supplier to the pharmaceutical trade. Regulation 6 allows the following categories of worker to possess drugs whilst acting in the course of their duties:

- police officers;
- police support employees;
- customs officers;
- postal workers.

The remainder of the Regulations give exemptions to members of the medical profession and states the necessity to keep records in relation to drugs and to patients who have been lawfully prescribed drugs by a medical practitioner. Any other person (other than those listed in the Regulations) is therefore acting unlawfully if they possess a controlled drug.

It is an offence under s 5(2) Misuse of Drugs Act for a person unlawfully to:

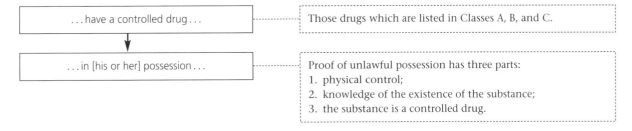

| ... have a controlled drug ... | Those drugs which are listed in Classes A, B, and C. |

| ... in [his or her] possession ... | Proof of unlawful possession has three parts: 1. physical control; 2. knowledge of the existence of the substance; 3. the substance is a controlled drug. |

9.13.3   The Three Parts of the Proof for Unlawful Possession

The following are the three parts required for proof of unlawful possession of a controlled drug. (The term 'part' is our own notation, not that of the law.)

Part 1—Physical control	The drug must be in the physical control of the suspect and the suspect must know where the drug is, though it does not have to be on his or her person. For example, if a suspect keeps drugs in a lock-up garage and gives the keys to an innocent person, the drugs remain in the suspect's control and possession but in the custody of the innocent person. However, if two people use a car and they both use drugs from the glove compartment, they both possess the drugs.
Part 2—Knowledge of the existence of the substance	The suspect must know of, or suspect the existence of, the substance in question. The substance could be in a cigarette packet or pouch, but under those circumstances you must show that the defendant not only had physical control over it, but that he/she knew it contained something as well.
Part 3—The substance is a controlled drug	The drug must be a controlled drug in Class A, B, or C.

As an example, imagine that whilst on Supervised Patrol you carry out a search of a man and a woman under the powers within the Misuse of Drugs Act 1971, and you find a cigarette lighter and aluminium foil with traces of brown powder on it in the man's pocket. After examination of the substance it is found to be heroin. To prove the offence of possession you must therefore show:

- that the foil was in his pocket;
- that he knew there was powder on the foil; and
- that after examination you had evidence that the powder was heroin.

9.13.4   Defences to Unlawful Possession of a Controlled Drug

Section 28 of the Misuse of Drugs Act 1971 provides a suspect with a potential defence in terms of satisfying Part 1 together with either Part 2 or Part 3 as described earlier. The flow charts below provide more explanation of the ways each part could be used in defence.

Part 1, remember, is about the suspect having **physical control** of the drug. His/her defence could be that he/she did not know it was there.

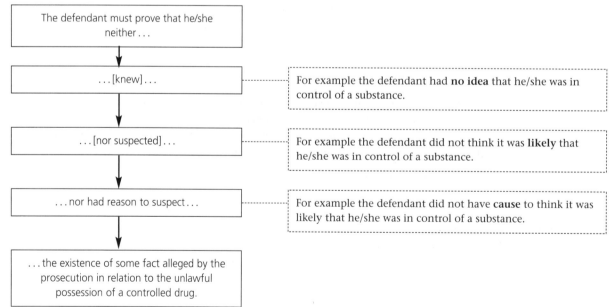

If the woman from our example above had slipped the aluminium foil into the man's pocket (before they were both searched) and the man **did not know** the woman had put it there, he could claim this defence.

In addition to Part 1, **either** Part 2 or Part 3 must be satisfied as part of the defence.

As explained above, **Part 2** is about the defendant's **knowledge of the existence** of the substance. A defence could be that he/she did not know about the existence of a controlled drug.

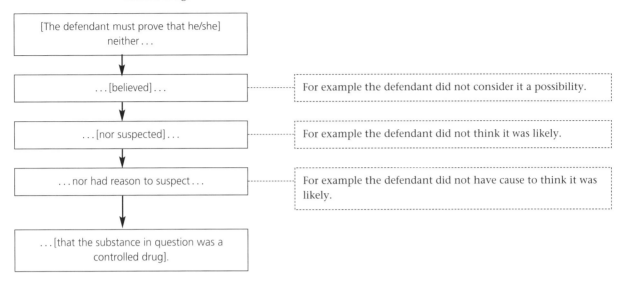

The man in our example who was subsequently found with the aluminium foil package in his pocket claimed that he did not know what the substance was, had never seen anything like it before, and would not be able to have a guess at what it was—he could claim this as a defence.

Part 3 is about the substance being a controlled drug. The defence could be that the defendant believed it was a drug he/she was lawfully entitled to possess:

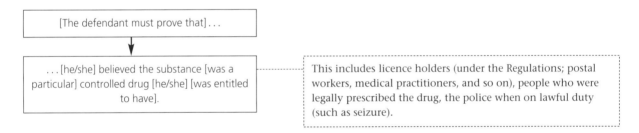

If the man (with the aluminium foil containing heroin in his pocket) held a licence under the Regulations to possess cocaine (unlikely, we know), and if he neither knew, nor suspected, nor had reason to suspect the substance was actually heroin (and not cocaine), he will have a defence, unless the prosecution can prove otherwise.

There are other circumstances which can also provide a defence (s 5(4), the Misuse of Drugs Act 1971), for example:

- parents temporarily possess drugs they have taken from their child (to prevent the child having unlawful possession);
- a member of the public finds a package of drugs and takes it to a police station.

The flowcharts below provide more details about these particular circumstances and the conditions that must be satisfied.

Preventing unlawful possession under s 5 of the Misuse of Drugs Act 1971 means:

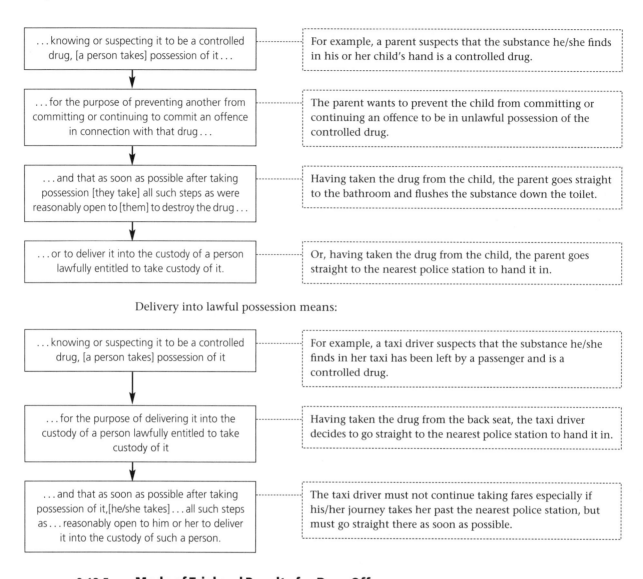

...knowing or suspecting it to be a controlled drug, [a person takes] possession of it...	For example, a parent suspects that the substance he/she finds in his or her child's hand is a controlled drug.
...for the purpose of preventing another from committing or continuing to commit an offence in connection with that drug...	The parent wants to prevent the child from committing or continuing an offence to be in unlawful possession of the controlled drug.
...and that as soon as possible after taking possession [they take] all such steps as were reasonably open to [them] to destroy the drug...	Having taken the drug from the child, the parent goes straight to the bathroom and flushes the substance down the toilet.
...or to deliver it into the custody of a person lawfully entitled to take custody of it.	Or, having taken the drug from the child, the parent goes straight to the nearest police station to hand it in.

Delivery into lawful possession means:

...knowing or suspecting it to be a controlled drug, [a person takes] possession of it	For example, a taxi driver suspects that the substance he/she finds in her taxi has been left by a passenger and is a controlled drug.
...for the purpose of delivering it into the custody of a person lawfully entitled to take custody of it	Having taken the drug from the back seat, the taxi driver decides to go straight to the nearest police station to hand it in.
...and that as soon as possible after taking possession of it,[he/she takes]...all such steps as...reasonably open to him or her to deliver it into the custody of such a person.	The taxi driver must not continue taking fares especially if his/her journey takes her past the nearest police station, but must go straight there as soon as possible.

9.13.5 Mode of Trial and Penalty for Drug Offences

Offences involving class A drugs are triable either way:

- Summarily; six months' imprisonment and/or prescribed fine.
- On indictment; seven years' imprisonment and/or fine.

Offences involving class B drugs are triable either way:

- Summarily; three months' imprisonment and/or fine.
- On indictment; five years' imprisonment and/or fine.

Offences involving class C drugs are triable either way:

- Summarily; three months' imprisonment and/or fine.
- On indictment; two years' imprisonment and/or fine.

> **TASK 10**
>
> Identify the common street names for the most common Class A, B, and C drugs in your policing area.

9.13.6 Power to Search

If you have 'reasonable grounds to suspect a person is in possession of a controlled drug', you can 'search that person' and his or her 'vehicle' and 'seize anything found' (s 23(2), Misuse of Drugs Act 1971).

9.14 Production, Supply, and Search for Controlled Drugs

Drugs legislation has been carefully worded so that it is not only the illegal end user of controlled drugs who is subject to prosecution, but also (and perhaps more importantly) those people involved in the supply of the drugs.

The offences of production and supply will be dealt with here; the legislation involved is from ss 4(2), 4(3), 5(3), 6(2), 8, and 28 of the Misuse of Drugs Act 1971.

9.14.1 Production of a Controlled Drug

Section 4(2) of the Misuse of Drugs Act 1971 states that it is an offence for a person to:

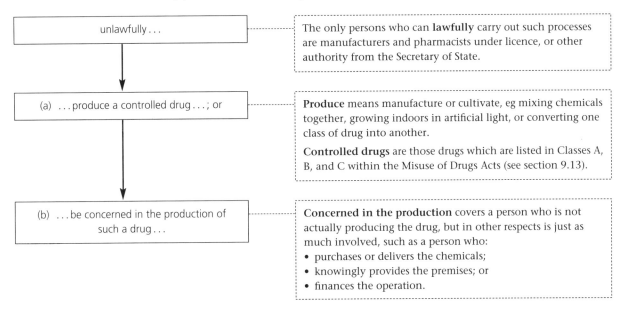

unlawfully . . .

> The only persons who can **lawfully** carry out such processes are manufacturers and pharmacists under licence, or other authority from the Secretary of State.

(a) . . . produce a controlled drug . . . ; or

> **Produce** means manufacture or cultivate, eg mixing chemicals together, growing indoors in artificial light, or converting one class of drug into another.
>
> **Controlled drugs** are those drugs which are listed in Classes A, B, and C within the Misuse of Drugs Acts (see section 9.13).

(b) . . . be concerned in the production of such a drug . . .

> **Concerned in the production** covers a person who is not actually producing the drug, but in other respects is just as much involved, such as a person who:
> • purchases or delivers the chemicals;
> • knowingly provides the premises; or
> • finances the operation.

Offences involving class A drugs are triable either way:

• Summarily; six months' imprisonment and/or prescribed fine.
• On indictment; life imprisonment and/or fine.

Offences involving class B drugs are triable either way:

• Summarily; six months' imprisonment and/or fine.
• On indictment; fourteen years' imprisonment and/or fine.

Offences involving class C drugs are triable either way:

• Summarily; three months' imprisonment and/or fine.
• On indictment; five years' imprisonment and/or fine.

This is a 'trigger' offence under s 63B of the PACE Act 1984; you can demand a sample from a person in police custody (see section 8.29 above).

9.14.2 Supplying a controlled drug

Section 4(3) of the Misuse of Drugs Act 1971 states it is an offence for a person to:

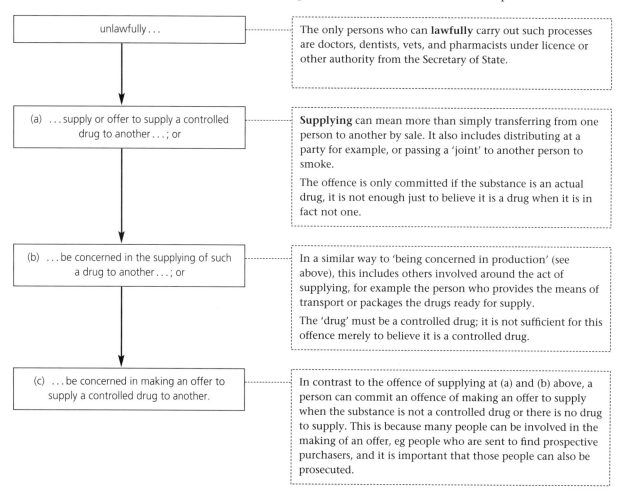

> unlawfully . . .

The only persons who can **lawfully** carry out such processes are doctors, dentists, vets, and pharmacists under licence or other authority from the Secretary of State.

> (a) . . . supply or offer to supply a controlled drug to another . . . ; or

Supplying can mean more than simply transferring from one person to another by sale. It also includes distributing at a party for example, or passing a 'joint' to another person to smoke.

The offence is only committed if the substance is an actual drug, it is not enough just to believe it is a drug when it is in fact not one.

> (b) . . . be concerned in the supplying of such a drug to another . . . ; or

In a similar way to 'being concerned in production' (see above), this includes others involved around the act of supplying, for example the person who provides the means of transport or packages the drugs ready for supply.

The 'drug' must be a controlled drug; it is not sufficient for this offence merely to believe it is a controlled drug.

> (c) . . . be concerned in making an offer to supply a controlled drug to another.

In contrast to the offence of supplying at (a) and (b) above, a person can commit an offence of making an offer to supply when the substance is not a controlled drug or there is no drug to supply. This is because many people can be involved in the making of an offer, eg people who are sent to find prospective purchasers, and it is important that those people can also be prosecuted.

Under s 4A of the Misuse of Drugs Act 1971, a court must treat this offence more seriously if it was committed on or in the vicinity of a school, or the suspect used a courier who was under the age of eighteen years.

Offences involving class A drugs are triable either way:

- Summarily; six months' imprisonment and/or prescribed fine.
- On indictment; life imprisonment and/or fine.

Offences involving class B drugs are triable either way:

- Summarily; six months' imprisonment and/or fine.
- On indictment; fourteen years' imprisonment and/or fine.

Offences involving class C drugs are triable either way:

- Summarily; three months' imprisonment and/or fine.
- On indictment; five years' imprisonment and/or fine.

This offence is also a 'trigger' offence under s 63B of the PACE Act 1984; you can demand a sample from a person in police custody (see section 8.29 above).

9.14.3   Possession with Intent to Supply a Controlled Drug

Section 5(3) of the Misuse of Drugs Act 1971 states it is an offence for a person to:

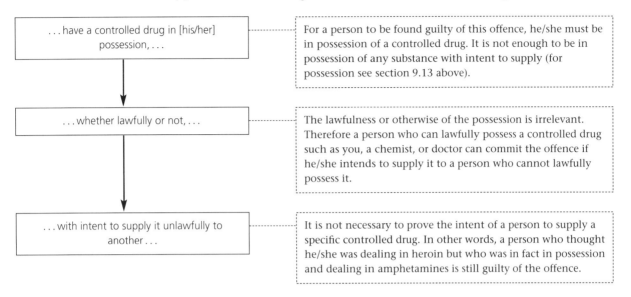

. . . have a controlled drug in [his/her] possession, . . .	For a person to be found guilty of this offence, he/she must be in possession of a controlled drug. It is not enough to be in possession of any substance with intent to supply (for possession see section 9.13 above).
. . . whether lawfully or not, . . .	The lawfulness or otherwise of the possession is irrelevant. Therefore a person who can lawfully possess a controlled drug such as you, a chemist, or doctor can commit the offence if he/she intends to supply it to a person who cannot lawfully possess it.
. . . with intent to supply it unlawfully to another . . .	It is not necessary to prove the intent of a person to supply a specific controlled drug. In other words, a person who thought he/she was dealing in heroin but who was in fact in possession and dealing in amphetamines is still guilty of the offence.

Offences involving class A drugs are triable either way:

- Summarily; six months' imprisonment and/or prescribed fine.
- On indictment; life imprisonment and/or fine.

Offences involving class B drugs are triable either way:

- Summarily; six months' imprisonment and/or fine.
- On indictment; fourteen years' imprisonment and/or fine.

Offences involving class C drugs are triable either way:

- Summarily; three months' imprisonment and/or fine.
- On indictment; five years' imprisonment and/or fine.

This offence is also a 'trigger' offence under s 63B of the PACE Act 1984; you can demand a sample from a person in police custody (see section 8.29 above).

9.14.4   Occupier or Manager of Premises Permitting Drug Abuse

Section 8 of the Misuse of Drugs Act 1971 states it is an offence for a person:

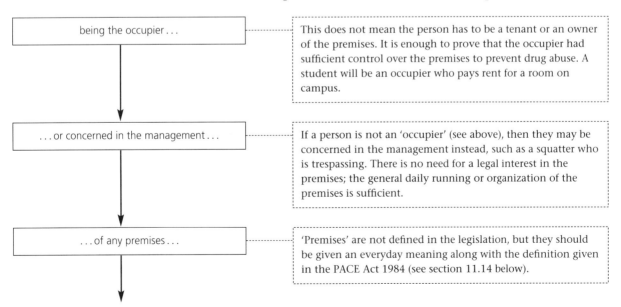

being the occupier . . .	This does not mean the person has to be a tenant or an owner of the premises. It is enough to prove that the occupier had sufficient control over the premises to prevent drug abuse. A student will be an occupier who pays rent for a room on campus.
. . . or concerned in the management . . .	If a person is not an 'occupier' (see above), then they may be concerned in the management instead, such as a squatter who is trespassing. There is no need for a legal interest in the premises; the general daily running or organization of the premises is sufficient.
. . . of any premises . . .	'Premises' are not defined in the legislation, but they should be given an everyday meaning along with the definition given in the PACE Act 1984 (see section 11.14 below).

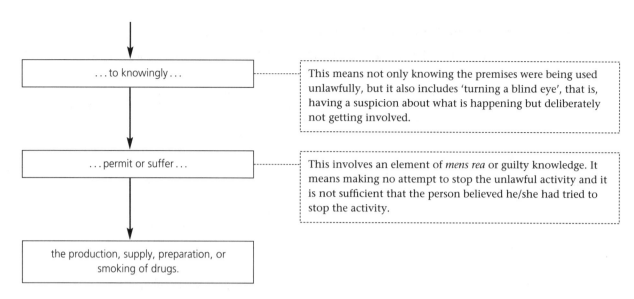

...to knowingly...	This means not only knowing the premises were being used unlawfully, but it also includes 'turning a blind eye', that is, having a suspicion about what is happening but deliberately not getting involved.
...permit or suffer...	This involves an element of *mens rea* or guilty knowledge. It means making no attempt to stop the unlawful activity and it is not sufficient that the person believed he/she had tried to stop the activity.
the production, supply, preparation, or smoking of drugs.	

More details of the type of drug-related activities and the possible role of the occupier of the premises are given in the table below.

Drug-related activity	Role of the occupier of the premises
8(a) production or attempted production of a controlled drug	Here the occupier or manager would need to know or 'look the other way' in relation to the production of a controlled drug, or perhaps he/she could be conspiring with the producer.
8(b) supply or attempt to supply a controlled drug to another	It is not necessary to prove that the occupier knew exactly which type of drug was being supplied, only that the substance was a controlled drug.
8(c) preparation of opium for smoking	The occcupier would be guilty of an offence if s/he permitted this activity, such as raw opium (obtained from the unripe seed pods of the opium poppy) being 'cooked' to make it suitable for smoking. At the time this was drafted, the legislators were particularly keen to outlaw this practice.
8(d) smoking of cannabis, cannabis resin or prepared opium.	The action of smoking must actually occur for the offence to be committed; it is not enough for the occupier or manager just to give permission for these activities to take place. The cleaner of premises which he/she knows to exist primarily for the smoking of cannabis would not be guilty of this offence because he/she is not occupying or managing the premises.

Offences involving class A drugs are triable either way:

- Summarily; six months' imprisonment and/or prescribed fine.
- On indictment; fourteen years' imprisonment and/or fine.

Offences involving class B drugs are triable either way:

- Summarily; six months' imprisonment and/or fine.
- On indictment; fourteen years' imprisonment and/or fine.

Offences involving class C drugs are triable either way:

- Summarily; three months' imprisonment and/or fine.
- On indictment; fourteen years' imprisonment and/or fine.

9.14.5 The Offence of Growing Cannabis

Section 6(2) of the Misuse of Drugs Act 1971 states it is an offence 'for a person to cultivate any plant of the genus Cannabis'. 'Cultivate' is not defined but would involve some sort of attention such as watering the plants. There is no need to prove that the defendant knew it was a cannabis plant.

This offence is triable either way:

- Summarily; six months' imprisonment and/or fine.
- On indictment; fourteen years' imprisonment and/or fine.

9.14.6 Defences to Drugs Offences

Section 28 of the Misuse of Drugs Act 1971 provides a defence to the following drugs offences:

- s 4(2) Production of a controlled drug;
- s 4(3) Supplying a controlled drug;
- s 5(3) Possession with intent to supply a controlled drug; and
- s 6(2) Unlawful cultivation of cannabis.

Refer to section 9.13 above for full details of this defence.

9.14.7 Stop and Search for Controlled Drugs

Drugs are **not** prohibited articles under s 1 of the PACE Act 1984, but s 23(2) of the Misuse of Drugs Act 1971 has its own power of search (for persons and vehicles) which states that:

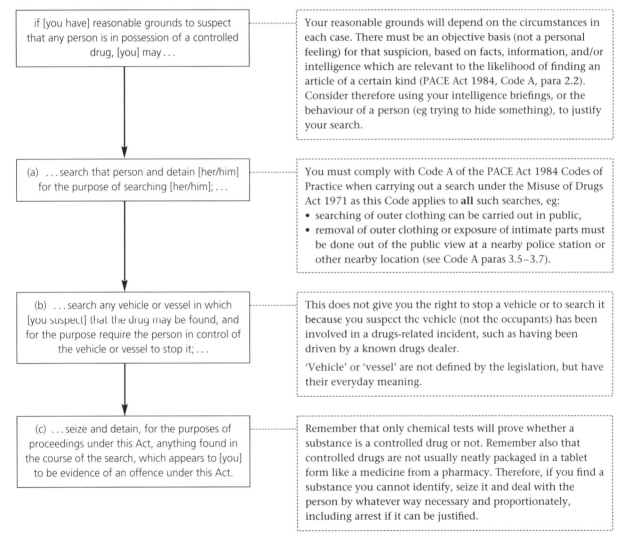

if [you have] reasonable grounds to suspect that any person is in possession of a controlled drug, [you] may . . .

Your reasonable grounds will depend on the circumstances in each case. There must be an objective basis (not a personal feeling) for that suspicion, based on facts, information, and/or intelligence which are relevant to the likelihood of finding an article of a certain kind (PACE Act 1984, Code A, para 2.2). Consider therefore using your intelligence briefings, or the behaviour of a person (eg trying to hide something), to justify your search.

(a) . . . search that person and detain [her/him] for the purpose of searching [her/him]; . . .

You must comply with Code A of the PACE Act 1984 Codes of Practice when carrying out a search under the Misuse of Drugs Act 1971 as this Code applies to **all** such searches, eg:
- searching of outer clothing can be carried out in public,
- removal of outer clothing or exposure of intimate parts must be done out of the public view at a nearby police station or other nearby location (see Code A paras 3.5–3.7).

(b) . . . search any vehicle or vessel in which [you suspect] that the drug may be found, and for the purpose require the person in control of the vehicle or vessel to stop it; . . .

This does not give you the right to stop a vehicle or to search it because you suspect the vehicle (not the occupants) has been involved in a drugs-related incident, such as having been driven by a known drugs dealer.

'Vehicle' or 'vessel' are not defined by the legislation, but have their everyday meaning.

(c) . . . seize and detain, for the purposes of proceedings under this Act, anything found in the course of the search, which appears to [you] to be evidence of an offence under this Act.

Remember that only chemical tests will prove whether a substance is a controlled drug or not. Remember also that controlled drugs are not usually neatly packaged in a tablet form like a medicine from a pharmacy. Therefore, if you find a substance you cannot identify, seize it and deal with the person by whatever way necessary and proportionately, including arrest if it can be justified.

If a person you are trying to search is obstructive and tries to prevent the search, he/she commits an offence under s 23(4) of the Misuse of Drugs Act 1971.

This offence is triable either way:

- Summarily; six months' imprisonment and/or prescribed fine.
- On indictment; two years' imprisonment and/or fine.

TASK 11

- Make a list of factors and circumstances that would provide reasonable grounds for suspecting a person is in unlawful possession of drugs with intent to supply.
- Consider what you would say to a person before carrying out a search under s 23 of the Misuse of Drugs Act 1971.
- Having found an unidentifiable substance, what are some of the reasons that would make it necessary to arrest the person?

9.15   Unlawful Personal Violence

This section covers several different types of offence:

- Common assault under s 39 of the Criminal Justice Act 1988.
- Common assault by beating (battery) under s 39 of the Criminal Justice Act 1988.
- Assault occasioning actual bodily harm under s 47 of the Offences Against the Person Act 1861.

This section contains material likely to be relevant to Phase 3 of the IPLDP and LPG 1 under the 'Crime' heading. The law regarding unlawful personal violence concerns two groups of offences, assaults and batteries, which each have separate legal meanings. An **assault** does not in law actually mean physical attack; instead it is any act, such as a threat made by an assailant, which makes a victim understand they are going to be immediately subjected to some personal violence. An example of this would be: 'I'm going to smash your head in!' A **battery**, on the other hand, is the actual use of force by an assailant on a victim such as a kick or a punch.

9.15.1   Common Assault

Common assault is an offence under s 39 of the Criminal Justice Act 1988. Common assault consists of either an assault **or** a battery (for more details on the distinction between these two, see below). If there is a serious outcome, then the injuries may constitute **actual bodily harm** (ABH) and the offender will receive a greater penalty if found guilty at court. If the outcome is even more serious, then the injuries may constitute **grievous bodily harm** (GBH).

First, we should look at the distinction between assault and battery. The case of *Fagan v MP Commissioner* [1969] 1 QB 439 has set a precedent for the definition of an assault.

9.15.2   Assault

An assault (s 39, Criminal Justice Act 1988) is:

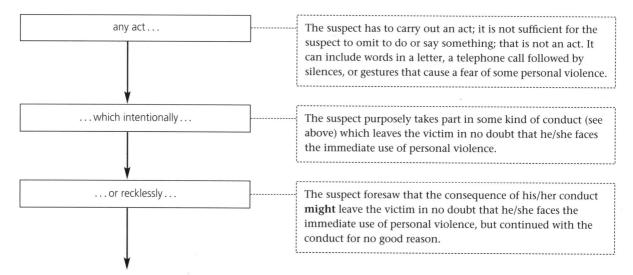

any act . . .	The suspect has to carry out an act; it is not sufficient for the suspect to omit to do or say something; that is not an act. It can include words in a letter, a telephone call followed by silences, or gestures that cause a fear of some personal violence.
. . . which intentionally . . .	The suspect purposely takes part in some kind of conduct (see above) which leaves the victim in no doubt that he/she faces the immediate use of personal violence.
. . . or recklessly . . .	The suspect foresaw that the consequence of his/her conduct **might** leave the victim in no doubt that he/she faces the immediate use of personal violence, but continued with the conduct for no good reason.

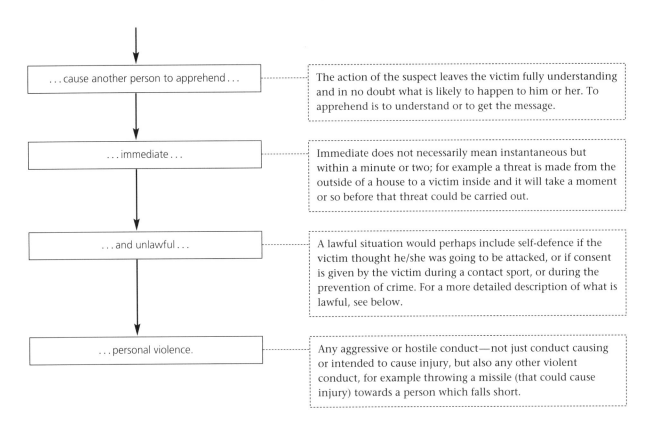

... cause another person to apprehend ...

The action of the suspect leaves the victim fully understanding and in no doubt what is likely to happen to him or her. To apprehend is to understand or to get the message.

... immediate ...

Immediate does not necessarily mean instantaneous but within a minute or two; for example a threat is made from the outside of a house to a victim inside and it will take a moment or so before that threat could be carried out.

... and unlawful ...

A lawful situation would perhaps include self-defence if the victim thought he/she was going to be attacked, or if consent is given by the victim during a contact sport, or during the prevention of crime. For a more detailed description of what is lawful, see below.

... personal violence.

Any aggressive or hostile conduct—not just conduct causing or intended to cause injury, but also any other violent conduct, for example throwing a missile (that could cause injury) towards a person which falls short.

9.15.3 Battery

A person commits a battery (s 39, Criminal Justice Act 1988) if they:

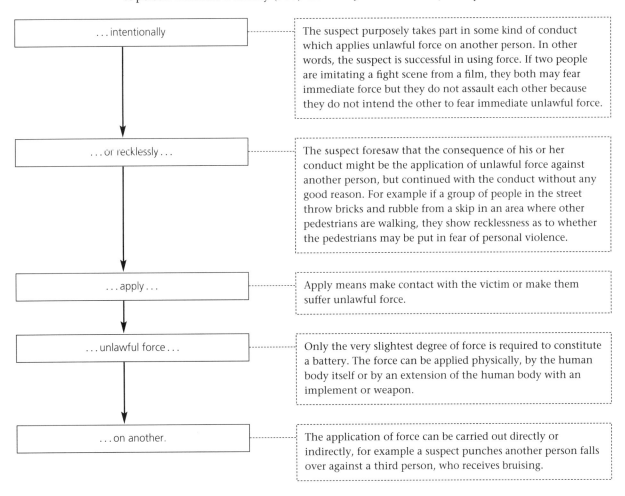

... intentionally

The suspect purposely takes part in some kind of conduct which applies unlawful force on another person. In other words, the suspect is successful in using force. If two people are imitating a fight scene from a film, they both may fear immediate force but they do not assault each other because they do not intend the other to fear immediate unlawful force.

... or recklessly ...

The suspect foresaw that the consequence of his or her conduct might be the application of unlawful force against another person, but continued with the conduct without any good reason. For example if a group of people in the street throw bricks and rubble from a skip in an area where other pedestrians are walking, they show recklessness as to whether the pedestrians may be put in fear of personal violence.

... apply ...

Apply means make contact with the victim or make them suffer unlawful force.

... unlawful force ...

Only the very slightest degree of force is required to constitute a battery. The force can be applied physically, by the human body itself or by an extension of the human body with an implement or weapon.

... on another.

The application of force can be carried out directly or indirectly, for example a suspect punches another person falls over against a third person, who receives bruising.

By now, you will probably have realized that most batteries are preceded by an assault, but not all of them. For example if a person is punched to the ground in the dark without anything being said, there has definitely been a battery, but because of the lack of light, it is unlikely there has been an assault, as the victim could not have been aware that immediate unlawful violence was about to be used against him/her.

9.15.4 Defences

There are several defences for the offence of battery, such as consent or the lawful application of force.

Consent could be given for being tattooed, having a piercing, or being operated on for a medical condition. Consent does not include:

- being reckless as to whether consent was or was not actually given, for example knowing an injury may occur and still taking a risk of causing it;
- submitting to an assault, for example by giving in;
- duress, which means giving in as a result of pressure or a threat.

Lawful sports such as boxing and rugby involve the participants in contact activities, and they consent to the injuries they may receive while playing within the rules of that sport. (If the rules are broken and the injuries are caused as a consequence, then this defence can no longer exist.)

Self-defence may also be used as a defence against the offence; the court must decide if the actions of the person defending him or herself were reasonable under the circumstances and not excessive.

Prevention of crime or lawful arrest can also be used as a defence; s 3(1) of the Criminal Law Act 1967 allows a person to use such force as is reasonable in the prevention of crime, or in effecting or assisting in the lawful arrest of offenders (see section 11.13.2). Similarly, s 3(1A) of the Criminal Law Act 1967 states that a defence will be available to a person who uses force on another:

- in the prevention of crime, or
- in defence of persons or property

if that other person is in a building having entered or attempted to enter as a trespasser, **unless**:

(a) the degree of force used was grossly disproportionate, and
(b) this was or ought to have been apparent to the person using such force.

In this section 'building or part of a building' shall have the same meaning as in section 9 of the Theft Act 1968 (see section 9.5.2.2).

Note, however, that as a result of s 58 of the Children Act 2004, a parent no longer has the legal right to apply moderate and reasonable physical chastisement to their children. In other words, if any injury is inflicted on the child, there is no defence at all.

TASK 12

Consider the following incidents:

1. You are called to investigate an incident in which very little force has been used upon the victim, who is therefore uninjured. What offence has been committed?
2. If you are called upon to investigate an incident where no force has been used upon the victim but the victim was left in no doubt that he/she was about to face unlawful personal violence, what offence has been committed?

The offence of common assault is triable summarily only and the penalty is six months' imprisonment. Note that this offence can be racially or religiously aggravated (see section 8.10).

9.15.5 Actual Bodily Harm (ABH)

The offence of Assault Occasioning Actual Bodily Harm (s 47 of the Offences Against the Person Act 1861) has been committed if there is a more serious outcome and the injuries of the victim (owing to the assault or battery) result in actual bodily harm. The aspects of intention or recklessness are the same for actual bodily harm as they are for common assault.

In this offence, the assault can be either an assault or a battery, as long as actual bodily harm has been caused. Actual bodily harm means any injury which interferes with the health or comfort of person in more than a trivial way. The injury must be real and it should be capable of being seen or felt by the victim (or by witnesses such as yourself). This includes psychiatric injury caused by an assault such as a threat which has put a victim in fear of immediate, unlawful violence. Similarly, a battery can be committed if the victim suffers some unlawful force such as a punch which causes the loss of a tooth.

In terms of intent, there is only a need to prove that the assault or battery was intended or that it was carried out recklessly. There is no need to prove that the accused intended to cause injuries amounting to actual bodily harm (or was reckless as to whether the injuries amounting to actual bodily harm would be caused).

This offence is triable either way:

- Summarily; six months' imprisonment and/or fine.
- On indictment; five years' imprisonment.

Note that this offence can be racially or religiously aggravated (see section 8.10 above).

Unlawful personal violence is a very common occurrence and you will be called upon to investigate such incidents with alarming frequency. The incidents may or may not be drink or drug related. The health and safety of you and the general public is paramount, therefore always consider whether the use of your personal protective equipment is required.

> **TASK 13**
> You attend a domestic crime incident involving two partners in a relationship. One of the partners complains that she has been punched by the other. How will you identify what type of assault has been committed?

9.16 Serious Offences of Personal Violence

This section covers the following serious offences of personal violence:

- Unlawful and malicious wounding or inflicting grievous bodily harm (inflicting GBH).
- Wounding or causing grievous bodily harm with intent to do grievous bodily harm or to resist or prevent arrest (referred to as 'GBH with Intent').
- Assaults on the police.
- Assault with intent to resist arrest.
- Obstructing a police officer.

9.16.1 Unlawful and Malicious Wounding or Inflicting GBH

Section 20 of the Offences Against the Person Act 1861 states:

> it is an offence unlawfully and maliciously to [either]
>
> - wound another person or
> - inflict grievous bodily harm [(GBH) upon another person].

To understand this offence, careful consideration needs to be given first to the meaning of the words unlawfully and maliciously.

Unlawfully means 'without lawful justification', as opposed to cases of lawfully-inflicted injury, as in some cases of self-defence.

Maliciously means:

- an actual intention to do that particular kind of harm; or
- recklessness (unreasonably persisting in taking that risk) as to whether such harmful consequences would occur as a result of the actions taken;

Note that:

- malice (ill-will or a malevolent motive) must be present, but is not limited to, nor does it require, any ill-will towards the injured person him or herself;
- a weapon need not be used;
- Some knowledge that there would be some kind of injury is required, but not necessarily foreseeing the degree of this injury.

We need to consider wounding and grievous bodily harm (GBH). **Wounding** must involve the breaking of all the layers of the skin. The bodily harm must be serious, but not necessarily dangerous or permanent. It is not necessary to cause the wound with a weapon (though of course this is often the case, for example using a deliberately smashed glass for the attack). **Grievous bodily harm** is not defined in the Act but in the case of *DPP v Smith* [1960] 3 All ER 161 it was agreed that it should be given its ordinary meaning which is 'really serious bodily harm'.

Examples of GBH include:

- injury resulting in some permanent disability, loss of function;
- visible disfigurement;
- broken or displaced limbs or bones, fractured skull;
- injuries with substantial blood loss, usually requiring blood transfusion;
- injuries resulting in lengthy treatment or incapacity;
- psychiatric injury (expert evidence is required).

(The list above is adapted from CPS, 2006.)

GBH does not have to include an assault or a battery (see section 9.15 above). For example, a person infecting his/her partner knowingly with the HIV AIDS virus while concealing the infection from the partner is committing the offence of grievous bodily harm. Telephone calls that would result in serious psychiatric injury to the victim can also amount to grievous bodily harm.

This offence is triable either way:

- Summarily; six months' imprisonment and/or a fine.
- On indictment; five years' imprisonment.

This offence can be racially or religiously aggravated, see section 8.10 above.

9.16.2 GBH with Intent

The full name for this offence is 'wounding or causing grievous bodily harm with intent to do grievous bodily harm or to resist or prevent arrest'.

Section 18 of the Offences Against the Person Act 1861 states it is an offence to:

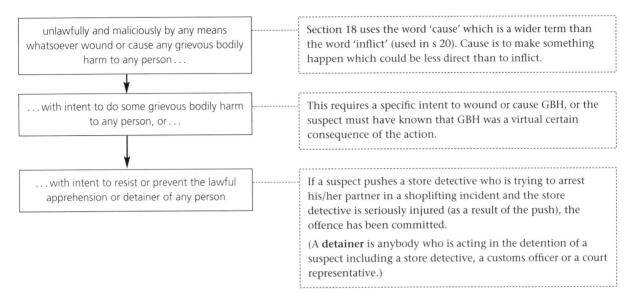

unlawfully and maliciously by any means whatsoever wound or cause any grievous bodily harm to any person . . .	Section 18 uses the word 'cause' which is a wider term than the word 'inflict' (used in s 20). Cause is to make something happen which could be less direct than to inflict.
. . . with intent to do some grievous bodily harm to any person, or . . .	This requires a specific intent to wound or cause GBH, or the suspect must have known that GBH was a virtual certain consequence of the action.
. . . with intent to resist or prevent the lawful apprehension or detainer of any person	If a suspect pushes a store detective who is trying to arrest his/her partner in a shoplifting incident and the store detective is seriously injured (as a result of the push), the offence has been committed. (A **detainer** is anybody who is acting in the detention of a suspect including a store detective, a customs officer or a court representative.)

The main difference between s 18 and s 20 offences is that s 18 offences have the element of intent (whilst s 20 refers to the concept of 'malicious'). Of course, intent is sometimes difficult to prove although there will be some obvious examples as in the use of a weapon.

This offence is triable on indictment only and the penalty is life imprisonment.

There was no perceived need to create a racially or religiously aggravated offence for this offence as the maximum sentence is already life imprisonment.

9.16.3 Assaults on Police Officers and Persons Supporting a Police Officer

Section 89(1) of the Police Act 1996 states it is an offence:

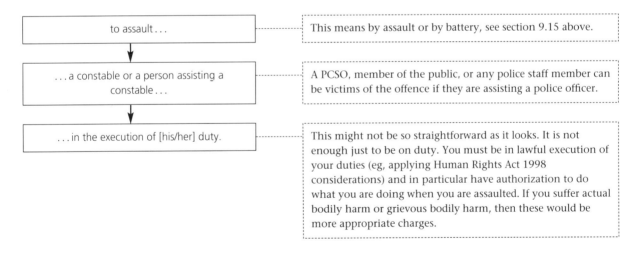

to assault . . .	This means by assault or by battery, see section 9.15 above.
. . . a constable or a person assisting a constable . . .	A PCSO, member of the public, or any police staff member can be victims of the offence if they are assisting a police officer.
. . . in the execution of [his/her] duty.	This might not be so straightforward as it looks. It is not enough just to be on duty. You must be in lawful execution of your duties (eg, applying Human Rights Act 1998 considerations) and in particular have authorization to do what you are doing when you are assaulted. If you suffer actual bodily harm or grievous bodily harm, then these would be more appropriate charges.

This offence is triable summarily and the penalty is six months' imprisonment and/or a fine.

9.16.4 Assault with Intent to Resist Arrest

Section 38 of the Offences Against the Person Act 1861 states it is an offence to:

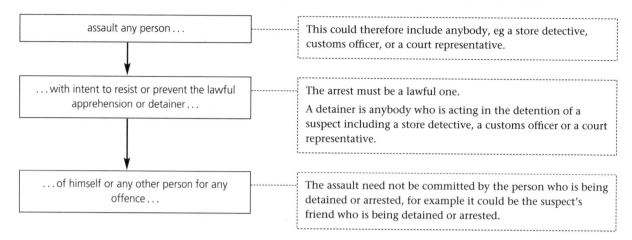

Even if the suspect believes the person making the arrest had no lawful power to do so, or the suspect believes he/she is innocent, this makes no difference to the offence.

This offence is triable summarily and the penalty is two years' imprisonment.

9.16.5 Obstructing a Police Officer

Section 89 of the Police Act 1996 states it is an offence for any person:

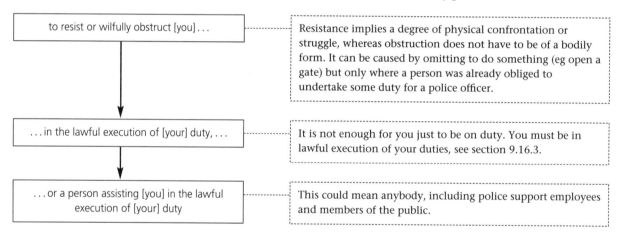

This offence is triable summarily and the penalty is one month's imprisonment and/or a fine.

TASK 14

You are deployed by your control room to the each of following incidents. Using the information you are given (and no more), decide what offence or offences may have been committed in relation to the injuries sustained by the victims. In some cases you may wish to give more than a single answer.

1. Two people are arguing in the street. The dispute reaches a point where one of the couple 'head-butts' the other, causing a severe nose bleed.
2. An apparently drunken man throws a glass bottle from a moving car in the direction of a woman waiting at a bus stop. The glass breaks on the frame of the shelter and a large fragment shatters off and hits her in the forehead, causing a deep wound which bleeds profusely. The woman's skull can be easily seen through the wound. Subsequently, the victim attended accident and emergency at a local hospital and had several stitches inserted.
3. CCTV images note a woman taking and secreting goods from a clothes store. A store detective follows the suspect out and into the street, stops the woman, explains who he, is and why he

is detaining her. She makes a sudden move, pushes the store detective backwards, and he falls over and grazes his hand.

4. After months of alleged harassment by local youths in the street outside her house, the occupant loses her temper, goes out to one of the youths and slaps him round the face, leaving a large red slap mark on his cheek.

9.17 Cruelty to Children and Police Protection Procedures

Children are sometimes exposed to significant harm by their parents, relatives, and other people involved in their care and supervision. The Children Act 1989 provides you with the powers to take children (under eighteen years of age who are at risk of significant harm) into police protection. However, the Home Office Circular 44/2003 states that:

Police protection powers should only be used when necessary, the principle being that wherever possible the decision to remove a child from a parent or carer should be made by a court (para 14).

Apart from in exceptional circumstances (for example, an imminent threat to a child's welfare), no child is to be taken into police protection until the **investigating officer** (see 9.17.3.1 below) has seen the child and assessed his or her circumstances.

Some of the legislation relating to children's safety and well-being is considered below, and this is followed by an account of the procedures to be followed by the police, to help protect children from harm.

Section 1(1) of the Children and Young Persons' Act 1933 states that it is an offence:

if a person who has attained the age of sixteen years and has responsibility for a child or young person under that age wilfully . . .

- assaults,
- ill-treats,
- neglects,
- abandons or
- exposes [him/her], or . . .

. . . causes or procures [him/her] to be . . .

- assaulted,
- ill-treated,
- neglected,
- abandoned or
- exposed . . .

. . . in a manner likely to cause [him/her] unnecessary suffering or injury to health including injury to or loss of . . .

- sight,
- hearing,
- limb or
- organ of the body . . .

. . . and any mental derangement.

This offence is triable either way:

- Summarily; six months' imprisonment and/or a fine.
- On indictment; ten years' imprisonment and/or a fine.

9.17.1 Cigarettes and Young People

As a police officer you have a responsibility to help prevent young people from smoking and gaining access to cigarettes (and rolling tobacco). Section 7(3) of the Children and Young Persons Act 1933 states:

> It is the duty of a constable [. . .] in uniform to seize any tobacco or cigarette papers in the possession of a person apparently under the age of sixteen years whom [he/she] finds smoking in any street or public place, and any tobacco or cigarette papers so seized will be disposed of [. . .] in a manner prescribed by the police authority.

It is also an offence to sell cigarettes to young people under the age of eighteen years. Section 7(1) of the Children and Young Persons' Act 1933 states:

> A person who sells to a person under the age of eighteen years any tobacco or cigarette papers, whether for [his/her] own use or not, commits an offence.

However, shopkeepers may be relieved to know that under s 7(1A) of the Children and Young Persons' Act 1933:

> It is a defence for a person charged with an offence under subsection (1) to prove that [he/she] took all reasonable precautions and exercised all due diligence to avoid the commission of the offence.

This offence is triable summarily and the penalty is a fine.

9.17.2 Injuries to Children from Heating Appliances

Carers have a responsibility to ensure that children are kept safe when heating appliances are in use. The legislation applies to people over the age of sixteen who are caring for children under the age of twelve. Section 11 of the Children and Young Persons' Act 1933 states:

> If a person [. . .] allows the child to be in a room containing an open fire grate or any heating appliance
>
> * liable to cause injury to a person by contact with it;
> * not sufficiently protected to guard against the risk of being burnt or scalded
>
> without taking reasonable precautions against that risk, and because of that the child is killed or suffers serious injury, [he/she] commits an offence.

This offence is triable summarily and the penalty is a fine.

9.17.3 Police Protection

The police can act to prevent further harm to a child. Whether or not a child would otherwise be likely to suffer significant **harm** will be a matter for you (as a police officer) to decide. The term is not specifically defined in the Act, but s 31 of the Children Act 1989 provides some guidance on the meaning of harm. The diagram below summarizes the different types of harm, and shows the many ways in which children can suffer harm.

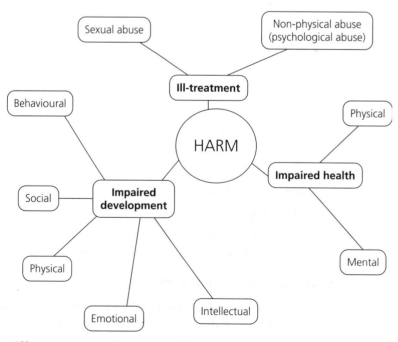

Different types of harm to children

9.17.3.1 Procedure for police protection

Section 46(1) of the Children Act 1989 states that:

where [you have] reasonable cause to believe that a child would otherwise be likely to suffer significant harm, [you] may . . .

(a) remove [the child] to suitable accommodation and keep [him/her] there; or
(b) take all reasonable steps to ensure that [his/her] removal from a hospital, or other place, in which [he/she] is accommodated, is prevented.

There are two separate and distinct roles for the police in relation to police protection: the **investigating officer** and the **designated officer** (s 46(1), the Children Act 1989). If you are the officer who initially takes the child into police protection, you will be given the title of investigating officer, and you would also undertake the initial enquiries. The designated officer will have at least the rank of inspector and will play a less active role in the investigation. His or her role is to have an independent overview of the circumstances in which the child was taken into police protection.

9.17.3.2 Suitable accommodation

A definition of suitable accommodation is given in the Home Office Circular 44/2003:

The term 'suitable accommodation' would normally mean local authority accommodation, a registered children's home or foster care. If the designated officer and social services consider it appropriate, the child may also be placed with relatives or other appropriate carers. The child may also be taken to hospital if [he/she] requires medical attention.

The circular also emphasizes that a child under police protection should **not** be brought to a police station unless there is absolutely no alternative.

9.17.3.3 The role of the investigating officer

According to s 46(3) of the Children Act 1989, the investigating officer must:

as soon as reasonably practicable after taking a child into police protection

(a) inform the local authority within whose area the child was found of the steps that have been, and are proposed to be, taken concerning [the child] under this section and the reasons for taking them;
(b) give details to the authority within whose area the child is ordinarily resident ('the appropriate authority') of the place where [he/she] is being accommodated;
(c) inform the child (if [he/she] appears capable of understanding) of:
  (i) the steps taken with respect to [him/her] and of the reasons for taking them; and
  (ii) the further steps that may be taken with respect to [him/her] under this section;
(d) take such steps as are reasonably practicable to discover the wishes and feelings of the child;
(e) ensure that the case is inquired into by an officer designated for the purposes of this section by the chief officer of the police force concerned; and
(f) where the child was taken into police protection by being removed to accommodation which is not provided:
  (i) by or on behalf of a local authority; or
  (ii) as a refuge . . . ,

secure that [the child] is moved to such accommodation [eg voluntary homes, private children's homes and foster parents].

In addition, the investigating officer must contact the parents or other responsible adults who have been caring for the child.

Under section 46(4) then:

as soon as is reasonably practicable after taking a child into police protection, [you] must take all reasonably practicable steps to inform:

(a) the child's parents;
(b) every person who is not a parent but has parental responsibility for [the child]; and
(c) any other person with whom [the child] was living immediately before being taken into police protection,

- of the steps that [you] have taken under this section with respect to the child,
- the reasons for taking them, and
- the further steps that may be taken with respect to the child under this section.

A child can be in police protection for up to seventy-two hours (s 46(6), Children Act 1989).

9.17.3.4 The meaning of 'parental responsibility'

In s 3(1) of the Children Act 1989 parental responsibility means:

all the rights, duties, powers, responsibilities and authority which by law a parent of a child has in relation to that child and [his/her] property.

Parental responsibility can be held by either the parents, the step-parents and in certain circumstances, by other people or bodies. The question of who has parental responsibility is dealt with in ss 2 and 3 of the Children Act 1989 which states that:

2(1) Where a child's father and mother were married to each other at the time of [his/her] birth, they will each have parental responsibility for the child.

2(2) Where a child's father and mother were not married to each other at the time of [his/her] birth:
   (a) the mother will have parental responsibility for the child;
   (b) the father will not have parental responsibility for the child, unless he acquires it in accordance with the provisions of this Act.

2(4) The rule of law that a father is the natural guardian of his legitimate child is abolished.

2(5) More than one person may have parental responsibility for the same child at the same time.

2(6) A person who has parental responsibility for a child at any time does not cease to have that responsibility simply because some other person acquires such responsibility for that child.

2(7) Where more than one person has parental responsibility for a child, each may act alone to meet that responsibility, but nothing in this Part affects the operation of any legislation which requires the consent of more than one person in a matter affecting that child.

2(8) The fact that a person has parental responsibility for a child does not entitle that person to act in a way that would be incompatible with an order made in respect of that child under this Act.

The spirit of the legislation is that all the parties including the parents, the child, and the local authority are to be kept informed and given reasons for any actions. The child's wishes must be listened to but do not necessarily have to be acted upon.

TASK 15

Jo is a single parent struggling to care for a four-year-old called Sam whilst employed part-time. Recently Sam has been ill, and although Jo's employer has been very understanding, Jo does not want to take any more time off work. Jo's parents often care for Sam while Jo is at work.

However, on one occasion the grandparents are unavailable to supervise Sam. Jo realizes that there is no food in the house and when Sam falls asleep, Jo decides to go to buy some food at the supermarket. During the journey, Jo's car breaks down.

Sam awakes and is distraught. Having heard the child screaming hysterically, the neighbours call the police and you attend. Although you can clearly hear Sam inside, all the doors and windows are shut and Sam refuses to open the door.

1. What power of entry, if any, is available to you?
2. What offence might you consider investigating Jo for?

9.18 Exposure and Voyeurism

Here, we will begin with the common law offence of 'outraging public decency', move on to consider exposure, and finally deal with voyeurism, more commonly known as the act of a 'Peeping Tom'.

9.18.1   Outraging Public Decency

The common law offence of outraging public decency states that it is an offence:

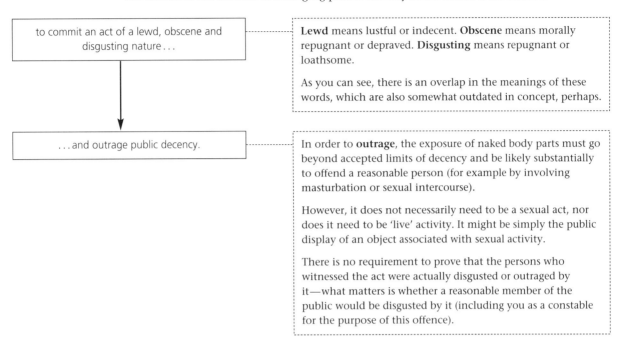

to commit an act of a lewd, obscene and disgusting nature . . .

Lewd means lustful or indecent. **Obscene** means morally repugnant or depraved. **Disgusting** means repugnant or loathsome.

As you can see, there is an overlap in the meanings of these words, which are also somewhat outdated in concept, perhaps.

. . . and outrage public decency.

In order to **outrage**, the exposure of naked body parts must go beyond accepted limits of decency and be likely substantially to offend a reasonable person (for example by involving masturbation or sexual intercourse).

However, it does not necessarily need to be a sexual act, nor does it need to be 'live' activity. It might be simply the public display of an object associated with sexual activity.

There is no requirement to prove that the persons who witnessed the act were actually disgusted or outraged by it—what matters is whether a reasonable member of the public would be disgusted by it (including you as a constable for the purpose of this offence).

For this offence:

- The public must have access to (whether they have a right or not) or be able to see the location, such as a private balcony in public view (*R v Walker* [1996] 1 Cr App R 111; *Smith v Hughes* [1960] 1 WLR 830).
- More than one person must have been able to witness the act.

This offence is triable either way:

- Summarily; six months' imprisonment and/or a fine.
- On indictment; unlimited powers of sentence.

9.18.2   Exposure

This offence (s 66(1), Sexual Offences Act 2003) is commonly referred to as 'flashing'. A person commits an offence if:

    (a) [he/she] intentionally exposes his/her genitals, and
    (b) [he/she] intends that someone will see this and be caused alarm or distress.

A person who exposes his/her genitals knowing this might be seen by others, does not commit this offence unless they have an **intention to cause alarm or distress.** For example, a 'streaker' intending to create amusement does not commit this offence. Also, on a site specifically set aside for naturism, a nudist does not conceal his or her genitals, but this is as a result of his or her beliefs and not for the purpose of onlookers becoming alarmed or distressed.

It is not necessary for a person to actually have seen the exposed genitals or to have been distressed as a result; the offence is committed regardless of whether a passer-by actually sees them or not.

This offence is triable either way:

- Summarily; six months' imprisonment.
- On indictment; two years' imprisonment.

9.18.3 Voyeurism

People who commit this offence (s 67(1), Sexual Offences Act 2003) are commonly known as Peeping Toms. In this category, there is a variety of offences, but most commonly you will come across the situation where a suspect secretly observes another undressing or having sexual intercourse (a 'private act') for the purposes of the suspect's own sexual gratification.

Section 68(1) of the Sexual Offences Act 2003 explains that for the purposes of s 67, a person does a **private act** if he/she is in a place which would reasonably be expected to provide privacy, such as in a home or hotel (but not on a beach or in a field) **and** the following conditions are met:

- [his/her] genitals, buttocks or breasts are exposed or covered only with underwear,
- [he/she] is using a lavatory, or
- [he/she] is doing a sexual act that is not of a kind ordinarily done in public.

The sort of act, known as a private act, would not include kissing or cuddling, but would include sexual intercourse or oral sex.

Under s 67(1) of the Sexual Offences Act 2003 a person commits an offence if:

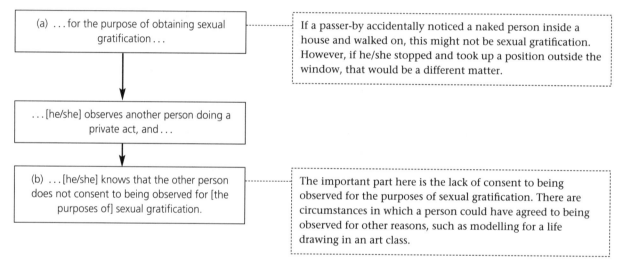

There is a form of voyeurism linked to 'dogging' (outdoor sexual activities). If the 'doggers' encourage people to watch, the offence of voyeurism is not committed because consent has been given. Other offences, however, may have been committed, depending on the particular circumstances.

In the other subsections of the Sexual Offences Act 2003, the offence of voyeurism includes a third party and their sexual gratification by means of equipment involved to record the private act.

9.18.3.1 Voyeurism using live link equipment

Under s 67(2) of the Sexual Offences Act 2003 a person (A) commits an offence if he/she operates equipment with the intention of enabling another person (B) to observe, for the purpose of obtaining sexual gratification, a third person (C) doing a private act, and A knows that C does not consent to the operation of equipment with that intention.

For example, a landlord commits an offence if he operates a webcam so that people on the internet can gain sexual gratification from viewing his tenant having sexual intercourse. The landlord must know that the tenant did not agree to this. Also, there is no need to prove that the landlord personally gained sexual gratification.

9.18.3.2 Voyeurism and making recorded images

Under s 67(3) of the Sexual Offences Act 2003 a person (A) commits an offence if:

- he/she records another person (C) doing a private act, with the intention that he/she (A) or a third person (B) will obtain sexual gratification looking at an image of C doing the act; and
- knowing that C does not consent to the recording of the act with that intention.

For example, an offence is committed by a person who secretly photographs another person masturbating in a bedroom and intends to show the photos to others for their sexual gratification. The photographer must know that the subject of the photos does not consent to the photos being taken with that intention. Proof that the intention was sexual gratification could be that the image was posted on a pornographic website or that it was offered for sale to an adult (pornographic) magazine.

9.18.3.3 Voyeurism and installing equipment

Under s 67(4) of the Sexual Offences Act 2003 a person commits an offence if:

- he/she installs equipment; or
- constructs or adapts a structure or part of a structure

with the intention of committing an offence (or enabling or another person to commit an offence) of simple voyeurism (s 67(1)).

For example, an offence is committed by a person who drills a spy-hole in a wall for the purposes of spying on someone for sexual gratification. The offence is committed even if the peephole is discovered before it is used. Note that a 'structure' (a site where the equipment is installed) can include a tent, vehicle, or vessel or some other temporary or movable structure.

Offences relating to voyeurism are triable either way:

- Summarily; six months' imprisonment.
- On indictment; two years' imprisonment.

TASK 16

On the drive back to their home-ground, some members of a rugby club team have taken to celebrating their wins by exposing their naked buttocks ('mooning') out of the rear window of the team bus. You have been tasked to deal with the most recent incident in the busy main high street, and are now considering what offence might have been committed. What is your conclusion?

9.19 Further Sexual Offences

Some sexual offences have already been covered earlier in this chapter. This part of chapter 9 covers the following offences:

- Sexual assault (touching) (s 3, Sexual Offences Act 2003).
- Sexual assault of a child under thirteen (s 7(1), Sexual Offences Act 2003).
- Sexual activity with a child (s 9(1), Sexual Offences Act 2003).
- Prostitution (s 1, Street Offences Act 1959).
- Kerb crawling (s 1, Sexual Offences Act 1985).
- Indecent photographs (s 1, Protection of Children Act 1978).

9.19.1 Consent

In many sexual offence cases, the defence will focus on the issue of consent. It is a defence if the suspect believes that consent was given. He (very rarely, she) would also have to prove that this belief was reasonable. In any prosecution the court will decide whether the belief was reasonable after considering the circumstances and the steps that the suspect took to obtain consent (s 1(2), Sexual Offences Act 2003).

The court will seek to establish whether the suspect made a conscious effort to:

- establish consent; and
- monitor the consent—the other person might change his/her mind and withdraw his/her consent, indicated by a change of physical expression or voice tone, for example.

Section 74 of the Sexual Offences Act 2003 states that a person consents if he/she agrees by choice, and has the freedom and capacity to make that choice. **Freedom to make the choice** means that the choice is not made under duress or through being put in fear of violence. **Capacity to agree** means the ability to decide either way, and to be able to communicate the decision. If a person is 'unable to refuse' through mental disorder or intoxication for example, he/she does not have the capacity to make the choice.

In order to increase the conviction rate for those guilty of sexual assault, the Sexual Offences Act 2003 introduced two sets of presumptions which courts can make in relation to the guilty knowledge of the defendant:

1. evidential presumptions about consent (s 75 can be rebutted by the defence); and
2. conclusive presumptions about consent (s 76).

9.19.1.1 Evidential presumptions about consent

Under s 75 of the Sexual Offences Act 2003 if it is proved in court that:

1. the defendant did the sexual assault;
2. any of the **circumstances** listed below existed; and
3. the defendant knew any of the circumstances listed below existed;

then the court will make the presumption that the victim did **not** consent.

The circumstances are:

- use of and fear of violence;
- unlawful detention;
- unconsciousness;
- inability to communicate from physical disability;
- substances non-consensually administered that are capable of stupefying or overpowering.

In order for the defence to rebut this presumption, the defendant will need first of all to satisfy the judge from evidence that there is a definite issue about consent that he/she wants to put to the jury. If the judge is persuaded that there are accountable issues, then it is for the defence to produce that evidence from the defendant, a witness, or the victim under cross-examination.

If the judge does not conclude that there is sufficient evidence from the defence, then the jury will be directed to find that the victim did not consent to the sexual assault and that the defendant could not have reasonably believed otherwise.

9.19.1.2 Conclusive presumptions about consent

Under s 76 of the Sexual Offences Act 2003 if it is proved in court that:

1. the defendant did the sexual assault; and
2. that any of the circumstances listed below existed

then the court will make the presumption that the victim did not consent to the sexual assault, and that the defendant did not believe the victim consented.

The circumstances are:

- The defendant intentionally deceived the complainant as to the nature or purpose of the relevant act, for example a person engages in a sexual activity having told the victim it was a necessary medical procedure.
- The defendant intentionally induced the complainant to consent to the relevant act by impersonating an individual known personally to the complainant, for example, during complete darkness or while the victim is blindfolded, the suspect engages in sexual activity while pretending to be someone with whom the victim would have consented to such activity.

These are important considerations if you gather evidence in connection with a prosecution for the sexual offences listed in section 9.19.

9.19.2 Sexual Assault (Touching)

Section 3 of the Sexual Offences Act 2003 states a person (A) commits an offence if:

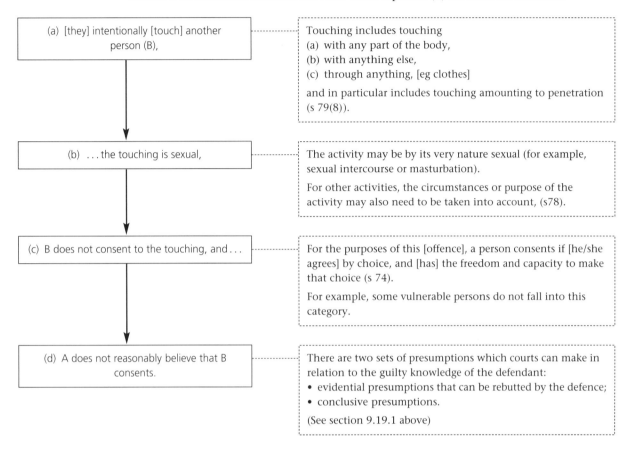

(a) [they] intentionally [touch] another person (B),	Touching includes touching (a) with any part of the body, (b) with anything else, (c) through anything, [eg clothes] and in particular includes touching amounting to penetration (s 79(8)).
(b) ... the touching is sexual,	The activity may be by its very nature sexual (for example, sexual intercourse or masturbation). For other activities, the circumstances or purpose of the activity may also need to be taken into account, (s78).
(c) B does not consent to the touching, and ...	For the purposes of this [offence], a person consents if [he/she agrees] by choice, and [has] the freedom and capacity to make that choice (s 74). For example, some vulnerable persons do not fall into this category.
(d) A does not reasonably believe that B consents.	There are two sets of presumptions which courts can make in relation to the guilty knowledge of the defendant: • evidential presumptions that can be rebutted by the defence; • conclusive presumptions. (See section 9.19.1 above)

9.19.3 Sexual Assault of a Child Under Thirteen

Section 7(1) of the Sexual Offences Act 2003 states that it is an offence if:

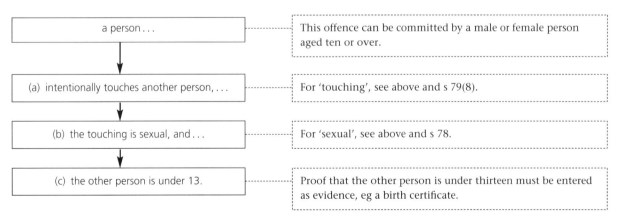

a person ...	This offence can be committed by a male or female person aged ten or over.
(a) intentionally touches another person, ...	For 'touching', see above and s 79(8).
(b) the touching is sexual, and ...	For 'sexual', see above and s 78.
(c) the other person is under 13.	Proof that the other person is under thirteen must be entered as evidence, eg a birth certificate.

This offence is triable either way:

• Summarily; six months' imprisonment and/or a fine not exceeding the statutory maximum.
• On indictment; fourteen years' imprisonment.

9.19.4 Sexual Activity with a Child

Section 9(1) of the Sexual Offences Act 2003 states that it is an offence if:

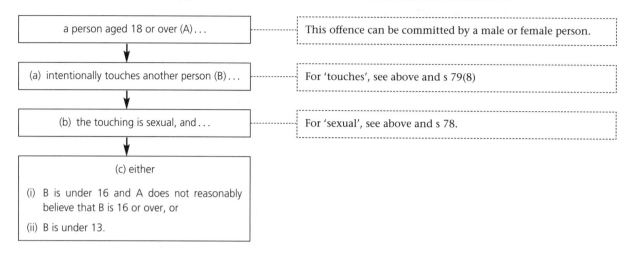

Note that:

- Proof that B is under sixteen must be entered as evidence, eg birth certificate.
- If B is aged thirteen to fifteen, there is a defence available if A reasonably believed that B was over sixteen.
- There is no defence available if B is under thirteen.

This offence is triable either way:

- Summarily; six months' imprisonment and/or a fine.
- On indictment; fourteen years' imprisonment.

9.19.4.1 Touching a child and penetration

Section 9(2) of the Sexual Offences Act 2003 states that it is an offence if the touching involved:

(a) penetration of B's anus or vagina with a part of A's body or anything else;
(b) penetration of B's mouth with A's penis;
(c) penetration of A's anus or vagina with a part of B's body; or
(d) penetration of A's mouth with B's penis.

Note that:

- Penetration is a continuing act from entry to withdrawal (s 79(2)).
- References to a part of the body also include references to a part that may have been surgically constructed (in particular through gender reassignment surgery) (s 79(3)).

If the touching of the child involved penetration as in s 9(2)(a)–(d) above, the offence is triable by indictment only, and the penalty is up to fourteen years' imprisonment.

9.19.5 Prostitution

Note that paying for sex is not an offence, for either party involved. Prostitution, per se, is not illegal but almost all 'public manifestation' of the trade is illegal. So, for example, it is an offence for a prostitute to loiter or solicit.

Section 1(1) of the Street Offences Act 1959 states it is an offence:

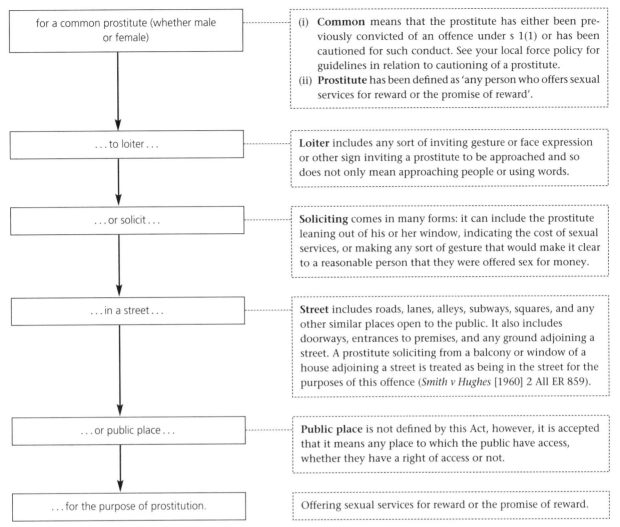

for a common prostitute (whether male or female)	(i) **Common** means that the prostitute has either been previously convicted of an offence under s 1(1) or has been cautioned for such conduct. See your local force policy for guidelines in relation to cautioning of a prostitute. (ii) **Prostitute** has been defined as 'any person who offers sexual services for reward or the promise of reward'.
...to loiter...	**Loiter** includes any sort of inviting gesture or face expression or other sign inviting a prostitute to be approached and so does not only mean approaching people or using words.
...or solicit...	**Soliciting** comes in many forms: it can include the prostitute leaning out of his or her window, indicating the cost of sexual services, or making any sort of gesture that would make it clear to a reasonable person that they were offered sex for money.
...in a street...	**Street** includes roads, lanes, alleys, subways, squares, and any other similar places open to the public. It also includes doorways, entrances to premises, and any ground adjoining a street. A prostitute soliciting from a balcony or window of a house adjoining a street is treated as being in the street for the purposes of this offence (*Smith v Hughes* [1960] 2 All ER 859).
...or public place...	**Public place** is not defined by this Act, however, it is accepted that it means any place to which the public have access, whether they have a right of access or not.
...for the purpose of prostitution.	Offering sexual services for reward or the promise of reward.

This offence is triable summarily and the penalty is a fine.

Finally, note that the law surrounding prostitution may change in the future as a result of the Government's 'Paying the Price' consultation.

9.19.6 Kerb Crawling

Section 1 of the Sexual Offences Act 1985 states that an offence is committed by any person who:

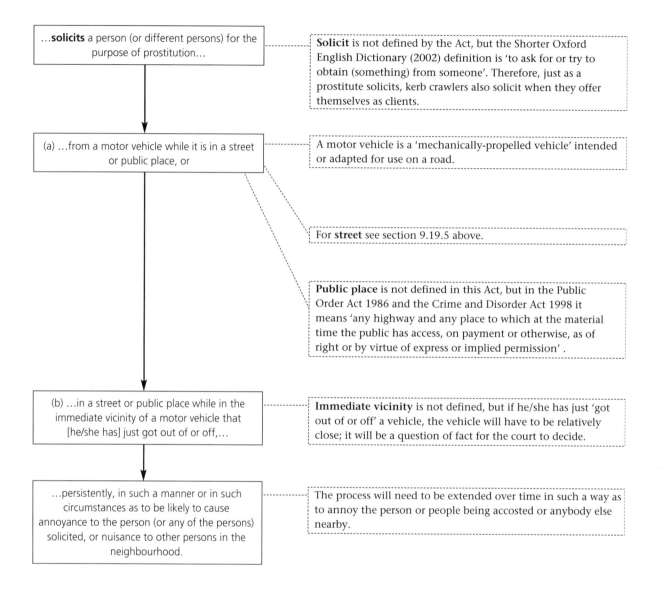

...**solicits** a person (or different persons) for the purpose of prostitution...

Solicit is not defined by the Act, but the Shorter Oxford English Dictionary (2002) definition is 'to ask for or try to obtain (something) from someone'. Therefore, just as a prostitute solicits, kerb crawlers also solicit when they offer themselves as clients.

(a) ...from a motor vehicle while it is in a street or public place, or

A motor vehicle is a 'mechanically-propelled vehicle' intended or adapted for use on a road.

For **street** see section 9.19.5 above.

Public place is not defined in this Act, but in the Public Order Act 1986 and the Crime and Disorder Act 1998 it means 'any highway and any place to which at the material time the public has access, on payment or otherwise, as of right or by virtue of express or implied permission'.

(b) ...in a street or public place while in the immediate vicinity of a motor vehicle that [he/she has] just got out of or off,...

Immediate vicinity is not defined, but if he/she has just 'got out of or off' a vehicle, the vehicle will have to be relatively close; it will be a question of fact for the court to decide.

...persistently, in such a manner or in such circumstances as to be likely to cause annoyance to the person (or any of the persons) solicited, or nuisance to other persons in the neighbourhood.

The process will need to be extended over time in such a way as to annoy the person or people being accosted or anybody else nearby.

This offence is triable summarily and the penalty is a fine.

9.19.7 Indecent Photographs of Children

Section 1 of the Protection of Children Act 1978 states that it is an offence for a person:

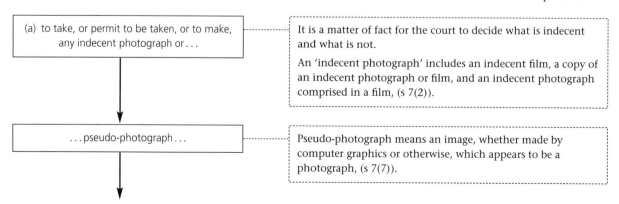

(a) to take, or permit to be taken, or to make, any indecent photograph or . . .

It is a matter of fact for the court to decide what is indecent and what is not.

An 'indecent photograph' includes an indecent film, a copy of an indecent photograph or film, and an indecent photograph comprised in a film, (s 7(2)).

. . . pseudo-photograph . . .

Pseudo-photograph means an image, whether made by computer graphics or otherwise, which appears to be a photograph, (s 7(7)).

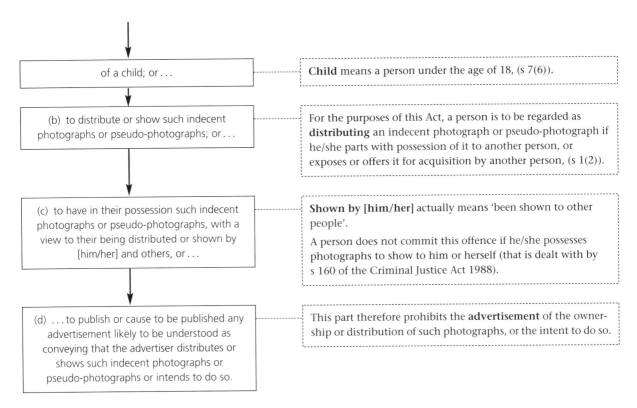

of a child; or . . .	**Child** means a person under the age of 18, (s 7(6)).
(b) to distribute or show such indecent photographs or pseudo-photographs; or . . .	For the purposes of this Act, a person is to be regarded as **distributing** an indecent photograph or pseudo-photograph if he/she parts with possession of it to another person, or exposes or offers it for acquisition by another person, (s 1(2)).
(c) to have in their possession such indecent photographs or pseudo-photographs, with a view to their being distributed or shown by [him/her] and others, or . . .	**Shown by [him/her]** actually means 'been shown to other people'. A person does not commit this offence if he/she possesses photographs to show to him or herself (that is dealt with by s 160 of the Criminal Justice Act 1988).
(d) . . . to publish or cause to be published any advertisement likely to be understood as conveying that the advertiser distributes or shows such indecent photographs or pseudo-photographs or intends to do so.	This part therefore prohibits the **advertisement** of the ownership or distribution of such photographs, or the intent to do so.

This offence is triable either way:

- Summarily; six months' imprisonment and/or a fine.
- On indictment; ten years' imprisonment.

Two defences to this offence are listed in s 1(4) of the Protection of Children Act 1978:

- the defendant had a legitimate reason for distributing, showing or having possession of the photographs or pseudo-photographs;
- the defendant saw the photographs or pseudo- photographs and did not know, nor had any cause to suspect them to be indecent.

9.19.8 Exceptions

Some exceptions are listed in s 1 of the Protection of Children Act 1978.

Exception 1A applies if the suspect can prove that the photograph was of a child aged sixteen or over, and that, at the time of the alleged offence, the child and the suspect:

(a) were married; or
(b) lived together as partners in an enduring family relationship.

Exception 1B applies if the suspect proves it was necessary to make the photograph or pseudo-photograph for the purposes of the prevention, detection, or investigation of crime, or for the purposes of criminal proceedings, in any part of the world.

TASK 17

1. You are on uniform patrol near a railway station and you notice a woman standing in the car park, for no apparent reason. As you approach the woman she walks away towards the town centre, but is back in the same place a few minutes later. Later on in the evening you see two cars stop by the woman and each time the male drivers or occupants of the cars talk to the woman and then drive off. What would you consider doing in these circumstances?

2. You are asked to attend the home of a fifteen-year-old girl. In discussion with you and her mother, the girl alleges that a family friend has been visiting the house on a regular basis, and on each occasion the family friend massages her genitals (but no penetration takes place). Could the family friend have a defence to any possible charge, if the allegations are substantiated? Would it make a difference if the young person was twelve years old?

9.20   Rape and Other Serious Sexual Offences

These offences are covered under the Sexual Offences Act 2003. In this section we will consider the offences of:

- Rape (s 1)
- Assault by penetration (s 2)
- Causing another person to engage in sexual activity without consent (s 4)

Remember that the question of consent is of paramount importance when considering whether a sexual act amounts to an offence, and hence re-read section 9.19.1 if you wish to remind yourself of some of the considerations involved.

9.20.1   Rape

Section 1 of the Sexual Offences Act 2003 makes it an offence for a person intentionally to penetrate with his penis the vagina, anus, or mouth of another person without that person's consent, when he does not reasonably believe that the other person consents. This offence can only be committed by a man, and hence the use of male personal pronoun.

Section 1 of the Sexual Offences Act 2003 states that 'a person (A) commits an offence if he':

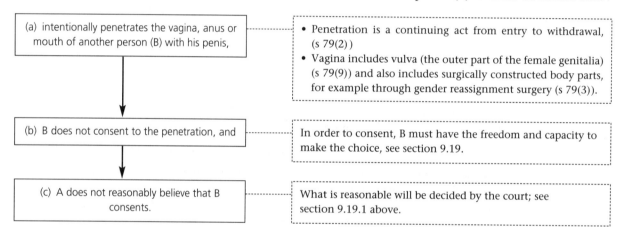

The offence of rape is triable by indictment only and the maximum penalty is life imprisonment.

9.20.2   Assault by Penetration

Section 2 of the Sexual Offences Act 2003 covers the situation where a person intentionally (and not just recklessly) penetrates the vagina or anus of another person. It can be committed by a male or a female. This offence is very similar to rape in terms of the guilty knowledge of the suspect, and evidential and conclusive presumptions must be considered (see section 9.19.1 below).

Section 2 of the Sexual Offences Act 2003 states that:

(1) A person (A) [male or female] commits an offence if:
   (a) he/she] intentionally penetrates the vagina or anus of another person (B) with a part of [his/her] body or anything else;
   (b) the penetration is sexual;
   (c) B does not consent to the penetration, and
   (d) A does not reasonably believe that B consents.

The points to prove in this offence are therefore:

- that the suspect intentionally penetrated the vagina or anus of another person, and
- the guilty knowledge that penetration occurred (outlined in evidential presumptions under s 75 and conclusive presumptions under s 76 (see section 9.19.1 above)).

This offence is triable by indictment only and the maximum penalty is life imprisonment.

9.20.3 Causing Another Person to Engage in Sexual Activity without Consent

Section 4(1) of the Sexual Offences Act 2003 states that:

(1) A person (A) commits an offence if:
  (a) [he/she] intentionally causes another person (B) to engage in an activity;
  (b) the activity is sexual;
  (c) B does not consent to engaging in the activity, and
  (d) A does not reasonably believe that B consents.

This offence is triable either way:

- Summarily; six months' imprisonment and/or a fine.
- On indictment; ten years' imprisonment.

9.20.3.1 Causing another person to engage in penetration without consent

Section 4(4) states that if the s 4(1) offence described above involves:

  (a) penetration of B's anus or vagina;
  (b) penetration of B's mouth with a person's penis;
  (c) penetration of a person's anus or vagina with a part of B's body or by B with anything else;
  (d) penetration of a person's mouth with B's penis;

then the offence is triable on indictment only, and the penalty is life imprisonment.

TASK 18

Many victims of rape will be concerned about their identity becoming known during the investigation and any subsequent court case. What legislation is available to provide anonymity in relation to complaints of rape and restrictions on evidence at trials for rape?

9.21 Damage to Property

The Criminal Damage Act 1971 lists several different offences and the following are covered here:

- Criminal damage (s 1(1));
- Criminal damage life endangered (s 1(2));
- Arson (s 1(3));
- Threats to damage (s 2);
- Possession with intent to damage (s 3).

Other offences covered here are:

- Causing damage to ancient monuments (s 28, Ancient Monuments and Archaeological Areas Act 1979).
- Graffiti (s 54(1), Anti-Social Behaviour Act 2003).

The kind of criminal damage that you will meet as a student police officer is usually graffiti and minor damage to fences, cars, and bus shelters. Occasionally, the damage can be much more serious, when, for example the damage has been caused by fire.

An understanding of the law surrounding damage to property will assist your achievement of the police action required to 'Conduct the Initial Investigation & Report of Volume Crime According to National Policing Plan' under the 'Investigation' PAC heading.

9.21.1   **Criminal Damage**

Section 1(1) of the Criminal Damage Act 1971 states that an offence is committed by:

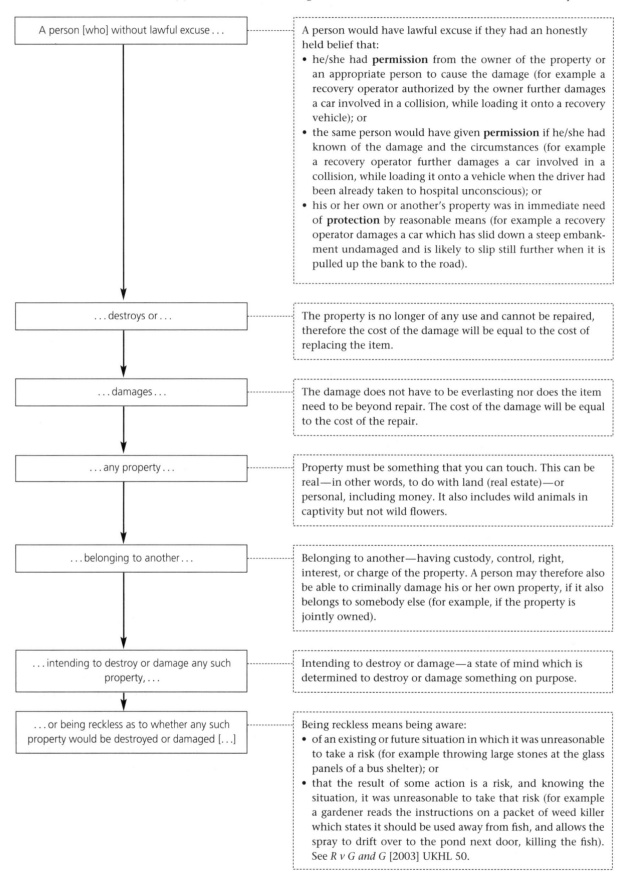

A person [who] without lawful excuse . . .

A person would have lawful excuse if they had an honestly held belief that:
- he/she had **permission** from the owner of the property or an appropriate person to cause the damage (for example a recovery operator authorized by the owner further damages a car involved in a collision, while loading it onto a recovery vehicle); or
- the same person would have given **permission** if he/she had known of the damage and the circumstances (for example a recovery operator further damages a car involved in a collision, while loading it onto a vehicle when the driver had been already taken to hospital unconscious); or
- his or her own or another's property was in immediate need of **protection** by reasonable means (for example a recovery operator damages a car which has slid down a steep embankment undamaged and is likely to slip still further when it is pulled up the bank to the road).

. . . destroys or . . .

The property is no longer of any use and cannot be repaired, therefore the cost of the damage will be equal to the cost of replacing the item.

. . . damages . . .

The damage does not have to be everlasting nor does the item need to be beyond repair. The cost of the damage will be equal to the cost of the repair.

. . . any property . . .

Property must be something that you can touch. This can be real—in other words, to do with land (real estate)—or personal, including money. It also includes wild animals in captivity but not wild flowers.

. . . belonging to another . . .

Belonging to another—having custody, control, right, interest, or charge of the property. A person may therefore also be able to criminally damage his or her own property, if it also belongs to somebody else (for example, if the property is jointly owned).

. . . intending to destroy or damage any such property, . . .

Intending to destroy or damage—a state of mind which is determined to destroy or damage something on purpose.

. . . or being reckless as to whether any such property would be destroyed or damaged [. . .]

Being reckless means being aware:
- of an existing or future situation in which it was unreasonable to take a risk (for example throwing large stones at the glass panels of a bus shelter); or
- that the result of some action is a risk, and knowing the situation, it was unreasonable to take that risk (for example a gardener reads the instructions on a packet of weed killer which states it should be used away from fish, and allows the spray to drift over to the pond next door, killing the fish). See *R v G and G* [2003] UKHL 50.

This offence is triable either way:

- Summarily; six months' imprisonment and/or a fine.
- On indictment; ten years' imprisonment.

Note that if the value of the property damaged or destroyed is less than £5,000, the offence is tried summarily only (s 22, Magistrates' Courts Act 1980) but it still remains an 'either way' offence.

> ## TASK 19
> Bob, after his arrest for being drunk and disorderly, smears his own excrement on the walls of the police station cell.
>
> Discuss whether this constitutes criminal damage.

9.21.2 Criminal Damage Life Endangered

The offence of 'criminal damage life endangered' is committed by a person who destroys or damages property intending (or being reckless as) to endanger life.

The following points explain the meaning of the term to 'endanger life':

- There is no requirement for there to be an attempt to kill; murder or manslaughter would be the more appropriate charge.
- There is no requirement for any actual injury to occur. For instance, the ex-employee of a garage owner damages the brake system on one of the vintage motorcycles owned by his ex-boss. By chance, the ex-boss decides to put it on display (and therefore not ride it for the foreseeable future) so, although no harm may actually come to the intended victim, the potential for harm exists.
- The actual damage caused must also be the cause of the danger; for example shooting at someone in a room through a window both endangers life and damages the window, but it is the shot, bullet, or missile that endangers the life, not the damage from the window. Therefore the offence here would not be criminal damage; however, another offence such as attempted murder may have been committed.

Section 1(2) of the Criminal Damage Act 1971 states that it is an offence for a person:

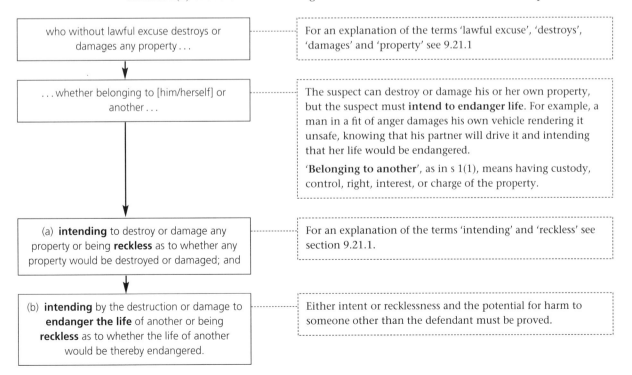

This offence is triable by indictment only and the penalty is life imprisonment.

9.21.3 Arson

Section 1(3) of the Criminal Damage Act 1971 states that an offence committed under this section by destroying or damaging property by fire shall be charged as arson. For a person to be found guilty of causing criminal damage by fire, at least some of the damage must have been caused by fire, but this does not include smoke damage. There must be an intent or an element of recklessness as to the use of fire in order for the offence to be proved.

This offence is triable either way:

- Summarily; six months' imprisonment and/or a fine.
- On indictment; life imprisonment.

9.21.4 Threats to Damage

This offence is covered in s 2 of the Criminal Damage Act 1971. There are two points to prove in relation to a threat. First, the conduct that is threatened must refer to damage, and the extent of the threatened damage must constitute an offence under s 1 of the Criminal Damage Act 1971. This can include acts of simple damage under s 1(1) as well as criminal damage where life is endangered under s 1(2). However, the offence of making threats to damage cannot be committed if the threat involves an element of recklessness as to whether the property would actually be destroyed or damaged (see section 9.21.1 for an explanation of 'reckless'). An example might include an angry person who shouts to a neighbour 'If your kid keeps throwing stones over the wall near my windows, I'll throw them straight back'; there is no threat to actually break anything, so this cannot amount to a threat to damage. In order to commit the offence of making threats to damage, there must be a stated intention to destroy or damage the property. The threat can be communicated in any way such as e-mail, text message, fax, letter, or phone call and it could be an idle threat; there need be no intention to actually carry it out. The recipient does not have to believe the threat will be carried out immediately (if at all), nor does the recipient need to be put in fear. In any prosecution it will be for the court to decide whether what was communicated had enough substance and immediacy to constitute a threat.

Note that in some circumstances considering an offence under s 4 of the Public Order Act 1986 (see section 8.12 above) might be more appropriate.

Section 2 of the Criminal Damage Act 1971 states it is an offence for a person:

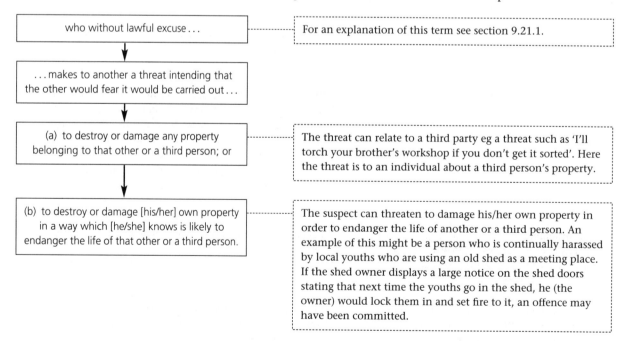

This offence is triable either way:

- Summarily; six months' imprisonment and/or a fine.
- On indictment; ten years' imprisonment

9.21.5 Possessing an Article with Intent to Cause Criminal Damage

This offence is covered in s 3 of the Criminal Damage Act 1971. The type of article involved here can be literally anything. The Law Commission, who advised on the Act, explained that:

> The essential feature of the proposed offence is to be found, not so much in the nature of the thing, as in the intention with which it is held (Law Commission No 29, para 59).

Section 3 of the Criminal Damage Act 1971 states it is an offence for a person who has anything:

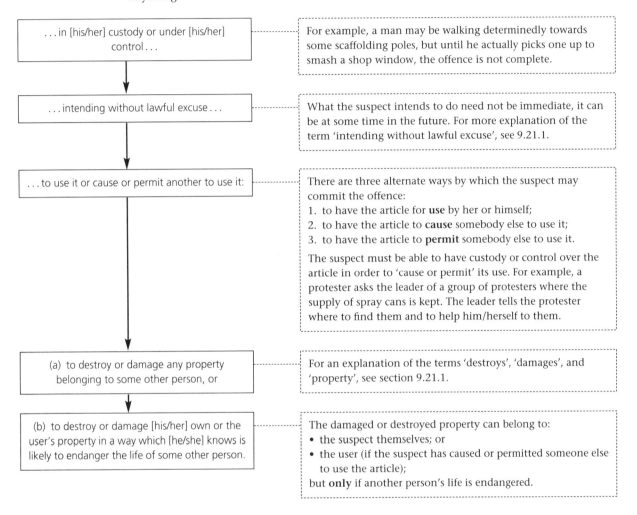

. . . in [his/her] custody or under [his/her] control . . .	For example, a man may be walking determinedly towards some scaffolding poles, but until he actually picks one up to smash a shop window, the offence is not complete.
. . . intending without lawful excuse . . .	What the suspect intends to do need not be immediate, it can be at some time in the future. For more explanation of the term 'intending without lawful excuse', see 9.21.1.
. . . to use it or cause or permit another to use it:	There are three alternate ways by which the suspect may commit the offence: 1. to have the article for **use** by her or himself; 2. to have the article to **cause** somebody else to use it; 3. to have the article to **permit** somebody else to use it. The suspect must be able to have custody or control over the article in order to 'cause or permit' its use. For example, a protester asks the leader of a group of protesters where the supply of spray cans is kept. The leader tells the protester where to find them and to help him/herself to them.
(a) to destroy or damage any property belonging to some other person, or	For an explanation of the terms 'destroys', 'damages', and 'property', see section 9.21.1.
(b) to destroy or damage [his/her] own or the user's property in a way which [he/she] knows is likely to endanger the life of some other person.	The damaged or destroyed property can belong to: • the suspect themselves; or • the user (if the suspect has caused or permitted someone else to use the article); but **only** if another person's life is endangered.

This offence is triable either way:

- Summarily; six months' imprisonment and/or a fine not exceeding the statutory maximum.
- On indictment; ten years' imprisonment.

9.21.6 Powers to Search

Under s 1(2)(a) of the PACE Act 1984 you have the power to search for articles made or adapted for use in the course of or connection with an offence under s 1 of the Criminal Damage Act 1971. It states that you:

(a) may search—
  (i) any person or vehicle;
  (ii) anything which is in or on a vehicle . . . for stolen or prohibited articles [and]
(b) may detain a person or vehicle for the purpose of such a search.

Prohibited articles include articles used in the course of or in connection with offences under s 1 of the Criminal Damage Act 1971, which are used to destroy or damage property.

Remember, that you must follow s 2 of the PACE Act 1984 and its Codes of Practice when conducting a search, and supply the person searched with the information contained in para 3.8 of Code A.

9.21.7   Damaging Ancient Monuments

It is an offence under s 28 of the Ancient Monuments and Archaeological Areas Act 1979 to damage certain monuments. An offence is committed by:

> a person who, without lawful excuse, destroys or damages any protected monument—
>
> (a) knowing that it is a protected monument; and
> (b) intending to destroy or damage the monument or being reckless as to whether the monument would be destroyed or damaged.

This offence is triable either way:

- Summarily; six months' imprisonment and/or a fine.
- On indictment; two years' imprisonment and/or a fine.

9.21.8   Graffiti

As graffiti is among the commonest forms of criminal damage, it is an offence to sell aerosol paint to children. Section 54(1) of the Anti-Social Behaviour Act 2003 states that it is an offence for a person to sell an aerosol paint container to a person under the age of sixteen. Section 54(2) states that:

> 'Aerosol paint container' means a device which—
>
> (a) contains paint stored under pressure, and
> (b) is designed to permit the release of the paint as a spray.

This offence is triable summarily and the penalty is a fine.

9.22   Criminal Attempts

A person planning a criminal offence might not actually commit the full offence. This could be because he/she lost his/her nerve or was disturbed, or simply found that his/her plans were impracticable. The offence of criminal attempts (s 1 of the Criminal Attempts Act 1981) enables courts to penalize criminals for carrying out an act just short of committing the full offence, even if he/she did not commit the full offence. The offence he/she attempts to commit must be an indictable offence. (Indictable offences are those offences which can be tried on indictment in a Crown Court or either way at a magistrates' court or a Crown Court (see section 5.12 above).) Summary offences cannot be attempted in terms of this legislation.

This offence is described under s 1(1) of the Criminal Attempts Act 1981:

> If with intent to commit the offence to which this section applies, a person does an act which is more than merely preparatory to the commission of the offence, [he/she] is guilty of attempting to commit the offence.

9.22.1   Criminal Intent

The suspect must have formed criminal intent (*mens rea*) in all three of the following areas:

The suspect must have the intent to:	Example
Commit the full offence.	The suspect intended to steal a car or intended to rob a person.
Take part in a series of events which will lead to a final outcome of committing the full offence.	The suspect made a point of collecting the tools together, going to a house, and forcing a window in order to break in.
Fulfil **all** the elements of the offence.	In order to attempt a theft, the suspect must have acted dishonestly with the intention of appropriating the property belonging to another with the intention of permanently depriving the other of it.

For a person to be found guilty of an attempt to commit an offence, the suspect must have more than an intention to do it. In this context, merely thinking about committing an offence, such as deciding upon what article to use and what time to carry it out, is not enough; the suspect must demonstrate his or her guilty intent by carrying out acts which are more than just preparing to commit the full offence. Therefore, it would not be enough if the suspect simply thought about setting fire to a rival's house and only considered the location of the required articles. If, on the other hand, the suspect went to the front door of his rival with cloth soaked in petrol and put it in the letter box and then used a lighter to attempt to light the cloth, this would show a clear intent to carry out the offence of arson. These acts would be more than merely preparatory and therefore constitute an attempt under the Criminal Attempts Act 1981.

9.22.2 Thorough Planning and Practical Preparation

Section 1(2) of the Criminal Attempts Act 1981 states that there must be evidence that the person actually planned to carry out the act him or herself rather than just planning it (in which case someone else could have carried it out):

> the person does an act which is more than merely preparatory to the commission of the offence.

Therefore, if there is something else to be done before the completion of the offence, it does not amount to an attempt. Similarly, the final act carried out by the accused must be in combination with all the other preparatory acts, and have no other aim than to complete the full offence. For example, a group of people may be seen getting out of a car and then standing close to a fenced enclosure that contains scrap copper and other metals. They cut a hole in the fence that would big enough for someone to climb through. On seeing a security guard, the group drives away from the scene and is stopped some miles away. One of the group still has some wire clippers in his pocket and another throws a pair of bolt croppers out of the van. They have done more than merely prepare to steal the metal; they have committed an attempt under s 1(1) of the Criminal Attempts Act 1981 (see *Davey v Lee* [1967] 51 Cr App R 303).

It does not matter (for the offence of criminal attempt) if the attempted offence would actually be impossible to carry out:

> A person may be guilty of attempting to commit an offence (to which this section applies), even though the facts are such that the commission of the offence is impossible (s 1(2)).

Section 1(3)(b)) states that if the person **believes** that he/she is committing an offence, he/she will still be regarded as having attempted it, even if it is proved later that it would not have been possible to commit the full offence. For example, a woman is paid money to travel from another country to the UK with a suitcase that she believes contains heroin. On arrival at the UK port her suitcase is searched and she admits to importing heroin into the UK. However, tests on the substance in the suitcase reveal it to be harmless vegetable matter, and not drugs. The offence of importation of controlled drugs has therefore not been committed, but the person has still attempted to commit the crime.

9.22.3 Offences Which Cannot Be Attempted in Terms of Criminal Attempts

Section 1(4) of the Criminal Attempts Act 1981 lists several categories of offence that cannot be 'attempted'. Summary-only offences cannot generally be attempted unless specifically stated in the legislation, such as attempting to drive whilst unfit through drink or drugs. 'Taking a conveyance without the owner's consent' is a summary-only offence and therefore cannot be attempted, which is why the (summary) offence of 'Interfering with vehicles' was created in the Criminal Attempts Act 1981.

However, there are a number of ways in which indictable offences cannot be attempted. These include:

- **conspiracy** to commit an indictable offence; that is, an agreement between people to commit an offence;
- **aiding, abetting, counselling, procuring, or suborning** the commission of an indictable offence; for example, a person knew all the circumstances surrounding a person's murder by the suspect and did everything apart from deliver the fatal kick to the head;

- **assisting** offenders; such as knowingly helping offenders avoid arrest or concealing information, perhaps by paying money to a witness to stop him/her giving testimony in any trial.

The mode of trial is the same as for the main offence:

- Either way offences; the same maximum penalty as the substantive offence when tried summarily.
- On indictment-only offences; the same maximum penalty as the substantive offence

---

TASK 20

Look at the following case relating to an attempt. The case subsequently went to appeal. Predict the result of the appeal and explain your reasoning.

A suspect was seen by a teacher in the lavatory block at a school. A cider can with the suspect's fingerprints was in one of the cubicles. The suspect's rucksack, containing a large kitchen knife, some rope, and a roll of masking tape, was found in some nearby bushes. The suspect was charged and convicted of attempted child abduction, the prosecution putting forward the argument that the suspect had been hiding in the lavatories to abduct a child.

The suspect appealed on the grounds that he had not attempted to commit the offence, (*R v Geddes* [1996] Crim LR 894).

9.23 Answers to Tasks

TASK 1

You probably considered the following:

(i)   Was the person dishonest?
(ii) Did s/he take the property?
(iii) Who did the property belong to?
(iv) Did the person show an intention never to give the property back to its owner?

TASK 2

The circumstances do not amount to an offence of robbery because violence was not used in order to steal. This is because Jo picked up the bag and attempted to run off with it and did not use force to steal it. Jo then picked up an item from the ground of the shopping centre and ran into Chris, causing her to fall over and break her arm, and it is only now that force is used. However, this force is used after the theft has taken place. Force was not used immediately before, at the time or in order to steal the bag and the goods and therefore robbery has not been committed.

TASK 3

(a) No burglary has been committed. Although Jo entered the storage warehouse as a trespasser, the intention was to sleep, not to commit any of the offences specified in s 9(1)(a) of the Theft Act 1968. Once inside the warehouse, Jo damaged the door, which is property. Jo also extracted electricity by using the fire, but neither damage nor abstraction are included in the acts listed under s 9(1)(b) of the Theft Act 1968 which is confined to theft and grievous bodily harm.

(b) The following offences are likely to have been committed:

- Burglary with intent to steal (s 9(1)(a), of the Theft Act 1968) as Terri entered as a trespasser with the necessary intent.
- Burglary (s 9(1)(b), Theft Act 1968) has also taken place as Terri having entered as a trespasser inflicts grievous bodily harm on the occupier.

- Aggravated burglary (s 10, Theft Act 1968) has taken place because whilst committing the s 9(1)(b) burglary, Terri was armed with a weapon of offence at the time of the search for something to steal.

TASK 4

1. Section 163 of the Road Traffic Act 1988 states that 'a person driving a mechanically propelled vehicle on a road must stop on being required to do so by a constable in uniform'.
2. This is covered under s 67 of the Road Traffic Act 1988.

You will be made an authorized examiner by your chief officer and as such you will have the authority to test a vehicle (and drawn trailer) on a road for the purposes of ascertaining compliance with:

- the construction and use requirements including lighting; and
- the requirement that the condition of the vehicle is not such that its use on the road would involve a danger of injury to any person.

This is described under reg 67 of the Road Vehicles (Construction and Use) Regulations 1986. All wheeled vehicles after 1 April 1980 should be equipped with a plate in a conspicuous and readily accessible location on a part not normally subject to replacement which clearly shows the:

- Vehicle Identification Number.
- Name of manufacturer.
- Type approval number (possibly on a separate plate).

The VIN should also be stamped on the chassis or frame and together these identifying features can be matched against details on PNC to enable identification of stolen vehicles.

TASK 5

National research in the late 1990s showed that the risk of theft of cars was greatest for:

- older cars;
- familiar makes of cars (for example, Fords);
- performance models.

The same survey showed that the type of car least likely to be stolen was a 'people carrier', such as the Ford Galaxy or Renault Espace. See <http://www.crimereduction.gov.uk/toolkits/vc020204.htm> for further details.

TASK 6

1. Yes, a horse box is a trailer.
2. No, a go-kart is not a motor vehicle adapted or intended for use on the road.
3. Yes, there is an intention to commit theft of the CD player which is 'anything carried in or on the motor vehicle'.
4. No, there is no intention to steal the vehicle, anything in or on it, or take it without the owner's consent.

TASK 7

The correct response is (iii) 'both'.

TASK 8

(1) In respond to this task you may have asked yourself a series of questions (Q) to establish whether an offence had occurred. We offer a number of possible answers (A) below.

(Q) Are they at the place of abode?

(A) If you are in fact talking to the prolific car thief, then the answer is 'no' as he/she is sitting outside the house and so he/she is not at his or her place of abode.

(Q) Has he/she 'control' over a pair of gloves, a large bunch of approximately forty car keys, and a short length of scaffold pole?

(A) Yes, they are on the passenger's seat and therefore the person has control over them.

(Q) Are the gloves, a large bunch of approximately forty car keys and a short length of scaffold pole 'any article'?

(A) Yes, they are.

(Q) Are the articles for use in the course of or in connection with any 'burglary, theft or cheat'?

(A) Clearly, these are articles often used for breaking into cars. (The short length of scaffold pole for example, can be used to break a steering lock.) However, it is not clear at this point whether or not the person has used the articles for any burglary, theft, or cheat, or whether he/she was going to use them so in the future. In order to be found guilty of going equipped the suspect must have some future intention to carry out a burglary, theft or cheat, and therefore this particular case would need further investigation.

(2) The correct response is (i), that is (a) and (b) only.

TASK 9

People enter the restaurant and order a meal.	There is an expectation on people when they enter a restaurant that they will pay for food which is prepared for them and served accordingly. By entering a restaurant therefore, people imply that they have the means by which to pay for goods which are provided and the intention to do so unless there is a special credit agreement whereby payment can be delayed until a later date.
	If people enter the restaurant with the appearance of paying customers (the false representation) but with an express intention not to pay for the meal they are about to consume (the property) or knowing they do not have the means to pay for it, they will commit a s 1 Fraud Act 2006 offence of 'fraud by false representation'. This is because the 'dishonest represenation' took place before the property was obtained.
Having ordered the meal, they wait at the table for it to be served.	When people enter a restaurant and order the meal, initially intending to pay but then change their mind about paying before it is obtained, then the offence is again one of s 1 'dishonest represenation' as once more they assume the role of paying customers (the false represenation) before the meal is obtained (the property).
The meal is served to the table.	When obtaining a meal at a restaurant, some of the charge is for the service that the customer receives. If the customer implies that he/she is an ordinary customer but intends not to pay for the service of the meal, then a s 11 Fraud Act offence 'obtaining services dishonestly' may be committed.
Having consumed the meal, they are expected to pay.	If people who enter a restaurant and intend from the start to pay for their meal, but change their minds after their meal is obtained, then the dishonesty has occurred after obtaining the property, so a s 1 Fraud Act offence has not been committed. However, because the meal was served to the table, a s 11 Fraud Act offence 'obtaining services dishonestly' may be committed.
They leave the restaurant.	If the people continue to make out they are ordinary customers, intending to pay, waiting for the bill for example, and then make off out of the restaurant at a convenient moment without paying, there is dishonesty but it takes place after obtaining the property and the offence is more likely to be s 3 Theft Act 1978, that is, 'bilking'. Seek the advice of a CPS representative in such cases for the most appropriate charge.

TASK 10

Some common street names are:

Amphetamines— speed, crystal, crank, meth, black beauties, bennies, uppers, dexies, 357 magnums.

Cocaine— crack, coke, booth, blow, railers, snow, ringer, divits, toot, cola, rocks, blast, white dust, ivory flakes, nose candy, mobbeles.

Heroin— china white, fix, horse, smack, whack, mother pearl, H, junk.

Cannabis— dope buds, bhang, goof butt, grass, hash, hay, hemp, herb, jive, pot, rope, stinkweed, stuff, tea, weed, wacky backy, whack.

TASK 11

Factors might include:

- Intelligence that drugs are being supplied or used in that particular area.
- Information on the descriptions of people supplying or using drugs in that area.
- Behaviour of the person—for example, is he/she trying to hide something? Or preparing to throw something small away so you do not see it?
- The physical demeanour and apparent mental state of the person—for example, does he/she appear to be drunk (without smelling of intoxicating liquor)?

Perhaps this is a good description of the consumption and effects of a class A drug?

'X' took his bottle from the corner of the mantel-piece and his hypodermic syringe from its neat morocco case. With his long, white, nervous fingers he adjusted the delicate needle, and rolled back his left shirt-cuff. For some little time his eyes rested thoughtfully upon the sinewy forearm and wrist all dotted and scarred with innumerable puncture-marks. Finally he thrust the sharp point home, pressed down the tiny piston, and sank back into the velvet-lined arm-chair with a long sigh of satisfaction.

In this case 'X' is Sherlock Holmes (Conan-Doyle, 1887).

What to say or to think about before carrying out the search:

- Purpose of the search;
- Entitlement to a copy of the record of search;
- Grounds for the search;
- Warrant card if you are not in uniform;
- Explain to the person that he/she is being detained for a search;
- Legal search power title you are using (s 23 of the Misuse of Drugs Act);
- Police station name;
- Your name.

You could call upon the following reasons to make an arrest:

- to enable the name or address of the person in question to be ascertained;
- to prevent him/her from causing physical injury to him/herself;
- to prevent him/her from suffering physical injury;
- to allow the prompt and effective investigation of the offence or of the conduct of the person in question;
- to prevent any prosecution for the offence from being hindered by the disappearance of the person in question.

TASK 12

1. Common assault by beating (battery).
2. Common assault.

If a person is assaulted he/she is the victim of common assault (remember that assault is the **threat** of violence or harm, not the harm itself). If force is threatened and then used, the offence is common assault by beating (battery). The suspect can only be charged or summonsed with common assault **or** common assault by beating (battery), not both.

TASK 13

You probably considered the following:

(i)   Through questioning you will be able to determine if the injury affects the health or comfort of the victim in more than a trivial way.

(ii)   Through questioning and observation you will be able to collect and collate evidence concerning the injury and whether it can seen or felt by the victim or witnesses (which include you).

(iii) If there is no evidence of the offence of **actual bodily harm** then consider **common assault** as an alternative.

TASK 14

The problem with these kinds of scenarios is that you lack all the other information that would actually be potentially available to you in a real incident. However, based entirely on the limited information available to you in the questions, the following are the possible offences that could be considered:

1. Section 47, Offences Against the Person Act 1861.
2. Sections 18 or 20, Offences Against the Person Act 1861. Until evidence is gathered from witnesses and an interview with the suspect is held, the offence could be either s 18 or s 20, depending on what the suspect intended.
3. Assault with intent to resist lawful arrest.
   Common Assault.
   Section 38, Offences Against the Person Act 1861.
   Section 39, Criminal Justice Act 1988.
4. Common Assault and Section 39, Criminal Justice Act 1988.

TASK 15

1. Under s 17(e) of the PACE Act 1984 you 'may enter and search any premises for the purposes of saving life or limb or preventing serious damage to property'.
2. It would appear that Jo has committed an offence under s 1 of the Children and Young Persons Act 1933. This is committed by any person who is sixteen years or over who has responsibility for a child under the age of sixteen years and who 'willfully assaults, ill-treats, neglects, abandons or exposes the child in a manner likely to cause unnecessary suffering or injury to health'. In these circumstances Jo has 'abandoned' Sam in a manner likely to cause unnecessary suffering or injury to health. It appears that, although an offence has been committed, the child is no longer in immediate danger and arrangements could be made perhaps with the neighbours or the grandparents for the child's safety while Jo is absent. If you had any reason to believe the child was in immediate danger you could consider taking Sam into police protection and arresting the mother. However, you must be guided by prosecution guidelines and you should seek the guidance of a CPS representative in relation to this matter. Whatever action you take, it must be proportionate.

TASK 16

Section 66 of the Sexual Offences Act only applies to exposure of a person's genitals, not the buttocks (although it is possible that 'mooning' may also result in exposure of the genitals, even though this was not intended). However, in any case the suspects might excuse themselves by stating that their intention was to entertain or amuse, not to alarm or distress.

In the common law offence of Outraging Public Decency, there must be a deliberate act that is lewd, obscene, or disgusting. In *R v Rowley* [1991] 4 All ER 649, Lord Simon decided that outraging public decency goes considerably beyond offending the sensibilities of 'reasonable' people.

Therefore you should seek advice from your local evidence review representative or CPS representative as to whether the common law offence might be committed by members of the rugby team and also consider public order offences as well, eg s 5 of the Public Order Act; non-intentional harassment, alarm, or distress.

TASK 17

1. You may consider investigating the woman under s 1(1) of the Street Offences Act 1959 as a 'common prostitute loitering or soliciting in a public place'. However, the Home Office recommends that a woman found soliciting in the street should be cautioned on two occasions before being prosecuted (and also see your local force policy). You may therefore consider speaking to the woman and, having found out her name and address, check whether she has been previously cautioned for soliciting. If it were apparent that she is a persistent offender you may need to consider further action. Otherwise you might consider cautioning her, ensuring of course that the caution is recorded in the appropriate place according to local procedures. In this way the fact that she has already been cautioned will be apparent to any subsequent police officer who may need to check.
2. In the case of sexual activity with a child under s 9(1) of the Sexual Offences Act 2003, there is a defence available if the family friend reasonably believed that the girl was over sixteen. If the girl was twelve years old or younger the defendant would have no defence.

TASK 18

Section 7 of the Sexual Offences (Amendment) Act 1976 provides anonymity for victims of rape, attempted rape, aiding, abetting, counselling and procuring rape or attempted rape, incitement to rape, and conspiracy to rape.

TASK 19

The excrement will not have destroyed the walls of the police cell but the walls will need to be cleaned therefore they will have been damaged. The cost of the damage will be equal to the cost of the cleaning operation. The suspect will need to be interviewed to prove or disprove whether he intended to damage the walls or was reckless as to whether or not the damage was caused. If the drunken state was self-induced, it will not be a defence.

TASK 20

The suspect had never had communication with any children nor made any contact with a child. As a result, the Court of Appeal concluded that the acts of the suspect were merely preparatory and that the suspect had not attempted to abduct any children.

10 | Road and Traffic Policing

10.1 Chapter Briefing

This chapter describes police procedures and duties relevant to road and traffic policing. You will probably be expected to demonstrate competence in many of the areas described in this chapter whilst on Supervised and Independent Patrol.

Much of the content of this chapter concerns legislation. As we explained in Chapter 2, we often provide a simplified and abbreviated version of the law, and use flow charts to explain points when appropriate. If you require more detail then you may need to consult the original legislation, other textbooks, or websites.

10.1.1 Aim of the Chapter

The aim of this chapter is to introduce you to the legislation and police practice when involved with road and traffic policing.

This chapter will enable you to:

- understand the legislation surrounding the use of vehicles;
- identify a number of common offences related to vehicles and to driving, and how to take the appropriate action according to the powers legally granted to you;
- develop the underpinning knowledge required for a number of NOS elements, one of the PAC headings, and entries for your Learning Diary Phase 3 and a CAR of your SOLAP.

10.1.2 Police Action Checklist

This chapter will assist in meeting the following requirements of the Police Action Checklist under the Road Policing heading:

- Check driving documents.
- Complete traffic documents—including HO/RT1/FPN(E)/CLE2/VDRS.
- Demonstrate correct administration of the appropriate tests for drink/drugs driving offences.

10.1.3 National Occupational Standards

This chapter will provide you with some of the knowledge required to demonstrate aspects of the following NOS elements:

National Occupational Standards Elements

2C1.1 Gather information and plan a response.
2C1.2 Respond to incidents.

10.1.4 IPLDP Phases and Modules

This chapter will provide you with resources to support the following Operational Module of the IPLDP:

OP 3 Respond to incidents, conduct and evaluate investigations.

It will also cover aspects of the following topic areas of Legislation, Policy and Guidelines of the IPLDP.

- Police Policies and Procedures (LPG 1.4);
- Road Policing (LPG 1.8).

Much of the content of this chapter relates to IPLDP Phase 3 Supervised Patrol and Phase 4 Independent Patrol.

10.1.5 SOLAP

The contents of this chapter are relevant to the 'knowledge' evidence requirement of CAR 2C1.

10.1.6 Learning Diary Phases

The contents of this chapter may provide you with stimulus material for completion of your Learning Diary (Phase 3) and the Traffic heading in particular.

10.2 Introduction

It is perhaps apocryphal to remark that the first time the middle classes encountered the police was in the introduction of traffic law in the first decades of the last century (see section 1.3). However, if we substitute the phrase 'otherwise law-abiding' for 'middle' in the sentence above, it may still be the case.

Most of us are law-abiding most of the time. We do not attack our neighbour as he or she passes in the morning, nor do we steal from, rob, knife, bludgeon, or attack our work colleagues. We do not routinely murder passers-by or members of our families or set light to public buildings. We may sometimes get drunk and fall over, or make inappropriate comments, or have an irrational hatred of garden gnomes but, generally speaking, most of us observe most laws, most of the time. Except, that is, when we are driving.

What happens when we get behind the wheel of a car? For a start, many of us routinely **drive too fast** for the legal speed limit. The following table gives the proportion of vehicles observed exceeding the speed limits in surveys conducted in Great Britain in 2004.

Vehicles exceeding the speed limit (%)

	Motorways	Non-urban dual carriageways	Urban 40 mph	Urban 30 mph
Cars	56	48	28	53
HGVs	2	80	26	54
Coaches/ buses	3	40	15	28

(Adapted from Department of Transport, 2005).

Of particular concern must be the majority of cars and HGVs that exceed the 30 mph urban speed limit, where, of course, there is a greater density of foot travellers and children.

The majority of urban accidents are caused by excessive speed, whilst other factors, including driver inattention, driving too close to the vehicle in front, not allowing for adverse weather conditions, and mechanical defect, often dominate motorway and rural collision statistics. Very few of us drive at the legal limit all the time, and those who do are often abused by those who do not. These are daily occurrences on any of our roads.

Poor maintenance of vehicles is also common and the reason for this is not hard to see. Fewer people these days seek to keep a car beyond five years, and possessing the same one for more than ten (unless a vintage vehicle) is unusual. Therefore, the argument runs, fewer people invest in maintenance skills and do-it-yourself repair. The complexity of modern vehicles, particularly in their electronic circuitry, also tends to make maintenance of vehicles the province of the specialist garage mechanic. The cost of repairs and maintenance, plus the fear of being ripped off by unscrupulous garages, make people increasingly reluctant to have their vehicles maintained routinely. It is only after a knock, or when an MOT is due, that most people have their vehicles serviced. This means that it is quite common to see vehicles with only one headlamp, tyre wear, or poor bodywork.

What has this to do with roads policing? In the pages which follow you will be learning the law about highways, driving, road traffic collisions (no longer called accidents), insurance, offences, driving standards, drink-driving, drug-taking and driving, and arcane subjects such as 'fireworks and highways'. Whilst all of this law and procedure is relevant to your function as a police officer, what is not quite so explicit is:

- how driving standards have fallen in the last ten years, particularly in courtesy and tolerance;
- how we have noted instead the appearance (at least in media reporting terms) of 'road-rage';
- how driving skills have become abraded over time without reassessment or re-tests for poor driving (even after conviction);
- how poorly many privately-owned (and some publicly-owned) vehicles are maintained and how, consequently, drivers are less aware of vehicle defects and safety rules;
- how many more vehicles are on the roads, especially in the congested South-East of England;

- how litigious drivers may be towards you and towards each other (especially as a result of 'no win, no fee' practice).

Bear in mind, as you read and learn from the following, and as you go out on Supervised Patrol, that it is often the case with British drivers of 'love me, love my car'. You may encounter more hostility and aggression among the nation's drivers than among its drunks. Sometimes, of course, they are one and the same.

Finally, we should perhaps note the link between road and traffic offences and other forms of criminality. Research by Rose (2000) demonstrated that 79% of disqualified drivers had a criminal record (four times the average). Approximately 50% of dangerous drivers had a previous conviction and approximately 25% were reconvicted within a year (three times the average). Drink drivers had less extensive criminal records than other groups of serious traffic offenders—40% had a criminal record, the average time since their last court appearance was eight years, and 12% had a subsequent conviction within a year. However, these figures are still twice the average. Similarly Junger et al (2001) identified links between 'risky' traffic behaviour and more general violent crime. All of this leads us to the notion of 'self-selecting' road and traffic behaviour that you might usefully consider as indicators of perhaps more serious criminal predisposition. For example, in a famous study, Chenery et al (1999) demonstrated the links between the relatively minor offence of illegal parking in disabled bays, active criminals, and illegal vehicles.

10.3 Powers to Stop a Vehicle and 'Using, Causing, and Permitting'

Whilst on foot or mobile patrol it will be necessary for you to investigate offences connected with the use of mechanically-propelled vehicles (such as cars) on the road. These offences may relate to the way in which the vehicle has been driven, or because you suspect the ability of the driver has been impaired through drink or drugs, or the condition of the vehicle needs examination. You may suspect the occupants of the vehicle to have been involved in committing other offences using the vehicle or you may wish to speak to them about other matters. For whatever reason, if the vehicle is in motion on a road, you will need to stop it safely in order to speak to the people inside. This process will necessitate you being on duty in full uniform to give a clear direction from a police vehicle or while you are on foot patrol.

The power to stop a mechanically-propelled vehicle on a road is contained under s 163 of the Road Traffic Act 1988, which states:

163(1) A person driving a mechanically propelled vehicle on a road must stop the vehicle on being required to do so by a constable in uniform or a traffic officer.

163(3) If a person fails to comply with this section, [he/she] is guilty of an offence.

This offence is triable summarily and the penalty is a fine.

There is a power of entry to premises for the purposes of arresting a person for this offence under s 17 of the Police and Criminal Evidence Act 1984 (see section 11.10 below).

10.3.1 Using, Causing, and Permitting

Many offences in road traffic law relating to vehicles can be committed not only by people who **use** the vehicle (such as the driver), but also by people associated with the vehicle who **cause** or **permit** its use (such as people who hold supervisory responsibilities and owners).

You need to have a clear understanding about the meanings of these terms. We illustrate the principles below, where an employer and employee are used as an example, but 'using', 'causing', and 'permitting' also occur in other circumstances, for example within families or between friends.

A useful definition to know is that of a motor vehicle, which under s 185 of the Road Traffic Act 1988 means 'a mechanically propelled vehicle intended or adapted for use on roads'. Note that 'motor vehicle' and 'mechanically propelled vehicle' are different, and that is because some mechanically-propelled vehicles are not intended or adapted for use on roads, such as Go-Peds, speedway motorcycles, and formula one racing cars.

10.3.1.1 Using

In road traffic law, the user of a vehicle is not always the driver of a vehicle, but can also be a person other than the driver under certain circumstances which are listed below. Also, the vehicle can be in use whilst parked and not being driven, or it can be in use whilst being towed.

The user of a vehicle can be:

1. The actual **driver** of a vehicle, including an employee driving a company vehicle for business purposes. The employee is likely to be held responsible if the vehicle was being used for purposes other than company business.
2. The **employer** of the driver (who is an employee if the vehicle is a company vehicle used on behalf of the company's business). The employer can be held responsible for committing the offence even if he/she is unaware of the defect on the vehicle. In some circumstances, both the employer and the employee can be held responsible.
3. The **owner** of a vehicle driven by another person with the owner present.
4. A person **steering** the vehicle, for example when it is being towed.

10.3.1.2 Causing

There are two elements in causing a vehicle to be used:

1. The 'causer' must have the **authority** to make a subordinate carry out a particular action. For example, the line manager of a transport company orders one of the company's drivers to make an urgent delivery using a particular company vehicle.
2. The causer must also have **knowledge** about the unroadworthy state of that vehicle.

If one of these elements cannot be proved, causing cannot be considered as an offence. However, the using of the vehicle can be considered as an alternative offence.

In some cases, the company can be held responsible for causing the use of an unroadworthy vehicle if the company director knows the vehicle is defective. Also, note that if a person tows a vehicle, then this person is causing that vehicle to be used on a road.

10.3.1.3 Permitting

There are two elements in permitting a vehicle to be used. The first requires a degree of permission as distinct from authority or control, and the second is a degree of knowledge about the vehicle's defect or lack of documentation.

1. A person permits a vehicle to be used when he/she is in a position to **allow** its use, or to forbid its use. Such permission can be given verbally or it can be written down. It can also be implied permission.
2. The second element of permitting involves **knowledge of** (or 'turning a blind eye' to) the unroadworthy state of the vehicle. Therefore an offence is committed by an employer who allows an employee to use a defective company vehicle for business purposes, but only if the employer knows about the defect.

However, many companies give a general permission to their employees to use company vehicles, including for private purposes. In these cases it is unlikely that the employer can be held responsible for permitting the vehicle to be used (depending on the circumstances).

If one of these elements cannot be proved, then the 'use' of the vehicle is an alternative to 'permitting' the use because there will be no requirement to prove the existence of a permission or knowledge of the defect.

It is also important to note that it will be for the courts to decide on a question of fact whether or not any or none of these offences has been committed, and under what circumstances. The descriptions above are general guidelines.

TASK 1

You see a Fordover car being towed by a van. You stop both vehicles. The car is not being steered by any person, and has many defects; locked steering; one wheel is not turning, seized brakes and the engine is not able to start.

- What offence (if any) is the van driver committing? Is the offence using, causing or permitting an unroadworthy vehicle to be on the road?
- What evidence will you need to prove this offence?

10.4 Driving Licences

Over the years, the Government has introduced new policies and procedures to improve driving and riding standards, such as up-dated driving tests and compulsory basic training for motorcyclists. There will obviously be members of the public who disregard these requirements or standards.

In the course of your Supervised and Independent Patrol it is inevitable that you will investigate and detect a number of possible driving offences relating to driving licences. This is an introduction to those offences.

The table below shows the age requirements for driving particular categories of vehicle.

Age requirement for driving

Vehicle category		Minimum age requirement
A	Motorcycles motorbikes	17
B	Cars and light vans	17
C	Large goods vehicles	21
D	Passenger-carrying vehicles	21
E	Trailers	18
F to K	Other vehicles	16
P	Mopeds	16

10.4.1 Information Contained on Driving Licences

Driving licences are made up of two parts: the photocard and the counterpart. Photocard full licences are pink (see below), but green for provisional licences. The driver number contains information about the driver.

How to interpret the driver number

The Driver Number is **GARDN 605109C99LY**

The first five characters of the surname	**GARDN**
The first and last digits are derived from the year of birth	605109 shows the year of birth is 1969
The second and third digits represent the month of birth and the gender of the licence holder	605109 shows that the person was born in May and is male. For females, 5 is added to the second digit so for a female born in May the number would be 655109, and for a female born in December, it would be 662109
The fourth and fifth digits show the day of birth	605109 shows that the date of birth was the 10th of the month
The first two characters of the final cluster represent the initials	C (if there is only one initial, **9** is used in place of a second initial)

The middle number of the final cluster is computer-generated, in order to avoid duplicate records	**9** (can be any digit between 0 and 9)
The final two letters are also computer-generated	**LY** in this case

Full details concerning the driving licence, including the meaning of the various symbols and codes, may be found at the DVLA website <http://www.dvla.gov.uk>.

10.4.1.1 The photocard

The following describes the main features of the front of the photocard.

The reverse of the photocard contains the following information.

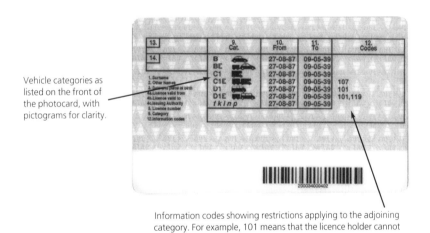

Information codes showing restrictions applying to the adjoining category. For example, 101 means that the licence holder cannot drive that category of vehicle for hire or reward.

10.4.1.2 The counterpart

The counterpart is a paper document showing additional information, such as vehicle categories the holder is entitled to drive provisionally, entitlement history (superseded categories), and endorsements. It is green and pink for both full and provisional licences (see below). Note that at the time of publication of this Handbook, it is proposed under the Road Safety Act 2006 that a computerized version of a driver's record will be made available to police officers for the purposes of investigating a criminal offence.

List of categories for which the holder is entitled to drive provisionally

The issue number on the counterpart will be followed by a letter

Superseded categories of vehicles

List of endorsement with dates and codes

(Image reproduced with the permission of the DVLA)

10.4.2 Requesting to See a Driver's Licence

Under s 164(1) of the Road Traffic Act 1988 you may require any of the following persons (**or their supervisors if they are provisional licence holders**) to produce their driving licences:

(a) a person **driving** a motor vehicle on a road,

(b) a person whom [you have] reasonable cause to believe to have been the **driver** of a motor vehicle at a time when an **accident** occurred owing to its presence on a road;

(c) a person whom [you have] reasonable cause to believe to have **committed an offence** in relation to the use of a motor vehicle on a road.

Under s 164(8) of the Road Traffic Act 1988 it will be a defence for that person to show that either:

1. he/she produced the documents **within seven days** in person at a police station (specified by her/him at the time of the request);

2. he/she produced the documents **as soon as reasonably practicable** in person; or

3. it was not reasonably practicable to produce the documents before the day on which written charge proceedings were commenced.

It will be a question of fact for the court to decide when is 'as soon as is reasonably practicable', given the circumstances of the case.

10.4.2.1 Requiring a person to state his/her date of birth

Under s 164(2) of the Road Traffic Act 1988 you may require the same people (see above) to state their dates of birth under the following circumstances:

1. they have failed to produce their licences;

2. they have produced licences:

   • which you have reason to suspect were not granted to those persons;

   • which were granted to those persons in error or which contain alterations;

3. they are the supervisors of learner drivers at the time of an accident or an offence, and you have reason to suspect that they (the supervisors) are under twenty-one years of age.

10.4.2.2 Offences relating to failing to produce a licence

Under s 164 of the Road Traffic Act 1988 it is an offence for a person to fail to:

- produce his/her licence and its counterpart; or
- produce his/her certificate of completion of a motorcyclist's training course; or
- state his/her date of birth.

Under s 164(7) of the Road Traffic Act 1988 a person does not commit the offence if he/she:

1. produces at the time (or within seven days) a current receipt for the licence (as a result of sending his or her driving licence to a court for points to be added); and
2. if required to do so, produce both parts in person immediately on his/her return, at a police station which was specified at the time he/she was stopped.

10.4.2.3 Failure to update a change of address on a driving licence

This is an offence under s 99(5) of the Road Traffic Act 1988 and the penalty is a fine.

10.4.2.4 Driving a vehicle that is not in accordance with a licence

Breaches of licence conditions, under-age driving, or no-licence driving are covered in s 87 of the Road Traffic Act 1988.

- It is an offence for a person to drive on a road a motor vehicle of **any** class **otherwise than in accordance with** a licence authorising him/her to drive a motor vehicle of that class [s 87(1)].
- It is an offence for a person **to cause or permit** another person to drive on a road a motor vehicle of any class otherwise than in accordance with a licence authorising that other person to drive a motor vehicle of that class [s 87(2)].

This offence includes circumstances where the offender is **driving under age.**

10.4.3 Seizing a Vehicle

Under s 165A of the Road Traffic Act 1988, you have the power to seize a vehicle if you have reasonable grounds for believing that the driver does not have a suitable licence or that the vehicle is not adequately insured. To seize a vehicle you must be in uniform and you must have already requested to see the driver's licence and counterpart or evidence of insurance, but the appropriate document has not been produced.

Before you seize a vehicle, you must **warn** the person driving the vehicle that you will seize it unless the person produces the required documentation immediately (it might not be practical to warn the driver; if so, this stage may be omitted) (s 165A(6)).

You can also seize a vehicle if, while in uniform, you have required a vehicle to stop, but it has **not stopped** or has not stopped long enough for appropriate enquiries **and** you have reasonable grounds for believing that the driver does not have a suitable licence or that the vehicle is not adequately insured. If you are unable to seize the vehicle immediately because the person driving it has failed to stop or has driven off, you may seize the vehicle at any time within twenty-four hours from the incident. In order to seize a vehicle you may enter premises (other than a private dwelling-house), if you have reasonable grounds for believing the vehicle to be present, using reasonable force if necessary. Note that a private dwelling-house does not include any outbuildings or adjacent land, so you may seize a vehicle from such areas.

10.4.4 Provisional Licence Holders

A provisional driving licence holder must **not** drive a vehicle unless he/she is accompanied and supervised by a **qualified driver** (see section 10.4.4.1). Details are provided in reg 16(2)(a) of the Motor Vehicles (Driving Licences) Regulations 1999.

There are exceptions; supervision is not required when:

- driving a motor vehicle of certain categories; for example three-wheeled vehicles;
- riding a moped or motor bicycle (with or without a side-car);

- driving a motor vehicle on an exempted island (except large goods vehicles and passenger carrying vehicles);
- driving a motor vehicle having just passed a test (having been given a certificate authorizing the person to drive the respective class of vehicle).

10.4.4.1 Meaning of qualified driver

The meaning of qualified driver is described in reg 17(1) and (2) of the Motor Vehicles (Driving Licences) Regulations 1999.

A qualified driver (for the purposes of reg 16):

- is twenty-one years of age or over;
- holds a relevant licence for the relevant category of the vehicle (a full British (including Northern Ireland) or a Community (EC) licence);
- has the relevant driving experience;
- has held the relevant licence for a continuous period of not less than three years.

10.4.4.2 Displaying learner driver plates correctly

A provisional driving licence holder must **not** drive a vehicle **unless** he/she displays 'L' plates on the vehicle in such manner as to be clearly visible to other road users from within a reasonable distance from the front and back of the vehicle. Details are provided in reg 16(2)(b) of the Motor Vehicles (Driving Licences) Regulations 1999.

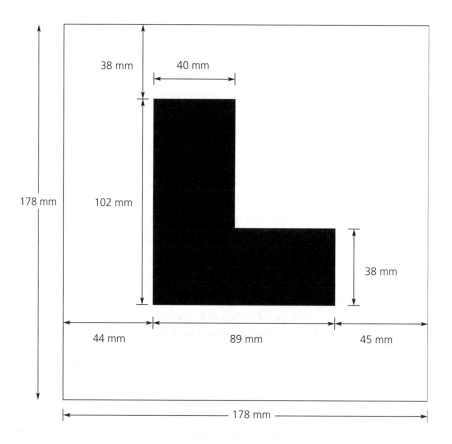

'D' plates can be displayed in Wales; however, if such a vehicle is driven in England these must be replaced with 'L' plates. The appropriate sizes and measurements of an 'L' Plate are shown in the diagram. The corners can be rounded, but the dimensions of the 'L' plate must be as shown.

10.4.4.3 Provisional licence holders and towing

A provisional driving licence holder must **not** drive a vehicle while it is being used to draw a trailer. Details are provided in reg 16(2)(c) of the Motor Vehicles (Driving Licences) Regulations 1999. There are exceptions, such as for provisional licence holders of certain categories such as articulated lorries.

10.4.5 Provisional Licence Holders for Mopeds or Motorcycles

As you might expect, riders of motorcycles with only provisional licences are subject to certain restrictions.

A Certificate of **Compulsory Basic Training** (CBT) is required by all motorcycle and moped provisional licence holders before they ride on a road (except during the training itself). The CBT lasts for two years and then has to be renewed. This legislation is described in s 97(3)(e) of the Road Traffic Act 1988.

Car drivers who passed their category B test on or after 1 February 2001 (giving full entitlement to ride mopeds) will have to complete a CBT before riding a moped unless they already have a valid CBT from other motorcycle training. Under these circumstances the CBT will not need renewing once it has been obtained.

No passengers may be carried on a moped or a motor bicycle (with or without a side-car) if the driver has only a provisional driving licence. Details are provided in reg 16(2)(b) of the Motor Vehicles (Driving Licences) Regulations 1999.

For a provisional licence holder a breach of these conditions amounts to an offence of driving otherwise than in accordance with a licence under s 87(1) of the Road Traffic Act 1988.

These offences are triable summarily.

10.4.6 Motorcycle Training and Licensing Arrangements

These arrangements are complicated and are summarized in sections 10.4.6.1 to 10.4.6.3 below.

10.4.6.1 Licence for Category P—Moped

- Limited to 50 cc/50 kph capacity/maximum speed. There is a minimum age requirement of sixteen years.
- **Car drivers** with a full Car Cat B licence automatically have a full Cat P licence, but if they passed their Cat B test on or after 1 February 2001, they still require CBT. The CBT Certificate does not have to be renewed.
- **New riders and drivers** need a provisional licence and CBT before riding on the road, (apart from riding on the road during training). The CBT certificate is valid for two years
- **Full Cat P holders** who have taken Cat P test since 1 December 1990 also need to complete CBT. The Certificate is valid for two years.

10.4.6.2   Licence for Category A—Motorcycle

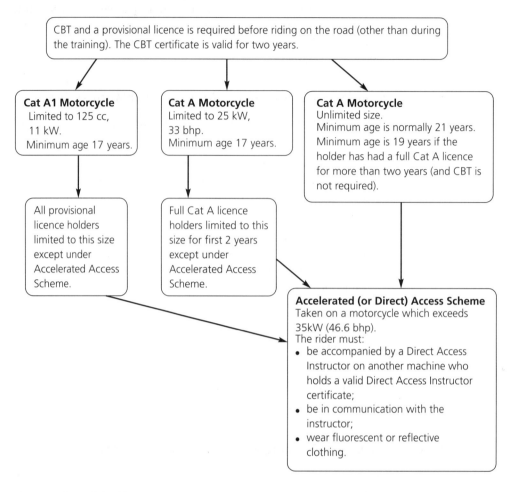

10.4.6.3   Motorcycles with sidecars

Provisional licence holders and full licence holders are restricted to a power/weight ratio of 0.16 W/kg for two years after passing a test.   .

The technical specifications (for example, the brake horse power (bhp), engine size, or power output) of the vehicle can be seen on a metal plate on the vehicle. They will also be outlined on the registration document of the vehicle.

10.4.6.4   'Mini-motos', 'go peds', and electrically assisted pedal cycles

The use of miniature motorbikes ('mini-motos') and petrol-driven scooters ('go peds') may pose potential risks to the health and safety of other road and pavement users and are considered by many members of the public as examples of anti-social behaviour. There have been a number of fatalities and serious injuries as the result of the use of mini-motos.

The Department of Transport have clarified that mini-motos and go peds are in fact 'lightweight powered motor vehicles' and must therefore comply with the usual road traffic and vehicle excise license laws. So, for example, it is illegal to use a mini-moto or go ped on the pavement under s 72 of the Highways Act 1835. Further information can be found in a government publication at the Department for Transport website <http://www.dft.gov.uk/transportforyou/roads/miniaturemotorbikesminiature6076?version=1>.

For case law on go peds, refer to *DPP v Saddington* [2000] The Times, November 1 QBD and *Burns v Currell* [1963] 2 QB 433, 440.

A distinction should be drawn between miniature motorbikes such as the mini-moto and electrically assisted pedal cycles. These are classified pedal cycles, and not motor vehicles, so long as:

- they are no heavier than 40 kgs;
- they are still capable of being propelled by pedals;
- their electric motor does not exceed 0.2 kilowatts and makes the cycle go no faster than 15 mph.

Similar exemptions are made for powered wheelchairs and powered scooters designed for people with disabilities.

TASK 2

1. Familiarize yourself with the form you would need to use to request a person to produce his or her driving licence within seven days.
2. What problems might there be in establishing the true identity of the person?
3. What safety measures will you undertake to make sure you have obtained the person's real name and address?

10.5 Insurance

All users of cars, motorcycles, and other vehicles are required by law to have a minimum level of insurance to cover eventualities such as injuries to others. This insurance covers the individual concerned in the case of financial payments to those injured during an accident. This section describes these requirements.

10.5.1 Third Party Motor Vehicle Insurance

Third party motor insurance is the minimum level of insurance allowed. This level of cover guarantees that injuries to other people (including passengers) or damage to other peoples' property (third parties) resulting from an accident caused by the insured person can be compensated. Additions such as cover for fire and theft are made at the discretion of the insured person. Fully comprehensive insurance goes further; it covers damage to the insured and his/her vehicle as well as cover for third parties, fire, and theft.

Sections 143(1) and (2) of the Road Traffic Act 1988 states it is an offence for a person:

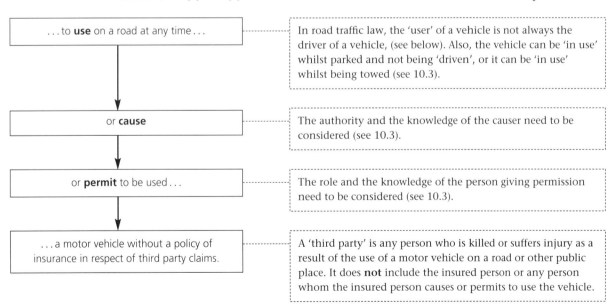

It is a defence (s 143(3), Road Traffic Act 1988) for a person charged with using a motor vehicle without third party insurance to prove that:

- the vehicle did not belong to him/her nor was it hired by him/her;
- he/she was using the vehicle in the course of her or his employment; and

• he/she had no reason to believe that the vehicle was not properly insured; an employee is unlikely to know about his or her employer's insurance arrangements.

10.5.1.1 Offence of keeping a vehicle which does not meet insurance requirements

This is covered in s 144A Road Traffic Act 1988 which states:

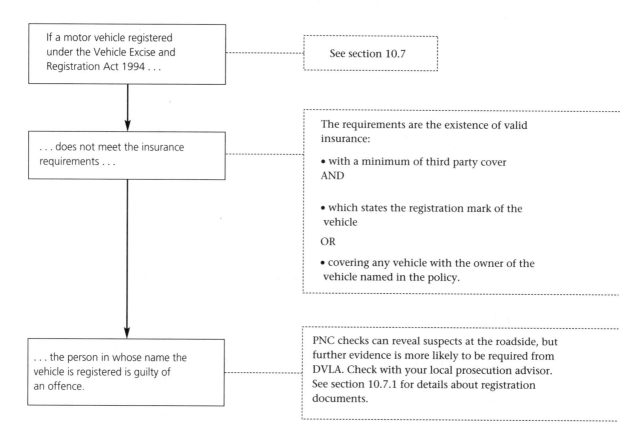

There are a number of exceptions to this offence which, if produced, must be substantiated. These exceptions include vehicles:

1. being driven by an owner who has deposited £500,000 with the Accountant General;
2. that are owned, for example, by councils, police authorities, NHS, Army or Air Force;
3. that are not kept by the registered keeper at the relevant time, for example, whilst lent to another person;
4. that are kept by the registered keeper, but are not on a road or other public place;
5. that are stolen and not recovered before the relevant time.

10.5.2 Key Features on a Certificate of Insurance

There are in excess of fifty companies in the UK offering insurance to drivers. An insured driver will receive a certificate of insurance from such a company which will include at least the following features:

Insurance Company Name and Address:
AAA Insurance Ltd.
The High Street
Maidbury MB1 1AB

Certificate number: 000/999/123   **Registration Number:** AA 00 AAA
Policyholder's name: Ava UNDERWOOD   **Expiry date:** Noon 16th April 2008

Permitted Drivers: Those specified including the policyholder must have a licence to drive the vehicle and must not be disqualified from driving it.

Limitations as to use: Use for social, domestic, and pleasure purposes including travel between the driver's home and place of work.

10.5.3   Requesting to See a Motor Insurance Certificate (section 165 of the Road Traffic Act 1988)

You may require any of the following persons to produce their insurance certificate (s 165(1), Road Traffic Act 1988):

(a) a person driving a motor vehicle [. . .] on a road; or

(b) a person whom [you have] reasonable cause to believe to have been the driver [. . .] at a time when an accident occurred owing to [the person's] presence on a road or other public place;

(c) a person whom [you have] reasonable cause to believe to have committed an offence in relation to the use of a motor vehicle [. . .] on a road.

You may also request him/her to provide his/her name and address and, if different, the name and addresses of the owner of the vehicle.

It is an offence under s 165(3) of the Road Traffic Act 1988 to fail to produce a certificate of insurance when required.

Under s 165(4) of the Road Traffic Act 1988 it will be a defence for that person to show that:

1. within seven days, he/she produced the documents in person at a police station that was specified at the time of the request;

2. he/she produced the documents in person as soon as reasonably practicable, or

3. it was not reasonably practicable for him or her to produce the documents before the day on which the written charge proceedings were commenced.

'As soon as is reasonably practicable' will be a question of fact for the court to decide given the circumstances of the case.

This offence is triable summarily only.

10.5.4   Seizing a Vehicle without Adequate Insurance Cover

You have the power to seize such a vehicle under s 165A of the Road Traffic Act 1988. Details of the procedure are described in section 10.4.3 above.

TASK 3

You stop a vehicle using your powers under the Road Traffic Act. The driver is very young. You establish from the Police National Computer that the vehicle he/she is driving has a large engine capacity.

- What questions would you put to the driver about his/her insurance policy?
- How would you check that the insurance company has been notified of the large engine capacity, and that the insurance cover is adequate?

10.6   Test Certificates

Certain categories of vehicle must have an MOT test certificate if they are to be used on the road. The type and age of vehicles requiring MOT certificates are given in s 47 of the Road Traffic Act 1988 which states that it is an offence for a person:

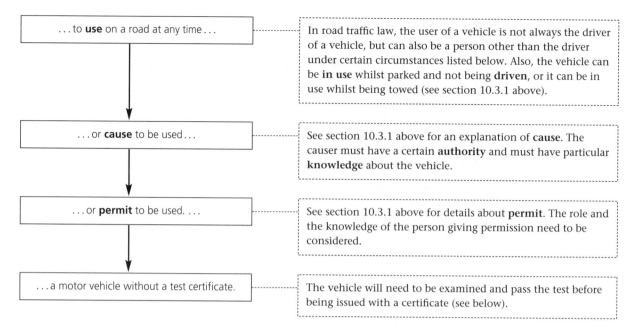

The following vehicles must be submitted for annual tests with effect from the **third** anniversary of their registration (s 47(2)):

- **passenger vehicle** with not more than eight seats (excluding the driver's seat);
- **rigid goods motor cars** (unladen weight not exceeding 1,525 kg);
- **dual-purpose vehicles**;
- **motorcycles** (including three-wheelers and mopeds);
- **motor caravans**.

However, other categories of vehicle must be submitted for annual testing from the **first** anniversary of their registration (s 47(3)):

- **passenger vehicles** with **more** than eight seats exclusive of the driver's seat (mainly public service vehicles, but also, for example, eleven-seat school mini vans);
- **taxis** licensed to ply for hire; and
- **ambulances**.

10.6.1 Exemptions from Having a Valid Test Certificate

There are the following exemptions under the Motor Vehicles (Tests) Regulations 1981:

- vehicles travelling to a pre-arranged test;
- where the vehicle has failed:
  - whilst being driven from the test; or
  - for the purpose of delivering it by previous arrangement to a place for work to be carried out; or
  - for the purpose of being broken up for scrap.

10.6.2 Date of Registration and Date of Manufacture

Under s 47(2) of the Road Traffic Act 1988 a test certificate must be obtained three years from the **date of manufacture** of the vehicle. This situation would include those people who live and work abroad and return to the UK. The date of manufacture of a vehicle shall be taken to be the last day of the year during which its final assembly was completed.

10.6.3 Requiring to See a Test Certificate

You may require any of the following persons to produce their test certificate (under s 165 of the Road Traffic Act 1988) and to give his/her address and the vehicle owner's name and address if different:

(a) a person driving a motor vehicle [. . .] on a road; or

(b) a person whom [you have] reasonable cause to believe to have been the driver of a motor vehicle [. . .] at a time when an accident occurred owing to its presence on a road or other public place; or

(c) a person whom [you have] reasonable cause to believe to have committed an offence in relation to the use on a road of a motor vehicle [. . .]

It is an offence to fail to produce a certificate of insurance when required (s 165(3), Road Traffic Act 1988).

It will be a defence under s 165(4) of the Road Traffic Act 1988 for that person to show that:

• within seven days, he/she produced the certificate in person at a police station that was specified at the time of the request;

• he/she produced the certificate in person as soon as reasonably practicable; or

• it was not reasonably practicable for him/her to produce the certificate before the day on which the summons proceedings were commenced.

'As soon as is reasonably practicable' will be a question of fact for the court to decide given the circumstances of the case.

This offence is triable summarily.

10.6.4 Key Features of an MOT Test Certificate

The following diagram illustrates the key features of the MOT certificate.

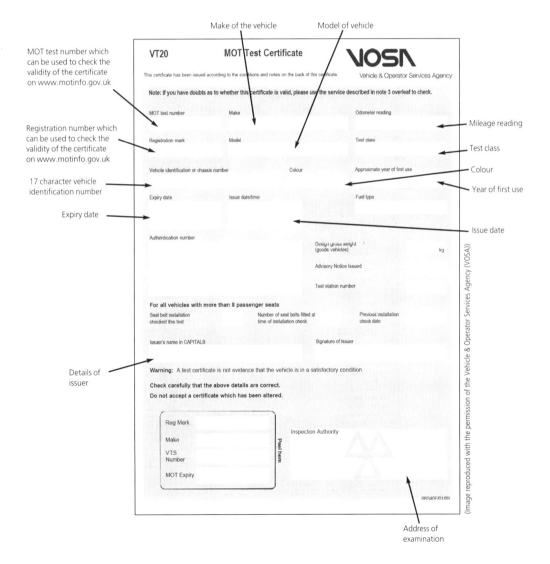

TASK 4

Whilst on Independent Patrol you have stopped a vehicle using your powers under the Road Traffic Act 1988 and have asked the driver to produce a valid test certificate.

- How are you going to obtain the date of first registration if it is a UK registered vehicle?
- What questions are you going to put to the driver to negate any defences?

10.7 Vehicle Registration and Licensing

When a vehicle is first registered, the Secretary of State issues a Registration Certificate, formally known as a Registration Document and assigns a registration mark (also known as an index number) to the vehicle.

Most vehicles used on a road are also subject to vehicle excise duty, otherwise known as road tax. The licence disc shows that road tax has been paid.

10.7.1 Registration Documents

The annotations below draw attention to just some of the information on the new style Registration Certificate. There is more, and all this information can be useful in the investigation of a number of offences.

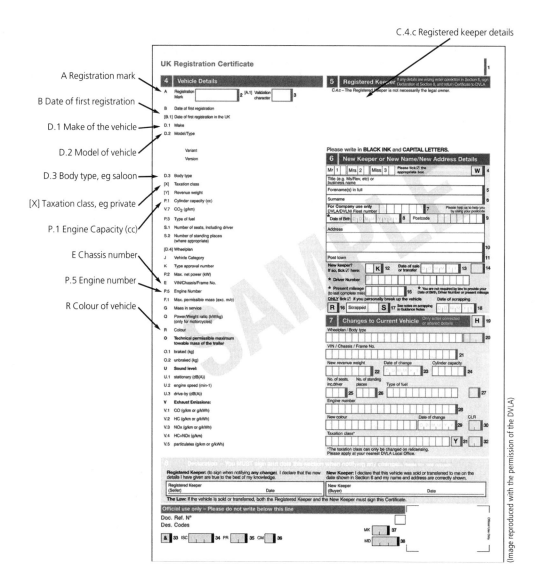

C.4.c Registered keeper details

A Registration mark

B Date of first registration

D.1 Make of the vehicle

D.2 Model of vehicle

D.3 Body type, eg saloon

[X] Taxation class, eg private

P.1 Engine Capacity (cc)

E Chassis number

P.5 Engine number

R Colour of vehicle

(Image reproduced with the permission of the DVLA)

10.7.2   The Layout of Registration Marks on Number Plates

You are familiar with number plates used on vehicles in the UK. The following system has been in use for several years.

(Image reproduced with the permission of the DVLA)

Local memory tag denoting where a vehicle is first registered. AB refers to Peterborough.

Age identifier which changes twice yearly in March and September. The number 51 refers to September 2001.

Random letters which will never include I or Q and which uniquely define the vehicle.

The number plate should use a standard font and the font should not be customized in any way.

Further details on number plates (including the use of a standardized font) may be found at the DVLA website <http://www.dvla.gov.uk/vehicles/regmarks/reg_marks_current_system.htm>.

10.7.3   Offences Relating to Vehicle Registration and Number Plates

It is an offence to **use a vehicle** on the road that is not properly registered (s 43C(1) of the Vehicle Excise and Registration Act 1994):

> A person is guilty of an offence if, on a public road or in a public place, [he/she uses] a vehicle [to which vehicle excise duty is chargeable or it is exempt from duty] and in respect of which:
>
> (a) the name and address of the keeper are not recorded in the register [meaning the car is registered and has a Registration Certificate], or
> (b) any of the particulars recorded in the register are incorrect.

Defences for this offence include:

- No reasonable opportunity for supplying the name and address of the keeper.
- Reasonable grounds for believing that the recorded particulars were correct.

For **registration documents**, it is an offence to fail to notify the:

- acquisition of the vehicle;
- disposal of the vehicle;
- a change of registered keeper's address;
- a change of vehicle details.

Most of these offences will be committed under the Road Vehicles (Display of Registration Marks) Regulations 2001 and the Vehicle Excise and Registration Act 1994.

It is also an offence to fail to produce a registration document when required to (s 28A(1), Vehicle Excise and Registration Act 1994):

> A person is guilty of an offence if s/he uses a vehicle in respect of which a registration document has been issued and fails to produce the document for inspection on being so required by a constable.

There are exceptions:

(a) the person produces the registration document, in person, at a police station specified by him/her at the time of the request; and
(b) he/she does so within seven days after the date on which the request was made or as soon as is reasonably practicable; or
(c) the vehicle is subject to a lease or hire agreement.

For **number plates**, the following are all offences:

- Having no number plate.
- Having an obscured number plate.
- Forgery of a number plate.
- Incorrect number and position of plates.
- Incorrect fitting.
- Incorrect layout of registration marks.
- Incorrect size and spacing of characters.
- Incorrect style of characters (they should use the font referred to in seven 10.7.2 above).

Most of these offences will be committed under the Road Vehicles (Display of Registration Marks) Regulations 2001.

These offences are all triable summarily.

10.7.4 Vehicle Excise Duty

Vehicle excise duty is the administrative name for road tax and not all vehicles are subject to this duty. Section 1 of the Vehicle Excise and Registration Act 1994 states that:

> ... every mechanically propelled vehicle used or kept on any public road [a road repairable at public expense] is subject to a charge of excise duty and [this] shall be paid in the form of a licence to be taken out by the person keeping the vehicle.

A **keeper** means a person who causes a vehicle to be on a public road for any period.

10.7.4.1 Exemptions from vehicle excise duty

There are approximately twenty categories of exempted vehicles (s 5(2), Vehicle Excise and Registration Act 1994), including:

- goods and passenger vehicles being used for current commercial purposes;
  Others include:
- fire engines;
- ambulances; and
- vehicles for disabled people.

For a full list visit <www.opsi.gov.uk/acts/acts1994/Ukpga_19940022_en_8.htm#sdiv2>.

10.7.4.2 Key features of a licence (tax disc)

The vehicle excise duty licence is commonly known as a tax disc. It displays information about the vehicle and the vehicle excise duty paid.

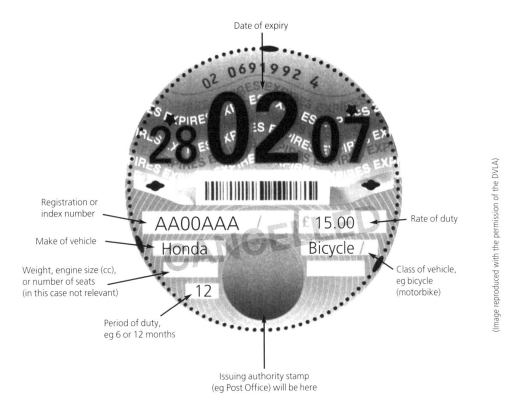

10.7.4.3 **Correct display of the vehicle excise duty licence**

The licence (tax disc) must be displayed in the vehicle to show that vehicle excise duty has been paid. It must be protected from the weather and exhibited so that it is clearly visible in daylight from the nearside of the road (reg 16, Road Vehicle (Registration and Licensing) Regulations 1971).

Required position of tax disc

Type of vehicle	Position for licence disc
Cars and most common vehicles	On or adjacent to the nearside.
Other vehicles	On the nearside in front of the driver or, if no driver's seat, towards the front between 2'6'' and 6' from the ground.
Solo motorcycles, motor tricycles, and invalid vehicles	On the nearside in front of the driving seat.
Motorcycle and side-car	On the nearside of the handlebars of the motorcycle or on the nearside of the side-car in front of the driving seat.

10.7.5 **Offences Relating to Vehicle Excise Duty**

It is an offence under the Vehicle Excise and Registration Act 1994 for a person:

- to use or keep on a public road a vehicle which is **unlicensed** (s 29);
- to **forge** or fraudulently use, alter, lend, or allow to be used by another person a vehicle licence (s 44(1));
- to use or keep on a public road a vehicle in respect of which vehicle excise duty is chargeable without there being fixed to and **exhibited** on that vehicle in the manner prescribed (below) a current licence for that vehicle (s 33).

TASK 5

When you are on Supervised Patrol in your BCU area and you see a vehicle not displaying a licence.

- How could you report the user or keeper of the vehicle?

> • What would you do if the driver or keeper of the vehicle is not present?
>
> Find out what forms you can use for these processes at your police station.

10.8 Construction and Use of Vehicles

The following section draws upon the Road Vehicles (Construction and Use) Regulations 1986.

Your responsibility to prevent crime does not only apply to preventing those crimes associated with theft or violence. Criminal acts can also be committed by people driving motor vehicles on the road, and the potential to cause danger to other road users is very high. You also have the responsibility to 'pursue and bring to justice those who break the law' and 'protect, help and reassure the community'. You will therefore be required to investigate offences in relation to the use of vehicles and to contribute to road safety campaigns in order to reduce still further the death toll on roads in the UK.

10.8.1 Authority to Examine a Vehicle Being Used on the Road

Under s 67 of the Road Traffic Act 1988 you will be designated as an authorized examiner by your chief officer of police. As an examiner you will be authorized to test a vehicle (and drawn trailer) on a road for the purposes of ascertaining compliance with:

- the construction and use requirements, [including lighting];
- the requirement that the condition of the vehicle is not such that its use on a road would involve a danger of injury to any person.

10.8.2 Tyres

The component parts of a tyre profile are shown in the diagram below.

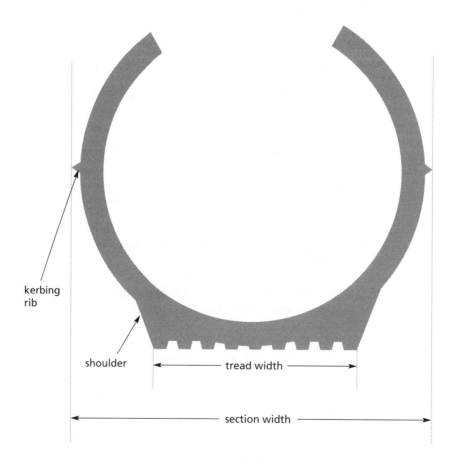

For the purposes of evidence-gathering, make a note of **all** identifying codes and features on the wall of a tyre, including serial numbers and characters relating to type of tyre. The photograph below shows a typical location for the numbers.

(Image © Kevin Lawton-Barrett)

In our example above we would note:

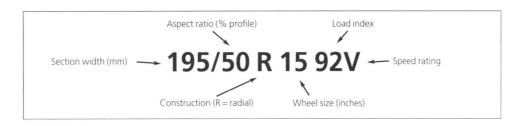

(You will find the full details of what each letter and number refers to at <http://www . blackcircles.com/general/sidewall>.)

10.8.2.1 Offences relating to the condition and maintenance of tyres

Regulation 27 of the Road Vehicle Construction and Use Regulations 1986 describes a range of tyre problems, relating to their condition and the circumstances in which they are being used. These regulations only apply to vehicles and trailers used on roads with pneumatic (inflatable) tyres. Some types of vehicles or circumstances are not subject to the regulations. A summary of the regulations and the exemptions is shown in the table below.

Regulations relating to the condition and maintenance of tyres

Regulations	Exemptions
The **type** of tyre must be: • the correct type for the vehicle, including taking into account the type of tyres fitted to the other wheels; • the correct type for the road conditions or purpose.	• Agricultural motor vehicles which have a maximum speed of 20 mph.
The tyre must not be **damaged** in the following ways: • cuts in excess of 25 mm or 10% of the section width of the tyre (whichever is the greater), measured in any direction on the outside of the tyre, and deep enough to reach the ply or cord; • lumps, bulges or tears caused by separation or partial failure of its structure; • exposed ply or cord. The tyre must be inflated to the correct **pressure** for the purpose.	• Agricultural trailers. • Agricultural trailed appliances. • Broken-down vehicles or vehicle en-route for breaking up or being towed at a maximum speed of 20 mph.
The tyre must not be so **worn** that the base of any groove which showed in the original tread pattern of the tyre is not clearly visible.	• Cars (and other passenger vehicles carrying no more than eight passengers). • Light goods vehicles and trailers.
The tyre must be correctly **maintained** so it is fit for the use to which the vehicle or trailer is being put, and must not have defects which might cause damage to the road surface or persons in the vehicle or road.	• No exemptions.

10.8.2.2 **Offences relating to bald tyres**

A tyre is said to be 'bald' if part of the original tread is no longer visible on the tread width (reg 27). The position of bald patches is significant. Bald patches on the central three-quarters of the tread width do matter, but bald patches on the outer eighth of each side of the tread width may not matter. (Furthermore, the tyres for some vehicles, such as motorcycles, are manufactured with no grooves or tread on the outer eighths of the tread width.) Clearly, you need to be able to accurately identify the central three-quarters and the outer eighths of the tread width for any tyre you examine.

Note that the tread width (the surface in contact with the road) is always less than the maximum width of the tyre (the section width).

To calculate the width of the central three-quarters of the tread width, see the diagram below, showing a new unworn tyre.

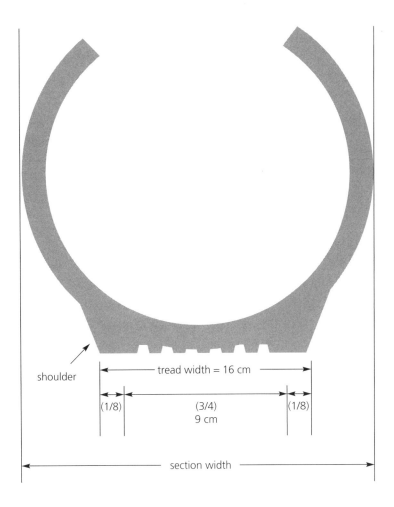

To calculate the central three-quarters of a tyre tread, using the tyre in diagram above:

1. Measure the breadth of the tyre in contact with the road (total width = 16cms).
2. Obtain the width of central three-quarters of the tyre by dividing the total width by 4, then multiplying by 3 (16cm/4 = 4cm, and then 4cm × 3 = 12cm).
3. Obtain the width of each of the two outer eighths of the tyre by dividing the total width by 8 (16cm/8 = 2cm).
4. Check that your calculations are correct by adding the value for the central three-quarters to twice the value for the outer eighth (12cm + 2cm + 2cm = 16cm, hence correct).

For **cars, light goods vehicles, and trailers**, if any groove or tread is less than 1.6 mm deep in the central three-quarters anywhere round the tyre, an offence is committed. Note therefore, that if the depth of any grooves is less than 1.6 mm in the outer eighths of the tread, no offence is committed. These outer areas can therefore be bald (see the diagram below, showing a tyre that is worn on the outer eighths, but which still has 1.6 mm of tread over the central three quarters of its tread width).

This 1.6 mm rule does not apply to agricultural vehicles or any vehicle which is:

* broken down or being towed;
* en-route for breaking up;
* being towed at a maximum speed of 20 mph.

For **other types of vehicles**, such as motorcycles, larger passenger vehicles, and larger goods vehicles, the specified groove depth is less. The groove depth over the central three-quarters of the tread must be at least 1.0 mm. If a tyre on one of these vehicles was originally manufactured with no tread pattern grooves in the outer eighths of the tread, then the outer eighths do not need to be considered (see the diagram below, showing a brand new tyre which has been manufactured with no grooves in the outer eighths of its tread width).

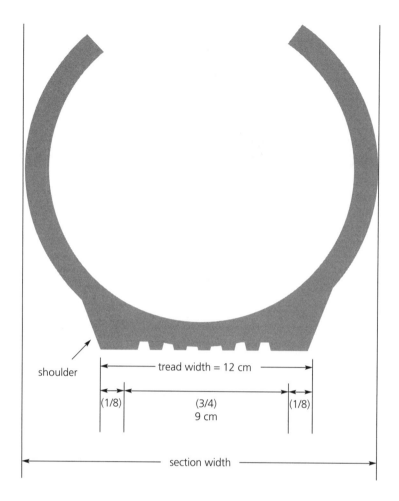

1. The tread width of this tyre is 12 cm.
2. We can calculate the central three-quarters as 9cm(12cm/4 = 3cm, and then 3cm × 3 = 9cm).
3. We can calculate the width of each outer eighth as 1.5cm(12cm/8 = 1.5cm).
4. The original tread pattern of a tyre did not extend beyond three-quarters of the tread width. If any groove which showed in the original tread pattern is less than 1 mm deep, an offence is committed.
5. The outer eighths (in this case 1.5 cm) do not need to be considered as they were not manufactured with grooves.

10.8.3 Danger of Injury from the Use of Vehicles or Trailers

A person is guilty of an offence under s 40A of the Road Traffic Act 1988 if they use, cause, or permit another person to use a motor vehicle or trailer on a road when the use of the motor vehicle or trailer involves a danger of injury to any person because of:

- the condition of the motor vehicle or trailer or of its accessories or equipment, or
- the purpose for which it is used, or
- the number of passengers carried by it or the manner in which they are carried, or
- the weight, position, or distribution of its load or the manner in which it is secured.

See section 10.3 for a discussion of 'use, cause, or permit'. Details of the types of situation that could lead to injury or the danger of injury are listed in the sections below.

10.8.3.1 Poor maintenance of a vehicle and some associated offences

The following examples are a sample of offences which can be committed in relation to poor maintenance of a vehicle. This list is by no means exhaustive. A general rule is to consider how a vehicle was first constructed. This will be a guide as to how the vehicle should be maintained throughout its life. If you examine a vehicle and a component part of it is missing or is not working, an offence is likely to have been committed.

- Using a vehicle in a **dangerous condition** such as the **bodywork** having jagged edges (reg 100(1)): obligatory disqualification if committed within three years of a previous conviction under s 40A, Road Traffic Offenders Act 1988, discretionary disqualification in any other case.
- The **wipers** and **washers** that are required to be fitted must be maintained in efficient working order and be properly adjusted (reg 34).
- An audible warning instrument (**horn**) must be fitted to any motor vehicle with a maximum speed of more than 20 mph (reg 37).
- The **braking** systems must be maintained in good and efficient working order and be properly adjusted, including the handbrake (reg 18(1)).
- **Exhaust** systems and silencers must be maintained in good and efficient working order, and must not be altered to increase the noise made by the escape of the exhaust gases (reg 54).
- **Motorcycle exhausts** must be the correct type (this applies only to a moped or motorbike first used after 1 January 85) (reg 579A (1) or (4)). The silencer should be either the original fitted by the manufacturer or a replacement marked with an approved British Standard marking. (A motorcycle should not be used on a road if the exhaust fitted is marked 'Not for road use' or similar.)
- Vehicle **emissions** must not contain any smoke, visible vapour, grit, sparks, ashes, cinders, or oily substance that causes (or is likely to cause) damage to property or injury or danger to other road users (reg 61). Your force may have instruments to test vehicle emissions.

10.8.3.2 Incorrect use of a vehicle and some associated offences

Loads carried by a vehicle must not be a danger or nuisance to any person or property. The weight, packing, distribution, and adjustment of a load must be taken into account (reg 100(1)). The load carried by a motor vehicle or trailer must be secured, if necessary by physical restraint other than its own weight, for example the luggage on the roof bars of a car must be tied down (reg 100(2)).

Passenger numbers must not exceed the number that seats allow (reg 100(1) and (3)). For example, passengers must not be carried in the rear of a small van with no fixed seating.

The **horn** (reg 99) must not be used when the vehicle is stationary (other than an emergency involving another vehicle, or when using a reversing alarm or boarding aid alarm). In addition, the horn must not be used by vehicles in motion on restricted roads between 2330 hours and 0700 hours

Excessive noise from motor vehicles on roads must be avoided by the exercise of reasonable care on the part of the driver (reg 97).

10.8.4 Offences in Relation to Parking and Braking

The **engine** must be turned off when the vehicle is stationary for any length of time (reg 98) in order to prevent noise or exhaust emissions. For example, a driver commits an offence by leaving the engine running whilst stationary in a confined space with other vehicles.

When leaving an **unattended motor vehicle** (quitting) the engine must be turned off and the parking brake applied, unless there is another person in the vehicle who is licensed to drive it (reg 107 and **s 42 of the Road Traffic Act 1988**). This would apply to a driver who parks outside a shop and runs inside to buy something, leaving the engine running.

Exceptions apply to emergency services vehicles and to vehicles that need to keep the engine running, for example to drive machinery such as a crane or to charge the battery.

10.8.5 Safety and Associated Offences

There are a number of considerations concerning the personal safety of drivers and passengers of vehicles.

10.8.5.1 Helmets

It is an offence under s 16 of the Road Traffic Act 1988 to drive or ride on a motor cycle on a road without suitable protective headgear. Helmets must:

- be securely fastened to the head of the wearer by means of straps or other fastening provided for that purpose (if it has a chin cup it must have an additional strap to go under the jaw);
- bear a mark indication in compliance with the British Standard/equivalent EU standard (or be of a type which, by virtue of its shape, material, and construction could reasonably be expected to afford protection similar to, or greater than a helmet which conforms to the latest British Standard 6658:1985 (or equivalent EU standard)).

There are some categories of persons who do not have to wear a helmet, such as:

- drivers of ride-on motor mowers;
- followers of the Sikh religion who wear a turban whilst driving or riding motorcycles;
- passengers in a sidecar;
- any person pushing the motorcycle on foot.

10.8.5.2 Motorcycle eye protection

There is no legal requirement that a visor or goggles be used at all. However, if eye protection is used and it does not meet the British Standards (BS EN 1938:1999) an offence has been committed under s 18(3) of the Road Traffic Act 1988.

10.8.5.3 Seat Belts

The requirements for the use of seat belts depend on the age of the person and where he/she is sitting (s 14(3), Road Traffic Act 1988). Details are shown in the table below (based on extracts from the Highway Code, 2004 and *Child Car Seats—The New Law 2006* available from <http://www.thinkroadsafety.gov.uk/campaigns/childcarseats/pdf/law-leaflet.pdf>).

Seat belt requirements

	Front seat	Rear seat	Who is responsible?
Driver.	Must be worn if fitted.	Not applicable.	Driver.
Child under 3.	Correct child restraint must be used.	Correct child restraint must be used.	Driver.
Child 3yrs up to 135 cms tall (or 12th birthday whichever comes first).	Correct child restraint must be used.	Correct child restraint must be used where seat belts fitted.	Driver.
Child aged 12 or 13 or younger child who is 135 cms or taller.	Adult seat belt must be worn if fitted.	Adult seat belt must be worn if fitted.	Driver.
Passenger aged 14 years or over.	Adult seat belt must be worn if fitted.	Adult seat belt must be worn if fitted.	Passenger.

Child restraints consist of four types as described in the table below:

	Child weight and age	Notes
Baby seats	Less than 13kgs (approx. birth to 9–12 months).	Rear-facing
Child seats	From 9–18kgs (approx. 9 months to 4 years).	Forward-facing

	Child weight and age	Notes
Booster seats	15kgs onwards (approx. 4 years and up).	May or may not have a back
Booster cushions	22kgs onwards (approx. 6 years and up).	Do not normally have backs

In some situations a seat belt does not have to be worn, such as:

- people engaged in deliveries (for example, delivering post or newspapers) or collections;
- people reversing a vehicle or supervising provisional licence holders while reversing a vehicle (or a manoeuvre which includes reversing);
- people in vehicles being used for police purposes (but consider your force policy in relation to people under arrest);
- taxi drivers while 'plying for hire', answering calls for hire, or carrying passengers;
- private hire drivers while carrying passengers for hire;
- persons in vehicles being used for fire brigade purposes;
- persons taking part in processions organized by, or on behalf of, the Crown;
- persons holding an exemption medical certificate from wearing a seat belt provided it is produced at the time or within seven days;
- conducting a driving test if wearing of the belt would be dangerous;
- the vehicle is driven under a trade licence for the purposes of investigating or remedying mechanical fault;
- where the seat belt is an inertia type which is locked as a result of being, or having been, on a steep incline;
- when disabled people are wearing a disabled person's belt.

10.8.6 Vehicle Identification Regulations for the Detection and Prevention of Crime

Under reg 67 all wheeled registered vehicles after 1 April 1980 should be equipped with a plate in a conspicuous and readily accessible location (on a part not normally subject to replacement) which clearly shows the:

- Vehicle Identification Number (the 'VIN' which is also stamped on the chassis or frame);
- name of manufacturer;
- type approval number (possibly on a separate plate).

These identifying features can be matched against details on PNC to enable identification of stolen vehicles (see section 9.6).

TASK 6

You stop a car using your powers under the Road Traffic Act 1988 as you suspect the vehicle may have a number of serious defects.

1. What are you going to say to the driver?
2. What process are you going to go through if you find a defect?

10.9 Lights on Vehicles

The following section concerns, in part, the Road Vehicles Lighting Regulations 1989.

There is a possibility of underestimating the importance of lights on vehicles when placed alongside other demands on your time, particularly when compared with incidents involving violent criminal activity. However, the position, style, maintenance, and colour of vehicle lights are very important for road safety.

Your many responsibilities include identifying vehicles with lights that are not working properly, testing and inspecting lights, and bringing the faults to the attention of the owner and/or driver.

Drivers are also expected to employ their lights with consideration towards other road users, and you can offer advice to drivers about how they use their vehicles' lights. No vehicle lights should be used in a way that causes undue dazzle or discomfort to other persons using the road.

To help you understand the extensive lighting regulations, a family saloon has been chosen as an example to illustrate the two main categories of lights on vehicles:

- **obligatory lights** that **must** be fitted and maintained; and
- **optional lights**.

> **TASK 7**
>
> List all the types of lights that you think are **obligatory** for a car. Now compare your list with the list in the section below (no peeping!).

10.9.1   Obligatory Lights

On the front of a car, the following lights are obligatory:

- Front position lights (side lights)
- Dipped beam headlights
- Main beam headlights
- Direction indicators

On the back of the car, the following are obligatory:

- Rear position lights
- Direction indicators
- Rear stop (brake) lights
- Rear fog light
- Rear registration plate lamp
- Rear reflector (agreed, not strictly a light, but is obligatory)

A 'hazard warning signal device' to operate the direction indicator lights on the front and back of the car is also obligatory.

These obligatory lights may be clustered as a group of lights underneath a plastic or glass cover; some **typical** arrangements are shown in the diagrams below.

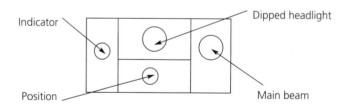

Scheme showing a front light cluster

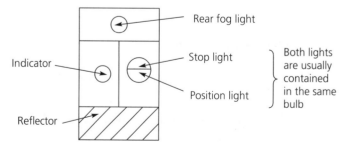

Scheme showing a rear light cluster

Remember, these are typical arrangements. There is in fact significant variation between makes and models of cars.

10.9.1.1 Position lights

These lights must be present on all four corners of a vehicle, and their purpose is to indicate the vehicle's presence and width to other road users. On the front of the car they are also known as side lights. They are white and not particularly bright, and they are often switched on by the first click of the switch near the steering wheel. On the back of the vehicle, the position lights are also known as tail lights. They are red, but not as bright as brake lights, and are operated by the same switch as the front position lights.

The position lights must be lit when the vehicle is moving at night (between sunset and sunrise) and when the vehicle is moving during the day if visibility is reduced. When the vehicle is parked at night, the position lights must be illuminated unless the vehicle is parked with its nearside against the nearside kerb on a 30 mph road with street lighting.

10.9.1.2 Dipped beam headlamps

These are strong white lights at the front of the car, and are also known as head lights. They shine forward to show the road ahead but they should shine downward and to the left of the vehicle to prevent oncoming vehicles being dazzled. They are often switched on with two clicks of the lights switch.

These lights must be lit when the car is being driven during hours of darkness, except when:

• driving on a 30 mph road with street lighting;
• the fog lights are illuminated.

They should also be used when the car is driven during the day in seriously reduced visibility. The head lights do not need to be illuminated if the car is being towed.

10.9.1.3 Main beam headlights

These lights are very bright white lights at the front of the car which shine straight ahead to illuminate the road over a long distance. They are usually operated with a pull or push of a switch near the steering wheel when headlamps are already on.

The main beam headlight switch must be wired so that they can be deflected by the driver in order to avoid dazzling oncoming traffic. The deflection switching mechanism should also switch on the dipped beam headlights as soon as the main beam headlights are deflected.

If the front fog lamps are on in seriously reduced visibility, there is no need to use the main beam headlights.

10.9.1.4 Direction indicators

These are found at each corner of the car (and sometimes at the sides) and they are used to indicate to other road users that the driver is intending to move the car to the right or left.

They must be amber and must flash on and off between sixty and 120 flashes a minute. They are usually operated by pushing a switch near the steering column upwards or downwards, and there must be an indicator near the driver to show that the indicators are being used.

10.9.1.5 Rear registration plate lamp

This is a small white light at the rear, shining on to the registration plate, and it automatically illuminates when the position indicator lights are switched on. The registration lamp should not shine directly into the eyes of the driver of the vehicle behind.

10.9.1.6 Rear fog lamps

These lamps are very bright red to help other drivers see the vehicle in conditions of reduced visibility. They are operated by an independent switch that will only work when the headlights are illuminated. They do not need to be used when the car is towing a trailer.

10.9.1.7 Rear stop lamps

These are also known as brake lights and are very bright red. They are positioned at the rear corners of the car and must operate when the braking system (eg foot brakes) of the car is applied. They warn other road users that the vehicle is slowing down or stopping.

10.9.1.8 Hazard warning signal device

This is not a lamp or set of lamps, but a switching device to enable all the direction indicators to flash at the same time. It is only to be used:

• when the vehicle is stationary to alert other road users of the obstruction; or
• on a motorway or dual carriageway to warn drivers behind of an obstruction ahead; or
• by the driver of a bus to summon help; or
• by the driver of a bus when children under sixteen are getting on or off.

The switch of this device must be in reach of the driver. The switch button surface often has a small triangle which will be illuminated when the hazard warning lights are switched on.

10.9.2 Optional Lamps

Some optional lamps are fitted to a vehicle which are **extra** or additional to those already fitted, but fulfil the same function as obligatory lights, for example, extra front position lights (sidelights), extra stop lamps, extra direction indicators, and extra dim/dipping and hazard warning devices. As these optional extra lamps have the same functions as obligatory lights: they must be maintained and in full working order, just like obligatory lights.

Other optional lamps include lamps such as reversing lights and front fog lights. They are not obligatory in type, and are put on the vehicle by the manufacturer or the owner to help the driver. There is no need for these lamps to be maintained and working, as they do not fall into any of the categories of obligatory lights. However, they must not be used in such a way that they cause undue dazzle or discomfort to other persons using the road.

10.9.3 Sunrise, Sunset, Lighting Up Times, and Hours of Darkness

To establish when position lamps or sidelights must be illuminated, published sunrise and sunset times may be consulted. Times can be found in diaries, the internet, or local publications such as newspapers and databases which your control rooms have access to.

> Remember: Sunset and Sunrise for Sidelights

For the purposes of finding out when dipped headlights must be illuminated, hours of darkness can be calculated by adding thirty minutes to sunset time and taking away thirty minutes from sunrise time, in other words half an hour after sunset and half an hour before sunrise.

> Remember: Hours of Darkness for Dipped headlights

10.9.4 Parking without Lights between Sunset and Sunrise

In certain situations, some categories of vehicle may park between sunset and sunrise without lights.

These categories of vehicle are:

• passenger vehicles which do not exceed eight passengers seats and the driver, such as most family **cars**;
• light goods vehicles, for example **vans**;
• motorcycles and invalid carriages.

The categories of vehicle listed above may park without lights between sunset and sunrise on a road with a speed limit of 30 mph or less, but only:

- in a designated parking area or lay-by; or
- if it is parked facing the right way on that road and no less than ten metres from a junction; or
- if it is parked on a one-way street, facing the right way (on either side of the road).

10.9.5 Legitimate Use of a Vehicle with Defective Lights

Vehicles with defective lights may be driven in some circumstances without an offence being committed. A vehicle may be used on the road with defective lights but only:

- between sunrise and sunset; and
- if the lights became defective during the journey, or if arrangements have been made to repair the fault.

Remember: the examples above relate to a family car only and therefore there are a number of other regulations regarding other forms of transport which you may have to identify in the future.

TASK 8

Consider each of the following statements in turn, and decide if each statement is true or false:

1. The term 'hours of darkness' refers to a period in time which is half an hour after sunset to half an hour before sunrise.
2. The legislation that covers the use of lights on vehicles is the Road Vehicles (Construction and Use) Regulations 1986.
3. The permitted flash rate of an indicator lamp fitted to a vehicle is between eighty and 100 pulses per minute.
4. Hazard warning signals on a vehicle may be used lawfully when the vehicle is being towed by another vehicle.
5. A defect occurring during a journey during daylight hours is a defence to a defective light fitted to a vehicle.
6. A reversing light is an optional lamp.
7. The term 'obligatory light' means a light that is required by the legislation to be fitted to a vehicle.

10.10 Pedestrian Crossings and Road Signs

Over the years, the number of road signs and regulations in England and Wales has increased greatly in an attempt to keep the road environment as safe as possible for all road users. These signs and regulations, however, are only of value if road users take notice of them. When you are considering enforcement of these regulations in the future, do not restrict your intentions only to detecting offences; remember, you are in a position to help the public develop road safety awareness.

10.10.1 Pedestrian Crossings

The table below shows the key characteristics of the three main types of pedestrian crossing described in the Zebra, Pelican and Puffin Pedestrian Crossings Regulations 1997.

Pelican	• Pedestrians have the opportunity to bring vehicles to a stop to let them cross. • Operated by pedestrian(s) pushing a button. • Vehicles are stopped by a set of regular traffic lights except that the sequence is different after the red light. The amber light flashes to indicate that vehicles may proceed, but only if the crossing is clear.
Puffin	• Sensors detect anyone waiting to cross and change the traffic lights accordingly for vehicles to stop. • The traffic light signal is the same as regular lights.

Zebra	• Not supported by traffic lights.
	• Pedestrians walk across a section of road indicated by alternate white and black stripes.
	• Drivers and riders of vehicles are warned of the presence of a crossing by two black and white striped poles with yellow flashing beacons on top, on each pavement.

10.10.1.1 Layout of crossings

The **limits of the crossing** are by marked out by two parallel lines of studs across the carriageway or, in the case of a zebra crossing, black and white stripes across the road. The **stop lines** for Pelican or Puffin crossings are shown by a solid line across the road before the first line of studs indicates the start of the crossing. Drivers and riders must not cross that line if there are pedestrians on the crossing or if the traffic lights are red.

The **give-way line** at the start of a zebra crossing is indicated by a broken white line across the road before the first line of studs. Drivers and riders must not cross that line if there are pedestrians on the crossing.

The controlled area of a crossing is a certain length of road adjacent to each side of a crossing. It is indicated by white zigzag lines painted next to the edge of the road and along the middle of the road. There may be between two and eighteen zigzags, depending on the road layout in the immediate vicinity. It is an offence to park in the controlled area for vehicles travelling in either direction. Overtaking in a controlled area when approaching a crossing is also an offence, but overtaking in the controlled area after a crossing is not.

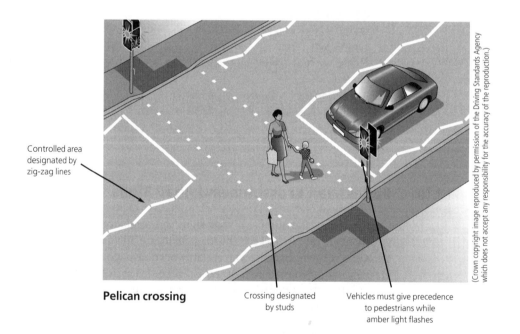

Controlled area designated by zig-zag lines

Pelican crossing

Crossing designated by studs

Vehicles must give precedence to pedestrians while amber light flashes

(Crown copyright image reproduced by permission of the Driving Standards Agency which does not accept any responsibility for the accuracy of the reproduction.)

10.10.1.2 The correct use of crossings

The regulations for the use of crossings are given in the Zebra, Pelican and Puffin Pedestrian Crossings Regulations 1997. The Regulations give rise to several offences which can be committed by the drivers of vehicles or by pedestrians on pedestrian crossings. Not all the offences apply to all types of crossings; details are provided for each offence.

Vehicles must not stop on crossings (all crossings)

Drivers must not stop their vehicles within the limits of a crossing, unless the way is blocked or it is necessary for them to stop to avoid injury or damage to persons or property (reg 18).

Pedestrians must not delay on crossings (all crossings)

'No pedestrian shall remain on the carriageway within the limits of a crossing longer than is necessary for that pedestrian to pass over the crossing [in a reasonable time]' (reg 19).

Vehicles must not stop in controlled areas (all crossings)

'The driver of a vehicle shall not cause it or any part of it to stop in a controlled area' (reg 20). This does not apply to pedal cycles or public service vehicles, or if the vehicle is beyond the driver's control. There are some other exceptions; a driver may stop in the controlled area in order to:

- allow pedestrians to cross or to prevent injury or damage;
- carry out building work;
- remove obstructions from the road;
- carry out maintenance of the road or crossing;
- make a right or left turn (regs 21–22).

Vehicles must stop at red/steady amber lights (pelican or puffin crossings only)

When vehicular traffic light signals at a pelican or puffin crossing are displaying the red light or a non-flashing amber light, the driver must stop (reg 23).

Vehicles must not overtake approaching a crossing (all crossings)

Whilst any motor vehicle (or any part of it) is within the limits of a controlled area and is proceeding **towards** the crossing, the driver must not overtake any stationary vehicles or vehicle approaching the crossing (reg 24).

Pedestrians have precedence over vehicles at crossings (zebra crossings only)

A pedestrian on a zebra crossing (not controlled by a constable in uniform or traffic warden) has precedence over approaching vehicles that are not yet on the crossing (reg 25). Where there is a refuge for pedestrians or a central reservation on a zebra crossing, each part of the crossing is treated as a separate crossing.

Pedestrians have precedence over vehicles at crossings during a flashing amber light sequence (pelican crossing only)

When the vehicular traffic light signals at a pelican crossing are showing the flashing amber signal, every pedestrian has precedence over approaching vehicles that are not yet on the crossing (reg 26).

The offences listed above are committed under the Zebra, Pelican and Puffin Pedestrian Crossings Regulations 1997, s 25(5) of the Road Traffic Regulation Act 1984, and Sch 2 to the Road Traffic Offenders Act 1988.

10.10.2 White Lines along the Centre of the Road

These are covered in reg 26 of the Traffic Signs Regulations and General Directions 2002. The lines may be continuous on both sides, or continuous on one side and broken on the other. The lines are used to indicate parts of the road where vehicles may not be permitted to stop or to cross the lines:

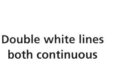  

Double white lines both continuous

Double white lines one continuous, one broken

(Crown copyright images reproduced by permission of the Department for Transport)

10.10.2.1   No stopping if there is a continuous white line

No vehicle is permitted to stop on any length of road with a continuous white line marked in the centre of the road. This also applies to roads with a broken line on one side, and applies to vehicles on either side of the road (reg 26(2)(a)). This regulation does not apply to dual carriageways or to vehicles used for fire brigade, ambulance, or police purposes.

Exceptions also apply for vehicles that have stopped in order to:
- allow passengers to board/alight from a vehicle;
- allow goods to be loaded or unloaded from the vehicle;
- facilitate building or demolition work;
- enable the removal of any obstruction to traffic, road-works, or public utility work.

Exceptions also apply for vehicles that:
- are required to stop by law or with the permission or direction of a constable in uniform or a traffic warden;
- are prevented from proceeding by circumstances outside the driver's control;
- have stopped to avoid an accident.

10.10.2.2   No crossing or straddling a continuous white line

No vehicle shall cross or straddle a continuous line when the line is to the **left** of the broken line or another continuous line (reg 26(2)(b)).

There are exceptions:
- when a vehicle is turning right;
- when the action is unavoidable, or to pass a stationary vehicle or to avoid an accident;
- to enable the vehicle to overtake a pedal cycle, horse, or road maintenance vehicle moving at a speed not exceeding 10 mph;
- to comply with the directions of a police officer or a traffic warden in uniform.

The above offences are committed under s 36(1) of the Road Traffic Act 1988, reg 10 of the Traffic Signs Regulations 2002, and Sch 2 to the Road Traffic Offenders Act 1988.

10.10.3   Disobeying a Traffic Sign

This only applies to signs of the prescribed type that have been lawfully placed on or near a road. Drivers are therefore under no obligation to heed informal signs erected by members of the public (s 36 of the Road Traffic Act 1988, for signs listed under reg 10 of the Traffic Signs Regulations and General Directions 2002).

Regulation 10 of the Traffic Signs Regulations and General Directions 2002 creates two lists of relevance to s 36 of the Road Traffic Act 1988:

List 1: signs which if contravened by a driver create an offence under s 36 of the Road Traffic Act 1988.

List 2: offences for which a convicted driver may be **disqualified** or his/her licence may be **endorsed**.

Examples of List 1

| Give-way sign | Indicator sign | Regulatory arrow sign | Stop sign manually operated |

(Crown copyright images reproduced by permission of the Department for Transport)

Examples of List 2

Red light of permanent or portable traffic signal

Stop sign · No-entry sign

(Crown copyright images reproduced by permission of the Department for Transport)

TASK 9

1. The following is a list of some of the **main** contributory factors leading to a fatal road accident or collision in 2005 (not all factors are listed here; we have omitted the 18% of fatal accidents that were attributed to the involvement of pedestrians). Put them in order, with the most frequently occurring first.
   (a) Road environment (eg road layout, slippery road)
   (b) Vehicle defects (eg defective tyres, defective brakes)
   (c) Injudicious action (eg exceeding speed limit, going too fast for conditions)
   (d) Driver/rider error or reaction (eg loss of control, failed to look properly)
   (e) Impairment or distraction (eg impaired by alcohol, illness, or disability)
   (f) Behaviour or inexperience (eg careless, reckless, or in a hurry; aggressive driving)
   (g) Vision affected (eg by road layout, dazzling sun)
   (Adapted from data provided in Robinson & Campbell, 2006).
2. List three ways that you and your colleagues might be able to help reduce the number of deaths in subsequent years.

TASK 10

For each of the following road traffic signs, find an image to show either the symbol for the sign or the sign as marked on the road surface itself.

1. Vehicular traffic entering the junction must give priority to vehicles from the right, for example, a mini-roundabout.
2. Priority is to be given to vehicles from the opposite direction.
3. Warning of a weak bridge.
4. Prohibition of vehicles exceeding a stated height.
5. Drivers of large or slow vehicles to stop and phone for permission to cross a level crossing.
6. Route for use by buses and pedal cycles only.

7. Route for tramcars only.
8. Stop sign, manually operated.
9. Convoy vehicle no overtaking.
10. Stop for road works.
11. Vehicles to stay to the right of a vehicle involved with mobile road works.
12. Zigzag lines for an equestrian (horse) crossing (also called 'pegasus') or toucan crossing (crossing for pedestrian and cyclists to use together).
13. Line markings across a junction at which a vehicle must give way.
14. Variations of double white line markings including the use of hatched areas.
15. Variations of yellow bus stop markings.
16. White lines and hatched areas dividing lanes or a main carriageway from a slip road (on motorways or dual carriageways).
17. Yellow grid markings within a box junction preventing entry without a clear exit.
18. Red light signal of permanent/portable traffic signals and green filter arrows.
19. Tramcar not to proceed further.
20. Intermittent red light signals at railway level crossings, swing bridges, etc.
21. Matrix prohibition.

10.11 Methods of Disposal for Motoring Offences

When investigating the kind of road traffic offences we have described so far, there are potentially several ways in which you can deal with the person who has committed the offence. Your decision will be based upon a number of issues, including your own force's policy and your own discretion (see section 5.7 above). The methods of disposal for such offences include:

- a verbal warning;
- the Vehicle Defect Rectification Scheme;
- a fixed penalty notice;
- reporting a suspect for the purposes of issuing a written charge;
- notice of intended prosecution.

10.11.1 Vehicle Defect Rectification Scheme

Drivers in possession of a vehicle found to be in an unsuitable condition can be given the opportunity to join the **Vehicle Defect Rectification Scheme**, or VDRS. This will depend upon both the circumstances of the offence and your discretion. The VDRS is a way of dealing with certain minor vehicle defects without the need to prosecute or issue a fixed penalty notice.

The advantages of this scheme include:

- the defects are rectified, which contributes to road safety;
- the offender does not have to go to court;
- better police and public relations; for many people, the only time they will come into contact with you is during the investigation of road traffic matters and VDRS is partly supportive rather than being wholly punitive.

When you consider using the VDRS you must:

- point out the offence to the person responsible for the vehicle;
- inform him/her that no further action will be taken if he/she agrees to participate in the scheme;
- continue to report the driver for prosecution, in case the defects are not rectified and the matter has to be taken to court;
- inform the driver that he/she does not have to participate, as VDRS is voluntary.

If the driver refuses to participate in the VDRS, you should then proceed with a fixed penalty notice, or a report for summons.

10.11.1.1 The VDRS timescale

To avoid the possibility of prosecution, the driver must complete the following within fourteen days of the ticket being issued:

1. Repair the defect or renew the faulty body part.
2. Submit the vehicle for examination at a Department of Transport approved testing station (an MOT testing station).
3. Have the VDRS form endorsed at the MOT testing station to confirm that the fault is rectified.
4. Forward the completed VDRS form to the Central Ticket Office within the time specified on the ticket.

If the driver fails to return the form within the time specified on the form, you may consider prosecution of the driver by way of summons, as if the driver had never been entered on the VDRS in the first place. The copy of the form will be returned to you after twenty-one days, to enable you to expedite the reporting process. You will then need to write a duty statement (see section 11.19 below) to include evidence relating to the offence, just in the same way that you would when reporting a suspect for the purposes of issuing a written charge (see section 10.11.3 below).

You will then be required to submit a case file including a report requesting a written charge to be issued which will outline the offences for which the driver was reported.

10.11.2 Fixed Penalty System

The fixed penalty system (Pt III, Road Traffic Offenders Act 1988) provides offenders with the opportunity to pay a fixed fine instead of going to court. It speeds up administrative processes for a number of traffic-related matters. Fixed penalty notices can only be issued to the person actually committing the offence or driving the vehicle involved; they cannot be used for people who cause or permit an offence (see section 10.3 above for 'cause' or 'permit'). In some circumstances the fixed penalty ticket can be issued by leaving the documents on the vehicle without the need for the driver to be present, such as a parking ticket affixed to a car's windscreen.

Fines for fixed penalty notices must be paid within twenty-eight days (to the Central Ticket Office in the area). If the fine is not paid within this time, it will be increased by 50% and recovered by the courts.

There are two kinds of fixed penalty notice:

1. **Non-endorsable fixed penalty notices (NEFPN)** are used for offences which do not add penalty points to an offender's driving licence such as offences relating to:
   * parking;
   * seat belt wearing; and
   * vehicle lighting.
2. **Endorsable fixed penalty notices (EFPN)** are used for offences which add penalty points to an offender's driving licence. Such offences include:
   * contravening a red traffic light;
   * failing to conform to a stop sign; and
   * driving a vehicle with defective tyres.

10.11.2.1 Issuing a non-endorsable fixed penalty notice

When you are in uniform and you have reasonable grounds to believe that a person is committing or has committed a fixed penalty offence, you may issue that person with a fixed penalty notice in respect of that offence (s 54, Road Traffic Offenders Act 1988).

If the driver is present you should:

1. Point out the offence.
2. Caution the driver using 'when questioned' and satisfy Code C10.2 (explaining to the suspect that they are not under arrest and do not have to remain with you, sometimes referred to as 'caution + 2'—see Chapter 11).
3. Question the driver and allow the driver to ask questions (in relation to the offence(s)).
4. Complete and issue the NEFPN.
5. Report the driver or owner for summons.
6. Use the 'now' caution (again, see Chapter 11).

If the driver is not present and the offence relates to the vehicle only you may attach a NEFPN to a stationary vehicle (s 62(1)). Note that it is an offence to remove or interfere with a fixed penalty notice fixed to a vehicle.

The flow chart below summarizes the process.

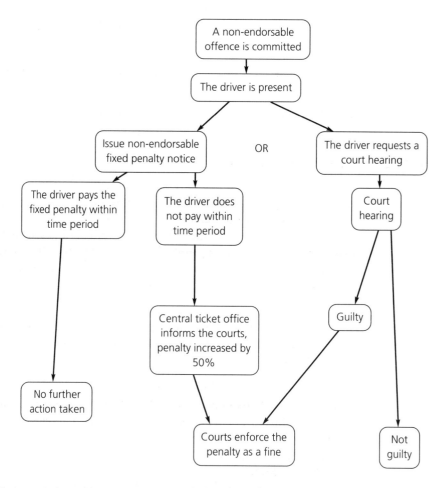

10.11.2.2 Issuing an endorsable fixed penalty notice

Where the penalty for the offence is obligatory endorsement, s 54 of the Road Traffic Offenders Act 1988 states that you may only issue an endorsable fixed penalty notice if:

- the driver produces a licence and its counterpart for inspection;
- you are satisfied on inspecting the licence and its counterpart that the driver would not be liable to disqualification;
- the driver surrenders his/her licence and its counterpart to you.

If the fixed penalty notice is not accepted by the driver, there is no further action to be taken on the street, and the driver will have to be reported and prosecuted.

The procedure for issuing an EFPN is as follows:

1. Point out the offence to the driver.
2. Caution the driver using 'when questioned' and satisfy the PACE 1984, Code C10.2 (explaining to the suspect that he/she is not under arrest and does not have to remain with you, sometimes referred to as 'caution + 2',—see Chapter 11).
3. Ask to see the driver's licence.
4. Question the driver and allow the driver to ask questions (in relation to the offence(s)).
5. Offer FPN in lieu of court.
6. Report the suspect for the purposes of issuing a written charge
7. Caution (use the 'now' form, see Chapter 11).

10.11.2.3 The significance of the driver's licence

If the driver does not have a driving licence available, you should issue a provisional fixed penalty notice instructing him/her to produce the licence for inspection at a police station of his/her choice within seven days.

If the driving licence contains **less than twelve points**:

- ask the driver to surrender the licence;
- issue a fixed penalty notice and give a receipt of the ticket to replace the driving licence;
- explain to the driver that he/she needs to pay within the specified time or face an increased fine (as for NEFPN; see the previous section).

If the licence contains **more than twelve points** a fixed penalty notice cannot be used; you must report the driver for prosecution.

10.11.3 Reporting for the Purposes of Issuing a Written Charge

If you choose to report a person for summons as the method of disposal, or the person elects to go on to the VDRS, or you issue a fixed penalty ticket, you will always need to go through the following process. This is because not everybody will have the defect rectified or pay the fixed penalty and there will instead be a written charge and a requisition will be issued to attend court. The process is as follows:

1. examine the vehicle or see the offence being committed;
2. decide what offence(s) was (were) detected (having gathered evidence in the usual way, that is using your senses, what you saw, felt, smelt, and so on);
3. point out the offence(s) to the driver;
4. caution the driver using 'when questioned' form of caution and ensure you meet the PACE Act 1984, Code C10.2 (explaining to the suspect that he/she is not under arrest and does not have to remain with you, sometimes referred to as 'caution + 2',—see Chapter 11).
5. write down questions and answers about the offences into your PNB, eg when the person last inspected the vehicle, how long ago he/she began his/her journey, was he/she already aware of the defect?;
6. offer your PNB to the driver to read and sign that the notes were a true record of the interview;
7. allow the driver the opportunity to have his/her vehicle rectified or pay the penalty notice;
8. report the driver for the offence by saying 'I am reporting you for the offence(s) of ...';
9. caution the driver (using the 'now' caution, see Chapter 11).

10.11.4 Notice of Intended Prosecution (NIP)

A Notice of Intended Prosecution (NIP) is a document that can be issued to a person suspected of committing certain road traffic offences (s 1, Road Traffic Offenders Act 1988). A NIP specifies the nature of the offence and the time and place where it is alleged to have been committed. It must be given to the offender (the driver or the registered keeper of the vehicle), at the time of the offence (or sent within fourteen days of the offence).

A person will not be prosecuted for the offences listed below in section 10.11.4.1 unless he/she has been:

- **warned** at the time of the offence of the possibility of prosecution (s 1(1)(a)); or
- **served a summons** within fourteen days of commission of the offence (s 1(1)(b)); or
- **given a notice** setting out the possibility of prosecution (Notice of Intended Prosecution) (s 1(1)(c)), specifying the nature of the offence, and the time and place where it is alleged to have been committed.

Verbal warnings can lead to difficulties such as the defendant not fully understanding what was said (see *Gibson v Dalton* [1980] RTR 410). In any court case it would be the responsibility of the prosecution to prove that the defendant understood the verbal NIP and therefore you should always consider sending a written NIP in addition to a verbal warning.

10.11.4.1 Offences requiring a NIP

The following offences require an NIP:

- Dangerous driving.
- Careless and inconsiderate driving.
- Dangerous cycling.
- Careless and inconsiderate cycling.
- Failing to conform with the indication of a police officer when directing traffic.
- Failing to comply with a traffic sign.
- Exceeding temporary speed restrictions imposed by s 14 of the Road Traffic Regulation Act 1984.
- Exceeding speed restrictions on a special road.
- Exceeding temporary speed limit imposed by order.
- Speeding offences generally.

10.11.4.2 Circumstances when a NIP is not required

Circumstances when a NIP is not required are listed in s 2 of the Road Traffic Offenders Act 1988 and include:

- incidents when the vehicle concerned is involved in an accident at the time or immediately afterwards; or
- a fixed penalty notice has been issued; or
- a provisional fixed penalty notice has been issued.

10.11.5   Flow Chart of the Investigative Process for Dealing with Motoring Offences

The following flow chart summarizes the investigative process for dealing with motoring offences.

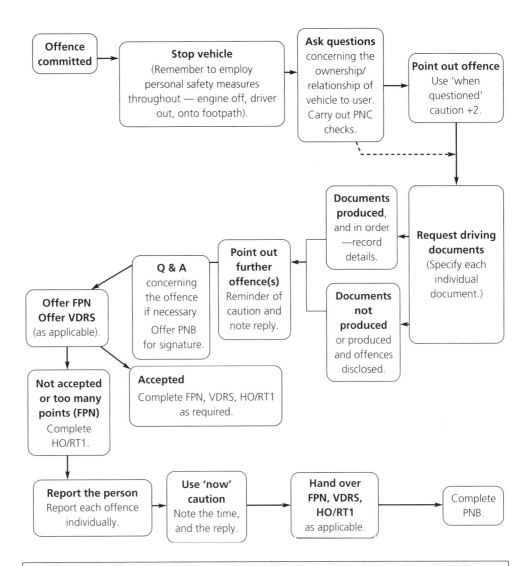

TASK 11

1. Write down the order in which you would investigate the following ways to deal with a motoring offence:
   - offences not covered by FPN/DRS;
   - driver unable to produce driving documents;
   - fixed penalty notices;
   - vehicle defect rectification scheme.

   Write down here how you will deal with the investigation of a road policing offence relating to driving documents and list the sequence of events, eg:
   - ask the driver of a vehicle to produce documents;
   - identify the offence.

2. Find out about and list the offences for which you can issue a non-endorsable fixed penalty notice.

10.12 Road Traffic Collisions (Section 170 of the Road Traffic Act 1988)

We often refer to collisions between vehicles (of various degrees of seriousness) as 'accidents'. Indeed the previous police term RTA (for Road Traffic Accident) has even entered the popular language. However, it is more common now in police circles to refer to road traffic **collisions** rather than accidents. This is partly to reflect that incidents of this kind are often due to driver error rather than simply a random accident. However, you are still likely to find 'accident' used frequently during training by other police officers and members of the public.

Regardless of whether we refer to the incident as an accident or a collision, it remains true that incidents of this sort are very common. Collisions also give rise to a large number of injuries. In 2004, there were 31 million vehicles in Britain and 207,000 injury accidents (Department of Transport, 2005). It is difficult to overstate just how dramatic these numbers are. It is as if the whole population of a town the size of Milton Keynes were to be injured every year, year after year.

The Road Traffic Act 1988 takes a common sense approach to collisions (referred to as accidents in the legislation) and dictates that the driver of a vehicle involved in a collision must stop and be prepared to provide details to anybody who reasonably requires information. This information might be needed for compensation claims for repairs or injuries or deaths.

During training you are likely to be tested on your detailed understanding of how these obligations are met, and what offences can be committed if they are not.

10.12.1 Reportable Accidents

A road accident requiring police involvement is usually a reportable accident. Although the meaning of the general term 'accident' is broad and hard to define, the meaning of the term 'reportable accident' is clearly defined in s 170(1) of the Road Traffic Act 1988. For an accident to be a 'reportable accident' **all** of the following criteria must be met; further details about each criterion are provided in subsequent sections:

> A reportable accident must:
>
> - take place on a road or other public place;
> - involve a mechanically-propelled vehicle;
> - result in damage to property or injury to a person other than the driver.

10.12.1.1 Location

Reportable accidents must take place on a road or other public place. If the collision takes place in any other location other than a road maintained at public expense, then you must gather evidence concerning the location in relation to its use, (that is, the frequency of use, used by whom, and under what circumstances) in order to prove it is a public place.

10.12.1.2 Type of vehicle

A reportable accident must be due to the presence of a mechanically-propelled vehicle. This includes vehicles intended or adapted for use on roads (cars, vans, and so on), as well as vehicles intended or adapted for use off road (for example dumper trucks and off-road motorbikes).

10.12.1.3 Damage or injury

The **damage** must be to another vehicle or object, such as a bicycle, road sign, or a garden wall. The damage can be to private property, but the accident itself must take place on a road or other public place. So if the vehicle leaves the road or other public place during the accident and ends up in a private dwelling or grounds adjacent to the road or public place, a reportable accident has still occurred. Damage does not have to be permanent or beyond repair, but the physical appearance must have been altered in some way.

Harm caused to farm animals and dogs during a reportable accident is classified as damage within the Act. Harm caused to cats or wild animals is not classed as damage for the purposes of this legislation.

The **injury** must be to another person, not just the driver of the vehicle. Injury includes shock as well as actual bodily harm. Note that if the only injury or damage caused is to the mechanically-propelled vehicle itself, its driver, or an animal in or on it, then the accident is not a reportable accident in terms of this piece of legislation.

10.12.2 Providing Information after a Reportable Accident

After an accident, the driver must **stop**, which includes remaining at the scene for as long as necessary to provide information to others (s 172(2), Road Traffic Act 1988). **Failing to stop at an accident** is a serious offence and is committed even if the person reports the accident to the police at a later time.

At the scene, the driver must provide particulars to anyone who has reasonable grounds for needing the information, such as the driver, rider, and passenger of any other vehicle involved, owners of property, pedestrians, or their representatives. The driver must provide:

- his/her name and address;
- the name and address of the vehicle's owner;
- the identification marks of the vehicle (for example, the vehicle registration number).

Failing to stop or report an accident is an **offence** under s 170(4) of the Road Traffic Act 1988. This offence is triable summarily and the penalty is six months' imprisonment and/or a fine and the offender may also be disqualified.

10.12.2.1 Reporting a reportable accident

Under s 170(3) and (6) of the Road Traffic Act 1988, if the driver of the mechanically-propelled vehicle does not give the information listed in section 10.12.2 above, then the accident must be reported as soon as reasonably practicable but not later than twenty-four hours after the accident (it is a matter for a court to decide what is 'reasonably practicable' for the circumstances). The driver must report in person to a constable or police station; it is not sufficient to telephone or send a fax or e-mail, nor should the driver just wait for the police to make contact.

10.12.2.2 Providing a certificate of insurance

Where personal injury is caused to a person other than the driver and the driver does not at the time produce a certificate of insurance, the driver has a further seven days to produce the relevant documents.

Failing to produce proof of insurance after an injury accident is an **offence** under s 170(7) of the Road Traffic Act 1988, unless the person concerned can subsequently produce the certificate (or other evidence) at a police station (specified by him/her at the time of the accident) within seven days of the accident.

This offence is triable summarily and the penalty is a fine.

TASK 12

Find out about your force policy concerning the procedures to be followed when attending the scene of a road traffic collision, especially on the way that you record your attendance.

Part of the policy may include the administration of a preliminary breath test to every driver involved in a collision. What legislation gives you the power to carry out such a policy?

What other computer checks are you going to carry out on the drivers involved?

10.13   Offences Involving Standards of Driving

Whilst investigating the consequences of a road traffic collision or the anti-social behaviour caused by a driver's careless or inconsiderate driving, you may need to consider the offences described in the following section. Standards of driving are first met whilst undertaking a driving test, but this minimum standard must be maintained for the rest of a person's driving career. Careless and inconsiderate driving can result in damage to property or injury to a person, but such poor driving can also be alarming, distressing, or annoying to members of the public. If vehicles are used in such a way you have a power to stop, seize, and remove the vehicle.

This section covers the following offences:

- Dangerous driving (s 2 of the Road Traffic Act 1988).
- Careless and inconsiderate driving (s 3 of the Road Traffic Act 1988).
- Causing death by dangerous driving (s 1 of the Road Traffic Act 1988).
- Causing death by careless or inconsiderate driving (s 2B of the Road Traffic Act 1988).
- Causing death by driving whilst unlicensed, disqualified or uninsured (s 3ZB of the Road Traffic Act 1988).
- Causing the death of another person whilst under the influence of drink or drugs (s 3A of the Road Traffic Act 1988).
- Wanton and furious driving (s 35 of the Offences against the Person Act 1861).
- Off-road driving (s 34 of the Road Traffic Act 1988).
- Careless and inconsiderate cycling (s 29 of the Road Traffic Act 1988).

10.13.1   Careless or Inconsiderate Driving

Legislation concerning careless or inconsiderate driving is described in s 3 of the Road Traffic Act 1988.

Section 3 states that an offence is committed by a person who . . .

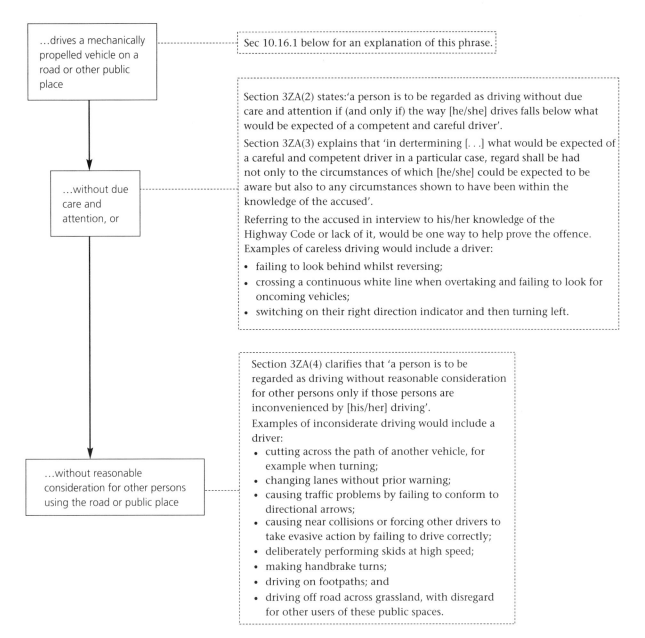

However, note the following:

- the offence applies only to mechanically-propelled vehicles;
- careless or inconsiderate driving is a question of fact for the court to decide;
- a driver can only be charged with careless or inconsiderate driving, not both.

This offence is triable summarily and the penalty is a fine. The driver may also be disqualified.

10.13.2 Dangerous Driving

There are two main causes of dangerous driving defined in s 2 of the Road Traffic Act 1988:

- by 'bad driving' due to the driver's style of driving;
- through driving a vehicle that is in a dangerous condition.

10.13.2.1 Bad driving

Section 2A(1) of the Road Traffic Act 1988 states that 'a person is to be regarded as driving dangerously if [...]':

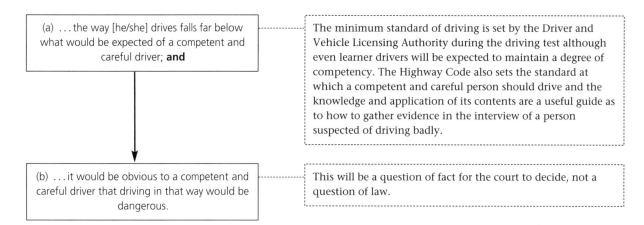

The following are examples of driving which may support an allegation of dangerous driving under s 2A(1):

- Racing or competitive driving.
- Speed which is highly inappropriate for the prevailing road or traffic conditions.
- Aggressive driving, such as sudden lane changes, cutting into a line of vehicles, or driving much too closely to the vehicle in front.
- Disregard of traffic lights and other road signs, which, on careful analysis, would appear to be deliberate; or disregard of warnings from fellow passengers.
- Overtaking which could not have been carried out safely.
- Where the driver is suffering from impaired ability such as having an arm or leg in plaster, or impaired eyesight.
- Driving when too tired to stay awake.
- Using a mobile phone whether as a phone or to compose or read text messages (*R v Browning* [2001] EWCA Crim 1831; [2002] 1 Cr App R (S) 88).

10.13.2.2 Dangerous state of a vehicle

Section 2A(2) of the Road Traffic Act 1988 states that:

> a person is to be regarded as driving dangerously [...] if it would be obvious to a competent and careful driver that driving the vehicle in its current state would be dangerous.

In determining the state of a vehicle for the purposes of s 2A(2), the load carried by the vehicle can be considered as well as the weight or height of the vehicle in relation to restrictions on the road. It is for the jury or magistrates to decide whether it would be obvious to a competent and careful driver that driving the vehicle in such a state would be dangerous. During evidence gathering (such as interviews of witnesses and suspects), use the Highway Code and Construction and use Regulations as a benchmark.

The following are examples of driving which may support an allegation of dangerous driving in relation to the state of a vehicle under s 2A(2):

- Driving a vehicle with a load which presents a danger to other road users.
- Driving with actual knowledge of a dangerous defect on a vehicle.

To summarize, whilst considering an offence of dangerous driving, it will be your responsibility to investigate the suspect in relation to whether:

- His/her driving fell far below the fixed and objective standard of a competent and careful driver; and
- it would be **obvious** to a competent and careful driver that driving in the way the defendant drove would be dangerous.

During the interview it is advisable to consider the wide range of defences that can be used to avoid prosecution for this offence. Care should be taken to collect evidence to contradict all of the defence strategies that might be employed by the defence counsel (see below).

If no one has died as a result of the incident, the offence of dangerous driving might be considered as an alternative offence.

10.13.3   Defences to Dangerous, Careless or Inconsiderate Driving

There are various defences that may be offered by a suspect in respect of committing the offences of dangerous or careless or inconsiderate driving (see 10.13.1 and 10.13.2 above). These are summarized in the table below:

List of defences

Automatism	Automatism is 'the involuntary movement of a person's body or limbs' (*Watmore v Jenkins* [1961] 2 All ER 868) which must occur very suddenly with little or no warning in order to claim the defence. It may include an epileptic fit or a sudden attack by a stinging insect, but (as a result of case law) will not include situations where a person falls asleep at the wheel or goes into a hypoglycaemic coma as a result of diabetes and continues to drive for a considerable distance.
Unconsciousness or sudden illness	This would include situations where a person suddenly becomes unconscious as a result of circumstances beyond his/her control, such as a stone being thrown from a bridge through the windscreen of the vehicle and hitting her/him on the head.
Assisting in the arrest of offenders	Here, the driver may have a defence (even though he/she was driving dangerously) if he/she could prove that he/she shunted another car off the road intentionally in order to help the police arrest people (in the shunted car) who had committed an indictable offence (*R v Renouf* [1986] 2 All ER 449).
Duress by threats	In order to claim this defence, the suspect must be able to show that he/she drove dangerously as a result of a threat. However, he/she must neither place him/herself voluntarily under the threat nor avoid the opportunity to escape from it.
Duress of necessity (of circumstances)	In order to claim this defence, the suspect must be able to show that he/she drove dangerously out of necessity in order: • to avoid death or serious injury to him/herself or anybody else; and that • he/she could not reasonably have been expected to act otherwise, as a result of the circumstances in which he/she found her/himself.
Sudden mechanical defect	If there is a sudden mechanical defect in the vehicle which causes the driver to totally lose control, this may be a defence. However, it does not apply if the driver is already aware of the defect or it could have been easily discovered by superficial examination, eg of tyres (*R v Spurge* [1961] 2 All ER 688).
Authorized motoring event	Person will not be guilty under ss 1, 2, or 3 of the Road Traffic Act if they drove in accordance with an authorization for a motoring event given by the Secretary of State (s 13(A), Road Traffic Act 1988).

The offence of dangerous driving is triable either way:

* Summarily; six months' imprisonment and/or a fine.
* On indictment; two years' imprisonment and/or a fine.

10.13.4   Other Offences Involving Dangerous Driving

There may be occasions when dangerous driving has taken place but you cannot use the Road Traffic Act 1988 as the basis of a prosecution, such as:

* when the driving was not on a road or other public place;
* when the vehicle used was not a mechanically-propelled vehicle (such as a bicycle or horse drawn vehicle);
* when the statutory notice of proposed prosecution was not given.

In these situations there is an alternative offence you might consider; s 35 of the Offences against the Person Act 1861 states that it is an offence for anyone having the charge of any carriage or vehicle to **cause** or **cause to be done bodily harm to any person** (hurt or injury calculated to interfere with the health or comfort of the victim):

453

- by wanton (deliberate) or furious driving, racing; or
- other wilful misconduct; or
- by wilful neglect.

The offence can only be committed if the driver has a degree of subjective recklessness; the driver must appreciate that harm was possible or probable as a result of his/her bad driving (*R v Okosi* [1996] CLR 666).

This offence is triable by indictment only and the penalty is two years' imprisonment. Disqualification is discretionary. Endorsement (3 to 9 points) is obligatory if committed in respect of a mechanically-propelled vehicle.

10.13.4.1 Riding a cycle carelessly or inconsiderately

It is an offence under s 29 of the Road Traffic Act 1988 for a person to ride a cycle on a road without due care and attention or reasonable consideration for other persons using the road.

This offence is triable summarily and the penalty is a fine.

10.13.5 Causing Death by Driving

The offences of causing death by dangerous driving, careless or inconsiderate driving, or whilst being unlicensed, disqualified, or uninsured are described in the table below.

Causing death by dangerous driving (s 1 of the Road Traffic Act 1988)	Causing death by careless or inconsiderate driving (s 2B of the Road Traffic Act 1988)	Causing death by driving whilst unlicensed, disqualified or uninsured (s 3ZB of the Road Traffic Act 1988)
An offence is committed by a person who		
causes the death		
of another person		
by driving a mechanically propelled vehicle		by driving a motor vehicle
dangerously	without due care and attention, or without reasonable consideration for other persons using the road	whilst committing an offence of: • driving otherwise than in accordance with a licence (s 87(1) RTA); • driving while disqualified (s 103(1)(b); • no insurance (s 143)
on a road or other public place.		on a road.
This offence is triable by indictment only and the penalty is: • Fourteen years' imprisonment. • Obligatory disqualification. • Obligatory endorsement—licence endorsed between three and eleven points.	This offence is triable either way and the penalty is: • Summarily; twelve months' imprisonment. • On indictment; five years' imprisonment. • Obligatory disqualification. • Obligatory endorsement—licence endorsed between three and eleven points.	This offence is triable either way and the penalty is: • Summarily; twelve months' imprisonment. • On indictment; two years' imprisonment. • Obligatory disqualification. • Obligatory endorsement—licence endorsed between three and eleven points.

There are two important points to note:

1. Causing death by driving whilst unlicensed, disqualified, or uninsured can only be committed whilst:
   - driving a motor vehicle only (see 10.3.1 above for the definition of 'motor vehicle')
   - on a road (see 10.16.1 above for the definition of 'road').
2. In all three offences, the death must be of a person other than the suspect. It is not relevant whether the deceased person was inside or outside the suspect's vehicle at the time of the incident.

10.13.5.1 Causing the death of another person whilst under the influence of drink or drugs

Section 3A of the Road Traffic Act 1988 states it is an offence:

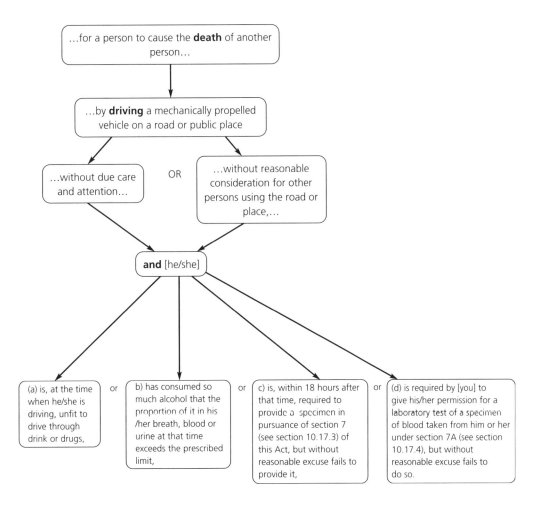

This offence is triable by indictment only and the penalty is fourteen years' imprisonment and/or a fine.

TASK 14

1. Which of the following have been held to be 'driving' in case law?
   (a) Letting a car free wheel down hill with the steering lock on. See *Burgoyne v Phillips* [1982] RTR 49.
   (b) A passenger in a car sees a friend walking along the roadside towards the car. To frighten the friend, the passenger pulls the steering wheel from the driver's grasp towards himself in order to make the car veer in that direction. See *DPP v Hastings* [1993] 158 JP 118.
   (c) A passenger in a car leans across the driver and steers the car while the driver manipulates the other controls. The driver's view forward is partially obscured by the passenger. After some distance, the car runs into a ditch while the passenger is steering. The passenger had been able to reach both the handbrake and the ignition key and knew the consequences

---

of using the various controls, but did not have access to the foot pedals. See *Tyler v Whatmore* [1975] RTR 83.
2. Where can dangerous driving and causing death by dangerous driving be committed?
   (i) Anywhere.
   (ii) On a road.
   (iii) In another public place.
   (iv) In a public place only
   Choose the correct answer from:
   (a) (i) only.
   (b) (iv) only.
   (c) (ii) and (iii) only.
   (d) All of the above.
3. In what locations does s 35 of the Offences Against the Persons Act 1861 apply?
   (a) A public place only.
   (b) A private place only.
   (c) A road only.
   (d) Anywhere.

10.13.6 Other Offences Involving Standards of Driving

Other offences relating to poor standards of driving are described in the Road Vehicles (Construction and Use) Regulations 1986. The term 'driving' has a wide meaning under s 192 of the Road Traffic Act; pulling up by the side of a road with the engine running, for example, could be considered as driving. The offences apply not only to the driver, but also to any person **causing or permitting** another to drive inappropriately. The following regulations are relevant to offences involving standards of driving:

- No person shall drive or cause or permit any other person to drive, a motor vehicle on a road if [he/she] is in such a position that [he/she] cannot have **proper control** of the vehicle or have a full view of the road and traffic ahead (reg 104). The obligatory penalty is an endorsement (three points) and a discretionary disqualification.
- No person shall open, or cause or permit to be opened, any **door** of a vehicle on a road so as to injure or endanger any person (reg 105).
- No person shall drive a motor vehicle on a road if the driver is in such a position as to be able to see directly or by reflection, a **TV or similar apparatus** except apparatus used to display information about the state of the vehicle or its location (satellite navigation), or devices to assist the driver to see the road adjacent to the vehicle (reg 109).
- Driving a motor vehicle on road while using a **hand-held phone (mobile)** is an offence, and also applies to similar devices with an 'interactive communication function'. (Communication by two-way radio, such as 'CB', is excluded from this offence, although the general need for safe driving still obviously applies.) Apart from applying to drivers, this offence can be committed by anyone supervising a driver with a provisional licence. Employers providing the employee with a company hand-held phone can be held liable if they fail to prohibit their employee from using it while driving on company business (reg 110). The obligatory penalty is an endorsement (three points) and a discretionary disqualification.

It is important to note that, as a member of the police service, you, together with members of other emergency services, are granted some exemptions from road traffic regulations. However, as a police officer you will be expected to drive at least as well as other motorists; you should aim to provide a positive role model for other drivers—look back at section 5.5 where we discuss personal authority. It is very important that your driving meets the standards prescribed by the level of your training and that you are fully aware of your force policies before taking on any emergency response.

TASK 13

1. What offences in this section might be considered for a person using a hand-held mobile telephone while driving, apart from the offence following from reg 110?
2. Apart from a driver using a phone, suggest some other circumstances or activities that might lead to a fall in standards of driving.

10.13.7 Off-road Driving

The law surrounding off-road driving is covered in s 34 of the Road Traffic Act 1988.

Section 34 states that an offence is committed by a person who:

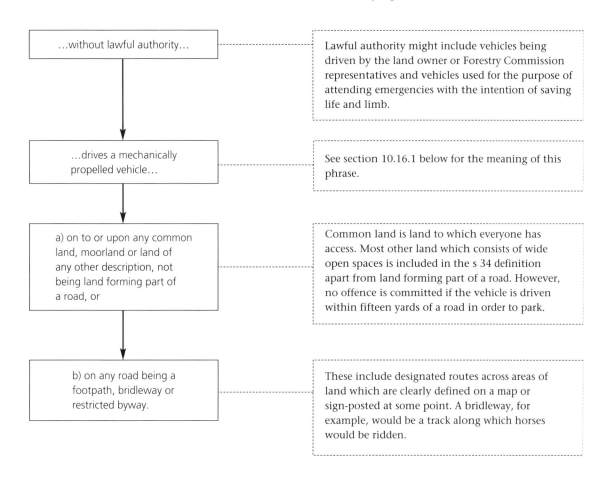

...without lawful authority...	Lawful authority might include vehicles being driven by the land owner or Forestry Commission representatives and vehicles used for the purpose of attending emergencies with the intention of saving life and limb.
...drives a mechanically propelled vehicle...	See section 10.16.1 below for the meaning of this phrase.
a) on to or upon any common land, moorland or land of any other description, not being land forming part of a road, or	Common land is land to which everyone has access. Most other land which consists of wide open spaces is included in the s 34 definition apart from land forming part of a road. However, no offence is committed if the vehicle is driven within fifteen yards of a road in order to park.
b) on any road being a footpath, bridleway or restricted byway.	These include designated routes across areas of land which are clearly defined on a map or sign-posted at some point. A bridleway, for example, would be a track along which horses would be ridden.

This offence is triable summarily only and the penalty is a fine.

10.14 Vehicles and Harassment

If you attend an incident where a group of people are racing in their cars and causing concern for other people in the area, what powers are open to you? You may have reasonable grounds for believing that an offence of careless and/or inconsiderate driving (under s 2 of the Road Traffic Act 1988) or driving a mechanically-propelled vehicle off-road (under s 34 of the Road Traffic Act 1988) has been committed. However, if the driving is causing (or is likely to cause), alarm, distress, or annoyance to members of the public, a power to seize the vehicle under s 59 of the Police Reform Act 2002 is available to you. You may take the following actions:

- **stop** the vehicle if it is moving; it is an offence to fail to stop;
- **seize** and **remove** the vehicle, after warning the driver;
- **enter** certain types of premises in order to stop or seize a vehicle;
- **use reasonable force** to carry out the above actions.

10.14.1 Warning the Driver Before Seizing a Vehicle

You cannot seize a vehicle unless you have issued a warning to the driver. You must normally warn him/her that you will seize the vehicle if the improper use continues. However, you do not have to warn the driver if:

- it would be impracticable to do so;
- you have already on that occasion given a warning;
- you have reasonable grounds for believing that such a warning has been given on that occasion by someone else;
- you have reasonable grounds for believing that the person is one to whom such a warning has been given (whether or not by you or another or in respect of the same vehicle or the same or a similar use) on a previous occasion in the previous twelve months.

10.14.2 Entering Premises to Seize or Stop a Vehicle

The term premises does not include a private dwelling or home, nor does it include any garage or other structure occupied with the dwelling house, or any land attached to the dwelling house. You must have reasonable grounds for believing the vehicle is on the premises.

10.14.3 Failure to Stop; the Offence, Mode of Trial, and Penalty

This offence is found in s 59(6) of the Police Reform Act 2002. It is triable summarily, and the penalty is a fine.

10.15 Driving Whilst Disqualified

Disqualification means that a licence is temporarily suspended, but revocation means it is effectively cancelled and the driver will have to pass a second driving test to obtain a full licence again.

10.15.1 Disqualification

Main ways in which a driver may be disqualified

Endorsement and penalty points	Penalty points are awarded according to the type and seriousness of the offence and are endorsed on the driving licence. When **twelve points** in a **three-year** period have been accumulated ('totted up'), the driver must be disqualified.
Discretionary disqualification	Where a person is convicted of certain offences which carry discretionary disqualification, such as a s 170 'failing to stop after an accident' offence, the court may disqualify for a period of its choosing (but not for an indefinite period).
Obligatory disqualification	The Road Traffic Act 1988 sets out minimum periods of compulsory disqualification for certain offences, such as drink driving. In some cases, the court can disqualify a person until he/she has retaken and passed the appropriate driving test again. In such a case, a disqualified person will become a provisional licence holder during the period leading up to the test. A failure to satisfy any of the requirements of a provisional licence means the person will commit the offence of disqualified driving.

A person is guilty of an offence under s 103(1) of the Road Traffic Act 1988 if:

... whilst disqualified from holding or obtaining a licence, [he/she] ...

(a) obtains a licence, or
(b) drives a motor vehicle on a road.

There are several forms of evidence you can use to prove that a driver is disqualified:

- A certificate of conviction under s 73 of the PACE Act 1984.
- The defendant's admission at interview.

- The defendant's admission in court.
- Evidence of a person who was in court when the original disqualification was imposed.

These offences are triable summarily. The penalties are as follows:

- Obtaining a licence while disqualified (s 103(1)(a)) a fine.
- Driving a motor vehicle on a road (s) 103(1)(b)); imprisonment for a term not exceeding six months and/or a fine, discretionary disqualification, and obligatory endorsement (six penalty points).

10.15.2 Revocation of Driving Licences

Section 3 of the Road Traffic (New Drivers) Act 1995 provides for the revocation of the driving licences of **new drivers** who have accumulated six or more penalty points within a period of two years, beginning on the day he/she passed his/her driving test.

A driver's licence may be revoked when:

- a licence holder is convicted of an offence involving obligatory endorsement; or
- a licence and counterpart have been sent to the fixed penalty clerk, and there are six or more penalty points to be taken into account.

The court (or the fixed penalty clerk) must send the licence and the counterpart to the Secretary of State who will then revoke the licence.

If a driver has had his/her licence revoked within the two-year probationary period, he/she reverts to the status of a learner driver and has to take a driving test again. He/she is not subject to a further probationary period if he/she passes this driving test.

A new driver who has had his/her licence revoked commits an **offence** if he/she drives without a new provisional licence or without 'L' plates and appropriate supervision (see section 10.7 above).

TASK 15

1. How could a disqualified driver or 'new driver' with a revoked licence conceal that he or she is disqualified?
2. What resources are available to you on Independent Patrol, if you need to establish whether a person is disqualified?

10.16 Drinking, Drug-taking, and Driving

The following section relates to ss 4, 5, and 6 of the Road Traffic Act 1988.

There are two main driving offences relating to driving whilst under the influence of drink or drugs:

- driving or attempting to drive a mechanically propelled vehicle while being unfit through drink or drugs (s 4, Road Traffic Act 1988); and
- driving or attempting to drive with alcohol in excess of the prescribed limit (s 5, Road Traffic Act 1988).

The key difference between these two offences is that for a s 4 offence the prosecution has to prove that the suspect's ability to drive was actually impaired, whereas for s 5 offences a high blood, breath, or urine alcohol level is the only evidence required.

10.16.1 Unfit to Drive through Drink or Drugs

The evidence of being unfit will be given by a police medical practitioner who will give the suspect a series of tests to indicate the level of impairment and his/her (in)ability to drive properly. The assessment will take place at the police station. In addition a specimen of breath, blood, or urine may be collected as well to prove the presence of the alcohol in the body.

Section 4 of the Road Traffic Act 1988 states that it is an offence for a person when:

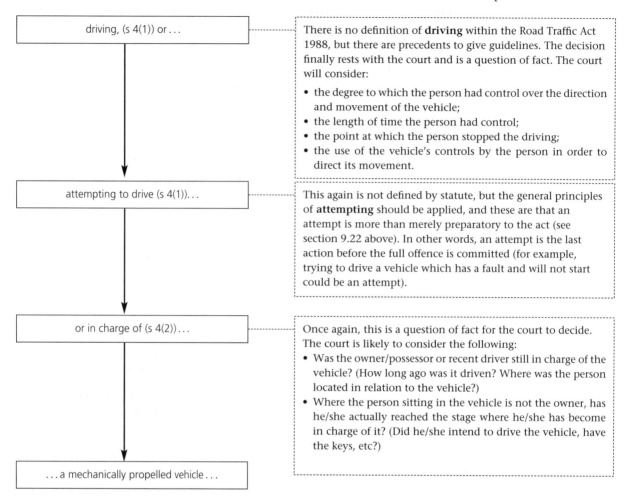

driving, (s 4(1)) or ...	There is no definition of **driving** within the Road Traffic Act 1988, but there are precedents to give guidelines. The decision finally rests with the court and is a question of fact. The court will consider: • the degree to which the person had control over the direction and movement of the vehicle; • the length of time the person had control; • the point at which the person stopped the driving; • the use of the vehicle's controls by the person in order to direct its movement.
attempting to drive (s 4(1))...	This again is not defined by statute, but the general principles of **attempting** should be applied, and these are that an attempt is more than merely preparatory to the act (see section 9.22 above). In other words, an attempt is the last action before the full offence is committed (for example, trying to drive a vehicle which has a fault and will not start could be an attempt).
or in charge of (s 4(2))...	Once again, this is a question of fact for the court to decide. The court is likely to consider the following: • Was the owner/possessor or recent driver still in charge of the vehicle? (How long ago was it driven? Where was the person located in relation to the vehicle?) • Where the person sitting in the vehicle is not the owner, has he/she actually reached the stage where he/she has become in charge of it? (Did he/she intend to drive the vehicle, have the keys, etc?)
...a mechanically propelled vehicle...	

This does not just mean a motor vehicle. A mechanically-propelled vehicle is not defined in law, but would include any vehicle which is powered by a mechanical means and does not have to be intended or adapted for use on the roads; it could include an off-road quad bike or scrambler.

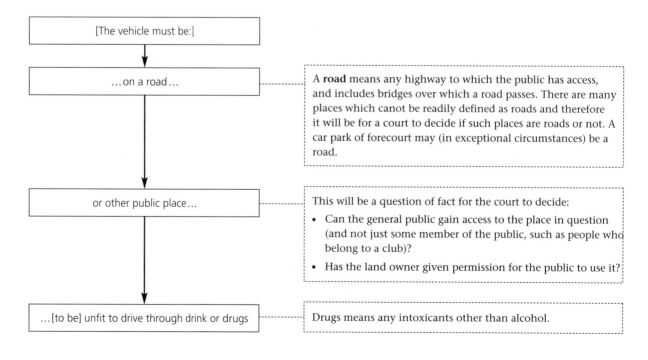

[The vehicle must be:]	
...on a road...	A **road** means any highway to which the public has access, and includes bridges over which a road passes. There are many places which canot be readily defined as roads and therefore it will be for a court to decide if such places are roads or not. A car park of forecourt may (in exceptional circumstances) be a road.
or other public place...	This will be a question of fact for the court to decide: • Can the general public gain access to the place in question (and not just some member of the public, such as people who belong to a club)? • Has the land owner given permission for the public to use it?
...[to be] unfit to drive through drink or drugs	Drugs means any intoxicants other than alcohol.

10.16.1.1 Possible defences to s 4(3) and (4) of the Road Traffic Act 1988

It is a defence if the suspect can prove that there was no likelihood of him/her driving (s 4(3)) so long as he/she remained unfit to drive through drink or drugs; for example he/she no longer had the vehicle's keys or he/she had taken a hotel room for the night.

The court may choose to disregard any injury to the suspect and any damage to the vehicle when deciding whether or not there was a likelihood of the suspect driving (s 4(4)).

These offences are triable summarily and the penalties are:

1. **Driving** and **attempting to drive** whilst unfit due to drink or drugs (s 4(1)):
   - Six months' imprisonment and/or a fine.
   - Obligatory disqualification.
2. **Being in charge of a vehicle** whilst unfit due to drink or drugs(s 4(2)):
   - Three months' imprisonment and/or fine.
   - Discretionary disqualification.

You have a power of entry under s 17(1)(c)(iiia) of the PACE Act 1984 to arrest a person under s 4 of the Road Traffic Act 1984. Remember, there is **no** need to administer a preliminary test for blood alcohol levels to a person before arresting him/her for this offence.

10.16.2 Blood Alcohol in Excess of the Prescribed Limit

There is no need to provide evidence that the suspect was unfit to drive for a s 5 Road Traffic Act offence. All that is required is a blood, breath, or urine test result showing that the level of alcohol in his/her body is above the prescribed limit. Section 5 of the Road Traffic Act 1988 states that it is an offence for a person to:

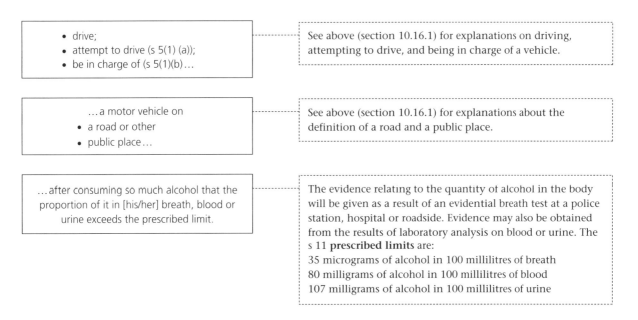

- drive;
- attempt to drive (s 5(1) (a));
- be in charge of (s 5(1)(b)…

See above (section 10.16.1) for explanations on driving, attempting to drive, and being in charge of a vehicle.

…a motor vehicle on
- a road or other
- public place…

See above (section 10.16.1) for explanations about the definition of a road and a public place.

…after consuming so much alcohol that the proportion of it in [his/her] breath, blood or urine exceeds the prescribed limit.

The evidence relating to the quantity of alcohol in the body will be given as a result of an evidential breath test at a police station, hospital or roadside. Evidence may also be obtained from the results of laboratory analysis on blood or urine. The s 11 **prescribed limits** are:
35 micrograms of alcohol in 100 millilitres of breath
80 milligrams of alcohol in 100 millilitres of blood
107 milligrams of alcohol in 100 millilitres of urine

It is a defence (s 5(2)) if a person can prove that there was no likelihood of him/her driving the vehicle at the time whilst he/she was over the prescribed limit (see section 10.16.1.1 above and also *Sheldrake v DPP* [2003] 2 All ER 497).

These offences are triable summarily and the penalties are:

1. **Driving** and **Attempting to drive** above the prescribed limit (s 5(1)(a)
   - Six months' imprisonment and/or a fine.
   - Obligatory disqualification.
2. **Being in charge of a vehicle** above the prescribed limit (s 5(1)(b)
   - Three months' imprisonment and/or a fine.
   - Discretionary disqualification.

10.16.3   Preliminary Tests

Preliminary tests are used to find out if it is likely that a drugs- or alcohol-related driving offence has been committed. They are referred to as roadside tests. These tests are covered in ss 6A, 6B, and 6C of the Road Traffic Act 1988. The three main types of preliminary tests are:

- a **preliminary breath** test to indicate whether the proportion of alcohol in the breath or blood is likely to exceed the prescribed limit (s 6A, Road Traffic Act 1988);
- a **preliminary impairment** test of whether a person is unfit to drive due to drink or drugs. This is done by observing the person's performance during a set of tasks or observing his/her physical state. You can only carry out such a test if you are approved for that purpose by the chief officer of the police force to which you belong (s 6B, Road Traffic Act 1988);
- a **preliminary drug** test to indicate the presence of drugs in a person's body by obtaining a specimen of sweat or saliva and testing it with an approved device (s 6C, Road Traffic Act 1988).

The preliminary breath test uses equipment commonly referred to as a 'breathalyser'. You will be given training in the use of preliminary breath test equipment (currently the Lion Alcolmeter 500). It is most important that you follow the manufacturer's instructions as well as force policy when using these devices.

If you make the requirement to a person to be tested on one or more grounds, you do not need to be in uniform. However, the police officer actually administering the test(s) must be **in uniform**.

You have a power of entry in order to administer preliminary tests under s 6E of the Road Traffic Act 1988:

(1) [you] may enter any place (using reasonable force if necessary) for the purpose of
   (a) imposing a requirement [for a preliminary test under s 6 (5)];
   (b) arresting a person under s 6D [(see the table in section 10.16.4 below];
      [but only] following an accident in a case where [you] reasonably [suspect] that the accident involved injury of any person [this applies to both (a) and (b)].

The following flow chart summarizes the circumstances for administering preliminary tests.

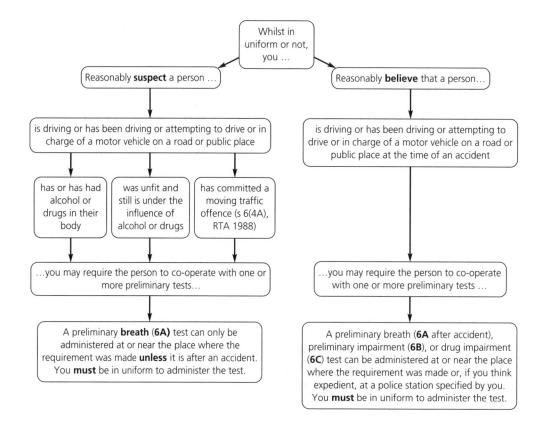

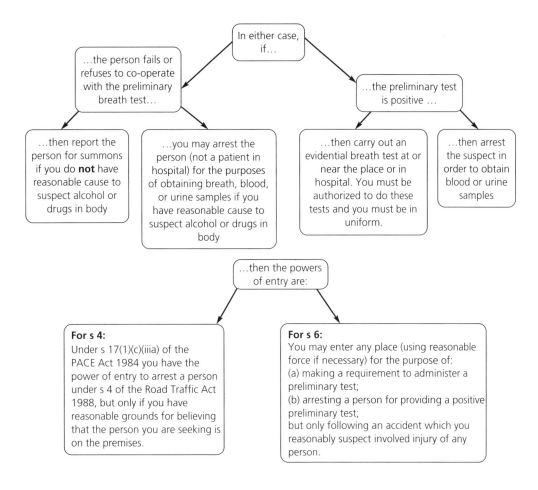

In either case, if...

...the person fails or refuses to co-operate with the preliminary breath test...

...the preliminary test is positive ...

...then report the person for summons if you do **not** have reasonable cause to suspect alcohol or drugs in body

...you may arrest the person (not a patient in hospital) for the purposes of obtaining breath, blood, or urine samples if you have reasonable cause to suspect alcohol or drugs in body

...then carry out an evidential breath test at or near the place or in hospital. You must be authorized to do these tests and you must be in uniform.

...then arrest the suspect in order to obtain blood or urine samples

...then the powers of entry are:

For s 4:
Under s 17(1)(c)(iiia) of the PACE Act 1984 you have the power of entry to arrest a person under s 4 of the Road Traffic Act 1988, but only if you have reasonable grounds for believing that the person you are seeking is on the premises.

For s 6:
You may enter any place (using reasonable force if necessary) for the purpose of:
(a) making a requirement to administer a preliminary test;
(b) arresting a person for providing a positive preliminary test;
but only following an accident which you reasonably suspect involved injury of any person.

It is an offence to fail to co-operate with the provision of a specimen for a preliminary test under s 6(6) of the Road Traffic Act 1988. This offence is triable summarily and the penalty is obligatory endorsement (four points) and discretionary disqualification.

10.16.4   Key Differences between s 4 and s 5 RTA 1988 offences

Key differences between s 4 and s 5 RTA 1988 offences

	s 4 'Unfit to drive'	s 5 'Over the prescribed limit'
Vehicle	Mechanically propelled vehicle (see 9.16.1 above)	Motor vehicle (see 10.3.1 above)
Arrest	**Not** required to be in uniform. The power is provided by s 24 of the PACE Act 1984 which requires you to have a reason why it is necessary, such as 'to allow the prompt and effective investigation of the offence'.	**Not** required to be in uniform when requiring co-operation for a preliminary test. **Must** be in uniform when administering preliminary test (except after an accident) or evidential test (the results of an 'evidential test' can be used as evidence in court to show the level of alcohol in a person's body).
	Preliminary test not required.	**Not** required to be in uniform for arresting a suspect for : • providing positive preliminary test, the result of which provides you with reasonable suspicion that the proportion of alcohol in the person's breath or blood exceeds the prescribed limit (s 6D(1), RTA 1988); • failing to provide a specimen for a preliminary breath test (s 6D(1), RTA 1988). However, you must suspect the influence of alcohol or drugs.

Key differences between s 4 and s 5 RTA 1988 offences (*continued*)

Power of entry	Power of entry to arrest under s 17(1)(c)(iiia) of the PACE Act 1984.	Power of entry to arrest under s 6E(1) of the RTA 1988, for the purposes of: • requiring preliminary test after an accident involving injury to any person; • arresting for providing positive preliminary test after accident involving injury to any person.
Offence	Unfit through drink or drugs proven by police medical practitioner or breath or blood or urine test results.	• Proportion of alcohol in breath or blood or urine exceeds the prescribed limit proven by breath or blood or urine test results. • Failing/refusing to provide a specimen.

10.16.5 Further Questions (and Some Indicative Answers)

In our experience, student police officers often have a number of questions concerning the circumstances surrounding testing.

FAQs

Question	Answer
How am I going to reasonably suspect or believe that a person may have excess alcohol in their body if I am not in the car with them?	For example, you might consider a person's driving to be erratic or too fast or ponderously deliberate and this gives you cause for suspicion. Although you must **not** administer **random** breath tests, you do have the power under s 163 of the Road Traffic Act 1988 to stop a vehicle. When you speak to the driver you might be able to smell intoxicating liquor on his/her breath.
If I suspect a person has been drinking and then request a preliminary breath test at the roadside, at what point to I caution the suspect in order to satisfy PACE Code C?	If you have a suspicion that a person has been drinking and therefore suspect he/she has alcohol in his/her body, you are not obliged to issue a caution. Once you have administered a preliminary breath test and the results of the test indicate a body alcohol level above the prescribed limit, it is at this point you are obliged to give a caution, as there are now reasonable grounds to suspect an offence has been committed (*Sneyd v DPP* [2006] EWHC 560).
What is a 'moving traffic offence' for the purposes of administering a preliminary breath test?	There are many, but one example would be an offence under the Road Traffic Regulation Act 1984: exceeding the speed limit. Therefore, if you saw a person speeding, that would give you a reason to administer a preliminary breath test.
What happens if a person fails to co-operate with a preliminary breath test on the basis that he/she has a medical condition?	If you reasonably suspect that the person has alcohol or a drug in their body or he/she is under the influence of a drug, you may arrest him/her and have his/her blood or urine tested. If you do not suspect alcohol or drugs, you cannot arrest him/her. Instead you should report him/her for the offence of failing to co-operate with a preliminary test.
What can I do if no one in a vehicle involved in an accident admits to driving?	First of all clarify who was in the vehicle at the time of the accident. Ask witnesses for help in this matter, but remember that you only have to **reasonably believe** that a person was driving a vehicle at the time of the accident to administer a preliminary test. Therefore you can test more than one person in the same vehicle. After an accident, there is an automatic requirement for preliminary tests. There is no need for you to suspect alcohol or drugs or a moving traffic offence.

TASK 16

Find out at your police station or from your force policies what preliminary test equipment is available for you to use and how you use it.

- Would you only be authorized to use equipment to test for breath alcohol or could you test for drugs as well?
- Who would be able to carry out a preliminary impairment test?

Find examples of moving traffic offences under the Public Passenger Vehicles Act 1981, the Road Traffic Regulation Act 1984, and the Road Traffic Offenders Act 1988.

10.17 Drink-driving and Admission to Hospital

This section is about investigating drink- or drugs-related driving offences in cases where the driver has been admitted to hospital after the accident (s 9, Road Traffic Act 1988). Once a person has been admitted to hospital, his/her doctor must agree to any tests you may wish to carry out, and of course the patient's welfare is paramount. A further complicating factor is that the suspect is also a patient and may be given drugs as part of his/her medical treatment. The presence of these drugs in the body may interfere with the accuracy of drink and drugs tests carried out as part of a police investigation.

Hospital is defined by the Act to mean an institution which provides medical or surgical treatment for in-patients or out-patients. The term **patient** is not defined and will be a question of fact for the court to decide, but, generally speaking, it will be a person who is currently on hospital grounds and either is receiving medical treatment or waiting to receive medical treatment.

10.17.1 Obtaining Breath/Blood or Urine Samples from a Hospital Patient

The regulations governing such procedures are given in s 9(1) of the Road Traffic Act 1988. You must get the agreement of the suspect's doctor before making any requirements, because the welfare of a patient is of primary importance.

The following paragraphs summarize the regulations.

10.17.2 Conducting Preliminary Tests

- Find the **doctor** in charge of the case (a nurse cannot give you permission to take samples from a patient).
- Ask for the **doctor's consent** to conduct a preliminary breath test, explaining the method of operating the particular device to be used. The doctor will give consent if the process is not prejudicial to care or treatment of the patient. You must obtain the doctor's consent before proceeding any further.
- Request the **patient's consent** to take part in the preliminary breath test.
- Carry out the **preliminary breath test** if the patient consents.

If the test is negative, you must explain to the patient that there will be no further action.

If the patient does not consent, then under s 6(6), Road Traffic Act 1988, 'a person commits an offence if without reasonable excuse [he/she] fails to co-operate with a preliminary test in pursuance of a requirement imposed under [s 6]'. If he/she does not co-operate with the test, you will need to report the person for the offence under s 6(6).

10.17.3 Evidential Tests

The results of evidential tests can be used as evidence in court, and the regulations concerning this type of testing are given in s 7 of the Road Traffic Act 1988.

If the result of the preliminary test is positive (or the patient fails to complete the test), you need to proceed to evidential testing. The outline procedure is shown below.

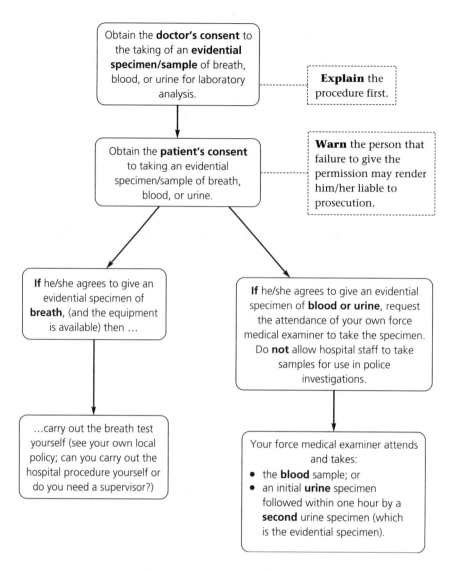

Obtain the **doctor's consent** to the taking of an **evidential specimen/sample** of breath, blood, or urine for laboratory analysis.

Explain the procedure first.

Obtain the **patient's consent** to taking an evidential specimen/sample of breath, blood, or urine.

Warn the person that failure to give the permission may render him/her liable to prosecution.

If he/she agrees to give an evidential specimen of **breath**, (and the equipment is available) then …

…carry out the breath test yourself (see your own local policy; can you carry out the hospital procedure yourself or do you need a supervisor?)

If he/she agrees to give an evidential specimen of **blood or urine**, request the attendance of your own force medical examiner to take the specimen. Do **not** allow hospital staff to take samples for use in police investigations.

Your force medical examiner attends and takes:
- the **blood** sample; or
- an initial **urine** specimen followed within one hour by a **second** urine specimen (which is the evidential specimen).

10.17.4 Unconscious Patients and Tests for Drugs or Alcohol

Once again you will you need to notify the medical practitioner in charge of the case of the unconscious driver of your proposal to take a specimen of blood, which is a process outlined in s 9(1A) of the Road Traffic Act 1988. Subsequently, if the medical practitioner in charge of the case does not object, you should request a police medical practitioner to take a specimen of blood from the person concerned (unless it is not reasonably practicable for the request to be made or for the police medical practitioner to take the specimen (s 7A(2)).

The police medical practitioner can take the specimen whether or not the unconscious person consents and provide the sample to you (s 7A(3)). The following is a summary of these procedures:

- Find the **doctor** in charge of the case (a nurse cannot give you permission to take samples from a patient).
- Ask for the **doctor's consent** to the taking of a sample from the unconscious person. The doctor will give consent if the process is not prejudicial to care or treatment of their patient. You must obtain the doctor's consent before proceeding any further.
- If the doctor consents, request the attendance of **your own force medical examiner** to take the specimen.
- The medical examiner attends and takes the specimen(s).

Under s 7A(4), a specimen shall not be subjected to a laboratory analysis unless the patient:

(a) has been informed that it was taken; and

(b) has been requested by you to give their permission for a laboratory analysis of the specimen; and

(c) has given his/her permission to do so.

10.17.5 Allowing for the Delay between the Offence and Taking Samples

It is assumed that the proportion of alcohol in the suspect's breath, blood, or urine at the time of the alleged offence would not have been lower than the level revealed in the evidential specimen. Generally, the court will accept that the levels of intoxicants in the body at the time of the evidential test are at least equal to the levels at the time the alleged offence was committed (s 15(2), Road Traffic Offenders Act 1988).

Sometimes, the accused will claim the '**hip flask defence**'. He/she will insist that he/she consumed alcohol or drugs after the offence but before the evidential sample was taken. The assumption under s 15(2) (see previous paragraph) cannot be made if the accused proves that he/she consumed alcohol before he/she provided the specimen (s 15(3), Road Traffic Offenders Act 1988) and after the time of the alleged offence. He/she might claim for example that he/she ran off after a collision and went for a drink before the police apprehended him/her. Or, having been given a preliminary test, he/she consumed intoxicants from a container in the vehicle, such as the proverbial (and sometimes actual) hip flask before the evidential specimen is taken. This is formally referred to as 'post-incident drinking'.

If a driver provides an evidential specimen and alleges he/she has consumed further intoxicants since the time of the alleged offence, the Forensic Science Service (FSS), or a private laboratory, may advise that **back calculations** could be used to establish that the driver was in excess of the legal limit when the offence occurred. These calculations are based on the rate of elimination of alcohol from the driver's body and the time elapsed since the offence and the subsequent consumption of alcohol.

Evidence for back calculations should be recorded on Form MG/DD/D at the police station. However, if this defence is not raised until later, the FSS should be provided with as much information as can be obtained from the case papers and the officer in the case.

The following information is relevant, where available:

- the type and quantity of alcohol consumed **before** the offence and, if possible, the times at which individual units of alcohol were consumed;
- the type and quantity of alcohol allegedly consumed **after** the offence but before the provision of a breath or laboratory specimen;
- **driver's** characteristics: weight, height, build, age, sex, and medical conditions;
- details of any **food** consumed six hours before the offence and the subsequent provision of a breath or laboratory specimen;
- details of any **medication** taken regularly or within four hours prior to drinking.

TASK 17

Whilst on Independent Patrol you are required to attend the accident and emergency department at the local hospital. At the hospital you make a lawful requirement for a sample of breath, blood, or urine from a patient who was the driver of a vehicle at the time of a collision. Unfortunately, whilst waiting for your medical practitioner to arrive, the patient is discharged from hospital and leaves the building.

Does the obligation to provide that sample still stand? Refer to *Webber v DPP* [1998] RTR 111 for your answer.

10.18   Offences Related to Highways

In this section we begin by examining the legal definitions of terms such as 'highway'. We then consider a number of offences relating to highways including 'causing danger on highways'.

10.18.1   Highways—Some Definitions

Legislation relevant to road and traffic policing often includes the words 'road' and 'highway'. It is important therefore to be very clear about the difference between these two when applying the law.

- A **highway** is a road, bridge, carriageway, cart way, horse way, bridleway, footway, causeway, church way, or pavement (s 5, Highways Act 1835).
- A **road** is any (length of) highway to which the public has access, and includes bridges over which a road passes (s 192, Road Traffic Act 1988).

There are also are number of other terms used in legislation:

- A **carriageway** is a way marked or arranged in a highway over which the public have a right of way for the passage of vehicles, but does not include cycle tracks (s 329, Highways Act 1980).
- A **bridleway** is a highway over which the public have a right of way on foot, on horseback, or leading a horse (s 329, Highways Act 1980).
- A **footpath** is a highway not adjacent to a road over which the public have a right of way on foot only (s 329, Highways Act 1980).
- A **footway** is a highway next to a road over which the public have a right of way on foot only (s 329(1), Highways Act 1980).
- A **street** includes roads, lanes, alleys, subways, squares, and any other similar places open to the public. It also includes doorways, entrances to premises, and any ground adjoining a street (*Smith v Hughes* [1960] 2 All ER 859).

10.18.2   Wilful Obstruction

Wilful obstruction is an offence under s 137 of the Highways Act 1980. It is an offence for a person:

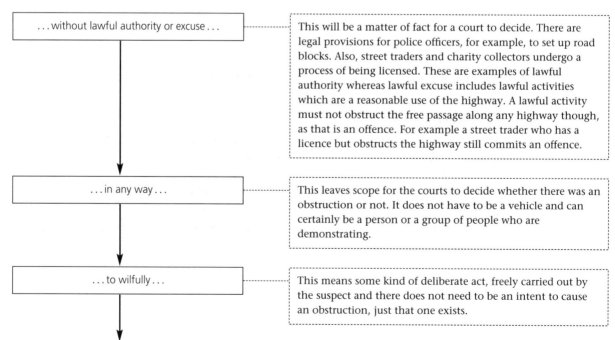

. . . without lawful authority or excuse . . .	This will be a matter of fact for a court to decide. There are legal provisions for police officers, for example, to set up road blocks. Also, street traders and charity collectors undergo a process of being licensed. These are examples of lawful authority whereas lawful excuse includes lawful activities which are a reasonable use of the highway. A lawful activity must not obstruct the free passage along any highway though, as that is an offence. For example a street trader who has a licence but obstructs the highway still commits an offence.
. . . in any way . . .	This leaves scope for the courts to decide whether there was an obstruction or not. It does not have to be a vehicle and can certainly be a person or a group of people who are demonstrating.
. . . to wilfully . . .	This means some kind of deliberate act, freely carried out by the suspect and there does not need to be an intent to cause an obstruction, just that one exists.

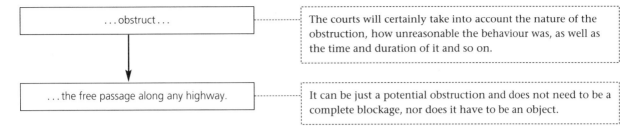

This offence is triable summarily, and the penalty is a fine.

10.18.3   Directing 'Unauthorized Campers' away from the Roadside

Section 77 of the Criminal Justice and Public Order Act 1994 provides local authorities with the procedure for removing persons and vehicles parked at the roadside. This includes verges, unoccupied property, or places where they are trespassing.

10.18.4   Vehicles or Trailers in a Dangerous Position on a Road

Section 22 of the Road Traffic Act 1988 states that it is an offence for 'a person in charge of a vehicle to cause or permit:

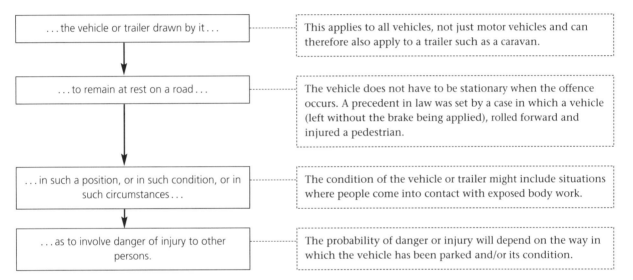

This offence is triable summarily, and the penalty is a fine.

10.18.5   Lighting Fires or Letting off Firearms near a Highway

Section 161 of the Highways Act 1980 prohibits any person (without lawful authority or excuse) from:

- **depositing** anything on a highway which leads to someone getting injured; or
- **lighting a fire** on or over a carriageway; or
- **discharging a firearm (or firework)** within 50 feet of the centre of a highway if it could injure a user of the highway.

This offence is triable summarily, and the penalty is a fine.

10.18.6   Interfering with Road Signs

On occasions people can cause potential danger to road users by interfering with road signs or vehicles. Section 22A of the Road Traffic Act 1988 states that:

a person is guilty of an offence if intentionally and without lawful authority or reasonable cause [they]

- [cause] anything to be on or over a road, or

- [interfere] with a motor vehicle, trailer or cycle, or
- [interfere] (directly or indirectly) with traffic equipment (defined below),

in such circumstances that it would be obvious to a reasonable person or bystander, that to do so would be dangerous. The reasonable person or bystander does not have to be a motorist (*DPP v D* [2006] EWHC 314).

Traffic equipment is defined as:

- anything lawfully placed on or near a road by a highway authority;
- a traffic sign lawfully placed on or near a road by a person other than a highway authority;
- any fence, barrier or light lawfully placed on or near a road [to protect street works or undertakings, or items placed] by a constable or a person acting under the instructions (whether general or specific) of a chief officer of police.

If the danger would have been **obvious** to a reasonable person, it is irrelevant that the suspect was unaware of it. This will be a question of fact for the court to decide given the circumstances. **Dangerous** means that injury to a person, or damage to property is likely to occur.

This offence is triable either way:

- On indictment; seven years' imprisonment and/or a fine.
- Summarily: six months' imprisonment and/or a fine.

10.18.7 Repairing Vehicles in the Road

The repairing of vehicles in the street is a relatively common occurrence but may give rise to nuisance to other residents and may even cause environmental damage.

Under s 4 of the Clean Neighbourhoods and Environment Act 2005, a person commits an offence if he/she 'carries out restricted works on a motor vehicle on a road'. In this case **restricted works** means works for:

- the repair, maintenance, servicing, improvement or dismantling of a motor vehicle or of any part of or accessory to a motor vehicle;
- the installation, replacement or renewal of any such part or accessory.

However, no offence is committed if the works:

- were **not** carried out in the course of, or for the purposes of, a business of carrying out restricted works or for gain or reward **unless** the works gave reasonable cause for annoyance to persons in the vicinity (our emphasis); or
- arose from an accident or breakdown and repairs were necessary on the spot or carried out within 72 hours.

TASK 18

Several complaints have been made by the residents in the neighbourhood of a club. They say that at closing time they have seen obstructions being placed in the roads nearby, traffic lights being tampered with, and the tyres of their vehicles being deflated.

- What offences might have been committed?

10.19 Answers to Tasks

TASK 1

As you approach and examine the vehicle, consider health and safety implications (see the answer to Task 6 below).

You would have to consider gathering the following evidence:

1. That the wheels of the Fordover turned round (including the one that appeared to be seized).

2. That the normal vehicular controls were operative including the locked steering.
3. That the brakes were capable of working and the engine could have started.

In such cases (where proof is required to determine whether or not a motor vehicle is still a motor vehicle for the purposes of the Road Traffic Act 1988), the best evidence would be more appropriately obtained by a thorough examination by a qualified and authorized vehicle examiner. Your local procedure will explain how the services of such a person can be obtained.

If the results of the Fordover examination reveal that it can still be classified as a motor vehicle, then the person towing the Fordover along with another vehicle will be using the Fordover.

TASK 2

1. The form you will need is an HO/RT/1 (Home Office Road Traffic Form 1), known colloquially as a 'Horti'.
2. Some of the problems associated with the use of this form include the following:
   • If the driver has not given you details of his/her true identity, you will probably not be able to find the driver again and he/she will continue to drive without the documents you have asked him/her to produce, thereby avoiding prosecution.
   • The driver may give you completely false details, allowing the possibility of avoiding prosecution.
3. Make checks of the details you are given:
   • Always check the driver and vehicle details with the PNC to establish if they match.
   • Use the PNC to provide a description if the driver has a criminal record.
   • Request further proof of identity, for example passports and credit cards.
   • Request a voters' register check.
   • Request telephone numbers and ask control room to call the numbers to verify the existence of the person.

There may be no need to use an HO/RT/1 if the person's verified address is nearby.

TASK 3

Questions to ask the driver might include:
• What is the name of your insurance company?
• What is the starting and expiry date of the policy you have?
• How much did the policy cost you?
• How is the cost being met?

Further questions to decide on would include:
• What vehicle is the person insured to drive?
• What type of vehicle is the person entitled to drive on such a policy including the engine size?
• What is the engine size of the vehicle that is being driven?
• Has the vehicle been modified in any way?

If you have a doubt that the engine size of the vehicle differs from the engine size described on the PNC, then request the vehicle to be examined by an authorized vehicle examiner.

On completion of your enquiries, contact the insurance company and speak to a police liaison representative of the company to determine exactly what type of vehicle the person is insured to drive.

TASK 4

Date of first registration can be obtained from the Certificate of Registration and/or the PNC.

Possible defences can be countered by asking the driver: What was the starting point of his/her journey? What is the destination of his/her journey?

If the answer to either of those questions involves the testing of the vehicle, then further questioning to counter the possible defences of vehicles travelling to a **pre-arranged** test and where the vehicle has **failed the test** may be necessary.

TASK 5

- Use your investigative skills to locate the user or keeper by accessing the PNC or undertaking house to house ('H2H') enquiries.
- Use a DVLA form CLE 2/8 found in a pad of forms which can be obtained from your stationary store or administration at your police station. There are a number of other ways of notifying DVLA of a vehicle not displaying a licence including completing and submitting an online form available from<http://forms.dvla.gov.uk/public/unlic_veh/report_online.dg .htm>.

TASK 6

As you approach the vehicle, think of health and safety implications and consider the potential problems associated with the:

- vehicle driving off;
- traffic passing by the location;
- engine running;
- driver making off;
- location of the ignition keys;
- handbrake not being applied.

A possible sequence is then as follows.

1. Speak to driver and introduce yourself.
2. Outline your reason for stopping the vehicle.
3. Ask the driver for his/her name and address and date of birth.
4. Ask the driver for his/her connection with the vehicle (is he/she the owner and/or driver?).
5. Ask the driver for details of his/her intended destination and the place where he/she began his or her journey.
6. Examine the vehicle whilst considering the potential health and safety implications associated with:
   - moving parts inside the engine compartment such as thermostatically controlled cooling fans;
   - high temperatures associated with parts such as brakes, exhaust systems, radiators, and engines;
   - harmful liquids such as hydraulic fluids, battery acid, anti-freeze, and hot engine coolant;
   - sharp objects such as exposed tyre cords or faulty bodywork;
   - movement of the vehicle and anything in, on, or under the vehicle;
   - movement of other vehicles and persons around you;
   - the surface upon which you and the vehicle are positioned and the existence of harmful objects or substances.
7. Note any possible offence(s) detected (in the usual way, through gathering evidence using your senses, that is, what you saw, felt, smelled, and so on).
8. Point out the possible offence(s) to the driver.
9. Caution the driver using the 'when questioned' form described in section 11.13 of this Handbook and ensure that you satisfy the PACE Act 1984, Code C10.2 (for example, explain to driver that he/she does not have to remain with you).
10. Write down questions and answers about the offences in your PNB, for example when the person last inspected their vehicle, how long ago did he/she begin her or his journey, was he/she already aware of the defect?
11. Offer the PNB entry to the driver to read and sign that the notes are a true record of the interview.

12. Report the driver for the offences.
13. Caution the driver.

TASK 7

How did your list compare?

Blue flashing lights ('beacons') are of obvious importance to the police and emergency services and their use is strictly controlled. No vehicle is permitted to use blue flashing lights other than if it belongs to a defined list (such as police vehicles). However, the number of types of vehicles so permitted continues to grow. A recent decision was to allow 'vehicles owned by HM Revenue and Customs and used in pursuit of serious crime to be fitted with blue warning beacons' (Explanatory Memorandum to the Road Vehicles Lighting (Amendment) Regulations 2005 No 2559).

TASK 8

1. **True**. The term 'hours of darkness' refers to a period in time which is half an hour after sunset to a half an hour before sunrise.
2. **False**. It is the Road Traffic Lighting Regulations 1989 as amended by the Road Vehicles Lighting (Amendment) Regulations 1994.
3. **False**. The correct rate is 60 to 120 pulses per minute.
4. **False**. The lawful circumstances are:
    (a) while stationary to warn other road users of a temporary obstruction;
    (b) to summon assistance to the driver, conductor, or inspector of a bus (PSV);
    (c) on a motorway or unrestricted dual carriageway to warn following drivers of the need to slow down due to a temporary obstruction ahead;
    (d) in the case of a school bus, while loading or unloading (or about to do so) passengers (under sixteen years of age) provided the bus displays the statutory yellow reflective signs indicating the presence of schoolchildren.
5. **True**
6. **True**
7. **True**

TASK 9

1. The order is as follows, with percentages for 2005:

Order	Factor	Percentage of fatal collisions/accidents*
d)	Driver/rider error or reaction (eg loss of control, failure to look properly)	64%
c)	Injudicious action (eg exceeding speed limit, going too fast for conditions)	32%
f)	Behaviour or inexperience (eg careless, reckless, or in a hurry; aggressive driving)	29%
e)	Impairment or distraction (eg impaired by alcohol, illness, or disability)	19%
a)	Road environment (eg road layout, slippery road)	12%
g)	Vision affected (eg by road layout, dazzling sun)	8%
b)	Vehicle defects (eg defective tyres, defective brakes)	3%

  * Note that column does not total 100% as some collisions/accidents have more than one contributory factor.

2. Some of the ways in which you might be able to help reduce the number of deaths in subsequent years are to be found in the Roads Policing Strategy agreed between ACPO, DoT and Home Office in 2005 and which can be found at: <http://www.acpo.police.uk/asp/policies/Data/acp_dft_ho_rp_strat_jan05.pdf>.

TASK 10

See the Highway Code for answers. The Highway Code is available online at <http://www.highwaycode.gov.uk/index.htm>. You can also practise your understanding online via the DSA website at <http://www.theory-tests.co.uk/home/>.

TASK 11

Offences not covered by FPN/VDRS	Driving documents	Fixed penalty notices	Vehicle defect rectification scheme
• Point Out Offence • Caution + 2 • Questions and Answers • Report the suspect • Caution (now)	Make requirement for each document to be produced **Produced** Examine and record details of any document produced in PNB **Not produced** • Point Out Offence • Caution + 2 • Questions and Answers • Complete + issue HORT1 • Report the suspect • Caution (now)	**NON-ENDORSEABLE FPN** Driver present • Point out offence • Caution + 2 • Question and answers • Complete and issue NEFPN • Report the suspect • Caution (now) Driver not present Complete and affix NEFPN to vehicle. **ENDORSEABLE FPN** • Point Out Offence • Caution + 2 • Questions and Answers • Offer FPN in lieu of Court • Report the suspect • Caution (now) **Accepted—D/L available** • less than 12 points and Driving Licence surrendered—Issue Full FPN • 12 points or more—Report the suspect **Accepted—D/L unavailable** Issue Provisional FPN Not accepted NFA on street	• Point Out Offence • Caution + 2 • Questions and Answers • Offer VDRS (voluntary) • Report the suspect • Caution (now) **Accepted** Issue VDRS **Not Accepted** NFA on street

List of offences for which you can issue a non-endorsable fixed penalty notice

Road Traffic Act 1988

14	No seatbelt—adult, front or rear
15(2)	No seatbelt—child in front of vehicle
15(4)	No seatbelt—child in rear of vehicle
16	No helmet—motorcycles
19	Parking LCV on verge or footway
22	Leaving vehicle in dangerous position
23	Unlawful carrying of passengers on motorcycles
24	More than one person on a pedal cycle

34	Driving a motor vehicle off-road
35	Failure to comply with traffic directions
36	Failure to comply with traffic signs
40A	Using vehicle in dangerous condition etc
41A	Construction & Use Regulations relating to brakes, steering, and tyres
41B	Construction & Use Regulations relating to weight (goods and passenger vehicles)
42	Other Construction & Use Regulations relating to lighting offences
87(1)	Driving other than in accordance with a Driving Licence
163	Failing to stop vehicle for constable in uniform
172	Failing to notify the police of driver's identity

Highways Act 1835
72	Cycling on the footway (not Scotland)

Highways Act 1980
137	Obstruction of highway by a vehicle

Road Traffic Regulation Act 1984
5(1)	Contravention of Traffic Regulation Order outside London
8(1)	Contravention of Traffic Regulation Order inside London
11	Breach of experimental traffic order
13	Breach of experimental traffic scheme inside London
16(1)	Use of vehicle against temporary prohibition/restriction orders at roadworks
17(4)	Contravention of motorway regulations
18(3)	Contravention of one-way traffic on trunk road
20(5)	Contravention of restriction/prohibition of use of vehicle on a particular road
25(5)	Breach of pedestrian crossing Regulations
29(3)	Use of vehicle in street playground
35A(1)	On road parking restrictions etc
47(1)	Failure to pay excess charge at parking place
53(5)	Breach of parking place Designation Order etc
53(6)	Breach of parking place Designation Order etc
88(7)	Contravention of minimum speed limit
89(1)	Speeding offences

Vehicle Excise and Registration Act 1994
33	Using or keeping vehicle without excise licence
42	Driving or keeping vehicle without registration mark
43	Driving or keeping a vehicle with obscured registration mark
43C	Using incorrectly registered vehicle

Road Vehicles (Display of Registration Marks) Regulations 2001
	Registration mark not in prescribed format

Greater London Council (General Powers) Act 1974
59	Parking on footways, verges, etc

Zebra, Pelican and Puffin Pedestrian Crossing Regulations and General Directions 1997
Reg 24	Overtaking a moving or stationary vehicle in controlled area of a crossing

TASK 12

The legislation that gives you the power to implement such a policy is s 6A of the Road Traffic Act 1988.

Whilst in uniform or not, if you reasonably believe that a person:

- is driving; or
- has been driving; or
- attempting to drive; or
- in charge of a motor vehicle

on a road or public place at the time of an accident, you may require the person to co-operate with one or more preliminary tests including a breath test. You must be in uniform to administer the test.

The other computer checks that you are likely to carry out on the drivers involved include:

(a) A PNC check to:
- discover if the driver is wanted, or disqualified from driving;
- ascertain if there are any reports regarding the vehicles being stolen;
- establish details of the keepers of the vehicles.

(b) Local checks regarding the drivers to determine whether their names and addresses are valid and/or if they are locally wanted on warrant.

TASK 13

1. Using a hand-held mobile telephone (mobile) while driving could easily amount to failing to have proper control of the vehicle, or even dangerous driving (see section 10.13.1.).
2. Other 'careless driving' activities may include lighting a cigarette, turning round and shouting at children, searching for a station on the radio, changing CDs, looking for sun glasses, looking in the mirror and applying make-up, or any other similar action that diverts the attention from driving.

TASK 14

1. (a) Held to be driving.
   (b) Not held to be driving.
   (c) Held to be driving.
2. (c) that is, (ii) and (iii) only.
3. (d) that is, anywhere.

TASK 15

1. Knowing that he/she was likely to be disqualified from driving, a person might contact the DVLA to obtain a duplicate licence before the court hearing and then submit one or the other of his/her licences and keep one which he/she could produce to you in the future. The person could obtain a stolen licence and produce it to assume the identity of another person (if it was an old style licence without a photograph).
2. As a result of the possibility of a disqualified driver or a new driver having had his/her licence revoked, producing a duplicate to you, it is important that you carry out PNC checks, local database checks such as the voters' register, and question the person about his/her identity to match the details given to you with the details held on police computer databases. Your local knowledge will be very important here as you will be able to ask about the description of localities and names of places to help verify the identity of the driver.

TASK 16

1. You can only carry out a preliminary impairment test if you are approved for that purpose by the chief officer of the police force to which you belong.

Currently there are two types of preliminary tests that can be administered to trigger further investigations into the possible level of intoxication of people in control of different forms of transport. One of these tests relates to the consumption of alcohol and the other to the use of drugs.

You will most probably receive training quite early on in the use of an Electronic Breath Screening Device (ESD) which will be a type approved by the Secretary of State. This training will enable you to administer preliminary breath tests for alcohol. The equipment is usually a hand-held device which will be issued to you during Supervised Patrol. There will be a need to change the mouthpiece into which the suspect will exhale breath each time you carry out a test and you will be trained in the procedure for assembling the equipment and interpreting the tests results.

A preliminary drug test on the other hand is a procedure whereby a specimen of sweat or saliva is obtained and, through the use of an approved device by the Secretary of State, an indication is given as to whether or not the person to whom the test is administered has a drug in his or her body. Currently, each force has different policies relating to which members of staff can carry out this procedure and therefore you may not be trained in the use of such a device straight away.

2. Moving traffic offences include:

- Contravention of traffic regulations, for example speed limits.
- Failing to comply with traffic signs and directions, for example traffic lights.

TASK 17

Yes, in such circumstances, the required sample may then be taken at a police station, regardless of whether an appropriate breath analysis machine is available. See *Webber v DPP* [1998] RTR 111.

TASK 18

Section 22A of the Road Traffic Act 1988 states that a person is guilty of an offence if he/she intentionally and without lawful authority or reasonable cause:

(a) causes anything to be on or over a road; or
(b) interferes with a motor vehicle, trailer or cycle; or
(c) interferes (directly or indirectly) with traffic equipment.

11

Detention, Arrest, and Collecting Evidence

11.1 Chapter Briefing

This chapter describes the legislation and police procedure surrounding the detention and arrest of people and the collecting of evidence. You are likely to undertake many of the tasks described in this chapter whilst on Supervised and Independent Patrol.

11.1.1 Aims of the Chapter

This chapter will enable you to:

- understand how respect for and understanding of human rights is a central requirement of modern day policing;

- appreciate the importance of the Police and Criminal Evidence Act 1984 (PACE) in governing your powers as a constable;
- understand how to deal with a number of aspects of handling suspects, including their identification by others;
- appreciate your right to enter buildings for the purposes of arrest or to save life;
- comprehend the powers to detain and arrest individuals (including new legislation introduced in 2006);
- search premises with or without a warrant;
- perform some of the regular duties of a police officer, such as the correct completion of your pocket notebook and the making of duty statements;
- comprehend the context of your role when attending a crime scene;
- develop the underpinning knowledge required for a number of NOS elements, several of the PAC headings and entries for your Learning Diary Phases 3 and 4, and the CARs of your SOLAP.

11.1.2 Police Action Checklist

This chapter will provide you with the underlying knowledge and theory to meet the following requirements of the Police Action Checklist:

11.1.2.1 Search

Conduct stops.
Demonstrate lawful search—persons.
Demonstrate lawful search—premises.
Demonstrate lawful search—vehicles.

11.1.2.2 Investigation

Demonstrate initial crime scene management.
Provide support and advice to victims and witnesses.

11.1.2.3 Disposal

Reporting for summons.
Make lawful arrests.
Convey a suspect into custody.

11.1.2.4 Custody office procedures

Present suspect to custody in accordance with force procedures.

11.1.3 National Occupational Standards

This chapter will provide you with some of the knowledge required to demonstrate aspects of the following NOS elements:

National Occupational Standard Unit Elements

1A1.1 Apply principles of reasonable suspicion or belief.
1A1.2 Use police actions proportionately.
1A1.3 Use police actions fairly.
AA1.1 Promote equality and value diversity.
2C3.1 Arrest, detain or report individuals.
2G2.1 Conduct priority and volume investigations.
2I2.1 Prepare to search vehicles, premises and open spaces.
2I2.2 Conduct searches of vehicles, premises and open spaces.
2K1.1 Escort detained persons.
2K2.1 Present detained persons for custody process.

11.1.4 IPLDP Phases and Modules

This chapter will provide you with resources to support the following Induction and Operational Modules of the IPLDP.

11.1.4.1 Induction modules

> IND 2 Foster people's equality, diversity and rights (particularly IND 2.1 Identify people's rights and their responsibilities).
>
> IND 10 Use police actions in a fair and justified way (particularly IND 10.3 Use police actions proportionately).

11.1.4.2 Operational modules

> OP 3 Respond to incidents, conduct and evaluate investigations.
> OP 5 Search individuals and premises.
> OP 7 Arrest and report suspects.
> OP 8 Escort suspects and present to custody.

11.1.4.3 Legislation, policy, and guidelines

Aspects of the following topic areas of LPG 1:

- Crime (LPG 1.1);
- Protecting People (LPG 1.3);
- Police Policies and Procedures (LPG 1.4);
- Non-Crime incidents (LPG 1.5).

Much of the content of this chapter relates to IPLDP Phase 3 'Supervised Patrol' and Phase 4 'Independent Patrol'.

11.1.5 SOLAP

The contents of this chapter are relevant to the 'knowledge' evidence requirements of CARs 1A1, 2C3, 2G2, 2I2, 2K1, and 2K2.

11.1.6 Learning Diary Phases

The contents of this chapter may provide you with stimulus material for completion of your Learning Diary (Phase 3) and the following headings in particular:

- Crime;
- Police policies and procedures;
- Stops and searches;
- Ethics and values of the police;
- Rights and responsibilities.

You may also find some content of this chapter relevant to your Learning Diary (Phase 1) under the heading 'Rights and responsibilities'.

11.1.7 IPLDP Learning Requirement

This chapter is relevant to the following sections of the IPLDP Learning Requirement: 1.18, 3.1, 3.2, 3.4, 3.6, 5.1, 5.3, 7.1, 7.4, and 7.8.

11.2 Introduction

In this chapter, we look in detail at what is involved in detaining a person, in arresting someone, and in collecting evidence—both from a crime scene and from people who were victims, witnesses, or perpetrators of a crime. Again, as we have commented throughout this Handbook, you will need to know your law, and the application of the law, in detaining a person, arresting someone, and so on, because only with a thorough knowledge of the law allied to a proper understanding of police procedure can you be sure that you are doing the right thing.

Before we go into the detail, let us have a quick knowledge check. Do you know when to make an entry in your pocket notebook (PNB)? Do you know when you have to use the caution? (Do you know the caution, come to that?) Do you know what to do when a suspect makes voluntary (unsolicited) comments about an offence (or other offences)? Do you know when you can arrest without warrant, or when you can enter property without a warrant? Do you know what is involved in making a search? What are your powers to seize and retain property? What happens when you take the suspect to the police station? Can you make a duty statement and do you know what it means? How do you 'dispose' of people who have been arrested?

If your answer to all or any of these questions was 'No', then this is a chapter you need to study well. We talked in the opening to Chapter 8 about the **proportionate use of powers** and the same general point is valid here as well. The exercise of your powers should be consistent with the Human Rights Act 1998 and the provisions of the Police and Criminal Evidence Act 1984. We put this into a dramatic context in chapter 12 and show you how to apply the logic of interviewing to the investigation of a crime. You have to be able to show that your use of your powers to detain, arrest, and gather evidence was justified and proportionate to what had taken place. It is not always easy to understand what the people upon whom you use your powers are thinking or feeling.

Over the years of your service, you will become very familiar with the layout of a police station, the location of the cells, the role of the custody officer, the procedures for taping and/or video-recording an interview using PEACE principles, the use of the caution, the making of statements, and the use of legal jargon. You will become so used to it in fact that much of it will become automatic to you. That is the nature of professionalism. However, do not assume that just because you have such familiarity with the criminal justice system that other people will. Some of your witnesses and victims might be anxious when first visiting a police station. Your suspects, some of whom will **not** be hardened criminals, may be anxious too, or confused, or disorientated. Neither victims, witnesses, nor suspects will have your easy familiarity with what goes on, and so you should remember to explain processes and to anticipate people's unease or discomfort. All this is part of being a professional and part of your response to people's right to dignity and respect. It is too easy to forget that people can be overwhelmed by the experience of being caught up in the ponderous machinery of criminal justice, and that they may often rely on you to be the centre of reassuring normality, to help them through it. As we show later in Chapter 12, the individual is more likely to respond to you if you show the acceptable, professional, and impartial face of policing and therefore, if a suspect, may start to talk; if a victim, may feel able to describe what happened; if a witness, may tell you what was seen, felt, smelled, touched, or tasted—all without being forced, intimidated, or humiliated.

Whilst you will learn specialist interview techniques and procedures (we cover some of them in the next chapter) as your training unfolds, you can offer such reassurance as we have described above from your first day in the police service. That professionalism of approach to all you do as a police officer is nowhere more important that when you are processing a person's arrest and detention. You are taking away a fundamental liberty, and you must be entirely conversant with your powers to do so. You must also understand the risk assessments which must be made when a person is detained, especially when there is a risk of self-harm. 'Death in custody' is a devastating occurrence to all concerned and treated as such by the IPCC investigators, and you do not want your actions to be the pretext or reason for any criticism of police procedure. Make sure you get it right. Errors or mistakes in process can be a gift to defence counsel; you do not want to lose a case because you had the details wrong. Worse, you do not want someone who is guilty to walk free, and possibly offend again, because of a procedural or technical lapse on your part.

11.3   The Human Rights Act 1998

The concept of human rights and the responsibilities of police officers in the preservation and maintenance of those rights runs throughout this Handbook. However, it is perhaps worth noting that recent legislation concerning human rights marked a significant mood change towards an emphasis on rights ('you shall') rather than the usual focus of the law on prohibition ('you shall not'). By this we mean that most laws, until recently, defined what constitutes wrong-doing and how law enforcers and the criminal justice system should respond to these crimes. Human rights legislation on the other hand stresses an individual's **entitlement** to expect certain fundamental rights as part of their social contract with the State and other forms of authority. The Human Rights Act 1998 is the prime example. It falls to public authorities such as the police (and by extension, to student police officers as a member of that police service) to maintain the fundamental rights of all individuals who come into contact with that authority.

So important is this emphasis on the proactive protection of human rights that some police forces, notably the Police Service of Northern Ireland, may even be described as 'human rights based'.

There are a number of NOS elements relevant to human rights and the student police officer, most notably the element:

National Occupational Standards Element

AA1.1 Promote equality and value diversity

This section provides background information relevant to performance criterion 1 of element AA1.1 (to 'act in accordance with relevant legislation, employment regulations and policies, and codes of practice related to promoting equality and valuing diversity'). As with the majority of NOS elements, direct observation by your assessor or other qualified witnesses is likely to form the main method of assessing this element.

The roots of the Human Rights Act 1998 are to be found in a set of articles containing rights agreed by the European Convention for the Protection of Human Rights and Fundamental Freedoms (or in short often referred to as 'the Convention'), which came into force in 1953 as part of the reconstruction of Europe after the Second World War.

There are two main features of human rights legislation. First, all new statute law must be compatible with the rights. Secondly, an individual may take a public authority to a UK court if the authority has not acted in a manner compatible with the rights.

11.3.1   What Are the Rights?

These are normally described in terms of the Article number:

Article number	Article title
2	Right to life
3	Prohibition of torture
4	Prohibition of slavery and forced labour
5	Right to liberty and security
6	Right to a fair trial
7	No punishment without law
8	Right to respect for private and family life
9	Freedom of thought, conscience and religion
10	Freedom of expression
11	Freedom of assembly and association
12	Right to marry

Article number	Article title
14	Prohibition of discrimination
16	Restriction on the political activities of aliens
17	Prohibition of the abuse of rights
18	Limitation on use of restrictions on rights

(You may be wondering what has happened to Article 1. As far as we need be concerned as student police officers, there is no Article 1. This is a technical aspect of the adoption of the European Convention.)

11.3.2 The Three Types of Convention Rights within the Act

There are three types of convention rights within the Human Rights Act 1998: absolute, limited, and qualified rights. We examine each in turn.

11.3.2.1 Absolute rights

Within these rights, the interests of the community as a whole cannot restrict the rights of the individual in any way. They are absolute.

Article number	Article title
2	Right to life
3	Prohibition of torture
4	Prohibition of slavery and forced labour
7	No punishment without law

11.3.2.2 Limited rights

These rights are not absolute because the articles are limited.

Article number	Article title
5	Right to liberty and security
6	Right to a fair trial

An example of a limitation is in Article 5; the right to liberty and security does not apply if the detention is lawful as a result of six listed arrest situations. One of these circumstances is when the arrest is made to ensure attendance in court if there is a reasonable suspicion that a crime has been committed, or to prevent crimes being committed.

A further example occurs within Article 6, where there is a right for both the public and the press to have access to any court hearing. However, this right is subject to certain restrictions in the interests of morality, public order, or national security, or where the interests of those under eighteen or the privacy of the parties require the exclusion of the press and public.

11.3.2.3 Qualified rights

These rights contain circumstances in which interference with them by the public authority is permissible if it is in the **public interest** and can be **qualified** for example to prevent disorder or crime, for public safety, or for national security

Article number	Article title
8	Right to respect for private and family life
9	Freedom of thought, conscience and religion
10	Freedom of expression
11	Freedom of assembly and association

However, a public authority (such as the police) may only interfere with one of these qualified rights under one of three circumstances:

- The interference is **lawful** and must form part of existing common or statue law (see section 5.11 above) such as the power to stop and search.
- The interference is made for one of the specifically listed **permissible** acts in the interests of the public so as to prevent disorder or crime for public safety.
- The interference is **necessary** in a democratic society because the wider interests of the community as a whole often have to be balanced against the rights of an individual, but it must be **proportionate**, not excessive or heavy-handed.

11.3.3   Applying the Human Rights Act to Everyday Policing

You may need to ask yourself the following questions in relation to an individual or group before you interfere with their qualified rights:

1. Are my actions **lawful**? Is there a common or statute law to support my interference with a person's rights?
2. Are my actions **permissible**? Am I permitted to interfere with a person's rights because it is in support of a duty such as the preventing of crime?
3. Are my actions **necessary**? Do the needs of the many outweigh the needs of the few, in other words, must I take into account the interests of the community and balance one individual's rights against another's?
4. Are my actions **proportionate**? Having considered everything, will my actions be excessive or could they be less intrusive and more in proportion to the outcome I need to achieve?

During training you may be given a mnemonic to use to help remember the questions you should ask yourself about any action you might take that affects human rights. These mnemonics vary from force to force from JAPAN (Justifiable, Accountable, Proportionate and Necessary) to PLAN (Proportionality, Legality, Accountability and Necessity) but in essence all refer to the criteria described above.

A standard that you will need to achieve in order to qualify as a police officer is NOS element AA1.1: to 'promote equality and value diversity' of people. (Note that Skills for Justice define people to include a 'child, adult, group, community or agency that [you] come into contact with, either directly or indirectly. It includes members of the public, individuals who are clients of the justice sector, and colleagues in the workplace'.)

This element has the following **performance criteria** (see Chapter 6) which expect you to:

1. act in accordance with relevant legislation, employment regulations and policies, and codes of practice related to promoting equality and valuing diversity;
2. act in ways that:
   - acknowledge and recognize individuals' background and beliefs;
   - respect diversity;
   - value people as individuals;
   - not discriminate against people;
3. provide individuals with the information they need to make informed decisions about exercising their rights;
4. provide information in a format appropriate to the individual;
5. take account of how your behaviour affects individuals and their experience of your organization's culture and approach;
6. seek feedback from individuals on your behaviour and use this to improve what you do in the future;
7. challenge people when they are not promoting equality and valuing diversity;
8. actively help others to promote equality and value diversity;
9. seek support from appropriate sources when you are having difficulty understanding how to promote equality and value diversity.

(Skills for Justice, 2007b).

TASK 1

How would you seek to meet the first bullet point of criterion 2, that is to 'acknowledge and recognize individuals' background and beliefs'? What evidence would satisfy the performance criteria for this?

11.4 The Police and Criminal Evidence Act 1984

We consider later in this chapter the powers that you have as an attested student police officer that enable you to arrest individuals, to search people and property, to enter buildings, and to seize objects whilst on Supervised or Independent Patrol. Many of these powers (and restrictions on their use) are to be found in the Police and Criminal Evidence Act 1984, (known as the PACE Act 1984). In this section we examine the PACE Act 1984 in more detail. It is important that you become familiar with the PACE Act 1984, and it is very likely that your police tutors will provide you with many opportunities to check your understanding. It also worth noting that there have been significant changes to the PACE Act 1984 as a result of the Serious Organised Crime and Police Act 2005. Note also that aspects of the PACE Act 1984 and its associated Codes of Practice may change during and after 2007 as part of the Home Office's 'Modernizing Police Powers' programme. For further information view the Home Office website <http://www.homeoffice.gov.uk/documents/cons-2007-pace-review>.

A good understanding of a number of sections of the PACE Act 1984 (and particularly, the associated Codes of Practice) is an essential prerequisite of meeting the whole of NOS Unit 1A1 and the NOS element 2C3.1:

National Occupational Standards

1A1   Use police actions in a fair and justified way.
2C3.1   Arrest, detain or report individuals.

The demonstration of a knowledge of the PACE Act 1984 in practical policing contexts is also an important milestone of the PAC—for example, the parts of the checklist concerned with your ability to search.

You are likely to encounter this subject matter when undertaking Phase 3 of the IPLDP and within LPG 1 under the heading 'Police Policies and Procedures' and specifically, parts of LPG 1.4(1) and LPG 1.4(8).

11.4.1 Key Features of the PACE Act 1984

Some key features of the PACE Act 1984 are shown in the diagram below:

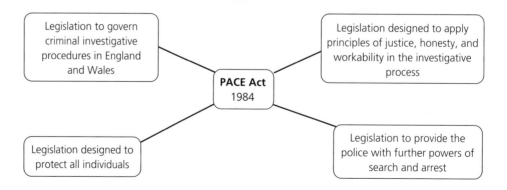

11.4.2 PACE Codes of Practice

The Codes are guidelines that regulate the investigative process. They are divided into seven main sections, and refer to contacts between the police and public in the exercise of the following police powers, which include searching, detaining, and questioning suspects:

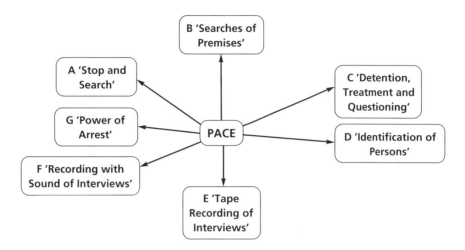

The Codes can be downloaded in full via the website <http://police.homeoffice.gov.uk/operational-policing/powers-pace-codes/pace-codes.html?version=1>

Note that the subsections of each code are numbered, for example 'Code C 10.1'. We use the same notation in the remainder of this and subsequent sections.

A brief summary of each code is provided here.

The PACE Act 1984 Codes of Practice

Code of Practice	Summary
Code A deals with the exercise by police officers of statutory powers of **stop and search**, and police officers and police staff of requirements to record public encounters.	This code provides guidelines on searching people who are not under arrest. It provides guiding principles for the justification needed to use a power of search, the circumstances in which the search can take place, and the responsibility of those making the search towards the individual. The code outlines considerations and recommendations for the protection of an individual's rights and leaves very little doubt about the extent of the search and where it can take place. In addition, the code outlines what documentation must be completed at the end of such a search or encounter.
Code B deals with **searches of premises** by police officers and the seizure of property found by police officers on persons or premises.	This code provides guidelines as to how a person's rights can be protected prior to a search of premises being made by police officers, in relation to the conduct of the search itself and the recording of such a search on its completion. It includes searches which are pre-planned and therefore use warrants issued by magistrates as well as powers of search which police officers are given for the purposes of making an arrest or to search in order to find stolen or unlawfully possessed property in premises and on persons.
Code C deals with the **detention, treatment, and questioning** of persons by police officers.	This code outlines the procedure for protecting a person's rights whilst they are in detention having been arrested and the care they must be given while in custody at a police station. It underlines the rights that detained people have whilst in police detention to communicate with other people including legal representation and sets out the process to protect those rights when being questioned whilst under arrest and not under arrest.
Code D deals with the **identification of persons** by police officers.	This code protects the rights of the suspect regarding their identification before they can be named and arrested, as well as the identification of those that have been arrested and are going to be identified by a witness. Such processes therefore include identification parade procedure and identification by body samples and fingerprints as well as showing witnesses photographs of suspects.

The PACE Act 1984 Codes of Practice (*continued*)

Code of Practice	Summary
Code E deals with **tape recording interviews** with suspects.	This code safeguards the rights of an individual while they are being interviewed and recorded on tape. It considers the necessity for the tapes to be handled in confidence and securely and allows for the process of taking breaks during the interview in order to further consider the rights of the individual. The code requires that the person is informed of the process through which they are being taken at every stage.
Code F deals with **visual recording with sound of interviews** with suspects.	This code outlines procedures that should take place while the interview of a person is being recorded both with sound and vision. At the time of going to print there is no statutory requirement on the police to visually record interviews.
Code G deals with the statutory **power of arrest** by police officers.	This code outlines procedures that you should adopt when arresting a person in order that their right to liberty is considered at all times. It defines what a lawful arrest is and that an arrest is made up of two parts. The first is the person's involvement in the commission of the offence and the second is a list of reasons why the arrest is necessary. It also describes the information to be given on arrest.
Code H deals with and **only** with, the **detention**, treatment and **questioning** of suspects arrested under s41 of the Terrorism Act 2000.	This code outlines the procedure for protecting a suspect's rights whilst they are in detention, but **only** when they have been arrested on suspicion of being a terrorist under s41 of the Terrorism Act 2000 and at no other time. Once the suspect has been charged with an offence, released without charge, or transferred to a prison, the code no longer applies.

11.4.3 Possible Consequences of Breaching One of the Codes

If a Code is breached there is a possibility of:

- disciplinary action, depending on the circumstances;
- a court deciding that your evidence is inadmissible;
- a court deciding that your evidence poses a threat to fairness;
- liability for civil or criminal proceedings.

> **TASK 2**
>
> Study the summaries of the Codes and for each one write down a brief description of a situation you have witnessed (for example, on Supervised Patrol) when the Code has been applied.
>
> The descriptions may provide you with knowledge evidence for Unit 1A1 in the CAR of your SOLAP.

11.5 The Pocket Notebook

Almost immediately you join your police force as a student police officer you will be issued with a pocket notebook. No doubt at the same time you will be given instructions on force policy concerning the keeping and use of the notebook, its surrender, the issuing of new notebooks and so on. However, there are a number of fundamental aspects of the pocket notebook common to virtually all police forces:

- it notes the start and finish time of each period of duty;
- it is used to keep a contemporaneous account (unless impossible) of information collected during an incident: for example, a statement made by a suspect or a description given by a witness;
- you are asked to note clearly where you have consulted with another police officer (for example your assessor whilst on Supervised Patrol) in the writing of an entry;
- the notebook may be used to increase the extent and accuracy of recall in court (see section 11.5.4 and Chapter 12);
- there is a need to ensure that the language you employ in writing the notebook is clear, factually based, and does not employ exclusionary language.

11.5.1 How to Use the Pocket Notebook

Although it may appear on the surface rather trivial, the importance of your pocket note book cannot be overemphasized. Your force places obligations upon you to record matters within it and, if you use it to give evidence, the courts have the opportunity to examine it. Therefore, a certain set of rules have been established in relation to its completion and if these rules are broken then the correctness or even the authenticity of the entries will be questioned.

We have already seen how a number of NOS elements are concerned with the need to keep accurate, legible, and complete records

---

Here are the **top 10 hints** to remember about a pocket notebook:

1. Carry it at all times on duty.
2. Use it to record evidence (**not** opinion, except in the case of drunkenness!)
3. Remember that it is a supervisor's responsibility to issue you with a new one when needed.
4. Always apply the **general rules** (see below).
5. It often contains other useful information.
6. You may refer to it while giving evidence (but see section 11.5.4 below).
7. Remember, it is police property.
8. Use it for drawing diagrams as well as writing.
9. On duty, do not use additional pieces of paper either to supplement your pocket notebook, or as an alternative.
10. Don't lose it!

The following table depicting a page from a pocket book outlines **general rules** that you should apply to its completion:

> If you do make a mistake, cross it out with a single line, ~~so it can be still read~~, then put your initials beside the deletion, and then write down the words(s) you wish to use straight after the ~~mistake~~ I.N.I.T.I.A.L.S.
>
> If you accidentally turn over two pages by mistake and leave some blank pages, draw a diagonal line across the blank pages and write 'omitted in error' across the page.
>
> Do NOT tear out or remove any of the pages or parts of the pages.
>
> Write all SURNAMES in BLOCK CAPITALS.
>
> Write down the names and addresses of victims, suspects and witnesses.
>
> Write down all identifying features such as serial numbers of property, including vehicles or documents, e.g. the registration numbers of vehicles.
>
> If you write down what a person says to you 'Then do so in direct speech!' and make sure that you record the conversation verbatim or word for word.

11.5.2 Example of a Pocket Notebook Entry

The following is an example of a typical pocket notebook entry.

01

<u>Wednesday 16th January (0000)</u>

	Duty 0600–1600 ———— Patrol ZZ 10
	Refreshment time 0900 and 1400
0545	Briefing at ZZ
0550	Collected keys for ZZ 10 patrol vehicle index number ZZ 00 ZZZ
0600	Checked vehicle seats and feet areas for property—no trace of any property
0605	Commenced patrol
0610	At the time stated on the date above, I was alone on mobile patrol in uniform travelling in an easterly direction along Sheerbury Road, Ramstone, approximately 50 metres east of the junction with Applebreaux Road, when I saw a Fordover motor vehicle, index number YY 00 ZZZ being driven in the same direction approximately 20 metres in front of me. There was a clear unobstructed view of this vehicle. I caused the vehicle to stop in Sheerbury Road, 20 metres west of the junction with Applebreaux Road and spoke to the driver who was the sole occupant of the car. The driver identified him/herself to me as First Middle <u>LASTNAME</u>, born 00/00/00 address 101 Hernegate Road,Ramstone, Kentshire.
Q	'May I see your driving Licence and insurance for this vehicle please?'
R	'Haven't got my insurance with me, but here is my driving licence.' Driving licence details LASTN0000FM9ZZZ
Q	'As a result of what you have just told me, I suspect you of failing to produce or not having a certificate of insurance for this vehicle.' I cautioned Mr(s) <u>LASTNAME</u> and said s/he was not under arrest and free to leave at any time.
Q	'Where is your insurance certificate right now?'
R	'It's at home, I think. It's been a while since I last saw it.'
Q	'What is the name of your insurance company?'

Example of Pocket Notebook Entry (*continued*)

R	'I can't remember that either.'
Q	'How much did you pay for the insurance?'
R	'Again, sorry, can't remember.'
Q	'How long have you owned this vehicle?'
R	'About a month.'
	PNC CRO check no trace LASTNAME. PNC vehicle check LASTNAME RO at address given. Voter's register check confirmed LASTNAME living at address I completed an HO/RT/1 form .
Q	'As you haven't been able to produce your insurance to me now, please produce your certificate of insurance and this form at a police station within 7 days Have you got any questions for me, and do you understand what you have to do?' LASTNAME made no reply.
Q	'I have been making a record of our conversation, would you please read these notes I have made, and if you agree they are a true record of what we have said, would you please sign my notes to that effect?' This is a true record. FM Lastname
Q	'As you have been unable to produce your certificate of insurance to me here, I am going to report you for the offence of failing to produce or not having a certificate of insurance for this vehicle. ' I cautioned LASTNAME and there was no reply. These notes were made at the time between 0610 and 0630. CL Underwood PC 118118
0630	Resumed patrol.
0900	Refs ZZ
0945	Resumed patrol.

11.5.3 Summary of the Rules

Pocket notebook rules can be summarized by the mnemonic No ELBOWS(S), commonly used in police training.

E	No Erasures
L	No Leaves torn out/Lines missed
B	No Blank spaces
O	No Overwriting
W	No Writing between lines
S	No Spare pages
	But
(S)	Yes Statements in 'direct speech'

11.5.4 Effective Use of the Pocket Notebook in Court

Courtroom skills, protocols, and behaviour are considered in detail in Chapter 12. However, it is worth noting at this point that you may well have to refer to your notebook when giving evidence in court, and if given permission to do so (although technically your notes themselves do not constitute evidence). There is a certain art to this. In a Police Research Series publication by Stockdale & Gresham in 1995 it was noted that:

While it was recognised that reference to notes was often essential, for a variety of very good reasons, many officers were criticised for being over dependent and for reading rather than referring to their notes. Such behaviour was judged to reduce the credibility of the police evidence and was held to be damaging to the prosecution case. (Stockdale, 1995, p 25).

TASK 3

Write down the reason why we should not refer in our pocket notebooks to the 'Christian name' of a witness.

TASK 4

Formulate a system for remembering the general rules concerning pocket notebook entries—for example, a mind map or mnemonic.

11.6 Cautions

From the moment you start dealing with anybody you suspect of committing an offence, you must remember that he/she has the right to certain information. Code C 10 of the PACE Act 1984 Codes of Practice outlines the necessity to give a suspect a warning or caution at certain points during the investigative process.

The type of caution given depends on the stage of the investigation. The caution may be given:

- at the very beginning of an investigation, when he/she is first arrested and interviewed, or interviewed without having been arrested. In this case use the **when questioned** caution;
- right at the end of the investigation, just before he/she goes to court (whether arrested or not), as a result of charge or reporting the suspect. In this case use the so-called **now** caution. This caution is his/her last chance to have what he/she says put on record before they go to court.

To summarize therefore, there are **two** different kinds of caution with an apparently very small difference between them. The difference is the words 'when questioned' and the word 'now'. In both cases you are warning them about how the words they say can be used as evidence. The difference is about the stage in the investigative process when a particular form of caution are given. The 'when questioned' caution is before the interview of the suspect, and the 'now' caution is right at the end of the investigative process. In both cases, whatever they say can be used in evidence.

11.6.1 The Three Parts to a Caution

There are three parts to a caution which we describe below (Code C 10.5):

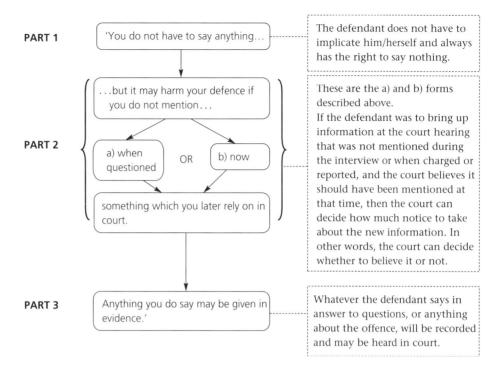

11.6.2   When to Caution a Suspect

The following describes the circumstances of when to caution a suspect (Code C 10.1):

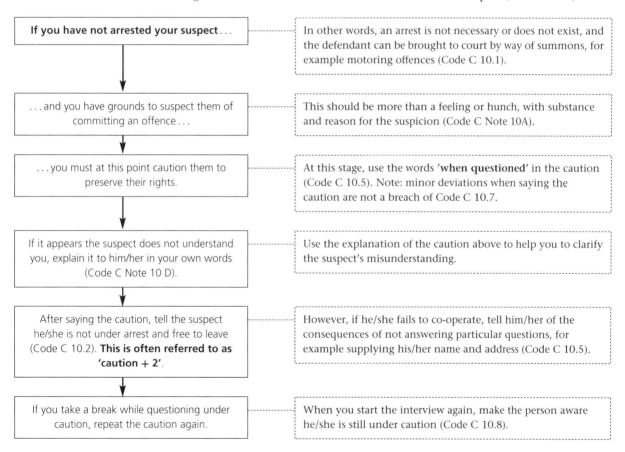

If you have arrested your suspect, you must caution him/her at the time of the arrest unless:

- it is impossible for you to do so because of his/her condition or behaviour for example he/she may be unconscious or fighting (Code C 10.4 and Code G 3.4);

- the suspect has already been cautioned before he/she was arrested, because he/she was suspected of committing an offence (Code C 10.4 and Code G 3.4).

11.6.3 There May Be No Need to Caution a Person

If you have not arrested your suspect, and your questions are for other purposes (Code C 10.1), you do not need to use a caution.

Examples of such situations are:

- When you ask for a driver's name and date of birth under the Road Traffic Act (see Code C 10.9).
- When you ask for a person's identity or the identity of the owner of a vehicle.
- When you ask a suspect to read and sign records of interviews and other comments (see Code C para 11 and Note 11E and 'unsolicited comments' in section 11.7 below).
- Whilst you carry out a search using an appropriate power and at the same time following the Codes of Practice.

11.6.4 Other Times when a Caution is Needed

You need to use a caution when informing someone that he/she may be prosecuted, for example:

- when you charge (a charge is a written accusation) a detained person with an offence or inform a person that he/she may be prosecuted (reported for summons). At this stage, use the word 'now' in the caution in section 11.6.1 above (see Code C 16.2);
- when you inform a person not under arrest that he/she may be prosecuted for an offence. At this stage, use the word 'now' in the caution (see Code C 16.2). This is not a requirement within the Codes of Practice, but if the 'now' caution is not given at this time, the court cannot draw its own conclusions if the defendant enters new information at the hearing. In other words, the court might be more likely to believe the new information (see Code C Note 10 G.) The advice is therefore to use the 'now' caution after informing a person they may be prosecuted.

11.6.5 Recording Evidence when Giving a Caution

Always write down in your pocket notebook (or on a record of the interview) when you give a caution. You must also record whether it was the 'when questioned' or the 'now' version (See Code C 10.13).

11.6.6 Caution after Charge

Having been charged with, or informed he/she may be prosecuted for an offence, a detained person may not be interviewed further unless the interview is necessary for the following reasons (listed in Code C, para 16.5):

- to prevent or minimize harm or loss to some other person, or the public;
- to clear up an ambiguity in a previous answer or statement;
- in the interests of justice for the detainee to have put to him/her, and have an opportunity to comment on, information concerning the offence which has come to light since he/she was charged or informed he/she might be prosecuted.

The caution that is given to a detainee before an interview takes place is often referred to as the 'restricted' caution as it is much shorter in length when compared to the 'when questioned' or 'now' cautions described in section 11.6.

Before any interview, the interviewer should:

(a) caution the detainee, using the words 'You do not have to say anything unless you wish to do so, but anything you do say may be given in evidence';
(b) remind the detainee about his/her right to legal advice.

11.6.7 A Word of Caution!

The caution is a necessary warning that must be given to a person to protect his/her rights and keep him/her informed of the consequences of what he/she says during an investigation. This can only be done if you have a thorough understanding of the 'when questioned', 'now' and 'restricted' cautions so that you can pass the meaning on to the suspect. The suspect can be made more aware of the importance of a caution if you are aware of it yourself.

TASK 5

Learn the cautions and when to use them!

You have arrested somebody. Firstly, decide which caution you will use at this stage. Secondly, after you have cautioned your suspect, he/she tells you that he/she did not understand what it meant. Write down how you would explain the caution to the suspect.

11.7 Unsolicited Comments by Suspects

Following a decision to arrest a suspect, they must not be interviewed about the relevant offences except at a police station (Code C 11.1). Bear in mind that an interview is defined to be the 'questioning of a person regarding his/her involvement in a criminal offence', which must be carried out under caution (Code C 11.1A).

So what do you do when a suspect who has been arrested suddenly says something that applies to the offence in question, or to another offence? After all, the comments may contain information that could be used in evidence.

Just because he/she has said it outside the context of an interview, are you required to ignore it? No, that is not the case; these are referred to as 'unsolicited' or voluntary comments and there is procedure laid down in the Codes of Practice for their recording and possible subsequent use in a court hearing. Unsolicited (or voluntary) comments by suspects are of two types; relevant comments and significant statements.

A **relevant comment** can be made by a suspect at any time, and includes anything which might be relevant to the offence (Code C 11.13 and Note 11E), for example:

That other person you've arrested, it was them that did it, you'll see, just ask the witness you've been talking to, they'll back me up, you'll see!

A **significant statement** includes anything which appears capable of being used in evidence against the suspect, and in particular an admission of guilt (Code C 11.4A). It may be part of a relevant comment and must be made by a suspect at any time in the presence and hearing of a police officer (or other police staff member), for example:

I wish I hadn't done it now, but I lost my temper, the knife was on the table and I just kept stabbing and stabbing!

11.7.1 Recording Unsolicited Comments

Write down any such comment made by the suspect in your pocket notebook (see section 11.5), noting when the comment was made, and then sign the entry. When practicable, ask the suspect to read the entry, and ask him/her if he/she agrees that it is a true record of what he/she said. If the suspect **agrees** that it is a true record, ask the suspect to endorse the record with the words 'I agree that this is a correct record of what was said' and to sign his/her signature (Code C Note 11E). If the suspect **does not agree** with the record, you should record the details of any disagreement. Then ask the suspect to read these details, and to sign to say that they accurately reflect his/her disagreement. You should also record any refusal to sign (Code C Note 11E.)

11.8   Identification of Suspects whose Identity is Unknown

A significant number of the incidents you will deal with on the street whilst undertaking Supervised or Independent Patrol will involve criminal offences which have been witnessed by members of the public. In many cases the witness can remember something about what the suspect(s) looked like, but the identity of the suspect is probably not known. The Codes of Practice outline a process to safeguard the rights of a possible suspect. The Codes specify that a record must be made of the first description of the suspect that is given by a witness, and describe the procedures for taking a witness to a particular neighbourhood or place to identify the suspect. Finally, if the witness is successful in pointing out the suspect to you, the circumstances under which the identification was made must be recorded in line with the precedent set in the case of *R v Turnbull* [1976] 63 Cr App R 132.

The following subsections provide more detail of the procedures involved.

11.8.1   Taking a Witness to a Place to Identify the Suspect

The only circumstance under which you can carry out such an identification is when the identity of the suspect is **not known,** and you have insufficient information available to you to justify his/her arrest. In other words you do not have reasonable grounds to suspect a particular person or group of people to have committed that offence (Code D 3.2).

Do not take a witness to identify a suspect who has already been arrested. In that case the suspect's identity is now regarded as being **known** (Code D 3.4). Other identification procedures are used once a suspect has been arrested—for example identification parades, video identification, and group identification.

11.8.2   The First Description

Where it is practicable, a record should be made of the witness's description before asking them to make any kind of identification (Code D3.2a). This first description must be **clearly** recorded in a visible and legible form which can be given to the suspect or the suspect's solicitor. Ideally, it should be recorded in your pocket notebook.

11.8.3   Support for the Witness During the Identification

Care must be taken not to direct the witness's attention to any individual, unless, taking into account all the circumstances, it cannot be avoided (Code D 3.2b). However, this does not prevent a witness being asked to look carefully at the people around or to look towards a group, or in a particular direction. This might be necessary to ensure that the witness does not overlook a possible suspect or to enable the witness to make comparisons between any suspect and others who are in the area.

The identification may be **compromised** if you specifically draw the witness's attention to the suspect (see Note 3F), or the suspect's identity becomes known before the procedure. Therefore do **not** point at the suspect and ask the witness to verify your choice.

11.8.4   More than One Witness

Witnesses should be taken **separately** to see whether they can identify a person independently. This may mean that you will have to call for other patrols to help you with the identification process (Code D 3.2c).

11.8.5   Recording an Identification

The student police officer or police support employee accompanying the witness must record as soon as possible in his/her pocket notebook full details of the action taken (Code D 3.2e).

The record should include:

1. The date, time, and place of the relevant occasion the witness claims to have previously seen the suspect.

2. Where any identification was made.
3. How it was made.
4. The conditions at the time (for example the distance the witness was from the suspect, the weather, and light).
5. If the witness's attention was drawn to the suspect.
6. The reason for this.
7. Anything said by the witness or the suspect about the identification or the conduct of the procedure.

11.8.6 Evidence to be Gathered from the Witness

The witness has had two opportunities to see the suspect. First, around the time the offence was committed, and secondly when you took the suspect to the neighbourhood of the incident. Always consider that the visual evidence from the first sighting may be disputed in court. You should try to minimize that possibility by applying the guidelines set by case law in *R v Turnbull* [1976] 63 Cr App R 132. A helpful way to remember the component parts of *Turnbull* (as it is commonly referred to in police circles), is to use the mnemonic ADVOKATE, an approach common within police training:

A Amount of time the suspect was under observation.
D Distance between the witness and the suspect.
V Visibility, for example what was the lighting like, what were the weather conditions?
O Obstructions to his/her view of the suspect.
K Known or seen before, does he/she know the suspect and, if so, how?
    If the witness has seen the suspect before is there:
A Any reason for remembering the suspect? This could be distinguishing feature or peculiarity of the person, or the very nature of the incident itself that made the person memorable. This can relate to previous or present sightings.
T Time lapse between the first and any subsequent identification to the police. This is not the time between first seeing the suspect and the writing of the statement.
E Errors between the first recorded description of the suspect and his/her actual appearance.

11.8.7 ADVOKATE in detail

In terms of the **amount of time the suspect was under observation**, consider the following:

• During the time that the witness saw the suspect carrying out the criminal act, for how long was he/she looking at the suspect?
• Record the total time but also identify how long the witness observed the suspect at specific moments throughout the entire period; it is highly unlikely a suspect will be standing in exactly the same position for the whole observation period.
• Was there a break (however brief) in his/her observation?
• What were the various distances involved (see below) and how long was the suspect observed for at that particular distance?
• Was it a frontal view, rear view, profile view?

In essence, the circumstances of an observation will alter from moment to moment and this needs to be recorded in detail.

In terms of the **distance between the witness and the suspect** consider the following:

• How far away was the witness from the suspect when the incident took place?
• If in the street, count kerb stones as a guide: they are usually one metre long.
• Record the distance between the suspect and the witness. The distance is likely to vary during the course of the observation and will rarely be one measurement.
• Record furthest distance, shortest distance, and timings involved at each level.
• Also record distances of obstructions.
• Where was the witness in relation to the suspect?

In terms of the **visibility**, consider the following:

- Was it day time or night time?
- Were the street lamps on?
- Was the witness wearing glasses or contact lenses?

Weather conditions must be included in detail, for example it is not sufficient to say 'It was raining':

- Was it heavy rain, drizzle, etc?
- Was sunlight a factor?
- Where was the sun in relation to the suspect and the witness?
- Were there shadows cast?
- Include, if possible, the distance of available visibility.

In terms of **obstructions to his/her view of the suspect** consider the following:

- Any obstruction between the witness and the suspect should be described in detail. It is insufficient to say, for example, that the view was obstructed by a hedge. How tall, how wide, how dense was it?
- Obstructions include glass and the glass would need to be described as well: the size, was it clean or dirty, frosted, open, closed, double glazed, was there glare from sun, etc?
- How did the obstruction actually obstruct the view of the witness and to what extent?

In terms of whether the **suspect is known or seen before**, consider whether there is an association between the witness and the suspect, for example a relationship, friendship, or do they work together? If there is an association then:

- How long has the witness known the suspect?
- **How** does he/she know the suspect?
- In **what** context and how well?
- **When** did he/she last see the suspect?
- Has his/her description changed in the interim period?

In terms of the existence of **any reason why the witness should remember the suspect** consider the following:

- This could be a distinguishing feature or peculiarity of the person, or the very nature of the incident itself that made the person memorable. This can relate to previous or present sightings.
- Was there anything unusual about the suspect's appearance (for example distinguishing features) or the prevailing circumstances?
- What, if anything, attracted the witness's attention?
- What has stuck in their mind?

In terms of the **time lapse** between the **first and any subsequent identification** to the police consider the following (note that this is not the time between first seeing the suspect and the writing of the statement):

- How much time elapsed between recording or obtaining a description and the sighting of the suspect?
- How much time elapsed between recording or obtaining a description and the subsequent identification?

In terms of **errors between the first recorded description of the suspect and his/her actual appearance** consider the following:

- Remember, you **must** have recorded a first description.
- Once the victim identified the suspect later on, what was the similarity between the first description and what the suspect actually looked like?

- Record any errors, or differences between the first description, and the actual appearance of the suspect when he/she was identified (for example a suspect is identified while wearing a black sweatshirt when the original description recorded a hooded top).
- You must record the difference to show integrity of the evidence.

One of the most important issues to consider when using this process of identification is the question of whether or not you had sufficient evidence upon which to justify an arrest prior to taking the witness to make an identification. If you had such evidence, then the courts may consider that an identification method relating to **known identity** of the suspect might be more appropriate.

Remember also that although you can ask a witness to look carefully at the people around at the time or to look towards a group or in a particular direction, you must **not** draw the witness's attention to the suspect.

> **TASK 6**
>
> You attend an incident involving criminal damage of property belonging to a householder. The victim tells you the incident happened five minutes ago and that he/she can positively identify the suspect. What are your actions going to be at this point and what are you going to say to the victim?

11.9 The Regulation of Investigatory Powers Act 2000

During your policing duties, it may be necessary to carry out the surveillance of suspects in order to obtain information about them. These activities are strictly regulated under s 26 of the Regulation of Investigatory Powers Act 2000 (RIPA).

Surveillance includes (s 48(2)):

(a) monitoring, observing or listening to persons, their movements, their conversation or their other activities or communications;
(b) recording anything monitored, observed or listened to in the course of surveillance; and
(c) surveillance by or with the assistance of a surveillance device.

If you do this without attempting to hide your presence and in uniform, it is considered as **overt.** In other words, you carry out actions which are undertaken in an open and obvious way. If, however, you undertake observations out of uniform when you cannot be recognized as a police officer, your actions are **covert** (s 26(9)). Covert surveillance requires authorization under the RIPA 2000.

There are two main types of surveillance:

- **Directed** surveillance which is carried out on people anywhere other than residential premises or vehicles;
- **Intrusive** surveillance which is carried out on people in residential premises or vehicles.

11.9.1 Directed surveillance

The following is the definition of the term 'directed surveillance' from s 26(2) of the RIPA Act 2000.

Surveillance is directed [...] if it is covert but not intrusive and is undertaken: (a) for the purposes of a specific investigation or operation;	This means a pre-planned event and not an immediate response to an incident.
(b) in such a manner as is likely to result in the obtaining of private information about a person (whether or not one specifically identified for the purposes of the investigation or operation); and	Carrying out surveillance of people while they carry out a criminal activity is unlikely to bring about the gathering of private information about them. However, surveillance of people who are not engaging in criminal activity is far more likely to result in obtaining private information about them.
(c) otherwise than by way of an immediate response to events or circumstances, the nature of which is such that it would not be reasonably practicable for an authorization under this Part to be sought for the carrying out of the surveillance.	Circumstances which occur before your eyes and happen at that very moment would not be termed as directed surveillance. For example, while on Independent Patrol, you observe a person on a building site loading material into a vehicle and decide to observe them, using cover until other patrols arrive to support you.

11.9.1.1 Directed surveillance and the use of overt CCTV

If CCTV is to be used for a covert pre-planned investigation, then authority should be sought. However, the normal use of CCTV for the purposes of crime prevention does not require authorization.

11.9.1.2 Authorization for directed surveillance

Authorization for directed surveillance is given by an authorizing officer. The authorizing officer will not be below the rank of superintendent and the authorization will be in writing and last for three months.

In urgent cases, oral authorizations may be given by a superintendent (lasting only for seventy-two hours from the time the authority was granted). The person to whom the authorizing officer spoke should make a written record as soon as reasonably practicable. Where a superintendent is absent and the case is urgent, written authority may be given by an officer not below the rank of inspector, which will again last for seventy-two hours. For both types of urgent authorization written authority should be sought from the superintendent prior to the expiry of the seventy-two hour period.

11.9.2 Intrusive Surveillance

This is described in s 26(3) of the RIPA Act 2000. Intrusive surveillance:

(a) is carried out in relation to anything taking place on any residential premises, or in any private vehicle; and
(b) involves the presence of an individual on the premises, or in the vehicle, or is carried out by means of a surveillance device.

Residential premises means premises 'occupied or used by any person, however temporarily, for residential purposes or otherwise as living accommodation (including hotel or prison accommodation that is so occupied or used)' (s 48(1)).

Private vehicle means 'any vehicle which is used primarily for the private purposes

• of the person who owns it or
• of a person otherwise having the right to use it' (s 48(1)).

Surveillance device means 'any apparatus designed or adapted for use in surveillance' (s 48(1)).

11.9.2.1 When surveillance ceases to be intrusive

Surveillance will cease to be intrusive without the presence of a person or a device on the relevant premises or vehicle(s) and under the following circumstances:

1. It is carried out by a device:
   - designed or
   - adapted principally for the purpose of providing information about the location of a vehicle (s28(4)(a)); or
2. It consists in any one-sided consensual interception (of a postal service or telecommunication system) where there is no intercept warrant (s 28(4)(b)); or
3. It is:
   - carried out by means of a device in relation to anything taking place on any residential premises or in any private vehicle, but,
   - carried out without that device being present on the premises or in the vehicle **unless** the device is such that it consistently provides information of the same quality and detail as might be expected to be obtained from a device actually present on the premises, or in the vehicle (s 28(5)).

In other words, when equipment is used in a remote location away from the premises or vehicle that is so powerful and accurate that the information received from it is as good as the information gathered from equipment on the premises or in the vehicle, then it is intrusive. If, on the other hand, a device is used that simply tracks the location of a vehicle, it is not intrusive but will remain 'directed' surveillance.

11.9.2.2 Authorization of intrusive surveillance

Intrusive surveillance is a highly specialized area of police work and will only be authorized if it involves serious crime. All intrusive surveillance operations will be authorized by a person holding the rank of chief officer (that is, assistant chief constable rank and above).

11.9.3 Covert Human Intelligent Sources (CHIS)

People who supply information about criminal activities in a secret or hidden way are called covert human intelligent sources (CHIS). They are also referred to as informants and the person to whom the information is supplied is often referred to as a handler. Section 26(7)(a) of the RIPA Act 2000 outlines the conduct of a CHIS (normally a paid informant) and states a person is a CHIS if he/she:

- establishes or maintains a personal or other relationship with a person for the covert purpose of facilitating the doing of anything [listed below], or
- covertly uses such a relationship to obtain information or to provide access to any information to another person; or
- covertly discloses information obtained by the use of such a relationship, or as a consequence of the existence of such a relationship.

We examine the role of the CHIS in more detail in Chapter 12.

11.9.3.1 Activities that amount to the use of a CHIS

Section 26(7)(a) of the RIPA Act 2000 outlines the activities that amount to the 'use' of a CHIS as:

> . . . any action for the purposes of inducing, asking or assisting a person to engage in the conduct of such a source, or to obtain information by means of the conduct of such a source.

Therefore, the cultivation, tasking, handling, and controlling of a CHIS is a specialized area of police work. Before considering the recruitment or use of a CHIS, you should make contact with your supervisors or intelligence units who manage and co-ordinate such activity.

11.10   Entry for Purposes of Arrest and to Save Life

The Police and Criminal Evidence Act 1984 gives you a power of entry to premises where you believe a person you are seeking to arrest is located. The list of offences for which you can enter to arrest has been recently extended under Sch 7 of the Serious Organised Crime and Police Act 2005.

You can also enter premises in order to save life.

11.10.1   Section 17 of the PACE Act 1984

Section 17 of the PACE Act 1984 states that:

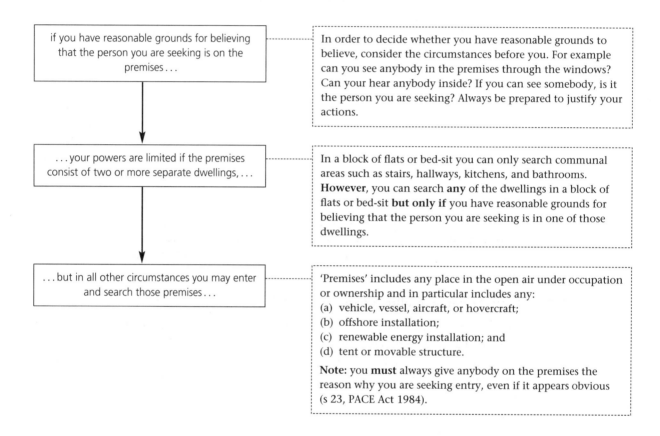

if you have reasonable grounds for believing that the person you are seeking is on the premises . . .	In order to decide whether you have reasonable grounds to believe, consider the circumstances before you. For example can you see anybody in the premises through the windows? Can your hear anybody inside? If you can see somebody, is it the person you are seeking? Always be prepared to justify your actions.
. . . your powers are limited if the premises consist of two or more separate dwellings, . . .	In a block of flats or bed-sit you can only search communal areas such as stairs, hallways, kitchens, and bathrooms. **However**, you can search **any** of the dwellings in a block of flats or bed-sit **but only if** you have reasonable grounds for believing that the person you are seeking is in one of those dwellings.
. . . but in all other circumstances you may enter and search those premises . . .	'Premises' includes any place in the open air under occupation or ownership and in particular includes any: (a) vehicle, vessel, aircraft, or hovercraft; (b) offshore installation; (c) renewable energy installation; and (d) tent or movable structure. **Note:** you **must** always give anybody on the premises the reason why you are seeking entry, even if it appears obvious (s 23, PACE Act 1984).

You may search and enter those premises for the purposes of:

Arresting a person during the execution of an arrest warrant issued in connection with or arising out of criminal proceedings.	Home Office Circular 88/1985, para 8 stated that this section 'is deliberately widely drawn and the words "in connection with" enable a constable to enter and search premises for the purpose among other things of executing a warrant for the arrest of a person for non-payment of a fine'.
Arresting a person during the execution of a warrant of commitment (ie a commitment warrant to prison).	A commitment warrant goes further than a default warrant (where an offender has defaulted on his/her payment of a fine and is being ordered to appear before a court to explain the reasons). It is a step beyond that and requires the offender to be taken straight to prison unless the monies are paid. It is a warrant issued under s 76 of the Magistrates' Courts Act 1980 (for failure to pay fines).
Arresting a person for an indictable offence.	Indictable offences are those offences which are: • 'Either-way offences' (which can be tried at magistrates' court **or** Crown Court), or • 'Indictable-only offences' (which can be tried at Crown Court only). (See the descriptions at the end of each relevant section in the Handbook when offences have been described.)

Arresting a person for an offence under s 163 of the Road Traffic Act 1988.	This section requires a person driving a mechanically propelled vehicle or riding a cycle on a road to stop if you require him/her to do so. Failing to do so is an offence for which you can use this power of entry to arrest if necessary. **Note** that you can only use this power when you are in uniform.
Arresting a person for an offence under s 4 of the Road Traffic Act 1988.	This is an offence of driving or being in charge of a mechanically propelled vehicle on a road or other public place when unfit through drink or drugs (see section 10.16 above). Under this section you can enter premises to arrest a person you have reasonable cause to suspect of committing the offence.
Arresting a person for an offence under s 27 of the Transport and Works Act 1992.	This is an offence for certain staff operating the railways and other guided transport systems when they are under the influence of drink or drugs. Under this section you can enter premises to arrest a person you have reasonable cause to suspect of committing the offence.
Arresting a person for an offence under any enactment contained in ss 6, 7, 8, or 10 of the Criminal Law Act 1977.	These offences include using violence to secure entry (s 6), trespassing with a weapon of offence (s 8), and entering and remaining on premises (squatting) (s 7) (see section 8.13 above). **Note** that you can only use this power when you are in uniform.
Arresting a person for an offence under s 4 of the Public Order Act 1986.	The result of the suspect's conduct in this offence is to bring about a feeling of fear or provoke a reaction of violence in the victim or recipient. **Note** that this power of entry does **not** extend to s 4A of the Public Order Act 1986 'intentional harassment, alarm or distress' offences (see section 8.12 above).
Arresting a child, in pursuance of s 32(1A) of the Children and Young Persons Act 1969.	Section 32(1A) gives you a power of arrest to arrest a child who is absent from care, but only if the child is in care having been remanded or committed to local authority accommodation under s 23(1) of the Children and Young Persons Act 1969.
Arresting a person for an offence under s 61 of the Animal Health Act 1981.	This offence relates to the control of rabies and sets out a power of arrest for you of any person you have reasonable cause to suspect to be committing, or to have committed an offence in relation to bringing animals into the UK. Under this section you can enter premises to arrest a person you have reasonable cause to suspect of committing the offence.
Arresting a person under s 1 of the Public Order Act 1936.	This offence, albeit not very common, involves the offence of wearing a political uniform in a public place or at a public meeting if it signifies their association with any political organization or with the promotion of any political object. The offence originates from the existence of extreme political organizations in the years before the Second World War.
Arresting a person for an offence under s 76 of the Criminal Justice and Public Order Act 1994;	This is an offence of failing to comply with an interim possession order of premises. This is an order made under the rules of court which bring about summary proceedings for the possession of premises which are occupied by trespassers. You are able to use these powers of entry to arrest a person who contravenes this order. **Note** that you can only use this power when you are in uniform.
Arresting a person for an offence under sections 4, 5, 6(1) and (2), 7, 8(1) and (2) of the Animal Welfare Act 2006;	These are offences relating to the prevention of harm to animals.
whom you are immediately pursuing;	This could include a person who had escaped from you or a colleague having been arrested, as well as a patient who has escaped from involuntary custody at a Psychiatric Unit. **Note**, however, that the chase must be under circumstances of hot pursuit, for example the person must have only just escaped from lawful custody or a hospital; it cannot be used after a period of days or weeks.
while liable to be detained in a prison, remand centre, young offenders' institution, or secure training centre;	This could include any person who has been placed in a secure detention centre as a result of a penalty placed upon him/her by a court. Circumstances could include perhaps an escape from the prison itself or whilst being transported in a vehicle between establishments.
while liable to be detained in pursuance of s 92 of the Powers of Criminal Courts Sentencing Act 2000 in any other place.	Under s 92 it is mandatory that any person aged 18 or under, found guilty of an offence for which the penalty has been fixed by law as life imprisonment, shall be detained at Her Majesty's prisons. He/she can be detained at other places than those listed above. If this person was to escape from such detention, then you can use this power of entry to recapture him or her.

11.10.2 Searching Premises for a Suspect

The power of arrest from the PACE Act 1984 also permits you to search premises in order to find that person, but you must not search for anything else, unless you have other justifications for searching. For example, if you have entered premises by force to search for and arrest an adult, there is no justification in looking in a bread bin because that person is not going to be located there.

11.10.3 Power of Entry and Breach of the Peace

You are entitled to enter either private or public premises in order to make an arrest for a breach of the peace or prevent one from happening. However, you should **always** make sure that the circumstance you are faced with really constitutes a breach of the peace as shown in *R v Howell* [1982] QB 416 (see section 8.11 above). Once the breach has finished, you should not remain on private premises but should be given the opportunity to leave. Nothing in s 17(6) of the PACE Act 1984 affects any power of entry to deal with or prevent a breach of the peace.

11.10.4 Power of Entry to Save Life and Property

Section 17(1)(e) of the PACE Act 1984 gives you the power to enter premises to save human life and limb and also to prevent serious damage to property (note, that s 17(1)(e) is not about arresting a person, just entry).

Unlike the rest of s 17(1), under part (e) you can enter and search even if you do not have reasonable grounds for believing any person is on the premises **provided** the entry is save life and limb or to prevent serious damage.

Further, and again unlike the rest of s 17(1), under (e) you can also enter and search all the flats within a block of flats and not just one of them, but only in order to save life and limb or prevent serious damage.

11.10.5 The Use of Reasonable Force to Secure Entry

Section 117 of the PACE Act 1984 states that:

> where any part of the PACE Act 1984 grants [you] a power . . . [you] may use reasonable force, if necessary, in the exercise of the power.

In a similar way to s 3 of the Criminal Law Act 1967, a court must decide that you honestly believed that the force you used was **reasonable**, and whether the circumstances surrounding the use of that force were proportionate to the amount of force you used. In other words, if you are met with force, you may have to equal that force to negate it, and then use even more force in order to take control. You will receive training on this subject as part of your personal safety training.

11.10.6 Health and Safety when Entering Premises

Health and Safety issues were examined in section 7.7 above. Consider the potential risks involved when using the PACE Act 1984 to search in unplanned situations, as you do not know who or what you will encounter. Note that it might not be necessary to enter premises immediately. It might be better to stay outside, watch the front and back, and secure the area until colleagues with appropriate equipment and resources arrive.

TASK 7

You and a colleague are required to arrest a person on suspicion of theft. You have followed the suspect to his/her house which has a front and rear entrance, but you lose sight of him/her at the last moment. In what way are you going to carry out the arrest in relation to the premises and what are your considerations at this time?

11.11 Arrest Without Warrant

It is no surprise that the right to liberty is an important principle within the Human Rights Act 1998 (see section 11.3 above) and your power to arrest and take away a person's liberty clearly challenges that right. It is obvious, therefore, that the proper use of your responsibility to arrest a person for the right reason and at the right time is paramount.

This, and the following sections, will assist you in providing evidence to meet NOS element 2C3.1:

National Occupational Standard Element

2C3.1 Arrest, detain or report individuals.

---

and in particular the following performance criteria:

- to 'check that there are the grounds and legal authority for your actions'
- to 'identify the individual subject to your actions in accordance with legislation and current policy'.

This section is also relevant to the PAC heading 'Disposal' and in particular 'make lawful arrests' and also contains material likely to be relevant to Phase 3 of the IPLDP LPG 1 under the 'Police Policies and Procedures' heading, particularly LPG 1.4(1).

The title of this section may need explaining. You may have heard the phrase 'the judge ordered a warrant for his arrest' used by the media when reporting, for example, the failure of somebody to attend court. In these circumstances a **warrant** (in the form of a document) is issued and it is the responsibility of the police, or in some cases a civilian enforcement officer, to serve the warrant on the person concerned (see section 11.12 below). However, the police also have powers to arrest without the need for a warrant, for example, in response to a public order crime. These powers are referred to as 'arrest without a warrant' and are the most common forms of street-level arrest that you are likely to use.

In the course of your duties whilst on Supervised or Independent Patrol, you may need to arrest without a warrant someone who you suspect of committing a criminal offence. Apart from the power to arrest for a breach of the peace (see section 8.11 above), and specific powers of arrest from other legislation, you also have a 'general' power of arrest without a warrant that stems from s 24 of the PACE Act 1984 (as amended by s 110 of the Serious Organised Crime and Police Act 2005). Using these powers, you may arrest a person whether you are in uniform or not, however, you may only arrest a person if, and only if, certain criteria are met. These criteria are discussed in the following sections.

11.11.1 The Two Conditions for an Arrest to be Lawful

The two conditions for an arrest to be lawful are:

1. that a person is about to commit an offence, or is in the act of committing an offence, or that there are reasonable grounds to suspect that a person is involved, or has attempted to be involved in the commission of an offence; **and**
2. that there are reasonable grounds for believing that the person's arrest is necessary.

So you must **not** arrest a person **only** because of his/her involvement, or suspicion of involvement in a criminal offence. You must make an arrest **only if it is necessary**. The reasons for which an arrest may be necessary are specified in s 24(5) of the PACE Act 1984 (as amended by s 110 of the Serious Organised Crime and Police Act 2005) and its Code G, para 2.9 (see section 11.11.4 below).

Before we look further at the power of arrest, it is important that you understand the term 'reasonable grounds to suspect', as it is a central component part of the power.

11.11.2 Reasonable Grounds to Suspect

It is important to bear in mind that although words such as 'suspicion', 'grounds', and 'belief' are in common usage they have particular meanings within the context of policing and the law. You may need to relearn some of the concepts in order that you can exercise your powers within the law—do not assume that they necessarily mean what you think they mean.

- Whether or not something is **reasonable** is a conclusion that one or more people reach in agreement as a result of personal experience or understanding. It is a practical, level-headed, and logical result.
- **Grounds** for something include a reason or argument for a thought to exist.
- To **suspect** something is to think that it is probably true, but you are not certain. To 'believe' something is a stronger and more concrete conclusion.

Therefore, in order to decide whether you have reasonable grounds to suspect, consider the offence you are investigating. Then consider the component parts of that offence, and whether or not a like-minded person would draw the same conclusion as you about the suspect and the offence. For example: did the person have the opportunity, the motive, the presence of mind, and the incentive to commit the offence? And did he/she have the means?

11.11.3 Involvement in the Commission of a Criminal Offence

The first condition for an arrest to be lawful is that you know, or have reasonable grounds to suspect, that a criminal offence is in the process of being committed or that is about to be committed. This is shown in the table below:

Level of involvement	Example
A person is **about to commit** an offence.	You are on duty, in non-uniform clothing, in an electrical store when you see a woman, who is obviously not a member of the shop staff, walk up to a display of MP3 players, select one, and put it under her coat. You see her walk towards the entry/exit of the shop, making no attempt to pay for the item. You stop her as she is about to leave the shop, as she is **about to commit** an offence. If it is **necessary**, you may arrest her (see section 11.11.4 below).
A person is **in the act of committing** an offence.	You are on duty, in non-uniform clothing, in an electrical store when you see a man walk up to a display of DAB radios, cut a security link, pick up a radio, and walk towards the door of the shop past the check outs, without paying for the radio. The store alarm is activated and the man continues to walk out of the shop. You decide the man is stealing the radio and stop him just outside the shop as he is **in the act of committing** the theft of the radio. If it is **necessary**, you may arrest him (see section 11.11.4 below).
You have **reasonable grounds** for **suspecting** a person to be **about to commit** an offence.	You are on duty, in non-uniform clothing, in an electrical store when you see a man walk up to a display of mobile phones. He has a rucksack on his back and appears extremely nervous. You see him take a metal cutter out of his rucksack. He then reaches out with the tool in his hand towards the security chain of the mobile and appears to be about to cut the chain when he is disturbed and puts the tool back inside the rucksack and walks away. A few seconds later the same man returns to the display of mobiles takes out the same tool, places the tool around the security chain, and sets off the alarm. At this moment you walk up to the man having decided you have **reasonable grounds** for **suspecting he is about to commit** an offence. If it is **necessary**, you may arrest him (see section 11.11.4 below).
You have **reasonable grounds** for **suspecting** a person **to be** committing an offence.	You are standing outside a store that sells electrical goods when you see a person standing just inside the store near the doorway. The person is carrying an unpacked, brand new DVD player underneath his arm with the lead and plug dragging behind. He also has a rucksack on his back and appears nervous. You see him use a tool to cut away the security tag from the DVD player which he throws in a bin by the door, and then starts to place the player in the rucksack. The person then walks towards the door as if to leave the store. You note the obvious facts:

Level of involvement	Example
	• the player should be boxed or at least in a bag supplied by the shop;
• the person carrying it should not be so anxious to quickly leave the shop especially with the lead dragging along the ground;
• the person should not have cut the security tag;
• he should not be placing the DVD player inside a rucksack.
You therefore form **reasonable grounds** for **suspecting** that he has been found **to be** in the process of committing an offence of theft of a DVD player. If it is **necessary**, you may arrest him (see section 11.11.4 below).

You may also arrest someone on suspicion of committing an offence on an earlier occasion.

Note that you do not have to be certain that:

- **The offence actually took place**. As an example, imagine that you are standing outside the shop mentioned in the table above that sells electrical goods when a male runs out of the shop carrying an unpacked, brand new DVD player underneath his arm with the lead dragging behind. The store alarm is activated. You therefore suspect that an offence has recently been committed.
- **The suspect is the actual person who carried out the suspected offence**. You run after the person but lose sight of him in a crowd. A short while later you are still without confirmation that a DVD player has been stolen from the store. You see a person fitting the description of the person you ran after earlier. You decide you have reasonable grounds for suspecting he is the same person that you saw earlier and reasonable grounds for suspecting the player has been stolen.

Remember, however, you must be certain that it is **necessary** to arrest the suspect, and have clear **reasons** in mind (see section 11.11.4 below).

In other situations, it will be clearer that an offence has definitely been committed. For example, a shop owner who deals with **every** sale in their shop sees a female walk up to a display of DVD players, pick one up, and walk towards the door of the shop without paying for it. The store alarm is activated. The shop owner decides she has stolen the player. The shop owner runs after the suspect and stops her. The shop owner calls the police and you attend to investigate the offence of theft.

In these circumstances, you may arrest (if it is **necessary**):

- **Anyone who is guilty of the offence**. For example, when you arrive at the shop, the shop owner tells you the circumstances in the presence and hearing of the suspect, and you therefore have information that an offence has been committed. The shop owner confirms an offence of theft has occurred.
- **Anyone who you have reasonable grounds for suspecting to be guilty**. For example, a shop owner who deals with **every** sale in his shop sees a female walk up to a display of DVD players, pick one up, and walk towards the door of the shop without paying for it. The store alarm is activated. The shop owner decides she has **stolen** the player. The shop owner runs after the suspect, but is unable to catch up with her. The shop owner calls the police and supplies a first description of the woman who stole the player. The description is passed to you and later during the day several miles away from the shop, you see a woman fitting the description given by the shop owner earlier. You decide therefore that you have reasonable grounds for suspecting her of the theft of the DVD player.

11.11.4 Reasons that Make an Arrest Necessary

Note at the outset that an arrest is not always necessary, and as a student police officer you will need to make decisions for each particular situation:

- what action to take when you first come into contact with the suspect—for example, when to caution, search, use personal safety equipment or techniques;

- whether to arrest, report for summons, grant street bail, issue a fixed penalty notice, or take any other action.

In section 11.11.1, we explained that there are two conditions which need to be satisfied before an arrest should be made. The first concerns the existence of an offence, and we discussed this in section 11.11.3. The second condition is that one or more of a number of **reasons** make the arrest **necessary** which are set out in the PACE Act 1984, Code G 2.9 (Code G is available at <http://police.homeoffice.gov.uk/news-and-publications/publication/operational-policing/PACE_Chapter_G.pdf>).

An arrest is deemed to be necessary if one or more of the following reasons apply:

(a) to obtain someone's name;
(b) to obtain someone's address;
(c) to prevent injury, damage, indecency, or obstruction;
(d) to protect a vulnerable person;
(e) to ensure prompt investigation;
(f) to prevent a suspect disappearing.

These reasons are now explained in more detail.

11.11.4.1 To obtain someone's name or address

You must always explain the consequences if the person refuses to provide his/her name or address, ie that it may lead to his/her arrest. Remember, this is not a power to arrest a person who simply refuses to give you his/her name or address. Instead, this is one of several reasons that make a person's arrest necessary.

You may arrest someone in a situation where:

(a) You do not know and cannot readily ascertain the person's name or address.

Do not just ask him/her for his/her name and address once, or in a manner that lacks confidence. Make it clear to him/her that you need his/her name and address and the reason why. Explain that you suspect that he/she has committed an offence and that you require his/her name and address in order that the process of investigation can be followed.

(b) You have reasonable grounds for doubting whether a name or address given by the person is real.

You **must** have a logical reason for not believing that the name or address he/she gave you is correct, for example:

- he/she cannot give you anything which identifies him/her with the name or address (for example a driving licence with a photograph);
- you suspect he/she is using the name or address of a close relative with the same details (which are therefore false);
- there is no record of the name or address he/she provided in the voters' register or telephone directory;
- you suspect his/her name or address is fictitious because it is the name or address of a famous person or character.

Code D provides more detailed information about the definition of a satisfactory address.

Examples of **unsatisfactory** addresses include:

- that of a person who is working in the UK and leaving very soon, never to return;
- that of a person of 'no fixed abode' who cannot supply any other permanent addresses;
- the address the person supplies does not exist;
- the existence of a person with a different name registered as a voter at the address he/she has given.

However, an address will be satisfactory if some other person (for example employer or relative) at that address will accept service of the summons on his/her behalf. This could be used by a person whose home address is not in the UK.

11.11.4.2 To prevent injury, damage, indecency, or obstruction

A reason for arresting someone could be to prevent the person:

- **Causing physical injury to any other person.** For example, if you were investigating an offence of throwing fireworks in a street or public place under s 80 of the Explosives Act 1875, you might reach the conclusion that the suspect may harm him/herself or somebody else.
- **Suffering physical injury themselves.** For example, if you were investigating a person for an offence of being a pedestrian on the carriageway of a motorway under s 17(4) of the Road Traffic Regulation Act 1984, you might reach the conclusion that the suspect may suffer physical injury him/herself from a passing vehicle which could leave the main carriageway.
- **Causing loss of or damage to property.** For example, if you were investigating a person for an offence of interference with a motor vehicle or trailer under s 9 of the Criminal Attempts Act 1981, you might reach the conclusion that the suspect might cause damage to a vehicle during the interference.
- **Committing an offence against public decency.** For example, if you were investigating a person for an offence of using profane or obscene language under the Town Police Clauses Act 1847, you might reach the conclusion that the suspect was committing an offence against public decency. However, this section can only be used when it is in the presence of members of the public who cannot avoid the suspect.
- **Causing unlawful obstruction of the highway.** For example if you were investigating a person for an offence of wilful obstruction of the highway under s 137 of the Highways Act 1980 and the suspect was stopping or slowing pedestrian or vehicular traffic on the highway, you might reach the conclusion that the person would need to be removed.

At this stage, do not lose sight of the need for reasonable grounds for believing that the arrest is necessary to prevent the person from causing one of these outcomes. Remember, this is not a power of arrest for a person who just carries out one of these actions. Instead, they are reasons that make a person's arrest necessary.

11.11.4.3 To protect a child or other vulnerable person from the relevant person

A reason for arresting someone could be if you were investigating a person for any offence and you suspected that the suspect was putting the health and safety of a vulnerable person or child at risk as a result of his/her conduct. An example would be that he/she was walking along the hard shoulder of a motorway with an elderly relative.

11.11.4.4 To allow the prompt and effective investigation of the offence or of the conduct of the person in question

There may be many reasons why you may feel that an investigation may be jeopardized if you do not arrest the suspect, such as where there are grounds to believe that the person:

- has made false statements—for example, dates of birth, denials of disqualification from driving;
- has made statements which cannot be readily verified—for example, ownership of property for which he/she has no records such as vehicle registration documents;
- has presented false evidence—for example, forged driving licences or MOT certificates;
- may steal or destroy evidence—for example, disposing of stolen property from a burglary;
- may make contact with co-suspects or conspirators—for example, a warning through the use of mobile telephones which would make the co-suspects more difficult to locate;
- may intimidate, threaten, or make contact with witnesses—for example in cases where the identities of the suspect and victim are known to each other.

This may include cases such as when you are considering an arrest in connection with an **indictable** offence (see sections 5.11 and 5.12 above) and there is an operational need to:

- enter and search any premises occupied or controlled by the person being considered for arrest: if you do not arrest him/her, you will **not** be able to use s 18 of the PACE Act 1984 to search his/her premises;
- search the person: if you do not arrest him/her, you will **not** be able to use s 32 of the PACE Act 1984 to search and seize property;

- prevent contact with others: if you do not arrest him/her, you will **not** be able to seek the authority to delay the notification of a person's arrest;
- take fingerprints, footwear impressions, samples or photographs of the suspect: if you do not arrest him/her, you will not be able to obtain forensic evidence from the suspect.

You may also need to arrest someone if there is a need to test him/her for drugs, thereby ensuring compliance with statutory drug testing requirements: if you do not arrest the person, you will not be able to use s 63B of the PACE Act 1984 to obtain samples from the suspect to ascertain whether he/she has taken a Class A drug.

11.11.4.5 To prevent any prosecution for the offence from being hindered by the disappearance of the person in question

This may arise if there are reasonable grounds for believing that:

- if the person is not arrested, he/she will fail to attend court—for example, there is currently a warrant for the arrest of the person for failing to appear at court and he/she has now committed another offence;
- street bail after arrest would be sufficient to deter the suspect from trying to evade prosecution—for example, the arrest and subsequent use of street bail would be beneficial and would make the suspect more inclined to answer to bail at the appropriate time and place.

11.11.5 Summary of Reasons That Make an Arrest Necessary

The reasons that make an arrest necessary can best be remembered by the mnemonic **ID COP PLAN**.

I	Investigation	To allow the prompt and effective **investigation** of the offence or of the conduct of the person in question.
D	Disappearance	To prevent any prosecution for the offence from being hindered by the **disappearance** of the person in question.
C	Child	To protect a **child** or other vulnerable person from the relevant person.
O	Obstruction	To prevent the relevant person causing an unlawful **obstruction** of the highway.
P	Physical Injury	To prevent the relevant person causing **physical injury** to him/herself or any other **person**.
P	Public Decency	To prevent the relevant person committing an offence against **public decency**.
L	Loss or damage	To prevent the relevant person causing **loss of, or damage** to, property.
A	Address	To enable the **address** of the relevant person to be ascertained.
N	Name	To enable the **name** of the relevant person to be ascertained.

11.11.6 Arrest Without Warrant: Other Persons

This section has described the reasons why you, as an attested student police officer (a constable), may arrest a person. However, others also have the ability to arrest.

Other persons (persons other than a constable) may arrest someone but only if a constable is not present to carry out the arrest (s 24A(3)(b) of the PACE Act 1984), and only if it is necessary in order to prevent:

- injury to the suspect;
- injury to another person;
- damage to property;
- the suspect escaping before a constable can arrest them.

Other persons (persons other than a constable) may also arrest without a warrant:

- anyone who is in the act of committing an indictable offence (s 24A(1)), such as a member of the public who sees a person in the act of shoplifting or burgling a house;

- anyone whom he/she has reasonable grounds for suspecting to be committing an indictable offence (s 24A(1)), such as a member of the public who sees a person climbing into a window of his/her neighbours' house and suspects this person to be committing burglary (without actually knowing if the person has the neighbours' permission to enter the premises);
- where an indictable offence has been committed (s 24A(2)), such as when a store detective observes a person taking property from a display and leaves the shop without paying. The next day, the same person returns to the shop and the store detective is positive it is the same person and decides to arrest him/her.

11.11.7 Summary

The power of arrest without warrant is governed by Code G of the PACE Act 1984 Codes of Practice. Remember that the arrest of a suspect is not mandatory in every case where an offence has been committed. There are other ways of processing a suspect who has committed an offence such as report for summons, grant street bail, or issue a fixed penalty notice. These are covered later in this Chapter. The power to arrest without warrant is no different from any other power that you have been given as a police officer. If you fail to observe the rights of an individual, your investigation will be discredited at the very best and in the worst case actually discontinued. Finally, remember, you can only use the power of arrest if it **meets the two criteria** in section 11.11.1 and is **necessary** for any of the reasons specified in section 11.11.4.

TASK 8

Think of a practical example for each of the offences of unlawful possession of drugs (section 9.13 above), criminal damage (section 9.21 above), theft (section 9.3 above), and a s 5 Public Order Act offence (section 8.12 above). Consider the circumstances under which you would arrest for these offences and what possible reasons you would have for believing that arrest to be necessary.

11.12 Warrants of Arrest

In section 11.11 above, we discussed your general power to arrest without a warrant. Occasionally, whilst on Supervised or Independent Patrol you may be required to arrest a person on the basis of a warrant.

A **warrant** is a formal written document of authority issued by a magistrate or judge which directs the person or group of people to whom it is addressed (normally, but not exclusively, the police) to carry out an action on behalf of the court. A warrant of arrest therefore authorizes the arrest of a named individual to take place.

The following warrants of arrest and committal may be executed by you even though the warrant may not be physically in your possession at the time, under **s 125 of the Magistrates Courts Act 1980**. The most common warrants that you are likely to be involved with are for failure to answer bail, non-payment of fines, non-appearance at court, and those associated with witnesses giving evidence at court.

11.12.1 Non-Payment of Fines

Section 76(1) of the Magistrates Courts Act 1980 states:

> Where default is made in paying a sum adjudged to be paid by a conviction or order of a magistrates' court, the court may issue a warrant of distress for the purpose of levying the sum or issue a warrant committing the defaulter to prison.

11.12.2 Non-Appearance at Court

Section 55(2) of the Magistrates Courts Act 1980 states:

> Where the court, instead of proceeding in the absence of the defendant, adjourns or further adjourns the hearing, the court may, if the complaint has been substantiated on oath, issue a warrant for [his/her] arrest.

11.12.3   Witness Warrant for Arrest

Section 97(2) of the Magistrates Courts Act 1980 states:

> If a justice of the peace is satisfied by evidence on oath that it is probable that a summons would not procure the attendance of the person in question, the justice may, instead of issuing a summons, issue a warrant to arrest that person and bring [him/her] before such a court, at a time and place specified in the warrant.

11.12.4   Warrant of Arrest for Material Witness in Committal Proceedings

Section 97A(5) of the Magistrates Courts Act 1980 states that if:

(a) a person fails to attend before a justice in answer to a summons under this section,
(b) the justice is satisfied by evidence on oath that [he/she] is likely to be able to make a statement or produce a document or other exhibit,
(c) it is proved on oath, or in such other manner as may be prescribed, that [he/she has] been duly served with the summons and that a reasonable sum has been paid or tendered to [him/her] for costs and expenses, and
(d) it appears to the justice that there is no just excuse for the failure,

the justice may issue a warrant to arrest [him/her] and bring [him/her] before justice at a time and place specified in the warrant.

TASK 9

First research and then describe in your own words the process for executing a warrant.

TASK 10

What is the 'European Arrest Warrant'? How does it work?

11.13   Making an Arrest

This section will deal with the process of making arrest and your responsibility towards the suspect in relation to protecting the rights of the suspect.

It will therefore cover:

- what information should be given to the suspect on arrest;
- how much force you can use when making an arrest;
- under what circumstances you can release the suspect before arriving at the police station;
- what you can and cannot ask the suspect before arrival at the police station;
- how long that journey should take;
- under what circumstances you can search the arrested person,
- when you should inform him/her that he/she is under arrest for a further offence.

Making an arrest is an important milestone to achieve with your Police Action Checklist. In particular the 'Disposal' heading of the PAC is relevant here and particularly the confirmation that you can make lawful arrests.

The relevant NOS element is:

National Occupational Standard Elements

2C3.1 Arrest, detain or report individuals.

This section will help you develop some of the knowledge and understanding required for 2C3.1 and in particular:

Legal and organizational requirements

1. Current, relevant legislation, policies, procedures, codes of practice and guidelines for conducting arrests, detentions and reporting procedures.
4. The legal rights of individuals who have been arrested, detained and reported.

Conducting arrests, detentions and reporting procedures

5. How to check there is sufficient evidence or legal authority for arrest, detention and reporting procedures.
10. When and how interviews may be conducted with a detained person to obtain urgent information.
11. The need to release individuals without delay where information is obtained which negates the need for arrest or detention.

The evidence for the achievement of this element will come from successfully conducting arrests whilst under supervision on at least five different occasions.

Finally, ensure that you read section 11.11 of this Handbook concerning your general powers of arrest before you undertake the remaining sections of this part of the Handbook.

11.13.1 Information to be Given on Arrest

Section 28 of the PACE Act 1984 states that:

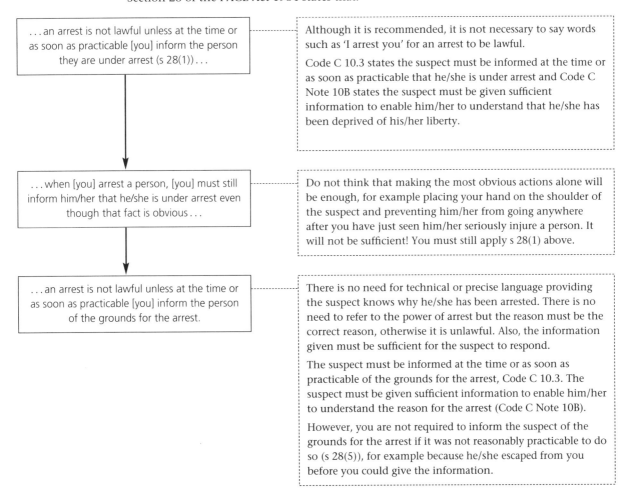

. . . an arrest is not lawful unless at the time or as soon as practicable [you] inform the person they are under arrest (s 28(1)) . . .	Although it is recommended, it is not necessary to say words such as 'I arrest you' for an arrest to be lawful.
	Code C 10.3 states the suspect must be informed at the time or as soon as practicable that he/she is under arrest and Code C Note 10B states the suspect must be given sufficient information to enable him/her to understand that he/she has been deprived of his/her liberty.
. . . when [you] arrest a person, [you] must still inform him/her that he/she is under arrest even though that fact is obvious . . .	Do not think that making the most obvious actions alone will be enough, for example placing your hand on the shoulder of the suspect and preventing him/her from going anywhere after you have just seen him/her seriously injure a person. It will not be sufficient! You must still apply s 28(1) above.
. . . an arrest is not lawful unless at the time or as soon as practicable [you] inform the person of the grounds for the arrest.	There is no need for technical or precise language providing the suspect knows why he/she has been arrested. There is no need to refer to the power of arrest but the reason must be the correct reason, otherwise it is unlawful. Also, the information given must be sufficient for the suspect to respond.
	The suspect must be informed at the time or as soon as practicable of the grounds for the arrest, Code C 10.3. The suspect must be given sufficient information to enable him/her to understand the reason for the arrest (Code C Note 10B).
	However, you are not required to inform the suspect of the grounds for the arrest if it was not reasonably practicable to do so (s 28(5)), for example because he/she escaped from you before you could give the information.

According to Code G 2 you are required to inform the arrested person of the relevant circumstances of the arrest in relation to both elements of s 24 of the PACE Act 1984.

That is, you are required to tell him/her:

- the circumstances surrounding his/her involvement or suspected involvement or attempted involvement in the commission of a criminal offence;
- and the reason(s) why the arrest is necessary (see section 11.11).

For example:

I have just seen you run out of the store with a brand new digital radio under your arm. I heard the store alarm sound at the same time and I therefore suspect that you have stolen the radio. I am therefore arresting you on suspicion of theft of the radio as the arrest is necessary to allow the prompt and effective investigation of the offence through the search of any premises occupied or controlled by you.

11.13.2 The Use of Force to Arrest a Person

You may need to use force to arrest a person, but the amount of force you use must be reasonable. Two pieces of legislation will help you here, s 3 of the Criminal Law Act 1967 and s 117 of the PACE Act 1984.

Section 3(1) of the Criminal Law Act 1967 states that...

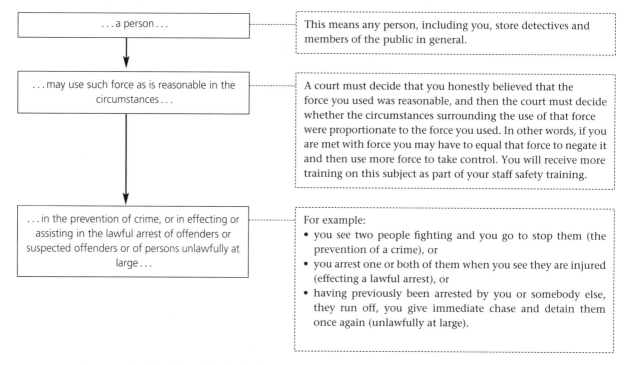

Section 117 of the PACE Act 1984 states that where any part of the PACE Act 1984:

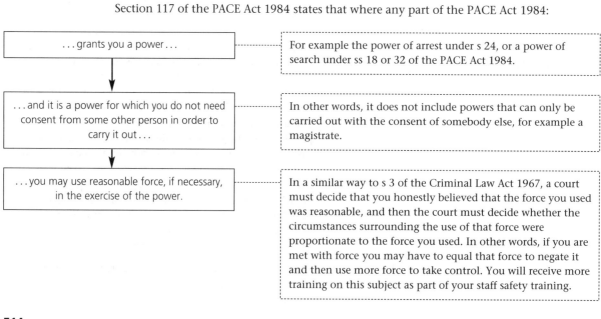

11.13.3 What to Do Immediately After an Arrest

First, do not forget to caution the suspect! (See PACE Act 1984, Code G 3.4 and section 11.6 of this chapter). Secondly, unless it is impracticable to do so, record in your pocket notebook (section 11.5):

- the nature and circumstances of the offence leading to the arrest;
- the reason or reasons why the arrest was necessary;
- the fact that you gave a caution;
- anything said by the person at the time of arrest.

11.13.4 Searching a Suspect after Arrest

Section 32(1) of the PACE Act 1984 states that you can search any person who has been arrested elsewhere than at a police station if you have reasonable grounds for believing that the arrested person may present a danger to himself or others. This is not a power to search everybody after arrest. You must have reasonable grounds for believing that the person to be searched may have concealed on them anything that would help them escape or provide evidence of an offence.

11.13.4.1 Searching persons

Remember, you must have reasonable grounds to search a person. Without those grounds you cannot carry out the search.

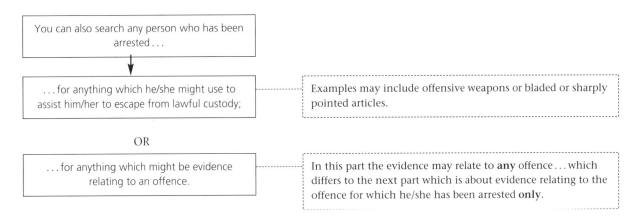

You can also search any person who has been arrested . . .

. . . for anything which he/she might use to assist him/her to escape from lawful custody;

Examples may include offensive weapons or bladed or sharply pointed articles.

OR

. . . for anything which might be evidence relating to an offence.

In this part the evidence may relate to **any** offence . . . which differs to the next part which is about evidence relating to the offence for which he/she has been arrested **only**.

When using these powers to search a person, you only have a power to search to the extent required to find the item you are seeking—for example if you are looking for a plasma TV, there is no reason to be looking in a trouser pocket. You cannot require him/her to remove any clothing in public other than an outer coat, jacket, or gloves, but you can search a person's mouth.

11.13.4.2 Searching premises

Under s 32(2)(b) of the PACE Act 1984 you may search premises, but only if the offence for which the person has been arrested is an indictable offence. However, you must have reasonable grounds for believing that there is evidence relating to that offence on the premises. You may **only** search for evidence relating to the offence for which the person has been arrested; it is **not** like a fishing trip when you try and catch any fish that happens to be there at the time.

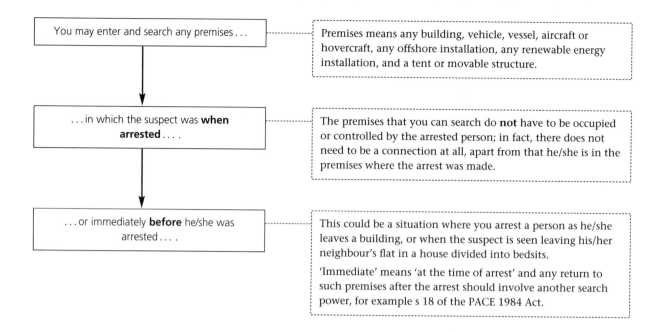

When using these powers to search such premises, you only have a power to search to the depth required to find the item you are looking for. For example, if you are searching for a stolen petrol generator taken from a building site, there is no justification for looking in a toilet cistern.

This also means that when, for example, using these powers to search a block of flats or a bedsit you must limit the power to search to:

- a dwelling where the arrest took place or the arrested person was immediately before the arrest, or
- communal areas, for example stairs, hallway, etc.

11.13.5 Permission is Withheld

If permission is not given to search then you may enter a premises by reasonable force, under s 117 of the PACE 1984 Act. This section applies to any part of the Act, including s 32 (see above).

11.13.6 Seizing Items

You can seize anything you find on the person or premises as a result of searching (under s 32), apart from items to do with legal privilege—for example letters from his/her legal representative (ss 19, 32(8), 32(9), of the PACE Act 1984).

11.13.7 Taking the Suspect to a Police Station

If someone is arrested (but not in a police station), they should be taken to a police station as soon as possible (s 30(1) of the PACE Act 1984).

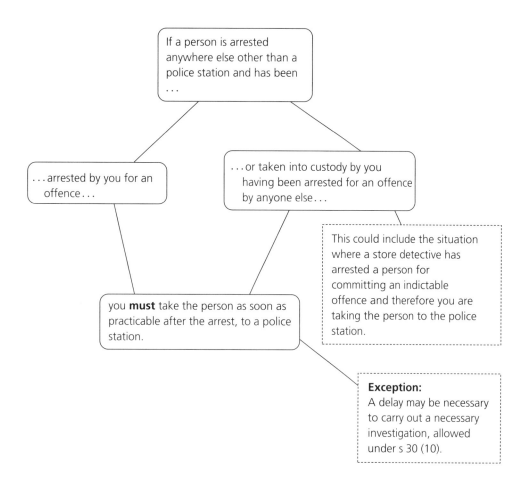

If a person is arrested anywhere else other than a police station and has been ...

... arrested by you for an offence ...

... or taken into custody by you having been arrested for an offence by anyone else ...

This could include the situation where a store detective has arrested a person for committing an indictable offence and therefore you are taking the person to the police station.

you **must** take the person as soon as practicable after the arrest, to a police station.

Exception:
A delay may be necessary to carry out a necessary investigation, allowed under s 30 (10).

This is not a situation where you should, or could take him/her as soon as practicable, but you **must**—you have no choice.

11.13.8 Discussing the Alleged Offence on the Way to the Police Station

This should be avoided, as any questioning of a person regarding his/her involvement or suspected involvement in a criminal offence is an interview which must be carried out under caution in a suitable place (PACE Act 1984, Code C 11.1A, see section 12.5 below).

However, if the suspect freely gives information to you without you having first asked a question, then follow the guidelines in relation to significant statements and relevant comments (see section 11.7, and how we use this during interviewing in Chapter 12).

11.13.9 Location for an Interview

After an arrest it is likely that you will conduct an interview with the suspect. Any interview should take place at a police station (PACE Act 1984, Code C 11.1A), but there might be reasons for conducting the interview elsewhere. This would apply if taking the suspect to a police station would cause a delay that could:

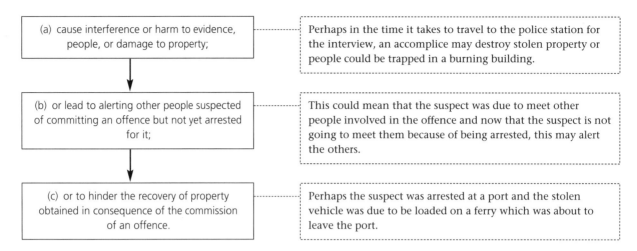

If any of these risks cease to apply, the interview should be stopped and moved to a police station. If the risks no longer exist and you continue the interview without moving to a police station, you may be jeopardizing the whole investigation. See section 12.5 below for a comprehensive description of conducting interviews.

11.13.10   'De-arresting' a Suspect

Any person you arrest elsewhere than a police station must be released if you are satisfied that there are no grounds for keeping him or her under arrest (s 30(7), PACE Act 1984).

For example, you initially decided that an arrest was necessary because the suspect did not give you his/her name, but on the way to the police station the person supplied his/her name to you. So there would be no need to continue to the police station as the reason for the arrest would no longer exist. Under these circumstances you are required to make a record of the release. Put a note in your pocket notebook outlining why the circumstances for keeping him/her under arrest no longer existed (see section 11.5 above for guidance on the pocket notebook).

11.13.11   The Suspect has Committed Further Offences

Section 31 of the PACE Act 1984 states that:

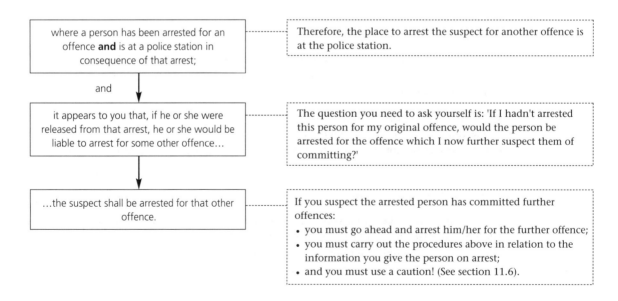

TASK 11

Look at the following set of circumstances and consider what you would say to the suspect in order to arrest him/her:

You are standing outside a shop that sells electrical goods when you see a person run out of the shop carrying an unpacked, brand new toaster under their arm with the lead dragging behind. The shop alarm is activated. During your briefing at your police station before commencing patrol you were made aware that this shop had suffered a number of walk-in thefts of small electrical items over the last few days. You therefore decide to arrest the person.

You say (on a bad day at the office):

Hey . . . you're not going anywhere, you've got to come with me, I'll tell you why later . . . for now just do as I say . . . have you got a problem with that? Got anything to say, well it doesn't matter if you have. Come on, give me that radio'.

Take a moment to write down what is wrong as far as the PACE Act 1984 and the Codes of Practice are concerned.

Next write down what you should have said to the person.

Undertaking this task will help you demonstrate the knowledge and understanding requirement of NOS Unit 2C3. It could also form the basis of evidence of the knowledge required for Unit 2C3 of the CAR in your SOLAP and in particular the 'legal and organizational requirements' evidence sections.

11.14 Search of Premises After Arrest

It is reasonable to suppose that few suspects are ever caught the first time they break the law. Equally, when suspects are arrested, there are few occasions when they are still in possession of the evidence connected with the crime for which they have been arrested. The PACE Act 1984 allows you to search premises of suspects who have been arrested for indictable offences in order to establish whether evidence that relates to that offence or a similar one is present.

This section will support you in developing the underpinning knowledge to achieve the PAC checklist heading 'Search' and in particular the ability to 'demonstrate a lawful s 18 PACE search'. The relevant NOS element is 2I2.2:

National Occupational Standard Element

2I2.2 Conduct searches of vehicles, premises and land.

Skills for Justice requires that evidence be provided from a minimum of two real searches for each type of search, ie two searches of vehicles, two searches of premises, and two searches of land. These searches must be real and not simulated.

11.14.1 A Search under s 18(1) of the PACE Act 1984

Section 18(1) of the PACE Act 1984 states that:

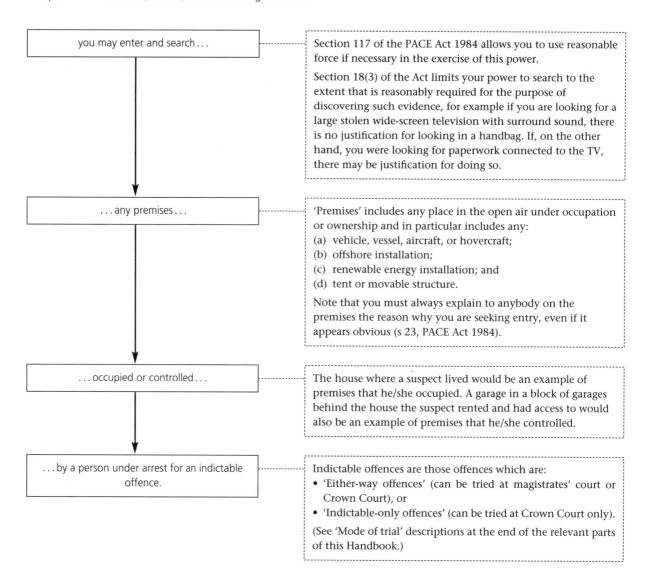

you may enter and search...	Section 117 of the PACE Act 1984 allows you to use reasonable force if necessary in the exercise of this power. Section 18(3) of the Act limits your power to search to the extent that is reasonably required for the purpose of discovering such evidence, for example if you are looking for a large stolen wide-screen television with surround sound, there is no justification for looking in a handbag. If, on the other hand, you were looking for paperwork connected to the TV, there may be justification for doing so.
...any premises...	'Premises' includes any place in the open air under occupation or ownership and in particular includes any: (a) vehicle, vessel, aircraft, or hovercraft; (b) offshore installation; (c) renewable energy installation; and (d) tent or movable structure. Note that you must always explain to anybody on the premises the reason why you are seeking entry, even if it appears obvious (s 23, PACE Act 1984).
...occupied or controlled...	The house where a suspect lived would be an example of premises that he/she occupied. A garage in a block of garages behind the house the suspect rented and had access to would also be an example of premises that he/she controlled.
...by a person under arrest for an indictable offence.	Indictable offences are those offences which are: • 'Either-way offences' (can be tried at magistrates' court or Crown Court), or • 'Indictable-only offences' (can be tried at Crown Court only). (See 'Mode of trial' descriptions at the end of the relevant parts of this Handbook.)

11.14.2 Evidence Requirements

Section 18 of the PACE Act 1984 states that you must have reasonable grounds to suspect that there is evidence on the premises that relates to that offence or to some other indictable offence connected with or similar to that offence. For example, if you arrest a suspect who was in the process of stealing a TV from a store, you may want to search his/her car for other stolen property which he/she has received and is in the process of selling. This would therefore be handling stolen goods and would be a similar offence to theft.

You may:

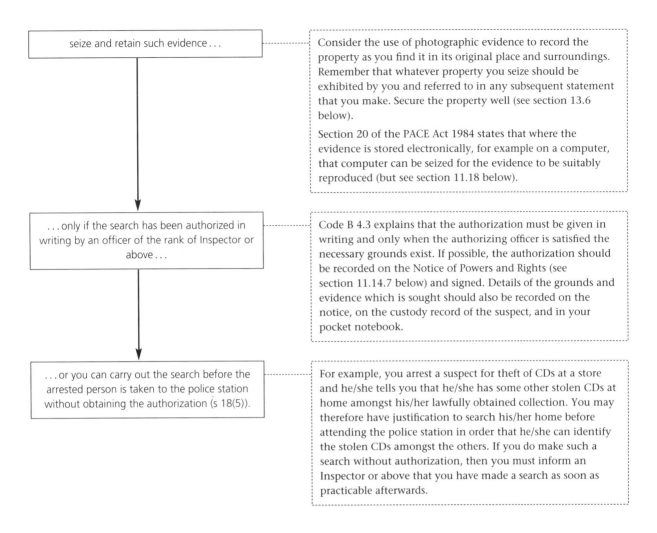

seize and retain such evidence . . .	Consider the use of photographic evidence to record the property as you find it in its original place and surroundings. Remember that whatever property you seize should be exhibited by you and referred to in any subsequent statement that you make. Secure the property well (see section 13.6 below). Section 20 of the PACE Act 1984 states that where the evidence is stored electronically, for example on a computer, that computer can be seized for the evidence to be suitably reproduced (but see section 11.18 below).
. . . only if the search has been authorized in writing by an officer of the rank of Inspector or above . . .	Code B 4.3 explains that the authorization must be given in writing and only when the authorizing officer is satisfied the necessary grounds exist. If possible, the authorization should be recorded on the Notice of Powers and Rights (see section 11.14.7 below) and signed. Details of the grounds and evidence which is sought should also be recorded on the notice, on the custody record of the suspect, and in your pocket notebook.
. . . or you can carry out the search before the arrested person is taken to the police station without obtaining the authorization (s 18(5)).	For example, you arrest a suspect for theft of CDs at a store and he/she tells you that he/she has some other stolen CDs at home amongst his/her lawfully obtained collection. You may therefore have justification to search his/her home before attending the police station in order that he/she can identify the stolen CDs amongst the others. If you do make such a search without authorization, then you must inform an Inspector or above that you have made a search as soon as practicable afterwards.

11.14.3 The Timing of Searches

Searches should be made at a reasonable hour. However, searches may be carried out at any time if the results of the search might otherwise be prejudiced (Code B 6.2).

11.14.4 Before Starting the Search

If the premises are occupied before the search begins (Code B 6.5) you should:

- identify yourself and state the purpose and grounds of the search;
- identify and introduce anybody with you.

11.14.5 Using Force to Enter

Reasonable and proportionate force may be used if necessary (Code B 6.6):

- if the occupier has refused entry;
- if it is impossible to communicate with the occupier.

11.14.6 Communication with People on the Premises during a Search

If you are in charge of the search, you should communicate with people on the premises (Code B 6.4) unless there are reasonable grounds for believing that alerting the occupier would frustrate the object of the search or put you in danger.

11.14.7 Documentation to be Left on the Premises after a Search

A copy of the Notice of Powers and Rights should be given to the occupier or left on the premises if they are empty (Code B 6.7). You will probably be given specimen copies of a notice to examine whilst training.

TASK 12

You are called to your custody area where your inspector is waiting to give you a signed 's 18' authority to search the premises of a person in custody for burglary of an electrical store which sells small electrical goods. The burglary took place yesterday and the person in custody was not in possession of any stolen property at the time of arrest.

- What are you considerations before leaving the custody area?
- What are you going to do on arrival at the premises to be searched?
- How will you conduct the search?
- What will you do before leaving the premises?

11.15 Search Warrants for Evidence of Indictable Offences

Section 8 of the PACE Act 1984 (extended by the Serious Organised Crime and Police Act 2005) provides the grounds and procedure to be followed when applying for a warrant to search premises in connection with an investigation into an indictable offence. It also provides a power to seize certain evidence.

Section 8 states:

> A justice of the peace may issue a warrant authorising you to enter and search premises . . . if there are reasonable grounds for believing [. . .]
>
> (a) that an indictable offence has been committed; and
> (b) that there is material on the premises mentioned [. . .] below which is likely to be of substantial value (whether by itself or together with other material) to the investigation of the offence; and
> (c) that the material is likely to be relevant evidence; and
> (d) that it does not consist of or include items subject to legal privilege, excluded material or special procedure material
>
> and that any of the following [**conditions**] apply in relation to each set of premises specified in the application:

Condition 1

It is not practicable to communicate with any person entitled to grant entry to the premises.

or

Condition 2

It is practicable to communicate with a person entitled to grant entry to the premises but it is not practicable to communicate with a person entitled to grant access to the evidence.

or

Condition 3

That entry to the premises will not be granted unless a warrant is produced.

or

Condition 4

That the purpose of a search may be frustrated or seriously prejudiced unless a constable arriving at the premises can secure immediate entry to them.

The 'premises' mentioned in part (b) above are:

- **one or more sets of premises specified in the application** (known as a 'Specific Premises Warrant'); or
- **any premises occupied or controlled by a person specified in the application**, including such sets of premises as are so specified (known as an 'All Premises Warrant').

Note that premises may be entered and searched on more than one occasion under the same application although the second and any more entries must be authorized by an officer of the rank of inspector or above.

Further, note that in the case of an application for an 'All Premises Warrant' the justice of the peace must also be satisfied:

(a) that because of the particulars of the offence, there are reasonable grounds for believing that it is necessary to search premises occupied or controlled by the person in question which are not specified in the application in order to find the material referred to; [or]

(b) that it is not reasonably practicable to specify in the application all the premises which [he/she] occupies or controls and which might need to be searched.

11.16   Power to Retain Property from a Detained Person

There will be occasions when it is necessary to seize and retain a suspect's property. This normally occurs when the property is potentially to be used as evidence against the suspect.

The main guidance is found in s 22 of the PACE Act 1984 although you will also be given detailed guidance by your police force when undertaking training. Note that s 22(4) states that 'nothing may be retained if a photograph or copy would be sufficient for that purpose' and so you must ensure that the property itself is required and that a photograph or copy would not be sufficient.

Section 22 also explains that the property 'may be retained so long as is necessary in all the circumstances' but does not elaborate further on the meanings of 'necessary' and 'circumstances'. However, common respect for the property rights of others (as described, for example, in the Human Rights Act 1998) would suggest that property should be returned as soon as possible when it is no longer relevant to an investigation. Your force is likely to have a 'Property Management Policy' that sets out the protocols for return (see, for example, Leicestershire Constabulary's at <http://www.leics.police.uk/files/library/documents/property_policy20060103.pdf>).

Section 22 describes two main reasons for seizing and retaining property.

(a) anything seized for the purposes of a criminal investigation may be retained . . .
  • for use as evidence at a trial for an offence, or
  • for forensic examination or for investigation in connection with an offence . . .

(b) anything may be retained in order to establish its lawful owner . . . where there are reasonable grounds for believing that it has been obtained in consequence of the commission of an offence.

When seizing and retaining property bear in mind the need to minimize contamination and to maintain a continuity record (see sections 11.18 and 13.6 of this Handbook) and also the rules concerning 'Retaining, Recording, and Revealing' (section 12.9).

TASK 13

Familiarize yourself with the forms used by your force that are used to record 'special' property (property relating to a crime) which you seize from a suspect, or 'special' property which you take possession of, having been abandoned or recovered from a criminal activity.

Once you have seized such property, where is it initially stored and, if required, where is it stored for longer periods of time?

What are your organizational procedures for retrieving exhibits in order to take them to court, for example, evidential recordings of interviews?

11.17   Presentation of Detained Persons to Custody Officers

The arrest of a person for an offence is a highly charged emotional event, and as a police constable you are required to maintain your professionalism throughout. An arrest is the start of a long process for the suspect, and you have a responsibility to preserve his/her rights throughout the whole detention process. Having deprived him/her of his/her liberty and therefore made it impossible for him/her to continue what he/she was doing previously, you have to prioritize your activities surrounding the detention, so that the suspect, and the incident you are investigating, receive the appropriate attention.

This section is relevant to the custody office procedures checklist in the PAC, in particular the requirement to 'provide grounds of arrest to custody officer' and 'search suspect and place in cell where appropriate' and the 'disposal' checklist in so far as it requires you to 'convey a suspect into custody'.

This section is also relevant to the following NOS elements:

National Occupational Standard Elements

2K1.1   Escort detained persons.
2K2.1   Present detained persons for custody process.
2K2.2   Conduct initial custody reception actions.

11.17.1   Arrival at the Police Station with an Arrested Person

When an arrested person reaches the boundary of a police station, he/she should be taken before a **custody officer** as soon as practicable after arrival (Code C 2.1A).

The time that the arrested person arrived at the police station is relevant because the he/she is only allowed to stay in custody for 24 hours after arrival. The arrival time is referred to as the **relevant time**. Therefore, make a note of this time in your pocket notebook.

11.17.2   The Custody Officer

A custody officer is a police officer of at least the rank of sergeant or a police support employee designated as a staff custody officer. His/her main duty is to ensure that all persons in police detention are treated according to the PACE Act 1984 and the Codes of Practice and that such treatment is recorded on a custody record.

You are required to inform the custody officer of the relevant circumstances of the arrest in relation to both criteria of s 24 of the PACE Act 1984, ie the suspect's **involvement in the commission of a criminal offence** and the **reason(s)** why the arrest was necessary (Code G 2.2, see section 11.11).

Here is an example of what you might say to the custody officer:

> At eleven hundred hours today I was on duty outside an electrical store in the High Street when I saw this person run out of the store with a brand new digital radio under his arm. I heard the store alarm sound at the same time and I therefore suspected that he had stolen the radio. I therefore arrested him on suspicion of theft of the radio as the arrest was necessary to allow the prompt and effective investigation of the offence through the search of any premises occupied or controlled by this person.

You should then remain with your arrested person during this initial custody process.

11.17.3   The Decision to Charge a Suspect

The custody officer must decide if there is enough evidence to charge your arrested person at this point (s 37(2), PACE Act 1984). If the custody officer decides there is not enough evidence to charge the suspect, he/she can still detain the arrested person if they have reasonable grounds for believing that detention without being charged is necessary to:

- secure or preserve evidence relating to an offence for which he/she is under arrest, for example to carry out searches for evidence;
- or obtain such evidence by questioning the suspect, such as by using a tape recording.

The time that the custody officer authorises the detention of the arrested person is important, as it is from this time that the **review times** of the detention are calculated. The reviews are carried out by an inspector not more than:

- six hours from the time of authorized detention; then
- nine hours after the first review; then
- at nine-hour intervals after that.

11.17.4 The Detainee's Rights After the Arrest

If the custody officer decides to detain your arrested person he/she must inform the detainee of the following rights which continue throughout his/her detention (PACE Act 1984, Code C 3.1):

1. the right to have someone informed of his/her arrest;
2. the right to consult privately with a solicitor and receive free legal advice;
3. the right to consult the PACE Act 1984 Codes of Practice.

The detainee must be given two written notices (Code C 3.2). The **first notice** sets out:

- the three rights noted above;
- the arrangements for obtaining legal advice;
- the right to a copy of the custody record;
- an explanation of the caution, for example what it means to him/her (see section 11.6 above).

The **second notice** sets out the detainee's entitlements while in custody, for example the provision of food and drink and access to toilets and so on.

The detainee will be requested to sign the custody record to confirm his/her decision about legal advice and informing someone of his/her arrest (Code C 3.5). The custody officer will also determine whether the detainee requires:

- medical attention, for example as a result of an injury or lack of medication;
- an appropriate adult, for example, the parent or guardian for a juvenile or, a relative or guardian for a mentally vulnerable person;
- help to check documentation, for example clarification of any of the rights;
- an interpreter, for example for non-English speaking detainees or those with speech or hearing impairments.

The custody officer will record his/her decision about the requirements on the custody record. The custody officer will also carry out an assessment of the detainee to determine whether he/she will be a risk to him/herself or others. Such assessment will include a check of the PNC and consultation with you as the arresting officer and appropriate health care professionals, for example custody nurses (Code C 3.6).

11.17.5 The Detainee's Right to Inform Someone of their Arrest

The detainee may inform one friend, relative, or interested person as soon as practicable (s 56, PACE Act 1984 and Code C 5.1). If the attempt fails, the detainee can have two other people contacted. In the case of a juvenile, the person responsible for his/her welfare **must** be informed of his/her detention. The detainee shall be given writing materials on request, and be allowed to telephone one person for a reasonable time.

The right to have someone informed of the arrest can be delayed, but only if the offence is an **indictable** one (see sections 5.11 and 5.12 above) or if there are reasonable grounds for believing that to allow the communication will lead to:

- interference with or harm to evidence or other people;
- alerting other people suspected of committing an indictable offence but not yet arrested;
- hindrance relating to the recovery of property.

The delay can only be authorized by an officer of at least the rank of inspector, and the delay must not be for more than thirty-six hours (s 56, PACE Act 1984 and Code C, Annex B).

A detainee's right to legal advice can be delayed (Code C, Annex B) but this is very rare. The decision must be taken by an officer of the rank of superintendent or above, who must have reasonable grounds to believe the solicitor for the detainee will pass on a message or act in some way which will lead to:

- interference with or harm to evidence or other people;
- alerting other people suspected of committing an indictable offence but not yet arrested;
- hindrance relating to the recovery of property.

11.17.6 Searching the Detainee

The custody officer has the power to search detainees, though he/she may ask you to carry out the search. The custody officer will decide the extent to which the search will be made (s 54(6), PACE Act 1984) but the search must not be intimate (it must not involve the physical examination of orifices other than the mouth). The search must be carried out by a constable of the same sex as the detainee (s 54(7)). However, a **strip search** can be authorized, but only if it is necessary to remove an article which the detainee would not be allowed to keep (Code C, Annex A 10), and if it is reasonably considered that the detainee has concealed such an article.

The search must be carried out:

- by an officer of the same sex;
- in an area away from other people;
- in a safe place with at least two other people present;
- with regard to sensitivity.

The following should also be noted:

- to assist with the search, the detainee can be required to lift his/her arms and stand with his/her legs apart;
- if anything is found the detainee should be asked to hand it over;
- the strip search should be carried out as quickly as possible.

All or any of the items found during the search may be recorded on the custody record. Clothes and effects can only be seized (s 54(3)) if the custody officer believes the detainee would use them to:

- harm him/herself;
- damage property;
- interfere with evidence;
- assist in escape;
- there are reasonable grounds for believing they may be evidence relating to an offence.

The custody officer is responsible for the detainee's possessions after the arrest (Code C 4.1). He/she must arrange the safekeeping of property which is taken from the detainee.

As you can see, making the arrest and bringing your suspect to the police station is just the beginning of an extended process, at the end of which the detainee may or may not be presented to the court. Whether he/she is presented to the court or not, each detained individual must have his/her rights protected and as the arresting officer you will be partly responsible for making sure the person you have arrested is allowed each of the rights they are entitled to.

TASK 14

Earlier you were standing outside a shop that sells electrical goods when you saw a male person run out of the shop carrying an unpacked, brand new DVD player with the lead dragging behind. The shop alarm was activated. During your briefing at your police station before commencing Independent Patrol you were made aware that this shop had suffered a number of walk-in thefts of small electrical items over the last few days. You therefore arrested this person and followed the PACE Act 1984 Codes of Practice accordingly. Having arrived at the police station, you are about to present the arrested person to the custody officer. Consider what you are going to say.

Completion of this task will help you towards achieving the knowledge requirements of CAR 2K2 in your SOLAP.

11.18   Attendance at Crime Scenes and Care of Exhibits

In this section we will introduce the procedures you may be involved with to protect evidence and minimize the risk of contamination when attending crime scenes during your Supervised Patrol. In section 13.6 we examine the broader subject of forensic investigation in more detail, including the types of evidence that you may encounter.

The material covered in this section is relevant to NOS element 2G2.1

National Occupational Standard Element

2G2.1 Conduct priority and volume investigations

---

and in particular the requirement to: 'identify and preserve the initial scene(s)' and 'identify and deal with evidence'.

The relevant knowledge and understanding from 2G2.1 is:

• how to maximize useful evidence and minimize loss of potential evidence;
• how to prevent the cross-contamination of evidence;
• the procedures for retaining and recording material in a durable and retrievable form;
• the reasons why the integrity and continuity of evidence must be maintained.

This section will also help you to satisfy the PAC requirement to 'correctly handle exhibits' under the general heading of 'Investigation'.

11.18.1   The Crime Scene

The crime scene is frequently the most important component of any investigation, because it is from here that physical evidence may be located which demonstrates guilt or innocence, which identifies suspects, and which corroborates or refutes statements made by witnesses. Early and effective protection of the crime scene ensures that the greatest amount of potential evidence is available for recovery and, therefore, maximises its value to the investigation.

11.18.1.1   What is a crime scene?

Crime scenes are not purely geographical locations to which we can apply an address, postcode, or map reference. Whilst it is true that homes, open spaces, and town centres have all witnessed much criminal activity, it is unduly restrictive to limit our consideration to just these areas.

Crime scenes can be physical places, as above, or vehicles or even people. Treating people as crime scenes may be potentially offensive to the families of victims, but it is vital that we consider people as sources of evidence and intelligence. This is to ensure that we effectively 'protect and preserve' such people, and recover from them the evidence or intelligence we need. A crime scene is not just a place; crime scenes are sources of evidence or intelligence. By using this definition, crime scenes can also be seen to include the intangible: computer hard drives, digital storage media, and the internet.

The first police officer who attends the scene (possibly as the result of an emergency call) is deemed to be the first attending officer (FAO). The FAO may be of any rank and position within the organization—indeed, it could be **you** whilst under supervision or whilst undertaking Independent Patrol.

11.18.2   Preserving the Scene—Safety First

The overriding principle applied to the management of crime scenes is that all attending officers rigorously ensure the safety of the public, their colleagues, and themselves. Any physical location in which an offence has occurred may include emotional, aggressive, or confused people who may represent a danger. In addition, damage to premises, such as by fire, may weaken the structure of a building, resulting in further hazards.

All physical evidence is expendable when balanced against human life. Hence the FAO should not preserve a crime scene to the extent that it causes unnecessary delay which results in aggravating a victim's injuries or leads to increased danger to life and limb.

This is not to say that one can disregard physical evidence during the life-saving process. After all, the FAO can advise the ambulance crew where not to tread and can carefully move furniture away from the victim to facilitate medical aid when necessary. However, if such actions are carried out, it is essential that moved items are left where they are and that all such activity is clearly reported to attending crime scene investigators (CSIs) early on in the investigation. Movement of furniture, switching on lights, and even opening doors represents contamination (in its loosest sense) and may take the item out of context. All these actions must be reported to the CSI and should be recorded in your pocket notebook (see section 11.5). All police officers attending crime scenes, including the FAO, should wear protective clothing for their own safety and to prevent the addition of misleading material to the scene.

11.18.3 Cordons

Once any victims have been treated and removed (or confirmed dead), the venue of the offence must be cordoned to prevent access by the public. The first few minutes after a major crime may be confusing and the FAO should control any person in the vicinity, including colleagues, and direct them to carry out urgent tasks since he/she is effectively the 'scene manager' at this time. The FAO should not be afraid of instructing superiors in this respect; if an action urgently needs completing then it must be done without delay and the superior officer should respect this.

The golden rule in cordoning is to make the cordon larger than you think is immediately necessary. The **inner cordon** (also known as the first cordon) must encompass specific areas:

- The venue of the offence.
- All possible routes into or out of the venue taken by the offender/s and victim/s.
- Any location where physical evidence may be found, for example: communal bins, under cars in the street, nearby gardens.
- Any location identified as routes, or as significant, by witnesses.

The cordon is erected using police tape and should be attached to fixed objects and made secure. Attaching the tape to potential evidence, for instance a parked car of interest, may erase evidence like blood stains and fingerprints because of the action of the wind, or people moving the tape. The presence of fixed objects must not determine the cordon size: if necessary, the tape can be affixed further out from the centre until poles are made available. Whilst putting this in place the officer must also control witnesses and keep them out of the freshly cordoned area. This is sometimes difficult.

Once the initial cordon is in place a **secondary cordon** (the outer cordon) can be installed. The outer cordon is placed to manage the public's access and view and is strictly a matter of control. If the public can see significant evidence then this cordon is too small. It also makes sense to position the cordon so that vehicles can turn around, minimizing local congestion.

The policy of some police forces is to position the cordons so that the area between the inner and outer cordon **might** contain material of importance to the enquiry. Typically this could be a discarded weapon, clothing, telephone kiosks, or shoe marks which are not within the inner cordon.

Once the inner cordon is in place, **nothing**—not even a patrol car—may leave it until sanctioned by a CSI, unless it is required to save life—for example, an ambulance or fire appliance. Vehicles moving through the cordoned area may damage vital evidence which has not yet been seen and recovered. Additionally, the offender may have leaned on a vehicle outside the venue of the offence when he made off, so CSIs may wish to examine every vehicle within the cordon or, on occasions, every vehicle in the street.

11.18.4 The Rendezvous Point (RVP)

The rendezvous point (RVP) is vital to the smooth running of the investigations at the scene, and should have been carefully chosen early on in the investigation. It may be required to hold a number of vehicles, rest stations, food vans, major incident vehicles, and even a command tent. RVPs should never be placed in a narrow street with restricted access. They should always be in a roadway or on land with good access which is unconnected to the investigation. When attending the scene of a suspicious explosion, care must be taken to search the RVP for secondary devices which have been deliberately placed to cause maximum casualties to the emergency services.

11.18.5 The Common Approach Path (CAP)

This is the route from the cordon's edge into the crime scene proper and should be guarded by a **scene control officer**. This may be you, whilst under supervision.

The CAP should **not** be the route likely to have been taken by victim or offender. Nor should it necessarily be the same route taken by the FAO (who was initially acting without full knowledge of the facts). If the scene is empty (there are no living victims on the crime scene), there will be more time to choose the most suitable route for the CAP.

The route of the CAP should minimize damage to potential evidence, particularly material which is small or almost two dimensional—such as shoe marks and blood. Wherever possible, the CAP should be laid on solid ground. This will help to prevent accidental concealment of evidence which might occur if personnel walked over a CAP consisting of softer materials such as grass and soil.

Ideally the CAP should be marked with tape but, in the early stages, this may not be possible. Attending personnel should not be tempted to anchor the tape with rocks and other debris in the vicinity, since one of these may have been a weapon.

Some of the problems associated with CAPs are:

- The eagerness to establish a CAP through the rear of the premises; entering the premises via a back door and searching for a key may destroy vital evidence.
- Choosing the route for a CAP in a flat, featureless field.
- There is only one entrance to the building.
- There is no available means to mark the CAP.

One of the early tasks of the CSI is to search the CAP for evidence. It is possible the CSI will want to move the CAP to another location as a result of finding material.

11.18.6 The Log

Perhaps the most important document at the crime scene is the log. This is a booklet or sheet upon which the details of all attending personnel are recorded. It must be copied and disclosed to the defence who will study it and compare it to statements and other scene logs (see section 12.9 below). In essence, it records any event that could have led to contamination of evidence. The log should contain details of:

- every person already at the scene when the FAO arrived;
- every person who subsequently attended the scene;
- every person who entered the inner cordon (for whatever reason);
- the time and date of their entry and exit;
- preferably, the reason for their attendance;
- preferably, a description of the CAP.

Failure to maintain the log may render some or all of the evidence removed from the scene unusable within the context of the CJS. It is the responsibility of the **scene control officer** and every individual to ensure the log is completed correctly. As a student police officer, ensure that you know who the scene control officer is when attending a crime scene under supervision.

11.18.7 Attending Personnel

You may observe some or all of the following when attending a crime scene.

11.18.7.1 The ambulance crew

They carry out an essential role and are to be allowed controlled access in order to save life. Ambulance crews are generally aware of how to behave in a crime scene but may have to be reminded not to touch anything needlessly and to show caution where they walk. Crews should be accompanied by the FAO who should take their names for later elimination (particularly of shoes, clothing, and fingerprints) and point out apparently significant evidence to be avoided.

11.18.7.2 The doctor

In cases involving fatalities, a doctor is not always necessary to carry out certification of death since some ambulance trusts have devolved this responsibility to their crews. If a doctor attends, he/she should wear protective clothing and carry out the minimum disturbance to the body that is necessary. The use of oral, rectal, or deep tissue thermometers is not generally permitted. The doctor is also requested not to turn the body nor search through clothing to view hypostasis or injuries (see section 13.6 below).

11.18.7.3 Other police colleagues

Other police colleagues (such as senior officers) are generally not allowed to enter the inner cordon unless:

• the offender is likely to be within and must be apprehended;
• they are saving life;
• they can assist in urgent and immediate acts to prevent loss of the scene (for example a fire);
• a dog is required to pick up a track from within the cordon.

In the case of deaths, there is no requirement for a senior officer to enter the scene once death has been confirmed, nor to confirm that a death is suspicious. In addition, it is not necessary to confirm observations made by other officers.

11.18.7.4 The CSI

The CSI will attend at the rendezvous point (see section 11.18.4 above) and, together with the FAO and other personnel, make a judgement as to how exactly to proceed. In general terms, the CSI's initial role is to gather information, start with photography where appropriate, advise detectives and uniformed police on the arrangements for any arrested persons, and call for assistance from colleagues. Once this has been achieved he/she may be in a position to examine the CAP, record and recover vulnerable evidence from it, and occasionally move the CAP to another location. It is common for the CSI to enter the scene with the doctor to certify deaths.

11.18.7.5 The Crime Scene Manager (CSM)

This person is appointed in a major crime enquiry to manage the crime scene and to deal with scientific resources. In some cases only one CSM may be appointed who will deal with all parts of the investigation. In a more serious or complex case there may be a number of CSMs and a crime scene co-ordinator (CSC). Typically, the CSM will be hands-on, but will be flexible enough to attend strategy meetings and deal with other issues.

11.18.7.6 Emergency personnel

A variety of emergency personnel may attend a scene. Whether they are recorded in the log (see section 11.18.6 above) depends on whether they enter the crime scene or assist elsewhere. The first five groups in the list below will also keep independent records of attendance for their own personnel.

List of emergency personnel

- The fire service
- EOD (in the case of explosions or suspected explosive devices)
- Coastguard and RNLI
- Mountain rescue and their dogs
- Lowland search organizations
- Borough or district surveyors
- Structural engineers
- Transco (for gas leaks)
- Scaffolding contractors

11.18.8 Fast Track Actions

In every major crime the Senior Investigating Officer (SIO) will consider fast track actions which may resolve the investigation rapidly. These decisions are taken after careful consideration, and are noted in the **policy file**. However, in the very early minutes of an investigation, some actions may be necessary to prevent the loss of evidence or facilitate the apprehension of a suspect. These can include the following:

- The use of a dog to track the offender, particularly if the scent is not contaminated. This may necessitate the dog's entry to the inner cordon. If you are involved with this, you should be guided by the handler.
- The immediate collection of evidence which is in danger of being lost, such as wadding and cartridge cases blowing down a street.
- Switching off a cooker if it may start a fire.
- Covering shoe marks and tyre marks in poor weather with boxes or bin lids taken from an area well away from the crime scene.
- An urgent search (sometimes called a **flash search**) of the street for evidence which has been discarded, especially when the area is busy.
- Controlling large groups of people in confined situations, such as a public house (pub), which may cause the loss (or gain) of fibre evidence.

In these circumstances care must be taken to make the right decision and, where necessary, protective clothing (at the least, clean medical-style gloves) should be worn to prevent contamination of the evidence. Police officers, including supervised student police officers, should be prepared to justify their actions (or lack of them) to the senior investigating officer.

11.18.9 Volume Crime Scenes

'Volume crimes' are crimes such as property crimes (for example, burglary) and certain forms of interpersonal crimes (such as assault).

At volume crime scenes you should bear in mind the points made above, but note that the actions of the CSI and others are likely to be less extensive. Officers will also try to minimize disruption to normal life in the immediate vicinity of the crime. If the CSI is delayed, a police officer (and hence you) may be required to carry out these actions:

- Close doors to control children and pets, instead of using cordon tape.
- Close windows and consider boarding up in inclement weather.
- Cover shoe marks inside with a chair (not a piece of paper which is more likely to be moved or trodden on).
- Bring broken glass and property inside, handling it by the edges and wearing gloves, as moisture makes fingerprinting difficult.
- Cover shoe and tyre marks with bin lids, trays, or boxes, even in sunny weather.
- Allow the victims to make drinks and food and facilitate this, unless doing so would damage good evidence or cause a health risk.
- Use the blanket or quilt to funnel any material on the beds to a corner of the room.

- If boarding-up is to be arranged, ensure the original window is left rather than being removed by the contractor.

Whilst these actions may help a victim's state of mind, there are other considerations which must be borne in mind. The most important is that adequate protection of moved articles should be carried out by wearing gloves and handling material carefully: **gloves do not prevent fingerprints from being destroyed**. Secondly, continuity must be considered, as the police officer who moves articles of interest should—technically—**exhibit** them. You should follow local protocols on this issue.

11.18.10 Exhibits and Exhibiting

According to common law 'it is within the power of, and is the duty of, constables to retain for use in court things which may be evidence of crime' (*R v Lushington ex p Otto* [1984] 1 QB 420). These 'things' can include physical objects, such as knives, and are often referred to as **exhibits** as they may be exhibited to the court. Under a Code of Practice within the Criminal Procedure and Investigations Act 1996 (CPIA), any police officer investigating alleged crimes 'has a duty to record and retain material which may be relevant to the investigation' (see section 12.9 below). Sections 21 and 22 of the PACE Act 1984 describe the powers of police to retain exhibits.

Any police officer or member of the public who produces or finds an article which may be used as evidence should exhibit it—that is, to formally record certain facts about the object. We look in detail at packaging of exhibits in section 13.6. In this section we outline the principles employed.

Packaging materials often have **labels** printed on the outer surface which can be used for noting facts; otherwise a simple label can be affixed. The **basic information** required is:

- Name of the person exhibiting.
- An exhibit number: normally the person's initials and a sequential number.
- A description, which should be brief and to the point (to prevent other people shortening the description for convenience). You should include index numbers or serial numbers for clarity.
- The date and time the exhibit was found.
- Where the exhibit was found.

It is the mark of a professional to make detailed notes about the exhibit to assist other investigators. If detailed and accurate records are not kept about the contents of a package, another person may be obliged to open it to check the contents. This is a possible source of contamination. In your detailed notes, you should record any identifying marks, the size of clothing, any damage or stains, any logos or identifying features, serial numbers, and describe the precise location of the exhibit and its orientation. A final search of any clothing should be made **after** the clothing has been placed in the bag, so any debris which falls from it is retained within the bag.

11.18.10.1 When should I sign an exhibit label?

The exhibit label records the **continuity** (or chain of custody) of the exhibit. Ideally, the chain should be unbroken from its seizure until it arrives at court. Every person who takes control of the exhibit should sign the label (and later write a statement) unless local protocols dictate otherwise. For instance, the movement of bulk quantities of exhibits is often recorded on a proforma by the driver, and major crime exhibits officers do not normally write a statement for every receipt of every exhibit.

If a police officer passes another a packaged exhibit for comment but it remains in his/her custody, the second officer need not sign the label. An example might be where he/she asks for a **casual** opinion:

- Have you ever seen one of these before?
- Is this a ball-peen hammer?
- Should I call this a herbal substance or dried plant material?

If a professional opinion is given, then the officer should sign the label and write a statement describing his or her actions. Finally, do not accept an unpackaged exhibit from anyone other than a member of the public. This is a potential cause of contamination.

11.18.10.2 Firearms as exhibits

It is not the purpose of this section to advise upon **firearms safety**, but safety must always be considered when dealing with firearms as exhibits. Firearms are excellent sources of evidence. As well as providing ballistic evidence, their smooth surfaces are good sources of fingerprints and DNA can be collected from their rough, control surfaces such as the grip, slide, and trigger. We consider this in more detail in section 13.6. We have already looked at the law surrounding firearms in section 8.22.

Chiefly, at scenes of crime:

- Treat every weapon as if it is loaded.
- Never handle or move a firearm.
- Never stand in front of a firearm.
- Never point a firearm at any person, even when safe.
- Never kick, move, or drop an article onto a firearm.
- Ensure every person who passes a firearm to you clearly demonstrates that it is safe and vice versa.
- Never make a weapon safe whilst pointing it at the floor or wall if it is possible that people may be below you or on the other side of a wall.
- Call for expert assistance—it is normal practice for a photographer or CSI to be present during the making-safe process by a firearms officer.
- Never convey a loaded firearm to the police station or laboratory unless this is necessary and suitable safety measures are in place.
- Never dry-fire a firearm or tamper with any controls apart from those necessary to make it safe.
- Never move a firearm by poking a pen, or any other object, into the barrel or trigger guard.

Above all: expect every firearm to be loaded and ready to fire.

In truth, very few guns can fire by being dropped or knocked since the majority of them have in-built safety features, but the consequence of a weapon firing by accident can obviously be serious.

11.18.11 Contamination

Certain forms of forensic evidence are, in all practical senses, incontrovertible (see section 13.6). Nonetheless, such evidence will be scrutinized by the defence in a criminal case in order to cast doubt on the **integrity** of an exhibit and have it disallowed by the judge. An effective defence team will look for:

- errors in continuity;
- errors in packaging and handling;
- any possible source of contamination.

Contamination is the transfer of trace evidence by any means other than by direct or indirect involvement with the crime. It can be accidental or deliberate. The term is also broadly used to describe damage to an exhibit or altering its state in some way that is not required for its preservation.

Proper packaging and storage can prevent contamination becoming an issue, and this is examined in detail in section 13.6. However, if you are required to package exhibits then the following general advice applies:

- Always use new paper and plastic bags, containers, and boxes and select the best material for the task.
- Damp or recently worn items of clothing should be packed in paper bags which allow the exhibit to breathe.

- Wet items should be brought to the attention of the CSI who will control the drying-out process. As a temporary measure, items can be stored in unsealed polythene bags sealed into a paper sack. However, items soaked with blood are best left to the CSI, as any folding of the exhibit may cause the transfer of blood onto other parts of the item.
- Always pack your own exhibits.
- Never deal with exhibits from two facets of the same offence, such as victim and suspect exhibits. Care should be taken when considering dealing with clothing from two people arrested together, for instance in the same vehicle.
- Store exhibits properly to prevent decay and damage.
- Do not package clothing from one person in an offence in a room that has previously been used for the sampling of another person.
- Never convey two people from the same offence in the same vehicle, even at separate times, until all parties have been forensically examined.
- Clean or wash down police vehicles which contain blood, once any forensic examination has been completed.
- Regularly and fastidiously valet patrol cars.
- Do not place a prisoner in a cell until it has been cleaned.
- Never package your search gloves with an exhibit; they are a source of your DNA as they are normally soaked in sweat.
- Always wear gloves and a face mask, as a minimum.

11.19   Duty Statements

As a student police officer you will, under supervision, increasingly become involved in incidents involving the investigation of criminal offences, subsequent arrests, and the presentation of suspects to the custody officer. Although you are involved as a trainee police officer in these incidents, you are, at the same time, a **witness to events.** As with all witnesses, you may be required to make a statement which is then a form of evidence. A shorthand term for witness statements by police officers is a 'duty statement'.

The diagrams that follow will help you learn how to complete a typical duty statement. (Some of the following is adapted from the unpublished document 'A Guide to Form MG11, General Rules for Completion' by Kent Police.)

MG 11

RESTRICTED (when complete)

WITNESS STATEMENT

(CJ Act 1967, s.9; MC Act 1980, ss5A(3) (a) and 5B; MC Rules 1981, r70)

URN

Statement of: *Charlotte Louisa UNDERWOOD*

Age if under 18: *Over 18* (if over 18 insert 'over 18')   Occupation: *Police Constable 118118*

This statement (consisting of 4 page(s) each signed by me) is true to the best of my knowledge and belief and I make it knowing that, if it is tendered in evidence, I shall be liable to prosecution if I have wilfully stated anything in it, which I know to be false, or do not believe to be true.

Signature: *C. Underwood*   Date: *01.03.(year)*

Tick if witness evidence is visually recorded ☐ *(supply witness details on rear)*

Duty Statements should commence with **time**, **day**, **date**, **location**, **officer status**, and details of other persons **present** (normally other colleagues), eg '*At 1600 hours on Wednesday 1st March (year) I was on uniformed mobile patrol in a marked police vehicle with PC 00000 when, as a result of information received, I attended 98 High Street, Maidbury, Kentshire. Upon my arrival . . .*'

OR

'*On Wednesday 1st March (year) I was engaged on plain clothed patrol alone in an unmarked police vehicle at High Street, Maidbury, Kentshire when at 1600 hours...*'

It is not necessary to include your name, title, number, or station at the start of the main body of text. Additionally, NEVER start a statement with '*I am the above named person ...*'

Use the 24 hour clock when making reference to timings. Do not use the phrase '*At approximately ... hours...*'; it should be either '*At*' or '*Approximately* ' but as a police officer, you should be specific and use '*At ... hours ...*'

When initially referring to other officers in your statement, record their ranks, numbers and surnames (in CAPITALS), eg '*I was in company with PC 66900 UNDERWOOD*'. Thereafter refer to them by way of rank and surname, eg *PC UNDERWOOD*.

Set the scene so the reader can form a mental picture of the layout of the area. Rather than saying that you '*noticed*' something, it is better to be more positive and say '*I saw ...*'.

Relevant conversation must be recorded in 'direct speech'.

Signature: *C. Underwood* PC 118118   Signature witnessed by: *N/A*

PTO

All continuation sheets (MG11a) should include your name in the 'Continuation of statement of…' section. Your rank and number should also be included.

Complete the 'page no … of …' section on each page (including continuation sheets—MG11a) and ensure these are correctly numbered.

MG 11A

RESTRICTED (when complete)

Continuation of Statement of: *Charlotte Louisa UNDERWOOD*   Page No 2 of 4

Arrests must be recorded in 'direct speech', eg '*At 1600 hours that same day I said to the SUSPECT "You match the description given by a shopkeeper of a person who has just stolen a radio from their store, and I am therefore arresting you on suspicion of theft of the radio from an electrical store".*'

There is no requirement to record the caution given in full but replies after caution should be recorded in direct speech, eg '*I then cautioned the SUSPECT to which he/she replied "You've got the wrong person".*'

OPINION is generally not permitted for inclusion in a statement, however, **expert** opinion **is** allowed and you are regarded as an expert witness in relation to providing evidence of drunkenness. Note: Opinion can and should be recorded in your PNB.

HEARSAY—Although there are exceptions, the basic definition of 'hearsay' is 'statements made other than in the presence and hearing of the accused'. If something is not said by the accused or in their presence and hearing, then it is 'hearsay'. However, you may be asked to include 'hearsay' in your statement for the following reasons: 1) It might not in fact be 'hearsay'; 2) The Criminal Justice Bill widens the admissibility of 'hearsay'; 3) It alerts the CPS to other possibilities of getting the same information in evidence. The CPS will edit 'hearsay' from your statement as appropriate. **N.B.** In any case, 'hearsay' **SHOULD ALWAYS be recorded in your PNB.**

Descriptions should be recorded **in detail**.

If you are not sure of a point of detail, then you must include this fact in your statement, eg '*I am not sure of the colour of the man's coat*'. This shows that you have considered the point even if you are unable to give details of it.

R v Turnbull 'ADVOKATE' requirements should be recorded **in detail**:

Amount of time you had the accused/suspect under observation?

Record the total time, but also identify how long you observed a person at specific moments throughout the entire period, ie it is highly unlikely a suspect and/or witness will be standing in exactly the same position for the whole observation period. Was there a break (however brief) in your observation? You should also include the various distances involved (see below), ie how long was the person observed for at that particular distance? Was it a frontal view, rear view, profile view? Basically, the circumstances of an observation will alter from moment to moment, and this needs to be recorded in detail.

Signature: *C. Underwood* PC 118118   Signature witnessed by: *N/A*

RESTRICTED (when complete)

Continuation of Statement of: *Charlotte Louisa UNDERWOOD*   Page No *3* of *4*

Distance between you, the suspect and/or witness

Record the distance between you, the suspect and/or witness. The distance is likely to vary during the course of the observation and will be rarely one measurement. Record furthest distance, shortest distance, and timings involved at each level. Also record distances of obstructions, etc—where are they in relation to you, the suspect and/or witness?

Visibility, ie what was the lighting like, what were the weather conditions?

Was it daytime or night-time? W ere the street lamps on? Weather conditions must be included in detail, eg it is not sufficient to say 'it was raining':Was it heavy rain, drizzle, etc? Was sunlight a factor? Where was the sun in relation to you, the suspect and/or witness? Were there shadows cast? Include distance of available visibility. Do you wear glasses or contact lenses? Were the witness and suspect at different heights?

Observation impeded in any way, such as by passing traffic or a press of people?

Any obstruction between you, the suspect and/or witness should be described in detail. It is insufficient to say, eg that the view was obstructed by 'a hedge'.The actual obstruction should be described, eg how tall, how wide, how dense? Obstructions include glass and the glass would need to be described, eg size, was it clean or dirty, frosted, open, closed, double glazed, glare from sun etc? How did the obstruction actually obstruct your view and to what degree?

Known or seen before, do you know the suspect and/or witness and, if so, how?

How do you know the person? In **what** context and how well? **When** did you last see him/her? Has his/her description **changed** in the interim period?

Any reason for remembering the suspect and/or witness?

This could be a distinguishing feature or peculiarity of the person, or the very nature of the incident itself that made the person memorable. This can relate to previous or present sightings. Was there anything unusual about the person's appearance (eg distinguishing features) or the prevailing circumstances? What, if anything, attracted your attention? What has stuck in your mind?

Time elapsed between the observation and the subsequent identification?

How much time elapsed between recording or obtaining a description and the sighting of the suspect? How much time elapsed between recording or obtaining a description and the subsequent identification?

E*rrors between the first recorded description of the suspect* and/or witness *and his/her actual appearance*

Any errors, or differences between the first description originally recorded / furnished by the witness and the actual appearance of the suspect when you arrested them, eg a suspect is arrested and is wearing a brown jumper when the original description recorded a long coat. You must record the difference to show integrity of the evidence. Remember, police officers are evidence gatherers, NOT prosecutors.

Signature: *C. Underwood* PC *118118*   Signature witnessed by: *N/A*

MG 11A

RESTRICTED (when complete)

Continuation of Statement of: *Charlotte Louisa UNDERWOOD*   Page No 4 of 4

Take pride and care in the completion of your statement to avoid errors Any errors you do make in the text should be corrected by striking the error through with ~~one line~~. This should then be initialled in the margin. You **must never** overwrite a mistake or use correction fluid. Any additions to the text should be initialled.

Always write in black ink.

When setting out your statement, you can make use of paragraphs, but do not leave a blank line in between. You do not need to 'rule off' an incomplete line.

Use proper grammar and sentence construction. Avoid abbreviations and the use of jargon. Write in plain English, so everyone can understand what you mean.

Surnames/family names should be written in CAPITALS. If you write entirely in capitals, then <u>underline</u> it. This applies to all names written in a statement to avoid ambiguity and misunderstanding by the reader.

Ensure that when you include a place/person's name that it is spelt correctly. Consider the effect on your credibility if important evidence such as a location or a person's name is spelt incorrectly.

Pages should be held together by use of a paper clip and not stapled.

EXHIBITS—Exhibit continuity can easily be explained. The first person coming into possession of the evidence after the offence or incident is the witness who will produce the item at court, and the exhibit MUST be given their reference number.

Once an exhibit has been given a reference, all witnesses who refer to the same exhibit will use that reference.

An example of the above is as follows:

1. A person called **A. Witness** sees a suspect being chased by **PC Charlotte L. UNDER-WOOD**. The suspect throws an MP3 player into a garden.
2. **PC UNDERWOOD** arrests the suspect and finds a similar MP3 player in his/her jacket. This MP3 player becomes **CU/1** as a result of using the officer's initials.
3. The person called **A. Witness** recovers the first MP3 player from the garden and gives it to **PC UNDERWOOD**. This MP3 player will be **AW/1** and signed by **A. Witness**.
4. **PC UNDERWOOD** takes possession of the MP3 player exhibited labelled and marked **AW/1** and signs the reverse of the label.
5. Both MP3 players will be taken to the owner to be identified. **PC UNDERWOOD** will make reference to both MP3 players, exhibits **CU/1** and **AW/1**, in a duty statement.
6. The owner's statement will include the identification of both MP3 players and the owner will sign both labels of exhibits **CU/1** and **AW/1**.

The witness should not make reference to producing the item but refer to it, ie '*I found an MP3 player in the garden which I handed to PC UNDER WOOD. C. Underwood PC 11818*'.

Signature: *C. Underwood* PC 118118   Signature witnessed by: *N/A*

Witness contact details

Home address: _c/o MAIDBURY POLICE STATION, HIGH STREET, MAIDBURY,_
KENTSHIRE .... Postcode: _MA5 9TF_

Home telephone No: _N/A_ .... Work telephone No: _01 1212999_

Mobile/Pager No: _N/A_ .... E-mail address: _118118@999.police.uk_

Preferred means of contact: _N/A_ ....

Male/Female (delete as applicable) .... Date and place of birth: _00.00.00_

Former name: _N/A_ .... Height: _5' 8"_ Ethnicity Code: _W1_

Dates of witness non-availability: ....

....

Witness care

a) Is the witness willing to attend court? Yes/No. If 'No', include reason(s) on form MG6. What can be done to ensure attendance?

....

b) Does the witness require 'special measures' as a vulnerable or intimidated witness? Yes/No.

c) Does the witness have any specific care needs? Yes/No. If 'Yes' what are they? (Healthcare, child-care, transport, disability, language difficulties, visually impaired, restricted mobility or other concerns?)

....

....

Witness Consent (for witness completion)

a) The criminal justice process and Victim Personal Statement Scheme (victims only) has been explained to me: Yes/No

b) I have been given the leaflet 'Giving a witness statement to the police — what happens next?'   Yes/No

c) I consent to police having access to my medical record(s) in relation to this matter: Yes☐ No☐ N/A☐

d) I consent to my medical record in relation to this matter being disclosed to the defence: Yes☐ No☐ N/A☐

e) I consent to the statement being disclosed for the purposes of civil proceedings eg: child care proceedings (if applicable):   Yes☐ No☐ N/A☐

f) The information recorded above will be disclosed to the Witness Service so that they can offer help and support, unless you ask them not to. Tick this box to decline their services: ☐

Signature of witness: _C. Underwood_

Statement taken by (print name): .... Station: ....

Time and place statement taken: _23.30 hrs. 13.11.(year) MAIDBURY POLICE STATION_

Side annotations:

NEVER include your home address or home telephone number on the rear of an MG11. Consider the potential consequences if a defendant obtained these details.

Record your business address in the 'Home address' section. Record this information in CAPITAL letters.

Endorse the 'home telephone number' section as 'N/A'.

Include the telephone number of your police station in the 'business telephone number' section.

The 'contact point . . .' section should be endorsed as 'N/A'—your contact details should already have been completed in the 'Home address' section.

Delete 'Male / female' as appropriate.

Include your 'Date and place of birth'.

Complete the 'Maiden name' section if appropriate or endorse as 'N/A'.

Your 'height' must be included.

The 'Identity Code' section must be completed. The 'Identity Code' is your ethnic appearance code.

The 'Dates to be avoided' section does not have to be completed. Your statement should be accompanied by a completed MG10 which records your availability status.

Witness Care and Witness Consent are not applicable to you.

The 'Statement taken by . . .' section should be endorsed as 'N/A'.

The time and location of statement completion should be recorded in your PNB.

11.20   Victim Personal Statements

Victims will often also be witnesses and so will complete a witness statement. A **victim personal statement (VPS)** consists of additional statements by the victim—they are not replacements for the evidential witness statement but provide extra information concerning how the crime has affected the victim and what support they need. VPSs can also be made by the relatives or partners of homicide victims or the parents or carers of children or adults with learning difficulties. You would normally take a VPS immediately after a witness statement and using the same MG11 form. This is known as a Stage 1 VPS. When a Stage 1 VPS is taken there should be a clear separation between the evidential part of the statement and the VPS. A caption should be inserted between the two to emphasize this separation. However, victims may choose instead to make a VPS at a later stage, known as a Stage 2 VPS. A caption should also be used to start a Stage 2 VPS to emphasize that it is a VPS and not an evidential witness statement.

The caption should read as follows (you will need to amend it according to whether it is a Stage 1 or Stage 2 VPS):

> I have been given the Victim Personal Statement (VPS) leaflet and the VPS scheme has been explained to me. What follows is what I wish to say in connection with this matter. [In addition to what I said in my previous victim personal statement]. I understand that what I say may be used in various ways and that it may be disclosed to the defence.

Although they can write anything they see fit, you can explain to victims that they may wish to write about one or more of the following:

- if they want to be told about the progress of their case;
- if they would like extra support (particularly if they are appearing as a witness at a trial);
- if they feel vulnerable or intimidated;
- if they are worried about the offender being given bail (for example, if the offender knows them);
- how the crime has affected them if they feel racial hostility was part of the crime;
- how the crime has affected them if they feel that they were victimized because of their faith, cultural background, or disability;
- if they think they will try to claim compensation from the offender for any injury, loss, or damage they have suffered;
- if the crime has caused, or made worse, any medical or social problems (such as marital problems);
- anything else they think might be helpful or relevant.

(adapted from Home Office, 2006).

11.21 Methods of Disposal of Criminal Suspects

This section describes the various methods of 'disposing' of a criminal suspect including directing him/her to court or by imposing penalties without going to court.

The methods of disposal described below are:

1. Written charge and requisition by a public prosecutor.
2. Penalty Notices for Disorder.
3. Juvenile warnings and reprimands.
4. Bail from elsewhere than a police station: 'Street bail'.
5. Charge.
6. Bail from a police station.
7. Police caution.
8. Conditional caution.
9. Refused charge.

11.21.1 Written Charge and Postal Requisition by a Public Prosecutor

In circumstances where a suspect is not arrested, but is suspected of committing an offence, criminal proceedings will be instituted by way of a written charge and issue of a postal requisition. An example of such criminal proceedings will be when you report a suspect at the roadside for a road traffic offence, or a suspect attends a police station voluntarily at your request. Once you have gathered your evidence in relation to the suspect, you will submit your case file. If a decision is reached to prosecute the suspect, a person authorized by your organization to institute criminal proceedings (a public prosecutor) will issue a writen charge to the suspect. This written charge will describe the offence for which the suspect is being prosecuted, including the title of the Act under which the offence was created. At the same time, the public prosecutor will issue a requisition which requires the suspect to appear before a magistrates' court to answer the written charge. The written charge and requisition will be served on the person concerned by post, and a copy of both will be served on the court named in the requisition. See section 10.11.3 for the process of reporting a suspect for the purposes of instituting proceedings by way of written charge.

11.21.2 Penalty Notices for Disorder

These provide offenders with an opportunity to pay a fine for an offence without going to court. The Penalty Notice for Disorder (PND) scheme has its legal basis in ss 1 to 11 of the Criminal Justice and Police Act 2001. It has been introduced as a response to the perceived need for a speedy and effective method for dealing with low-level, anti-social, and 'nuisance' offending. As with the Fixed Penalty Notice (FPN) system for motoring offences that we described in Chapter 10, this scheme allows offenders to pay a fine without having to go to court.

The key aims and objectives of the scheme are:

- To reduce the amount of time that police officers spend completing paperwork and attending court, while simultaneously reducing the burden on the courts.
- To increase the amount of time officers spend on the street and dealing with more serious crime.
- To offer operational officers a quick and effective alternative means of dealing with low-level, anti-social, and nuisance offending.
- To deliver swift, simple, and effective justice that carries a deterrent effect.

Under the Criminal Justice and Police Act 2001 the following procedures are adopted.

1. If you have reason to believe that a person has committed a penalty offence, you may give that person a penalty notice for that offence (see your local policy for the minimum age of the recipient).
2. The notice may be issued either:
   - on the spot by an officer in uniform; or
   - at a police station by an authorized officer (in the majority of cases, this takes place in the custody area of a police station, by the custody officer, after the person has been investigated).
3. The issue of a penalty notice gives the recipient the opportunity to pay the penalty, in order to discharge liability to conviction for the offence.
4. Once the notice has been issued, the recipient may elect to either:
   - pay the penalty; or
   - request a court hearing.
   He/she must do one or the other within 21 days of the date of issue; and
5. Failure to do either may result in:
   - the registration of a fine of one and a half times the penalty amount as a fine against the recipient; or
   - court proceedings against him/her.

The Anti-Social Behaviour Act 2003 also provides for penalty notices to be issued for disorder in respect of graffiti or fly-posting.

11.21.2.1 Offences included in the scheme for which the penalty is £80

The table below summarizes which offences may be dealt with by an £80 fine under the FPN scheme.

Offence	Legislation
Wasting police time/giving false report	S 5 of the Criminal Law Act 1967
Using public electronic communications network in order to cause annoyance, inconvenience, or needless anxiety	S 127(2) of the Communications Act 2003

Offences included in the scheme for which the penalty is £80 (*continued*)

Offence	Legislation
Knowingly giving a false alarm to a person acting on behalf of a fire and rescue authority	S 49 of the Fire and Rescue Services Act 2004
Causing harassment, alarm, or distress	S 5 of the Public Order Act 1986
Throwing fireworks	S 80 of the Explosives Act 1875
Drunk and disorderly	S 91 of the Criminal Justice Act 1967
Selling alcohol to person under 18 (anywhere)	S 146(1) and (3) of the Licensing Act 2003
Purchase of alcohol by a person under 18	S 149(1) of the Licensing Act 2003
Selling Alcohol to a drunken person	S 141(1) of the Licensing Act 2003
Purchase or attempting to purchase alcohol on behalf of a person under 18 (includes licensed premises and off-licences)	S 149(3) and (4) of the Licensing Act 2003
Consumption of alcohol by persons under 18 or allowing such consumption	S 150(1) and (2)of the Licensing Act 2003
Delivery of alcohol to under 18 or allowing such delivery	S 151 of the Licensing Act 2003
Obtaining alcohol for a person who is drunk	S 142 of the Licensing Act 2003
Destroying or damaging property under £500	S 1 of the Criminal Damage Act 1971
Theft (retail) under £200	S 1 of the Theft Act 1968
Breach of fireworks curfew	Reg 7 of the Firework Regulations 2004 under s 11 of the Fireworks Act 2003
Possession of a category 4 firework	Reg 5 of the Firework Regulations 2004 under s 11 of the Fireworks Act 2003
Possession by a person under 18 of an adult firework in public	Reg 4 of the Firework Regulations 2004 under s11 of the Fireworks Act 2003

11.21.2.2 **Offences included in the scheme for which the penalty is £50**

The table below summarizes which offences may be dealt with by a £50 fine under the FPN scheme.

Offence	Legislation
Trespassing on a railway	S 55 of the British Transport Commission Act 1949
Throwing stones at a train	S 56 of the British Transport Commission Act 1949
Drunk in the highway	S 12 of the Licensing Act 1872
Consumption of alcohol in designated public place, contrary to requirement by constable not to do so	S 12 of the Criminal Justice and Police Act 2001
Depositing and leaving litter	S 87(1) and (5) of the Environmental Protection Act 1990
Consumption of alcohol by a person under 18 in a bar	S 150(1) of the Licensing Act 2003
Allowing consumption of alcohol by a person under 18 in a bar	S 150(2) of the Licensing Act 2003
Buying or attempting to buy alcohol for a person under 18	S 149(1) of the Licensing Act 2003

11.21.3   Power to Photograph Persons Away from a Police Station

Section 64A (1A) of the Police and Criminal Evidence Act 1984 states that a person may be photographed elsewhere other than at a police station (for example, on the street):

(a) with the appropriate consent [of the person concerned]; or
(b) if the appropriate consent is withheld or it is not practicable to obtain it, without [his or her consent] **if:**

- arrested by you for an offence;
- taken into custody by you after being arrested for an offence by a person other than another police officer;
- he/she has been made subject to a requirement to wait with a community support officer;
- he/she has been given a penalty notice for disorder or a penalty notice for truancy or a road policing offence by you whilst in uniform;
- he/she has been given a fixed penalty notice by a community support officer;
- he/she has been given a fixed penalty notice by an accredited person (a person outside of the extended police family).

Section 64A(2) of the Police and Criminal Evidence Act 1984 states when you are proposing to take such a photograph you may-

(a) for the purpose of doing so, require the removal of any item or substance worn on or over the whole or any part of the head or face of the person to be photographed; and
(b) remove the item or substance if the requirement is not complied with.

However, if a person declines to remove in public religious garments covering part of the head then you should consider taking the person out of public view so that a photograph can be made in private.

11.21.4   Juvenile Warnings and Reprimands

This is a new system of pre-court actions aimed at diverting children and young people (ten to seventeen years) away from their offending behaviour and avoiding them entering the court system (ss 65–66 of the Crime and Disorder Act 1998). The final warning scheme has replaced police cautioning for juveniles. The aim of the system is to end repeat cautioning and to provide progressive and effective interventions to help prevent re-offending.

A **reprimand** is a formal verbal warning given by a police officer to a young person who admits guilt for a minor first offence. Sometimes the young person can be referred to the Youth Offending Team (YOT) to take part in a voluntary programme to help him/her address the offending behaviour.

A **final warning** is a formal verbal warning given by a police officer to a young person who admits guilt for a first or second offence. The final warning triggers an automatic referral to the YOT where the young person is assessed to determine the causes of the offending behaviour and a programme of activities is identified in an attempt to address them.

Both the reprimand and final warning are designed to divert young people from the criminal justice system. If they do go to court for a further offence, the court will take the reprimand and final warning into account when deciding on the appropriate sentence for the offence. The court may only in exceptional circumstances give a conditional discharge if a final warning has been given within the last two years.

11.21.5   Bail Elsewhere than at a Police Station—'Street Bail'

Under ss 30A–D of the PACE Act 1984, street bail is a discretionary power which allows police officers to release an offender on bail (without taking them to a police station), on the condition that the offender must attend a specified police station at a later specified date.

Benefits for the police include:

- A reduction in the amount of time travelling to and from the police station.
- Better opportunities for planning the investigation and work caseload.

- Less time waiting at the police station to progress the investigation.
- Better opportunities for appropriate representation on answering bail.

Benefits for the suspect include:

- There is less of a need to travel to a police station.
- There is no need to spend time in detention whilst awaiting representation.
- It is more likely that time spent in detention is focussed on the investigation and not awaiting representation.

For legal representatives, parents, and appropriate adults, there are better opportunities to plan and prepare for attendance.

Street bail enables 'front-line' officers to apply their discretion at the point of arrest. There are four key considerations for you:

- the **nature** of the offence;
- the **ability** to progress the investigation at the station;
- **confidence** in the suspect answering bail;
- the **level** of awareness and understanding of the procedure by the suspect.

Your decision to grant street bail should follow the normal arrest procedures in s 24 of the PACE Act 1984 (see section 11.11 above). Statements concerning guilt are not relevant to the decision to grant bail—interview and examination of evidence will take place in more detail when the person answers bail.

Whilst on the street ask yourself the following questions when deciding to grant street bail:

1. **What type of offence has been committed?** There is no definitive list of offences to which street bail can be granted. It is a matter for the police officer's discretion. However, it is unlikely that street bail would be granted in relation to a serious offence.
2. **What impact has the offence had? That is:**
    - How has the offence impacted on the victim and those others involved?
    - What impact has it had on the offender?
    - **How serious is the offence?**
3. **Would a delay in dealing with the offender result in loss of vital evidence?** It might be necessary to take an arrested person to a police station to preserve and examine forensic evidence which could be lost if the suspect is released.
4. **Is the arrested person fit to be released back onto the streets?** A drink driver or those with mental health problems, for example, may not be in a fit state to be returned to the streets. In the case of a juvenile, consideration must be given to the welfare of the child.
5. **Does the arrested person understand what is happening?** This particularly applies to vulnerable people who would normally require the assistance of an appropriate adult (mentally disordered or mentally vulnerable people and juveniles), but may also include those suspected to be under the influence of drink and/or drugs.
6. **If released on bail, is the arrested person likely to commit a further offence?** You should not grant street bail if there are reasonable grounds to believe that the arrested person might continue to commit that or another offence if released, for example where fighting is involved.
7. **Am I satisfied that the arrested person has provided a correct name and address?** You must not grant bail if you are not satisfied that the identification and address details provided are correct.

If you are satisfied that street bail is appropriate you should explain the decision to the offender, and issue him/her with a street bail notice. The offender should be released as soon as possible.

It is important that the arrested person understands that:

- he/she is not being legally discharged;
- court proceedings or other disposal further action may be taken against him/her; and
- he/she is required to attend a police station at a later, specified date.

A verbal explanation of the points above should be given to the person granted street bail, even though it is also clearly stated on the notice to be handed to the arrested person. No requirement other than attendance can be imposed as a condition of bail.

11.21.5.1 Length of time for street bail

The length of time for street bail is partly determined by the time it takes for you to carry out investigations, but you should also be guided by your force policy (your force might well have maximum periods that can be specified).

11.21.5.2 Failure to attend the police station to answer street bail

You have the power to re-arrest without warrant those who fail to answer bail at the specified time (s 30A of the PACE Act 1984).

11.21.5.3 Attaching conditions to street bail

Section 30A (3A) of the PACE Act 1984 states you 'may impose, as conditions of the bail, such requirements as appear to you to be necessary to secure that the person':

- surrenders to custody;
- does not commit an offence while on bail;
- does not interfere with witnesses or otherwise obstruct the course of justice, whether in relation to [him/herself] or any other person.

However, when issuing street bail, the following conditions **cannot** be imposed on a person as a provision for his/her surrender to custody:

1. a recognizance (a declaration by the bailed person which is 'recognized' as an obligation such as a recorded promise of appearance);
2. a security (a declaration by the bailed person or anyone on his/her behalf, to forfeit property such as cash, for non-appearance);
3. a provision of surety or sureties (the bailed person provides details of a person or persons who will be responsible for his or her appearance).
4. a requirement to be a resident of a bail hostel (an establishment provided by the National Probation Service for prisoners who are soon to complete a prison sentence).

Section 30B (4A) states that if conditions are attached to the bail, the notice given to the suspect must specify:

- the requirements of the conditions;
- the opportunities to vary the conditions;
- the police station at which the conditions can be varied.

Section 30D (2A) states that 'a person who has been released on bail under section 30A may be arrested without a warrant by [you] if [you have] reasonable grounds for suspecting that the person has broken any of the conditions of bail'.

11.21.6 Charge

A charge is a formal accusation that a person has carried out something illegal and will be required to stand trial in a court of law. A person will be notified of such an allegation by way of a written notice.

Code C, paras 16.1–16.3 of the PACE Act 1984 states that:

> When the officer in charge of the investigation reasonably believes there is sufficient evidence to charge a person with an offence, [he/she] *shall without delay* [. . .] inform the custody officer who will be responsible for considering whether the detainee should be charged.

> When a person is detained in respect of more than one offence, it is permissible to delay informing the custody officer until the above conditions are satisfied in respect of all the offences.

As soon as there is sufficient evidence for a prosecution to succeed, the custody officer will decide whether or not the person should be charged with the offence, or released with or without bail. If the person is classified as a 'person at risk', then any action taken should be taken in the presence of an appropriate adult. When charged, he/she (or the appropriate adult) should be given a written notice which shows:

1. the particulars of the offence (that is, the precise offence);
2. the name of the police officer in the case;
3. the reference number of the case.

The notice should also begin with the following words:

> You are charged with the offence(s) shown below. You do not have to say anything. But it may harm your defence if you do not mention now something which you later rely on in court. Anything you say may be given in evidence.

A person who is to be charged or informed that he/she may be prosecuted for an offence, should be cautioned using the caution as outlined above (see also section 12.5).

11.21.7 Bail from a Police Station

Bail is a process of attempting to ensure that a person appears at a specified time at a specified place, such as a police station or court. For example, there may be further evidence to collect before a person can be charged with an offence; the custody officer can bail a person to return to the police station at a later date to be charged. Additionally, once a person has been charged with an offence, the custody officer must release the person on bail (unless the person comes within the terms of the Bail Act 1976; in these circumstances, the person will be kept in custody and be brought before a magistrates' court).

There are four main reasons for bail that you will encounter on a regular basis:

1. Continued detention in police custody cannot be justified; the offender may be bailed under s 34(5) of the PACE Act 1984 to return to the police station. Conditions **cannot** be attached to the bail under this section.
2. Insufficient evidence to support a charge; the offender may be bailed under s 37(2) of the PACE Act 1984 to return to the police station. Conditions **can** be attached to the bail under this section (for example, not to return to a crime scene).
3. Consultation with the CPS is required to agree charges; the offender may be bailed under s 37(7) of the PACE Act 1984 to return to the police station. Conditions **can** be attached to the bail under this section, for example not to communicate with a co-suspect.
   Section 46(1)of the PACE Act 1984 states you may

   > arrest without a warrant any person who, having been released on bail [...] subject to a duty to attend at a police station, fails to attend at that police station at the time appointed for [him/her] to do so.

   Section 46A (1A) of the PACE Act 1984 also states any person

   > who has been released on bail under section 37[(2) or (7)] [...] may be arrested without warrant by [you] if [you have] reasonable grounds for suspecting that the person has broken any of the conditions of bail.

4. Once a person has been charged with an offence, he/she may be bailed to court under s 38(1) of the PACE Act 1984. Conditions **can** be attached to the bail under this section, for example not to communicate with a co-suspect.

Bail after charge may also be refused by the custody officer after taking into account factors such as the seriousness of the offence. In that case, the suspect will be taken before the next available court.

11.21.8 Police Caution

A **police caution** is a formal warning given by a senior police officer or by another police officer on the instructions of a senior police officer. Do not confuse this with the other forms of caution that we discussed in section 11.6. A police caution can be only given to an adult who has admitted guilt for an offence. The police caution is administered where that person could have been charged or prosecuted for the offence and is only given for minor or less serious offences. The police caution is recorded on the PNC and can be taken into consideration by the court if that person is convicted and sentenced for a further offence.

11.21.9 Conditional Caution

One of the changes following the Criminal Justice Act 2003 was to introduce a new statutory system of cautioning, to be called **conditional cautions**.

As the term suggests, conditional cautions are cautions with attached conditions for the offender. They do not replace the non-statutory police cautions described above, but can be used where they be might an appropriate and effective way of addressing the offender's behaviour, or making reparation for the effects of the offence on the victim and others. Failing to comply with the conditions attached to the caution will result in criminal proceedings and the caution being cancelled.

Conditional cautions can be given by a police constable, an investigating officer, or a person authorized by the prosecutor to offenders **over the age of eighteen** provided that five requirements are fulfilled.

1. The officer has **evidence** that the person has committed an offence.
2. The relevant prosecutor decides that:
   (a) there is **sufficient** evidence to charge the person with the offence; and
   (b) a conditional caution should be given.
3. The offender **admits** the offence to the authorized person.
4. An **explanation** of the effect of a caution and the warnings about the consequences of failure to observe the conditions has been given to the offender.
5. The offender **signs**
   • a document that sets out details of the offence;
   • an admission;
   • consent to the caution; and
   • consent to the attached conditions.

Note that s 24A of the Criminal Justice Act 2003 states that if you 'have reasonable grounds for believing that the offender has failed, without reasonable excuse, to comply with any of the conditions attached to the conditional caution, [you] may arrest [him/her] without warrant'.

11.21.10 Refused Charge

If there is insufficient evidence to charge a detainee, the custody officer will release the person without charge. If this is done without bail, the process is called 'refused charge'.

TASK 15

Find out about your force's policy in relation to:

1. Written charge and requisition by a public prosecutor.
2. Penalty Notices for Disorder.
3. Juvenile warnings and reprimands.
4. Bail from elsewhere than a police station—street bail.
5. Charge.
6. Bail from a police station.
7. Police caution.
8. Conditional cautions.
9. Refused charge.

Research what offence, if any, a person commits if s/he does not return on bail to a police station or fails to surrender to custody at a court after having been bailed.

11.22　Answers to Tasks

TASK 1

You may have considered a number of possible scenarios that might take place on Supervised Patrol. Remember that these rights extend to suspects as well as victims and witnesses. For example, you may be involved in the arrest of an individual whose grasp of spoken English is poor or non-existent, and subsequently involved in the procedures used when suspects have difficulty communicating in English. Skills for Justice indicate that for this element, evidence must come from real-life situations. Your assessor may well be able to observe directly your actions in this case but you would also need to provide evidence of your knowledge and understanding—for example, through evidence in your SOLAP cross-referenced to your learning diary or pocket notebook.

TASK 2

Your answers may include the following:

Code A—You may have seen searches of people being conducted under a number of powers. Bear in mind that s 1 of the PACE Act 1984 is one power amongst others and the remainder are listed in Annex A of the PACE Act 1984 Codes of Practice. You may therefore have seen searches taken place under s 23 of the Misuse of Drugs Act, s 47 of the Firearms Act, and s 1 of the PACE 1984 Act.

Code B—You may have seen searches of premises take place in order to arrest a person using s 17 of the PACE Act 1984. You may also have observed searches of premises at the time of an arrest under s 32 of the PACE Act 1984 and after arrest you may have witnessed searches of premises taking place under s 18 of the PACE Act 1984. You may also have seen a warrant executed and all these searches would have been carried out under the guidance of Code B.

Code C—You may have observed people interviewed at the roadside, suspected of committing road traffic offences and the interview recorded in an officer's pocket notebook. You may also have seen suspects interviewed contemporaneously perhaps as a result of their involvement in a road traffic collision.

Code D—You may have seen the identification by a witness or victim of a suspect take place in the local neighbourhood of an offence soon after it takes place. You may also have observed an identification parade in which a witness was requested to make a choice concerning the identity of a suspect in an offence.

Code E—You may have seen suspects being interviewed at the police station which were recorded on tape and the steps taken to respect their rights—for example, the offering of a service to give the suspect the opportunity to have a copy made of the tape.

Code F—You may not have seen suspects' interviews visually recorded with sound as there is no statutory requirement to record interviews this way; however your force may be doing so and you may have seen this take place.

Code G—You may have seen suspects arrested and this should have occurred as a result of a set of circumstances described in section 11.11. You will also have seen them cautioned at the time of arrest.

TASK 3

We should use 'first' or 'given' name rather than 'Christian' name. The latter is a reflection of a time when the assumption was made that all UK residents subscribed (at least notionally) to Christianity as a religion.

TASK 4

The use of 'Mind maps' as tools for learning and analysis was pioneered by Tony Buzan and others. The website <http://www.ssdd.uce.ac.uk/learner/studyskills/mindmaps.htm> has some useful advice on the application of Buzan's ideas.

TASK 5

There are many examples but you might have considered the following:

> The caution means that you have the right to silence and you do not have to say anything or give any reply to any question put to you. However, if you choose not to say anything during the investigation and then you decide to say something during the court proceedings instead, the court has the opportunity to deal with this fresh evidence as they choose. Having said all that, anything that you do say during the investigation can also be given to the court for consideration.

See Chapter 12.

TASK 6

You probably considered the following:

(i) Obtaining a first description from the alleged victim and recording this description.
(ii) Asking if the victim would consider accompanying you to other locations in order to attempt an identification.
(iii) Explaining to the victim that during that process you cannot direct the victim's attention to any individual.
(iv) Explaining to the victim that during the process he/she should look carefully at the people in the vicinty.

TASK 7

You probably considered the following:

(i) How can you secure all entrances so that the person does not escape (for example, through the back door)?
(ii) Should and can you obtain further support from your colleagues to achieve this?
(iii) With the back door secured, knock on the door or ring the bell to locate the suspect.
(iv) If there is no response consider what reasonable grounds you have for believing the suspect is on the premises—for example, can you see the suspect through the window, and have you had the entrances and exits under continuous observation since you saw the suspect enter the premises?
(v) Is this now taking the form of a pre-planned event for which should you consider calling for further assistance? For example, by requesting colleagues with appropriate equipment to order to enter the premises by force and maintaining your and others' health and safety?

TASK 8

Whatever your examples were in relation to unlawful possession of controlled drugs, criminal damage, theft, and s 5 Public Order Act offences, they should all have consisted of the following:

- a person's involvement, or suspected involvement, or attempted involvement in the commission of a criminal offence; **and**
- the reasonable grounds for believing that the person's arrest is necessary.

TASK 9

- **Locate the person** who is subject of the warrant through the use of intelligence, a stop check, the PNC, or your local force database.
- **Identify yourself**, then confirm the identity of the person, and then arrest and caution the person.
- When you arrest a person on warrant and you are not in possession of that warrant, you must show him/her the warrant **as soon as practicable** on the demand of the person arrested.
- **Endorse the back of the warrant** (also known as 'backing up').
- **Record the event** in your PNB.
- **Send** the 'backed up' warrant to the appropriate court as per your local procedures.

TASK 10

The European Arrest Warrant (EAW) is an EU-wide arrest warrant which allows for the extradition of a suspect (of a serious crime) from a participating EU country.

The important and relevant feature of the EAW is that application for a person to be 'surrendered to answer a warrant' is made from a judge in one country to a judge in another (where the suspect is). The process is therefore within the criminal justice systems of either country. Previously, 'extradition' was highly politicized and people or cases were subject to long delay, political processes, appeals, and so on. The aim of the EAW is to speed things up. It is debatable whether this is yet the case. Further details may be found at <http://www.eurowarrant.net/>.

TASK 11

You probably considered the following:

(a) When you arrest a person, you must inform him/her that he/she is under arrest (s 28(2) and Code G 2.2).
(b) An arrest is not lawful unless at the time or as soon as practicable you inform the person of the ground for the arrest (s 28(3)).
(c) You are required to inform the arrested person of the relevant circumstances of the arrest in relation to both elements of s 24 of the PACE Act 1984 (Code G 2).
(d) You are required to caution a person you arrest (Code G, para 3.4).

In the second half of the task your answer was probably along the following lines:

> I have just seen you run out of the store with a brand new DVD player under his/her arm. I heard the store alarm sound at the same time and I suspect that you have stolen the player. I am therefore arresting you on suspicion of theft of the DVD player as your arrest is necessary to allow the prompt and effective investigation of the offence, and also, because you were running away, to prevent any prosecution for the offence from being hindered by you leaving the area. You do not have to say anything. But it may harm your defence if you do not mention when questioned something which you later rely on in court. Anything you do say may be given in evidence.

TASK 12

You probably considered the following:

(i) Is there a door key in the prisoner's property that you can take in case there is no one at the premises to allow you entry?
(ii) Is the 's 18' authorization signed and is it in your possession?
(iii) At the premises follow the PACE Act 1984 Code of Practice in relation to the searching of premises:
  - identify yourself and state the purpose and grounds of the search;
  - identify and introduce anybody with you.
(iv) Limit your search to the extent that is reasonably required for the purpose of discovering evidence from an electrical store.

(v) A copy of the 'Notice of Powers and Rights' should be given to the occupier or left on the premises if they are empty.

TASK 13

'Suspect's special property' (also known as 'prisoner's special property') will be property that relates to a crime and which you suspect the detained person to be in possession of unlawfully. The property may consist of one item or many and could include property which you suspect to be stolen but could also be other property, such as an offensive weapon, a suspected illegal substance, or items of clothing which are taken for forensic examination.

Special property which you take possession of under any other circumstances will include property that is not in possession of the detained person but which may have been abandoned by him/her after committing the crime, such as a TV which has been taken from a house and then left in the front drive by the suspect(s) because it is too heavy to carry.

It will be necessary to record both categories of 'special property' on a form which may be contained in the same 'book' of forms or separately. The form in each case will require similar information to be entered:

- Sequential number (to be attached to the property for the purposes of recognition).
- Name of the person from whom it was taken.
- Address of the person from whom it was taken.
- Place where taken.
- Details of the police officer who took possession.
- Exhibit reference (if known).
- Description of article(s).
- Reasons for taking into police possession.
- Proposed method of disposal.
- Current location of the property (see 'transit store' below).

Once the appropriate special property form has been completed and a copy attached to the property for the purposes of recognition, your force will have its own procedure for the storage of property. In the majority of cases, if you do not have access to the main property store because it is closed, at night-time for example, then the property will have to be placed in a 'transit store' (a smaller secure cupboard) before it is transferred by the property officer to the main store.

TASK 14

You probably considered the following:

> I have just seen this person run out of a store with a brand new DVD player under his/her arm. I heard the store alarm sound at the same time and I suspected that this person had stolen the player. I therefore arrested this person on suspicion of theft of the DVD player and the arrest was necessary to allow the prompt and effective investigation of the offence, and because this person was running away, to prevent any prosecution for the offence from being hindered by the person leaving the area

TASK 15

Bail to a police station: Section 46A of the PACE Act 1984 states that 'where a person is bailed to return to a police station [you] may arrest without warrant a person who fails to attend at the appointed time'.

Bail to a court: Section 7(3) of the Bail Act 1976 states that 'where a person has been bailed to a court [you] may arrest without warrant if [you] have reasonable grounds to believe the person is not likely to surrender to bail, likely to break their conditions or has broken their conditions'.

12 | Intelligence and Criminal Investigation

12.1   Chapter Briefing

In this chapter we start by examining the forms of intelligence available to the police and set these in the context of the National Intelligence Model. We then look at a number of aspects of criminal investigation, including the use of interviews, the need to 'record, retain, and reveal' certain materials, and preparing and submitting case files. Finally we illustrate some of the issues surrounding giving evidence in court.

12.1.1   Aim of the Chapter

The aim of this chapter is to examine in detail the place of open and closed intelligence when used to support policing objectives, and to provide the background you need to meet the more general requirement to conduct investigations and, if required, to present evidence to a court.

This chapter will enable you to:

- understand the meaning and importance of intelligence in a policing context;
- appreciate the place of the NIM in policing;
- develop your skills in interviewing;
- identify case papers relevant to your investigation;
- understand when 'bad character' evidence may be used;
- develop your ability to give evidence in court;
- appreciate how CPIA affects the way you conduct investigations;

- develop the underpinning knowledge required for a number of NOS elements, several of the PAC headings, and entries for your Learning Diary Phase 3 and the CARs of your SOLAP.

12.1.2 Police Action Checklist

This chapter will provide you with some of the underlying knowledge and theory to meet the following requirements of the Police Action Checklist.

12.1.2.1 Investigation

- Interview—conduct a witness interview using the PEACE model.
- Interview—conduct a suspect interview using the PEACE model.

12.1.2.2 Finalize Investigations

- Prepare for court or other hearings.
- Present evidence to court or other hearings.

12.1.3 National Occupational Standards

This chapter will provide you with some of the knowledge required to demonstrate aspects of the following NOS elements:

National Occupational Standards Elements

2G2.1 Conduct priority and volume investigations.
2G4.1 Finalise investigations.
2H1.1 Plan and prepare interviews with victims and witnesses.
2H2.2 Conduct interviews with victims and witnesses.
2H2.3 Evaluate interviews with victims and witnesses.
2H2.1 Plan and prepare interviews with suspects.
2H2.2 Conduct interviews with suspects.
2H2.3 Evaluate interviews with suspects.

12.1.4 IPLDP Phases and Modules

This chapter will provide you with resources to support the following Operational Modules, and Legislation, Policy, and Guidelines of the IPLDP:

OP 2 Obtain, evaluate and submit information and intelligence to support local priorities.
OP 3 Respond to incidents, conduct and evaluate investigations.
OP 6 Prepare, conduct and evaluate interviews.
OP 9 Prepare and present case information, present evidence and finalise investigations.

The aspects of Legislation, Policy, and Guidelines are:

- Crime (LPG 1.1);
- Investigation and Interview (LPG 1.7).

12.1.5 SOLAP

The contents of this chapter are relevant to the 'Knowledge' evidence requirements of CARs 2G2, 2G4, 2H1, and 2H2.

12.1.6 Learning Diary Phases

The contents of this chapter may provide you with stimulus material for completion of your Learning Diary (Phase 3) and the following headings in particular:

- Crime;
- Police policies and procedures;
- Investigation and interview.

12.1.7   **IPLDP Learning Requirement**

This chapter is relevant to section 7.2 of the IPLDP Learning Requirement.

12.2   **Introduction**

The chapter is concerned with intelligence (both open and closed forms) and the process of criminal investigation, including interviewing and giving evidence in court. We have included intelligence and investigation in the same chapter as they are often linked in practice.

The ability to undertake the successful investigation of volume crimes is considered to be a fundamental skill of a police officer, but is perhaps also one of the more demanding parts of the role. It is perhaps a cliché to say that 'all police officers are also investigators' but it is certainly true to note that the development of investigative skills will feature extensively in your training. Past inadequacies in police investigation of crime are well documented (eg Macpherson, 1999) and recent years have seen determined efforts by the police (often centred on the work of NCPE under the leadership of Sir David Phillips) to improve the levels of knowledge and skills of all investigators.

You may encounter the IPLDP 'Crime Investigation Model' during Phases 3 and 4 of training if your force uses IPLDP nomenclature. The IPLDP Crime Investigation Model consists of seven stages: instigation, initial response, investigative assessment, suspect management, evidence assessment, charge and post charge activity, and finally court (Home Office, 2004c).

In other chapters we have already examined many aspects of the IPLDP's seven stages and we discuss most of the remaining ones in the sections that follow. However, during initial training you may also be taught a model of investigation drawn from the NCPE Practice Advice on Core Investigative Doctrine (Home Office, 2005e) which posits five groups of tasks: initial investigation, scene management, further investigation, investigative and evidential evaluation, and finally, suspect and case management. There are a number of activities within these groups of tasks, which we have interpreted below.

The links between Core Investigation Doctrine and NOS Units

Core Investigative Doctrine Activity	Example of activity	Linked NOS Units
Initial Report	Control room instruction, incident log, etc	BE1
Police Response	Risk assessment, recording the incident, etc	BE1, 2H1, 2I1, 2I2, 2C1
Scene Attendance	Provide immediate support to victims, etc	AF1, 4G4
Crime Scene Assessment	CPIA 1996, protecting the scene, minimising contamination, etc	2C1
Witnesses	Identify and question witnesses, CCTV, etc	2G2
Information/Intelligence	Force intelligence reports, CHIS, etc	2G2
Suspect?	Initial lines of enquiry, description, names, etc	2G2
Enquiries to trace offender	PNC, NDNAD	2G2
Arrest	Arrest strategy, PACE Act 1984/SOCPA 2005 powers of arrest, etc	2C3
Searches	Legal authority, seizure of items, proportionality, etc	2J1, 2J2
Custody Procedures	Escort to custody, give grounds for detention, etc	2K1, 2K2
Interview(s)	PEACE, interview strategy, etc	2H1, 2H2
Charge, Caution, Bail, NFA (No Further Action), etc	CPS charging standards, prepare case files, evaluate investigation, etc	2J1, 2G4, 2J2

(Adapted from Home Office, 2005e)

The Core Investigative Doctrine informed the development of PIP Level 1 (see section 6.9 above) which you are also expected to attain before the end of your initial training.

Whichever model of investigation you are asked to apply, remember that you will at the same time be collecting evidence towards the achievement of the NOS. Undertaking investigations provides many opportunities for doing so. For example, when you respond to an incident you will be completing your pocket notebook and be recording statements which can be used towards showing achievement of a number of Units.

An important change in recent years is an attempt to 'recast' the process of investigation as a 'seeking after the truth' rather than the 'building of a case' against a suspect from the outset. (This is not to say that case building does not feature in investigation; it is just that it should not be the focus.) What this means in practice is that you will be expected to pursue just as vigorously those reasonable lines of enquiry which point towards the innocence of the suspect(s) as you do to those that point towards guilt and to be **seen to have done so**. We have reflected this more modern approach to investigation throughout the remainder of this chapter in a number of key ways: our approach to describing intelligence, our case study description of interview and giving evidence at court, and our decision to introduce you to the complex area of 'disclosure'.

Finally, note that the following legislation is relevant to undertaking investigations:

* The Criminal Justice and Public Order Act 1994 (CJPOA)
* The Police and Criminal Evidence Act 1984 (PACE) and Codes of Practice 2004
* The Criminal Procedure and Investigations Act 1996 (CPIA)
* The Human Rights Act 1998 (HRA)
* The Regulation of Investigatory Powers Act 2000 (RIPA)
* The Serious Organised Crime and Police Act 2005 (SOCPA)

12.3 The National Intelligence Model

In this section, we will examine in detail the **National Intelligence Model (NIM)** and how it relates to the wider needs of the police for useful, accurate, and timely intelligence concerning criminal activity. An understanding of the NIM is an important requirement on student police officers, and it features either explicitly or implicitly within many parts of the IPLDP, including PIP Level 1, the IND modules and particularly the OP 2 module. The NIM was launched by NCIS in 2000, and police forces throughout England and Wales are expected to adopt the model in their day-to-day work.

12.3.1 Intelligence

The NIM has obviously some connection with the concept of 'intelligence'. Intelligence, in the investigative context, may be considered a form of information, but of a special kind—that is, it is information which has taken on **meaning**. For example, we may have information concerning an increase in the number of thefts of radios from cars in a particular area. If we link this information to a change in payment policy by a local drug dealer (who is now accepting goods in lieu of money in payment for drugs) we begin to derive intelligence from the information.

Whilst in an open society, information is freely available, most criminal intelligence is not. In fact, criminals will usually go to some lengths to prevent knowledge about what they do leaking out. Criminals will often seek to protect key questions about a crime or a criminal, such as:

* Who did it?
* Who is going to do it?
* When?
* Where?
* How?
* Why?

Finding out about criminal intentions before a crime is committed, or using covert (hidden) methods after a crime has been committed, is an aspect of **intelligence-led policing** (ILP).

Perhaps a more detailed practical example will help at this point. In one county, the police suffered from a series of crimes, where luxury cars were stolen from forecourts, taken to a criminal dealer (often called a fence) and quickly disposed of in Europe. This was a major criminal business and very lucrative, resulting in millions of pounds for the dealers. Conventional policing would usually concentrate on making it harder to steal the cars and then target the thieves. Intelligence-led policing does not rule out such preventive or investigative methods, but would bring the disciplines of **assessed intelligence**, **crime analysis**, and a **targeting 'package'** to bear on the crime series, and to focus initially on the dealers rather than the thieves. In the case above, within six weeks, intelligence identified the major dealers, an operation was mounted, and three dealers were arrested and charged. The evidence against them, including some of the tracked stolen cars, was convincing and each received a custodial sentence. In the interim, the conduit or route for stolen luxury cars was blocked, and it was a relatively simple matter to clean up the front end of theft, since the thieves had no one to whom they could go with their stolen vehicles, and they made the mistake of then trying to sell the cars cheaply to undercover police officers.

You will have noticed that a number of words in the case study have been highlighted. This is because these are key concepts in intelligence-led policing which we consider below. Before that, we need to look at the central reasoning behind intelligence-led policing and that is found in the National Intelligence Model, usually referred to as the NIM.

12.3.2 The NIM

All police forces now employ the NIM and use it widely for intelligence purposes, but also in other parts of policing, because the NIM is considered by many to be an effective **business-process model**. Note however, that the way in which the NIM has been implemented in particular forces does vary (John and Maguire, 2004) and what follows may not describe exactly what happens in your own force.

The following is a diagram of the model.

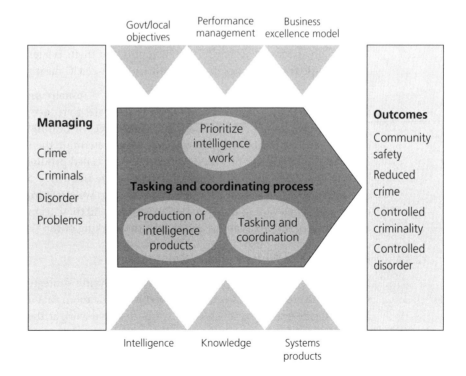

You can find a comprehensive description of the NIM at <http://www.acpo.police.uk/asp/policies/Data/nim2005.pdf>.

At first sight, the model looks daunting and appears to be very detailed, but if we examine each component in turn, it should become clearer. The model is **linear**, which means that you read it mainly from left to right, but the key part is in the centre: the **Tasking and Co-ordinating Process**. The intelligence requirements, such as identifying hot spots of crime, or information about a series of burglaries, are prioritized according to what has to be done, and in what order. (Remember that the **Basic Command Unit** (BCU), which polices a geographical area, will have priorities determined by force need, local need, and availability of resources.) Once the priority of the intelligence—**who, when, where**—has been decided, the information stream flows into a Tasking and Co-ordination Group (known as a **T&CG**) where it joins **assessments** and **profiles**. These are derived from the intelligence, and build on what is known in order to assess how complete the intelligence picture is, and provide profiles of the crime or the criminal. It is the task of the T&CG, comprising the senior management team, intelligence specialists, and crime analysts, to determine what the operational responses should be to the crime or criminality.

In the NIM model, above and below the Tasking and Coordinating Process are factors which impact on how the intelligence is used and what the T&CG will decide to do. The **government objectives** might be raising the profile of thefts from cars, dealing with anti-social behaviour, investigating domestic violence, or dealing with public order issues. These would be national objectives rather than those specific to the BCU, which is where **local objectives** come into play. The local community will have views on what their priorities are: problem families, problem estates, local disorder, and so on. These views will have been canvassed both by the police, through community liaison officers, and through local government councillors, local authority officials, and other parts of local government. All will be conveyed to the area or BCU commander (usually a superintendent) through routine meetings and consultations, and will be arranged into local objectives. This means that the Senior Management Team, the **SMT**, should be aware of their targets and priorities as part of the assessment process in the T&CG.

12.3.3 The T&CG

The intention is that the full picture is considered at the frequent T&CG meetings, of which the crime intelligence is only a part. For example, there would be some tensions if a T&CG decided to recommend an operation targeting thefts from cars when local priorities were largely focussed on alcohol-related violence. That said, operational command rests with the BCU Commander, and it may be that disrupting car thefts is a temporary but urgent priority. These are the types of issues that are dealt with at a T&CG meeting.

The long-term **performance objectives** for the BCU (usually on a yearly basis) will also be taken into account. These may be to develop strategies to reduce all crime locally, and would include reducing burglaries by a specific percentage, or dealing with anti-social behaviour, or arrest rates, or 'brought to justice' data. These determine the BCU Commander's strategic approach, to which will be added constant inputs, called **products**, which consist of what is known about the crime area, the crime type or the frequency of such crimes, the **analysis** of crimes and what **system products** (such as what we know from databases on crimes and criminals) are relevant to the operational planning. All these technical factors help to produce the profiles we looked at above and inform the working of the T&CG.

12.3.4 Links with the Wider Policing Role

It sounds highly complex (and some parts of planning strategies against crimes are indeed very difficult) but the NIM is meant to be the engine room that drives the policing machine. Police officers undertake much of their non-reactive work at the direction of the T&CG, so that policing in the area, in theory, is co-ordinated, specific, and focussed. The NIM seems to work, at least in parts, and its results are at least measurable (but see section 5.9 above on policing plans).

Underpinning this central process are assumptions of what policing is about, within the paradigm of the NIM. The **business** of policing, within this model, is shown on the left hand side of the NIM. This involves the management of crime, criminals, local disorder, enforcement community issues, and the reduction of the opportunities to commit crime. This reminds the T&CG—and any larger strategic grouping—of the purpose of the NIM; the outcomes (shown on the right of the diagram). If crime is managed adequately through the T&C process, then the argument goes that the community will be safer, crime will be reduced, criminals will have been arrested or their activities disrupted, hot spots will have been managed, and potentially dangerous offenders will have been controlled, or their capacities blunted. We refer you again to John and Maguire (2004) for a recent analysis of the NIM.

12.3.5   The NIM in Practice

To illustrate the way in which the model works, rather than simply describing its components, we will track through a crime from start to finish.

Suppose we receive reports of an 'artifice burglary'. In this context 'artifice' crime is when a criminal (or criminals) turn up unannounced on a person's doorstep and use trickery to gain admission (for example, pretending to be somebody from one of the public amenities). Whilst the householder is distracted in some way, the criminal, or an associate, steals something of value, usually cash or goods which can be 'fenced' rapidly for cash. The usual victims are elderly people living alone (in fact, statistically, **very** elderly), and a clever, plausible artifice burglar could easily commit ten offences in the same locality in a day. Not all artifice crimes are reported, either because the victim is unaware at first that the burglary has occurred (it might be some days before an object is noted as missing), or because the victim is reluctant to be involved with the police. Artifice burglars usually commit **series offences** (or perhaps, more accurately, 'spree offences') that is, the crimes usually take place one after another. This is often because the net haul from each residence entered is relatively small.

The reports of artifice burglary enter the T&CG process as so-called **knowledge products**, and a key early requirement will be for analysts to give an **assessment** of the criminal's **modus operandi** (often abbreviated to MO): where the victims have been targeted, the methods and tricks used to gain entry, types of theft, and so on. This builds an initial picture. The T&CG may then task police staff responsible for gathering intelligence to find out whether there is access to this type of criminal (perhaps through a regular fence), and whether there is knowledge locally of such individuals. As distinct from usual burglary (where the burglar's home and the crime scenes are usually just a few kilometres apart), artifice burglars do not tend to 'work their own patch', perhaps because they run the risk of being recognized and they may already have police records for deception or theft.

The T&CG will assign a **priority** to the investigation of the artifice burglary and will commission further work, which will include checking the force's criminal databases, matching any other likely series offences elsewhere in the force area, or in neighbouring forces. Analysts may note, for example, that the offences have all taken place within half a mile of a railway station, in which case the force may approach British Transport Police for help and any CCTV footage may be scrutinized.

Suppose the frequency of artifice burglaries increases, and an old person becomes ill by the shock of what happened (quite a common occurrence). This may increase the perceived need to catch the perpetrators. Therefore, at the next T&CG meeting, the priority level of the case will be raised and operational plans will be developed to attempt to further tackle the problem. Possibly at the back of the BCU Commander's mind will be the government's **objectives**, the feelings about the nature of the crime locally, media pressures, and the chances of catching whoever is involved.

Now imagine that a CHIS (a police informant, normally paid for information) gives useful information to his/her handler and a report is submitted. It is assessed by the research and development unit and compared with other intelligence. We now have a name, a preferred location, and a clear idea of the MO. An operation is mounted, two people are arrested, and a case is prepared. The final **outcome** could well be a prison sentence but equally, a caution, a fine, seizure of assets, or community service. Other outcomes might include displacing the activity of artifice burglars elsewhere, a **crime reduction** (prevention) strategy, contact between the police and the local community for safety awareness, and probably some useful media coverage.

The NIM process has led to an assessment of the nature of the crime, to tasking the intelligence-gathering parts of the force and giving the crime a priority level in the midst of competing claims for attention. The newly-acquired intelligence was assessed and used to develop a package of operational measures through the T&CG, and the resulting police action was both disruptive of the crime type and possibly also contributed to community reassurance.

In a force which follows NIM principles, and practically all forces do, this would be a simple example of the **business process model of policing**, but the same principles will operate whether it is people vandalizing cars or a serious crime enquiry, such as the systematic robbing of cash machines (ATMs).

TASK 1

Now it is your turn; using the NIM, describe what would happen if the BCU Commander wanted to deal with:

- A crime hot spot involving alcohol-fuelled violence?
- A spate of break-ins into vehicles?
- A series of attacks on students to steal credit cards?

What factors do you think would influence the prioritizing of the crimes? What would you expect the crime analysts to provide? How would you task the collection of intelligence? What operational considerations would there be? How would you describe a good outcome?

12.3.6   Components of Intelligence

We turn now to consider some of the components of intelligence: sources, source-handling, surveillance, research and development, the intelligence 'target package', and some of the laws and rules around what you can and cannot do with intelligence. Some of the material may not appear immediately relevant to the work of a student police officer but you will discover its importance as you move through your training, and particularly so when you are engaged on Supervised Patrol and undertaking the IPLDP OP 2 module.

Before reading the remainder of section 12.3, you may wish to look again at section 11.9 above which outlines some of the legal considerations when employing intelligence.

12.3.6.1   Sources

The police usually call an informant or source a **CHIS**, which stands for Covert Human Intelligence Source. Criminals use many more descriptions (mostly unflattering) such as 'grass', 'snout', and 'nark'. Many police intelligence sources are themselves criminals, and we need to look closely at what constitutes a source. Members of the public who volunteer information about criminals or crimes are not generally defined as sources. However, if they have access to hidden criminal intentions or plans, such people are then regarded as sources. As we noted at the beginning of this discussion about intelligence, criminals will go to some lengths to hide what they are doing or planning, and normally the only people with real access to this process are fellow criminals. The exception to this is the **undercover police officer**, see section 12.3.10 of this chapter.

The law is clear about what constitutes a source. Under s 26(8) of the **Regulation of Investigatory Powers Act 2000** (known to the police as **RIPA**), a person is a source if he/she:

establishes or maintains a personal or other relationship with a person for the covert purpose of facilitating the doing of anything falling within:

- covertly uses such a relationship to obtain information or to provide access to any information to another person, or

- covertly discloses information obtained by the use of such a relationship, or as the consequence of the existence of such a relationship.

This probably needs some explanation. In essence it means that a CHIS is someone who cultivates someone else to obtain information, or who provides access to information, or who discloses information. Notice that the words criminal or unlawful are not used here. This is because the information need not necessarily be criminal, at least to start with. It is the **covert** part which is important. (Covert refers to a relationship with the police as well as actually or potentially with a criminal.) Thus, people like solicitors or bank officials who pass details of suspicious activity to the police are not sources because they are working in an open relationship with the police. But what does covert actually mean? In general terms it usually means hidden, but the RIPA has an exact legal definition (s 26(9)(b)–(c)):

- A purpose is covert in starting or sustaining a relationship if it is conducted in a manner which is calculated to ensure that only one of the parties to the relationship is unaware of the purpose; and
- A relationship is used covertly, and information obtained is used or disclosed in a manner that is calculated to ensure that one of the parties to the relationship is unaware of the use or disclosure in question.

What this means in straightforward terms is that someone working as a CHIS for the police (or any other law-enforcement agency), is aware of the relationship with the police. But, the person being cultivated or from whom information is obtained because of that relationship, does not know that the CHIS is informing the police. This can be confusing, as we are in the realms of 'he knows that she knows that he knows'.

As an alternative, consider this as a working (but strictly speaking, 'non-legal') definition: a CHIS is tasked by the police to cultivate or sustain a relationship with someone. That someone does not know about the police involvement.

Any use or conduct of a CHIS by the police will always require **authorization** granted by a senior police officer (usually a detective superintendent or higher) who is the **force authorizing officer**, also answerable to a **surveillance commissioner** within whose national remit this falls. In other words, if you set up a covert relationship with a source, tasking that source to obtain information from someone who does not know about the police involvement, you will need sanction from the force authorizing officer. The authorization (or 'authority') will normally last twelve months, but, as we shall see below, the relationship between the source and the police will be carefully monitored.

12.3.6.2 Source-handling

Not just anyone can handle a CHIS. Most forces would use a qualified and experienced detective constable **source-handler**, probably paired with another (perhaps less experienced) handler. The good practice of having two handlers is so that CHISs, who can be manipulative and who can bring agendas of their own to relationships with the police, have less chance of exerting control over their handlers. There are many examples of handlers being 'turned', exploited, or dominated by a clever, plausible source, especially when the relationship is laxly or ineptly overseen by the handler's supervisor (usually a detective sergeant). Having a pair of handlers makes it more difficult for a CHIS to dominate or take control of the relationship. Also, two can share the responsibility of handling, welfare issues, and recording of meetings with a CHIS. Sometimes, especially when meetings or intelligence taskings are urgent, there have to be 'singleton' meets between one handler and a source, but most forces recommend that this should never be routine.

Handlers are usually detectives who have undergone an intensive training programme lasting several weeks in which the participants learn (through scenarios and role play), how to:

- handle devious, dishonest, manipulative, and fantasizing sources;
- how to task informants;
- how to meet securely; and
- how to keep control.

TASK 2

What qualities do you think would make a good source-handler? Discuss this with your colleagues and produce a list of attributes, skills, and competences necessary to handle a covert source with access to criminal information.

12.3.6.3 Restrictions on the use of sources

We have already noted that the RIPA governs the definitions of a source and what is meant by covert, but the Act also determines the legal and practical parameters for handling a CHIS. We do not need to go into all the detail of the Act here, but you should know that there are special safeguards for vulnerable or young people, and a regular audit of authorizations by a surveillance commissioner, appointed nationally under a chief surveillance commissioner. Attention is drawn throughout the Act to **proportionality** and the articles in the Human Rights Act 1998 legislation, particularly the right to a private life. The RIPA provides the necessary framework for the ethical and legal use of CHISs by properly trained source-handlers who are aware of their powers (but will not abuse them), as well as ensuring that the risk of exploiting a source in a criminal network, for example, is proportionate to the expected gain. To make this a little more concrete, you would not use a source with excellent access to the upper echelons of criminality in order to find out who the local graffitists are. You would not use a CHIS when the information required can be gained in other ways or put a CHIS into physical danger without carefully assessing the risk.

So far we have looked at the **NIM**, the **RIPA, sources**, and **source-handlers**, but what happens to the intelligence that a CHIS acquires and passes to his/her handler?

12.3.7 Intelligence 'Packages'

Handlers submit reports detailing the intelligence that they have obtained from their CHIS. They write a separate note detailing the meeting itself, which goes to their supervisor. The intelligence is passed, in its raw state, to the **Research and Development (R&D)** unit where the intelligence is assessed against what is already known, compared with the bigger picture and sanitized (see section 12.3.7.1 below).

Intelligence packages (the term comes from the idea of bundling different items together) may then be constructed. These can be highly accurate pictures of how particular crimes are mounted in a given locality, by whom, with what success, how the acquisitions from the crime are fenced, how money is laundered and by whom, what the likelihood is of repeat victimization, and intelligence on how the crime series is likely to develop. That perhaps would be an ideal package; many lack such detail and are much more likely to combine hard intelligence with some speculative hypothesis setting and testing. Any best guestimates should be clearly designated as such: as non-specific and unevidenced supposition.

The intelligence package is fundamental to police operational planning at the T&CG (and above) level. Note also that intelligence packages are not only put together as a response to crime but may also be used to support other policing objectives. An example might be in policing operations for public order. It could be problematic to deploy just twenty police officers to supervise demonstrations in excess of 8,000—within which might be hostile and antagonistic groups. Conversely, providing 600 public-order equipped police officers to control a crowd of fifteen might not only be wasteful but also be viewed as oppressive. A good intelligence package would assist the police in estimating both the likely size of the demonstration and the possibility of disorder arising. The accuracy of the intelligence-led prediction is what matters and this is what the intelligence package aspires to do: to provide the right level of detailed, meaningful information as will make the use of resources and tactics proportional, economic, and effective in any police operation that may follow.

12.3.7.1   Sanitizing intelligence

Sanitizing removes any features of the intelligence that could identify the source, or the circumstances when the intelligence was obtained. For example, no R&D staff would allow a report to go into circulation which began:

> At five thirty p.m., on Tuesday 15 August, 'Fat Jimmy' saw the well-known criminal Sam 'Toucan' Befalonte in the *Three Feathers* pub in Harpenden, when he told Jimmy the following . . . .

Such obvious indicators could quickly identify the source, compromise his/her access, and, at worst, may lead to violence against the source. Sanitizing the report does not dilute the intelligence but offers some security to those engaged in its acquisition.

12.3.7.2   Intelligence reports

Intelligence is usually reported, on forms called '**5x5x5**'. (The numbers refer to 'qualities' of the intelligence, measured in three categories, using an ordinal scale of 1 to 5. For example, in terms of a CHIS they refer to the reliability of the CHIS, the importance of the intelligence, and the level of security to be implemented.) These forms are a major part of the intelligence inflow into R&D. It is the task of R&D to ensure that the reports of value are circulated to those who need to know, which in the majority of cases will be the T&CG. Reports dealing with a common theme, collated from a number of sources can be circulated as a single composite intelligence item (further protecting each source). Occasionally, reports from 'quality' sources with access to particularly important intelligence will go higher in the organization, which makes the sanitizing process all the more important. The more people who know about a piece of intelligence, the more likely it is that there will be a leak, and consequently a danger to the CHIS who originally reported it. There is a 'need to know' principle common to many policing activities, and this applies to protecting sources because the police want the source to continue his/her covert relationship with the target. R&D staff may return to the handler(s) with requests for further work, directions to pursue, and more targets; a productive source will be heavily tasked.

At some point on the distribution chain (this varies from force to force), analysts will examine the intelligence and match it with what is known. It will be another piece in the jigsaw. In some forces, this happens with the raw intelligence, in others with the sanitized version. Either way, the assessed intelligence helps to fill out the picture which the analysts are trying to create. As we noted above, the R&D unit in turn will try to gather enough intelligence to construct a 'targeting package' for the T&CG to consider.

Much will depend at what level the CHIS is operating. In the glossary in Chapter 1, we described Level 1, Level 2, and Level 3 crime and criminals:

Level 1	Local BCU-based crime, 'volume' crime.
Level 2	Across the force, often into neighbouring forces, often serious and organized.
Level 3	National or international crime, always serious and organized.

An illustrative example of the different levels can be found in drugs crime. Level 3 will be importation and distribution, level 2 will be major 'dealing' and level 1 will be local dealing and/or use of the drug.

The NIM uses these categories of offender to indicate the relative scale of the criminality. At level 3, the criminality is national or international and requires national and international law enforcement agencies to combat it. Level 2 will cross force or regional boundaries and is usually of a serious and/or organized nature. Our artifice burglar example, which we looked at above, is level 2 because the criminal crosses internal force boundaries and may stray into another force's territory. Criminals, of course, do not recognize these boundaries; however, there is at least some evidence that some criminals deliberately exploit the differences between forces to avoid being caught by either. Level 1 is local, operating at BCU level or on a neighbourhood basis.

The point about the classification is about resources. A single BCU does not have the resources to cope with, say, a group of criminal associates mounting robberies from ATMs (cash machines) across the force area. In such instances, there is a need for a force-level response, which is usually co-ordinated and directed centrally. It is important to note that the NIM principles continue to apply. Most forces will have a **tactical level T&CG** which will deal with serious level 2 crime. Level 3 crime is dealt with by national agencies such as the Serious Organised Crime Agency (SOCA), in co-operation with its international counterparts. Whether on a national, regional, or local scale, the use of assessed intelligence to inform operational decision-making works on the same principles.

We might note, in passing, that the national intelligence agencies link closely with the police at Level 3. HM Revenue and Customs, for example, has an investigation branch (now in the Serious Organised Crime Agency, at least in part) which uses intelligence-led principles to track illegal importations (of any kind: drugs, people, contraband), whilst the Security Service (MI5) uses intelligence to counter threats to national (internal) security. It is interesting to note, in the Home Office Codes of Practice to the RIPA, that many government agencies may use CHISs to gain intelligence. Agencies and departments include the Inland Revenue, the Ministry of Defence, the Departments of Health, Trade and Industry, Work and Pensions, the Environment Agency, the Armed Forces, and the Food Standards Agency. It is not just the police who are governed by the RIPA; any agency needs to observe its requirements and have a responsible authorizing officer to use a CHIS.

TASK 3

We noted above that a police CHIS is often a criminal because it is usually through criminals that access can be gained to other criminals. What do you think the problems might be for a police force when recruiting and using an active criminal as a CHIS? (In some other countries, the use of CHISs is unlawful.) Aside from the ethical and moral considerations, what practical difficulties might there be? How might they be met and overcome?

12.3.8   Problems when Using Sources

In Task 3, you might have referred to the difficulty of using an active criminal as a source. If a CHIS takes part in an organized crime, or is involved in criminal planning, these are, of course, offences for which the CHIS could be charged and brought before a court. A further difficulty is found in whether, to obtain the intelligence they need, the police have to allow a crime to go ahead and let their source take part. Evidently, any ban on using an active criminal as a source would render the whole exercise pointless. Without the intelligence which the source provides, the police would not be able to target the crime.

The practical solution to this is in designating the CHIS as a **participating informant**. This does not mean that the source will not be charged if he/she is involved in a crime, but that **a plea of mitigation** may be made to the judge at any criminal trial. This is not done in open court because of the risk to the source, so a judge will have a private discussion with the police and the Crown Prosecution Service to decide if the source's evidence is admissible and the judge alone will decide whether or not to pass a more lenient sentence on the CHIS (if found guilty) in view of the source's co-operation with the police. This is a problematic judicial area, and some defence lawyers argue that it prevents due process for their clients. The police and the Crown Prosecution Service usually adopt what they see as a pragmatic approach: if there is a risk to the source, the chances are that the prosecution will be withdrawn and charges dropped. The principle here is that it is better not to proceed with a prosecution and retain a source who can be used again rather than expend a valuable source of criminal intelligence for one prosecution. No one can pretend that these are easy judgements, but the decision is the judge's alone. If the judge decides not to allow the evidence of a participating informant unless he/she is identified in open court, then the CPS will drop the case. Behind all this is the need to protect the source: consider the point of view of the source; would you stand up in court and give evidence of your involvement in a crime and accept a possibly long sentence simply because you had a relationship with the police and hoped for a light sentence?

Confidentiality protects the source; sources are meant to be informed of this at the outset of their relationship with their handlers. They are also told that there is no automatic right to be exempt from criminal charges if they engage in crimes whilst acting as informants. **Participating** brings its own difficulties which the source needs to be aware of. As the police put it, there is no 'get out of jail free' card to be waved in court.

12.3.9 Motivation of Informants

This is an appropriate stage of section 12.3 to consider why criminals decide at the outset to become covert human intelligence sources. We need to look at motivation, and, to do so, we need to think about the psychology involved.

TASK 4

Before we go on, discuss what you think makes someone decide to be a source for the police. Why would you betray your criminal colleagues (who may be friends of long-standing or family members) and tell the police what was being planned? How do you keep it up, week after week, month after month? How do you manage the clandestine meetings with your handler without someone spotting you? How do you keep the secret of your relationship over what could be years?

It should be noted at the outset that this is a very under-researched area and hence what follows should be treated with some caution. With this caveat we may explore some possible reasons for becoming a CHIS. The following table, constructed from data to be found in Billingsley et al (2001), is a typical set of research findings:

Stated reason	Proportion of sample (%)
Financial	26.7
Dislikes that crime	14.2
Reduced sentence	13.3
Revenge	12.5
Right side of the law	7.5
Looking for a favour	7.5
Friendly with officer	6.7
Police pressure	3.3
Take out competition	2.5
Part of a deal	1.7
The challenge	1.7
Gratitude	1.7
Enjoyment	0.8

Hence many sources, when asked why they decided to be a CHIS, will suggest that they do it for the money. Informants are paid for their intelligence; the better the intelligence, the more they will be paid. But these are not huge sums; the Treasury and public service accountability ensure that. In fact, a CHIS might make more money from the very criminal enterprise he/she is reporting on. We must therefore look a little deeper into what might motivate the source and be sceptical of the possibly glib 'cover' explanation that there is a financial motive.

Motivation is psychologically complex and will always have a bearing on the value of the intelligence gained and any selectivity on the part of the CHIS in providing intelligence. There have been occasions when an experienced and 'lifestyle' criminal has informed on other criminals threatening his/her dominance, in order to leave the field clear for his/her own criminal activities. So too, a level 2 criminal is often not averse to informing on level 1 activity to reduce pressure and keep the police away from his/her criminal enterprises. **Revenge** is often cited in the research as a strong motive, especially when the informant has been 'bested' by another criminal. **Envy** of a successful criminal's lifestyle, **anger** at being the one caught for a previous crime, **resentment** that a major criminal player always seems to get away with it, and **jealousy** at not having been allowed to join in another's crime can all be cited as reasons for a decision to inform.

It often seems that there are as many motivations as there are sources, and the handler needs to determine what the potential source's primary motive or motives might be (even before recruitment takes place). We can occasionally overlook the fact that sources are human: they want affection, praise, contact, reward, encouragement, and a sense of being valued. Handlers can provide all these things for a source, but there is a danger that a source might become too emotionally dependent upon a handler and be unable to function adequately (in other aspects of life) without the handler's help. Doctors, psychiatrists, and counsellors also recognize this dependency from their patients and clients, but their professionalism means that they attempt to keep a distance and remain objective. Handlers have to do the same but under more difficult clandestine circumstances.

The professionally detached, objective, and neutral source-handler nonetheless still feels the pressure of dealing with sources in fragile emotional states. Other sources may have motivations of greed, vanity, a distaste for the crimes which the target criminal is engaged in (people trafficking, for example), or disgust at a criminal's sexual perversions. There is a contemporary case in which the motivation of the source was to inform on her brother, a prominent local criminal, because she (a mother with two young children) suspected that he was an active paedophile and had seen him downloading child pornography on his computer.

We have established that there are complex reasons why criminals become sources and that handlers have to analyse carefully what they are told by the source to determine the real motivation. This is not always easy to do, especially if sources are effective dissemblers (many are, or they would not obtain good intelligence). A handler needs to assess whether the strength of the emotion, which may have been a primary motivation at the outset, is enough to sustain the source throughout the long period of gathering intelligence.

12.3.10 Undercover Officers and 'Test Purchase' Operations

Before we leave covert human intelligence sources and look at other forms of intelligence gathering, we need briefly to look at the role of undercover police officers and the kinds of intelligence operations with which they are involved.

We discussed earlier the type of people who become a CHIS and concluded that most were active criminals or were involved in some way with criminality. Police officers who go undercover are CHISs but are not normally criminal, of course. A highly trained police officer can work to penetrate a group of criminals, for example, posing as a drugs importer or a supplier of documentation (such as passports). The same legal principles surround this use of a police officer as surround other CHISs. The risk must be proportionate to the outcome—in other words, you would only use an undercover officer for very serious crimes, such as high profile robberies, conspiracy to murder, importing considerable quantities of class A drugs, and so on. The risk assessment must be very detailed and every possible permutation of danger, risk or accident carefully anticipated.

All operations using an undercover officer require authorization, sometimes from ACPO ranks if the deployment is dangerous or difficult. Officers cannot sustain this undercover role for long; they need to be re-integrated into the police force before they are compromised, exhausted by the continuous strain, or, as the police describe it, 'turned or burned'. This requires fastidious timing by the handler and supervisors, since the sustainability of the operation is short.

A specialist undercover role, into which police officers can slide in and out, are **test purchase** operations. This is when a police officer poses as a potential buyer of some illegally acquired item such as drugs, contraband, or luxury goods. The problem for many criminals is converting goods or items they have illegally acquired into the most CRAVED item of all—cash (see section 5.13 for an explanation of CRAVED). They need to be able to sell on whatever they have to someone else. Police officers can pose as purchasers, given specialist training. The whole transaction is monitored carefully (there are surveillance teams deployed and uniformed officers on hand) and when the moment is right, the dealer or seller is arrested and charged. The reason that police officers are used extensively on such 'sting' operations is that they only need to appear once in one location. The advantage from the policing point of view is that the criminal is caught in flagrante. This may result in a guilty plea at court and saves time, both for the police and the criminal justice system.

> **TASK 5**
>
> What do you think are the qualities and competences of a good undercover officer? What might be the problems, both logistical and operational? What would you think about when planning a test purchase operation?

12.3.11 Other Forms of Intelligence-Gathering

Thus far, we have concentrated on covert human intelligence sources to gather the material needed to meet at least one of the requirements of the NIM. We now look briefly at other forms of intelligence-gathering and examine how useful or limited they are in assisting policing operations. We shall look at **surveillance**: **human**, **technical**, **directed**, and **intrusive**. A word of caution: whilst it is appropriate to describe generally what is involved in these intelligence-gathering techniques, the detailed nature of such operations will not be discussed, and for obvious reasons. Details will be given to you as a student police officer as and when appropriate.

12.3.11.1 Human surveillance

Human surveillance, in its essence, is one person covertly following another. Familiar as a concept from countless films and television dramas, it is the scene when the hero, ill-disguised and looking shifty, follows about six paces behind the villain, who is often so stupid that he does not realize when the hero is breathing down his neck. Real life is not like that, particularly in the generally mundane world of crime in the UK. Human surveillance is complex, and the teams who undertake it are highly trained.

What we should establish early on, then, in any surveillance operation, is the appropriate methodology and how it can blend with the background. A great deal of operational planning goes into surveillance operations, in which the awareness of the target, or quarry, is a key factor. Some criminals use sophisticated 'dry-cleaning' techniques to shake off surveillance, though by doing so, of course, they demonstrate that they probably have something to hide. Shaking off surveillance is not that easy, but compromises sometimes happen and the operation has to be aborted.

Another factor taken into account during the extensive planning is the location in which surveillance will take place. A tightly-knit rural community is an example of a difficult location for a surveillance team. Strangers and unknown cars 'show out' (may be very noticeable) in a small village (and even in a quiet residential street), and it is not unknown for villagers to ring the uniformed police who arrive to arrest the surveillance team. Careful briefing and professional deployment should ensure that this does not happen, but blending into a landscape is not easy. A housing estate is another example of a location where surveillance can be compromised; it may be that car ownership in deprived areas is not high, so new-looking cars may stand out, as can pairs of people sitting, apparently idly, in the front seats of a vehicle. Different, but equally complex problems present themselves in busy high streets, where the presence of many pedestrians means that keeping the target in sight is fraught with difficulty, especially when there are many shop entrances offering temporary concealment.

12.3.11.2 CCTV

The simplest and most obvious form of surveillance is the ubiquitous CCTV camera, over-looking public and private premises, inside shops, malls, walkways, in town centres, banks, building societies, railway stations, pedestrian precincts, airports and yes, even in police stations. CCTV cameras have become so commonplace that we are hardly aware that they are there. Yet, on an average shopping trip to a town, you might expect to be photographed about fifty-seven times in an hour. The benefit of CCTV is that it gives twenty-four-hour coverage of a location and its images are retrievable within a time period; the disadvantage is that CCTV is itself fixed—cameras cannot follow a target or detach themselves from a wall to see what is going on elsewhere. So we need to make a distinction between the value of fixed surveillance and mobile surveillance, as well as between 'open' surveillance and covert surveillance. The CCTV camera is usually easy to spot, so an aware criminal will note where the cameras are and by-pass them or take care to wear something which disguises his/her features. This will be familiar to you from the countless grainy videos of bank robbers or hold-ups in post offices, in TV programmes such as *Crimewatch*.

Because the CCTV cameras are on fixed sites and no disguise of them is attempted, they are principally operated by local authorities or store security officers. The police can have access to film from these cameras (as in the Jamie Bulger case, when two young children enticed away and murdered a young child) and CCTV images have an important role to play in preventing crime and in providing evidence in any criminal proceedings. It is unusual for the police themselves to operate fixed cameras (except speed cameras).

12.3.11.3 Covert surveillance

The Regulation of Investigatory Powers Act 2000 (RIPA) governs the use of concealed cameras and of eavesdropping devices. The definition of covert is very similar to that which we encountered with CHIS, but this time it refers only to surveillance:

> If, and only if, it is carried out in a manner that is calculated to ensure that the persons who are subject to surveillance are unaware that it is or may be taking place (s 26(9), RIPA 2000);

and surveillance is later defined (in s 48(2)) as including:

- monitoring, observing, listening to persons, their movements, their conversations or their other activities or communications;
- recording anything monitored, observed or listened to in the course of surveillance; and
- surveillance by or with the assistance of a surveillance device.

The Act divides surveillance into two types: directed or intrusive. The distinctions are important because of the different levels of authorization which are needed for such actions to be lawful. (Look back at section 11.9 for a summary of what follows.)

Directed surveillance is essentially the covert targeting of an individual with the intention of obtaining private information. There are principles about liberty and freedom here to which the police are expected to subscribe, especially if, in the process of undertaking the surveillance, there is an infringement of the 'right to privacy and family life' (Sch 1, art 8 of the Human Rights Act 1998, deriving from the European Convention on Human Rights, see section 11.3 above). The RIPA provisions are intended to ensure that what the police are doing is proportionate and justified. Student police officers should perhaps remember the JAPAN principles in this context: justification, authorization, proportionality, auditable, and necessary. An example of directed surveillance might be the installation of a concealed camera in a tree opposite a criminal's residence; the camera would act as a 'trigger' to alert surveillance teams that the target was moving. This is not intrusive and could be authorized by a superintendent.

Intrusive surveillance entails some sort of interference with property or possessions, such as residences or vehicles. Part 3 of the Police Act 1997 gives chief constables the power to authorize intrusive surveillance operations that require 'entry on or interference with property or wireless telegraphy', but any intrusive surveillance operation usually involves consideration of both Acts—the RIPA 2000 and the Police Act 1997. An example of intrusive surveillance would be a covert entry into a property to install a listening device on a telephone landline. Since there is a danger that the device will record innocent conversations on the telephone by people other than the target, the authorization has to be at a higher level (chief constable) and overseen more systematically by a Surveillance Commissioner.

Authorization for directed surveillance can be given by a police officer not below the rank of superintendent, in writing, and valid for three months. Authorization for intrusive surveillance is, as we have noted, to be given in writing by the chief constable, will be valid for three months, and must be approved by a Surveillance Commissioner. There are different rules and obligations in cases of urgency, which need not be dealt with here. Authorities are in any case scrutinized (usually monthly in the case of intrusive surveillance) by a Surveillance Commissioner who can quash an authorized operation and demand the destruction of any intelligence obtained, if the Commissioner is not satisfied that the grounds were reasonable and the justification proportionate.

Why so complex and so carefully overseen? The purpose behind all of this is to ensure that the police (and other agencies) operate in a system which is open to both scrutiny and monitoring, in compliance with the Human Rights Act. Ultimately, they are safeguards against any abuse of the powers granted to law-enforcement agencies by the citizens whom they protect.

The intelligence which is gained has to be of sufficient quality to justify the risks taken in its collection. Making this judgement is not always straightforward because there is an element of speculation in any attempt to gather intelligence. There have been examples of criminals only talking about their plans in the open air, so they can be seen but not heard. Other instances include conversations with loud background noise.

Properly safeguarded, meticulously planned, using officers with highly developed professional skills in effective and imaginative operations, covertly gained intelligence can be an important dimension of policing. Many of the serious and organized crime investigations which result in a successful prosecution have their origins in good intelligence. Very few investigations into level 2 crime (and many investigations into level 1 crime) would be effective without intelligence, and certainly much police time would be ill-directed and fruitless. Intelligence is not the only tool available, and you will have seen in other sections the parts played by forensic investigation and others. Remember that assessed and prioritized covert intelligence is only one component in the NIM; so it is with policing.

12.4 Open Sources of Intelligence

We should not think that the only sources of information or intelligence about crimes or criminality are covert or clandestine. There are 'open' (or 'overt') sources.

TASK 6

Can you think of some open sources of intelligence?

The first and most obvious source of 'open' intelligence about crime and criminality is likely to come from the **general public**. People notice all kinds of things and should be encouraged to report to the police if what they see is odd, suspicious, or out of character.

There is much to be gleaned about the lifestyles of criminals from simple observation or from engaging members of the public in conversation. Criminals live in the community, in houses or flats; they have to go shopping, drive, wear clothes, socialize, enjoy their leisure; they may have families, hobbies, or interests which may have nothing to do with crime. Profiles can be built up of criminals' daily habits: where they buy newspapers, where they go for a drink, which supermarket they shop in, what cars they drive and where they buy them, where they buy clothes, which gym they use, where they go for holidays (and with which travel agent), and so on. Think of neighbours, garages, newsagents, dog walkers, joggers, parking attendants, crossing attendants, fitness instructors, and the like. Remember the RIPA 2000, though; you must not treat such people as sources or informants.

Other sources of information may be obtained from **police interviews** (either with the criminal or with others who know the criminal) and, whilst this is covert in a conventional sense, there is advantage in letting colleagues know that you are interested in a particular individual and would welcome any useful information which they might pick up in the course of such interviews. The same applies of course to police patrols, which should spend some part of their duty deployment on open observation and interaction with the public (even though they will tell you that the whole shift is spent responding to 999 calls).

Do not ignore information which may be obtained from **prisons**. Although the gathering of intelligence in prisons is subject to strict protocols and risk assessments, there is likely to be much miscellaneous and open information about criminal targets of interest which comes from prison visits, interviews, preparations for release, and so on.

You might note the details in your local **newspapers** as well. Most provincial newspapers are served by a small army of volunteers who send in reports every week on the events in their localities, and, whilst there is much that is not relevant, it is sometimes possible to pick up open references to criminal targets.

There are some other sources too which, whilst not 'open' in the sense of being available to anyone to tap into, nonetheless may provide you with useful information about a criminal target. These sources include **other police forces**. A word of caution here. You are probably aware of the Bichard report published in 2004.

What Sir Michael Bichard concluded was that police forces should routinely communicate information which, though itself trivial or incomplete, may have a bearing on the activities of someone in another police force area (Bichard, 2004). As we have noted elsewhere, the infrastructure for such information exchange is not yet in place. Nonetheless, you might give thought to routine enquiries with other forces perhaps including those where your target has worked, or was born, or was married or where his or her holidays are taken.

Lastly, there is information which is obtained under the provisions of the **Proceeds of Crime Act 2002**. Part of this Act, designed to seize illegally-gained money and assets from criminals, places an obligation on occupational groups such as bank managers and solicitors to report the handling of sums of money for which there is little or no justification. A bank manager, noting the sudden deposit of large sums in cash, is meant to report this fact to the authorities. There could be an innocent explanation such as a win at the races (but proof may be required), or it could be the profits from a drugs deal. The information you obtain from such officials can be privileged, but that does not mean that it cannot be used to build up a picture of, or even a circumstantial case around, your criminal target.

We should like to make a couple of important points: there is no justification for gathering information about someone unless there is a criminal justice reason for doing so. You cannot just decide that, because your neighbour is noisy, you want to devote time to gathering information about her. That would not be an appropriate (or proportionate) use of your time, and could well be construed as abuse of your 'office of constable' (technically misfeasance, see section 5.4 above). In other words, there has to be a reason which will stand up to scrutiny for gathering information about someone. Even if the target is demonstrably criminal, you still have to remember proportionality and the JAPAN principles. If you do not, and, incidentally, you do not discuss what you are doing with your sergeant or inspector, you could be open to charges of harassment.

12.5 Interviewing

In this section, we will examine in detail what is involved in interviewing people and the recommended methods for conducting interviews. Under the IPLDP you will undertake extensive study and practice of interviewing procedures and techniques, and the codes and legislation that surround them. In your Learning Diary (Phase 3) under the heading 'Investigation and interview' you may find opportunity to record some of your reactions to this part of Chapter 12.

Many laws regulate the process of police interviews, in order to protect the person being interviewed. Unquestionably, there are many instances in the past of the police abusing their powers to question suspects (some of the motivation for which we saw in the so-called 'noble cause corruption' discussed in section 5.4). This could range from oppressive behaviour used to obtain confessions under duress, to a lack of safety provisions when interviewing someone who was vulnerable, perhaps because of a disability or learning difficulty. Certainly laws such as the Police and Criminal Evidence Act 1984 have gone some way to reassure the public, lawyers, academic commentators, and the police themselves that interviewing is now more tightly controlled, more ethical, and often more effective. However, the test is always **whether the evidence obtained from interviewing will stand up to scrutiny in court,** and that is what should perhaps always be at the forefront of your mind when you conduct an interview.

The modern approach to police interviewing in the UK is to see it as a process of establishing the truth. This sounds obvious but it does in fact represent a marked change in emphasis from the past. It is not a case simply of 'points to prove' but is much more akin to the 'inquisitorial approach' to justice that we discussed in section 5.8.

Remember too that interviewing is not just about suspects; it involves interviewing witnesses and victims of crime as well. Different approaches can be adopted, depending on the nature of the interview being conducted.

> **TASK 7**
>
> Can you think of one very clear difference between interviewing suspects and witnesses?

You might have said that witnesses and victims (unless you believe they have committed offences) are not interviewed under caution, but that suspects are.

There is much law involved in police interviewing and in this section we cover the basics, sufficient for the student police officer. In addition, it is recommended that you familiarize yourself with the following:

- Sections 76 and 78 of the PACE Act 1984, including provisions under Code C, Code E, and Code F.
- Part III and ss 34, 36, and 37 of the Criminal Justice and Public Order Act 1994 (CJPOA) including 'special warnings', which we will discuss later.
- Criminal law relating to the offence(s) with which suspects are charged (including the Theft Act 1968 and Offences Against the Person Act 1861).
- The Human Rights Act 1998.
- The Criminal Procedures and Investigation Act 1996 (CPIA).
- The Youth Justice and Criminal Evidence Act 1999 (especially on 'vulnerable witnesses' and 'intimidated witnesses').

There are other laws with specific provisions which we will refer to later, but those noted above are the principal sources for the legality of what you do when interviewing; the observance of which will give you confidence in presenting your evidence in court. You must make sure you know the PACE Act 1984, CPIA 1996, and the CJPOA 1994 very well indeed, or you may make mistakes which may render parts of the evidence against a suspect void or inadmissible. Worse still, a guilty offender may not be prosecuted on a technicality (potentially an error made on your part during the interview process) and be free to offend again, or an innocent person may be wrongly charged and convicted. So the message is very firmly that you have got to get it right. That is what this section is about and it will guide you into getting it right every time; you have to know the law governing interviews so well that it is second nature to you, and no one can do that learning for you.

12.5.1 The Importance of Interviewing

Interviewing witnesses, victims, and suspects will be a core part of your role as a police officer and something which you will do nearly every day. Why is it so important? The short answer is that **interviewing is the way in which you obtain important evidence or information in relation to something which has happened.** It may or may not be a crime. It is a formal, recorded process. At a police station (where the majority of formal interviews of suspects take place), interviewing will involve a custody officer, working with you and the duty inspector (whose authority will be needed to retain a suspect without charge in custody beyond a certain point). The evidence of a witness or victim may be vital in obtaining a conviction. You cannot hope to get a full picture of the event without talking to them and getting their side of the story.

12.5.2   A Case Study

We are going to change the format slightly from this point. We will follow a single criminal case through the interview stages and stop every now and again to draw out a point or explain a principle. It might help you to have copies of the PACE Act 1984 and the CJPOA 1994 to hand while you work through this part of the chapter. Copies of both are available from <http://www.opsi.gov.uk/legislation/index.htm> by following the relevant links.

> You are on Supervised Patrol when you receive a call to proceed to Mortesbury's supermarket on the outskirts of town where alleged shoplifters have been detained.
>
> When you arrive there, chaos reigns. Three store detectives are holding three people by the arms, there is a pile of goods on the floor, supermarket managers and check-out staff are milling about and several dozen spectators are watching what is going on, and everyone is shouting at once.
>
> You and your colleague restore order, and calm things down.

What is your next priority? You need to find out what has happened. This is **not** an interview; it is ascertaining if a crime has been committed. Your priority is to identify possible suspects and witnesses and to eliminate from your enquiries those who were not involved or who did not see what went on (and the chances are that these will include most of those present, including (probably) the store managers and most of the check-out staff). You should seek to reduce the people around to those who have been directly involved. This is not as easy as it sounds. People can become over-excited when they think they have witnessed a crime (especially one like this: carried out apparently in front of many people, and no violence used) and will be keen to give you their (derivative) account. You need to exercise judgement in establishing who was a **material witness** to the event (who actually saw it) and who was not. Take full details (ensuring you include identifying particulars).

Remember too, that you need to think about compliance with the Criminal Procedures and Investigation Act 1996 (CPIA) because there have been occasions when police officers have not recorded 'relevant material', to the detriment of the prosecution of offenders. You must make sure that you have made an entry about **all** the witnesses in your PNB, and that your colleagues have made notes in their PNBs about any actions, statements, comments, or relevant material. It may not be used by the defence, but it could be. The case would be potentially undermined if the defence asked you, in court, what was said by one material witness and there was no record of what was said in your PNB. We look at the need to 'record, retain and reveal' in section 12.9 in this chapter. Refer to section 11.5 to refresh your memory about the PNB and its importance.

You end up with the three store detectives, three alleged suspects and a female member of the check-out staff who raised the alarm.

Are there any other sources of potential evidence? You might have considered CCTV, both internally and externally. You would seek to obtain any film from the store manager as soon as is practicable. Let us pause a moment here. The same applies to CCTV under the CPIA as applied to material witnesses. You are not simply looking for evidence of the crime, but for any relevant material, which may support the defence case. You would ensure that you viewed the CCTV there and then, and, if it contained relevant material, you would seize the tape and 'bag' it in accordance with the rules about the preservation of evidence (see section 13.6 in the next chapter). This would apply even if the CCTV did not show the crime itself, but only the suspects in the supermarket.

The story unfolds:

Lisa Ship, a check-out operator, became suspicious when the three suspects joined her customer line, all holding large shopping bags, but paid only for small items in cash. She wondered why they had not gone in the 'baskets only' queue and why they were wearing bulky coats on such a warm day. She told her supervisor, who alerted security staff, and the trio was stopped as they left the store. Each appeared to have a bundle of branded supermarket goods for which they could produce no sales receipts. The store detectives agreed that each of the suspects had concealed items within their clothes and inside their shopping bags. The cost of the goods was calculated to be £240 and included spirits, electronic goods, and luxury items. The supermarket has a policy of always prosecuting for theft and the store manager is insistent that you arrest the suspects.

What do you do now? For the moment, politely ignore the advice of the store manager. He is not helping you. However, you have enough **prima facie** evidence to arrest the suspects on suspicion of theft. That said, you want to explore this further and see what other evidence there may be, perhaps in the vehicle(s) which the suspects used to get to the supermarket car park. (Do you have the power to search their vehicle(s)?)

You should also take the details of all those involved in identifying and detaining the suspects, including Ms Ship and the store detectives.

Are details needed from anyone else? You should take the details of Ms Ship's supervisor, for it was the latter who played a decisive part in alerting the supermarket security staff. You might also spend a moment ascertaining if anyone witnessed the detention of the suspects by the store detectives (to ensure that the detention was proportionate, not accompanied by violence and was effected outside the store so that there is no possibility that the suspects could plead that they were trying to get to a pay-point inside the store). If you do identify someone who can testify independently to the detention, ensure that you record all their details in your PNB.

As to the power to **search** the suspects' vehicle(s), under the PACE Act 1984 you are lawfully able to do this. Section 32(2) states that a constable shall have power to search any premises in which the suspect was present before the offence for which he/she was arrested. This would cover any vehicle used by the suspects to travel to the supermarket and therefore you would be exercising your powers lawfully if you searched the suspects' vehicle. (See Chapters 8, 9, 10, and 11 for further details concerning powers of search and arrest.)

The story continues:

In fact, when you search the single car in which the suspects visited the supermarket, you find some new, still-packaged electronic goods from Curret and Lixon, the high-street store. None of the suspects can produce receipts for the expensive cameras, CD players, and mobile phones which were hidden under a blanket in the boot of the suspects' vehicle.

You and your colleague decide that you now have enough evidence and that you will take all three suspects to the police station for questioning.

What should you be thinking about at this point? Identification of the suspects would be a priority if you have not already asked them for their names and addresses. You should also let your station know that you are bringing the suspects in. You might also request (or carry out yourself, if you have direct access to the databases) a **criminal records check** on each of the suspects. Additionally, you need to interview witnesses, either in their place of work—somewhere quiet—or at home, or at the police station. You need to conduct these interviews relatively quickly because they are a basis for your subsequent investigations. You might also consider whether or not you should caution the suspects now, and if you did, for what purpose. **What is the caution?** We covered this in section 11.6, but here is a reminder:

> You do not have to say anything. But it may harm your defence if you do not mention when questioned something which you later rely on in court. Anything you do say may be given in evidence (PACE Code C10.5).

As we noted in section 11.6, it is possible that some people, particularly those who do not have English as their first language, may not understand the caution when formally made. You have an obligation under PACE (Code C10.7 and Note 10D) to ensure that the detained person comprehends the caution. However, this may not be appropriate at the time of arrest and a full explanation of the caution may only be possible at the time of interview.

When in doubt, try to get an interpreter fluent in the suspect's own first language (you may need an interpreter in the interview process as well).

Let us make a check of what you should have done up to this point in the case. This is to ensure that we have covered everything before taking the arrested suspects to the police station:

- Have you made arrests?
- Have you ensured that the detained people are under control and properly supervised?
- Have you kept the supermarket staff away from the arrested people and established the circumstances of the offence?
- Have you separated the offenders?
- Have you ensured, if appropriate, that you have viewed the CCTV for any relevant material?
- Have you obtained details of the suspects?
- Have you done the same with witnesses?
- Have all details been entered in your PNB?
- Have you explained the arrest procedure to the people you have detained? (Make sure that they understand why they have been arrested and your powers to do so.)
- Have you undertaken a PNC and other data checks on the arrested people?
- Have the suspects been searched? (Remember that you can only search persons of the same sex as you. Request a colleague of the appropriate gender if you have male/female suspects.)
- Have you seized evidence? Remember that you have to obtain a 'Void Receipt' from staff of the goods allegedly stolen. The Void Receipt will give a list of the items and their values. This will help the interviewer later on if there is a delay with statements. The receipt can also be exhibited later in court—useful when there are many items.

12.5.3 The Case Continues

In this section we continue the case introduced in section 12.5.2 and move on to discuss questioning and interviews.

> Because there are three suspects, you call for back-up to transport them to the station. You have 'bagged' the evidence ready for forensic examination. A crime scene investigator will also examine the suspects' vehicle. On the way back to the station, the suspect in your car seems willing to co-operate and she answers your questions freely, including implicating the other two in organized thefts from supermarkets and other stores across the town over the last month. When you reach the station, you hand the suspect over to the custody officer and write up your PNB with an account of what was said in the car.

Are there any problems with doing this? Yes there are. Questioning suspects about the offences after they have been arrested and before arrival at the police station is likely to render your evidence inadmissible and risks the whole case. It is bad practice to question in this way. However, if the suspect makes a statement voluntarily ('outside the context of an interview, but which might be relevant to the offence'), you should record it in your PNB. The PACE Act 1984, Code C Note 11E advises you that the suspect should be asked to endorse your PNB with the words 'I agree that this is a correct record of what was said.' (See also the PACE Act 1984, Code C, para 11.13, see section 11.7 above for more details).

The following then takes place:

> The custody officer accepts all three suspects and authorizes detention. You now have to think about interviewing each of the suspects and each of the witnesses. Ten minutes after reaching the station, you and a colleague go into the interview room and tell the first suspect that she has 'no chance of getting off', so she might as well confess to the whole thing. She starts to cry, so you turn off the tape-recorder in the interview room and tell her to 'pull herself together'. She asks for a solicitor but you tell her she cannot have one until she has answered your questions. You bellow at her to assert your authority.

What has gone wrong here? The first thing to say is that your behaviour might be considered oppressive. You cannot bully the suspect, nor can you deprive her of the right to a legal representative. You do not yet have the full picture of what happened, so phrases such as 'no chance of getting off' are completely inappropriate. You do not turn off the tape recorder just because she has started to cry, but it would be common decency (if not quite a human right) to ask her if she would like a few minutes to compose herself. She may be crying because of your bullying manner (which is one reason why interviews are recorded).

Not only have you not prepared yourself properly for the interview, you are rushing the whole thing. Any one of the errors you have made above may be enough to get the case thrown out—long before it arrived at court.

Let us start again. What is the purpose of the interview? The PACE Codes of Practice set out what an interview is:

> An interview is the questioning of a person about his or her involvement in a criminal offence or offences, which (by virtue of paragraph 10.1 of Code C) is required to be carried out under caution.

The reason why you want to interview is that it is the best method to obtain accurate and reliable information from suspects, victims, or witnesses in order to discover the truth about events or matters which you are investigating as a police officer. There are some important principles involved, which we will now take some time to look at in detail.

12.5.3.1 General rights of the suspect

First, the suspect has rights. In addition to the normal rights of being treated with dignity, fairness, and objectivity, those rights include the presence of a legal adviser during interview. In the case of a vulnerable person, an 'appropriate adult' should also be present; we look at this in more detail later. The suspect should have his/her rights explained, and this should be reinforced by providing the suspect with a written explanation. The suspect should be assessed as 'fit for interview'; you need to consider whether the suspect is ill or hurt or suffering from a psychological condition. Normally a doctor or custody nurse will ascertain fitness for interview, but it can be done on the person's own say-so, supported by the custody officer's own observations. You should explain to the suspect what is going to happen and how things will proceed. Remember that most people will not know what is happening; they may never have been in a police station before or have never given a statement under caution or have never been formally interviewed. If you explain what is going to take place, you are more likely to reassure and relax the person whom you are interviewing. If you do all this in a friendly and non-threatening manner, you are half way to a co-operative interview. Remember, creating an environment that encourages the interviewee to talk is a primary aim of the interview process.

12.5.3.2 Preparing for the interview

Even before all this, you should have made some preparations. Can you really interview effectively if you have not made a plan? Are you sure that you have all the available evidence? Have you got the witness statements? What is the detained person suspected of? Have you used the caution? (A word of advice: you cannot go wrong if, at each interview session, you remind the suspect of the caution and repeat it.) Do you know what route you want the interview to follow? What do you still need to know?

Remember that, if an offence has actually occurred, you have to prove two things:

1. **Criminal intent** (*mens rea*): What was in the suspect's mind at the time? Why did he/she commit the offence?
2. **Criminal action** (*actus rea*): What did he/she actually do? How did he/she do it?
   (See section 5.10 above for further details.)

The interviews which you plan should be geared towards the outcome of these proofs (or, if the course of the interviews suggests otherwise, to 'no charge').

It is worth bearing in mind some essential principles before you plan your interviews:

- All interviews should be approached with an open mind. You should not allow yourself to use the interview process to prove some preconception of your own.
- The information you obtain should be tested against what you already know or what you can find out subsequently.
- You are free to ask questions in an interview to establish the truth. You are not constrained by the rules applied to lawyers in court.
- You do not have to accept the first answer you are given. If you think that the interviewee may be covering something up or not telling you the whole truth, you are perfectly entitled to probe further. Case law has established that questioning is not unfair just because it is persistent and robust.
- Even when a suspect exercises his/her right to silence (which we deal with in more detail later), you still have the right to put questions to him/her. Indeed, if you do question properly and this is recorded, the jury may draw inferences from the suspect's silence if it chooses to.
- Vulnerable interviewees must be treated with particular care and respect.
- You must understand what you are doing with the interview and why.

In other words, there is no substitute for careful and detailed planning for the interview. You cannot rush in, as we saw in our case study and hope to get anywhere near the truth of what happened. You need to be as prepared and well acquainted with all the known facts before you start interviewing as you are when you put together the subsequent case file.

One of the first things you need to decide is what potential offence or offences you are investigating. In our example, the first possible offence is **theft**, so ensure that you are familiar with the provisions of the Theft Act(s). However, since two or more people may have conspired together to commit a crime, you might also be looking at **conspiracy**— but this will need long conversations with your colleagues and the Crown Prosecution Service, because conspiracy is notoriously hard to prove.

Decide what contribution the interview is going to make to your investigation of theft. You must also consider:

- What do you not know?
- What do you need to know?
- Are you certain that you understand what happened at the scene?
- Do you have your witness statements?
- Have you checked on the property which appears to have been stolen from Curret and Lixon and which you found in the boot of the suspects' car? If the property is identified as stolen, is there any additional evidence you need from Curret and Lixon, such as descriptions of the possible perpetrators or additional CCTV footage?
- Do you know who the suspects are?
- Have they been fully identified?
- Do any of them have previous convictions?
- Do any figure on the force's intelligence database? Are they suspected of other crimes elsewhere?
- Decide what the legal requirements are in the interview. Are you fully up to speed with the PACE Act 1984, especially the Codes of Practice?

- What about the role of the defence solicitor or legal adviser?
- Are you fully prepared to encounter this person?
- What have you decided to disclose? What are you going to withhold (and have you justification in mind against a legal challenge)?
- What are your points to prove?
- Have you thought about possible defences which the suspects could offer?
- What will you do about challenging them?
- Finally, what practical arrangements have you thought about?
- Where will you interview?
- Which suspect will you begin with?
- Will you have a colleague in the interview with you?
- Have you obtained the designated tapes for the recording?
- Have you discussed with the custody officer how long you intend to interview and have you planned for breaks?

12.5.4 'PEACE'

To assist you with structuring the interview, police forces have adopted the '**PEACE**' approach (see Clarke, 2001 for an evaluation of the use of PEACE by police forces in England and Wales).

PEACE (which more strictly should be PPEEACCCE) is an acronym which stands for:

P	Planning and Preparation
E	Engage and Explain
A	Account, Clarification and Challenge
C	Closure
E	Evaluation

You will often hear the process referred to in your force as the 'PEACE interview'.

Let us look at an overview of each of the elements of PEACE (adapted from Murphy, 2005) before going back to our case study. The detail will depend on whether we are interviewing suspects or co-operative witnesses.

12.5.4.1 PEACE Planning and Preparation

The following are likely to be involved:

- Your objectives—what you hope to achieve and how you intend to achieve them. Remember, the emphasis is to establish the truth.
- Knowing the law; research the law and recent stated cases, eg intention, effect of drink/drugs on intention, recklessness, etc.
- Possible defences, eg statutory defences, reasonableness, mistake, coercion, duress, self-defence, etc.
- Possible mitigating and aggravating factors.
- Pre-interview disclosure to solicitors or legal representatives.

12.5.4.2 PEACE Engage and Explain

In this stage of a PEACE interview, the following are likely to be involved:

- Establishing a rapport; introductions, concerns, and considerations (how long will this take?), creating a compatible atmosphere, establishing common ground, use of appropriate humour.
- Reasons for interview; in the case of a suspect, offence explained, grounds for arrest and interview, opportunity for the suspect or co-operative witness to put his/her account of what happened, the opportunity for you, the police officer, to put 'your' account, to seek the truth.

It is after this stage that you would formally start the interview.

There are many technical requirements at this stage that you will be trained in which subscribe to the requirements of the PACE Act 1984 and other legislation and codes.

The **tapes** which are used to record the interview will be sealed when you collect them and take them to the interview room. The tapes must be shown to the suspect so that they can see they are sealed, new and have therefore not been tampered with.

Two tapes will be recording simultaneously; at the end of the interview one will be sealed (the master tape) and not opened until the court hearing. The other tape (the working copy) will be used to transcribe the interview. The suspect must be informed that when the tape recorder is first switched on there will be a continuous sound from the machine during which time nothing can be recorded, while the tape is winding on past the start of the tape.

You need to record the following information in your pocket notebook or on the paper seals that will be wrapped around the tapes at the end of the interview (see Code C 11.7, PACE Act 1984):

- the time, day, date, location;
- the name, rank, role of the interviewer;
- the name, address, date of birth of the interviewee;
- the persons present;
- a description of room and equipment layout.

At the start of the interview you need to caution the interviewee (see Code C, para 11.4) and check his/her understanding and read out any significant statements made prior to interview. Further details concerning taped interviews may be found in the ACPO Investigation of Volume Crime Manual, Appendix H (ACPO, 2001).

12.5.4.3 PEACE Account, Clarification, and Challenge

This is the main part of the interview:

- First ask for a 'free' account given without interruption.
- Now develop the account; phase the incident then move systematically from one phase to another, clarify or seek greater detail. You may need to bear in mind *Turnbull* and the ADVOKATE checklist (see section 11.8 above).
- Summarize the account and then select topics to examine in greater detail that are relevant, in dispute, and checkable. Does the account make chronological sense?
- Seek new/additional information. Summarize each topic and if possible achieve commitment and agreement. (Note that you may also be taught about the Cognitive Interview memory enhancement techniques during your PEACE training, particularly in the context of co-operative witnesses, but we do not cover this in the Handbook. However, see the answer to Task 7.)
- Clarify and challenge, but restrict challenge to: checkable facts, inconsistencies, provable and admissible facts. When challenging, do not criticize or accuse, but instead seek an explanation—ask for explanation especially where discrepancies emerge.
- Throughout, anticipate intervention by the solicitor who might well be employing 'active defence' (Ede and Shepherd, 2000). Adopt appropriate strategies for no comment interviews (see below).
- Is a special warning needed? (see 12.5.11 below).

12.5.4.4 PEACE Closure

You should check the following points before finishing the interview:

- Have you reviewed the suspect's account in the interview in full?
- Has the suspect the chance to correct, confirm, deny, alter, or add to the interview?
- Have you covered all the questions you wish to ask?
- Has the suspect provided all the information?
- Have the suspect or solicitor any questions?
- Explain what will happen in the future.

You can now formally close the interview.

As with formally starting the interview, there are a number of requirements to be met. You will be taught these as part of your training. This stage is likely to include recording the time when the interview finishes and sealing the master tape in the presence of the suspect.

Further details concerning taped interviews may be found in the ACPO Investigation of Volume Crime Manual, Appendix H (ACPO, 2001).

12.5.4.5   **PEACE Evaluation**

This occurs after the interview has been closed. You should ask yourself the following:

- Have you discovered other reasonable lines of enquiry for fast-track response such as an alibi?
- Have you discovered other forensic opportunities?
- Have you achieved your objectives?
- Does the interview add to your investigation as a whole?
- Will adverse inference apply?

Assess your personal level of skills and knowledge (an opportunity for Learning Diary entries). Have the requirements of the CPIA 1996 been satisfied?

12.5.5   **PEACE Applied to the Case Study**

We have already established some of the elements of preparation and planning which go into the interview process. In this case, there are three suspects who must be interviewed.

In which order will you take the suspects for interview? You could decide on any order, perhaps beginning with the oldest, but, if you remember, one of the suspects began to volunteer statements about the crime and her two associates on the way to the police station in your car. It would make sense to begin with her. You should now know her age and this will help you determine the best time for the interview and whether an appropriate adult is needed. You may also consider whether there are any cultural or behavioural considerations such as how you address the suspect. The best way is to ask the suspect directly since this will provide an easy ice-breaker at the beginning of the interview. You will also need to find out:

- What are her personal circumstances?
- How does she know the other two suspects?
- What is her educational background and intellectual ability—is any shortfall here an indication of vulnerability?
- What have background checks revealed about the suspect's previous history?
- Has there been any previous involvement with the police?
- Have you allowed enough time for the interview?

It is often a process that is open-ended (you cannot predict how much or how little the suspect will say), but you should build in appropriate breaks (this is important, so that neither of you is exhausted by the process). Make sure that you have all the equipment you need and that you are familiar with the place where the interview will take place. For example, you will need the explanation form about custody, the Medical Release Authorization forms (showing that the suspect is fit for interview), and the requisite audio or video tapes for the interview room. If you intend to interview with a colleague, make sure that you have agreed how to partition the questioning, and who takes the lead. If it is you who leads, arrange when your colleague will take over the questioning and what topics will be covered by whom.

There is no obligation on you to **disclose** any of your evidence at this stage, but it is often pragmatic and sensible to disclose some. This is of particular point when dealing with the suspect's legal adviser, who will challenge you to justify the detention of his or her client. In our case study, you might disclose the 'flagrante' detention and arrest of the suspects at the supermarket and the possession of goods which the suspects cannot account for. You would not necessarily reveal the recovered property from the car, nor would you reveal the identity of the witnesses. Expect to be challenged robustly by the solicitor however; his/her aim will be to get you to reveal everything you have against the suspect. We talk about tactics in dealing with the legal adviser later on. You can read more about disclosure in section 12.9.

It is advisable to have a **written plan**. If you have a particularly good memory, you may decide not to take notes into the interview with you. However, there are very few of us that could achieve this, and you might want a copy of the PACE Act 1984 Codes for reference, as well as a written plan of how you want the interview to go, noting the following:

- the range of topics you want to cover;
- the points needed to prove the possible offence(s) under investigation;
- evidence that the suspect committed the offence(s) and the specific parts of the criminal law under which the suspect may be charged.

A written plan helps you keep track of what has been covered and what remains to be explored. It will also help you if the suspects' accounts contradict each other or vary significantly from what you currently believe to be the facts.

Remember though: your interview plan is relevant material, as defined by the CPIA 1996 and must therefore be retained as disclosable information (see section 12.9 below).

12.5.6 The Case Study Continues

You made such a mess of it earlier that we are taking the interview away from you and giving it to two experienced police officers, Pc Alison Wyatt and Pc Jon Singh. We will let you listen in to how they conduct their respective interviews, but you must stay alert because we are going to ask you questions from time to time about what is going on. We join our two police officers as, well prepared and well planned, they go into the interview room.

> The first suspect, Nicola Kew, aged 28, is brought in and is clearly very nervous. She is hesitant, somewhat scared, and her body language suggests that she is very ill at ease. She twists her hands to and fro, shifts her position often, looks trapped by something she may not understand and speaks in a very quiet voice, licking her lips frequently. She has been crying.

The interviewing officers need to take this into account. Remember 'engage and explain' in the PEACE mnemonic described above. Research and experience has shown that the sooner an interviewee feels at ease (not the same as comfortable) with the interviewer, the better the interview works. You need to appear relaxed yourself and be willing to explain what is going to happen. Nicola may not have been in a police station before, nor perhaps had a formal interview ever in her life. It could be all very alien to her, as though she is caught in a process where she cannot do anything for herself; it is all happening **to** her; she feels helpless.

> **Interviewer:** Good afternoon, I'm Pc Alison Wyatt and this is Pc Jon Singh. What would you like us to call you?
> **Suspect (faintly):** I'm ... you can, um, call me Nic.
> **Interviewer:** That's short for Nicola, isn't it?
> **Suspect:** Yes, Nicola Kew.
> **Interviewer:** OK, Nic. You look thirsty. Would you like a cup of tea or a glass of water or something?
> **Suspect (gratefully):** Oh a cup of tea would be great, thanks.
> **Interviewer:** How do you take it? Milk? Sugar? I gave up milk once, but I couldn't hack it so I went back to milk.
> **Suspect (smiling):** Milk, no sugar, please.

Consider this exchange carefully. The interviewer is polite and relaxed, and shows interest in how the suspect is feeling. She introduces herself by full name (given name as well as family name) and invites the suspect to say how she wants to be addressed. Notice the suspect's hesitation and nervousness in her reply. Notice too how the interviewer picks up on the offer of a shortened form of the suspect's name and how she makes it into a friendly gesture, followed by concern for the suspect's comfort. The little anecdote about giving up milk is an 'ice-breaker'. It shows that the interview is not likely to be oppressive or threatening (it may even be more like a conversation), and gives a touch of humanity to the interviewer who comes across as more of a real person. And in this case it seems to work, because the suspect is smiling as she gives her drink order.

It is important to note that at no time has Pc Wyatt lost control of the process, nor has she compromised her dignity. Instead, she has made friendly overtures which have relaxed the suspect who is now much more likely to talk openly and freely. Had Pc Wyatt been overbearingly formal or pompous or 'stand-offish' in her attitude to the suspect, the latter may well have clammed up completely. These gambits may seem trivial matters, but research suggests that they do seem to work.

Remember: your goal at the outset is to create an atmosphere in which the suspect (or any other interviewee) will **want to talk to you**. That does not mean that you have to be over-friendly or gushing, but emphatically that you are relaxed and conversational, so that the suspect becomes so too. You might like to consider the personal style of the interviewer in terms of transactional analysis. (See section 7.18 above).

One of the things you may not have noticed is that Pc Wyatt had picked up on the body language which Nicola Kew was showing. The officer could see the nervousness and anxiety and that is why she made an effort to reassure Nicola. These behavioural signs or 'leakages' are usually described as **non-verbal communication** (NVC).

Some words of warning: NVC is not recorded in a PACE interview unless commented on, as, for example, a shake of the head or a nod. You should not ascribe depths of insight to NVC; the leakage is an indicator, no more, and it is difficult to separate signs of stress that are from simply being interviewed by the police from those down to lying. Beware of those who tell you that hand gestures are 'windows on the soul'; they are not. (Unfortunately, these kind of scientifically unjustified 'tips and tricks' used to feature in police training in the past.) In particular, using 'body language' in an attempt to identify deception or lying is problematic and you should certainly not believe some of the more popular accounts (see Vrij, 2000 for a comprehensive consideration of this). There is another danger with placing too much reliance on postures or physical signs: it can lead to **stereotyping**. You must be alert to 'ethnocentrism' in your interpretation of non-verbal communication; you should not centre your understanding of gestures or attitude, for example, on purely British or Western interpretations. A refusal to make eye contact or sometimes adopting a posture of humility, say, is characteristic of some ethnic groups, which has to do with cultural attitudes to authority, **not** to guilt or remorse.

Back to the interview. **What should Pc Wyatt, and her colleague, Pc Singh, do now that Nicola Kew has her cup of tea and is slightly more relaxed?**

I am sure that you referred back to PEACE to remind you that we have entered the 'engage and explain' part of the process. Pc Wyatt has made a good start with engagement, but if she is to calm Nicola Kew's nerves, the officer must go on to explain what is going to happen:

> **Pc Wyatt:** Now, Nic, I'm going to explain what this is all about and cover why you're here, what we will ask you about and the things which will happen afterwards. [For the benefit of the tape, Nicola Kew's solicitor has entered the interview room and has sat down beside her. I will ask the solicitor to identify himself.]
>
> **Solicitor:** I am David Evan Williams, Duty Solicitor.
>
> **Pc Wyatt:** The time is 1423. I shall resume my explanation of the interview process and why Nicola Kew is here. Nic, you have been arrested on suspicion of theft from Mortesbury's supermarket. This means that my colleague Jon and I must ask you to tell us what happened at the supermarket this morning. Under the law, you are entitled to have a legal adviser present when you are interviewed, and that is Mr Williams here. Also, the law says that we must record the interview, which is why that tape recorder is on the desk. This is to make sure that everything is fair and properly done in accordance with the law.

Solicitor (interrupting): Which is also why I'm here, to advise you.

Pc Wyatt: Exactly. Mr Williams will already have talked to you about what is going to happen and you should listen carefully to his advice. Pc Singh and I will ask you questions about this incident. Either Jon or I may take notes as well as having the tape on. We may show you things and ask you to identify them. These are called 'exhibits'. We may also ask you to write a statement and sign it. This should be in your own words. What we would like you to do is to tell us what happened and why. We need to know the truth about today's incident and hope that you will be able to fill in the details for us. We will stop for a break after about an hour, and you are free at any time to consult with Mr Williams. All we'd ask is that you tell us when you are going to do this, because we need to stop the tape. Your conversations with Mr Williams, as I'm sure he has told you, are confidential, which means that Jon Singh and I are not allowed to hear what is said. Do you understand what I've said so far?

Suspect (Nicola Kew): Yes.

Pc Wyatt: Thank you. Here is a card which explains what I've said, which you can keep and look at whenever you want. [I am handing Nicola Kew an aide mem card in accordance with the PACE Act 1984, Code E.] What the card tells you is that this is a police interview which is being recorded. My colleague and I must interview you under caution. Do you know what that means?

Nicola Kew: Yes.

Pc Wyatt: Good. Nicola Marie Kew, you do not have to say anything. But it may harm your defence if you do not mention when questioned something which you later rely on in court. Anything you do say may be given in evidence.

Do you understand the caution, Nic?

Nicola (hesitantly): Um, I think.. um some of it, that...

Pc Wyatt: That's OK. Let me put it this way. You don't have to answer my questions. However, if this matter goes to court at a later date, and you tell the court something in your defence, for example an innocent explanation of what took place at the supermarket, and they think you could reasonably have told me here today, they may not believe you, and that could harm your defence. Also everything we are saying in this room is being recorded and we could use all of this conversation as evidence at court if required.

Nicola: Yeah, I get it now.

Pc Wyatt: Good, it is important to me that you do understand it, so I am going to ask you some quick questions to make sure, is that OK?

Nicola: Sure.

Pc Wyatt: Nicola, do you have to speak to me in this interview?

Nicola: No.

Pc Wyatt: That's right, however, what may happen, for example, if you gave an innocent explanation about what happened at the supermarket at a court, in your defence, but didn't mention it here, in this interview if it was reasonable to do so?

Nicola: Well, the court may not believe me, and that could harm what I am saying at court.

Pc Wyatt: OK, so could we use everything said in this interview as evidence if it went to court?

Nicola: Yes, you could.

Pc Wyatt: Thank you. It's clear to me that you understand the meaning of the caution, now Nic, I am going to ask you some questions about this morning. Take your time and think about your answers, OK?

Nicola: (nervously): OK.

We have given the transcript of the preliminaries here in some detail because it is important for you to understand what is going on, and how Pc Wyatt is building on the good **rapport** (engagement) with the suspect with which she started.

We have also introduced the solicitor (Mr Williams) because it is Nicola's right to have a legal adviser present. Notice that David Williams described himself as a '**duty solicitor**'; this means that he comes from a retained panel of solicitors available to advise arrested people who do not have a solicitor of their own or, if they do, that person is not available for the interview. He may or may not know Nicola, but his role is to do what any other solicitor or accredited legal representative would do: advise his client in her best interests. (This does not always mean that he advises her to be silent; sometimes an admission of guilt is better for the client, especially if there is strong or irrefutable evidence or strong **mitigation**—an excuse or reason for what has been done. We look at the solicitor's role and interaction with you in detail later.)

You should have observed that Pc Wyatt recorded the solicitor's entry on the tape and had him identify himself. This helps to make the tape clear and comprehensible when it is replayed (especially in court), but also helps to underline that Pc Wyatt is in charge. It is she who controls the interview process.

Note too that Pc Wyatt tells Nicola why she is there and what the law says. Nicola does not need to know the details of the PACE Act 1984 or any other law, but she **does** need to know why she is in the police station, why she has been arrested, and why she is being interviewed under caution. I know that we have rather laboured the point about recasting the caution in more common language, but this is to try to encourage you to see this process through the eyes and feelings of the person being interviewed. By the end of training **you** will know the procedure well and be very familiar with what happens, but most people will not be at all familiar with it.

Why the emphasis on **procedure**? Partly this is to reassure the person being interviewed (in the 'explain' part of PEACE, described earlier), but it is also partly to ensure that the detail of the law is followed. Notice how carefully Pc Wyatt explains what will happen to Nicola and that Nicola must tell her story in her own words. You should have picked up that Pc Wyatt explains that Nicola will be shown exhibits (without saying what they are) and that she may be asked to make a statement. Observe too that Pc Wyatt explains the concept of 'legal confidentiality' very simply, and that she reinforces what she has said with a written document. Did you notice how many times Pc Wyatt is careful to check that Nicola understood what was going on, and that her re-explanation of the caution responds directly to Nicola's expression of uncertainty about understanding?

We have devoted considerable time to looking at these preliminaries, but it has been found to be beneficial to establish an appropriate tone, mood, and format for an interview from the very start. Time spent now on relaxing the suspect, engaging with him or her, explaining what is going to happen, and following procedure properly, may well prove productive later, as well as not giving the defence solicitor any irregularities to use in the defence of his client.

12.5.7 The Questioning Continues

> **Pc Wyatt:** Nic, you were stopped by Mortesbury's security staff leaving the supermarket this morning and you had things from the shop which you didn't pay for. Can you explain to me how this happened and what you did?

Much is contained in this opening question which we need to look at. First of all, Pc Wyatt is giving the context for the interview (Nicola has apparently committed a theft and has been caught in possession of the stolen goods). Also, Pc Wyatt is asking an **open question** (it cannot be answered with a simple yes or no) which invites a response. The reason that Nicola is in the police station is reinforced and the nature of any police charges arising from the incident is indicated.

What do you think Nicola's response will be? What do you think the solicitor will say? Nicola's response may surprise you (see below). The groundwork which Pc Wyatt has undertaken in making the opening stages of the interview relaxed and unthreatening, starts to pay dividends, as Nicola is invited to talk about things from her own point of view. The solicitor could challenge her and suggest to his client that she does not reply, but in this instance it is unlikely. He is much more concerned at this stage to find out what the strength of the case is against her. He might intervene later if she is likely to incriminate herself, but even then he may not. Much depends on **the strength of the evidence**, which the solicitor wants to test.

> **Nicola:** Yes. I um...I had to do what Alan said. He uh..., he said he'd bloody kill me if I didn't um...go with him on this one and he's nearly done it before [crying] hitting me and stuff and and I was scared. I've never done anything like this before and I've never been in trouble with the police until now, but I didn't have any, any choice. You don't know Alan. He seems so normal most of the time but for no reason he'll just go bloody mad and smash things up and if you're in the way you get smashed up too.
>
> **Pc Wyatt:** Who is Alan, Nic?
>
> **Nicola:** Alan Stacker, the man who was with me at Mortesbury's and who got arrested too.
>
> **Pc Wyatt:** Was anyone else involved, Nic?
>
> **Nicola:** Yeah, that wanker Bolgomov.
>
> **Pc Wyatt:** Who's he?
>
> **Nicola:** Sergei Bolgomov. He follows me about. I don't like him. Alan said he'd be good to have along when we did the supermarket and he's been living in a squat down at Ledbury. I hate him. He's always, you know, um...undressing me with his eyes sort of thing and watching me all the time. He's a bloody creep. I don't know why Alan wants him along. He can hardly speak any English and he's just a thug.

Let us pause a minute and look at what is going on here. Nicola has said that she was pressured or intimidated by Alan Stacker into 'doing' the supermarket.

Is this a confession? What is the law about forcing someone to do something criminal against their will? Notice that Pc Wyatt did NOT say 'Alan is Alan Stacker isn't he?', because this would have been a **leading question** which tried to put words into Nicola's mouth. Instead, Pc Wyatt quietly asked who 'Alan' was, and let Nicola implicate the man in the incident. Notice too that Nicola alleged that Stacker is capable of violence and that she has been the victim of his anger. (You would need to explore this further to see if there might be other, more serious, charges against Stacker, but that might be much later in the process.)

Then Pc Wyatt asks if anyone else was involved; she does not ask, 'Who is the third man who was with you?' because again that would be a leading question. Nicola then implicates Sergei Bolgomov as the third participant in the theft. There are some helpful details about him, such as his poor English (implications for when he is interviewed?) and his living in a squat. This might suggest that he is not in the UK legally, or that he is 'of no fixed abode', which may make full identification difficult. What Nicola has said provides the interviewers with several new leads and these will inform and help to structure the interviews with the two male suspects later.

If you were Pc Wyatt, what would be your next question? The next question would probably be: 'Tell me about the supermarket business, Nic'. Remember the temptation to ask leading questions? The solicitor would no doubt have intervened if Pc Wyatt had said 'So you're admitting you went to Mortesbury's with the intention of stealing?', because again, it is a leading question which invites Nicola to incriminate herself. It is far better to let Nicola say things in her own words because there is little doubt now that she wants to talk about what happened.

As well as inviting Nicola to talk about the crime, Pc Wyatt will be keen to find out what was in Nicola's mind at the time (the *mens rea*; one of the points to prove, see above and section 5.10), and she could do this by asking any of a number of 'open' questions, such as:

'What were you feeling when you went into the supermarket?' or
'What were you thinking when you were inside Mortesbury's?' or
'How did you feel when you went to the check-out?'

This is what Nicola actually said in reply to Pc Wyatt's question:

> **Nicola:** It was all Alan's idea. He'd met this bloke in a pub who'd said he was in the market sort of thing for anyone with booze and new cameras and the latest phones and all that kind of thing. And Alan said that nicking this sort of stuff was easy, especially if we went as a couple because we'd look as though we were shopping. I didn't want to do it and I've never been in trouble with the police before but Alan said that we wouldn't be caught if we were cool. He said that he and Sergei were going to do over Curret and Lixon's because they had good stuff there you could sell off and I didn't have to come but I **did** have to go to the supermarket because two men shopping alone might be suspicious. I said again that I didn't want to and Alan went mad. He um…he hit me and said that he'd fucking kill me if I didn't do it with him because there was no money coming in now I'd lost my poxy job and how could he get a drink if he didn't have any sodding cash. So I said yes, more to stop him hitting me again than because I wanted to. This morning, we drove there in Alan's car and just went in. Alan said go for the small spirits and razors and stuff and to push them inside my coat or in the bag. So I did. I was sort of hoping we'd get caught. I don't know. I just want to get away from him because he's mental. I don't want to be hit again. Look.
>
> **Pc Wyatt:** Nicola Kew is showing me a large bruise on her left breast and left collar bone.
>
> **Nicola:** That's what he did last night, the bastard. I can't bear this any more. [crying] Oh God what have I done?
>
> **Solicitor:** I think I should speak to my client privately.
>
> **Pc Wyatt:** Of course. This interview is suspended. The time is 1505.

This is a confession, because Nicola has described the *mens rea* and the *actus rea* in her own words. She described how she was pressured into agreeing to steal from the supermarket by Stacker and what her method was to steal the items. There are other things happening in this statement too. Nicola had commented that 'a man in a pub' had offered to act as a 'fence' (a receiver of stolen goods) for anything of value which Stacker could steal, and Nicola has implicated both Stacker and Bolgomov in the theft of goods from the high street store, prior to the supermarket visit. It suggests too that Nicola was innocent of the high street theft.

However, none of this will be left to chance, and Pc Singh will be asked to check out what evidence there is from CCTV of the theft at Curret and Lixon's. If CCTV showed Nicola taking part, then there would have to be a **challenge** to her evidence (she might be blaming the others in an attempt to exonerate herself). However, the bruises and the circumstantial account, including her state of mind, seem to be truthful. Never assume this, though; you have to test the account by challenging it in the details.

There appears now to be further detail around the allegation that Stacker has attacked Nicola (the evidence of severe bruising, which he may or may not have done: you do not know either way for certain), and the police officers would certainly follow this up in their interview with Stacker, perhaps with a view to bringing charges of assault against Stacker. The request from the solicitor for time alone with his client for confidential discussions is immediately respected by Pc Wyatt, though we should note that the break is convenient for the police as well, with so many leads from this statement to follow up.

Why do you think that the solicitor intervened at this point in Nicola's narrative? The answer is in two parts. First, Nicola has admitted her part in the theft and it is probable that the police will prefer charges against her. Secondly, the solicitor will be thinking that, although guilty, his client could be let off lightly because of the intimidation by Stacker. The solicitor will want to follow this up in private with her. Also, Nicola has perhaps realized the implications of all she has said to the police officers (her comment 'Oh God, what have I done?') both in admitting her guilt and in implicating Stacker. It is also likely that she realizes that she has now suggested far graver charges against Stacker, and that she may have to make a statement to that effect. You may have noticed that what began as a simple interview about a straightforward arrest for theft is developing complexities. That is not just to furnish us with a comprehensive example. Such developments often happen in interviews and you should be at least attuned to the possibility that it will happen. Notice too that Pc Wyatt made no attempt to interrupt Nicola at any point. She let the suspect talk about what had happened in her own way and did not seek to lead, guide, or otherwise influence her. This demonstrates good **listening skills** (see section 7.18 above).

We need to stop for a moment at this point too, because we need to discuss some of the things which are going on and what procedures and actions must now follow. Nicola has confessed to having committed a crime. What she has said fits the legal definition of a confession as 'any statement wholly or partly adverse to the person who made it, whether made to a person in authority or not and whether made in words or otherwise' (paraphrased from the PACE Act 1984, s 82).

Nicola has made a statement which is **adverse** (that is, it goes against her). Her solicitor will probably argue that the commission of the crime was 'under duress', but that is a matter for the courts to consider, if the police press charges against her and if the CPS decides that the case should go to court. Nicola has also implicated others in the commission of the crime and these 'leads' will be the focus of further police enquiries. Additionally, Nicola has alleged that Alan Stacker has assaulted her, occasioning actual bodily harm, which must be investigated further by the police.

We must also note the likelihood of a **significant statement** being made when the interview resumes. This means that it is something which (along with **silence**) could be **used in evidence against the suspect**. The term derives from Part III of the Criminal Justice and Public Order Act 1994:

> A significant statement or silence is one which appears capable of being used in evidence against the suspect, in particular a direct admission of guilt, or a failure or refusal to answer a question or to answer it satisfactorily which may give rise to an inference

We will look at **silence** and **refusal to answer** later on. Nicola has admitted guilt and Code E of the PACE Act 1984 also applies to her; her admission is 'a significant statement'. What does this mean? The Codes of Practice state that, at the start of every interview, after caution, and before any questions about the offence are put to the subjects, 'any significant statement must be put to them'. They must be given the opportunity to confirm or deny that earlier statement and must be asked if they wish to add anything. Anything said which is pertinent to the offence, but which falls outside the definition quoted above, is classed as 'a relevant comment'. The best advice is that if you are in any doubt as to whether a comment made is significant or relevant, put it to the suspect at the start of the interview.

In our case, it would be put to Nicola by Pc Wyatt when the interview starts again after the recess. Certainly, Nicola's solicitor will be expecting Pc Wyatt to do so; failure to do so will breach the Codes of Practice, upon which the solicitor is keeping a close eye. After such a break Code C 10.8 requires the person being questioned to be reminded that they are still under caution and if there is any doubt, for the caution to be repeated.

It is good practice anyway for Alison Wyatt to use the opening of the second part of the interview to **summarize** what Nicola has said and to invite Nicola to comment on the accuracy of the summary. This shows that Pc Wyatt and her colleague have been listening carefully to what Nicola has said, have realized the significance of what she has said, and have reflected back to the speaker how important her words are. It is also a reassurance tactic for the interviewee herself, showing that she is being taken seriously (think how important that would be in a rape case, for example).

We cannot reproduce the whole of the interview with Nicola Kew here: it would take too long and some of it was repetition or elaboration of what we already know, but there are a couple of points to emphasize before we leave Nicola (either still in custody or released on police bail). Pcs Wyatt and Singh shared the subsequent questioning, and they challenged Nicola politely but robustly about the minimal part she appeared to play in the theft at the supermarket. The police officers were mindful, as we noted above, that Nicola could be transferring all the blame to the two men in an attempt to exonerate herself or to play down her part. After the challenge, both officers are more convinced that Nicola is telling the truth and that she was forced to take part in the crime against her will. It was fear of Stacker's violence which compelled her to participate.

The officers explored further Nicola's allegations of violence against her by Stacker and asked her if she would make a statement. She consulted her solicitor who agrees that she may do so. There are two separate processes at work here. First, Nicola writes out a statement about her part in the supermarket robbery, and signs it. Then secondly, as a victim, she makes a statement about Stacker's violent assault on her. Although she had been under caution during her interview about the theft, she was not cautioned when making the victim statement.

It is time for **closure.** There is not much more now to be gained from continuing the interview with Nicola Kew. She is getting tired and starting to repeat herself, the solicitor is becoming impatient to talk to her again and the two police officers have all they want from the interview process for the moment. It is time to draw proceedings to a close, but there are some legal requirements to be met first. Nicola must be asked whether she wants to add to or clarify anything she has said before the interview tape machine is switched off. Pc Wyatt needs to tell her what will happen to the tapes, reinforcing this by providing a written explanation, and Pc Wyatt must state the time before switching off the machine.

TASK 8

Do you know the procedures for the tape recordings? Summarize them now.

Copies of the recording are made under strictly controlled conditions: one copy will remain with the case file, another will be provided to Nicola herself and an extra copy will be made available to the solicitor if he continues to act for her. The master (original) tape is sealed and remains in the possession of the designated responsible person in your force. Some forces are content to allow that to be the custody officer; others have a specific person who will have had nothing to do with the case. The **continuity of evidence** chain is very important in this respect (see sections 11.18 and 13.6 of the Handbook).

The two police officers must make an effort to sustain the good rapport that they have spent so long building up. They may need to interview Nicola again, especially if any new evidence emerges from the other interviews or from further police enquiries, and it is important to part from Nicola in a relaxed but professional manner. Pc Wyatt made a point of telling Nicola that she will not be detained any longer and explained what enquiries the police still had to make. Pc Wyatt also made sure that Nicola could go from the police station to a place of refuge where Stacker could not pursue her, supposing that Stacker was released. (The officer responsible in the BCU for domestic violence was fully briefed during the recess.) The last thing to be done before Nicola can go is that Pcs Wyatt and Singh sign the tape labels and seal the tapes in Nicola's presence, witnessed additionally by the solicitor.

What part of the PEACE process still has to be completed? It is the **Evaluation** phase. Pc Wyatt conducted the interview with professional skill and has obtained an admission of guilt as well as evidence of the more serious involvement in crime of the two male suspects. However, both she and Pc Singh will want to consider their performance. Referring to their plan, they will assess whether or not they met the aims and objectives of the interview, looking at what they did well, things they might have done better and areas which, next time, they would seek to develop or improve. This self-critical process is important if the officers are to learn from what they have done and become even more professional in their conduct of interviews. Assume that you are an uninvolved student police colleague of Pcs Wyatt and Singh, but that you observed those parts of the interview with Nicola Kew which we have looked at above.

What comments would you make to Pc Wyatt about how she performed, what she could have done better, and where she needs to think about development needs? You might have drawn attention to the late arrival of the solicitor. Why had the introductions begun before he had come into the interview room? Were the tapes running? Were introductions properly made? Did Wyatt deal adequately with the solicitor? When should Singh have taken over the questioning? Next time, for example, they might think about rotating the questioning at an earlier point instead of leaving all the early moves to Pc Wyatt. But against that you have to balance how well and quickly Pc Wyatt established a rapport with Nicola Kew, and how there could have been a danger of disrupting that 'engagement' if questioning had switched to a male colleague. Finally, would Nicola have spoken to a male officer about being attacked by Stacker in the same way that she did with Pc Wyatt? (Again, think of a rape case and whether the victim might be more comfortable talking to a female about what happened.)

If you were in the position of Pcs Wyatt and Singh, what would be your next moves? The chances are that you would want to interview Alan Stacker, possibly arranging for colleagues (with an interpreter) simultaneously to interview Sergei Bolgomov. You would want to do the same with Stacker as you did with Kew, exploring the ground in a logical way and inviting the interviewee to tell it in his own words what had happened. You would want to check the facts of his story against those you had from Nicola Kew and how they matched with the independent facts. In the back of your mind as you prepare for the interview with Stacker will be the need to raise **TICs**.

Can you remember what these are? This was described in the glossary in Chapter 1 and is shorthand for 'taken into consideration', and is an invitation to a suspect to talk about other offences which he or she may have committed. Pc Wyatt is pretty sure that Stacker and Bolgomov stole from the high street store and Nicola had mentioned in the car on the way to the police station that crimes involving the two men had been going on for about a month. The police would want to match that against what they know of crime patterns in the last month and would consult their intelligence colleagues.

Precisely the same process as we saw for the interview with Nicola will be followed for Stacker. Let us eavesdrop on the opening:

> **Pc Jon Singh:** This is an interview with [Stacker's voice: Alan Maurice Stacker, aged 39, date of birth 16 April 1968]. Present are Mr Stacker, Mr Stacker's solicitor.
> **Solicitor:** Michaela Mary O'Connor, Duty Solicitor.
> **Pc Jon Singh:** and Pc 11267 Jon Singh and Pc 10899 Alison Wyatt as interviewing officers. The time is 1625. Mr Stacker, what would you like us to call you?
> **Stacker:** Piss off.
> **Pc Singh:** We'll stay with Mr Stacker then . . . .
>   [The caution follows.]
> **Pc Singh:** Do you understand the caution Mr Stacker?
> **O'Connor:** My client understands.
> **Pc Singh:** Thank you Ms O'Connor, but I should prefer to have confirmation from Mr Stacker himself. Did you understand the caution, Mr Stacker?
> **Stacker:** Piss off.
> **Pc Singh:** Mr Stacker, you were detained this morning outside Mortesbury's supermarket in Pound Lane Estate. You had possession of supermarket goods for which you had no receipts or proof of payment. How do you account for that?
> **Stacker:** No comment.
> **Pc Singh:** I am showing Mr Stacker some of the goods alleged to have been taken by him without payment. Mr Stacker, can you account for your possession of these two bottles of rum?
> **Stacker:** No comment.
> **Pc Singh:** Mr Stacker, it has been established that your fingerprints are on the bottles, so we can prove that the bottles were in your possession. Additionally, I have witnesses who are prepared to testify that these bottles were recovered from an inside pocket of

> your jacket where you had concealed them. I shall prove that these were Mortesbury's goods for which you had not paid. Can you account for your fingerprints?
>
> **Stacker:** No comment.
>
> **O'Connor:** Where is this taking us Pc Singh?
>
> **Pc Singh:** I have put a serious allegation of theft to your client, Ms O'Connor, and have invited him to account for his possession of bottles of spirit. This is not an unreasonable line of questioning.
>
> **Stacker:** I'm saying nothing.

This is not going well, is it? What are the problems here? You would swiftly point out that Alan Stacker shows none of Nicola Kew's co-operativeness, and also that Stacker's solicitor is hostile to the line of questioning pursued by Pc Singh. Pc Singh himself is doing his job perfectly well; he is polite, logical, and relaxed. It is the scenario which most police interviewers dread: Stacker is not prepared to volunteer anything except abuse, hostility, and the stonewall tactic of 'no comment'. He is definitely not a subject prepared to come half way towards the officer and has no intention of being co-operative. However, you should remember that interviewees can sometimes move from refusal to co-operation within the course of an interview. It is important to persist.

What should Pc Singh do? He should proceed with his questioning as planned. He probably picked up from the pre-briefing with Stacker's solicitor that she would advise her client to make no comment to any of the points put to him. Certainly, the line taken by the solicitor suggests that Stacker has been briefed to say nothing and that Ms O'Connor intends wherever possible to disrupt the interview or discommode the interviewer. However, Pc Singh has another tack which he can take. Listen:

> **Pc Singh:** Under Part III of the Criminal Justice and Public Order Act 1994...
>
> **O'Connor:** Spare us the legalese, Constable!
>
> **Pc Singh:** Ms O'Connor, your interruptions are not helpful and you appear to be attempting to disrupt this interview. I must ask you to restrict yourself to comments which are relevant to your client. I repeat, Mr Stacker, that under Part III of the Criminal Justice and Public....
>
> **O'Connor:** For God's sake!
>
> **Pc Singh:** ...Act 1994, I have to bring to your attention the definition of a significant statement or silence. The law says this: [he quotes the section]. Do you understand what this means, Mr Stacker?
>
> **Stacker:** No comment.
>
> **Pc Singh:** It means that the court can make an inference about your silence and your refusal to answer my questions. I remind you also of the terms of the caution with which I began this interview.
>
> **Stacker:** No comment.

Pc Singh has quite properly drawn the attention of both Stacker and the solicitor to the implications of refusal to answer questions, and, by invoking the caution again, reminds both that 'it may harm [Stacker's] defence'. There are clear indications that Pc Singh is calm and continues to be in control of the situation (note his polite reprimand to the solicitor and subsequently her more subdued jeering), and that he does not appear to be panicking that Stacker is refusing to answer the questions.

The common tendency is to confront the solicitor or to start rushing the interview. **This must be avoided**. It is very important that the questions continue to be open and to proceed logically through the planned structure for the interview. You should not slide into the temptation to ask **closed** questions (requiring a yes or no reply) nor to speed up, allowing little time to answer. These would all be products of unease because the interview is not going as well as you hoped. Finally, you should not ask the suspect to justify why he is not answering the questions nor show any reciprocal hostility to him or to the solicitor. The simple advice in this situation is to adhere to the PEACE model of interviewing and not be thrown by the suspect's refusal to answer your questions.

It is time to visit the interview again, this time after half an hour has elapsed. The case study continues:

Pc Singh: Let me summarize then. You went to the supermarket with the intent to steal small, easily-portable items with a view to selling them on to a man you met in The Flying Horse, Mickey Dawson. That person has told us that he regularly receives stolen goods from you and from your associate Sergei Bolgomov. We have CCTV coverage of you leaving the premises of Curret and Lixon in the High Street and have recovered from your car items identified by the store manager at Curret and Lixon as having been stolen earlier today. Your fingerprints are on the bottles of spirit taken without payment from the supermarket and on two of the unopened packages of cameras stolen today from Curret and Lixon. How do you account for these facts?

Stacker: (yawning) No comment.

O'Connor: Oh come on, Singh, we've been over this ground time and again and you are getting nowhere.

Pc Singh: It is Constable Singh, Madam. Now Mr Stacker, I want to move on now to a more serious charge. It has been alleged that you attacked Nicola Kew last night in her house, an assault which occasioned actual bodily harm. Do you want to tell me about this assault?

Stacker: The bitch! Did she say that? I'll kill her, the stupid cow!

O'Connor: Mr Stacker, you mustn't . . .

Pc Singh: Do I understand you to be making threats to kill, sir?

Stacker: No! I do not mean that! I mean, I only smacked her once, maybe twice to get her to pull herself together and it was only a tap like, nothing hard, but Christ! To say that I caused her bodily harm, that's just . . .

O'Connor: I need time to consult with my client.

Pc Singh: Just a moment, Madam. Do I understand you right, Mr Stacker? You said you hit Nicola Kew last night?

Stacker: Just tapped her on the chest, not really hit hard or anything.

Pc Singh: You have told me that you hit Nicola Kew in the chest. Where exactly? Show me on your own chest. Mr Stacker is indicating an area around his left breast and left collar bone.

O'Connor: Pc Singh, may I ask for a moment to consult with my client?

Pc Singh: Let me summarize what has been said before I agree to that, Ms O'Connor. I'm sure you'll agree that this admission is very serious and we should be absolutely clear what we are talking about here. Mr Stacker, you have made the significant statement that last night you attacked and injured Nicola Kew, striking her with your fist . . .

Stacker: Hand!

Pc Singh: . . . striking her with your hand. Do you want to add anything to what you have said? Can you tell me why you did it?

Stacker: She kept on and on about not wanting to do the supermarket today and I just couldn't stand her whining bloody voice any longer and I wanted to shut her up, the daft bitch. That idiot Sergei just sat there laughing all the time. Fat lot of help he was. We'd have got clear of the supermarket if he hadn't stuffed that bottle in his trousers.

Pc Singh: We shall adjourn for thirty minutes to give you time to consult your legal adviser, Mr Stacker. The time is 1715.

An 'ambush' question like this—perfectly proper within the context of the interview—has slipped under Stacker's defences and clearly caught him unprepared. Stacker then admitted the offence and the mens rea was his irritation that Nicola would not join him in stealing from the supermarket. Stacker was unprepared for the sudden change of tack and a new line of questioning and forgot to brazen it out with his repeated 'no comment'. Once he had committed himself on record, there was no going back. (His admission also suggests that Nicola Kew was telling the truth in her interview.) The chances are that, on resumption of the interview, Stacker will be charged with ABH as well as with theft, and he faces the prospect of a prison sentence, if found guilty. The solicitor may try bargaining (admitting the lesser charge of theft) but the police are unlikely to accept that and will discuss with the CPS whether the evidence of ABH is enough to take to court. The officers were quite correct to stop the interview to allow Stacker time to talk to his solicitor, but notice that Pc Singh did not accept an adjournment until he had had Stacker's confirmation of what happened. The fact that Stacker indicated where he had hit Nicola (and that Pc Singh mentioned it on tape) will be material evidence against him at any trial.

On resumption of the interview, Pc Singh must give Stacker the warning that he has made a 'significant statement' and invite him to confirm or deny the statement.

It is a good result for Jon Singh, arising not by chance but through patient, probing questions and his interview planning. Notice how he began by summarizing the lesser charges against Stacker before going on to address the ABH charge, and notice too how he continually asked Stacker to confirm what he had said, incidentally getting additional evidence as he did so, such as confirmation of the area of Nicola's body which Stacker struck. Singh's persistence with the PEACE model, the open structure of his questions, all contributed to the admission.

We need now to think about, and discuss in more detail, the role of the legal adviser or defence solicitor, and how you can prepare your responses to 'active defence'.

12.5.8 Dealing with the Solicitor

The PACE Act 1984 Codes of Practice Code C, Note 6D states that:

> The solicitor's only role in the police station is to protect and advance the legal rights of his client. On occasions this may require the solicitor to give advice which has the effect of his client avoiding giving evidence which strengthens the prosecution case.

It sometimes difficult for a police officer, particularly a student police officer who is by definition early in his/her career, to accept that a solicitor's advice can stop a suspect giving details about a crime, or an admission of guilt in committing a crime. Similarly, a solicitor may advise a client (as we saw with the opening of Alan Stacker's interview in Section 12.5.7) not to make any comment at all, though, as we have seen, the law and the caution now reflect the fact that a jury may adversely interpret a suspect's silence in the face of reasonable questioning and where that suspect relies on evidence in court which he/she could have provided to a police officer when questioned.

Nonetheless, as a student police officer you may often hear more experienced police officers argue that the there is not a 'level playing field' with the accused, particularly when a legal adviser specifically advises the suspect not to give confirming evidence of involvement in a crime.

What can you do? Let us start with the solicitor's role and then look at your relationship with the solicitor both before and during interview of the suspect (the solicitor's client). Your role is to investigate the offence and to prove or disprove the suspect's involvement. You are not the judge and jury; it is not for you to pronounce on the suspect's guilt nor to administer punishment.

Remember what we said at the beginning of the interview process? You seek the truth about what happened. It follows that you must regard the defence solicitor as part of the criminal justice system, not as an obstruction to your search to establish the facts.

That said, a solicitor may adopt an 'active defence' role which may look like this:

[In a corridor near the interview room].

Solicitor: You are Pc Singh?

Pc Singh: I am.

Solicitor: You have arrested my client, Sergei Bolgomov?

Pc Singh: I have, with my colleague, Pc Wyatt, and we are preparing to interview Mr Bolgomov in connection with an alleged theft.

Solicitor: I am Peter Jones of Jones, Gateweigh and Bord, Solicitors.

Pc Singh: I know who you are, Mr Jones.

Jones: What evidence do you have to justify the detention of my client?

Pc Singh: Your client was detained at Mortesbury's supermarket this morning in possession of items for which he had not paid and could...

Jones: How do you know he hadn't paid?

Pc Singh: ...could not account for. Because he had no receipts for the goods in his possession.

Jones: What if someone else had the receipts?

Pc Singh: Our enquiries have not confirmed that.

Jones: So it is possible that others have the necessary receipts? Why in that case do you want to interview my client?

Pc Singh: As I've explained, it is to explore with him his account of what happened this morning

Jones: You realize that he cannot speak much English?

Pc Singh: Yes, we have arranged for an interpreter to sit in on the interview.

Jones: What is the evidence that he did not intend to pay?

Pc Singh: That is something I intend to ask him.

Jones: Who else was involved?

Pc Singh: Other suspects are in detention, Mr Jones, but I am not prepared at this stage to identify them to you until I've heard Mr Bolgomov's account.

Jones: One of them is Alan Stacker isn't it?

And so on. What the solicitor is trying to do here is find out what the police case is against his client and to challenge the evidence before the interview begins. This serves two purposes. The first is that the solicitor can ascertain what the strength of police evidence is and therefore advise his client whether to admit the offence or not. If the evidence looks weak or merely circumstantial, the solicitor will probably advise his client to remain silent or not to volunteer information. If the evidence is very strong (as it is in this case) the solicitor may opt for the 'active defence' of admitting a lesser charge in exchange for mitigation or seek to blame the crime on others, or depict his client as the non-English speaking tool of unscrupulous others. Secondly, the solicitor is trying to find out what the police line of questioning will be and if he can, to head off any lines of enquiry which will be difficult for his client, whilst at the same time suggesting to the police officer in charge of the case that he/she will have a hard time proving an offence.

In addition, the solicitor will closely monitor (as we saw above) the interview process itself because, however overwhelming the evidence, a flaw in police procedure can mean the dismissal of charges against the solicitor's client. The defence solicitor will always be looking for a flaw in procedure, or the overlooking of something which should have been properly undertaken. This is one of the reasons why you need to know the law and the associated police procedures very well indeed. The solicitor's tactic is: if you cannot fault the evidence, fault the way it was obtained, or fault the process which led to the charging of his client. If all that fails, it was someone else's fault. Peter Jones, evidently, will go for Stacker as the perpetrator.

Notice that Pc Singh was well prepared for this encounter and, as we expected, is calm and self-possessed in the face of the solicitor's persistent questioning. Notice too, that the solicitor tries all sorts of different tacks, such as switching abruptly from one kind of questioning (about evidence) to another (that Bolgomov does not speak English well) and you can see that at the same time, Pc Singh has intelligently anticipated these questions and has firm answers ready.

Mr Jones wants to know what Pc Singh's case is against his client and displays at least one of his strategies when he tries to find out who else has been charged with the offence(s). Pc Singh quite properly withholds this information until Bolgomov has had the opportunity to give his account, but it is clear that one of Peter Jones's options is to suggest that his client, imperfectly understanding what had been said to him, was exploited by unscrupulous criminals.

All this takes place before the interview begins. In a well-planned meeting, the encounter between the police officer and the defence solicitor will take place in a quiet room, uninterrupted. Sometimes though, the encounter will take place in a corridor with others passing by, with all the noise and disruption you associate with a busy police station, even with other conversations taking place around you, or the encounter may be in or near the cells where the suspects have been detained. These are not ideal circumstances because you as the interviewing officer may feel rushed or ill-prepared. If you are, **the solicitor is likely to attempt to take advantage** of this. The solicitor may even pressure you into saying more than you meant to about the case, thus handing him valuable material in defence of his client. You have to remember that this is not personal, it is business. Let us look at what you can say and what you do not have to divulge at this stage.

First of all, it is the custody officer who has made contact with the solicitor, following a request from the detained suspect. You need to tell the custody officer that you are the point of contact for the defence solicitor, and ensure that you do not leave prisoner handover documents or witness statements attached to the custody record. Do not brief the defence solicitor on the phone; tell her/him that you will make yourself available when the solicitor attends at the police station.

The solicitor will require information from you before you commence the interview, so that the client may be properly advised. You should plan, as Pc Singh did, what you are going to disclose. Ask yourself these questions (and make sure that your answers are robust):

- What evidence do I have?
- What evidence shall I disclose immediately?
- What evidence shall I withhold?
- When will I disclose this evidence in the interview process?
- Can I justify withholding this evidence?

You, as the investigator, can decide what the impact will be of disclosing too much or too little. You should not be defensive and disclose only in answer to the solicitor's questions. You increase the likelihood of a 'no comment' interview if you are perceived by the defence solicitor to be reluctant to disclose evidence unless you are really pushed. On the other hand, you would not want to disclose evidence which has come from an **intelligence source**, or through **surveillance** operations or vital **forensic evidence**, or details which relate to **a particular MO** until you have to and disclosure becomes inevitable, see section 12.9 below.

Expect the defence solicitor to persist in questioning your motive for withholding evidence because he/she will claim not to be able 'properly to advise the client'. If you can justify your decision to withhold, you should avoid becoming drawn into a confrontation with the solicitor. This refusal to follow the solicitor's lead also applies if the solicitor asks for your views on the likely outcome for his/her client. You have to **stay in control** of the process. The more you know the case, and the more you know and understand the law, the more confident you will be in dealing with any legal adviser.

12.5.8.1 Briefing the solicitor

Explain exactly how you intend to conduct the encounter and say that you will answer the solicitor's questions when you have completed the disclosure (see section 12.9 below) of your evidence. Brief at a pace which enables the solicitor to take notes and bring him/her up to date with the welfare of the client. Outline the case you have against the suspect and brief on the evidence you have and upon which you intend to base the interview. Do it chronologically and in a structured manner (straightforward if you have prepared a plan for the interview, of course). Then you can invite questions; the solicitor will want to know about everything you know in relation to the case. The solicitor will encourage you to divulge every piece of evidence in your case, and will often include the common 'catch-all' question, such as: 'Officer, have you disclosed all the evidence in this case?', sometimes phrased as 'Officer, is there any evidence which you are withholding?'. You should have anticipated this question and be ready with your prepared and credible reply.

Listen to Pc Singh's response to the solicitor:

> **Jones:** You're deliberately holding some evidence back, aren't you?
>
> **Pc Singh:** Evidence is being withheld at this stage but I am not prepared to discuss it with you. I fully accept that you will want to advise your client at the time this evidence is disclosed, but I have given you enough in my disclosure briefing for you to advise your client for the purpose of the forthcoming interview.

There are two major warnings which you must heed in briefing the solicitor: **never overstate or understate your evidence**. You should avoid like phrases such as 'your man is right up against it on this one' or 'there is not much in the way of evidence as yet'. Either phrase will (quite rightly) provoke the solicitor and it is likely that he/she will comment like this:

> **Solicitor:** Your comment about being 'right up against it' is outrageous, inappropriate, and highly prejudicial to my client. I am making a note about your attitude and I shall raise it both with your superiors and with the CPS.
>
> or:
>
> **Solicitor:** If, as you have just said, the evidence is thin for the detention of my client and you evidently lack proof that he committed the alleged offence, why are you proceeding with the interview? Is there any point in your interviewing my client at all if you have not a shred of reason to hold him here? I demand that my client is released at once.

Not what you want to hear either, since in both instances you have surrendered control of the briefing and you could be on the way to losing the case entirely.

Most defence solicitors, particularly those who are duty solicitors, will have a good understanding and plenty of experience of the PEACE interview model and the approaches which an interviewing officer will adopt. He/she will know that you will try to build a rapport with the suspect to get him/her to talk to you, but do not expect the solicitor to help you or assist with the process. For example, you might (as Pc Wyatt did) select a non-contentious or non-challenging topic to encourage the interviewee to open up. Unless it directly relates to the suspect's welfare, be prepared for the solicitor to challenge its relevance. The maxim here is not to choose a vague subject which you cannot pursue in the face of the solicitor's challenge and from which you will have to back down.

The point is that the solicitor is monitoring **you** as closely as he/she is monitoring the client. If you let your feelings show because the solicitor or interviewee is frustrating your efforts, this will help them. Remember how calm Pc Singh was when the solicitor challenged him? You should be aware that the solicitor is looking for precisely the weaknesses we have advised you against, so that he/she can take over or disrupt what you are trying to do.

The Codes of Practice give you (and solicitors) some guidance on what is acceptable behaviour by the solicitor and what is unacceptable.

A legal adviser **may:**

- seek clarification of an issue or question;
- advise the client not to answer a question;
- challenge an improper question or the manner in which it is put; or
- wish to offer the client further advice.

A legal adviser **may not:**

- answer questions on the client's behalf;
- provide the client with written responses to quote.

The solicitor has to have **grounds to intervene** and disrupt your interview. If you ask any leading questions or adopt a threatening or bullying manner, or seek to offer the suspect a lighter sentence in exchange for giving more evidence, the solicitor will intervene (and rightly so). If, however, you are acting fairly, proportionately, and properly, the solicitor's grounds for intervention are much reduced. It is unlikely that you will ever meet solicitors who behave so inappropriately that you have to exclude them from the interview (though it has happened) but you may encounter a solicitor who becomes so disruptive that you have to deal with them or lose the interview. Let us see how this may work:

> **Pc Singh:** Mr Bolgomov, please tell me how you travelled to the supermarket this morning.
>
> **Jones:** Do not answer.
>
> **Pc Singh:** What did you do when you got to the supermarket?
>
> **Jones:** My client went to buy razor blades.
>
> **Pc Singh:** Mr Bolgomov, I'd like you tell me why you had four bottles of whisky hidden inside your jacket.
>
> [*Pause*]
>
> **Pc Singh:** Mr Jones, I am asking your client for an account of what happened this morning and on three occasions you have disrupted the interview by telling him not to answer, by answering on his behalf and telling him not to answer by shaking your head.
>
> **Jones:** Just doing my job, Constable.
>
> **Pc Singh:** No, Mr Jones. You are not giving the interpreter time to translate my question and you are not giving Mr Bolgomov time to formulate his answer. My questions are relevant and I shall continue to ask them.
>
> **Jones:** Oh, very well.
>
> **Pc Singh:** I should like you to stop interrupting after every question and allow me to conduct this interview properly.

Remember that this is all on tape, and the court may take a very dim view of a disruptive solicitor. It may even prejudice his client's chances. Few solicitors, once challenged in this way, will persist so brazenly, though they may well continue to use the tactics in a muted or less systematic way. You will have made your point and be on record as having done so, politely and proportionately.

The final point to make in your dealings with a defence solicitor is that it is only another part of the interviewing process. If you know the law, know your evidence, and if you have planned your interview properly, you will be confident and not likely to be pushed around by a highly skilled or manipulative solicitor. In other words, you will have anticipated difficulties before they arise and you will be fully capable of dealing with them when they do.

12.5.9 Meeting the Needs of all Interviewees

There are times when you may be interviewing (as witness, victim, or suspect) a 'vulnerable person'. There is no specific definition of a vulnerable person, but the PACE Act 1984, Code C 1.4 suggests that, if an officer has any suspicions, or is told in good faith, that any person of any age may be mentally disordered, mentally handicapped, or mentally incapable of understanding the significance of questions put to them, then that person shall be treated as a vulnerable person requiring the additional presence of 'an appropriate adult'. This extends, obviously, to children under the age of seventeen and further to any person who, because of an impairment such as a serious visual handicap, deafness, illiteracy, or who has difficulty in articulation because of a speech impediment, may find an interview problematic. It is usually the custody officer who considers whether an appropriate adult is required, not you as the interviewer.

However, you should be prepared for an additional person to be present at your interviews and acting on behalf of the person being interviewed. The legal adviser does not play this role; the appropriate adult is a completely separate person. Legal advisers seldom have experience or expertise in dealing with impairment or mental handicap and his/her role is confined to the **legal** interests of the person as client.

The PACE Act 1984, Code C 1.7, sets out the categories of person who can be an appropriate adult, and their duties are also described. The appropriate adult for a **juvenile** is, first, a parent or guardian, or, if the juvenile is in care, a suitable representative from the care authority or voluntary organization. Failing the availability of any of these, a social worker may stand 'in loco parentis' (instead of a parent). As a last resort, any responsible person aged eighteen or over who is unconnected with the police in any way, may be an appropriate adult. The PACE Act 1984 does not define what is meant by responsible, but it will not include the juvenile's friends nor anyone with a criminal record.

For a person who is **mentally disordered** or **mentally handicapped**, an appropriate adult is a relative, guardian, or other person responsible for their care and custody, or someone who has experience of dealing with mentally handicapped people (such as an approved social worker as defined by the Mental Health Act 1983, or a specialist social worker). Again, anyone connected with the police is not eligible. Failing either of these two categories, some other responsible person aged eighteen or over and unconnected with the police in any way, may be the appropriate adult.

As well as the custody sergeants or custody officers, you as an interviewer should be alert to the special circumstances involved in interviewing a person with a physical or mental impairment. You should always try to ascertain the nature and extent of the impairment if you can and if the individual is willing to divulge it. Remember that the PACE Act 1984 'allows you to proceed on an assumption', either because you have been told or because you suspect an impairment. This obviously needs careful and sensitive handling. Do not say to someone (witness, suspect, or victim) 'Are you deaf?' in a challenging way. Try instead saying 'Do you have a physical impairment we should be aware of?' or more neutral language of this kind. Make arrangements for a **signer** to attend the interview if the individual is profoundly deaf or if there are problems with lip-reading. Do not shout or raise your voice with deaf people, but ensure that they can see your face in order to lip-read. Ensure you speak one at a time. Attract their attention by lightly touching the sleeve. You may also suggest these things to the legal adviser.

It may be difficult to arrange Braille texts in order for blind people to make statements, but it may be a good initiative for you, in consultation with your force diversity team, to establish whether there are Braille texts available which explain, for example, suspect's rights, the caution, and the management of tapes after interview. If there are none, you should arrange that some are made. The local branch of the Royal National Institute for the Blind would help you if asked. You need to be aware that not all blind people can read Braille.

Other impairments may be more difficult to deal with, such as speech impediments, but as general advice be sensitive to the individual's needs and requirements and do your best to meet them. What should guide your actions and approach to any of these situations is the simple question: 'Have I done all I can to ensure that this person is not disadvantaged in any way because of a disability or impairment?' If your answer to this is 'yes', then you have taken all reasonable steps. No one should be placed at a disadvantage in a police interview because of physical or mental impairment; the criminal justice system is not well served unless this principle is upheld.

The appropriate adult does not have a passive role, sitting in the interview as a mere observer. The custody officer should read from the custody record the following to anyone acting as the appropriate adult:

> Where you are present at an interview, you are not expected to act simply as an observer. The purpose of your presence is to advise the person being questioned, to observe whether or not the interview is being conducted properly and fairly, and to facilitate communication with the person being interviewed.

The appropriate adult will be invited to sign the custody record to show that he/she understands the responsibilities involved. You would be well advised as interviewer to check that this has been done. If it has not, you should remedy that, and obtain a voluntary signature from the appropriate adult before the interview begins. A couple of other practical points: you may assume that such interviews may take longer, especially if there is interpretation involved, for example by a signer. The same applies to interviews at which a language interpreter is used. Even simple questions have to be translated from English into the other language and the reply translated into English. Allow at least twice as long as normal for this, and do not hurry the process or become impatient. The disadvantage, perhaps, is that in a suspect interview, the suspect has much longer to consider a reply. An advantage may be that you could use that delay profitably by observing the suspect's NVC and monitoring the suspect's demeanour, always allowing for cultural and linguistic diversity.

12.5.10 Intelligence Interviews

An often-overlooked by-product of a formal police interview is the 'intelligence interview'. In order to establish the definition of an intelligence interview, you might have referred to the section which discusses intelligence acquisition in depth, or reasoned that someone being interviewed who has access to criminal intelligence might be worth questioning further. Two things apply here:

- An intelligence interview is a separate process from your interview, and must be undertaken by specialist intelligence officers.
- You have nothing more to do with the intelligence process apart from alerting your intelligence section to the potential of the interviewee.

The intelligence interview and your interview must be kept separate and distinct from each other. The intelligence interview is ring-fenced and, on the **need-to-know principle**, you should not have any further dealings with the matter.

An intelligence interview is the process through which the police attempt to gather criminal intelligence on the activities and lifestyle of the interviewee and others. The process must be separate from the criminal investigation. All police officers should be alert to the potential for an intelligence interview and carefully note those people (known as 'subjects' in this context) who would have access to information about Category B targets, nominals, associates, or offenders whose criminality comes within the force's strategic intelligence requirement. The access which the subject has should be reported to the BCU Intelligence Unit and arrangements made for the Unit to conduct an interview at an appropriate point. In many forces, the intelligence interview is conducted by a field intelligence officer (FIO) from the BCU Intelligence Unit who may go on to be the principal informant handler, sometimes in conjunction with a colleague who may become the co-handler.

However, some forces have concluded that the potential exposure of the covert identity of an informant handler in the cells or in interview rooms, where they may be seen by other criminals in transit, is too great a risk. Instead, the exploratory intelligence interview is carried out by a trained intelligence analyst or researcher, who does not work 'in the field' and therefore runs less risk of being exposed to possible recognition by other criminals. This is not just a protective measure for the officer, but has a very real impact on the security of the potential informant. It is more professional to use a 'back office' member of staff (properly trained in interviewing and in the intelligence requirements, including the RIPA 2000) to conduct the initial approach than to use a functioning field intelligence officer. The potential informant may be reassured by such professionalism and therefore more likely to co-operate.

As a student police officer you are unlikely to be involved in the detail of any of this, but you should know that it is going on. Any interview conducted whilst the subject is in custody (and this is often the only opportunity for a secure approach) must be recorded on the custody record, but without specific reference, of course, to the purpose. The record will simply record transfer of custody from one police officer to another. The intelligence interview should not be recorded, nor should any others be present, to enhance the confidentiality of the process. Any information obtained as a result of the interview will be recorded on a 5x5x5 (the intelligence report form, see section 12.3.7.2 above), but the provisions of the RIPA 2000 must be adhered to. It is highly unlikely that any intelligence interview of a juvenile would be undertaken since the safeguards around juvenile informants are very stringent.

Should you subsequently re-interview someone who has been the subject of an intelligence interview, no reference should be made to that interview in the presence of others or while the interview tapes are running, since this will be potentially disclosable (see section 12.9 below). Under some circumstances, intelligence officers can offer inducements, such as the provision of 'texts' for informants or the trading of charges in exchange for intelligence. We are in somewhat un-researched territory here, and there is ambiguity around the nature of the trading. The point is that you should be aware that this goes on and that it is a function of the wider intelligence and investigation picture, to which you can contribute positively. You are advised by most forces not to speculate about any intelligence interview with others who do not need to know, and not to discuss any trading of charges which result. All you need to understand is that any trading will be on the authority of a BCU crime manager (usually a detective inspector) and is lawful under the RIPA 2000. However, it is not appropriate for you to make any offer to a suspect, even if the individual has admitted guilt or has proffered intelligence useful to the force. Leave that to the intelligence section.

12.5.11 Special Warnings

Under ss 36 and 37 of the Criminal Justice and Public Order Act 1994 (CJPOA), there are occasions when you will be obliged to issue a 'special warning' to a suspect who has been caught directly in the commission of a crime (in flagrante or 'red-handed'). If a suspect has given a reasonable account of the fact in question, do not use a special warning. Inappropriate use of the special warning can be interpreted as oppressive behaviour.

TASK 9

Write down when you think the special warning should be used. Before caution? During the 'engagement' phase? At the end of the interview, as things are being brought to a close?

Many police practitioners argue that the best place to use a special warning is in the **'challenge'** phase of the PEACE interview (see section 12.5.4.3), after the suspect has had a full opportunity to account for what happened, but has not done so. The special warning should include the following points, put in language which the suspect will understand:

- what offence is being investigated;
- what particular fact you want the suspect to account for;
- that you believe that the fact arose because the subject was involved in the offence;
- that a proper inference may be drawn if the suspect fails to account for that specific fact;
- that a record of the interview is being made.

Sections 36 and 37 are very specific and the codes of practice outline the nature of the warning that must be given in order for an adverse inference to be drawn later. Officers must correctly apply the legislation open to them. In the context of our extended case study interviews about the supermarket thefts, it might appear like this:

> **Pc Singh:** Mr Stacker, I have asked you before how you account for your fingerprints being on the two bottles of spirits taken without payment from Mortesbury's stores this morning. You were arrested on suspicion of theft and that has been part of the focus of this interview. I have to tell you now that I am not satisfied with your response, which has been 'no comment' and I have to ask you again if you will explain why it is that your fingerprints appear on bottles from the supermarket. I believe that you stole those bottles and I must remind you that a proper inference may be drawn by the court if you cannot, or will not, account for your fingerprints. You should be reminded that this interview is being taped.

You can imagine the likely intervention of the solicitor at this point. Nonetheless, Pc Singh has properly administered the special warning and he has covered the five essential points. Any continued silence or refusal to answer will be considered carefully by the court and an adverse impression may be created.

After some time, during which Stacker persisted with his formula of 'no comment', Pc Singh said this:

> **Pc Singh:** Very well. It is clear to me that you refuse to answer the questions I have put to you about the existence of your fingerprints on bottles of spirits from the supermarket. I continue to believe that you stole the bottles and the fact that you refuse to account for your fingerprints has been recorded. I drew your attention to the circumstances around this fact and your solicitor advised you not to answer. I want to turn to another part of the events of this morning, and must tell you that the special warning now no longer applies. Do you understand what I have said?
> **Stacker:** Piss off.
> **O'Connor** (solicitor): My client understands, Constable Singh.
> **Pc Singh:** I would rather he said so himself.

Notice here that Pc Singh has indicated that he is moving to another part of the evidence to ask questions and that the special warning no longer applies. This is very important, not just because extended special warnings can be interpreted as oppressive behaviour on the part of the police, and it must be administered appropriately and proportionally, but also because this stops Stacker or his legal adviser claiming at a later date, or in court, that Stacker continued to answer questions because he thought he had to. Not that Stacker did answer the questions under the special warning, but the point is that **this is a very specific use of questioning, on a specific fact, and cannot be extended to other parts of the interview**.

Of course, when Pc Singh comes to the matter of other supermarket goods in Stacker's possession and not paid for, or the goods hidden in the back of his car which have been stolen from Curret and Lixon, Pc Singh may have to administer the special warning again. Remember that the special warning comes in the challenge phase of the interview, must include the five points, and must be ended with a specific comment to the suspect when the time has come to move on to other things. The court will draw the necessary inference from Stacker's refusal to account for the facts in question.

Just to recap: a **significant statement** is when you draw the suspect's attention to what he/she has said (or failed to say) in a statement, and you give him/her the opportunity to confirm or deny what was said. A **special warning** is when you want to challenge an account or a silence about a particular fact. Two useful flow charts about the use of special warnings follow, which you could use in the interview and which can remind you about the provisions of ss 36 and 37 of the CJPOA 1994.

Section 36 of the CJPOA 1994 states that if:

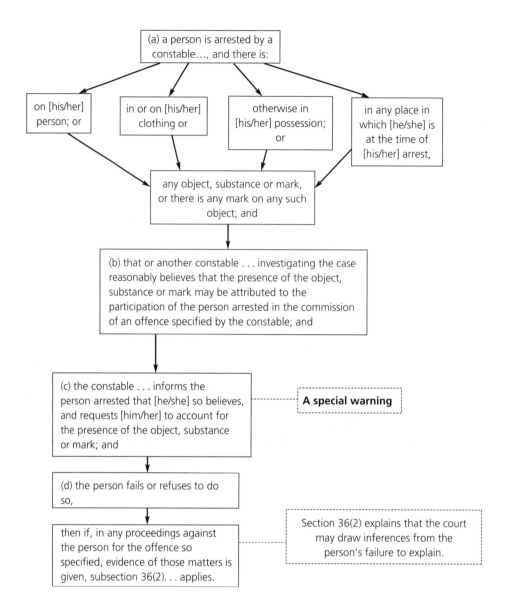

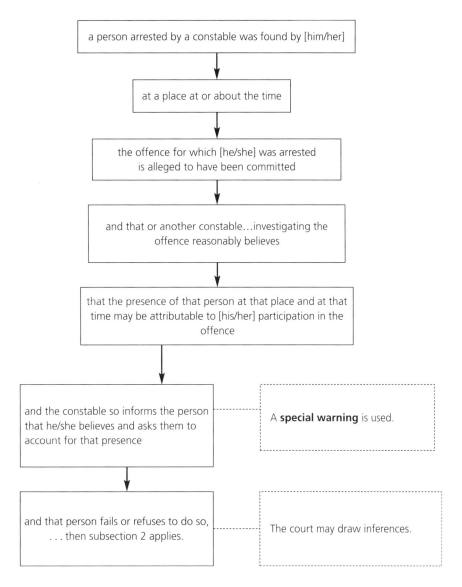

12.5.12 Summary

Let us sum up the main points from this long discussion about interviewing.

Every interview is different and every witness, victim, or suspect will behave differently. You have to be prepared for these differences and plan accordingly. Nearly all witnesses will co-operate, unless they are frightened, confused, or intimidated; you need to be able to cope with that, just as you do when interviewing victims. Both witnesses and victims are better interviewed away from a police station and in surroundings which are quiet and reassuring. Your skills of empathizing and reassuring will be needed throughout the process.

Your role as an interviewer is to help establish the truth; the suspect must explain his/her role in the event or act under investigation. You can help him/her do this by engaging with the suspect from the opening stages, having carefully explained what is going to happen. The more detail you obtain in the suspect's own words, the more you can refute denial of guilt, and the easier it will be to detect if he/she is lying, evading, or telling you only half a story. Equally, the more detail you obtain, the more a suspect may be exonerated and his/her innocence established.

Careful planning and preparation for a police interview is essential. You are well advised to follow the PEACE model of interviewing, though you may expect a solicitor to challenge you when you seek to engage with his/her client. If a suspect refuses to speak or takes (with or without legal advice) refuge in silence, your methodology must not change. You must continue to ask open questions, give the suspect time to answer, and always guard against allowing yourself be drawn into using only closed questions, or losing your temper or abandoning the interview. Remember that the courts can take a negative view of a suspect's silence and may draw adverse inferences from his/her refusal to answer reasonable questions. The qualities of persistence and resilience are key to making you a successful interviewer.

Be confident and positive in dealing with legal advisers; remembering that they are there to do a job (protecting their client's interests) and that it is a part of their professional business. It is not personal. As long as you conduct yourself in a professional and competent manner, you have nothing to fear, and remember that you are entitled to ask robust and persistent questions in an interview.

Finally, remember that a good interview may often be the deciding factor in a successful investigation, and from that, a successful court case.

12.6   Preparing and Submitting Case Files

The interview record that we discussed in section 12.5 will be one of the case files that will be used in any subsequent prosecution. There will be numerous other case files involved, including charge sheets, lists of exhibits (normally forensic evidence), and so on. Successful investigations require the preparation and submitting of good quality and accurate case files. We recognize that paperwork is rarely popular, but all officers acknowledge the particular importance of case files. Do not regard case file preparation as a mere technical exercise—the successful prosecution of a person who is guilty of a serious offence may depend on your ability to work with these files.

Before the introduction of the IPLDP, shortcomings in the training of student officers in the skills of case file preparation were noted by a number of forces (Cambridgeshire Constabulary, 2005). You are likely to find the subject dealt with extensively during the latter half of your training. There are a number of NOS Units and elements directly concerned with this aspect of your training, notably:

National Occupational Standards Elements

2G4.1 Finalise investigations.

2J1.1   Prepare case files.

2J1.2   Submit case files and progress enquiries.

The PAC under the 'Finalise Investigation' heading also lists 'Complete pre-charge files', 'Complete post-charge files', and 'Complete summons files'.

In addition to any notes and training you may receive from your force, you could also download and read section 1 of the 2004 edition of the Prosecution Team Manual of Guidance available from <http://police.homeoffice.gov.uk/news-and-publications/publication/operational-policing/prosecution-manual-intro.pdf>.

You may sometimes hear case files referred to as 'MG files'. This is because you will be using nationally produced forms which have the prefix MG Examples include MG4, 'Charge Sheet' and MG11 'Key witness statement(s)'.

You will be given training by your force on case file preparation and the roles of others who also share responsibility, such as the CPS. Detailed explanations of the processes involved would be inappropriate for a Handbook of this kind. Instead we have produced (using the Prosecution Team Manual of Guidance mentioned above) a list of the MG forms that you are likely to require in two different circumstances:

- straightforward cases (that is, without complications such as certain sensitive disclosure issues) and where a guilty plea is entered;
- contested ('not guilty' pleas) or Crown Court cases.

The likely case file forms in each eventuality are summarized below (CPS, 2004).

12.6.1 Straightforward and 'Guilty Plea' Cases

12.6.1.1 Pre-charge expedited report

For charging decision—to custody officer or Duty Prosecutor:

- MG 3—Report to Crown Prosecutor (for offences where CPS decides to charge).
- MG 11(s)*—Key witness statement(s) or Index (if visually recorded)(if witnessed by police, use the MG11 of one officer).
- MG 15—SDN or verbal summary of admissions. (SDN can be written on officer's MG11).
- Phoenix print (suspect pre-cons, cautions, etc).

(*Include details of pre-cons for witnesses who have provided Key MG11s if case involves a remand in custody.)

Once a charging decision has been made, the Pre-charge Expedited Report becomes the Post-charge Expedited File for court. Further upgrading is not required if the case is disposed of at the first court appearance. If a 'not guilty' plea is entered or the defendant elects Crown Court, prepare a Full File.

12.6.1.2 Post-charge expedited file

For EFH court hearing:

- MG 1—File front sheet.
- MG 4—Charge sheet.
- MG 5—Case file summary (unless the statements cover all elements of the case).
- MG 6—Case file information (if there is information for the investigator to record).
- MG 10—Witness non-availability (PYO only).
- MG 11(s)*—Key witness statement(s) or Index (if visually recorded).
- SDN—may be written on MG15, MG5, or MG11 of officer.
- Phoenix print (suspect pre-cons, cautions, etc).

Where applicable, also include the following:

- MG 2—Initial witness assessment.
- MG 3—Report to Crown Prosecutor (for offences where CPS decide charge).
- MG 3A—Further report to Crown Prosecutor.
- MG 4A—Conditional bail form.
- MG 4B—Request to vary police conditional bail.
- MG 4C—Surety/Security.
- MG 7—Remand application.
- MG 8—Breach of bail conditions.
- MG 11—Other witness statements already taken.
- MG 13—Application for order on conviction.
- MG 18—Offences taken into consideration (TIC).
- MG 19—Compensation form (plus supporting documents).
- Copy of documentary exhibits/photos.
- Police racist incident form/crime report (in racist incident cases).

12.6.2 Contested ('Not Guilty' Pleas) or Crown Court Cases

12.6.2.1 Pre-charge evidential report

For charging decision—to custody officer or Duty Prosecutor:

- MG 3—Report to Crown Prosecutor (suggest charges).
- MG 5—Case summary (unless the statements cover all elements of the case).
- MG 6—Case file information.
- MG 11(s)—Key witness statement(s) or Index (if visually recorded). If witnessed by police, use MG11 of one officer, summarize evidence of others.
- MG 12—Exhibits list.
- MG 15—Interview record: SDN/ROTI/ROVI (SDN can be on MG5, officer's MG11 or MG15).
- Crime report and incident log.

- Any unused material which might undermine the case (disclosure schedules are not required at this stage).
- Copies of Key documentary exhibits Phoenix print (suspect pre-cons, cautions, etc).

Once a charging decision has been made, the Pre-charge Evidential Report becomes the Post-charge Evidential File for court.

Further Upgrading may also be required. Where it is clear that the case will be heard in the Crown Court, or a not guilty plea is likely, a Full File should be prepared and submitted with the MG3.

12.6.2.2 Post-charge evidential file

For EAH court hearing:

- MG 1—File front sheet.
- MG 3—Report to Crown Prosecutor.
- MG 4—Charge sheet.
- MG 5—Case file summary (unless MG11(s) cover all elements of case).
- MG 6—Case file information (if there is information for the investigator to record).
- MG 10—Witness non-availability.
- MG 11(s)—Key witness statement(s) or Index (if visually recorded).
- MG 12—Exhibits list. Copies of Key exhibits/photos.
- MG 15—Interview record—SDN/ROTI/ROVI (SDN can be on MG5, officer's MG11 or MG15).
- Phoenix print (suspect pre-cons, cautions, etc).

Where they are also applicable, include the following:

- MG 2—Initial witness assessment.
- MG 3A—Further report to Crown Prosecutor.
- MG 4A/B/C—Bail/surety/security.
- MG 7—Remand application.
- MG 11—Other witness statements already taken.
- MG 13—Application for order on conviction.
- MG 18—Offences TIC.
- MG 19—Compensation form plus supporting documents.
- Police racist incident form/crime report (in racist incident cases).

12.6.2.3 Upgrade to full file

For Crown Court or contested cases:

- MG 6C—Schedule of non-sensitive unused material.
- MG 6D—Schedule of sensitive material.
- MG 6E—Disclosure officer's report.
- MG 9—Witness list.
- MG 11—All other statements.
- Custody record.

Where applicable, also include the following:

- MG 2—Initial witness assessment.
- MG 6B—police officer's disciplinary record.
- Phoenix print (witness pre-cons, cautions, etc, see the JOPI).

12.7 Evidence of Bad Character

We are about to consider the detailed process of giving evidence in court. However, before we do so it is useful to examine a significant change to the law in recent years in the area of 'evidence of bad character'. This also relates to case files, covered in section 12.6. You will probably look at bad character evidence as part of your training as it features in IPLDP

Operational Module 9 'To prepare and present case information, present evidence and finalise investigations' and under LPG 1.4 'Bad character evidence'.

In this section we provide an overview of bad character evidence introduced by the Criminal Justice Act 2003 which is relevant to the student police officer. The NCPE have produced Practice Advice on Evidence of Bad Character on behalf of ACPO which you may wish to consult via your police force (it is not a publicly available document). If you need the full details then the CPS website on bad character evidence is a good starting point and is publicly available: <http://www.cps.gov.uk/legal/section13/chapter_u.html>.

The new law clarifies when a non-defendant's bad character and a defendant's bad character can be used in criminal cases. For the bad character of a **non-defendant** to be utilized in criminal cases, either the defence or the prosecution must make an application for leave to the judge under s 100 of the Criminal Justice Act 2003. The judge must then decide whether that bad character can be brought up in the case, ie whether it is admissible under either of three conditions, which we list below. Case law already shows that judges are unlikely to allow such evidence to be introduced unless it really is of significant value to the issues in the case (See *R v Bovell* [2005] 2 Cr App R 4012005). The main principle influencing s 100 of the Criminal Justice Act 2003 is to protect witnesses and victims from having their previous history brought up unless it is truly considered relevant to the case.

12.7.1   The Definition of Bad Character

The definition of bad character provided under s 98 (see below) is wide enough to cover behaviour **not** amounting to crimes as well as obvious instances such as previous convictions. The law makes it clear that reprehensible behaviour falling short of a conviction also counts as bad character. For instance, someone may show a propensity to be violent if he/she gets drunk on a regular basis and has altercations with his/her loved ones. This may become relevant in a case of assault against a family member irrespective of whether he/she has been convicted in relation to that previous behaviour.

Bad character is defined by s 98 of the Criminal Justice Act 2003 in the following way:

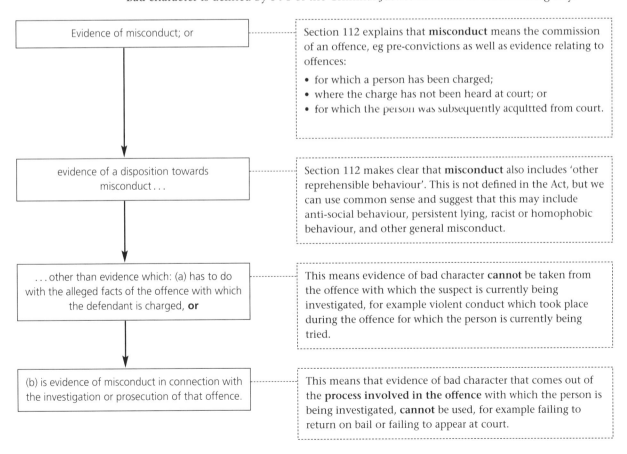

| Evidence of misconduct; or | Section 112 explains that **misconduct** means the commission of an offence, eg pre-convictions as well as evidence relating to offences:
• for which a person has been charged;
• where the charge has not been heard at court; or
• for which the person was subsequently acquitted from court. |

| evidence of a disposition towards misconduct . . . | Section 112 makes clear that **misconduct** also includes 'other reprehensible behaviour'. This is not defined in the Act, but we can use common sense and suggest that this may include anti-social behaviour, persistent lying, racist or homophobic behaviour, and other general misconduct. |

| . . . other than evidence which: (a) has to do with the alleged facts of the offence with which the defendant is charged, **or** | This means evidence of bad character **cannot** be taken from the offence with which the suspect is currently being investigated, for example violent conduct which took place during the offence for which the person is currently being tried. |

| (b) is evidence of misconduct in connection with the investigation or prosecution of that offence. | This means that evidence of bad character that comes out of the **process involved in the offence** with which the person is being investigated, **cannot** be used, for example failing to return on bail or failing to appear at court. |

The implication of bad character evidence is that police officers should record matters contemporaneously, and provide such intelligence to the relevant department. One day such information could be crucial to a criminal investigation. When dealing with criminal cases, officers should always consider whether relevant bad character exists. Form MG16 will need to be completed in order to notify the CPS of any relevant bad character, and officers should also consider raising relevant bad character with the defendant in interview.

12.7.2 Introducing Evidence of the Bad Character of the Defendant

Section 101(1) of the Criminal Justice Act 2003 lists the seven circumstances where evidence of the defendant's supposed bad character is admissible. This does not require leave of the judge, but does require the prosecution to give notice to the defence regarding the bad character they propose to use about the defendant. They will need to provide this to the defence so that the latter can consider in some cases making an application to the judge to disallow its use.

Seven circumstances where evidence of bad behaviour may be admissible

Section 101(1) of the Criminal Justice Act 2003	Comments and explanations
(a) all parties to the proceedings agree to the evidence being admissible;	That is, the defence and prosecution agree. Perhaps unlikely.
(b) the evidence is adduced by the defendant [him/herself] or is given in answer to a question asked by [him/her] in cross-examination and intended to elicit it;	Called a 'waiver by the defendant'. This would include for example, situations where suspects introduce evidence of their own bad character brought up during interview. It can also happen that during cross-examination the defendant chooses to reveal something of bad character; eg 'I couldn't have been there because I was in prison at the time'.
(c) it is important explanatory evidence;	So, for example, in the case of disqualified driving, evidence is submitted to the court that the defendant had been previously disqualified from driving.
(d) it is relevant to an important matter in issue between the defendant and the prosecution . . .	Defined as 'a matter of substantial importance in the context of the case as a whole'. This part is a major break with previous practice and should be read in conjunction with s 103, that is whether a defendant has a propensity to: • habitually commit crimes of the kind with which they are charged; • be untruthful (eg previous convictions for perjury).
(e) it has substantial probative value in relation to an important matter in issue between the defendant and a co-defendant;	In this instance, a co-defendant may wish to provide evidence of the defendant's bad character, thus trying to prove that it was less likely that he/she committed the offence, and more likely it was the other defendant.
(f) it is evidence to correct a false impression given by the defendant, or	Here the prosecution may wish to introduce evidence which is relevant, in order to correct a false impression that the defendant has given in relation to his/her character, eg saying that he/she is known for his/her honesty, when in fact he/she has previous convictions for deception.
(g) the defendant has made an attack on another person's character.	In this instance, the defendant attacks another person's character by accusing him/her of committing an offence or behaving in a reprehensible way (whether true or not). Note that this also applies at the time the defendant was being charged or interviewed under caution—hence include such an attack in the records kept.

Finally, note that there are also guidelines concerning exclusions to bad character evidence and non-defendant bad character evidence that you will find detailed via the CPS website given above.

> **TASK 10**
>
> Find out which MG form is used to place evidence of bad character into the case file of the defendant.

12.8 Giving Evidence in Court

Now we have come to the stage where the final phases of the investigative process will be played out: the magistrates' or Crown courts. You may wish to re-read section 5.12 on the CJS at this point.

Remember that a magistrates' court hears all criminal cases in its particular area (called the petty sessional area) and the majority of cases do not progress further; the offender is tried and either punished or acquitted. Serious criminal offences may be referred to trial at a Crown Court, but they are always presented first at a magistrates' court to decide if there is sufficient evidence to support a trial at the higher court. A magistrates' court can consist of a bench of magistrates (lay persons, unpaid, who are Justices of the Peace) or a stipendiary magistrate who is a legally-qualified and paid practitioner. Some courts have both at different times.

Perhaps describing this as a 'stage' is apt: the course of events in a magistrates' court, and more so in a Crown Court, do bear a striking resemblance to scenes in a theatre; the participants perform a very particular role.

Actors in the Court

Participants and others	Description of the role
The Magistrate(s)	Concerned local citizens who act 'for the people' in hearing petty offences or the evidence of crimes.
The Stipendiary	The paid professional dealing with local offences.
The Clerk	The paid professional who knows the law and advises the lay magistrates.
The Accused	In the dock and trying to create the best possible impression, whether guilty or not.
Prosecution	The retributive voice of the people; a professional lawyer (Crown Prosecution Service).
Defence	The upholder of justice acting for the client(s); equally a professional lawyer or solicitor.
The Public	The 'theatre audience' (but can be the families of victims, or relatives of the accused, so having an interest in the outcome).
The Judge	In a Crown Court, a professional lawyer whose legal experience qualifies him/her to assume the role of objective and dispassionate 'arbiter'. Judges have seen all the legal tricks and heard all the courtroom arguments before, but some remain curiously innocent of many of life's common features. It is not uncommon for example, for some judges to ask questions such as 'What is an iPod?'
The Jury	In a Crown Court, brought together for a trial at which the defendant has pleaded 'Not Guilty', the representatives of the people upon whom all those present want to make an impression; the jury is nominally 'twelve good persons and true' drawn from any walk of life.
Witnesses	Sometimes overwhelmed by the big occasion and can be inhibited by the battery of legal representatives from both sides; sometimes play the role of rabbits caught in headlights. At other times, witnesses are specialists with expert knowledge (for example, pathologists or forensic scientists) who are well used to appearing in court.
The Media	Usually at big trials, but there are also court reporters at the petty level; also claiming to represent the people and apt to raise the drama as many levels as possible.

This is the cast of players, with the first seven likely to appear at the magistrates' court (where the drama is often brief and low-key) and the remainder at the Crown Court, where the drama can be prolonged and at fever pitch. Add to this heady mix the panelled court room, the eighteenth-century costumes and wigs, the rituals, and the ceremonial, and you have a stage set.

It may be considered somewhat trivializing or even inappropriate to ask a student police officer to view the enactment of justice as a play and the venue as a stage set. However, in our experience such an analogy helps police officers understand the culture of the courtroom and emphasizes the inherently adversarial nature of the courts in England and Wales. By understanding the dynamics of the court room you will be better able to support justice.

12.8.1 The Role of the Police Officer in Court

Appearance in court in whatever capacity requires you to give as much attention to planning and preparation as you would for a police interview, which we covered in section 12.5. You certainly cannot just turn up at court on the day and expect to recall the criminal investigation with accuracy, or perform your role as a witness in a professional fashion.

You are there to give evidence as a police officer, probably as the officer in the case. Later in your career you may attend court as an expert witness (for example, in the forensic recovery of data from a computer hard drive), but at this stage you have no more privileged status than any of the other witnesses. However, you will be more familiar with court procedures than the non-specialist witnesses, and you know more about the case being tried (or you should) than anyone else present.

12.8.2 Evidence

You will be asked to think about the nature and types of evidence during your training, for example in LPG 1.7 'Investigation and Interviews'. Evidence is information which is presented to a court so that it may decide upon a fact (did the accused do this act by this means?). In the sense that we use the word throughout this Handbook, evidence is almost always linked with crime in some way. Evidence is usually regarded as consisting of four kinds:

- **oral** (also called verbal or spoken);
- **real** (an article, object, or thing with material existence—that is, it can be produced in court);
- **documentary** (a document, paper, or record, which can be electronic);
- 'hearsay evidence'.

Oral evidence is the most common form of evidence presented to a court. A witness will say 'I saw him push the block over the parapet of the bridge', or 'I heard her scream and then felt a hand on my bottom', or 'The drink tasted bitter, which it hadn't before I went to the lavatory'. It is what has been directly experienced by someone on the spot at the time that the alleged offence was committed, and it must relate directly to the individual who is giving testimony. In other words, a witness to an act must have perceived that act directly, through his/her senses. The witness must have seen, heard, felt, tasted, or smelled whatever is being witnessed.

Real evidence, as we have noted, is any article or thing which can be produced for the court, however small and however large. Real evidence can range from microscopic bloodstains or particles of explosive, through to objects which the court will have to see in situ (such as a large lorry, a crash site, or piece of machinery). Real evidence has to have a material existence independent of anything else. Its link to the accused generally has to have supporting testimony, such as 'This is the iron bar which I saw the accused waving and then tried to take away from him', or 'These bloodstains were recovered from the clothing worn by the accused at the time of his arrest and which match the blood type of the man found lying in the stairwell'. It is common to have to explain in court the significance of a piece of real evidence, especially when using something obscure as evidence which is not within everyone's common experience, such as an explosive detonator used to trigger a bomb or the motherboard from a computer.

TASK 11

Can you think of potential problems associated with the use of, and production in court of, 'real evidence'?

You might have referred to the 'continuity of evidence'. You will remember from many examples in this Handbook that this is a mundane but vital part of case preparation. There must be an auditable trail from the moment that the article produced as real evidence is discovered or recovered until it is produced in court. This is also referred to as the chain of evidence and it simply means that the prosecution can prove that the article was held securely from its discovery or recovery and that it was not tampered with, modified, or changed in any way. It is the responsibility of the reporting or arresting police officer to ensure the secure retention of exhibits and their production to the court. In complex cases, there will be an exhibits officer appointed to the case, and in some police forces, there is a designated specialist who safeguards specialist materials such as forensic items or CCTV footage (see section 13.6).

Documentary evidence is something written which is produced in court. The medium through which it is written can vary from a Last Will and Testament on parchment with spidery copperplate writing, to the use of a credit card on line to download child pornography. The rules about the legal status of documents are complex but the general point to make is that the document should be produced by the person who created it and who can testify to its contents. This is not always possible (the makers of wills have a regular habit of dying) but courts can sometimes invoke the services of handwriting experts who can testify that, within limitations, the author of one particular document is likely to be the author of another particular document.

This becomes even more complex when it comes to electronic text, and specialists differ over degrees of certainty about the authorship of, for example, web documents, if they are not signed or copyrighted. Some documents will be seized as evidence by the police and will then be submitted to the court—the classic example is a suicide note—and of course the points made above about 'continuity of evidence' apply just as much to documents as to real evidence. A physical document is real evidence, but is separately classed because of its referential nature and because often authorship can be proven (which is more difficult say, with a common-pattern kitchen knife).

'**Hearsay evidence**', as indicated by its name, is evidence provided by one person about what another person said. Hearsay can also include documents whose existence cannot be proven by the author, or whose contents cannot be similarly proven. It is generally inadmissible in court because of the potential for ambiguity or malice ('Someone told me that he confessed' is not evidence.)

TASK 12

There are a number of exceptions to this last statement. Can you think what they might be?

12.8.3 Our Adversarial Justice System

We tend to think that the only criminal justice system which works is our own. It can therefore come as a surprise to find that other countries' police forces believe precisely the same about theirs. The system used in England and Wales is the adversarial system, whilst elsewhere in Europe, in France or The Netherlands for example, the system used is called inquisitorial. In some European countries, and elsewhere in the world, guilt is presumed and innocence has to be proven, whereas in the UK, we presume innocence and expect the prosecution to prove guilt. In some countries, there is no jury system, only a panel of judges, so the courtroom dramas which we began by describing simply do not apply. In other countries, the questioning of the accused is undertaken not by a prosecuting counsel but by an investigating judge; correspondingly, the role taken by defence counsel is of much lower profile (and of lesser significance) than it is here.

You will have noticed that we have excluded Scotland and Northern Ireland from this discussion. This is not because they do not embrace the British criminal justice system, but because they have their own laws which differ from those in England and Wales to some degree. In Scotland, for example, the police caution is different; no legal adviser may be present as of right at a police interview and there is a verdict intermediate between 'Not Guilty' and 'Guilty' which is 'Not Proven'. Rather than make exceptions throughout this discussion about the criminal justice system, we shall address the England and Wales model (which of course is very similar in structure to that used in Scotland, Northern Ireland, the US, Canada, Australia, and so on: similar, but not identical).

The adversarial model requires that a person, the defendant, is accused of an offence and that he/she is tried by a court (usually in open session) which is required to prove the defendant's guilt beyond reasonable doubt. The prosecution is conducted on behalf of the Crown (often referred to in written case law as 'R', meaning 'Regina' or 'Rex' (the Queen or King respectively), depending whether there is a King or Queen on the throne at the time the case is heard. The Crown Prosecutor is a lawyer employed by (or, rarely, retained by) the Crown Prosecution Service. The defendant is normally represented by a lawyer, usually a barrister, who is also called 'defence counsel', or generically 'the defence'. However, the defendant can choose to conduct his/her own defence, although this is rare.

At its simplest, what the prosecution tries to establish is that the offence actually happened and that the accused defendant was the person who did it. The defence challenges the prosecution's proofs and, increasingly, where proof is very strong (such as in DNA evidence), attempts to fault the process by which his/her client has ended up in court. The defence will challenge in order to suggest:

- that the alleged offence did not take place (such as in a rape case);
- or, if it did, that the defendant did not do it;
- or, if the defendant did it, then there were justifiable reasons for having done it, such as self-defence;
- or, if the defendant did commit the crime and there is little to be said in mitigation (excuse), something was wrong in the process which ended with the defendant in court.

In the US, they put it slightly differently: if you can't win on the facts, argue the law; if you can't win on the law, argue the facts; if you can't win on either; delay.

In terms of the last of these, it is the role of the defence counsel to expose flaws in the prosecution case if it is helping his/her client to do so. Again, this is business; it is not personal, though many student police officers appear to dislike or despise these aspects of the defence counsel's role, believing such approaches to be morally ambiguous. This misses the point: the defence will do anything it can to belittle and undermine the evidence and the testimony of witnesses. This can be by direct 'counter-proof', by making evidence or testimony appear shaky, by challenging the veracity or integrity of a witness, by making the witness appear vague, contradictory, or uncertain, or by attacking the legal process and exploiting loopholes in the law; especially if the law has been badly 'framed' or written.

A minor example can illustrate this last point quite graphically. A solicitor nicknamed by the media as 'Mr Loophole' specializes in defending the rich against charges of drink-driving or speeding. He has specialized in helping film directors, footballers, and others able to afford his £10,000 a day retention fee, to 'get off' the charges they have faced. The solicitor concerned rejects any suggestion that he should feel guilty about this:

> The laws I argue have been put in place by our democratically elected parliament . . . It is not me who is to blame. If they [the prosecuting authorities] did their jobs properly, nobody would ever get off.

All I am doing is protecting people from the police not doing their job properly (Mr Loophole, cited in Jenkins, 2005).

So there is a sense in which we can say that the police have to get it absolutely right every time, whilst the defence does not. There are arguments about moral rightness in both this and in many other examples, but the essential fact remains that defence lawyers will naturally exploit every loophole, every aspect of a process which has been blurred or not properly followed and every shortfall in police procedure which they can find. As a student police officer and subsequently as a qualified police officer you may not agree with this approach but we would argue that morality has very little to do with the day-to-day administration of justice. That is why our emphasis is always upon your getting the procedure right first time, and every time thereafter.

In the dramatic setting of the court, the contest is played out between these two adversaries or opponents; the defence and prosecution lawyers, who must comply with the rules of evidence. The prosecution has a duty to ensure that all relevant evidence is disclosed; the defence has no such obligation. In a magistrates' court, the bench (lay or stipendiary) and in a Crown Court, the jury, will decide on the basis of the evidence that has been given whether the accused is guilty or not. The magistrates' clerk and the judge, respectively, ensure in their courts that the rules of evidence are followed. If the accused pleads guilty, there is, self-evidently, no need for a jury and hearings or trials are thereby much shortened.

Evidence is usually presented in court in the form of the testimony of a witness. As we noted above, witnesses give evidence of what they heard, saw, smelled, tasted, or felt. Sometimes, an expert witness (usually, one with a special kind of knowledge) may be asked to give an opinion, such as a pathologist giving an opinion on the cause of death in a murder case, but ordinary witnesses, including police officers, will seldom be asked for an opinion.

12.8.4 Giving Evidence as a Police Officer

You will experience, from an early stage in your training as a student police officer, what it is like to give evidence in court. You will give evidence at both a magistrates' and a county court. You will be assessed against the NOS in terms of the standards that you reach, most notably Unit 2J2. Giving evidence also features as one of the PAC headings, a key aspect of qualifying to undertake Independent Patrol.

An important point to note at the outset is that, although you are a police officer and although you have powers which are not granted to the ordinary citizen, you are not treated any differently from any other witness. You have no special status because of your profession or role. The only major departure from other witnesses will be your familiarity with the court and its rituals and procedures, based on your knowledge of what goes on in the criminal justice system, your studies, your knowledge of the law, your experience, and perhaps this Handbook.

You will soon become experienced at court, but do not expect your subsequent court appearances to be frequent. Most police officers, unless they become SIOs or computer specialists or perform similar roles, actually will not appear in court that often. After qualifying as a police officer (to some extent, opportunities for you to experience court during training are contrived or constructed) you may not attend court again for years. In some forces, officers have served whole careers without going to court to give evidence. In others, police officers appear more frequently, and, correspondingly, are more used to what goes on in the theatre of the courts. It is also likely that the further you progress through the ranks, the less likely you are to give evidence in court, unless you are a detective working on volume crime issues on a BCU, or involved in some major police operation which requires your appearance. It is something of an irony that you are more likely to go frequently to court if you remain a constable than if you become a superintendent.

The reasons behind this diminishing frequency of court appearances are complex and will divert us if we spend too long on them, but we should note that there are now a higher proportion of 'guilty' pleas at court than there used to be, even ten years ago, probably because of advances in DNA evidence and the routine taking of non-intrusive buccal (mouth) swabs for DNA from detained persons. Also, the Auld Review into criminal justice (2001) cleared away many of the petty offences which used to necessitate court appearance, particularly at magistrates' courts, and replaced them with statutory fines or penalties. Examples include speeding offences recorded by fixed cameras and other motoring offences such as having no vehicle excise duty. Such penalties are generated automatically, and fines levied directly on the offender, without the intervention of the courts. In other words, there are fewer reasons now for police officers to go to court than there used to be. Some older officers recall having to go to a magistrates' court on a fortnightly basis and sometimes a weekly one. However, court appearances now by police officers tend to include the more serious offences and crimes which attract higher penalties. This means that you may go to court less frequently, but when you do go to court, it will be probably for a substantial criminal trial. There is therefore all the more reason for you to get it right.

If you are what is termed 'the officer in the case' (that is, you made the arrest, the charge, the interview and prepared the case papers for the CPS, or you were in charge of a team of people who did this), you have to do more than just give evidence. On the contrary, you will have a great deal to do, from liaising with the CPS lawyer(s) on the case to arranging for witnesses to attend. You will also be responsible for any exhibits in police possession to be made available to the court. In a real sense, the success of the case will depend very much on how well prepared and organized you are.

You are not normally allowed to speak to the accused, unless you have permission from the CPS lawyer and you will not be allowed to sit in the courtroom once your case has begun. You will have to wait until summoned, along with the other witnesses in the case. Do not expect your case to be heard quickly: many commentators acknowledge the slowness of the criminal justice system in this country and it may be for any number of technical or procedural reasons that the case is put back, postponed, rescheduled, or otherwise not heard on that day. Being 'warned for court' can be a frustratingly long and drawn-out process. Remember too that delay serves the purposes of the defence team. The longer a case is delayed, the fainter the witnesses' recollections and the less detail people can remember about the case. Most magistrates and judges are wise to this defence tactic and will deal with it brusquely after a reasonable period, but some will not. Be prepared for this; be prepared to talk to the CPS lawyer about making a protest if the defence appear to be postponing or prolonging matters unnecessarily. Justice may have to proceed with ponderous and deliberate consideration, but that is no reason for an unreasonable delay in a case.

12.8.5 Giving Evidence

Your evidence, and that of other witnesses, is given from the witness box (often surprisingly small and modest in reality, unlike those you may have seen on TV or film). You should face and direct your evidence to the judge or to the bench. When you are asked a question, you should face the questioner, but your answer should always be delivered to the bench or to the judge.

12.8.5.1 The oath

Evidence must be given on oath by any witness or defendant at a statutory legal process (magistrates' court, employment tribunal, judicial enquiry, Crown Court, Parliamentary Select Committee enquiry, and so on). This is enshrined in law (the Perjury Act 1911 and the Oaths Act 1978), which requires that a person must be sworn in the particular form or manner which is binding on his/her conscience. There are prescribed forms for those who profess a religious belief and for those who profess no belief, with which you should be familiar.

The essence of the oath is that you, the witness, will 'tell the truth, the whole truth and nothing but the truth', under the provisions and strictures of your religious belief or through a secular (non-religious) attestation.

Taking the Oath

Belief system or religion	Wording of the oath
Most Christians	'I swear by almighty God . . .'
Hindus	'I swear by the Gita . . .'
Muslims	'I swear by Allah . . .'
Sikhs	'I swear by Guru Nanak . . .'
All non-believers, most Buddhists, some Quakers, Jehovah's Witnesses, and others.	'I do solemnly, sincerely and truly declare and affirm . . .'

Those adhering to a religious belief touch or hold (covered or uncovered) their respective Holy Books when giving the oath, but there may be other observances involved such as a ritual washing (cleansing of the hands or mouth for example) or taking the oath in front of a picture (such as that of the Dalai Lama for Buddhists). Whatever the variation invoked by the individual, the taking of an oath obligates the individual to tell the truth, both before his/her religion and before the law. The law is clear: lying on oath is perjury, which is a criminal offence. Offenders will certainly be punished, because the law takes this offence very seriously.

12.8.5.2   Introducing yourself

When you, as a police officer, have given the oath appropriate to your belief or non-belief (the affirmation is, for shorthand, still called 'the oath'), you should introduce yourself, giving your rank, police number, name, and the police station where you are based, thus:

> I am Police Constable 10899 Alison Wyatt of Carlton Road Police Station in Hemel Keynes.

12.8.5.3   Giving your evidence

In most straightforward cases, you may be asked by the Prosecuting Counsel (CPS) to give your evidence directly. That means that you will give a detailed and accurate chronology of events, without any prompting from the prosecution, like this:

> I am the officer in this case. On Tuesday 25 July at 1040 hours, whilst on patrol in Hemel Keynes, I was directed to Mortesbury's supermarket on the Pound Lane Estate where the accused, Alan Maurice Stacker, was being held with others by security personnel from Mortesbury's on suspicion of having taken items without payment. I questioned the accused, who was unable to account for his possession of two bottles of spirits . . . .

In more complex cases, and always at a crown court, you will give your evidence in response to questions from prosecuting counsel. Again, the chronology of events is likely to be followed, but the prosecuting counsel will seek to draw out detail from you, like this:

> **Jane Hervey-Richards (CPS):** Constable Wyatt, at what point did you first become aware that Alan Stacker, the accused, was responsible for planning the thefts, with his co-accused, from the supermarket?
>
> **Pc Alison Wyatt:** This was revealed in a police interview, on the same day, with Nicola Kew, who made a statement alleging that the accused had planned the thefts, and giving circumstantial detail of how this was to be done.
>
> **JH-R:** My Lord I refer you to Exhibit 19 in your second bundle, the taped interview with Nicola Marie Kew. Now, Constable Wyatt, what happened when Ms Kew made this allegation?

Note here, in our fictionalized trial transcript, that the prosecution and defence will always refer to exhibits by number and that the taped interview with Nicola Kew is part of the prosecution's case against Stacker. Of course, had it only been the supermarket theft which was being considered, the case would probably have been heard at a magistrates' court. However, the prosecutor referred the exhibit number to 'My Lord' which suggests that the trial is being heard by a judge at county court or at Appeal. Also, you should have noted that the evidence from Pc Wyatt is being elicited by prosecution questioning rather than the officer giving a direct statement: so likely to be in the Crown Court, not the magistrates' court.

If you want to refer to your pocket notebook (PNB) in court, you should ask for permission to do so. (The PNB is described in section 11.5). The PNB entry may have been disclosed in evidence and the court will follow your reading of it. This may lead the defence to ask you to explain the manner and time of your notes, and whether your notes represent a 'contemporaneous account' (you did it there and then) or whether you wrote up your PNB afterwards. Provided that the writing up was reasonably soon after the event, this should be acceptable, but if there is a significant time lag (say two days or longer), you should expect the defence to question you very closely and probably in a hostile manner.

Sometimes, if your PNB entry has not been submitted in evidence, the court and both prosecution and defence will want to examine your PNB entry physically. This may make you nervous, but do not be: you were there and you recorded the event, not them. Just make sure that your grammar and spelling are up to scratch and that your handwriting is at least legible.

You could be tempted (or worse, advised by 'experienced' colleagues) to try to learn your evidence by heart and then quote from memory in the witness box when you are giving your evidence. This is most inadvisable. For a start it will sound rehearsed and artificial. Secondly, the defence will try to jog you off course with questions so that you lose your thread and flounder. This can be embarrassing for you and tedious for the court. Worst of all, it suggests that you do not have the confidence to rely on your recall of events. There is nothing wrong with referring to your PNB entries, and if you do so confidently and with permission, you will continue to look and sound professional. After all, the lawyers constantly refer to their notes and so does the judge or stipendiary, and that means that there is no reason why you should not do the same. However, you should not rely on your PNB exclusively. The court will not have a good impression of you if you merely read your notes. How much better it would be if you gave your evidence clearly and confidently, referring only now and then to points in your PNB to refresh your memory or to quote some complex fact.

12.8.5.4 Cross-examination

Once you have concluded your evidence (either directly or in response to the prosecution's questions), the defence may wish to ask you questions. This is called cross-examination and has to do with the questioning 'crossing' from one side of the adversarial contest to the other.

By now you should know what the defence's tactics are likely to be in the case, but try to be prepared too, for the unexpected:

> **Charles W Money (defence):** Constable Wyatt, what formal training have you had in interview techniques and did that training, if indeed you had it, cover the use of oppressive interrogation?

Watch the answer here; because the defence has used a common tactic of double questioning, as well as launching straight into querying the police officer's qualifications. This is Pc Wyatt's calm response:

> **Pc Wyatt** [turning to the judge]: I was trained in cognitive interview techniques at the Bramshill Police College in August last year, in addition to the basic and advanced interview courses run by my own force in February and April of the same year.
> [turning back to Mr Money]: Would you repeat the second part of your question, sir?

Note her politeness and refusal to be flustered or stampeded by the defence's approach. In fact, the completeness of her first reply will have established her as a professional and credible witness and the defence may seem merely querulous (questioning for its own sake). The judge may intervene to ask Mr Money where this is leading if the defence persists in this deliberately provocative tone and innuendo.

Particular care needs to be taken with questions which appear innocent but which are barbed—as here where Mr Money plants the suggestion of oppression. There are questions where the answers are of the 'damned if you do and damned if you do not' kind. Never be hesitant about asking the defence (or anyone else) to repeat a question which you did not hear, did not understand, or which you want clarified. It also gives you a moment extra to think. However, that does not mean that you should challenge every question put to you by the defence. Do not try to be too 'clever' (remember the effect you are having on the jury as a competent professional?), but do be aware of trick questioning and defence ploys.

You might have noticed how Pc Wyatt 'collects' the question from the lawyer and delivers her answer directly to the judge, before politely asking Mr Money for the second part of his question. This shows that Pc Wyatt has been attentive, brief, and to the point and is not to be hurried into giving confused (or confusing) answers to compound or complex questions. She is creating a good impression, which will add to her confidence. Always deal with multiple questions one at a time.

The defence would normally approach you with more caution than that shown by Mr Money, taking you back over the evidence and probing for any weakness which may be favourable to the defendant. There will be occasions when your evidence **is** favourable to the defendant (think of the statements made in interview by Nicola Kew and how they would support her defence's case that she was forced by Alan Stacker into illegal acts against her will) and, naturally enough, the defence will want to give prominence to any evidence which helps the defendant. You should expect to be questioned about how you conducted the investigation, the evidence you have already given, and any additional facts which you have not already given. Do not be defensive; rather be confident and positive. This is your case and you know it well.

There will be times when, at the end of the cross-examination, the prosecutor will come back to ask you further questions. These will be designed to clarify any confusion or to point up a particular fact or issue. New evidence cannot be introduced at this stage.

Stay where you are (in the witness box) until the magistrate or judge tells you to stand down. You may then stay in the court to hear the rest of the case, because you can only be released if the magistrate or judge gives you permission. In other words, you have to stay put until you are told that you can go (you may be re-summoned to give evidence). At no time during this period should you speak to any witnesses who are still waiting to be called.

Let us now look at your role, and your planning and preparation before you go to court. You need to:

- review the case, re-read the case papers, re-read your PNB;
- familiarize yourself with the rules of evidence (particularly on hearsay evidence and opinion);
- check that everything in the case is administratively in order, including labelling the exhibits;
- go and look at the court premises, familiarize yourself with the layout, sit through part of a case;
- speak to the CPS lawyer who will be prosecuting;
- think about what will happen and prepare yourself to deal with it;
- re-read this part of the Handbook!

Now, let us go into some detail. You are there because this was your investigation into a crime and, as a result of your work, a person has been charged and brought before the courts. The hearing in the magistrates' court, the committal for trial at the Crown Court, and the criminal justice system has swung into action because of the work you have carried out in 'the discharge of your office of constable'. Your job in court is the next phase of the investigation in a sense, because it is the calling to account of the case against the accused and a consideration (a weighing) of the evidence. You are there to help the court to reach a decision based on the evidence placed before it. You do this by presenting your part in the process which brought the accused to the dock.

You are not there to secure a conviction: that is the role of the Crown Prosecutor from the CPS. You are not there to decide on guilt or innocence: that is the role of the magistrates or the jury. You are not there to impose punishment: that is the role of the bench or the judge. Your job is to explain what part you played in this story, to tell what you have done, heard, seen, or recorded, as clearly and as concisely as you can. You must do it honestly, without exaggeration, remembering that you are sworn to uphold the law. That said, the facts alone are not enough. Juries and judges are human and are apt to be influenced by impressions almost as much as by the facts.

12.8.5.5   Creating an impression

The impression which you create in court, as we have noted above, will have an influence on your credibility. There are a number of factors which build an impression in the minds of those observing and listening to you giving your evidence. Imagine the situation:

> **L Eagle (prosecuting):** Tell the court, Sergeant Ambles, what happened next.
>
> **Sergeant Harry Ambles:** Well, John, when I got down to the edge of the like disco area, there was your man bigging it up and asking all comers like if they wanted a piece of him and he said 'You're having a laugh' and I turned round to him and said 'You're nicked' and this other bloke says 'Nah' and he said to him 'You're a cocky sod ain't you?' and swung a punch like, so I stopped the music sort of thing and took them all in.
>
> **LE:** Then what?
>
> **H Ambles:** We got down the station and Pete Finch was on custody, no, hang on a minute, it was Debbie Johnson, I think. Just a sec. (He consults his PNB). I got it down here somewhere.
>
> **Lady Justitia Foreall:** Sergeant, have you or have you not a record of this very confusing scene? Whom did you arrest? On what charge?
>
> **SHA:** Sorry your Worship, I've got it on a bit of paper somewhere, I arrested the bloke in the dock, 'Smasher' Higgins. We know him all right, he's got a record as long as your arm. Put him away twice myself.

It is clear that the sergeant is disorganized, over-familiar, too prone to use slang expressions, and fails to untangle the various threads of who said what to whom (too many 'he's'). This exchange is deliberately exaggerated, of course, but the poor impression which the sergeant gives is not just of himself, but also of his police force and of the police in general. No one listening to this exchange would give the police officer any credibility and the probability is that the jury (it is at a Crown Court, is it not, despite Ambles misaddressing the judge?) would be even more confused than the learned judge. You might have noticed too that, unprofessionally, Ambles reveals that Higgins (apparently the accused) has a police record and has served a prison term, which is information supplied gratuitously (without being asked) and which is likely to prejudice the case against Higgins. It does not fit the 'bad character' rules which we looked at earlier in section 12.7. The defence counsel would almost certainly have intervened at this point and lodged a strong objection to the 'evidence' being given. In sum, Ambles has no sense of where he is, no understanding of the effect that his disorganization is having on those around him, and he is dangerously close to contempt of court.

You need to convey to the court that you are properly organized and have all the facts of the case available to you. Remember that this is not the same as learning your evidence word for word. You can consult your PNB for facts, figures, dates, times, and exact words, but the reassurance which comes of thoroughly knowing the case and all the components of it is immense. You want to show that you are confident and at ease. Using the correct terminology will help: calling the Judge 'My Lady' or 'My Lord' and the lawyers on both sides 'Ma'am' or 'Sir' creates the impression of a person who understands the rules of the ceremonial game. ('Your Worship' is for the magistrates' court, but even there, 'Sir' or 'Ma'am' will do; certainly not 'Susie'...) No one would advise you to talk like a legal text book when giving your evidence but you should be careful about using jargon or slang expressions. Not only will some of these not be understood but they can give the impression of someone who is too relaxed, complacent even, for the surroundings and the occasion. Formal events like this tend to require more formal (but not stilted) language. The language of 'street cred' should be used sparingly, and then only when expressing the flavour of an idiom, such as the language used by the accused.

You need to look as smart as you sound. It would be easy for us to ignore this aspect through some sense of 'politeness'. However, the court is no place for a police officer witness with unpolished shoes, unkempt hair, a sloppy uniform, or badly creased clothes. A smart uniform, polished shoes and neat hair can seem petty restrictions, but they help you assert your authority (see section 5.5 above). The smartness also aids your confidence when you are in the witness box.

Watch your attitude to both the defendant and your evidence, because you must avoid any suggestion of prejudice. Lawyers from both sides will tell you that an obvious bias against a defendant on the part of the police officer in the witness box will actually aid the defence. More importantly, it will be deeply unhelpful to the prosecution case.

Finally, watch what you say. The temptation is always to say too much and to keep on talking. Instead, keep your answers to questions short and to the point:

> **Jane Hervey-Richards (CPS):** Constable Wyatt, were you shown the effects of the assault which Ms Kew says was perpetrated by the accused?
>
> **Pc Alison Wyatt:** Yes I was. This was at first during the initial interview, when Ms Kew showed me an extensive and fresh bruise to her left upper breast area and left collar-bone.
>
> **JH-R:** What did you do next?
>
> **AW:** I arranged for the Force Medical Officer to examine Ms Kew and to give a view on the cause of the bruising.
>
> **JH-R:** With what result?
>
> **AW:** The Force Medical Officer concluded that Ms Kew had been assaulted.
>
> **JH-R:** My Lord; I refer to the statement taken from Dr Salim Khan, Force Medical Officer, which is in bundle 6, document 44A.

Notice that Pc Wyatt gives clear answers, but does not elaborate (she knows that the prosecution or, equally, the defence will follow up with another question if there is more to be said). Note too that she does not try to give a medical opinion or to paraphrase Dr Khan's evidence or statement. This is because Pc Wyatt has no medical qualifications and she knows that she cannot speak with any authority. All she can say is that the FMO's view was that Nicola Kew had been assaulted because that is what Dr Khan had told her. The temptation to use someone else's evidence in your answers is strong, especially if you know the case well and have carefully read all the statements and written evidence, but you must resist the temptation. Confine your answers, as Pc Wyatt does, to what you know to be fact and what happened in the story you are unfolding for the court.

Another point: do not use long words or over-formal constructions. The lawyers and the judge will probably understand you if you do, but some members of the jury may not. You might look as though you are trying too hard to impress if you say something like this, especially if your grasp of the meaning of words is a little shaky:

> I proceeded in a southerly direction towards the connurbative encompassment of commercial premises which is characterized by the soubriquet of 'shopping mall'. The chronological observation which was then essayed by myself was recorded contemporaneously as 1345 hours, British Summer Time. It was at that juncture that I espied the trio of adult males engaging in what I deemed to be behaviour which warranted a sufficiency of explanation as to make my legitimated suspicions subside . . . .

Perhaps all you needed to say was:

> I was on patrol in the Shopping Mall at 1345 when I saw three men behaving suspiciously, so I challenged them.

Even this is fairly formal, but it has the great merit of being brief. Remember the impression you are creating. Do you want to be seen as pompous or as a concise, well-prepared professional?

We looked at cross-examination in outline earlier. How would you respond if you were the object of this defence argument?

> **Charles W Money:** I put it to you officer, that this whole case is a tissue of invention from beginning to end. You have said that the defendant assaulted Nicola Kew with his fists on the evening of May 16, but that is not true is it?
> **Pc Wyatt:** It is true, sir.
> **Money:** I'll tell you what is true. It is true that you and your colleague decided between you that you didn't have enough evidence against the defendant to put him away this time, didn't you? You have lied in evidence, you have lied about the events and you have lied about framing the defendant for something he didn't do!
> **Pc Wyatt:** None of those things is true. I have told the truth.
> **Money:** You're lying now!
> **Pc Wyatt:** No, sir, I am not.
> **The Judge:** Mr Money, I am growing tired of this. Kindly make your point now, or move your questioning to something we all understand.

You will recall (or if not, you will soon experience) abuse from people you have arrested, or when you have intervened in a fight, or when you have tried to sort out a domestic quarrel. You will have been called names, spat at, sworn at, jeered, and belittled. If you kept your temper then, keep it now. The defence is trying to provoke Pc Wyatt, to probe beneath her calm and to make her lose her temper.

You will experience, at some point in your career, an attack on your integrity. If you lose your temper or reply in kind, your credibility as a police officer on oath in court is in danger of collapse. If you flare up that easily, the jury might think that maybe you did hit the accused as is counter-alleged or that you ran away from the gang fight outside the night-club.

Police officers can be subject to more personal scrutiny than any other witness likely to appear. Your record, your training, your job performance, even your personal life, will be closely investigated by the defence before the trial takes place. Anything which can undermine your credibility or make the jury dubious about how reliable your testimony is, will be fair game to the defence, and a defence lawyer will not hesitate to confront you with it when you are being cross-examined. Remember how Money asked Pc Wyatt about her interview training? Or how he suggested that she had 'cooked up' the case against Stacker, by colluding with her colleague and with Nicola Kew?

TASK 13
How should you respond when your training, your integrity, and your standing as a police officer is so fundamentally challenged?

Perhaps one rule to adopt is not to be provoked. If you remain calm and collected, you will impress those watching and listening with your professionalism.

12.8.6 Summary

This section has been largely about your role in presenting evidence as a police witness in court and all the procedures and protocols involved. We have noted that you are less likely to go to court as often as your more experienced colleagues have done in the past, but that when you are actually called to court, the crimes on trial are likely to be the more serious ones.

We have explained the importance of preparation and planning, including referring to your pocket note book. We have looked at the various roles played by prosecutor, defence, and judge and how the impression you convey can be very important to the case.

There is much in this section that you will need to refer to again and again until it is embedded in your knowledge, but we must emphasize that there is no substitute for familiarizing yourself directly with court procedure at all levels (magistrates' court and Crown Court) by visiting them and observing the procedures live.

12.9 Record, Retain, and Reveal

We look in this section at the need to 'record, retain, and reveal' information that you gather in the course of your duties as a police officer.

First a cautionary note. It is easy for student police officers to become cynical about the area of police work that is described in this section and see it as yet another way in which the odds are stacked against the police. However, there is an alternative way of viewing what follows, which is to acknowledge that it is simply a reflection of the need to conduct investigations as a search for the truth. We mentioned this at the beginning of this chapter. This aim is perhaps best achieved by following all reasonable lines of enquiry, whether they point towards the guilt or the innocence of the suspect.

We have made a number of references earlier in this chapter and elsewhere in the Handbook to evidence that you will gather (including witness statements), forms that you will complete, and other information that you will be responsible for collecting. In many cases these materials will be an important element in the decision to prosecute a person for a crime. They could also be influential in somebody's decision to plead guilty to a charge (as so-called 'advanced information' which is provided in advance of a 'guilty' or 'not guilty' plea).

In general terms, a consequence of the rules of evidence is that all police officers have a responsibility to record and retain relevant material obtained or generated by themselves or others during the course of the investigation, even if it is not subsequently used by the prosecution. If relevant material is not recorded, or recorded wrongly, or not retained then it is 'lost' to the defence and hence has not been properly shared with them, through the CPS. This could be a serious loophole that the defence may exploit.

What follows is more detailed guidance for you in terms of the relevance, recording, and retaining of material in the course of your initial investigation of a crime or arising from being an officer involved in a response to an incident. We call this the '3 Rs' of Record, Retain, and Reveal (this is an approach common in national police training). The content of this section is drawn largely (but not exclusively) from the Criminal Procedure and Investigations Act 1996 more commonly known as the CPIA and its associated Code of Practice (which we refer to as the Code).

Before we examine the 3 Rs in detail we will first illustrate the importance of this topic with an example.

12.9.1 First Officer at the Scene

Consider the following set of circumstances that take place when your tutor takes you to observe a court case in your local magistrates' court. The prosecution counsel opens the case by outlining the circumstances in which a major public disturbance has taken place outside a nightclub in Maidbury town centre. The incident was witnessed by a number of people. Officers from the nearby police station and surrounding areas attended the scene. A person was arrested and the arresting officer consequently provided a statement regarding the arrest and, eventually, a number of statements were taken from independent witnesses who provided good evidence of the assault by the defendant. The decision to prosecute is made and a case file is built, the suspect is subsequently charged and bailed to court.

So far, so good. You observe the one and only witness who now gives evidence for the prosecution, and is then cross-examined by the defence counsel. Next, the arresting officer is asked to take the witness stand and the prosecution ask the officer to outline the evidence of the arrest. Afterwards, the defence counsel rises, and says:

> Officer, I have only two questions for you...we will hear shortly from my client that there were several other police officers at the scene of the alleged assault. Who were these other officers and why are they not giving evidence today?

The arresting officer addresses the magistrates and replies:

> There were approximately 10 officers at the scene; I do not know their names and they weren't called to court today because I didn't record all their names.

The defence then turns to the arresting officer and says:

> Officer, the last witness has told this court that when you arrived at the location, you had a conversation with her about what actually happened. Where are your notes of that conversation?

The arresting officer addresses the magistrates and replies:

> I have no record of the conversation, I remembered the name and address and then a statement was taken later.

The defendant now takes the stand and tells the court the reason for the assault was self-defence and that the arresting officer was completely wrong about how drunk the defendant was. The defence counsel asks his client if there is anybody who can corroborate what she is saying and the defendant replies that if the other police officers and witnesses were at court, they would be able to say exactly the same thing.

The focus of the solicitor has now switched from what his client actually did at the scene (which is what you are probably thinking is the most important issue), to attack the credibility of the police by some other means.

The defence now apply to stay the proceedings on the basis that their client is being deprived of the right to a fair trial under Sch 1, art 6 of the Human Rights Act 1998 (see section 11.3), as the prosecution have effectively prevented them from access to a number of witnesses who are crucial to the defence of their client.

The magistrates retire to deliberate. You may think at this point that whether the application is successful or not, much time and effort has been wasted and there is even the danger that the case may be lost.

12.9.2 Record

It is the responsibility of the officer in charge of the investigation to ensure that the material is **recorded** in a durable or retrievable form, for instance, in writing, on video or audiotape, or on computer disk.

As the example illustrates, you will need to identify and record all relevant material. It is important to note that relevant material has a much wider meaning than, for example, the term evidential material. Taking the term relevant material in reverse order, the Disclosure Manual (CPS, 2006 and henceforth referred to as the 'Manual') suggests the following (in our words):

- **material** refers to information and objects obtained in the course of a criminal investigation;
- these materials are **relevant** when they have a bearing on any offence under investigation or any person being investigated, or on the surrounding circumstances of the case.

Material here has a wide meaning, not only including objects such as written materials and video tapes but also information given orally. Note that investigation also has a wide meaning. The Code defines investigation as:

- investigations into crimes that have been committed;
- investigations whose purpose is to ascertain whether a crime has been committed, with a view to the possible institution of criminal proceedings; and
- investigations which begin in the belief that a crime may be committed, for example, a surveillance operation is part of an investigation even if it is directed to a target without there being a specific offence in mind.

The difficulty for you with this lies in recognizing what does and what does not have bearing on an investigation and any possible criminal case that follows. You will often need to make such a decision very quickly. You should also note that the responsibility to record and retain relevant material does not just relate to prosecution material, but also to material which may assist the defence. It is impossible to second-guess a defence at this time and you must remain aware of the possibility that the defence may wish to call you as a witness or potential witness for them (as happened to the police officer in our fictional example above). The following is a list of material which you and colleagues are required to record and retain, as described in paragraph 5.4 of the Code of Practice of CPIA:

1. **Crime reports** (including crime report forms, relevant parts of incident report books, and your PNB).
2. **Custody records.**
3. Records which are derived from **tapes of telephone messages** (for example, 999 calls) containing descriptions of an alleged offence or offender.
4. **Final versions of witness statements** (and draft versions where their content differs from the final version), including any exhibits mentioned (unless these have been returned to their owner on the understanding that they will be produced in court if required).
5. **Interview records** (written records, or audio or video tapes, of interviews with actual or potential witnesses or suspects).
6. **Communications between the police and experts** such as forensic scientists, reports of work carried out by experts, and **schedules** of scientific material prepared by the expert for the investigator, for the purposes of criminal proceedings.
7. **Records of the first description of a suspect by each potential witness** who purports to identify or describe the suspect, whether or not the description differs from that of subsequent descriptions by that or other witnesses.
8. Any **material casting doubt on the reliability of a witness.**

There is a particularly important point concerning witnesses. In the case of *R v Heggart & Heggart* (CA, November 2000), it was determined that any potential witnesses known to exist by the police, but who were not interviewed by them, were to be treated as witnesses whose evidence the courts must assume would either undermine the prosecution case or assist the defence case. Therefore, in the example of the court case above, a record should have been made of any witness details and what they observed in relation to the incident at the scene. There is, however, a notion of proportionality here. If an incident happens at a football match with 25,000 spectators then you would not be expected to record details of all 25,000.

12.9.3 Retain

Material relevant to an investigation is required to be **retained** for specified periods of time. These periods of time are dependent upon a number of factors such as whether or not the case continues to court and if so, whether acquitted or the length of sentence following conviction. This is explained in more detail in para 5.8 of the Code.

12.9.4 Reveal

Your main responsibilities as a student police officer are to record and retain all relevant information and make it available when required. Responsibility for revealing relevant unused material to the prosecutor is achieved through use of the unused material schedules. The type of offence under investigation and procedures within your host force will determine whether this is a responsibility for yourself or another individual. However, it does not automatically follow that all this information will by necessity be revealed to the defence. Tests will be applied.

12.9.5 A Further Example

We can illustrate the principles of the 3 Rs by means of an example. Consider the situation where you have collected CCTV recordings of an incident involving assault outside a nightclub in the centre of town. In terms of the 3 Rs you would view the tape in terms of whether it contains relevant material with a bearing:

- on the offence under investigation; or
- any person being investigated; or
- on the surrounding circumstances of the alleged offence.

That much is obvious. However, remember that the test of relevance here applies to both the potential **defence** in a case as well as the prosecution. The tape is relevant material if it is of potential use to either party involved in any subsequent prosecution. You may have started viewing the tape for evidence on who hit whom, with what force, and at what time and so on. Perhaps there is nothing of relevance in these respects. However, the tape may show one of the individuals under suspicion talking to a bouncer outside the club. This is potentially relevant as an alibi for the suspect. So the tape is **relevant material**, and hence it must be retained and recorded into a durable and retrievable format. If the tape also becomes **evidential**, it will be exhibited and form part of the prosecution case; if the tape is relevant and **non-evidential**, its contents will be described on Form MG6C (see section 12.8). However, if the tape has been considered to be **non-relevant** (at that time), there is no legal requirement to retain it, but a summary of what the tape contained should be made.

This is complicated, but as police officer acting as an investigator, your obligation, under the statute, code, common law, and any operational instructions, is to record or record and retain material where you have any doubt as to whether the material may be relevant.

12.9.6 Disclosure

Disclosure is a term used in policing and legal circles and according to the Manual (drawing on the CJA 2003 amendments) it refers to:

> providing the defence with copies of, or access to, any material which might reasonably be considered capable of undermining the case for the prosecution against the accused, or of assisting the case for the accused, and which has not previously been disclosed.

Hence it occurs, for example, after a not guilty plea, which is one of the triggers for disclosure to come into play. Pertinent information has already been shared with the defence and now the question settles on the material which the prosecution has decided not to use.

However, the word is possibly confusing to you in initial training as you will not actually be personally disclosing anything to the legal representatives of the accused. Perhaps a better word is the term 'reveal' that we use above. Put this way, you or the Disclosure Officer reveal to the CPS the unused relevant material, whilst the CPS decides on what will be disclosed to the defence. Just because it is revealed does not mean that it will be disclosed.

Relevant material is defined in the Code as:

anything that appears to an investigator, or the officer in charge of an investigation or the disclosure officer to have some bearing on any offence under investigation or any person being investigated or on the surrounding circumstances unless it is incapable of having any impact on the case.

Unused material is defined by the Manual as:

material that may be relevant to the investigation that has been retained but does not form part of the case for the prosecution against the accused.

You should learn about disclosure at some point during your training (it is part of the IPLDP module LPG 1.7).

We should point out at this stage that some of the intricacies of disclosure are both detailed and complex and beyond the scope of this Handbook. However, a useful resource to learn about the detail of disclosure is to download the Disclosure Manual via the CPS website at <http://www.cps.gov.uk/legal/section20/chapter_a.html>. Be warned though, it runs to many pages, and the internet version does not contain the chapters of the full Manual that deal with sensitive matters such as CHIS. The full unexpurgated version should be available from your force.

Note that certain materials should not be initially disclosed to the defence, due to their sensitivity. These include materials which are marked confidential and use, for example, Form MG6D (see 12.10 below). An example would be a document providing personal details of a CHIS (see section 12.3 above) or a person giving information through the Crimestoppers scheme.

You will learn about the particular procedures involved for disclosure in your force during training. You will also learn about the role played by disclosure officers, the CPS, and the legal representatives of the suspect in the process of disclosure. Disclosure officers (who are members of police staff but not necessarily police officers) for example, will, amongst other tasks, examine the material that is retained for the investigation and disclose unused material to the accused. You might be designated as a disclosure officer yourself and apply the necessary disclosure tests, but not until you have more experience.

TASK 14

If you were the officer giving evidence in the court case above, what actions should you have taken to meet the requirements of disclosure?

TASK 15

In order to undertake the following task you may need to consult the Manual of Guidance referred to above or your own force documentation.

1. In the section above, reference is made to material that is relevant but non-evidential and will therefore not be used as evidence. In relation to the disclosure process, what title will this material be given?
2. Who is responsible for examining the records created during the investigation with a view to revealing the material to the prosecutor?
3. How is unused material revealed to the prosecutor, and how must it be described?

12.10 Hearsay

In everyday language, 'hearsay' is a reference to rumour or speculation which is often unreliable. Generally, therefore hearsay cannot be used as evidence in court **but there are many exceptions to this.** This section is concerned with some of these exceptions.

In legal terms, s 114 of the Criminal Justice Act 2003 defines hearsay evidence as 'any statement not made in oral evidence in the proceedings'. However, the same Act also changed the law relating to the admissibility of hearsay evidence in criminal proceedings. The new hearsay rules applied from April 2005. Essentially, the old law was criticized for being too complicated, difficult to obtain (because it was in different Acts of Parliament or case law), and inflexible. In *R v Sparks*, (1967), the court would not allow a defendant to adduce evidence at his trial for indecent assault, the fact that the alleged victim had described the attacker to her mother in circumstances that showed that it probably was **not** the defendant who committed the crime. The judgment indicated that the hearsay rule was inflexible, and Sparks was not able to lead significant evidence in his defence because of it. He was convicted of the crime.

The new law can be seen as a major shift in attitudes towards hearsay evidence. There are now four gateways to admissibility of hearsay evidence.

These are where:

(1) The Criminal Justice Act 2003 or any other Act indicates so. This will include for instance where a witness may have given evidence to police but now cannot attend court for various reasons such as illness, death, or being in fear;
(2) Any of the common law exceptions have been preserved by the Criminal Justice Act 2003. This will include confession evidence and many other areas;
(3) All parties to the proceedings agree to the evidence being given;
(4) The court thinks in the interests of justice it should be admitted.

Parts 1 and 2 effectively allow for many of the old exceptions to be admissible in proceedings, but there are some significant differences. The new law now allows for **verbal hearsay** to be admissible, whereas before it was limited to certain circumstances.

Part 4 is particularly welcome by the prosecution. It is clear that if evidence is hearsay, but does not fit any of the recognized exceptions, then it could **still be admissible** if the court thinks it is in the interests of justice to admit it. This section is known as the 'safety valve' and will potentially be capable of admitting relevant evidence even if it does not quite fit recognized exceptions.

For student police officers, it is essential that you record what happens contemporaneously, and you record what witnesses and victims say to you. It is possible that what they say to you may be admissible under these provisions. Of course, if you have not recorded anything, then the prosecution will not even be able try to get the evidence in. You do not need to learn all of the hearsay provisions, but merely record (in your PNB) what is said to you.

Defence and prosecution may also agree upon hearsay evidence being led at trial. Both parts 3 and 4 make it clear that when submitting evidence in the form of statements or cases, officers should also include hearsay evidence so that proper consideration can be given to the issues.

12.11 Answers to Tasks

TASK 1

You should consider where the hot spot is. Is it in a town centre? Close to a series of pubs or clubs? When does it happen? Would a police presence act as a deterrent? Who is likely to have brought the incidents to police attention? What would be the feelings and fears of the local community?

Are the vehicle owners reporting the crime? What is taken? Is there a pattern? What is the location? Are particular kinds of cars targeted? What preventive action would help (for example, leafleting car owners, warnings in the media not to leave valuables on view, posters of the 'Watch out! There's a thief about!' variety, and CCTV coverage)?

Are the credit card thefts seasonal (that is, do they happen in the summer, at the start of a new term, at the approach of Christmas)? What is the MO? What do students do about it? Is violence involved? How is the crime reported? Are women students more at risk than men? Are there criminals on the database who specialize in this sort of crime? What preventive action might you recommend? (**Hint**: think about crime prevention, raising awareness, liaison with college and university authorities to put cash points on campuses, credit card theft prevention schemes, talking to the banks, posters near ATMs (cash machines), security awareness, CCTV, and so on.)

You can see from these suggestions what sorts of questions are involved. A T&CG has to consider all the angles, all the permutations, as well as assess the intelligence, commission more work, and decide what to do operationally. It may be months or even years before you attend a T&CG, but if you understand how the process works, you will understand why you are tasked and how your work will feed into the NIM.

TASK 2

You may have come up with a list like the following (which is not exhaustive!):

integrity;
honesty;
patience;
attention to detail;
strong-minded;
not easily diverted;
experienced;
knowledgeable about crime and criminals;
ordinary/normal in appearance, so can blend into a crowd;
reticent or discreet;
firm sense of duty;
objective;
understands the 'bigger picture' of force needs and intelligence requirements;
adaptable (can think on his/her feet);
flexible;
professional in the relationship (courteous but not close);
willing to work long or unsocial hours;
resilient;
stable as a personality;
good listener;
empathetic ('emotional intelligence').

These qualities, skills, or attributes are not common in such combinations. A good source-handler can be trained to a high pitch, but there must be strong character traits already there upon which the training can build. You can see, I hope, that being a source handler is not something you can waltz straight into doing; it takes someone with considerable investigative experience and 'life skills' to do well in the role.

TASK 3

This is discussed in the text immediately after the question. In addition, you might like to look at the work of Dunnighan and Norris in respect of the use of informers (Dunnighan and Norris, 1996 and Dunnighan, 1999).

TASK 4

We discuss this task in the text that follows. Motivation is notoriously difficult to understand and identify, and particularly so with informants. As we have noted, most informants are themselves criminals and we have several layers to peel back. As Canter and Alison (2000) noted, the motivation that a person may put forward for their actions is not necessarily the most useful for understanding that person's actions and is only one of a number of possible explanations.

TASK 5

You could indicate resilience, self-sufficiency, strong professionalism, the ability to work alone, the ability to pass yourself off as something you are not, the focus and concentration to know what intelligence is needed, a very good relationship and trust with your handler, and a personal inclination towards the clandestine.

Logistical and support problems include a good cover story (both for the criminal target and to explain the officer's absence back in the force), payment, nothing to identify the officer as from the police (in clothing, residence, possessions) career-planning, reassuring family members, diverting curious colleagues, and so on. There are a host of problems associated with going long-term undercover and a team of people are used to support the lone officer.

In **planning a Test Purchase (TP) operation**, you would have to think about the original intelligence and its reliability, the patterns of movement (and MO) of the target criminal, when to insert the TP officer, how to monitor what is happening, how to intervene and disrupt or arrest, and whether you have the authorization to proceed.

'The battle is the pay-off' for that specialist form of intelligence: the risks taken are in proportion to the expected result. Quantifying the participation of a police officer in such undercover operations is fairly easy (and thus dear to the hearts of those who think policing is about counting), but other forms of intelligence-gathering are less amenable to the bean-counter's mentality.

TASK 6

We discuss open forms of intelligence in the text that follows the task. Open sources of intelligence have grown rapidly in recent years, largely as a result of the availability of electronic resources such as the internet. Whereas in the past we might need to search manually through paper copies of newspapers and magazines selling used cars for evidence of possible 'ringing' now we can use the search facilities available on most websites. Indeed, the widespread availability of information is causing some concern with the advent of crimes such as identity theft (putting aside the obvious general desire to maintain personal privacy). As an experiment, try to find out as much about yourself as you can by using freely available internet resources. For example, start with <http://www.192.com> and enter your own name. You may be surprised at what you (and others) can find out.

TASK 7

This is discussed in the paragraphs that follow. One major difference is that with co-operative witnesses (remember that some may be friends or associates of the suspect and hence not co-operative) we may be able to employ the 'cognitive interview' (CI) technique. Although CI may be part of your PEACE training it is not often used by police officers investigating volume crimes. CI uses memory-enhancing techniques such as context reinstatement which involves recreating the other events that were also encoded at the same time (or before or after) the event that we are interested in. You are probably familiar already with this idea—for example, what techniques do you use to locate misplaced keys or your wallet? If you want to know more about the cognitive interview and other interview techniques then *Investigative Interviewing—Psychology and Practice* by Rebecca Milne and Ray Bull is a good start (Milne, 1999).

TASK 8

The procedure is described in the paragraph that follows, although you will no doubt be issued with detailed guidance and instructions when you reach this stage of training.

TASK 9

The next paragraph contains our advice. Suggested wording and more guidance on special warnings may be found in Appendix H of the ACPO Investigation of Volume Crime Manual (ACPO, 2001).

TASK 10

You should have discovered that Form MG16 is used.

TASK 11

We provide some suggestions immediately after the task.

TASK 12

The exceptions usually agreed to be taken as evidence are declarations on the point of death, and statements made as confessions.

TASK 13

We suggest later that you do not let yourself be provoked. Different police officers have different strategies to achieve this. Some mentally count to three before responding to allow themselves time to compose a calm response.

TASK 14

When you attend an incident, you are a potential witness, not necessarily only for the prosecution, but also for the defence.

When you arrive at the scene of an alleged disturbance and you do no more than establish that your colleagues dealing with the incident require no further assistance, then record that fact in your PNB.

If there are groups of people milling around you may decide to stay in the area in case of any further trouble. If that is the case, then make a short note to that effect.

If you are present and involve yourself in assisting an arresting officer, then make an entry to that effect.

If you talk to witnesses or potential witnesses, record their details and record what they observed in relation to the incident.

TASK 15

1. Unused material.
2. A disclosure officer is responsible for examining the records created during the investigation (and any criminal proceedings arising from the investigation).
3. It is revealed to the prosecutor on Schedules MG6C and MG6D (forms from the Manual of Guidance series of forms). It must be described in sufficient detail and with sufficient information to enable the prosecutor to make an informed decision as to whether or not the item contains anything which might undermine the prosecution case.

13 Critical Incidents and Forensic Investigation

13.1 Chapter Briefing

This chapter is concerned with the police response to critical incidents, such as dealing with major incidents and emergencies. We also examine forensic investigation, which is an important element in many successful investigations of crime. Throughout, we link both subject matters to your own training as a student police officer.

13.1.1 Aim of the Chapter

The aim of this chapter is to assist in the development of your knowledge of critical incident management (including missing persons and suspicious deaths) and to help extend your understanding of forensic investigation, and the role it plays in policing.

This chapter will enable you to:

- understand the meaning and importance of critical incident management;
- follow the procedures given to you by your force in the case of missing persons;
- understand the police approach to the process surrounding sudden death;
- have a comprehensive understanding of the basis of forensic investigation, how it supports police investigation, and your role in evidence protection and collection;
- develop the underpinning knowledge required for a number of NOS elements, several of the PAC headings and entries for your Learning Diary Phase 3, and the CARs of your SOLAP.

13.1.2 Police Action Checklist

This chapter will provide you with the underlying knowledge and theory to meet aspects of the following requirements of the Police Action Checklist.

13.1.2.1 Investigation

- Demonstrate initial crime scene management.
- Conduct the initial investigation and report of missing persons.
- Conduct the initial investigation and report of sudden death.
- Demonstrate correct handling of exhibits.

13.1.2.2 Custody Officer Procedures

- Obtain fingerprints.
- Obtain DNA sample.

13.1.3 National Occupational Standards

This chapter will provide you with some of the knowledge required to demonstrate the following NOS elements:

National Occupational Standards Elements

2C1.2 Respond to incidents.
2G2.1 Conduct priority and volume investigations.

13.1.4 IPLDP Phases and Modules

This chapter will provide you with resources to support Operational Module OP 3 'Respond to incidents, conduct and evaluate investigations' (and particularly OP 3.2 to 3.6 inclusive).

It will also provide guidance on the following topic areas of LPG 1:

- Policies and Procedures (LPG 1.4);
- Non-crime Incidents (LPG 1.5);
- Investigation and Interview (LPG 1.7).

Much of the chapter relates to IPLDP Phase 3 (Supervised Patrol) and Phase 4 (Independent Patrol).

13.1.5 SOLAP

The contents of this chapter are relevant to the 'knowledge' evidence requirements of CARs 2C1 and 2G2.

13.1.6 Learning Diary Phases

The contents of this chapter may provide you with stimulus material for completion of your Learning Diary (Phase 3) and the following headings in particular:

- Crime;
- Police Policies and Procedures;
- Non-crime Incidents;
- Investigation and Interview.

13.1.7 IPLDP Learning Requirement

This chapter is relevant to sections 6.2 and 6.6 of the IPLDP Learning Requirement.

13.2 Introduction

In this chapter we examine three important aspects of your training as a police officer: responding to incidents, dealing with the particularly challenging incidents of missing persons and suspicious deaths, and finally understanding the importance of forensic investigation and the procedures and processes that surround it.

13.3   Critical Incidents

As a student police officer, much of your Supervised Patrol will be spent dealing with **incidents**, or events, of one kind or another. This will range from handling minor disputes through to the complexities of a homicide. It is likely that, as you gain experience and specialist skills (see Chapter 14), you will attend incidents which are increasingly complex. You will use your skills across a range of events, perhaps in public order, firearms, hostage negotiation, or arresting and interviewing a serial rapist. That said, you could be caught up in, and be expected to control effectively, almost **any** incident from the moment you go out on the streets wearing a police uniform. The public will see the uniform, not knowing how long you have served, and there will be an expectation that you will take charge and resolve the problem, whatever it is, effectively and immediately. This is why, throughout your student officer training, great emphasis is laid upon your use of common sense, 'life skills', or 'nous'; it can be described in many ways.

You will practise and rehearse many times the effective ways in which you can intervene to resolve a problem before it gets out of hand, such as a domestic dispute, a quarrel between neighbours, drunken aggression amongst clubbers, breaking up a fight, dealing with a shoplifter, or calming people down who have been involved in a minor road collision. You will learn to defuse, control, restrain, or manage any of a great variety of incidents. But what about something you cannot control on your own, or something which has the potential really to get out of hand?

TASK 1

What would your first responses be, for example, if you were the first police officer to arrive at:

- A serious road collision?
- The site of a plane crash?
- The scene of a brawl in which someone had been knifed?
- An accident on a railway line?
- A robbery scene where people had been injured?
- A burning house where people are trapped on upper floors?
- A situation where a person has taken a child hostage?

What would your **responsibilities** be, as opposed to your instincts? What would you be expected to do? Is there an order in which you should do things? Have you priorities at the scene? What might they be? What communication is needed and with whom?

These incidents are all critical, that is they are of a major or significant dimension and they **have the potential to escalate beyond your control**. What you do as first police officer on the scene is crucial to the proper, managed outcome of the incident. Short of doing nothing, the worst thing you could do, probably, is rely on your instincts.

Let us discuss why. Suppose you turn up to a club where there is a brawl in progress, involving several dozen people; fists are flying, boots going in, staggering, screaming, bloodied people are rushing up to you and there is general din and mayhem. Control of the scene is not best effected by you wading into the middle of the fracas and grabbing the first brawler whom you can see. You are likely to provoke more violence and get hurt yourself. You are not much use lying on the ground trying to cover your kidneys while all hell breaks loose around you. Another example: suppose you turn up to a burning house and, heroically, you plunge straight in, clamber upstairs and try to save everyone from death by burning. Without the proper apparatus, or an understanding of the 'seat' of the fire and the imminence of collapse or otherwise of the building, you may become a victim yourself instead of rescuer. Just like throwing yourself into a river to save someone if you cannot swim, entering a burning building without fire fighting training and the proper equipment and knowledge will make you a liability, not a help.

This is hard. As a police officer, you have a duty to protect life and it is in most people's instincts to rush to the help of others. The rule is: only to try to rescue someone from a life-threatening situation if, and only if, you do **not** endanger yourself or others. If people are being hurt in a brawl, your first instinct will be to wade in and stop it. That is fine if you have support from colleagues and you can together take control and calm everything down, but not if you are on your own. If you try to break up fighting groups alone, you stand a very good chance of being hurt yourself. On occasions you have to be **counter-intuitive**, that is, you have to go against your instincts and allow your mind to rule and control your emotions. You need to **assess** what the situation is, calmly and rationally. You need to **communicate** as quickly as possible what you think is going on. You should **prioritize** your (and others') actions. Remember, in some situations, you may be overwhelmed by offers of help from well-intentioned people—though probably not when a large-scale fight is going on—and you need to do the same for them as you have done for yourself: **calm down, think, act rationally, and retain control**. Panic is infectious and can spread quickly through a large gathering. Think of crowd control at a football match or at an open-air concert, where panic can turn a mass of people into an uncontrollable mass; people can fall and be trampled; old people and young children may be crushed. You must retain control of people's movements, even at a relatively limited incident. Use volunteers to direct and contain people's movements, or to direct traffic and evacuation until professional police help arrives. In one well-known incident, a messy road traffic collision involving pedestrians outside a school, a single police officer was assisted immeasurably by a bus-load of rugby players in shepherding people to safe exits, in keeping back crowds of sightseers, and in directing traffic until police reinforcements and ambulances arrived. Police and other emergency service support can be delayed because of passers-by wanting to look at what is going on. People's curiosity is often an impediment to scene management, and you should be prepared always to handle such onlookers and get them away from the incident.

There is another and very important reason why the area itself must be controlled. It could be a **crime scene** (see section 11.18 above). Your role in controlling access, preservation of evidence, and the bringing of authority to a probably chaotic scene, is of absolutely **vital importance**, otherwise crucial evidence could be lost, overlooked, or damaged. We look at this in detail in the final section of this chapter.

We have discussed your first actions when attending an incident; indeed, a calm and authoritative police presence is often enough to prevent an incident becoming critical, but not always. How can you prioritize you actions?

Refer again to the scenarios offered above. Let us take the hostage-taking episode as our example to examine in detail.

TASK 2

What would be your list of things to do in priority order at such an incident? (Assume that back-up will be with you within ten minutes.) You have one other police officer to assist you. The hostage-taker appears to have barricaded himself into a semi-detached house in a cul-de-sac. About a dozen people are milling about, and the event has been described to you by two very excited and incoherent witnesses. Other emergency services (fire and rescue service, ambulance) are also on their way, with an estimated time of arrival of fifteen minutes.

Write down what you would do, in what order, to:

- contain the scene;
- protect life;
- manage the incident;
- prepare for the arrival of your supporting police officers.

Of course, this all assumes that there is no imminent danger to you or to anyone else. However, it is possible that the hostage-taker has been seen with a weapon. If a knife or something similar has been credibly witnessed, your primary concern will be those inside the house who may be threatened or at risk. This makes communication with the hostage-taker a vital early step. Suppose the information suggests that the hostage-taker is armed with a gun, or that witnesses have heard shots? Your responsibility now is to get everyone back out of the line of fire and far enough away not to be hit by stray rounds or ricochets. That may mean a larger evacuation and a larger 'sterile' cordon around the site. It also means that you must not expose yourself, or anyone else, to danger. All this information needs communicating urgently to your control room, because it is certain that firearms officers will attend, if the alleged perpetrator appears to be armed.

What you will need to keep in your mind throughout is that **you are in control** (as '**Silver**', the forward Commander) until you are relieved by someone of superior rank. We will go on later to describe how a large-scale incident of this kind is handled once support arrives, but meanwhile, you and any accompanying colleagues are 'it'. Remember too that you may be at a crime scene, so **preservation of evidence** and keeping the scene clear and untouched is very important. (That is why any rendezvous point (RV) for vehicles bringing support or assistance needs to be kept well back from the scene. In an armed emergency involving firearms or the risk of violence, you would not let other emergency services go forward into the 'line of fire' either. Look again at section 11.18 above.)

All this sounds complicated and difficult to remember in the urgency of dealing with an incident which is critical and which could become a major crime. However, there are ways in which you can keep priorities and procedures firmly in your mind, always assuming that you act calmly, positively, purposefully, and promptly.

13.3.1 CHALET

Let us go back a little first, and recap what we have discussed. We noted above that any incident has the potential to 'go critical'. We can define a critical incident, then, as 'any incident or event which requires **mutual aid**, or help from partner organizations such as the other emergency services'. More recent thinking suggests that a critical incident may be one in which there is a strong public perception about **vulnerability**, such as a missing person. The police may appear vulnerable too, if they are not seen to act decisively and effectively.

Procedures are well defined (after all, the police have plenty of experience in dealing with critical incidents, and nothing is likely to happen to you which has not happened similarly before). You need to learn and keep in your mind the mnemonic **CHALET**.

This means that you initiate action the following way:

> C Casualties (how many? where? what injuries?)
> H Hazards (actually **present**, such as fire, bare or exposed electrical wires, flood water, chemicals or hazardous substances, or **potential**, such as gas cylinders near heat sources, spilled fuel, overhead power lines, firearms)
> A Access (how to enter the site, RV points)
> L Location (where is the incident? Are precise map references needed?)
> E Emergency services (Are people hurt? Is there a fire? Are they already on the scene or are they needed? Is there a bomb or other explosive substance?)
> T Type of incident (vehicles in an accident, buildings in danger of collapse, affray in progress, underground tunnel collapse, public order, civil emergency, armed siege).

(Note that 'SAD CHALET' is also sometimes used as a mnemonic. In this case the 'SAD' part normally stands for 'Survey, Assess, and Disseminate'.)

We noted above that the police and the other emergency services are well used to dealing with critical incidents, and indeed every force and every emergency service will have **contingency plans** to deal with things which go wrong, or which threaten to get out of hand. Some of these plans will be legal requirements under the **Civil Contingencies Act** 2004. (You can find a full copy of the Act at <http://www.opsi.gov.uk/acts/acts2004/20040036.htm> and a guide via the PNLD website.)

There are **generic plans** (that is, all forces will have them, as will all emergency services) for the following types of critical incident:

- aircraft crash
- bomb or suspect device
- casualty bureau for major emergency
- contamination of food products
- disaster, including civil emergency
- evacuation
- gas emergency
- hazardous substances
- hostage or siege incident
- hostage involving kidnap
- maritime incident
- major fire or conflagration (including evacuation)
- rail incident
- transportation of irradiated fuel

Only the police will carry a constant alertness to the possibility of the commission of crime. Is the blaze deliberate or accidental? (Fire and Rescue Service experts will find out, not you.) Was this really a traffic accident or did someone throw something from a motorway bridge? Was one of the drivers drunk or under the influence of drugs? Did that person fall or was she pushed? Did someone tamper with this equipment? Is this a natural or a suspicious death? You should look for any **triggers** of suspicion, and be alert to any **signatures**, or characteristic signs, that there is something wrong. Examples might be stray remarks by witnesses, such as 'Funny thing; that man hanging round all morning', or something present at the scene or nearby such as an empty wallet or purse, which might suggest that all is not what it seems.

The critical factor in any incident is that you **take charge**, demonstrating those **leadership** skills and capability in a crisis which were looked for when you applied to join the police in the first place. Much of your training will seek to develop your skills as a leader and will focus upon what you are expected to do in any given situation (developed in more detail in Chapter 14 and which we looked at in Chapter 4). But no one expects you to be super-human, which is why we set you the next task.

TASK 3

What are the problem-solving and decision-making models used in your police force? What models will you be taught during training?

13.3.2 The 'Golden Hour'

The first period of any incident at a crime scene or at a critical incident is often described as 'the golden hour'. It is actually unlikely that you will be on your own for that long, unless the incident is in a really remote and inaccessible place, or there are corollary problems such as a natural disaster of some kind, where access roads are blocked and your support is experiencing severe difficulty in getting through to you. The golden hour is normally a shorthand reference to the need to preserve a scene quickly so that evidence can be gathered before it is disturbed, where forensic evidence can be gathered while fresh (bloodstains undiluted by rain, bodies examined before rigor mortis), witnesses interviewed whilst recollections are still clear, for example. You may be relieved by a senior officer quite quickly, but you may not. If you are not, the golden hour is down to you and your colleagues (if any). Listen to what you are being told by witnesses and evaluate that information against what you know. An example of this came from the Soham murders, in which it was shown (much later) that Ian Huntley, a school caretaker at a school in Soham village, Cambridgeshire, had murdered two young girls. The first alarm that was raised was the disappearance of the two girls. Imagine that you were the first police officer to respond to the alert. What triggers or signatures would you expect?

Your notes might include questions about what you were told. How long had the girls been missing? Was it normal for them to wander off without telling anyone? Were they going anywhere specific, such as to a shop or to visit a relative or friend? Had there been any difficulty at home, such as a row or a quarrel because one of them had been forbidden to do something? Had anyone seen anything suspicious? Did the girls have a favourite 'bolt hole' to which they would go if they thought they were in trouble? Did either have a special or particular friend? Did they have mobile phones? Where did they like to go for a walk or to 'hang out'? What were they wearing? Are there any recent photographs? Remember that in instances like this, parents, guardians, or carers might well be distraught with anxiety and worry. It is not unusual for anxiety to turn to anger. Expect anger, but do not be deflected by it. Be calm and in control. Remember too that this might not just be a matter of a missing person or persons; it might be a homicide (as Soham was), abduction, or kidnapping.

Among signatures might be a suspicious eagerness on the part of someone to help. Huntley, the murderer, spent much time in the initial searching for the two girls; volunteering to search himself, being conspicuously present around the police search teams for days, and eager to be informed of progress. This can be (though by no means always will be) an indicator of guilt or complicity, and is characteristic of a type of murderer who is excited and stimulated by the purposeful activity which his/her act has caused. This is, however, a very complex area of human psychology and we are not recommending that you adopt some of the more populist approaches around 'reading a signature'. Instead you might you might want to undertake further reading, perhaps starting with Blackburn (1995). What we are saying is that you should be attentive to these possibilities and keep a proper record in your PNB.

13.3.3   The Command Sequence

Throughout any initial stages of an incident, you must keep reporting what is happening to force control, so that those controlling the larger picture are fully informed about development or progress. There are good reasons why a central focus is sustained in such incidents. The first is a matter of **resources**. Much support is likely to be coming your way but it has to be mobilized. In the case of missing persons (especially when there may be other, criminal, factors), search teams are being called out, assessments of transport needs are being made, command and control, strategic, and tactical responses are all being set up, and the control room is alerting other emergency responses—including in some cases, the invoking of 'military aid to the civil power' (MACP), where specialists such as explosives ordnance (bomb-disposal), helicopters, search and rescue, engineers, nuclear, chemical, and radiological detection and containment units, and a host of others, may be called on.

Another factor is **co-ordination of control of the incident** in terms of what is done. Resources should not be committed too early, unless there is a clear picture of what is happening on the ground (see where you fit in?), because deployment is not only expensive, but over-resourcing is wasteful and inefficient. Police officers rushing (or, more properly, 'proceeding') to an incident cannot be deployed elsewhere, even though something equally dramatic and important could be happening. Swamping a site with everything from armed officers to dog teams, from underwater search teams to the Royal Engineers, could be wasteful if the incident turns out to be trivial.

The third factor is related to both preceding ones; it is **risk assessment**. When in possession of all the known facts, a senior officer (from a Duty Inspector up to Chief Officer rank) can make a risk assessment of the situation. He/she will ask questions (sometimes directly of you if you are still acting as 'Silver') such as: How many are injured? What access is there to the site? What is making the situation worse (spreading fire, rising flood water, gathering crowds)? Who is there now? Who is expected? Can the situation/incident/event be contained? Where are the other emergency services? What are witnesses saying? Do you have reason to believe that this is a crime scene? If so, what sort of crime? Is a senior investigating officer (SIO) en route or at the scene? What deployment has there been of scenes of crime officers (crime scene investigators or CSIs)? Is an armed response needed? Note here that deployment of armed officers is usually a top level command decision ('**Gold**'), made by a chief superintendent or chief officer.

The purpose of a risk assessment is to allow the right proportion of response in the right sequence. The assessment is about allocation of resources and the intensity of the required response, in addition to deciding who else should be there. Let us look at an example.

Four years ago, there was extensive autumnal flooding in some southern counties of England following a prolonged period of very heavy rain. River levels were dangerously high, many flood plains were already inundated, and there was a risk of widespread evacuation from premises in the path of further flooding. The strategic command of the incident was co-ordinated by the police, as is usual in the UK in civil emergency, supported by other services.

Levels of response

GOLD	strategic command of the incident, usually at police headquarters or at a designated strategic police command centre.
SILVER	tactical police command at a forward point closer to the scene of immediate crisis.
BRONZE	(often called Operational Response Commanders or ORC), local particular response at the crisis point itself (for example cordons or firearms), often carried out by a number of people rather than one designated commander.

This structure was common across several South-Eastern forces, each of which was in contact with the others, because there might be a need for **mutual aid**, where the police of one force go to the aid of another—usually in specific numbers.

At **Gold Command**, a number of senior representatives from a range of services were present, each with the power to deploy resources, under the chair of a chief police officer (ACC, DCC, or chief constable, depending upon relative severity and availability). In this instance, there were senior officers from Fire and Rescue, the Ambulance Service, health, housing, and the county council or unitary authority. In addition there were representatives from the regional water company, specialist surveyors, power companies (power lines were being brought down by high winds), and various parts of the armed forces, including the Royal Engineers, signallers, and the Royal Air Force, whose aircraft were being deployed.

This structure was replicated, on a smaller scale and at tactical level in **Silver Command**. The equipment, machinery, crews, vehicles, and those engaged in the actual operations on the ground were located at **Bronze** or the **ORC** 'forward control point' (FCP).

TASK 4

What do you think the problems could be with such structures?

Make a list of what could go wrong and what would avoid problems.

Your list might include something like this:

Potential problem	Resolution
Confusion about who is in charge	One command giving orders (GOLD)
Who does what?	Clarity around division of responsibility; obvious who does what
Overlapping of responsibility	See above
Duplication of tasks	Clarity at all levels of response
Gaps in knowledge	Expertise available at all levels
Uncoordinated response	Co ordinated through GOLD and passed down the 'chain of command'
Decisions made in a vacuum	Access to all information at all levels
Lack of prioritization	Continuous risk assessment
Orders not getting through	Continuous communication at all levels
Overlooking a vital component	Representatives of specialist areas all available to cover potential gaps
When to deploy what?	Decision taken at GOLD, controlled and timed at SILVER, executed at ORC

This tiered structure is considered by many in the police service to work effectively (and has been exhaustively tested) at local or force level and also at national level, as you will see when we come to look at a terrorist incident below.

You may feel that you are only a small and insignificant cog in this machinery, but that is not the issue. The issue is that everyone has an important part to play (the chain is only as strong as its weakest link), and the professional execution of each of those roles, from the chief constable at GOLD through to the Pc on the ground in front of the unfolding incident, is what matters. And the incident itself can be a civil emergency (such as the flooding crisis) or a major crime of very large dimensions; command is exercised in the same way, and co-ordination is properly structured. So, when you are at your first incident and all around you seems chaotic and purposeless, be patient. You know that control is developing behind you, with the correct risk assessment and the proportionate deployment of resources. As we have discussed, **your role is to contain and control the incident**, **on the spot, there and then**. Let others worry about resources and deployments.

13.3.4 Media Interest

At any critical incident, there is one common factor which we have not yet considered: media interest. Newspapers, radio, and television have apparently inexhaustible appetites for crime stories; sometimes critically, sometimes supportively, always dramatically (it is their job). Media interest can be as broad as the spectrum of policing itself, from the use of sniffer dogs to drive-by shootings, from bank robberies to terrorism. Just think of the police dramas on TV and the exciting flavour which seems to infuse all police work (including tangled personal relationships with almost everyone). When did you ever see a police officer on TV painstakingly construct a case file in close co-operation with the CPS? Probably never, and for obvious reasons.

This quest for the news story has produced an edgy, sometimes fraught, relationship between the media and the police: on the one hand the media are helpful distributors of appeals for information in complex crimes, or to publicize missing person enquiries; on the other they can be irritatingly vacuous and superficial in their endless desire for headlines. Leishman and Mason (2003) consider the relationship between police and the media in more detail and more complexity.

From your point of view, attending and trying to control a critical incident, the intrusion of the media, looking for a good story, is at best a distraction and at worst an obstacle. You should never be tempted to stop what you are doing to give press or broadcast interviews. Your headquarters will have a media services unit trained to do just that. Some BCUs have media relations staff as well. It is not that you should be 'muzzled', but that you may inadvertently be misleading. You do not have the full picture. It is unlikely that you are experienced in appearing in the media. The short and simple guide is: do not talk to the media, refer them always to media services. Photo opportunities for you and temporary fame can come later.

Let us look at an example of a case where media coverage could bring both advantages and disadvantages, and incidentally look at some of the elements involved in a critical incident. A sixteen-year-old boy has been reported missing by his mother. Checks with his school showed that he never turned up that morning, despite having left his house at the normal time and in school uniform. His whereabouts are unknown and he may have been missing for as much as ten hours before his absence was reported.

Remember the kinds of questions we looked at when visiting the parents of a missing child? In this case, it is a sixteen-year-old, but the law would treat this as a missing child. This is important because one of the first things to be done in a '**misper**' (missing person) enquiry is to make a risk assessment. The disappearance of a child can never be a low risk; it must always be medium or high. There is an urgent need, then, to assess whether the boy might be, or might become, the victim of a serious crime or be at risk of suffering serious harm. The likelihood is that this case would rapidly become a major incident if other factors indicated some form of **vulnerability**. We look in more detail at missing persons in the next section of this chapter.

In our example, we shall assume that the boy had recently become moody and depressed. There were hints that he may have been subject to some bullying at school. He is asthmatic and needs regular medication. He is a keen shot and has his own shotgun, properly licensed, for use on the farm where he lives. He had a quarrel with his father the night before because the boy wanted to attend a party in a neighbouring town, but his father had refused. There is a history of the boy acting rebelliously and his father only reluctantly granting limited freedom.

TASK 5

Given the above, what lines of questioning would you follow? What essential information must you obtain?

You might note that there are a number of vulnerabilities, or potential areas for concern, in this case. The boy needs regular medication: has he taken that medication with him? Are there medical factors which will make his condition worse (such as dust allergies or stress-induced attacks of asthma)? Can the condition in any way be life-threatening? Is his shotgun (and any other weapons on the farm) accounted for? If not, what is missing? Can an estimate be made of how much ammunition may have gone missing? How was the boy able to leave the house apparently normally for school without anyone noticing that he might be carrying a gun? Has the boy mentioned any particular individuals in connection with the apparent bullying at school? Has the boy said anything about revenge or getting his own back? What about the quarrel with the father? Was it more violent or tense than the usual family falling-out? Had the boy said anything to indicate that he contemplated any further action (such as saying 'I'll get even, you wait!' or 'I'll make you sorry for this')? What occasioned his depression and anxiety? Was he struggling with his school work? Are exams imminent or results due? Has he a close companion with whom he has had a quarrel? Has he ever talked about suicide or mentioned that, for example, life was not worth living? Does he have a religious belief or strong ethical principles? Has he taken drugs? Has he ever been in trouble with the police?

You can see that the **lines of enquiry** which the answers to these questions would provoke might take you into an investigation of crime, into the possibility of suicide and, if any gun is missing, into a major search operation or a serious crime investigation. There are, for example, instances both in the US and in Europe of so-called 'spree killings' where a young person takes a weapon into a school and shoots teachers or fellow students, and/or uses the weapon to commit suicide. At this age, and in this vulnerable or confused state, the boy might be emotionally and physically capable of causing great harm to himself or to others and the subsequent operation would reflect the gravity with which the case is treated. Knowing what has to be done, and what resources to commit, depends very much on the **initial questioning** and the lines of enquiry which emerge.

The media will almost certainly have discovered some of what has happened and will be anxious for the story. Remembering the guidance given above about referral to the force media team, it might be necessary to obtain a photograph of the boy for the newspapers and television stations to carry in their bulletins. Essentially, you need the media to co-operate and to publicize the request for information, such as 'Has anyone seen the boy? This is what he was wearing and what he looked like. These are his favourite places. These are his favourite activities.'

What can happen is that the media may decide that this case is of major public interest in which case they will visit the area in numbers and will approach the parents and relatives (who are often in a vulnerable state themselves, with worry and fear), or the school, where other children may be interviewed. There is a danger that this may get out of hand, and the media may besiege the family at its home or individual members at work, as well as potentially hindering the police operation. It is a fine line to tread between invoking the help of the media and coping with the news frenzy which may develop. That is another reason why relations with the media are best handled professionally by headquarters, rather than by the untrained on the spot. What usually happens in major cases is that the police will convene (and hope to manage) a **press conference**, or series of conferences, to brief on the information required and to report progress. Again, it is a fine line, calling for some acute judgements, whether the family of the missing person is involved in press conferences.

The media will demand their presence, but sometimes family members can be very fragile emotionally. Whilst it makes good television or newspaper pictures to see frightened parents crying, it might not advance the police operation or help the family.

We have looked in some detail at missing person incidents, not only because such incidents may be those in which you may be involved early in your career, but also because such incidents are good examples of the elements involved in critical incident management. We return to missing persons as a separate topic in section 13.4. It is time now to look at larger and sometimes more serious incidents and what is done about them, bearing in mind that the principles of incident management have not changed; only the scale has changed. When the Pan Am 103 aircraft exploded in December 1988 over Lockerbie in Scotland, debris was scattered over several miles of countryside, as well as within the village of Lockerbie itself. Nonetheless, the area was declared a crime scene and was treated in the same way as any other crime scene except that the scale of the incident required the provision of mutual aid.

13.3.5 Disasters

The UK seldom has natural disasters on the scale experienced elsewhere in the world (flooding and hurricanes are relatively mild, compared with, say, the Caribbean in the hurricane season or Bangladesh in the monsoon season), and this country's temperate climate is normally equable. Some isolated or freak weather conditions do occur: the winters of 1947 and 1962–3, the autumn storms of 1953 on the east coast, the hot, dry, and very long summer of 1976, the prolonged February freeze in 1987, the flood in Boscastle in 2004; but we do not anticipate such conditions as in any way likely. This can cause unpreparedness, and consequently the country can experience greater disruption than if the weather conditions or natural disaster were more frequent or predictable. A good example of this is how we deal with heavy snowfall. Canadians and Norwegians, for instance, know that every year (global warming permitting), they will have several metres of snow during the winter months, and prepare for it. Vehicles have snow tyres or snow chains fitted in good time, shops and city centres invest in subterranean heated malls, in the countryside children can ski at a very young age, and roads are kept clear of trees or other obstacles. Both countries invest in efficient snow ploughs—and plenty of them—and people understand the cold, so they dress and act accordingly.

The UK, with the exception of northern Scotland, does not get snow regularly, and it always seems to catch us out. However, whatever the weather, policing must be maintained, and you may well be involved in civil emergencies as a result. Genuinely heavy snow and severe cold can disrupt travel, isolate communities, bring down power supplies, and cause burst pipes. People may die if they are ill-equipped to deal with it. What happened in New Orleans and the southern US, during September 2005, was a graphic demonstration of what happens when relief supplies, aid, food, transport, power, sanitation, and the restoration of order cannot reach the stricken area from outside—and this after at least six days' warning of the arrival and probable course of **Hurricane Katrina**. The rapid degeneration of law and order which occurred, the rise of looting, the increase in gun crime and general violence (at least in parts of the city), were all symptoms of a society under severe pressure. If such a natural disaster happened here, you could anticipate at least some of the same sort of chaos, because this was not a specifically American phenomenon.

Let us look at a **man-made disaster**. We can choose any one of the recent spate of fatal train crashes across England as an example. The causes of train crashes are usually found to be:

- driver error;
- mechanical failure;
- signalling problems;
- poor track maintenance.

A train crash usually involves derailment, injury, fire, and sometimes death. Train crashes often happen in inaccessible places, which can pose logistical problems in gaining access, escorting uninjured passengers to safety, and bringing out the wounded for treatment. A train crash will engage all emergency services as well as specialists from the railway companies, involving heavy lifting equipment and metal cutting tools.

> **TASK 6**
>
> Imagine that you are on Independent Patrol in a police vehicle and you receive an urgent call to attend a reported train crash in a cutting in deep countryside. What will be your priorities when you reach the scene? What actions should you take to manage this critical incident from your arrival?

You probably answered that your first priority is to take control of the crash site until help arrives. However, you should **not** attempt any entry to the crash site itself until you have been told that the electrical power has been turned off, that trains approaching the site have been stopped, and that it is safe to continue. Your force control centre should be co-ordinating such action, but it is imperative for your own safety, and for that of other people, that you do not engage in any action which may result in further injury or loss of life. Remember our examples about fire and flood above: your response may need to be counter-intuitive and it must be focussed upon safe procedures. You will be in constant communication with your control centre and with colleagues on their way to the site.

All incidents which happen on railway property are the responsibility of British Transport Police (BTP) which extends up to and includes the investigation of homicide. (See the ACPO guidelines on the protocols for this available from your force.) However, it is likely that you and your colleagues will be first on the scene and you will have to take charge until relieved by BTP officers, or superior officers from your own force.

The **standard procedure for site management**, which we looked at earlier, extends to a train crash:

- control access;
- clear, or arrange to be cleared, a reception area for emergency services;
- preserve the scene (there may be evidence of a crime, for example, an obstruction placed on the line which caused the crash);
- secure an inner cordon around the site until the arrival of BTP officers;
- once relieved, continue to secure an outer cordon;
- once you have been assured that the power is switched off that section of railway line and that oncoming trains have been halted, you may approach the crash site.

You should be wearing high visibility clothing. Note the weather conditions, as you may need a torch and hazard lights (indeed, getting lighting to the crash site should be an early priority). You should not go anywhere near the live rail or overhead power cables unless absolutely necessary, even though you know that the power has been switched off. Then you can go to the carriages to help rescue the injured and escort passengers to safety, but remember that the carriages themselves may be unstable or dangerous. When in doubt wait for assistance, particularly the specialist assistance of the Fire and Emergency Service and the railway company.

A related critical incident which you may have to attend is a single death or injury on a railway line. You should be aware that bodies on or near railway lines will often be dismembered. They are there because of an accident (for example at a railway crossing), or from suicide, or as the result of a crime. The same procedures as outlined above must be observed. You should not approach a body or injured person until the power has been switched off (touching a body still in contact with a live rail, for example, could electrocute you). The third rail can carry up to 740 volts of direct current and is enough to kill you. Sometimes it may be imperative to move a person from contact with the live rail before power can be cut. In such cases, you must take extreme care and use a non-conducting material, such as a dry wooden pole, to push the casualty clear of the line. It is always better to leave such actions to experts or specialists if you can.

The same CHALET principles (see section 13.3.1 above) will apply whatever the crash site, and wherever it happens. The surrounding circumstances may, of course, complicate what you have to do, in terms of scale, access, site control, preservation of evidence, and local hazards.

13.3.6 Major Crimes

Critical incident management extends to **major crime**; indeed the distinction between a critical incident and a major crime is often blurred (one can precede the other), but the principles we outlined earlier remain the same. The additional burden when attending a major crime scene is clearly the preservation of evidence, whatever the scale of the crime itself (remember Lockerbie, which we noted above).

Many of the elements involved in investigating major crime have been covered elsewhere in the Handbook and we do not repeat them here, but some context for major crime will help, as will some common agreement on what a major crime is. Let us begin with a **working definition:**

> A major crime is an illegal act involving violence, requiring a significant investment of police resources and is one which will entail, upon conviction, a substantial prison sentence.

Major crime therefore covers those offences involving homicide, attempted murder, threat or conspiracy to murder, rape, grievous bodily harm with intent, and robbery involving the use of firearms or serious assault.

> **TASK 7**
> What do you think will be the characteristics of such investigations? What external factors will play a part?

You may have noted that major crime investigations are often long-term and complex (though not always), especially when dealing with 'stranger murders' or 'stranger rapes' (fairly uncommon, but the task which takes the time is identifying the perpetrator, who may have no known connection with the victim). Teams of police officers can be involved in the early stages, both uniformed (for house-to-house enquiries, for example) and detective officers (for investigating all leads, conducting interviews and so on), and the whole investigation is headed usually by a specially-trained **senior investigating officer** (SIO), usually of detective inspector or detective chief inspector rank.

You could note too that crimes of violence attract considerable **media** interest and widespread publicity which, whilst helpful in publicizing the crime, can adversely affect an investigation. The public, alerted by the publicity surrounding, say, a murder, can have its confidence in the police dented if the crime is not detected and 'brought to justice'. Indeed, a measure of public confidence in the police is how quickly a serial rapist (one who offends more than once and with different victims) is caught or how effectively a case is brought against a murderer. Another point to note is that these crimes are very serious; a force's reputation can rest on how well and how efficiently such serious crimes are detected and resolved. Think of the difficulties which faced the MPS in terms of credibility in the unsolved murders of, say, Rachel Nickell and Stephen Lawrence.

Most police forces have specialist (often centrally-based) departments or units which deal with major violent crime investigations. Such crimes are on the increase. The murder rate among young men in England and Wales, for example, has almost doubled since 1981. Fifty-one men aged twenty to twenty-four in every million are murdered, and the overall rate for male murder is seventeen per million per year, double the nine per million for women. Factors which have influenced this increase could be alcohol and the availability of weapons, including guns and knives, but simplistic conclusions of this sort are difficult to justify. Fifty years ago there were about 350 homicides a year in England and Wales. In 2002–3 there were 923 recorded murders, 818 attempted murders, and 18,031 threats or conspiracies to murder. The 'average' murder rate, if we can conceive of such a thing, is about 700 substantiated offences per year, ranging from more than 200 in Greater Manchester to one in the City of London, in a single year. Let us not lose perspective though: there are more homicides in the city of Johannesburg every year than in the whole of England and Wales. Indeed, in South Africa as a whole, there are 20,000 murders each year. This may be small comfort, but the likelihood is more than 40% that you will assist in the investigation of violent crimes during your career in the police, and that this may well become something in which you later specialize.

Before we go on, you need to know that **murders are classified** as follows:

Murder Classifications

Category A	A major crime of grave public concern: for example where the victim is a child or where multiple murders, or the murder of a police officer occurs.
Category B	A 'routine' major crime where the offender is not known.
Category C	A major crime where the identity of the offender is known.

The importance of these classifications from your point of view is the resources which the force puts into their investigation. As we have noted above, Cat A and Cat B murders will be led by an SIO who will probably be centrally based, while a Cat C murder could be investigated by detectives in a local BCU. However, there are variations on these basic categories, and a Cat C murder can often turn out to be more complicated than first thought, so that a largely local response is not always appropriate.

The ACPO **Murder Investigation Manual** (MIM) offers an investigative model which most police forces will follow as a template for enquiries into a major violent crime (ACPO, 1999). The model consists of five stages (fast track, theoretical process, planned method of investigation, suspect enquiries, and disposal), but for the purposes of this Handbook, we shall be concerned with only the first stage. Stage One in the MIM covers the initial police response to the reporting of the crime and the priority actions which follow, including crime scene and evidence preservation.

You are called to a crime scene. When you get there, a bedsit in a part of town with many multiple-occupancy dwellings, you find the body of a young woman on the floor. There is a lot of blood everywhere. Curious and worried onlookers are present. The landlord of the property, who discovered the body, is nervously waiting for you just inside the bedsit door. He says that he heard a disturbance and a lot of screaming. When he used his master key to open the door, this is what he found. He has not touched anything.

> **TASK 8**
>
> What do you do to ensure proper incident management, remembering Stage One of the MIM is 'crime scene and evidence preservation'. What are your tasks in priority order?

You would probably note that the first priority is not to let anyone else over the threshold of the crime scene, and that might well extend to the area outside the bedsit, to include stairs, stairwell, communal areas, and adjoining corridors or passages. You would clear people away, including the landlord and close off the scene as swiftly as possible. You would enter the room yourself, principally to ascertain if the presumed victim is still alive. If she were still alive (you would follow the Airways, Breathing, Circulation (ABC) procedures); your duty is to support her until the paramedics arrive. Your CAP (see section 11.18 above) into the crime scene will be that which others will follow and you would ensure that nothing else was touched.

Remember that the priority is the **preservation of life** followed by the **preservation of evidence**. You would be in urgent communication with your force control centre, describing what you can see, the location, and any other relevant requirements, such as the attendance of paramedics, an ambulance, and a doctor. You would request the attendance of CSIs and probably the duty SIO or duty detective officer, since it is evident that a violent crime has been committed. It might or might not be murder, but that will determined by the subsequent investigation.

Then what? If you have a colleague with you, you could share the note-taking, including the names and addresses of all those present, whether they have volunteered as witnesses or not. (Bear in mind the need to 'record, retain, and reveal' that we discussed in Chapter 12.) You would find out from the landlord (whose details you have also recorded) information about the victim and any information about visitors to her that day, including of course any information about the other person or persons present at the apparent altercation which the landlord heard. You would log your actions and begin arranging the CAP to the crime scene. You would note anything which you observed (such as a murder weapon, scattered possessions, blood splashes, and so on).

In other words, we are back to the **golden hour**, that crucial early period where evidence (including forensic evidence) can be gathered while still fresh and witnesses interviewed while their recollections are clear and unhampered. Getting your part right in this process could mean the difference between a guilty person being arrested and convicted, or someone literally getting away with murder because the crime scene has been disturbed and contaminated.

It might be helpful at this stage to review and itemize the actions you must take as first officer at the scene, recalling that your objectives are to protect the scene and preserve evidence, and to ensure the safety of police officers and others at the scene (look back at section 11.18 and forward to section 13.6):

- Cordon off the scene; prevent unauthorized entry. Make the cordon as wide as practicable to sustain; it can always be reduced later.
- Do not enter the scene yourself, except to preserve life.
- Create a CAP for all who come to the crime scene, ensuring that this path does not trample on evidence or compromise the crime scene in any way. You should use this route too.
- Begin a 'scene attendance log' in which you record all authorized persons who come to the site.
- Do not cover bodies; if in public view, remove the public or screen off the view.
- Record witness details and any comments they make. Listen to them.
- Make a record if anything was disturbed or moved.
- Consider whether you need assistance to preserve the scene.
- Continue to be in communication with the force control centre and keep them informed of what you are doing and why. Explain if you think you will need specialist help, or a doctor, or other emergency services.
- Remain calm, be positive, manage the situation until help arrives.

The process of crime scene preservation and the consequent forensic investigation is examined in more detail in the final part of this chapter.

13.3.7 Terrorism

Now we raise the criticality of an incident even further and consider how you manage an incident related to terrorism. A **working definition** of terrorism might look like this:

> The use or threat of violence (often extreme violence) to further or to publicize a political or extremist belief.

There are modifications which we can make to this definition, and you can perhaps think of ways we could refine the term 'extreme violence', but it will do for the moment. If you are interested further in what constitutes terrorism then Matassa, in Newburn, 2003 is an excellent starting point. The first thing we need to discuss is whether terrorism is a crime. Legislation about terrorism in the UK is increasingly detailed and extends beyond the act of violence itself to membership of proscribed groups, training and 'acts preparatory', the commissioning, construction, carriage or possession of an explosive or other device designed to take life or cause maximum damage and disruption.

The specialist details of this are best left to those whose policing job it is to counter terrorism, but all police officers have a duty to prevent terrorism, and so you should keep a lively interest in the legislation surrounding terrorism, especially where it augments your police powers.

There are two ways in which you could be involved in dealing with terrorism:

- attending a scene where there is a suspect device;
- attending a scene where there has been a terrorist attack.

13.3.7.1 Suspect devices

This could be a bomb, an incendiary device (one designed to start or sustain a fire), or any of chemical, biological, radiological, or nuclear (CBRN) devices, with or without explosive triggers.

The first point to make is that you cannot tell which it is by looking at it, nor would you necessarily know what you were dealing with, even if you could see the mechanism or contents. The cardinal rule is: **do not touch it**. Your role in managing this ultra-critical incident as the first police officer on the scene is to create as wide a space around the suspect device as is practicable and to get people out of the area. **Public safety** is your highest concern. Whilst the requirement to preserve evidence is high, this is secondary to public safety at all times. Your response will involve all the things we have looked at above, from clearing the scene to ensuring that you remain in constant communication with the force control centre. Until your force knows what it is dealing with, it cannot tell what resources are needed, and what specialist help to call in.

Bomb alerts can be major commitments of police and other emergency service resources, and terrorists know that hoaxes can be just as disruptive (in the initial stages at least) as the real thing. Nonetheless, your duty is preservation of life, which means that you have to assume that every suspect device has the potential to kill and injure; you cannot afford to take chances.

A helpful mnemonic is this:

> **B** Buildings: evacuate
> **O** Occupants: get them out and away
> **M** Move people right away from the scene
> **B** Back off: there could be secondary devices or other targets
> **A** Accurate information relayed back to control
> **L** Locate witnesses
> **E** Evacuate the neighbourhood of the device
> **R** RV points for support arriving
> **T** Tape off a cordon at the most practicable distance

As a rule of thumb on this last point, cordons for small objects (up to briefcase size), should be a minimum of 100 metres. For larger items (up to and including cars), the cordon should be a minimum of 200 metres, and for very large objects (such as vans or heavy goods vehicles), the cordon should be a minimum of 400 metres. There are rules about the colour of cordon tapes, but that should not bother you in the initial stages. Be aware that streets crowded with buildings provide the blast with a corridor which channels its energy; personnel are better behind 'hard cover' like concrete buildings rather than in view of the suspected device. Do not place the public or colleagues behind or beneath glass windows and panels, however far away from the device they might be.

If you do these things sensibly and well, you will make it much easier for the support coming in behind you, which will include a raft of specialists.

To expand a little on what you should do at the scene of a suspect device, think about these actions. It may be necessary to establish why the object itself is suspicious. Did anyone see it being installed or placed? Are there descriptions of the person(s) who placed it? What alerted people to the suspect device? You must make sure that the device is not touched, handled, or lifted. Hand-held radios or mobile phones must not be used within ten metres of the object, while vehicle-based radios must not be used to transmit within fifty metres of the object. You should mark out the CAP to the object, consistent with your overriding priority of public safety. You must pass as much information about the object as possible, concentrating on what size and shape it is, whether there are electrical components on view, if it smells, and whether there are stains or similar on it. Control will also want to know precisely where it is (especially if there is a wider evacuation going on outside your immediate cordon), when it was discovered, by whom, witness details, and any other relevant information.

Thereafter, specialist assistance will determine if the device is viable or not. Lives have been saved in the past through prompt and effective action by the first officers to arrive at the scene.

13.3.7.2 The scene of a terrorist attack

If you are first to arrive at a scene after a device has exploded, you should expect the kinds of chaos you associate with the disaster scenes we discussed above. There will possibly be devastation, wreckage, smoke, flames, badly-injured people, dead bodies (and parts of bodies), panic, noise, and confusion. Your role is the same, in principle, as that discussed for attending a train crash or major road traffic accident: take charge, clear those who can walk out of the area, close off the area with a cordon, attend to the injured if you can, remember that you are dealing with a crime scene. In addition to the CHALET principles we discussed earlier in section 13.3.1, another mnemonic may help:

> **I** Identify the source of threat or suspicion
> **C** Communicate all available details to force control
> **I** Investigate the circumstances
> **C** Contain the threat to people where possible
> **L** Lead and reassure people at the scene
> **E** Ensure that major incident procedures are put in hand

The most extreme form of terrorism is a CBRN device, because of the potential for devastation and very widespread loss of life. Such devices are still rare, but they have been known. In 1993, a small and secretive Japanese sect, called AUM, released small quantities of diluted Sarin gas inside a crowded Tokyo subway in the morning rush-hour. Twelve people died and a much larger number required hospital treatment for their injuries. Had the gas been in concentrated form, the Japanese authorities believe that thousands could have died, because of Sarin's extreme toxicity.

The same factors apply for dealing with a CBRN incident that apply to any suspect device. Can you remember what they were?

> **TASK 9**
>
> Note your priority actions now in response to (a) a suspect device and (b) a detonation. What should you do when you arrive and thereafter?
>
> How could you recognize a chemical, biological, radiological, or nuclear attack?

There are some safety triggers which you must look out for. The process is called **Steps**, and is in three parts.

Step	Scenario	Actions required
Step 1	**One** casualty or one person collapsed	Approach the site using the usual procedures
Step 2	**Two** casualties or collapsed people	Approach with caution and do not discount any possibility. Report your arrival and be careful that you do not touch any object. Update your report continually
Step 3	**Three** or more casualties or people in collapsed positions	**Do not enter** the scene. Create an RV point outside the area and await instructions

For step 3, you should provide a CHALET assessment if you can, but the rule is never to compromise your own or colleagues' safety. Again, this can be a hard call, especially if people inside the incident area are calling for help and your every instinct is to go in and help. If there has been a CBRN attack, then you will simply become another casualty if you go in. Other colleagues may come in to recover you and suffer themselves. The only safe option is to stop and wait, whatever your emotions tell you. CBRN materials are difficult to identify positively without very advanced training and highly sophisticated detection equipment. As first responder, you may not be able to identify the nature of the threat but you might be able to identify its location. If the device is still intact you would deal with locating and describing it in the same way that you would deal with hazardous materials in a civil emergency.

If you receive reports of groups of people suddenly collapsing or suddenly feeling unwell, or there is reported a strong or noxious smell, or people suddenly experience skin blisters, you could be in the presence of a chemical attack. (Alternatively, a tanker carrying cleaning materials could have jack-knifed and spilled its load. If the latter, more innocent explanation, do ensure that your force control centre is updated by you before you approach the tanker.)

You will remember from the newspapers and television, the disturbing scenes which followed the terrorist attack on the Twin Towers in New York and on the Pentagon in Washington, DC on 11 September 2001, or again in London on 7 July 2005, particularly at the scene of the explosion on the bus but also at the site of the tube train explosions. Nothing prepares you for the emotional impact of such scenes, and the overwhelming emotion which many police officers experience when first responders at a major disaster is helplessness. It all looks so chaotic, so awful; how can anything you do be of the slightest use? Where do you start with the bodies and the injured? How can you clear a path through that debris? Who knows how many bodies are under that collapsed building? You feel as though you want to cry. This Handbook cannot offer you solutions to such destruction and outrage. All we can do is indicate how you could help and what your professional response should be—and that will remain largely theoretical until you have your first experience of such scenes.

It has been said (and in our view rightly) that what distinguishes a police officer from the general public is not his/her exercise of powers, his/her uniform, or his/her knowledge of the law, but **knowing what to do in an emergency**. That professional response is what marks you out and what gives you the authority to act when all around you is panic and helplessness. It does not matter whether 'the right thing to do' is as small as giving first aid at a road traffic collision or as significant as coping with the aftermath of a terrorist bomb; what matters is that you made a difference by bringing calmness to chaos, order to disorder, method to mayhem. Ultimately, that is your professional role and the role of your many police colleagues, in managing a critical incident.

13.4 Missing Persons

Every year, in England and Wales, about 200,000 people go missing. Many are found very quickly, others are found dead after many weeks, and some are never found. The police become involved when a report is made of a missing person, and will take action (often extensively) if there is reason to suppose that the missing person is in some way **vulnerable**. This can entail a considerable expenditure of resources and time, including rural and urban searches, dragging of waterways, and exhaustive enquiries, when the chances are that no crime has been committed. You are likely to be involved in a search for a missing person during your initial training as a student police officer, and almost certainly a number of times during your police career.

Searching for missing persons is part of the **police emergency response** for civic and societal purposes, rather than law enforcement. For all that, criminal angles can, and do, emerge. The missing person may have been abducted, there may be criminal involvement (perhaps through drugs dealing), the victim could have been murdered and the body concealed, or the missing person might have been targeted for some other reason, such as a forced marriage. Not all disappearances attract media attention, or the presumption of a crime; but missing children often spark intense media interest, as do those involving young women.

All forces have a proportion of missing persons ('**mispers**') every year; some entail extensive searching, some develop into criminal investigations, and some involve vulnerable adults, such as those who are mentally ill or elderly and confused. A small proportion are found dead, and this can involve the force's major crime unit (or equivalent) extensively, especially if the missing person has been murdered or if the circumstances suggest a suspicious death. The salient point here is that the force commits considerable resources, either from BCUs or from central units, in responding to misper reports, and it may be that, on occasions, responses are disproportionate. Certainly, they are very expensive, both in time and in resources.

The national policy on the police response to misper was extensively redrafted in the light of the Soham (Cambridge) murders in 2002. That case highlighted how reliant smaller police forces were on 'mutual aid' for mounting large-scale searches, and is cited as part of the argument for more radical amalgamations of police forces into larger organizations capable of mounting such searches independently. Where criminal aspects (such as abduction, kidnap, and murder) are involved or suspected, there are distinct impacts on the force's investigative capability. It is interesting to note the Belgian experience in this field.

The Belgian Federal Police have a missing persons department ('Chiffres Disparitions'), set up in 1995 in the wake of the disappearance of six children. It co-ordinates the work of the 189 Belgian police districts (broadly equivalent to our BCUs, if a little smaller) when people are reported missing. The Belgian Federal Police note that they have about 1,200 reports of missing person each year, and over 90% of these turn up in due course. However, the Belgians use a sophisticated checklist and risk assessment system which, they claim, is a reliable indicator as to whether the police should launch a full-scale search or not.

Briefly, the Belgian assessment requires detailed answers to three questions:

1. **Who is missing?**
   The profile of the misper, behaviour patterns, family knowledge, movements.
2. **Is it worrying?**
   Standards for concern include:
   • Persons under twelve years old.
   • Persons with mental or physical disabilities.
   • Persons dependent on essential medication or treatment.
   • Circumstances of the disappearance that may suggest life-threatening danger.
   • As previously, but person may be victim of a possible crime.
   • Completely contradictory of normal behaviour.
3. **What happened?**
   Accident, crime, suicide, prepared departure, quarrels, family tensions. How? When? Where?

Much of the Belgian work is straightforward and commonsensical, but it can serve as a helpful risk assessment model in conjunction with your individual force policy.

We now return to a standard missing person enquiry and look at what is needed as the case unfolds. The requirements of each case are special to the individual who has gone missing, but there are standard considerations (some of which we have indicated above). In the first place are the **personal circumstances**, any of which may indicate the vulnerability of the subject:

- Age (under eighteen is technically and legally a child)?
- Any drugs or alcohol dependency?
- Essential medication (for example, diabetes, epilepsy)?
- Is he/she on the Child Protection Register?
- Is there a suggestion or belief that the individual might not have the physical capability to be safe in an unknown environment or might be unable to interact safely with others (suffering from such conditions as amnesia, dementia, visual impairment)?
- Is there any known or suspected mental impairment or psychological disorder which might increase the risk of harm to him/herself or others?

The next consideration is the **circumstances of the disappearance**. You need to build a picture, as we did in the example of the sixteen-year-old above, of the person who has gone missing. Enquiries should cover:

- Any employment problems?
- Any emotional problems in relationships?
- Any financial problems (is money missing? Did the person take credit cards or cash when he/she disappeared? What is the state of the person's finances?)
- Any family problems or recent history of conflict or abuse?
- Weather conditions (may also have a bearing on the subsequent search).
- Was the person subject to bullying or harassment (racial, sexual, homophobic, or community)?
- Is the disappearance out of character or has it happened before?
- Is there any suspicion of self-harm or harm to others?
- Is there any evidence or suspicion to suggest abduction (for example of a child by an estranged parent)?
- Has the person been engaged in, or have a history of involvement in, crime?
- Is the person normally resident abroad and believed to have gone missing while in the UK?
- Is the person normally resident in the UK and believed to have gone missing while abroad?
- Is there any suggestion of, or evidence indicating, that the disappearance was planned (packed cases, closed, and emptied bank accounts)?
- Is there any evidence of violence or struggle at any scene of the disappearance (such as struggle to avoid being pulled into a car)?

(Some of the above, and some of what follows, is drawn from ACPO, 2005.)

Remember too to think about **the person giving you the information**. Sadly, there have been a number of occasions when someone's disappearance is reported by the person who caused the disappearance in the first place, and we noted above in the Soham case, how eager Huntley was to assist with the search for the two girls (whom he had already killed and whose bodies he had concealed).

Finally, in a misper operation, there are **practical considerations** about the nature and extent of the police operation:

- Make a thorough search of the person's house, garden, and any adjoining premises. Remember that children can hide themselves in very small spaces.
- Look at personal papers belonging to the individual who has gone missing, especially diaries, work schedules, planners, and financial information. You may need to retain these as evidence.
- Check with the work place or school for absence records.
- Try to establish recent movements and behaviour.
- Check on police databases, locally and nationally.
- List any drugs, medication, or other health issues.
- List relatives, friends, contacts, and work colleagues/fellow students.
- Obtain recent (and likeness) photographs.

- Prepare a search of the surrounding area, concentrating first on 'habitual haunts' (where the person liked to go) and then on hazardous places, such as pools, streams, caves, empty buildings, and so on.
- Prepare to widen the search systematically, including making house-to-house enquiries.
- Prepare publicity and contact with the media (remembering caveats about referral to your media specialists at HQ).

If, for any reason, the circumstances of the disappearance are suspicious, the police will work on the assumption that a crime has been committed and therefore the scene of the disappearance must be preserved for evidential and investigative purposes.

TASK 10

If the missing person enquiry becomes prolonged, what national guidance can you obtain in order effectively to process the investigation?

13.5 Procedures Surrounding Sudden Death

We have considered in this chapter a number of examples of when you may encounter death and injury as the result of critical incidents. However, you will also experience attending scenes where there is a dead person who may well have died through natural causes such as illness and old age. The local police station may be called by the neighbour of an elderly person to report that they have not seen their neighbour for some time or that there are other circumstances which give them cause for concern.

Of course, these situations are not restricted to the elderly; you may have the particularly distressing task of attending a scene of the death of a child or young person. Many deaths occur in hospital and you will not normally be involved with these. Deaths which occur outside of the hospital environment and are in some way unexpected are referred to in police circles as 'sudden deaths'. Any sudden death will be subject to some form of investigation but of course this does not mean that they have happened because of some kind of criminal activity. The procedure to follow for sudden deaths will vary from force to force although all subscribe to certain basic principles.

1. Ensure your own safety before approaching, as the scene of a death can be dangerous.
2. Establish and use a CAP (see section 11.18) to preserve the scene.
3. Beware of bodies connected to electrical systems, as well as toxic fumes, poisons, firearms, needles, and body fluids.
4. Touch nothing until you have made a visual inspection.
5. Is there a chance the person is still alive; can you administer first aid and is an ambulance required?
6. Consider that any death may be the result of crime if it is in any way suspicious.

Next, begin a PNB entry (see section 11.5) which records the following information:

- the location and position of body;
- any physical evidence in the immediate area;
- a general description of the body, including any visible injuries;
- the evidence of any witnesses;
- the identity of the deceased, if known.

You will need to call a doctor (or arrange for one to be called) either to provide medical advice or to certify that 'life is extinct'. The procedure to be followed depends on whether the death was expected or unexpected.

Procedures are shown in the flow chart below:

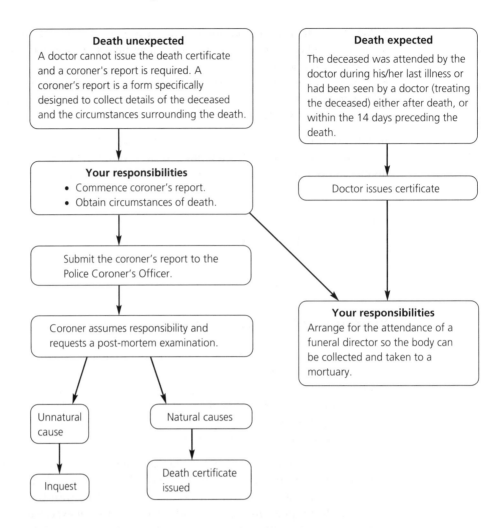

Certainly in the case of 'unnatural causes' a police investigation would ensue, although in most cases of this kind it would already be underway.

13.6 Forensic Investigation

In this section we examine those aspects of forensic investigation that are relevant to your initial training. Forensic investigation is used for a number of reasons in policing and criminal investigation and we look at some of these in section 13.6.5. This means that we will explore not only the subject of forensic investigation itself (and its relationship with forensic science) but also your specific roles in assisting the crime scene investigator, such as 'bagging and tagging' evidence and collecting evidence from suspects.

13.6.1 Introduction

Unapologetically, we devote considerable length to this part of Chapter 13. Our reasons are simple: an understanding of forensic investigation and how you support that process is vitally important in terms of both convicting the guilty and exonerating the innocent. This importance is reflected in the IPLDP; there are a large number of learning outcomes that relate to forensic investigation in the modules OP 3, LP 1, and LPG 2.

13.6.2 Locard's Principle and Individualization

We take a knife from a drawer and replace it. In so doing, material (for example, sweaty deposits from our fingertips) is transferred from the hand to the knife and may remain there, for a little time at least. Material is also transferred from the knife to our hand—for example, particles of dust or even tiny fragments of the wooden handle. Edmond Locard

(1877–1966) is credited with the development of this **Principle of Exchange.** His assertion was that material from the crime scene would be found on the suspect and vice versa. This is commonly expressed as: 'every contact leaves a trace'. As a simple example, this could mean that the offender could leave fingerprints, blood, and shoe marks at the crime scene and might take away glass fragments on his/her clothing.

Locard's principle has been a mainstay of forensic investigation, but not all of these contacts can actually be proven because the quantities of the physical material transferred may be so minute that they defy the ability of current technology to locate them. The principle is really inductive reasoning by another name and hence cannot be considered a scientific law in the Popperian sense (look back at section 4.13). This, however, until relatively recently, did not much concern the courts. The fingerprint, for example, is still assumed to be unique. In practice, Locard's Principle manifests itself in reverse in forensic investigation—it tends to use the transfer as demonstration of contact. First, there are the so-called traces that include debris like glass, paint flakes, hairs, and fibres. Traces can also include saliva, blood, and other DNA rich material which are often classified separately. Secondly are 'impressions' which include 'prints' made by fingers, shoes, tools, typewriters, and printers. Note also, that Locard's principle is not restricted to these traditional and tangible examples: it can also be extended to intangible digital data held by electronic media, such as computers, discs, and mobile phones. Trust in the principle requires a leap of faith, but even after assuming we can find the transferred material or impressions, we then need to show that it came from the source we are concerned with. This brings us to the concept of **individualization** or uniqueness.

The Latin root for unique is 'uno', which means one. Despite what we may think or believe to be true, no two things can actually be identical, apart from at an atomic or molecular level. Thus everything we are concerned with in Forensic Investigation should be considered as unique, or a one-off. This represents another leap of faith on the part of the investigator and forensic scientist because this concept, again, is not strictly a scientific law. If you are interested, it cannot be considered to be a scientific law because there is no way it could ever be falsified. However, as with Locard's Principle, the CJS does not consider this a particular problem (and it is doubtful whether it has ever featured in deliberations in the courts).

Many objects which appear to be identical are markedly different, and those that are very similar (perhaps too similar to measure) become visibly or measurably unique during use. This unique quality is brought about by the development of **individual characteristics**. The majority of industrial processes impart very similar characteristics to the same products. In commerce, this is a matter of quality control which ensures the product is fit for purpose and conforms to standards to ensure safety and homogeneity.

Consider a standard 'slot' screwdriver:

- The shaft is typically cylindrical and appears identical in each screwdriver made on the production line.
- The tip is hammered flat and a subsequent sharpening process grinds the blade tip to preset dimensions, creating an edge which is generally very similar in every screwdriver.

The end products of the manufacturing process are thousands of screwdrivers which are—to unaided eyes—identical in every way. During subsequent use (and misuse) each screwdriver develops unique characteristics, which provide the means for the forensic scientist to tell them apart, or individualize them.

Any thing or person which can be associated with its source is said to have individual characteristics, for instance: a fingerprint to a finger, a tool-mark to a tool, and so on.

There are different types of characteristics:

- **Class characteristics** are qualities produced by a controlled process, typically a manufacturing process; for instance, the manufacture of a screwdriver, where each one is similar to the naked eye.

- **Sub-class characteristics** are the features on a batch of screwdrivers, particularly those which differentiate them from other batches. These features may be imparted by poor quality control or minute changes in settings, grinders, and so on.
- **Individualization** follows from the premise that two items are derived from a common source, but that damage caused to the screwdriver during use individualizes it. Any marks it makes can be matched with the screwdriver in question.

Locard's principle holds well for situations such as the use of a well-used screwdriver to force a window frame, but it is not a panacea ('instant answer') for difficult criminal investigations. Essentially, there are further issues to be investigated before the principle can be properly employed in the investigative context:

- Who owns the screwdriver?
- Who was holding the screwdriver when it forced the window?
- Indeed, where is it now?

Clearly, owning the screwdriver is not an offence. Using the screwdriver to force the window is an offence, but was the screwdriver borrowed or stolen to commit the crime? Investigators frequently say that they wish to 'put the suspect at the scene'. Whether this is a screwdriver alone or the screwdriver attached to the offender **at the time of the offence** is for you to consider and discuss.

Locard's principle is primarily used to create physical links between the differing parts of an investigation. This is set out in its simplest form below.

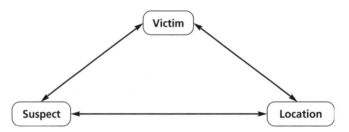

The links are normally created by forensic scientists by comparing a 'questioned sample' with a 'control'. For instance: the Crime Scene Investigator will recover control samples from the crime scene, perhaps a sample of paint and a tool mark, and will aim to have these compared to the questioned sample which might be a screwdriver you have taken from a suspect. A control in crime scene investigation terms comes from a known source.

Clearly, the link may be between two or more people, a suspect and the scene only, or any permutation of these. A chief aim of forensic investigation is to locate and recover the physical material which will allow the links to be made. Although any police officer may be involved in searching a crime scene—whether a place, person, or thing—the majority of scenes are examined by specially trained Crime Scene Investigators (CSIs). The best links are two-way instead of one-way, and may be referred to sometimes as 'best evidence'.

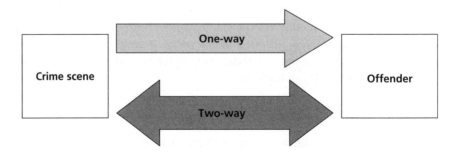

Locard's principle does not cease to apply after the commission of the offence. All trace material or articles which leave an impression continue to change: fibres on the guilty party are lost, shoes continue to wear out, screwdrivers become blunter, DNA decays. The objective of the police is, therefore, to intervene as quickly after the crime as possible to recover the potential evidence and stop it changing further.

13.6.3 The Role of the Crime Scene Investigator (CSI)

The CSI serves a number of roles within the police service. (As we have noted elsewhere, some forces continue to use the term Scenes of Crime Officer (SOCO), but CSI is now mostly accepted.) The CSI is typically the first port of call for all enquiries regarding forensic science such as taking samples from suspects and victims and, principally, the examination of crime scenes. Chief amongst the CSI's crime-based activities are:

- the locating, assessment, and recovery of physical evidence (including fingerprints) from crime scenes such as burglary, murder, arson, and theft;
- the photography of crime scenes and articles or people associated with crime, such as weapons, injuries, victims, and suspects;
- the packaging, storage, and documentation of recovered material;
- attending post-mortem examinations if required;
- provision of advice to police officers and investigators on matters related to physical evidence, photography, and laboratory submissions;
- gathering intelligence in support of the NIM, whether the spoken word, or personal observations, or physical material for use in databases (see section 12.3).

CSIs also carry out their activities at non-crime related events such as:

- the investigation, photography, and scene analysis of some sudden deaths, most suicides and fatal industrial accidents on behalf of HM Coroners and in support of Health and Safety Executive investigations;
- maintenance of equipment on area (such as cameras for photographing prisoners);
- the recording of loss through fire (especially at high-value scenes prior to arson being ruled out).

The majority of CSIs in the UK Police Service are police support staff. They are attached to a force's Scientific Support Department which includes other complementary services such as a photography unit, fingerprint bureau, and a laboratory for the enhancement of fingerprint evidence.

13.6.4 Forensic Science

Forensic science is commonly described as the application of scientific disciplines to the legal system. The fields of science so employed are many and varied: from archaeology through every conceivable speciality to zoology. Any scientific discipline may have a function to play in the investigation of offences and it is the experts in these fields who produce the evidence the investigator requires by **interpreting** the material provided to them.

13.6.5 Employing Forensic Investigation

Forensic investigation is often concerned with two main forms of (largely physical) evidence:

1. **Corroborative evidence** material that will confirm or refute a hypothesis about the crime, for instance that a powder is, or is not, heroin.
2. **Inceptive evidence** which identifies an unknown, for example a person.

The investigator may employ forensic investigation and forensic science in a variety of ways when considering these two main forms of evidence. These include:

- **Describing the *modus operandi*** (MO). The attending CSI can help form a hypothesis of the method used by the offender to commit the crime. This is an early stage in the forensic investigation. These data can be analysed for patterns to link offences. For example, scientists may analyse a fire scene to establish the MO for an arson or the events which caused a road crash.
- **Answering investigative questions** in order to progress an enquiry. For instance whose DNA is this? Is there a connection between the weapon used in this crime and this suspect?

- **Establishing that an offence has occurred**. By examining exhibits it may be shown that an offence has been committed, for instance the analysis of a white powder; the classification of a firearm; the calculation of alcohol in urine or blood.
- **Identifying an offender or suspect**. In the right context, DNA and fingerprint evidence can identify the offender, normally they identify suspects.
- **To corroborate or refute witness statements**. This is particularly useful when applied to very specific issues raised during interview.
- **To establish a physical link between suspect, crime scene, and victim** although the route for this may be circuitous, for instance linking the suspect to a weapon and the weapon to the incident.
- **To identify an individual**. Fingerprints and DNA (and some other techniques) can be employed to identify people, including suspects, arrested persons, or found bodies.
- **To further inform an enquiry**, often by clarifying issues or providing some form of descriptive information or intelligence. An example would be a specialist helping to identify the make and model of a vehicle involved in a hit-and-run RTC.

13.6.6   Forensic Science Laboratories and Forensic Scientists

It is the responsibility of the forensic scientist to analyse and test materials supplied by an investigation in order to determine facts about the case. This evidence may point to the guilt or innocence of a suspect, and this should never be a consideration for the scientist. There are a number or important principles which the scientist is bound by, and chief amongst these is the concept that—although paid by the police in this instance—scientific responsibility is to discover the truth in an unbiased way. Some might say that this is the essence of science itself. It is, as we have seen in Chapter 12, also the essence of a police investigation, and the primary focus of the criminal court.

In order to provide an efficient and effective service to the police, your scientist expects:

- Unbroken continuity.
- Correct packaging with intact integrity seals.
- Utmost care in preventing contamination.
- A clear communication which explains the investigative need and describes the perceived relevance and place of the evidence.
- Up-to-date information whenever the investigation changes tack and clear guidance on any deadlines, such as bail dates or court appearances.

The scientist also needs you to understand that **forensic evidence is context sensitive**. This means that the information or a statement provided by the forensic scientist is based upon the place the evidence occupies within the investigation. It is the investigator's responsibility to communicate this information clearly to the scientist in order to achieve the best—and most relevant—results. Some examples of context are:

- A fingerprint found near the point of entry in the female toilets of a burgled pub was found to belong to the barman. The context of this apparently innocent mark changed when, during interview, he categorically denied ever having been in the toilet.
- Blood on a suspect's clothing was explicable because he had provided first aid to a victim when flagged down in his car. Crucially, the person who stopped him for assistance had disappeared. Upon closer analysis it was apparent that the blood must have spattered onto his clothing during the commission of the offence.

In order to provide the correct information and to explain its importance to the case, the **Forensic Science Service** (FSS) provides a form called the MG FSP which, if followed closely, will guide the investigator through the submissions process. Different police forces have different systems and policies regarding the submission of exhibits to laboratories. It is in your interest to ensure that you follow the procedure laid down by your force; you otherwise risk problems in any subsequent prosecution.

13.6.7   Time and Date Stamping

Some evidence may occur in a form which shows it was created during the commission of the offence—this is potentially of great value. Examples include:

- The distribution of blood, particularly that found on the suspect, might indicate he/she was present during an assault, and even distance and position in relation to **the** victim.
- The presence of unusual stained glass from a broken church window on the suspect's upper clothing may indicate they were present when **the** window was smashed.
- Locating the residue from burnt firearm propellants (Firearm Discharge Residue or FDR) on a suspect may show they were present when **a** firearm was discharged.

Note that in the examples above the words 'the' and 'a' are highlighted. The DNA within the victim's blood and the unusual glass on the suspect may show he/she was present at the specified offences during their commission. Finding firearm discharge residue (FDR) on a suspect does not actually prove that the suspect fired the specific gun during the specific offence in question.

Pinning suspects down in interviews can, however, be used to reinforce many forms of evidence. CSIs and forensic managers prefer absolute statements from suspects because this can make the context of the evidence stronger. There are two important points here:

1. When a laboratory result is received (either in statement form or by other means) officers must consider their interview strategy, that is, how best to employ the information received. This is an example of forensic science driving the investigation forward.
2. If a suspect or other person makes an early statement, this information should be carefully considered: it may be of value to the scientist and must, at least, describe any admissions made by the suspect.

In a simplified example, where a man is suspected of a shooting, the forensic manager and scientist will weigh the value of the firearm discharge residue evidence after interview thus:

Weak

I regularly use a firearm for sport

I used a firearm last week

I have never used a firearm

Stronger

Clearly, if it is actually the case, it is preferable for the suspect to deny the use of firearms on any occasion, which weakens the value of his statement if FDRs are found. If this were the case, consideration must be given to his activity in recent days:

- Has he been in the vicinity of a firearm which has been used?
- Was he arrested by an officer who recently used a firearm, say, for sport?
- Was he conveyed in a vehicle which had contained people who were contaminated with firearms residues?
- Was he arrested by an officer who was environmentally contaminated through using firearms at work?

The forensic scientist would need to know this sort of information so that an informed assessment may be made about contamination. This in turn may impact on the guilt or innocence of a suspect.

13.6.8   Seizing Exhibits

We looked first at seizing exhibits in section 11.18. It might be worth looking back at that section before you read the remainder of this section.

When an exhibit is taken from a crime scene or a person, it is often described as **seizing**. The rights of the police in this respect are described in Chapter 11. Although most exhibits are never examined at a forensic laboratory, police officers must always consider that they **may** be needed for later analysis, so all personnel must take care not to contaminate exhibits and must package and record them correctly.

When taken, the exhibit must be named and numbered. The exhibit number is typically made up of the officer's initials and a number is allocated using the following method:

- In an enquiry where PC Alison Brown takes an exhibit she would call her first exhibit AB/1, her second exhibit AB/2, and so on.
- In the next enquiry, she would call her first exhibit AB/1 and so on.
- If she returned to the first enquiry, she can restart at AB/3.

However, if she returns to an enquiry and has no idea what number to allocate (although she should refer to her PNB) she might elect to use AB/100 or a similarly high number, because duplicating exhibit numbers in an enquiry can cause great confusion, particularly when statements are received from the laboratory.

TASK 11

How is this problem avoided in your force?

Exhibit names should be brief and to the point, to prevent other people shortening them. Extra, expansive descriptions of the article can be made in the PNB or special documentation (such as an exhibits book).

It is important to note that recent developments in evidence-tracking databases may mean that your force has elected to change the standard exhibit numbering system, so that the first exhibit seized at the beginning of the year would be AB/1, but the sequence of numbers would continue to rise throughout the year instead of restarting at AB/1 for every enquiry.

13.6.9   Types of Physical Evidence

Physical evidence can be divided into a number of groups, and different authors have varying opinions on the approach that should be adopted. We have chosen a relatively simple method for classifying types of physical evidence.

13.6.9.1   Trace materials

Trace material can be any material transferred from the suspect to the crime scene (or a victim) and vice versa. It includes common materials such as glass fragments and paint flakes transferred during property crimes to the more exotic, such as pollens, soils, and even insects or their fragments. Do not allow your imagination to be limited to any specific groups: creativity is a vital element in investigation.

Glass is manufactured in different ways in order that it can be used for different purposes; this provides us with varying degrees of discriminatory power (that is, the ability to distinguish one object made of glass from another). The addition of colourants and physical processes can make this outwardly common material very useful in the right criminal circumstances.

Glass is a mix of silica, sodium carbonate, and calcium compounds which are smelted to form the base material to which physical processes or chemical additives are applied, imparting a number of properties. Police officers often encounter the following types of glass in an investigation:

- **Plain window glass**: sometimes called 'float glass', which is the most common window glass manufactured today. The molten glass is poured on to a bath of molten tin and when it cools, it forms flat sheets.
- **Container glass**: which includes bottles, drinking vessels, and computer screens.
- **Toughened glass**: which is inherently strong and difficult to break—as used in telephone kiosks and the side windows of vehicles. When it breaks it forms thousands of cube-shaped granules. Toughened glass breaks easily if struck with force near the edge, particularly by a sharp object.
- **Laminated glass**: where two sheets sandwich a plastic filling. This prevents the pane shattering and it retains its position in the frame. Windscreens and many low level windows are constructed in this way.
- **Optical glass**: found in lenses.
- **Mirrors**.

Glass carries special health hazard warnings: obviously the shards may be exceptionally sharp and small and in some applications are very dangerous. Always wear goggles and gloves when dealing with broken glass. Large, unsupported broken windows are a particular hazard if they are not laminated, and can collapse and **kill** without warning. Fortunately there are very few non-laminated large panes still in existence because of their inherent dangers and subsequent legislation governing glazing practices.

Glass found on the suspect or other articles can be compared to samples recovered from the broken window frame by a variety of chemical and physical techniques. Where the glass is unusual (perhaps very old or specially coloured) the scientist may provide a forensically important statement.

Glass can be **broken** in a variety of ways and different authors have different views on classification. In a criminal context, glass is typically broken by slow moving to fast moving objects, by some form of stress, or by heat or by an explosion. Frequently, the cause is deduced at the scene, but windows and glass objects can be reconstructed in order to demonstrate the cause, point, and direction of the breakage.

One of the most valuable attributes of breaking glass is a process called **backward fragmentation**, where a breaking window throws out fine particles of glass. These may land on the offender in a characteristic way, which can demonstrate he/she was in the vicinity of the window when it broke. Part of this process involves the development of fractures through the glass, either radiating from the point of impact or running concentrically around it. The edges (viewed 'end on') of some of these fractures can assist in determining from which side a window was broken.

Soils are found nearly everywhere, but they can vary significantly over short distances because of a number of important geological and geomorphological ('rock shape') factors, such as the source rock contributing to the soil. The scientist examines the source minerals, amounts of organic material, and grain size of the sample. Of particular note are areas where the soil has been modified by the inclusion of chemicals, waste material, and industrial processes. Soil is sampled during exhumations to demonstrate that any suspected toxins have not leached into the coffin and body of the deceased.

Soil's main general limitation is difficulty in showing that it came from a very specific location (perhaps a few square metres of a field) related to the offence unless that location is, perhaps, inaccessible to anybody innocently passing the site.

Fibres can be natural, man-made, or mixed. They are frequently transferred from clothing, seats, and carpets on to receptive surfaces, especially when the contact has been violent or has occurred over a long period. There is some police reluctance about using fibres as a form of evidence because they are (wrongly) thought of by many to be very similar and common. However, manufacturers use different fibre mixes and dyes for a variety of reasons and these features mean that a garment or other fabric may have an unusual or characteristic mix. Man-made fibres, in particular, can survive conditions which cause decay in natural materials like wool and cotton.

Paint is applied to window and door frames, manufactured objects, and cars as a protective or cosmetic coating. Its chemical components are designed to give the paint specific properties, such as rust-proofing, weatherproofing, fungal resistance, and even an identification measure. These elements and the enormous variety of colour and finish types ensure that any surface which has been chipped or scraped may be examined and compared with paint fragments found on a suspect's clothing, tools, or other objects in his/her possession.

Since paint on houses is applied over time according to individual tastes and changing fashions, the profile of the layers of coatings on, say, a forced window frame, can be unique. The more layers of paint on an object, the more likely its profile will be unique. Unusual colourings or paint types can also be very useful.

Vegetative material can often be used by forensic botanists to identify the species of a plant from small fragments of leaf, stem, seed, flower, or wood. Palynologists can identify the species of plant from the pollen they leave behind. If the knowledge of both scientific specialists is pooled or synthesized, the source species of vegetable material is likely to be accurately identified. In many circumstances, an association between scene and suspect can be made by the mix of vegetative materials, and if this is linked with other forms of evidence such as paint the results can be powerful.

Note should be made of the fact that many plants occur naturally in specific locations owing to climate, soil type, and plants' relationships with animal and insect species, so plant material can also identify a broad location, such as heathland, deciduous forest, proximity to the sea, and so on. Of further note is the fact that plant material, especially wood, is used in thousands of domestic and industrial applications, and some of these require unusual imported species. The treatments carried out on woods for cosmetic or protective purposes may also be valuable to the investigator.

Insects, apart from the common pest species, are sensitive to their food source and climate. As a result, many species are found in limited ranges and, when insects are identified during forensic investigation, they may be helpful in determining materials or the movements of vehicles and people. Forensic entomologists can also use known data on insect life cycles—especially that of blow flies—to identify when a body became available for them to feed upon. It is possible that this information may be of value when attempting to determine the time of death.

13.6.9.2 Impressions

These are the marks left by shoes, tools, fingers, stamping machines, printers, and typewriters. Whilst these can be a direct 'stamped' effect, many are made up of irregular scrapes and smudges and even cutting or drilling marks.

Shoe marks or **footwear marks** are a useful but potentially short-lived form of evidence. Footwear is readily modified by use when people walk over surfaces which scratch and tear the soles or add particles such as glass and stones. The resultant damage to the soles occurs at random and is, therefore, unique to every shoe. When a shoe leaves an impression at a crime scene the mark left is readily comparable to the shoe in question. However, the shoe (and the suspect) must be located and recovered before the relevant damage (to their shoes or footwear) is further eroded.

Marks can be on a flat, two dimensional surface, or they can be impressed into a soft substrate to form a three-dimensional pattern. Importantly, the surface must be fine enough to receive the mark: soft clay is clearly better than shingle.

Trainers in particular are readily identifiable (either from databases or by an expert in the field) and this data can be used for intelligence purposes in order tentatively to link crime scenes. The addition of MO, times of offence and target properties can make such databases invaluable.

In theory, marks should be present at almost every crime scene since almost all offenders will walk within the venue. Always be aware of this and take care where you walk. Remember the discussion in section 11.18 about the Common Approach Path (CAP) to a crime scene.

A variety of techniques can be used to recover the marks: photography, casting, lifting, or removal of the surface upon which the mark rests.

Tool or **instrument marks** are marks imparted to receptive surfaces by the application of force. Typical examples are those where an offender has forced a window or cash box. The marks can be made in a variety of ways:

- Levering to force open a window, door, or cashbox; one edge of the target surface acts as a fulcrum and both this and the moving part will be marked.
- Cutting; the action caused by scissors, wire cutters, and bolt croppers.
- Drilling; the waste material from drilling can bear the impression of the cutting edge of the drill bit.

The actions used will impress into the surface (or cut into it) the shape of the tip or cutting edge of the tool which, like a shoe, has been individualized through its previous use.

Stamps, dyes, and **manufacturing marks** are impressions into a surface, similar to tool or instrument marks, and can be made by any item. This includes plastic label printers, metal numbering dyes, franking machines, rubber stamps, and other such devices. All are modified by accidental damage and ageing.

Any material which is set in a mould or extruded also takes on an impression of the mould or extrusion head, particularly where debris has built up. Examples include copper pipes, plastic bags, and plastic components. Many of these latter marks are visible as lines and dimples and, if invisible, can be viewed using microscopy or polarized light. The sequence of manufacture of rolls of bags, in particular, can be demonstrated by the scientist and may help to show that an offender stole a bin bag (from a particular place), for instance, to carry away goods from a burglary.

Vehicle tyres leave impressions, and tyres are modified during use by the surfaces over which they pass. Inclusions such as glass, and gravel also affect the impression left by the tyre. Tyre impressions are found in soft soils, on roads, smooth concrete floors, glass, and paper—particularly at 'ram raids'. The pattern can be two or three dimensional depending upon the solidity of the surface but the surface must be fine enough to receive the impression. In addition, the impression may be of a rotating tyre or it may be of a skidding tyre. The laboratory can assist in identifying the make of tyre from a recovered print which may include or exclude vehicles from the enquiry.

A full circumference of a car tyre is 3.14 times the diameter, so a car tyre 50 cm in diameter needs over 150 cm to leave a full print of one rotation. (Finally, that geometry you did at school has proved useful!) As a result, you must never assume that only part of a print needs to be preserved, always preserve as much as possible for your CSI.

Bite marks are valuable sources of evidence. The position, number, layout, orientation, and cutting surfaces of teeth make our dentition highly individual. It is the role of the odontologist to compare marks found on victims and in foodstuffs with the teeth of the suspect. This is carried out by taking a three-dimensional impression and comparing it with photographs or with impressions of the damage or injury.

Whenever bite marks are located always consider that DNA may be present. Older bite marks on skin may be visible under ultraviolet (UV) lighting and can be photographed some time after the incident. The apparent lack of a bite mark is not, therefore, a 'lost cause'.

Typewriters, printers, and **copiers** can also provide useful evidence. The fonts chosen by typewriter manufacturers can be identified when found on letters or other material, even with the demise of the traditional typewriters in favour of computers. A targeted search of premises can be made to locate a particular design of typewriter. When the metal letters, golf ball, or daisy wheel are damaged or aged they take on individual characteristics which are easily compared with characters contained in documents you may be considering as evidence.

Any fault which develops in computer printers may also be compared with suspect documents, especially when 'banding' occurs in large blocks of colour or across text. Currently, research is underway to link printers (without faults) to specific pages of text. Photocopiers superimpose an image of the glass screen, or platen, on the copies they produce. The more damage (or dried correction fluid) on the platen, the better the evidence. Paper feeders and rollers may also impart marks. Modern copiers (and all printers) are digital, which means that the pages which have been printed are digitally stored within the device's limited memory some time after printing.

13.6.10 Fingerprints

About 5% of the human body is covered in a horny layer of skin bearing ridge detail. This is found on the fingers, palms, soles, and toes. Every finger and toe print on every person is considered by the CJS to be unique. The prints left by any part of the hand or foot are, therefore, capable of identifying an individual with certainty. The ridges form classifiable patterns on the horny layer which are clearly visible to the naked eye. Upon close examination it is apparent that the ridges are not uniform lines: they split (bifurcate), they start and stop, and the lines sometimes cross over. These features are normally referred to as 'minutiae'.

The ridges develop in the womb and remain identical until death—or well past death if the body is preserved sufficiently. The only difference, between the patterns on the foetus' fingers and those when fully grown are size and the effects of ageing or injury. The ridges on the fingers and toes are thought to have three main functions:

- to increase friction for gripping;
- to allow sweat to dissipate along the furrows;
- to permit more nerve endings to be present in the corrugated skin.

Humans are still physiologically quite primitive and react in primitive ways: when nervous, our hands and feet sweat more, which is part of the 'fight or flight' response to stimuli. Poor quality marks can sometimes be left by nervous offenders with very wet fingers, but crucially, as the offender moves through a building, the hands dry out sufficiently to leave marks of good quality further inside the scene. Because of this, it is always better to preserve a **whole crime scene** rather than just the point of entry. Similarly, a suspect in custody may be nervous which can cause difficulties when taking fingerprints for later comparison. You are reminded to thoroughly and repeatedly dry the suspect's fingertips to prevent sweat smudging inked marks.

Fingerprints are found on all the surfaces we touch, but only if the surface texture is fine enough to receive them. The easiest test to determine whether a non-porous surface might yield fingerprints or not is to scratch it gently with a nail: if the nail makes a noise, then the surface might be unsuitable. A completely smooth surface will be silent. Clearly, this practice should be carried out with caution, and never at serious or major crime scenes.

CSIs locate marks in one of three ways:

- They can see visible marks, also called **positive** or **patent** marks, which are then photographed, and others are three-dimensional, normally called **plastic**.
- They can search invisible or **latent** marks with a torch and by dusting with powders using a fine brush. This is the commonest process; the fabric of the building can be examined, and bulky items can be left in place. After visualizing the mark, it should be photographed and, where appropriate, lifted with an adhesive material and placed on to an acetate sheet, or other substance as appropriate.
- They presume marks may be present and remove the article of interest for later chemical or physical enhancement. Occasionally, laboratory services are taken out to complex scenes where the fabric of the building is searched using chemicals and light sources.

Laboratory analysis normally involves employing different wavelengths of light which cause the mark to fluoresce, or by the application of chemicals which react with the non-aqueous components of the print. (Sweat is approximately 98.5% water and the remainder is made up of other components such as salts, fats, and amino acids.)

Whilst CSIs routinely 'dust' smooth non-porous surfaces, it should be borne in mind that many other surfaces may yield marks, such as textured plastics, polythene bags, paper, smooth wood, and even wall coatings. The majority of marks at scenes or on exhibits are invisible, or latent, which means they are easily damaged by clumsy actions. Police officers first on the scene should always wear gloves and handle potential exhibits by their edges. Since the majority of fingerprints are invisible, or latent, you should never assume that fingerprints are absent simply because you cannot see them.

13.6.10.1 National Automated Fingerprint Identification System

Note at the outset that the PACE Act 1984, Code D applies when fingerprinting detainees (see section 8.29 above). You can read this in full at <http://police.homeoffice.gov.uk/news-and-publications/publication/operational-policing/PACE_Chapter_D.pdf>.

In the UK the prints taken from prisoners in custody (so-called **Tenprints**) are input to the National Automated Fingerprint Identification System (NAFIS) which was fully rolled out to forces in 2001. In turn, marks recovered by CSIs from crime scenes, or developed by in-house laboratories, are scanned into NAFIS. The two parts of the database are employed to cross-check by:

* searching existing tenprints against scene of crime marks and vice versa;
* searching new scene of crime marks with the rest of the scene of crime collection to establish links;
* searching new tenprints against the tenprint collection to verify the identity of prisoners when they have a criminal record.

However, it is a fingerprint expert who actually carries out the identification procedure and makes a statement, because a computer obviously cannot form an opinion.

NAFIS is a computer, but it is not infallible; the adage 'rubbish in, rubbish out' still stands. A poorly taken set of prisoner's fingerprints may not identify someone at a crime scene, so it is a responsibility of all police officers to take the very best fingerprints on every occasion. In addition, it is a common misconception that a NAFIS search is carried out nationwide for every crime scene mark found. The amount of traffic this would generate would overwhelm the system, so searching is targeted depending upon the severity of the crime and whether or not specific intelligence points to the offender coming from another area.

One Southern English police force benefited from using intelligence to identify possible regional locations for many offenders involved in minor crimes of violence and criminal damage surrounding the importation of alcohol and cigarettes. It was noted that many offenders had accents from the North-East and North-West of the UK, and subsequent targeted NAFIS searches paid dividends. The same technique can also be used for vehicle registrations since some parts of these are regionally based.

13.6.11 Biological Material Yielding DNA

As with fingerprints, note that the PACE Act 1984, Code D applies when sampling detainees for biological material. Biological material that yields DNA is of major interest to the forensic investigator, and by extension to you, the police officer concerned with the investigation. Examples of such material include blood, saliva, semen, hairs with a root, and many other secretions such as ear wax and mucus. Indeed, nearly every cell and every secretion from the human body has the potential to provide DNA. You should be aware however, that all such biological material can also be very easily contaminated by victims or by police officers through talking, coughing, sneezing over, or mishandling the material.

Every cell in the human body—with a few exceptions—contains a nucleus and within the nucleus are chromosomes. Chromosomes are made up of genes which instruct the body to manufacture proteins and therefore govern the biological and physical processes within the cell and, consequently, the body. Individual genes are constructed from DNA. Many texts refer to DNA as the 'blueprint' for humans and other living things but you should note that **DNA Fingerprinting** is not to be taken literally—you cannot establish fingerprint patterns through DNA analysis.

Every nucleus contains a copy of the DNA for the entire organism, so a cell from the cheek contains exactly the same material as a white cell from the blood. Since it is the blueprint for humankind, a large proportion of DNA is the same in every human, but small differences occur which account for variations, like hair and eye colour, and invisible characteristics like genetically-related illness.

Amongst this important variable material are sections of DNA called Short Tandem Repeats (STRs) which are commonly referred to as 'junk DNA'. The junk DNA is highly variable between individuals and, as a result, can be used to differentiate between people. Clearly, there is no mileage in employing common genetic material in order to identify suspects because it is shared between so many people.

A DNA hit is a calculation concerning a selection of a person's STRs and is supplied by the scientist as a match probability. If the match probability is one in a billion it means that there is a one in a billion chance that another person **selected at random** has the same profile. It does not mean that there is a one in a billion chance that the suspect is innocent, nor does it mean that one in every billion people shares the same profile. These errors are called **fallacies** (see section 4.13). If the DNA recovered for analysis is degraded through age or lack of proper handling, the match probability applied to the comparison may be reduced, which can cause some concern, but remember that other evidence should be used to support the prosecution case.

DNA is typically found on articles or at scenes yielding blood, semen, saliva, hair with roots, some bodily secretions, and pieces of body tissue. It is important to treat all body fluids as potential health hazards. Not only do people need protecting from the biological material (which might contain pathogens or disease-carrying bacteria): the biological material also needs protecting from us, since our own DNA can easily contaminate it.

At the laboratory the DNA is removed from the swab or material upon which it is found, then copied many times using a process called Polymerase Chain Reaction to ensure enough is available for analysis.

The term **DNA LCN** means that only a very small amount of DNA is available ('low copy number'). If the quantity of DNA recovered is very low (or where it is believed some **may** be present), extra cycles of the PCR copying process are carried out to ensure enough is present for subsequent analysis. This has yielded sufficient DNA for analysis from a number of unexpected sources (according to the FSS) such as tools, clothing grabbed by the suspect, and weapons.

Mitochondrial DNA (Mt DNA) is a different form of DNA which can be extracted from bone, hair, faeces, and teeth. Mitochondrial DNA is doughnut-shaped and is found within all cells in organelles called 'mitochondria' which break down sugars (like glucose) for energy. The advantage to investigators is that the doughnut-shape makes the DNA more resilient to external influences so it may last many years. It does, however, have limitations in that it cannot uniquely identify a person: only the maternal line. This means, for example, that you share your Mt DNA with:

• your brothers and sisters;
• your mother and her siblings;
• your grandmother and her siblings; and
• if you are female, with your children.

If you are male your children do not share any of your Mt DNA.

Mt DNA can be beneficial when applied to the study of old and degraded samples where normal (nuclear) DNA is unavailable. It was famously used by the FSS to identify Tsar Nicholas II and Tsarina Alexandra, whose bodies (along with 3 children) were found near Yekaterinburg, Russia, in 1991 (the royal family having been killed by the Bolsheviks in 1919).

Y STRs are a variable genetic feature found on the Y chromosome. The male or Y chromosome is found only in men and can be used to determine paternal ancestry by studying a specific set of STRs. Since females have no Y chromosome to pass on to a son, Y chromosomes only pass from father to son. In Western culture (though not in Iceland), this is traditionally paralleled by the transfer of the surname; hence Y chromosome analysis has gained commercial popularity as a genealogical tool and may assist in some investigations. The value of Y STRs is, of course, diminished in males whose paternity is not ascertained.

13.6.11.1 The National DNA Database

The National DNA Database (NDNAD) is a database of the DNA of persons who are arrested, cautioned, convicted, and charged for recordable offences. The NDNAD is the property of the police but is managed by a custodian, currently the Forensic Science Service (FSS). The database stores all DNA recovered from crime scenes (where applicable) and all people who have been sampled subject to legal and operational criteria. The 2005–2006 NDNAD Annual Report shows that there are in excess of 3.7 million subject samples retained on the database and 382,000 samples taken from crime scenes.

The simple elegance of the system is based upon the theory that many offenders in minor crimes will either cease their criminality, or will continue as volume crime offenders or will step up their activity to more serious offences. Very few armed robbers, for example, when arrested, are found to be free of a criminal record. By taking the DNA sample of relatively new or volume crime offenders, the police effectively 'bank' this for the future, in the same way that they do with fingerprints. There may also be a deterrent effect. We put to one side however, the concerns over the civil liberty implications surrounding the NDNAD.

Each time a new crime scene or suspect sample is received it is entered in the database and cross-checking occurs. The results have been noticeable; in 2000 there were some 8,612 DNA detections, rising to 19,800 in 2005. The functionality of the system is similar to NAFIS in that it also identifies linked crimes. Whilst this may not seem to be a vital ability, consider **the case of John Wood:**

> A man sexually assaulted two young girls in 1988 in Canterbury, Kent. He was not apprehended at the time. Later, in 2001, a John Wood was arrested for shoplifting only £10 worth of groceries in Derbyshire. The arresting Pc took his sample in accordance with local instructions and the DNA taken from Wood was matched to DNA found at the crime scene in Canterbury. The Pc was, therefore, directly credited for Wood's arrest and for the detection of the Canterbury offences. Wood admitted the offences and was sentenced to fifteen years.

13.6.12 Toxicology

The poison, alcohol, or drug content within a person's body may be crucial to an investigation for a number of reasons: to calculate whether they are over the drink-drive limit; to establish that alcohol or drugs may explain behaviour such as violence or drowsiness; or to establish cause of illness and death.

Roadside breath tests and those carried out by an Intoximeter are still the most common forms of toxicological measurement carried out by the police, but these are normally used as screening tests prior to a full laboratory analysis (see section 10.16 above). A variety of field-test kits and covert-sampling devices can be employed to screen for drugs but, ultimately, the opinion of an expert toxicologist should be sought to provide evidence suitable for a prosecution. Do bear in mind that some policies exist, particularly for marijuana possession, that if the suspect makes a guilty plea, he/she will merely be cautioned. Elaborate analysis is not therefore required (or at best, not embarked on), since the case will not go to court.

In driving cases, you should use the laboratory submission forms MG/DD A to E. In cases where a back calculation is required (to establish a previous level of alcohol in a suspect, see section 10.16 above), police officers should **always** seek the advice of a CSI based at the BCU (or a Scientific Support Unit adviser) since the forms required for such a calculation can be quite complex. Regardless of this, always try to seize original bottles and glasses marked up to show what the suspect claims to have drunk, but bear in mind that a 'gulp' or 'swig' is not a scientifically-accepted measurement of alcohol consumption!

Commonly, blood or urine are the substances sent for analysis but other samples from the body tissue and eyes of deceased victims may be used depending upon the circumstances. Remember; toxicology samples must always be treated as a potential health hazard.

13.6.13   Digital Evidence

Digitally-stored data is retrievable from hard drives, discs, CDs, DVDs, mobile phones, telecoms equipment, credit cards and credit card reading devices, video systems, and any other electronic recording or processing device. These sources of data can provide evidence of the commission of a crime. Typically, these tasks are not the domain of CSIs; the analysis of digital data and associated equipment is the province of specialist computer crime units, fraud departments, or telecoms experts.

Special protocols exist for the seizure of digital evidence in every force in the UK; make sure you are aware of the procedures used in your force. We provide an overview of the particular issues surrounding the seizure of electronic equipment below in section 13.6.20.

13.6.14   Documents and Forensic Investigation

Under the term 'documents', forensic investigators normally include all letters, paperwork, invoices, cheques, transfers, application forms, handwriting, and any other printed material, whether by typewriter, computer printer, photocopier, or other device.

Document analysis can be carried out in a number of ways, some examples are:

- **'Impressed' writing** enhanced using Electrostatic Document Apparatus (ESDA). Typically this situation arises when a pad of paper is used, and an impression of writing on one page may be found on others below it.
- **Handwriting analysis**: the comparison of material obtained during the investigation with samples provided by a suspect.
- **Printers** and **typewriters**: the suspect printer or typewriter is compared with a specimen document. The presence of printer-head faults, 'banding' or damage to typefaces can be reproduced under laboratory conditions and compared with the suspect document.
- **Physical features** of paper can be compared, such as tear marks, staple holes, and altered text.

Other document features such as watermarks, obliterations, security features, paper types, security inks, and concealed marks and 'reactive fibres' can be analysed in a number of ways using microscopy and a Video Spectral Comparator to enhance images and features using a variety of wavelengths of light.

13.6.15   Mechanical Fits, 'Jigsaw', or Physical Matches

This is a form of evidence which is of exceptional power in many police enquiries. It is an extended application of the theory that all things are unique and can be individualized (see section 13.6.2). In its simplest form, if an object breaks into two or more parts, and if those parts are found separately and can be **reconstructed** as 'a fit', then they must all originate from the same source. For example, small fragments of a blade were found in the chin of a deceased male. Later, another male was found in possession of a damaged craft knife. The blade of his craft knife and the metal fragments were reconstructed.

13.6.16   Firearms and Forensics

First, a note on safety. If you are required to attend the scene of a shooting incident you must be sure in your mind that there is no danger from the offender. If you find shotgun cartridges at the scene or nearby inform your colleagues, since the offender may have reloaded. Key factors that need to be considered include:

1. Has he/she been taken into custody?
2. Has he/she made off from the scene? (But how reliable is this informant?)
3. Has he/she been incapacitated and disarmed?

If the offender is still at the scene and the incident is running you should identify the rendezvous point (RV or RVP, see sections 11.18 and 13.3 above) and go there unless instructed otherwise.

Consider the contamination issues regarding vehicles, prisoners, and colleagues. Make your concerns clear. If you are tasked to deal with the suspect you will contaminate him/her if you have been to the scene—voice your concerns.

Firearms, particularly relating to the law are covered in sections 8.22–8.27 above. Here we consider firearms in relation to forensic issues. In terms of their structure, there are two broad categories of firearms that will concern us here; smooth bore and rifled bore weapons. **Smooth bore** weapons have a barrel which is smooth inside to enable the easy passage of shot. Although normally associated with lead shot, as used in sport shooting, these weapons can fire a single lead slug. Generally, smooth bore weapons have a limited range, but find popular use in crime because accuracy is not required due to the spread of shot. For **rifled bore** weapons the inside of the barrel is rifled or grooved in a spiral pattern to impart a spin to the bullet. This gives the bullet stability that increases accuracy and range. The number of grooves in a barrel is normally between two and sixteen and they can twist clockwise or anti-clockwise.

Calibre is the measurement of the diameter of the barrel. In rifled weapons this figure is normally expressed in metric or imperial figures. eg 7.62 mm, 9 mm, .38, .357. The units are readily convertible between the two measuring systems. In Britain and the US, calibre is measured differently for smooth bore weapons owing to the inability of engineers in the past to be accurate to hundredths of one inch. The calibre denotes the number of lead spheres, each exactly fitting the barrel, which would together weigh one imperial pound. So, a twelve-bore (UK) or twelve gauge (US) is a barrel diameter that would fit 12 balls of lead each weighing approximately 1.33 ounces.

13.6.16.1 Ammunition and forensics

In a typical **bulleted cartridge** the bullet, made of lead, is at the front of the assembly, whilst behind it is a quantity of powder stored in a brass cartridge. At the closed end of the cartridge (the head) is a quantity of primer, a sensitive powder which is ignited by the action of the trigger and, hence, the firing pin. This causes the burning of the main powder charge and the resultant forcing of the bullet through the barrel. For the CSI and scientist the potential evidence is described in the following table.

Potential evidence available from the bulleted cartridge components

Bulleted cartridge component	Available evidence
Cartridge case	The actions of loading, firing, and ejecting the cartridge will scratch the polished brass casing and leave comparable marks upon it. These marks are caused by the magazine (if used), the ejector, extractor, breech face, and firing pin. Since bullet, cartridge design, and extractors vary, it may be possible to identify the type of weapon from which the cartridge was ejected. Manufacturer's details, calibre, and type of round are normally engraved on the head stamp (base) of cartridges.
Bullet	This will normally identify the calibre of the weapon used, and since there is huge variation in bullet design, specialist rounds and sometimes the type of weapon can be identified. Most importantly though, is the scratched impression on the bullet of the rifling grooves from within the barrel. Variations in the twist (left or right) and the number of grooves may assist in the identification of the make and model of the gun used, and can be compared to a suspect weapon. Even badly deformed bullets are useful to the scientist.
Powder	During burning, the powder gives off quantities of smoke and particulates which are emitted from the muzzle. Minute particles of the bullet, unburnt powder, and other debris are ejected in several directions. Some also contain small particles of lead, barium, and antimony which form small granules. These firearm residues can be found on the clothing, face, and hands of the offender and other people and items in the vicinity. Swabbing kits are available to retrieve this material. Suspects should be swabbed as soon as possible because the residues fall off easily.

For bulleted cartridges, the cartridge and bullet design vary for a number of reasons, such as:

- type of weapon (rifle, revolver, etc);
- type of loading system;
- type of firing mechanism (pinfire, needle fire, rimfire, centrefire);
- manufacturer;
- function of the bullet (anti-personnel, tracer, armour piercing).

A typical **shot cartridge** contains primer, charge, shot, wadding, and the outer case. The primer and propellant are stored in a brass cup at the base, and the rest of the assembly is stored in a tube made up of plastic or compressed card. The controlled explosion forces all the shot and wadding through the barrel. Different manufacturers place different types of wad in various positions within the cartridge depending upon the function of the shot, but the main function of wadding is to act as a shock absorber to prevent the spherical shot being deformed since a non-spherical shot would tend to stray from the intended path. For the CSI and scientist the potential evidence is summarized in the following table.

Potential evidence available from the shot cartridge components

Shot cartridge component	Available evidence
Cartridge case	This is normally retained in the weapon until reloading, however they may be ejected by automatic or self-loading weapons. It can be used to establish the bore of the weapon and the manufacturer and type of cartridge. Scratches on the brass base and the impression of the firing pin and breech face can be compared to suspect weapons. In automatic weapons marks from the extractor, ejector, and magazine may be found.
The shot	The size of the shot may eliminate some types of catridge. The spread of the shot is useful in establishing the range of the weapon (when the possible use of a 'choke' is taken into consideration).
Powder	Firearms residues are available.
Wadding	The presence of wadding indicates that a shotgun has been discharged. It can frequently give an indication as to the bore of weapon used, and a hint as to the cartridge manufacturer. Plastic wadding fired from a sawn-off weapon can sometimes be compared to the finish at the sawn-off muzzle end: if the finish is poor the wadding may bear scratches which can be reproduced during controlled tests. Wadding is normally badly deformed during discharge, so irregular lumps of plastic, felt, or cork at the scene should be collected and preserved.

13.6.16.2 Laboratory examinations of firearms evidence

The most frequently asked questions at the laboratory are:

- Is this a firearm as defined by the Act(s)? (See sections 8.22 to 8.27).
- Is this an imitation firearm? (See section 8.27).
- What weapon fired this bullet (or cartridge case)?
- Did **this** weapon fire **this** bullet or (cartridge case)?
- How far was the weapon from the victim?
- Can this weapon fire accidentally?
- Do these swabs/items of clothing bear firearm discharge residues?
- Which is the entry wound/exit wound on this victim?

(Adapted from a number of unpublished Forensic Science Service publications.)

13.6.17 Taking Samples from People

Note at the outset that when taking forensic samples from suspects you must follow the procedures set out in the PACE Act 1984, Code D. This is covered extensively in section 8.29 above.

As noted earlier, people are sources both of **evidence** (potentially to be used in court) and **intelligence** (for example, to provide leads in an investigation). Hence there are a number of reasons for taking samples from people:

- to prove or disprove their involvement in the offence;
- to corroborate or refute statements;
- to show a link between them and another person, or them and the scene or an exhibit;
- to establish drug, toxin, or alcohol levels in the body;
- to further inform the enquiry;
- to provide a reference sample (DNA, fingerprints, or footwear impressions) for direct comparison, for elimination, or for a database.

When taking samples from people always use brand new, unused packaging equipment as using old equipment usually causes contamination. Specific kits are available, for example, for the sampling of hair or urine. Make sure that you use the appropriate kit.

Material found upon them can include debris and DNA-rich material in or on any part of the body, including:

- foreign blood, saliva, and semen, which are sources of DNA;
- firearm and explosive residues;
- trace material such as glass, paint flakes, fibres, grease, or soil;
- bite marks, weapon marks, and bruises;
- chemicals, such as alcohol, toxins, and drugs within the blood and urine, or chemical traces upon the skin;
- DNA and fingerprints;
- handwriting characteristics.

Although the sampling of suspects (whether arrested or not) must be carried out under the PACE Act 1984, Code D, there is no PACE requirement for those people (usually, but not exclusively, victims) who provide samples to support investigations. This means it is not always necessary for a police surgeon or other medical practitioner to take some samples. Police officers do, however, have to behave towards victims and volunteers in accordance with the Human Rights Act 1998. This is an important consideration when arriving at a scene or dealing with a victim who attends the police station where no CSI or medical assistance is immediately available.

TASK 12

Consider what you might do if:

- A woman attends the police station and claims to have been 'date-raped'. GHB and Rohypnol (examples of so-called 'date rape' drugs) are rapidly excreted from the human body. Would you find a 'urine module' and request an immediate urine sample? How might this affect potential DNA evidence?
- You attend a robbery and a man says he bit the offender. He can still taste blood in his mouth. Would you ask him to spit into a sterile bottle?
- A victim claims a man sexually assaulted her and ejaculated over her hand. Would you glove or bag her hand, or even take a swab from it (if trained)?

13.6.17.1 What Samples Should Be Taken?

The types of sample taken from victims and suspects will depend on the nature of the criminal offence. The following table describes the minimum samples for consideration (represented by a tick in the table). Note that the PACE Act 1984, Code D and the Human Rights Act 1988 must be complied with and you should note your reasons for taking a particular sample in each case.

Chapter 13: Critical Incidents and Forensic Investigation

Minimum samples

	Cheque or other fraud. Hate mail	Burglary or other property crime	Sexual assault or rape (a special kit may be used)	Theft from motor vehicle with damage caused	ABH and other assaults	Homicide (the sexual offences kit is often used for victim and suspects)
Blood and/or urine for toxicology			✓		✓	✓
Clothing (inner)			✓		✓	✓
Clothing (outer)		✓	✓	✓	✓	✓
DNA	✓	✓	✓	✓	✓	✓
Fingerprints	✓	✓	✓	✓	✓	✓
Hair (combing)		✓	✓	✓	✓	✓
Hair (pulled/cut)		✓	✓	✓	✓	✓
Handwriting sample	✓					
Photographs of injuries		When relevant	When relevant	When relevant	When relevant	Effectively mandatory
Sexual offence kit			Mandatory			✓
Shoes		✓	✓	✓	✓	✓
Blood and/or urine for toxicology			✓		✓	✓

13.6.17.2 The sampling procedure for taking evidence from people

Whenever you take a sample from a person, you must be PACE Act 1984 and Human Rights Act 1988 compliant. The PACE Act, Code D is covered in detail in section 8.29 above. Inform your CSI when samples have been taken, so that correct storage and subsequent preservation can be arranged.

Here we deal with victims, who normally volunteer samples, and suspects who are dealt with under the PACE Act 1984, Code D. Typically, if you require a sample from one person or place you should ensure a corresponding sample is recovered from elsewhere for comparison.

Always wear gloves as a **minimum** form of protection. For serious offences, or where health warnings exist, officers should wear protective clothing to protect them and the evidence from contamination. It is essential that brand new, clean packaging equipment is used. There are two main types of sample:

An **intimate sample** is defined by the PACE Act 1984, Code D as:

> a dental impression or sample of blood, semen or any other tissue fluid, urine, or pubic hair, or a swab taken from any part of a person's genitals or from a person's body orifice other than the mouth.

The mouth is not included chiefly because swabs from the inside surface of the cheeks are used for DNA analysis. An orifice includes the ears and nose as well as the genitals and anus.

A **non-intimate sample** is defined by the PACE Act 1984, Code D as:

> a sample of hair, other than pubic hair, which includes hair plucked with the root, a sample taken from a nail or from under a nail, a swab taken from any part of a person's body other than a part from which a swab taken would be an intimate sample, saliva, a skin impression which means any record taken in any form and produced by any method, of the skin pattern and other physical characteristics or features of the whole, or any part of, a person's foot or of any other part of their body.

Swabs from the body include skin swabs from hands and face as well as elsewhere. Skin impressions include ear prints, lip prints, and prints of the skin. Non-intimate samples may be taken at a police station from a detainee using reasonable force, subject to proper documentation.

Clothing and **footwear** can be used as a source for samples, for the following purposes:

- for the recovery of fibres, hair, and particulate material and traces, wet or dry blood, and chemicals;
- for comparison use as a control of the fibre mix and to recreate impressions left by clothing or shoes on vehicles following RTCs and at scenes;
- damage to clothing may assist in describing weapons used on a victim;
- damage to fibres may indicate proximity to fire or explosion.

When taking clothing from suspects and victims, it is essential that the subject stands on a clean paper sheet which catches any debris which may fall. Material recovered from the floor of custody areas or medical facilities is not suitable for laboratory examination since it has no provenance. The majority of force quality control systems will prevent the submission of such articles.

Ensure any samples from the skin, hands, head, and mouth are taken first in order to prevent material from those areas contaminating the clothing or vice versa-for example, pulling a sweater covered in glass over the head which does not contain glass is contamination, so deal with the head hair first.

Remove the clothing in a logical manner and exhibit and package each piece separately in front of the subject. A final search of pockets may be carried out within the bag to prevent the unnecessary loss of material.

There may be a shoe-mark intelligence system operating within your force; you should follow the accepted procedure. It is inadvisable to scan or copy shoes which may be needed for the analysis of trace materials and DNA, since the action of using the scanner may contaminate the shoes or cause the loss of material.

Finally, ask the person to brush off his/her bare feet onto the paper sheet before stepping off, since material on the sheet will adhere to sweaty feet. The paper sheet on the floor is now an exhibit, so treat it with necessary care before it is despatched for analysis.

Without fail, make notes about the condition of clothing: its size, the presence of blood, colour, logos, and any damage. This prevents the need for another person to open the packaging in order to screen or describe the contents.

Head hair samples can be used for the following purposes:

- for the recovery of fibres, hair, and particulate material and traces, wet or dry blood, and chemicals;
- for comparison use as a control of the subject's hair (structure, length, colour, and treatments) when found at scenes or on other people;
- for DNA from a hair root.

Head hair may contain glass, plant material, foreign hairs, and so on. Deal with the head hair before the clothing in order to limit contamination by or from other samples (this is especially important in offences where windows have been smashed.) Hair samples must be taken over a sheet of pre-folded paper which catches debris. The technique in many police forces is as follows:

- Holding a piece of pre-folded paper, at least A4 size, comb the person's hair from front to back all over the head so that debris falls onto the paper. Continue until no more debris is found. Clearly, this is not easy when the person is not compliant. Exhibit the paper containing the debris and the comb.
- For matted hair, or dreadlocks, wear a glove and gently brush the hair with your hands and even a new small hairbrush if possible (with care.) Exhibit the paper containing the debris, the glove, and the brush.
- Hats should be exhibited first where they are worn.
- Where religious head coverings are worn, such as turbans, ask permission from the person first and, time permitting, make arrangements for alternative head coverings prior to removal.

- Blood or other matted material in the hair should be cut out over a sheet of pre-folded paper. Exhibit the cut section, paper, and the scissors.
- When you have finished, a 'control' of head hair is required and ideally this is pulled out so it contains the root material. Take at least twenty-five hairs including all colours and length variations.

Swabs from the skin can be used as a source for samples, and may show the presence of blood, saliva, or chemical residues such as explosives traces. Generally, this is best left to a CSI (particularly explosive and firearm traces and the photography of blood) or a medical examiner, but do not permit unnecessary delays to occur.

If the target substance is **wet**, for example from blood or saliva, or wet or greasy, like oils and paints, follow this procedure:

- Wearing surgical gloves, take a sealed sterile swab and break it from its tube. Swab the stain gently to soak the tip. Do this as often as required on as many stains as possible. Seal each swab in its container. Write the details and area swabbed on the container's label.
- Wet another swab with the water provided and swab an area of skin which is not contaminated with the target material. This is a control of the surface to show background chemicals. Seal the swab in its container. Write the details and 'skin control + water' on the container's label.

If the target substance is **dry**, like blood or paint, follow the procedure given above, but moisten the tip of the sterile swab with sterile water before you collect any samples. Swab the stain gently to discolour the tip.

DNA will be present in some of the types of samples described above. However, you will also be trained to take samples from people that will subsequently only be used for **DNA analysis**. In general terms, the subject should not eat, drink, or smoke for at least twenty minutes before the test. This allows the mouth to regenerate dead or damaged cells. Open the pack—which contains a buccal swab kit and a hair sampling kit—and check its contents. Always wear the gloves provided and once the pack is open discard it in its entirety if any part is dropped or if you cough or sneeze over it. Never use a swab picked up from the floor. Carry out the sampling process and, lastly, complete the associated paperwork, which saves time; since, if you fill in the paperwork first and then drop a swab, you must fill in a new form. Then seal everything into the 'tamper-evident' bag so that the forms can be read through the bag. Follow your force's protocols for subsequent handling and storage.

Under the PACE Act 1984, the subject may refuse a buccal swab, in which case he/she may elect a hair sample which is pulled to include the root. The hair sampling site can be chosen by the subject on condition that it is not in an intimate area.

Samples from people must be correctly **stored and transported.** Blood, semen, and saliva contain DNA and should be frozen immediately. Where DNA is not required, for instance for the comparison of paints and oils, it is best practice to air-dry them securely or to freeze them if this is not possible.

Fingerprints are a useful and non-invasive form of evidence. You will be specially trained so that you can fingerprint suspects and victims. Your force will use one of these methods at police stations:

- Livescan—a digital finger and palm scanning device.
- Ink—the traditional copper plate and printers' ink system.

In addition, there are simpler, portable systems—an ink pad or peel-apart pre-inked strips—which are used to eliminate the victim's prints at the scene.

Tooth impressions or bite marks may contain DNA found in the saliva which is normally present; you must consider how this DNA evidence is going to be preserved. A registered dentist is required under the PACE Act 1984 to take impressions of a suspect's teeth. Contact your CSI or Scientific Support Unit for advice.

Other body impressions may also be required at times. Consult your CSI for other impressions of the body.

Handwriting samples are used most effectively when a variety of material is submitted for comparison. This can include:

- samples produced in front of a police officer;
- material sourced from the suspect's home address, work, or other places (such as diaries, letters, general paperwork) which is identifiably written by the suspect. This is referred to as 'course of business' handwriting;
- material as above which is assumed to have been written by the suspect (but of poor value).

When taking a handwriting sample, the suspect must be given a well-used ballpoint pen and must write the sample material in the same format as the document under consideration as possible evidence: if the document is in capitals, then the sample piece must be in capitals, and so on. If the offence was committed on a specific form, ask the supplier to give you a bundle and use these too. Dummy cheques are available from your CSI or Fraud Unit (which may be combined with your Computer Crime Unit) if necessary. Ask the suspect to write out the contents of the document a minimum of five times (unless this would be unreasonable). For cheques, at least fifteen samples are needed. Each time the suspect completes a sample, remove it so that he cannot see the style in which he has previously written. Never allow the suspect to see the original document in question; always dictate. The suspect should sign and date every page.

Under no circumstances ask the suspect to write 'The quick brown fox jumped over the lazy dogs.' This sentence is of no use, since a person's writing style is partly determined by the letters before and after every other letter.

When a suspect is identified, the investigator should exploit any fingerprints on paper or probable DNA on envelope flaps and stamps.

13.6.18 Sampling from Crime Scenes

Different forces employ a variety of Crime Scene Investigation staff whose chief role is the recovery of physical material from crime scenes, but there are many occasions where a police officer may seize exhibits in the course of duty. Such instances include:

- where the officer is part of a search team;
- where there is no apparent evidence save for one or two items which can be safely recovered without a CSI (such as documents, cheques, or a single moveable shoemark); note that local policies must be followed;
- where the CSI is unable to attend;
- where evidence may be lost if not recovered immediately (such as a shotgun cartridge on a windy day).

13.6.18.1 Recovering 'controls'

Where a simple control of material is needed, including from a single building or site or vehicle window, or a single set of paint controls from a car involved in a RTC, a police officer may gather the control samples. For anything else, consult a CSI.

Glass controls should be taken as follows:

- Glass must always be taken from the frame which supports it because glass on the ground has no provenance. Where no glass remains you must satisfy yourself, the **scientist** and a potential **jury** that the glass did, indeed, originally come from the frame.
- Take a minimum of six pieces of glass and mark the inside or outside of each with a pen or 'chinagraph' pencil. Sample from all around the break. Wear thick gloves and goggles as a Health and Safety minimum.
- Where a toughened glass window has broken, merely remove the cube-shaped debris from around the hole.

- If a large laminate window has broken, the slabs can be extremely dangerous. You must sample the complete thickness, not only the dusty ground glass on the surface. Consider that shoe marks may be present on the glass.
- Place the fragments into a suitable sturdy box with **every** edge sealed with tape. Fragments must not puncture or escape through the box. An outer polythene bag is essential.
- Apart from in vehicle windows, always measure the window void and its exact position above the ground and provide this as a plan drawing.

Paint controls should be taken as follows:

- Never use adhesive tapes to recover paint samples.
- If there is a tool mark present, you should consider calling a CSI.
- On window and door frames, slice out a section (at least 20 mm) of the paint (and preferably include some base material) with a sharp knife. Use a new knife. Do this from several areas around the damage.
- Place the fragments into a paper fold and then put into a polythene bag.
- Remember, if you are considering paint samples there may be tool marks—you may need a CSI anyway.
- On vehicles, cut out a 10p sized section of paint, all the way to base metal (include filler where present) from several places near to, and remote from, the damage in question. Repeat the process where foreign paint is found.
- On vehicles with damaged panels the paint sometimes falls away in rectangular slabs. If so, take them from the car, not the ground beneath it.
- Because paint is brittle it may lend itself to a mechanical fit. In this case the entire object and all the chipped paint are required.

13.6.19 Packaging Techniques

Using the correct packaging prevents damage and contamination and is, effectively, a demonstration of the care and skill which went into the seizure of the exhibits. Always follow local force protocols, which are based on those laid down by Forensic Science laboratories. Specifically, guidance can be found in the FSS publication *The Scenes of Crime Handbook* (not publicly available, although your force should have copies).

13.6.19.1 Types of packaging and how to use them

The following table summarizes the types of packaging available and common techniques used when employing them. Note that some of the terms used in the table are explained later.

Types of packaging

Packaging	Procedure
Paper bags	• Place the article within and fold the top down twice, approximately 25 mm (one inch) per fold. • Seal over the joint with a signature seal (an adhesive label) bearing your signature, name, and number. • Completely seal the entire join between folds and bag and attach an exhibit label if required.
Polythene bags	• Attempt to locate and use a tamper-evident bag. • If a tamper-evident bag is unavailable, use a plain bag. • Place the article within. • Tent a signature seal over the top. • Tent a line of tape over the top along the entire open edge and attach an exhibit label if required. • Pinch the ends of the tape and cut off, about 10 mm from the bag. • Be cautious of packaging documents in plain bags: they should be packed in stout card folders or boxes to prevent people leaning on the documents or writing over them.
Nylon bags	• Place the article in a nylon bag, 'swan neck', tie the top, and seal. ('Swan neck' is a secure closure for a bag. The method is to twist the neck of the bag until it resembles a rope, loop this over itself in to an inverted U shape, then secure with tape or a cable.) Note the cable tie should not have 'teeth' which may puncture the bag. Place this bag into a polythene bag, swan neck, and seal. Use a nylon bag for hydrocarbons (such as petrol) and a nylon bag within a polythene bag for non-hydrocarbons (such as methylated spirits, alcohol, and acetone).

Types of packaging (*continued*)

Packaging	Procedure
	• If you are unclear as to whether you are packaging a hydrocarbon or not, use a nylon bag within a polythene bag. • Place the entire package into a rigid container, seal, and label. • These articles should not be stored in proximity to other samples.
Boxes	• Signature seal and seal with tape around all edges. Special perforated inserts are available for securing the item with string or cable ties. If you do not have this, simply puncture the box, but sign and seal over the holes.
'Paper folds'	• These are required for the safe collection and storage of dry materials such as powders, paint fragments, and hair combings. They are not adequate for storing glass. Always pre-fold the paper before use and work the debris down into the greyed section before re-folding. Seal into a suitable polythene bag. (See diagram below).

The following is a common technique used to construct a 'paper fold' container.

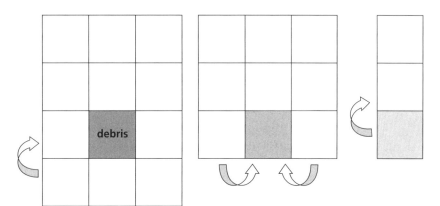

1. Work the material into the grey area and fold the base up

2. Fold in the left and right sides

3. Fold the base upwards and tuck the last fold in

(Image © Kevin Lawton-Barrett)

A Nylon bag 'swan necked' prior to securing with a cable tie

13.6.19.2   **How to package items of forensic importance**

Bedding and recently worn clothes or shoes must be sealed into paper bags which allow them to breathe. Sealing articles which are even slightly damp into plastic encourages the growth of mould and bacteria. You should also:

• Affix a health hazard warning where any biological material may be present or where it is known or believed that articles have come from a possibly contaminated source (eg a known drug addict).

• If needed, affix an exhibit label. If bags are not pre-printed, it is advisable to write the exhibit details on the bag as a fail-safe measure.

Articles that are **slightly wet or soaked with liquids** (including blood) need to be dried. Contact a CSI without delay for advice and assistance with drying. You should also:

• Avoid the temptation to fold clothes bearing wet blood as this causes the blood to transfer to other parts of the article.

• In an emergency, consider sealing into a polythene sack for transport but make contact with a CSI as a matter of priority. The sack should be sealed into a robust paper sack for protection.

Articles which may bear **flammable substances** should not be stored in paper bags because flammable chemicals (accelerants) will evaporate through paper sacks and be lost as well as contaminating other material in storage and transit. Where biological material is also believed present, consult your CSI since DNA may be destroyed. It is likely that the CSI will recommend immediate transport to a laboratory.

Sharps, bladed weapons, screwdrivers, and **other pointed objects** represent a very serious health hazard. Hypodermic needles are rarely dispatched to laboratories. You should:

• Always use a sharps storage pack for needles. Consider disposing of the needle in a sharps-bin prior to packaging the syringe. However, do not do this in major crime but take advice.

• Always use a knife tube for blades, but if unavailable, consider a clean, unused, sturdy box.

• Screw thread knife tubes are also inherently dangerous: never hold your palms over the ends since the screwing action 'jacks' the knife through the end of the tube if too much pressure is exerted.

• It is best practice to signature seal and tape the joints between the two halves of knife-tubes and sharps-packs prior to packaging in a polythene bag.

• If wet blood or water is present, the articles should be air dried first or frozen, but consult your local force policy. If a syringe contains liquid local policy may require it to be decanted into a bottle. In this case consult a CSI.

Firearms represent a serious and immediate high risk hazard. Student police officers must never handle or package a firearm without training: previous military expertise is not sufficient. It is best practice to call for the assistance of a Firearms Officer and CSI to properly record the making-safe process. Firearms are first made safe and then sealed into boxes (unless they are of no forensic interest, for instance when a firearm owner is considered unfit to continue possessing a firearm and the weapon is being removed to the police station for safety).

Bottles and **glasses** may have sharp edges; think health and safety, and follow these procedures:

• To protect fingerprints or DNA, bottles and glasses must be immobilized in a sturdy box.

• Signature seal and seal with tape around all edges. Special perforated inserts are available for securing the item with string or cable ties. If you do not have this, simply puncture the box, but sign and seal over the holes.

• When providing bottles and glasses for back calculation alcohol analysis ensure they are marked up to show the levels the suspect claims to have drunk and package securely in a box to prevent breakage.

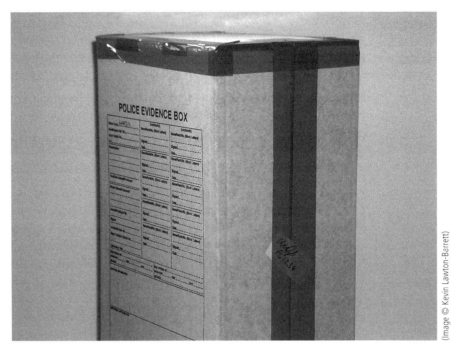

(Image © Kevin Lawton-Barrett)

Police evidence box

Urine samples may be required in a crime investigation or are taken from drivers under the Road Traffic Act 1988. Custody officers have access to 'RTA type' urine kits which contain a special preservative—use this kit unless local policies dictate otherwise. In other crime, the subject is asked to urinate into a plastic pot which is then decanted into a suitable bottle containing a preservative. Ensure the bottle is properly secured and place in a rigid outer container. Some urine collection pots bear a temperature gauge to ensure that the sample came from a living person, rather than from, say, a supply secreted for the purpose (those of you who have seen the film *Withnail and I* will understand why).

TASK 13

Discuss the following questions with a BCU CSI or your trainers:

1. At a major crime scene, what are the usual problems with the common approach path and cordons?
2. What is the best form of evidence? A fingerprint or DNA? (They should all have different views, based almost entirely upon the context of the evidence they have found in the past.)
3. What is worse, genuine contamination of an exhibit, or the suspicion of contamination?

13.6.20 Attending a Venue Containing Digital Media

The most common message given to people who are experiencing problems with electronic equipment is to turn the device off. Whilst this is a sensible precaution for our own domestic equipment, police officers should never turn off digital equipment at a crime scene or other site without first seeking professional advice from an expert. (There is, however, a notable exception to this rule, if you encounter computers executing certain routines. You should also be wary of the possible existence of an Uninterruptible Power Supply (UPS). These exceptions will be explained to you during training).

Digital equipment includes computers, Palmtops (a kind of PDA), mobile phones, PDAs, electronic organizers, satellite navigation equipment, credit card skimmers, and an array of domestic devices that include timers and programmers (such as modern washing machines). Storage media includes floppy discs, CD ROMs, DVDs, memory sticks, flash cards, and portable hard drives.

To an extent digital evidence includes nearly any electronic device of any description, since so many contain clocks and programmers.

13.6.20.1   Computers

Where a seizure is **planned,** the Computer Crime Unit should be contacted in advance for advice and, where necessary, attendance at the scene. Computer Crime personnel are specially trained to recover data and present it in a form acceptable to the CJS.

Where a seizure is **unplanned,** contact should be made with the Computer Crime Unit for advice. In the meantime:

- do not turn on or off any device;
- do not touch any key or the mouse;
- do not interrupt the power supply (there are, however, exceptions to this general rule, particularly if the computer is executing a program that is formatting the logical drives—see your local force policy on this);
- do not interfere with any other device on a network;
- do not use the telephone system in any scene;

but

- **do** photograph the screen, if it is displaying;
- **do** photograph or sketch the device and any associated cabling where practicable.

Even reasonably unsophisticated criminals may have sufficient ability to booby trap their computers so that the machines can execute certain procedures when interfered with. (Be particularly aware of wireless networks.) Whilst data can sometimes be recovered even after deletion, causing deletion to happen is a form of contamination and **must** be avoided if at all possible.

Computer and storage media analysis can provide evidence on:

- deleted files and images;
- e-mails;
- images and text, whether downloaded or created locally;
- address books and contact details;
- times and dates of activity;
- hidden files and data.

13.6.20.2   Small portable devices

These include items such as USB pens, digital cameras, PDAs, and organizers. If these are unconnected to other devices the Computer Crime Unit may suggest a simple seizure, but seek advice and check policy. Remember that these devices can still communicate with other systems through Bluetooth and Infrared, and wireless receivers and transmitters. Do not view call lists, pictures, or any other files on portables.

13.6.20.3   Mobile phones

Mobile phones are seized from nearly every major crime scene and every prisoner, and your force will have specific policies relating to their seizure and packaging. This may include storage in special packaging to prevent them communicating with the network. Mobile phones and the network supplier's databases contain an enormous amount of information relating to calls, texts, and even their movement through the cellular network—so-called Cell Site Analysis. Do not view call lists, pictures, or any other files on mobiles.

13.6.20.4   Transport and storage of computers and other large items

You must follow your local policy during all seizures and storage, particularly relating to packaging.

When carrying computer equipment it is difficult to transport such equipment without touching the surfaces. The outer skin of most computers is mildly textured and commonly will not yield marks (in volume crime) but the screen and areas which are not normally seen, such as the inside, under the support foot and at the rear, are often very smooth. However, remember that polythene bags will obliterate fingerprints if they touch the smooth surfaces.

In serious or major crimes great care must be taken: remember that the whole device may be required for DNA and fingerprint analysis.

13.6.21 Attending Crime Scenes with Fatalities

At any scene of a sudden death it is essential that student police officers and constables are never afraid to ask questions and, above all, if **you** believe an incident is suspicious it is **your responsibility** to say so. If you do not understand something then ask. Senior officers may thank you for it.

A senior police colleague recounts the following story to every new group of student police officers he trains.

> After the death of a child in London, the body was returned to a hospital in the county concerned for a post mortem examination. During the initial stages a new Pc asked: 'do bodies change colour after death?' The answer was: 'yes, in fact they change colour quite a lot due to hypostasis, decay and even mummification.' Later he asked if dead bodies could heal themselves. The curious pathologist answered that this was not possible and, incidentally, why was he asking? The answer was that the new Pc had seen the deceased in London, where the child appeared Caucasian and had a hole in its forehead, yet here at the post mortem was an apparently Asian child and there was no hole. The hospital had handed the wrong child to the police.

The story may be apocryphal but the moral of the story is not: ask questions.

In particular, if you are in early attendance at a scene of a fatality, ask yourself:

- Is the event which probably caused death at this scene likely or possible?
- If it is a suicide, were the means available to the victim?
- Was the victim physically capable of the act?
- Is there any sign of a struggle?
- Is anything apparently missing?
- Is there evidence of a forced entry?
- Does the position or state of the body logically fit with the information received?

13.6.21.1 Certifying death

Where there might be the slightest chance a victim is alive, seek medical assistance. If a victim has been beheaded you may presume death has occurred, however in other cases a medical professional is required to attend the scene. (This author, on one occasion reluctantly called a police surgeon to a skeleton.) See section 13.5 for the procedures in the case of sudden death.

13.6.21.2 Hypostasis

When people die, their blood settles to the lowest parts and enters the skin where it creates a port-wine coloured stain. This is also known as post mortem lividity or livor mortis. Where a body is upright, blood drains to the lower parts of the limbs and lower cheek and ear.

In addition to this discoloration, wherever pressure is exerted on the skin, the blood will not enter. As a result, the deceased's skin may take on an impression of the surface beneath it (for example from a tiled floor). The patterns of clothing on the victim or where seams are found may also be very clear.

After some time (around three to four hours), the blood solidifies into a clot and can no longer move, so if the body is subsequently moved the signs of hypostasis will no longer be on the lower or underside parts of the body.

13.6.21.3 Rigor mortis

After death, chemical changes in the muscles gradually cause them to stiffen. The process normally begins in the head and works down the body. In very general terms it might start after four hours and disappear after twenty-four hours (when the body begins biologically to break down), however, the process is dependent upon a number of factors, not least of which is the ambient temperature (it is faster at higher temperatures). Crucially, immediately after death the body becomes limp and will relax into position, and if left for a number of hours, rigor mortis will stiffen it in that position. If subsequently moved, the body will not be correctly orientated.

13.6.21.4 Body temperature

The core temperature of the deceased will equalize with the ambient temperature (so it will usually cool down) after death and then, due to decay and insect activity, the body temperature may increase. The relationship between the lowering of the core temperature to the ambient temperature is well documented but not so reliable that the pathologist can give an estimate of the time of death to within a few minutes—as commonly seen on television. The ambient temperature, amount of clothing, and general health of the victim may all affect the temperature drop.

13.6.21.5 Suicide by cutting

Where a suicide victim has stabbed him/herself or severed an artery, often in the throat, wrist, or groin, one would normally expect to see tentative cuts—minor cuts carried out prior to the lethal wound.

TASK 14

Answer the following questions and instructions to gauge your recall and learning of the whole of the 'Forensic Investigation' part of Chapter 13. Some of the questions simply require you to locate the information in the chapter. Other questions are more demanding. You may also find that an informal meeting with your local CSI is of benefit when you are Supervised Patrol at your BCU, or whilst on a course.

1. Who is credited with the development of the Principle of Exchange?
2. List three types of trace evidence or material which might be found at a burglary.
3. List three types of impressions.
4. List three sources of DNA.
5. List three things an investigator might employ forensic science for.
6. What is inceptive evidence?
7. In an emergency, can you lawfully ask a victim to provide a urine sample if s/he tells you s/he was the victim of a drug-induced rape?
8. You are tasked to attend a crime scene and take a control sample of glass. How many pieces should you take? From where? What should you mark on them?
9. You are taking a DNA sample from an arrested person. You drop the swab on the floor. What action do you now carry out?
10. Which PACE Act 1984 Code applies to fingerprinting suspects?
11. What does Mitochondrial DNA establish: male or female lines?
12. Imagine you have a quantity of fine debris you wish to store. Taking a sheet of A4 paper, make a paper fold to retain it. Now check your attempt against the diagram in section 13.6.19.1.
13. Clothing thought to be contaminated with hydrocarbons (like petrol) is packed into what sort of bag?
14. When can you effectively presume death has occurred?
15. What does FSS stand for?

13.7 Answers to Tasks

TASK 1

We were interested in your initial responses to this challenging question. Your answers could well have been 'I do not know' which would have been entirely understandable. (In fact your trainers might be more worried if you claim already to know the answers to these questions.) The rest of this section of this chapter is concerned with providing you with some pointers to possible answers.

TASK 2

Your list could read something like this:

- clear the immediate scene; note any injuries to anyone;
- ensure that the area around the house (the 'stronghold') is evacuated and 'sterile';
- move people as far from the scene as possible;
- continue to ask for information on what has happened;
- calm the hysterical or over-excited;
- create one way into the incident and one way out;
- clear a wide area to receive the support which is coming (keep arriving vehicles away from the scene itself);
- keep in constant communication with your control centre, making sure that they know what is happening and what you are doing;
- use your colleague pro-actively to control the immediate area, to talk to witnesses, to communicate with the incoming support;
- find out all you can about the alleged hostage-taker, including name and any relationship with anyone likely to be inside the house with him;
- make notes, keep a careful log of what has taken place to the best of your knowledge, recording names and addresses of witnesses (see section 12.9 above);
- if it is safe to do so, try to open a dialogue with the hostage-taker, making sure that he understands that you are a police officer;
- emphasize that your aim is to end this incident peacefully and without anyone getting hurt.

Compare this list to the one you will be probably be given during your training. No doubt there will be many points in common.

TASK 3

The usual model taught during police training adopts a six-stage process, starting with defining the problem:

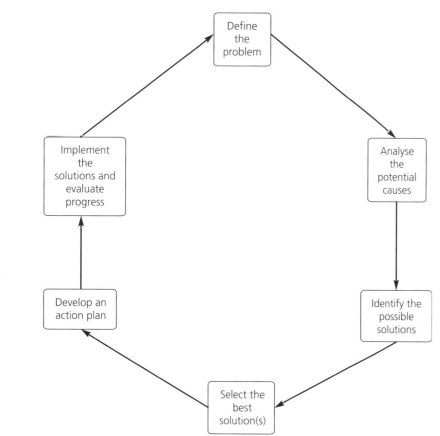

As an example, imagine you are asked to deal with a spate of thefts from cars in your area. Car radios have been targeted and the usual means of entry is by smashing a window of the car. Each stage of the model could be as follows.

Define the problem

This might appear deceptively simple—an increase in thefts from motor vehicles. However, beneath this there are a number of questions to consider.

How do we know there has been a significant increase in thefts from cars? Usually a problem of this kind is identified by analysis of reported or recorded crime and often by comparison with previous months or this time last year. (Some crime is known to have seasonal variations which are taken into account when trend spotting. For example, interpersonal crimes such as personal violence tend to peak during the summer months.) However, comparisons month on month, or year on year need careful scrutiny. If last year at this time there were an average of four such crimes but this year there are six is that level of increase a 'problem'? On the other hand if last year there were an average of twenty but this year there are thirty then we have ten more victims and so this increase would appear significant. However, in each case the percentage increase is the same: 50%.

Given that it is a genuine problem, and not random fluctuations, how do we then define it in such a way that we can start the process of analysis? In our case we may say that it is not so much the 'underlying' rate of this type of crime **but the fact that it has suddenly increased** to a much higher level that is the problem. This is not to suggest, however, that there is an 'acceptable' rate of any level. At this stage a useful 'trick' is often used. Rephrase the problem so that it becomes an action, a 'how to' rather than a bald statement of fact. In this case the problem is 'How do we tackle the increase in thefts from cars in this area?'

Analyse the potential causes

Note at this point that pinning the causes on general issues such as unemployment or a breakdown in society is not usually helpful. Instead, we are engaged in a form of hypothesis setting and testing. Bear in mind, however, what we had to say in section 4.13 above about logical fallacies when attempting to derive cause from effect. In our example, there are a number of possible hypotheses, of which the following are just some:

- Existing local criminals have 'graduated' to this crime. But why is this? Is this an example of displacement where, because of police action against another crime problem, criminals have gone for 'softer' targets instead? Or is it as the result of a change of policy of a drug dealer who will now accept goods in lieu of cash for drugs? Tasking a CHIS through your force procedures (see Chapter 12) might help you to establish whether this is the case or not.
- A person has been released from prison and has resumed his usual activity of stealing from cars. The prison release intelligence that your force has access to should help here.
- There has been a change in local circumstances, increasing the 'availability' of cars as the objects of crime. For example, has the temporary closure of a controlled car park meant that car owners are parking in less secure locations?

The situation can be very complex and you may wish to look at the Home Office crime reduction problem-solving website <http://www.crimereduction.gov.uk/learningzone/lz_learning. htm#theory> for some possible approaches to analysing the causes of your particular problem. There is also an abundance of literature on 'Problem Oriented Policing' (POP) which you might find useful. You will find some publications listed below in Bibliography and References.

Identify the possible solutions

It is not likely that there will be a single 'magic bullet' that will solve the problem, but rather a combination of approaches. For example, the CHIS might provide information about who is involved and why which we could follow up by using surveillance (but see Chapter 12 and section 11.9 on the RIPA 2000). We could also consider 'target hardening' where we take, or encourage action, to make breaking into cars less attractive—for example, by increasing awareness amongst drivers, by introducing CCTV, by increasing the number of police patrols, and so on. Finally, your policing partners will be important in terms of identifying possible solutions (you might well have been working from the outset with other CDRP agencies).

Select the best solution(s)

When identifying possible solutions from the list drawn up in the previous stage we will need to take into account a number of factors. These include:

- How effective the solution is likely to be. Do not confuse effectiveness with efficiency. Our proposed solution may be very efficient but hardly effective at all.
- The practicalities of the solution. You may have found the perfect solution, but if it costs too much in time or money then it is not going to happen and particularly so if the problem is not one of the policing priorities for your BCU (see section 5.9).
- The wider impact of the solution. This needs to be thought through, particularly in terms of police and community relations.
- The possibilities of displacement. You have solved your problem but only to discover that, at least in part, it manifests itself in another way or in another place.
- How long the problem is likely to stay 'cured'. It is easy to condemn police managers who seem obsessed by short-term solutions that will have an impact on next month's crime figures or that will produce an answer for the BCU commander at the next public meeting. However, long-term solutions are difficult to identify and in most cases out of the reach of individuals or even governments.

However, the best solutions are not always the most obvious or 'dramatic' (in the sense of making arrests). For example, in our case it might be that we concentrate at least in part on the other end of the problem, namely the drug dealer accepting radios in lieu of cash. There is a limit to the number of car radios he could use in his own vehicle and also a limit to the number of 'friends' that he can sell on to. The vulnerability here is his fencing of the car radios. If we can put pressure on car boot sales, second hand retailers, and pubs and clubs then this pressure will be transferred down the chain, via the dealer, to the 'supplier', in this case those undertaking the thefts.

Develop an action plan

The solution or solutions can usefully be divided up into more manageable tasks. Think about using the SMART approach to developing the action plan (see the glossary in Chapter 1). List also those other individuals and agencies that we need to be involved in implementing the action plan.

Implement the solutions and evaluate progress

Evaluating progress is sometimes methodologically difficult. Whereas in academic research we can establish 'control groups' and the like to measure the changes, you have no such luxury.

TASK 4

We list possible problems below the task.

The 'Gold, Silver, Bronze' system has come under critical scrutiny in recent years. We mentioned the Soham murders earlier in the section. In his subsequent report into the investigation of the murders, Sir Ronnie Flanagan made the following observation:

> Ironically, the overlaying of the Gold, Silver and Bronze command structure on this operation contributed to a lack of clarity of command of the incident, particularly in relation to the role of the SIO and was subject to comment in the internal review (Flanagan, 2004, p 13).

The report also contained a recommendation that the system when applied to homicide be clarified.

TASK 5

We provide some suggestions in the paragraphs that follow the task.

Although it is beyond the scope of this Handbook (and not something that you are likely to encounter unless you become an SIO) you might like to research the CATCHEM (Central Analytical Homicide and Expertise Management) database. Research conducted on child murder with a sexual motive revealed complex mathematical relationships between places of abduction, and aspects of the offender. This is described in Aitken et al (1995). One inferential model the authors describe suggests that, in the case of a boy victim, aged 0–ten who had been abducted, there are high probabilities that the offender lives within five miles of the contact point (75% chance) and is aged twenty-one + (77%).

The pioneering work of Aitken et al continues to be developed and extended by, amongst others, the Serious Crime Analysis Section of NCOF.

TASK 6

We discuss appropriate responses later.

We were not exaggerating when we discussed the extent of media interest earlier. In the case of the Watford train crash in 1996, Hertfordshire police reported that media interest in the incident commenced within five minutes of the crash happening (Moses, 1997).

TASK 7

Suggested answers are given in the remainder of the section.

We mentioned the CATCHEM database in our earlier response to Task 5. The research used has now been applied to the more general crime of homicide (Francis et al, 2004).

For example, if the victim is aged eighteen–twenty-four, male, ethnically of Asian background, unemployed, and 'stabbed in a rage' then the model predicts that the offender is over twenty-one (68% likelihood), also Asian (55%), and an acquaintance of the victim (60%).

TASK 8

You might like to look back at section 11.18 for an in-depth description of the CAP and other means of protecting the scene.

TASK 9

(a) You should remember from the discussion earlier that you are **not** there to identify what type of device it is. Your role is to contain the scene, evacuate anyone within the cordon and manage the site until help arrives. You should be communicating to the force control centre all that you see and learn, including location of the device and its description.
(b) Think about secondary devices. Think about containment and the ICICLE principles.

Further advice from the UK Government concerning CBRN and 'aimed at those responsible for the safety of others in businesses and other public/private sector organisations' may be found at <http://www.mi5.gov.uk/output/Page46.html>.

TASK 10

ACPO guidance can be found at <http://www.acpo.police.uk/asp/policies/Data/missing_persons_2005_24x02x05.pdf>.

TASK 11

The majority of investigative bodies in the UK use the simple format described here, namely AB/1. Your force might operate a different system, particularly in the light of the development of exhibit-tracking databases. The reason many people sanction a large jump in exhibit numbers when they return to an inquiry is to prevent confusion. You can never understand how serious this confusion might be until it happens to you!

When exhibiting drugs, in particular, this issue becomes even more difficult. If you search premises and find a box containing ten wraps of drugs, bear in mind that the wraps may be 'sub-exhibited' at a later stage—even on your behalf and without your knowledge. Thus the box may be AB/1, the wraps AB/1A to AB/1J and the contents of the wraps could become AB/1A/1 or similar. Imagine the confusion later. One system to prevent this is to exhibit the box as AB/1, then the wraps as AB/2 and so on. This at least reduces the future problem. Seek advice and follow your local force policy in this respect.

TASK 12

In all these instances you could **lawfully** have taken the evidence. If you elected not to do so the evidence would quite possibly be lost.

It is acceptable, in an emergency and when a CSI or medical assistance is not available, for anyone to take a sample from a victim in a case such as this. Clearly, the dignity and psychological well-being of the victim must be uppermost in your mind, but there are occasions when decisive action will benefit the investigation. Crucially, you would have to have the right sterile equipment for the task and you would preferably have received prior training.

Many police forces have evidence kits at the front counter for just these unlikely situations. Out on Supervised or Independent Patrol these kits may not be available and you may have to 'make do', but remember: immediate actions like these can be required at any time.

TASK 13

1. Common Approach Paths sound simple but raise many problems, not least of which is where to put them. Essentially, they should be on a hard surface and should not be the likely route that the offender or victim took to, or from, the crime scene. The next issue is: how can you mark them out on a windy day without anything to secure the tape? You cannot really do this until assistance arrives. Ask your CSI what happened at their last few incidents. They will probably be able to explain that, with hindsight, the FAO could have employed better tactics.
2. Fingerprints are assumed to be unique, but there is disagreement over this issue since it is difficult to actually **prove** this point in a scientific sense. Our DNA is unique, too, but many people feel more comfortable with DNA because it has been the subject of much recent research. The best evidence, ultimately, only occurs where the context for it is right, thus on one occasion DNA can be of no use, whilst the next day it is very powerful.
   If speed is the best measurement, then fingerprints win since the turnaround for a fingerprint in an emergency can be a few hours, at most, from any point in the UK by using Livescan or digital transmission techniques. The best that DNA can manage is around twelve hours. To improve this, DNA can now be analysed at the crime scene in a special vehicle and the results can be up-linked to the FSS by BT communications systems.
3. If your CSI **knows** contamination has occurred he/she can warn the scientist and, occasionally, there may be a way to overcome the problem. If there is a **suspicion** or **accusation** that it has occurred then there may be no resolution, particularly if the Crown is 'ambushed' in court. By ensuring rigorous standards at the scene (or elsewhere) and by admitting we have made a mistake the prosecution might be able to rebut these accusations. The most important point is that we never allow contamination to occur, but if it does we inform the CSI or scientist immediately.

TASK 14

Answers are as follows.

1. Edmond Locard.
2. Fibres, glass, paint, soil, pollen, fibres, etc.
3. Tool marks, shoe marks, impressions from stamps and dyes, extrusion marks, finger marks, clothing, gloves, etc.

4. Blood, semen, ear wax, mucus, saliva, etc.
5. A possible list:
   - Describing the modus operandi (MO).
   - Answering investigative questions.
   - To establish that an offence has occurred.
   - To identify an offender or suspect.
   - To corroborate or refute witness statements.
   - To establish a physical link between suspect, crime scene, and victim.
   - To identify an individual.
   - To further inform an enquiry.
6. That which identifies an unknown, eg a person.
7. Yes. There is nothing to stop you asking for a sample in an emergency (and assisting in its collection). However, respect the human rights of the individual concerned and matters of common decency.
8. Six pieces from the frame (around the hole) and mark the inside or outside of each.
9. Destroy the entire kit.
10. Code D.
11. Mt DNA comes from the female line, ie from your mother.
12. Compare the result to the text.
13. Nylon. Nylon bags are crinkly: remember 'Nylon is Noisy'.
14. When a person is decapitated.
15. See the glossary in Chapter 1. Forensic Science Service or the Forensic Science Society (sometimes FSSoc).

14 | Developing as a Police Officer

14.1   Chapter Briefing

You will naturally be concerned at the outset of training with the successful completion of your two-year probationary period. However, towards the end of your training (or in some forces, in the second year of training) you may be asked to consider the possibility of undertaking a specialist role within your force. Even if this is not the case, you may well be thinking of the prospects for promotion. This chapter will be of value to you when you begin to consider your career development within the police service.

14.1.1   Aim of the Chapter

The aim of this chapter is to assist you in your future development within the police service.

This chapter will enable you to:

- understand the variety of policing roles open to you after Confirmation;
- appreciate the need to maintain and, where appropriate, further develop your skills;
- understand the process of promotion within the police and the new roles and responsibilities you will be asked to adopt if you are promoted;
- develop the underpinning knowledge required for an NOS Unit and a CAR of your SOLAP and future entries in your PDP.

14.1.2   National Occupational Standards

This chapter will provide you with the knowledge required to demonstrate aspects of the NOS Unit AE1 to 'maintain and develop your own knowledge, skills and competence'.

14.1.3 IPLDP Phases and Modules

This chapter will provide you with resources to support some aspects of the Induction Modules IND 3 'Develop one's own knowledge and practice' and IND 4 'Develop effective relationships with colleagues'.

The relevant IPLDP Phase is Phase 4 (Independent Patrol).

14.1.4 The SOLAP and the PDP

The contents of this chapter are relevant to the 'knowledge' evidence requirements of CAR 4C1. After you are Confirmed your SOLAP is likely to be succeeded by a PDP as part of the PDR process. If this is the case, then you might find some of the material in this chapter useful in terms of personal development planning for the future.

14.1.5 IPLDP Learning Requirement

This chapter is relevant to the following sections of the IPLDP Learning Requirement: 2.5, 2.6, 4.2, and 4.8.

14.2 Introduction

This chapter is about you: your aptitudes and preferences and where you want to go in the police. There is no point in our being prescriptive, because we cannot determine what you want to do, or whether you will achieve your ambitions. You may want to be a chief constable/commissioner of the Metropolitan Police Service, or you may want to be a specialist in computer crime. You might want to work with police dogs for the rest of your career or command a BCU. Only you can decide. You know that you will need certain skills and competences for each role, as we have noted throughout this Handbook. You may also need some luck: being in the right place at the right time and taking advantage of the opportunity offered.

> **TASK 1**
>
> As a first step towards considering the rest of your time in the police service, write down where you want to be in three years', five years', and ten years' time.

These timings are deliberate. Within three years of completing your probation, you could be a sergeant or you could be a specialist constable. Within a further two years, you could be an inspector or overseeing the work of a specialist unit. After ten years, you could be a superintendent, commanding a BCU or heading a major investigation, a highly specialized officer such as a source handler or a tactical adviser to a firearms incident commander; you could be in another career entirely, having left policing. As we will see in the remainder of this chapter, the possibilities are numerous: there are at least twenty-five separate roles you could perform as a constable, at least nine as a sergeant and at least ten as an inspector. The options narrow as you move up the promotion ladder, but at the same time you increase your breadth—of experience, of command, of determining tactics, of playing a part in managing policing, and of developing the staff who work for you.

It may be that what initially attracted you to policing is not what you end up doing at all. This is because, as you study and learn more about the police, you find that there are other jobs which attract you and about which you knew very little when you joined. A survey in 2004 of newly-joined probationers in an English police force suggested that most male recruits wanted to be responsible for patrol cars and most female recruits wanted to undertake foot patrol in town centres. They were surveyed again after six to eight months; by which time the gender difference had become blurred. Most officers, irrespective of gender, now wanted to work in crime investigation or uniformed patrol and only a few wanted to join Traffic for roads policing. Many were attracted by community policing and some had already decided that Public Order was what they wanted to be involved with. The point is that choices were now clearer to them and they were now making informed decisions about where they wanted to go and what they wanted to specialize in. Even that choice is not irrevocable: there are many opportunities to change work streams as you progress, and we shall look at some of them later on.

Of course, your choices are often guided by your tutors and more experienced officers. They can show you what a specialist or generalist choice entails, and it may be that you have been influenced by their enthusiasm for what they do. Equally, a cynical, disengaged, or uninterested instructor can put you off a particular job for a long time, if not for ever. Just remember those people who influenced you at school and in higher education: there can be positive or negative influences at work, as in any area of your life.

This is not entirely about your choice alone. You are now a crown servant, a sworn officer, and the force to which you belong may determine (at least in the immediate term) the broad parameters of what you do. Your force would probably argue that this is because there is a balance to be struck between its needs and yours (organizational or individual). If your police force is short of foot patrol officers, or there is an urgent need for people to staff a crime desk, you may find yourself being nudged (sometimes none too gently) in a particular direction. That is a fact of life: the decisions about your posting are taken with the needs of the whole force in mind, and your preferences may come second. However, if you have a strong desire, say, to become a detective, it will not be long before opportunities arise and, in time, the force will be likely to accede to your wishes when its own needs have been met. This may sound somewhat provisional. You have a career plan, but it is being pushed to one side, perhaps to answer an expedient need for uniformed responses in a BCU, which may not be your first choice. What kind of career planning is that? However, you know that some policing is reactive (for example public order, murder investigations, a spate of violent robberies) and the police response cannot always be predetermined or governed by the early availability of intelligence. Sometimes, especially in a public order situation, the usual response is to put bodies in uniform on the street. Unless there is a serious and continuing crisis, your deployment in response to a particular situation will be short-lived. It is important then, that you do not lose focus on what it is that you actually want to do. Facilitating your career moves is the shared role of your supervisor and the force's HR team, but the major part is yours to play. And bear in mind that you will not be very popular if you change your mind too frequently or do not make a proper attempt at a job which you find uncongenial at first.

Let us suppose that you work for a well-resourced, forward-thinking, and lively police force and you have enjoyed every task set for you during your training as a student police officer; you have done well, have obtained good assessments, and your personal development portfolio is bulging with development opportunities and positive experiences. Your probation is over; you are Confirmed, there are no foreseeable staffing crises, and you have been told that you can choose where you go next. What do you do now?

14.3   Generalist or Specialist?

One of the first decisions will be whether to specialize or generalize. You should refer to the Integrated Competency Framework for the constable role at this point, and remind yourself what is involved in reaching the required standard for the generic role. We discussed this in Chapter 6, and you will find the ICF at section 6.3 and again at 6.5.

You will have noted that you should have the 'core responsibilities' competences to complete the administration procedures associated with the role and that you maintain the standards of professional practice, you work as part of a team, you can provide first aid when required, and you comply with Health and Safety legislation. You make the best use of technology (both in IT and telephony) and you promote equality, diversity, and human rights in all your working practices, as well as being part of an organizational response which recognizes the needs of all communities. You employ an effective problem-solving approach to all community issues in which you become involved and you make good use of intelligence to support the policing objectives of your force.

In addition, you will have attained the **behavioural competences** as follows:

- respect for race and diversity   A
- team working   C
- community and customer focus   C
- effective communication   B
- problem-solving   C
- personal responsibility   B
- resilience   A

(You will remember that these grades represent **levels of difficulty** or sophistication in your achievement of the necessary competence. There could be a higher requirement of you in some roles as a constable than there are for sergeants or inspectors in those competences.)

Thus equipped, you should be ready to take on any general task as a constable and to serve anywhere in the force where you are needed. For some people that is enough and they are perfectly happy refining these competences and behaviours, building experience, and interacting with the public on a daily basis. There is absolutely nothing wrong with wanting to be really good at the core basics of the job, and some officers will never want to move away from this generic role for their entire careers. That said, we doubt if any force will let an officer remain in this position without encouragement, at the very least, to pass on the knowledge he/she has accumulated to new recruits. Over time, those performing the general role of constable may be asked to become tutor constables (called assessor constables in some forces) or work in a local Professional Development Unit (PDU). And this makes sense, because it is important that the knowledge and experience gained from doing the job of a constable is passed on to others.

In some police forces, it is assumed that the generic role of constable means that the postholder can go anywhere and do anything. Whilst it would be welcome to have a constable who is able to take on a wide spread of tasks and responsibilities, it is perhaps wasteful to assume that the same individual can meet *any* challenge, no matter how specialist or demanding. An example may be in posting a constable to perform a role in Finance or in Human Resource Management, a practice not unknown in the past.

TASK 2

Can you say what the pitfalls and problems might be in such a practice?

You may have noted that many jobs in Finance or in HR are actually highly complex and require specialist skills and training. Without an accounting qualification, for example, an individual may make damaging errors in budget setting or out-turns or any of the complex processes involved in properly-audited financial transactions. Similarly, whilst it is possible for a non-specialist to try drawing up contracts, establish grievance procedures, or terminate someone's employment, the legal consequences could be serious if they get it wrong. At worst, a well-meaning but amateur interpretation of employment law could cost the force a significant sum if it subsequently loses an employment tribunal.

What such forces are subscribing to in allowing those without specialist qualifications to undertake specialist 'non policing' roles, is the 'myth of omnicompetence'. This refers to the prevalent (but probably waning) belief that a generalist can do anything. It is true that a generalist can try, but it is highly likely that the result will be a muddle or a mess. It is not fair on the individual and often sets him/her up to fail. After all, such forces would not allow an officer to carry firearms unless properly trained, or to investigate a 'Cat A' murder without the right qualifications and experience, so why should using police officers generally to fill specialist 'civilian' or non-sworn posts be any different?

At the same time, we have to be aware of the tendency to over-specialize. This carries to an extreme the idea that you need complete experts in every field and no one can be a generalist in modern times.

> **TASK 3**
>
> Can you think of other competences which 'amateur' people can acquire where performance does not have to be at a high level to be effective?

Your list might include driving skills (though these can always be improved and extended), or the ability to research through the internet, liaison skills in partnership working, or the use of technical equipment such as CCTV or handheld filming (for example, at demonstrations), or diversity awareness (another core competency), or keyboard skills or team-working, and so on.

What we are arguing here is that there is a tension between the generalist and the specialist, but that neither has the monopoly on effectiveness. One simple rule of thumb is that specialist knowledge can be acquired by the generalist, but the process often turns the generalist into a specialist. Alternatively, where highly specialized knowledge is required, and the post is not a sworn one (in other words, it does not have to be filled only by a police officer), the best solution often is to employ a member of the support staff whose specialist skill it is.

14.4 Specialization

Suppose that you wish to specialize whilst a constable.

> **TASK 4**
>
> Write down the range of jobs and roles which you think are on offer. Try to be as specific as you can.

Essentially there are three areas of policing: Investigation (which includes specialist intelligence), Patrol Policing, and Community Policing. You will have been exposed to the work of all these major divisions of policing during your initial training and, if you have been particularly astute, you will have noted the names of those who trained you, or presented their work to you, so that you can make follow-up enquiries about what interests you. We now examine each of the three areas in turn, beginning with Investigation.

14.4.1 Investigation

A decision to follow the **investigative route** does not mean that you are closing off the other avenues for ever. It is quite common to move in and out of roles and across the streams of central police work, but as a rule you will stay within the detective branch or department if you specialize. In many forces, the route to becoming a skilled investigator, whilst by no means limited to CID, is through service on an investigation team based locally in a BCU. In some forces, this is called a 'tactical criminal investigation department' or TAC CID. Your first sustained course of learning will be when you are enrolled for the Professionalising the Investigative Process (PIP) level 2 programme, in which you will study and practise to become an accredited (and later an advanced) investigator. Some police forces introduce the PIP level 2 programme during initial training itself, so that student police officers emerge with a level 2 PIP qualification as they enter mainstream policing, after two years. Level 1 PIP is linked with the IPLDP and the NOS units for initial policing and so you automatically achieve level 1 if you successfully complete your initial training. You will learn interviewing techniques, investigation methods and models, law, case files, major and serious crime procedures, and put your skills into practice in the investigation of crimes of all types, ranging from petty theft to 'Cat C' murders. You can find out more about the level 2 PIP programme by visiting the website <http://www.deliveringchange.org>.

Should you stay with this kind of work, you may move to internal force departments such as a central unit investigating level 2 serious crime, or you may join a specialist homicide team, investigating 'Cat A' and 'Cat B' murders, manslaughter, or GBH. In time, you could seek transfer to the Serious Organised Crime Agency (SOCA) and work on level 3 crime nationally (as we noted in Chapters 12 and 13). As a specialist (or even as a generic) detective, you will have promotion streams within the 'crime group' to detective sergeant, detective inspector, and so on. Few forces now require you to come out of the investigative stream to secure promotion.

14.4.2   Patrol Policing

If you decide that **Patrol** is your preferred interest, there are plenty of roles to take, from Traffic to Tactical Operations, from Firearms to Public Order. In this type of work, yours is the face and figure most seen by the public, and you will be at the forefront of visible uniformed policing. As we have seen with investigation, you will still have much training in prospect and a systematic development route to specialize within Patrol. Currently though, there are few training programmes which deliver advanced qualifications in Patrol, but a number of police forces are researching and designing possible ways to do this, some in conjunction with Skills for Justice and the NPIA. One of the things you should consider, before opting to go into the Patrol stream, is what opportunities there are for you to obtain further qualifications, and to find out whether there is a partnership programme with academic institutions. If Patrol is a 'default option' in your force, in which there is little evident development and no deliberate or systematic learning processes, you might want to think twice before committing yourself. If, on the other hand, your force is pursuing such partnerships, links, and development opportunities, you will find that Patrol is far from a backwater and may be the most vibrant and innovative part of your force. It very much depends on your local circumstances.

There is no doubt that Patrol can be an immensely satisfying part of policing: you will often be the first officer attending a crime scene (with all the responsibilities we outlined in Chapter 13, in terms of the 'golden hour' and your vital role in the preservation of life and the preservation of evidence), and you will have a major part to play in policing demonstrations, large gatherings, public events, and disorder. Your contact with the public will be an integral part of the reassurance agenda and you will be foremost in the policing of volume crime and public disorder. That said, it is also the most physically demanding of all police roles, and you will also be in the forefront of dealing with violence, collisions, tragedies, and human disaster. The dynamic risk assessments for many of the roles in Patrol will be crucial to the safety of you, your colleagues, and the public, and you should not underestimate the strains and stresses of front-line police work, particularly in the role of firearms officer.

14.4.3   Community Policing

Community policing is different again. Here, you will work with smaller teams, and often bridge the space between Patrol and Investigation. You will learn new skills and your development will probably be geared to specializing in one of a number of roles. For example, you may opt to work as a **Community Liaison Officer** (CLO), in which case you will begin to know the leaders and members of groups within your local community and you will help to develop sophisticated partnership working arrangements to meet community needs. Diversity skills will be to the forefront, as will the accumulation of intelligence on crime in the community. You will often be the first port of call from your detective colleagues when investigating crime within your area, and your advice will be needed, and usually respected and acted upon, especially when there are local sensitivities, such as minority ethnic communities or the investigation of a homophobic crime.

A **Family Liaison Officer** role is also specialist and of key importance within community policing. You will be trained in negotiation, mediation, and some group management techniques so that your work with families (usually the victims or witnesses of crime) is as productive, reassuring, and positive as possible. You will be the focus for the family in the wake of a crime, especially a crime of violence, and will help them through the difficulties of the search for the offender, arrest, and charge, and you will support the family through the subsequent court proceedings. In a very real sense, you will be the 'face of policing' to that family, and often it will be you who helps them provide vital evidence. An FLO played a leading part, for example, in obtaining evidence in the Lyn and Megan Russell murders in Kent in 1996. This was a particularly disturbing crime, in which Mrs Russell and her daughter Megan were attacked with a hammer or similar instrument and beaten to death. Another daughter, Josie, was attacked and badly injured, but not killed. In the investigation which followed, the skills of the FLO in gaining Josie's trust and confidence were integral to the successful prosecution of Michael Stone for the murders.

Working closely with the community is, for many officers, what policing is about and where its greatest rewards are. This is not to say that the work is easy, and to gain the community's trust and respect means working long hours, having highly developed personal skills, and understanding how community dynamics and partnerships work. The development of neighbourhood teams based on BCUs, in which there may be a mix of police officers, PCSOs, Special Constables and members of other agencies, is a pointer to the importance of local, citizen-focussed, engagement. Should you opt for a community policing role, you may well find yourself in time supervising the work of others, and/or managing a neighbourhood policing team. Many officers find this a deeply satisfying activity and are reluctant to leave it. Other work, such as crime reduction, schools' liaison and working with crime reduction partnerships, in areas like youth offending, also have considerable rewards for persistence, professionalism, and receptivity; but some of the results in reducing crime are long-term. What communities appear to dislike is the frequent change of police personnel, when it takes time to build relationships. If you opt for community policing, you need to be aware that it is often for the long haul.

14.5 Maintaining and Developing Your Skills

It is important that, in whichever of the 'strands' of policing you choose to follow, you continue the practices which you learned during your time as a student police officer. This principally means that you sustain your competencies and add to them through the accumulation of experience, and that you continue to update your **professional development portfolio** (**PDP**, also known as 'personal development programme' and a variety of other names). The PDP is not only considered by some to be good practice (it encourages you to reflect on what you are doing and to think about what you have learned) but you will also need your PDP to give evidence of your competencies and experience when you seek promotion. If your ambition is to become a sergeant in the shortest permissible time, two years from the end of your Confirmation, you will need to evidence your exceptional capabilities to perform at the next rank. Part of that evidence will be in your PDP and part in the tasks you have undertaken and excelled at. Whenever possible you should talk to those already holding the substantive rank and find out what they do and why. You will also need to look at the competences and role requirements of the generic sergeant role and any specialist functions which a supervisor performs. If you can, you should seek opportunities to 'act up' in the rank, perhaps by supervising a patrol of constables on occasions, or by seeking temporary promotion whenever it is offered. It is helpful here to understand a difference here in terminology: **acting rank** means that you do it for a short time on a probably casual basis. **Temporary rank** means that you perform the role of that rank for a period of at least three months, and you receive the pay of that rank.

It is not a requirement in the police service, as it is in the Armed Forces, to spend some time in the acting rank before being eligible for consideration for promotion. However, the opportunity for people to act up in the rank above is often a good opportunity for them to show that they can do the next job; it accretes experience in the role and gives the opportunity for assessors to make judgements on a person's actual performance rather than simply on potential.

Whether you seek promotion early or not, you have an obligation to sustain your **continuous professional development** (CPD). The nature of this CPD varies from force to force; in some it means gaining the necessary experience and qualification through training (such as in Firearms Teams to gain authorization as a Firearms Officer); in others it can mean pursuing further study which links your professional development with an academic partner, resulting in a further academic award. Examples range from a two-year occupation-based Foundation Degree, or vocational qualifications such as an NVQ or SNVQ, or a modern apprenticeship through to a higher award such as a BSc (Hons) in Policing or a Master's degree. Some forces do all of these, and this breadth is strongly encouraged by Skills for Justice which seeks to develop the skills and capabilities you will need as you progress in policing (laterally or vertically). Your force is likely to have a number of academic partners through whom further professional study may be pursued. If not, there are plenty of institutions which advertise their courses or programmes in publications such as *Police Review*, or through the NPIA's period bulletins.

Note that you will probably need permission to engage in further study, since the force has to balance your CPD with the demands of your current job and it will tend to look with disfavour on something which may add up to twenty-five hours to your working week unless it can be justified in both organizational terms (it helps the police through your increased professionalism) and individual aspiration. You may find a marked reluctance to let you study the function of the comma in late eighteenth-century literature by research thesis. Also, of course, if your agreed further study is directly related to your policing function, the chances are that the force will pay the tuition and allied fees and allow you some duty time to study. But always check first. Many police officers take a short break between ending initial training and embarking on further study for qualifications, because they feel they need to consolidate, through experience, what they have learned. This is probably good practice, and helps to prevent you from becoming a perpetual taker of courses or perceived by others as a 'study programme addict', as well as reinforcing your learning. This prescription cannot apply to all, of course, and some people thrive on the accumulation of knowledge, in which case it would be inappropriate to hold them back artificially.

14.6 Promotion

Let us return to your possible ambition to become a sergeant.

> **TASK 5**
>
> Do you know the formal qualification for being a sergeant or inspector? Write down what you know about the examination route and what is involved.

You should have noted the **OSPRE®** (an acronym for the Objective Structured Performance Related Police Promotion Exam) system which, currently at least, is the official and nationally recognized route to eligibility for promotion to sergeant and inspector. OSPRE®, a registered trade name owned by the **Employers' Organisation**, is the title for examinations conducted under the auspices of the Police Promotion Examinations Board. It is most unlikely at the moment that any police officer will obtain substantive promotion to sergeant without having passed both Part 1 and Part 2 of the sergeants' qualifying OSPRE® examination. The same applies to promotion from sergeant to inspector. However, passing both parts of the examination at either level is still no guarantee of promotion. Some forces will not have vacancies at the respective ranks, others may require you to go through a formal interview process as well, in which case the PDP plays a vital part in evidencing your fitness to take the rank above.

Each OSPRE® examination is in two parts, as we have noted above, and it is worth spending a few moments looking at what each part of the examination entails.

Until 2004, the pass requirement was a **norm-referenced** figure. This meant that there was a set percentage of those taking the examination who could pass. It was then changed to an **absolute standard**, which means that however many candidates reach the pass-mark, all will be deemed to have passed rather than simply a proportion of them. Some consider this fairer, as it does not penalize those who reach the standard but cannot proceed because of the limits built into norm-referencing. The pass marks are currently 55% for Part I and 45% for Part II of the sergeants' OSPRE and 65% and 45% respectively for the inspectors' OSPRE.

Part I of the **OSPRE**® **examination** takes the form of a multiple choice paper for both sergeants and inspectors. The time allowed is three hours and there are 150 questions. The syllabus is divided into four categories:

* Crime
* Evidence and Procedure
* Road Policing
* General Police Duties

The syllabus is cross-referenced to the **Blackstone's Police Manuals** and includes **topics** such as:

* Criminal conduct
* Homicide
* Misuse of drugs
* Offences against the person
* Sexual offences
* Theft
* Criminal damage
* The courts
* Summons and warrants
* Police bail
* Youth justice
* Evidence
* Police station procedure (including custody)
* Driving offences
* Drink-driving
* Insurance
* Fixed penalties
* Police legislation
* Human rights and policing powers
* Community safety (including anti-social behaviour)
* Public disorder and terrorism
* Firearms
* Civil disputes
* Discrimination and equality

Part 2 for both sergeants and inspectors is based on the **behavioural competences** in the **Integrated Competency Framework** (with which you are already familiar), each assessed at different levels according to rank. However, only seven of the twelve are specifically examined in Part 2 for sergeants and eight for inspectors. As you can see in the table below, some are common competencies, others relate to the role:

ICF behavioural competences

Generic behavioural competency	Sergeant	Inspector
Community and customer focus	level B	level B
Effective communication	level B	level B
Maximizing potential	level B	level B
Personal responsibility	—	level A
Planning and organizing	level C	level B
Problem-solving	level B	level B
Resilience	level A	—
Respect for race and diversity	level A	level A
Strategic perspective	—	level C

You will understand that there are different thresholds of competency at sergeant rank and at inspector rank, as well as different expectations of attainment. However, if you want to gain promotion within the police, you have to start here. In OSPRE® Part II, the examination is based around performance and response to a series of scenarios which test the behavioural competences at each level.

It is important to note that, as with many professional qualifications, there are some issues over the extent to which the OSPRE® coursework and examinations, train and assess officers in terms of the knowledge and skills applicable to the work required and demonstrate that candidates are ready for the practicalities of their profession. Recently, the OSPRE® system has been the subject of some debate (for example, in the pages of *Police Review*) and some forces have been piloting the substitution of a localized assessment (probably based on a portfolio of evidence), to replace Part II. However, so far OSPRE® has continued to be preferred to any of the proposed alternatives. This all underlines the need for you to sustain the process you began in your initial training of:

- recording experiences and learning;
- reflecting on the learning;
- evidencing your competences;
- keeping detailed notes on the variety of policing experiences which you encounter;
- showing how your skills have developed;
- and ensuring that entries are continually made in your PDP.

It will serve you well when you come to be considered for the next rank. You can read the preparation notes, commentaries, and tests which are published regularly for all the OSPRE®-type examinations in *Police Review*.

14.7   Interviews for Promotion

It would be appropriate here to think briefly about the recurrent feature of nearly all selection processes in the promotion stakes: the **interview**. Whilst there are plenty of critics of the interview system, especially of its subjectivity and the often ritualized formality of the process, nothing more substantial or satisfactory has yet been devised which can reproduce the impression which an individual can give when questioned. There are species of commercially-available **psychometric tests**, which seek to assess you and your responses to a number of more or less complex case studies; there are **verbal and numerical reasoning tests** which try to establish how good (or not) you are at understanding words and figures; and there are batteries of tests of both Intelligence Quotient and Emotional Intelligence (IQ and EI respectively) which are claimed to measure your capacity for reason or your capacity for empathy. It may be traditionalist, elitist, and even discriminatory, but the interview process is more popular—and more trusted—within the police force (post initial selection) than most of these alternative tests of ability.

TASK 6

Your turn: what constitutes a good interview performance by the candidate for promotion?

You may have referred to the importance of creating a good first impression; being smart, well turned out, formal without being 'stand-offish', attentive and eager without being unctuous. You may have gone on to talk about being well-prepared, anticipating some of the obvious questions which a panel will ask, carefully marshalling the evidence of your competencies and your track-record and thinking about how you will convey how utterly suitable you are to go to the next rank. You might have listed listening skills, brief but cogent answers, and the need to impress the panel with your competence. You may have warned against seeming to be arrogant when you want to convey confidence, seeming to be disorganized when you want to appear calm, and seeming to be thrown by a question for which you had not prepared an answer. Indeed, nearly every self help book on interview techniques seems to concentrate on what you should **not** do rather than on what you should.

However, there are some tips, based on experience, which can make the difference between success and failure at an interview.

14.7.1 What Does the Interview Panel Want to Know?

The interview panel often wants to know:

- Can you do the job or a substantial percentage of it?
- Are you willing to put in the effort to make the job or role a success?
- Are you manageable?

You need to be able to assure the members of the panel that you meet most of the competences required. You can do this by demonstrating:

- detailed examples of past performance (ensure they are relevant);
- how you solved a problem and what steps you took to do so;
- evidence how you meet the competencies for the next rank (and showing that you know and understand those competencies well);
- that you have the potential to go beyond the formal requirements;
- that you are eager to learn (no one expects you to be perfect);
- that you have good related qualifications or professional knowledge or training.

14.7.2 'Body Language' and the Interview

The first impression you give as you walk in the door could be the most lasting. Perhaps we should not be influenced by a person's body language but undoubtedly at least some of us are. We should also perhaps be aware of cultural differences that may lead to a misunderstanding of body language. This is a complex subject, and here we offer some simple advice concerning the unintentional 'negatives' and the intended 'positives' of body language.

14.7.2.1 Unintentional negatives

- frowning, grimacing, sniffing, biting or chewing your lips: these can all be read by others as symptoms of unease, discomfiture, or puzzlement (the opposite of the impression you want to give);
- folded arms (seen by some as a defensive posture);
- tapping your fingers or drumming with a pen (viewed by some people as a sign of nervousness or impatience);
- nodding too much (perhaps impatience and an over-eagerness to speak);
- putting hands behind your head (suggests to some arrogance or over-assuredness).

14.7.2.2 Intended positives

- firm handshake (pump twice or three times, no more);
- eye contact (do not stare unblinkingly but be aware of cultural differences);
- smile frequently, but not 'mechanically';
- take a moment for thought, but try not to break eye-contact with at least one of the panel;
- tilt your head slightly to one side when you respond to questions (this suggests to some that you are thinking and listening);
- adopt an upright, alert posture (but not stiff, otherwise you suggest rigor mortis);
- mirror all positive body language across the table (in other words, watch the body language of the panel members and **subtly** reflect it back to them).

You should be aware of your body language and a tendency to 'leak' information which you would rather conceal, such as nervousness or apprehension. An interview is often a nerve-racking process but if you are aware of your leakage, you can control some of it most of the time. As an exercise, try a short mock interview with a friend or colleague, getting the second person to note your body language and feed the results of the observation back to you. You will be surprised how much escaped your consciousness.

14.7.3   Questions and Answers

Always listen carefully to the question and then answer it. This sounds obvious, but many candidates fail promotion interviews by giving the answer which they have prepared rather than answering the question which has been asked. **Your answers should be brief, thorough, and to the point**. Do not waffle or start on long pointless anecdotes. Try to keep your thread. Limit yourself to about two or three points in each answer. The panel will ask follow-up questions if they are interested in what you have to say, so do not try to say everything at once.

Further, consider illustrating your points with examples (members of an interview panel are likely to find concrete examples easier to follow than abstract descriptions). Beware of using too much specialist jargon. Most of the panel will understand you, but you cannot guarantee that. The police service is peculiarly prone to the use of acronyms but they are not all shared or understood. If you begin your reply with 'I saw the IP during the cas.evac and rep'd on the PR what the FME had said, before asking the FCC for an ARV...', you could lose your audience, or worse, look at though you are trying too hard to impress.

Whatever the line of questioning, you must get three basic points across to the promotion panel. These are:

- That you can work unsupervised.
- You can be trusted.
- You are, nonetheless, a team player.

Use your examples and case studies of your achievements to emphasize these points. Throughout your interview, avoid politics and name-dropping: doing so will alienate the panel and make them think that you are perhaps a pretentious and manipulative person.

14.7.3.1   Difficult questions

Every promotion interview panel will pose tough questions to probe your claims of experience, knowledge, or qualifications, and a good interview candidate anticipates as much as possible what these questions will be, and prepares answers for them. Your questioners are looking for drive, initiative, motivation, leadership and communication skills, determination, reliability, and pride in the work. Your answers must demonstrate how you have these attributes. Let us look at some sample questions at police promotion interviews:

- What have you done that shows initiative?
- Have you ever had to deal with an awkward colleague?
- Tell me something you have done that you are not very proud of.
- What part of being a sergeant do you think is most crucial?
- What would you do if your patrol encountered a fight outside a pub and one of your officers was injured?
- How do you react to criticism?
- What orders would you give if one of your patrol crews reports a multiple vehicle traffic accident?
- How would you respond to a complaint about one of your constables?
- What would you do if you heard one of your officers make a sexist comment?

After listening carefully to the question, you can help yourself by reflecting back to the questioner some of the question structure (it also helps you to focus your answer), such as:

> I respond to criticism by treating it as a learning experience, and so I make sure that I take what is said on board and use it to modify my actions.

Another tack is to put a positive spin on the question (especially if it asks you to be self-critical), perhaps by saying:

> We all do things sometimes which we're not proud of. The important thing is to understand why you reacted that way and treat it as an experience which will guide you in the future. I remember one occasion when I did not intervene to challenge a colleague who said women were not physically up to front-line policing. What I should have said was. . . .

Another form of questioning is what is called **quick fire**. The panel members ask you questions in a short, brisk fashion. Your answers should reflect the tempo and practical nature of the question. An exchange might run like this:

Q. *How long does it take you to do an appraisal?*
A. In short, about three hours, depending on the difficulty I'm dealing with.

Q. *One of your officers is always ringing in sick. What do you do about it?*
A. Visit the person, find out what's wrong and use the positive attendance management process. I'm not medically qualified, so I'd rely on expert opinion.

Q. *What three things must you think about at a crime scene?*
A. Communicate, preserve life, preserve evidence.

Q. *You're just finishing a long shift and a report comes in about a suspected rape. You could go to the scene, but it's going home time.*
Do you leave it to the incoming sergeant?
A. No, my duty says I must attend, but having done all I can to secure the scene and set up the support mechanisms for the victim, I'll choose the right moment to go off duty.

Hammered at you relentlessly over fifteen or twenty minutes, this kind of questioning can be a nervous and exhausting experience for you. The interviewers are testing your response to stress and decision-making, but they are also probing for signs of weakness. Had you agreed that you would just go home when your shift finished, the chances are that you would have not been promoted this time around, especially since you are expected to show enthusiasm and professionalism in the next rank. Although the questions are short and your answers equally brief, you should expect a battery of follow-up questions: 'Why do you say that? How would you do this? What if the relief sergeant didn't show up? What if the sick officer tells you that her illness is chronic and comes under the auspices of the Disability Discrimination Act? What would you do next? What if your appraisal is challenged? How would you react to one of your officers taking out a grievance against you?'

14.7.4   Success and Failure

If you pass the OSPRE® tests, if your portfolio of evidence is comprehensive and well-presented, and if you perform well at the interview process, you may still not get through to secure that promotion. (If you do, of course congratulate yourself and move on.) If you have failed to get through on this occasion, always think of it as a temporary setback. Nearly all promotion panels will feed back to you on your performance, so this should be seen as an opportunity to get it right next time. For example, the panel might say that you lack experience or exposure to crime prevention techniques, or you have not had an operational role on a BCU since probation, or that you need some more work on demonstrating leadership skills. Take these points on board and do something about them, and as soon as possible. The reason to hurry is that you need to act before the opportunity to improve goes out of your head or is replaced by the day-to-day business of your job. Also, in larger forces, the promotion boards may sit as often as twice a year, which gives you about four months to remedy your shortfalls before you are applying for the next board. Time may be of the essence. Also of course, you will be showing how positively you respond to constructive criticism and how effectively you have moved to put remedies in place. These will be plus points on the next round.

When you receive your feedback, remember to ask questions, such as:

• What other areas for improvement should I think about?

- What did I not evidence well?
- What should I have done to make you select me for promotion to sergeant?

Some forces operate a mentoring scheme. If you can secure the services of a **mentor** (usually a senior officer), you can run your interview performance past him/her and ask for some objective advice. Mentors will **not** coach you, but will indicate courses of action which you are free to accept or reject.

As you move up the promotion ladder in your own force (or if you move, on promotion, to another force), it might be worth seeking a mentor elsewhere. That is, try to obtain a mentor within the police service, but not in any force you have served in or are serving in. Sometimes an internal mentor is not always able to work outside his/her own force priorities in advising or counselling you.

If your performance shortfall can be remedied by some **training** (for example, to bring your knowledge of first aid up to speed, or to refresh your knowledge of procedures in a custody suite), make sure that you consult your local training officer or talk to your force training team(s). They may be able to point you in the direction of good self-tutoring packages, e-learning, or information resource. There may even be a training programme which you could sit in on and refresh your skills. (If this means time away from your primary tasks, make sure you have agreement to absent yourself.)

Begin preparation for the next promotion board process as soon as you can. Get a friend or colleague to look through your portfolio for you, picking out examples of how you meet the competences for the next rank. They may spot things you missed. Consult existing holders of the rank and find out what kinds of experience are persuasive for the promotion board. Submit your new application in good time, with refreshed text and evidence, concentrating especially on those areas where the promotion board had seen a shortfall last time. Remember 'the Five Ps': **prior preparation prevents poor performance** (or vulgar variants on this advice) and the better you are prepared, the more confident and assured your performance at the next board will be. Do not give up. Sooner or later you will make it to the next rank; if not in this force, then in that one, always assuming you have the skills and behaviours required for the job.

14.7.5 Other Opportunities

Structures exist to 'fast-track' officers with the potential for early promotion and there are nationally-accepted learning programmes which are designed to develop officers for upward movement.

TASK 7

Do you know what they are?

You might refer to the **High Potential Development Scheme** (HPDS) which is designed to accelerate the development of officers from quite early in their police careers. Typically, an officer who applies for, and is accepted upon, HPDS is expected to undertake a demanding programme of study and research, culminating in a higher education Master's degree. HPDS students are encouraged to think critically about the police service and their own roles within it, and to reflect upon the societal, demographic, and political changes which impact upon policing. A review of HPDS in 2006–2007 has resulted in fewer people having the opportunity to enter the scheme, and endorsement by the Force of your enrolment is now a must.

Additionally, there are development programmes run by NPIA for the police in which leadership is emphasized. These are:

- **CLDP: the core leadership and development programme** (mostly for inspectors in early promotion to leadership roles).
- **SLDP: senior police leadership programme** (mostly for chief inspectors and superintendents in their first command roles).

- **SCC: strategic command course** (mostly for superintendents and chief superintendents who are judged to have the potential to become chief officers).

Other sponsored development programmes can be used for police officers, such as **Common Purpose, Young NODE**, the **Royal College of Defence Studies (RCDS)**, and the **Windsor Leadership Trust**. Attendants on such programmes also, typically, include ambitious civil and public servants, members of the armed forces, and 'high fliers' from the private sector. Such development opportunities are being added to all the time, and the best advice we can give to the aspirant to early command is to familiarize yourself with what is on offer, either through your own force resource centres or through the Bramshill Police Staff College in Hampshire. Be warned though: standards are very high on these flagship programmes, and you will need to be able to demonstrate exceptional potential to be considered.

14.8 Roles and Responsibilities of Ranks Above Constable

We consider in this section the roles and requirements for the ranks above constable. This is not to prescribe your route to promotion, but rather to suggest to you that each step up in the police service brings new challenges and new opportunities. You should be aware of what they are before you start your bid for promotion.

14.8.1 Becoming a Sergeant

The sergeant rank is the first management rank in the police, though it is often described as supervisory rather than management. Formally, a sergeant is expected to supervise the work of those in his/her team, to deal with any people management issues, and to appraise performance.

These are the **core responsibilities** of the generic rank of sergeant:

14.8.1.1 Personal responsibilities

As a sergeant you will be expected to:

- Complete administration procedures.
- Maintain standards of professional practice.
- Make best use of technology.
- Promote equality, diversity, and human rights in working practices.
- Work as part of a team.

14.8.1.2 Managing and developing people

You will be expected to:

- Carry out performance reviews.
- Delegate work to others.
- Develop individuals and teams to enhance performance.
- Supervise the work of teams and individuals.
- Address disciplinary and unsatisfactory performance procedures.
- Deal with grievances.
- Manage the welfare needs of individuals.
- Supervise Health and Safety.
- Provide first aid.

14.8.1.3 Intelligence

In terms of intelligence, you will need to:

- Conduct 'intelligence-driven' briefing, tasking, and debriefing.
- Use intelligence to support policing objectives.

The **behavioural competencies** we have looked at already in our consideration of the OSPRE® examinations, but you might usefully look back at those now to refresh your memory.

699

Much of what **others** do makes up the sergeant's supervisory portfolio. This can be especially difficult if a person moves from being part of a team to becoming its leader. The nature of friendships can change, and camaraderie can be lost if the one-time team player and friend is suddenly the boss. It is actually considered good practice in many police forces to move a newly-promoted sergeant to another section or even to another BCU to ensure that such difficulties are avoided. The sergeant is expected to be objective and rigorous in assessment, which is easier to do with a team of people with whom you have not socialized in the recent past.

Most forces have a programme of training and learning for the newly promoted sergeant, to cover matters such as enhancing team performance, tasking, briefing and debriefing, administration and supervision, as well as an introduction to management. Sometimes, these learning programmes are integrated with the duties and responsibilities of the custody officer (since this is often the first uniformed role which promoted sergeants take on; not unrelated to the fact that custody is currently unpopular as a sergeant's role).

It is worth looking at one or two of the core responsibilities and spelling out what is involved in a little more detail. The two areas we shall examine are **delegation** and **the development of others**.

First though, try the following task.

Delegation is an activity which some find painful. It means passing some of your work downwards to let others complete it for you. Some people cannot delegate at all (and as a consequence, can sometimes make poor leaders). There are several emotional activities taking place at the same time, and it is worth unpicking some of them.

The first component of delegation is **trust**: you trust your staff (under supervision) to deliver what you want. By pushing some of your work tasks downwards, you spread the load and give members of the team a chance to deliver against performance. At the same time, you are signalling to the team that you trust them, indeed, rely on them, to deliver.

However, the second component is that you have to assign some measure of **responsibility** to the individual or small team, to whom you have delegated. Perhaps one of the worst actions you can do is delegate and then not give autonomy in how the work is delivered. This can be compounded by over-intrusive supervision. No one likes to feel that they have been entrusted with a job or part of a job, only to have you breathing down their necks at every opportunity and saying do this, do that. Remember that delegation entails trust. That may mean letting people make mistakes and then your stepping in to help them remedy what went wrong. Treat each error as an opportunity for learning rather than blame. This is not just management speak: people learn from doing, and will learn the more willingly if they are not given criticism every time they get a small or trivial part wrong. You should be aware that many employees in the police service believe that large parts of the service are still rooted in a 'blame culture', which means that people learn negatively rather than positively. It is a bit like saying 'This is what I **don't** want you to do' rather than saying 'This is what I want you to do'.

That is not to say that you should condone serious mistakes when you are a supervisor, or excuse people who make mistakes through inadvertence or ineptitude. Ensure that your initial explanation is clear and your instructions precise. Make it plain to the team or individual that what you are doing is trusting them to deliver on the task because you think they are ready to take on the responsibility and you are confident that they will deliver. Watch what happens but only interfere if it really is going badly wrong.

The logical extension of **staff development** is that you will lose the staff. Accept this at the outset, and give yourself a timetable by which the development can be achieved, and then you will not be surprised when the individual outgrows what you can give him/her. Remember how it happened to you? Did your tutor constable or your trainer let you grow in the role of a police officer, encouraging and giving you opportunities? Or did your supervisor criticize your efforts and predict that you will never come to anything? The first is an empowering, positive developer of staff, the second is somebody who is unable to accept that people change and develop.

TASK 10

What is different about the job of a detective sergeant (DS)? Write down some job-specific activities which a DS would have and which would not necessarily be common to, say, a patrol sergeant or a sergeant in a custody officer role.

A detective sergeant has responsibility for ensuring that investigations are effective and professional and that all work in support of a criminal investigation is properly carried out. There may be some overlaps with other sergeants' roles, particularly in managing police operations, though with the investigative stream, operations are more likely to be covert than not. The same roles for delegating work, managing staff, and dealing with the problems and rewards of human resource management are common threads, given a particular spin by the detective role.

Unlike a uniformed sergeant, whose teams generally work specific shifts, time at work is more loosely defined in investigation, and one DS role which is implicit is in managing the workload of the detective teams, especially on a major enquiry where the desire to do a good job can result in significant overtime payments (not popular with senior management because of cost) or breaches of the Working Time regulations (not popular with senior management because it breaks the law).

We have dipped into parts of the police sergeant's role and commented on various aspects of the job. It is important to emphasize that these are well-known elements of a range of managerial or command roles, and are just as important for an inspector, chief inspector, superintendent, or chief officer (and their support staff counterparts) as they are for sergeants. This brings us to consider an inspector's role.

14.8.2 Becoming an Inspector

We noted above the change which results from promotion from constable to sergeant.

TASK 11

What do you think will be the changes involved in promotion from sergeant to inspector? Try to be specific.

Inspector is the first command rank and the first role to carry the designation 'senior officer'. It is the rank for which payment of overtime ceases, and it is assumed that you maintain this role out of professional pride as well as for the financial reward—a rather scant comfort when your sergeants and constables can earn more than you do while putting in the same or fewer hours. Police pay and the differences in salary are outside the scope of this Handbook, even though they will of course matter to you. If you have reached the rank of inspector, whether as a detective or as an operations officer in uniform, it is assumed that you have the capability to have a tactical overview of policing operations, that you can handle the responsibility of a wide range of police work—anything from writing tactical appreciations to handling a major series of investigations. Let us begin by looking at the generic role requirements and post profiles for an inspector.

Some aspects of overseeing and supervision are extensions of the sorts of work which sergeants do. New generic 'core responsibilities' include the ability to implement plans for change, participate in meetings, supervise the work of teams and individuals, and monitor and evaluate PDRs. For the first time, there is a responsibility for operating budgets (and thereby a financial accountability for public funds) and there are two new behaviours—'strategic perspective', where the individual inspector will be expected to attain a 'C' grading, and 'personal responsibility', where an 'A' grading is expected. A level of public and personal accountability, both for team and for individual performance, now goes with the rank of inspector. There is a higher public profile through attending meetings, and a greater measure of managerial responsibility through the overseeing of the PDR work of the inspector's sergeants. As we noted earlier, while the focus and variety of work decreases with rank, the responsibilities increase and the remit to deliver widens. If we take all this as implicit in the role of inspector, what sorts of jobs do you think an inspector might do?

If you looked at the Integrated Competency Framework roles, you will have noted that inspectors could expect to serve as:

- bronze or ORC (see13.3.3) commander (firearms incidents and other crises);
- community inspector;
- detective inspector;
- DI (Special Branch);
- operations inspector;
- patrol inspector;
- Senior Investigating Officer (SIO);
- Unit Executive Officer;
- Negotiator (though this is often additional work to the 'day job' and is usually unpaid);
- Area Intelligence Officer.

There are a number of variations on these within different police forces, but in general terms, these are the kinds of activities that you could expect to be doing if you were promoted to inspector.

As you can see, the remit for the role has widened considerably, and you are now expected to have responsibility for, and deliver a core part of, the policing business. For example, as a detective, you might now head a high profile investigation, or series of investigations within your BCU, or you might have trained to become a Senior Investigating Officer (SIO) for major investigations such as a Cat A or Cat B homicide or series of rapes. In Patrol, you might be responsible for a whole geographical area of the BCU, or for the effective deployment of traffic patrol vehicles on your force's strategic road network. In Special Branch, you might be tasked with the threat assessment of, and consequent security measures to protect, some important person living in your force area, such as a politician or member of the Royal Family. As an operations inspector, you could be dealing with the deployment of resources to contain a public order situation, or you might be co-ordinating the actions of officers to police inner-city unrest.

The variety is wide, and the responsibility which falls on you, the inspector, is heavy. You will no longer be operating day-to-day on the 'front line', yet the safety of quite large numbers of police officers, not to mention the safety of the public at large, is now in your hands. You are perhaps one or two steps removed from direct policing operations on the ground, but in place of that practical hands-on element comes public accountability. The inspector role is sometimes called 'up, down and sideways' because of the number of people to whom and for whom an inspector is responsible.

> **TASK 12**
>
> What do you think are the crucial parts of the SIO role?

You could have referred to the context of the crime investigation and the sorts of crime which require a SIO to take the lead. It is sometimes 'serious and organized' when a SIO is involved, but in practice, it is really the major crimes such as homicide (including manslaughter) and series rape. The SIO is the pivotal figure in the investigation, managing everything from family liaison to progress reviews, from house-to-house enquiries to the following-up of all leads, as well as the interviewing of witnesses, victims, and suspects. This is not a job that every detective could do, even with the requisite training and experience, because there are certain personal qualities such as resilience, detachment, objectivity, and persistence which make a good SIO. Some of these must be to some extent inherent within the individual, rather than acquired.

In small forces, SIOs are often detective inspectors; in larger or metropolitan forces, the SIOs are usually detective chief inspectors and, rarely, detective superintendents. (This will become even rarer since the National Centre for Policing Excellence (now part of NPIA), now 'owns' SIO training and licensing on behalf of the police service. An SIO 'licence' will be given only to those officers who habitually or usually investigate major crime as part of their remits.)

> **TASK 13**
>
> Whatever the rank, the salient characteristics of the role will be the same. Can you make a list of what these characteristics might be?

You might have replied with some or all of the following:

- managing family liaison;
- managing the initial responses to a major investigation;
- managing the ongoing investigation;
- facilitating closure of the investigation;
- maintaining effective relationships with the media;
- obtaining and managing the use of finance and resources;
- representing the police at partnership meetings and meetings with other agencies;
- adopting a problem-solving approach to community issues.

These are the core elements of being an SIO, though there are other competencies with which you are familiar, as they stem from the generic role. You will see that the competencies for the SIO are tightly organized around the management and progress of an investigation. Forces invest a good deal (of time, of money, or selection, of training) in producing and sustaining their SIOs, and they do not do it lightly.

> **TASK 14**
>
> What reasons are there for a force to make such a substantial investment in SIOs?

Your answer probably focussed on what an SIO is for. Forces are judged as effective, efficient, and professional on the basis of how quickly and competently a murderer or rapist is caught and brought to justice. Nothing is as certain to undermine a force's reputation as a poorly executed investigation into a crime which scares the public.

14.8.3   Becoming a Chief Inspector

Let us now look at the next rank to which our developing police officer aspires, that of chief inspector.

703

It will be obvious that the range of responsibility widens significantly at the chief inspector rank. A chief inspector is more likely to take charge of a major incident, a major event, a major public order event, and a major crime investigation. As we noted, large forces 'default' to chief inspectors as their SIOs, and this is very often the rank you find at the top end of specialist crime knowledge or specialist squads. Typically, chief inspectors will have served more than fifteen years in the police, some as many as twenty-five years. It is a fairly rare person who becomes chief inspector within seven or eight years, but it is not unknown.

The same core responsibilities that we found with inspectors are defined, though there is now a higher level of expectation about attainment. So too, expectations around behaviours are higher, even though the behaviours themselves are given somewhat low scores; this is mostly to do with the greater range of duties which operate at chief inspector rank. You should be aware that there is no national examination for chief inspector (or superintendent and chief superintendent come to that), though the Government has been consulting about the creation of a qualification for superintendents, especially for those who will command a BCU. Nothing is yet decided, but any outcome is likely to incorporate parts of the Leadership programme for senior officers. Currently, most forces rely on a complex interview and portfolio process in which candidates for promotion must evidence their fitness to perform at the next rank. That said, there is no consistency across England and Wales when it comes to the promotion of inspectors to chief inspectors, or beyond, and it is very much left to individual forces to decide whom they want in key senior roles. The framework for such national standards is implicit in the national occupational standards and in the integrated competency framework, but at the time of writing, no progress has been made in creating a core national assessment standard for chief inspectors. Let us glance at the core responsibilities briefly and then at the behaviours.

A chief inspector should be able to chair meetings, manage organizational change, maintain standards of professional practice, delegate work to others, and manage the performance of teams and individuals. In addition, CIs are expected to monitor and evaluate PDRs, promote equality, diversity, human rights, health and safety as well as manage the welfare needs of others, deal with grievances, and discipline issues or unsatisfactory performance.

Exploitation of intelligence opportunities and the best use of technology and problem-solving approaches are seen as part of the CI's battery of skills, whilst some skills in the management of finance and budgets are measured.

As far as behaviours are concerned, the individual scores have not risen. However, there is such a wide range of required behaviours across such a wide spectrum of activities, that while the levels for leadership, working with others, and achieving results are either 'As' or 'Bs', it is not as easy to reach the standards as might be supposed. In addition, the behaviours have developed towards working in partnership, inter-agency liaison, and a results-driven performance regime. It is clear that the bar has been raised. More is expected of CIs than inspectors, and the criteria for measurement have expanded in parallel with the expectations of the role.

These are the specific roles which a chief inspector will undertake, as opposed to the generic areas we have already examined and itemized:

- Criminal Justice Unit CI;
- detective chief inspector;
- DCI (Special Branch);
- operations chief inspector;
- Silver Commander.

You can see from this list that many specialisms have dropped away. For example, a detective chief inspector may have expertise in fraud investigations, but the average DCI will oversee many other kinds of criminal investigation of which fraud may only be a part. Essential core detective skills, the capability to manage a team, responsibility for a large tranche of policing business, and the delivery of required outcomes are what define (but do not limit) the spread of a chief inspector's range. This is the case whether it entails a complex investigation for a DCI or the command of an emerging situation on the ground as Silver Commander of an incident. You might at this point refresh your memory of the roles of Silver and Gold Commander which we looked at in Chapter 13. An operations chief inspector based on a BCU, for example, may be responsible for all uniformed operations which take place on a day-to-day basis within the BCU's geographical area, whereas a DCI might bear parallel responsibility for all detective-led investigations for the same BCU. Alternatively, the DCI and CI posts may be within specialist groups, based centrally or at Headquarters. It is not unusual for a large force to have 'Heads of Specialist Training' at DCI and CI rank, whilst, as we have seen, SIOs in large forces are almost always at DCI rank. Another role which has emerged in recent years is that of **critical incident chief inspector** (or inspector, in some forces), where a cadre of trained senior officers respond to critical incidents, ranging from searches for missing persons through to the immediate scene-management in the aftermath of terrorist incidents.

14.8.4 Lateral Development

Although we have looked so far at the ways in which a police officer may move upwards, through the ranks, you must not lose sight of the need for lateral development (through the increase in a range of skills or the accretion of valuable experience, allied to qualifications and professional recognition) of police officers within a particular skills set. It is as true of the police service as it is of the other emergency and armed services that recognition tends to come through promotion, but it is equally the case that recognition can come through the acquisition of fundamental skills even though the rank may be lowly. We are acquainted, for example, with a number of detective constables who have PhDs in Criminology and Law, or Masters' degrees in Investigative Science. They would be listened to with as great a respect for their chosen expertise as someone who had mere rank.

It is time now to turn our attention to **command rank**, and look at the ranks which carry autonomous responsibilities for the delivery of very large, strategic parts of policing, in ascending order: **superintendent**, **chief superintendent**, and **chief officer**. This is not because we expect you to get there quickly (though you may) but rather to provide an insight into the experience and qualifications of those who command you. Think of what follows when you next meet your BCU Commander.

14.8.5 Becoming a Superintendent

At one time, there was little distinction between the ranks of superintendent and chief superintendent, even though the roles performed by each rank were carefully distinguished. From 1994 until around 2004, in the wake of reforms to police ranks suggested by Sir William Sheehy, there was no distinction *in rank* between inspector and chief inspector, and between superintendent and chief superintendent. The latter pair was distinguished by the terms 'Range 1' superintendent and 'Range 2' superintendent, but gradually the old rank distinctions returned, as did the distinct rank of deputy chief constable. We shall assume that, even if your force persists with the designations 'Range 1' and 'Range 2' superintendent, there is in essence a difference between the functions of a superintendent and those of a chief superintendent. As a student police officer you are still likely to come across more experienced police officers who lived through the 'Sheehy era'.

As we noted for chief inspectors, appointments to the rank of superintendent and chief superintendent are by examination. Most forces will have a 'gateway' interview process followed by a panel interview (which is likely to include the chief constable), eligibility for which is probably predicated on a portfolio of evidence, itself based on the competencies for the rank. Note that when discussing chief inspector selection, the Government is considering the notion of some kind of formal qualification for the superintendent rank. By the time you are eligible for superintendent, the process may well have become regularized.

> **TASK 16**
>
> In more general terms, what do you think are the essential differences between a chief inspector and a superintendent?

You would almost certainly point to the range of responsibilities and the autonomy of command as being the essential distinctions between the two ranks, but there is often a blurring between the roles of a highly specialist DCI and a generic detective superintendent. However, by the time you reach these ranks, the definitions and role responsibilities might well have changed. You will not want to go to a Handbook to understand the nuances between 'commanding' and 'being in command'. There are changes in core responsibilities as well as in function which we might note, as well as increases in the behavioural scores. So, noting the generic core responsibilities for a chief inspector which we considered above, add the following for a generic superintendent:

- develop and maintain quality assurance systems;
- evaluate and improve organizational performance;
- develop management teams;
- enable the organization to retain personnel from all communities;
- select required personnel.

and in terms of behaviours:

- strategic perspective   **B**
- openness to change   **B**
- community and customer focus   **B**
- problem solving   **B**
- planning and organizing   **B**

You can see from this that the role of superintendent has developed a wider spectrum of responsibility and that there is autonomy of (and therefore individual accountability for) command. A superintendent will run a distinct part of police business, in which he/she will be responsible for the management of senior teams and for meeting targets. When the superintendent is the uniformed commander of a small BCU, the entire performance and efficiency of the BCU is his/her responsibility. Although the tendency amongst larger, amalgamated forces is for a chief superintendent to be the commander of a larger BCU, superintendents are often responsible for a geographically distinct part of that BCU under the chief superintendent's overall command.

For the first time, the role of superintendent entails responsibility for the selection of staff. This does not necessarily imply that a BCU commander or head of squad can cherry-pick his/her staff, but rather that there will be consultation and some degree of negotiation over who is wanted and who can be given up in exchange. This means that the ability to choose appropriate staff in any given set of circumstances is important. Also, a superintendent is expected to innovate, and to think of and implement changes which improve the organization. Most superintendents and chief superintendents are very experienced and nearing the end of their service, so they will know the force well and the individuals within in it very well indeed. Obviously, this can be a harder process for someone who has fast-tracked through the ranks. That said, an acute superintendent, though young in service, would be well aware of who performs well, and who less well, and would be able to bring this judgement to bear in the matter of choosing staff. A superintendent will have a strategic perspective on the force as a whole rather than on one part of it, and will be intensely aware of the pressures to deliver results. For the first time, the superintendent will be fully cognizant of the external political and social pressures which impact on policing, and will be in a position to gather a team in which he/she is confident in the context of those pressures. One of the privileges of command (as well as its fundamental pressure) is that the buck stops with the person who makes the decision. Other core responsibilities concerning people management include performance appraisal, grievances, development, and discipline, as well as the retention of staff. It is not enough to get people into the force;

the command structure must ensure that people are retained, developed, and progressed within the profession.

A word or two about the chief superintendent role before we consider chief officers. Just as the superintendent rank is about command, it might be fair to say that the chief superintendent rank is about co-ordination of commands. Indeed, in some police forces, the rank of chief superintendent is designated as co-ordinator. Sitting directly below chief officers, the chief superintendents in a police force will be the expert practitioners, with enormous experience in a variety of roles, and with a profound understanding of the strengths and limitations of the force. It will be the chief superintendents in a large force to whom chief officers delegate, and with whom they will discuss the management of their portfolios of police work. Unlike their police staff counterparts, most chief superintendents will still do duty at nights and at weekends, usually as duty gold commander, responsible for the deployment of staff to, and effective containment of, an incident, sometimes in co-ordination with other emergency and civil agencies.

14.8.6 Becoming a Chief Officer

Potential chief officers are selected from among the ranks of existing superintendents and chief superintendents, and are invited to take part in a national two-day selection and aptitude process called PNAC: the **Police National Assessment Centre**. Successful candidates are then enrolled on the Centrex (now NPIA)-delivered **Strategic Command Course** (SCC) at the Bramshill Police Staff College in Hampshire; this course involves a modular form of learning which extends over a minimum of six months, during which potential chief officers work in teams to consider the society in which they live and work, strategic leadership, politics, criminology, and a variety of other subjects and themes.

Graduation from the SCC does not guarantee success at the next rank, because there is open competition for each chief officer post and each successive 'graduate year' competes with students from the previous SCCs in chasing the advertised posts for assistant chief constables in England and Wales. (There are some exceptions to this, including posts in Scotland and with the Police Service of Northern Ireland, and within the London Metropolitan Police.) It is pretty rare for an emerging SCC graduate to be offered the first ACC post applied for. Most candidates for ACC posts will go through three or four interviews before obtaining a position within a police force. One of the characteristics of such interviews is that they are held by the local police authority rather than the police service, and candidate have to impress the lay members of the authority that they are the right person for the job. Do not think that this is easy. Being an accomplished police officer does not necessarily prepare you for a buffet lunch with members of a police authority, during which you may be quizzed on everything from fly-tipping to stab-proof vests.

There are essentially three chief officer ranks. In ascending order, they are:

- assistant chief constable (ACC);
- deputy chief constable (DCC);
- chief constable.

(Practice differs in the MPS; their equivalent of ACC is commander, whilst a DCC is a deputy assistant commissioner (DAC), and the equivalent rank to chief constable is assistant commissioner (AC). There are two further ranks in the MPS; deputy commissioner and commissioner. These are the highest police ranks in the country.)

Chief officers belong to the **Association of Chief Police Officers** (ACPO), which itself acts as the voice of the strategic end of the police service. Each chief officer will be expected to take some form of national portfolio, through which that chief officer will contribute to the development of police thinking across a host of issues. Current portfolios range from roads policing to counter-terrorist strategies. The range encompasses all aspects of policing but also includes society's attitude to crime, studies of criminality, law, criminal justice, and social order.

Should you be in the position of an ACPO having to lead on one of these topics (or in a support role to a more senior chief officer), you will be expected to bring together people from different parts of society—not just police officers—to ensure that you have the fullest possible picture. On drugs rehabilitation, for example, you would expect to consult those involved directly in drugs rehabilitation which may involve doctors and other workers in the medical professions, social workers, housing, and the probation service as well as those other agencies and academics playing a prominent role in counter-drugs strategies. As an ACPO officer you would also be expected to speak with authority to the media on your portfolio.

Within your force, you will also have a portfolio, which is likely to be different from the national one. Most forces of substance have between four and six ACCs, who will rotate between the commands of local policing, operations, support services, and investigations. The titles accorded to these divisions of the policing task vary from force to force and we cannot offer definitive descriptions of an individual ACC's portfolio here, except to say that the portfolio will range across the delivery of policing and will require the post-holder to undertake (in consultation with his/her senior staff) strategic planning and delivery of major parts of the police business.

You should be aware that both ACPO as a body and the chief officer structure generally in police forces in England and Wales have been subject to criticism over the last few years.

TASK 17

Have you any ideas what that criticism could be? Try to itemize some elements about which you have heard or read, relating to the top command of the police service.

You might have referred to some or any of the following; for ease of reading, the standard or recurrent criticisms of chief officers and ACPO are in bold and our commentary follows in normal type:

- **The selection process for chief officers merely clones officers in the image of those undertaking the selection. What you then get is a perpetuation of a particular kind of police officer or a particular mind-set.** The PNAC process has been extensively revised in recent years to try to design out such cultural stereotyping, with, it has to be said, only mixed success. There is still an insufficient proportion of female and minority ethnic community officers in ACPO ranks.

- **ACPO ranks are police butterflies. They flit from subject to subject and from portfolio to portfolio, never stopping long enough in one place to experience the consequences of what they have put in place.** There is some truth in what is a widespread mythology about chief officers. They have to be as responsive to major changes as the rest of us, and often have less control over what happens than they would like. ACCs do move from portfolio to portfolio, often with about two years' service in each role. This may not be enough to see through the cycle of change which they may initiate. On the other hand, more than three years in one post tends to limit the marketability of the ACC, either further within the force or elsewhere in the larger police service. It is a fine judgement, and few forces would claim to have it right yet.

- **ACPO has no teeth. As a negotiating body for the senior strategic end of the police service, it should work with the Home Office and the HM Inspector of Constabulary as an equal partner, but is too often supine or passive, and allows itself to be dominated by a vigorous HMIC or Home Secretary.** These are matters of perception which vary according to the portfolio, and the robustness with which the police service approaches any particular issue. In some areas (counter-terrorism, for example) ACPO can be resolute. In others, it can seem weak or vacillating. In one area especially this weakness seems to be evident, that of the measurement of performance. Not all things which the police do are measured, but those which are measured tend to receive disproportionate attention. In a whole raft of subjects, ranging from a lack of distinction between homicide categories to no qualitative measures for serious crimes, ACPO has remained relatively silent.

- **Finally, chief officers are too much like politicians and not enough like police officers. They have forgotten what it is to be like on the front line, or trying desperately to cope with too few resources.** It is probably true of a number of ACPO officers that they thrive on the jockeying for prominence on the national stage, or the internal politics of command, but this is by no means true of the majority. A degree of politicking goes with the job of chief officer, and you cannot hope to do the job properly without negotiating, mediating, persuading, cajoling, and influencing. This is especially true of a chief officer's relationship with his/her police authority, and with the partners and agencies which make up many of the force's strategic alliances. Not to be able to do these things well would be unhelpful to the force.

Where there continues to be ambiguity is in the nature of police leadership, the question of whether policing should be a profession, and whether a chief officer needs to be sworn. There are already some chief officers who are support staff (mostly in specialist areas like HR, Finance, or Information Services), but no appointments to ACPO ranks have yet been made from anyone outside the police service. The Government has been consulting on this for some time and we have yet to see a comprehensive response from ACPO to Home Office proposals to recruit from outside the police force. One important development occurred in April 2007, when a 'civilian' was appointed Chief Constable of the Civil Nuclear Fuel Constabulary. In fact the CNFC is a highly specialized service which does not require its Chief Constable to have been a police officer. However, a precedent may have been set.

Finally, a word about job security at the chief officer level. Remember that the appointments are made by the police authority, and some ambiguity exists in that sworn officers (who are Crown servants) are also employees of the Police Authority, within whose remit is extension or cessation of contract. It is most unusual for chief constables to be appointed for a single term exceeding five years. Additionally, the Home Secretary has taken powers to dismiss chief constables who fail to meet the standards expected of them. It is not usually possible to make it to the top within the same force. The HMIC and the Home Office encourage chief officers to move forces at the DCC level or, if DCC rank is reached in one force, the rank of chief constable must be sought in another force.

This chapter has been about how you could develop as a police officer, whether by increased lateral specialization in a role or by a programme of promotion until you reach chief officer rank. Such a course will usually take you a minimum of thirteen years and perhaps as long as twenty-five, so be prepared for the long haul if you want to get to the very top.

However, there are one or two further areas to consider before we move on.

> **TASK 18**
> Try to answer this question: Am I prepared to serve in the police for the next thirty to thirty-five years?

If you replied 'yes', you may well be in a minority. Many studies of attitudes to, and expectations of, work, suggest that people no longer expect or want a long career within one kind of organization. The single major exception is medicine, but all other professions report that young people come to them for periods of five to ten years and then move on to something new. The evidence suggests that people may spend some time accumulating capital in a private enterprise role and then move into the caring professions or public service of some kind, before, in a third or fourth phase, concentrating on developing in creative or artistic ways. This means that career paths are interruptible, and that breaks may be built in by the individual. The pensions problems which have characterized the early years of the new century also may impact on what young people want from their careers.

What this means for the police service is that individuals may be content with up to ten years' service and no more. They will leave variously at the rank of constable, sergeant, or up to superintendent (if fast-tracked), with a number of marketable skills. What then happens to the longer-term posts at the top end of the organization, and to those specialist posts such as computer crime? The Government appears to be arguing that such posts could be filled from outside the police service, an argument which is supported by the longitudinal studies of work preferences. We may begin to see people entering the police service at the rank of chief inspector or above.

What may happen instead is a qualifications route to chief inspector or superintendent, which looks for evidence that the competences for the role are met, and where other areas of experience can be regarded as valid. For example, in the matter of leadership, you might find that someone who has served in the armed forces meets the general competency requirement and requires only some on the job training to meet the police specific competences. Alternatively, someone who has held a financial shares portfolio in the city, or who has held a post as a senior teacher may equally be able to show the general competencies.

There is, though, a second element which modifies all this: the matter of demography. This is the study of population profiles with special reference to age. The whole of Europe is ageing, and the trend appears to be worldwide. The first point is that, in the developed world, people are living longer. Better health, fitness, nutrition, lifestyles, and so on, have raised the expectation of life by some six years for men and ten years for women. People are having children later in life than they used to, and we are having fewer children. What this produces over a generation or two is an inverted triangle in the demography: more and more older people supported by an ever smaller workforce.

In Poland, for example, the percentage of the population which will be aged sixty-five or over by 2025 is nearly 22%. In Britain in 2025, there will be three people of working age for every person aged sixty-five or over, compared with four to one at present. This country will certainly top the quarter of the population which is greying by 2025 (Duncan, 2005). Since the working population is largely responsible for the health or otherwise of pension schemes—especially as currently practised in the police service—an ageing population may constitute an unfair burden on the few left to work. The alternative is one which the Government is considering at the time of writing, to extend the retirement age. If the population as a whole is living longer, it may be that a longer period may be spent in productive work, and thus the old style retirement ages of sixty for women and sixty-five for men may no longer be appropriate.

This may also have an impact on the police service. Most constables and sergeants retire after thirty years' service, or aged fifty-five, whichever comes first (though they can opt for annual renewal of service or take part in the 'thirty plus' scheme), while inspectors and higher ranks usually have to retire by sixty years old. (Note that the arrangements for the police pension scheme, and the duration of the job to thirty-five years, changed after 5 April 2006 and this may affect you.) If the population as a whole works longer, this may mean that the current thirty year rule (thirty-five for those joining after 5 April 2006) will disappear and officers may be able to work until sixty-five or seventy. If so, what health implications are there in staying on longer? Can a sixty-year-old constable chase and apprehend a young criminal with the same persistence as his/her younger counterparts? Is it fair to ask the officer to do this? Does it mean that latter-end careers for police officers will be spent in so-called 'safe' activities? If so, what are the implications for the achievement of targets and measures? Alternatively, will there be a fitness and general health requirement to be satisfied if police officers wish to remain on active service? Who will draw it up and monitor it? How will this affect the short-term portfolio emerging in the younger generation? Might there simply not be enough people in the future to resource the police service? Might we have to turn to initiatives centred on the roles of community support officers and wardens to make up the shortfall in police officers? Where does that leave the trained police officer? What effect will this have on the Criminal Justice System?

All we can be certain of is that the future of policing is not certain. There are going to be complicated demographic issues, affecting types of crime as well as types of policing. Recruitment of police officers is going to have to be more imaginative and innovative than it is at present. The police service will be fishing in an increasingly diminishing pool of talent, and will have to offer something out of the ordinary to attract even the minimum number of young people into policing, whilst competing with those employers who can offer more money and better prospects. There is an argument that policing itself must become a profession, but there is as yet no consensus on how this change may be brought about, though Skills for Justice has taken the initiative.

14.9 Answers to Tasks

TASK 1

No doubt you wrote down your own aspirations. However, were they rank specific ('I want to be a sergeant') or were they role specific ('I want to be a detective')?

TASKS 2 & 3

We discuss possible answers to these tasks in the paragraphs that follow the task.

You would not be alone in speculating about the 'tension' in policing between moves towards generalization (the PCSO) and other moves towards specialization (the PIP Level 3 SIO). In a wide-ranging article, the distinguished academic Professor Tim Newburn offered the following predictions about policing in the UK:

- greater emphasis on professional training, including continuous professional development;
- a progressive shift away from the notion of omni-competence toward specialization;
- significant changes to the nature of recruitment to the police service, including multi-point entry;
- changes to the rank structure, including the introduction of advanced practitioners;
- increasing use of non-sworn specialists;
- further expansion in the numbers of non-sworn personnel with limited powers;
- much greater emphasis on the citizen or consumer;
- restructuring of the police organization at both national and local levels.

(Newburn, 2005)

You might be interested in looking back at this list in a year or two.

TASK 4

You should have a list which exceeds ten roles. The list which follows is not exhaustive (some forces have roles which other forces do not), but it gives you an idea of the spread of roles available to you:

- authorized firearms officer
- community constable
- crime reduction/architectural liaison
- dog handler
- intelligence (research and development)
- intelligence: source handler
- roads policing
- schools involvement
- search specialist
- family liaison officer (SLO)
- community liaison officer (CLO)
- crime desk
- detective (fraud, computer crime, serious crime, major crime, tactical CID, special branch)
- leading a neighbourhood team (see 14.3.3)
- tactical adviser (firearms, public order, etc)
- tutor constable
- youth offending team
- air operations
- trainer/teaching staff
- tactical operations and public order

- patrol
- wildlife and the environment.

TASK 5

We provide a detailed answer immediately after the task. Be aware that the whole system for promotion is under review. This is particularly the case in terms of promotion from constable to sergeant. You may like to read the Police Federation article 'OSPRE® needs to adapt or die' available at <http://www.polfed.org/0304promotion-and-selection.pdf>. Some of the Federation's recommendations have been implemented since the article was written (Munro, 2004).

TASK 6

Some suggestions are provided immediately after the task. There are also numerous books and websites with both general advice about interviews, and particular advice concerning police promotion.

TASK 7

We list and describe some of the schemes available.

TASK 8

You might have noted the fact that the sergeant has responsibility for team performance as a whole as well as for the individuals within that team. The sergeant will be held responsible for any shortcomings in performance, and accountable for the team's collective and individual achievements or mistakes. Additionally, the sergeant now assesses individual performance and reports on it (Appraisal or Performance Development Review, PDR), and is expected to develop the staff who make up the team, deal with grievances, and sort out unsatisfactory performance.

TASK 9

We discuss these topics in the text that follows. In 2004, a Home Office report suggested that the majority of police officers who left policing did so citing poor management as the reason. You can read a media report here: <http://news.bbc.co.uk/1/hi/uk/3691821.stm>.

TASK 10

You would obviously concentrate on supervising investigation and detection. A DS would have to have the competences of the generic sergeant role, but would additionally:

- allocate investigative work to a detective team or individual;
- manage scene preservation;
- monitor and evaluate the quality of investigations;
- plan and manage searches;
- recruit covert human intelligence sources (CHIS, see Chapter 12);
- monitor and evaluate interview processes;
- plan, manage, and evaluate police operations.

TASK 11

We discuss this later.

You were probably taken by surprise with the comment about pay. On 1 September 2005, a sergeant on point 4 (the highest point) would be paid £35,991 per annum. An inspector on promotion is paid £41,034. (Both figures are for outside London). However, sergeants are paid additional sums at 'time plus a third' for overtime which can easily close the gap.

TASK 12 & 13

We discuss these tasks in the paragraphs that follow the task.

The qualities of the SIO might mean something different. In 2000, Smith and Flanagan published a report which analysed the qualities of the SIO and identified three particularly important areas:

- investigative ability: this includes the skills associated with the assimilation and assessment of incoming information into an enquiry and the process by which lines of enquiry are generated and prioritized;
- knowledge levels: this relates to the different types of underpinning knowledge an SIO should possess;
- management skills: this refers to the different types of management skills an SIO should possess. They encompass a broad range of skill types that were further sub-divided into people management, general management, and investigative management.

(Smith and Flanagan, 2000)

The report is now a little out of date perhaps, especially with the advent of PIP Levels 2 and 3, but is still worth reading. It is available at <http://www.homeoffice.gov.uk/rds/prgpdfs/fprs122.pdf>.

TASK 14

How much does it cost to train an SIO? This is actually a more interesting question than it seems. We do not know very clearly how much it costs to train you. One estimate put the cost of training a pre-IPLDP student police officer at about £27,000 up to independent patrol (evidence submitted to the Morris Inquiry, 2004), less than half-way through training.

TASK 15 & 16

See the possible responses that follow the tasks.

All this discussion concerning the demands of progressing through the ranks may have begun to depress you by now, so it is time for a digression into history.

A little known experiment in policing in the US in the 1970s, which became known as 'team policing', involved the elimination of the existing rank distinctions between patrol and detectives altogether. It also involved all police officers working out of uniforms:

> The new, non-traditional uniform consisted of a forest green sport coat blazer worn over black slacks, a white shirt, and a black tie (Johnson, 2005).

The experiments were considered a failure and were abandoned after two to three years. However, team policing possibly laid the foundations for what is now almost the orthodox policing model in the US, that is Community Policing.

TASK 17

We list them below the task. A famous book on chief constables is Reiner (1991). However, you might want to first read Reiner's *The Politics of the Police*, now in its third edition, as a more general introduction to this whole subject.

TASK 18

Surprisingly, the precise current average length of service in the police is not known. In a reply to a parliamentary question in the House of Commons in September 2005 Hazel Blears responded:

> Information on length of service on leaving is collected in groups of years. This means average length of service of a police officer on leaving is not available. (Blears, 2005).

Appendix

Police and Criminal Evidence Act 1984, Code D, Sections 4 to 6

Section 4 Identification by Fingerprinting and Footwear Impressions

(A) Taking fingerprints in connection with a criminal investigation

(a) General

4.1 References to 'fingerprints' means any record, produced by any method, of the skin pattern and other physical characteristics or features of a person's:
(i) fingers; or
(ii) palms.

(b) Action

4.2 A person's fingerprints may be taken in connection with the investigation of an offence only with [his/her] consent or if paragraph 4.3 applies. If the person is at a police station, consent must be in writing.

4.3 PACE, section 61, provides powers to take fingerprints without consent from any person over the age of ten years:
(a) under section 61(3), from a person detained at a police station in consequence of being arrested for a recordable offence, see Note 4A, if [he/she has] not had [his/her] fingerprints taken in the course of the investigation of the offence unless those previously taken fingerprints are not a complete set or some or all of those fingerprints are not of sufficient quality to allow satisfactory analysis, comparison or matching.
(b) under section 61(4), from a person detained at a police station who has been charged with a recordable offence, see Note 4A, or informed [he/she] will be reported for such an offence if [he/she has] not had [his/her] fingerprints taken in the course of the investigation of the offence unless those previously taken fingerprints are not a complete set or some or all of those fingerprints are not of sufficient quality to allow satisfactory analysis, comparison or matching.
(c) under section 61(4A), from a person who has been bailed to appear at a court or police station if the person:
(i) has answered to bail for a person whose fingerprints were taken previously and there are reasonable grounds for believing [he/she is] not the same person; or
(ii) who has answered to bail claims to be a different person from a person whose fingerprints were previously taken;
and in either case, the court or an officer of inspector rank or above, authorises the fingerprints to be taken at the court or police station;
(d) under section 61(6), from a person who has been:
(i) convicted of a recordable offence;
(ii) given a caution in respect of a recordable offence which, at the time of the caution, the person admitted; or
(iii) warned or reprimanded under the Crime and Disorder Act 1998, section 65, for a recordable offence.

4.4 PACE, section 27, provides power to:
(a) require the person as in paragraph 4.3(d) to attend a police station to have [his/her] fingerprints taken if the:
(i) person has not been in police detention for the offence and has not had [his/her] fingerprints taken in the course of the investigation of that offence; or
(ii) fingerprints that were taken from the person in the course of the investigation of that offence, do not constitute a complete set or some, or all, of the fingerprints are not of sufficient quality to allow satisfactory analysis, comparison or matching; and

(b) arrest, without warrant, a person who fails to comply with the requirement.

Note: The requirement must be made within one month of the date the person is convicted, cautioned, warned or reprimanded and the person must be given a period of at least 7 days within which to attend. This 7 day period need not fall during the month allowed for making the requirement.

4.5 A person's fingerprints may be taken, as above, electronically.

4.6 Reasonable force may be used, if necessary, to take a person's fingerprints without [his/her] consent under the powers as in paragraphs 4.3 and 4.4.

4.7 Before any fingerprints are taken with, or without, consent as above, the person must be informed:

(a) of the reason [his/her] fingerprints are to be taken;

(b) of the grounds on which the relevant authority has been given if the power mentioned in paragraph 4.3(c) applies;

(c) that [his/her] fingerprints may be retained and may be subject of a speculative search against other fingerprints, see Note 4B, unless destruction of the fingerprints is required in accordance with Annex F, Part (a); and

(d) that if [his/her] fingerprints are required to be destroyed, they may witness their destruction as provided for in Annex F, Part (a).

(c) Documentation

4.8 A record must be made as soon as possible, of the reason for taking a person's fingerprints without consent. If force is used, a record shall be made of the circumstances and those present.

4.9 A record shall be made when a person has been informed under the terms of paragraph 4.7(c), of the possibility that [his/her] fingerprints may be subject of a speculative search.

(B) Taking fingerprints in connection with immigration enquiries

Action

4.10 A person's fingerprints may be taken for the purposes of Immigration Service enquiries in accordance with powers and procedures other than under PACE and for which the Immigration Service (not the police) are responsible, only with the person's consent in writing or if paragraph 4.11 applies.

4.11 Powers to take fingerprints for these purposes without consent are given to police and immigration officers under the:

(a) Immigration Act 1971, Schedule 2, paragraph 18(2), when it is reasonably necessary for the purposes of identifying a person detained under the Immigration Act 1971, Schedule 2, paragraph 16 (Detention of person liable to examination or removal);

(b) Immigration and Asylum Act 1999, section 141(7)(a), from a person who fails to produce, on arrival, a valid passport with a photograph or some other document satisfactorily establishing [his/her] identity and nationality if an immigration officer does not consider the person has a reasonable excuse for the failure;

(c) Immigration and Asylum Act 1999, section 141(7)(b), from a person who has been refused entry to the UK but has been temporarily admitted if an immigration officer reasonably suspects the person might break a condition imposed on [him/her] relating to residence or reporting to a police or immigration officer, and [his/her] decision is confirmed by a chief immigration officer;

(d) Immigration and Asylum Act 1999, section 141(7)(c), when directions are given to remove a person:
- as an illegal entrant,
- liable to removal under the Immigration and Asylum Act 1999, section 10,
- who is the subject of a deportation order from the UK;

(e) Immigration and Asylum Act 1999, section 141(7)(d), from a person arrested under UK immigration laws under the Immigration Act 1971, Schedule 2, paragraph 17;

(f) Immigration and Asylum Act 1999, section 141(7)(e), from a person who has made a claim:
- for asylum
- under Article 3 of the European Convention on Human Rights; or

(g) Immigration and Asylum Act 1999, section 141(7)(f), from a person who is a dependant of someone who falls into (b) to (f) above.

4.12 The Immigration and Asylum Act 1999, section 142(3), gives police and immigration officers power to arrest, without warrant, a person who fails to comply with a requirement imposed by the Secretary of State to attend a specified place for fingerprinting.

4.13 Before any fingerprints are taken, with or without consent, the person must be informed:

(a) of the reason [his/her] fingerprints are to be taken;

(b) the fingerprints, and all copies of them, will be destroyed in accordance with Annex F, Part B.

4.14 Reasonable force may be used, if necessary, to take a person's fingerprints without [his/her] consent under powers as in paragraph 4.11.

4.15 Paragraphs 4.1 and 4.8 apply.

(C) Taking footwear impressions in connection with a criminal investigation

(a) Action

4.16 Impressions of a person's footwear may be taken in connection with the investigation of an offence only with [his/her] consent or if paragraph 4.17 applies. If the person is at a police station, consent must be in writing.

4.17 PACE, section 61A, provides power for a police officer to take footwear impressions without consent from any person over the age of ten years who is detained at a police station:

(a) in consequence of being arrested for a recordable offence, see Note 4A; or if the detainee has been charged with a recordable offence, or informed [he/she] will be reported for such an offence; and

(b) the detainee has not had an impression of [his/her] footwear taken in the course of the investigation of the offence unless the previously taken impression is not complete or is not of sufficient quality to allow satisfactory analysis, comparison or matching (whether in the case in question or generally).

4.18 Reasonable force may be used, if necessary, to take a footwear impression from a detainee without consent under the power in paragraph 4.17.

4.19 Before any footwear impression is taken with, or without, consent as above, the person must be informed:

(a) of the reason the impression is to be taken;

(b) that the impression may be retained and may be subject of a speculative search against other impressions, see Note 4B, unless destruction of the impression is required in accordance with Annex F, Part (a); and

(c) that if [his/her] footwear impressions are required to be destroyed, [he/she] may witness their destruction as provided for in Annex F, Part (a).

(b) Documentation

4.20 A record must be made as soon as possible, of the reason for taking a person's footwear impressions without consent. If force is used, a record shall be made of the circumstances and those present.

4.21 A record shall be made when a person has been informed under the terms of paragraph 4.19(b), of the possibility that [his/her] footwear impressions may be subject of a speculative search.

Notes for guidance

4A References to 'recordable offences' in this Code relate to those offences for which convictions, cautions, reprimands and warnings may be recorded in national police records. See PACE, section 27(4). The recordable offences current at the time when this Code was prepared, are any offences which carry a sentence of imprisonment on conviction (irrespective of the period, or the age of the offender or actual sentence passed) as well as the non-imprisonable offences under the Vagrancy Act 1824 sections 3 and 4 (begging and persistent begging), the Street Offences Act 1959, section 1 (loitering or soliciting for purposes of prostitution), the Road Traffic Act 1988, section 25 (tampering with motor vehicles), the Criminal Justice and Public Order Act 1994, section 167 (touting for hire car services) and others listed in the National Police Records (Recordable Offences) Regulations 2000 as amended.

4B Fingerprints, footwear impressions or a DNA sample (and the information derived from it) taken from a person arrested on suspicion of being involved in a recordable offence, or charged with such an offence, or informed [he/she] will be reported for such an offence, may be subject of a speculative search. This means the fingerprints, footwear impressions or DNA sample may be checked against other fingerprints, footwear impressions and DNA records held by, or on behalf of, the police and other law enforcement authorities in, or outside, the UK, or held in connection with, or as a result of, an investigation of an offence inside or outside the UK. Fingerprints, footwear impressions and samples taken from a person suspected of committing a recordable offence but not arrested, charged or informed [he/she] will be reported for it, may be subject to a speculative search only if the person consents in writing. The following is an example of a basic form of words:

'I consent to my fingerprints, footwear impressions and DNA sample and information derived from it being retained and used only for purposes related to the prevention and detection of a crime, the investigation of an offence or the conduct of a prosecution either nationally or internationally. I understand that my fingerprints, footwear impressions or DNA sample may be checked against other fingerprint, footwear impressions and DNA records held by or on behalf of relevant law enforcement authorities, either nationally or internationally.

I understand that once I have given my consent for my fingerprints, footwear impressions or DNA sample to be retained and used I cannot withdraw this consent.'

See Annex F regarding the retention and use of fingerprints and footwear impressions taken with consent for elimination purposes.

Section 5 Examinations to establish identity and the taking of photographs

(A) Detainees at police stations

(a) Searching or examination of detainees at police stations

5.1 PACE, section 54A (1), allows a detainee at a police station to be searched or examined or both, to establish:
  (a) whether [he/she has] any marks, features or injuries that would tend to identify [him/her] as a person involved in the commission of an offence and to photograph any identifying marks, see paragraph 5.5; or
  (b) [his/her] identity, see Note 5A.
  A person detained at a police station to be searched under a stop and search power, see Code A, is not a detainee for the purposes of these powers.

5.2 A search and/or examination to find marks under section 54A(1)(a) may be carried out without the detainee's consent, see paragraph 2.12, only if authorised by an officer of at least inspector rank when consent has been withheld or it is not practicable to obtain consent, see Note 5D.

5.3 A search or examination to establish a suspect's identity under section 54A(1)(b) may be carried out without the detainee's consent, see paragraph 2.12, only if authorised by an officer of at least inspector rank when the detainee has refused to identify [him/herself] or the authorising officer has reasonable grounds for suspecting the person is not who [he/she] claims to be.

5.4 Any marks that assist in establishing the detainee's identity, or their identification as a person involved in the commission of an offence, are identifying marks. Such marks may be photographed with the detainee's consent, see paragraph 2.12; or without [his/her] consent if it is withheld or it is not practicable to obtain it, see Note 5D.

5.5 A detainee may only be searched, examined and photographed under section 54A, by a police officer of the same sex.

5.6 Any photographs of identifying marks, taken under section 54A, may be used or disclosed only for purposes related to the prevention or detection of crime, the investigation of offences or the conduct of prosecutions by, or on behalf of, police or other law enforcement and prosecuting authorities inside, and outside, the UK. After being so used or disclosed, the photograph may be retained but must not be used or disclosed except for these purposes, see Note 5B.

5.7 The powers, as in paragraph 5.1, do not affect any separate requirement under the Criminal Procedure and Investigations Act 1996 to retain material in connection with criminal investigations.

5.8 Authority for the search and/or examination for the purposes of paragraphs 5.2 and 5.3 may be given orally or in writing. If given orally, the authorising officer must confirm it in writing as soon as practicable. A separate authority is required for each purpose which applies.

5.9 If it is established a person is unwilling to co-operate sufficiently to enable a search and/or examination to take place or a suitable photograph to be taken, an officer may use reasonable force to:
  (a) search and/or examine a detainee without [his/her] consent; and
  (b) photograph any identifying marks without [his/her] consent.

5.10 The thoroughness and extent of any search or examination carried out in accordance with the powers in section 54A must be no more than the officer considers necessary to achieve the required purpose. Any search or examination which involves the removal of more than the person's outer clothing shall be conducted in accordance with Code C, Annex A, paragraph 11.

5.11 An intimate search may not be carried out under the powers in section 54A.

(b) Photographing detainees at police stations and other persons elsewhere than at a police station

5.12 Under PACE, section 64A, an officer may photograph:
  (a) any person whilst detained at a police station; and
  (b) any person who is elsewhere than at a police station and who has been:-
    (i) arrested by a constable for an offence;
    (ii) taken into custody by a constable after being arrested for an offence by person other than a constable;

(iii) made subject to a requirement to wait with a community support officer under paragraph 2(3) or (3B) of Schedule 4 to the Police Reform Act 2002;

(iv) given a penalty notice by a constable in uniform under Chapter 1 of Part 1 of the Criminal Justice and Police Act 2001, a penalty notice by a constable under section 444A of the Education Act 1996, or a fixed penalty notice by a constable in uniform under section 54 of the Road Traffic Offenders Act 1988;

(v) given a notice in relation to a relevant fixed penalty offence (within the meaning of paragraph 1 of Schedule 4 to the Police Reform Act 2002) by a community support officer by virtue of a designation applying that paragraph to [him/her]; or

(vi) given a notice in relation to a relevant fixed penalty offence (within the meaning of paragraph 1 of Schedule 5 to the Police Reform Act 2002) by an accredited person by virtue of accreditation specifying that that paragraph applies to [him/her].

5.12A Photographs taken under PACE, section 64A:

(a) may be taken with the person's consent, or without [his/her] consent if consent is withheld or it is not practicable to obtain [his/her] consent, see Note 5E; and

(b) may be used or disclosed only for purposes related to the prevention or detection of crime, the investigation of offences or the conduct of prosecutions by, or on behalf of, police or other law enforcement and prosecuting authorities inside and outside the United Kingdom or the enforcement of any sentence or order made by a court when dealing with an offence. After being so used or disclosed, they may be retained but can only be used or disclosed for the same purposes, see Note 5B.

5.13 The officer proposing to take a detainee's photograph may, for this purpose, require the person to remove any item or substance worn on, or over, all, or any part of, [his/her] head or face. If they do not comply with such a requirement, the officer may remove the item or substance.

5.14 If it is established the detainee is unwilling to co-operate sufficiently to enable a suitable photograph to be taken and it is not reasonably practicable to take the photograph covertly, an officer may use reasonable force, see Note 5F.

(a) to take [his/her] photograph without consent; and

(b) for the purpose of taking the photograph, remove any item or substance worn on, or over, all, or any part of, the person's head or face which [he/she has] failed to remove when asked.

5.15 For the purposes of this Code, a photograph may be obtained without the person's consent by making a copy of an image of [him/her] taken at any time on a camera system installed anywhere in the police station.

(c) Information to be given

5.16 When a person is searched, examined or photographed under the provisions as in paragraph 5.1 and 5.12, or [his/her] photograph obtained as in paragraph 5.15, [he/she] must be informed of the:

(a) purpose of the search, examination or photograph;

(b) grounds on which the relevant authority, if applicable, has been given; and

(c) purposes for which the photograph may be used, disclosed or retained.

This information must be given before the search or examination commences or the photograph is taken, except if the photograph is:

(i) to be taken covertly;

(ii) obtained as in paragraph 5.15, in which case the person must be informed as soon as practicable after the photograph is taken or obtained.

(d) Documentation

5.17 A record must be made when a detainee is searched, examined, or a photograph of the person, or any identifying marks found on [him/her], are taken. The record must include the:

(a) identity, subject to paragraph 2.18, of the officer carrying out the search, examination or taking the photograph;

(b) purpose of the search, examination or photograph and the outcome;

(c) detainee's consent to the search, examination or photograph, or the reason the person was searched, examined or photographed without consent;

(d) giving of any authority as in paragraphs 5.2 and 5.3, the grounds for giving it and the authorising officer.

5.18 If force is used when searching, examining or taking a photograph in accordance with this section, a record shall be made of the circumstances and those present.

(B) Persons at police stations not detained

5.19 When there are reasonable grounds for suspecting the involvement of a person in a criminal offence, but that person is at a police station voluntarily and not detained, the provisions of paragraphs 5.1 to 5.18 should apply, subject to the modifications in the following paragraphs.

5.20 References to the 'person being detained' and to the powers mentioned in paragraph 5.1, which apply only to detainees at police stations, shall be omitted.

5.21 Force may not be used to:
(a) search and/or examine the person to:
(i) discover whether [he/she has] any marks that would tend to identify [him/her] as a person involved in the commission of an offence; or
(ii) establish [his/her] identity, see Note 5A;
(b) take photographs of any identifying marks, see paragraph 5.4; or
(c) take a photograph of the person.

5.22 Subject to paragraph 5.24, the photographs of persons or of [his/her] identifying marks which are not taken in accordance with the provisions mentioned in paragraphs 5.1 or 5.12, must be destroyed (together with any negatives and copies) unless the person:
(a) is charged with, or informed [he/she] may be prosecuted for, a recordable offence;
(b) is prosecuted for a recordable offence;
(c) is cautioned for a recordable offence or given a warning or reprimand in accordance with the Crime and Disorder Act 1998 for a recordable offence; or
(d) gives informed consent, in writing, for the photograph or image to be retained as in paragraph 5.6.

5.23 When paragraph 5.22 requires the destruction of any photograph, the person must be given an opportunity to witness the destruction or to have a certificate confirming the destruction provided that [he/she] so requests the certificate within five days of being informed the destruction is required.

5.24 Nothing in paragraph 5.22 affects any separate requirement under the Criminal Procedure and Investigations Act 1996 to retain material in connection with criminal investigations.

Notes for guidance

5A The conditions under which fingerprints may be taken to assist in establishing a person's identity, are described in section 4.

5B Examples of purposes related to the prevention or detection of crime, the investigation of offences or the conduct of prosecutions include:
(a) checking the photograph against other photographs held in records or in connection with, or as a result of, an investigation of an offence to establish whether the person is liable to arrest for other offences;
(b) when the person is arrested at the same time as other people, or at a time when it is likely that other people will be arrested, using the photograph to help establish who was arrested, at what time and where;
(c) when the real identity of the person is not known and cannot be readily ascertained or there are reasonable grounds for doubting a name and other personal details given by the person, are [his/her] real name and personal details. In these circumstances, using or disclosing the photograph to help to establish or verify [his/her] real identity or determine whether [he/she is] liable to arrest for some other offence, e.g. by checking it against other photographs held in records or in connection with, or as a result of, an investigation of an offence;
(d) when it appears any identification procedure in section 3 may need to be arranged for which the person's photograph would assist;
(e) when the person's release without charge may be required, and if the release is:
(i) on bail to appear at a police station, using the photograph to help verify the person's identity when [he/she answers] bail and if the person does not answer bail, to assist in arresting [him/her]; or
(ii) without bail, using the photograph to help verify [his/her] identity or assist in locating [him/her] for the purposes of serving [him/her] with a summons to appear at court in criminal proceedings;
(f) when the person has answered to bail at a police station and there are reasonable grounds for doubting [he/she is] the person who was previously granted bail, using the photograph to help establish or verify [his/her] identity;
(g) when the person arrested on a warrant claims to be a different person from the person named on the warrant and a photograph would help to confirm or disprove [his/her] claim;
(h) when the person has been charged with, reported for, or convicted of, a recordable offence and [his/her] photograph is not already on record as a result of (a) to (f) or [his/her] photograph is on record but [his/her] appearance has changed since it was taken and the person has not yet been released or brought before a court.

5C There is no power to arrest a person convicted of a recordable offence solely to take [his/her] photograph. The power to take photographs in this section applies only where the person is in custody as a result of the exercise of another power, e.g. arrest for fingerprinting under PACE, section 27.

5D Examples of when it would not be practicable to obtain a detainee's consent, see paragraph 2.12, to a search, examination or the taking of a photograph of an identifying mark include:
  (a) when the person is drunk or otherwise unfit to give consent;
  (b) when there are reasonable grounds to suspect that if the person became aware a search or examination was to take place or an identifying mark was to be photographed, [he/she] would take steps to prevent this happening, e.g. by violently resisting, covering or concealing the mark etc and it would not otherwise be possible to carry out the search or examination or to photograph any identifying mark;
  (c) in the case of a juvenile, if the parent or guardian cannot be contacted in sufficient time to allow the search or examination to be carried out or the photograph to be taken.

5E Examples of when it would not be practicable to obtain the person's consent, see paragraph 2.12, to a photograph being taken include:
  (a) when the person is drunk or otherwise unfit to give consent;
  (b) when there are reasonable grounds to suspect that if the person became aware a photograph, suitable to be used or disclosed for the use and disclosure described in paragraph 5.6, was to be taken, [he/she] would take steps to prevent it being taken, e.g. by violently resisting, covering or distorting [his/her] face etc, and it would not otherwise be possible to take a suitable photograph;
  (c) when, in order to obtain a suitable photograph, it is necessary to take it covertly; and
  (d) in the case of a juvenile, if the parent or guardian cannot be contacted in sufficient time to allow the photograph to be taken.

5F The use of reasonable force to take the photograph of a suspect elsewhere than at a police station must be carefully considered. In order to obtain a suspect's consent and co-operation to remove an item of religious headwear to take [his/her] photograph, a constable should consider whether in the circumstances of the situation the removal of the headwear and the taking of the photograph should be by an officer of the same sex as the person. It would be appropriate for these actions to be conducted out of public view.

Section 6 Identification by body samples and impressions

(A) General

6.1 References to:
  (a) an 'intimate sample' mean a dental impression or sample of blood, semen or any other tissue fluid, urine, or pubic hair, or a swab taken from any part of a person's genitals or from a person's body orifices other than the mouth;
  (b) a 'non-intimate sample' means:
    (i) a sample of hair, other than pubic hair, which includes hair plucked with the root, see Note 6A;
    (ii) a sample taken from a nail or from under a nail;
    (iii) a swab taken from any part of a person's body other than a part from which a swab taken would be an intimate sample;
    (iv) saliva;
    (v) a skin impression which means any record, other than a fingerprint, which is a record, in any form and produced by any method, of the skin pattern and other physical characteristics or features of the whole, or any part of, a person's foot or of any other part of their body.

(B) Action

(a) Intimate samples

6.2 PACE, section 62, provides that intimate samples may be taken under:
  (a) section 62(1), from a person in police detention only:
    (i) if a police officer of inspector rank or above has reasonable grounds to believe such an impression or sample will tend to confirm or disprove the suspect's involvement in a recordable offence, see Note 4A, and gives authorisation for a sample to be taken; and
    (ii) with the suspect's written consent;
  (b) section 62(1A), from a person not in police detention but from whom two or more non-intimate samples have been taken in the course of an investigation of an offence and the samples, though suitable, have proved insufficient if:
    (i) a police officer of inspector rank or above authorises it to be taken; and
    (ii) the person concerned gives [his/her] written consent. See Notes 6B and 6C.

6.3 Before a suspect is asked to provide an intimate sample, [he/she] must be warned that if [he/she] refuses] without good cause, [his/her] refusal may harm [his/her] case if it comes to trial, see

Note 6D. If the suspect is in police detention and not legally represented, [he/she] must also be reminded of [his/her] entitlement to have free legal advice, see Code C, paragraph 6.5, and the reminder noted in the custody record. If paragraph 6.2(b) applies and the person is attending a station voluntarily, [his/her] entitlement to free legal advice as in Code C, paragraph 3.21 shall be explained.

6.4 Dental impressions may only be taken by a registered dentist. Other intimate samples, except for samples of urine, may only be taken by a registered medical practitioner or registered nurse or registered paramedic.

(b) Non-intimate samples

6.5 A non-intimate sample may be taken from a detainee only with [his/her] written consent or if paragraph 6.6 applies.

6.6 (a) under section 63, a non-intimate sample may not be taken from a person without consent and the consent must be in writing. A non-intimate sample may be taken from a person without the appropriate consent in the following circumstances:

    (i) under section 63(2A) where the person is in police detention as a consequence of [his/her] arrest for a recordable offence and [he/she] has not had non-intimate sample of the same type and from the same part of the body taken in the course of the investigation of the offence by the police or [he/she] has had such a sample taken but it proved insufficient.

    (ii) under section 63(3)(a) where he is being held in custody by the police on the authority of a court and an officer of at least the rank of inspector authorises it to be taken.

(b) under section 63(3A), from a person charged with a recordable offence or informed [he/she] will be reported for such an offence: and

    (i) that person has not had a non-intimate sample taken from [him/her] in the course of the investigation; or

    (ii) if [he/she has] had a sample taken, it proved unsuitable or insufficient for the same form of analysis, see Note 6B; or

(c) under section 63(3B), from a person convicted of a recordable offence after the date on which that provision came into effect. PACE, section 63A, describes the circumstances in which a police officer may require a person convicted of recordable offence to attend a police station for a non-intimate sample to be taken.

6.7 Reasonable force may be used, if necessary, to take a non-intimate sample from a person without [his/her] consent under the powers mentioned in paragraph 6.6.

6.8 Before any intimate sample is taken with consent or non-intimate sample is taken with, or without, consent, the person must be informed:

(a) of the reason for taking the sample;

(b) of the grounds on which the relevant authority has been given;

(c) that the sample or information derived from the sample may be retained and subject of a speculative search, see Note 6E, unless their destruction is required as in Annex F, Part A.

6.9 When clothing needs to be removed in circumstances likely to cause embarrassment to the person, no person of the opposite sex who is not a registered medical practitioner or registered health care professional shall be present, (unless in the case of a juvenile, mentally disordered or mentally vulnerable person, that person specifically requests the presence of an appropriate adult of the opposite sex who is readily available) nor shall anyone whose presence is unnecessary. However, in the case of a juvenile, this is subject to the overriding proviso that such a removal of clothing may take place in the absence of the appropriate adult only if the juvenile signifies, in their presence, that [he/she] prefers the adult's absence and the adult agrees.

(c) Documentation

6.10 A record of the reasons for taking a sample or impression and, if applicable, of its destruction must be made as soon as practicable. If force is used, a record shall be made of the circumstances and those present. If written consent is given to the taking of a sample or impression, the fact must be recorded in writing.

6.11 A record must be made of a warning given as required by paragraph 6.3.

6.12 A record shall be made of the fact that a person has been informed as in paragraph 6.8(c) that samples may be subject of a speculative search.

Notes for guidance

6A When hair samples are taken for the purpose of DNA analysis (rather than for other purposes such as making a visual match), the suspect should be permitted a reasonable choice as to what part of the body the hairs are taken from. When hairs are plucked, they should be plucked individually, unless the suspect prefers otherwise and no more should be plucked than the person taking them reasonably considers necessary for a sufficient sample.

6B (a) An insufficient sample is one which is not sufficient either in quantity or quality to provide information for a particular form of analysis, such as DNA analysis. A sample may also be insufficient if enough information cannot be obtained from it by analysis because of loss, destruction, damage or contamination of the sample or as a result of an earlier, unsuccessful attempt at analysis.

(b) An unsuitable sample is one which, by its nature, is not suitable for a particular form of analysis.

6C   Nothing in paragraph 6.2 prevents intimate samples being taken for elimination purposes with the consent of the person concerned but the provisions of paragraph 2.12 relating to the role of the appropriate adult, should be applied. Paragraph 6.2(b) does not, however, apply where the non-intimate samples were previously taken under the Terrorism Act 2000, Schedule 8, paragraph 10.

6D   In warning a person who is asked to provide an intimate sample as in paragraph 6.3, the following form of words may be used:

'You do not have to provide this sample/allow this swab or impression to be taken, but I must warn you that if you refuse without good cause, your refusal may harm your case if it comes to trial.'

6E   Fingerprints or a DNA sample and the information derived from it taken from a person arrested on suspicion of being involved in a recordable offence, or charged with such an offence, or informed [he/she] will be reported for such an offence, may be subject of a speculative search. This means they may be checked against other fingerprints and DNA records held by, or on behalf of, the police and other law enforcement authorities in or outside the UK or held in connection with, or as a result of, an investigation of an offence inside or outside the UK. Fingerprints and samples taken from any other person, e.g. a person suspected of committing a recordable offence but who has not been arrested, charged or informed [that he/she] will be reported for it, may be subject to a speculative search only if the person consents in writing to [his/her] fingerprints being subject of such a search. The following is an example of a basic form of words:

'I consent to my fingerprints/DNA sample and information derived from it being retained and used only for purposes related to the prevention and detection of a crime, the investigation of an offence or the conduct of a prosecution either nationally or internationally. I understand that this sample may be checked against other fingerprint/DNA records held by or on behalf of relevant law enforcement authorities, either nationally or internationally. I understand that once I have given my consent for the sample to be retained and used I cannot withdraw this consent.'

See Annex F regarding the retention and use of fingerprints and samples taken with consent for elimination purposes.

6F   Samples of urine and non-intimate samples taken in accordance with sections 63B and 63C of PACE may not be used for identification purposes in accordance with this Code. See Code C note for guidance 17D.

Bibliography and References

ACPO (1999), *National SIO Development Programme Murder Investigation Manual* (London: Stationery Office Ltd).

____ (2001), *ACPO Investigation of Volume Crime Manual* (London: Stationery Office Ltd).

____ (2005), *Guidance on the Management, Recording and Investigation of Missing Persons* (London: Stationery Office Ltd).

Aitken, C, Connolly, T, Gammerman, A, Zhang, G, and Oldfield, R (1995), *Predicting an Offender's Characteristics: An Evaluation of Statistical Modelling. Police Research Group Special Interest Series* 4 (London: Home Office).

Alderson, J (1998), *Principled Policing: Protecting the Public with Integrity* (Winchester: Waterside Press).

Alegre, S, and Leaf, M (2003), *European Arrest Warrant: A Solution Ahead of Its Time?* (London: Justice).

Anderson, DM and Killingray, D (eds) (1991), *Policing the Empire* (Manchester: Manchester University Press).

Auld, Lord Justice (2001), *A Review of the Criminal Courts of England and Wales* (London: Stationery Office Ltd).

Banton, M (1964), *The Policeman in the Community* (London: Tavistock).

Bayley, DH (1994), *Police for the Future* (Oxford: Oxford University Press).

BBC (2002), *Doctors and Nurses 'Most Respected'* available at: <http://news.bbc.co.uk/1/hi/uk/2014128.stm> (Accessed 20 March 2006).

Beattie, JM (2001), *Policing and Punishment in London, 1660–1750: Urban Crime and the Limits of Terror* (Oxford: Oxford University Press).

Benner, P (1984), *From Novice to Expert* (Menlo Park CA: Addison-Wesley).

Berne, E (1968), *Games People Play: The Psychology of Human Relationships* (Harmondsworth, Middlesex, England: Penguin Books Ltd).

Bichard, Sir M (2004), *Return to an Address of the Honourable the House of Commons dated 22nd June 2004 for the Bichard Inquiry* (Report HC 653, London: The Stationary Office).

Billingsley, R, Nemitz, T, and Bean, P (2001), *Informers: Policing, Policy, Practice* (Collompton: Willan).

Blackburn, R (1995), *The Psychology of Criminal Conduct: Theory, Research & Practice* (Chichester: Wiley & Sons).

Blears, H (2005), *House of Commons Hansard Written Answers for 12 September 2005* (pt 93) available at <http://www.parliament.the-stationery-office.co.uk/pa/cm200506/cmhansrd/cm050912/text/50912w93.htm> (Accessed 2 January 2006).

Bloom, BS (1964), *Taxonomy of Educational Objectives: Handbook 1/Cognitive Domain* (London: Longman).

BNP (2005), *Rebuilding British Democracy* (British National Party General Election Manifesto 2005) available at: <http://www.bnp.org.uk/candidates2005/manifesto/manf6.htm> (Accessed on 2 January 2006).

Bowers, KJ, Hirschfield, A, and Johnson, S (1998), 'Victimisation Revisited: A Case Study of Non-residential Repeat Burglary in Merseyside', British Journal of Criminology 38 (3) pp 429–52.

____ Johnson, SD, and Pease, K (2004), 'Prospective Hot-Spotting: The Future of Crime Mapping?', British Journal of Criminology 44(5) pp 641–58.

Bowling, B, and Foster, J (2002), 'Policing and the Police', in Maguire, M et al (eds), *Oxford Handbook of Criminology* (3rd edn, Oxford: Oxford University Press).

Brogden, M, and Shearing, C (1993), *Policing for a New South Africa* (London: Routledge).

Button, M (2002), *Private Policing* (Cullompton: Willan).

Cambridgeshire Constabulary (2005), *Local Performance Plan 2003—2004* available at <http://www.cambs.police.uk/caminfo/plansandreports/lpp0304/best_value_statutory_report.asp> (Accessed on 30 November 2005).

____ (2007), *Cambridgeshire Policing Plan 2006–2007* available at <http://www.cambs.police.uk/information/plansreportspolicies/reports/cpp2006_2007.pdf>.

Canter, D and Alison, L (2000), *Precursors to Investigative Psychology. Criminal Detection and the Psychology of Crime* (Aldershot, England: Ashgate).

Centrex (2005), Level 1 Investigator Professional Development Portfolio.

Chan, JBL (2003), *Fair Cop: Learning the Art of Policing* (Toronto: University of Toronto Press).

Chenery, S, Henshaw C, and Pease, K (1999), *Illegal Parking in Disabled Bays: A Means of Offender Targeting.* Police and Reducing Crime Briefing Note 1/99 (Home Office, London).

City & Guilds (2005), *For the Attention of the Police/Community Justice NVQ Co-ordinator* (NVQs in Policing).

Clarke, C and Milne, R (2001), *A National Evaluation of the PEACE Investigative Interviewing Course* (Home Office Report PRAS/149).

Clarke, RV (1999), *Hot Products: Understanding, Anticipating and Reducing Demand for Stolen Goods*. Police Research Series Paper 112 (London: Home Office).

Coleman, R, (2004) *Reclaiming the Streets: Surveillance, Social Control and the City* (Cullompton: Willan).

Conan-Doyle, Sir A (1887), *A Study in Scarlet*.

——— (1894), *The Adventure of Silver Blaze* available at <http://etext.virginia.edu/toc/modeng/public/DoyBlaz.html>.

Copi, IM (1982), *Introduction to Logic* (London: Macmillan).

Cottrell, S (2003), *The Study Skills Handbook* (Basingstoke: Palgrave Macmillan).

Cozens, C and Tryhorn, C (2005), 'Police Data Sold to Newspapers', *The Guardian*, 16 April 2005.

CPS (2004), *Prosecution Team Manual of Guidance 2004 Edition* available at <http://police.homeoffice.gov.uk/operational-policing/prosecution-manual-guidance>.

——— (2006), *Disclosure Manual* available at <http://www.cps.gov.uk/legal/section20/chapter_a.html#178>.

——— (2006), *Offences Against the Person, Incorporating Charging Standard* available at <http://www.cps.gov.uk/legal/section5/chapter_c.html#10>.

Crawford, A, (2003), 'The Pattern of Policing in the UK: Policing Beyond the Police' in T Newburn (ed) (2003), *Handbook of Policing* Chapter 7.

Crawshaw, R, Devlin, B, and Williamson, T (1998), *Human Rights and Policing; Standards for Good Behaviour and a Strategy for Change* (The Hague: Kluwer Law International).

Critchley, TA (1978), *A History of Police in England and Wales*.

Daly, M (2003), 'My Life as a Secret Policeman' available at <http://news.bbc.co.uk/1/hi/magazine/3210614.stm>.

Davis, M (1996), 'Police, Discretion, and the Professions', in J Kleinig, *Handled with Discretion: Ethical Issues in Police Decision Making* (Maryland: Rownman & Littlefield Publishers).

Delattre, EJ (2002), *Character and Cops: Ethics in Policing* (4th Edn), Washington, DC: AEI Press).

Department of Transport (2005), TSGB 2005 Traffic speeds—data tables, available at <http://www.dft.gov.uk/pgn/statistics/datatablespublications/roadstraffic/speedscongestion/tsgbchapter7trafficspeedsdat1877>

Dobash, RE, Dobash, RP, Cavanagh, K, and Lewis, R (2000), *Changing Violent Men* (London: Sage).

Duncan, G (2005), 'All Around the World, the Future is Grey', *The Times*, 24 October 2005, p 37.

Dunnighan, C and Norris, C (1996), 'A Risky Business: Exchange, Bargaining and Risk in the Recruitment and Running of Informers by English Police Officers', Journal of Police Studies, 19 (2), pp 1–25.

——— and ———, (1999), 'The Detective, The Snout, and the Audit Commission: The Real Costs in Using Informants', The Howard Journal 38 (1), pp 67–86.

Ede, R and Shepherd, E (2000), *Active Defence: Lawyer's Guide to Police and Defence Investigation and Prosecution and Defence Disclosure in Criminal Cases* (London, Law Society Publishing).

Edexcel (2005), *NVQs in Policing Guidance for Centres*.

Edwards, S (1989), *Policing Domestic Violence* (London: Sage).

Ekblom, P (2001), *The Conjunction of Criminal Opportunity. A Framework for Crime Reduction Toolkits*. Home Office Policing and Reducing Crime Unit, Research Development and Statistics Directorate available at <http://www.crimereduction.gov.uk/learningzone/cco.htm> (Accessed 9 February 2003).

Elliott, J, Kusher, S, Alexandrou, A, Dwyfor Davies, J, Wilkinson, S, and Zamorski, B (2003), *Review of the Learning Requirement for Police Probationer Training in England & Wales* (University of East Anglia & University of the West of England).

Emsley, C (2003), 'Policing since 1945', in T Newburn (ed), *Handbook of Policing* (Cullompton: Willan).

——— (1996), *The English Police: A Political and Social History* (2nd edn, London: Longman).

——— (2003), 'The Birth and Development of the Police', in T Newburn (ed), *Handbook of Policing* (Cullompton, Willan).

Facione, PA (1998), *Critical Thinking: What It Is and Why It Counts* (Santa Clara University) available at <http://www.calpress.com/pdf_files/what&why.pdf> (Accessed 22 March 2006).

Farrall, S and Gadd, D (2004) *Evaluating Crime Fears: A Research Note on a Pilot Study to Improve the Measurement of the 'Fear of Crime' as a Performance Indicator* Evaluation, Vol. 10, No. 4, pp. 493–502

Feldberg, M (1985), 'Gratuities, Corruption and the Democratic Ethos of Policing: The Case of the Free Cup of Coffee', in FA Elliston and M Feldberg (eds), *Moral Issues in Police Work* (New Jersey: Rowman & Allanheld Publishers) pp 267–76.

Felson, M (2002), *Crime and Everyday Life* (London: Sage).

Flanagan, Sir R (2004), *A Report on the Investigation by Cambridgeshire Constabulary into the Murders of Jessica Chapman and Holly Wells at Soham on 4 August 2002* (HMIC).

Francis, B, Barry, J, Bowater, R, Miller, N, Soothill, K, and Ackerley, E (2004), Using Homicide Data to Assist Murder Investigation, Home Office Online Report 26/04 (London: Home Office).

Garb, M, Erzen, B, and Jelušíc, L (2004), 'Police in Peace Operations: The Case of Missions in South East Europe and the Case of Slovenian Peace-Keepers', in G Mesko et al (eds), *Dilemmas in Contemporary Criminal Justice*.

Gelles, R and Cornell, C (1990), *Intimate Violence in Families* (London: Sage).

Grace, S (1995), *Policing Domestic Violence in the 1990s*, Home Office Research Study 139 (London: HMSO).

Haigh, J (2006), 'Forensic Science and the Legal Process' available at <http://www.maths.sussex.ac.uk/Staff/JH/Fslp/FSLPnotes.pdf>.

Hanmer J, Griffiths S, and Jerwood, D (1999), *Arresting Evidence: Domestic Violence and Repeat Victimisation*, Police Research Series Paper 104 (London: HMSO).

Hanvey, P (1995), *Identifying, Recruiting and Handling Informants*, Home Office Police Research Group Special Interest Series Paper 5 (London: Home Office).

Hay, D and Snyder, F (eds) (1989), *Policing and Prosecution in Britain, 1750–1850* (Oxford: Oxford University Press).

Health and Safety Executive (2006), Publications available at <http://www.hse.gov.uk/pubns/index.htm>.

Heaton, R (2000), 'The Prospects for Intelligence-led Policing: Some Historical and Quantitative Considerations', Policing & Society 9, pp 337–55.

Hebenton, B and Thomas, T (1995), *Policing Europe: Co-operation, Conflict and Control* (London: Macmillan).

Highway Code (2004) available at <http://www.highwaycode.gov.uk>.

HMIC (1999), *Police Integrity, England, Wales and Northern Ireland: Securing and Maintaining Public Confidence* (London: HMSO).

——(2000), *Calling Time on Crime* (London: HMSO).

——(2000a), *Domestic Violence: Break the Chain. Multi-Agency Guidance for Addressing Domestic Violence* (London: HMSO).

——(2000b), *Domestic Violence: Revised Circular to the Police*. Circular No 19/2000 (London: HMSO).

——(2001), *Policing a New Century: A Blueprint for Reform* (London: HMSO).

——(2002), *Training Matters* (London: HMSO).

——(2003), *Safety and Justice. Domestic Violence Consultation Paper*. (London: HMSO).

——(2004a), *Building Communities, Beating Crime. A Better Police Service for the 21st Century* (London: HMSO).

——(2004b), *Campaign to Warn of Net Paedophiles* (London: HMSO).

——(2004c), *Initial Police Learning and Development Programme (IPLDP) Version 1* (London: Home Office).

——(2004d), *Initial Police Learning and Development Programme Force Learning and Assessment Manual* (London: Home Office).

——(2004e), *Violent Crime Unit, Domestic Violence Strategies—A Guide for Partnerships* (London: HMSO).

——(2005a), *Inspection of Kingston upon Hull BCU Humberside Police July 2005* available at <http://inspectorates.homeoffice.gov.uk/hmic/inspections/bcu/humberside/bcu05-hull-humberside.pdf?view=Binary>

——(2005b), *Police National Computer Data Quality and Timeliness Second Report on the Inspection by HM Inspectorate of Constabulary* (London: HMSO).

——(2006), *PNC Compliance Report—City of London (Aug 2005)* (London: HMSO).

Home Office (1997), *Police Health and Safety. Volume 2: A Guide for Police Managers* (Police Policy Directorate, London: Home Office).

——(2005a), *Home Office Counting Rules for Recorded Crime* (London: HMSO).

——(2005b), *Initial Police Learning and Development Programme (IPLDP)* Letter to Chief Police Officers 7 November 2005 (London: Home Office).

——(2005c), *IPLDP Central Authority, Practitioner Guidance, Community Engagement & Professional Development Units* (London: Home Office).

——(2005d), *IPLDP Guidance for Chief Officers and Police Authorities Version 2* (London: Home Office).

——(2005e), *PIP Guidance for Completion of the Professional Development Portfolio Investigators and Assessors* (London: Home Office).

——(2005f), *Rationale for Changing the Overall Module Structure of the IPLDP*, IPLDP Central Authority Executive Services (London: Home Office).

——(2005g), *The National Community Safety Plan 2006–2009*, Annex A: 'The National Policing Plan', pp 28–9, para 12 (London: HMSO).

——(2006), 'Making a Personal Victim Statement' available at <http://www.cjsonline.gov.uk/downloads/application/pdf/victimstate.pdf>.

Hoyle, C (1998), *Negotiating Domestic Violence* (Oxford: Clarendon Studies in Criminology).

Ingleton, R (2002), *Policing Kent 1800–2000* (Chichester: Phillimore & Co Ltd).

Inness, M (2004) 'Crime as a Signal, Crime as a Memory', Journal for Crime, Conflict and the Media 1 (2) pp 15–22

—— (2005) 'What's your problem? signal crimes and citizen-focused problem solving', Criminology & Public Policy 4 (2), pp 187–200

Jenkins R (2005), 'How Mr Loophole Overtakes the Law', *The Times*, 10 December, p 41.

Jewkes, Y (2003), 'Policing Cybercrime' in T Newburn (ed), *Handbook of Policing* (Cullompton: Willan).

—— (2003) (ed), *Dot Cons: Crime, Deviance and Identity on the Internet* (Cullompton: Willan).

John, T and Maguire, M (2004), 'Rolling out the National Intelligence Model: Key Challenges', in K Bullock and N Tilley (eds), *Crime Reduction and Problem-Oriented Policing* (Cullompton: Willan).

Johnson, R (2005), 'The Psychological Influence of the Police Uniform' available at <http://www.policeone.com/police-products/apparel/uniforms/articles/99417/>.

Johnston, D and Hutton, G (2005), *Blackstone's Police Manual, Volume 2: Evidence and Procedure* (Oxford: Oxford University Press).

Jones, T and Newburn, T (1998), *Private Security and Public Policing* (Oxford: Clarendon).

Junger, M, West, R, and Timman, R (2001), 'Crime & Risk Behaviour in Traffic', Journal of Research in Crime & Delinquency 38(4), pp 439–59 (London: Sage Publications).

Kelly, L (1999), *Domestic Violence Matters: An Evaluation of a Development Project*, Home Office Research Study 193 (London: HMSO).

Kent, JR (1986), *The English Village Constable 1580–1642: A Social and Administrative Study* (Oxford: Clarendon).

Kleinig, J (1996) (ed), *Handled with Discretion* (Lanham: Rowman & Littlefield).

Klitgaard, R (1988), *Controlling Corruption* (Berkeley, USA: University of California Press).

Knutsson, J (2004), 'Police Use of Firearms a Constant? The Swedish and Norwegian Experience', in Mesko et al (eds), *Dilemmas in Contemporary Criminal Justice*.

Kolb, D (1984), *Experiential Learning: Experience as the Source of Learning and Development* (New Jersey: Prentice Hall).

Lee, M and South, N (2003), 'Drugs Policing', In T Newburn (ed), *Handbook of Policing* (Cullompton: Willan).

Leishman, F and Mason, P (2003), *Policing and the Media: Facts, Fictions and Factions* (Cullompton:Willan).

Levi, M (1997), 'Violent Crime', in M Maguire, R Morgan, and R Reiner (eds), *The Oxford Handbook of Criminology* (2nd edn, Oxford: Oxford University Press).

Loader, I and Mulcahy, A (2003), *Policing and the Condition of England: Memory, Politics and Culture* (Oxford: Oxford University Press).

Luft, J (1970), *Group processes: An Introduction to Group Dynamics* (Palo Alto, CA: National Press Books).

Macpherson, Sir W (1999), *The Stephen Lawrence Inquiry: Report of an Inquiry by Sir William Macpherson of Cluny* (Cm 4262) (London: HMSO).

Matassa, M and Newburn, T (2003), 'Policing and Terrorism', In T Newburn (ed), *Handbook of Policing* (Cullompton: Willan).

Mawby, RI (1999), 'Police Services for Crime Victims', In RI Mawby (ed), *Policing Across the World: Issues for the Twenty-first Century* (London: UCL Press).

—— (2003), 'Models of Policing', In T Newburn (ed), *Handbook of Policing* (Cullompton: Willan).

McNee, D (1983), *McNee's Law* (London: Collins).

Mesko, G, Pagon, M, and Dobovšek, B (2004) (eds), *Dilemmas in Contemporary Criminal Justice, Policing in Central and Eastern Europe* (Slovenia: The University of Maribor Press).

Metropolitan Police (2006), *The History of the Metropolitan Police* available at <http://www.met.police.uk/history/definition.htm>.

Miles, A (2005), 'One Rule for Them, 1000 New Ones for Us', available at <http://www.timesonline.co.uk/tol/news/politics/article586778ece>.

Miller, J (2003), *Police Corruption in England and Wales: An Assessment of Current Evidence*, Home Office Online Report 11/03 available at <www.homeoffice.gov.uk/rds/pdfs2/rdsolr1103.pdf>.

Milne, R and Bull, R (1999), *Investigative Interviewing—Psychology and Practice* (Chichester and New York: John Wiley & Sons).

Morgan R and Newburn, T (1997), *The Future of Policing* (Oxford: Clarendon Press (Oxford University Press)).

Morris, W, Burden, A, and Weekes, A (2004), *The Case for Change: People in the Metropolitan Police Service* (Morris Inquiry) available at <http://www.morrisinquiry.gov.uk/report/default.htm>.

Morton, J (1993), *Bent Coppers: A survey of police corruption* (London: Little Brown and Co).

Moses, D (1997), *The Watford Rail Incident Inter-Agency De Briefing Report* available at <http://www.herts.police.uk/FOI/Significant_Information/r_Watford%20rail_%20crash-%20REDACTED.pdf>.

Munro, T (2004), 'Ospre Needs to Adapt or Die,' Police Federation Magazine, March, pp 11–13.

Murphy, R (2005), *Investigative Interviewing for Patrol Officers Level 1* (unpublished).

National Police Training (1995), *Police Probationer Training Foundation Course Notes* (Police Central Planning & Training Unit, a division of National Police Training).

Newburn, T (1999), *Understanding and Preventing Police Corruption: Lessons from the Literature*. Police Research Series Paper 110 (Home Office: London).

____ (2003) (ed), *Handbook of Policing* (Cullompton: Willan)

Newburn, T (2005), *A Force for Change*. Police Federation Magazine, August, pp 12–13.

Neyroud, P and Beckley, A (2001), *Policing, Ethics and Human Rights* (Cullompton: Willan).

Neyroud, PW (2003), 'Policing and Ethics', in T Newburn (ed), *Handbook of Policing* (Cullompton: Willan).

Nicholas, S, Povey, D, Walker, A, and Kershaw, C (2005), *Crime in England and Wales 2004/2005* (Home Office Statistical Bulletin 11/05).

Nolan, Lord (1995), *First Report of the Committee on Standards in Public Life* (Cm 2850-I) (Stationery Office).

Norfolk Constabulary (2006) *Training and Development* available at <http://www.norfolk.police.uk/article.cfm?catID=818&artID=7419&bctrail=0>.

Nozick, R (1974), *Anarchy, State and Utopia* (Oxford: Blackwell (2003 print)).

Office of Public Services Reform (2004), available at <http://www.cabinetoffice.gov.uk/opsr/documents/pdf/customer_satisfaction_final.pdf>.

Osterburg, J, and Ward, R (2004), *Criminal Investigation*, (4th edn, Cincinnati: Anderson).

Patten Commission (1999), *A New Beginning: Policing in Northern Ireland. Report of the Independent Commission on Policing for Northern Ireland*.

Pease, K (1997), 'Crime Prevention', in M Maguire, R Morgan, and R Reiner (eds), *The Oxford Handbook of Criminology* (2nd edn, Oxford: Oxford University Press).

____ (2002), 'Crime Reduction', in M Maguire, R Morgan, and R Reiner (eds), *The Oxford Handbook of Criminology* (3rd edn, Oxford: Oxford University Press) pp 947–79.

Peters, R (1973), *Authority, Responsibility and Education* (London: Allen and Unwin).

Phillips, C (2002), 'From Voluntary to Statutory Status: Reflecting on the Experience of Three Partnerships Established under the Crime and Disorder Act 1998', in G Hughes, E McGlaughlin, and J Muncie (eds), *Crime Prevention and Community Safety: New Directions* (London: Sage).

Plotnikoff, J and Woolfson, R (1998), *Policing Domestic Violence: Effective Organisational Structures*, Police Research Series Paper 100 (London: HMSO).

Popper, K (1990), *Conjectures and Refutations: The Growth of Scientific Knowledge* (London: Routledge).

Rawlings, PJ (2002), *Policing: A Short History* (Cullompton: Willan).

Reid, J (2007) *Common values for the police service of England and Wales. A Message from the Home Secretary*. Letter sent to all police services on March 6th 2007 (London: Home Office). Available at <http://police.homeoffice.gov.uk/news-and-publications/publication/police-reform/policing-values-letter> (accessed 30 March 2007).

Reiner, R (1991), *Chief Constables* (Oxford: Oxford University Press).

____ (1997), 'Policing and the Police', in M Maguire, R Morgan, and R Reiner (eds) (2002), *The Oxford Handbook of Criminology* (2nd edn, Oxford: Oxford University Press).

____ (2000), *The Politics of the Police* (3rd edn, Oxford: Oxford University Press).

Reynolds, EA (1998), *Before the Bobbies: The Night Watch and Police Reform in Metropolitan London, 1720–1830* (London: Macmillan).

Robinson, D and Campbell, R (2006), *Contributory Factors to Road Accidents*, Transport Statistics: Road Safety, Department for Transport.

Rogers, A (1996), *Teaching Adults* (2nd edn, Buckingham: Open University Press).

Rose, G (2000), *The Criminal Histories of Serious Traffic Offenders*, HORS 206 (London Home Office).

Rothschild, J (1993), *Return to Diversity: A Political History of East Central Europe Since World War II* (Oxford: Oxford University Press).

Rowe, M (2002), 'Policing Diversity: Themes and Concerns from the Recent British Experience', in Police Quarterly, Vol 5, No 4: pp 424–46.

Safer London Committee (2005), *Transcript of Item 5—Scrutiny on Planned Civil Defence and Recovery in Response to a Catastrophic Event in London*, available at <http://www.london.gov.uk/assembly/past_ctees/safe_lon/2005/mar0905/minutes/safelonmar09trans.pdf> (accessed 16 April 2005).

Scarman, Lord (1981), *Report into the Brixton Disorders* (Cmnd, 8427).

Shearing, C and Stenning, P (1981), 'Modern Private Security: Its Growth and Implications', in M Tonry and N Morris (eds), *Crime and Justice: An Annual Review of Research Vol 3* (Chicago: University of Chicago Press).

Shepherd, E (2001), *SE3R A Resource Book* (East Hendred Forensic Solutions Ltd).

Sherman, LW (1985), 'Becoming Bent: Moral Careers of Corrupt Policemen', in FA Elliston and M Feldberg (eds), *Moral Issues in Police Work* (Towota, New Jersey: Rowan and Allanheld).

Shorter Oxford English Dictionary (2002) (5th edn, Oxford: Oxford University Press).

Simmons, AJ (2001), *Justification and Legitimacy. Essays on Rights and Obligations* (Cambridge: Cambridge University Press).

Skills for Justice (2003), *Integrated Competency Framework*.

____(2004), *Skills Foresight 2004: Identifying the Current and Future Skills Needs of the Police Sector*.

____(2005), *Policing as a Profession—Managing the Professional Workforce*.

____(2006), *National Occupational Standards* <http://www.skillsforjustice.net/template01.asp?pageid= 37>.

____(2007), *Unit 2C1* <http://www.skillsforjustice.com/websitefiles/NOS_POLICE06_2C1.doc>.

____(2007a), *Unit AB1* <http://www.skillsforjustice.com/websitefiles/NOS_POLICE06_AB1.doc>.

____(2007b), *Unit AA1* <http://www.skillsforjustice.com/websitefiles/NOS_POLICE06_AA1.doc>.

Smith, MJ and Tilley, N (2005), *Crime Science: New Approaches to Preventing and Detecting Crime* (Cullompton: Willan Press).

Smith, N and Flanagan, C (2000), *The Effective Detective: Identifying the Skills of an Effective SIO*, Police Research Series Paper 12 (Home Office).

Stockdale, J and Gresham, P (1995), *The Presentation of Police Evidence to Court*, Police Research Series Paper 15 (Home Office).

Sussex Police (2006), Freedom of Information Act Previous Requests, available at <http://www.sussex. police.uk/foi/request_faq_lists.asp?id=Professional%20Standards>.

Svensson, R (2002), 'Strategic Offences in the Criminal Career Context', British Journal of Criminology 42, pp 359–411.

Taylor, D (1999), Cannabis Cautioning Notice Pilot Program Training Module—Bunbury and Mirrabooka, 5–6 (Alcohol and Drug Coordination Unit).

Taylor, M (1986), 'Learning for Self-direction in the Classroom: The Pattern of a Transition Process', Studies in Higher Education 11(1), pp 55–72.

Thames Valley Police (2005), *Join Us: Training to Be a Police Officer* available at <http://www.thames valley.police.uk/recruiting/police/pol5.htm>.

Tilley, N and Laycock, G (2002), *Working Out What to Do: Evidence-based Crime Reduction*, Crime Reduction Research Series Paper 11 (Home Office: London).

Townsend, M (2006), 'Row over Second Jobs for Police Deepens', *The Observer* 5 February.

Vrij, A (2000), *Detecting Lies and Deceit: The Psychology of Lying and Implications for Professional Practice* (Chichester: John Wiley and Sons).

Waddington, PAJ (1999), 'Domestic Violence and the Social Divide', in Police Review, 26 March.

____(1999a), *Policing Citizens* (London: UCL Press).

____Stenson, K, and David D (2004), 'In Proportion: Race, and Police Stop and Search', British Journal of Criminology 44, pp 889–914.

Wadham, J (2004), Conference on Data Protection and Information Sharing, 15 July 2004 (London).

Walker, A, Kershaw, C, and Nicholas, S (2006) *Crime in England and Wales 2005/06* Home Office Statistical Bulletin

Wall, D (ed) (2001), *Crime and the Internet* (London: Routledge).

Wilson, JQ (1996), 'On Deterrence', in J Muncie, E McLaughlin, and M Langan (eds), *Criminological Perspectives. A Reader* (London: Sage).

Wolfenden Report (1957), *Report of the Committee on Homosexual Offences and Prostitution* (Cmnd 247) (London: HMSO).

Woolcock, N (2006), 'Forces Fail the Equality Test as Women and Blacks Quit', *The Times*, 16 January.

Wright, A (2002), *Policing: An Introduction to Concepts and Practice* (Willan Publishing).

Zedner, L (2002), 'Victims', in M Maguire, R Morgan, and R Reiner (eds), *The Oxford Handbook of Criminology* (3rd edn, Oxford: Oxford University Press).

Index